HANNO-WALTE

A HISTORY

of

ARCHITECTURAL THEORY

FROM VITRUVIUS TO THE PRESENT

TRANSLATED BY
RONALD TAYLOR, ELSIE CALLANDER AND ANTONY WOOD

PRINCETON ARCHITECTURAL PRESS

English language edition first published in 1994 by
Princeton Architectural Press
37 East 7th Street
New York, New York 10003
and
Zwemmer, an imprint of Philip Wilson Publishers Ltd
143-149 Great Portland Street, London WIN 5FB

© 1994 Zwemmer
This edition published with the assistance of the Getty Grant Program
10 09 08 07   6 5

First published by Verlag C.H. Beck, Munich in 1985 under the title
Geschichte der Architekturtheorie: Von der Antike bis zur Gegenwart
© C.H. Beck'she Verlagsbuchhandlung (Oscar Beck), München 1985

ISBN (Princeton Architectural Press)
       1 56898 001 9 (hardback)
       1 56898 010 8 (paperback)

Library of Congress Cataloging-in-Publication Data

Kruft, Hanno-Walter
    [Geschichte der Architekturtheorie. English]
    A history of architectural theory : from Vitruvius to the present
    Hanno-Walter Kruft: translated by Ronald Taylor, Elsie Callander, and
    Antony Wood.
        p.   cm.
    Includes bibliographical references and index.
    ISBN 1-56898-001-9 (Princeton), — ISBN 1-56898-010-8 (Princeton :
    pbk.). — ISBN 0-302-00603-6 (Zwemmer), — ISBN 0-302-00622-2
    (Zwemmer : pbk.)
        1. Architecture—Philosophy. 2. Architecture—Historiography,
    I. Title.   II. Title. Architectural theory.
    NA2500.K7513   1994
    720'.1—dc20   93-50746
                                                        CIP

Designed by Cole design unit
Original cover design by Allison Saltzman
2007 paperback cover design by Deb Wood
Typeset in Monophoto Garamond Stempel by Lasertext Ltd, Stretford,
Manchester
Printed and bound in the United States

For a free catalog of other books published by Princeton Architectural Press,
call toll free (800) 722-6657
Visit Princeton Architectural Press on the World Wide Web at
www.papress.com

Contents

Preface

It was only possible to write this book with a certain professional insouciance, not to say naïveté. Only after part of the manuscript had already been written – fortunately – did it dawn on me that an historical survey of architectural theory measured by the present state of our knowledge was a premature undertaking, and one probably beyond the power of a single individual. As I worked on, my task became like an obstacle race, and I must leave it to better-informed judges than myself to decide which obstacles I have avoided and which I have failed to clear.

The book owes its existence to one simple stimulus, that students of architecture, reflecting on the nature of their studies, were beginning to ask questions about the theory underlying their subject, and about the history of that theory. I could give only incomplete answers to their questions, and there was nothing to meet their justifiable request for a historical survey.

From 1972 onwards, I gave a series of lectures and seminars at the Technische Hochschule in Darmstadt on the history of architectural theory, and in the course of these I became more and more aware of the desirability of such a survey. The present book is the product of this experience. My initial idea of being able to draw to a large extent on existing secondary literature for individual sections proved illusory, since I found to my surprise that for many aspects of the subject there was no such literature. The more closely I studied what literature there was, the more necessary I found it to go back to primary sources, and my perusal of these served to raise doubts and suspicions about the secondary material available. So I realised that any acceptable survey of the subject would have to be based on the original sources, and from this point on I made it a principle not to write on anything, if I could help it, that I had not consulted in the original.

This could have led me to throw in my hand, for it involved studying rare, valuable and not easily accessible first editions, and had it not been for the generous assistance of a number of libraries, the whole project would have foundered. In the end, with the help of the superlative resources of the Hessische Landesbibliothek in Darmstadt, the Bibliotheca Hertziana and the Bibliotheca Apostolica Vaticana in Rome, the Zentralinstitut für Kunstgeschichte and the Bayerische Staatsbibliothek in Munich, the Oettingen-Wallerstein Library in Augsburg, and other institutions, I managed to trace most of the source material in first or early editions. My thanks are due in the first instance to all these bodies.

While at work on individual chapters of the book, I sought the specialist advice of colleagues and asked them to read parts of the manuscript. I have greatly profited from their criticisms, particularly those of scholars at the Bibliotheca Hertziana in Rome.

A special problem was to decide how to present the material in a reasonably concise and readable form without oversimplifying it. I can scarcely imagine that anyone will read the book from cover to cover – rather, that interest will focus on a particular question and the reader will then pursue this question forwards and backwards in time.

It has not been my aim to offer a complete bibliography, but rather to deal with the particular primary texts that I considered essential. Any notion of a complete coverage of the literature was out of the question, and would have swamped the idea of a survey in a sheer mass of material. Such an ideal is attainable for specific periods, as is shown by Johannes Dobai's monumental volumes on the literature of the art of Neo-classicism and Romanticism in England; yet these not only aroused my admiration, but also served as a warning against attempting anything comparable. Instead, I set out to draw attention to the most important and most representative figures. I have aimed at a balanced selection, though I am well aware that by choosing other sources, I could have emphasised different features. In the last analysis one cannot avoid the banal conclusion that one can only write about what one knows, or believes one knows.

Having embarked on a history of architectural theory based on primary sources, I am conscious of my debt to earlier scholars who have produced historical surveys of writings on art, above all Julius von Schlosser. A history of architectural theory comparable to his work has, however, never been written. My own work has naturally drawn on the work of Rudolf Wittkower, Emil Kaufmann, Nikolaus Pevsner and other distinguished scholars when dealing with particular periods. At the same time the observant reader will observe that my judgements sometimes differ considerably from theirs. My concern has been, not to discuss interpretations of the various theories of architecture, but to offer a critical account of the theories themselves; and it is from these theories, rather than from any preconceived intellectual schema, that this particular history of ideas is distilled.

I have been well aware that in individual fields there have almost always been greater experts than I, pursuing an overview, could be; but at the same time this very overview has given me insights into connections that generally escape the specialist. This, in retrospect, provides the main justification for my work.

Illustrations play an important part in architectural theory, and this book contains a selection of such illustrations. In the course of consulting primary source material, opportunities arose to prepare a large number of photographs of original illustrations, of which only a few could be reproduced here.

The bibliography has been kept within limits, and the source material listed is that which forms the subject of this book. Secondary literature on individual theorists and specific problems is quoted only in the notes and not repeated in the bibliography. I consulted more primary and secondary sources than I have discussed and cited, but the titles selected will provide a general survey and give the reader suggestions as to how to proceed further. Most readers will also welcome the fact that I have quoted details of modern reissues of primary sources, where these are known to me.

I owe a debt of gratitude to many friends and colleagues for discussions, advice and help, only a few of whom I can mention here: Hans Belting, Munich; Adrian von Buttlar, Kiel; Christoph Luitpold Frommel, Rome; John Herrmann, Boston; Julian Kliemann, Florence; Heiner Knell, Darmstadt; Georg Friedrich Koch, Darmstadt; Magne Malmanger, Oslo; the late Wolfgang Müller-Wiener, Istanbul; Christof Thoenes, Rome. Nor can I begin to assess the value of the stimulation that I have received from friends in totally different disciplines.

I am grateful to the technicians in the photographic laboratories of the Institut für Kunstgeschichte at the Technische Hochschule Darmstadt and the University of Augsburg for their careful processing of the photographs.

H.-W. K.

Foreword to the English edition

The text follows that of the third printing of the German edition published by Verlag C.H. Beck, Munich (1991), with occasional amendments. The main text of the 1991 printing by Beck remained substantially unaltered from the first edition, the book's reception having indicated no major lacunae. I have taken the opportunity to update the notes where it was most necessary. I have removed from bibliography and notes German-language translations not relevant in the present edition, and my publishers have added a list of English-language translation of sources. The Supplement to the Bibliography contained in the third German printing, set out in the same way as the main bibliography, is here included.

Extended quoted passages appear in the main text in English translation (in most cases in versions specially prepared for this volume), with texts in the original language in the end-notes. My British publishers have taken great pains to achieve this arrangement systematically and have often supplied and translated from original texts where I quoted from published German translations in the original edition of this book. I should particularly like to thank Lisa Adams for her help in providing my British publishers with original Latin, Greek and Italian texts where necessary, and either locating standard English translations of them or supplying new ones.

Spelling and capitalisation of cited material, including titles, follow original sources. For the English version of my text I am most grateful to Ronald Taylor, Elsie Callander and Antony Wood, assisted by Margaret Curran, who succeeded in transforming the sometimes heavy German sentences into what seems to me excellent English. And I am deeply indebted to Alastair Laing, and also to John Newman, Jeremy Melvin and Alexandra Wedgwood, who all contributed their individual knowledge and skills towards preparation of the final text.

H.-W.K.

Publisher's note

We regret to record the author's untimely death, on 10 September 1993, while this book was going to press.

Introduction: What is architectural theory?

It would be possible to produce a more or less objective definition of the concept of architectural theory, but it would run the risk of turning out to be unhistorical, since it would assume a constancy of meaning that the term might not have; the criteria for such a definition require historical legitimation, but this can only be provided for one period at a time. Moreover, such a definition quickly assumes a categorical character; that is, it would be taken as the measure of anything and everything that has been called, or has claimed to be, architectural theory. The longer one studies the subject the clearer it becomes that an abstract, normative definition of such a kind is both impracticable and historically indefensible.

However, it is possible to arrive at a much narrower definition if the history of architectural theory is taken as the sum of what has been consciously formulated as such, i.e. as the history of thought on architecture as recorded in written form. At first sight an insistence on written sources may not appear to be essential, since one could well conceive of a theory that was not written down but still revealed itself in built architecture. The same applies to written sources that have been lost, as is the case with the entire architectural theory of Antiquity, with the exception of Vitruvius. In such a case one has to ask to what extent a theory can be extrapolated from the surviving architecture. And here no consensus of opinion is possible, as is seen from the various attempts to interpret Greek and Gothic architecture, which ultimately tell us more about the position of the interpreter than about what is being interpreted. All architecture is based on principles of one kind or another, but these by no means need to be articulated. Technically, one can reconstruct these principles, but one cannot re-experience the state of mind behind them. Gothic architecture, for example, has been interpreted in diametrically opposed ways, ranging from pure functionalism at one extreme to transcendentalism at the other. We find ourselves in an area close to the history of style and the general history of art. In a nutshell: historical analyses of architecture are rarely unambiguous in respect of the theories that lie behind them. What comparative analysis provides us with is a knowledge of certain architectural conventions. In principle, a theory of architecture has no need to be recorded in writing, but the historian is dependent on such records. Hence for practical reasons, architectural theory is synonymous with its writings.

Yet even if the concept is restricted in this way, architectural theory remains an aspect of a historical process of which the observer himself is part. Just as there are no objective criteria for a definition of the concept, so also there is none for the formation of judgements.

This leads to the need to understand historical systems in terms of their own premises and their own aims, before we can make comparisons and sketch lines of development that allow us to conclude that there are indeed constant factors present – or perhaps only historically determined modes of regarding them. Each theoretical system has to be judged according to its own objectives, and we have to ask, first: what is its aim? and second: for whom is it intended?

An evolutionist or positivist concept of development does not seem to me to be tenable. Developments are usually the result of new needs or new technologies, though they may also be the expression of purely intellectual ideals. By no means can one assume that the onward march of historical development is accompanied by a rise in the quality of architectural theory; in fact, intellectual stagnation and loss of sophistication can often be observed. The existence of natural laws must not be taken for granted, nor can they be deduced, in my view, from the experience of history. Thus developments in architectural theory cannot reasonably be reduced to formulae, in the way that has become such a popular art-historical approach since Wölfflin advanced his 'basic concepts'.

The above pragmatic definition is probably the only one open to the historian. But a further difficulty arises. Theoretical concepts of architecture may be found in very complex literary contexts; attention can hardly be restricted to sources that deal with no other theme, for observations on the subject are often to be found incorporated in more general discussions of artistic theory, in which architecture is but one aspect, as part of some wider issue, such as the idea of proportion. We thus find numerous theories of architecture contained within general discussions of artistic theory, especially when the emphasis is on producing comprehensive categories embracing all the arts. Artistic theory, and aesthetics, of which it is a branch, are an aspect of epistemology. The sources of our knowledge about architectural theory are thus polyvalent, and there is no justification for limiting the scope of enquiry. Even works on the subject in a narrower sense have their aesthetic, philosophical and ideological foundations, which need to be taken into account if the historical position of these works is to be established. In practice this cannot always be done, since many writers on architecture do not display a philosophical dimension.

The other side of the subject concerns what attitude to adopt towards the practical issues involved in architecture – questions of construction, materials, use and so on – which also have their place in architectural theory since they constitute the premise for any theoretical discussion. Here it has to be decided to what extent, if at all, such specialised studies of technological and constructional problems should be brought within the framework of a book such as this. For our particular purposes, which are primarily concerned with ideas and motivations, it is necessary above all to decide how important such technical matters are to particular theories.

The majority of programmes that purport to be theories of architecture seek to combine aesthetic, social and practical considerations in an integrated whole; the emphasis being either theoretical or practical, according to whether the author directly tackles the question of the purpose and possibilities of architecture, and thereby promotes change in it, or whether – often with scant interest in theory – his intention is to provide a handbook of practical building instructions, frequently in the form of a compilation of examples. It depends to a large extent on whether the author is an architect himself, and on whom he is writing for. Exemplary compilations of this kind are generally lavishly illustrated, with specimens of actual buildings or ideal designs by the author himself, and often have a prescriptive tendency. Because of their practical value, they have been far more popular than the more fundamentally theoretical works by writers who were often not architects themselves, and whose treatises contained no illustrations. Architectural pattern-books, some of which may dispense with an explanatory text altogether, must certainly be regarded as belonging to the subject.

The practical aspect made it possible for individual topics, such as the Classical orders of architecture, the theory of proportion, or the study of specific buildings or parts of buildings – such as country villas or portals – to be treated separately, and a great deal of the literature of architectural theory is in this category. There was, however, a danger of this resulting in the theoretical context being overlooked, and the part being mistaken for the whole. This applies particularly to works on the Classical orders published in Northern Europe.

Bearing all this in mind, we may now be in a position to offer a practical definition of our subject as follows: architectural theory comprises any written system of architecture, whether comprehensive or partial, that is based on aesthetic categories. This definition still holds even if the aesthetic content is reduced to the functional.

In view of the changes in the way architectural theorists have understood their activity, any attempt to arrive at a narrower definition would hardly serve any useful purpose; and even the above definition leaves open the question of the line dividing it from aesthetics and artistic theory on the one hand, and from pure technology on the other. Moreover, there are close links between architectural theory and other historical disciplines, in particular archaeology, the history of architecture and the history of art; literary figures may also draw on such material, as Francesco Colonna and Rabelais did. A particularly interesting area of overlap is the political and social utopia, in which ideas about society can be expressed in the form of ideas about architecture. The most important discipline, however, remains that of archaeology, which has been an essential element of architectural theory since the Renaissance. It has to be remembered that men such as Palladio, Piranesi and even Henri Labrouste were practical architects, theorists, and archaeologists rolled into one. Right down to the period of Neo-classicism, the publication of archaeological discoveries did not spring primarily from their antiquarian interest, but from their presentation as norms, or as models susceptible to adaptation to changed uses.

In the nineteenth century in particular, the history of architecture was made into a vehicle of architectural theory, the most extreme representatives of this programmatic systematisation being probably Fergusson and Choisy. Historicism would have been unthinkable without the models provided by the history of architecture; both historical material and historical arguments have been deliberately adduced with contemporary debates in mind, from the so-called 'battle of styles' through Sigfried Giedion to Postmodernism.

The history of art can influence architectural theory by reviving the memory of historical theories that are then taken up by architectural theorists. Emil Kaufmann, for example, exercised considerable influence through his rediscovery of so-called 'Revolutionary architecture'; Rudolf Wittkower's *Architectural Principles in the Age of Humanism* (1949) is a similar case in point. The role of the historian in such instances is, or should be, strictly defined, for although he may trace the history of architectural theory, he cannot advance a theory of his own without exceeding his brief as a historian. The way in which others, architects and theorists, may use his work is something which his work may reflect but which he cannot determine. He shares the responsibility for the uses and abuses of history, so that objectivity must be his goal, even though he can never attain it.

In order to appreciate how architects saw their task it is of great importance to understand the theoretical foundation of architecture at the time, and how this had evolved. Theories of architecture always belong to a historical context which is in part causative. New systems emerge from debates on older systems; there is no such thing as an entirely new system, and if a system claims to be such, it is either stupid or dangerous. Thus architectural theory and the history thereof are synonymous, to the extent that the present position always represents a phase in a historical process.

Some knowledge of the theory of his subject is a prerequisite for the practising architect who wishes to understand the principles according to which he is working; and for the clarification of his own views it is necessary, or at least useful, for him to know how others handled the same or similar problems. An architecture with no theoretical basis will either issue in arbitrariness or become stereotyped.

What is the relationship between architectural theory and the built architecture of its time? Is the theory an *ex post facto* set of reflections complementing, justifying, and intellectualising what has already been built; or does it lay down programmes and requirements for architecture to fulfil? In fact it oscillates between the two. On the one hand, in a passive sense it represents what Marxists would call the 'superstructure' of architecture, and could be discarded without making any difference to the buildings that already exist; on the other hand, it is the practical manifesto of the tenets of architectural theory. Examples could be quoted to illustrate both points of view, but neither position reflects either the actual or the desirable relationship between architecture and architectural theory.

The most brusque rejection of the notion of the influence of theory on practice came from Emil Kaufmann in 1924:

> The idea that theory or criticism has an influence on artistic creation is untenable. The latter owes its origin to a given set of feelings, a particular temperament, the whole pattern of intellectual assumptions of a period, and many other factors besides, but never ever to contemporary lucubrations about it. Rather are these as rooted in their own time as artistic creation itself; they are as unfree, as much a product of conditioning, as the latter.... Artistic theory is itself no more than an expression of the spirit of the age, and its significance does not reside in the fact that it points the way for its own age, but in its serving subsequent generations as a monument to past ideas.[1]

Kaufmann never repeated these extreme views. At almost the same time Paul Valéry was pondering the fluctuating relationship between theory and practice in his dialogue *Eupalinos* (1923), in which he came to the conclusion that 'when they attain their most extreme formulation, theories may on occasion provide weapons for use.'[2]

Today it is hardly possible to deny that the whole of architecture from the Renaissance to Neo-classicism would have looked completely different had it not been for the influence of Vitruvius. The study of Classical architecture and the study of Vitruvius might complement each other but they also went their own ways. Most sixteenth-century editions and commentaries on Vitruvius make it clear that study of the text had become an end in itself, and was rarely verified by reference to extant Antique buildings. Let us take a relatively insignificant example of Vitruvius's influence on European architecture. In his description (I. 1) of the architect's training, Vitruvius refers to the need for a knowledge of history, illustrating this by the example of caryatids. When, in the sixteenth century, it was felt desirable to provide an illustration to this passage in editions of Vitruvius, the caryatids of the Erechtheum on the Acropolis in Athens were still unknown. Maybe the Captives on Michelangelo's Tomb of Pope Julius II and in Marcantonio Raimondi's engraving represent a reflection of the passage in Vitruvius. The connection becomes undeniable when in the first French edition of Vitruvius (1547) Jean Goujon provides an illustration of this point, and three years later – putting Vitruvius into practice, so to speak – designs his caryatid gallery for the Salle des Caryatides in the Louvre. By including Goujon's design in his commentary on Vitruvius (1648), Charles Perrault showed that he had understood the allusion to Vitruvius as it had been intended. In the twentieth century, the theories of Le Corbusier on domestic architecture and town planning, for example, were published before they were put into practice.

But there is a certain ambiguity in the influence of theory on built architecture. It can lay down norms which make it almost impossible to produce really bad architecture; at the same time, making aesthetic conventions normative can stifle, or at least hamper, creativity. Operating from false or biased premises, architectural theories can make stipulations whose implementation has disastrous results, as with the reduction of architecture to function, or the concept of zoning in modern urban planning.

It is only in dialogue with each other that architectural theory and architecture itself can flourish. The former can be a statement, a codification of practice, or a programme; and the quality of the corresponding architecture serves as a gauge of the usefulness of the theory. It must be possible to check architectural theory by reference to actual buildings. And may one also conclude that good architecture is – or even has to be – always capable of justification in terms of some theory? A number of great architects have recognised this reciprocal relationship and left a body of theoretical work in addition to their architecture – Palladio and Frank Lloyd Wright, for example – and one will never fully understand their buildings if one is not acquainted with their theoretical work, and vice versa. But one must beware of laying down the law in such matters. Only under certain historical circumstances have architects been able to express their ideas in theory; in the fifteenth century it was the Humanists who wrote about architecture, in the eighteenth century it was mainly the dilettanti. As long as he operates within the norms of his day, the individual architect has no need to advance theories of his own, any more than a theorist is under a compulsion to put his theories to the practical test himself. There is no simple causal relationship between architecture and architectural theory.

Over the ages architectural theory has been coloured to varying degrees by political ideologies; in extreme cases it may even become an ideology in itself. Here too there is no straightforward correspondence between theory and practice. As in France at the time of Colbert, architectural theory may fulfil a normative, official function, yet retain a certain intellectual freedom. In totalitarian states, as the twentieth century has shown, it becomes degraded, in the cause of uniformity – *Gleichschaltung*, to an ideological tool, and pseudo-theories are advanced to complement inferior art. In such communities the important corrective influence of art criticism is also suppressed. Yet even here there is no certainty of cause and effect, as the case of Italy under Fascism shows. The part played in architectural theory by political and ideological factors can only be established in certain historical situations, or possibly only in particular cases. One must steer clear of generalisations.

Architectural theory, moreover, must be viewed, as a matter of principle, in its historical context. Any survey of it that takes the form of a history of abstract systems, divorced from their historical background, as histories of philosophy and aesthetics frequently do, is unhistorical and of scant value. An aesthetic idea is not important in itself; what is important is when, under what circumstances, and in what context it was conceived.

It is necessary to mention the multifarious historical connections of architectural theory here, even though it has not been possible to give them sufficient weight in a survey such as this. In many cases I have had to content myself with passing references. On the other hand, there is a danger that a history of architectural theory may get taken over by the history of aesthetics, technology, society, culture, and so on, as happened to Miloutine Borissavliévitch in his *Les théories de l'architecture* (Paris, 1926).

Methodologically speaking, there are various ways in which the subject can be presented. It would be possible, for example, to deal with it in chapters devoted to proportion, symmetry, the Classical orders, ornament, functionalism, organic architecture, and other basic concepts. Such a procedure would, however, be open to the objection that the import and historical significance of each such concept within the system in which it appears could hardly be appreciated. Investigations into the history of individual concepts may be of some benefit, but there is a danger that the concepts in question may be detached from their historical context. Edward Robert De Zurko's *Origins of Functionalist Theory* (New York, 1957) is a case in point. Systems of architectural theory are most properly understood as entities and as part of a historical sequence. We must first understand the system on its own terms, before moving to a critical assessment of it. This allows us both to engage with it directly, and to perceive the historical basis on which subsequent systems arise. To do justice to a system, one has to measure it against its own claims before pronouncing a critical verdict on it. This method also takes account of the shifts of focus within architectural theory that have occurred over the centuries: in the sixteenth century, for instance, interest centred on the Classical orders, while in the 1920s the focus of attention was popular housing.

The methodology of this book has been kept as undogmatic as possible, with judgements based on historical comparisons rather than on any personal ideological position. There are, of course, limits to such attempts at objectivity, and individual sympathies and intellectual affinities cannot be kept entirely out of the picture, but it has been far from my mind to proclaim a personal credo of architectural theory. As far as possible the emphases have been laid where the age or a particular theorist laid them, and how to determine the boundaries between architectural theory and adjacent topics have been decided from one case to the next. There can be no question of an exhaustive treatment of the subject, but most of the names and theories cited do have a representative character. Nevertheless, it remains open to question whether such a survey as this can ever achieve the balance that it aims for, the more so since it is the first attempt of its kind.

The arrangement of the book follows conventional lines, based on chronological, national and usually also linguistic criteria. National and linguistic factors, indeed, play a more important role than would at first be expected, even in the twentieth century, with its international trends. The chosen form also has the advantage of setting the individual chapters in a historical continuum. At the same time the arrangement of contents and chapter-headings is intended to make it clear that the conventional pattern of historical epochs and stylistic concepts is of only very limited use for our purposes.

The scope of this book is governed by the fortuitous preservation of written documents and our knowledge of these documents. Thus by starting immediately with Vitruvius, I am conforming to the imperatives of the written record, even though we know that Vitruvius drew on earlier theoretical works which have not survived.

I have been at pains to keep closely to the actual texts of the writers whose work I discuss, for the original language proves to be extremely important, not only for terminology but also for trains of thought. Translations can frequently misrepresent or confuse the original meaning, hence specialised terminology has been retained in the original language, whilst extended quotations, given in this English edition of my book in translation, are also given in the original language in the end-notes.

Most architectural theories are intended for the age in which they are written, but their influence may also be felt at a far later date. Vitruvius, for instance, was of virtually no consequence to Classical Rome, and his meteoric rise to fame began only in the fifteenth century. The impact and influence of individual theorists is of central concern to the history of architectural theory, but it has hitherto only been possible to chart it in small areas. The limited availability of the relevant texts long made it difficult or impossible to deal with the subject on a broad canvas. Only in recent years has the publication of numerous facsimile editions facilitated the study of original texts.

I am well aware that my book is not free from historical, geographical and personal presumptions. It is the work of a German who has tried to think as a European. In the narrower sense its subject is Western architectural theory – non-European or non-American ideas of architecture have not been covered. That particular attention has been paid to Southern, Western and Central Europe is to a large extent a reflection of the course that original ideas have actually taken: Eastern Europe and Scandinavia were tributaries of the systems described here until the early twentieth century. As to North America, fed initially from European sources, its architectural theory began to go its own way in the nineteenth century, so that coverage of that country begins with Thomas Jefferson; whereas Latin America, for example, still has no body of theory of its own to show. There are, however, gaps for which I can find no real explanation. Was there really no worthwhile contribution to architectural theory in Italy in the nineteenth century?

The four apparent digressions from the central theme (Chapters 5, 9, 17 and 20) might seem at first sight to be departures from the principles enunciated above; but they have their relevance, especially in the periods when the subjects in question were at the height of their importance, and they could not reasonably be omitted.

As I see it, the experiments being made in contemporary architectural theory have their roots in history. Down to the middle of the twentieth century this book seeks to preserve a historical framework, but the debates that have taken place since the end of the Second World War are still too recent and too inconclusive to be assessed with historical objectivity. I see myself both as a participant in these developments and as a critical observer of them. I should therefore like to ask that the fragmentary impressions I give in my final chapter be read in a different frame of mind from the rest of the book.

1. Vitruvius and architectural theory in Antiquity

Vitruvius's *De architectura libri decem* is the only major work on the architecture of Classical Antiquity to have survived. Great significance thus attaches to it, and this has been enhanced in the light of history in that the whole literature on architectural theory from the Renaissance onwards has been based on Vitruvius or on a dialogue with his ideas. Without a knowledge of Vitruvius it is impossible to grasp any of the discourse on architectural theory from the Renaissance onwards – at least up until the nineteenth century.

Vitruvius was not the first to write on architecture, but all earlier writings on the subject have been lost. These Greek and Roman treatises, some of whose titles are known, were descriptions of individual buildings or dealt with specific problems, such as the proportions of temples.[1] It is the task of archaeological research to lay bare Vitruvius's relationship to the sources he used but only mentioned in passing (Book VII, preface), and to the actual buildings of Antiquity. For the subsequent history of architectural theory, Vitruvius's *Ten Books on Architecture* can and must be taken as a whole, although this work's patchwork character and erratic terminology – partly due to confused translations from Greek into Latin – cannot be ignored. Indeed, obscure passages in Vitruvius are largely responsible for similar obscurities and debate in subsequent architectural theory.

Vitruvius was the first – as he himself proudly maintained (Book IV, preface) – to cover the entire field of architecture in systematic form. Later works, such as the compendium by M. Cetius Faventinus (?third century), the *De diversis fabricis architectonicae,* or the Late Imperial work of Palladius (Rutilius Taurus Aemilianus), *De re rustica,* are direct or indirect complications from Vitruvius[2], and have little significance for architectural theory.

Few biographical[3] details are known about Vitruvius. It would have been useful to know something about his travels and his knowledge of the buildings he mentions. Since only his family name is known, but not his *praenomen* nor his cognomen, unproven identifications have been proposed, the main one being with a Roman noble from Formia named Mamurra.[4] Attempts to reconstruct his biography must be judged with equal caution. Vitruvius served in the Roman army under Julius Caesar, building siege machines and perhaps bridges, and after Caesar's death (44 BC) he was involved in the construction of the Roman water supply under Octavian. He retired about 33 BC, and through the good offices of the by then Emperor Augustus's sister Octavia, received a pension which ensured him a care-free old age. Thielscher places his birth in 84 BC, and if this date is accepted, he would have begun working on his treatise on architectural theory at the age of fifty-one, just as he was entering retirement. The period during which the *Ten Books on Architecture* were written must have fallen between 33 and 14 BC, on external evidence.[5] The prefaces to the books, setting out basic principles, were probably composed later, and the order in which he wrote the books themselves is not entirely clear.

It emerges from several of Vitruvius's own statements that he was not a successful architect. He mentions only one building of his own, the basilica in the provincial town of Fano. He enjoyed no recognition as a creative architect. His treatise was intended to increase awareness of the importance of architecture, and to constitute a lasting memorial to himself (prefaces of Books II and VI).

The treatise *De architectura libri decem* is divided into ten books, each of which has a preface that is loosely related, if at all, to the book in question, as well as giving a summary of the previous book. The prefaces should be seen as forming a whole, and contain fundamental statements about the aim of the treatise and the author's image of himself.

The contents of the ten books are as follows:

Book I   The education of the architect; basic aesthetic and technical principles; subdivisions of architecture – buildings, horology, mechanics; public edifices and domestic architecture; town-planning.

Book II   The evolution of architecture; building materials.

Book III   Temple construction.

Book IV   Types of temple; the Orders; the theory of proportion.

Book V   Communal buildings, with special reference to theatres.

Book VI   The private house.

Book VII   The use of building materials; wall painting and colours.

Book VIII   Water and the provision of water supply.

Book IX   The solar system; sundials and water-clocks.

Book X   The construction of machinery and mechanics.

In the prefaces various issues are discussed, bearing on three types of subject:

a)   Vitruvius as a person;

b)   the function of the treatise;

c)   problems of architecture in general; and here Vitruvius succeeds in bringing his conception of architecture into line with the contemporary ideology of the state.

The treatise is dedicated to the Emperor Augustus (Book I, preface). The composition of the book and its dedication are described by Vitruvius himself as tokens of gratitude for the pension awarded to him. The author, who describes himself in the preface to Book II as small, old and ugly, seeks to commend himself to Augustus through this work, possibly in the hope of receiving building commissions. In order to put his honesty and discretion in a good light, he tells the story of the architect Deinocrates, who appeared dramatically before Alexander the Great disguised as Hercules, in an attempt to secure the commission to execute a design he had brought with him.[6] Alexander is said to have rejected the design, but to have entrusted to Deinocrates the building of Alexandria in Egypt. Vitruvius deprecates such methods of obtaining commissions and the favour of rulers, but would 'hope to gain your approval with the help of my knowledge by the publication of this text-book'.[7] With his *Ten Books*, he would like to ensure the acclaim of posterity (Book VI, preface).

Vitruvius sees the aim of his treatise on several levels. Following the dedication and expression of thanks for the provision for his old age in the preface of Book I, a definition of the treatise is addressed to Augustus:

I have observed that you have already built much, are continuing to do so, and I will appreciate that you will also direct your efforts in the time that remains to you to the construction of public and private buildings, to be handed down to posterity as a fitting record of the greatness of your deeds. I have drawn up clearly defined rules, so that by studying them closely you will be able to judge for yourself the quality of the buildings you have already created and of those to come, for in these books I have laid down all the principles of architecture.[8]

Vitruvius was thinking, however, of a wider circle of users and was directly addressing the people for whom houses were built (architects, surprisingly, he was addressing only indirectly through the programme of training he had devised for them), for whom private building was to be made possible without an architect.[9] Finally he states: 'Hence I thought I should compose with the utmost care a comprehensive work on the art of building and its methods in the belief that the future will not be ungrateful for this service to the world.'[10]

Vitruvius discusses methodological and linguistic aspects of the presentation of his material in various passages. In the first chapter of Book I he apologises for his clumsiness of language, adding however: 'But I promise and hope in these books to present the meaning of my art and the principles involved in it clearly and with the greatest authority, not only for builders but for all educated people.'[11]

In the preface to Book V he stresses the desirability of brevity and conciseness, but recognises the difficulty that his terminology is remote from ordinary speech and might be difficult to understand. For this reason he points to the importance of clear and succinct conceptual definitions, an aim he himself fails to fulfil in key passages.

In the preface to Book VII Vitruvius argues for originality and against artistic and literary plagiarism. In order to present his own work to the best advantage, he lists the sources he used,[12] citing them only very selectively, however, so that his own originality is open to question.

In the preface to Book VIII Vitruvius surveys the significance of the four elements and the pre-eminence of water, to which subject the book is devoted. In the preface to Book IX he emphasises the importance of mathematics and geometry, and outlines a model of the cosmos, which turns into practical instructions for clock-making.

In the preface to Book X Vitruvius discusses the relationship between estimates and actual building costs and suggests making architects who exceed an estimate by more than twenty-five per cent liable to make good the surplus out of their own pocket.

As to architectural theory, Vitruvius asserts that the organisation of his work and the arrangement of its contents are systematic. This is in fact true only of practical matters. The theoretical backing appears only sporadically, after its exposition at the beginning of Book I.

In the first chapter of Book II Vitruvius gives his theory of the origins of architecture, the primary motivation for which he sees as the protection of man from the elements. The first houses, he writes, were imitations of natural formations (leaf huts, swallows' nests, caves), since 'men are by nature given to imitation and ready to learn.'[13] He asserts that architecture was the first of the arts or sciences to emerge, and hence has a prima facie claim to primacy among the arts.[14]

The invention of the 'rules of architecture' is mentioned almost en passant. After evolving various types of house, men were led on 'by dint of observations made in their studies from vague and uncertain judgements to fixed rules of symmetry.'[15] Vitruvius does not pursue the idea, but the 'rules' appear here as relative sizes arrived at empirically and so the seed is planted for the controversy about 'arbitrary beauty' that took place in the French Academy at the end of the seventeenth century.

In contrast to the relativity of the rules of architecture indicated here, Vitruvius endows them with claims to absolute validity; in the first chapter of Book IX in an account of the cosmos and the planets he describes the universe as an architectural design, in which the laws of the cosmos and of architecture are clearly regarded as identical.[16] This view-point was to become fundamental to the claims later made for architecture, God being seen as architect of the world (*'deus architectus mundi'*) and the architect as a second god (*'architectus secundus deus'*).[17] Vitruvius himself, however, drew no conclusions from this concept, nor did he integrate it into a system.

In the first chapter of Book I Vitruvius builds up a detailed profile of the professional architect. The architect must be a master of *fabrica* (craft) and *ratiocinatio* (theory). *Ratiocinatio* is a concept characterised by scientific content.[18] Vitruvius demands a broadly ranging education for the architect, on the grounds that architecture makes varied demands on its practitioner. The architect must be skilled in writing, in order 'to be able to render his memory more reliable by the use of notes';[19] he must be a good draughtsman and have a command of geometry, in order to make correct perspective drawings and plans. A knowledge of the laws of optics is necessary for the correct use of light. Arithmetic is necessary for the calculation of costs and also of proportions. Historical knowledge is required if the architect is to understand ornament and its meaning. Philosophy should set its stamp on his character. An understanding of music is desirable for its application to tensions in siege machines and for the building of theatres. Medical knowledge is called for in order to take account of the requirements of climate and of health in building. Vitruvius further stipulates a basic knowledge of building law and of astronomy.

For Vitruvius a lengthy schooling in sciences and humanities is thus an essential part of an architect's training, which alone can lead to the *summum templum architecturae.*[20]

In the second chapter of Book I Vitruvius sets out and defines the fundamental aesthetic principles of architecture. Here, from the theoretical point of view, lies the heart of the treatise. The fundamental concepts contained in this chapter underlay all discussion of architectural theory right up to the nineteenth century. They must therefore be considered in detail. The subject at issue is the whole scope of *ratiocinatio*, the intellectual apprehension of architecture.

Architecture, as Vitruvius states in the third chapter, must satisfy three distinct requirements: *firmitas, utilitas* and *venustas. Firmitas* (strength) covers the field of statics, construction and materials. *Utilitas* (utility) refers to the use of buildings and the guarantee of successful functioning. *Venustas* (beauty) includes all aesthetic requirements, that of proportion above all. With reference to public buildings, Vitruvius relates these considerations to each other as follows:

> These [public facilities] must be built in such a way as to take account of strength, utility and beauty. The demands of strength will be met when the foundations are sunk to bedrock, and the building materials, whatever they are, are carefully chosen without trying to save money; those of utility when the layout of the sites

is faultless and does not make their use difficult, and when their arrangement is convenient and in each case suited to its particular situation; and those of beauty when the work has an elegant and pleasing appearance and the relative proportions of the individual parts have been calculated with true symmetry.[21]

The basic category of *venustas* is divided into six basic concepts, of which only one (*distributio*) also comes under *utilitas*; Vitruvius sometimes gives these ideas Latin names, and sometimes, where there is patently no Latin equivalent, Greek:

1) ordinatio (τάζις, taxis).
2) dispositio (διάθεσις, diathesis).
3) eurythmia.
4) symmetria.
5) decor.
6) distributio (οἰκονομία, oeceonomia).

Vitruvius's definitions, which cause difficulties in understanding these concepts, are given below, with interpretations.[22]

1. *Ordinatio* is the detailed proportioning of each separate part of a building, and the working out of the general proportions with regard to *symmetria*. The latter is achieved by means of *quantitas*, which the Greeks call *posotes*. *Quantitas* is the taking of units of measure [*moduli*] from the building itself, and the creation of a harmonious whole from the individual parts.[23]

Ordinatio is the result of consistent proportioning of a building as a whole and in detail. This proportioning is based on *quantitas*, the module taken from the structure itself (which presupposes that the structure has been planned by means of a basic module-unit). The theory of proportion is not expounded by Vitruvius at this point.

2. *Dispositio* is the fitting arrangement of parts, and the elegant effect of the building achieved through *qualitas*. The various types of *dispositio*, which the Greeks call 'forms' (ἰδέαι, ideae) are: *ichnographia*, *orthographia*, and *scaenographia*. *Ichnographia* is the competent use of rules and compasses, by which ground plans are laid out on site. *Orthographia* is the representation of the front elevation of the building and its appearance drawn according to rules, in proportion to the proposed structure. *Scaenographia* is the delineation of the façade and the receding sides of the building, the lines all meeting at the point of the compass [the vanishing point]. These three all spring from *cogitatio* (reflection) and *inventio* (invention). *Cogitatio* is the laborious and painstaking effort expended to make the imagined effect pleasing. *Inventio* is the solving of difficult problems and the discovery of new things by the application of a lively intelligence. These are the goals of *dispositio*.[24]

Dispositio denotes the design of a building (in plan, elevation and perspective) and its execution, for which *ordinatio* is clearly a necessary premise, while the execution must be carried out with *qualitas*, a concept which is given no further definition. Reflection (*cogitatio*) and invention (*inventio*) are required for the drawing up of a design.

3. *Eurythmia* implies an appearance that is graceful and agreeable in the way in which its individual elements are arranged. It is achieved when these are of a height proportionally suited to their breadth and of a breadth suited to their length; when, in short, they all correspond *symmetrically*.[25]

Eurythmia is the result of proportion applied to a building and of the effect of such proportion on the beholder. It corresponds more or less to the modern conception of harmony.

4. *Symmetria* is the harmony arising out of the assembled parts of a building, and the correspondence of the separate parts to the form of the building as a whole in a fixed proportion. As in the human body *eurythmia* takes its symmetrical quality from the forearm [cubit], foot, palm, finger [inch] and the other parts, so it is with buildings. Particularly in the case of sacred buildings, symmetry is calculated either from the thickness of the columns, or from a triglyph, or from the module [Greek: *embater*].[26]

By 'symmetry' Vitruvius means the harmony of the parts in relation to the whole within the total design, as measured by a module, his term corresponding to the present-day concept of proportion.

The concepts of *ordinatio*, *eurythmia* and *symmetria* are different aspects of the same aesthetic phenomenon; *ordinatio* might be described as the principle, *symmetria* as the result, and *eurythmia* as the effect.

Such compartmentalisation is only to a limited extent meaningful, and leads to conceptual confusion, which Vitruvius himself did not escape, and has led to endless arguments and misunderstandings in commentaries on him.

5. *Decor* is the correct appearance of a building, composed according to precedent [*auctoritas*] from approved elements. It is achieved by following convention, which the Greeks call *thematismos*, or by following common usage, or Nature. Convention is obeyed when buildings that are erected to Jupiter Fulgor, to the Heavens, to the Sun, or to the Moon, are hypaethral (open to the sky), for the appearance and effects of these gods we witness in the light of the open sky. Doric temples are to be built to Minerva, Mars and Hercules, for it is fitting that temples without ornament should be put up to these gods, in keeping with their virile nature. Temples in Corinthian style will have qualities more suited to Venus, Flora, Proserpina and the Nymphs of Springs, since buildings of more slender proportions, embellished with flowers, leaves and scrolls (volutes), seem to express their delicate nature more appropriately. The construction of temples in the Ionic style to Juno, Diana and Bacchus and other similar gods will be appropriate to their intermediate position, in that their character will avoid the severity of the Doric style on the one hand and the delicacy of the Corinthian on the other.[27]

Decor concerns the appropriateness of form and content, not of applied embellishment. The use of the Orders comes under this heading. The attribution of specific qualities to specific orders points beyond aesthetics to the signification of architecure, that is, to architectural iconology.

6. *Distributio* is the advantageous management of materials and site, along with care and economy in the calculation of building costs... A second stage in *distributio* is reached when important buildings are erected for heads of households or for those with great wealth, or for dignified officials such as orators. Town houses obviously call for a different kind of construction from those which receive the products of country estates; different kinds of houses are required by money-lenders and others again by men of taste. For the powerful, however, whose thoughts govern the state, buildings must correspond to their special needs. In a

word, the *distributio* of buildings must be designed to suit their occupants.[28]

Only the second half of this definition comes into the category of *venustas*, whereas the first belongs rather to that of *utilitas*. The relationship between buildings and occupants anticipates a concept that was elevated into a system in the Enlightenment, that of *architecture parlante*, according to which architecture should be the expression of its function or of the status of its occupants.

Vitruvius's six fundamental concepts fall into three groups:

1. *Ordinatio, eurythmia* and *symmetria* denote the various aspects of the proportions of a building.

2. *Dispositio* refers to the artistic design, for which *cogitatio* and *inventio* are necessary.

3. *Decor* and *distributio* concern the appropriate use of the Orders and the relationship between house and occupant.

Vitruvius sees proportion as a prerequisite for *ordinatio, eurythmia* and *symmetria*, but does not define it when he introduces these concepts.[29] For Vitruvius proportion is not an aesthetic concept; it is purely a numerical relationship, not the effect arising from its application. Vitruvius's key statements on proportion are contained in the list in the first chapter of Book III, in which he broaches the subject of temple-building.

> The planning of temples is based on symmetry, to whose laws architects must conform with painstaking exactitude. It derives from proportion, which the Greeks call *analogia*. Proportion is present when all the parts and the building as a whole are based on a selected part used as a measure [*commodulatio*]. From this symmetries are calculated. For without symmetry and proportion no temple can have a rational design, unless, that is, there is a precise relationship between its parts, as in the case of a well-built human body.[30]

In this passage architectural proportion is defined in three ways:

1) By the relationship of the parts to each other.

2) By reference of all the measurements to a common module.

3) By analogy with the proportions of the human body.

This laid the seeds of the dual form of the concept of proportion, which has largely dominated discussion of architectural theory ever since Vitruvius: proportion as a relationship of absolute numbers, and proportion derived from analogy with the human body – anthropometric proportion.

Next, Vitruvius lays down fundamental rules of proportion for the human body,[31] according to which the length of either the face or the nose – three nose lengths being equal to one face length – is taken as a module. He applies these anthropometric proportions to painting and sculpture, but goes on immediately to say: 'Similarly, the parts of temples must be in complete and harmonious proportion to the whole, which is the sum of those parts.'[32]

In the sentences that follow, Vitruvius attempts to combine the human body and the geometrical forms of circle and square, and thus to establish a connection between man, geometry and the number. So-called 'Vitruvian man' is thus described in this passage:

> Similarly, in the human body the central point is naturally the navel. For if a man lies flat on his back with arms and legs outspread and a circle is described with the point of a compass placed where his navel is, the fingers and toes of his hands and feet will touch the circumference of the circle. And just as the human body

will give a circle, it will also give a square. For if we measure from the soles of the feet to the top of the head and then compare that measurement with the span of the outstretched arms, width and height will be found to be equal, as in an area set out with a builder's square.[33]

The graphic interpretation of this figure or figures has preoccupied nearly all commentators on Vitruvius. We shall return to this point later.

In order to substantiate the connection between the proportions of the human body and numbers, Vitruvius claims that all measurements (inch [finger], palm, foot and cubit [forearm]) are derived from the human body and that ultimately the perfect number ten, the decimal system, corresponds to the number of fingers (cf. also the fact that Vitruvius's books are ten in number). Vitruvius takes the number six to be another perfect number. The sum of the two perfect numbers, ten plus six, makes, he states, of sixteen the most perfect number of all.

At the end of the chapter, Vitruvius sums up as follows:

Hence if it is agreed that number is derived from the parts of the body, and that there is a correspondence between the various parts of the body and its overall form in fixed proportion, it follows that we must acknowledge our debt to those who, in constructing temples to the immortal gods, so ordered the parts of their buildings that by means of proportion and symmetry the arrangement of both the separate parts and the whole design should be harmonious.[34]

Nowhere does Vitruvius give a general theory of proportion with numerical values. Only when he is describing the '*genera*' of temple types (IV.i)[35] does he offer concrete proportional numbers, which again are substantiated by analogy of columns with the human body. Thus the Doric column is supposed to correspond to the male body, taken as six foot high; hence the height of the Doric column, including the capital, should be six times its lower diameter. In accordance with the proportions of the female body, he gives the ratio of one to eight (lower diameter to height) for the Ionic column, adding, however, that both Orders were given more slender proportions in later periods: the Doric one to seven, the Ionic one to nine.

It must be noted that the so-called Orders in the sense of the Renaissance canon do not feature in Vitruvius's writings. The concept of Orders represents a systemisation undertaken after Alberti, which has ever since been identified with Vitruvius's *genera*.[36]

In Vitruvius, proportions have empirical values derived from the human body, i.e. not absolute values. Hence in considering proportional relationships in private houses, Vitruvius can recommend deviations from proportion to take account of optical distortions (VI.ii):

Where therefore the system of symmetries has been decided on and the dimensions worked out by calculation, then [the architect] must use his judgement to make special provisions for the nature of the site, either in its use or appearance, by making modifications [*temperaturas*], so that by additions or subtractions made to its proportions [*symmetria*] the building appears correctly shaped and nothing is lacking in its final aspect.[37]

It must be noted that in his treatment of individual building-types Vitruvius loses sight of the fundamental concepts and aesthetic principles he has worked out in the second chapter of Book I, which he had claimed to be universally binding. The conceptual structure seems to be superimposed; Vitruvius did not feel the need to apply his criteria to specific buildings or types of building. Thus one cannot speak of a unified or systematic architectural theory in Vitruvius, except in a very limited sense.

Vitruvius's statements on particular aspects of building and existing structures, which make up the main body of his treatise, are of particular importance for archaeology, but are also of great significance in the subsequent history of architecture. From the moment of his canonisation in the Renaissance, his treatise was consulted for countless building projects and, misunderstood to a greater or lesser degree, exerted enormous influence over built architecture.

Any description of Vitruvius's 'system' can largely omit his discussion of the practical aspects of building, so that his 'rules of building' need not be summarised here. However, all such discussion in Renaissance and baroque treatises must be understood against the background of Vitruvian statements. In specific cases it is thus necessary to refer back to Vitruvius's text.

Clock-making and the construction of machinery, regarded by Vitruvius as branches of architectural theory, were looked upon up to the Renaissance as a single category.

Editions

Bodo Ebhardt's *Vitruvius. Die zehn Bücher der Architektur des Vitruv und ihre Herausgeber*, Berlin 1918 (reissued New York 1962) lists editions of Vitruvius up to 1918. The *Regesto cronologico e critico* compiled by Laura Marcucci in *2000 anni di Vitruvio (Studi e documenti di architettura*, no. 8, Florence 1978, pp. 29ff) goes up to 1976. There is still no completely satisfactory critical edition. For the Latin text: *Vitruvii de architectura libri decem*, edited by Valentin Rose, Leipzig 1899.

The most serviceable edition is the bilingual one by Frank Granger, *Vitruvius on Architecture*, Loeb Classical Library, 2 vols, London and Cambridge 1931 (frequently reprinted). Hermann Nohl's *Index Vitruvianus*, Leipzig 1876; reissued Darmstadt 1965) and a concordance[38] published in 1984 make Vitruvius's texts easier to use. Morris Hicky Morgan's posthumously published English translation (1914), illustrated but entirely unannotated or explained, is still available in paperback: Vitruvius, *The Ten Books of Architecture*, New York 1960.

2. The Vitruvian tradition and architectural theory in the Middle Ages

The influence of Vitruvius in Antiquity was very limited. His ambition to establish critical norms for architecture was not fulfilled in the age for which he wrote. This was partly because his treatise did not come to grips with current building problems such as the technique of building with tiles, vault construction and multi-storeyed structures;[1] or at least it did so only peripherally. Vitruvius had no influence on the architectural practice or thinking of the early Imperial era; only Pliny the Elder quotes Vitruvius as a source reference for the thirty-fifth and thirty-sixth books of his *Naturalis historia*; this, however, only in connection with his statements on painting and types of stone. To the later Imperial era belongs the *Compendium* of Faventius, and borrowings by Palladius, as well as passing references in Sidonius Apollinaris (c. 430–85 AD) and Cassiodorus Senator (c. 490–583 AD);[2] but these references are in a rhetorical context. We know nothing about the dissemination of Vitruvius's text in Antiquity.

Concrete interest in Vitruvius can be demonstrated only from Carolingian times, increasing in the High Middle Ages, and leading in the Renaissance to a degree of fame[3] that Vitruvius can hardly have dreamt of. The peculiar fate of Vitruvius's treatise has been aptly characterised as follows: 'In the history of art there is probably no other example of a systematic textbook aiming at contemporary influence, missing its target, and yet achieving such overwhelming success centuries after its appearance.'[4]

It has been widely assumed[5] that use was made of Vitruvius in the most important of the early medieval encyclopedias, the *Etymologiae* of Isidore of Seville (c. 560–636). In fact Isidore draws on the Roman encyclopedias of Marcus Terentius Varro (particularly the *Antiquitates*), which had been used by Vitruvius, but which have survived only in fragments. When one reads Isidore's exposition of the basic principles of architecture in the nineteenth book of the *Etymologiae*, it is clear that he can scarcely have based them on Vitruvius.

He proposes three components of architecture: 'There are three parts to a building: *dispositio, constructio, venustas*.'[6] Isidore's definitions of *dispositio* and *venustas* will suffice to illustrate his distance from Vitruvius: '*Dispositio* is the surveying of a site, or of the floor and foundations'[7]; '*Venustas* is whatever is added to buildings for the sake of ornament or decoration.'[8] Isidore's use of concepts which are apparently Vitruvian does not correspond in content to Vitruvius's definitions.

In the fifteenth book of the *Etymologiae*, which is concerned with architecture and surveying, Isidore gives no sign of having made use of Vitruvius. There are numerous references to the architecture of Antiquity, most of them displaying misunderstandings. It is interesting in this connection to note that five Orders seem to have been known to Isidore. Here is a typical passage, on the Orders:

> Columns, which are so-called because they are tall and round, support the whole weight of the building. The old ratio of columns was that the width was one-

third of the height. There are four types of round columns: Doric, Ionic, Tuscan and Corinthian, which differ from one another in height and diameter. A fifth kind is that called Attic, which is square or broader, and formed from brick piers.[9] That Hrabanus Maurus (780–856) has been enlisted as a proof of medieval recognition of Vitruvius, using this sentence quoted from his work *De universo libri XXII*: '*Aedificiorum partes sunt tres: dispositio, constructio, venustas*' (XXI.ii)[10] points rather to direct dependence on Isidore of Seville.

The use of Vitruvius in Carolingian times was probably less extensive than has sometimes been assumed. A mention of Vitruvius in a letter from Einhart to his pupil Vussin[11] is evidence of a purely philological interest; Einhart was having difficulty with the *verba et nomina obscura* in Vitruvius and recommended Vussin to consult Virgil for the meaning of the term *scenographia*. There is no reason to infer from this that he had been concerned with the architectural theory of Vitruvius.[12] The possible use of Vitruvius by Einhart in the building of his basilicas in Steinbach and Seligenstadt[13] is conjectural. The number of surviving Carolingian manuscripts of Vitruvius is extremely small;[14] commentaries on Vitruvius from this time are not recorded. It is worth noting, however, that a Vitruvius manuscript of the ninth or tenth century contains illustrations which show engagement with Vitruvius's practical discussion of architecture (Vitruvius Codex in Sélestat[15]); these do not relate, however, to the passages intended by Vitruvius for illustration – his illustrations have not survived – but to the component parts of the Orders; the explanatory texts are simplified paraphrases of Vitruvius (*Plate 1*)[16]. These illustrations do not in fact reflect a knowledge of either Classical or contemporary architecture; they belong 'to the no-man's-land between the literary and the architectural transmission of Classical antiquity'.[17] The fact that Vitruvius's passage on the proportions of the human body (Vitruvius, III, i. 2) is written out in full is worth noting;[18] 'Vitruvian man,' however, is not depicted. Peter the Deacon (b. 1107) produced an excerpt from Vitruvius's treatise at Montecassino, selecting the same extract on the proportions of the human body[19] as the Sélestat Codex. It was recently convincingly suggested that the originals of these illustrations were produced at the court of Charlemagne in Aachen, and the illustrations of the Sélestat Codex are even attributed to Einhart himself;[20] at the same time the similarity between the Ionic capital illustrated and the capitals of the pilasters of the gatehouse at Lorsch was pointed out.[21]

The influence of Vitruvius on Ottonian architecture has been plausibly demonstrated in the case of St Michael's, Hildesheim.[22] The oldest surviving Vitruvius manuscript, in the British Museum,[23] has a provenance going back to Goderammus, Prior of St Pantaleon in Cologne, whom Bishop Bernward of Hildesheim appointed as first Abbot of St Michael's in 996. If Bernward (d. 1022) did in fact play a prominent part in the planning of St Michael's, and with his scholarly bent took his own manuscript of the *Liber mathematicalis* of Boethius (Hildesheim, Cathedral Treasury) and the Goderammus Vitruvius as the basis of the design (construction began in 1001), here would be a unique case of thoroughgoing understanding of Vitruvius and the use of him in an actual building.[24] This would presuppose an understanding of Vitruvian principles sufficient to have extracted a method of proportional thinking from the formal vocabulary of Classical architecture, and a thoroughgoing adaptation of it to the needs and vocabulary of Ottonian architecture.[25]

Before we consider Western writings of the High Middle Ages on architecture, a literary form of architectural commentary should be briefly mentioned, which was probably nurtured by Hellenistic and Roman models concerned with painting (Flavius Josephus, Statius, Pliny the Younger, and Lucian),[26] and which reached its heyday under Justinian: *ekphrasis.*[27]

From the wealth of Byzantine ekphrasis,[28] we may cite the justifiably celebrated appreciations of the Hagia Sophia in Constantinople. The fourth- and fifth-century building, which was destroyed in the Nika Insurrection (532), was replaced by the new building of Anthemios of Tralles and Isidoros of Miletus[29] between 532 and 537. An earthquake in December 557 caused the dome to collapse the following year. By 562 it had been replaced by a ribbed dome and was reconsecrated on 24 December 562. Both the construction and partial reconstruction fell within the reign of Justinian (527–65), and became the subject of ekphrasis, which throws considerable light, not just on the architectural history, but also on the architectural aesthetics of the time.

The sixth-century lawyer and historian Procopius from Caesarea, a contemporary of Justinian, completed an extensive work (c. 560) on the comprehensive building activities of the Emperor under the title 'Buildings' (περι κτισματων) towards the end of Justinian's reign.[30] The book tends to be flattering to Justinian, just as Vitruvius's treatise had been to Augustus: its explicit aim is to ensure that Justinian will be acclaimed by posterity as a builder.[31] Beginning with Constantinople, Procopius presents all Justinian's building enterprises throughout his empire. He starts with the Hagia Sophia.[32] Procopius presents the Emperor in an active role, particularly in the appointment of the two engineers (μηχανοποιοι) Anthemios of Tralles and Isidoros of Miletus, whose personal significance for both design and execution he emphasizes. Anthemios is shown as the designer-architect. In spite of its rhetoric, Procopius's ekphrasis embodies a clear-cut concept, in which architectural description and aesthetic effect are combined. His observations express great breadth of vision, as when he describes the urban context of Hagia Sophia:

> So the church affords the most magnificent sight...for it reaches up to the sky and, as if keeping aloof from other buildings, looks down on the whole city from on high; it both adorns the city because it is part of it, and at the same time, although it is part of it and stands within it, the church basks in its own beauty, for it towers so high that from it there is a bird's-eye view of the city in the distance below.[33]

This goes far beyond a concern with liturgical functions.

Procopius singles out the balanced proportions in the plan and in the masses (ἁρμονία τοῦ μέτρου), in which nothing is exaggerated and nothing is lacking, a formulation which almost anticipates Alberti.[34] It is proportion, he says, more than mere size, that gives the building its distinction. The floating effect of the central dome and the calculated use of the incidence of light are described in detail. The effect on the observer, who is equally fascinated by the whole and by detail, is thus analysed:

> All these elements fit together miraculously on high, suspended from each other in mid-air and supported only by those closest to them, giving the whole work a single, most remarkable harmony; yet the spectator is not allowed to linger long on the details of any one of the elements, for each attracts the eye away from what it was looking at and onto itself with the greatest of ease.[35]

Decoration and liturgical function are described by Procopius in the same way, so that a complex picture is presented to the reader. The description ends with anecdotes about the providential intervention of the Emperor at critical points in the history of the building.

A poem on the Hagia Sophia by Paul the Silentiary was recited a few days after the reconsecration at the beginning of January 563.[36] Paul the Silentiary goes even further than Procopius in portraying the visual charms of the building and its decoration. He enumerates the related types of marble and their places of origin, and vividly describes the lighting arrangements after the onset of darkness. As a poet, he gets carried away by his own descriptions, but a present-day reader gains a precise idea of the aesthetic chain of associations that occurred to a cultured and sensitive contemporary observer of the Hagia Sophia.

Later descriptions, such as the anonymous *Narratio de S. Sophia* dating from the eighth or ninth century,[37] add to the legendary aura surrounding the building. The design is revealed to the Emperor by an 'angel of the Lord'. Alongside the almost transcendental description of the building, however, we find precise technical detail on such things as the use of iron clamps and the removal of scaffolding.

The Byzantine ekphrases of the Justinian period show a sympathetic link with Antiquity only in literary form, not in architectural perception. This is not accidental, since Byzantine architecture first emerged under Justinian or, to put it another way, the 'first medieval architectural system' was created[38] in his reign.

In connection with these descriptions of the Hagia Sophia, a further architectural parallel must be mentioned, which first becomes tangible here, and was to be of prime importance for the whole conception of architecture during the Middle Ages, the Counter-Reformation and the Baroque, although its full extent is not easy to appreciate today. This is the parallel with Solomon's Temple in Jerusalem, as it was known from Old Testament descriptions (I. Kings 5 and 6; Ezekiel 40–42). At the consecration of the Hagia Sophia in 537, Justinian is supposed to have made the statement, 'Solomon, I have surpassed thee', which, however, comes not from the ekphrases but from another source.[39] It has recently been demonstrated that the Justinian building with its first dome corresponded in the dimensions of its plan and height to the traditional proportions of Solomon's Temple, in which the ratio of length to width and of width to height was $3:1$ and $1:1.5$.[40] The wide divergence in outward appearance between the Hagia Sophia and the Temple of Solomon should not come as a surprise, in view of the abstract nature of medieval notions of imitation.[41] Efforts to reconstruct the appearance of Solomon's Temple, with direct repercussions on the design of contemporary architecture, begin with the Counter-Reformation. We shall return to this topic later.

A series of Western writings of the High Middle Ages that deal wholly or in part with architecture is concerned with specific buildings.[42] Since they may go beyond this to make statements about architecture itself, we shall mention a few of the most important of them.

The third book of the history of the Benedictine Abbey of Montecassino begun by Leo of Ostia (c. 1046–1115)[43] describes in detail the building that took place under Abbot Desiderius. The reconstruction and decoration give evidence of a far-reaching artistic policy. The Abbot himself travelled to Rome to buy marble. Building was begun in 1066, 'and carried out from the start by the most skilled builders' ('*conductis protinus peritissimis artificibus*');[44] while construction was still proceeding, the Abbot engaged mosaic artists from Constantinople, in order to resurrect an art that had been neglected in the West for five hundred years. He had some of his young monks trained in crafts. The chronicler appends an exact description of the building, with measurements. The unity of conception behind both architecture and decoration in the mind of the builder is very evident, despite the use of artists of completely different origins.

Among the most astonishing of medieval utterances on architecture are the writings of Abbot Suger of Saint-Denis (1081–1151), which cannot be traced back to any known theoretical forebears, not even to Vitruvius. The case of the creator of a building describing how it was built is historically virtually unique, and it is to be explained as a mixture of apologetics (in answer to Cistercian puritanism) and the personal vanity of the author.[45] Suger accounts for the partial rebuilding of the abbey church of Saint-Denis (1140–44) by the need for more space on feast days; the retention of the Carolingian nave and the addition of a new choir and atrium presented Suger with an aesthetic problem, which he clearly recognised when he described himself as 'concerned about the consistency and coherence of the old work and the new' ('de convenientia et cohaerentia antiqui et novi operis sollicitus').[46] Suger does not deal with how the plan was arrived at, so no master-mason is named. Suger merely mentions, almost as if it were self-evident, that the twelve pillars of the choir denote the Twelve Apostles, in accordance with a widespread iconological tradition.[47] When crises in manpower and materials arise in the course of building Suger repeatedly invokes divine intervention, which surrounds the process of building and his own personality with a supernatural aura. Suger's special concern was to furnish his church with precious liturgical accoutrements, and in so doing he does not conceal the fact that rivalry with the furnishings of the Hagia Sophia in Constantinople is at the back of his mind. He counters the imagined reproach that precious materials are an end in themselves with a tag from Ovid, 'the work surpassed the material' ('materiam superabat opus') and with theological cunning he argues that precious stones and gems contribute 'by analogy' ('analogico more') to meditation.[48]

Suger's writings may have been inspired by Byzantine ekphrasis, but they have been convincingly classed with a type of memorial[49] of which the treatise of the monk Gervase on the rebuilding of Canterbury Cathedral is another example.

This treatise, entitled 'Gervasii Cantuariensis tractatus de combustione et raparatione Cantuariensis ecclesiae',[50] was described in the mid-nineteenth century as 'the most important document of medieval architectural history'.[51] Little is known of its author, the monk Gervase (c. 1141–1210) of Canterbury Cathedral. When his treatise is compared with Suger's writings, it is his precise use of building terms and establishment of aesthetic criteria for architecture that make his work extraordinarily 'modern' from the standpoint of present-day architectural history. After the burning down of Canterbury Cathedral in 1174, French and English architects ('artifices Franci et Angli') were consulted as to whether reconstruction or a completely new building was to be preferred, and finally the 'artifex subtilissimus', William of Sens, was commissioned to direct operations for a new building.[52] Gervase, who knew the original building well, gives a detailed description of the old cathedral before embarking on an account of the new (1174–85). The comparison of the two buildings is based on specific architectural features, but despite all his restraint, one has the definite impression that the aesthetic sympathies of the author are more with the new building. A few sentences from his comparison are here quoted:

> But now the difference between the two works must be mentioned. The shape of the old and new piers is the same, as is their thickness, but their length is different. That is to say, the new piers were lengthened by about twelve feet. The treatment of the old capitals was plain; the new ones are subtly carved... There [in the old building], a wall built above the piers divided the transept from the choir, but here [in the new], there is no division and the arms of the transept seem to meet the choir as one, in the keystone in the middle of the great vault, which rests on the four main piers...[53]

Whereas in Suger's accounts there emerges no clear dividing line between the person commissioning a new building and the designer of it, in Gervase a few decades later there can be detected a clear awareness of the technical and aesthetic competence of the *artifex*, with whose role the author identifies. In Gervase's comparison between the old and new cathedrals it is possible that conversations he had had with William of Sens and his successor, William the Englishman, are reflected.[54] Gervase's text is the most direct written evidence we have informing us about the thinking of early Gothic architects.

A knowledge of Vitruvius, albeit rather indirect, is indicated in the description of the human body in the *Liber divinorum operum simplicis hominis* by the mystic Hildegard von Bingen (1098–1179).[55] It is apparent that the text relating to 'Vitruvian man' is known to the author: 'For the height of a man is equal to his breadth when his arms and hands are extended on both sides from his chest.'[56] The human figure is thereupon interpreted as a mirror of the cosmos, Hildegard continuing: 'for in like manner the firmament has its length equal to its breadth...'[57] The tripartite division of the face[58] also indicates a knowledge of Vitruvius.

The representation of man (microcosm) and macrocosm in a manuscript of Hildegard's *Liber divinorum operum* from the first half of the thirteenth century[59] has clear analogies with 'Vitruvian man' (*Plate 2*). This is even more the case in a representation of the *aer*, the lower air, in a manuscript of the *Liber pontificalis* from the end of the twelfth century (*Plate 3*)[60] which probably derives from a passage in one of Hildegard von Bingen's texts.[61] These layers of meaning played an important role in medieval thinking, and even in large-scale works of sculpture, as has been shown by the head fragment from the west jube of Mainz Cathedral.[62]

There was probably an application of the Vitruvian legacy in the case of the plan of the church of Cluny III.[63] Whether this was a special case or a widespread occurrence (at least among the Cluniacs) remains an unanswered question.

Sicardus, bishop of Cremona (d. 1215), in his work on the church building and its liturgical functions, *Mitrale, sive de officiis ecclesiasticis summa*,[64] gives a symbolic interpretation of church-building and its various elements which is a typical theological interpretation of architecture, quite lacking in architectural or aesthetic ideas. The architectural form of the church is traced back to the Ark of the Covenant and Solomon's Temple, as images of the *ecclesia militans* and the *ecclesia triumphans* respectively. The bedrock is Christ, above which lie the foundations, representing the Apostles and Prophets. Every single architectural element from portal to roof tiles is interpreted as a component of the *ecclesia universalis*. The church building becomes an ordered, functioning mirror of the living members of the Church. Such iconological treatment is frequent and of central importance in medieval architectural literature,[65] but architectural symbolism goes far beyond aesthetics and architectural theory, and so this kind of approach will not be considered further here.[66]

The importance of scholastic philosophy and its premises for both the scientific and the theological understanding of architecture during the thirteenth century has often been emphasised.[67] Geometry and arithmetic were given a special role in the interpretation of the cosmos. The importance of number as the principle underlying cosmic order had been elaborated in Antiquity in Pythagorean, Platonic and Neoplatonic philosophy. St Augustine drew on this tradition in his treatise *De musica*, in which he demonstrated how musical harmony conforms to mathematical rules. In the opinion of St Augustine, music and architecture are sister arts, both based on number, which ranks as the source of all aesthetic perfection.[68] In *De libero arbitrio*, St Augustine even describes form as the result of number: 'They have forms, because they have numbers' ('*formas habent quia numeros habent*').[69] Through St Augustine aand Boethius, who further developed this theory, a system of aesthetics based on numerical proportions acquired binding force for the Middle Ages. From the second quarter of the twelfth century onwards, mathematics and geometry became basic principles of theological interpretation at Chartres. Thierry of Chartres explained the mystery of the Trinity by the geometrical demonstration of the equilateral triangle; the relationship of God the Father to the Son was explained by the square.[70] For the theologians of Chartres the cosmos was a work of architecture, God himself its architect, and the mathematical ratios relating to the structure of the cosmos, music and architecture identical.[71] The Cistercian poet-philosopher Alanus ab Insulis (c. 1120–1202), who was closely associated with the ideas of the Chartres school, described God as '*mundi elegans architectus*', and the '*universalis artifex*', who constructed the '*palatium mundiale*'.[72] The idea of God as the builder of the world was also current as a pictorial image.[73] The Gothic cathedral has been construed as the 'model of the medieval universe'.[74]

Such philosophical and theological ideas provided the intellectual basis of the geometry of medieval masons' lodges, although the nature and scope of this are not at all clear, in spite of everything that has been written on the subject.

Before we tackle this problem, attention should be drawn to the position of architecture in the most important of the encyclopedias of the High Middle Ages, the *Speculum majus* of Vincent de Beauvais (c. 1190–1264).[75] Architecture is discussed in the second book of the *Speculum doctrinale*, devoted to the '*artibus mechanicis*'. The sections on architecture are compilations, partly taken over verbatim from Vitruvius and from the late Antique encyclopedia of Isidore of Seville.[76] The recurrence here of the Vitruvian components of architecture is evidence of a knowledge of Vitruvius's text, rather than of his architectural theory, exercising a determining influence in the thirteenth century.[77] Vitruvius's significance for the High Gothic has been overrated.[78] Whether the only surviving masons' lodge-book of the Middle Ages does in fact presuppose a real knowledge of Vitruvius, as has been assumed, is open to doubt.

The lodge-book of Villard de Honnecourt (active between roughly 1225 and 1250)[79] is strictly speaking the only manuscript of the High Middle Ages exclusively devoted to architecture that has a didactic purpose. Begun as a pictorial pattern-book by the much-travelled architect Villard de Honnecourt, it developed in his hands and those of his two successors into a written embodiment of lodge traditions,[80] which, however, by the very nature of its compilation is not composed methodically and survives in an incomplete form.

On the second page Villard speaks directly to the reader of the manuscript and defines his aims:

> Villard de Honnecourt greets you and begs all those who are engaged in the various kinds of work contained in this book to pray for his soul and to remember him. For this book will greatly aid you in learning the principles of masonry and construction work. It will also teach you how to render something accurately and how to do line drawing, according to the rules and precepts of geometry.[81]

The requirements for the education of the architect (although neither this nor any equivalent term is actually used) are as all-embracing as in Vitruvius. Villard himself had clearly taken both the *trivium* and the *quadrivium*.[82] Nevertheless, it is misleading to call Villard the 'Gothic Vitruvius'.[83]

It should be stressed that Villard's lodge-book did not have literary origins; it was rather a case of a text being added to a sketchbook. Only the section on lodge geometry (*Plate 6*; Hahnloser, plates 39–41) shows any formal correspondence between illustration and text, and this section probably depends on Roman traditions, as represented by the so-called '*Gromatici veteres*'.[84]

In his critical edition of Villard's lodge-book Hans R. Hahnloser has reduced his drawings and texts to seven headings: 1) architectural drawings; 2) applied architecture; 3) masonry and geometry; 4) carpentry and timber frames; 5) the human form; 6) representations of animals; 7) draughtsmanship ('*portraiture*'). In his architectural drawings Villard provides a comprehensive set of procedures, to the extent that all the elements of a church are represented – in plan and elevation, and in the depiction of detail down to the spire – the only methods of depiction not shown being isometry and sections.

The section on draughtsmanship ('*portraiture*') is the most important in the whole of the lodge-book. In his plate 36 Villard introduces this concept as follows (*Plate 4*): 'Here we begin the method of depicting [a figure] through drawing, as is taught in the art of geometry, in order to facilitate work...'[85]

Though a geometrical system is used here in relation to human and animal forms, it must be explained that, in contrast to the proportional figures of Antiquity, these figures are now not distillations of the measurements of organic forms, but autonomous geometrical figures (square, circle, triangle and pentagon) projected onto organic forms. The interpretation of bodies as triangles indicates contours and directions of movement but neglects the plasticity of the body and the relationship of its limbs to one another.[86] A reflection of Antique tradition, probably handed down via Byzantium, is still visible in the division of the face in terms of nose-lengths, but here geometrical form is independent of the form of the head. As Erwin Panofsky has demonstrated, such geometrical grids applied to organic form were actually used; for in a roughly contemporary stained glass window in Rheims Cathedral the geometrical grid corresponds exactly with one of Villard's heads.[87] Strange to say, the use of such a geometrical schema for architecture is found solely in the roofing of a gatehouse and in the plan of a Cistercian church (*Plate 5*), which bears the inscription: 'Here is a longitudinal church designed for the Cistercian Order.'[88] The plan is in fact developed entirely from a bay of the aisles used as the module. All the elevations offer only limited support for the theory that medieval buildings were built with plans or elevations developed out of a limited number of geometric formulae.[89]

Medieval lodges, lodge rules and the so-called lodge secrets have only a very limited place within the framework of the present work. Concern with these areas was largely a matter of historical interpretations projected onto the Middle Ages by Freemasonry and Romanticism, in order to find confirmation of their own ideas through a correspondingly interpreted past. The unravelling of such layers of interpretation, which sought to trace back to the Gothic functionalist aesthetic and 'organic' structures (Viollet-le-Duc) or backward-looking social utopias (Ruskin), and to find the roots of the mysteries of all-pervasive geometrical building rules, is by no means yet over.

The Gothic masons' lodge[90] and its 'secret' have largely lost their mystery; the 'secret' was perhaps never more than the geometrical representation of an irrational numerical proportion.[91] The role of 'measurement and number' proved, on critical examination of the sources, to be no more than the application of a given state of knowledge in mathematics and geometry to practical building tasks.[92] The use of *ad quadratum* and *ad triangulum* methods of design is not recorded until the late fourteenth century.[93] A series of stonemasons' books, partly in manuscript and partly printed, of the late fifteenth and sixteenth centuries contain practical building precepts and are not to be taken as compendia of architectural theory. We shall nonetheless touch briefly on the most important of these writings, since they embody the tradition of Gothic masons' lodges, which was apparently set down in writing at a relatively late date.[94]

The earliest of these sketchbooks would seem to be an unpublished pattern-book from the mid-fifteenth century, now in the Nationalbibliothek in Vienna. Besides the lodge rules, it contains a technical treatise in which very varied buildings are discussed, including utilitarian structures such as bridges and dams.[95]

A short work by Hans Hösch of Gmünd,[96] *Geometria Deutsch*, from the last third of the fifteenth century, intended for the use of artists, gives guidelines for the construction of geometrical figures under nine heads.

In 1486 there appeared the first printed stonemasons' book; its author was the Cathedral Architect of Regensburg, Matthäus Roriczer, and its title *Büchlein von der Fialen Gerechtigkeit* ('Little Book on the Correctness of Pinnacles').[97] In this short work a geometric method of design for the construction of Gothic pinnacles is demonstrated, 'on the basis of geometry', by means of increasingly complex methods of squaring the circle. One or two years later Roriczer published his *Geometria Deutsch*,[98] with guidelines similar to Hösch's for the construction of geometrical figures. At about the same time as Roriczer's *Büchlein von der Fialen Gerechtigkeit* there appeared a *Fialenbüchlein* by Hans Schmuttermayer[99] of Nuremberg, which set out similar geometrical principles for the same element of architecture.

A stonemasons' book of 1516, known only from two transcriptions of the late sixteenth century, by Lorenz Lacher (Lechler), was written as 'instruction' for his son Moritz.[100] Lacher's work is considerably more comprehensive than the pinnacle books of Roriczer and Schmuttermayer, and deals with all the components of a church, beginning with the design of a choir. As his predecessors had with pinnacles, Lacher uses a system of squares and circles for the whole of a building; he demands 'accuracy of measurements from beginning to end'[101] as a prerequisite of design.

Alongside these stonemasons' books concerned with monumental masonry, there also appeared special pattern-books on ornament, such as the pattern-book of leaves (1435) by Hans Boeblinger the Elder (c. 1412–82), now in the Bavarian National Museum in Munich.[102] It is striking that all these fifteenth-century pattern-books originated in South Germany. Whether these late Gothic stonemasons' books [103] are any evidence for ways of thought and design in the thirteenth century must remain an open question; Walter Ueberwasser has attempted to bridge the gap of two centuries between them and Villard de Honnecourt.[104] At all events, these stonemasons' books represent an older tradition, and probably also regionally conditioned modes of thought, completely untouched by the new departures in architectural practice and theory that were taking place in Italy.

Before turning to the architectural theory of the Early Renaissance, we must revert to the question of the transmission of Vitruvius. In Italy, Vitruvius clearly played a marginal role in the High Middle Ages. Attention was redirected to his treatise only through the early Humanists Petrarch and Boccaccio. A Vitruvius manuscript of the fourteenth century in Oxford bears marginal notes by Petrarch, and it has been assumed that Vitruvius was consulted by Petrarch in connection with the rebuilding of the pope's palace in Avignon.[105] Boccaccio possessed a Vitruvius manuscript, which he quotes profusely in his *De genealogia deorum*.[106] While it is unclear whether Cennino Cennini relies directly on Vitruvius in his work on the proportions of the human body in his late fourteenth-century treatise on painting,[107] Filippo Villani compares the painter Taddeo Gaddi with Vitruvius a decade later on account of his depiction of architecture in paintings.[108] Vitruvius had been relatively well known to the early Italian Humanists since the middle of the fourteenth century, so that the legend of the 'discovery' of a Vitruvius manuscript in Montecassino by the Humanist Poggio Bracciolini loses some of its credibility, especially since it was recorded that the latter was resident in Constance in 1414 and probably only 'found' the Codex Harleianus in St Gallen, where it had been preserved, in 1416.[109] There was thus no break in the transmission of Vitruvius during the Middle Ages.

In the fifteenth century there was a considerable dissemination of the knowledge of Vitruvius, as the numerous manuscript copies from this period make clear.[110] We know from various sources that Vitruvius was now not read only for antiquarian or literary reasons, but was also consulted on specific questions of building. Thus Antonio Beccadelli records in his biography of Alfonso of Aragon that the latter had 'sent for Vitruvius's book on the art of building' when he embarked on the reconstruction of the Castelnuovo in Naples (1442/43).[111] Pope Pius II (Enea Silvio Piccolomini) names Vitruvius in his *Commentarii* in connection with the building of Pienza (1459–64).[112] Other kinds of artists besides architects read Vitruvius in the first half of the fifteenth century, as Lorenzo Ghiberti's *Commentarii* show.[113] Ghiberti evidently had in his possession a medieval Vitruvius manuscript, which he partly translated, probably in connection with a planned treatise on architecture, which he never in fact wrote.[114] His translation of Vitruvius seems to have formed the basis for another by Buonaccorso Ghiberti (1451–1516), which used as models for its illustrations some found in the Latin

Vitruvius manuscript of Lorenzo Ghiberti, which in its turn seems to have gone back to a Carolingian original, comparable to the Sélestat Codex.[115] This translation was never published, however.[116] It has been recently demonstrated that Vitruvian proportions were drawn on by Lorenzo Ghiberti in his *Stephanus* (1427/28).[117]

Interest in Vitruvius during the Early Renaissance started with the Humanists, but soon spread to architects, and other kinds of artists and their clients, who were united by a common new interest in the architecture of Classical antiquity, for which Vitruvius was the only literary source.

Varied as medieval writings on architecture are, it may be noted that only in very rare cases were they produced by practising builders. The preponderance of the philosophical, theological and geometrical aspects of the subject clearly shows that concern with architecture was nourished from heterogeneous sources. The Middle Ages neither could nor did produce an architectural theory of its own, since as an *ars mechanica*, architecture occupied a relatively low position in the hierarchy of knowledge.[118] The name of Vitruvius is the only continuous thread that runs through the literature, but it cannot be concluded from this that Vitruvian theory had currency during the Middle Ages. It was not until the early Humanists that the significance of Vitruvius's system came to be recognised, and from their endeavours arose the first systems of architectural theory since Classical antiquity, which though not replacing Vitruvius, to some extent far surpassed him in intellectual significance.

3. Leone Battista Alberti

Medieval writing on architecture ranges from the descriptive to the speculative, the encyclopedic to the practical. It was not until the Early Renaissance, when the arts were breaking loose from their subservient function and winning a measure of autonomy, that the need to reflect on their function and principles emerged. Art became a mirror of measurable reality; consequently, its laws had to be identical to those of the physical world or behave in a similar way. Definitions and classifications meant the description and prescription of rules.

In the early phase of Humanism, artists and craftsmen, schooled in the medieval tradition, were not yet taking part in this intellectual development to the extent that they could fulfil a requirement of this kind. Hence it is not unexpected to find that the first systematic exploration of the visual arts and architecture, before artists and architects themselves were able to formulate and systematise their ideas in words, was made by a prominent Humanist.

Leone Battista Alberti (1404–72)[1] wrote the key theoretical works of the first half of the fifteenth century not only on painting and sculpture but also on architecture. Born in Genoa on 14 February 1404, the illegitimate son of the exiled Florentine Lorenzo di Benedetto Alberti and the Genoese Bianca Fieschi, he spent his childhood in Venice. During the years 1416–18 he received a humanistic education in Padua from Gasparino Barzizza. Then he studied canon law, physics and mathematics in Bologna, but did not take his doctorate in canon law until 1428 because of family problems and illness. As a student he distinguished himself by literary works, a Latin comedy *Philodoxeos*, and a series of writings in the vernacular. A lifting of the ban on his family allowed Alberti to return to Florence after 1428, but it is not entirely clear where he was between 1428 and 1432. He was probably travelling through France, Germany and Belgium in the service of Cardinal Albergati. From 1432 until 1434 Alberti lived in Rome as secretary to the Patriarch of Grado, Biagio Molin; in the same year he obtained his first church benefice as Prior of San Martino, Gangalandi. At the Roman Curia he met a circle of important Humanists, including Bruni, Poggio and Biondo. His earliest study of the architecture of Roman antiquity and of Vitruvius probably dates from this stay in Rome. Within a short space of time Alberti wrote *Della famiglia* (1434). He reached Florence in 1434 in the retinue of Pope Eugenius IV, and there he became closely associated with the circle of artists centring upon Brunelleschi and Donatello. In 1435 he completed *De pictura* in Latin; this he translated into the vernacular in 1436 and dedicated to Brunelleschi. In 1436 he followed the papal court first to Bologna, then in 1438 to Ferrara, where the Council of the Eastern and Western Church was taking place. In 1439 he returned to Florence, and in the same year finished *Intercenales*, begun during his student days in Bologna, dedicating it to the mathematician Toscanelli.

In 1443 Alberti returned to Rome, where he lived and worked until his death in April 1472. Repeated journeying took him to Rimini, Florence and Mantua. He advised Pope Nicholas V on his building plans for Rome and completed a number of his most important aesthetic and mathematical works, the *Descriptio urbis Romae, De statua* and *Ludi rerum mathematicarum*. The ten books of *De re aedificatoria* were completed in 1452. It was not until the last twenty-five years of his life that Alberti was vested with tangible architectural responsibilities: in 1447 by Nicholas V, as superintendent of the restoration of important buildings of Antiquity, and after 1450 with commissions in Rimini, Florence and Mantua. In his last years Alberti was much occupied with literary productions, satires, and works on mathematics and ethics (including *De iciarchia*, 1468), in Latin and the vernacular.

Alberti's short work *Descriptio urbis Romae* should be seen in the historical context of guides to the marvels and sights of Rome, but it shows a completely new approach in developing a system of coordinates centred on the Capitol, giving an exact determination of the position of every topographical feature of the city. It is an excellent example of Alberti's gift for conceptual abstraction.

For an adequate evaluation of *De re aedificatoria*, which took shape between 1443 and 1452,[2] a thorough knowledge of Alberti's philosophical and aesthetic positions is necessary; but in spite of extensive literature on the subject,[3] there has been no satisfactory clarification of its mélange of Aristotelian and Neo-Platonic thought, Ciceronian rhetoric, and the philosophy of the time (e.g. Nicholas of Cusa).[4] The question as to whether Alberti's treatise forms a theory in its own right still produces varying answers.[5] To describe it as 'a hotch-potch inspired by Vitruvius'[6] is going rather too far. The very juxtaposition of Alberti and Vitruvius reveals the extent to which Alberti strove for the systematic assimilation of his material.[7] The connection between Alberti's treatise and Vitruvius in both form and content is obvious in such matters as the division into ten books, and in his use of historical facts, technical detail, the theory of the Orders, the adoption of Antique building types, and in general terminology. But Alberti approached Vitruvius critically when it came to the information that the latter supplied about Antique architecture:[*]

> There was not the least Remain of any ancient Structure, that had any Merit in it, but what I went and examined, to see if any Thing was to be learned from it. Thus I was continually searching, considering, measuring and making Draughts of every Thing I could hear of, till such Time as I had made myself perfect Master of every Contrivance or Invention that had been used in those ancient Remains; and thus I alleviated the Fatigue of writing, by the Thirst and Pleasure of gaining Information.[8]

Alberti's criticism of Vitruvius is fundamental, especially with regard to the obscurity of his terminology:

> It grieved me that so many great and noble Instructions of ancient Authors should be lost by the Injury of Time, so that scarce any but *Vitruvius* has escaped this general Wreck: A Writer indeed of universal Knowledge, but so maimed by Age, that in many Places there are great Chasms, and many Things imperfect in others. Besides this, his Style is absolutely void of all Ornaments, and he wrote in such a Manner, that to the *Latins* he seems to write *Greek*, and to the *Greeks*, *Latin*: But indeed it is plain from the Book itself, that he wrote neither *Greek* nor *Latin*,

[*]Quotations from *De re aedificatoria* in this chapter are in James Leoni's English translation of 1755.

and he might almost as well have never wrote at all, at least with Regard to us, since we cannot understand him.[9]

Although Alberti takes over Vitruvius's basic principles of architecture – *firmitas, utilitas, venustas* – his own aesthetic ideas are radically different. Alberti does not stop, as Vitruvius does, at the description of phenomena, but inquires into the principles that underlie them.

In the introduction to his work – in contrast to Vitruvius, Albertie does not have a preface before each book of it – Alberti defines the task of architecture and the architect in terms of social commitment, of service to humanity. He thus defends architecture's pre-eminence among the Arts:

> But if you take a View of the whole Circle of Arts, you shall hardly find one but what, despising all others, regards and seeks only its own particular Ends: Or if you do meet with any of such a Nature that you can in no wise do without it, and which yet brings along with it Profit [*utilitas*] at the same Time, conjoined with Pleasure [*voluptas*] and Honour [*dignitas*], you will, I believe, be convinced, that Architecture is not to be excluded from that Number. For it is certain, if you examine the Matter carefully, it is inexpressibly delightful, and of the greatest Convenience to Mankind in all Respects, both publick and private; and in Dignity not inferior to the most excellent.[10]

Alberti's definition of the architect anticipates his later definition of architecture, but goes beyond that to contribute to the self-image of the Renaissance architect, in distinguishing his calling from that of the craftsman (*faber*):

> For it is not a Carpenter or a Joiner that I thus rank with the greatest Masters in other Sciences; the manual Operator being no more than an Instrument to the Architect. Him I call an Architect, who, by sure and wonderful Art and Method, is able, both with Thought and Invention, to devise, and, with Execution, to compleat all these Works, which, by means of the Movement of great Weights, and the Conjunction and Amassment of Bodies, can, with the greatest Beauty, be adapted to the Uses of Mankind.[11]

The role of the architect in society is pitched high.

> The Conclusion is, that for the Service, Security, Honour and Ornament of the Publick, we are exceedingly obliged to the Architect; to whom, in Time of Leisure, we are indebted for Tranquility [*cum amoenitate*], Pleasure and Health, in Time of Business for Assistance and Profit; and in both, for Security and Dignity.[12]

If Alberti then stresses the idea of lasting fame, by doing so he clearly defines the role of the architect as that of a responsible shaper of the human environment.

In the structuring of his treatise, Alberti starts with the idea that a building is *a kind of body*, consisting of lines and materials, in which the lines are produced by mind, the material obtained from Nature.[13] Alberti builds up his treatise logically, beginning, after some basic definitions of architecture, by discussing materials and construction, then types of building and their functions, and finally the subjects of ornament and beauty. The Vitruvian concepts of *firmitas, utilitas* and *venustas* determine the structure of Alberti's exposition of architecture.[14]

Book I: Definitions (design).
Books II and III: *Firmitas* (materials and construction).
Books IV and V: *Utilitas* (building types and their uses).

Books VI–IX: *Venustas* (ornament; sacred, public and private buildings; the theory of proportion).

Book X: General conclusions.

Alberti's treatise, written in Latin, is not primarily for architects, but for the circle of Humanist patrons desiring a set of criteria for their building projects. The impetus for its composition probably came from Lionello d'Este.[15] Alberti's republicanism becomes evident in his whole approach, though he tries to conceal it behind a 'neutral' conception of different political systems, adherents of all of which might use his treatise. Alberti tells even the tyrant how to build his palace.

A first draft of the work was presented to Pope Nicholas V in 1452. In his introduction to the first edition of 1485, Angelo Poliziano points out that Alberti was still revising the text at the time of his death. His intention was to dedicate it to Lorenzo the Magnificent.

Alberti's definitions, which go far beyond Vitruvius, show his system most clearly. He thus defines the architectural drawing: 'we shall call the Design a firm and graceful pre-ordering of the Lines and Angles, conceived in the Mind, and contrived by an ingeneous Artist.'[16]

With a consequentiality foreign to Vitruvius, Alberti names six fundamental elements of architecture: region (*regio*); site (*area*); subdivision or plan (*partitio*); walling (*paries*); roofing (*tectum*); openings (*apertio*).[17]

The most significant of Alberti's reflections under these headings are those on plans (I. 9). As criteria for the quality of a plan, he names purpose – better to be understood as 'function' (*utilitas*), dignity (*dignitas*) and attractiveness or amenity (*amoenitas*). Here Alberti integrates the criteria of functionality, aesthetics and use.[18] The same chapter contains his analogy of house and state, the state being regarded as a great house and the house as a small state. The two are held together by the organic concept that 'as the Members of the Body are correspondent to each other, so it is fit that one Part should answer to another in a Building; whence we say, that great Edifices require great Members.'[19] The organic nature of Alberti's conception of architecture is shown in the requirement: 'Let your Building therefore be such, that it may not want any Members which it has not, and that those which it has, may not in any Respect deserve to be condemned.'[20]

Alberti is aware of the danger of the ossification of architectural norms, and counters this with the demand for *varietas*, so as 'to avoid falling into the Error of Excess, so as to seem to have made a Monster with Limbs disproportionable...'[21] Such formulations show Alberti's desire for *varietas*,[22] in the sense of keeping architectural alternatives open: 'And these ought to agree one Member with another to perfect and compose the main Design and Beauty of the whole...'[23]

The difficulty in assessing Alberti results from his discerning admiration of Antiquity and, as is yet to be shown, from his unlimited faith in the validity of mathematical proportions on the one hand; and on the other, from the fact that for him Classical antiquity is not simply the unsurpassable and normative, for he believes in the possibility of developing further in the tradition of the Ancients, in order 'to produce something of our own Invention, and to endeavour to acquire equal or greater Praise than they did.'[24]

There is a certain inconsistency in Alberti's outlook in that he deals, like Vitruvius, exclusively with Antique forms of building, yet he sometimes takes a totally un-Vitruvian standpoint, in for example stating that the wall, and not the support, is a fundamental element of architecture: 'a Row of Columns being indeed nothing else but a Wall open and discontinued in several Places.'[25] Yet the proportions of a wall are calculated from those of Antique columns. For Alberti, pillars and columns are not mutually exclusive alternatives, since they are both derived from the wall.[26] Rudolf Wittkower's very strictly conceived limitations of pillars to archivolts and columns to architraves[27] are possibilities for Alberti, not fixed rules.[28] The fact that elsewhere he declares the column or support to be the structural skeleton (*'ossa'*)[29] of architecture, and at the same time describes the column as the most important architectural ornament (*'primarium ornamentum'*),[30] bridges the gulf between his own approach and that of Antiquity.

Like Vitruvius, Alberti believes that architecture has its origins in *utilitas*, but he subdivides Vitruvius's concept of *utilitas* according to the functions of different types of building. He distinguishes between buildings that merely serve *necessitas* (the needs of life), others that serve *opportunitas* (fitness for a given purpose), and other that serve *voluptas* (passing enjoyment).[31] The *varietas* afforded by different solutions of building tasks is seen by Alberti as the desirable expression of human individuality, to be ranked higher than mere fulfilment of function. Alberti roots architecture firmly in human individuality and the structure of society.

> So that if upon considering the various Sorts of Buildings, we should say, that some were contrived by Necessity, some by Convenience, and some by Pleasure, it might, perhaps, be no ill Definition of the Matter. Yet when we take a View of the great Plenty and Variety of Buildings all about us, we easily perceive that all were not erected merely upon those Accounts, or for one Occasion more than another, but that this great Variety and Difference among them, are owing principally to the Variety there is among Mankind. So that, if according to our Method we would make a careful Enquiry into their Sorts and Parts, it is here that we must begin our Disquisition, namely, from the Nature of Mankind, and wherein they differ from one another; since upon their Account it is that Buildings are erected, and for these Uses varied: So that having thoroughly considered these Things, we may treat of them more clearly.[32]

Alberti discusses both public and private buildings, treating the question of appropriateness for the individual within the framework of the community as a primary one. Size and ornament of a building should be apt to the function of the building and appropriate to its occupants; function (*utilitas*) thus acquires an influence over the aesthetic criteria of *venustas*, but the latter are not absorbed in the former.[33]

Alberti deals with more strictly aesthetic questions in the second half of his treatise, especially in Book IX. Chapter 5 of Book IX constitutes the theoretical centre of the work, in which the key definitions of beauty (*pulchritudo*) and ornament (*ornamenta*) are given.[34] Here too Alberti sets out from an organic way of regarding architecture, in terms of the body:

> I now come once more to those Points which I before promised to enquire into, namely, wherein it is that Beauty and Ornament, universally considered, consist, or rather whence they arise. An Enquiry of the utmost Difficulty; for whatever the Property be which is so gathered and collected from the whole Number and

Nature of the several Parts, or to be imparted to each of them according to a certain and regular Order, or which must be contrived in such a Manner as to join and unite a certain Number of Parts into one Body or Whole, by an orderly and sure Coherence and Agreement of all those Parts: Which Property is what we are here to discover; it is certain, such a Property must have in itself something of the Force and Spirit of all the Parts with which it is either united or mixed, otherwise they must jar and disagree with each other, and by such Discord destroy the Uniformity or Beauty of the Whole.[35]

Alberti is aware of the relativity of 'beauty', but attempts to refer it back, in neo-Platonic fashion, to a fixed criterion, 'a certain inborn insight'.[36] Applied to architecture: '...the Judgment which you make that a Thing is beautiful, does not proceed from mere Opinion, but from a secret Argument and Discourse implanted in the Mind itself...'[37]

Alberti names three criteria of beauty: 1) number (*numerus*); 2) proportion (*finitio*); 3) distribution (*collocatio*). The sum of these concepts, for Alberti, is harmony (*concinnitas*), the key aesthetic concept of his architectural theory.

Alberti's observations on number are derived from Nature. He notes the rule of odd and even numbers in Nature, and applies this as a law to architecture:

The first Thing they observed, as to Number, was that it was of two Sorts, even and uneven, and they made use of both, but in different Occasions: For, from the Imitation of Nature, they never made the Ribs of their Structure, that is to say, the Columns, Angles and the like, in uneven Numbers; as you shall not find any Animal that stands or moves upon an odd Number of Feet. On the contrary, they made their Apertures always in uneven Numbers, as Nature herself has done in some Instances, for tho' in Animals she has placed an Ear, an Eye, and a Nostril on each Side, yet the great Aperture, the Mouth, she has set singly in the Middle.[38]

Albert recognises a series of optimal numbers, which 'stand nearer to nature' (4, 5, 6, 7, 8, 9, 10), and have a corresponding significance for architecture. On the other hand, 'irrational' numbers, which are only arrived at by geometrical means, play a smaller part because of their incommensurability.[39]

Alberti's conception of proportion (*finitio*), which corresponds roughly to *symmetria* and *eurythmia* in Vitruvius, covers the modern idea of proportion, but in a broader sense. Alberti's definition of proportion is as follows: 'a certain mutual Correspondence of those several Lines, by which the Proportions are measured, whereof one is the Length, the other the Breadth, and the other the Height.'[40]

In Alberti's opinion, proportions are immutable, like the laws of Nature. Adducing Pythagoras he states: 'It is absolutely certain that Nature always remains the same in all respects.'[41] Alberti stands in a tradition running from St Augustine to Boethius when he identifies the laws of proportion in architecture with the theory of harmony in music; indeed, he actually transfers the theory of harmony from music to architecture.[42] *Harmonia* in music and *finitio* in architecture are subject to the same *natural* laws. Here Alberti is clearly standing for the existence of fixed rules.

Distribution (*collocatio*) is likewise traced back to Nature; the concept defines the position of parts of a building relative to one another. The natural laws already observed by Alberti in the case of numbers lead him here to demand architectural symmetry (in the modern sense); 'So agreeable it is to Nature, that the Members on the right Side should exactly answer the left:'[43] Here Alberti requires symmetry as if it were a law of Nature, which Claude Perrault was to formulate in a completely different context at the end of the seventeenth century as *'beauté positive'*.

For Alberti, beauty (*pulchritudo*) arises from the conjunction of *numerus, finitio*, and *collocatio*. Instead of the concept of beauty he employs 'harmony' (*concinnitas*); in other words beauty for him consists in *concinnitas*. His definition runs:

> we may conclude Beauty to be such a Consent and Agreement of the Parts of a Whole in which it is found, as to Number, Finishing and Collocation, as Congruity, that is to say, the principal Law of Nature requires.
>
> (*'pulchritudinem esse quendam consensum et conspirationem partium in eo, cuius sunt, ad certum numerum finitionem collocationemaque habitam, ita uti concinnitas, hoc est absoluta primariaque ratio naturae, postularit.'*)[44]

Concinnitas is the absolute and supreme law of Nature, the *absoluta primariaque ratio naturae*, 'and runs through every Part and Action of Man's Life and every Production of Nature herself, which are all directed by the Law of Congruity...'[45] With his concept of *concinnitas*, Alberti equates the laws of Nature with the law of beauty and that in turn with the laws of architecture. *Concinnitas* stands above Nature; it is the governing principle of creation.[46]

The application of *concinnitas* to architecture rests for Alberti on the observation and imitation of Nature, whose multiplicity of phenomena he sees reflected in architecture in the different Orders:

> And considering that one Building differed from another, upon account of the End for which it was raised, and the Purpose which it was to serve, as we have shewn in the foregoing Books, they found it necessary to make them of various Kinds. Thus from an Imitation of Nature they invented three Manners of adorning a Building, and gave them Names drawn from their first Inventors. One was better contrived for Strength and Duration: This they called *Doric*; another was more taper and beautiful, this they named *Corinthian*; another was a Kind of Medium composed of the other two, and this they called *Ionic*. Thus much related to the whole Body in general.[47]

The fact that Alberti sees architecture as analogous to the infinite multiplicity of phenomena in Nature prevents his rules from being hardened into dogma. Alberti's prescriptions set out possibilities of building, but there are alternatives which he cites himself in some cases.

Alberti's conception of beauty transcends aesthetics. For him beauty possesses an active moral quality, it is a protective power...Alberti utters the bold thought:

> But beauty will have such an Effect even upon an enraged Enemy, that it will disarm his Anger, and prevent him from offering it any Injury: Insomuch that I will be bold to say, there can be no greater Security to any Work against Violence and injury, than Beauty and Dignity.[48]

Alberti has no canon of the Orders as such. He treats the Orders he knows in Book VII. 6, but he divorces the use of them from the Vitruvian system of *decor*, from their innate appropriateness to the kind of building in question. He is the first to recognise the Composite order – he calls it the *'genus italicum'* – but he does not seem to recognise the Tuscan order as an independent one.[49] Evidence of concrete interest in the Orders is scanty in Alberti, and it is thus very unlikely that a work, *I cinque ordini architettonici*, long attributed to him, is actually by him.[50]

Alberti's concept of ornament or adornment (*ornamentum*) is less developed than Vitruvius's. For Vitruvius the question of *decor* consists in whether the form is appropriate to the content, not in whether ornament is applied or not. For Alberti, ornament or adornment is something superimposed, in the modern sense:

> If this be granted we may define Ornament to be a Kind of an auxiliary Brightness and Improvement to Beauty. So that then Beauty is somewhat lovely which is proper and innate, and diffused over the whole Body, and Ornament somewhat added or fastened on, rather than proper and innate.[51]

Here Alberti is taking the momentous step of describing ornament no longer as an integral part of architecture but as a specious addition. He anticipates the trend towards an ever-widening divergence between form and decoration, until the demand is made for ornament to vanish completely from architecture.[52] The concepts of *decor* or *decus*, significantly, appear only rarely and peripherally in Alberti, whereas the term *ornamentum* is very frequent.[53]

Alberti concurs with Vitruvius, however, insofar as the use of ornament is concerned, when he takes as his criterion its appropriateness to the function of a building or of a building to its occupant. Only ornament befitting the status of the occupant can be judged good.[54] For example:

> Between a House in Town and a House in the Country, there is this further Difference, besides what we took notice of in the last Book, that the Ornaments, for that in Town ought to be much more grave than those for a House in the Country, where all the gayest and most licentious Embellishments are allowable.[55]

Alberti draws a more ambitious picture of the professional formation of the architect than does Vitruvius, although he renounces the need for some of the detailed knowledge that Vitruvius demands.[56] Alberti conceives of a good architect as being in the nature of a spiritually highly prepared scholar. An architect is the representative of an élite:

> Doubtless Architecture is a very noble Science, not fit for every Head. He ought to be a Man of a fine Genius, of a great Application, of the best Education, of thorough Experience, and especially of strong Sense and sound Judgement, that presumes to declare himself an Architect. It is the Business of Architecture, and indeed its highest Praise, to judge rightly what is fit and decent: For though Building is a Matter of Necessity, yet convenient Building is both of Necessity and Utility too: But to build in such a Manner, that the Generous shall commend you, and the Frugal not blame you, is the Work only of a prudent, wise and learned Architect.[57]

The architect should absorb whatever seems to him might serve as a model, and imitate it. Alberti is not thinking of wholesale copying, but rather a thorough understanding and recreation of principles, which must always rest on the laws of Nature.

For Alberti the most important elements in the formation of an architect are painting and mathematics. Painting – or rather, drawing – is of particular importance in his eyes, because he believes that the architectural idea is crystallised in the drawn design. In both his theory and practice, design and execution were divorced from one another. For him, mathematics is indispensable, in order to establish proportion (*finitio*), without which no *concinnitas* is possible.

When Alberti began working on his treatise,[58] he had no experience as an architect. Only when he was near to finishing the first draft of *De re aedificatoria* in 1452 did he begin to receive commissions.

The relationship between Alberti's theory and his own architectural practice has been very variously judged. The fact that with him theory preceded practice might suggest seeing the latter as a built embodiment of the former, a line of approach followed pre-eminently by Rudolf Wittkower.[59] By contrast, in recent times Hellmut Lorenz[60] has been the main representative of the tendency to see Alberti's treatise as the work of a Humanist historian, to which no significance should be attached in the assessment of his own buildings.[61] Such a view of Alberti is supported by the fact that in his theoretical work he treats only the architecture of Antiquity, and does not mention contemporary exercises such as church façades, which make up the core of his own (later) work.[62] Nevertheless, it seems questionable as to whether such a wedge should be driven between his theory and his practice as to talk of 'fundamental incompatibility'.[63]

Paul von Naredi-Rainer has demonstrated how Alberti's conception of *concinnitas* was realised in his own buildings.[64] Richard Krautheimer has shown that Alberti's S. Andrea in Mantua is based on the '*templum Etruscum*' described by Vitruvius (IV. 7) and that in planning it he overcame cruxes in the text, for which he had supplied his own interpretations (*De re aedificatoria* VII. 4), by recourse to Roman buildings with which he was familiar.[65] In a letter of 12 October 1470 to Ludovico Gonzaga, Alberti comments on his own design for S. Andrea: 'This form of temple has been called a shrine [*sacrum*] by the ancient Etruscans…'[66] Alberti believed that in Mantua he was building a tunnel-vaulted Etruscan temple with subsidiary transverse tunnel vaults. Out of this historical misunderstanding arose a spatial conception that was to have a decisive influence on Western church-building for several centuries.

Alberti's buildings are certainly not devoid of any connection with his theory, but he did make use of the licence that he conceded intellectually to the architect to create new resolutions of Classical models and theoretical principles.

Alberti's treatise never attained the widespread impact that Vitruvius, Serlio and Vignola enjoyed for centuries. Making high claims for what architecture should be, his book was nevertheless of little use as a practical handbook for the architect, since it did not treat specific buildings originally and lacked illustrations.[67] In the theoretical domain, however, Alberti's treatise is perhaps the most significant contribution ever made to the literature of architecture.

Editions

Alberti's writings in the vernacular are available in a critical edition: Leon Battista Alberti, *Opere volgari*, ed. Cecil Grayson, 3 vols, Bari 1960–73.

The most convenient edition of the shorter works (*Della pictura libri tre, De statua*), with German translation, is Leon Battista Alberti, *Kleinere kunsttheoretische Schriften*, ed. Hubert Janitschek, Vienna 1877 (reissued Osnabrück 1970). For the *Descriptio urbis Romae*, the following editions should be consulted: *Codice topografico della Città di Roma*, Vol. IV, ed. Roberto Valentini and Giuseppe Zucchetti, Rome 1953, pp. 209–22;

L. Vagnetti, *'La "Descriptio Urbis Romae".
Uno scritto poco noto di Leon Battista Alberti'*,
Quaderno, no. 1, Università degli Studi di
Genova, Facoltà di Architettura, 1968, pp. 25–
88.

The treatise on architecture *De re aedificatoria* first appeared in print in Florence in
1485 (*editio princeps*). A facsimile of this
edition was published in Munich in 1975, and
on it is based the *Alberti-Index*, a concordance
compiled by Hans-Karl Lücke, Index Verborum, 3 vols, Munich 1975 ff. The first Italian
translation, which was also the first illustrated
edition, was produced in Florence by Cosimo

Bartoli in 1550. The most important modern
edition (Latin text with Italian translation)
is: Leon Battista Alberti, *L'architettura*, ed.
Giovanni Orlandi, 2 vols, Milan 1966 (vol. I,
pp. xlviii ff. lists all earlier editions and
translations). James Leoni's English translation
of 1726 (3rd ed. 1755) was reissued in facsimile,
Alberti. The Ten Books on Architecture, ed.
Joseph Rykwert, London 1955; New York
1986 (the English text quoted in the present
work). A modern English translation: L.B.
Alberti, *On the Art of Building in Ten Books*,
trans. Joseph Rykwert and others, Cambridge,
Mass. 1989.

4. Quattrocento theory after Alberti

With his treatise on architecture Alberti created a foundation of theory not to be surpassed by any of his contemporaries. His aesthetic categories were addressed to his own day, but his typology of buildings referred back to Roman antiquity, and he offered no directly practical models. His 'scientific' conception of architecture, his linguistic decision to use humanistic Latin, and a lack of clarity, must have led other authors to approach architecture in a more 'contemporary' way.

Such attempts naturally led away from the systematic architectural treatise to more diverting forms of presentation. Writing in the vernacular was a necessity, in order to reach a wider public. One must assume that it was as a direct reaction to Alberti that Filarete, the first architectural writer after him, preferred 'to describe the methods and measurements of building', and this he did, with his practical capability and experience, in the vernacular, referring those 'who consider themselves more skilful and learned' to the 'above-mentioned authors', namely Vitruvius and Alberti.[1]

Antonio Averlino, who adopted the surname Filarete (φιλαρετής, Friend of Virtue), was born in Florence around 1400, where he trained as a goldsmith and bronze-founder, possibly in the workshop of Ghiberti.[2] The latter part of his life was spent in Rome (c. 1433–c. 1448), where in 1445 he completed his chief sculptural work, commissioned by Pope Eugene IV, the monumental bronze door for St Peter's. From 1451 he was engaged as engineer and architect in the service of Francesco Sforza, Duke of Milan. His most important commission was the planning and construction of the Ospedale Maggiore (1456–65). His treatise on architecture was probably written in the years 1461–64.[3] We know from a letter of recommendation from Filarete's friend Filelfo (Francesco da Tolentino) of 30 July 1465 to Georgios Amoirukios, a doctor living in Constantinople, that at this time Filarete was seriously considering travelling to Constantinople.[4] Nothing is known about whether this journey took place, or of the time and circumstances of Filarete's death.

His treatise on architecture is written in the narrative form of a dialogue, and describes in daily stages the planning and building of the fictitious town of Sforzinda. The work has with some justification been termed a 'diary novel'.[5] The dedication of manuscripts to Francesco Sforza and Piero de' Medici[6] reveals that Filarete, whose career as an architect was not especially successful, was hoping to secure commissions as a result of his treatise; it did not, however, achieve this end. Although his treatise was used around 1490 by artists in the Milanese orbit (Amadeo, Francesco di Giorgio, Leonardo, Bramante, Cesare Cesariano),[7] his work remained unpublished and so had only limited influence. No systematic study of it was possible, until the editions published in recent times.

Formally speaking, Filarete's treatise is divided into twenty-five books of varying length. His ideas are not expounded as a system but introduced in loose narrative form.[8] His choice of the dialogue form and significant criteria of his treatise have been traced back to Platonic dialogues such as *Timaeus* and *Laws*.[9] The treatise begins as courtly table talk in which the architect instructs an assembled company about the principles of architecture. The narrative then turns to the foundation and stage-by-stage building of the town of Sforzinda: the description of this is interspersed with accounts of hunting excursions and inspections. In the course of excavations for a port to serve Sforzinda – in Book 14 – a 'Golden Book' is discovered, containing a description of Plusiapolis, a town situated in Antiquity in that spot. Filarete's friend Francesco Filelfo[10] translates this book, the contents of which are from then on interwoven with the account of Sforzinda. The architect of the city of Plusiapolis, mentioned in the '*libro d'oro*', is Onitoan Nolivera, an anagram for Antonio Averlino. The buildings of Plusiapolis are reconstructed from illustrations in the Golden Book, and several display many points of agreement with the designs which, according to the narrative, had already been made for Sforzinda before the discovery of the Golden Book – for example the plans for the cathedrals of Sforzinda and Plusiapolis.[11] It is thus clear that Filarete is claiming to realise the norms of Greek antiquity in his own designs. The account of the foundation of the city breaks off at Book XXI. Books XXII-IV concern drawing, painting and sculpture. Book XXV describes the buildings in Florence and Milan constructed for the Medici.

Filarete initially promises a systematic presentation of his material, stating his intention of treating first the origin of measurements and of the house, then the planning of a town, and finally the various types of building of Antiquity and his own time,[12] but he does not keep to this scheme. Basing his ideas on Vitruvian and Albertian concepts, he claims that architecture was born of '*necessitas*'. The human need for a dwelling is, in his opinion, analogous with that of eating.[13] Vitruvius's account of the origin of the house is linked by Filarete with the Christian tradition: after the Expulsion from Paradise, Adam became the builder of the first, or primal hut. Filarete gives us the earliest known representation of the primal hut. He shows how Adam forms a shelter for himself from the rain with his arms (*Plate 7*); there follows the depiction of a tent-like dwelling, and of huts with roof-beams resting on forked tree-trunks (*Plate 9*).[14] Later Filarete explains that these tree-trunks also led to the development of the column,[15] and gives as an illustration of this the framework of the primal hut, consisting of four vertical trunks forked at the top – the prototype of the column – with horizontal trunks resting upon them (*Plate 8*).[16] According to Filarete, the height of the uprights was measured in terms of human stature, and so the proportions of the primal hut are commensurate with those of the human body. Thus Filarete's archetypal dwelling acquires the status of a major architectural statement. It not only marks the origin of architecture itself, but it also embodies already the concepts of proportion and the Orders. Yet Filarete did not claim, as Laugier was to do in the eighteenth century, the primal hut as the norm for all architecture. In Filarete's work, the proportions of the human figure become the decisive scale of reference. He is the first representative of pure anthropometry: 'architecture is derived from man, that is from the human body, its limbs and proportions.'[17] The head as the noblest part of the human body becomes the standard unit of measurement, the module. Filarete relates the Orders to human stature in twofold fashion, linking their origin with that of the primal hut. He proceeds on the basis of five different kinds of human proportions, differentiated by their *qualità*: 'as far as I can discern, the qualities of human measurement are five.'[18] These five *qualità* are for him the axiomatic basis of the five Orders, but only the three Greek ones, Doric, Ionic and Corinthian, interest him. He arrives at very idiosyncratic distinctions between them, according to which the Doric column ('*misura grande*') is nine '*teste*' high – the ideas of man and column, head and capital, are interchangeable in Filarete's work[19] – the Ionic ('*misura piccola*') seven, and the Corinthian ('*misura mezzana*') eight.[20] The Doric order is for Filarete historically the earliest, and the most perfect. Adam as the image of God is for him the model for the Doric order.[21] Later the Orders appear in a clear hierarchy as a reflection of social structures. The Doric order befits the *signore* alone, while 'the other, inferior ones are for the *signore*'s use [*utilità*], requirements and service.'[22]

The proportions of the Orders given by Filarete represent a reversal of Vitruvius's specifications. Examination of his illustration of the Orders (*Plate 10*)[23], however, shows that what he depicts as Doric has no historical precedent but corresponds rather to the Composite order, while the Corinthian is depicted with unfluted shaft and rather simplified capital, and only the Ionic bears some relation to its prototype, with its voluted capital. Behind this distortion of Vitruvian typology lies, not archaeological ignorance, but the drive to express a Christian message. Filarete speaks in general of the squatness of temple proportions in Antiquity, which he interprets as the expression of man's prostration before the gods, whereas the Christian church, with its greater verticality, sought to elevate the human soul in contemplation towards God: 'And whereas they generally built them [their temples] squat, we, on the other hand, build ours tall.'[24] Filarete's treatment of the Orders is a typical attempt of his to link Graeco-Roman with Christian ideas, the latter clearly looking back to the Gothic.[25]

Filarete's total anthropometrism is obvious from his use of the concept of Vitruvian man (encompassment of the human figure in circle and square) – which he does not, however, illustrate – to base even the basic geometric shapes on human proportions: '... whatever it may be, the circle, the round, the square, and every other measurement derive from man.'[26]

Alberti's notion of *varietà* as the expression of human individuality leads Filarete to the further claim that, just as one human being differs from another, so each building is unique: 'You will never see any building, or... house or dwelling that exactly resembles another either in appearance, in form or in beauty.'[27] At the same time he formulates – for the first time, as far as the present writer can see – the possibility of limitless rows of identical houses: 'if he wished, man could build houses that resembled one another in form and appearance, so that they all looked alike.'[28] But he stigmatises this as an offence against the divine plan of Creation!

Filarete's anthropomorphic ideas turn in yet another direction, that of architecture as a living organism. Architecture, for him, is not only derived from human proportions but actually resembles the human organism in a more intimate way. Architecture lives, sickens and dies, as man does. What was for Alberti an analogy is transformed by Filarete into an exact representation of things as they are:

> I will show you that a building is really a living being, and you will see that it thus needs nourishment in order to live, just as man does, that it sickens and dies, and also, that it can be cured of illness by a good doctor... You might say that a building does not sicken and die like a man, and I would reply that indeed it does just that: it falls ill when undernourished, that is, when it is not maintained, and little by little falls into decline, just as a man, when he goes without food,

will eventually drop dead. A building does just the same. But if it has a good doctor when it falls ill, that is, a master-builder who repairs and cures it, it will stay in good condition for a long time.[29]

Filarete carries the verisimilitude of his organic conception so far as later to designate the client as father and the architect as mother of a building. The architect should develop his design in his own mind, 'ponder upon it, and give free reign to his imagination for seven to nine months over it.'[30]

Filarete's organic theory implies a kind of functionalism. This is most evident in his distinction between various types of private dwellings, which he enumerates as palaces for the nobility, and differing sorts of house for burghers and craftsmen, those of 'bassa condizione' and the poor.[31] Being reduced to the purely functional, however, the last-mentioned interest him little, 'because they don't require great expense or skill.'[32]

The clear separation of the architectural design from the actual construction of the building, already realised by Alberti, is linked in Filarete's mind with the ideal of the acquisition of great social prestige for the architect. The latter is both man of science and Humanist, and eats at table with the Duke, who respects his architectural ideas and causes them to be translated into a (fictitious) reality.[33] The intrinsic worth of the artistic design (disegno), as opposed to the process of construction, could scarcely be more clearly stated than in the distinction made by Filarete in calling the disegno for his town 'Averliano', and the town built from it 'Sforzinda'.[34]

Filarete's 'Sforzinda' is the first thoroughly planned, and what is more illustrated, 'ideal town' of the Renaissance.[35] It was to be built, however, not in a vague future but in the immediate present: the foundation stone is said to have been laid on 15 April 1460. Filarete plans not only its shape and layout, but above all its siting in the landscape, which he sets out in drawings[36] (Plate 11). Reference is repeatedly made in the text of the dialogue to the drawings. They are not mere 'illustrations' for the reader, but the direct product of the architect's invention. Filarete's drawings thus acquire autonomy, or even priority, vis-à-vis the text. The importance of drawings in Filarete's work opens up a new possibility for later architectural theory, that of the text becoming quite secondary to illustrations, or even disappearing altogether.

Sforzinda is a town with a centralised octagonal layout and a radial street pattern (Plate 12). In the heart of the town is a central square flanked by markets, the ducal palace and the cathedral.[37] Astonishingly, Filarete proceeds to describe and illustrate numerous individual buildings without indicating their location in the town. This is the case, for example, with the citadel, which is otherwise described in detail.[38] The individual buildings allegorically described by Filarete take up much space, and are sometimes far removed from known buildings of the Renaissance (Plate 13). The main tower of the citadel designated as 365 feet in height and with 365 windows (alluding to the number of days of the year),[39] is clearly reminiscent of Far Eastern pagodas; a connection with Hindu architecture has even been seriously considered.[40] There is, however, no mention of Asiatic sources in the treatise, and even Filarete's possible journey to Constantinople could only have taken place after its completion.

Towards the end of the work, Filarete allows his imagination free rein, in the manner of science fiction. He describes as his own invention a revolving tower in Plusiapolis, surmounted by an equestrian monument revolving with it, to the son of Zogalia (anagram for Galeazzo Sforza).[41]

In Filarete's most extreme project, the House of Vice and Virtue,[42] architectural allegory attains the dimensions of *architecture parlante* (*Plate 14*). A cylindrical building crowned with a monumental statue of Virtue reflects, in its inner compartmentalisation and means of circulation, a programme of educational instruction. Seven rooms must be traversed to learn the seven Liberal Arts, and the seven storeys correspond to the four Cardinal and the three Theological Virtues, or the Seven Deadly Sins, etc. Architecture becomes the external representation of an educational idea. Filarete's conception strikingly anticipates that of the Frenchman Ledoux for his salt-mining town of Chaux. With his perspective section of the building (fol. 144r; *Plate 14*) Filarete creates a new form of architectural representation.[43]

Filarete's treatise contains many contradictions. He presents himself as an exponent of the Renaissance, but his thought and style are still thoroughly pervaded by medieval notions.[44] On the other hand, his utopia, in the totality of its planning and its ideas of the division of human labour prefatory of the production line,[45] has eerily far-sighted elements. Whether one may see in Filarete's treatise a plea for a Christianised Greek antiquity as opposed to Alberti's Roman-oriented approach[46] is questionable, for Filarete also bases himself almost exclusively on Roman models. The literary form of the utopian novel allows him to exaggerate theoretical positions and architectural ideas to the point of scurrility. But it is in the very extremism with which he states his ideas that his contribution to the Renaissance understanding of architecture lies.

A synthesis and extension of the ideas of Alberti and Filarete is offered by the *uomo universale* Francesco di Giorgio Martini (1439–1501), well known as a painter, sculptor and architect,[47] but as an expositor of architectural theory only recently at all thoroughly investigated. He bears the stamp of his Sienese origins and the time he spent at the courts of Urbino and Naples. His role as referee in the construction of the cathedrals of Milan and Pavia (1490), and his meeting with Leonardo da Vinci, certainly influenced his later theoretical standpoints, whilst Leonardo, in his turn, became familiar with Francesco di Giorgio's architectural theory. Influence was mutual.

Francesco di Giorgio's architectural manuscripts were written between the 1470s and the 1490s. Their relative chronology has been greatly clarified in the last few years, but to what extent they are in his own hand remains controversial.[48] The treatises remained unpublished in his lifetime, but were nevertheless extensively used by the architects of the late fifteenth and the sixteenth centuries (Fra Giocondo, Peruzzi, Serlio, Pietro Cataneo and Palladio). The *Architettura civile e militare* first appeared in 1841 in the context of a military history of Italy.[49] An annotated edition of the two main redactions of the treatise, with facsimiles of the manuscripts, was produced in 1967 by Corrado Maltese. This edition was the first to afford a true insight into Francesco di Giorgio's architectural thinking. A translation of Vitruvius by Francesco di Giorgio, first published only recently, provides further insights into the genesis of his theoretical ideas.[50] We are not in this context concerned with the complicated problems of the chronology or language of Francesco's manuscripts, but we shall try to outline his ideas from a study of both main redactions of his treatise.

The first redaction is considered to be that known as the *Codex Saluzzianus 148* in the Biblioteca Reale in Turin, entitled *Architettura, ingegneria e arte militare*.[51] The contents of the treatise are unsystematically organised, and it begins directly with the building of fortifications, an activity to which Francesco di Giorgio especially devoted himself from the 1470s onwards. His debt to Vitruvius and his basic theoretical approach are abundantly clear from the outset, where he refers to Vitruvius in saying that every art and calculation (*'ragione'*) should be derived from the well-proportioned human body. The organic terms in which his theory is couched are evident when, for example, he speaks of the 'body of the town' to which the fortress as *'più nobile membro'* should be attached like a head, and in illustration of this he appends a town plan on which a male human figure is superscribed, with the fortress placed upon his head (*Plate 15*).[52] Francesco di Giorgio compares the ruler to the doctor, an analogy he has obviously taken from Filarete, whose ideas he directly embodies in his illustrations. However, the anthropometric approach is not maintained consistently, for a few lines later he writes of geometrical plans for the town without fitting them into any analogy with the human body. Yet he begins the following chapter on the town with a description of 'Vitruvian man', in which circle and square are brought into conformity with the human body. The accompanying very rough drawing[53] is probably the first surviving illustration of Vitruvius's text (III. 1. 3; *Plate 16*). The underlying anthropometric bias is confirmed in the introduction to the chapter on temple-building, where it is stated that all architectural measures and proportions are derived from the human body. The reflections here on the architect's professional image are a paraphrase of Vitruvius,[54] as is the very incidental mention of aesthetic principles,[55] which obviously do not interest him. Alberti's treatise was not yet to hand when this version was written. It is striking that Francesco di Giorgio immediately followed a survey of types of temples of Antiquity with a description of churches of *'moderne formazioni'*. Once more the plan is inspired by the proportions of the human body and the chancel is compared to the head: 'And basilicas having the proportions and shape of the human body, as a man's head is the most important part of the latter, so the chancel must be the most important part, and head, of the church.'[56]

This relationship too is illustrated.[57] Polygonal and circular temples are explained in detail in text and pictures. Again, in the chapter on the Orders, Francesco di Giorgio offers a graphic interpretation of Vitruvius's *genera* (IV. I). He actually derives the Orders in his drawings from the proportions of the human body, and explains fluting as being based on the number of human ribs.[58] Subsequent chapters continue the same basic thinking, containing specifications and models of geometry, particular kinds of buildings, and the construction of machines.

A supplement to the treatise forms a separate compendium of the architecture of Roman antiquity. Francesco di Giorgio expresses his fear that many buildings of Antiquity may soon disappear, and his desire to preserve them in drawings. The exemplary character of the buildings of Antiquity for him is indisputable when he defines the motive behind his treatise as the 'burning desire to recreate them'.[59] Some fantastic reconstructions are offered, such as those of the Capitol and the Palatine (*Plate 17*).[60] Here the manner in which Francesco di Giorgio pursues perfect symmetry, both as regards the exterior and in plan, is striking, for such consistency is unexpected before the Cinquecento. A number of Classical rotundas appear in the form of reconstructions,[61] as models for Bramante's *tempietto* of S. Pietro in Montorio[62] (*Plate 18*). These drawings, forming no part of any system, were obviously intended for publication. They form the first Renaissance compendium of architecture of the Classical world.

The later redaction of the treatise, entitled *Architettura civile e militare*, is a more systematic work. The manuscript in the National Library of Florence was probably completed in 1492.[63] The treatise is in seven books, a preface and an epilogue:

Book I.   Preconditions for building. Advice of materials.
Book II.   House and palace construction. Methods of discovering a water supply.
Book III.   Citadels and town-planning.
Book IV.   The construction of temples.
Book V.   Forms of fortification.
Book VI.   Harbour construction.
Book VII.   Machines for transporting materials, etc.

In the preface Francesco di Giorgio states his basic theoretical position. His starting point is a study of the texts and monuments of Antiquity, of which he speaks proudly of 'having seen and considered the majority' in Italy.[64] He complains of the difficulties of understanding the terminology of Antiquity, and intends to clarify these by reference to extant buildings ('concordando il significato col segno'[65]). Vitruvius remains his chief source, but he refers also to 'alcuni moderni', whom he feels, however, are already superseded. Francesco di Giorgio is of the opinion that architecture has only recently been rediscovered ('ritrovata'), along with its 'fondamenti, regule e conclusioni',[66] and maintains that modern architecture is full of errors and false proportions. His intellectual frame of reference has broadened considerably since the earlier redaction of the treatise, as is evident when he expressly refers to Platonic and Aristotelian philosophy, and takes the view that man is an 'animale sociabile' (Aristotle: 'ζῷον πολιτικόν') as the starting-point of his architectural theory.[67] In this lies an innate kinship with Alberti.

In Book II he argues for construction governed by climate, following Vitruvius (IV. I. I), but at the same time implicitly challenging the idea that architecture can be based completely on norms. For house-building he evolves a typology that goes beyond Filarete's, distinguishing five basic types of house, which he illustrates with many variations: houses for farmers, craftsmen, scholars, merchants and the nobility.[68] The layout of each house corresponds to its functions. The craftsman's house, for example, will have the workshop situated under the living area so that the craftsmen and his clients can work and transact their business undisturbed by the family.[69] Like Alberti, he makes no distinction in his treatment of the building of palaces for such different political systems as a republic or an autocracy, but like him believes personally in an ideal republic.[70]

In Book III, on citadels and town-planning, Francesco expands ideas already put forward in the first redaction of the treatise. Now, however, he makes the analogy not only between man and architecture but also between man and the cosmos, thus forming a bridge with the intellectual world of the High Middle Ages: 'man, called a little world, contains in himself all the general perfections of the whole world.'[71]

Against this background his statement that 'columns, particularly, have all the proportions of a man'[72] does not appear so arbitrary. The square becomes the navel of the town, whence all food is distributed. The analogy drawn by Alberti between town and house is referred back by Francesco di Giorgio to the proportions of the human body, which itself contains the principles of cosmic order.

In Book IV, on the construction of temples/churches, the old contradiction between basic geometrical shapes and anthropometric proportions recurs when Francesco di Giorgio declares the circle to be quite simply the perfect basic plan.[73] As further possible kinds of plan he stiltedly suggests the rectangle, and the combination of circle and rectangle.

He evolves a theory of the origins of architecture in connection with the Orders, but in contrast to Filarete, he does not start from the premise of the original correspondence of the proportions of column and man, but from that of their gradual approximation.[74] He claims to have achieved, by careful measurement, his own proportions for column and capital, superimposing human and architectural measurements, arriving by such a comparison at a *regola generale* which corresponds to Vitruvius's column proportions.[75] But Francesco extends the anthropometric principle still further by deriving the proportions of the entablature in temple architecture from those of the human head[76] (*Plate 19*). In every detail of the temple building he is able to trace and measure the proportions of the human body. For an example of a church with a rectangular plan he utilises the experience he has gained in designing S. Maria delle Grazie al Calcinaio in Cortona, c. 1484–90 (*Plate 20*).[77] Comparing this building with the module-systems described by Francesco – he uses modules of $\frac{1}{7}$th and $\frac{1}{9}$th – Henry Millon has convincingly demonstrated the architectural application of the module system.[78] It must, however, be admitted that Francesco starts in practice with a given module-grid into which the human figure is fitted, and not vice versa.[79]

In Book V Francesco illustrates and describes in detail and at first hand a great variety of plans of fortifications, a sphere of work that he was mainly active in for Federico da Montefeltre, as he liberally acknowledges.[80] In this redaction of his treatise, however, as regards this class of building, he gives up the strained analogy with the human body. At the end of this book he mentions the part played by *disegno* in the architectural design: a drawing has the task of conveying what is not directly communicable in words but lies in the *discrezione* and in the *giudizio* of the artist.[81] In Book VI he explains even more clearly the primary role of the illustrations in his treatise, noting that architecture consists not only of *concetti della mente*, but that these must be translated into *disegno*.[82] He insists on the marriage of architectural principles with talent and experience. Whereas in Filarete's treatise text and illustration are rather rigidly yoked together, presupposing a stark differentiation between the artistic design and its realisation, in Francesco's there is total unity between the two. His claim at the end of his epilogue, that 'without a drawing [*disegno*] one cannot express and clarify one's idea [*concetto*]'[83] marks a clear break with Alberti's Humanistic literary approach. Francesco as a theorist remains the practitioner with a pen in his hand, assuming the daunting task of reconciling his practical experience with the axiom that all architecture has developed from human measurements. More thoroughly than any other writer, he succeeds in applying an anthropometrically obtained module to architecture,[84] although with a metaphysical basis. Formally speaking, his idea is a forerunner of Le Corbusier's *modulor*.

Closely linked to the later redaction of Francesco di Giorgio's treatise is a recently published manuscript attributed to Baldassare Peruzzi.[85] If all the texts previously ascribed to Francesco di Giorgio are indeed his work, this manuscript is nothing more than a compilation based largely on Francesco, and is thus scarcely likely to be by Peruzzi.

Leonardo da Vinci (1452–1519) has only limited significance in architectural theor since his projected comprehensive treatise on architecture did not proceed beyond the stage of scattered jottings.[86] His practically-oriented approach is, however, especially worthy of note, since it synthesises ideas by Vitruvius, Alberti, Filarete and Francesco di Giorgio. We know that he possessed Alberti's treatise in the 1485 edition,[87] and that he annotated a manuscript of Francesco di Giorgio's and made excerpts from it,[88] which show an interest in the purely practical information, not in the theoretical framework. His well-known drawing of 'Vitruvian man' (*Plate 21*)[89] is part of a single sheet, and can therefore be related only to a limited extent to his projected treatise. Heydenreich has indicated the systematic approach behind Leonardo's sketches of centrally-planned buildings, and has assumed that the treatise, besides its theoretical part, was to have had an 'anthology of architectural models'.[90] If this assumption is correct, Leonardo's treatise would have been comparable with Francesco di Giorgio's. However, for chronological reasons it is not to be presumed that Leonardo was led to his project by Francesco di Giorgio. Most of his sketches date from the 1480s, whereas Francesco's manuscript was probably not in his possession until after the latter's death in 1501.[91]

Leonardo's ideas on architecture are most clearly expressed in the town plans and expositions of them that he set down on paper under the impact of the great plague of 1484/85, which caused the death of around one-third of the population of the duchy of Milan. These papers of Leonardo's are to be found in Codex B of the Institut de France in Paris, which also contains some of Leonardo's studies for sacred buildings. Here Leonardo expounds a radically new concept of town planning based on the principles of decentralisation, urban development, and hygiene. He presents the grid plan of a riverside town crossed by canals.[92] A typical passage, referring to an illustration of street crossings on different levels (*Plate 22*), runs as follows:

Streets *m* are six *braccia* higher than streets *ps*, and every street must be 20 *braccia* wide and have a gradient of half a *braccio* from the edge to the centre. In this centre there should be placed at intervals of one *braccio* respectively, openings of one *braccio* in length and one finger in width, through which rain water can run away into the drains which are laid at the same level as the lower streets *ps*. At each end of the aforementioned street should be a six *braccio* wide portico on columns. And you must understand that anyone who wishes to traverse the whole area on the upper-level streets can use them for this purpose, as likewise he who wishes to do so on the lower level.

No carts or other similar vehicles may pass through the upper streets, for these shall be reserved for the sole use of the better sort of people. Carts and other conveyances shall, however, pass through the lower streets for the supply and provision of the common people.

Each house must have its back to the next, with the lower level street between, and provisions shall be brought in through the entrances *n*, such as wood, wine and the like. Middens, stables and other foul-smelling places shall be emptied through underground passages. The distance between one portico and the next shall be 300 *braccia*, each portico receiving its light from openings in the street above. At every portico there must be a wide flight of spiral steps in a round casing, because if it is square, the corners tend to be used as privies. At the first bend there shall be a door leading to the public middens and urinals, and these steps afford access from the upper street to the lower. The upper streets start outside the city gates, and by the time they reach the gates their height is six *braccia*. The site thus described should be near the sea or some large river, so that the city's sewage and waste products, flushed out by water, may be washed away.[93]

The premises behind Leonardo's planning here prove to be unmistakably functional: priority is given to the separation of different types of traffic, and to sanitary arrangements. At the same time this concept of town planning seems to reflect the class structure of the inhabitants.[94] Leonardo is probably the first architectural writer to have expressed his repugnance at the cramped conditions and the stench and filth of the city, and to have contrasted these with the peaceful, contemplative life of the countryside. City-dwellers are for him 'full of never-ending illnesses'.[95]

Leonardo's ideas, far ahead of his time, are expressed in both designs and words. His design for a conical building which he calls 'a place where one preaches'[96] resembles an Expressionist sketch, and has the shape of a hollow globe, in the geometric centre of which, raised on a pillar, stands the pulpit, evidently so that the preacher is equidistant from all his audience.

Many town planning directions are phrased in the form of aphorisms, for example: 'The street shall be as wide as the average height of the houses'.[97] Practical and aesthetic considerations concur in the sentence 'A building must always be free-standing so as to reveal its true shape [*la sua vera forma*].'[98]

Leonardo's extant notes are very practically orientated, and might rate him the label of a functionalist *avant la lettre*, but one must reckon with a theoretical and aesthetic framework which he lacked time to formulate in words.

On the fringes of architectural theory is the *Hypnerotomachia Poliphili* by the Dominican friar Francesco Colonna (1433–1527).[99] There has been much speculation about the identity of the author, but certainly he belonged to the North Italian Humanist circle.[100] His long life was spent in the narrow triangle of Venice, Padua and Treviso.[101] The *Hypnerotomachia* is an allegorical novel in the tradition of the *Roman de la Rose* and of Boccaccio's *Amorosa visione*, and is told in the form of a recounted dream.[102] Julius von Schlosser has even described the book as a 'romanticised commentary on Vitruvius'.[103]

The involved allegorical plot of the 'Love Struggle in a Dream' cannot be related here.[104] The dream journeyings of Polifilo, in pursuit of his beloved Polia, are the framework for lengthy descriptions of architecture, enriched by literary fantasy. In the context of Antiquity falling into decay, architecture becomes a vision composed of experience and history, now attainable only in dream.[105] The tale is told in an artificial language, a 'kind of relatinised vernacular',[106] enriched with numerous Hellenisms. The author sets his dream in the year 1467, but his borrowings from Alberti (1485) and from a Latin translation of Filarete[107] acquired in 1492 by the friary of SS. Giovanni e Paolo, to which Francesco Colonna belonged, are clearly detectable.[108]

Despite the exceptionally fine woodcuts, probably based on drawings by the author,[109] which make the book one of the treasures of fifteenth-century printing, the text of the publication was a failure, since it was practically unreadable. Although Albrecht Dürer seems to have procured a copy in Venice in 1507,[110] the *Hypnerotomachia* only gained wide currency in the sixteenth century in France, through French translations.[111] In order to explain Colonna's very individual attitude to architecture in his descriptions and woodcuts, a few of them may be briefly examined.[112]

In a valley lying between high mountains, Polifilo is suddenly confronted by a towering construction of incredible height, which is described as an enormous stepped pyramid, on top of which stands an obelisk, crowned by a revolving brass statue of Fortune[113] (*Plate 23*). The monument is higher than Olympus or any peaks of the Caucasus, the length of the base of the 'immense and terrible pyramid of marvellous and exquisite symmetry' being given as six *stadia* (approximately 900 metres); 1,410 steps lead up to the obelisk, which is larger than all other known examples. In his description the author displays his antiquarian knowledge of obelisks, and a signed inscription by a Libyan architect is supposed to add verisimilitude to his account, which is probably based on a combination of descriptions of the mausoleum at Halicarnassus and the Tomb of Augustus in Rome.[114] Colonna paints a heightened picture of an Antique monument, which overwhelms his hero, putting him in a state of physical excitement and making him sob.

Further on his journey Polifilo comes across a monumental elephant carved in obsidian, carrying a green obelisk on its back.[115] This striking image was turned into a (somewhat chastened) reality by Bernini's monument in front of S. Maria sopra Minerva (1666–67) in Rome.[116]

Colonna devotes nearly twenty pages to the description of a door and its decoration.[117] Its geometrical construction is minutely described, the terminology largely borrowed from Alberti.[118] When Colonna states that 'the main rule of architecture is quadratura', and derives harmony and 'its admirable composition' from it,[119] he is echoing, as is Francesco di Giorgio, the late medieval system of setting out by the square.

The high-point of these architectural descriptions is that of the Temple of Venus Physizoa[120] (*Plate 24*). Again, the geometrical construction of this domed rotunda is described;[121] formally it is modelled on the late Antique structures of S. Constanza and S. Stefano Rotondo in Rome.[122] The architectural form of the temple, '*per architectonica arte rotondo*', is the setting for an initiation rite into the kingdom of Venus. A Dominican could only permit himself to express such pagan images in a dream.

Polia leads Polifilo into a *Polyandrion*, a temple set by the sea, containing many human graves (*Plate 25*), which is now ruined, but which has a powerful effect on the visitors as a vestige of man's early past ('*primaevo*') and as 'a worthy monument of great things for posterity'.[123] The text and accompanying woodcut convey a feeling of the romance of ruins, the thrill of the greater world of an unspecified past. The architecture of ruins becomes a reminder of a Golden Age, the emblem of a backward-looking utopia.[124]

Polifilo and Polia are finally united on the island of Cythera. This '*perameno loco*' (Colonna's italianisation of the *locus amoenus*) – 'pleasant place' – is a circular island laid out concentrically, where nature and architecture combine in planned unity.[125] Colonna is here probably imitating ideas of the Platonic Atlantis, on which 'greater and lesser girdles of water and land in turn encircle a central eminence';[126] the completely circular form of the *locus amoenus* as an island was also, however, current in medieval iconography.[127] In the centre of the island stands an amphitheatre, an imitation of the

Colosseum in Rome. In Colonna's description of Cythera, elements of the ideal state, the *locus amoenus*, and the kingdom of Venus are superimposed to form a perfect harmony between Nature and architecture. The regular form of Colonna's Cythera lies half-way between Filarete's Sforzinda and the island utopia imagined by Thomas More and Campanella.

Anthropomorphic architectural ideas run through the whole of Colonna's romance, often with clear reference to the figure of his beloved Polia. Thus a mausoleum can remind him of Polia's breasts.[128]

The work is full of echoes of Quattrocento architectural theory, here assuming an occult character. The whole world of Antiquity, which is seen as perfect, merges with the initiation rites of the cult of Venus, and finds its reflection in dream architecture set in a romanticised utopian domain, poised between learned antiquarianism and megalomaniac urges. It is this new mode of feeling for architecture that constitutes the significance of the *Hypnerotomachia Polifili* for us today.

The theoretical works of Bramante, the foremost architect of the High Renaissance, must be considered as lost, to the extent that they existed at all.[129] Bramante's *Pratica* seems to have been devoted mainly to the theory of architectural proportion. A programmatic engraving made by the engraver Bartolomeo Prevedari in 1481, however, from a drawing by Bramante,[130] represents the fragmentary section of a centrally-planned building in perspective form, and from what is shown, it is possible to deduce the form of the whole building.[131]

The eye-catching inscription '*Bramantus fecit in Mediolano*' has no doubt the unabashed aim of recommending Bramante as an architect as well as an expert in perspective. Recently it has been convincingly argued that Bramante is the author of the small work by a certain '*Prospectivo Melanese, Depictore*', *Antiquarie Prospettiche Romane*[132] (*Plate 26*). What is particularly interesting about this poem on monuments of Roman Antiquity, published around 1500 and dedicated to Leonardo, is the woodcut of the title-page, depicting the naked figure of the author kneeling in a circle, measuring geometrical shapes with compasses. Carlo Pedretti has used a letter from Guglielmo della Porta to Bartolomeo Ammannati to illuminate the meaning of this figure. The letter states that Bramante had urged every architect coming to Rome to follow the example of the serpent and slough off his clothes, and with them all that he had learnt elsewhere.[133] In his nakedness the architect goes back to geometry, perspective and Antiquity. With his move to Rome, Bramante broke completely with the architectural past, as symbolised in the woodcut, and became a reviver of Antiquity, and his work was soon to be placed on a par with its original monuments by, for instance, Serlio and Palladio. Serlio defined Bramante's significance, clearly marking a distinction from the Early Renaissance, by saying 'that he revived good architecture, which had lain buried since the Ancients until that time.'[134]

The only surviving statement by Bramante directly about architecture is his submission for the vaulting of the crossing of Milan cathedral, which he made along with others by Leonardo and Francesco di Giorgio.[135] Bramante's report, drawn up around 1488–90,[136] possesses exceptional conceptual clarity and rigour. That he gives prime consideration to statics (*forteza*) is hardly surprising, considering the complexity of the constructional problem. In second place, however, he places stylistic *conformità* with the rest of the Gothic building, in this echoing Alberti and showing astonishing historical sensitivity. Only after these considerations come the criteria of lightness of construction and finally of beauty. Bramante's suggestions for a square drum later found expression in the illustrations to Vitruvius by his pupil Cesariano.

The Franciscan friar and professor of mathematics, Luca Pacioli (c. 1445–post 1514), offers a remarkable synthesis of the ideas current at the end of the Quattrocento. Probably born in Borgo S. Sepolcro, Pacioli was a pupil of Piero della Francesca, and in the course of his career had close contact with Alberti, Bramante, Francesco di Giorgio and Leonardo da Vinci. Both a mathematician and a theorist about art, he was first and foremost a compiler, who was also not averse to plagiary. He neglected the duties of his order, and basked in the glory of the lecture circuit at numerous universities (Perugia, Naples, Padua, Pisa, Bologna). He was possibly the object of Dürer's mysterious visit in 1506 to Bologna, where he was lecturing at the time.[137]

His treatise *Divina proportione*, published in 1509,[138] is addressed to a wide circle of those interested in philosophy, perspective, painting, sculpture, architecture, music and mathematics.

Its first part deals with the *divina proportione*, the Golden Section, and Part II, rather loosely connected with it, is a hastily written survey of '*norma e modo... de l'architettura*'. Part III is an Italian translation of Piero della Francesca's *Libellus de quinque corporibus regularibus*, without Pacioli's naming his teacher as the author;[139] the illustrations of this section come from Leonardo da Vinci. Although Pacioli, following Euclid, takes the Golden Section as the *divina proportione*, it must be noted that, contrary to what is generally believed, during the Renaissance this proportional relationship played a subordinate role, and preference was given to integral arithmetical ratios.[140] The first two parts of the book are consequently unrelated, and Pacioli in his 'Architectural treatise' scarcely refers back at all to the Golden Section. The treatise and its contents are conventional in treatment, with a noticeable tendency towards the prescriptive, and a preponderance of theory over practice. Proportion and *proportionalità* emerge as the single key architectural concept. Combining the ideas of Vitruvius and Francesco di Giorgio – without naming the latter – Pacioli derives every measurement and form in architecture from the human body; in it are revealed the 'intrinsic secrets of Nature'.[141]

The concept of the town adumbrated by Francesco di Giorgio, with the citadel as head, in analogy with the proportions of the human body, is repeated. On the other hand, circle and square are retained as 'the most important shapes [*figure*]', and the notion of Vitruvian man is put upon a procrustean bed to derive these from proportions of the human body.[142] The proportions of the human head are derived from the equilateral triangle, a procedure which had already been employed by Villard de Honnecourt.[143] Pacioli leaves proportions with irrational number ratios to 'sound judgement' ('*degno arbitrio*'), simply stipulating *grazia* when calculating them.[144]

In general Pacioli's understanding of the Orders follows Vitruvius, but he adds psychological characteristics: the Ionic order for him expresses melancholy, the Corinthian, joy.[145] He discusses special theoretical problems with the Orders, but produces no rules actually applicable to built architecture. The treatise is of a rather improvised, fragmentary nature, a fact acknowledged in the dedication, and which he claims he will rectify by a more comprehensive work, never, however, written.[146]

Luca Pacioli, like Francesco Colonna, turns the theory of proportion into an esoteric doctrine, a '*secretissima scientia*', as the title of *Divina proportione* proclaims. The age of a relatively unfettered approach to Vitruvius and the architecture of Antiquity was over by around 1500. After that the trend is towards the normative and the doctrinaire.

By the end of the Quattrocento, the need was already being felt for a clarification of architectural concepts. Francesco Mario Grapaldi wrote *De partibus aedium*, which appeared in many editions between 1494 and 1618,[147] to try to meet this need, but the work is difficult to use because architectural terms with their historical explanations are not arranged in alphabetical order. There is a complete lack of any fundamental theoretical concepts. However, this first 'Dictionary of Architecture' was successful, as is shown by the number of editions it went through.

The Humanist Paolo Cortesi (1471–1510), in his essay *De cardinalatu* (Book II, Chapter 2),[148] expressed incisive views on one particular type of building, namely the palace. He describes the site and layout of a palace from a functional point of view, and recommends the imitation of models from Antiquity. Of particular interest is his interpretation of the two different sets of rules to which ornament is subject, depending upon whether it is external or internal. His ideas about exterior ornament are landmarks in the history of architecture, and clearly mark off the High Renaissance from the Quattrocento.[149] From his reading of Alberti, Cortesi comes to the conclusion that a palace with a magnificent and imposing façade can intimidate a rebellious mob and prevent them from plundering it. For the interior decoration of a palace, didactic sets of murals are recommended. Cortesi's text is an important document for our understanding of Italian palace-building in the High Renaissance.[150]

The surprising lack of evidence for any practicable prescription for the five Orders in the High Renaissance, before the publication of Book IV of Serlio's treatise in 1537, can now be partly remedied by a recently published manuscript from the Bibliothèque Nationale in Paris.[151] This manuscript, apparently written in Siena after 1520, and probably the copy of an earlier one, is connected with Peruzzi, and represents an important source for Serlio. Text and illustrations of this treatise reveal the existence of routines for handling the five Orders, and presuppose earlier craft-oriented attempts to arrive at their proper measurements. The craft-oriented nature of the treatise is revealed at the outset in the first comment on the Tuscan order, since the anonymous author starts with the assumption of a predetermined measurement for the diameter of the column, from which the dimensions of other architectural members can be calculated by subdivision: 'Note that you can have the column any height you choose; and divide it into six parts, which thus gives you its dimensions.'[152]

It is difficult to understand why such prescriptions for the Orders were never published, especially as the need for them is evident from the flood of editions of Serlio, Blum and Vignola once they saw the light of day.[153]

Editions

Filarete. The late nineteenth century saw a dubious partial edition, consisting of a partial Italian text and a partial German paraphrase, *Antonio Averlino Filarete's Tractat über die Baukunst neben seinen Büchern von der Zeichen-* *kunst und den Bauten der Medici*, ed. Wolfgang von Oettingen (*Quellenschriften für Kunstgeschichte*, N.F. vol. III), Vienna 1890. A technically excellent facsimile edition of the most important manuscript (Biblioteca Nazionale, Florence, Codex Magliabechianus II. 1. 140) with an English translation was published by John R. Spencer: *Filarete's Treatise on Architecture*, 2 vols, New Haven–London 1965 (vol.: *Translation*; vol. II: *Facsimile*; cf. the review of the translation by Peter Tigler in *The Art Bulletin*, XLIX, 1967, pp.352–60). The first annotated critical edition appeared in 1972: *Antonio Averlino detto il Filarete, Trattato di architettura*, ed. Anna Maria Finoli and Liliana Grassi, 2 vols, Milan 1972 (vol. I contains the illustrated pages of the Florentine Cod. Magl. II. 1. 140, although not nearly so well reproduced as in Spencer's edition).

Francesco di Giorgio Martini, *Trattati di architettura, ingegneria e arte militare*, ed. Corrado Maltese, transcription by Livia Maltese Degrassi, 2 vols, Milan 1967. *Il Codice Ashburnham 361 della Biblioteca Medicea Laurenziana di Firenze, Trattato di architettura di Francesco di Giorgio Martini*, 2 vols, facsimile and critical edition, ed. Luigi Firpo and Pietro C. Marani, Florence 1979; this facsimile is of excellent quality, and the philological transcription of the text is more reliable than in the Maltese edition.

Francesco Colonna, *Hypnerotomachia Poliphili*. Critical edition and commentary by Giovanni Pozzi and Lucia A. Ciapponi, 2 vols, Padua 1964. A reissue of an English translation of 1592: *Hypnerotomachia: The Strife of Love in a Dreame*, New York 1976.

Fra Luca Pacioli, *Divina Proportione*, Italian text with German translation and commentary by Constantin Winterberg (*Quellenschriften für Kunstgeschichte*, N.F., Vol. II), Vienna 1889. A selection with notes, containing Part II, the *Trattato de l'architettura* in full, in Arnaldo Bruschi and others, *Scritti rinascimentali di Architettura*, Milan 1978, pp. 55 ff. An English translation was announced in July 1991: *The Divine Proportion*, New York.

5. Vitruvian tradition in the Renaissance

As has already been shown, it was not Poggio Bracciolini's legendary 'discovery' of the Codex Harleianus in St Gallen in 1416[1] that focussed attention once again on Vitruvius; knowledge of Vitruvius had been relatively widespread – at least in Italy – since the time of the early Humanists, Petrarch and Boccaccio. Vitruvius formed the naturally accepted background to fifteenth-century Italian architectural theory, which, as we have seen, interpreted him extraordinarily freely. Linguistic and terminological difficulties, however, revealed the need for serviceable editions and comprehensible translations. Francesco di Giorgio, who makes frequent reference to Vitruvius in his own treatise, translated Vitruvius[2] into Italian in the 1470s. A number of other translations dating from the end of the fifteenth and beginning of the sixteenth centuries were never published.[3]

The late Quattrocento's preoccupation with Vitruvius centred in particular on the Vitruvian image of man as the measure of proportion (Vitruvius III. 1). In his *Architettura*, Francesco di Giorgio refers to this passage of Vitruvius, supplementing his remarks with a freehand illustration, and immediately goes on to say that the city and its buildings should follow the same rules.[4] Leonardo da Vinci, who had in his possession a manuscript of Francesco di Giorgio's text,[5] evidently used the Vitruvius passage verbatim when he made his well known drawing of Vitruvian man (*Plate 21*) and inscribed it with an Italian paraphrase of the Vitruvian text.[6] Leonardo combined the diagrams of the *homo ad circulum* and *homo ad quadratum* into one figure, whereas the later illustrators of Vitruvius separated them. It is possible that Leonardo's drawing formed a component of the architectural treatise which he planned but never executed, and for which other material exists.

Whereas the fifteenth century maintained a flexible stance towards Vitruvius, the sixteenth century saw the emergence of an increasingly dogmatic attitude. Editions and translations of, and commentaries on, Vitruvius became widely established as the vehicles of architectural theory, and even newly composed treatises fell under the influence of Vitruvius, who increasingly came to be regarded as normative. Sixteenth-century architectural theory developed against a background of 'Vitruvianism'. For this reason, it will be necessary to characterise the numerous editions of Vitruvius.[7]

The first printed edition of Vitruvius, edited by Giovanni Sulpicio of Veroli, was probably published in Rome in 1486;[8] appended to it is the text of Frontinus's *De aquaeductibus urbis Romae*. Although Sulpicio based his edition on a number of manuscripts of Vitruvius, it was soon seen to be unacceptably corrupt. Nevertheless, there were a number of reprints (Venice, 1495; Florence, 1496) and the 1496 edition includes five basic illustrations (an illustration of a compass card and various geometric patterns).[9]

Whether Fra Giocondo of Verona was involved in an edition published in Venice in 1497 is uncertain.[10] In 1511, however, there appeared a lavish edition by Fra Giocondo which provided a reliable text, contained an alphabetic index, and above all contributed to the understanding of the work by the inclusion of one hundred and forty woodcuts.[11]

In his dedication to Pope Julius II, Giocondo not only indicates the textual criteria for his edition; he also plays upon the preamble to Vitruvius's first book by drawing a parallel between Julius II and Augustus as great builders: 'You have surpassed not only the leaders of our time, but also those of the past in the number and magnificence [of your buildings].'[12]

Fra Giocondo's illustrations[13] had a decisive influence on the majority of later editions of Vitruvius, both in the passages selected for depiction and as models. For example, Giocondo illustrates the stories of the Caryatids and conquered Persians, whose effigies were introduced into architecture as supports of entablatures as a visible reminder of their punishment,[14] although Vitruvius (I. 1) relates these stories merely as an example of the necessity of historical knowledge in the formation of an architect. There is probably not one later edition of Vitruvius that forgoes the opportunity of illustrating this essentially peripheral passage. Were it not for the interest in this passage and the illustrations of it, the introduction of caryatids into Renaissance architecture would scarcely be explicable, since the Caryatids of the Erektheion in Athens only became known (other than through Roman copies) through eighteenth-century publications on Greece.

The methods of architectural representation described by Vitruvius (I. 2) as *ichnographia*, *orthographia* and *scaenographia* are illustrated by Giocondo as plan, elevation and perspective view.[15] Vitruvian man (III. 1) is reproduced by Giocondo in two illustrations[16] which provide the starting-point for almost all later illustrations of the passage (*Plate 27*). Giocondo is the first to illustrate the basilica at Fano described by Vitruvius (V. 1), though he provides only a plan.[17] This remote building of Vitruvius, to which he refers in his text, plays an important role in all illustrations of Vitruvius.[18]

Fra Giocondo's magnificently printed but costly edition of 1511 paved the way for smaller, cheaper editions which followed after an interval of a few years. The first of these editions appeared in Florence in 1513, again with Frontinus as an appendix, though this is not illustrated.[19] This edition is dedicated to Giuliano de' Medici. The woodcuts are considerably reduced in size, they are coarser in appearance, and some are printed the wrong way round (*Plate 28*). Compared to the 1511 edition, the only new woodcut to have been added is a depiction of Halicarnassus, which Vitruvius (II. 8) discusses when explaining the different types of masonry.[20]

Around 1514, the Humanist Fabio Calvo produced a translation of Vitruvius for which Raphael was meant to provide the illustrations.[21] Evidently because these illustrations were never executed, this translation was never published.[22] It would have been the first illustrated translation to result from the modern-style collaboration of a 'team' of Humanists and artists (Calvo, Fulvio, Raphael and Fra Giocondo).[23] The influence of Vitruvius on the Raphael circle emerges particularly clearly in the famous letter written by Raphael, with Baldassare Castiglione, to Leo X.[24] This letter is important above all for the light it sheds on the writers' understanding of Antiquity.

An Italian translation with an extensive commentary was produced in 1521 by the painter-architect and pupil of Bramante, Cesare Cesariano (1483–1543).[25] Cesariano based his translation on the Latin edition of 1497 and Giocondo's edition of 1511. The peculiarity of Cesariano's edition – reflected both in his illustrations and in his commentary – lies in the fact that his knowledge of Classical and Renaissance architecture was limited to North Italy. Cesariano saw his task as being 'to reconstruct Antique architecture by linking Roman prototypes with familiar buildings which appeared to have something in common with what was said in Vitruvius's text'.[26] His illustrations display the formal vocabulary of the North Italian Renaissance. As usual, the Caryatids and Persians[27] appear first, as illustrations to Vitruvius I. 1, but in an ornamental style that made them readily adaptable for contemporary use. Cesariano's extremely detailed notes appear in smaller type-face around the text itself. The Vitruvian terms *ichnographia*, *orthographia* and *scaenographia* (Vitruvius I. 2) are illustrated by Cesariano with a plan, section and triangulated elevation of Milan Cathedral,[28] which he well knew to be of Northern origin (*Plate 29*). Concerning the triangulation, he remarks in his commentary: 'And this is almost the same system as that used by the German Architects in the Arch-Cathedral of Milan'.[29] Cesariano's depiction of Halicarnassus[30] (Vitruvius II. 8) can be traced back to Giocondo's modest illustration of 1513, but its magnificence is more reminiscent of a North Italian ideal city from the end of the Quattrocento (*Plate 30*).

Cesariano devotes a detailed commentary and two full-page illustrations to Vitruvian man (Vitruvius III. 1). The explanatory notes accompanying the illustrations are, however, not entirely clear.[31] It is possible that Cesariano was familiar with Leonardo's version.[32] He is clearly still drawing on medieval cosmology[33] when he explains his depiction of the *homo ad circum*: 'And in the above illustration of the human body, through [the study of] whose geometrical limbs we shall learn how to, as we say, commensurate everything else on earth'.[34]

In an illustration elucidating Vitruvius's comments on the three Orders (*Plate 31*) (Vitruvius IV. 1), Cesariano indicates possible alternatives in the proportions; here too he makes use of the decorative style prevalent in fifteenth-century Lombardy.[35] This is the first time the Orders are brought together in one diagram, in the form which later became very widespread as a result of the work of Serlio and Vignola.

Vitruvius's basilica at Fano (*Plate 32*) (Vitruvius V. 1) is here depicted for the first time in plan, section and elevation.[36] Not only the design for the façade of the Santa Maria di San Satiro in Milan, attributed to Bramante (c. 1480, Louvre), and the façade of the cathedral at Carpi (1515), attributed to Peruzzi, but also what may have been projects by Cesariano himself for San Celso in Milan, have all quite plausibly been suggested as models here.[37] In his illustration Cesariano demonstrates the relevance of a classical type of construction, as he interprets it, for his own age. He remarks accordingly: 'In this passage Vitruvius has supplied the means of constructing all the above mentioned buildings [i.e. basilicas].'[38]

Despite its lavish and costly format, Cesariano's translation and commentary proved influential, not only because the Italian translation made the Vitruvian text accessible, but also because the commentary and illustrations established a direct link with current practice. To the historical understanding of Vitruvius Cesariano made no contribution, but he did promote the application of Vitruvius to contemporary building projects. Although the historical unreliability of his work cannot have escaped any sixteenth-century reader with a modicum of learning, his illustrations later superseded those of Giocondo in influence.

In 1523 a reissue of Giocondo's edition of Vitruvius of 1513 appeared in Lyon, the title-page of which promises a number of completely new illustrations,[39] which however turn out to have been copied from Cesariano's 1521 edition. The 1523 edition offers a curious mélange of Giocondo and Cesariano illustrations. In the case of

Vitruvius's definition of *ichnographia, orthographia* and *scaenographia* (Vitruvius I. 2), it offers both Giocondo's illustrations and those of Cesariano, i.e. the drawings of Milan Cathedral,[40] though without explanatory notes. The captions merely state that the drawings have been executed '*germanico more*'. The Halicarnassus illustration follows Cesariano, whilst the diagrams of 'Vitruvian man' and the basilica of Fano follow Fra Giocondo.[41] The speed with which the publishers wished to get this edition onto the market is evident. Although the format is almost identical with that of the 1513 edition, it is obvious that the printer in Lyon did not have access to the blocks used for the Florentine edition, with the result that all the woodcuts (not just the Cesariano copies) had to be made from scratch, with a reduction in quality. Such was the haste that one illustration was even printed upside down.[42]

In 1524 an allegedly new translation by Francesco Lutio of Castel Durante (hence his name Durantino)[43] was published in Venice. In fact, however, this folio edition borrows the text of Cesariano's translation of 1521 and was illustrated re-using the blocks of Giocondo's 1511 edition, which had also been published in Venice.

The year 1526 saw the publication for the first time of a summary of Vitruvius in dialogue form, in Spanish.[44] The author of this edition, Diego de Sagredo, is prompted, whilst explaining the term 'baluster', to develop the ideal of specifically Spanish national architectural form. This marks the first step in the direction of the discussion which was to take place later, particularly in France, about a 'national' Order. Epitomes of Vitruvius such as this, with illustrations based on Giocondo and Cesariano, enjoyed increasing popularity, and were in circulation in several languages.[45]

In 1536, Giovanni Battista Caporali of Perugia (1476–1560), extensively criticising his predecessors, particularly Cesariano, produced a new translation of the first five books of Vitruvius with commentary.[46] In fact, in both his text and his commentary, as well as in his illustrations, he adhered to a large extent to the so-criticised Cesariano.

In subsequent decades the Vitruvius editions of Fra Giocondo of 1511 and of Cesariano of 1521 were plagiarised, and published in some cases under other names. It was predictable that there would be resistance to this trend from Humanist quarters.

In 1531 the architect Antonio da Sangallo the younger, frustrated at the inadequacy of existing editions of Vitruvius, planned a new translation, which, however, never materialised. All that has come down to us is his programmatic foreword.[47] At the outset he remarks, provocatively, that Vitruvius had not been understood up to that time. Since, he says, existing 'copies, or rather, editions' ('*trascrizioni overo stampazione*') have been 'ignorantly produced' ('*fatte igniorantemente*'), he promises to return once again to the oldest manuscripts and not rely on existing editions. It is necessary, he states, to investigate Vitruvius's sources, and above all to check his statements against the actual buildings of Antiquity.

Parts of Sangallo's text anticipate the programme of the Vitruvian Academy, established in Rome in 1542. To this Academy, which had grown up around Cardinal Bernardino Maffei, belonged the Frenchman Guillaume Philander, who published a commentary on Vitruvius in 1544; the young architect Vignola; and, most importantly, the Sienese Humanist Claudio Tolomei, who set out the Academy's programme in a letter to Count Agostino de' Landi on 14 November 1542.[48]

Tolomei begins by calling for an annotated critical edition of the Latin text. Since Vitruvius had illustrated his text, this new edition should also be illustrated, but not in the misleading way Fra Giocondo had done. Furthermore, this edition should have appended to it an explanatory index of terms. On the basis of this edition, a new translation '*in bella lingua toscana*' should be produced, and also provided with a terminological index. The next task would be to check Vitruvius's statements against extant examples of Classical architecture – a task already accomplished by Alberti, though his name is not mentioned. This procedure leads Tolomei on to develop the gigantic plan of a complete corpus of the architecture of Classical Antiquity, to be based on uniform measured drawings in Roman feet (with their equivalents in contemporary measurements), this publication to be illustrated with plans, elevations and all necessary details. This corpus of Classical architecture is to be followed up with analogous complete publications of Classical sculpture, vases, inscriptions, paintings and medals. Tolomei counters the objection that a project of this kind might be overambitious and might never be completed, with the argument that if 'many fine minds' ('*molti belli ingegni*') could only come together, the whole project could be completed within three years.

Tolomei approached Vitruvius from the standpoints of both textual criticism and archaeology. For the Vitruvian Academy this was the spur to a systematic reappraisal of Classical architecture. The Academy's ambitious project came to nothing; not even a new edition of Vitruvius was produced. The only outcome was the publication in 1544 of Guillaume Philander's commentary on Vitruvius,[49] which projected sixteenth-century ways of thinking and seeing on to Vitruvius, and can scarcely be regarded as fulfilling the intentions of the Academy.

This failure of the Vitruvian Academy meant that the editions of Vitruvius that continued to be produced in quick succession were all still based on Fra Giocondo or Cesariano. The breakthrough of the Renaissance in France and Germany created the need in these countries also for translations of Vitruvius's text. The first French translation appeared in 1547 in Paris, translated by the French Humanist Jean Martin, and partially supplied with new illustrations by the sculptor Jean Goujon.[50] This translation is based on Fra Giocondo's edition with assistance from Cesariano's. The plates derive from both Giocondo and Cesariano,[51] but for the first time the plan and depictions of tragic, comic and satirical stage-settings from Sebastiano Serlio's second book of *Regole generali di architettura*, published in 1537,[52] are used as illustrations of Vitruvius's specifications for the theatre (Vitruvius V. 6, 7).

Goujon's illustrations are of exceptional elegance. His rendering of the Caryatids and Persians (Vitruvius I. 1)[53] far surpasses Fra Giocondo and Cesariano in its Classical spirit.[54] The conception of a monumental rostrum supported by caryatids, which Goujon executed in 1550/51 in the so-called Caryatid Hall of the Louvre,[55] could scarcely be explained without Vitruvius's text and Goujon's illustrations of 1547. In this connection, the question of whether Roman copies of the Caryatids from the Erektheion at Athens might also have been used as stylistic models is of secondary importance.[56]

The illustrations of the *homo ad quadratum* (Vitruvius III. 1)[57] are based on Cesariano, but the first figure shows that Goujon is considerably more interested in the proportions of the human body, whilst the inscribed circle within the square in the second figure may be taken as an imperfectly understood allusion to the *homo ad circulum*.

In a fold-out plate[58] Goujon depicts the five Orders alongside one another, as

Serlio had, but unlike Serlio he indicates how the diameters vary for columns of the same height (*Plate 33*). Goujon is the first to give detailed depictions[59] of the construction of the volutes on Ionic capitals; these can probably be traced back to contact with Philibert Delorme, to whom Goujon makes explicit reference in his epilogue. It should be noted that in Jean Goujon, who describes himself as, '*studieux d'architecture*', we have for the first time an illustrator who addresses himself directly to the reader.[60] Dispensing with a commentary, Martin's translation was inevitably difficult to understand, yet it managed to hold its own in France until the publication of Claude Perrault's annotated translation of 1673, which was to have such far-reaching influence.

In Germany, the first translation of Vitruvius appeared in 1548. The Humanist-trained doctor and mathematician Walther Ryff (Rivius) had already published a Latin edition in Strassburg in 1543, before producing his annotated German edition in 1548.[61] The Strassburg edition was based on Fra Giocondo's text and its illustrations were taken from Giocondo and Cesariano.[62] Rivius's principal source for the 1548 edition was Cesariano's translation and commentary of 1521, but he also drew on other editions and writings on architecture which he mentions in his foreword.[63] Rivius skilfully won himself a readership scarcely familiar even with such terms as 'architect' and 'architecture'. On the title-page he addresses himself to 'all ingenious craftsmen and masters: stonemasons, builders, gunsmiths and armourers, water- and mining-engineers, painters, sculptors, goldsmiths, cabinet-makers, and all those who make cunning use of ruler and compass.' In his introduction he states 'the little word Architecture' should be taken to mean 'an art such as is so embellished with a variety of other Arts that he who is practised in this art [is able] to devise and build into the Work, justly and with sound understanding, everything that may be of temporal and bodily service to us, for our needs, pleasure, and use.'[64] Rivius emphasises contemporary kinds of building even more directly than Cesariano; in addition to churches, he mentions buildings for 'civil policy and governance' ('*Bürgerliche Policey und Regiment*'), courts of justice, town halls, arsenals, treasuries and hospitals, royal and princely palaces, 'and all common – and particularly citizens' – dwellings' ('*und aller gemeiner und sonderlicher Bürgerlichen wonung*'). The illustrations[65] are taken mainly from Cesariano, but those of Marcantonio Raimondi, Dürer, Serlio and others are also used. A striking feature is the stylistic assimilation to German Late Gothic. If, for example, the depiction of Halicarnassus (Vitruvius II. 8)[66] is compared with Cesariano's original, it can be seen that the architectural language of fifteenth-century Lombardy has been transposed to that of Nuremberg Late Gothic. The commentary also has a bias towards Nuremberg civil life (*Plate 34*). The villas described by Vitruvius (VI. 6) become 'country buildings' ('*rustici aedificii*') in Cesariano (VI. 9), and thence 'cottages, granges, farmhouses;' ('*veldwonungen, Meyerhöfe und Beurische wonungen*'), or simply 'farms' ('*bawrenhöff*') in Rivius.[67] In his commentary, Rivius likewise devotes space to Black Forest houses and Scandinavian timber-frame construction.[68]

In translating Vitruvius, Rivius was faced with the difficult task of rendering Vitruvius's terminology – which he describes as 'somewhat dark and difficult, and not universally comprehensible' ('*etwas dunckel und schwer und nit allenthalbe verstendlich*') – into a language that had no suitable terminology available. By means of his commentary, however, he was able to make himself better understood than Jean Martin had been able to do a year previously.

A partial translation of Vitruvius, with illustrations, was produced in 1558 by the Mantuan painter and architect Giovanni Battista Bertani (1516–76);[69] Bertani's main preoccupation in this translation is to clarify 'obscure and difficult passages' in Vitruvius (e.g. *peripteros*, *scamilli impares*, etc). As a visible demonstration of his study of Vitruvius, he erected in front of his house in Mantua an Ionic column decorated with vine leaves, and another in section, marked with the Vitruvian proportions.[70] A treatise published by Francesco Salviati in 1552 is devoted to a correct description of Vitruvius's specifications on the construction of the volutes on an Ionic capital.[71]

The ten-part treatise by Giovanantonio Rusconi (c. 1520–87), planned in the mid-sixteenth century but only published in 1590 by Giovanni Giolito under the title *Della architettura... secondo i Precetti di Vitruvio... libri decem*, represents an exceptional case in the Vitruvian literature of the sixteenth century.[72] Rusconi left only the illustrations, whilst the text was put together by the publisher in the form of an Italian paraphrase of Vitruvius.[73] The illustrations, some of them employing the revolutionary new device of axonometric projection, represents a curious mélange of contemporary architecture and reconstructions of the Antique. Rusconi takes Vitruvius's account of the primal hut (II. 1) as a cue for an extensive survey of timber-frame construction, half-timbering, and masonry – a sort of pictorial encyclopaedia of the building of houses in Portugal, Spain, France, Germany, Poland, and Russia right up to the Black Sea.[74] In general, his illustrations display an unusual degree of independence compared to all earlier Vitruvian editions and commentaries, and they reveal a marked anti-classical attitude (*Plate 35*).

Aside from the translations of Vitruvius published just before the middle of the sixteenth century, it may be said that an impasse had now been reached as far as new editions and critiques of Vitruvius were concerned. The misinterpretations of Fra Giocondo and Cesariano had become a part of Vitruvius himself. It was only with Daniele Barbaro's ambitiously conceived commentary on Vitruvius, illustrated by Andrea Palladio, in 1556 that a decisive step was taken towards overcoming this stagnation. This new phase of exploration of Vitruvius will best be discussed in relation to Palladio. Vitruvius prescribed the basic lines of architectural theory right up to the eighteenth century, but his treatise was never again to dominate architectural thinking as exclusively as in the first half of the sixteenth century. The architectural treatises of Serlio, Vignola and Palladio could not displace the Vitruvian text from which they evolved even in the second half of the sixteenth century, but from then on they held equal rank alongside it.

6. Sixteenth-century codification

None of the writings of the Quattrocento nor the editions of and commentaries on Vitruvius from the first half of the Cinquecento answered the needs of architects seeking instruction or suggestions for practical building tasks. The work that dealt in most detail with the problems of current architectural practice, the treatise of Francesco di Giorgio, was unpublished and after Bramante had appeared in Rome, the style in which it was dressed made it unacceptable. The governing principles of architecture had been set out by Alberti within the framework of an overall world order, by Francesco di Giorgio within a totally anthropometric context, and by Filarete and Francesco Colonna within the concept of a utopia. These conceptions were available in a great variety of interpretations, but were scarcely of use to an architect with a commission to fulfil.

This was the problem tackled by Sebastiano Serlio (1475–1553/4). He sought to furnish practical rules for architecture, not for 'great minds' but so that 'any average [person] would be capable [of understanding them]'.[1] He avoided theorising, and even brought it into some disrepute; with regard to perspective, he wrote that he wished to impart only as much theory as an architect needed, and that as briefly as possible, and to refrain from philosophising about it and defining it.[2] Filarete and Francesco di Giorgio had already written their treatises in the vernacular, with illustrations constituting an indispensable element. Serlio went one step further. His pictorial compendium of architecture, using highly succinct and comprehensible language, provided, even for his less educated fellow-practitioners, direct aid at the drawing board. This approach made his treatise, along with Vignola's of a slightly later date, one of the most influential of all publications on architecture.

Sebastiano Serlio,[3] born in Bologna in 1475, received his original training as a painter from his father Bartolomeo. He began his career as a perspective painter in Pesaro (1511–14). From 1514 up to the Sack of Rome (1527), Serlio was working in Rome as assistant to Baldassare Peruzzi, who was planning to write an architectural treatise, the preliminary drafts of which he bequeathed to Serlio. The latter made no attempt to conceal this fact, which resulted in accusations of plagiarism from his contemporaries. Serlio became an architect under Peruzzi. He spent the years 1527–40 in Venice and the Veneto, during which time he became acquainted with various North Italian Humanists and artists, without achieving any notable success as an architect. This period saw the genesis of a plan for a large-scale architectural treatise of his own, which he published book by book from 1537 onwards. The dedication of the third volume to François I in 1540 brought him an invitation to France, where he spent the rest of his life (until 1553/4). Under François I he worked mainly in Fontainebleau as Royal Painter and Architect, but even then his achievements as a practising architect were limited. He devoted himself chiefly to the preparation of his treatise for publication. After the death of François I in 1547 he was ousted from his post at court by Philibert Delorme. Some time before 1550 he moved to Lyons where he spent his last years in poverty, still working on his treatise.

As Serlio states in the preface to the fourth book of *L'architettura*, which was the first to appear, he originally planned a total of only five books.[4] He did in fact leave nine, of which only Books I to V and the *Libro Extraordinario* were published in his lifetime, parts of Books VI to VIII being sold in manuscript to the art-dealer Jacopo Strada, who published Book VII in Frankfurt in 1575. The two extant drafts of Book VI were not published until 1967 and 1978. Part of Book VIII was published in 1969.

Because Serlio decided on publication of individual books by instalments, and because the sequence in which these were published had momentous consequences for their afterlife, we shall list them here in order of publication.[5]

Book IV:	*Regole generali di architettura sopra le cinque maniere degli edifici... con gli essempi dell' antichità, che, per la magior parte concordano con la dottrina di Vitruvio*, Venice, 1537.
Book III:	*Il Terzo libro... nel quale si figurano e descrivono le Antichità di Roma...*, Venice, 1540.
Books I and II:	*Il Primo libro d'architettura...* [Geometry, together with] *Il Secondo libro (Prospettiva)*, Italian text, with French translation by Jean Martin, Paris, 1545.
Book V:	*Il Quinto libro d'architettura... nel quale si tratta di diverse forme de' tempi sacri...*, French translation by Jean Martin, Paris, 1547.
Libro Extraordinario:	*Extraordinario libro di architettura nel quale si dimostrano trenta porte di opera rustica mista...*, Lyons, 1551.
Book VII:	*Il settimo libro d'architettura... nel quale si tratta di molti accidenti che possono occorrere all' Architetto...*, Italian-cum-Latin edition, Frankfurt, 1575.[6]
Book VI:	*Sesto libro. Delle habitationi di tutti li gradi degli homini*: Ms in the Bayerische Staatsbibliothek, Munich, Cod. Icon. 189; facsimile edition, Milan, 1967, with commentary by Marco Rosci; Ms in the Avery Library, Columbia University; published by Myra Nan Rosenfeld, New York, 1978.
Book VIII:	*Della castrametatione di Polibio ridotta in una cittadella murata...*; Ms in the Bayerische Staatsbibliothek, Munich, Cod. Icon. 190; partially published by Paolo Marconi, 'Un progetto di città militare. L'VIII libro inedito di Sebastiano Serlio,' *Controspazio* I (1969), n. 1, pp. 51–59; n. 3, pp. 53–59.

In some editions the *Libro Extraordinario* is quoted as Book VI, which has led to misunderstanding. Most books came out in Dutch, French and German translations soon after they first appeared, which proves their widespread success in northern Europe.[7] The lavishness of the original publication in single folio volumes, together with the great demand for the work, gave rise to the need to make Serlio's treatise available in more accessible form; this was first done by the Venetian publisher Francesco de' Franceschi in 1566 in a combined edition of Books I to V, with the *Libro Extraordinario*, with a dedication to Daniele Barbaro.[8] The same combination, with the addition of Book VII, which had been first published in 1575, was edited by Giovanni

Domenico Scamozzi and was printed four times in Venice between 1584 and 1619. This edition contains the *Libro Extraordinario* confusingly numbered 'Sesto Libro'. Serlio was translated into Latin in 1569; there was even an Italian-Latin edition in 1663. Of the various German translations, the most significant was the edition that appeared in Basel in 1608.[9]

Book IV, the first to be published, on the Orders, was the most important in Serlio's view, and 'more necessary than the others for an understanding of the different types of building and of their ornaments'.[10] It contains the theory of the five Orders (*Plate 36*), here systematised for the first time.[11] The Orders (Tuscan, Doric, Ionic, Corinthian and Composite) are defined in terms of column heights as integral multiples of their lower diameters, pedestals being also thus defined. This was the origin of the rigid proportional system governing columns, unknown to Classical antiquity or the Quattrocento. The stress laid by Serlio himself upon the theory of the Orders ('with these one embraces almost the whole art [of architecture] through an understanding ['*per la cognitione*'] of its diverse aspects'), and the separate publication of the book devoted to it, founded a tradition codified in innumerable books on the Orders, especially in northern Europe, in the sixteenth century, reducing architectural theory to the theory of the Orders and instructions on their use.

Basing himself explicitly on Vitruvius's prescriptions of propriety in the use of the Orders, Serlio stipulates adjustment to the needs of 'these modern times', saying that 'our Christian customs' have to be respected.[12] The Orders are subordinated to their context in both sacred and profane domains. The Order used for a house has to reflect the characteristics of its inhabitants: 'I will give them to men according to their status and their profession.'[13] The Tuscan order is to be preferred for all kinds of fortified buildings, the Doric for building connected with Christ, soldierly and virile saints (Peter, Paul and George), and private houses belonging to warriors and powerful individuals; the Ionic is intended for female saints 'who led matronly lives' and 'men of letters, who led quiet, rather than vigorous lives'; the Corinthian for the Virgin Mary, saints who have led stainless lives, monasteries, and private individuals distinguished by lives of chastity; the Composite order, defined by Serlio somewhat hesitantly as 'virtually a fifth type' and as a hybrid form, is regarded by him as being particularly apt to Roman triumphal arches and the highest registers of a building. He feels the need to apologise for the omission of this order in Vitruvius, 'who was unable to include everything.'[14]

In spite of the prescriptive nature of Serlio's theory of the Orders, it must be acknowledged that he constantly returns to the discretion of the architect ('*arbitrio*') and to architectural licence ('*licentia*'). Thus he suggests the mixing of Tuscan forms ('*opera Rustica*') with Doric and Ionic elements, the former representing for him 'the works of Nature' ('*opera di natura*'), the latter 'the works of the human hand' ('*opera di mano*').[15] With such allusions to the '*libertà*' of the architect, Serlio, in spite of his concern to establish rules, nonetheless transcends them, and thus becomes the founder of Mannerist architectural theory.[16] The use of hybrid Orders is justified by the striving for architectural originality ('*novità, & le cose non troppo usate*').[17] Serlio sees many of his designs as an indulgence towards fashion in architecture; thus he justifies his portal designs in the *Libro Extraordinario* by saying 'most men more often than not enjoy something new'.[18]

In his preparedness to consider regional variations in architecture, too, Serlio shows that he is not aiming to establish an absolute set of architectural rules, irrespective of context; thus already in Book IV he gives detailed consideration to the constructional peculiarities of Venice ('*costume di Venezia*').[19]

From the very first he reveals a not uncritical attitude towards Vitruvius. He is constantly remarking on the divergence between Vitruvius's statements and the extant buildings of Classical antiquity, and hence allows himself to differ from him.[20] Serlio even maintains a critical distance from his own rules in admitting that there are only 'a few places in architecture that can be given more or less fixed rules',[21] and he leaves deviations from them to the '*giudizio*' of the architect.

In an appendix to Book IV, on the painting of buildings, he discusses interior decoration and grotesques, which, he maintains, should always be subordinate to the architect's overall plan. In the painting of façades he is in favour of monochrome decoration 'so as not to break up the architectural order' ('*per non rompere l'ordine dell' Architettura*'), while for interiors he advocates illusionistic frescoes in extension of the room, following Vitruvius.[22]

Book III of Serlio's treatise on Roman architecture, published in 1540, is also of cardinal importance. It is the first coherent publication on Classical architecture; Francesco di Giorgio's anthology of the buildings of Antiquity had not been published. Serlio was in no doubt about the exemplary nature of the architecture of Classical antiquity; he does not establish grounds for this but commences with a description of the 'most beautiful building' of Antiquity, namely the Pantheon in Rome. Echoes of theoretical discussions can be heard when he speaks of the 'many members, such that all correspond to the body' ('*molti membri, così ben tutti corrispondono al corpo*'), and describes its '*rotondità*' as 'the most perfect form'.[23] Serlio clearly has a tendency towards a holistic conception of architecture which allows him to place 'a few modern works built in our time' alongside the buildings of Classical antiquity.[24] The buildings in question are those of Bramante, Raphael and Peruzzi; the only Quattrocento building that he finds worthy of reproduction is the Villa Poggioreale in Naples. Some of the woodcuts published by Serlio are of prime value as evidence, for example Bramante's plan for a round courtyard at San Pietro in Montorio 'although it was not actually built, since [what was built] was instead matched to the existing fabric',[25] or the plans of Poggioreale.[26]

In his reconstructions of the buildings of Classical antiquity Serlio is less fanciful than Francesco di Giorgio, but the trend towards total symmetry is evident here also. The explanatory texts contain numerous measurements of buildings and confirm his claim to have everywhere 'diligently measured' the buildings.

It is striking to find in Serlio the beginnings of a relativist view of history; he not only illustrates an Egyptian pyramid on the basis of an account by Marco Grimani,[27] but offers in an appendix to Book III a postscript on 'some marvels of Egypt'. Serlio goes back from the Romans by way of the Greeks to the Egyptians, and regrets the loss of 'works of the Greeks', even conceding 'that perhaps they were superior to those of the Romans', whereas he describes the 'most marvellous works of Egypt' as 'dreams and chimeras'.[28] Serlio displays here an astonishingly developed historical consciousness, and prepares the way for the argument over the relative superiority of Greek or Roman civilisation which became so crucial in the eighteenth century.

Books I and II, on geometry and perspective, published in 1545, have a strictly practical bearing 'on the needs of the Architect' ('*al bisogno dell' Architetto*'), but in the preface to Book II we find Serlio's very telling proclamation of the connection between painting, perspective and architecture: the architect, he says, has an absolute need of perspective, and he points out that the most important architects 'of our century, in which good Architecture has begun to flower', began as painters. As examples he mentions Bramante, Raphael, Peruzzi, Girolamo Genga, Giulio Romano and himself.[29] One can detect here in Serlio a 'pictorial' approach to architecture, which is more concerned with effect than with conformity to unseen rules. Thus it is significant that Serlio devotes a volume to perspective, but not to proportion. Proportion is made, in the context of the Orders, into a useful set of rules which need not necessarily be adhered to at all times.

In an appendix to Book II, following Vitruvius V. 7, Serlio deals with the three types of stage-set for comedy, tragedy and satire.[30] Serlio's prescription of these types and his illustrations of them have been extremely influential in the history of the theatre. The *scena comica* is characterised by a contrast of styles, 'an open [i.e. Antique] portico – a modern [i.e. Gothic] work' ('*portico traforato – opera moderna*') and should have, inter alia, an *hosteria*; whereas the *scena tragica* must have only noble buildings, since tragedies will be played out only in the houses 'of Lords, Dukes, great Princes, even Kings'. The *scena satirica* is the setting for actions involving 'country folk' and should be a landscape, enlivened with 'a few rustic huts' ('*alcune capanne alla rustica*'). Since Serlio evolved his types of setting in conjunction with a particular form of stage, they acquired a great importance in the Cinquecento.[31]

Book V on church building, published in 1547, deals mainly with centrally-planned buildings, particularly rotundas, 'because the circle is the most perfect form of all'.[32] This for Serlio is axiomatic. Individual elements of his designs, however, have extremely pragmatic origins: the first building to be presented was to have niches on the exterior in order to save materials, and the level of the church was to be raised by at least five steps, because experience had shown him that the level of the surrounding ground would rise in course of time. Serlio produces a repertoire of nearly every conceivable round, polygonal or oval design.

The *Libro Extraordinario*, published in 1551, with its illustrations of fifty portals, is even more markedly a pattern-book, in which concessions are deliberately made to fashion. Serlio apologises for 'so much ornamentation, so many cartouches, scrolls and superfluous things' with the reminder that he is currently working in France.[33]

Book VII, published posthumously in 1575, is a conglomerate of designs for villas, palaces, windows, buildings on irregularly shaped sites, restorations, etc. In his designs for villas especially, Serlio offers a great variety of ideas, going far beyond what was actually feasible in the mid-Cinquecento. In some passages he expresses unconcealed criticism of French customs, to which he was himself subject on occasion. He illustrates some of the fireplaces at Fontainebleau and calls the mixture of Orders 'a hybrid work' ('*opera bastarda*'), the work of masons, which he sees as inconceivable in 'good architecture'. [34] His suggestions for the restoration of medieval houses are particularly illuminating. The examples[35] he describes all show that he makes as few alterations as possible to their structure, to which he then concedes *commodità*, but that he gives them modern façades and puts the entrances in the centre, regardless of the layout of the rooms behind them; the asymmetrical placing of medieval doorways is an eyesore to him, 'something that is very contrary to Architecture'.[36] Here again we see the importance for Serlio of visual impact, which takes precedence over functional considerations and even over the relationship between exterior and interior. He is concerned with architecture not as it is, but as it looks.

Aside from some attempts in the unpublished treatises of Francesco di Giorgio, Book VI, known in manuscript from an earlier version in New York and from another in Munich prepared for the printer, which were not published until 1978 and 1967 respectively,[37] is the first systematic exploration of the problem of private house-building. Whereas Filarete was not interested in houses for people of 'low degree', Serlio designs a typology 'of dwellings for all classes of men' (*Plate 37*). He evolves the building of houses from their practical function, as had been customary since Vitruvius. He distinguishes several grades of poverty for the various classes, and begins with designs for the lowest social stratum, the poor peasantry. Then follow designs for the 'ordinary peasant' and 'rich peasant'. He goes through the same sequence for craftsmen and merchants; then follow the town and country houses of the nobility, culminating with princes and kings. Serlio also offers variations, taking into account differing site conditions and national building practices ('*costume di Franza*'): these include numerous designs for terraced houses, and designs for Italian and French dwellings on identical plans. The 'French' designs are Late Gothic in style, although Serlio tries to introduce Renaissance detail.[38] A typical example of this procedure is his design for the house of a Paris merchant. In his designs for palaces Serlio offers ideal plans with large, sometimes circular, inner courts, such as have hardly ever been built.

In Book VI, Serlio expresses reservations with regard to Vitruvius and counters him with rules which he says he has gained from his own experience; he claims 'a certain licence' ('*qualche licencia*'), especially for his work in the north, not least because he has noticed that 'works with a certain freedom' ('*le cose licenciose*') please many more than those that follow the rules; apart from that, he says, 'more works with a certain freedom than those governed by Vitruvian rules'[39] are found in Europe. Serlio proves to be a pragmatist with regard to Vitruvius as to all theory.

Book VIII, for unknown reasons not published by Jacopo Strada, is mainly known through a transcription by Serlio in the Staatsbibliothek in Munich.[40] The manuscript combines a commentary on Polybius with archaeological notes by Marco Grimani on a Roman city he had examined in Dacia, Machiavelli's *Arte della guerra* (1521), and Dürer's treatise on fortification.[41] It is not primarily a treatise on the building of fortifications but on fortified urban sites. Serlio's plans are set out on a rigid grid system (*Plate 38*). Archaeological reconstruction is really a pretext for a modern city plan. The book not only contains instructions for the building of fortifications, but also provides detailed designs for all the civic buildings of a town. Serlio's Book VIII should thus really also be seen in the context of Renaissance ideal city planning. A more thorough assessment cannot be given until the whole book has been published.

Serlio has been reproached for derivativeness, plagiarism and lack of critical judgement.[42] He propounded no all-embracing theoretical system, and did not deduce things from certain 'absolute values'.[43] He should, however, be judged according to what he actually did: he produced pattern-books that could be used and rules which could be applied, and took account of social conditions and national customs. His strength lay in his systematic approach to particular kinds of building, and this was the basis of his enduring international following. Serlio has had a more powerful influence on built architecture – particularly outside Italy – than any architectural writer before or after him.[44] On the other hand, by failing to offer general definitions of architecture, and by structuring his material in separate publications, Serlio was to a considerable extent responsible for architectural theory breaking up, or being reduced to distinct and separate themes. Serlio was stimulating, and he was not normative. Therein resided his strength and his weakness.

Serlio soon found followers – not only through the publication of his fourth book, which was the inspiration for a whole series of books on the Orders, but also with that of his third book, on Roman antiquity, which also included some contemporary buildings. Thus in 1552 Antonio Labacco, a pupil of Antonio da Sangallo the Younger, published a book of plates of ancient Roman architecture,[45] in which he claimed a design for a round church as his 'own invention', but which was revealed to have been plagiarised from his teacher.[46]

Around the middle of the century Pietro Cataneo of Siena, about whose life little is known – all we do know is that he worked on various Sienese fortifications in the Maremma[47] – embarked on a comprehensive architectural treatise similar to Serlio's. In 1554 he published *I quattro primi libri di architettura* (Venice, 1554), and there followed a version extended to eight books under the grandiose title of *L'architettura* (Venice, 1567). This treatise, particularly in its later version, partially consists of rather petty criticism of Serlio, but there are also new departures which deserve mention.

For the first time, we find town-planning described as the central task of architecture: 'The finest aspect of architecture will certainly be that which deals with cities.'[48] Book I deals in detail with the criteria for the choice of site in the building of cities, going on to argue typologically in favour of square and preferably polygonal plans. Considerations of fortification are predominant.[49] Cataneo favours a chequerboard system, the cathedral and the most important buildings occupying positions on a central square. For him the city is a body, with limbs which it is natural to want well-proportioned. Both Ancient and Christian Rome are criticised, since neither the Roman Forum nor St Peter's lies in the centre of the city. He evolves special plans for ports, which are on the one hand reminiscent of similar solutions in Francesco di Giorgio, and on the other hand correspond in structure to the plan of an army camp, which he illustrates in the second edition of his treatise.[50] Francesco Laparelli's plan for La Valletta (1565/66)[51] is a realisation of proposals such as those made by Cataneo in his treatise.

Cataneo's third book, on church-building, has aroused special interest from time to time (*Plate 39*). He argues for a plan in the shape of the Latin cross because it indicates the death of Christ the Redeemer.[52] This has been connected with Counter-Reformation tendencies in church-building, which found particularly clear expression in the later *Instructiones* of Carlo Borromeo.[53] But this is to overlook the fact that in his illustration Cataneo was clearly going back to the models supplied by his compatriot Francesco di Giorgio, and that the impetus derived from the analogy of the plan with the perfectly-proportioned human body. Cataneo combines anthropometric proportion with Christian content, seeing perfect proportion in the body of Christ: 'It happens that no human body since that of Jesus Christ, leaving aside His divine goodness, has ever been perfectly proportioned'.[54] Otherwise, Cataneo's attachment to centrally-planned structures remains complete.

In his 1567 edition Cataneo introduces his consideration of churches with a detailed typology of the plans of Antique temples. He describes the 'different forms of temples, ancient as well as modern' as of equal validity.[55] In Book V he deals with the Orders, and here his thinking is totally determined by the analogy with the proportions of the human body. With unusual frankness Cataneo goes so far as to state that much of the architecture of Antiquity is 'incorrect', and that it must not be regarded uncritically.[56]

Book VI deals with the quality and use of water, Book VII with the theory of geometry, Book VIII with perspective, which Cataneo regards as particularly important for the architect, who must make his *concetto* clear by means of perspective drawing.[57] Just as he does the architecture of the Classical world, so Cataneo regards Vitruvius with a critical eye, removing a knowledge of philosophy, astrology, music and law from the latter's requirements for the education of an architect with the ironic observation: 'how brief human life has become'.[58]

The disintegration of architectural theory into separate elements, whose linkage with an overall system is often no longer recognisable, is the chief development of the sixteenth century. This is particularly true of the work of Jacopo Barozzi, known as Il Vignola[59] (1507–73). Like many of his contemporaries, he began as a painter and only came to architecture through studying the Antique. His membership of the Vitruvian Academy instituted in 1542 probably sparked off or reinforced his interest in theoretical problems. His architectural work sprang chiefly from commissions from Pope Julius III and Cardinal Alessandro Farnese. From his years of apprenticeship as a painter Vignola had been concerned with perspective, which found its theoretical expression in a posthumously-published treatise on the subject.[60]

Vignola's *Regola delli cinque ordini d'architettura*, which was probably first published in 1562, instituted a new type of architectural textbook.[61] It cannot be called a treatise in the full sense, since the text is completely overshadowed by the plates, which speak for themselves. Apart from the dedication (to Alessandro Farnese) and a very brief introduction, the work consists exclusively of plates; the explanatory text is incorporated in them. This work by Vignola was the most widely used architectural textbook of all up to the nineteenth century, and to some extent into the twentieth century, forming one of the universal bases of courses of architecture. About two hundred and fifty editions are extant in nine languages. Vignola's book is widely dismissed today as doctrinaire and dead, but such an assessment misses his actual intentions and fails to account for his work's extraordinary success. In order to understand his purpose, it is best to study the edition of the *Regola* that he published himself, which is available in a modern facsimile edition.

Vignola presupposes a knowledge of previous architectural treatises. Above all he must be viewed in the light of Serlio, who began the tradition of an isolated treatment of the Orders with the separate publication of his fourth book in 1537. Vignola, however, takes this a step further, by not even writing a comprehensive book on the Orders, but instead demonstrating through his plates a method of his own devising of constructing them:

> As I said, my intention has been to be understood by those who already have some familiarity with the art, and for this reason, presupposing them to be already known, none of the names of the individual members of these five Orders is given.[62]

Vignola is chiefly concerned to evolve a universally valid method of obtaining exact measurements for the five Orders. He does not adduce mathematical or geometrical laws, but measurements from the buildings of Antiquity, in which the proportions 'by common consent appear the most beautiful';[63] thus he takes his specifications for the Doric order from the Theatre of Marcellus in Rome. Vignola's proportions are obtained empirically. Only for the Tuscan order does he use Vitruvius's specifications as a basis, as he knew no building of Antiquity of this Order in Rome.[64] In order to make his measurements correspond to his rules, he makes allowances for stonemasons' inaccuracies, which allow him to adjust his findings to his *regola*. This is the point where empiricism stops and Vignola's dogmatism begins.

Vignola summarises his measurements of Antique architecture in a 'brief, easy and quick rule', which may also serve 'any [one of] average intelligence... in a single glance, without a great deal of trouble'.[65] He does not use any of the then current measuring systems, but makes the module into the *misura arbitria*, which can be of any size one likes. Even with the module, Vignola was not looking for theoretical underpinning, but simply for a means of simplifying the calculation of the measurements of the parts of the Orders. He was not seeking to lay down the law, but to provide a method of construction supported by aesthetic experience; it was Vignola's successors who codified his system of proportions. But it was predictable from the very disposition of the book that his method would harden into dogma.

In order to account for Vignola's enormous success, a short explanation of this method must be given.[66]

Whereas Serlio started from the module, and suggested a different method of assembly for each Order, employing complicated fractions and sometimes non-whole numbers, many of which anyway failed to correspond with his illustrations, so that they were only of limited use in practice, Vignola started from the opposite, extremely practical stand-point, that the overall size of buildings generally comes first, and made the overall size of the Order the basis of his calculations (*Plates 40, 41*).

He lays down that in all the Orders the height of the entablature is a quarter, and that of the pedestal a third, of the height of the column. The heights of pedestal, column and entablature are always in the ratio of 3:12:4. In the case of an Order without pedestal, the ratio between the height of the column and that of the entablature is 12:3. In other words, Vignola starts with a nineteen- or fifteenfold division of the total height. Only after this step, which is the same for all Orders, does differentiation come. And the module does not make its appearance until this point in his scheme. The module is defined by Vignola, as by most of his predecessors, as the radius of the lower shaft. His empirically obtained ratios of module to column height run as follows for the various Orders: 14 (Tuscan), 16 (Doric), 18 (Ionic), 20 (Corinthian and Composite). Any given column measurement – $^{12}/_{19}$ths or $^{12}/_{15}$ths of the total height of the Order – must always be divided by these numbers; the correct proportion for the individual Orders is then automatically obtained. From the module measurements, which are further subdivided into *parti*, the proportions of bases and capitals are obtained.

Since relatively complicated fractions result from these calculations, Vignola simplifies the process by giving formulae for each of the Orders, by means of which the size of the module may be calculated from the overall height of the Order. The respective formulae for each Order are: $22\frac{1}{6}$ (Tuscan), $25\frac{1}{3}$ (Doric), $28\frac{1}{2}$ (Ionic), 32 (Corinthian and Composite). One has only to divide the overall height of the Order by these numbers to obtain the module measurement in each case. The proportions prescribed for pedestal, column and entablature for all the Orders, and between the different Orders, then result automatically. Vignola treats the openings of arcades of whatever Order as being in the ratio of $1:2$.

The striking success of Vignola's method is ascribable to the fact that the numbering of each plate in modules or fractions of a module is compatible with any given system of measurement. Once, starting with a desired height, the module has been fixed, each individual measurement can be obtained by multiplication, using the numbers of the *Regola* tables.

Vignola facilitates the use of his *Regola* by presenting each Order in a fixed sequence: 1) colonnade; 2) arcade; 3) arcade with pedestal; 4) pedestal and base alone; 5) capital and entablature alone.

On the title-page of his book Vignola looks out at us as an architect-instructor, flanked by Theory and Practice.[67] At the end, Vignola gives more advice on the construction of tapered columns and Salomonic columns.[68] Supplementary plates showing his own designs for doorways and chimney-pieces were not part of the original concept.

Vignola's work underwent substantial revision in the course of numerous editions and translations, ranging from lavish polyglot productions with supplementary plates of historic buildings[69] to cheap pocket editions.

Vignola himself had based his *Regola* on an empirical aesthetic; it was inevitable that once it came to be applied without questioning his data, it would be taken as normative. This is in fact what transpired, and is the sole reason why Vignola has been misunderstood as the great dogmatist of architecture. This misunderstanding applies, however, only to Vignola's own intentions, and not to the influence that he has in fact exerted.

Serlio and Vignola both became prisoners to dogmatising tendencies, which they perhaps might have foreseen, and which even to this day cast a negative shadow over their theoretical work.

Editions

There is no extant critical edition of Serlio. Even the two de luxe editions of Book VI (1967 and 1978) contain no transcription of the text. For practical purposes a facsimile reprint of the 1619 edition can be recommended: *Tutte l'opere d'architettura et prospettiva di Sebastiano Serlio Bolognese... diviso in sette libri* (Venice 1619), facsimile reprint Ridgewood, N.J., 1964; also a facsimile reprint of the 1584 edition, with an introduction by Fulvio Irace: Sebastiano Serlio, *I sette libri dell' architettura* (Venice 1584), 2 vols, Bologna 1978. A facsimile reprint of the English edition of 1611: *The Five Books of Architecture*, New York 1982.

Pietro Cataneo, *I quattro primi libri di Architettura* (Venice 1554), facsimile reprint, Ridgewood, N.J., 1964; and *L'architettura* (Venice 1567), facsimile reprint, Bologna 1982.

Jacomo Barozzio da Vignola, *Regola delli cinque ordini d'architettura* (without place and year), facsimile reprint with introduction by Christof Thoenes, Vignola 1974.

7. Palladio and the North Italian Humanists

When Serlio went to Northern Italy and there conceived and began publication of his treatise on architecture, he encountered an intellectual climate in which profound discussion of architecture was much cultivated. Here was a circle of Humanists, with whom Serlio came in contact during only one phase of his life, while for Andrea Palladio it was decisive for his theoretical thinking.

The stonemason Andrea di Pietro della Gondola (1508–80) is a representative of Humanism not only by reason of his nickname, 'Palladio'; for all his innate gifts, the contribution of his patrons to his intellectual and artistic formation should not be underestimated.[1] In his early years he was fostered by Giangiorgio Trissino and Alvise Cornaro, and in his maturity by Daniele Barbaro; these patrons enabled him to travel to Rome and other centres of Antiquity and worked on architectural projects with him. As a result of his artistic ability, Palladio became the exponent of this group, capable of giving form to what his patrons could only begin to conceive of. It is thus necessary to give a brief outline of the ideas and concerns of these patrons of his, inasmuch as they are to some extent elaborated in his own system.

Giangiorgio Trissino (1478–1550),[2] later celebrated by Palladio as 'the splendour of our age',[3] was a scholarly, dry writer who tried to revive the literary forms of Antiquity, as for example in his *Sofonisba* (1524), an attempt at the revival of Greek tragedy. Between 1528 and 1548 he worked on a heroic epic conceived on the principles of Aristotle's *Poetics* and modelled on Homer's *Iliad*, entitled *L'Italia liberata dai Goti*, which contained a symbolic plea to Charles V to liberate the Eastern Roman Empire from the heathen. In *L'Italia liberata* Trissino draws upon his encyclopaedic knowledge, and so we find in the work, inter alia, passages on architecture. A description of the courtyard of a palace runs as follows:

> A cloister runs around the little courtyard
> Its spacious arches resting on round pillars
> Whose height is equal to the pavement's width;
> Their thickness is their height by eight divided.
> Each column has a silver capital
> Whose height repeats the measure of its thickness,
> Whereas the shaft stands on a metal base
> Which is again exactly half as high.

Translated by R. Wittkower[4]

Here we have a description of a modular architecture based on column height or diameter. This text is recited by one 'Palladio'; from this epic character with a name from Antiquity, Andrea di Pietro della Gondola received his Humanistic sobriquet around 1540.[5]

In the 1530s, when the relationship between Palladio and his friend and patron Trissino was developing, the latter designed and built his villa in Cricoli at the gates of Vicenza.[6] This '*villa suburbana*' was used for Humanistic gatherings in which Palladio participated, and possibly had the function of an academy with a regular teaching syllabus (philosophy, astronomy, geography and music).[7] The villa in Cricoli has a completely symmetrical structure, and draws upon Roman garden loggias known to Trissino from the Villa Farnesina and from Serlio's subsequently (1540) published woodcut of a loggia of the Villa Madama or of its model.[8] For Palladio Trissino's villa, along with that erected by Falconetto and Alvise Cornaro in Padua ten years previously, represented a first encounter with High Renaissance architecture in the Roman idiom. He visited Rome for the first time in 1541, accompanied by Trissino.

Trissino's theoretical preoccupation with architecture would seem to fall within the period when he was constructing his villa. His surviving fragment on architecture must be presumed to date from 1535–37.[9] It contains, however, hardly anything more than the announcement of a manifesto for a treatise. Starting from Vitruvius, and very critical towards Alberti, he draws up quite a different list of architectural definitions and concepts. The very first sentence states explicitly: 'Architecture is an art concerning the habitation of men, that provides a basis for utility and pleasure.'[10] Human habitation is to the fore, and the architect's primary task is to ensure '*utilità*' (the Vitruvian *utilitas*) and '*dilettazione*' (pleasure) for the occupier. Behind the concept of '*dilettazione*', clearly narrowed down to the viewpoint of the occupant, lies Vitruvius's *venustas*, as Trissino later indicates; his term refers to '*simmetrie*' and '*ornamenti*'.[11] '*Utilità*' is chiefly understood as public and private security ('*sicurezza*') and convenience ('*commodità*'). The Vitruvian *firmitas* appears as '*durabilità*', dependent on and subordinated to '*utilità*'. It becomes obvious that Trissino is more interested in the utilitarian value of architecture than in its structural or aesthetic elements.

Trissino conceives his treatise from the proposition that knowledge of Antiquity has been lost and Vitruvius has been misunderstood. He maintains that Alberti has omitted many points in his treatise, and on the other hand that much in it is superfluous. Trissino begins with reflections on the security of city sites, enumerating a set of historical examples. But at this point the fragment breaks off. It is hardly long enough to tell us to what extent Trissino coloured Palladio's views. Nevertheless, the emphasis given to '*commodità*', to which Palladio was to keep returning, is certainly a point upon which the pragmatic thinking of Trissino in these matters influenced his protégé.

Through Trissino, Palladio made the acquaintance of (Ludovico) Alvise Cornaro (1484–1566), who had been living in Padua since 1490, and is to be seen as a typical representative of those aristocratic Venetians who left Venice for the mainland and there cultivated a particular lifestyle.[12] Cornaro combined a Humanist existence as it is reflected in his then famous text *Discorsi intorno all vita sobria*, with extremely practical activity. As a landlord he undertook the draining of marshlands, and in treatises and reports he wrote about the deepening of the Venice lagoon and waterways, and the cathedral of Padua. Evidence of his important role as patron remains to this day in the form of his Paduan residence near Sant' Antonio, where he gave shelter to artists such as Ruzzante and Giovanni Maria Falconetto.[13] The garden loggia built by Falconetto in 1524 is one of the earliest High Renaissance buildings showing Roman influence in Northern Italy. In addition, Cornaro was himself active as a practising architect; recently he has been credited with the famous Odeo Cornaro and the Villa dei Vescovi in Luvigliano.[14] In the first book of his treatise Palladio remembers Alvise Cornaro as a 'gentleman of excellent judgement, as one recognises from the most beautiful loggia and exquisitely decorated rooms built by him at his residence in Padua'.[15] Cornaro also left two drafts of an architectural treatise which is of some importance.[16] It was probably written around 1555.[17]

Cornaro's treatise is expressly addressed to city-dwellers who use architects, and not to architects, and deals exclusively with dwelling-houses because these are required in large numbers and indeed together make up a city. He does not write on theatres, amphitheatres, baths or the Orders 'because there are already plenty of books on them'.[18] Cornaro adopts a pragmatic and distanced stance towards existing architectural theory. Not only a certain irony, but even a critique of the aesthetic principles of his time is apparent in such a statement as: 'and furthermore, a building can be both beautiful and convenient, and be neither of Doric nor of any other Order...'.[19] citing San Marco in Venice and Sant' Antonio in Padua as examples, which betokens a positive attitude towards medieval architecture. He does not speak of founding new towns because these never come about, nor about types of buildings no longer in use, about which the 'divino Vitruvio' and the 'gran Leon Baptista Alberti' have already, he maintains, written enough. He writes about the building of new houses and also methods of improving old houses, and touches on the problem of sanitation for the first time in architectural theory. (Serlio's Book VII, with comparable suggestions, did not appear until 1575). For Cornaro aesthetic value is less important than convenience. *Commodità* becomes the decisive criterion in architecture even more emphatically than with Trissino: 'I shall always lavish more praise on a building that is straightforwardly beautiful but perfectly convenient, than on one that is exquisitely beautiful, but inconvenient.'[20]

Vitruvius's text seems to Cornaro corrupt, full of lacunae, and obscure in its terminology; for this reason he uses terms in everyday use; '*et userò parole et vocaboli, che hora sono in uso*'.[21] Palladio was to express himself to the same effect in the preface to his first book: 'I shall make use of those terms that craftsmen commonly use today.'[22] Cornaro gives his fellow-citizens practical advice of a technical, economic and aesthetic nature for the building of their houses. The fact that he restricted himself to the dwelling-house as the most important architectural form must have been a considerable spur to Palladio, who regards the house as the prototype of all buildings and begins his treatise (in Book II) with the dwelling-house.

Cornaro's manuscript was known to Palladio.[23] His sense of reality is frequently present in Palladio's utterances. The priority Cornaro gives to '*commodità*' is not a fundamental rejection of the '*veri fondamenti*' of architecture, which he himself discusses,[24] but an ironical detachment from them. In a late letter to Daniele Barbaro, any theoretical statement which cannot be turned into practice is dismissed as vain.[25]

Daniele Barbaro (1513–70), a slightly younger contemporary of Palladio, exerted a decisive influence on him in his mature period, both in intellectual discussions and as a builder.[26] Barbaro and Palladio met around 1550, at about the time of Trissino's death. Barbaro was one of the foremost Humanists of Northern Italy in the mid-Cinquecento. He founded the botanical garden in Padua, and from 1548 to 1550 was the Venetian ambassador at the English court. On his return, the rank of Patriarch of Aquileia was conferred on him, which enabled him to lead the retiring life of a scholar. Aristotle, whose *Rhetoric* and *Nicomachean Ethics* he edited in 1544, was a particular influence on this thinking.

Around 1547, before he met Palladio, he had already begun a new translation of Vitruvius, which occupied him for nine years. Barbaro's translation of Vitruvius with a commentary is the most conscientious and thorough of the whole sixteenth century. Its illustrations are mainly based on drawings by Palladio,[27] who had clearly discussed Vitruvius's text at length with him. The first, very lavish edition of this translation appeared in 1556 (*Plate 43*). In 1567, the Venetian publisher Francesco de' Francheschi published simultaneously a Latin and Italian edition considerably expanded in commentary and illustrations, for which the German Giovanni Chrieger (Johann Krüger) provided woodcuts. The originals for the newly-added woodcuts were again drawn by Palladio, as can be seen from their only slightly altered re-use in his *Quattro libri* (1570). In accordance with the wishes of the publisher, these editions are *in forma commoda* and were no doubt less expensive; the woodcuts are inferior in quality to those of the 1556 edition.[28] Since Barbaro adds many new insights in these later editions, they are the preferred texts for his understanding of Vitruvius.

Barbaro elucidates his ideas on architecture in his commentary, which proceeds separately from Vitruvius's text in a manner comparable to that of Claude Perrault a hundred years later (1684). In the preface he formulates the Aristotelian principle of experience: 'All art is born of experience'.[29] Barbaro's method is correspondingly deductive, proceeding from one definition to the next. He explains his understanding of architecture in his commentary on Vitruvius I. 3. Art and architecture create – according to the same principle as Nature, which is understood to be rational. The relationship of human intellect to the principle of Nature is analogous to that between a work of art and Nature: 'the principle of art, which is the human intellect, closely resembles the principle that moves Nature, which is an intelligence.'[30]

Architecture is thus not a literal imitation of Nature, but the adoption of its prime principle. Art and architecture are determined by '*ragione*', they are '*scienza*', knowledge. For Barbaro the science of architecture lies in proportion. Vitruvius's discussion of proportion (III. 1) does not add up to a complete system; Barbaro uses his commentary to evolve his own system of proportion in detail.[31] From the theory of proportion there emerge for him the 'innumerable precepts of architecture'. The architectural design takes shape in the '*disegno*', which is defined as the 'quality, and the form, that were in the mind of [the maker] [*artefice*]'.[32] Finally, the geometry underlying proportion is for Barbaro 'the mother of *disegno*', the basis of all architectural rules.[33]

For him form is a result of applied reason, i.e. applied proportion. Material is for him pure being ('*lo essere*'), architecture ('*il bene essere*') is the ordering of material by reason, i.e. its proportionality. Barbaro speaks of 'defects of the material',[34] which will often not correspond to the requirements of art. Material is clearly subordinate to form; ideas such as truth to material are completely alien to this way of thinking. This explains how it was possible for Palladio to face his materials (his columns, which appear monolithic, are in fact built up of bricks and then stuccoed over). For Barbaro, architecture is a science, aiming at absolute truth, touching here on the Platonic ideas[35] of the good, the true and the beautiful. Thus architecture impinges on the realm of ethics. It is significant that the '*Regina virtus*' is later to be enthroned above the personifications of geometry and architecture on the title-page of Palladio's *Quattro libri* (*Plate 46*).

Experiences from Palladio's built architecture have clearly crept into his illustrations to Barbaro's edition of Vitruvius (*Plates 44, 45*). Thus in an elevation of a dwelling-house of Antiquity he shows a temple-like portico with Corinthian columns (Book VI). On the one hand, the temple is thus derived from the typology of the house, and on the other, a form known till then only from Antique temples is legitimised in its profane application to his own architecture. The relationship of Palladio's illustrations to Barbaro's commentary still needs close examination.[36] Barbaro sees in Palladio a continuation of Antiquity. He praises his 'beautiful drawings [*disegni*] of plans, elevations, and sections, as in the execution of many and superb buildings in his native region, and elsewhere, that rival those of Antiquity, enlighten his contemporaries, and will be cause for marvel to all those who will see them hereafter.'[37]

A tangible reflection of Barbaro's and Palladio's joint edition of Vitruvius is the villa of Daniele and his brother Marcantonio at Maser,[38] which Palladio was commissioned to build about the same time as the first edition was published (1556). Barbaro's ideas of '*proporzionalità*' are realised in the manner in which the rooms are grouped in the villa.[39]

Shortly before his death in 1568, Barbaro published a treatise on perspective, intended chiefly for painters, sculptors and architects.[40] In certain respects this is an extension of his commentary on Vitruvius. Thus Vitruvius's statements on stage design are elucidated with the aid of Serlio.

One other sequence of events may not have been without influence on Palladio and the North Italian Humanists above-mentioned. In 1534 the church of San Francesco della Vigna in Venice was begun, to plans by Jacopo Sansovino. Because of differences of opinion over the proportions of the design, the Doge Andrea Gritti commissioned the Franciscan Francesco Giorgi (b. 1460) to write a memorandum on the proportions of the building.[41] Giorgi had won renown in 1525 with a comprehensive work on the 'Harmony of the Universe'[42] in which he had developed a Neoplatonic-cum-Pythagorean theory of proportion. In his memorandum of 1535[43] he gives proportional relationships which can be reduced entirely to the numerical musical ratios of octave $(1:2)$ and fifth $(2:3)$. Giorgi attempts to reconcile the specifications of Plato's *Timaios* with those of the Old Testament on the proportions of the Ark of the Covenant and the Temple of Solomon. He also uses concepts of Francesco di Giorgio Martini in the analogy of choir and nave to human head and body. Giorgi's memorandum was appraised by Titian as painter, Serlio as architect, and by the Humanist Fortunio Spira. Subsequently, Palladio had the task of building the façade of the church.

In 1554 Palladio paid his last visit to Rome, accompanied by Daniele Barbaro. The fruit of this stay was a guidebook to ancient Rome, written by Palladio and published in the same year, *L'antichità di Roma* (Venice, 1554), in which he tried to conjure up the cityscape of ancient Rome, and at the same time advance beyond the traditional miracle-ridden guides to the city.[44]

At about the time when he was working on the illustrations to Barbaro's commentary on Vitruvius, Palladio decided upon the publication of his own treatise on architecture.[45] The first four books, *I quattro libri dell'architettura*, appeared in 1570 in two instalments: 1) *I due primi libri dell'architettura*; 2) *I due libri dell'antichità*. Following Vitruvius and Alberti, Palladio probably planned a total of ten books. The preface to the first book contains an announcement of the total contents, but without any division of the material into individual books:

I will deal first with private houses, and then with public buildings: I will deal briefly with roads, bridges, squares, prisons, Basilicas (that is, places of justice), Hospitals, Stadia (places where men took exercise), Temples, Theatres, Amphitheatres, Triumphal Arches, Public Baths, Aqueducts, and finally, how to fortify Cities and Ports.[46]

The preparation of the whole set of books was well advanced, and the manuscript was allegedly even ready for publication at the time of Palladio's death.[47] A large proportion of the intended drawings has been preserved, but the manuscript has been lost and was never published.[48]

In order to make a just assessment of the fragment constituted by the *Quattro libri*, it is necessary to imagine the project as a whole. At all events a considerable preponderance of the total work was concerned with the architecture of Antiquity. *I quattro libri* enjoyed great success from its first publication, finding wide currency in numerous reprintings and translations in the seventeenth and eighteenth centuries. Facsimiles of the 1570 edition are easy to come by today. A critical edition has recently become available (see Editions).

Since its first publication, Palladio's treatise has been read not only as a historical source,[49] but for its immediate message. Goethe, who made an intensive study of Palladio, acquired a copy in Padua on 27 September 1786. Three days later he wrote from Venice to Frau von Stein: 'I found the book in Padua, now I'm studying it and it is as if scales have fallen from my eyes; the mist is clearing and I am recognising objects. It is also great as a book.'[50] For Goethe, Palladio provided a decisive stimulus on the path of self-discovery, a bridge on his way to Classicism. In his mention of the quality of the work as a book, Goethe is alluding to the extraordinary beauty and clarity of the woodcuts based on Palladio's drawings, and to the setting of the text. In this respect Palladio's treatise, along with the *Hypnerotomachia Polifili* of 1499, is the most beautifully produced book of the Renaissance.

Its contents are as follows:

Book I: Instruction on materials, the construction of a house from the foundations to the roof; general prescriptions, valid for both public and private building; prescriptions for the five Orders.

Book II: The dwelling-house in town and country (the villa).

Book III: Streets, bridges, squares and basilicas.

Book IV: Antique temples, in Rome, Italy, and outside Italy.

One of the features that run through the *Quattro libri* is the self-confidence of the author. He addresses the reader in the first person. He refers to his journeys and his measurements of Antique buildings, and on the basis of his experience claims competence to supply rules for both his contemporaries and posterity:

I also set myself the task of giving all the necessary advice that should be heeded by all those fine minds [*belli ingegni*] desirous of building both elegantly and well... I dare say that I have shed so much light on Architectural matters, that those who come after me will be able, with my example, to exercise the perspicacity of their own lucid minds.[51]

In his preface Palladio justifies a return to Antiquity by stressing how far ahead of their successors the Romans were in matters of art. As far as he is concerned, Vitruvius is of less importance than the actual architecture of Antiquity, measured drawings of which for him provide the main basis for the architecture of present and future. Wherever surviving Antique monuments or Vitruvius supply inadequate information for a given building task, he fills the gap with his own architecture. Palladio does not see himself as an imitator, but as a continuator of Antiquity. His own buildings are not merely possible solutions to problems, he also publicises them 'for the use of others too'.[52] To a large extent he rejects contemporary architecture, today described as Mannerist, with reference to its 'strange abuses, barbaric inventions, and unnecessary expenditure' and to artificial ruins. In contrast to the modish Serlio, Palladio is firmly orientated towards Classicism. His language is clear and terse – 'I will avoid being long-winded'[53] – and he uses terms that are universally comprehensible.

In his aesthetic ideas Palladio is largely dependent on Vitruvius and Alberti. His categories of *utilità* (which he sees as synonym for *commodità*), *perpetuità* and *bellezza* are Vitruvian. His definition of beauty as 'a correspondence of the whole to all the parts, of the parts to each other, and of those parts to the whole'[54] is taken from Alberti. A building is a self-contained, well-defined body. Palladio's interest, however, lies not in the mental grasp of a building but in the perception of it. In his discussion of the misuses of architecture (I. 20), Palladio's closeness to Barbaro is apparent. Architecture is 'the imitation of Nature', it demands 'simplicity' in order to reach its goal of being 'almost another Nature'. Beautiful building implies also true and good building.[55] Here Palladio clearly speaks for the Neo-platonic notion of the unity of the good, the true and the beautiful. Anything that goes against reason also runs counter to Nature, to the 'universal and necessary rules of art': cartouches, broken pediments, etc.[56] For Palladio, architecture is rational, simple, Classical.

Palladio takes the Orders as fixed by Serlio and Vitruvius as axiomatic. Again, Vitruvius's argument is of less importance for him that his own measurements. More clearly than Serlio, he establishes precise proportional relationships based on the use of modules between the Orders, the proportions within each kind of column and intercolumniations. Palladio follows Vignola's *Regola* (1562)[57] down to the very form of his illustration. Palladio's undogmatic stance vis-à-vis Antiquity is apparent in one detail here: he observes that the Doric columns of Antiquity frequently have no bases, but decides in favour of the use of an Attic base, 'which will greatly increase its length'.[58]

The second book, with which Palladio's discussion of building types begins, is concerned with dwelling-houses in town and country (the villa). Almost without exception it is his own buildings that are cited and illustrated. The strong influence of Trissino is felt here, and even more that of Cornaro, when Palladio gives primacy to the criterion of *commodità*. In a very individual way *commodità* is associated by Palladio with the problem of *decor* and beauty, the last two seeming to be subordinate: 'So one must call that house convenient [*commoda*] which is in accord [*conveniente*] with the quality of the person who lives in it, and whose parts correspond to the whole and to each other.'[59]

Palladio now makes an analogy between the concept of *commodità* and the human organism (II. 2). Functional and aesthetic considerations are combined; the most beautiful parts of a building are displayed, the ugly but necessary parts hidden. The organic and aesthetic correspondence of individual parts to each other and to the whole is repeatedly emphasised by Palladio. Yet as an experienced architect he knows that the architect's ideas must often be subordinated to the wishes of the patron. He makes the pragmatic statement: 'But it is often necessary for an Architect to comply with the wishes of those responsible for the expense, rather than with that which ought to be observed.'[60] This sentence is much milder than what he had originally written.[61]

Palladio is thoroughly aware of the innovatory nature of his designs. He stresses the difficulty of asserting his 'new fashion' against the 'old fashion of building without grace'.[62] His reconstructions of the Antique house largely correspond to those in Barbaro's commentary on Vitruvius of 1567. In his own plans he takes over from these individual elements such as the atrium or, with reference to the Greek house (*Plate 47*), a separate range for guests (in the Palazzo Porto-Festa, Vicenza; the guest range was never built).[63] Actually, in the case of Palazzo Porto-Festa, Palladio is following the Roman palace tradition of the Bramante period (Raphael's house; the Palazzo Vidoni-Caffarelli).

In the section concerning the situation of villas (II. 12), Palladio sketches a brief picture of their purpose: agricultural profitability, physical invigoration, facilities for study and contemplation, are to be combined without any awkwardness. Functional and aesthetic considerations complement each other. Wherever possible, a villa should be built on a hill, for this is healthy and handsome; and situated on a navigable river, for this is convenient, saves transport costs, and looks well, etc. Its situation in relation to the surrounding landscape is decisive for a villa's design, which indeed is a response to the nature of the site. Palladio's comments on the Villa Rotonda make this particularly clear (*Plate 48*):

> The site is one of the most pleasant and delightful that can be found, because it is on a gently rising hill, which is watered on one side by a navigable river, the Bacchiglione, and on the other surrounded by more very pleasant hills that give the effect of a great Theatre. They are all cultivated, and abound in the most excellent fruits and the best vines. One enjoys the most beautiful views on all sides, some near, some far, some that end with the [distant] Horizon, and for this reason, porticos have been built on all four sides.[64]

A villa's porticos serve *ornamento* by indicating the social status of the occupant, and at the same time *commodità*. Palladio justifies the use of the portico not only with reference to the 'grandeur and magnificence of the thing', but also with the consideration that the Romans used them in their public and probably also their private buildings.[65] Since, along with Barbaro, he believes in the derivation of all building types from the dwelling-house, no problem exists for him in transferring such building forms to the private town house (*palazzo*) and villa.

In Book III Palladio proceeds to public buildings (roads, bridges, squares and basilicas), regarding this as the beginning 'of my Antiquities'.[66] Palladio refers pointedly to the drudgery of the work of taking measurements, and of the ensuing nocturnal labours, in order to obtain a complete picture from fragments. For him the latter activity is not so much a purely archaeological procedure; it is more an endeavour to proffer 'the utmost usefulness' (*'utilità grandissima'*) to 'students of architecture', because anyone who measures good models is enabled to learn a great deal in a short time.[67] His apparently antiquarian attitude is addressed to the present and the future. The buildings of Antiquity appear exemplary to Palladio in so far as their functions agree with present needs. With a change of function, Palladio demands a new form. This becomes clear in the case of the basilica, for whose Roman and contemporary manifestations he establishes completely different types, by reason of their distinct functions.[68] He states:

> The basilicas of our own time differ in this respect from those of Antiquity: the latter were built upon or on a level with the ground: while ours have an upper floor containing shops displaying the wares of various crafts...[69]

He refers to the Salone in Padua and finally, with great self-confidence, to his own Basilica in Vicenza, which, he says, has no need to fear comparison with Antiquity, and which he counts among the 'most beautiful buildings that have been erected since Antiquity'.[70] Palladio confronts Antiquity on equal terms. He regards his own building activity not as a revival of Antiquity, but as a continuation of it.

Book IV deals with temple-building in Antiquity. In the second chapter Palladio gives his views, in his succinct manner, on the aesthetic bases of this building task, with reference, of course, to the present. The basic geometrical forms of circle and square are for him the most beautiful, the circular because it is an image of the circular movement of the cosmos. His arguments concern both form and content: the rounded shape is simple, uniform, equal, strong and spacious', it makes visible the 'Oneness, the Infinite Essence, the Uniformity, and the Justice of God.'[71]

In his specifications for the appropriate use of the Orders (*decor*), Palladio concurs with Vitruvius and Serlio, but does not take over Serlio's rather contrived adaptation for Christian use.

Considering his preference for basic geometrical forms, resting primarily on formal aesthetics, there seems to be a gap in the argument when he continues without transition: 'Those churches built in the form of a Cross are also very praiseworthy'. and for this quotes only the iconological reference to the Cross of Christ, stating laconically: 'And this is the form I used for the Church of S. Giorgio Maggiore in Venice.'[72] Here a nod towards Counter-Reformation ideas is perceptible, and these become even more apparent in the course of his later recommendations of the purity of white as appropriate for churches, when he says that 'if you were to paint them, those pictures would not go well whose meaning alienated the soul from the contemplation of Divine things; therefore, we must not depart from gravity in our Temples.'[73]

Here Palladio is in line with the resolutions of the Council of Trent.[74] His own church buildings, such as San Giorgio Maggiore and Il Redentore, Venice, are to be seen against this background. The Redentore combines a centrally-planned choir, in keeping with the ideas of the Renaissance, with the required nave. With the same justification as Serlio, Palladio ranks Bramante's tempietto of San Pietro in Montorio with the temples of Antiquity, because 'Bramante was the first to bring good and beautiful Architecture to light, that from Antiquity until that time had been hidden.'[75]

Palladio relies to a large extent on the communicative power of his woodcuts. These are provided throughout with indications of measurement – uniformly in Vicenzan feet – which underlines the systematic nature of his didactic intentions. Palladio does not offer a cohesive system of architectural theory – it is not only the fragmentary nature of the *Quattro libri* that rules this out – rather, he is concerned to lead the reader to the principles of good architecture by the observation of concrete instances. One has the feeling that Barbaro's ideas of proportion form the background to his views, but nowhere does Palladio express himself coherently on the subject of proportion.[76] Like Barbaro, he believes in rules for architecture, but as a practising architect he accommodates his own ideas to the wishes of his employers, and his thinking accords primacy to *commodità*.

After the appearance of the *Quattro libri*, Palladio's composition of the further projected books[77] was interrupted by illustrated commentaries on Caesar (1575) and (unpublished) Polybius,[78] which attest to his interest in military architecture. Like Serlio, he takes the form of the Roman *castrum* (*Plate 49*) as his starting-point, and in his commentaries and illustrations he describes 'all the sites, of cities, mountains and rivers'.[79]

Editions

I dieci libri dell'architettura di M. Vitruvio tradutti e commentati da Monsignor Barbaro, eletto patriarca d'Aquileggia, Francesco Marcolini, Venice 1556.

I dieci libri dell'architettura di M. Vitruvio, tradotti & commentati da Mons. Daniel Barbaro, Venice 1567 (ed. Manfredo Tafuri, Milan 1987).

M. Vitruvii Pollionis De Architectura Libri Decem, Cum commentariis Danielis Barbari, Venice 1567.

Andrea Palladio, *I quattro libri dell' architettura*, ed. Licisco Magagnato and Paola Marini, Milan 1980. A facsimile reprint of Isaac Ware's translation of 1738: *The Four Books of Architecture*, New York n.d.

8. The Counter-Reformation, Baroque and Neo-classicism

The importance of the Counter-Reformation for architecture and architectural theory in the second half of the sixteenth century has to this day not been adequately explored. While the relationship between the Counter-Reformation and Mannerism[1] and the influence of the Council of Trent (1545–63) on treatise literature and the visual arts have repeatedly been investigated,[2] architecture and architectural theory have always remained on the side-lines in this connection. This was partly because the Council, which passed the decree on the worship of saints, relics and images in its last session of December 1563,[3] did not make any direct pronouncement on architecture. Whereas the Council resolved that all works of art, whether inside or outside the church, required episcopal authorisation before they could be displayed, and religious representations should contain nothing false, nothing profane, nothing immoral, nothing absurd, nothing deviating from the straight and narrow',[4] there were no strictures regarding architecture. The effect of the Council of Trent's resolutions, whose goals were reactionary and propagandistic, is not only apparent in their interpreters, such as Giovanni Andrea Gilio and Gabriele Paleotti;[5] artists were also psychologically affected by them, as is shown in the well-known letter of Bartolomeo Ammannati to the Florentine Accademia del Disegno (1582),[6] in which he repudiates his earlier work as 'the grossest and gravest error'; in another letter just before his death to Grand Duke Ferdinando de' Medici, he describes himself as 'exceedingly grieved to have been, in my life, the perpetrator of such statues',[7] and asks for his nude figures to be clothed or totally removed.

Counter-Reformation attitudes are not reflected so directly in architectural theory. The intellectual return to Early Christianity and Scholasticism is apparent in isolated cases in certain building projects, such as the restoration of the Cathedral of Mantua, begun in 1545 by Giulio Romano, whose colonnades, architrave, and flat ceiling of the nave refer back to Old St Peter's.

There is only one known case of the Council's resolutions being applied to architecture in definite written form. In 1577 the Archbishop of Milan, Cardinal Carlo Borromeo, nephew of Pope Pius IV and particularly active[8] during the last session of the Council, published his *Instructiones fabricae et supellectillis ecclesiasticae*,[9] which although addressed only to his own diocese, gained currency throughout Europe. It is not an architectural treatise in the strict sense, but rather an exposition of points that the Archbishop of Milan had to attend to in his church visits and building projects.[10] Nevertheless, the *Instructiones* give clear expression to the Counter-Reformation's attitude to church-building.

Striking is the tendency, that runs all through the *Instructiones*, to create a feeling of awe and reverence in the beholder. As far as possible, it is recommended, a church should be situated on a hill. If it is built in a flat location, it should be raised on a plinth three to five steps high. Interference caused by noise from outside or by profane activity should be avoided. Hence a church should always be completely free-standing and separated by a few paces from other buildings.[11] The size of a church will depend on the requirements of ceremonial masses; in order to ensure fitting solemnity on these occasions, Borromeo specifies a required surface area per head.[12]

Although a plan may be *multiplex* in form, Borromeo gives unequivocal priority to the Latin cross as the *insignis structura* of the Cross of Christ, referring thus to early Christian Roman basilicas. The Renaissance idea of a centrally-planned building is implicitly rejected by Borromeo; he gives the Roman cross preference over the Greek, and condemns the circular form as heathenish.[13]

Borromeo places much emphasis on the aesthetic effect of the façade; all exterior embellishment and iconography – restricted to a cycle on the life of the Virgin – are concentrated on it, no artistic decoration being permitted on the other sides.[14] Borrromeo is in favour of an atrium before the façade, or at least a portico using a giant Order.[15] He prescribes that windows should have no scenic representations in stained glass, but should allow the light to enter through plain glass.[16] He goes on to give precise instructions for church furnishings and iconographical programmes.

In his last chapter Borromeo summarises his requirements in a direct paraphrase of the Tridentine decree of 1563 as follows:

> Nothing is to be made, carved, inscribed, depicted, or expressed in the fabric or ornament of any work, whatsoever it be, that is foreign to Christian piety and religion, or that is profane, ugly, sensual, lewd or obscene.[17]

Columns are permitted only because they are necessary for the *firmitas* of the building, but are now completely subordinated to the *architectonica ratio*.[18]

It would be no overestimation of Borromeo's *Instructiones* to see in them a considerable contribution to the genesis of the Baroque in architecture. The requirement of magnificence, the emphasis on the façade, the subjection of all furnishings and decoration to an overall plan – towards a theologically motivated *Gesamtkunstwerk* – are constituent elements of the Baroque. This is true at least of sacred architecture. It is still not clear through what channels this attitude spread. At all events, early Jesuit architecture – such as Il Gesù, Rome and St Michael, Munich – to some extent played an intermediary role.[19] The two treatises by Pellegrino Tibaldi, who worked for Borromeo, were only recently published.[20]

The effects of the reforms of the Council of Trent on aesthetic theory in general must be recognised as having been very varied, and cannot be discussed here.[21] Leaving aside Carlo Borromeo's *Instructiones*, and the commentary on Ezekiel by Villalpando (discussed in Chapter 18), a general tendency can be detected to subject architecture and all the plastic arts to external criteria that, although not uninfluenced by post-Tridentine attitudes, are more particularly indebted to Neoplatonism, which was not widespread until the end of the Cinquecento. Cardinal importance is attached to the concept of *disegno*,[12] which unites architecture, sculpture and painting. It is symptomatic that architecture is treated along with the plastic arts in many sixteenth-century works. Giorgio Vasari (1511–74), himself a painter, architect and theoretician, was already following this course in his well-known collection of the lives of artists, first published in 1550 and considerably expanded in 1568, which is preceded by a detailed 'Introduction to the three arts of *disegno*'.[23] Vasari places his account of architecture before that of the plastic arts, referring to Vitruvius's and Alberti's ideas on historical development.[24] However, he does not claim any superior worth for architecture as a result of such historical priority.[25] Within the framework of his 'Introduzione' Vasari does not develop any cohesive theory of architecture, but deals merely with varieties of stones – as part of a study of materials – and the Orders. What is particularly striking here is that alongside the canon of the five Orders he places the '*lavoro tedesco*', the Gothic, whose ornamentation and proportion he sees as quite distinct from those of both Antiquity and his own day.[26] Vasari describes the '*lavoro tedesco*' not as an '*ordine*' but as a '*maniera*', and attributes its evolution to the Goths. Describing the impact of the buildings, he writes that they appear to consist of paper rather than of stones or marble.[27] He makes no secret of his aversion when he speaks of 'a plague of buildings' flooding all Italy.[28] Vasari nevertheless perceives the Gothic an an autonomous style. He is a Vitruvian inasmuch as utility and beauty are for him inextricably linked in the form of a good building,[29] and he stands completely in the Renaissance tradition in his analogy of the human body with architecture.[30]

The intimate connection of architecture with the plastic arts also became apparent in the Florentine 'Accademia del Disegno' founded by Vasari in 1562.[31] It is nevertheless striking that throughout the Cinquecento no architectural theory as such was formulated in Florence, despite the fact that the Medici from Cosimo I onwards consistently pursued an absolutist policy towards architecture.[32]

Benvenuto Cellini (1500–71) left the beginning of an architectural treatise,[33] in which architecture was classed as the '*figliola seconda*' of sculpture, and reproaches were levied against Serlio for his plagiarism of Peruzzi. The content of Cellini's text is conventional.

At the beginning of the 1570s Giovanni Antonio Dosio (1533–c. 1609) was working on an architectural treatise,[34] which was supposed to be based mainly on illustrations, on the model of Serlio's, only considerably more precise. A series of drawings of Roman antiquities give an idea of Dosio's project.

The more extensive *Libro delle antichità di Roma*[35] of Pirro Ligorio (1513/14–83), known in several versions but never published, is an attempt to present a whole corpus of Roman antiquity, in which architecture is only one element. Ligorio's work comes close to the principles of the Vitruvian academy, without actually setting out from primarily architectural theoretical considerations.

A fragment has recently been published of an architectural treatise by Gherardo Spini,[36] who as a member of the Florentine Academy wrote in 1568/69 three books of a large-scale work dedicated to Cosimo de' Medici. Little is known of Spini's life. At the beginning of the treatise he describes himself as thirty years old, and later reveals that he has travelled widely in Bohemia and Austria. A rational, scientific mode of thought prevails throughout; he himself stresses his mathematical background. His work contains a few new lines of thought which make him unique for his time, and which partly anticipate concepts of the French Enlightenment.

Spini divides architecture into *fabbrica* and *ornamento*; here he is in line with Alberti, but his separation of the carcase of the building from the ornament applied to it is more extreme than Alberti's. Spini develops a new historical vision, a novel conception of architectural history, when he credits the Greeks with its high-point and with the creation of '*regole infallibili*'.[37] Accordingly, the Orders are reduced to three (Doric, Ionic and Corinthian), whose original state of perfection is to be re-established.

Here Spini strikingly anticipates the thinking of Roland Fréart de Chambray.[38] Spini has pronounced hatred for Gothic architecture, which he calls monstrous, lacking in dignity, German and 'without any rule or order'.[39]

Spini is a typical representative of the Renaissance, in assuming regularity of proportions and their analogy with the human body. Yet, it sounds strange when he justifies the carcase of a building by its necessity (*necessità*) alone, and describes it as 'the naked expression of truth' to which are added 'eloquence and its ornaments'.[40] Ornament is something 'applied', yet a building without *decoro* – the term is used by Spini as a synonym for 'ornament' – is quite lacking in dignity – like an 'outlaw'.[41]

The heart of Spini's theory is a doctrine of mimesis, according to which architecture and invention must never depart from the direct imitation of Nature. Even ornaments are subjected to this mimesis. Spini arrives at a design of the primal hut, and of various forms of wooden beams and roofs, of which he gives detailed interpretations as prototypes of the Orders (*Plates 50, 51*). These he also takes as mimetic of their constructionally interpretated 'prototypes', any deviation being understood to be an abuse and a violation of Nature. This thinking brings Spini very close to the theories of Antoine Laugier around the middle of the eighteenth century.

Spini's early rationalism is a striking exception in the Renaissance. It does not appear that there was any direct knowledge of his text in the French Enlightenment.

In the 1580s Bartolomeo Ammannati (1511–92) was engaged on a work on the ideal city, but he completed only an extensive typology of buildings. He wrote no coherent text, and the work remained unpublished.[42]

A similarly structured book by Vasari's nephew Giorgio Vasari il Giovane (1562–1625), under the title *Città ideale*, dates from 1598, and was never published either.[43] It contains a typology of models for buildings public and private, 'that may be required in the construction of a beautiful and thoroughly well-ordered city'.[44] Beyond a dedication to Grand Duke Ferdinando Medici I and an address to the reader, the book contains only brief notes. In certain details the use of Filarete, Francesco di Giorgio and Pietro Cataneo may be detected. The writer's ideal city, which he situates in the plain,[45] is clearly derived mainly from Cataneo (*Plate 52*). The younger Vasari, along with Serlio, was one of the first to show interest in the question of low-cost housing (*Plate 53*). He evolved a rational type of semi-detached house for manual workers, designed to obviate the disadvantages of two families sharing a house for economic reasons.[46]

The concept of *disegno* as a Neoplatonic Idea of form had the potential of subordinating architecture to painting in a hierarchy of the arts. This indeed was the outcome in the work of the Milanese painter and theorist Gian Paolo Lomazzo (1538–1600), who in his *Trattato dell'arte della pittura* (1584) and his *Idea del tempio della pittura* (1590) sought to prove the absolute priority of painting.[47] He proceeded to do this by means of the concept of proportion, in which according to him 'the rules of Nature' ('*ordine de la natura*') and 'the rules of theory' ('*ordine della dottrina*') meet.[48] The intellect plans according to the same principle as Nature. The idea of proportion, which he links with painting, is synonymous for him with the concept of beauty. In Neoplatonic thought the Beautiful and the Good are inextricably bound up together. But Lomazzo goes one step further in asserting that nothing can be convenient and useful if it is not at the same time beautiful, i.e. well-proportioned.[49] Since proportion reflects the '*ordine de la natura*', it follows for him that all beautiful, useful and enjoyable objects must please all men everywhere.[50] Lomazzo's speculative argument springs from medieval scholasticism, as is quite evident when for 'true proportion' he reverts to triangulation.[51]

The concept of *disegno* received theological dignity in the work of Federico Zuccaro (c. 1540–1609), who, as founder of the 'Accademia del Disegno' in Rome in 1593, gave the latter its status and presented in his *L'Idea de' pittori, scultori et architetti* (1607) a survey of Aristotelian and Scholastic ideas.[52] For him the Idea is 'internal *disegno*, form, idea, order, rule, limit, and object of the intellect in which things understood are expressed';[53] *disegno interno* is a kind of universal formula, to which the sciences, arts and moral categories are subordinate. *Disegno esterno* (what we should call 'drawing') is form become manifest in its abstract state, not its material substance.[54] With unusual rigour Zuccaro rejects the sciences, especially mathematics, as the basis of the Arts,[55] thus removing from architecture the basis which from Early Renaissance times had never been questioned. Zuccaro had as early as 1594 imposed his idea of *disegno* on the Accademia del Disegno of Rome, which was concerned to find a definition of architecture; he described painting as the mother and daughter of architecture, clearly rejecting Vitruvian definitions,[56] and went so far as to find no use for the sciences. This extreme position was bound to provoke a reaction from architects forced on to the defensive and deprived of their firm base. The response was to come from Vincenzo Scamozzi.

But before we turn to Scamozzi, let us briefly refer to a work which pertains to the history of the utopian state, but extends into architectural theory by reason of its detailed description of an ideal city: the *Città del Sole* by the Dominican Tommaso Campanella (1568–1639).[57] On the one hand, the 'Sun State' is in the tradition of the political utopias of Plato, Thomas More and Ludovico Agostini;[58] on the other, it is a concrete answer to the economic and political conditions of Southern Italy, of which Campanella was a native.[59] The Sun City is located by Campanella on the island of Taprobana (Ceylon). It is a city situated on a hill, with seven encircling walls, named after the seven planets; the diameter of the city measures two miles, its perimeter seven miles. The walls of the city are interconnected by four gates at the North, South, East and West. On top of the hill and in the centre of the innermost ring, in a spacious square, stands a round temple opened to the outside by the disposition of its columns. The building is lit from a single source of light in the crown of the cupola. Under the cupola stands the altar. But 'Nothing is to be seen on the altar but two globes, on the larger of which all the Firmament is represented, and on the second the Earth. One beholds on the interior surface of the great dome all the stars of heaven from the first to the seventh magnitude, each named and with three verses juxtaposed describing the influence it exerts on earthly things.'[60] The city is the expression of the cosmic conception of the world and of a cosmic religion. The concentric circles of the walls, with the round temple in the middle, epitomise the Renaissance conception of an ideal city.

On both sides the city walls carry an encyclopedic sequence of images. The natural sciences, ranging from mathematics through geography to the history of science, together with any inventions considered by the all-knowing government to be worthwhile, are depicted in monumental 'Agit-prop' style.[61]

This *orbis pictus* is explained by teachers, 'and it is usual for the children to learn by the age of ten, with no great effort and as if it were a game, all the sciences and yet with historical exactitude'.[62] In Campanella the ideal city is not merely the expression of a formal ideal, but at the same time the visual translation of a notion of world and society, with a pedagogical and propagandistic influence on the inhabitants. The idea of a totalitarian state is directly reflected in the Sun City. Lenin, indeed, derived ideas from the monumental propaganda of Campanella's 'Città del Sole'.[63]

Neoplatonic and Aristotelian tendencies in general aesthetic theory, as found in Lomazzo (1584, 1590) and Federico Zuccaro (1607), were also immediately reflected in pure architectural theory, and in the most comprehensive work that had so far been published in the field. Vincenzo Scamozzi (1548–1616), the much travelled and most successful architect in the generation following Palladio's death,[64] alludes in the title of his work *L'idea della architettura universale* (1615) to the treatises of Lomazzo and Zuccaro. At the same time the title holds the ambitious claim to be a comprehensive exploration of architecture. The title-page of the work (*Plate 54*) shows a self-portrait of Scamozzi, surrounded by a Neoplatonic inscription distinguishing between the '*corporis effigies*' and the '*intus effigies*' – between theory and experience. The cultured author – '*liberalium artium expers*' – who describes his labours beneath and publishes his work himself, addresses the reader with unusual directness.

By his own account Scamozzi worked on the book for twenty-five years.[65] That is to say, he must have begun writing it around 1590. In 1584, probably in collaboration with his father Giovanni Domenico Scamozzi (1526–82), he had already produced a detailed index to Serlio's works and a *Discorso* on architecture,[66] in which fundamental standpoints of his later work are foreshadowed, for example the emphasis on the scientific character of architecture and its position of priority among the other arts. A six-point programme for architecture corresponds by and large to the disposition of the later work.

In the preface to the first book, Vincenzo Scamozzi gives a synopsis of the whole treatise, with its planned ten books.[67] Through the tenfold division of contents Scamozzi consciously aligns himself with his predecessors Vitruvius and Alberti, and their aspirations. In the event, however, only Books I–III and VI–VIII appeared in print.

Scamozzi lists the overall contents of the work as follows:

Book I: Architecture's rank as a science; the architect's education.
Book II: The geographical and topographical conditions of architecture.
Book III: Private buildings.
Book IV: Public buildings.
Book V: Sacred buildings.
Book VI: The Orders.
Book VII: Building materials.
Book VIII: Construction, from the laying of the foundation-stone to roofing.
Book IX: *Finimenti* (finishing and embellishments).
Book X: Alterations and restoration.

In the mixture of pride and self-pity which pervades the work he describes his project, which he calls 'completed and perfected in all its parts' as 'a work of Daedalus'.[68] Publication of the missing books was clearly prevented by his death.

The text of the book is dauntingly erudite, pedantic and lengthy. Yet it does not offer a really coherent system of architectural theory, nor is this only because of its fragmentary nature. His basic attitudes are recognisable, but overall Scamozzi makes eclectic use of the entire history of architectural theory and practice. As the last and distinctly belated representative of the Renaissance, Scamozzi draws together a résumé of ideas that have been overtaken by events. As a guardian of Renaissance ideas, he articulates his unease about the incipient Baroque in violent invective. Writing as a cultured man for cultured readers – in his preface to the reader he addresses the '*studiosi lettori*' – he takes architecture as a science, its law as 'reason' ('*ragione*'). In fact, Scamozzi clings to the medieval cultural distinction between the *artes liberales* and the *artes mechanicae*, but at the same time, linking architecture to mathematics on the level of design and concept, frees it from the *artes mechanicae*. In his eyes, architecture is the worthiest and most important of all the sciences; it alone serves the adornment of the whole world, it gives order (*ordine*) to all things.[69] In his aesthetic concepts Scamozzi shows total adherence to Vitruvius, but the overriding claims of all-pervasive reason are evident, inasmuch as even the concept of *decoro* points back to the fact 'that all the parts are made with the use of reason'.[70]

Both geographically and historically, Scamozzi unfolds an extensive architectural panorama. As far as his own time is concerned, he claims unconditional priority for Italy, while the rest of the world known to him is 'very far behind our own Italy'.[71] With Scamozzi, design becomes a totally scientific process. Invention is applied mathematics, form is established in *disegno*, the architect is an encyclopedist.

Scamozzi seems to have been the first to recognise, or at least to formulate, the political ambivalence of the architect. He sees the alternatives of either serving 'an absolute ruler' or living 'in simple liberty and according to one's own free-will'. He considers service to an absolute ruler justifiable when the latter is virtuous and generous, but proves himself a republican at heart: 'otherwise it is much better that man lives in freedom...'[72]

Scamozzi's own wide reading in philosophy, history and aesthetics is evident throughout the work. Wherever he adopts or contradicts ideas, he nearly always gives chapter and verse in the margin. In architectural theory he knows nearly all the texts, printed and unprinted, up to his own time. He even draws on French and German authors: Hans Blum, Philibert Delorme, Hans Vredeman de Vries, Jacques Androuet Ducerceau, and Albrecht Dürer.[73] Scamozzi was the first to attempt a reconstruction of Pliny the Younger's Villa Laurentina,[74] which was henceforth to play an important role as an architectural problem.[75]

Scamozzi retains the phraseology of essential Renaissance formulae, for example in the analogy of the human body with architecture; he paraphrases 'Vitruvian man'. But here again, he finds only geometrical laws: 'thus one sees the extent to which Geometry embraces the human body.'[76] In his illustration, a geometrical grid is imposed on Vitruvian man (*Plate 55*). Architecture is separated from the plastic arts. Whereas the latter rest on the imitation of Nature, the architect creates with his intellect, and makes designs using basic geometrical forms;[77] on these rests the *idea* of the architect who is expressly compared with the mathematician and the philosopher.[78] Architectural designs must be simple and easy to understand, and above all based on the right angle; the circle and other regular forms may also be used. Therein consists concordance with

Nature. Undulating lines, layered surfaces, and non-right-angle corners are for him a violation of Nature and Reason, and contribute to 'ugliness to the sight'.[79] Here is a complete rejection of the embryonic Baroque.

The priority Scamozzi claimed for Italy in architecture is presented in the second book (on climatic conditions) as determined by Nature. If Europe is perceived as the mother of all men and Italy as the centre of Europe, Italy maintained precedence *à ragione* over all the other parts of the world.[80] Vitruvius (VI. 1) had based Rome's claim to world supremacy on similar notions. According to Scamozzi, the climatic disadvantages of other countries exercise an effect on their inhabitants and on their architecture. Thus the Germans are labelled 'late developers' (*'huomini di tardo ingegno'*).[81]

Scamozzi gives a detailed account of the planning of towns and fortifications. At one time the design of Palmanova, one of the few ideal cities of the late Cinquecento to be realised, was attributed to him. Even though it has recently emerged that the design was probably not executed by Scamozzi, but was the result of the collaboration of several designers,[82] in my opinion Scamozzi's design for Palmanova, which was however rejected by the building commission, exists in the form of his well-known design for an ideal city[83] (*Plate 56*). Although Palmanova is not mentioned in his description of the ideal city, under the item 'Palma Città nova' in the index Scamozzi gives the page reference to his description of the former. Scamozzi was unable to gain acceptance for his chessboard layout, which clearly links up with Cataneo, in the face of the opposition of the pure military architects, who preferred a radial system.[84]

In his third book, on the building of domestic architecture, Scamozzi restricts himself exclusively to palaces and villas. In many details he is dependent on previous writers. For example, his reconstruction of the 'Greek' house is but a variant of Palladio's plan.[85] Like Palladio, Scamozzi takes the opportunity of including a series of his own designs in this book.

In the sixth book, on the Orders, Scamozzi's rationalism is particularly evident. Whereas the concept of *ordine* in earlier architectural theory denoted merely the *genera* of Orders, it takes on a double meaning with Scamozzi. For him, *ordine* is the ordering of the *màcchina del mondo* which emerged from Chaos in accordance with Reason, and architecture, 'as the handmaiden of illustrious Science, requires order'.[86] 'Order' for him is the rational working principle of the world and Nature, to which the architectural 'Orders' are also subject. Although he bases his presentation of the five Orders on Serlio (*Plate 57*), whom, like Vignola, he criticises over points of detail, he goes far beyond these writers in asserting that the five Orders are rooted in the laws of Nature, that they are God-given and immutable. Their number is limited to five:[87] thus the canon established by Serlio and systematised by Vignola has become absolute. Scamozzi's rigid prescriptions may actually have been directed against Philibert Delorme, who had attempted in his *L'Architecture* (1567) to extend the canon of the Orders by the addition of a sixth, 'French', order. According to Scamozzi, the proportions of columns must follow pure numerical proportions;[88] the claims of architecture to embody reason are so pressing that irrational numbers are banished from it.

Scamozzi's sixth book, like Serlio's fourth, was also separately published, but never had any broad impact.[89] It is significant, however, that a French edition appeared in Paris in 1685, at the height of the conflict between Blondel and Perrault.[90]

Book VII, on materials, contains the most lucid treatment of the connection between materials and form of the entire Renaissance. Material, Scamozzi states, lacks form by its very nature. However, different materials have properties (*habilità*) which allow particular things to be made of them. One cannot produce any form with any given material. In the case of a form bound to a specific material, the latter could only take one form. Nevertheless, he states, form exists in its own right, material as such is without form. Only when it is shaped into form does material realise itself.[91] This thinking is based on Neoplatonism, and can be compared to the ideas already expressed by Daniele Barbaro. But Scamozzi seems to envisage something like 'truth to materials' when he requires that the architect should not force a substance: 'It is not very laudable for an architect to attempt, as it were, to do violence to the material, in the sense that he always seeks to subordinate Nature's creations to his own will, in order to give them the forms that he desires'.[92] Here Scamozzi takes up a position between theory and experience, which seems to anticipate the arguments of the Werkbund and the Bauhaus. But Scamozzi's position is unequivocal; the architect designs forms according to scientific and mathematical criteria, using materials whose specific qualities he takes into account. He plainly indicates that locally available materials should be used.[93]

Scamozzi's treatise proceeds from the general to the particular. Whereas Palladio had described the erection of a building from the foundations to the roof in the first book of his *Quattro libri*, Scamozzi does not do so until the end, in his eighth book. He aspires to *architettura universale*. Not only does he describe all the tasks and formal problems of architecture, he also displays a highly developed historical awareness, which is also reflected in his travel diaries.[94] The exponent of a completely rational architectural dogmatism, he reflects his own position in history, which he contemplates with detached interest. This explains how he came to sketch Gothic cathedrals in France with astonishing precision.[95] He writes in his diary about the cathedral of Meaux: 'In this place the cathedral is rather beautiful in the form of a cross, with five aisles, of which we have drawn the plan and given the measurements'.[96] Scamozzi sketched the plan and the elevation of the façade, with measurements. Basel Cathedral and its bridge over the Rhine arouse his interest in a similar fashion.

Scamozzi's works exude a sober and diligent straightforwardness, which rests on the rationalist's belief in progress, firm in the knowledge that he can contribute 'some happiness to man in this world'.[97] He represents at one and the same time the end of the Renaissance, reaction against the 'Mannerist' aesthetics of Lomazzo and Zuccaro, abjuration of the embryonic Baroque, and the proclamation of a new Classicism.

It is a curious fact that Italian architecture of the Early and High Baroque never received a systematic theoretical defence. Aesthetic theory as articulated in the first half of the seventeenth century to a large extent ran counter to the actual evolution of architecture and the plastic arts. The Accademia di San Luca in Rome must be regarded as once more the forum of contemporary argument.[98]

Such argument only ceased as a result of the dominating status of Giovanni Pietro Bellori (1613–96) in the Academy, who may be regarded as the lucid exponent of 'Baroque Classicism'. Bellori's aesthetic outlook is of outstanding importance not only for Italy but also for France, where he was influential through his contacts with Poussin and Roland Fréart de Chambray. In 1664 Bellori delivered a crucial lecture to the Academy under the title '*Idea del pittore, dello scultore, e dell' architetto scelta dalle bellezze naturali superiore alla Natura*' ('The idea of the painter, sculptor and architect selected from natural beauties and [thus] superior to Nature') which he placed at the beginning of his work on the lives of artists in 1672.[99] As with Zuccaro, architecture is incorporated into a general theory of art, but Bellori represents a changed position, one of a Neoplatonic stamp, which the opening sentences of his lecture spell out:

> The highest and eternal Intellect, the author of Nature, in fashioning his marvellous works looked to Himself on high and constituted those primal forms called Ideas, so that every species was expressed by its primal Idea, forming the wonderful context of created things. But the celestial bodies above the moon, not subject to change, remain beautiful and [well-]ordered, so that from their measured spheres and from the splendour of their aspects we come to recognise them as perpetually most perfect and most beautiful. Sublunary bodies, on the contrary, are subject to change and deformity...[100]

For Bellori, art consists in the approximation to the inner Idea, which is of divine origin. It is its task in this connection to 'improve' on Nature, which is subject to all the changes of this sublunary world. The Idea is not given to man a *priori*, however, but is derived from the contemplation of Nature. God himself, as the 'good architect', created the 'sensible world' on the model of the 'ideal and intelligible world'.[101] The idea of the *mondo ideale* he regards as having been rediscovered by Antiquity, hence it is to be imitated. His idea of architectural evolution culminates in the postulation of numerical, immutable laws:

> As for Architecture, let us say that the Architect must conceive a noble Idea, and fix it in his mind, so that it serves as law and reason for him, his inventions consisting in the order, disposition, measure, and harmonious proportion of the whole and of the parts. As regards the decoration and ornamentation of the Orders, he will certainly find the Idea established and confirmed by the examples of the Ancients, who gave form to this art as a result of a long study. When the Greeks defined them and gave them the best proportions, later confirmed in the most learned centuries, and by the consensus of successive wise men, they became the laws of a marvellous Idea and a supreme beauty. There being only one [kind of] beauty for each species, it cannot be altered without being destroyed.[102]

Bellori returns to the Vitruvian categories in a completely different way from Zuccaro. Bellori sees the arts as having declined with the fall of the Roman Empire, and after the fresh start made by Bramante, Raphael and Michelangelo, the prevailing subjectivism appears to him both a formal and intellectual degeneration. It infuriates him that every Tom, Dick and Harry can come up with some new idea of architecture and display it for all to see in public squares and façades. Without naming any names, he is addressing the architects of the High Baroque, whom he reproaches with ignorance:

> Not only do they deform buildings, cities themselves, and memorials, they make crazy angles, fragmented and twisted lines, they distort bases, capitals and columns with flourishes of stucco, trivialities, and disproportionate elements; and yet Vitruvius condemns such novelties.[103]

Bellori clings to the imitation of Nature and Antiquity: in the process of selection – he refers to the celebrated story of Zeuxis and the maidens – the artist approximates to the Idea and improves on Nature. Bellori rejects an imitation of Nature which does not go beyond itself as 'too natural', citing Caravaggio as an example.[104] Because Antiquity has already taken the path of selection towards realising the Idea, Bellori accepts it as normative, and regards it as standing above Nature. He strikes a curious balance between the study of nature and ideality;[105] his quest for archetypes is at the same time a search for norms for the present. But his position has a metaphysical basis, whereas analogous tendencies in absolutist France were the expression of state authority, with its desire for regimentation. It should not be forgotten, however, that Bellori's *Lives* are dedicated to Colbert.

Though one cannot say that no literature on architectural theory appeared in Italy in the seventeenth century, it is true that the Baroque was given no theoretical formulation. Most Italian authors hold backward-looking or Renaissance-oriented positions, and great architects like Borromini were more concerned with publishing their works than with theoretical reflection.

The standpoint of an aristocratic client is clearly embodied in the *Discorso sopra l'architettura* by Vincenzo Giustiniani, a Genoese of Venetian family living in Rome, best known as an art collector, which was probably written in the first decade of the seventeenth century.[106] His architectural principles have a direct link with those formulated by the North Italian circle of Humanists gathered around Giangiorgio Trissino and Alvise Cornaro two generations earlier. Like them, Giustiniani places the functional categories of *comodità, sodezza* and *sicurezza* to the fore, at the same time stressing the importance of *simmetria necessaria* and *debita proporzione*, which however are once again recommended for practical reasons.[107] He emphasises the correspondence of interior and exterior, and deals at length with the various ways of adorning a façade. At the same time, architecture is understood in its functions of 'private convenience [*comodità*]' and 'general public ornament of city and country'.[108] From these preliminaries, he goes on to considerations of town planning. Extensive theoretical and practical knowledge is demanded of the client.

Since Palladio and Scamozzi the criticism of abuses (*abusi*) in architecture had become a regular part of treatises. In 1625 the Sienese mathematician and doctor Teofilo Gallaccini (1564–1641) completed a *Trattato sopra gli errori degli architetti*, which did not however appear in print until 1767.[109] This treatise, reminiscent of Scamozzi in its rationalism, is directed, without naming names, against architectural Mannerism and the Early Baroque, but beyond this contains certain insights that ensure a place for Gallaccini in the history of architectural theory. He distinguishes pragmatically between errors which may be committed before, during and after building. For him architecture is 'imitator of the works of Nature'.[110] Crucial errors may be made before building, in the choice of site and materials, and in design. In order to avoid such mistakes as far as possible, Gallaccini pleads for local building legislation which would lay down the precise tasks of architects and workmen. Here he invokes Antiquity, and the monastic schemata of the Carthusians and Capuchins.[111]

Gallaccini writes with specialised knowledge about mistakes made in establishing foundations. Among errors that may be committed in building, the most interesting to us are those arising from the failure to take account of optical foreshortening (*Plate 58*). The constant target of his criticism is St Peter's, whose dome seems to him to be set too low. He insists that the observer's point of view should have been considered, and the springing of the dome set higher.[112] It is not numerically defined proportion that is decisive for Gallaccini, but apparent proportion based on optics. In this he is truly Baroque.

Like Palladio and Scamozzi, he turns against broken pediments and in general against any use of architectural forms contrary to the rules. He takes very seriously Vitruvius's specifications for *decoro*. Nothing must be missing and nothing superfluous, every member must of necessity (*necessità*) be in its right place.[113] He claims that the non-observance of rules and *decoro* leads to deformation and is against reason. Like Scamozzi he argues that 'where one does not observe order there is confusion, and where there is confusion there is deformity, and where there is deformity there can be no perfection of any kind'.[114] No one who violates the 'sound reason of Architecture' deserves the name of architect. Gallaccini is against the divorce between architecture and decoration. For him *decoro* constitutes the essence of a building; it is determined by *necessità*, and is thus an integral part of it.

Gallaccini's illustrations were revised for their belated publication by the Venetian architect Antonio Visentini (1688–1782),[115] and furnished with Rococo embellishments. The arguments Gallaccini had put forward against Mannerism and the Early Baroque were eminently suitable for criticism of the Rococo 150 years later. Thus, following on from Gallaccini's, Visentini published a treatise of his own in 1771,[116] extending the fight to the High Baroque and Rococo. Asserting that he does not see himself as a reformer, he states his aim of contributing to a national resurgence of architecture ('in order to revive perfect Architecture...'), the model for which he sees in the 'excellent architecture of Greek and Rome'.[117] The argument paves the way for Neo-classicism.

The majority of seventeenth-century Italian architectural treatises are compilations, manuals in cheap editions for an unsophisticated readership. This is true of the treatises of Pietro Antonio Barca (1620), Gioseffe Viola Zanini (1629), Giovanni Branca (1629), Carlo Cesare Osio (1641), Constanzo Amichevoli (1675) and Alessandro Capra (1678).[118] These on the whole modest publications enjoyed a fairly widespread circulation, as their repeated printings show. In the words of his first publisher, Branca aims at nothing more than a '*commentàrio portabile*' in which the 'general rules' are all gathered together so that with their help an approach can be made to the 'reading of serious authors'.[119] Viola Zanini repeats the Vitruvian categories and offers a somewhat unoriginal but later much quoted exposition of the Orders. Osio's treatise mainly offers rules of geometry, but endeavours to give the concept of *ordine* an ethical dimension; actually he achieves nothing more than instruction in the use of columns. Capra's subtitle announces a study of '*Architettura familiare*' (1678), in which he aims to give 'true rules' covering 'the usual things that are frequently put into practice'.[120] Appropriately, he names his five books on civil architecture after the five Orders. In the *Libro primo corrispondente all' Ordine Toscano* he deals with questions of soil and increased agricultural productivity. The Composite order serves him as a pretext for pumps and hoists. His work is less an architectural treatise than a manual for farmers in the Cremona area.

None of these treatises contributes much towards a theory of the Baroque. It is regrettable that neither from Bernini nor from Borromini nor Pietro da Cortona do we have any cohesive thoughts on architecture. Although Pietro da Cortona jointly published a treatise with the Jesuit Giovanni Domenica Ottonelli on abuses in painting and sculpture (1652),[121] in which a Counter-Reformation attitude is evident, only to a very limited extent can his views on architecture be inferred from it.[122] In Bernini's statements on architecture, which hardly add up to a self-contained system, Renaissance ideas are still apparent, for example his repeated analogy of architectural with human proportions. Thus he states in Paris in July 1665: 'And the whole art of building consists in taking proportions from the human body. That is why sculptors and painters are usually the best architects, because dealing with the human body is their livelihood'.[123]

Francesco Borromini, two of whose works intended for publication (on the Oratorio di S. Filippo Neri and S. Ivo alla Sapienza) appeared in 1720 and 1725,[124] does not represent in his commentaries – and we speak only of the *Opus Architectonicum*, on the Oratory (edited by Virgilio Spada), since the work on S. Ivo contains no commentaries – any definite 'Baroque' position either, but views rather like those expressed by Bellori to the Academy. Like Bellori, he perceives architecture as an imitation of the constructive principles of Nature. The 'lowliness of my style'[125] can hardly be held to account for his reticence. He describes his Oratorio di S. Filippo Neri as 'son of the church' (the pre-existing Chiesa Nuova), and argues that his façade is 'like a daughter of the façade of the church, that is smaller, less ornate, and of inferior materials';[126] and in so doing associates himself with sixteenth-century notions of *decoro*. He explains the fact that the façade is placed along the side of the oratory by saying that he had been trying to show the importance of the Congregation, and so had resolved 'to deceive the view of the passer-by'.[127] This regarding architecture as a matter of optical effects and façades seems to him a matter of course.

It is possible Borromini may have felt that his treatment of Antique forms was to some extent legitimised by the publications of Giovanni Battista Montano (1534–1621), of which he demonstrably made use.[128] In his reconstructions and designs Montano arrived at proto-Baroque creations, in which perspective effects are introduced, whose potential applications Borromini was the first to recognise.[129]

The only seventeenth-century Italian architectural theory after Scamozzi truly deserving of the name is the work of the Theatine father, Guarino Guarini (1624–83) of Modena.[130] Guarini published works on theology, mathematics and architectural theory, his architectural activity being concentrated mainly in Turin, with buildings also in Modena, Paris, Messina and Lisbon.

After a thorough study of Borromini's works, with which he became acquainted during his novitiate in Rome, Guarini approached architecture through mathematics, whose fundamental importance for architecture he repeatedly stresses. He gives prominence to the surveying of buildings and geometrical projection. In 1674 in Turin he published his treatise *Modo di misurare le fabbriche*, and in 1676 the *Trattato di fortificazione*.[131] He worked on his architectural treatise in the last years of his life; it was unfinished at his death, but the extant parts including the illustrations seem to have been taken to their final form by Guarini himself. In 1686, three years after his death, there appeared a collection of plates[132] of his depictions of the Orders and of his own architectural works. The first complete edition of the whole treatise, or as much of it as was in existence, was published in 1737, edited by the architect Bernardo Vittone (1702–70).

Guarini, an exceedingly methodical and at times somewhat schematic theoretician, possessed a thorough knowledge of the literature of mathematics and architectural theory. He comments on his Italian predecessors, but the French writers Philibert Delorme and Roland Fréart de Chambray, and the Spaniard Caramuel, against whose *Architectura civil recta y obliqua*,[133] published in 1678, he waged a polemic, almost play a greater part in his thinking.

Like most theoreticians since Vitruvius, Guarini perceives architecture as a science. The architect must be broadly educated in the arts and sciences, particularly mathematics and geometry; for 'Architecture, as a faculty that in all its operations uses measurements, is dependent upon Geometry.;[134] but in spite of its rationality, it must appeal to the senses. Guarini's emphasis on geometry brings him very close to Fréart de Chambray, who in 1650 had described geometry as 'the basis and the general store of all the arts'.[135] Following Alberti, Guarini distinguished very sharply between design ('*idee, o sia disegno*') and execution ('*esecuzione*').[136] The six Vitruvian criteria of architecture (Vitruvius I.2) Guarini reduces to four, which he interprets not in relation to architecture but to *disegno*, the drawn design clearly being of primary importance. The concepts taken over from Vitruvius are *sodezza* (strength); *eurythmia*, interpreted by Guarini as *ornamento*; *simmetria*, explained as proportion; and *distribuzione*, which he takes in the French sense, to mean the proper and convenient arrangement of rooms.[137] It is striking that Guarini mixes fundamental categories such as *sodezza* with aesthetic concepts. The Vitruvian concepts of *ordinatio, dispositio* and *decor* are obviously understood as synonyms by Guarini, and hence superfluous. The structural (*sodezza*) and the functional (*distribuzione*) points of view are paramount in Guarini: 'Architecture is concerned above all else with convenience ['*comodità*'].[138] For Guarini architecture cannot be beautiful unless it takes account of *utilità*. It adjusts to national customs and individual needs. This viewpoint brings Guarini very close to the French theorists of the seventeenth century.

Towards Antiquity and the theories of his predecessors, Guarini is detached and critical. Antiquity is not the standard model, the rules of Vitruvius and Vignola are not unconditionally binding. He maintains a view of architectural evolution according to which the habits and needs of men change, and architecture has to adapt to these changes. The military architecture of his time is completely different from that of Antiquity by reason of new weaponry, and civil architecture is similarly subject to changes. Guarini plainly states: 'Architecture can correct the rules of Antiquity, and invent new ones.'[139] In this formulation, presenting an exact reverse of the abstract, dogmatic, and backward-looking position of Fréart de Chambray, architectural theory can be seen taking a decisive step out of the ossification in which it had been caught since the late Renaissance; one may see it as the Baroque's theoretical self-justification.

This is no plea for complete freedom from rules. Guarini is aware of the sensuous appeal of architecture, but on the other hand he declares his allegiance to the 'true proportion'.[140] The goal of architecture remains that of giving concrete form to 'true symmetry', but it is permissible to deviate from it when it cannot be directly conveyed to the senses, in which case the architect may make an optical compromise, by means of his knowledge of perspective, through addition or subtraction. The precepts of Gallaccini can be apprehended here, though he is not named. At all events, Guarini maintains, the exact proportions must be established before they are deviated from. A preoccupation with the optics of the beholder, so fundamental to the Baroque, leads Guarini, almost incidentally, to justify the handling of *non-finito* in painting and sculpture as follows: 'Whence we see that painters and sculptors make images and statues rough and only sketched out to be seen from a distance, [and that] they look better than if they were highly finished.'[141]

Guarini's fundamental treatment of architecture is to be found in the first three chapters of the *Modo di misurare le fabbriche*. He goes on the reflect that in order to present his ideas, the architect needs drawing materials, and immediately embarks on a detailed discussion of drawing implements.[142] He then does the same for geometry, so important for the architect, which leads him from a textbook exposition of the principles of levelling and geometrical projection to geodesy, which discussion takes up most of the rest of the work.[143] In his eyes geometry is uppermost in the process of design.

Statements embodying Guarini's totally practice-oriented attitude towards architecture are to be found rather at random. For example, his requirements for a satisfactory plan are that rooms should be of different sizes according to their function, that doors should make an enfilade, and that each room have at least two windows; doors should be as near as possible to the outside wall, in order not to hinder the placing of beds;[144] from the outside a building must appear completely symmetrical. Guarini does not yet use the modern concept of symmetry developed by Perrault about this time, but speaks of the 'proper correspondence'.[145]

The sense of architectural evolution that permits the establishment of new rules brings Guarini to the espousal of aesthetic relativism. He sees the difficulty of defining sources of aesthetic pleasure ('*diletto*'), since these are subject to changing fashions. The architecture of Roman antiquity displeased the Goths, just as Gothic architecture displeases his own time.[146] Hence – as with Philibert Delorme – the number of the Orders themselves is not restricted to five: their number can be added to, their proportions can be changed. In the end Guarini gives only *regole generali*; his position is in many respects comparable to that of Claude Perrault. Guarini allows three varieties of each of the Doric, Ionic and Corinthian Orders. The 'Latin' Orders, the Tuscan and Composite, he sees as subsumed by the Greek. This is reminiscent of Fréart de Chambray, whose antipathy towards the Latin Orders he does not, however, share. He gives surprisingly precise specifications for the proportions of the Orders, being clearly afraid of excessive licence in their use. It is astonishing to us that Guarini gives the status of an Order to the 'Gothic': he speaks, as Caramuel had not long before him, of the '*ordine Gotico*',[147] describing its 'lovely slenderness... [so] completely contrary to Roman architecture'.[148] With great sensitivity he describes the floating, diaphanous quality of Gothic architecture, mentioning numerous examples from Spain, France and Italy that have left their mark upon his own architecture.[149] He has reservations about the Gothic masons' excessive license in proportions, but calls them 'ingenious builders'.[150] Guarini finally goes so far as to propose an academic debate as to whether Roman or Gothic architecture has the higher goals.[151] Guarini takes a decisive step towards making a positive evaluation of the Gothic possible again.[152]

Schematic as he is from time to time, Guarini accepts 'three varieties of column' for the Gothic as well as in the case of the Greek Orders, and significantly, he represents them on a plate that also includes contemporary forms of pediments (*Plate 59*). He specifically stresses that the *frontespizio ondato* was not known to Antiquity, and he defends the *frontespizi spezzati*[153] branded by Palladio as an architectural abuse. He derives the '*ordine Corinto supremo*', the spiral column with undulant entablature, from the Temple of Solomon (*Plate 60*).[154] Here he is probably drawing on experience going back to his travels in Spain and his meeting with the Spanish Benedictine monk Fray Juan Ricci, who in 1663 wrote a *Brebe tratado de Arquitectura acerca del orden Salomónico Entero*.[155]

Guarini is eclectic in his thinking,[156] but he brings into his theory, fragmentary as it is, so much experience and sense of reality as to make him alone in the seventeenth century in daring, in some measure, to forsake Renaissance positions and to advocate a Baroque synthesis of geometrical patterns, sense experience and innovatory forms. His plates, evidently prepared by himself for publication, are unfortunately without commentary. Competent interpretations in theological, iconological and architectural terms might perhaps have been expected of Guarini.

To the end of the seventeenth century belongs a treatise on perspective by the Jesuit father Andrea Pozzo (1642–1709),[157] which does not altogether fall within the framework of architectural theory. In *Perspectiva Pictorum et Architectorum* (published in Rome in two volumes, 1693–98) Pozzo is exclusively concerned with the representation of architecture: he wishes to convey to his readers 'the most expeditious [*sbrigato*'] way of rendering all architectural designs in perspective', as he states in the subtitle in Italian. Architecture itself is taken in his work as given, but its representation cannot, he says, be beautiful unless it itself is so: 'The perspective rendering of Buildings, with which we are now dealing, will be devoid of beauty and proportion if these are not inherent in the Architecture.'[158] Represented and real architecture are perceived as two separate things. However, maintains Pozzo, a good painter must be good at perspective; and if this is so, he will also be a good architect. His book is a didactic introduction to the perspective drawing of architecture. It begins with the square, progresses to complex forms and bodies and ends, significantly, with stage-sets. In the second volume Pozzo mainly presents his own designs, and here also their perspective depiction interest him most. His words in connection with his alternative designs for the façade of San Giovanni in Laterano (1699), 'to the extent that they vary in the architecture, they vary also in the perspective rendering of it',[159] clearly show that for him the dividing line between architecture and *quadratura* has become fluid. Here lies the point of departure for the view of architecture held by Ferdinando Galli Bibiena and his family in the first half of the eighteenth century.

An important book of plates of Roman Baroque architecture was produced in three volumes between 1702 and 1721 by the publishing-house of Domenico de' Rossi;[160] it contains the earliest reproductions of measured drawings of the buildings and much of the architectural detail of the Roman Baroque. Although the *Studio d'architettura civile* ... furnishes no contribution to architectural theory, it nevertheless became the most important source for the international spread of Roman Baroque, and contributed considerably to its international character at the beginning of the eighteenth century.

Editions

Vincenzo Scamozzi, *L'idea della architettura universale*, Venice 1615 (facs. editions Ridgewood, N.J. 1964; Bologna 1982). The first editions in English, 1690, 1708.

Guarino Guarini, *Architettura civile*, 2 vols, Turin 1737; facs. edition, London 1964. Critical edition: Guarino Guarini, *Architet-* *tura civile*, ed. Nino Carboneri and Bianca Tavassi La Greca, Milan 1968.

The first part of Andrea Pozzo's *Perspectiva Pictorum et Architectorum* (Rome 1693) is available in a facsimile reprint of the English-and-Latin edition of 1707: Andrea Pozzo, *Perspectives in Architecture and Painting*, New York 1989.

9. The theory of fortification

For Vitruvius, as for the Early Renaissance, fortification and the science of siege-devices and defensive machines formed an integral part of architecture. The technological revolution in artillery at the end of the fifteenth century, consisting in the systematic use of cannon fired by means of gunpowder, and the use of iron as opposed to stone cannonballs, necessitated a radical change in fortifications, the conventional forms of which no longer stood up to the new weapons; the superiority of the cannon became abruptly clear from the Italian expedition of Charles VIII of France in 1494. Until these developments took place, the occupations of architect and engineer were inseparable; the terms were interchangeable. The new technology, however, necessitated specialisation; cooperation between engineers and the military increased, soldiers became engineers and began to write treatises on fortification. By about the middle of the sixteenth century, the separation of military and civil architecture was largely complete.[1]

The hiving-off of military architecture, and the implicit disdain of it as a form of engineering, contributed to the virtual exclusion of this type of construction and its theory from the history and theory of architecture. As far as the history of art was concerned, it became a part of 'military science'.[2] This historical attitude is questionable, for it overlooked the interdependence of fortification and town-planning, and ignored the aesthetic premises implicit in fortification. These interconnections have only recently become a focus of attention once again, and are now rearousing interest in military architecture.[3]

Yet the separation of civil architecture and fortification was never a complete one; this is demonstrated by the treatises of Pietro Cataneo (1554 and 1567) and Vincenzo Scamozzi (1615). Despite the necessarily practical emphasis on fortification, aesthetic considerations were never completely abandoned, even where justified on functional grounds. For these reasons, it seems appropriate to give a brief survey of the theoretical literature on fortification.

In the Early Renaissance, Flavius Vegetius Renatus's Late Antique treatise on warfare, *Epitoma rei militaris* (c. AD 400), was widely read and, thanks to numerous manuscript copies and printed editions in the fifteenth century, was known throughout Europe.[4] The fourth book deals with siege warfare, and the first six chapters of this book are devoted to the fortification of towns. For a time, Vegetius enjoyed as wide a circulation as Vitruvius.

As late as the mid-fifteenth century, a treatise on the art of warfare could still be thought of largely as a philological work, as indicated by Roberto Valturio's *De re militari libri XII*, which relies entirely on Classical authors and the Church Fathers.[5] Valturio's work was the first printed (1472) military treatise.

For Alberti, Filarete and Francesco di Giorgio, fortification is part of a global conception of architecture, but Francesco di Giorgio's treatises clearly reveal his special interest in this type of construction; Francesco was the leading designer of fortifications of his time. Yet it is clear that the theoretical integration of fortification into anthropometric schemata took second place to practical considerations in the later versions of Francesco's treatise *Trattato di architettura civile & militare*.[6] His designs show the special way in which he was forced to react to the new developments in siege technology. As a result, one of the main areas dealt with in his treatises falls within the field of engineering. This also sets Francesco in a Sienese tradition. In the mid-fifteenth century, his fellow-countryman Jacopo Mariano, known as Il Taccola (1381–c.1453–58), had already compiled an extensive compendium on mechanical engineering, *De machinis libri X*, comprising compilations of drawings in which military machines figure prominently (mss. in Munich and Florence).[7] Taccola's work had a great influence on Francesco di Georgio and on the whole course of mechanical engineering in the sixteenth century.

During the sixteenth century, military architecture is largely a reply to the prevailing state of ballistics. Walls become lower and towers turn into bastions. The construction of bastions occupies a central place in treatises such as Giovan Battista della Valle di Venafro's *Vallo. Libro continente appartenentie ad Capitani*[8] and Niccolò Machiavelli's *Arte della guerra*.[9] Although Machiavelli was opposed in principle to any kind of fortification, since, he claimed, a submissive army made such fortification otiose, nevertheless, on a specific level, he does discuss Polybius's specifications for Roman camps,[10] a subject later also explored by Serlio and Palladio.

The year 1527 saw the publication of Albrecht Dürer's treatise on fortification, strictly speaking the first treatise dealing exclusively with this subject.[11] It is unlikely that Dürer's preoccupation with military architecture dates back to his travels to Italy; it was probably first triggered off by the siege of Hohenasperg in 1519, which he had observed with his friend Willibald Pirckheimer. What prompted the writing of his treatise was clearly the advance of the Turks – then occupying Hungary – the need to repel whom Dürer explicitly mentions. It is therefore natural that the work should be personally dedicated to the hard-pressed Ferdinand I, proclaimed king of Hungary and Bohemia in 1526.

Dürer's treatise employs a dual approach. On the one hand Dürer develops various alternatives for the construction of bastions to defend existing cities; this is the contemporary aspect. At the heart of his treatise, he outlines a utopian city, in which the nature of the fortifications merely serves as a spur to the depiction of a social structure organised on the ground (*Plate 61*). Dürer does not speak of a city; he calls it instead a '*fest schloß*' ('fortified citadel'), which he envisages building in the shape of a square beside a river and in a plain.[12] The only source mentioned by Dürer is Vitruvius,[13] but even this reference remains vague. Dürer first describes a system of ditches and ramparts, in the centre of which lies the '*gefierter Platz*' ('square') and the palace, also erected on a quadrangular plan. There follows a detailed division of the rest of the town's surface area. Related trades are placed side by side; smiths are to be housed near foundries, etc. The town hall and the houses of the nobility are sited near the royal palace. The whole system of organisation is hierarchical and functional. Dürer thinks of every function of the city, right down to the taverns. He formulates the idea behind his organisation as follows:

> The king shall not let people live in this citadel who are not useful, but only capable, god-fearing, sage, manly men of experience, skilled in arts, good craftsmen, who will serve the citadel, who can make guns and use them.[14]

In an astonishingly far-sighted, economically and socially pragmatic way, Dürer advocates the use of the unemployed poor in the building of fortifications, people who would otherwise have to be supported by charity; providing them with a daily wage will stop them begging, and in this way their inclination to revolt will be suppressed. In support of his argument, Dürer cites the otherwise pointless waste of resources involved in the building of the Egyptian pyramids.[15] The construction of fortifications thus performs as a job-creation scheme.

It is unlikely that Dürer drew any formal inspiration from earlier Italian architectural theory for his quadrate town plan, since that theory advocated polygonal or star-shaped plans. A possible source for Dürer – as for Machiavelli, Serlio and Palladio – could have been Polybius's *Castrametatio*. Any indication in this direction is, however, lacking. What is more likely is that Serlio went back to Dürer for the reconstruction of Polybius in his sixth book.[16] It may here be recalled that a Latin edition of the first of Hernando Cortès's letters to the Emperor Charles V concerning the conquest of Mexico was published in Nuremberg in 1524[17] and that these letters were accompanied by a woodcut depicting the Aztec capital Tenochtitlan (*Plate 62*). This woodcut was probably known to Dürer. The island-city laid out on a square-shaped grid cannot be dismissed as a possible source for Dürer's plan.[18] Quadrate town plans such as those of Francesco de Marchi, Cataneo and Ammannati are found in the second half of the sixteenth century, and presuppose Dürer's design. The Black Forest town of Freudenstadt, designed by Heinrich Schickhardt and begun in 1599, clearly goes back to Dürer's project.[19] Another derivative of Dürer's design may perhaps be seen in the plan drawn up in 1638 for the town of New Haven in Connecticut. It has recently been claimed that Utopian town plans such as Johann Valentin Andreae's 'Christianopolis' (1619) and Villalpando's reconstruction of Solomon's Temple may have influenced the plan for New Haven,[20] but Dürer's project is much closer to it.

The fortified outpost sited in a narrow pass between mountain and sea which Dürer presents next, describing it as a '*feste Clause*' (fortified pass), displays totally fantastic features. Dürer develops the pure circle into a '*Zirkularbefestigung*' (circular fortification) of huge proportions. The use of a basic geometric shape is taken to be as self-explanatory as it is in the case of the town plan. Military reasons for its choice are not adduced.

At the end of his treatise, Dürer offers suggestions for the strengthening of older fortifications. The practical nature of these proposals links up with the proposals for bastions set out at the beginning.

Dürer's precepts on fortification are a combination of practical observations on fortifications with utopian notions of the ideal city. This combination appears again and again in treatises in fortification, and here is another reason why the science of fortification must be included in architectural theory.

A codification of contemporary knowledge of ballistics is to be found in the work of the mathematician Nicolò Tartaglia, who in 1537 published his *Nova scientia*, followed a year later by *Quesiti et inventioni diverse*.[21] In these works Tartaglia presents detailed calculations of trajectories; he is regarded as 'the father of ballistics'. Although his works contain no theory of fortification, they became the basis of defensive architecture in the sixteenth century. In the 1550 edition of the *Nova scientia* Tartaglia provides a remarkable frontispiece (*Plate 63*). Euclid opens the only door to a closed walled circle; within the walled circle, Tartaglia stands surrounded by the Liberal Arts, demonstrating the trajectory of a cannonball. Aristotle opens the door to a second, smaller walled circle; behind him stands Plato holding a pennon bearing the legend *'Nemo huc Geometrie expers ingrediat'* ('Let no one enter here save the expert in geometry'). Philosophy sits enthroned above the smaller walled circle. The entire layout resembles a fortified town such as we are familiar with from numerous sixteenth-century illustrations. The only way into the internal part is via geometry; the picture has a double meaning.

The tendency to specialisation that characterised military as opposed to civil architecture emerges particularly clearly in Giovanni Battista Bellucci (1506–54) of San Marino, who was first a merchant and came into contact with architecture relatively late in life through marriage to a daughter of Giorolamo Genga. In the service of Cosimo de' Medici he became one of the leading military architects of his time.[22] Bellucci left several unfinished drafts of a treatise on fortification, numerous copies of which were in circulation and use in the sixteenth century but which did not appear in print until 1598, in a corrupt version under the name Belici.[23] In addition to a diary,[24] an autograph abridgement of the treatise dated 1545 is now available in a critical edition.[25]

Bellucci writes in the terse style of a soldier with little time to spare. He regards a knowledge of ballistics as fundamental in fortification. He subdivides the different types of fortification into *reale* and *non reale* according to the calibre of the guns that are deployed on them, shot weighing over 8 *libre* (approximately 6 pounds) being classified as *reale*, under 8 *libre* as *non reale*.[26] This classification according to calibre of cannon was a subject of constant debate in the sixteenth century. Bellucci confines himself to his own time, for which, he claims, the older rules of the art of fortification are no longer valid.[27] Bellucci writes from personal experience of the factors of time, weather and supplies of material and labour. In his opinion, the academically trained mind cannot fulfil the requirements of military construction. The drawing of the plan must be entrusted to a 'soldier who, through his experience of war, can plan well'; the execution of the construction may, he says, be entrusted to a 'reliable captain, a master-builder, who has sound architectural principles...'[28] The construction of fortifications can, in Bellucci's experience, only be carried out by a team. Aesthetic considerations take second place to practical; he speaks of the 'wantonness of the ornament', without, however, completely excluding it from the architecture of fortification.[29]

Bellucci's treatise is the first work by an engineer specialising exclusively in fortification in which the image of the universal architect is called into question. Technological developments to a large extent proved Bellucci right. The artillery-led conception of fortification spread rapidly across Europe. In Italy Giovanni Battista Zanchi was the first to publish a compendium of this kind (1554),[30] which was translated into French two years later by François de la Treille without mention of his source.[31] In 1559 the Englishman Robert Corneweyle adapted the French text – again without giving precise details of his source – in preparation for an English edition, which, however, remained unpublished.[32] All these texts advocate polygonal layouts with corner bastions, and demonstrate the weakness of solutions based on squares.

Pietro Cataneo, whose treatise (1554) is generally classified with the literature on fortification, again attempted a wider synthesis. Although he gives priority to fortification and town planning, it seemed more appropriate in this book to present Cataneo in another context.[33]

The path embarked on by Bellucci was pursued in particular by Francesco de Marchi of Bologna (1504–76), who was employed mainly in the service of Pope Paul III and in the Netherlands.[34] De Marchi worked over twenty years on his *Architettura militare*. According to his own statements, the work was begun before 1545 in Rome; one plan for fortifications is dated Brussels, 27 September 1565.[35] Parts of the work, in particular the plates, were printed and even plagiarised whilst the author was still working on the book. A complete edition was published only in 1599, over twenty years after his death.[36]

Like Pietro Cataneo, de Marchi alternates between town planning and fortification. In his foreword he addresses the reader as 'soldier', and like Bellucci, of whose treatise he made a copy,[37] he advocates that it should be primarily the soldier experienced in artillery who has the deciding voice in the planning of fortifications.[38] He envisages the planning of fortifications and town as a collaborative task: the architect drawing the plans and supervising construction, and a soldier deciding on location and form; a doctor being consulted about climatic conditions and the quality of provender, an agriculturist about food supplies, a mineralogist about deposits of raw materials, an astrologer about the best time to begin work, etc.[39]

Planning is a product of cooperation between architect and professional soldier. De Marchi, however, brings aesthetic criteria decisively into play in advocating geographical situations in which '*l'arte*' can be expressed in the design, and in which it does not have to be dictated by the site. De Marchi wishes to see the functional and aesthetic aspects being made to coincide:

> However, skilful and ingenious soldiers and architects, in a similar situation, will be able to build both impregnable and beautiful works, in accordance with the dictates of the site, that will comply with the rules of art, positioned and executed by a man of skill and ingenuity.[40]

He respects asymmetrical fortifications, but thinks they should be 'symmetrical, or as nearly so as possible'.[41] For him, geometric regularity remains the clear objective of all designs, and this is clearly reflected in most of his own.

De Marchi's first book, which has no illustrations, is, along with Cataneo's first book, the earliest cohesive account of town planning. In contrast to Bellucci, de Marchi provides historical examples. Alongside the notion of the Vitruvian-style architect with an all-round education, he places the 'uneducated man' who, through experience and a love of the subject, wins the right to work as a planner, and even to write about architecture: 'However, with love, enjoyment and long experience, even without education, it is possible to write sincerely and without sophistication about worthwhile things, as I myself have done'.[42] De Marchi here lays down the professional profile of the practically-trained engineer, who ousts the architect from certain areas of his work. The fact that this claim is also translated to the level of theory hastens the separation of civil and military architecture.

De Marchi's third book consists of 161 plans of fortifications and cities in both fictitious and real geographical situations, accompanied by explanatory notes. It is the most comprehensive compendium of the sixteenth century. There is a clear preference for regular geometric designs with a radial system of streets in the interior. De Marchi's long years of service in the Netherlands result in a curious combination of Northern and Mediterranean architectural forms (*Plate 64*). Northern Gothic and Italian Renaissance styles appear side by side on radial or grid-shaped layouts, in an almost historicist manner.

The siege of Malta by the Turks in the summer of 1565 prompted de Marchi to bring forward a plan for a new fortified town on the island, that had actually been previously drawn up in Brussels, on 27 September 1565, but which was nonetheless to underlie Francesco Laparelli's designs for Valletta.[43] Another plan for an actual geographical situation relates to a town on Monte Argentario in southern Tuscany.[44]

De Marchi regards his plans as models for towns and fortifications 'which will be of use, if not in their entirety, at least in part'.[45] Whether de Marchi achieved this objective remains to be investigated. A discourse on artillery is appended to the treatise as a fourth book.

The treatise published in 1564 by Girolamo Maggi (1523–72) and Jacomo Fusto Castriotto (c.1510–63) represents an interesting attempt to set the engineering element of fortification within a Humanistic framework.[46] The core of the treatise is the work of Castriotto, a fortifications engineer who worked in Italy and France, whilst the introductory sections and commentaries, which help give the tersely military text some background of learning, were added by the Humanist-trained jurist Maggi.[47] Maggi presents himself as the actual author, but has the honesty to indicate the true authorship of the various parts of the text by name. How Maggi came to be in possession of Castriotto's texts and drawings is not quite clear, but the fact that the book was published one year after Castriotto's death is probably no accident.

Castriotto,[48] who was a friend of Bellucci, clearly had in mind a very practical treatise on fortification, including a section on the construction of siege forts. Maggi provides an introductory passage – sprinkled with quotations and historical digressions – in which he expounds on the various elements of human coexistence, such as family, house, neighbourhood and city, giving precedence as he does so to questions of social structure over considerations of fortification. Maggi rejects town plans based on square or triangular designs, which he describes as 'the most imperfect',[49] and inveighs repeatedly against Dürer, to whose work he evidently had access.[50] Castriotto advocated either circular shape or regular polygons for fortifications and cities[51] and recommended curved walls, claiming them to be more resistant. He thus arrived at a circular town plan, with a radial street-pattern and octagonal ramparts (*Plate 65*).[52] Interestingly, however, the groups of buildings summarily indicated in each block all differ from one another. Castriotto went on to present a number of projects for fortifications or siege-forts, some of which he had actually executed, others merely planned, e.g. his fortifications for Sermoneta,[53] and his plans for the siege of Mirandola in 1552.[54] Both writers go into much detail about topography and the technical problems of sieges. In the third book of the treatise, Maggi provides a résumé of a number of works by other writers, which are only loosely related to the main subject.[55] Maggi's contributions are in parts rather stilted. The usefulness of the treatise lay exclusively in Castriotto's instructions on engineering.

The treatises on fortification[56] written in Italy in the second half of the Cinquecento and at the beginning of the Seicento hold less interest as regards theory. To 1570 belongs a work by Galasso Alghisi[57] of Carpi. Although Alghisi starts off from the self-evident premise that the nature of fortification is determined by artillery, he soon lapses into a tedious polemic against Maggi and Castriotto, and in the end becomes the victim of a geometric formalism, which basically allows only the circle as the basis of any plans. He rejects square-shaped designs and those with sharp-angled bastions. The second book, which contains designs for layouts with between five and twenty-seven bastions, in each case plotted within a circle, reveals particularly clearly the schematism involved, which Alghisi formulates as follows: 'Because all buildings are no more than the sum of *disegno*, architecture, arithmetic, geometry and perspective.'[58]

Only recently has a manuscript compendium on military architecture by Galeazzo Alessi (1512–72) come to light, dating from the last few years of the author's life (c.1564–70), giving a brief résumé of the state of fortification theory.[59] Alessi bases his account especially on Maggi and Castriotto, and on Alghisi. Whether Alessi's treatise contains any originality will not be known until its publication.

The use of the circle as a basis for design completely dominates architectural discussion at the end of the Cinquecento. Towns are planned radially.[60] Thus Bonaiuto Lorini (c.1540–1611) published a radial plan with nine bastions and an internal arrangement of piazzas[61] like the one actually realised by himself and Giulio Savorgnano in Palmanova (from 1593).[62] Lorini's treatise displays another interesting feature in that he, as a practitioner, offers advice for the calculation of time and cost (Book II) and for the modernisation of outdated fortifications using existing masonry to a large extent (Book IV).

Around 1600 *architettura civile* and *architettura militare* appear to have equal status. Pietro Sardi puts them on a par with each other as '*due Arti*'.[63] With the decline in the military importance of fixed fortifications in the seventeenth century, treatises also lose something of their gravity, and the illustrations occasionally take on an idyllic character.[64]

In the German-speaking world, no important contribution had been made to the theory of fortification since Dürer's short treatise.[65] It was only at the end of the sixteenth century that an important German treatise was again published, which may indeed be regarded as the most significant of its time: that of the much-travelled and widely employed municipal architect of Strassburg, Daniel Speckle (also known as Specklin, 1536–89).[66] The *Architectura von Vestungen*, new editions of which continued to be published up into the eighteenth century, appeared in the year of his death.[67]

Speckle writes his treatise from a strongly national motivation as is clear from his preface. He wishes to prove that the Germans are not completely without imagination, and that their invention of printing and of a '*grausam Geschütz*' ('fearsome artillery') shows them to be 'the greatest in the world' in these fields.[68] He attacks, above all, the Italian theorists for their academic disputes, declaring their rules to be outmoded and openly ridiculing their approach ('when someone has no Latin, he cannot understand it, and so has no business to talk about it'[69]). He demonstrates the urgency of fortification, as Dürer had done, by reference to the Turkish threat. Speckle claims to be familiar with fifty or sixty types of fortification, but restricts himself to a few only. He writes in German and avoids foreign words, 'so that every German – such as I too have the honour to call myself – can understand'.[70]

Speckle tackles his subject as a practitioner, and a marked sense of realism runs through his whole treatise. In the first part he deals with fortifications in the plain, in the second with those in hilly and mountainous terrain, in the third with equipping fortifications. For Speckle too, mathematics and in particular geometry, together with mechanics and practical expertise, form the basis of fortification. Accordingly, he first provides an introduction to geometry. He completely rejects the triangle as a basis for plans, and, beginning with the square, discusses the advantages and disadvantages of the various polygonal forms. In his view, defensive capability increases in proportion with the number of bastions. In Speckle too, there is no separation of fortification and town planning. The twenty-eighth chapter of the first part of the treatise contains the essence of Speckle's thinking on town planning. He starts with a description of a regular plan with six bastions, of which he gives a perspective view and which reveals the priority he accords to defensive considerations.[71] He then describes in great detail an ideal type of town plan with eight bastions (*Plate 66*), in which his political and social ideas are revealed. In the tradition of all military architects of the second half of the sixteenth century, he uses a strict radial pattern. Around the central square are sited church, royal palace, town hall and staple inn. Religious, secular and economic power are concentrated in this area. The military, on the other hand, are removed to the areas around the bastions. It is interesting that Speckle expressly sets civil law above martial law.[72] Speckle aims overall at a very ordered community: 'mercenaries should be done away with'.[73] Defensive considerations determine the city to the last detail. Thus he writes of private dwellings:

> Wherever possible every house should be of proper stone, or at least the lower storey, cellars should all be vaulted, and all houses should be on the same level and of the same height; they should all be roofed with tiles rather than shingles. They should all be provided with strong doors, and have bars over the windows, and all the streets should be paved, so that, even if an enemy were to capture such a citadel, each house could be defended with projectiles and ammunition.[74]

In principle, Speckle here adumbrates a plan for an ideal city such as was realised a few years later in Palmanova.

In the second part of the treatise Speckle presents plans whose form is dictated by terrain. He describes *inter alia*, in great detail, the Turkish siege of Malta (1565) and the rebuilding of Valletta, and in so doing provides us with one of the most detailed plans we have of Francesco Laparelli's project.[75] In the same part Speckle also provides examples of fortified passes and mountain castles. The engravings by Matthäus Greuter are of excellent quality, and very evocative.[76] Particularly noteworthy is Example No. 7, described by Speckle as a '*wunderbarlich Hauss*' (*Plate 67*). Atop a rock edged like a diamond is placed a 'glorious pleasure house' ('*ein herrlich lustig Wohnung*').[77] Such flights into the Utopian and fantastic are rare in Speckle. He owes the success he enjoyed in his time to his practical instructions, offered with the experience of a very knowledgeable, though not learned, man.

France in the sixteenth century was largely dependent on Italy as far as fortification was concerned.[78] It was only at the end of the century that a number of treatises appeared displaying some degree of independence. The Lorrainer Jean Errard of Bar-le-Duc (1554–1610/11), whose treatise on fortification was completed in 1594 but not published until 1600, is regarded as the '*père de la fortification française*'.[79] Structurally, this treatise bears some resemblance to Speckle's. In the first part, Errard deals with general problems of fortification, in the second with regular polygonal layouts ranging from the hexagon to the twenty-four-sided polygon, in the third with irregular layouts, and in the fourth with fortifications whose shape is dictated by terrain. In 1597 the Frenchman Claude Flamand, employed partly in German service, published a treatise on fortification[80] dealing not only with geometry and fortification, but also with siege warfare itself. Both Errard and Flamand are characterised by their practicality.

Jacques Perret's work is purely a collection of plans, which, although depicting various polygonal types of fortification, essentially contains plans for ideal cities based on radial and octagonal grids.[81] Perret first presents a number of plans for fortifications with four, five or six bastions, providing a plan and aerial view of each. In each case the nature of the internal design is derived from the number of bastions. A sixteen-sided town plan enclosing a citadel provides Perret with the opportunity to develop a layout in the form of a *'quadrature parfaite'*.[82] Around a central square occupied only by a fountain, Perret lays out a chessboard pattern of blocks of houses; the communal buildings are sited on the outer edge, near the ramparts, there are no churches. In the centre of the citadel stands a *'grand pavillon'* several storeys high, intended for the commander, affording a view over the whole fortification.

Perret's thinking in geometric patterns and grids is revealed even more clearly in a twenty-three-sided fortification with citadel (*Plate 68*), within which he lays out a radially arranged city composed of eight large segments.[83] The design of the city, reminiscent of a textile pattern, interests him far more than its practical functions. In the centre of the octagonal main square stands a rectangular *'grand pavillon Royal'* (*Plate 69*), a curious Utopian multi-storey block which, according to Perret's specifications, could house five hundred people. The idea of this high-rise building, dominating the town, must have greatly fascinated Perret; at the end of the treatise he describes and illustrates the building, sited amongst gardens and pavilions, in great detail.[84] The purpose of the building, which has a total of twelve storeys, is not clear. Perret does mention a central kitchen and communal areas, but says nothing about the social composition of the five hundred inhabitants he envisages. The ground plan, with its absence of load-bearing internal walls, clearly shows that his project had not been thought out at all with a view to construction. Perret is more interested in the view, and in the fireworks that can be set off from the roof terrace. Perret's plans and illustrations are not genuine utopian cities embodying a particular view of society.

Some seventeenth-century writings on fortification are the work of mathematicians, philologists and theologians. In the Romance countries, there is a veritable burgeoning of literature on fortifications written by *abbés*.[85] On the one side there is theory, completely detached from practice, and playing with pure forms; on the other, straightforward rule-books by soldiers whose activities occasionally extend into town-planning. Thus the work of the military engineer Sébastien Le Prestre de Vauban (1633–1707) was influential well into the eighteenth century.[86] His fort at Neubreisach (Neuf-Brisach) in Upper Alsace (1699) is again laid out like a plan for an ideal city. His posthumously published notes,[87] however, form part of military history.

From the late fifteenth century to the early seventeenth century, the theoretical study of fortifications overlaps with and touches upon problems of architectural theory in general, and it is for this reason that the most important representatives of this period whose views extend beyond pure engineering and fortification have been presented here.

10. France in the sixteenth century

The beginnings of architectural theory in France were at first shaped exclusively by Italian ideas.[1] Since the end of the fifteenth century, Italian artists, particularly sculptors, had worked in France or exported their sculptures there,[2] but in most cases they settled into a pre-existing historical environment or one that was dominated by the Flamboyant style. Architecture absorbed Italian Renaissance influences only hesitantly, and at first only in decoration.

Around 1500, Fra Giocondo gave a lecture on Vitruvius in Paris. In 1512 a French edition[3] of Alberti's Ten Books on Architecture was published. The considerable importance of Serlio in and for France has already been mentioned; he showed himself willing to accommodate French building practice in the books he wrote whilst in France. The most important mediator in the transfer of Italian thought to France was undoubtedly Jean Martin, the translator of Francesco Colonna's *Hypnerotomachia Poliphili* (1546), the first two books (1545) and fifth book (1547) of Serlio's treatise, Vitruvius (1547), and Alberti (published posthumously in 1553).[4]

In the last half of the sixteenth century there were already signs of a reaction against the dominant Italian influence in French art and thought. A number of the leading French architects spent several years of their lives in Rome, studied Classical architecture at first hand, and struck out on a path to an autonomous 'French' theory of architecture. The most important names here are Jacques Androuet du Cerceau, Philibert Delorme and Jean Bullant.

Jacques Androuet du Cerceau (c.1520–84)[5] appears to have spent some time in Rome during the 1540s in the entourage of the French ambassador, Georges d'Armagnac. From 1549 onwards, he began to achieve recognition through the publication of sets of engravings, but nothing has survived of the few buildings that he constructed.

In 1549 du Cerceau published a collection of engravings on Roman triumphal arches,[6] followed in 1550 by another on temples. Although his books are the first by a Frenchman to have resulted from direct contact with Roman architecture, du Cerceau's purpose is not to produce detailed illustration of Classical architecture; instead he mixes Roman antiquity with Lombard Renaissance architecture and his own creations. He is clearly keen to highlight his own – by which he also means independent French – buildings, explicitly stating in the title of his book on triumphal arches that they are 'partly invented by himself, partly taken from the Antique' (*'partim ab ipso inventa, partim ex veterum sumpta'*).

In 1559 du Cerceau published his *De architectura* (*Livre d'architecture*),[7] in which, in the dedication to Henry II, he clearly states that the aim of his book is to put an end to the appointment of foreign artists. The book is devoted to domestic architecture – in its structure it is reminiscent of Serlio's unpublished sixth book – and offers a typology of buildings for intending patrons of modest, average or substantial means (*'petit, moyen, ou grand estat'*). In fact, however, du Cerceau provides only designs for bourgeois and aristocratic patrons (*Plates 70, 71*). He provides plans – in a few cases for all storeys – elevations, and occasionally also sections and isometric projections. The vocabulary of style is French, only the details are borrowed from the Italian Renaissance.

In 1561 there followed a second book in which du Cerceau provides designs for chimneypieces, windows, doors, fountains and tombs, without explanatory notes.[8] In 1582 a third book, on the construction of country houses, was published.[9] This is similar in structure to the first book, and the designs which it contains are as far removed as can be imagined from the typical Italian villa.

The establishment of the autonomy of French architecture is the goal of the most famous of du Cerceau's publications – the two volumes on the '*plus excellents Bastiments de France*'.[10] Using the example of château construction, du Cerceau gives an account of French architectural development, making use of the opportunity to publish his own plans for the châteaux at Verneuil and Charleval. Apart from being of enormous value as a source for architectural history, this work shows that du Cerceau's aim was not so much a theoretical study of architecture nor a systematic application of Classical or Italian Renaissance architecture to France, as legitimisation of French developments and provision of models for the future. His own designs display a bizarre Mannerist eclecticism.

Jean Bullant (1520/25–78) lived in Rome at the same time as, or a little later than, du Cerceau.[11] His activity as an architect, and in particular his part in the construction of the château of Ecouen, have to date not been conclusively determined. In 1564 he published a book on the Orders entitled *Reigle géneralle d'architecture des cinque manières de colonnes*[12], in which he uses measurements which he himself took in Rome, and attempts to bring these into line with Vitruvius's specifications. Unlike du Cerceau, Bullant is a partisan of Classical Roman architecture. In identifying the human body as a model for, and analogue to, architecture, he is making use of the ideas of Alberti and Daniele Barbaro. Bullant's *Reigle géneralle* is the first French book on the Orders, and, as indicated by the new editions of 1568 and 1619, did meet a need. It is largely independent of Serlio's fourth book (1537).

Although he was a few years older than du Cerceau and Bullant and had been in Rome before them (1533–36), it was only towards the end of his life that Philibert Delorme (d. 1570),[13] who was born in Lyons in 1510, began to exploit his experience of Classical antiquity. Delorme was the most important practising architect in sixteenth-century France, and his architectural theory is the product of a combination of practice and reflection on that practice. Delorme began elaborating his architectural theory at a time when his great commissions (château d'Anet, the Tuileries) were either completed or well advanced. At any rate, it was in his case the personal experience of having fallen into disfavour (after the death of Henry II in 1559) and of being condemned to idleness and resignation, that prompted the formulation of his architectural theory. Although an Italian, Primaticcio, had supplanted him as royal architect, his theory does not display the explicitly anti-Italian features of du Cerceau's. Even Serlio, at times a rival to Delorme, is treated with fairness by him. In any case, his work for Catherine de Médicis and the dedication of his theoretical work to this Florentine queen of France would, of course, hardly have admitted of a pointedly anti-Italian stance.

In 1561 Delorme published a thin folio volume entitled *Nouvelles inventions pour bien bastir et à petits fraiz*. In 1567 followed his main theoretical work *Le premier tome de l'architecture*,[14] to which the *Nouvelles inventions* were appended in later editions. Delorme was the first Frenchman – and the only non-Italian in the sixteenth century – to attempt a comprehensive theory of architecture, instead of merely producing another pattern-book or book of Orders. Delorme worked contemporaneously with Palladio, but the latter's *Quattro libri* were published only in the year of Delorme's death. It is fascinating to see how Delorme steers architectural theory in a new direction.

Delorme followed the same principle of presentation as Palladio, namely the erection of a building from its foundations to the roof. He displays a keen sense of the status of the architect, playing the 'true architects' off against 'those who give themselves the name' and who 'should rather be called master masons'.[15] The architect must combine knowledge of scientific disciplines with that of practical requirements. He is perceived as analagous to the divine Creator.

The image of the professional architect as a figure with an all-round education was completely new for France, where architecture had hitherto been a craft activity. Although Delorme omits the knowledge of law, rhetoric and medicine required in the Vitruvian canon, he does call for an extensive knowledge of geometry.

The contents of Delorme's nine books are as follows:

Books I and II   The architect-client relationship; selection of the site; importance of climate.
Books III and IV   Mathematics, geometry.
Books V–VII   The rules of the Orders.
Books VIII and IX   Individual architectural elements.

Delorme wrote at a time when he was in disfavour, without work and in a mood of resignation. His concern is to protect the architect from the client; yet he also warns the client to beware of waste and fraud. The goal of the architect is – as it already was to Vitruvius – posthumous fame, hence commissions from kings, princes and great nobles are regarded by Delorme as particularly desirable.

Delorme works on the supposition that 'the use of geometric forms' ('*usage des traits Géométriques*') almost automatically brings with it 'convenience' ('*commodité*').[16] He therefore warns the architect to beware of the frequent demand made by patrons to incorporate existing – irregularly-shaped – constructions into his plans. But in case of necessity Delorme demonstrates how a site of irregular layout may be made on the basis of an axially symmetrical design.[17] An aesthetic requirement appears here to be the precondition of the functional one.

In his third and fourth books, Delorme develops in great detail various systems of vaults and stairs, combining French medieval building traditions and the contemporary science of geometry.

In his rules for the Orders, Delorme falls back on Vitruvius and Serlio, but also makes his own measurements of Classical architecture. Like Vignola, he chooses the Theatre of Marcellus in Rome as a model for the Doric order. He does not prescribe any absolute standard proportions, but does attempt to give his rules religious sanction, taking up the notion of God as the Architect of the World, the proportions of which are comprehensible only with the help of His inspiration.

A new feature of Delorme's rules for the Orders is the introduction of a sixth – 'French' – order. He starts by referring to the Classical derivation of columns from trees – a notion adopted shortly before him by Bernard Palissy[18] – and arrives at the almost neo-Gothic vision of a portico composed of tree trunks, giving the impression of '*quasi une petite forest*' (*Plate 72*).[19] The Classical orders, Delorme maintains, were evolved from Nature, so why should France not be able to develop its own order? This argument from evolution is followed by another practical, though historically inaccurate consideration: Delorme assumes that Greek marble columns were monoliths; the stone available in France, on the other hand, says Delorme, can only be used in drum form to build columns (*Plate 73*). This leads him to call for the insertion of bands at the joins in order to conceal the fact. The 'French' order disguises a supposed necessity; formally speaking, Delorme could justify his proposal by reference to Classical precedents.[20] His French order is, in fact, merely another version of the five Orders, in which bands are added to the shafts.

Delorme himself used his new order in the chapel of Villers-Cotterêts and at the Tuileries. The first real example of the trend towards national forms of the Classical orders is to be found in the 'baluster order' of the Spanish architect Diego de Sagredo (1526).[21] Delorme's simple adaptation of the Orders was merely an interlude, but the idea of a 'French' order remained active in France and had repercussions throughout Europe.[22]

In the technical field, particularly in the *Nouvelles inventions*, Delorme developed bold ideas, for example that of a great royal 'basilica' to be spanned by a flat wooden vault. In the later books, Delorme uses a grid developed from the module (basal radius of a column) for examples of the use of proportion. He appears to have used Francesco di Giorgio for the establishment of the proportions of a façade.[23] At various points in his work, particularly in the dedication (to Catherine de Médicis) and in the foreword, Delorme alludes to an intended second part of the treatise, in which he will provide a theoretical explanation of his teachings on proportion. Delorme envisages deriving the 'divine proportions' from the Old Testament: from the dimensions of Noah's Ark, the Ark of the Covenant, and Solomon's House and Temple.[24] A theory of proportion derived systematically from the Bible would have been something new, but Alberti had already, *en passant*, attempted to bring his teachings on proportion into line with the Old Testament details of Noah's Ark by reference to contemporary theology, according to which Noah's Ark was modelled on the human form.[25] Francesco Giorgi had also made reference to these precedents in his assessor's report on S. Francesco della Vigna in Venice.[26] The tradition became established with the publication of Juan Bautista Villalpando's commentary on Ezekiel in 1604.

At the end of Delorme's treatise there are allegorical woodcuts of the good and bad architect (*Plates 74, 75*).[27] The bad architect has no eyes, ears or nose; he stumbles through the countryside, in the background of which a castle and medieval village are depicted as architectural forms that are to be superseded. The good architect is dressed as an academic. He has three eyes: one to observe God and the past, one for the present, and one for the future. Delorme gives him four hands, and his feet are winged. A cornucopia and a spring denote his wisdom. The setting is a fertile garden. A ruin represents Antiquity, a church and palace the architecture of the present.

Delorme's treatise, like Palladio's, remained incomplete. Delorme is the first to anchor French national characteristics into a theoretical system. His theological speculations may be a reflection of Counter-Reformation tendencies.

Notions of an 'ideal' architecture extend into literary circles in sixteenth-century

France, as demonstrated by the fictional description of the abbey of Thelema by Delorme's friend François Rabelais (c.1494–1553).[28] In the first book of his novel *Gargantua and Pantagruel* (published 1532–64), the former Franciscan friar, later Benedictine monk, and finally doctor and secular priest, describes the 'anti-monastery' of Thelema, built by Gargantua for Frère Jean des Entommeures as a mark of gratitude for the latter's exploits in war. Rabelais was thoroughly conversant with Vitruvius and Alberti, and with Francesco Colonna's *Hypnerotomachia Poliphili*. In 1534 and 1535 he was in Rome, in the entourage of Cardinal Jean du Bellay, and from January to April 1534 he was joined there by Philibert Delorme, whom he later mentions (in the fourth book, 1552) as an interpreter of Vitruvius and '*grand architecte du roy Mégiste*' (i.e. Henry II). Rabelais planned to produce a topography of Ancient Rome but ceded this project to Bartolommeo Marliani of Milan, whose work he published in Lyons in 1534.[29] In the autumn of that year, after Rabelais' return from Rome, the first book of *Gargantua and Pantagruel*, which contains the description of the abbey of Thelema, was also published.

The 'abbey', situated on the banks of the Loire, has been described as an 'anti-monastery' because the rule according to which it is run is 'contrary to all others'. This rule is '*Fay ce que vouldras*' ('Do as you please').[30] This is no plea for lawless immorality: it is a product of the Humanist conviction that 'free persons who are well born, well educated and conversant with polite society, have by nature in them an instinct and a spur which drives them to virtuous deeds'.[31] Rabelais envisages an ideal courtly society housed in an ideal architectural setting. He is the first in France to combine ideal architecture and Utopian society, a society such as one finds in Baldassare Castiglione's *Cortegiano* (1528).[32] The rule is that 'only beautiful, well-formed, good-natured persons of each sex will be admitted'.[33] The educational ideal is formulated as follows: 'They were so well instructed that there was not one amongst them that could not read, write, sing, play several musical instruments, speak five or six languages and compose in these in verse and prose'.[34]

This aristocratic society lives in the ideal building of Thelema (= will). This is a huge hexagonal construction on the south bank of the Loire (*Plate 76*) 'a hundred times more magnificent than Bonnivet, Chambord or Chantilly'.[35] In the six symmetrical wings of the building, each side of which is 312 paces long, there are 9,332 dwellings on six storeys. The storeys are linked not only by spiral staircases but also by a riders' ramp. Six round corner towers are named after the points of the compass – an allusion to Vitruvius. In the north-west wing there are six libraries on each of the six storeys, divided according to language: Greek, Latin, Hebrew, French, Tuscan and Spanish. In the south-west wing there are 'beautiful spacious galleries all painted with pictures of heroic deeds of ancient times, of stories and descriptions of the world'.[36] In the middle of the great courtyard stands a fountain adorned with the Three Graces which can be traced back directly to a woodcut in the *Hypnerotomachia Poliphili*. French customs are reflected in the interior decoration and the layout of the grounds around the 'abbey'.

Serlio's reconstruction of the port of Ostia has been suggested as a possible model for Thelema;[37] however, a more plausible explanation for the hexagonal shape of the plan and the striking repetition of numbers and dimensions which are divisible by six or produce six when their digits are added together (eg a dimension of 312 paces) is to be sought in the great significance attached to the number.[38] In Vitruvius (III. 1) six was the mathematician's perfect number; six is also half of the number of twelve, which characterises the heavenly Jerusalem of the Apocalypse. The earthly Thelema would then, in Rabelais' ironic view, be 'half' a heavenly Jerusalem, as it were. On the other hand, the compact centrality of the hexagonal shape links up with the conception of the ideal city known since Antiquity[39] and rediscovered in the Renaissance, in particular by Filarete.

The land of Gargantua and Pantagruel is Utopia. Thelema is, as it were, a Utopia within a Utopia. It does not possess the grandeur of Thomas More's or Tommaso Campanella's social vision, but it has remarkable visual quality, in which the influence of Philibert Delorme may surely be seen.

11. The Classical synthesis in seventeenth-century France

The course of French architectural theory in the seventeenth century runs parallel to the consolidation of French absolutism and reaches its peak in the reign of Louis XIV. National characteristics and a close connection with the practicalities of building are central in French architectural theory; questions of cost, comfort and inhabitants' social status are of primary importance. Books on the Orders and treatises on domestic building are particularly in demand. In this connection a treatise by Pierre Le Muet (1591–1669) merits attention. Le Muet[1] began as a collaborator of Salomon de Brosse; he himself was mainly concerned with the building of houses and castles, but few of his own buildings remain. Apart from two books on the Orders, which are simply French adaptations of Vignola and Palladio,[2] Le Muet published a book on domestic architecture which continues in the tradition of Serlio's sixth book and Du Cerceau's *Livre d'architecture* (1559) but has a more developed methodology than either: the *Manière de bien bastir pour toutes sortes de personnes* (1623).[3]

In the dedication to Louis XIII, Le Muet declares his aim as being to use his knowledge to '*assister le public*'.[4] In his preface to the reader, he names '*necessité*' as the mainspring of architecture; he accords the functional aspect prime place, not only from the point of view of historical evolution but also from that of significance. His intention is 'to work more and more for the common weal in all that concerns my employment and my profession'.[5]

His '*Sommaire discours*' is brief; Le Muet repeats the Vitruvian concepts, but with a new emphasis. He requires *durée* (Vitruvius: *firmitas*), *aisance ou commodité* (Vitruvius: *utilitas*), *la belle ordonnance* (Vitruvius: *venustas*), *la santé des appartements* (a partial aspect of *utilitas*).

Commodité requires that a room with a width of 22–24 feet should have a length of 34–36 feet. Large rooms should be in the proportion of 1:2, small rooms should be square. In small rooms the fireplace should not be positioned in the middle of the wall but two feet to the side of it, leaving room to install a bed.[6]

The aesthetic concept of *belle ordonnance* consists in 'symmetry, which must be balanced either horizontally or vertically'[7], i.e. in proportion. It is an echo of Alberti, for it means that all the parts should be in proportion to the whole and in relation to each other.

Le Muet's practical advice relates to house-building. He proceeds in a very systematic manner, starting from given dimensions for each plot, ranging from 12 feet in width and 21–25 feet in depth, up to 101 feet in width and 45 feet in depth. He develops thirteen types of house in all, offering up to five alternatives for each plan (*Plate 77*). Le Muet mostly gives plans of several storeys and the exact purpose of individual rooms. His practical sense is shown also in the fact that he presents the cheap and popular half-timber technique and describes and illustrates roof-timber construction.

Le Muet reflects seventeenth-century Parisian building practice, but strikes a new note in architectural theory. Although we have here, as with Serlio, a pattern-book, the fact that alternatives are offered shows a new approach. Le Muet takes immediate account of needs and circumstances. Considerations of *commodité* are to the fore, those of *belle ordonnance* secondary.

His own designs shown in a second volume of *Manière le bien bastir* published in 1647, with *Augmentations de nouveaux bastiments faits en France par les ordres et desseins du Sieur le Muet*, are also almost exclusively concerned with house- and palace-building. The title-page of this second part, in the edition of 1681 (*Plate 78*), shows a figure of Fame having taken from her lips one trumpet with a plate from the first part attached to it, to sound a second in praise of *Les Oeuvres du S.r Le Muet*. This illustration shows nonetheless that 'fame' can also be won by concern with simpler tasks such as houses, a notion that would have been totally alien to Renaissance artists.

Practical building handbooks and rule- and pattern-books were clearly in demand in France in the first half of the seventeenth century. But no new system of architectural theory emerged. In 1631 Alessandro Francini, a native of Florence but engaged in French service, published a collection of forty doorways,[8] in which the thirty found in Serlio's *Extraordinario Libro* (Lyons 1551) are adapted to suit the taste of the time, although Francini does not acknowledge his debt. In 1648 Delorme's *Premier tome de l'architecture* was reprinted. In addition to books on the Orders and collections of designs (executed and unexecuted) – Antoine Le Pautre published his works complete with descriptions in 1652[9] – authors who were not experts in the field also began to write technical building treatises: Louis Savot, a doctor, wrote on the techniques of construction and the calculation of building costs in his *Architecture françoise des bastiments particuliers* (1624),[10] giving a surprisingly comprehensive survey of the previous literature on architecture.[11] The role of non-architects was to be of growing significance for French architectural theory in the later seventeenth century.

This is already true of the aesthetic theory of Roland Fréart de Chambray (1606–76),[12] whose training was in mathematics, geometry and perspective. From 1630 to 1635 Fréart de Chambray was resident in Rome, where he established friendly relations with Charles Errard, the future director of the Académie de France in Rome, and with Nicolas Poussin. In 1640, along with his brother Paul, the sieur de Chantelou, who was to act as Bernini's personal escort during the latter's sojourn in Paris in 1665, Fréart de Chambray was sent to Rome with the mission of urging Poussin to return to Paris, in which he was only temporarily successful (autumn 1640–autumn 1642). In Rome Fréart already belonged to the circle of proponents of Classicism, as represented by Bellori in theory and Poussin in practice,[13] against the High Baroque. It was logical that Fréart de Chambray and his brother Fréart de Chantelou should ally themselves subsequently with the artistic policies of the administration of Colbert, to whom Bellori dedicated his biographies of artists.

In 1650 Fréart published a French translation of Palladio,[14] and more importantly the *Parallèle de l'architecture antique avec la moderne*, illustrated by Charles Errard, on which he had been working since his stay in Rome in 1640.[15] He expressed the same classicising principles in a later treatise of 1662.[16] The *Parallèle* is dedicated to his brothers Jean and Paul Fréart. In the dedication Roland gives an account of his mission to Rome to see Poussin, '*le Raphael de nostre siècle*',[17] and his encounter with the architecture of Antiquity.

The *Parallèle* takes the form of an anthology of quotations from previous architectural theorists on the Orders. What is new here is the distinction made between three Greek and two Latin orders. The three Greek orders (Doric, Ionic and Corinthian) are for him 'the flower and perfection of the Orders' and contain 'not only all that is beautiful, but also all that is necessary in Architecture'.[18] In his eyes they correspond to the three possible ways of building, the *trois manières: la solide* [Doric], *la moyenne* [Ionic], and *le délicate* [Corinthian]'. Beauty ('*la beauté véritable et essentielle*') consists above all in '*symétrie*', which is defined as 'the union and general accord of all parts together, making a kind of visible harmony',[19] in other words, Alberti's harmony of the parts among themselves. *Symétrie* here corresponds to the modern concept of proportion. Since the Greek orders possessed all possible perfection, the whole development of architecture is seen as a process of degeneration. For Fréart the only possibility of correct architecture lies in a return to the principles of the Greeks, as he understands them, though he had no personal knowledge of Greek architecture. As a mathematician, he regards these principles as geometrical and reducible to a few basic elements; for him it is simplicity of principles that constitutes perfection:

> For the excellence and perfection of an art does not consist in the multiplicity of its principles; on the contrary, the simpler and fewer these are, the more is art to be admired: and this we see in the rules of Geometry, which is the basis and general font of all the arts, out of which they have been drawn, and without the aid of which it is impossible that art should exist.[20]

Imitation of the Greeks and observance of geometrical principles lead to a doctrinaire Classicism, which in a sense anticipates Winckelmann's later requirement: 'The only way for us to become great, even inimitable, if this is possible, lies in the imitation of the Ancients [i.e. Greeks]',[21] in which Greek art was to be a lodestone in the quest for a national German style; something similar was aspired to by Fréart de Chambray in connection with France.

Fréart's elevation of the Greek orders into the three principles embracing all beauty in architecture has little to do with genuine archaeological enthusiasm for Greece or with the Greek versus Roman debate of the eighteenth century, but is rather an aesthetic construct. For Fréart, perfection lies in the historically elusive origins of architecture, which he ascribes to the Greeks, and all subsequent architecture, particularly that of the present, is a falling away from their principles; the idea that was to a large extent to dominate aesthetic theory in France in the eighteenth century[22] may legitimately be spoken of as a quasi-reversal of the notion of progress.

The Roman orders (Tuscan and Composite) are, for Fréart, corruptions of the Greek. He develops a positive hatred of the Composite order, which for him is 'the most irrational' and unworthy of the name of 'Order', 'since it has been the cause of all the confusion that has crept into Architecture'.[23] Any concern with this order, according to him, is 'sterile study and a waste of time'.[24]

The main part of the *Parallèle* is concerned with the positions held by the ten authors quoted along with Vitruvius (Palladio, Scamozzi, Serlio, Vignola, Barbaro, Cataneo, Alberti, Viola, Bullant and Delorme). To the dogmatism of architectural principles is added a hierarchy of their interpreters. Virtuvius is unassailable; Daniele Barbaro, as his most important interpreter, becomes the oracle.

Fréart gives the Corinthian order a special place as the 'flower of Architecture, and the Order of Orders' because it was used in the Temple of Solomon (*Plate 79*), for which he quotes Villalpando's commentary on Ezekiel as his authority.[25]

Fréart's principles of architectural theory are characterised by a claim to absoluteness analogous to that of the emerging absolutist state in France; the hierarchy imposed on the sources he uses is reminiscent of the centralist structure of the absolutist administration itself. His values are given no theoretical basis. His theory is the product of an intellectual, mathematical mode of thought, a philosophical basis is absent. Here lies a considerable difference from the position represented by Bellori in Rome.

On 10 August 1665, Roland Fréart de Chambray was introduced by his brother to Bernini, to whom he took the opportunity of presenting a copy of the *Parallèle*. Bernini, who as an architect incarnated a Classicising but undogmatic position, was guarded in his reaction to this judgment of the Baroque, which was already familiar to him, and which he was bound to apply to himself. Paul de Chantelou reports:

My brother handed him his *Parallèle de l'Architecture*. At first he refused to accept the book: Monsieur had already given it to Mr Paul and Mr Matthias and one copy in the house was enough. But when I assured him that my brother would deem it an honour to be allowed to make him a present of the book, he finally accepted it and expressed his best thanks.[26]

The rationalist conception of architecture of the mid-seventeenth century is particularly evident in the frontispiece (*Plate 80*) of a book on the Orders, consisting only of Plates, by the engraver and theorist of perspective Abraham Bosse (1602–76).[27] His *Traité de manières de dessiner les ordres de l'architecture antique* (1664) gives an allegorical treatment to hierarchically arranged architectural concepts. Under an Ionic aedicula, enthroned in a large niche on a high pedestal, is a helmeted goddess with the attributes of lion and spear; on the pedestal beneath her is the inscription *La raison sur tout* (Reason over all). In side niches in the rear wall, she is flanked by the figures of 'Le Solide' and 'La Agréable'. A flight of steps with the inscription 'Le Commode' leads up to the aedicula, on whose flanking parapets stand Theory and Practice. The Vitruvian categories of *utilitas* (*le commode*), *firmitas* (*le solide*) and *venustas* (*la agréable*) are thus all subjected to *raison*. The functional aspect – without it *raison* is not attainable – is of paramount importance. The aesthetic principle, now only tolerated in the background as *La Agréable*, is looking through a telescope into the future – an image rich in implications. The supreme law of architecture is *raison*.

12. The foundation of the French Academy of Architecture and the subsequent challenge to it

In the visual arts, the foundation of national academies went hand in hand with the consolidation of absolutism in France. In these fields programmes prescribed and commissioned by the king were carried out. In sixteenth-century Italy, academies had been associations of artists who made their own statutes and chose their own members.[1] In France the founding of the academies was ordained by the state, which laid down statutes and appointed members. Enlightenment and centralised Absolutism formed an unholy alliance in the creation of these national academies. After 1635, when Richelieu founded the Académie Française to oversee the French language, other academies were systematically founded to cover virtually all the arts and scholarship and bring them under state control: the Académie de Peinture et de Sculpture (1648), the Académie de Danse (1661), the Académie des Inscriptions et Belles-lettres (1663), the Académie des Sciences (1666), the Académie de France à Rome (1666), the Académie de Musique (1669).

The Academie Royale d'Architecture, founded by Colbert in 1671[2], completed this system of academies. Its members and director, appointed by the king, could not work independently; the sessions were attended by a representative of Colbert, who since 1664 had held the office of 'Surintendant et ordonnateur général des bâtiments, arts, tapisseries et manufactures de France'.[3] The Académie d'Architecture had a multiple task: in the weekly sessions (at first there were two a week), it had to discuss architectural themes and arrive at a resolution. These sessions usually began with the reading aloud of earlier architectural theorists. It was the task of the Académie d'Architecture to establish binding architectural doctrine, which was expounded in public lectures on two days a week (under François Blondel on Tuesdays and Fridays) for the education of young architects. This practice made the Académie Royale d'Architecture the first institution to practise systematic architectural teaching, and thus the forerunner of faculties of architecture. The complementary subjects prescribed were geometry, arithmetic, mechanics, hydraulics, military architecture and perspective. A Rome scholarship was awarded for the best student performance.

The Académie also functioned in an advisory capacity for inquiries from the provinces. Finally, members discussed their own projects. Louis Hautecoeur sums up its functions as follows:

> The Academy ruled over architects, students, contractors, royal buildings, provinces, towns. It was a mighty instrument in the service of the central power.[4]

The Académie d'Architecture was in existence from 1671 until 1793. Its minutes were published by Henry Lemonnier.[5] In 1671 the Académie consisted of eight members, including director and secretary;[6] in the following years there were some minor additions to staff. Minutes of the sessions were signed by all those present. Guests who were not members of the Académie were allowed to take part in certain sessions. Thus in several minutes we find the signature of Claude Perrault,[7] who was never a member of the Académie. In 1699 a change in the composition of the membership took place: henceforth there were seven architects, *de première classe*, one professor of architecture, a secretary, and seven architects *de seconde classe*. In addition, the right to participate in sessions was extended to '*officiers en charge des bâtiments*'.

The task of the Académie consisted in the passing of resolutions which were eventually to be incorporated into a normative architectural aesthetic, perhaps even result in the establishment of a national French order,[8] an idea which Philibert Delorme had already tried to initiate and put into practice. It is clear that, as in the case of Fréart de Chambray, the principles on which the Académie's discussions were based were derived from philosophy and the natural sciences, and were not specific to architecture: in the spirit of Descartes' rationalist philosophy, the basic principle of all discussion is *raison*. Only mathematics can guarantee *certitude*, while geometry is the basis of all beauty.[9] *Bon sens* (good sense) saves the architect from mistakes. Experience serves as a control for *raison*. In addition there is an absolute belief in the authority of Antiquity. At first architectural theory in the Académie follows in the wake of literary theory as it was formulated by Boileau and La Bruyère.[10] The belief was held that greatness and perfection could be achieved only by imitating Antiquity. La Bruyère establishes the connection with architecture as follows:

What was no longer to be seen save in the ruins of ancient Greece and Rome has – become modern once more – burst out in our porticoes and peristyles. In just the same way, in writing there is no way of achieving perfection and – if such a thing is possible – surpassing the Ancients, other than by imitating them.[11]

Hence the Académie cultivated the reading aloud of Vitruvius and Renaissance authors, who were seen in a strict pecking order: Vitruvius, Palladio, Scamozzi, Vignola, Serlio, Alberti, Viola, Cataneo.

Medieval architecture is judged as absolutely '*insupportable*', Michelangelo is held responsible for the '*libertinage*' in architecture which reached its highest point in the excesses of the Italian Baroque (Borromini, Guarini). This architecture is accounted the expression of individual fantasy. In France what is needed is an '*ordre général*', the expression of a '*beauté universelle*'.[12] These are the basic positions of the Académie, and Colbert repeatedly pressed for them to be prescribed in a standard form.

The study of the architecture of Antiquity was made considerably more difficult by the lack of accurate surveyed buildings and contradictions in existing publications. For this reason Colbert had in 1669, even before the foundation of the Académie, sent the architect Mignard to take accurate measurements in Provence. In 1674 Desgodets was sent to Rome for the same purpose (of which more will be said later). The lack of uniformity in earlier data on the Orders was to be solved by imitating the best buildings of Antiquity, a principle which Vignola had already quoted when establishing his *Regola*.

In 1671 Colbert announced a competition with a prize of 3,000 livres for the design of a 'French' order.[13] This was becoming an urgent problem, as the design of the third storey of the Cour carrée in the Louvre, the Composite order having already been used for the second storey, was now being discussed. Claude Perrault suggested the use of caryatids, which was accepted. The question of a new Order, however, was regarded as one of the most important tasks of French architecture; for, argued François Blondel, following Delorme, just as the Romans had added two new orders to the three original Greek ones, it must also be possible to establish a new Order for the present day, provided the rules of proportion were adhered to.[14] This requirement was fundamental to progressive thinking in French architecture. Participation in the competition in France and Italy was keen. The winner was Colbert himself.

But the Académie did not work as swiftly and resolutely as Colbert wished; the questions under consideration were discussed entirely for their own sake, which says much for the moral integrity of its members. This tendency was clear from the outset. In the inaugural session on 31 December 1671, François Blondel suggested discussing the question of *bon goût* in architecture at the next session.[15] On 7 January 1672 the Académie did not reach any definition or resolution, merely stating that work possessing *bon goût* would be bound to please, but not, conversely, that all that pleases would necessarily possess *bon goût*.[16] A week later it was provisionally agreed that *bon goût* was whatever pleased *intelligent* people.[17]

The question of good taste, one of the key points of aesthetic discussion in the Enlightenment, proved to be an insoluble problem for the members of the Académie, imbued as they were both with the ideals of the Enlightenment and with respect for Authority. If the subjectivity of taste was acknowledged, according to the motto *De gustibus non disputandum*, that would have made it possible for the champions of relativity in aesthetic criteria to breach the norms which it was one of the objects of the Académie to establish. That was why the question of taste was linked to the social structure, to the authority of *personnes intelligentes*. Antonio Hernandez aptly describes this polarity: 'Rationalism and belief in authority had to fight it out even within the Academy.'[18]

François Blondel's lectures at the Académie, which began in 1671 and took place parallel with the Académie's sessions, are not to be considered as the definitive utterance of the Académie that Colbert was expecting. Nevertheless, it is in the lectures of Blondel that the position of the Académie is made most clear.

François Blondel (1617–86), from a family of court officials, was by training primarily an engineer and mathematician.[19] He travelled as a tutor and in a diplomatic capacity in Italy, Greece, Turkey and Egypt. No architectural works by Blondel are known before he was appointed director of the Académie d'Architecture by Colbert. At about the same time he was made 'directeur général des travaux de la ville de Paris'. His only extant executed building is the Porte Saint-Denis, erected in 1672. Blondel wrote on the classics and history, a mathematical textbook (*Cours de mathématique*, Paris, 1683) and a work on ballistics (*L'Art de jeter les bombes*, Paris, 1683).[20] The lectures he delivered to the Académie were published in five parts under the title *Cours d'architecture* between 1675 and 1683.[21]

It is important to emphasise that Blondel came to architecture via mathematics and that his adversary Claude Perrault approached architecture as a physiologist. This shows, remembering also Fréart de Chambray, that the most important architectural theorists of French absolutism were scientists.

Blondel's *Cours* is dedicated to the king. In the dedication his academic function is defined: 'to teach publicly the rules of this art, as taken from the teaching of the greatest Masters and the example of the finest Buildings that remain to us from

Antiquity.'[22] At the same time it is the task of architecture to surpass Antiquity. In his preface Blondel unfolds the programme and the educational function of the Academy. In his inaugural lecture delivered to the Académie on 31 December 1671, the 'Discours' which precedes the work, Blondel states that the Académie is to give back to architecture the lustre it enjoyed in Antiquity, and to work for the glory of the king.

Blondel's ideas on architectural evolution differ from the backward-looking ones of Fréart de Chambray. Blondel believes in progress towards perfection, and for him architecture did not reach consummation in Antiquity, on the contrary, new forms can be invented. Thus he justifies the demand for a national French order.

Blondel's *Cours* is not a completely systematic presentation of his architectural theory but a printed set of lectures, which nevertheless contains the first didactic formulation of architectural theory. From the outset Blondel's conception of architectural development admits of no rigid dogmatism such as is found in Fréart de Chambray. He inquires into the genesis and development of architectural forms, into the origins of architecture, and in the Vitruvian tradition establishes the motive of shelter for the primal dwelling. What is new in Blondel is the idea of various stages of architectural development among different peoples; such an idea might have been expected from the far-travelled Blondel with his wide experience of diverse national cultures. The earliest consideration, 'as to this day among the least civilised people', was protection against wind and rain.[23]

For Blondel everything stands in need of justification. The proportions of the Orders are seen in the light of the analogy with the human body,[24] as had been usual since Vitruvius. The columns themselves, with their capitals, are interpreted as converted grave steles with urns on top of them[25] (*Plate 81*), and again the Orders are seen as being in a supposed evolutionary sequence: the Doric is the oldest, then comes the Ionic. The Corinthian order, according to Blondel, was at first identical to the Ionic, the voluted capital having merely been replaced by a leafy capital.[26] He states the Tuscan order was invented by the Lydians in Etruria, while the Composite order was not an order at all but a modern designation for a variety of Antique precedents.[27] Supporting himself by referring to Serlio, Blondel comes to accept varying proportions within the same Order, that is, becoming increasingly slender, starting with the free-standing column, then the one placed before the wall, the engaged column, and finally the engaged column attached to a pilaster.[28] Blondel postulates the continued development of forms; those that were laid down in Antiquity are not unchangeable. For the present time he even advises against the use of Antique forms in certain cases.[29]

In his long-winded lectures on the individual Orders, Blondel adheres to the authors as ranked hierarchically by the Academy. His interpretations of the Orders are also conventional:[30] Tuscan = gigantic; Doric = Herculean; Ionic = womanly; Composite = heroic; Corinthian = virginal. Like Vignola he uses the radius of the lower end of the column as a module.

At the beginning of the first book, Blondel thus defines architecture: 'Architecture is the art of building well. A building is called good when it is solid, convenient, healthy and pleasing'.[31] These categories of the *solide, commode, agréable* and *sain* correspond to a great extent to those of Pierre le Muet (*durée, commodité, belle ordonnance, santé*), save that the aesthetic one – merely labelled *agréable*, which links it up with Abraham Bosse's inscribed engraving – appears strangely colourless.

At the end of Book IV Blondel presents his own sole building, the Porte Saint-Denis (1672) (*Plate 82*), which he also uses as the frontispiece to the whole book, and describes as 'perhaps one of the greatest works of this kind in the world'.[32] He draws attention to the quotations from Antiquity in its decoration, and stresses his adherence to exact proportions.[33]

Blondel's approach in the first parts of his *Cours d'architecture* has few surprises – it is only in the fifth part, in the polemic waged against Claude Perrault, that Blondel makes his personal contribution to theory. The fifth book is devoted to proportion. While Blondel uses the general heading '*proportion*', he does not adhere to Vitruvian usage in his terms *eurythmie, symétrie,* and *bien-séance*. For Blondel *eurythmie* is '*l'aspect agréable & de bonne grace*' of a properly proportioned building.[34] *Symétrie* lies in the relationship of the parts to the whole, Blondel perceiving this by analogy with the human body; this implies a turning against Perrault, who contested the analogy. Blondel's concept of *symétrie* nonetheless remains rooted in the Vitruvian tradition, close to the modern concept of proportion. *Bien-séance* is the 'beauty governing with nicety the outward appearance of a building' ('*beauté réglant avec justesse l'aspect d'un ouvrage*'),[35] in other words it corresponds to Vitruvius's concept of *decor*. For Blondel the proportions of a building are just as unchangeable as those of the human body. Blondel bases his argument mainly on Alberti.[36] Blondel's evolutionary way of thinking does not on the other hand allow him to describe Antiquity as absolutely normative. Thus for example he discovers mistakes in the proportions of the Pantheon.[37] Blondel does, however, reject the position represented by Perrault of seeing in works of art only 'the effect of genius and experience'.[38] He cites a text published in 1679, *Architecture harmonique* by the musician René Ouvrard (1624–94),[39] which is also directed against Perrault, maintaining the analogy between architecture and the human body, and calling for the identification of the theory of harmony in music with the theory of proportion in architecture, in the sense of a 'marriage of music with architecture'.[40] Perrault had disputed this identity and taken only musical harmony as embodying a law of Nature.

For Blondel a normative theory of proportion remains indispensable. He regards it as being one of the criteria of architecture which have 'a sure and real foundation in Nature'.[41] While conceding unreservedly that there are areas of architecture which do not rest on natural laws but on custom, he denies that this is the case with proportion,[42] which for him remains a law of Nature as 'the cause of beauty in architecture'.[43]

Blondel believes that proportions derived from Nature are to be found even in the Gothic style. Using Cesariano's commentary on Vitruvius (1521), he attempts to demonstrate them from the example of Milan Cathedral.[44] This position – the projection onto the style of proportions postulated as occurring in Nature – allows Blondel to give a positive evaluation of the Gothic, and even to find it beautiful: 'One will find in it a large number of recurring proportions, which are doubtless accountable for its beauty, and for the pleasure that one takes in looking at it.'[45]

Blondel tries to combine the concept of progress with a normative aesthetic. From these conflicting aims and from the quarrel with Perrault which began while the *Cours* was in course of publication, a number of contradictions arise. While Blondel does not represent the abstract dogmatism of a Fréart de Chambray, he is yet the exponent of a cerebral conception of architecture, which leads to a cold and rigid monumentality, as is demonstrated in his Porte Saint-Denis.

As a physiologist, his adversary Claude Perrault (1613–88)[46] was a representative of epistemological empiricism, as taught mainly by John Locke, who denied the existence of innate ideas and compared the original state of the mind to a *tabula rasa*, on which external and internal experience ('sensation' and 'reflection' respectively) is written. Locke was resident in France from 1675 to 1679 and he may have met Claude Perrault.[47]

Claude Perrault, elder brother of Charles Perrault (b. 1627), taught physiology and later pathology at the University of Paris from 1651/52; in 1666 he was made a member of the newly founded Académie des Sciences (Blondel became a member in 1669). In the Academy he conducted anatomical demonstrations and published their results. He also published, partly on Colbert's instructions, books on medicine, machine-building and zoology. Apart from a few early indications,[48] no concern with architecture is noticeable until the 1660s. In 1664 he produced his first design for the façade of the Louvre. The Louvre colonnade was to be his major architectural achievement.

In the same year 1664, Colbert commissioned Perrault to undertake a new translation of Vitruvius; it should be remembered that until that time only one French translation of Vitruvius existed, that of Jean Martin, dating from 1547, which was full of errors and had no commentary. Perrault's very painstaking translation, complete with textual criticism and an extensive commentary, appeared in 1673.[49] The Académie d'Architecture founded only two years previously had no influence on Perrault's translation, waiting until Perrault's edition actually appeared before it came to grips with Vitruvius.[50]

In 1683 Perrault presented his own body of theory in the guise of a conventionally structured treatise on the Orders.[51] The manuscripts or proofs of this work seem to have been at Blondel's disposal when he took issue with Perrault in the fifth book of his *Cours d'architecture*, also published in 1683.

Perrault's translation of Vitruvius was read aloud in the Academy between 1674 and 1676.[52] While the minutes at one point record 'some difficulty with one of the notes',[53] the explosive material in the commentary was obviously not immediately realised. Perrault's commentary has been described as a 'total revolution in architectural aesthetics'.[54] It is a strange irony of history that the work was commissioned by Colbert and that this 'revolution' was played out in footnotes. Recently, however, Perrault's revolutionary stance has been played down, in favour of greater emphasis upon the conventional aspects of his work.[55] The fact that in his commentary Perrault was not just interested in historical interpretation, but wanted to have an immediate effect on the architecture of his time, is apparent in the frontispiece, in which he depicts his Louvre façade and his design for a triumphal arch for the Place du Trône (*Plate 83*).[56]

Both in his commentary on Vitruvius and in his *Ordonnance* Perrault undermines Vitruvius's aesthetic architectural principles and those of his successors. His most important point of attack is the concept of proportion. Antiquity, he maintains, has its own rules and proportions, which depend on the type of construction ('*massif*' or '*délicat*')[57] in question. For Perrault, proportions are not a law of Nature as they were in previous architectural theory, and so were not to be perceived as normative, but as '*établies par un consentement des architectes*', determined by custom and tradition.[58] Proportion is relativised to become an empirical concept and as a result, the core of all earlier architectural theory is called into question. But Perrault goes even further. He establishes a list of the essential criteria of architecture in order of priority. He distinguishes between two basic principles of aesthetic judgment, which he designates as positive and arbitrary:

> The whole of Architecture is founded on two basic principles, one of which is positive and the other arbitrary. The positive foundation of Architecture is use and the end to which a building is put, and so covers *Solidité* [solid construction], '*Salubrité*' [health], and *Commodité* [fitness for use]. The foundation that I call arbitrary is Beauty, which derives from Authority and Usage: for although Beauty to some extent also derives from a positive foundation, consisting of appropriateness governed by reason, and the fitness of each part for the use for which it is intended...[59]

The positive principle which makes concepts previously not understood as specifically aesthetic (Vitruvius's *firmitas* and *utilitas* are equivalent to Perrault's *solidité*, *salubrité* and *commodité*) the basis of beauty thus becomes a part of beauty itself (*beauté positive*). For Perrault it is this *beauté positive* that is fundamental, while *beauté arbitraire* denotes the artist's field of action,[60] which is, however, limited by custom. The use of a building ('*usage*') becomes the decisive factor of its beauty: 'the use for which everything is intended, according to its nature, must be one of the principal causes on which the beauty of the Building must be based.'[61] The concept of *usage*, whose importance had been stressed in France since the sixteenth century, is elevated for the first time by Perrault into an aesthetic premise.

The concept of *symmetry*, which had corresponded in Vitruvius and in architectural theory up to this point to the modern concept of proportion, undergoes a bifurcation with Perrault that was to have momentous consequences. In the translation of Vitruvius I. 2, Perrault renders the Vitruvian concept of *symmetria* by the word *proportion*, and explains in a note:

> the word symmetry has another meaning in French; for it signifies the correspondence in a building between right and left, high and low, front and back, whether in size, shape, height, colour, number, or placing – indeed in everything that can make one part resemble another; and it is rather odd that Vitruvius never spoke of this kind of Symmetry, which accounts for much of the beauty of Buildings.[62]

Perrault is here setting out the modern concept of symmetry, which for him constitutes an important part of *beauté positive*. Alberti was already familiar with the phenomenon in his discussion of the theory of *numerus* (*De re aedificatoria* IX. 5), but he grounded this on the way in which right mirrors left in the human body. Since Perrault rejects such a justification for proportion, he cannot use it to make the case for symmetry either. The concept of symmetry, already used in the modern sense by Le Muet and Savot,[63] becomes with Perrault an indispensable requirement in building, with the same fundamental importance as *solidité, salubrité* and *commodité*; in other words, it is a component part of *beauté positive*. Thus symmetry, in the modern sense of axiality, is given theoretical anchorage as a decisive, almost indispensable criterion for beauty. Symmetry, which has been known in practice since Antiquity, becomes a dogma of Classicism.[64]

The other part of the concept of symmetry, the one which until then in the Vitruvian tradition had been synonymous with proportion, and for which Perrault now employed the word *proportion*, as something arrived at by agreement no longer belongs to *beauté positive*, but solely to *beauté arbitraire*. With Perrault the original concept of symmetry is split into two parts: the modern concept of symmetry as a component part of *beauté positive*, and the concept of proportion as a component part of *beauté arbitraire*.

Perrault's concern is not to abolish the concept of proportion but to make it less absolute. It is not *certaine proportion* that is important for him, but the *grâce* that may be attained by acceptable modifications in proportion: 'grace of form is nothing other than its pleasing modification, on the basis of which pure and surpassing beauty can be established'.[65] If grace is to be assured, only limited deviations from proportion are possible. Within such limits, buildings of varying proportions may be perceived as equally beautiful; but in addition there is a need for *bon goût*.[66] *Bon goût* rests on the knowledge of both types of beauty, the positive and the arbitrary,[67] while *bon sens* is restricted to judging *beauté positive*.

Perrault is able to cite the differences in column proportions in Antiquity and the varying specifications for them of earlier authors in support of his opinion, but in a passage on the misuse of alteration of proportions he maintains that changes in 'things so firmly established in the opinion of everybody' are ridiculous.[68]

Perrault does indeed remove the normative aesthetic basis of the theory of proportion, but at the same time he sanctions contemporary practice by laying down limits of *convenance*. In his *Ordonnance* he suggests simple rules with average whole number values for the individual Orders, which ensure a certain amount of room for manoeuvre for the architect. One could, speaking metaphorically, say that Perrault's theory of the Orders, compared with earlier theories, resembles a ship that was formerly anchored and now weighs anchor; but ship and crew remain the same.

Perrault reckons with a gradual change in *bon goût*, and hence in proportion. Blondel believes in a further development of forms, with the theory of proportion remaining constant. In this debate there are surprising *rapprochements* in spite of methodological differences.

In the argument as to whether Perrault's coupled columns on the Louvre façade are admissible, he appeals to modern taste, which he claims is different from that of Antiquity and which he derives from the nationally esteemed Gothic:

> The taste of our age – or at least of our nation – differs from that of the Ancients; it may be that in doing so it has something Gothic about it: for we have in common the air, the day, and the freedom. This has brought us to invent a sixth way of arranging these columns, namely to couple them and link them two by two.[69]

Blondel also derives from the Gothic the laws of Classical proportion.

In his illustrations[70] to Vitruvius, Perrault sometimes uses other men's ideas, but without naming his sources at the appropriate place; thus his illustration of the huts on the Black Sea and in Phrygia is copied from the Rusconi illustration.[71] His plan of the 'Greek House' (*Plate 84*) is a paraphrase of the plans published by Palladio.[72]

Perrault's most successful achievement was to break up the old concept of 'symmetry', and to give his own the force of dogma as a *beauté positive*. Less successful was his attempt to dismiss its old connotation, proportion, as a *beauté arbitraire*, and thus destroy the consensus over the aesthetics of architecture (though in practice he was himself constrained by custom). Most of his contemporaries repudiated him or passed him over in silence.[73] It was only at the beginning of the eighteenth century, when the subjectivity of *bon goût* was maintained, that his ideas became vulgarised. Perrault's arguments for the arbitrary nature of proportion were known in the Académie d'Architecture even before the publication of his commentary on Vitruvius; the question as to whether proportion was a *règle positive* or *arbitraire* being discussed as early as 21 January 1672.[74] The Académie never reached any conclusion on the matter. This says a great deal for its enlightened liberalism, although Blondel's antagonism was never in doubt.

The conflict between Blondel and Perrault was not limited to architecture, but it was symptomatic of a wider dispute. It was repeated in literary theory with very similar arguments. Here Blondel's position was represented by Nicolas Boileau (1636–1711), who makes unmistakable allusions to Claude Perrault in his *Art poétique* (1674).[75]

Charles Perrault (1628–1703), Claude's younger brother and the well-known author of fairytales, took his brother's position in the literary debate. Charles had been trained as a lawyer but worked until Colbert's death as *'Premier commis de la surintendance des bâtiments du roi'*, and was well versed in the controversy about architectural theory. In his *Parallèle des Anciens et des Modernes* (1688–97)[76] he put forward a similar point of view for literature to that of his brother for architecture. Like him he sought to demonstrate the superiority of the moderns over Antiquity, also making use of the distinction between 'positive' and 'arbitrary' beauty to do so. He uses his brother's arguments, however, with a different emphasis. When talking of architecture he one-sidedly stresses the solid, the functional, and the magnificent (*'magnifique'*) as components of *beauté positive* in contradistinction to Claude, who in order to prove the superiority of the moderns ascribed special significance to *beauté arbitraire*, because it allowed free play to the artistic imagination.[77]

The discrepancies and contradictions in earlier measurements of the architecture of Antiquity, which Claude Perrault and others had uncovered, induced Colbert to send an architect to Rome in 1674 to take new, accurate measurements of Antique buildings. His choice fell on the young Antoine Desgodets (1653–1728),[78] who had entered the French building administration at an early age and had attended Blondel's lectures at the Académie since 1672. Desgodets left for Rome in 1674 along with scholarship winners from the Académies but was taken prisoner by pirates during the voyage and was held for sixteen months in Algiers before reaching Rome. In Rome he remained a further sixteen months, during which he measured twenty-four monuments; on the way back to Paris he also measured the Amphitheatre in Verona. Desgodets must have worked with incredible speed and precision, and did all the final drawings himself, a fact that he stresses. Back in Paris he presented his drawings to the Académie d'Architecture, whose reaction was guarded;[79] with a subsidy from Colbert and a royal patent they appeared in print in 1682. Desgodets' *Les édifices antiques de Rome*[80] has remained his masterpiece; it represents an important step in the direction of scientific archaeology.

The lavish presentation and the exactness of the drawings are however not an end in themselves. In the dedication to Colbert, the enormous pride of architects under Louis XIV is brought out, the king being described as putting the Roman emperors in the shade with his building prowess.[81] The exactness of his measured drawings indirectly serves the same goal. Desgodets believes in the 'Mystery of Proportion' in architecture,[82] to which the Ancients were particularly close and which he hopes to penetrate by the accuracy of his measurements. Desgodets was thus using empirical methods in an attempt to attain proportions perceived as absolute, instead of through a pre-existing theory of proportion with a purely mathematical basis, as employed by his teacher Blondel, who was uninterested in exact measurements of Antique architecture, since they set him at odds with his axiomatically based theory of proportion.[83]

Desgodets worked with concordances of earlier measured drawings of buildings (Palladio, Labacco, Fréart de Chambray and Serlio), in all of which he demonstrates inaccuracy. He proceeds on strict principles, adhering exclusively to the surviving buildings of Antiquity and ignoring the reconstructions of his predecessors. As a standardising system of measurement he uses the Paris foot and the module (the radius of the lower column). His comments on individual buildings are restricted to brief historical and technical or descriptive data, and discussion of the earlier measured drawings. Desgodets is proud of the accuracy of his measurements, which he has repeatedly verified in order to attain 'certitude'.[84] That this very accuracy immediately occasioned charges of pedantry and excess is clear from his own statements. In fact, the origin of modern archaeological surveys may be seen in his method. He arranged his work according to the grandeur 'and beauty of the buildings',[85] beginning with the Pantheon, to which alone he devotes twenty-three plates. Although his work met an urgent demand and enjoyed the patronage of Colbert, it was ignored by the Académie for over a decade. Nevertheless, both Blondel and Perrault made use of it.[86]

In spite of active collaboration in the work of the Académie d'Architecture, Desgodets' path was made difficult. He was not made a 'first class' member until 1718, and finally a year later, a professor of architecture, an appointment he held until his death in 1728. Although no executed buildings by him appear to be known, he left two unpublished theoretical works: a treatise on the Orders and the text of the lectures he delivered at the Académie between 1719 and 1728.[87] Desgodets' treatise on the Orders is conventional and based on Vignola. The most interesting of his lectures are those in the second, unfinished part, entitled Traité de la commodité de l'architecture, concernant la distribution et les Proportions des Edifices', in which he develops a general typology of buildings from selected examples.[88] In spite of his belief in the authority of Antiquity, Desgodets' attitude to Vitruvius was markedly detached, and in his designs of churches he approached a nationally interpreted Gothic.[89].

Another protégé of Colbert's, a prolific if unoriginal literary figure, was André Félibien (1619–95), who was secretary of the Académie d'Architecture from its foundation.[90] Félibien steered a liberal middle course between Blondel and Perrault. In 1676 he published the first of many editions of his much-used compilation Des principes de l'Architecture, de la Sculpture, de la Peinture.[91] Following Perrault, ornament is made dependent on considerations of space and cost:

> In building, one must always have regard to Solidité, Commodité and Beauté; as far as Ornaments are concerned, one uses them as one sees fit, according to the arrangement of the site and the money that one wants to lay out.[92]

Félibien appends a glossary of the terminology of architecture and the visual arts. Under the entry 'Symétrie', for example, it may be seen how Perrault's definition of the French concept of symmetry prevailed against the Vitruvian. 'One says: These two statues are in the same proportion, and not: in the same symmetry.'[93]

Félibien's son Jean-François published a collection of biographies of architects[94] in 1687, extending from Antiquity up to the fourteenth century, compiled entirely from earlier literature. Exactly a hundred years later there appeared a collection of architects' lives in continuation of it by Antoine-Nicolas Dézallier d'Argenville,[95] which starts with Brunelleschi and attempts, in the very structure of the work, to demonstrate France's pre-eminence in architecture.

The 1680s saw a gradual dilution of the Classical tendencies in the Académie d'Architecture that Colbert and Blondel had had in mind. The protagonists of the foundation years died in quick succession – Colbert in 1683, Blondel in 1686, Claude Perrault in 1688. Under Blondel's successor Philippe de la Hire (1640–1718) priority was given to the technical problems of building. His lectures at the Académie were never published.[96] In the discussions that he led at the Académie, a primary concern with practical questions is apparent. Greater importance was attached to *distribution* than to *décoration*. In the session of 29 March 1700 there were readings from Palladio and a discussion of his villas in Vicenza, and the conclusions of the Académie on the matter were revealed as follows:

> all of which demonstrates that the buildings are not appropriate for France, where the convenience of the interior is commonly put before the appearance of the exterior; upon which the assembled company resolved that when building it is no less important to dispose the rooms skilfully than it is to adorn the façades finely.[97]

At first sight the *Cours d'architecture* by Augustin-Charles d'Aviler (1691),[98] which underwent regular revision in the eighteenth century in the various editions published by P.-J. Mariette[99], appears to be a new French edition of Vignola's *Regola*. D'Aviler had been in the service of Jules Hardouin-Mansart and had a Classical temperament, as is apparent from his regarding Vignola as the best architectural theorist among the moderns, and his aligning himself mainly with the views of Blondel. He adopts Blondel's account of the evolution of the column from the grave stele and repeats the well known analogies between architecture and the human body. D'Aliver tacks onto his treatise on the Orders illustrations of works by Vignola and Michelangelo, the latter of whom he ventures to criticise on account of the liberties he has taken. By way of Philibert Delorme's French order, which he merely describes as a 'column with various stringed patterns' ('*colonne avec diverses bandes*'),[100] he goes on to discuss a series of column forms (*Plate 85*), which he defines as '*extraordinaries et symboliques*', as distinct from '*colonnes ordinaires*'.[101] In putting forward these types of columns, along with suggestions for pedestals, balusters and panelling, d'Aviler employs the stylistic vocabulary of the day throughout, although in fact he ought to have condemned them as *licences*.

In 1693, as the second volume of his *Cours*, d'Aviler published a *Dictionnaire d'architecture*,[102] which constitutes one of the first systematic lexica of architecture, after that of Grapaldi. In some of the definitions the influence of Claude Perrault is evident, whose redefining of proportion and symmetry had by then clearly become to a large extent common currency. On *Simmetrie* he writes:

> It is the equal correspondence in the parts of a building, either in height, or in breadth, or in length, in order to form a beautiful whole...and *Simmetrie respective* is that in which the opposite sides match one another.[103]

On proportion:

> it is the appropriateness of the dimensions of the members in each part of a building, and the relationship of the parts to the whole.[104]

D'Aviler hastens to add that there were considerable differences of opinion about the correct way of adjusting to optical distortions in the perception of proportion, and refers, without taking sides in the matter, to Blondel and Perrault.

In 1770/71 C. F. Roland Le Virloys attempted to replace d'Aviler's successful *Dictionnaire* with a three-volume, heavily illustrated dictionary, covering the terminology used in all leading European languages,[105] but operating with a rather infelicitous mixture of concepts and names.

In the same year, 1691, in which the first volume of d'Aviler's *Cours d'architecture* was published, there appeared a work by Pierre Bullet (1639–1716), one of Blondel's pupils and a member of the Académie, *L'architecture pratique.*[106] Bullet was a practising architect; his treatise is little more than a manual on geometry for builders. His sharp polemic against Louis Savot, his emphasis on experience and architectural practice, and his comments on architectural theory in general show a certain weariness with theoretical controversy. His only assertion with regard to architectural theory is: 'The theory of Architecture is an accumulation of principles that lay down, for example, the rules of analogy, or the science of proportion, to compose that harmony which so pleasantly strikes the eye.'[107] He solves aesthetic problems with easily grasped aphorisms: thus he classes *bienséance* as 'character fitting to the end that one has in view.'[108] Bullet's book is straightforward and easy to use, scantily illustrated, and ran to several new editions during the eighteenth century.

Around 1700 the architectural debate reached a wider public. A work by the Parisian treasury official Michel de Frémin, written from a very rational layman's viewpoint, *Mémoires critiques d'architecture contenans l'idée de la vraye & de la fausse Architecture*, was published in 1702.[109] The fact that the book is addressed to a particular circle of readers – 'persons of not out of the ordinary intelligence' ('*personnes d'un génie un peu court*')[110] – is already apparent in its taking the fashionable form of an epistolary novel. Frémin strives to attain a basic definition of architecture. With the incisive reasoning of a treasury official, he insists first and foremost on functional considerations, relegating aesthetic categories somewhat contemptuously to a subordinate rule. For him architecture comprises all buildings from the shepherd's hut to the ruler's palace.[111] He disapproves of architectural compilations which treat partial aspects of architecture as if they were the whole. He attacks treatises on the Orders in particular, for in his eyes they are only 'the least part' of architecture.[112]

He gives the following portentous definition of architecture: 'Architecture is an Art of building having regard to the thing itself, the person for whom it is built, and the site'.[113] For Frémin, *objet* denotes precise knowledge of the intended functions of buildings as a prerequisite for planning. *Sujet* is the 'exact propriety and correspondence' ('*juste convenance, & un rapport régulier*') to be attained in a design, starting from a given *objet*.[114] The aesthetic factor is reduced here to the orderly arrangement of functions. By *lieu* Frémin means a thorough investigation of the harmonisation with surroundings and adjacent buildings, calculation of the availability of light and the incidence of wind.[115] He assumes that the first men to build houses employed the 'rational procedure' ('*ordre de la raison*') that he outlines. He calls it a positive crime not to think of the *comfort* of a house before one dreams of making it 'pleasing' ('*agréable*').[116]

In a surprising animadversion against post-Renaissance architecture, he exemplifies his rational architectural criteria by Gothic buildings, Notre-Dame and the Sainte-Chapelle, and plays them off polemically against the 'bad architecture' of Saint-Eustache and Saint-Sulpice.[117] For Frémin, ornament, seen purely as additive, must be entirely subordinate to function, to 'the relationship that is natural and suited to the purpose (take careful note of my terms) for which the Building is intended.'[118]

The viewpoint of Frémin, a layman and an outsider, typical of the Englightenment, and ignoring the discussion of aesthetic norms, is characteristic of the age. It very quickly found its way into professional architectural theory and even into the Académie d'Architecture.

13. Relativist architectural aesthetics, the Enlightenment and Revolutionary architecture

The *Nouveau traité de toute l'architecture* by the abbé Jean-Louis De Cordemoy, first published in 1706, occupies a key position in French architectural theory at the beginning of the eighteenth century.[1] Little is known about Cordemoy himself except that he was a canon of the abbey of Saint Jean-de-Vigne at Soissons.[2] Cordemoy took his chief bearings from Frémin's treatise of 1702 and from Claude Perrault, whose theory of positive and arbitrary beauty he does not, however, mention.

Cordemoy structures his treatise around the Vitruvian-sounding concepts *ordonnance, disposition (distribution)* and *bienséance*, but uses these terms in a very restricted sense. *Ordonnance* is the theory behind the use of the Orders, which, although rehabilitated after their treatment by Frémin, are nevertheless regarded as dependent on function: '*Ordonnance* is that which gives to all parts of a building the appropriate dignity that is proper to their use.'[3] In keeping with seventeenth-century French tradition, *disposition (distribution)* is defined as 'the suitable arrangement of these same parts'.[4] Particularly revealing is the role allocated to the aesthetic aspect, to *bienséance*: 'that which ensures that this *Disposition* is such that nothing will be found that is contrary to Nature, to custom, or to the use of things'.[5]

The definition of *bienséance* has become a purely negative one; *bienséance* is not – in Perrault's terms – a positive aesthetic quantity: it has become dependent on custom and function. In Cordemoy's view, consideration of the social status of clients is also included in *bienséance* – a reflection of earlier precepts concerning *decor* – but the term is now reduced to an equal footing with *usage* and *commodité* as one of the prerequisites for beauty in a building.[6]

Cordemoy, together with Frémin, is one of the precursors of modern functionalism. It is characteristic that he should find symmetry, established by Perrault as a positive beauty, difficult to reconcile with the requirements of *commodité* and *usage*.[7] He does not, however, venture to question the concept of symmetry itself. He proposes a style of architecture based on simple geometric forms, favouring rectangularity and flat roofs, and shunning acute angles and curved surfaces. He calls for overall unity of structure but at the same time for independence of the separate parts of a building (*dégagement*). He values Greek and Gothic architecture equally highly for their clear expression of function. This leads him to propose a Graeco-Gothic style of architecture in which a Gothic building (he uses the example of a church) is to be achieved in Classical Greek forms. He envisages the west towers of a cathedral being built using the Classical orders. Unfortunately, he provides no illustration of his Graeco-Gothic vision. Following d'Aviler's example (1693), a *Dictionnaire de tous les termes d'architecture* is appended to the treatise.

Cordemoy had as little real knowledge of Greek architecture as Fréart de Chambray when he wrote of Greece in his treatise of 1650. He saw Antiquity, *la sainte Antiquité*, through the eyes of Perrault, and, as a cleric, based himself mainly on early Christian architecture. He would have had the pier-and-arch constructions of St Peter's and the buildings modelled on it replaced by buildings based on the column-and-architrave model, thus bringing about a renewal in church architecture. Cordemoy did achieve some success with his ideas, as is demonstrated by Boffrand's chapel in the château de Lunéville.[8] His influence on eighteenth-century architectural theory, and particularly on Desgodets, de la Hire, Boffrand and Laugier, was considerable,[9] and he ought therefore to be accorded a substantially more important rôle than hitherto.[10]

At the time, however, Cordemoy immediately encountered strong opposition, in particular from the military engineer Amédée-François Frézier (1682–1773), who, in a series of articles published between 1709 and 1712 in the Jesuit monthly journal, the *Mémoires de Trévoux*, employed various historical and technical arguments to discredit him.[11] Frézier's attacks and Cordemoy's ripostes focused exclusively on sacred architecture, with Cordemoy, as a theologian, supporting his case with somewhat unfair quotations from the Church Fathers.

Frézier subsequently accepted some of Cordemoy's theoretical ideas but, after the publication of Laugier's *Essai sur l'architecture* (1753), which took its bearings from Cordemoy, he once again challenged the latter's position using technical arguments. Frézier's own theoretical work has to date been largely ignored. His main work, running to three volumes, was published between 1737 and 1739.[12] Frézier's theoretical position steers a course between Claude Perrault and François Blondel: on the one hand he advocates a relativist aesthetic, and on the other he calls for an *architecture naturelle* with fixed rules and close reference to Nature. He expounds his *architecture naturelle* using the example of huts on the French Caribbean islands, which he had got to know during a voyage to South America. His interpretation of the Orders is taken from François Blondel; his call for a return to the 'simplicity of primitive times' is directed at the 'improper ornaments' (*ornements déplacés*) of the Rococo. For him, the principle of true beauty lies in the imitation of Nature,[13] a position which brings him close to Laugier's theory.

The path that Frémin had already embarked on and which was pursued to some extent by Cordemoy, namely that of writing as a layman for laymen, and thus popularising theoretical discussion, reaches a climax in a treatise by Sébastien Le Clerc,[14] in which architectural theory is presented as a suitable topic of conversation for polite society.[15]

Le Clerc deals with the aesthetic side of architecture only: '*la beauté, le bon goût, et l'élégance*'.[16] He does not concern himself with simple buildings, only with those that are '*magnifiques, nobles et pompeux*'.[17] He regards Perrault's relativist aesthetic as self-evident. What matters is effect; the Orders become badges of social status; decoration and furnishings are detached from architecture proper. Le Clerc speaks disparagingly of positive forms of beauty; he is interested only in the arbitrary ones, which are determined by *bon goût*. He practically abolishes the science of proportion, declaring that: '*Proportion* is not to be understood as a purely rational relationship in the manner of geometry, but rather a fitness of the parts founded in the good taste of the architect.'[18] In Perrault, proportion, as an arbitrary beauty, was determined by tradition and custom; in Le Clerc, it is the product of a subjectivised taste. Each Order therefore admits of a range of proportions.[19] Le Clerc proposes a separate French order, with a capital composed of fleurs-de-lys, palm leaves and a cock – symbolising France – and a frieze decorated with a sun motif, as an allusion to the glory of Louis XIV.[20]

To *bon goût* corresponds the *plaisir* of the beholder. Sensory perception is the judge of beauty. Both concepts are regarded as subjective by Le Clerc; *bon goût* thus becomes a personal judgement based on taste and is no longer, as in the discussions of the Académie under Blondel, the result of agreement by members of a privileged section of society. The finest taste creates the greatest individual pleasure. Personal taste is the arbiter of what is permissible, pleasure the criterion of beauty.

Even the Académie d'Architecture in Paris and the Académie de France in Rome could not escape this 'subversive' but extremely popular mode of thinking. In line with Colbert's views, the *pensionnaires* of the French Academy in Rome were charged with studying Classical architecture, as Desgodets had done, and making it fruitful for French architecture. Now, however, a young architect such as Gilles-Marie Oppenordt (1672–1742), who spent the years 1692 to 1699 in Rome as just such a *pensionnaire*, could interpret the 'finest *monuments*' to include those of the Roman Baroque, and draw these with the approval of the director.[21] The Académie had scarcely begun its work when its students started to find beautiful just what it had been set up to combat. Oppenordt's enthusiasm for Borromini would have seemed like rebellion in the eyes of the Académie. Oppenordt did not become a representative of French Classicism but went on to be one of the great creators of the Rococo.[22]

In accordance with the task it had been set, the Académie d'Architecture repeatedly returned to the theoretical discussions which were supposed to lead to the establishment of binding architectural doctrine. Thus in May and June 1712, the question of *bon goût*, which had already occupied the Académie in 1672, was taken up once again. On 30 May 1712, agreement was reached on the following definition: '*Bon goût* in architecture consists in that which manifests the simpler relationship in all its parts, and which, communicated more easily to the mind, satisfies it more deeply.'[23] It is obvious from this definition, which takes account of the importance of the effect on the observer, that new ways of thinking had gained acceptance even in the Académie. At the next two sessions of the Académie, de la Hire, François Blondel's successor as director, lectures on *bon goût*, examining buildings 'that are the most advantageous of all times'.[24] Taste is subordinated to function. Although not made totally subjective as in Le Clerc, it undergoes a clear reinterpretation, away from aesthetics and in the direction of dependence on function.

In 1734 the Académie was called upon to bring its findings together and publish them in one work.[25] On 5 April 1734 it approved definitions of four fundamental concepts in the theoretical discussion: *bon goût, ordonnance, proportion* and *convenance*. The definitions were as follows:

Bon goût consists in harmony or agreement between the whole and its parts. The harmony that gives a work the quality of *bon goût* depends on three factors, which are *ordonnance, proportion* and *convenance*.

Ordonnance is the *distribution* of the parts, exterior as well as interior. It will depend on the size of the building and the use for which it is intended.

Proportion is the yardstick for the appropriate dimensions which must be given to the whole and to the parts, in accordance with their uses and their locations. It is almost always based on ideal Nature, whose wisdom it makes us imitate.

Convenance is submission to received and established uses. It provides the rules by which to put everything in its due place.[26]

Bon goût here appears as the highest theoretical concept, almost comparable to Alberti's *concinnitas. Ordonnance, proportion* and *convenance* are all defined in terms of use (*usage*), i.e. of the function of architecture. This latter concept, on the other hand, is no longer subject to definition. *Usage* is evidently whatever is required of architecture in any given case: practicality, comfort, fashionableness, etc. Basic aesthetic concepts become dependent on the utility value of architecture. The definitions of the Académie abolish the notion of normative architectural doctrine.

On 12 April 1734, only one week after these definitions were approved, Germain Boffrand (1667–1754) presented to the Académie his *Dissertation sur ce qu'on appelle le bon goust en architecture,*[27] which appeared at the beginning of his *Livre d'architecture* of 1745.[28] Boffrand was a very successful architect,[29] a 'first-class' member of the Académie d'Architecture since 1709, and since 1732 'Inspecteur général des Ponts et Chaussées'. He had had a Humanist education, and published his architectural treatise in a bi-lingual version in French and Latin ('*opus Gallicum et Latinum*'). Boffrand's *Livre d'architecture* essentially contains descriptions of his own buildings and projects, prefaced by '*réflexions sur les principes généraux de l'architecture*',[30] which consist of the discourse on *bon goût* already mentioned and some '*Principes tirés de l'art poétique d'Horace*'. Boffrand's style is that of an enlightened and humorous theorist, and he touches on all the great themes of the contemporary debate. For him, as for all his contemporaries and for the Académie, *bon goût* is the central concept. But he is opposed to making the idea of taste entirely subjective (*chacun à son goût*) and describes the common definition of it as a *je ne sçais-quoi qui plaît* as vague.[31] For Boffrand, *bon goût* is 'a faculty that distinguishes the excellent from the good', a product of reflection by 'more enlightened men'. This view ties in with the attempts at definition made by the Académie in 1672, but Boffrand also links the concept of *bon goût* – as in the Académie's definition of 5 April 1734 – to the fundamental principles of architecture (*belles proportions, convenance, commodité, sûreté, santé, bon sens*). The principles of architecture, in Boffrand's argument, have been developed over centuries, and without them, *bon goût* is impossible. Taste thus becomes a correlate of the level of civilisation. *Bon goût* is only possible where the principles of architecture have been mastered – a view that restores some measure of objectivity to this concept. For Boffrand, *bon goût* is more than a quality of either architect or observer; it becomes a quality of the building itself. For without the principles of architecture, no building can be '*réputé de bon goût*'.[33] Boffrand does not regard the principles of architecture as constants, but as subject to development. They have their origins in Nature, but are further developed by *réflexion* and *expérience*. Nature is brought nearer to perfection through Art. Level of enlightenment and experience also help to determine *bon goût*.

Boffrand takes up the idea, already formulated by François Blondel, that architectural development varies according to the level of civilisation reached and the climatic conditions present. He does not believe that the path taken by Antiquity is the only path; he believes, in regard to French Gothic, that 'other principles arose, also derived from the bosom of Nature',[34] and he derives the Gothic style from the paradigm of the French forests. Antiquity, says Boffrand, had a unique opportunity to perfect the arts, and that is the reason for its superiority.[35]

The concept of function, upon which so much stress had been placed since Cordemoy and which the Académie too had underlined, reappears in Boffrand, though in a less emphatic form. Regarding the architectural principles which he says are necessary, Boffrand writes: 'insofar as it relates to the whole, each part should be proportionate, and have a form appropriate to its use'.[36]

According to Boffrand, a totally individualised concept of *bon goût* results in the predominance of fashion ('*La mode le tyran du goût*'), which, he says, proves a great hindrance to the perfection of art.[37] Fashion corrupts the principles of architecture. It is the task of the Académie to guard these principles and ward off the *folles nouveautés* of fashion.[38] He points to the degeneration of architectural ornament, and holds that adherence to principles always brings with it a '*noble simplicité*'.[39] Boffrand's *noble simplicité* signals the *edle Einfachheit* of Neo-classicism.

There is another concept that Boffrand appears to have been the first to introduce systematically into architectural theory: that of *caractère*. According to Boffrand, every house should, from its external construction to its internal furnishings, clearly express the *caractère* of its builder.[40] In his above-mentioned lecture on the application of Horatian poetic ideas to architecture, Boffrand goes even further, requiring that every building should express its function: 'Different Buildings should, by their arrangement (*disposition*), their construction, and by the way in which they are decorated, proclaim their destination to the observer.'[41]

A building should express the *caractère* of the occupant or its function. Architecture has an effect, it speaks to the observer. This concept of *caractère*, nowadays felt to be ambivalent, remained current throughout the eighteenth century. The language used has assumed a psychological character centred on the observer; it becomes the medium of expression for subject-matter that no longer belongs to the field of aesthetics. The language of form and *bon goût*, however, continue to be determined by aesthetic principles, which in turn must be governed by function. With the concept of *caractère*, Boffrand provides the basis for ideas central to 'Revolutionary architecture' and so-called *architecture parlante*. The role of the aesthetics of effect, which derives from rhetoric, emerges particularly clearly in Boffrand. This idea exerts an increasing influence on the eighteenth-century debate over architectural theory. The monumental designs produced by Boullée, pupil of Boffrand and J. F. Blondel, embody these ideas of a visual rhetoric. In his own buildings and plans, Boffrand arrived at a Palladian-style Classicism. A particularly characteristic example of his work is the plan for a hunting lodge at Bouchefort, which was designed for Max Emmanuel of Bavaria (1705)[42] and which in its overall circular layout may perhaps be regarded as a precursor of Ledoux's plans for Chaux (*Plate 86*).

Reaction against the anti-Classical tendencies of the Rococo begins to emerge across a wide front in France from the 1740s onwards. There is a return to the argument between Blondel and Perrault. One important authority for the retracing of aesthetic criteria to objective premises is the *Essai sur le beau* by the Jesuit priest Yves André (1675–1764),[43] postulating a *beau essentiel* and a *beau naturel*, independent of human opinions. Where architecture is concerned, André holds a view based largely on Perrault.

He distinguishes between fixed and variable principles in architecture, corresponding to Perrault's 'positive' and 'arbitrary' beauty. In the former category he includes, for example, geometry and symmetry, in the latter, proportion.[44]

The new direction in theoretical thinking emerges most clearly in the writings of Charles-Étienne Briseux (1660–1754), who in the course of his long life completed the transition from Rococo architect to dogmatist of a new Classicism. His importance as a practising architect is secondary to his significance as a theorist.[45] In 1728 he published a two-volume work containing designs and technical advice on house-building, the title of which clearly signals a determination to supplant Pierre Le Muet's work published one hundred years before (1623).[46] Briseux's sole concern in this work is to be of service to private house-builders. In his plans, each of which is based on a given site, Briseux sets out to show how convenience and aesthetics can be reconciled with the conditions imposed by the site and building regulations (*Plate 87*). The five-part treatise deals first with questions of construction and the qualities of materials. The main body of the treatise consists of fifty-nine '*distributions*' with 142 commented plates. Briseux deals only with Parisian town houses, so that even the houses occupying the smallest sites have several storeys. For each house Briseux provides a plan of the ground floor and a uniform plan for the upper storeys. He provides designs for occupants of all social classes as well as combinations of business premises and residential buildings. His plans are extremely functional, the precise purpose of each room being indicated in captions. The use of embellishments is very restrained.[47] In the later sections of the treatise, Briseux gives a survey of geometry, how to measure construction, and, most importantly, the then current Parisian building regulations. This first, little-known treatise by Briseux is an important source of information on eighteenth-century Parisian residential architecture.

In 1743 there followed a pattern-book for one of the building types fashionable in the first half of the eighteenth century: villas (*maisons de plaisance*).[48] The prospective builders to whom Briseux addresses himself are amateurs, and his illustrations are of importance as encouragements to the reader. In his designs Briseux takes every liberty allowed him by the Rococo. The accompanying text does not contain any coherent architectural theory, but in a number of passages the influence of Père André's *Essai sur le Beau*, published two years before, is detectable. Thus Briseux demands a Classical allure for a building as a whole, requiring in relation to the adornment of a façade that 'The Decoration of this should present a natural beauty, as noble as it is simple, satisfying the eye by symmetry alone', and stipulates ornament that is 'appropriate and devoid of confusion'.[49] Briseux prefaces his work with an uncommented frontispiece depicting a '*Temple de l'Architecture*' (*Plate 88*), with the personification of Architecture sitting enthroned in a Minerva-like pose in the broken pediment of a Rococo pavilion. At the end of the work, Briseux provides patterns for panelling, rocailles, *agrafes* (ornamental keystones) and balustrades, of a kind that were shortly to come under savage attack.

Briseux's last work, which he published in 1752 at the age of ninety-two,[50] shows his reversion to normative Classicism. The very title – *Traité du Beau Essentiel dans les arts* – betrays reference to Père André, although Briseux does not follow the latter in his support of Perrault. Briseux returns to the dispute between François Blondel and Claude Perrault and seeks to refute Perrault using arguments similar to those that

Blondel had already employed. He regards beauty as founded mainly on proportion; he is aware that no binding rules of proportion have as yet been discovered, but the idea of fixed proportions becomes a postulate for him: 'It is true that it has not so far been possible to determine unalterable [proportions], but all authors are agreed on the necessity of adhering to them'.[51] Perrault is blamed for the decline of architecture in France; even the Académie, claims Briseux, ceased, after Blondel's death, 'to teach the fundamental principles of architecture.'[52]

The laws of beauty are to be derived from Nature, which prescribes the harmonious proportions common to music and architecture. These proportions appear, as they did to Renaissance theorists, as a Natural law, as 'a common principle, that renders them pleasing or displeasing, and that the soul, the Judge of all sensations, receives through each sense as agreeable or disagreeable impressions, in a uniform way...'.[53]

Briseux's starting-point is that proportions and their effects are the same for every human being. There is no room for individual taste, for proportion as an 'arbitrary' beauty. To the objection that there does seem to be such a thing as individual taste, Briseux replies that the proximity of human beings to Nature, as it were, varies; they differ in their physiological disposition and their knowledge. But *sensations* ... originally and essentially, 'are identical in everyone'.[54] Briseux argues in the spirit of the Enlightenment, using the tools of epistemology and physiology; everything has the ring of scientific deduction about it. That is why his theory has been called 'physiological aesthetics'.[55] So far does he pursue his rationalist aesthetic that he requires, over and above receptivity to architecture through the senses, intellectual comprehension of its underlying rules, and he scoffs at the ignorance of 'partisans of taste devoid of any principles'.[56] Knowledge renders the observer capable of identifying the cause of beauty and of verifying the principles that underlie it. One may well admire Blondel's Porte Saint-Denis, but to understand it one must read the explanation given in his treatise.[57]

Thus for Briseux, architectural theory is a means of raising the consciousness of and educating a non-expert public. Sensory experience is not enough for him; he demands intellectual verification and debate. Both realms, however, afford *plaisir*: 'If the mind has not received instruction, it contents itself with the enjoyment of pleasure from the senses alone; but if it has been educated by precepts, it can appreciate the same pleasure by examination and discussion.'[58]

Briseux represents a peculiar synthesis of the theory of the elder Blondel and the Neo-classical tendencies of the mid-eighteenth century, managing even to incorporate into this synthesis the theory of *caractère* propounded a few years earlier by Boffrand. This occurs almost casually. It is extremely interesting to compare his new requirement regarding the adornment of facades with that quoted earlier: 'The objects with which one seeks to decorate a façade must not only be appropriate to its character, but must appear useful and necessary, and merit their place there...'[59]

In the book's marginal decorations and vignettes, on the other hand, the Rococo vocabulary continues to predominate, though the now proscribed asymmetrical forms are avoided. Briseux takes works by Palladio, Scamozzi and François Blondel as models, along with some of his own designs in which there is a very restrained use of ornament. In his depiction of the Orders he predictably follows Vignola, Palladio and Scamozzi. At the end of the work, however, are once more illustrations of panelling and balustrades in pure Rococo idiom. Briseux is a transitional figure: as a designer, he is bound, to a large extent, to the stylistic vocabulary of the first half of the century; as a theorist, he is a pioneer of Neo-classicism.

A comparable though more influential position in the history of architectural theory is occupied by Jacques-François Blondel (1705–74).[60] This younger Blondel came from a family of architects; his family relationship to the elder François Blondel is unclear. Only a few of Blondel's executed buildings are known, and his importance lies mainly in his role as a teacher. In 1743, in the face of opposition from the Académie d'Architecture, he opened a private school of architecture, which, although very successful in its teaching, did not manage to make its way financially. Its students included Boullée, Ledoux and de Wailly. In 1755 the younger Blondel became a member of the Académie, and from 1762 he was professor of architecture, thus following in the footsteps of the elder Blondel.

Jacques-François Blondel left an exceptionally extensive literary legacy.[61] Several years before the appearance of Briseux's treatise he had published a two-volume work on villas (*maisons de plaisance*).[62] This treatise operates on the same level as Briseux's. Blondel calls for a close relationship between interior and exterior, in which the 'exterior decoration announces the interior *distribution* of the building'.[63] This more or less corresponds to Boffrand's view, though this was not put down in writing until some years later. Blondel writes consciously about architecture 'in the Modern taste'[64] and addresses himself to amateurs intending to build. Though still fully representative of the Rococo, he complains about clients' tendency to follow fashion, and the confusion to which this leads in ornament, demanding for the latter a 'general rule' ('*ordonnance générale*').[65] The impact of the book derived mainly from its plates. The first volume provides plans for buildings with their respective gardens, the second mostly contains designs for interior decoration.

In 1752 Blondel began publication of a large-scale work on the buildings in and around Paris, which he had already been working on for Mariette; he added his own commentary to the previously unaccompanied plates. Though this was originally envisaged as an eight-volume work, only four volumes were actually published.[66] In 1771 Blondel began publishing the lectures which he had given at his school of architecture since 1750. This work, consisting of six volumes of text and three of plates, was completed by Pierre Patte after Blondel's death.[67] Patte was responsible for the last two volumes, which are devoted to the technical side of architecture. Blonde's *Cours d'architecture*, the title of which is taken from the elder Blondel, is the most comprehensive and extensive body of architectural teaching produced in the eighteenth century, and the longest architectural treatise published up to that time.

Blondel conceals his true identity behind the figure of a fictitious publisher (M.R.***), and apologises for errors and repetitions.[68] He claims that there has to date been no comprehensive work covering all the fields of architecture. This gap is to be filled by his *Cours*. Beyond this he expects his book to have an effect in the French provinces, where schools of architecture are to be set up,[69] and have in some cases already been set up, on the lines of his school in Paris.[70]

Blondel starts his lengthy preamble with an outline of architectural history, followed by reflections on the '*utilité de l'architecture*'. In its basic features, Blondel's architectural teaching shows a clear reversion to earlier architectural theory. Like Briseux, Blondel takes the science of proportion as a 'necessity' in architecture, and, without naming Perrault, describes those who regard proportion as arbitrary as 'superficial men'.[71] He considers, like the elder Blondel, that architectural proportion is derived from Nature. On the other hand, he reverts to Renaissance theory when he interprets architectural proportion and form anthropomorphically. He was obviously familiar with Francesco di Giorgio's theory (*Plate 19*); this is demonstrated particularly clearly in a comparison of the Tuscan entablatures proposed by Palladio, Scamozzi and Vignola.[72] Having superimposed a human profile onto these, he assesses each of them according to the degree of correspondence between the profile and their structure, with Vignola getting the best rating (*Plate 89*). Francesco di Giorgio had undertaken a very similar interpretation of forms of entablature.[73]

Blondel's reversions to earlier architectural theory should not, however, be overemphasised. At the core of his teaching lie themes and concepts that clearly indicate his position between Rococo and Classicism.

Blondel takes up and elaborates Boffrand's theory of *caractère*. *Caractère* is the expressive function of a building. Blondel gives long lists assigning particular *caractères* to particular types of building: he associates temples with *décence*, public buildings with *grandeur*, monuments with *somptuosité*, promenades with *élegance*, etc.[74] Every building type has its own *caractère*, which belongs to a hierarchy. The highest *caractère* is that of *sublimité*, and is reserved for basilicas, public buildings and the tombs of *grands hommes*.[75] For Blondel, the use of ornament is not an arbitrary matter; it must be determined by expressive function. The concept of *caractère* leads Blondel to another, over-arching idea: that of 'style'. *Caractère* produces *style*. *Caractère* is the expression of function, *style* the effect. *Caractère* is *naïf, simple, vrai*; *style* is *sublime, noble, élevé*.[76] Expressing his opposition to arbitrary adornment, Blondel demands the *grand goût de la belle simplicité*,[77] which becomes one of the central catchwords of Neoclassicism. Blondel believes there is a 'true style' in architecture. True architecture has

> throughout its component parts, the style that is appropriate to it, completely unadulterated; it presents a definite character, each member firmly in its place, inviting only the ornament that is necessary for its embellishment.[78]

Blondel is aware that differences in national and cultural conditions lead to differences in style, but set against the background of *vrai style*, the autonomy of these variations is undermined:

> Egyptian architecture was more astonishing than beautiful; Greek architecture more regular than ingenious; Roman, more learned than admirable; Gothic, more solid than satisfying; finally, our French architecture is perhaps more well-contrived than truly interesting.[79]

These comments of Blondel mark the entry of the modern concept of style into architectural theory.

The 'true architecture' which Blondel calls for is pleasing to all. The prerequisite for the achievement of this goal is the cultivation of *goût*. Blondel assumes the existence of both an inherent and an acquired taste ('*goût naturel*' and '*goût acquis*').[80] In addition, he distinguishes between a '*goût actif*' and a '*goût passif*'. Active and acquired taste requires knowledge of the rules of Art and comparative study of the works of the great masters.[81] Taste must be perfected through the observation of Nature and the universe. Only in this way is the *vrai style* to be attained. Blondel agrees with Boffrand that taste rejects fashion in architecture. In his continuation of Blondel's work, Pierre Patte distinguishes between *goût antique* and *goût moderne*, by which he means seventeenth-century Baroque Classicism and Rococo, himself espousing 'modern' decoration.[82]. In his reversion to Renaissance ideas and to French Baroque Classicism, and in his allusion to a new kind of architecture distinguished by *caractère* and *vrai style*, Blondel is a crucial intermediate figure between older, Vitruvian architectural theory and 'Revolutionary architecture'. His students were clearly particularly receptive to certain parts of his architectural typology, for example his presentation of 'monuments built for magnificence', in which category he includes triumphal arches and gates, monuments erected in royal squares, obelisks and theatres.[83] His lectures on the Orders, which were necessarily based on Vignola, were probably received as more academic in nature. A certain remotenes and graphic austerity also characterises the majority of the illustrations in the *Cours d'architecture*.

As a good educationalist, Blondel seems to have recognised early on the need for some kind of manifesto-like compilation of his teachings. As early as 1754, he published a serviceable octavo-size summary of his teaching programme, 'in order to give more portable form to a work which should be useful to our pupils'.[84] Here Blondel describes his experiences of the last decade in the elaboration and communication of a workable theory of architecture, at the same time uttering the key concepts of his architectural theory in epigrammatic form, and giving concise explanatory definitions for them in footnotes. It was probably these definitions that students learned by heart. We are told, for example, that proportion is the 'most interesting part of architecture';[85] that ornament can be 'generally allegorical, symbolic or arbitrary';[86] symmetry is 'indispensable in buildings of importance',[87] and so on. In a clear attack on the functionalist views of the first half of the century, Blondel declares that the question of the decoration of a building has absolutely nothing to do with that of its *commodité* and *solidité*,[88] thus reverting to an autonomous aesthetic. Familiarity with architectural history, together with a good knowledge of the history of architectural theory, are for Blondel essential components of architectural training,[89] and accordingly he completes his 'study guide' with a 'critical' bibliography of architectural theory.[90] He also wrote important entries on architecture to Diderot and d'Alembert's *Encyclopédie*.[91]

Blondel's most faithful student was Pierre Patte (1723–1812),[92] and it was he who completed Blondel's *Cours d'architecture*. Patte wrote a great deal on architecture,[93] generally adopting the same line as Boffrand and Blondel; only on the subject of town planning did he evolve any original viewpoints of importance. The latter are hidden away in an unlikely place – a treatise on French monuments to Louis XV,[94] a remarkable work in several respects. It documents the great growth of interest in monuments which occurred around the middle of the eighteenth century. As a preamble to his treatment of the monuments to Louis XV, Patte gives a wide-ranging survey of the history of monuments to great men since Antiquity,[95] and he ends the work with a detailed description of the competition to design a square in Paris containing a monument to Louis XV.[96] Patte locates the competing entries together on a street-map of Paris, clearly testifying to his interest in the urban context of the designs (*Plate 90*). They include *ronds-points* surrounded by buildings with a central monument (e.g. Polard's entry), which may be regarded as formal precursors of Ledoux's plans for Chaux (*Plate 91*). The great significance attached to monuments, and their decisive influence on the character of the city, seem to signal the advent of the Revolutionary architects, for whom monuments, albeit different in content, were to become the highest kind of architectural challenge. His map of Paris incorporating the various competition designs prompts Patte to expound his own ideas on urban development, using Paris as an example – an undertaking in which he is also encouraged by Laugier's statements on the city, to which he explicitly refers.[97] Patte envisages an efficiently functioning city, conveniently laid out. But he rejects any kind of geometric grid.

It is not necessary, if a city is to be beautiful, that it should be parcelled out with the cold symmetry of Japanese and Chinese cities, and that it should always be an assemblage of houses arranged regularly in squares or parallelograms...[98]

Patte warns against 'monotony and excessive uniformity in the overall plan ['*distribution totale*'].[99] The different quarters of a city should display *variété* and should not resemble each other. A traveller should not be able to take in the city at one glance but should be constantly stimulated by novelty and variety. Patte's text sometimes reads like prophetic criticism of Le Corbusier's 'Ville Contemporaine' of 1922 or his 'Plan Voisin' for Paris.

Although he elaborates extensive plans for urban development[100] – a concern now appearing for the very first time on the architectural scene – Patte is proud of the current state of architecture as a standard: 'Never before has the true taste for Antique architecture been so widespread... The houses of ordinary people are today decorated with a nobility that was not always possessed in the past by the palaces of the great.'[101]

In his *Mémoires* (1769), Patte repeated his urbanistic approach. In this work, ideas about town planning based on climatic, geographic, sanitary and traffic considerations form the basis of his architectural philosophy.[102] Although he still mentions regular urban layouts such as the hexagon and octagon, Patte no longer takes such regular schemes as his starting-point.[103] His arguments are both geographically and historically wide-ranging; thus he states his preference for the bazaars of the Near East over the market-places of Europe.[104]

In his aesthetic statements, Patte already occupies an intermediate position between the straightforward practitioners of the *goût grec* and the Revolutionary architects, as when he stipulates that private houses be simple and forego the use of columns; *magnificence*, according to Patte, is reserved for the dwellings 'of the Supreme Being, and of Princes and Ministers'.[105] He continues to regard proportion as one of the mainstays of architecture, in support of which he characteristically cites Palladio, Vignola and Scamozzi.[106] In his practical arguments in support of a particular type of street, he gives equal consideration to questions of traffic, safety and sanitation.[107]

Patte treats the subjects of building materials and foundations in particular detail, so that his treatise here takes on the character of a modern textbook. One long chapter is headed 'Instructions to a Young Architect'. The treatise concludes with accounts of historical construction, such as that of the Louvre colonnade.

Like his teacher Blondel, Patte must be considered a significant transitional figure between Rococo and Neo-classicism.

With *Architecture moderne ou l'art de bien bâtir* (1764) Charles-Antoine Jombert attempted to capitalise on the success of the works on *maisons de plaisance* by Briseux and Blondel.[108] Jombert's treatise consists essentially of plans for town and country houses by the architect Tiercelet, acquired by Jombert's father in 1726 and first published in 1728. The arrangement of these plans is comparable to that adopted by Pierre Le

Muet one hundred years earlier. Jombert, however, shapes his work into a general architectural treatise tailored to Parisian conditions and concentrating on practical matters.

By the mid-eighteenth century it is hardly possible any longer to speak of a uniform theory of architecture. What may be observed is the coexistence of different, sometimes heterogeneous, trends. Common to all is an Enlightenment attitude and an anti-Rococo position. Alongside a reorientation towards a normative Classical style, there is a Rousseauist school of thought which seeks to derive every architectural tenet directly from rationally justifiable archetypes. In 1750 Jean-Jacques Rousseau published his prize essay *Discours sur les sciences et les arts*, from the competition set by the Dijon Academy, in which he evokes mankind in a blissful primaeval natural state. The most important representative of Rousseauism in architectural theory is the abbé Marc-Antoine Laugier (1713–69). Laugier was a cultivated and many-sided man of letters. As a Jesuit and successful, though over-revolutionary, royal preacher, later a Benedictine monk, publisher of the *Gazette de France*, historian and diplomat, Laugier had a varied career.[109] As an architectural theorist, he was, like his exemplar, Cordemoy, a layman. Of his extensive writings,[110] those on architecture are the *Essai sur l'architecture*, first published anonymously in 1753, and the *Observations sur l'architecture* (1756).[111]

In the *Essai*, Laugier expounds his basic principles of architecture. He declares that there are already sufficient treatises in existence dealing with the Orders and proportion; he sees them, however, as being based on a slavish imitation of Antiquity, and constituting nothing more than commentaries on Vitruvius[112] – with the sole exception of Cordemoy. Reviews of the first edition of the *Essai* accused Laugier of plagiarising Cordemoy,[113] a charge which he seeks to refute in the second edition of 1765. Like Père André and Briseux, Laugier believes in an absolute, 'essential' beauty, independent of custom and convention. He believes this beauty is to be found in Nature alone; it is from Nature that all rules are derived, but all architectural rules so far proposed seem to Laugier to be 'rules of chance' ('*règles au hazard*').[114] Architectural principles are imitations of the processes of Nature. Just as Rousseau envisages a blissful primitive condition, so Laugier posits a primitive hut as the origin of all possible forms of architecture (*Plate 92*).[115] The notion of the primitive hut had been current in architectural theory since Vitruvius, but up to Laugier's time it had been looked on in a purely evolutionary sense as the starting-point of architecture.[115] With Laugier, the primitive hut acquires a new significance: it becomes the principle and measure of all architecture. Column, entablature and pediment are all seen as originating in the primitive hut. Laugier remarks of the erection of the primitive hut, with a certain theatricality: 'and there is man housed' ('*& voilà l'homme logé*').[117] He regards its architectural elements as natural, rational and functional. The wall becomes nothing more than a '*licence*', no longer a constituent part of architecture. The pilaster is a deceitful imitation of the column, a 'bastard' of architecture; arcades are totally proscribed. For Laugier the primal hut embodies all structural logic. Hence he continually reduces all those concepts which have acquired a separate identity in earlier architectural theory to their rôle in the totality of a building, structural justification being the deciding factor in each case. He regards the Orders, the number of which he considers not to be limited to five, not as ornamental features but as constituent parts of a building.[118] Thus he is able to incorporate the use of the Orders into his structural logic, at the same time overcoming the dichotomy between structure and applied ornament. Proportion embraces not just the Orders but the entire structure of a building, as well as its internal divisions and even the selection of the Orders in accordance with the *caractère* of the building.[119] Determination of proportion is, in Laugier's view, a matter for the philosopher rather than the architect.[120] One important purpose of proportion is to provide confirmation of the repeatedly emphasised commensurability of the real world. The doctrine of *caractère* is accepted as a matter of course by Laugier. In his proposals for a 'French' order, he states that such an Order must be consonant with the *caractère* attributed to the French by the whole of Europe: 'and being regarded as the nation with the most exquisite wit and the lightest morals, we must make the French Order the lightest of the Orders.'[121]

Laugier measures all architecture by his own concepts and can scarcely imagine that anyone could think differently. On the one hand he aims at a reduction in the number of architectural elements, as dictated by structural logic, and on the other, he returns, in the case of church architecture, to an almost Renaissance-like way of thought, regarding 'all geometrical figures' as suitable for plans[122] without asking himself whether and in what way they accord with the principles embodied in the primitive hut. He is ecstatic at the idea of a church on a plan in the form of an equilateral triangle. In the *Observations* he applies these geometric designs to secular buildings also, suggesting for example a hospital based on a St Andrew's cross.[123] The choice of geometric plans is not an arbitrary one: it must always be *raisonnable* and determined by the *caractère* of a building. Laugier does not, however, explain how *caractère* and geometric shape are related. These are the musings of a layman; none of them, understandably, is illustrated.

The doctrine of *caractère* clearly goes back to Boffrand; the concept of structural logic, which is regarded as a natural principle, is linked to a claim to truth in architecture. Terms such as *architecture vraie* and *crime* are moral categories. Architecture becomes an ethical issue. One here senses the closeness of Laugier's thought to Rousseau's. In the proposition that truth of architecture lies in its structural logic, Laugier formulates a new concept of functionalism superseding that which had been current at the beginning of the century and had been orientated towards *usage* (function understood in terms of use). Laugier thus becomes one of the initiators of the nineteenth- and twentieth-century debate about functionalism.[124] Similar ideas were evolved at the same time, but much more systematically, by the Franciscan Carlo Lodoli.

Laugier finds his 'natural principles' exemplified by the English landscape garden, and derives from the latter certain ideas about Nature which he would like to see applied to town planning: the city as a park, as a forest, exhibiting at one and the same time symmetry and variety, as well as '*confusion*' and '*tumulte dans l'ensemble*'.[125] Laugier was probably the first to criticise the planning of Paris.

Laugier rejects French Classicism and becomes instead an enthusiastic discoverer of the Gothic style, in which, despite its ornamentation, he sees a partial realisation of his architectural ideas. His appreciations of Gothic buildings, with their descriptions of the incidence of light and of the constantly changing vistas, are emotive in character. In his description of Strasbourg Cathedral he goes as far as to claim that 'There is more art and genius in this single creation than in all the marvels that we see about us'.[126]

Against the background of Rousseauism, Laugier's brilliantly and lucidly written *Essai* quickly attained a wide readership. Blondel recommended it to his students only one year after it was published, though he dismissed it twenty years later as a passing vogue.[127] Two years after its publication (1755) an English translation appeared, and in 1756 a German translation. Goethe's father had a copy of the 1758 edition in his library, and also owned a copy of the *Observations* published in 1765.[128] Goethe was undoubtedly influenced by Laugier in his description of Strasbourg Cathedral (1772), though he disparagingly refers to him as a 'philosophising expert of the new French school', according to whom 'the first man, turned inventor in the face of necessity, drove four posts into the ground, strung four poles across them and covered these with branches and moss.'[129] Even during his Italian journey Goethe still could not entirely escape Laugier's thinking, reproaching Palladio for using engaged columns, and applying to him the moral judgments of truth and falsehood.[130]

Laugier's influential, unillustrated, pocket-sized treatises command a unique position. Alongside them one may observe, around the middle of the century, a growing interest in the purely emotive depiction of architecture. In the latter half of the century the trend towards pictorial architecture became the norm, particularly in the case of 'Revolutionary architecture'.[131] The part played by the engravings of Jean-Laurent Legeay (c.1710–post-1786) and the influence of these on Piranesi and the Revolutionary architects have no doubt been overestimated.[132] But Legeay's work does manifest an architectural approach in which the architect is concerned exclusively with effect, architecture itself taking second place. If, as is supposed, Legeay occasionally taught at Blondel's school of architecture,[133] one may assume that he had direct contact with the Revolutionary architects.

The somewhat younger Marie-Joseph Peyre (1730–85)[134] was a product of Blondel's school of architecture and may have been influenced by Legeay. Having won the *grand prix* of the Académie d'Architecture in 1751, he was awarded the scholarship to go to Rome in 1753. Two generations before him, Gilles-Marie Oppenordt had taken the finest monuments of Rome to be those of the High Baroque; Peyre, on the other hand, has eyes for almost nothing but the architecture of Imperial Rome. For him this period of Antiquity once again becomes the paragon: he sees in it the *belle ordonnance* and even the *distribution*, that the French regarded as their own great contribution to architectural theory, already realised.

The fruits of Peyre's stay in Rome were published in 1765 in the form of a large book of plates entitled *Oeuvres d'architecture*, which was followed in 1795 by a posthumous volume published by his son.[135] Peyre shows his own architectural projects elaborated in Rome directly alongside their Antique models. With his fellow stipendiaries Moreau and De Wailly,[136] he took measurements of the Baths of Diocletian and Caracalla, but when it came to publication, he produced totally symmetrical and scaleless reconstructions of them.[137] Unlike Desgodets, Peyre is not interested in actual measurements or individual architectural elements, but concentrates on overall symmetry. He regards his own projects as forming part of this Roman tradition: 'I have tried to imitate the various projects included in this work, the most magnificent kind of buildings built by the Roman Emperors.'[138] He believes that the possibilities for the imitation of Roman architecture have not yet been exhausted. The Imperial Baths and the Villa

Hadriana 'offer us fine models, which no-one hitherto has made sufficient attempt to imitate.'[139]

A project for a single building containing 'academies and all that is necessary for the education of the young'[140] displays the perfect symmetry discerned in the Roman Baths, but attempts to surpass the Antique model by a combination of architectural structures (*Plates 93, 94*). The didactic style and utopian character of the conception foretoken Revolutionary architecture, in particular Ledoux. The inner building is to serve for intellectual instruction, the outer buildings for entertainment, bodily exercises, and sport.

Peyre takes the Roman buildings to be perfect also in their *distribution*. He regards them as constituting an undisputed model in this regard as well; all one need do is adapt the buildings of Antiquity to contemporary use, '*de les adapter à nos usages*'.[141] Thus a mortuary chapel is modelled on the tomb of Caecilia Metella in Rome, Peyre commenting that it is possible nowadays to build 'in our own way' ('*selon nos usages*') 'monuments to the glory of great men'.[142]

In his project for a cathedral comprising two palaces – for the archbishop and the canons – which was entered for the Concorso Clementino of the Accademia di San Luca in Rome in 1753 (*Plate 95*), Peyre borrows Bernini's colonnades of St Peter's in order to delimit a 'sacred zone', on the model of the Antique *temenos.*[143] Peyre actually justifies formal recourse to Bernini by reference to Antique tradition. The astonishing monumentality of Peyre's design and the totality of its symmetry, taking in the back and front of the entire project, can only be appreciated when it is compared with the other designs in this *concorso*.[144]

Peyre's plan for the 'Palace of a Sovereign' includes colonnades, a theatre, and even a triumphal arch.[145] This design is a kind of super-Versailles based on the Roman Baths.

In Peyre, imitation of Antiquity is overlaid with the new ideas of *caractère*, to which he had been introduced by the lectures of the younger Blondel. The *caractère* of buildings has a directly associative and emotional effect; it can create an impression of 'terror, fear, respect, gentleness, tranquillity, voluptuousness', etc.[146] Certain types of building become symbols of their function by virtue of their *caractère*. Peyre carries over the concept of *caractère* wholesale into the realm of psychological effect, which is produced in architecture ideally conceived, to be taken as pictorial composition rather than reality. Scale and feasibility become unimportant. The monumentality and awe-inspiring nature of Peyre's designs are striking indeed; his attempt to outdo Antiquity brings him close to the ideas of the Revolutionary Architects. Peyre's architectural language is confined by a strict Classicism; but some of his designs display an unornamented, planar treatment foreshadowing Ledoux.[147]

Peyre did not intend that his work should be the vehicle for the exposition of any 'principles of architecture';[148] nevertheless, his illustrative work became the Revolutionary Architects' major point of reference.

Another pupil of Blondel, Jean-François de Neufforge, was responsible for the publication of a huge collection of designs in a ten-volume work entitled *Recueil élémentaire d'architecture* (1757–80). This work, consisting of nine hundred or so plates, is a compendium of every kind of structure; and from the point of view of form in places already foreshadows the work of Ledoux.[149] The *Recueil* is a pattern-book, covering everything remotely connected with building, from garden design to interior decoration, sometimes with bifurcated designs presenting alternative proposals for the same thing. Fantastic pyramids and obelisks and bizarre plans characterise many of the designs, yet Neufforge's plans do not have the intoxicating effect of those of Peyre.

Nine years before the Revolution, the effect of architecture on the human senses becomes – significantly – the subject of an investigation entitled *Le génie de l'architecture ou l'analogie de cet art avec nos sensations* by the architect Nicolas Le Camus de Mézières.[150] Le Camus investigates the fundamental concepts of architectural theory from the point of view of their effect, thus taking up themes raised by Le Clerc, Boffrand, Peyre and others. He assumes, for example, that proportion has a direct effect on the human senses; there occur 'affections of the heart'.[151] He bases himself on the Baroque doctrine of the affections, making direct reference to the teachings of Le Brun,[152] who had propounded a mechanistic theory of expression according to which emotional states could be gauged with scientific accuracy from facial expressions. Le Camus applies this mechanistic approach to architecture, stating that 'each object possesses its own character',[153] thus placing the theory of *caractère* on an objective footing. The *caractère* of a building, which is determined by the characteristics of its occupant or by its function, exercises the same effect on every observer – one is here reminded of Briseux. Le Camus takes the idea further, extending his mechanistic doctrine of effect to the sphere of colours and sounds, positing synaesthetic analogies between proportion, musical harmony and colour – one of the favourite concepts of late eighteenth-century art theory. Le Camus makes reference to Ouvrard's theory – of which the elder Blondel had already made use – and to the 'colour keyboard' of the Jesuit Père Castel.[154]

Le Camus employs the concept of proportion but no longer takes it to mean an arithmetic or geometric relation, but rather a harmony of solid masses, which, he says, is determined by the *caractère* of the building and drawn directly from Nature.[155] The doctrine of *caractère* is thus projected back onto Nature, a crucial premise for the thinking of the Revolutionary architects. Le Camus for example describes the '*caractère majestueux*', the '*genre terrible*' – probably taking up Edmund Burke's concept of the Sublime (1757); his definition of the *genre terrible* already has a Boulléean ring about it: 'The genre of the terrible is the effect of grandeur combined with might. The terror inspired by a scene of Nature may be compared to that produced by a dramatic scene.'[156] A fossil-like reminiscence of the theory of the Orders surfaces in the prescriptions relating to *caractère* when Le Camus recommends the Doric order for the '*genre martial*'.[157]

A belated, not to say anachronistic, note is sounded in Ribart de Chamoust, *L'Ordre François trouvé dans la nature* (1783).[158] Just as Laugier believed he had discovered a timeless functionalist system in Nature in the form of his primal hut, so Ribart de Chamoust observes in Nature groups of three trees with trunks entwined with foliage, and identifies in them the French order, the search for which had been going on since the sixteenth century (*Plate 96*). He draws an analogy between the three tree-trunks and the Three Graces, identifying these with the three Gallic goddesses.[159] This French order is reserved for public buildings, and private buildings of especial '*grandeur*' and '*magnificence*'; it is finally equated with Divine Wisdom,[160] and the book culminates in a design for a Temple of Holy Wisdom. This is a centrally-planned octagon, in which the piers – inspired by Perrault's twinned columns in the Louvre colonnade – are made up of groups of three columns.

The *Lettres sur l'architecture des anciens et celle des modernes* (1787) by Jean-Louis Viel de Saint-Maux represent a break with previous architectural theory.[161] Throughout his series of letters, the author pursues a single basic aim, that of proving that the architecture of Antiquity evolved from ritual, earth-bound ideas related to fertility, the seasons and the cosmos. Knowledge of the liturgical origins of architecture has been lost, claims Viel de Saint-Maux. The architectural language of Antiquity was, he claims, symbolic and expressed the forces of Nature and the attributes of the Creator.[162] The symbolism is straightforward and associated with the world of agriculture. Viel de Saint-Maux rejects the whole of architectural theory since Vitruvius as an aberration. His language is polemical, at times incantatory. Vitruvius's work is described as an 'unintelligible work, which could be of use only on Robinson Crusoe's island.'[163] Agriculture becomes the paradigm for architecture. Stress is laid on common features in the architecture of primitive agricultural peoples. The Classical temple is seen as originating in monoliths, set out in accordance with the number of planets, months and days, in such a way as to represent the course of the sun.[164] The fully-developed temple becomes a replica of the heavens.[165] Capitals are seen as an expression of the 'causes of Nature and the genius of each people.'[166] Architecture becomes a 'poem to fecundity' and a 'theological construction'.[167] Votive altars, aromatic plants and perfumes are all brought into the symbolism of architecture.[168] Viel de Saint-Maux would like to see a return by his own age to this symbolic language. The Romantic idealism of this was something onto which it was very easy to superimpose the then current ideas of *caractère*. Viel de Saint-Maux therefore ranks among the most important forerunners of Revolutionary architecture.

Charles-François Viel (1745–1819)[169] was evidently a relation, perhaps even a brother, of Jean-Louis Viel de Saint-Maux. Charles-François is a typical representative of strict Classicism, as demonstrated in particular by his *Décadence de l'architecture* (1800).[170] In this work he attacks Rococo and the frivolous adoption of principles of seventeenth-century France and Antiquity. His own designs are distinguished by their severity and almost total lack of ornament, for example, window-openings without architraves, simply cut into the wall. An interesting earlier project for a '*Monument consacré à l'histoire naturelle*'[171] is that dating from 1776 and published, with an accompanying text, in 1779. Dedicated to Georges Buffon, the author of the great *Natural History*, the project is for the erection of a 'monument' intended both to honour Buffon and to house the natural history museum founded by him, with the addition of a tree nursery and zoo. This museum as monument is an interesting precursor of the Dulwich Picture Gallery. Beyond its function as a museum-cum-memorial, Viel would also like his building to convey the 'grand idea' of the 'multitude of objects, of Nature and its immensity'.[172] Even more explicitly, he wishes the building 'by its grandeur and magnificence to announce the Temple of Nature and to be its sanctuary.'[173] The *caractère* of his design is described as 'sublimity' and 'grandeur'. At the same time, Viel is at pains to evolve an educational programme for the public; hence his suggestion that the animals in the zoo may be used as models by artists.[174] Viel hastens to assure the reader that he has not planned a gigantic project, but one conceived 'for possible execution'.[175] The impact of the severe design is therefore due more to the institution of columns than to its monumentality. A striking feature of Viel's design and commentary is an expressive intention which, though already prefatory of the thinking of the Revolutionary architects, remains faithful to the Classical vocabulary of form and attaches importance to feasibility.

To understand so-called 'Revolutionary architecture' aright, it is necessary to be familiar with the formation of the ideas that gave rise to it from the beginning of the eighteenth century onwards. The exaggerated interest of the twentieth century in the phenomenon has led to its isolation, and consequently to historical misinterpretations which claim to see in 'Revolutionary architecture' a break with tradition and something akin to the origins of modern architecture. The unfortunate term 'Revolutionary architecture' has also contributed to this process, despite the fact that these architectural ideas are not an expression of the French Revolution of 1789 and were not evolved by Revolutionaries, but originated much earlier. They are the product of Royalists, who after the outbreak of the Revolution could no longer find employment and lived in fear of their lives. At any rate, their 'revolutionary' element lies not in political upheaval, but in the view that existing ideas must be pushed to their extreme with logical rigour. It is therefore important to be familiar with the various currents of the eighteenth-century theoretical debate upon which Revolutionary architecture builds, and which it to some extent takes over and exaggerates.

It was Emil Kaufmann who 'discovered' and named Revolutionary architecture. His writings from the 1920s onwards directed attention to the phenomenon, starting with Ledoux.[176] The rediscovery of Boullée's drawings and treatise, and their exhibition and publication after the Second World War, were very influential.[177] The attempt to draw parallels between French and Russian Revolutionary architecture, which actually highlights the inappropriateness of the sobriquet for the movement, has reawakened interest in the subject.[178]

Étienne-Louis Boullée (1728–99), who was originally trained as a painter and later became a pupil of both Jean-François Blondel and Legeay, left behind only a small number of buildings and some interiors for private houses.[179] The various posts that he held in building administration, and his admission to the Académie d'Architecture as a first-class member, evidently provided him with the material means to enable him to retire from architectural practice in 1781 and begin working on projects of which there was no likelihood or indeed any intention of execution.

As a result, Boullée's importance lies mainly in his *Essai sur l'art* and the designs executed in connection with this between 1781 and 1793. In his will (1793) he bequeathed the manuscript and drawings to the French nation. The treatise first appeared in print in 1953.[180] A futher group of drawings was rediscovered in Florence.[181] An extensive literature has now grown up around Boullée.[182]

The *Essai* is prefaced by a motto which conveys the essence of Boullée's conception of architecture: '*Ed io anche son pittore*' ('And I also am a painter'). The form of words is borrowed from a similar saying of Correggio's, which Boullée also quotes. The motto should not be taken simply as an allusion to Boullée's training as a painter; the same thought is to be found in Ledoux's 'If you wish to be an architect, begin as a painter.'[183] Architecture is presented as a picture created by the effect of solid bodies; Boullée repeatedly speaks of '*tableaux*' and '*images*' whose effect is interpreted in 'poetic' terms.[184] The designs are not intended for execution; nor are they simply an end in themselves. They are rather a collection of examples to be stored in an imaginary architectural museum: 'In time, one would have a museum of architecture containing all that could be expected of the art from those cultivating it.'[185] The didactic and moral intentions are unmistakable. The size of the drawings, their fine detail and the partial use of colour cross the dividing-line between a simple design and an architectural composition, thus departing from the usual format for a published treatise.

With his *Essai* Boullée seeks to win public recognition 'by efforts useful to Society';[186] he is particularly keen to reveal the 'poetry' inherent in architecture. He calls for architecture with a poetic *caractère*, particularly in the case of public buildings:

Yes, I believe that our buildings, above all our public buildings, should be in some sense *poems*. The images they offer our senses should arouse in us sentiments corresponding to the purpose for which these buildings are intended.[187]

Boullée's emphasis on the impact of architecture on the senses corresponds to the theory propounded not long before (1780) by Le Camus de Mézières. The term *usage* (here translated as 'purpose'), which at the beginning of the century denoted the execution of a function, and in Laugier denoted structural logic, acquires in Boullée a meaning very close to that of *caractère*, appearing sometimes to be almost synonymous with it. Boullée logically recognises the need for a theory of solid bodies that will define characteristics of the latter and their effect on our senses, 'their analogy with our system.'[188] He virtually defines the nature of architecture as the realisation of the pictorial power of solid bodies: 'to present images through the disposition of solid bodies'.[189] Building itself becomes for Boullée a 'secondary art';[190] the main significance of his theory lies in its investigation of the pictorial effect of solid bodies, by which he means only regular geometric bodies, since these, by virtue of their regularity and symmetry, impart 'the image of order'.[191] From all this one may better understand why Boullée describes himself as a 'painter'.

Returning to the old dispute between François Blondel and Perrault, Boullée sides with Perrault in rejecting the analogy of music and architecture, but claims on the other hand that the principles of architecture emanate directly from Nature – though he does not identify these principles with those of Blondel. Boullée introduces new principles which were implicit in Perrault: *régularité, symétrie* and *variété*. Together these make up *proportion.*[192]

Boullée's concept of proportion, however, has nothing in common with the idea of proportion established in the seventeenth century: 'I understand by the proportion of a solid body, an effect that arises from regularity, symmetry and variety'.[193] Proportion is thus no longer an arithmetic relation – regardless of whether its beauty is 'positive' or 'arbitrary' – but is rather a combination of elements producing a certain effect. The elements in this combination are defined by Boullée as follows: *régularité* produces the beauty of forms, *symétrie* 'their order and cohesion', *variété* 'the aspects by which they are diversified to our eye.'[194] From all these results the harmony of solid bodies, i.e. proportion.

The most perfect solid, according to Boullée, is the sphere, which he describes as 'the image of perfection'; it combines, he says, perfect symmetry and regularity with the greatest *variété.*[195]

Boullée repeatedly describes proportion as 'one of the chief beauties of architecture',[196] and as flowing from Nature.'[197] His concept of it represents a reinterpretation of Perrault's distinction between proportion and symmetry – proportion in the true sense being here excluded, so that the concept moves straight towards the modern concept of symmetry. For Boullée, order can result only from symmetry. Proportion becomes a vague notion of harmonious order between regular, symmetrical bodies and masses. Proportion is, as it were, eliminated from Boullée's concept of *proportion*. Here is to be found a perplexing change in terminology: for Antiquity and the Renaissance, symmetry means proportion; in Boullée, the concept of proportion almost corresponds to that of symmetry. Since Antiquity, proportion had always taken the human body as its basis, and thus established an idea of human scale. With the disappearance of proportion, the idea of scale also automatically disappears from architecture. This has profound consequences for the subsequent stages in Boullée's thinking.

The analogy between regular solids and their effects on the human senses is described by Boullée as *caractère*: 'And I call *caractère* the effect which results from this object in any sort of impression.'[198] Boullée gives the concept of *caractère*, in the sense in which he had become familiar with it in particular through his studies under the younger Blondel, a new interpretation. That he should describe it as an 'effect' is a consequence of Le Camus de Mézières' arguments; that he should link it more to the effect of regular solids than to the expression of architectural use is what constitutes the crucial difference. Boullée regards the regularity and symmetry of solid bodies as epitomising Nature. He therefore includes the total effect of Nature in his definition, and seeks in his designs to do nothing less than create 'great pictures of nature' ('*grands tableaux de la nature*').[199] Architecture thus becomes for him the only art that 'sets Nature to work'.[200]

Boullée's design for a cathedral intended for the celebration of the feast of Corpus Christi clearly illustrates this (*Plate 97*). The building is to have a '*caractère de grandeur*', an '*important caractère*', and is to be set out in a '*noble et grande disposition*' on a site dominating the city. It is to be set amongst flowers and avenues of trees, their scents being offered up to the Deity like incense. Nature, the seasons, and the location are all included in the *caractère* of the building and therefore also in the design. Nature is at its best in summer, hence the designation of the building for a feast-day occurring at this time of year.[201] For Boullée the concepts of Nature and of the Deity are identical; revelation takes place in the architectural '*image*'. Architecture becomes a 'setting to work' of Nature, the architect he who 'sets Nature to work'.

In his cathedral project Boullée seeks to create an 'imposing picture' in honour of the Deity; the size of the temple 'should offer the most striking and greatest image of existing things'.[202] It should be a reflection of the universe.

Immensity, beauty and symmetry are inseparable in Boullée's eyes: 'so it is true that the great is necessarily allied with the beautiful.'[203] Great size is a sign of 'superior qualities'. In order to heighten this effect, Boullée employs rows of columns, pointing to similar use of them by the Greeks; finally, he calls for the effective use of lighting, as a contribution to the overall effect. A traditional idea like that of the Orders is not totally excluded from his designs, but is subordinated to the symbolism of his doctrine of *caractère*.

Boullée's designs all tend towards monumentality in both size and appearance. Sepulchral monuments, the function of which is 'to perpetuate the memory of those to whom they are dedicated',[204] play an important part in his work. He considers that the Egyptian pyramids, with their 'sad image of arid peaks and immutability', are particularly good at achieving the desired 'poetry of architecture'.[205]

The culmination of these designs and descriptions is the monument to Newton (*Plate 98*). The description of it takes the form of a hymn: 'Sublime spirit! Vast and profound genius! Divine being! Newton...you ascertained the shape of the Earth, and I have conceived the idea of enveloping you in your discovery...'[206]

The huge sphere represents the Earth and Newton's discoveries. The cenotaph – Newton is buried in Westminster Abbey – is the only 'material object'. During the day, the night sky will be reproduced in the interior of the sphere thanks to holes bored into its dome; at night, the interior will be lit up by a huge lamp. Around the outside of the building, circles of trees revive the Imperial Roman tradition of the Mausolea of Augustus and Hadrian. Boullée sums up the effect of his design as follows: 'the effects of this great picture are, as one sees, produced by Nature'.[207]

Boullée must have known that his design went beyond the structural possibilities of the day,[208] yet he did not consider this detrimental to it. The Newton monument, which is practically without function – it is not even a tomb, only a memorial – is the clearest expression of Boullée's intentions: the less purpose a building has, the more purely may a geometric idea be developed. The Enlightenment saw in Newton its spiritual lodestar. The monument to Newton is dedicated not to Newton's person, but to all that which is associated with his name. The quasi-religious reverence of the Enlightenment for Newton is exemplified in Alexander Pope's epitaph to him written in 1732:

Nature and Nature's law lay hid in night:
God said, Let Newton be! and all was light.

A design for a 'Temple of Reason', not mentioned in the *Essai*, takes the spherical idea even further. A smaller, lower half-sphere, laid out within as an artificial landscape, is covered over by a larger half-sphere.[209] In the centre of the site stands a statue of Diana of Ephesus, the goddess of Nature and Fertility. The Temple of Reason thus becomes a Temple of Nature as well.

The fortifications and bridges that Boullée describes in his *Essai* clearly illustrate his poster-like treatment of the doctrine of *caractère*. Fortifications in his scheme should present an image 'of strength' by the depiction of unconquerable-looking soldiers and shields in relief on the outer walls. This kind of architecture is imbued with *caractère, parlante*, and – intimidating.

The fascination of Boullée resides in his designs: in their systematic use of the geometric form; in their expression of ideas with scarcely any vestige of practical application; in their monumentality and superhuman scale. Boullée's is an architecture *per se*, which requires only depiction, and not execution. For Boullée, monumentality is not a form of megalomania but an expression of the sublimity of Nature, whose magnitude is reflected in the magnitude of the architecture. Without this world-view, typical of the later Enlightenment, all reference to Boullée becomes empty game with forms. Many architects of the twentieth century, familiar only with the forms employed by Boullée and not with his ideas, fall prey to this error. It is, to put it plainly, absolutely fundamental to Boullée's designs that they remained *tableaux*. Boullée's architectural theory was a radical extrapolation of then current ideas, which had lost contact with reality.

In his time, Boullée exerted considerable influence as an academic teacher;[210] but after his death his teachings fell into oblivion until their rediscovery in this century.

Claude-Nicolas Ledoux (1736–1806), Boullée's junior by eight years, was also a product of J.-F. Blondel's school.[211] He enjoyed success as an architect in Parisian high society, for which he completed numerous commissions, the most important being those for Madame du Barry. Appointed inspector of the royal saltworks in Franche-Comté in 1771, he began in 1775 to construct the saltwork town of Chaux (Arc-et-Senans); in 1784 he was commissioned to build the toll-houses (the Barrières) around Paris, a task cut short by the Revolution. Ledoux narrowly escaped the guillotine. Imprisoned from 1793 to 1795, he later became an admirer of Napoleon. From the 1770s he was preparing a large-scale architectural treatise, a small part of which he succeeded in publishing in 1804.

The forty toll-houses with a linking wall encircling Paris were looked upon as bastions of the monarchy: '*Le mur murant Paris rend Paris murmurant*'. The sharp criticism levelled against them by Ledoux's contemporaries did at least acknowledge their novelty: 'The architecture of these Barrières is cubic and angular. Their style has something severe and threatening about it.'[212] The decision of the Convention to convert these 'stones...heaped up by tyranny' into monuments to the Revolution[213] was never realised.

Ledoux's treatise *L'architecture considérée sous le rapport de l'art, des moeurs et de la législation*[214] is difficult to read, written in an emotive, meandering style, its meaning often unclear. Nevertheless, it is possible to discern in it the outline of an architectural system. Of the planned five-volume work, which was also to have contained a universal history of architecture, only a fraction was actually written. At no point in his treatise does Ledoux try to pass himself off as anti-Royalist; the work is dedicated to the Tsar of Russia, who was one of the first to subscribe to the work. The motto on the title-page of 1804, *Exegi monumentum* (Horace), indicates Ledoux's self-assurance.

The introduction to the work contains Ledoux's basic views on architecture. His plan is to elaborate an architectural system covering all existing architectural tasks. He assumes a given social structure within which his proposed improvements will be implemented. His designs are directly related to the 'social order': 'I have included all the kinds of buildings demanded by the social order'.[215] Architecture reflects the social order: 'The house of the poor man, by its modest exterior, enhances the splendour of the mansion of the rich.'[216]

The architect is given a directive role within the social order. He has political, moral, legislative, religious and governmental responsibilities.[217] His position is viewed in quasi-spiritual terms. The architect 'purifies' the social system: 'The craftsman is the machine of the Creator; the man of genius is the Creator himself.'[218] As in Rousseau, morality means 'active religion'.[219] The architect becomes an educator; architecture is the instrument he uses to educate. The novelty of Ledoux's approach lies not in his pioneering of a social revolution, but in his new interpretation of the role of the architect within the social order.

Ledoux no longer recognises a hierarchy in the various building tasks as did his teacher Blondel; for him the only difference between them lies in their scale and *caractère*. The poor man's house and the rich man's palace have become building tasks of equal status: 'The artist cannot always offer those gigantic proportions that overawe us to the eye; but if he is a true artist, he will not cease to be so while he builds a woodman's cabin.'[220] Architecture should express the laws of social coexistence; in his ideas Ledoux shows himself to be an adherent of Rousseau's theory of the Social Contract (1762):

> If society is founded on mutual need commanding reciprocal affection, why should we not bring together this analogy of sentiment and taste, which honours man, in private houses?...The *caractère* of monuments, like their nature, serves the propagation and purification of morals.[221]

Caractère transcends its function as a means of expression and becomes an educational tool. Ledoux's thinking is revealed particularly clearly in the example of the 'Oikema' or Temple of Love. The Oikema is a brothel with an educational function. The act and sight of vice, so Ledoux believes, evoke a sense of human degradation and lead one back on to the path of virtue.[222] With its windowless external walls and its portico, Ledoux's building looks like a temple set in a beautiful landscape,[223] but its phallus-shaped plan betrays the building's function.

Ornament is permitted by Ledoux when justified by the *caractère* of a building. This results for the most part in the disappearance of all architectural ornament. Ledoux moreover recognises the aesthetic appeal of undecorated geometric forms and unbroken lines. He speaks of 'unity of thought' defined as follows:

> Unity, type of the beautiful, *omnis porro pulchritudinis unitas est*, consists in the close relationship of the mass with details and ornaments, in the non-interruption of lines, so that the eye is not permitted to be distracted by detrimental accessories.[224]

Ledoux employs leading terms from the architectural theory of Classicism, but gives them a content consonant with his own view of architecture: *variété* confers on every building the physiognomy appropriate to it; *convenance* is the taking into account of social status, site, function and cost; *bienséance* is primarily the expression of the content of the building (*caractère*), as well as a rather obscure 'analogy of proportions and ornaments'; *symétrie* is derived from Nature, contributes to *solidité*, and balances one thing against another, but does not exclude the irregular in the shape of the picturesque and the bizarre; *goût* conveys pleasure and is the means by which ideas are clarified.[225] Here Ledoux becomes wholly unclear.

As in Boullée, proportion practically disappears as an aesthetic concept. *Solidité* appears, curiously, as a product of *symétrie*, the meaning of which is similar to that in Boullée. The emphasis on immensity as an end in itself is absent from Ledoux. Common to both Ledoux and Boullée is the disregard for function in the sense of the practical value of architecture, in other words the disregard for precisely that which, under the terms *usage* or *commodité*, had hitherto been such a decisive factor in French theory. Architecture becomes the medium of expression for particular content, an educational instrument; it is often, however, scarcely habitable or serviceable any longer, as is shown in numerous designs.

Ledoux developed most of his ideas working out his ideal design for the saltwork town of Chaux, where between 1775 and 1779 he had begun construction of the salt works themselves, along with administrative and residential buildings (*Plate 99*). His second partially executed circular plan, in the centre of which stands the 'Director's House', in the present writer's opinion forms part of a series of designs based on the idea of a circular layout with a building in the centre, e.g. the hunting pavilion in

Boffrand's plan for Bouchefort (1705) or the monument to the king in Patte's plan for a Place Louis XV (*Plates 86, 91*). In the plan for the royal saltworks at Chaux, the idea of absolutist monarchy, represented by the Director, is adapted to a factory settlement. Most of Ledoux's ideal plans date from a time when construction had been abandoned. Ledoux arrives at a project for a garden city, but the saltworks remain the central feature. Chaux was, however, increasingly used as a pretext for the design of a utopia.

The rejection of the city, as the cause of all civilisation's ills, can be traced on the one hand to Rousseau but probably also to François-Noel Babeuf (1764–97), a puritanically-minded revolutionary who rejected cities because of the inequality suffered by their inhabitants and regarded them as the source of vice.[226] Almost exactly the same phraseology is to be found in Ledoux. The fact that Ledoux, imprisoned as a Royalist in 1793, should at the end of his career have adopted the ideas of a man executed in 1797 for being too revolutionary, is not without historical irony. However that may be, it should not be assumed that these ideas were part of the original plans for Chaux.

In his later years, in the course of evolving his aesthetic ideas of *caractère*, Ledoux lights upon the notion of equivalence – if not of equality – in architecture. Ledoux is fully aware of the significance and novelty of this step: 'For the first time one will see presented on the same scale the magnificence of the tavern and that of the palace...'[227] Equality in Ledoux is a 'moral' equality[228] within the 'social order', not the *égalité* of the French Revolution. The Orders are no longer badges of class but may also appear in purely functional buildings, where this is justified by their *caractère*.

Ledoux's ideas about society are thoroughly Romantic, as demonstrated in his emotive illustration '*L'abri du pauvre*', in which a naked man sits under a tree by the sea looking up at the gods in heaven (*Plate 100*). Ledoux explains: 'this vast universe which astounds you is the house of the poor man, the house of the rich man, which has been plundered.'[229] Similarly, Ledoux explains the plan for Chaux, consisting of two semi-circles extended by an inserted section, by reference to the course of the Sun.

Ledoux's plans and views of Chaux, and his individual designs and descriptions, contradict each other at certain points, owing to the fact that they were drawn during different phases of planning or at different stages in the development of his utopian vision.[230] A few designs for individual buildings will be singled out here as typical examples. Ledoux shows his seriousness in his theory of the equality of all building tasks by providing plans of houses for manual workers and clerks. These houses, however, merely serve as an excuse to depict geometric solids, the choice of shape in each case being justified by reference to their *caractère*. Thus the 'House of a Hoopmaker' consists of two cylinders intersecting at right-angles (*Plate 101*); a circular opening affords a view straight through the house.[231] The all-round impression of rings created on the outside announces to the observer that this is the house of a maker of hoops for salt casks. In the 'House of the Inspector of the River Loue' the stream is simply made to run directly through the house.[232] The *architecture parlante* of the houses displays the occupations of their inhabitants to the outside world. In drawing up these plans, Ledoux shows the same predilection as Boullée for simple geometric bodies, seeking in each case to make these accord with the required *caractère*. In the necropolis for Chaux, Ledoux comes particularly close to Boullée's way of thinking: a great hollow sphere, half-sunk into the ground, is linked with the idea of the Roman catacombs. As a 'view' of this project, Ledoux provides a picture of the earth suspended in the clouds and surrounded by the other planets.[233] The crucial feature of this style of architecture is its symbolism.

The well-known spherical 'House of the Field Watchmen' does not form part of the plans for Chaux, but was included in a project for a château at Maupertuis which Ledoux was commissioned to design in 1780;[234] the spherical house was never built. The building sits, like a spacecraft at rest, in a hollow in the landscape. It has no windows; access to it, via ramps placed against the walls on four sides, is through openings remarkably resembling extended versions of Venetian windows. The section of the building shows particularly clearly how all functional considerations – in terms of suitability for habitation – have been sacrificed to the symbolism of an ideal architecture. Recourse to basic geometric forms as the basis of architecture had been accepted as a matter of course since the Renaissance, but the geometric form had never before acquired a legitimate independent status as a symbol or been detached from the other fundamental principles of architecture. Like Boullée's Newton monument, but on a smaller scale, the 'House of the Field Watchmen' translates the form of the sphere, as a replica of the universe and the most perfect of solids, into an architectural design – one which has attracted especially trenchant criticism.[235]

Although individual points in this criticism should be rejected, it is nevertheless true that the process of reducing architecture to mere geometry remains questionable. In addition, one may ask whether such use of the sphere is appropriate in this project. Boullée's intentions in designing his monument to Newton can be understood, but one feels that Ledoux's treatment only results in the trivialisation of an important idea. This is even more true of designs such as A.-L.-T. Vaudoyer's 'House of a Cosmopolite',[236] in which, despite a more house-like *disposition*, even the remotest trace of *bon goût* seems to have been lost.

Ledoux's importance for the later planning of ideal cities (Owen, Fourier, Pemberton, Howard) is clear. His reduction of architecture to basic geometric forms and his almost total renunciation of decoration make him – provided his theoretical premises are ignored – regardable as a forerunner of Loos and Le Corbusier.

Ledoux's idea of *caractère* appears ambivalent to us: *caractère* should express the function of the building yet not in a practical or structural sense, but symbolically, in a way that evokes associations and at the same time fulfils a set of heuristic objectives. The usability of a building is subordinated to this expressive task, internal functions often being neglected or sacrificed. *Caractère* takes precedence over *usage*. The latter concept, central to French architectural theory in the first half of the eighteenth century, disappears almost totally in the work of the Revolutionary Architects. Architecture becomes a language of signs, which celebrates itself. It is understandable, therefore, that no attempt actually to execute these designs was ever made. Execution would have denied the whole idea. The fascination lies in the extent to which the idea is taken; the idea has become pure image, but never architecture.

The idea of *caractère* and *architecture parlante* was predestined to trivialisation. With the designs of architects such as Jean-Jacques Lequeu[237] and others, *mauvais goût* marched in triumph over the ruins of a theoretical edifice that Colbert had sought to erect, and that had begun to crumble even as it was built.

14. Germany and the Netherlands in the sixteenth century

In the Age of Dürer, Germany and the Netherlands had their first episodic and personalised encounters with the thought of the Italian Renaissance. The sole German contribution to architectural theory at this time was Dürer's treatise on fortification (1527);[1] while Central Europe as a whole blindly succumbed to the influence of Serlio and the effect of piecemeal publication of his treatise, beginning with Book IV on the Orders (1537). Book IV was translated into Dutch in 1539 and into German in 1542, and spawned a series of works, particularly in Germany, which reduced architectural theory to treatises on the Orders alone. Most of these *Säulenbücher* were the work of men who had no direct personal knowledge of Antiquity or the Renaissance, but took what they knew from Serlio.[2] This led to a kind of 'second-hand' architectural theory derived, not from a personal experience of the Antique, but from books and collections of engravings; the result followed laws of its own, occasionally with bizarre consequences.

The first two treatises of this kind were written in Dutch; they were the work of Pieter Coecke van Aelst (1502–50) and appeared in 1539. One of them, a short work called *Die inventie der colommen*,[3] which draws in the main on Vitruvius, Cesariano's commentary on Vitruvius (1521), and on Diego de Sagredo's *Medidas del Romano* (1526),[4] was the result of a journey to Italy during which Coecke became acquainted with the architectural theories of the Renaissance; it is addressed primarily to painters, sculptors and stonemasons. The second work was the above-mentioned Dutch translation of Serlio's Book IV, with the title *Generale reglen der architecturen*,[5] although Serlio's name is nowhere mentioned. Both the translation and the illustrations stay very close to the original, and there is as yet no attempt to adapt Serlio to the stylistic preferences of Northern Europe.

In 1537 the versatile German Humanist Heinrich Vogtherr (1490–1556) wrote his *Kunstbüchlein*, lamenting the contemporary decline of art and offering his pattern-book as an encouragement to better things.[6] The book is intended for painters, wood-carvers, goldsmiths and other craftsmen, but its final pages contain architectural details which show that Vogtherr apparently envisaged a Renaissance architecture with elongated forms derived from late Gothic, its scope restricted to ornament and to individual architectural members.

Alongside these derivatives of Serlio there emerged an attempt to adapt Vitruvius to the needs of Northern Europe. Of particular importance in this connection is Walther Rivius, or Rhyff (d. 1548), a physician and mathematician from Nuremberg, who published a Latin edition of Vitruvius in 1543 and a German translation, with commentary, in 1548.[7] Rivius had an extensive knowledge of published Renaissance writings on architectural theory, and a year before his translation of Vitruvius he published a substantial volume of texts and commentaries on the subject, in German, from mainly Italian sources.[8] The work gives the impression that Rivius was anxious to display his wide reading for the benefit of his linguistically less-gifted contemporaries, and it is perhaps not surprising in such an age that he should make only general mention of his sources,[9] without specific references, giving the impression that he himself was the originator of the ideas he expounds.

Rivius concentrates on the subjects of perspective and geometry, taking over to a large extent the text and illustrations of Serlio's Books I and II, which had been published in 1545, but passing over Book IV, which had been available in German translation since 1542.[10] Following Alberti, he also deals with perspective and the theory of proportion in painting and sculpture. Book II is devoted to ballistics and artillery, and is based largely on the work of Tartaglia, 'the father of ballistics.'[11] An excursus headed 'On the laying out, construction and fortification of towns, castles and settlements', a title patently indebted to Dürer, contains a dialogue between an experienced architect (*Architekt*) and young builder (*Baumeister*) in the course of which, distinguishing between his own activity and that of a mere craftsman, the architect tells his young friend: 'There is a great difference between a true architect [*Architekt*] or master builder [*Bawmeister*] and a common builder [*Werckmeister*], or one who merely directs the erection of a building, as I shall now proceed to make somewhat clearer to you...'[12] The work has, however, an ambiguous purpose, addressing itself both to architects, as 'artists' in the broadest sense, and to craftsmen.[13]

Rivius gives detailed attention to the planning of Milan and Turin, and at the end of Book II there is a section on battle orders, such as one finds in the appendices of Italian treatises on fortification. Book III deals with geometric methods of measurement, and the treatise is rounded off with a discussion of weights and measures. The mathematician Rivius's work is thus anything but a systematic theory of architecture; rather, it is a compendium of information on applied geometry and ballistics – as a pattern-book it could have been only of limited value. In any event, it does not appear to have been widely known.

Many treatises on perspective had appeared in Central Europe in the wake of Dürer's *Underweysung der Messung mit dem Zirckel und Richtscheyt* of 1525,[14] among them Hieronymus Rodler's popularisation of that work, published in 1531.[15] The only aspect of interest in these works as far as architectural theory is concerned is their method of constructing space with a central vanishing-point. Rodler's designs vary in style from Late Gothic to a somewhat eccentric version of the Renaissance idiom, and unsurprisingly, rapidly acquired the status of potential models.

After the middle of the century treatises on geometry and perspective, some consisting merely of plates, often assumed peculiar forms, coming to resemble sheets of engraved ornament and exercising some influence on architecture. Notable among these are the 'constructivist' publications[16] of Lorenz Stöer,[17] Johannes Lencker[18] and Wenzel Jamnitzer,[19] in which geometry and perspective become a pretext for strange prismatic forms and unstable constructions. Indeed the importance of engraved ornament, particularly of the grotesque, must not be underrated,[20] particularly since these were soon to merge with the *Säulenbuch* tradition.

Serlio's treatise on the Orders became known in Germany chiefly through the *Säulenbuch* of Hans Blum, born in Lohr on the Main, who spent most of his life in Zurich.[21] Little is known about Blum's life, although we do know that he visited Rome.[22] His work first appeared in Latin (Zürich, 1550), then in Germany (Zürich, 1555),[23] with further editions, including Dutch, English and French translations, being published up to the second half of the seventeenth century.[24] Blum was the originator of the Northern

European treatise on the Orders, which is distinguished by the fact that the Orders are treated in isolation (*Plate 102*), independent of their architectural context.[25] Blum's procedure is identical to that in Serlio's Book IV, but owed its particular success to the inclusion of a table of ratios which made it possible to arrive straightaway at actual dimensions for the parts of any Order, whatever its given height (inclusive of the base).[26] This actually anticipates Vignola's *Regola*, but in Blum the height of the entablature varies, as do other individual measurements from one Order to another, so that as far as practical application went, his work could never emulate Vignola's.[27] Around 1558 Blum published a further treatise called *Architectura antiqua*,[28] also derived from Serlio, which was frequently appended to later editions of his *Säulenbuch*. In many of Blum's plates details from Serlio are printed the wrong way round, which shows again how mechanically he appropriated material from his source.[29] As Erik Forssman has acutely observed, the importance of Blum's work lies in his representation of 'the column independent of any structure, bearing no load and no longer part of any Classical temple, sufficient unto itself and simply a symbol of dignity.'[30]

A substantial set of engravings which adapts the Orders to Northern European taste is the *Architectura der Bauung der Antiquen ...* by the Dutchman Hans Vredeman de Vries (1527–1606),[31] who acknowledges Vitruvius, Serlio and Ducerceau as his masters.[32] It was in Ducerceau that he found the use of national and geographical or climatic criteria, and this led him to call for an architecture which took account of the particular conditions in the Netherlands, '... but in these Netherlands of ours, things are different, that is to say in Cities that do great business, because sites are restricted and expensive, one must build high for men to be able to practise their profession, by seeking maximum light up high.'[33]

It is a matter, Vredeman continues, confident of his principles, of 'knowing how to accommodate the spirit of Architecture to the country's nature and customs.'[34] This justifies the application of Northern European ornamentation to the Classical orders, 'for it is no bad thing to decorate the old with the new, within reason.'[35] Forssman strikingly calls this 'the Northerner's attack on the cold marble shaft, mastering material, with no Classical qualms'.[36]

Vredeman's works are addressed not only to architects and builders but also to cabinet-makers and other craftsmen, since Vredeman regards them as being relevant to the use of wood and other materials. In his *Architectura* he puts forward five different ways of using and decorating each Order, but unlike Blum, he incorporates the Orders in designs for complete buildings. In formal terms these designs are far removed from their Italian models, but take their lead from them where the rules of *decor* are concerned – fortifications must be Tuscan, for instance. But Vredeman also extends the Classical theory of *decor* based on Vitruvius, and links it to early Baroque notions of the brevity and transience of earthly life. In his set of engravings called *Theatrum Vitae Humanae* (1577) he pairs the Ages of Man and the Orders of architecture with one another,[37] with the Orders in reverse sequence: the Composite order corresponds to Childhood (one to sixteen years), the Corinthian to Youth (sixteen to thirty-two), the Ionic to the Mature Woman (thirty-two to forty-eight), the Doric to the Mature Man, and the Tuscan to Old Age. To these are added a sixth Order, the 'Ruin', the Order of Death (*Plate 103*). The Orders are invested with a new symbolism elaborated on the rules of *decor*, transformed into ethical and philosophical terms – a proceeding that reappears in the work of Dietterlin.

Thus Vredeman's approach to architecture subsequently dissolved into a series of unrealistic, originally pragmatic-seeming tableaux, most conspicuously in his last work, the *Perspective*, published shortly before his death.[38] These highly unusual perspective drawings portray a world of loggias, piazzas and vaulted halls, totally foreign to the confined circumstances of his native Netherlands, and make free use of Late Gothic forms.

Hans Vredeman de Vries's ideas and designs were popularised by his son Paul, who published *Architectura, die köstliche unnd weithberumbte Khunst* by both his father and himself.[39] Among these are five plates by Paul Vredeman portraying buildings using the five Orders, to each of which have been added allegorical figures depicting the five Senses: Sight is represented by the Tuscan order, Hearing by the Doric, Smell by the Ionic, Taste by the Corinthian, and Touch by the Composite (*Plate 104*).[40] Hans Vredeman's experiments with garden designs on the basis of the Orders reflect a similar arbitrary approach to this play with allegory.[41]

The outstanding German work on the Orders was the *Architectura* (1593–98)[42] of the Strassburg painter Wendel Dietterlin (1550/1–99).[43] Strictly speaking, this is neither a textbook nor a pattern-book but a series of variations on the theme of the Orders, as seen through the eyes of a painter. The Orders serve as the pretext for a series of fantastic engravings, which are among the outstanding artistic achievements of the late sixteenth century.[44] From the formal point of view Dietterlin stands in the tradition of Serlio and Blum, using a module system similar to Blum's and proceeding, like him, from a given overall height (*Plate 105*). He first determines the height of the base and entablature of each Order (including the capitals in the entablature) leaving the shaft as merely what is left after the other parts of the Order have been removed. Dietterlin has thus no conception of the column as an organic member of the whole.

Dietterlin's work, divided into five books, each devoted to one Order, and comprising 209 full-page engravings, a short preface, an index of technical terms and brief comments on the individual Orders, is essentially a collection of plates. Most of the plates are without text. Exactly as the full title of the work promises, each book, depicting its particular Order, goes on to illustrate the appropriate windows, chimneypieces, doors, portals, fountains, and epitaphs. The preface refers to conceptions of *decorum* and proportion, and warns against 'conspicuous ugliness and deformity' ('*mercklicher ungestalt und deformitet*'),[45] but Dietterlin makes no attempt to curb his wild imagination in his designs.

In his symbolic interpretation of the Orders Dietterlin links up with Vredeman de Vries, but goes further than the Netherlander, in superimposing Christian interpretations onto Classical mythology. He takes for granted the use of Northern forms of ornamentation, claiming that the Tuscan Order, for example, can be traced back to a giant called Toscano, 'who was called a father of the Germans'.[46] Following Serlio, Dietterlin associates the Tuscan order with the rustic world of farm-buildings, but we also find Bacchus and Saint Michael associated with this Order, although the former belongs properly with the Ionic and the latter with the Doric. The Doric order is seen as that of 'bold heroes'; here we find the *strong* Saint Christopher, together with Christ displaying his wounds. But later in the work the distinctions between the Orders become blurred – a 'Doric' illustration (Dietterlin's Plate 187), for example, appears under the Composite order. In fact, only to a very limited extent can one account for the illustrations in terms of the spirit of the Orders.[47] Late Gothic portals (his Plate 197) are subsumed under the Composite order. At the end, as in Vredeman, there is an allegory of Death, which Dietterlin does not, however, designate as an Order. Nor does he adopt Vredeman's analogy of the Ages of Man, with the decay of architecture to the state of 'Ruin', but depicts the victory of death over all things human, with quotations from Michelangelo in his figures (*Plate 106*).[48] The idea of *decorum* stimulates in his mind chains of associations which are sometimes converted into architectural terms, but in which these are also transcended as elements of an all-embracing artistic vision. One senses that the Orders are being given new layers of meaning, which, however, only serve in their turn as pretexts for imaginative flights of draughtsmanship. Dietterlin's *Architectura* raised the *Säulenbuch* to the rank of an autonomous work of art. Architects found it hard to understand and of little practical value – hence its limited success.[49]

The only field in which such a work could have had any influence was in that of ornament; but for this it was too complicated and too expensive. For these reasons Daniel Meyer, a Frankfurt painter – or his publisher – produced a popular version of Dietterlin's work in 1609 (*Plate 107*).[50] After a preamble in the style of the didactic religious literature of the time, and acknowledgement of the renowned Wendel Dietterlin as his model, the author goes on to explain that

> firstly, Dietterlin's work is not of such a kind as to be useful for everybody, especially as the designs ['*inventiones*'] are somewhat complicated, laborious and demanding, which not everyone will find acceptable, and which not everyone can translate into or put to practical use ['*ad usum*']. Secondly, as it stands, it is a large and expensive work, for which reason not everybody has the opportunity to own it. And thirdly, since the world constantly yearns after new fashions, the designs it contains are now regarded as familiar and old-fashioned. The present work, on the contrary, consists to a large extent of such slight, frivolous, yet decorative designs as have been so far possible to assemble and as are attractive to the eye, as well as being largely directed to the needs of the modern world.[51]

This quotation is highly revealing both from the point of view of the work's value as a practical handbook and in the context of the fickle, fashion-centred aesthetics of the time. The Orders are no longer mentioned in the title and make their appearance, in an almost unrecognisable form, only at the end of the work. Meyer's sole purpose was to make Dietterlin's *inventiones* available in inexpensive form, and as he hucksteringly proclaimed, by putting two on each sheet, he was able to offer a bargain of a hundred designs on fifty sheets.[52] But he did not have Dietterlin's exuberant imagination, and his engravings are generally lacking both in artistic invention and in refinement of taste (*Plate 107*). Although the word 'architecture' still figures in the title, the work has virtually no relevance to architecture in the structural sense; architecture, in fact, has become a pretext for the ornamental and the grotesque, and the only place where Meyer's designs could be realised would be the cabinet-maker's workshop. Meyer's *Architectura* marks the culmination of a particular line of development in architectural theory. By issuing his chapter on the Orders in isolation, Serlio laid the foundation for the publication in Northern Europe of *Säulenbücher* which, like that of Blum, presented the Orders detached from any architectural context; for Dietterlin the Orders are invitations to free-ranging interpretations purely imaginary and artistic in inspiration. Meyer then removed the actual Orders altogether, leaving a collection of ornamental designs. The coherence of architectural theory was destroyed, which is why *Säulenbücher* are to some extent only peripheral to our subject.[53] Most of these books are conventional in nature and set out, following Vredeman and Dietterlin, to adapt the Orders to the decorative apparatus proper to the style of the age. Such is the *Architectura Von den funf Seulen*...(1600) by Gabriel Krammer of Zürich (*Plate 108*), a collection of engravings published by Marco Sadeler, with no accompanying text.[54] In his anonymously published *Seulen-Buch Oder Gründlicher Bericht Von den Fünf Ordnungen der Architectur-Kunst* (1672) Georg Caspar Erasmus, a Nuremberg cabinet-maker, swathes the Orders with auricular ornament,[55] appropriately concluding his work with furniture designs.

To a large extent the information contained in architectural books, particularly *Säulenbücher*, in Germany in the second half of the sixteenth century is secondhand. But towards the end of the century people felt a desire to visit Italy and see the Classical sources themselves. In 1598 Heinrich Schickhardt (1558–1634), the Württemberg court architect, made a private journey to northern Italy and kept a diary with sketches made on his travels, largely of Renaissance buildings.[56] In 1599 he began work on the town of Freudenstadt, in the Black Forest, to a plan based on Dürer's treatise on fortification; and in the autumn of that year accompanied Duke Frederick I of Württemberg and his retinue on a longer journey through Italy, which took him as far as Rome. He published the drawings that he made on this journey in 1602,[57] the focus of interest again being the architecture of the Renaissance. As a German architect's view of Italy around 1600, this work deserves to be better known. A further sketchbook of Schickhardt's is devoted entirely to drawings of buildings designed by Palladio and to sketches in the Palladian manner; on it Schickhardt has written: 'This little book should be held in high esteem after my death, and preserved on my account.'[58] Schickhardt's well-stocked library contained almost all the important sixteenth-century treatises on architecture and fortification, as we know from the catalogue of it which has been preserved; from it we also learn that he was a friend of Dietterlin's as well as of the military architect Bonaiuto Lorini, the designer of Palmanova.[59]

Elias Holl (1573–1646), the most important late Renaissance architect in Germany, made a journey in 1600 from his native Augsburg to Venice, but merely notes in his autobiography that he had 'seen in Venice all the fine and wonderful things that were also to be beneficial to me in my future architectural activity.'[60] His unpublished manuscript on geometry and measurement deals only with matters of engineering, and puts forward no aesthetic principles.[61]

15. The German-speaking regions in the seventeenth and eighteenth centuries

We shall not deal here with the countless treatises on the Orders to be found in the German-speaking world in the seventeenth and eighteenth centuries. Many of them forsake architectural theory altogether, and are rather pattern-books for joinery, in which the Orders are purely ornamental. Others attempt rigidly to inculcate Vignola's rules for the Orders, with scarcely any advance on their model.[1]

In this chapter we shall endeavour to restrict discussion to those writings in which a systematic idea of architecture is to be found. The awareness of Italy displayed by Heinrich von Schickhardt and Elias Holl did not find written expresssion until a generation later in the comprehensive oeuvre of Joseph Furttenbach (1591–1667),[2] a merchant and the city architect of Ulm. At the age of sixteen Furttenbach was sent to Italy to be trained, remaining there ten years and pursuing diverse interests. His preoccupation with architecture and stage design was sparked off primarily by a year of study with Giulio Parigi in Florence. Throughout his career, Furttenbach combined his activity as the owner of a trading company with commissions carried out for the city building administration and extensive architectural writings. Even the notes that he made in Italy were published in book form soon after his return to Ulm, in 1627.[3] This account of Italy is unsystematic, but shows a marked interest in contemporary buildings. Thus he describes the palaces of the Strada nuova in Genoa 'in the most well-adorned modern style' ('*zierlichster Architectura alla moderna*') in detail, considering them to be unequalled in Europe.[4] He even illustrates one of these palaces, stating that the disposition of the rooms is governed by ventilation and optical axes ('*Durchsehung aller Zimmer*').[5] The style of illustration and the text suggest that Furttenbach was already using Peter Paul Rubens's *Palazzi di Genova* (1622),[6] although he does not cite it, just as in later works he also fails to give his sources in most cases. In his preface Rubens had told the reader: 'But private architecture, which of course in its totality makes up the body of a city, should not be ignored, especially as the convenience of the buildings nearly always goes hand in hand with their beauty and good form.'[7]

Rubens's credo could be a rubric for Furttenbach's work. He is not a Palladian like Schickhardt, but takes up Italian Renaissance architecture in a both geographically and temporally broad span, attempting to make it a model for Central European requirements.

Furttenbach was exceedingly prolific,[8] although not particularly original, as an author of books on architecture. He neither formulated nor represented a self-contained system of architectural theory; the attitude that comes through in his books is that of a businessman, realistic and practical. The Thirty Years War, during which most of his writings appeared, left little mark on them.[9] His most important works are *Architectura civilis* (1628),[10] *Architectura universalis* (1635),[11] *Architectura recreationis* (1640)[12] and *Architectura privata* (1641).[13] Already in the preface of his *Architectura civilis*,

Furttenbach declares himself a follower of Italian models: 'Because it is indeed known to all the world that the most prized buildings, those richest in art, the most noble and strong, are to be found in Italy rather than anywhere else in the whole of Europe.'[14] In his own designs Furttenbach attempts to reconcile Italian and German customs and building practice.[15]

Functional considerations are uppermost in Furttenbach. He states of his designs for rulers' palaces that their interiors should be 'well laid out and distributed with art, and their rooms adapted to the respective needs of business and relaxation.'[16] Furttenbach proceeds from a functional disposition in plan, whilst keeping the appearance of the building as a whole in view:

> But my intention is to show and demonstrate, on the basis of correct principles, the chief purpose [of building] in accordance with the overall symmetrical arrangement, namely how to dispose the rooms internally within the body of the building (this is the main purpose and by this means one may perceive the correct end result of the operation).'[17]

Furttenbach seems to be reverting here to Pierre Le Muet's *Manière de bien bastir* (1623), although he does not cite this work. His attitude to the authors he does use is summary: he mainly uses them for their exposition of the *principia Architecturae* and their exposition of the Orders, thus avoiding the need to do so in his own words.[18] Occasionally he refers to Vignola's *Regola* – to which he obviously had access in an expanded edition – not however for its authority on the Orders, but so that 'the lover of such ornament may study and learn from it all he wishes.'[19]

Furttenbach's writing is pedantic, vain and self-consciously cryptic. He attempts to display sophistication by using Italian terminology, and he constantly quotes his own example. The buildings he publishes are mostly unidentified, or identified only by allusion. The very first 'princely palace' (*fürstlicher Palast*') that he publishes in the *Architectura civilis* is introduced simply as one 'of the finest princely palaces to be found in Italy at this time':[20] he means the Pitti Palace in Florence.

In his descriptions of façades, Furttenbach frequently uses the terms 'bold' and 'heroic'. One should not however read any aesthetic or symbolic implications into these words, for Furttenbach also speaks of 'heroic galleries' (*heroische Galeeren*'),[21] so that the meaning of these words is reduced to 'large' or 'splendid'.

Furttenbach's approach is by different building types. This is particularly apparent in *Architectura universalis*, in which his discussion includes building types not often discussed in his time, such as schools, hostels, barracks, prisons and hospitals.[22] His projects are extremely functional in conception. Thus he evolves a three-storey 'burgher's house' (*bürgerliches Wohnhaus*') in which the object of every room is precisely defined (*Plate 109*). Furttenbach even goes so far as to include the furnishings of several rooms in his plans.[23]

In Furttenbach's *Architectura recreationis* projects for houses and *Schlösser* are presented, in which particularly close attention is devoted to garden layouts. He gives examples of how outmoded *Schlösser* can be adapted to contemporary taste and new requirements, how 'to set about restoring a house with well-appointed rooms at the least expense'.[24]

Furttenbach's mode of thought is most apparent in *Architectura privata*, concerning his own house in Ulm. He gives a precise description of the site, the garden, the incidence of light into the rooms, and exact reckonings of building costs by areas; he establishes the relation between the size of rooms and the cost of heating them. Alongside these functional considerations, we find somewhat unrelated descriptions of ornamental detail. The three lower storeys of the house consist of business and living rooms, while the upper storey contains rooms devoted to his collections, in which the well-educated Furttenbach displays himself as a 'Humanist': armoury, cabinet of curiosities, and library. The description goes into great detail.[25] It is part of his programme to hang in the great entrance hall (*Laube*) plans of Ancient and Modern Rome by Pirro Ligorio, Antonio Tempesta and Mathaeus Greuter. The cabinet of curiosities is a burgherly version of princely collections of art and rarities. In the centre of the room, however, is a large model devoted to Furttenbach's architectural interest. The garden, including its plants and a grotto of shells, is described and illustrated. The *Architectura privata* is a reflection of the burgher's way of life, setting out to be taken as a model in its solid and calculating love of comfort.

Reckoning with the *Architectura navalis* (1629) and *Architectura martialis* (1630) too, Furttenbach covered all fields of architecture in his writings. In collaboration with his son, known as Joseph Furttenbach the Younger, who died prematurely in 1655, he published a series of shorter works between 1649 and 1651, in which designs and sketches of father and son are mixed.[26] There are no writings dating from his last years.

In the final analysis, Furttenbach's books are in the Serlio tradition, inasmuch as they attempt to provide architects and their clients with models or guides for all kinds of building. This function of architectural publications is predominant in the German-speaking world throughout the seventeenth century, which period, strictly speaking, sees no new ideas.

Furttenbach had a series of direct or indirect successors.[27] His pragmatically orientated approach could serve as a direct practical guidance in building, as is seen for example in the *Bürgerliche Wohnungs Bau-Kunst* (1673) by Daniel Hartmann,[28] a native of Basle, who addresses stonemasons, bricklayers, carpenters, and particularly aspiring master-builders. Hartmann here gives five proposals for a building on a corner site, in what he calls the 'German manner' ('*Teutsche Manier*'), in which his plans vary with the differing fenestration according to the compass direction that the building faces. After some basic instructions on geometry, he presents his project in all constructional details, whilst his alternative proposals are limited to plans. Hartmann's approach is reminiscent of Pierre Le Muet's (1623), circumscribed though it is by a Germanic ingenuousness. In order to claim a certain multiplicity of purpose for his designs, he states in the last sentence of his text that anyone is at liberty 'to change the existing plans either for himself or according to the client's wishes, and to make mere grocers' shops, farmhouses, barns or stables out of them.'[29]

Johann Wilhelm's *Architectura civilis* (1649)[30] is exclusively concerned with timber construction, particularly roof trusses. Wilhelm regards his successful book, with its very practical instructions, which ran to several editions, as the transmission of building expertise that had been interrupted by the Thirty Years War. In his dedication to the city fathers of Frankfurt,[31] Wilhelm offers a strange mingling of his own experience and of what he has gathered from the writings of others. It is odd, to say the least, that his very title-page should so strongly stress the idea of fame ('Through building one's name is made immortal...') ('*Durch Bauen wird der Nam unsterblich aufferbauet...*'), considering it was only a year since the end of the great war.[32] His confused view of history is apparent in such statements as that 'in this last [Holy] Roman monarchy, Greek architecture too reaches the summit of its dignity.'[33] Wilhelm's work is one of the first books to deal with half-timbering. A later publisher exploited the success of *Architectura civilis* to publish a second part, which however is not by Wilhelm.[34]

The painter and art historian Joachim von Sandrart (1608–88) pursues a completely different purpose in the second part of his *Teutsche Academie*[35] and other writings. This is a kind of encyclopedic history of art, of a prescriptive nature. Both text and illustrations are to a large extent pure compilation, with no sources being given.[36] Sandrart's eighteenth-century editor, Johann Jacob Volkmann, aptly describes his purpose: 'Sandrart's intention was to present the best models of the old and new architecture in plate form, and to give some information about them, regarding the theory or the rules of art as a secondary purpose.'[37] Sandrart opened up Classical architecture for Germany. Each historical example is intended as a model, and to make an impact *per se*. Sandrart makes this clear in the first plate of the second part of the *Teutsche Academie*, depicting the suckling Roman she-wolf on a pedestal bearing the title of his book.

Sandrart's plates give a broad overview of Roman Antiquity, the Italian Renaissance and Roman Baroque, with the beginnings of which he had come into contact during his prolonged stay in Rome. The Middle Ages are totally omitted. He attaches particular importance both in text and illustrations to Palladio as a model.

The *Werk von der Architektur* by Prince Karl Eusebius von Liechtenstein (1611–84)[38] was not intended for publication. The prince, a committed collector, builder and architect, left these notes as guidelines for his heirs. What is illuminating in this piece of writing by a cultured dilettante is above all its way of looking at architecture from the standpoint of an aristocratic patron. In his eyes giving expression to the renown of the builder justifies any expense. Architecture is seen by him only in the light of the needs of a princely household. He covers churches, country *Schlösser* and town palaces, going into detail on their furnishings, in which art collections play a prominent part. Architecture without use of the Orders, which he sets out in a doctrinaire revision of Vignola, is valueless as far as he is concerned. Purely utilitarian architecture 'without ornament and with plain walls' ('*ohne Zierdt mit glatter Mauer*') is for him 'to be totally shunned and despised and is unworthy of attention or remembrance, simply common work like the common houses of which the whole world is full.'[39] Reading such a text, no doubt written in Eusebius's later years, one well understands how welcome the *Fürstlicher Baumeister* (1711 and 1716) by Paul Decker must have been.

In Duke Henry of Saxony's *Fürstliche Bau-Lust* (1698) festive and ephemeral architecture of all kinds is reproduced after his own designs, the use of personal emblems interesting him especially.[40]

No really new position emerges either from the writings of Georg Andreas Böckler (1617/20–87)[41] who worked mainly in Frankfurt and Ansbach and was in contact with Furttenbach, and whose treatises are based on the publications of Blum, Abraham Bosse, Le Muet and Fréart de Chambray. His *Compendium architecturae civilis* (1648),[42] which appeared in the year of the Treaty of Westphalia, was intended to contribute to the rebuilding of Germany after the devastation of the Thirty Years War. His *Architectura civilis nova antiqua* (1663)[43] presents a comparative treatment of the Orders. His posthumous translation of the first two books of Palladio's *Quattro libri* (1698)[44] sets out, with a comprehensive commentary, to adapt Palladio to the requirements of the German landed gentry. In two further books Böckler deals with military architecture.[45]

His best known work is the *Architectura curiosa nova* (1664),[46] in five parts, which is mainly a collection of plates. The first three parts contain designs for fountains, the last two for palaces and *Lusthäuser*. The book was a speculative venture on the part of the publisher, Paulus Fürst. The illustrations are intended to provide those intending to build – assumed to be exclusively from the nobility – with a European range of models. Böckler provides scantly and sometimes erroneous texts, and writes of 'many ornamental and artistic fountains to be found here and there in Italy, France, England and Germany at the present time, surveyed and drawn with great taste, and with a short description of each.'[47]

A few lines further on however, he gives credit to 'various authors'. Indeed, this work is a hastily produced compilation of pirated engravings after Giovanni Maggi and others, mostly without acknowledgement.[48] In the preface to part four, reference is made to existing literature on theoretical questions, without any original point of view being discernible: 'What architecture or the art of building is, and what it consists of, is not in fact our concern here, especially as this question is already dealt with in depth and in detail in the old and also the new writers and architects who are highly experienced in the matter.'[49]

Although the plates are sometimes indifferently executed (and inverted in relation to the originals), and the text contains serious errors – fountains by Bernini are attributed to Giovanni Maggi, the name of the builder of Aschaffenburg Castle, Georg Ridinger, is garbled as Friedtinger, etc. – the publisher's speculation was successful. The work appeared in a Latin translation and in a second edition.[50] Although works such as this had international pretensions, they are manifestly provincial in content and commentary.

Alongside them, however, there are works in which an attempt is made to treat architecture from a Christian point of view, in the spirit of the Counter-Reformation. This is true for example of the Dutch poet, painter and architect Salomon de Bray (1597–1664), who prefaces the *Architectura moderna ofte Bouwinge van onsen tyt* published by Cornelis Danckert with an attack on Vredeman de Vries,[51] in which he traces architecture back beyond Vitruvius to the Old Testament, Noah's Ark and Solomon's Temple. The Corinthian Order, described by Vitruvius (IV. 1) as having been discovered by Callimachus, is here said to originate from Solomon's Temple and the architect Hiram of Tyre. Thus architecture becomes the manifestation of Christian religious certainty. Salomon de Bray here takes up an idea of Philibert Delorme, which the latter intended to develop in the planned second part of his *Architecture*,[52] and at the same time he makes use of the reconstruction of Solomon's Temple in the commentary on Ezekiel by the Spanish Jesuit Juan Bautista Villalpando and Jerónimo Prado (1596–1604),[53] in which the Corinthian Order is demonstrated to have been the Salomonic (see Chapter 18). For De Bray the Orders are codified variants of rules developed by different nations at different times.

A synthesis of such 'Christian' architectural theory with the 'heathen' ideas based on Vitruvius was attempted by the mathematicians Nicolaus Goldmann (1611–65)[54] and his editor and commentator Leonhard Christoph Sturm (1669–1719).[55] The former, a native of Breslau who later taught in Leyden, published several works on geometry.[56] His main work on architectural theory, *Die Vollständige Anweisung zu der Civil-Bau-Kunst*, was completed just before his death[57] and published posthumously, edited from his papers by Leonhard Christoph Sturm while he was professor of mathematics in Wolfenbüttel (1694–1702).[58] The long Baroque title announces not only the treatment of the Orders according to the 'most excellent rules' ('*auserlesensten Reguln*') of Vitruvius, Vignola, Scamozzi, Palladio, and Villalpando, but also 'a detailed presentation [*weitläufftige Vorstellung*] of Solomon's Temple'.

Sturm's dedication stresses the 'rational way of building' which 'cannot deny its origins in the Temple of Solomon'.[59] Vitruvius is given a subordinate position: 'The latter [Vitruvius] took his architecture from the Temple of Solomon, as the proper original source, uniting with it at the same time the streams of ancient Roman wisdom.'[60] Sturm, who had already presented a reconstruction of Solomon's Temple in 1694,[61] reinforces the important role that Salomonic architecture already had for Goldmann himself in an extensive discussion of Villalpando's reconstruction of it.

As mathematicians, Goldmann and Sturm are at pains to be accurate and honest. Hence a bibliography of the texts used by Goldmann is placed at the beginning of the work. There is a table of contents, and short synoptic definitions of terms are given in five languages.

The authors recognise in the Orders architectural principles of organisation, not merely forms for applied decoration: 'Many splendid buildings are erected in which almost no columns or arches are used.'[62] The mode of thought is analytical, the procedure eclectic, the proposed goal being: 'to combine at once the lightness of Vignola, the show of Palladio, and the accurate measurements and fine distribution of Scamozzi.'[63] Proportion – termed '*symmetry*' – is regarded as the most important element of the art of building, but at the same time surrounded by an aura of mystery: 'For the great architects seems to have been at pains to preserve silence on this matter.'[64] Sturm describes as his own work all the plates to Goldmann's text, and the 'improvement' of Villalpando's reconstruction of Solomon's Temple.

The Vitruvian concepts of *firmitas, utilitas* and *venustas* are retained in the terms '*starck*', '*bequem*' and '*zierlich*', but are rooted in the Bible. '*Werckmeister*' (builders) are relegated to their proper place as executants, since left to themselves, they 'spoil architectural effect with far too much unnecessary decoration.'[65] The art of building is elevated to the rank of science – in line with Scamozzi, indeed, to the science of mathematics – yet the medieval scholastic tradition is still apparent when the practice of it is reduced to an *ars mechanica*.[66]

The authors set out their findings as points to be followed, but are modest enough to request the reader 'not to take our writings as Holy Writ'.[67] As mathematicians they give tectonics (*firmitas*) priority over functional and aesthetic criteria.[68] Aesthetic effect is for them the result mainly of the 'play of proportions' ('*Spiel der Proportionen*') – Sturm has some knowledge of the Perrault-Blondel debate – which 'can at once bowl one over and give one pause for thought.'[69] The direct impact of mathematical norms on the beholder is in no doubt. Art must follow Nature, but is able to bring a 'better order' ('*bessere Ordnung*') into its 'carelessnesses' ('*Unachtsamkeiten*'), 'for regardless of the fact that a garden or grove which has run wild looks pleasant, it is nevertheless certain that when the trees are regularly spaced by means of a thread and are of the same height, then Nature is made more attractive still.'[70]

Here speaks French rationalism. The theory of musical harmony, held from the Renaissance up to Ouvrard and Blondel, is repeated, but enhanced by the proportions of Solomon's Temple. The proportions given by Vitruvius are expressly described as being derived from Solomon's Temple.[71]

The 'sacred art of building' ('heilige Baukunst') is revealed by God in Solomon's Temple; the 'heathen' ('heidnische') art of the theory of the Orders is subordinated to it.[72] These ideas are based totally on Villalpando. The Orders are ranked in a strict hierarchy, divided into 'inferior' ('niedrige') and 'exalted' ('erhabene'): the 'inferior' and the 'masculine' ('männliche') are the Tuscan and the Doric, the 'exalted' and the 'feminine' ('weibliche') are the Ionic, Composite ('Roman') and Corinthian. The last Order occupies the highest position because it is that of Solomon's Temple. For the proportions of the Orders, Vignola's module system is broadly adopted, simplified in order to avoid 'really awkward numbers' ('gar unbequem Zahlen').[73]

The third and fourth books are devoted to the disposition of plans and a typology of buildings. The examples given show clearly what a dominant role was played by the classicising views of Vincenzo Scamozzi.

An appended 'Compendium of Goldmann's *Civil-Bau-Kunst*' and an *Architectura Parallela* offer tabulated comparisons of the ratios between the various parts of the Orders as given by Serlio, Palladio, Vignola, Scamozzi and Goldmann.

A section headed *Erste Ausübung der Vortrefflichen und Vollständigen Anweisung* ('The first practical use of the excellent and complete instructions'), which was written for the second edition of the *Civil-Bau-Kunst*, is likely to be mainly or wholly from the pen of Leonhard Christoph Sturm. In the preface he rebuts the accusation that the fourth book dealt 'mostly with old-fashioned designs... that are out of place in building as it is practised today'.[74] Sturm concedes that the 'practical requirements [*Commodität*] of German buildings', because of climatic and social conditions, are different from those of Italian buildings, but insists that it is only in Italy that one can learn 'what makes a building beautiful'.[75] In the course of the *Erste Ausübung*, however, he meets the wish for examples adapted to contemporary taste.

The core of the *Erste Ausübung* consists in an attempt to open up the possibility of a new, sixth, and indeed 'German' order[76] (*Plate 110*). Sturm rejects earlier French attempts under Louis XIV to invent a new Order as 'futile' ('vergeblich'), since they had all made the mistake of aiming to surpass the Corinthian-Salomonic order. He requires an Order that can be incorporated in proportion and meaning into the existing system, and that corresponds to the German national character. He places this Order between the Ionic and the Composite (Roman), so as to form three coupled groups of Orders, in which the heights of the columns are each the same multiple of the module (Tuscan and Doric × 16, Ionic and German × 18, Composite and Corinthian × 20). He believes that with this system he has at the same time demonstrated the German Order to be the ultimate possible one.[77] In fact his 'German' Order is merely a fashionable blend of Ionic and Doric elements.

A frontispiece opposite the title-page of the *Erste Ausübung* (*Plate 111*) illustrates the use of Sturm's German Order. In order to be sure that his intentions are understood, he feels obliged to give an 'explanation of the engraved title-plate' (*'Erklärung des Kupfer-Tituls'*) on its verso.

The significance of Goldmann and Sturm in the German-speaking world is similar to that of Scamozzi in the Italian. Theirs is a comprehensive, mathematically-based theory, which, however, derives its ultimate sanction from the Bible. Contradictions were inevitable, given the areas of conflict between the two authors, between the Enlightenment and religiosity, between the Baroque and Classical norms. In numerous publications on different kinds of building and constructional problem, Sturm recycled for the market the conclusions of Goldmann's *Civil-Bau-Kunst*.[78] A missionary fervour seems to have been behind the repeated compilation of tables and concordances, such as the *Vademecum Architectonicum* (1700).[79] In 1714 Sturm published a text on palace-building[80] in which he prescribed the norms for the German, as opposed to the French apartment. He attacked the German High Baroque as just exemplified by Paul Decker. In two further works Sturm attempted to work out criteria for the building of a specifically Protestant type of church.[81]

Sturm's works published at the beginning of the eighteenth century represent stylistic standpoints of the previous century. The French-oriented *Theatrum architecturae civilis* by the Bayreuth court architect, Carl Philipp Dieussart,[82] which went through several editions, and contains sections on building materials, a comparative treatment of the Orders, and prescriptions for particular architectural members, was similarly backward-looking.

The *Novum Architecturae Speculum* by Nikolaus Person (d. 1710), Electoral Engineer, engraver, and publisher in Mainz, belongs to the genre of the all-purpose architectural pattern-book.[83] The compilation, quite unsystematically put together, and devoid of any coherent text, offers views of late seventeenth-century buildings in Franconia and the Rhineland, which at least have considerable value as visual evidence, together with architectural details for the most part copied from d'Aviler's *Cours d'architecture* (1691) and other sources.[84] In the tradition of Furttenbach, Person supplies models for every possible type of building. A plate showing 'all kinds of country church and chapel' (*'allerhand Landtkirchen und Capellen'*) is immediately followed by another of a powder magazine.[85] There are special sections on machines and garden designs, with their own title-pages. The so-called *'Auer Lehrgänge'* of the Baroque architects of the Vorarlberg (compiled c. 1710) had a comparable function. These are a compilation of textual excerpts, and plans and elevations serving as typological models and teaching materials, derived from d'Aviler, Pozzo, and others.[86] Such manuscript volumes for family and guild use were probably not intended for publication, but show clearly how literature on architecture was used in a particular region. The *Auer Lehrgänge* originated in the circle of the architect Caspar Moosbrugger, and offer a unique insight into the working processes of a great team of architecture entrepreneurs of the South German Baroque.

Among German eighteenth-century treatises on the Orders should be mentioned the remarkable attempt of the Augsburg painter Johann Georg Bergmüller in his *Nachbericht zu der Erklärung des geometrischen Maasstabes der Säulenordnungen* (1752) to derive all the Orders, including their proportions, from the Doric.[87]

The most significant architectural publication of the German Baroque does not present itself in the form of a 'theory', but is one of the most lavish volumes of plates produced in the early eighteenth century. The *Fürstlicher Baumeister*[88] of Paul Decker (1677–1713) is only a fragment of a broadly conceived typology of architecture, which was intended to consist exclusively of ideal designs studied from every angle.

An undated *Ausführliche Anleitung zur Civilbaukunst*[89] ('Thorough introduction to domestic architecture') is based mainly on d'Aviler and Sturm and is indebted stylistically to Decker's teacher Andreas Schlüter; it must predate the *Fürstlicher Baumeister*. The *Ausführliche Anleitung* is purely a book of engravings, with an occasional commentary on the plates. It is unsystematic and clearly unfinished, and seems to have been interrupted by work on the *Fürstlicher Baumeister*, and not to have been published until after Decker's untimely death, from his papers. The first two sections are concerned mainly with architectural members and ornaments and the different parts of a building, while the third contains the beginnings of a systematic treatment of building types (*Plate 112*). Decker shows a burgher's house and a most opulent merchant's house, before quickly passing on to the palaces of noblemen and their country seats. His interest is mainly in buildings for show for the aristocracy, and this is even more apparent in the *Fürstlicher Baumeister*.[90]

The frontispiece of the *Fürstlicher Baumeister* (*Plate 113*), which is copiously explained by Decker, shows the arts conceived as a unity, but at the same time the subordination of painting and sculpture to architecture. The self-esteem of Baroque architecture is seldom so evident as in Decker's 'Explanation of the frontispiece', so I quote it here in full:

> So that the Reader who is so inclined may understand a little of my ideas from the engraved frontispiece at the beginning of this Work, this is the first thing his eye lights on: the Deity, with a flame on her head, here lowers herself on clouds, in a glory; in one hand she holds a sceptre as Ruler of the World, and a panel on which there is a drawing of a building: with the other she is handing a pair of compasses and a set-square to the figure of Architecture standing by her side, showing that she is implanting in her the appropriate understanding and wisdom for the fitting and comely execution of all sorts of tasks. Architecture is accompanied by a Genius carrying a level and holding another panel with the plan of a building; the Genius is looking at a quadrant lying at his feet. Painting, as Architecture's true helpmate, kneels beside Architecture, and round her lie her usual and familiar instruments. The tripod on which the said Arts make the Deity a fragrant offering is intended to show that these noble Arts are dedicated to God and cause all kinds of structures to be erected in His honour, such as temples, schools, altars, etc. Beside the tripod is an old man with a mirror in his hand, who represents the Wise Guidance through which one attains to the Arts. Beside him Sculpture hastens to the scene, holding in her arms a model of a statue, as a sign that buildings are best adorned and enlivened by statues. Next to the Deity are two angels in a glory, carrying a Crown of Stars to show that not only did truly great Virtuosi achieve esteem and honour in their lifetime, but that their fame remained immortal after their death. Above them is another angel in a glory carrying in one hand a cornucopia with various fruits, and in the other a golden chain with valuable medals hung on it, meaning that truly great Virtuosi, by their skill, win the grace of great lords, and often acquire riches and satisfaction for themselves. In the distance on one side is depicted a pantheon, and on the other a pleasance.'[91]

Strictly speaking Decker's work is not architectural theory, since it does not contain a system expressed in words. It must be reiterated, however, that one can barely speak of the verbal expression of Baroque architectural theory. Decker's plates with their descriptions speak for themselves, like those of Borromini; Guarini's *Architettura civile* had not yet appeared.

Without actually referring to contemporary French theory in so many words in his preface, and without naming names, Decker makes it clear that he is conversant with it. French Baroque classicism was hardly compatible with his own Roman Baroque inclinations. Nevertheless he tries, in the design for a palace that takes up the whole of the first part of the *Fürstlicher Baumeister*, to express the 'high character' of the person for whom it was to be built, and the 'magnificence' of the State, and to show the 'rules of symmetry' ('*Reglen der Symmetrie*').[92] Decker here uses concepts central to French architectural debate.

In the body of the book Decker presents a palace of medium size, from overall design down to the furnishing of individual rooms; for 'this is the type that is the most common and most frequently met with'. He announces a similar presentation of a royal palace as the second part of the work. The fact that a general typology of architecture was in his mind becomes apparent when he announces 'pleasances, gardens, orangeries, grottoes and grotto-buildings' in a third part, in a fourth 'designs for churches and chapels', and in a fifth 'town-halls, schools, hospitals, stock-exchanges, arsenals', etc.[93] Since Decker intended to have highly detailed illustrations of outstanding graphic quality, it was inconceivable from the outset that the work would ever be finished. The first part of the *Fürstlicher Baumeister* alone consists of fifty-nine plates, all based on Decker's drawings. What was new in Decker's approach was his attempt to present his architectural ideas in their totality, from structural design, through the programmatic decoration of the interiors, down to the furniture. Decker is the Baroque architect who, in the spirit of his frontispiece, is master of all forms of artistic activity. Accordingly he changes the scale of his presentation, so that the first part of the *Fürstlicher Baumeister* could have been taken almost as a set of designs for a particular building. The totality of his architectural vision accurately reflects the needs of his time. Schloss Pommersfelden, begun in the same year as the publication of the *Fürstlicher Baumeister*, shows how accurately Decker foresaw the trends in German princes' zeal for building. In the painted domes of his ceiling designs he was already making use of Andrea Pozzo's treatise on perspective.[94] In 1713 an appendix to the first part of the *Fürstlicher Baumeister* appeared, complementing the palace designs with those for parks, triumphal arches, towers, columns and garden buildings. Designs for grottoes and wells are in keeping with ideas that were taking form at the same time in Kassel-Wilhelmshöhe; in these areas Decker's designs are strikingly Borrominesque.

The second part of the *Fürstlicher Baumeister* (1716), which appeared three years after Decker's death in 1713, is incomplete in every respect. The publisher refers the reader to the works of Leonhard Christoph Sturm, although the latter represented the previous century. The design of the 'Royal Palace' (*Plate 114*) is not here worked out in detail as was the palace of the first part; it might be classified as something between the palace of Schönbrunn and the Würzburg Residenz, taken to the extreme. The large folio format of the volume accommodates a folding plan, which opens out to the astonishing width of over two metres. With elaborate allegorical fountain designs,

Decker attempts to put Bernini's Fountain of the Four Rivers in the Piazza Navona in the shade.

Decker's beautifully printed work is a highly typical document of the boundless zeal for building of Baroque princes in Germany. As one leafs through the plates, the effect is a kind of architectural intoxication, in which the author overestimates his powers, just as his potential patrons are invited to exceed their own. The occasional impact of publications such as those of Sturm and Decker on built architecture can be demonstrated particularly clearly in the case of their contribution to the staircases of Balthasar Neumann.[95]

The tradition of Andrea Pozzo, in which interest inclines more to the depiction of architecture than to architecture itself, is reflected in Germany not only in translations of his work, but in further developments that border on the absurd. In the extensive oeuvre of the Nuremberg mathematician Johann Jacob Schübler (d. 1741), his two-part *Perspectiva, pes picturae* (1719/20),[96] which actually claims to be a continuation of Pozzo's work,[97] is typical of this tendency. In his over-intellectualised conception of art Schübler goes even beyond Goldmann and Sturm, who were also mathematicians, in declaring 'that everything in painting and drawing that conflicts with the principles of mathematics, and that cannot be demonstrated by them, has every reason to be rejected.'[98] The role of perspective, which is of course what is intended here, is given almost absolute priority when he states that 'without perspective not the slightest visible object can be represented without error'.[99]

For Schübler, knowledge of perspective (for the purposes of architectural drawing) is inextricably bound up with architecture. Via the requirement of correctness in perspective he comes to that of correctness in architecture. He comes to the conclusion that: 'with all its accuracy, perspective can never conceal the errors of Antique and Modern architecture; rather, it makes them apparent to the eyes of all men. Hence in such a situation it is above all the symmetry in every part of the invention that should be well observed…'[100] Schübler even manages to establish his concept of the role of perspective by means of the design of Solomon's Temple – with reference to Villalpando. Schübler provides elaborately contrived, allegorical frontispieces with lengthy explanations, even in the middle of the work, in order that the reader 'may rest a little and take pleasure in other thoughts'.[101] The first part of the *Perspectiva* is basically structured like Pozzo's treatise, but uses 'newly invented' (*'neu invenirte'*) architectural examples as illustrations. The second part is devoted to the correct depiction of architecture with regard to perspective, including that of the shadows that are cast. With visible enjoyment of his own ability, Schübler now presents ever-more complicated situations; almost by the by, he designates 'the noble art of painting as a daughter of Reason'.[102] At the end of the work there are two illustrations in 'longimetric' perspective (*Plate 115*), from unlikely viewpoints looking down through a building from a vertiginous height.[103] Schübler comments: 'The longer one continues to look at this, the more satisfaction sweeps over the emotions.'[104] His illustrations serve him as a proof that 'the science of optics is to be counted among the most refined of art's devices for human entertainment.'[105]

The course embarked on by Pozzo and continued by Ferdinando Galli Bibiena ends up at the absurd stage, in Schübler, of looking at architecture only from the point of view of the depiction of perspective, in other words, only of effect. Schübler's

Perspectiva is one of the most rare and sophisticated of eighteenth-century works on the fringes of architectural theory.

The best-known architectural treatise of the Baroque period, the *Entwurff einer Historischen Architectur*[106] by Johann Bernhard Fischer von Erlach (1656–1723), is only a fragment.[107] Fischer started this work in 1705 'as an innocent pastime',[108] and gave the Emperor Charles VI the text in manuscript with proofs of the engravings in 1712; the work eventually appeared in print in 1721.[109] Fischer's work is as lavish as Decker's, but pursues completely different objectives. It too is primarily a collection of plates with brief expositions of their subject-matter. The *Entwurff einer Historischen Architectur* has been called the 'first comparative history of world architecture'.[110] An attempt at something like this had already been made by Vincenzo Scamozzi (1615), but his horizons were restricted to the West. The problem of comparing architecture of different cultures and different stages of development had been considered by François Blondel the Elder (1675), but in the firm conviction that architecture had unalterable norms.

Fischer von Erlach takes his comparative history of architecture, which includes the Near and Far East, out of the context of pure architectural theory, in which the tentative beginnings of Scamozzi and Blondel had remained. He does not address himself primarily to scholars, however, but is concerned to 'delight the eye of the connoisseur and to inspire artists to invention'.[111] The historical examples are intended to 'serve to promote both knowledge and the arts'.[112] Fischer accepts in architecture 'different national tastes' ('*Geschmack der Landes-Arten*'), and 'custom not bound by rules, wherein a nation's judgement cannot be contested any more than its taste'.[113] Fischer von Erlach has in mind of course the multi-nation state of the Danube monarchy; and as Imperial Court Architect, one of his chief concerns was to create an 'Empire style' (*Reichsstil*). Nevertheless, he holds fast to 'certain general principles... which cannot be forgotten without manifest harm. Symmetry is one of these...'[114] Fischer accepts a pluralism of historical styles. He is too much a figure of the Enlightenment, however, and too much a normative thinker, to subscribe to wholesale relativism in a historicist sense.

Fischer sees his work as an 'outline' ('*Entwurff*'), as a collection of examples of 'world architecture', not as a coherent history of development. Just how strong is his historical awareness is apparent in his method of historical recontruction, where 'truth' is his paramount concern. He uses findings from excavations, Antique texts, commemorative coins, and accounts of journeys, to serve his purpose alike, sometimes in startling anticipation of modern archaeology. Even in the dress of the figures represented in his engravings, Fischer strives for historical accuracy.

The *Entwurff* is divided into five books. The first deals with Solomon's Temple, the Seven Wonders of the world, and Jewish, Assyrian, Egyptian and Greek architecture; the second is concerned with Roman architecture; the third with Islamic and Far Eastern; the fourth with his own designs; and the fifth with Antique vases. The frontispiece shows an exedra in a mixture of Antique and Baroque styles, with a pedestal bearing the inscription '*Essai d'une Architecture Historique*', over which flies Fame borne by Time.

On a map of the Eastern Mediterranean region, reconstructions relating to this area are depicted in little. Fischer von Erlach begins his 'General idea of types of buildings of different times and nations' ('*generale Idee von den Bau-Arten unterschiedener*

Zeiten und Völker') with Solomon's Temple, whose reconstruction he takes from Villalpando, in a slightly altered perspective. In the tradition of Villalpando–de Bray–Goldmann–Sturm the Corinthian Order is said to have been first derived from Solomon's Temple through the Phoenicians and Greeks.[115]

Fischer gives a fairly accurate account of the sources he has used, especially at the beginning of his work, at the end of each explanation of a plate.[116] He often digresses considerably from his models, however. For example, he is the first to reconstruct the Tower of Babel correctly as ziggurat. He has an astonishing intuitive sense of history. Only when the sources let him down completely, as for example in the case of the Temple of Nineveh or the Golden House of Nero (the *Domus Aurea*) does he take over the reconstructions of others unaltered or allow his own imagination free rein (*Plate 116*). Thus his reconstruction of the *Domus Aurea* looks more like a variation on the Escorial than a Roman palace.

His reconstructions are extremely imaginative. This may be seen, for example, by comparing his 'Seven Wonders of the World' with his source, Martin van Heemskerck's *Septem Orbis Miracula*, which were engraved by Philipp Galle in 1572.[117] Even architectural visions such as Deinocrates' project of a city on Mount Athos in the form of a male statue (Vitruvius II, preface) are represented by Fischer pictorially. As to his reproductions of Classical Greek buildings, it should be remembered that the major publications of Greek remains only began to appear a generation later, so that he was dependent on scantily illustrated travel accounts such as those of Spon and Wheler (1679). Just how skilfully he turned to good account the information provided by travellers is shown in his reconstruction of the Palace of Diocletian in Spalato/Split, which goes far beyond the Spon-Wheler sketch, to approach Robert Adam's reconstruction published in 1764. His plate of the ruins of Palmyra is based on a drawing of 1711 by the Swede Cornelius Loos.[118] On the other hand, missing from Fischer are major monuments of Roman architecture (the Pantheon, etc.), a gap that he justifies by pointing out the availability of good existing books by other authors which 'were prepared with equal diligence' (*'mit gleichem Fleiss gemacht worden'*).[119] At the beginning of the examples of Islamic architecture Fischer shows a bath and a mosque from Hungary, which was reoccupied by the Habsburgs only at the end of the seventeenth century, and granted an independent administration in 1711; this shows a modern tolerance towards the heterogeneous building traditions of the multinational state.

Fischer von Erlach was the first to represent Chinese architecture in a European architectural survey (*Plate 117*). The source he used was the account by the Dutchman Jan Nieuhof of the Dutch East India Company's embassy to Peking in 1656, which was published in 1670.[120]

The representation of his own buildings in the fourth book was part of a firm tradition in architectural writings since the Renaissance, in which writers elevated their designs into models. But they too look like syntheses of 'historical architecture'. Fischer's concern was in fact to create a Holy Roman Imperial architecture for the Habsburgs, in which history gave his own designs legitimation and continuity. Fischer's view is for the first time world-ranging. The comparable, but national pretensions of French architecture under Louis XIV appear diminished by comparison with the scope of Fischer's aspirations.[121] And Fischer makes no reference to French architectural examples.

Although Fischer's *Entwurff einer Historischen Architectur* is not a system of architectural theory in the strict sence, it is a bold attempt to make the vision of a world system of architecture the basis of an individual conception of architecture. His Karlskirche in Vienna exemplifies how such an approach can work in practice.

In the wake of Decker's and Fischer von Erlach's works came individual publications on palaces and gardens, which thus likewise became potential models – for example the succession of sets of engravings by Salomon Kleiner (1703–61) of the Schönborn family's *Schlösser*, Gaibach, Seehof (outside Bamberg), Favorite (outside Mainz), Göllersdorf and Pommersfelden.[122] These pure collections of views are an indirect contribution to architectural theory, in that they give some idea of how buildings appeared to their contemporaries. The same might be said of the *Morceaux de caprices, à divers usages* by François Cuvilliés (1695–1768)[123] (who despite his Flemish origin and French training must be counted as belonging to the Bavarian Rococo), which is otherwise a pure pattern-book of *boiseries*, furniture, wrought-ironwork, candelabra, chimneypieces, etc.; although his son, incorporating these into the *Architecture Bavaroise*, which includes real and ideal designs for buildings by his father, was to broaden its scope.

Such writers as Decker and Fischer addressed themselves to court circles. Alongside their works, however, appeared others on 'citizens' building', of which those by Johann Friedrich Penther and Lorenz Johann Daniel Suckow are noteworthy. The *Bürgerliche Baukunst* by Johann Friedrich Penther, a professor and senior building official from Göttingen, is despite its length only a fragment of a larger project.[124] Penther is a very conscientious but somewhat pedantic author; his German thoroughness goes with a certain narrowness of intellect. His theoretical and aesthetic ideas have been taken from the writings of others. The first volume of his work consists exclusively of a lexicon of architectural terms in several languages, and the subsequent volumes on private buildings, the Orders, and public buildings, consist of schoolmasterly paragraphs and tables. The value of the work lies in its practical prescriptions. His conception of '*bürgerliche Baukunst*' embraces all kinds of building, hence numerous depictions of contemporary German *Schlösser* are to be found amongst his plates.

Suckow writes more narrowly on *bürgerliche Baukunst.*[125] He prefaces his work with economic considerations on the role of architecture, which he sees as the rational expenditure of public money or princely revenues on crafts and 'all kinds of manufactured goods' ('*alle Arten von Fabriken*')[126] put into a building. In his theoretical approach Suckow displays an odd synthesis of older German architectural theory in the tradition of Goldmann and Sturm with French functionalist ideas which had prevailed in the first half of the century since Cordemoy. Suckow proceeds from general instruction in the use of materials, making a causal connection between the nature of materials, construction, and function, which he regards as essential to beauty. He introduces the French concept of *usage* into his theory, which he calls 'purpose' ('*Absicht*'). Whatever is not functional is in his eyes not 'beautiful' ('*schön*'), but merely 'ornamental' ('*zierlich*'). This is true for example of the Orders, which are for him nothing but 'ornamented supports, whose business it is as supports to hold a load from falling'.[127] Totally in line with Perrault's concept of symmetry as 'positive beauty', Suckow requires that all parts of a building, 'at least those that are most noticeable...are symmetrically placed'.[128] The usefulness of Suckow's work also lay in the paragraphs of practical advice for building craftsmen.

Texts on the art of *bürgerliche Baukunst* were very much in demand in the second half of the eighteenth century. Johann David Steingruber's *Practische bürgerliche Baukunst* (1773) classifies the art of civil building as a branch of mathematics, and seeks to counter the French manner of construction with examples suited to Germany, but he offers only two examples of *bürgerliche* buildings designed down to the last detail.[129]

A very systematic work in its posing of theoretical and aesthetic questions is the *Anfangsgründe der bürgerlichen Baukunst* by the former Jesuit Johann Baptist Izzo (German edition 1773, Latin 1784).[130] It is based on the Vitruvian concepts of *Festigkeit, Bequemlichkeit*, and *Schönheit (firmitas, utilitas, venustas)*; appended is instruction in how to set about designing a building (*Baurisse*). Under the heading of *Festigkeit* Izzo gives a survey of construction, statics and the use of materials. His exploration of the concept of function in architecture (*Bequemlichkeit*), in which he also deals with hygienic, psychological and social factors, is particularly penetrating. Here Izzo goes far beyond all earlier attempts at definition and anticipates modern views. Here is his paragraph 114:

A building (see paragraph 3) is convenient when the whole and the individual parts are so disposed that the purposes for which the client has intended them can be achieved easily, without obstacles and without vexation. But can all this be achieved in a building in which one is constantly struggling against ailments or is always worried about one's health? In which one hasn't sufficient light, which is so essential to most human activities? In which, on account of the awkward distribution of its parts, one is plagued by the weather getting through, fatigue, foul smells, and other inconveniences? In which one can pass from one part to another only by lengthy detours?[131]

Izzo dissociates himself from functionalism understood purely in terms of structure, as in Laugier.[132]

Aesthetically, Izzo turns away from the relativism of Perrault and demands normative but simple proportions that have an immediate effect on the beholder and arouse 'great sensuous pleasure' ('*große Wollust*').[133] Izzo makes an attempt, in the eighteenth-century debate about taste, to bridge the divide between normative aesthetics and sensualism (paragraph 197):

This distribution of the parts and of the whole will be the more beautiful and arouse the greater pleasure in the beholder, the more easily the eye notices and distinguishes it; inasmuch as only what engages and pleases the senses is perceived as beautiful.[134]

For Izzo 'true beauty' ('*wahre Schönheit*') lies in proportion, but he also allows 'apparent beauty' ('*scheinbare Schönheit*'), as long as the prerequisites of *decor* are adhered to;[135] i.e. as long as the social status of the occupants or the building type determines architectural ornament.

While Izzo's plates are still wholly Baroque, his text is one of the most interesting of the late eighteenth century. He prepared a school edition himself in 1777.[136]

In 1792 Franz Ludwig von Cancrin published a textbook on *bürgerliche Baukunst*, based on Suckow,[137] in which functionalist positions are carried still further so that it is even stated that beauty is not absolutely necessary for perfection in architecture.[138] The usefulness of Cancrin's work lies in the fact that it attempts functional definitions for all types of building. It ends with instruction in how to design buildings (*Erfindung der Gebäude*), which however consists only of formulaic rules.

Johann Joachim Winckelmann (1717–68), in his *Geschichte der Kunst des Altertums* (1764), pursues an evolutionary historical approach not dissimilar to Fischer von Erlach's comparative history of architecture, relating directly to the present.[139] Winckelmann, though excluding architecture in his celebrated work, is nonetheless clearly following the tradition of the elder Blondel, whose *Cours d'architecture* he had excerpted.[140] Winckelmann grounds his evolutionary history of art in climatic, natural and social factors, seeking thus to gain an insight into the individuality of different artistic cultures. He perceives, however, an ideal moment in Classical Greece, and to the ancient Greeks he accords the greatest proximity to the 'essential' ('*Wesentliche*') and the 'true' ('*Wahre*'). Hence their art is presented as 'a model to be rehearsed' ('*zum Ausüben vorgetragen*').[141] In them he finds 'grandeur' ('*Großheit*') and 'simplicity' ('*Einfalt*'),[142] which he had already sworn by in his earlier work *Gedancken über die Nachahmung der Griechischen Wercke in der Mahlerey und Bildhauerkunst* (1755), as 'noble simplicity' and 'calm grandeur' ('*edle Einfalt*' and '*stille Größe*').[143] These aesthetic concepts place him in the tradition of the French and English Enlightenment.[144] Winckelmann is attempting to set up Greek idealism as the norm against the decline in art such as he sees in late Antiquity and the Baroque. In contrast to the French, he finds his norm not in Roman but in Greek art.

Winckelmann's personal knowledge of Greek architecture was limited to the Temples of Paestum. Archaeology was still in its infancy in his day, so that he could derive no support from that quarter. However, he recognises the importance of the architectural way of seeing: 'It all depends on the kind of eye with which one looks at things.' Travel literature, he maintains, has taken too little account of art; a man such as Desgodets has done nothing more than take measurements: 'Someone else must teach by general observations and precepts.'[145] Thus Winckelmann is restrained in his statements about architecture, but clings to the Classical tendencies of the French tradition: 'In architecture the beautiful is more widespread because it consists mainly in proportions: for a building can be beautiful by this alone, without embellishments.'[146]

Winckelmann's most important contribution to architecture is his *Anmerkungen über die Baukunst der Alten*[147] ('Observations on Ancient Architecture'), which arise out of a text (that he does not quote) by Friedrich August Krubsacius.[148] His starting-point is his experience of the Temples of Paestum, but he proceeds to a general treatment of architecture *per se*.[149] He distinguishes between the *Wesentliches* (essential) and *Zierlichkeit* (the ornamental): 'The essential comprises partly the materials and the method of building, partly the form of a building and the necessary parts thereof.'[150] Materials, construction and building typology constitute the 'essential' in architecture. Winckelmann links beauty with the ornamental (*Zierlichkeit*), by which he understands not just any old use of ornament, but one closely bound up with 'the essential: a building without ornament is like health in poverty... and when ornament allies itself with simplicity in architecture, beauty is the result: for a thing is good and beautiful when it is what it ought to be. Hence ornament in a building should remain consistent with its ultimate purposes both general and specific... and the larger a building, the less does it require ornament...'[151]

Winckelmann assumes a relative absence of ornament at the origins of architecture.

This leads him to a decisive aesthetic revaluation of the Doric order, but then, considering the (Doric) 'ancient temples of Pesto', he states that the emphasis of the columns 'is not ornamental'.[152] This shows clearly the aesthetic difficulties that an eye accustomed to Roman architecture had to overcome when faced with original Greek buildings.

For Winckelmann the 'overloaded ornament' ('*überhaufte Zierate*') of Late Antiquity and the Baroque led to 'pettiness in architecture' ('*Kleinlichkeit in der Baukunst*') and to decline. This attitude is very close to academic trends in France, with which he was familiar from his reading. Although the personal experience underlying his references to the Greeks in architecture was as yet fragmentary, it nevertheless represents a considerable step forward from the abstract hellenism of Fréart de Chambray a century earlier. At the same time, at the height of the Greek-Roman debate, Winckelmann takes up a position against the 'Roman' Piranesi in favour of the Greeks, thus making a decisive contribution to a new understanding of Greece.[153] What is surprising is that Winckelmann uses empirical arguments to call in question the anthropometric origin of the proportions of the Orders as expounded by Vitruvius (*Geschichte der Kunst des Altertums*, V. 4). His understanding of architecture never takes firm shape.

The most important contribution in German to the theory of art during the second half of the eighteenth century is the *Allgemeine Theorie der schönen Künste* by the Swiss Johann Georg Sulzer (1720–79),[154] who spent most of his life in Prussian state service. Sulzer's work, which covers the plastic arts, architecture, poetry and music, is in the form of a lexicon of terms, so that there is no systematic presentation of his 'system'. Sulzer's presentation was influenced by the model of Diderot's and d'Alembert's *Encyclopédie* (1751–72), to which he contributed, and his search for an aesthetic system by the philosophy of Christian Wolff and Alexander Gottlieb Baumgarten, whose *Ästhetik* (1750–58) makes him the real founder of this modern branch of philosophy. Baumgarten's interest in the sensuous perception of works of art and their effect – and here one only has to think of French approaches to architectural theory of the first half of the eighteenth century – had an especially profound influence on Sulzer.

Architecture is measured – like the plastic arts, poetry and music – more according to its socially educative effect than to its intrinsic aesthetic quality. Sulzer discusses this in his 'preface'. He sees the task of the arts as contributing to the 'cultivation of moral feeling' ('*Pflege des sittlichen Gefühles*') by means of the beautiful:[155]

> From frequently repeated enjoyment of pleasure in the Beautiful and the Good arises the desire for these, and from the adverse impression made on us by the Ugly and the Bad results an antipathy towards anything that is against the moral order.[156]

The impact of art should produce the 'universal achievement of human happiness'.[157] This idea brings Sulzer close to the position which Shaftesbury and English idealism had worked towards in Britain, and which in France had been developed by Ledoux, though his treatise was only published in 1804. Direct mutual influences are unlikely. Sulzer stresses that he is not writing as an art-lover but as a *Philosoph*, nor is he seeking to provide artists with rules.[158] Sulzer's position is that of a representative of 'Baroque classicism'; he opposes the emerging *Sturm und Drang*, which partly explains the sharply critical reactions of Johann Heinrich Merck and Goethe.[159]

Sulzer's conception of architecture can be grasped most clearly in his explanation of the term *Baukunst*.[160] He classifies architecture among the 'fine arts' (*'schöne Künste'*); starting with the concepts of 'necessity' (*'Notdurft'*) and 'solidity' (*'Festigkeit'*), he immediately moves on to write of their 'effect' (*'Wirkung'*): 'Admiration, awe, rapt attention, solemn emotion...these are effects of genius guided by taste.'[161] Similar formulations can be found in Boffrand and Blondel the Younger with regard to *caractère*, a concept that of course Sulzer also takes up. Sulzer next develops an organic-cum-functionalist theory based on the model of Nature and the human body:

> Every organised body is a building; each of its inner parts is completely appropriate to the use for which it is intended; but all the parts together are unified in the closest and most convenient relationship; the whole has in its own way the best outward form and at the same time is attractive by reason of good proportions, precise harmony of the parts, and lustre and colour.[162]

Sulzer emphasises the importance of landscape and climate for architecture. But he takes these ideas, which are based on Winckelmann, further by establishing a causal connection between 'a national state of mind' (*'Gemüthszustand einer Nation'*) and its architecture. From this he derives the requirement of State supervision and legislation for architecture. The training of the architect should be the responsibility of the State; for architecture, he maintains, does honour to its nation and fulfils an educative function. Ledoux put forward similiar ideas, but placed a higher value on the political role of the architect.

Sulzer is very close to Winckelmann in the evolutionary ideas that he applies to architecture. The object is 'to enter into the true taste of Antiquity'.[163] He again echoes Perrault in distinguishing between necessary and arbitrary rules for architecture; 'correctness, regularity, coherence, order, uniformity, and eurythmy' (*'Richtigkeit, Regelmäßigkeit, Zusammenhang, Ordnung, Gleichförmigkeit, Eurithmie'*) being classified as necessary rules, and proportion, for example, as arbitrary.

In Antique architecture Sulzer finds 'a noble simplicity and grandeur of form' (*'eine edle Einfalt und Größe in den Formen'*); he sees the Italian Renaissance as combining 'grandeur and splendour with simplicity' (*'Größe und Pracht mit Einfalt'*), and the French way of building as possessing 'less grandeur and simplicity, but rather more ornamentality and attractiveness' (*'Größe und Einfalt, aber mehr Zierlichkeit und Annehmlichkeit'*). These observations lead him to a conclusion which implies a kind of classicising historicism:

> If it is asked which architectural style is the best, the answer might run: for temples, triumphal arches and large monuments the Antique style is best; for palaces, the Italian, but combined with Greek precision; but for dwelling-houses, the French way of building.[164]

A considerable role is assigned to monuments in Sulzer's educative programme.[165] His rejection of the Middle Ages, especially his attitude to the Gothic, which he declares is a synonym for 'barbaric taste' (*'Barbarischer Geschmack'*),[166] places Sulzer in stark opposition to the reassessment being undertaken at around the same time by Goethe in his first essay on Strasbourg Cathedral (1771/72).

Sulzer's 'theory' is a synthesis of English and French ideas of the Enlightenment.[167] His bid to establish a comprehensive German terminology of architecture (*'Außenseite'*, 'exterior side', for *façade*, etc.) is not very successful. However, pirate editions, and new editions expanded to include Friedrich von Blankenburg's *Literarische Zusätze*,[168] show that Sulzer's *Allgemeine Theorie* corresponded to a widespread need and that it exerted a considerable influence into the nineteenth century, despite its repudiation by the adherents of the *Sturm und Drang* and the early Romantics.[169]

The encounter with mid-eighteenth-century Italian and French architectural theory is particularly apparent in the works of Christian Traugott Weinlig (1739–99), who arrives gradually, in a series of letters written from Rome between 1767 and 1769,[170] at a synthesis of the functionalist position of Lodoli – probably by way of Algarotti – and the primeval hut theory of Laugier. Weinlig is obviously moving away from the Classical theory of the Orders towards an evolutionary theory deriving from Laugier, in which primacy is given to material considerations. In many ways Weinlig anticipates Gottfried Semper.[171] He goes so far as to state that systematisation of the Orders and adherence to rules in architecture have been the cause of its decline: 'Perhaps the systematising works of Vignola, Scamozzi, Branca and others also contributed in no small measure to this decline of architecture.'[172]

Karl Philipp Moritz (1756–93), a friend of Goethe's but intellectually independent, made an original contribution to architectural theory with a late work partly compiled from his own earlier publications, *Vorbegriffe zu einer Theorie der Ornamente* (1793).[173] Moritz expounds a provocatively formulated functionalist standpoint: 'The most beautiful capital does not bear or support any better than the plain shaft; the most sumptuous cornice covers and warms no better than the flat wall'.[174] For Moritz the justification of architectural ornament lies exclusively in its educative effect; according to him, it can 'delight the soul through the eye and imperceptibly influence the refinement of taste and cultivation of the spirit.'[175]

Moritz's work bears the strong imprint of eighteenth-century French ideas. He sees the function of ornament as 'indicating and describing the essence of what is ornamented, so that we as it were recognise it and find it again in the ornament.'[176] In contrast to the Revolutionary architects, however, he finds the language of the *architecture parlante* of ornament constructional rather than expressive; for him the capital is the 'visible sign of pressure' (*'die sichtbare Spur des Drucks'*).[177] In his interpretation of the Orders he adumbrates a logical development according to which the Tuscan and Doric, because of their compactness, simply carry their entablature, whereas the Ionic and Corinthian, 'taller and more slender' (*'schlanker und aufgeschossner'*), raise theirs up.[178] For him the Corinthian order signifies upward striving, the Ionic the expression of gentle counter-pressure. This is a sensitively psychological interpretation of the Orders.

Moritz anticipates later ideas in condemning undulation in architecture on the ground that it expresses movement – and hence he finds it beautiful in ship-building, whereas he would like to see the solidity of architecture expressed in straight lines.[179] He agrees with the Revolutionary architects in seeing 'grandeur' (*'das Große'*) and 'the sublime' (*'das Erhabene'*) in uniformity and repetition.[180] His definition of architecture performs the mental acrobatics of combining Functionalist, Classicist and Enlightenment standpoints: 'The longer one contemplates a building, the more it should engage the eye by its noble functionality, by the beautiful symmetry of its parts, and by the occupation that it gives to reflective reason.'[181] Here Briseux and Winckelmann, Lodoli and Boullée, are all to be heard speaking at once. The close contact between Moritz and Goethe in Rome may also perhaps help to explain Goethe's change of mind in matters of architectural theory.

French influence on German architectural theory of this period is most clearly to be seen in an anonymous text of 1785, *Untersuchungen über den Charakter der Gebäude.*[182] The author is a practised spokesman for the aesthetics of effect. For him architecture is not imitation of Nature; on the contrary, it is its task to depict for us 'the condition of men'.[183] The impact a building makes is its *character*. The author describes not only the various architectural characters (the Sublime, the magnificent, the rural, the Romantic), but examines the use of the architectural forms by which each character is expressed and its impact achieved. It is not the functional reflection of the interior in the façade that gives character, but the appropriate use of formal means, for example roof shapes, and sizes of doors and windows. A building's setting in a landscape is also made to serve character. Social status and the psychological condition of the occupants of a building are revealed in a building's character to a greater extent than its function. The author does not shrink from stating: 'A magnificent house always signifies a happy man.'[184]

'Unity of form', which results from unity of mass, is required for the expression of each character – except for the Romantic. The expression of the Sublime requires a greater mass – this is reminiscent of Boullée – and here the author of the *Untersuchungen* is at pains to make a distinction between the concepts of mass, the 'colossal' ('*Colossalgröße*') and the 'gigantic' ('*Riesenmäßig*').[185] As with Boullée the concept of proportion disappears before that of mass, and architectural ornament and the Orders are a secondary component of architecture, serving only to underline the character expressed by mass.[186] By the almost experimental method of juxtaposing buildings of the same size but different ornament the author believes in the possibility of arriving at rules for the correct use of ornament (*Plate 118*). Thus he compares three alternative proposals for a building with a colonnade in front, differing only in its intercolumniation, and from this he extrapolates the rule: 'The richer the form of the colonnade, the more it draws our attention away from the mood of the building. It is striking but not moving. Gentle characters, and all those which are designed to arouse admiration and quiet reflection, are not compatible with the employment of numerous columns. The latter are more appropriate for lively, magnificent and heroic characters.'[187] Since their proportions can be anything one likes for this author, anyone looking at his illustration may be tempted to think of Paul Troost's 'Haus der Kunst' in Munich.

In an allusion to Winckelmann's ideas, he speaks of 'simplicity of ornament' ('*Einfalt der Verzierungen*'), since: 'all that is superfluous is ignoble' ('*alles Müßige ist unedel*'); the '*stille Größe*' ('calm grandeur') of a building, he maintains, is attained through uniformity.[188] This is very close to the ideas of Ledoux. The notion of the educative effect of architecture on the beholder and user is also present.

This engaged text, rich in ideas, often citing Peyre and already taking issue with Hirschfeld's *Theorie der Gartenkunst*, is perhaps the clearest German parallel to so-called Revolutionary architecture of France. Yet the author cannot have known the writings of Boullée and Ledoux, which were for the most part written later and published considerably later. His book is typical of the rapid diffusion throughout Europe of ideas that had evolved in Paris before they took definitive written form. It may be surmised that he spent some time in Paris at the beginning of the 1780s.[189]

The writings of Johann Wolfgang von Goethe (1749–1832) on architecture clearly reflect his personal development from *Sturm und Drang* to Classicism, and show that experience of architecture had a profound effect on his life, comparable to that reflected in Winckelmann's descriptions of sculpture. His early essay *Von deutscher Baukunst* (1771/72)[190] takes a determined stand against French Classicism, personified for him by Marc-Antoine Laugier. His attempt to see Strasbourg Cathedral as a German achievement in a national sense picks up earlier French interpretations – including Laugier's of course – of the Gothic as a French national style. Goethe takes issue with the negative yardsticks used to judge the Gothic, that he could find for example in Sulzer; finding that 'the countless parts' ('*die unzähligen Teile*') merge into 'whole masses' ('*ganze Massen*'), and experiencing their effect in Strasbourg Cathedral as 'simple and great' ('*einfach und groß*').[191] In other words, Goethe is here applying criteria derived by Winckelmann and his predecessors from the Antique to the Gothic!

Strangely Herder, in printing Goethe's essay in his anthology *Von Deutscher Art und Kunst* (1773), decided to couple it with a translation of the *Saggio sopra l'architettura gotica* by the Milan mathematician Paolo Frisi,[192] in which the latter attempts to demonstrate the aesthetically inferior quality of Gothic architecture in terms of its construction.[193] Frisi would have been more compatible with Sulzer.

Goethe's Italian journey (1786–88) brought him face to face with Palladio and Vitruvius, and with Roman and Greek architecture. Seeing through the eyes of Laugier, whom he had only recently attacked, he believes he can recognise the contradiction inherent in 'combining columns with walls' ('*Säulen und Mauern zu verbinden*'); but Goethe immediately recognises Palladio as a 'man of inner greatness' ('*von innen heraus großen Menschen*') who, with his pilasters and half columns, 'out of truth and falsehood creates a third entity, whose borrowed existence entrances us.'[194]

In Paestum and Sicily Goethe takes the almost painful step towards the understanding of Greek architecture, which Winckelmann had been unable to take. On his first visit to Paestum Goethe finds himself 'in a wholly alien world' ('*in einer völlig fremden Welt*') but recognises the aesthetic relativism of his feelings:

> For as the centuries evolve from the serious to the pleasurable, they form man as they do so, indeed they create him thus. At the present time our eyes and through them our whole inner being are drawn towards and decisively influenced by more slender architectural forms, so that these dumpy, skittle-shaped, densely serried masses of columns appear to us cumbersome, even monstrous.[195]

In Sicily Goethe has his 'Greek' experience; he reads Homer, works on a tragedy on the theme of Nausicaa, and learns to understand the stages of development of Greek architecture. From Naples he undertakes a second excursion to Paestum, which now appears to him as 'the last, and I might almost say the most wonderful, idea that I am now taking northwards with me in its entirety.'[196]

Goethe returned from Italy a Classicist. His essay *Baukunst* of 1788 shows that he has worked through Greek architecture and at the same time that he has distanced himself from the Gothic: 'Unfortunately all Northern adorners of churches sought their greatness in multiplied minuteness.'[197] The second essay entitled *Baukunst*, written in 1795, shows a marked reconciliation with the ideas of the French Enlightenment. As architectural preconditions Goethe stipulates materials, function and aesthetic effect. He introduces a very interesting new criterion into his reflections, the movement of the human body through architecture, and comes to the conclusion that a blindfold man could feel a 'well-built house' as such.[198] Goethe's ideas on materials do not lead him to require 'truth to materials', but he arrives instead at the Classical doctrine of mimesis: 'As long as only the immediate function was envisaged, and materials were allowed to control what was built rather than to be controlled, no art was possible...'[199]

For Goethe the imitation of material characteristics is totally permissible, just as he expressly approves of the combination of columns and pilasters with walls. He opposes the 'purists', 'who would like to turn everything to prose, even in architecture.'[200] Like the Revolutionary architects, he stresses the poetry in architecture: 'It is the poetical part, the fiction, that makes a building into a work of art.'[201]

Like the Revolutionary architects, and Sulzer as well, Goethe acknowledged in architecture a profound educative function. Thus in *Wilhelm Meisters Wanderjahre* (1821) he describes the urban settlement of the 'pedagogic province': 'The outside of the buildings expressed their purpose unequivocally, they were dignified and stately, beautiful rather than magnificent. Next to the more noble, sober ones in the centre of the town more cheerful buildings were pleasantly situated, until finally neat suburbs in an appealing style stretched towards the fields, before finally petering out as little garden houses.'[202] It would not be out of place to illustrate this text with Ledoux's designs for Chaux. Goethe also agrees with Ledoux that the high social standing of artists should be architecturally expressed: 'Artists must live like kings and gods: how else can they build and decorate for kings and gods?'[203] Hence Goethe has the pupils in his 'pedagogic province' participate in building activities. Goethe's frequent contact with Clemens Wenzeslaus Coudray, the *Oberbaudirektor* invited to Weimar in 1816, may here be recalled; he had studied under Durand in Paris[204] and may have made Goethe familiar with the ideas of Revolutionary architecture.

Goethe had an outstanding knowledge of the literature of architecture, as is clear from his notes for an architectural library (1797),[205] and from the contents of his own library.[206]

Fifty years after his essay *Von deutscher Baukunst* he published a new one under the same title, which shows a new approach to his youthful position. Here Goethe treats the completion of Cologne Cathedral with reserve: for him the main thing is 'the historical aspect of this whole affair' ('*das Geschichtliche dieser ganzen Angelegenheit*').[207] He looks at the Gothic as a Classicist:

> Thus we contemplate with enjoyment certain of the masses of those Gothic buildings, whose beauty seems to originate from symmetry and the proportion of the whole to the parts and of the parts among themelves, and that are worthy of attention notwithstanding the hideous ornament that overlays them...[208]

Goethe neither could nor would go along with Romantic enthusiasm for the Middle Ages. His grasp of history was sound, but he clings to Winckelmann's evolutionary, normative ideas, stating in his introduction to the *Propyläen* (1798): 'One of the most striking signs of decline in art is the jumbling together of different forms of it'.[209] Goethe's natural closeness to Winckelmann is particularly apparent in his essay *Winckelmann und sein Jahrhundert* (1805). His ideas on architecture belong to the eighteenth century. New approaches were being articulated during his lifetime, but his acknowledgement of them was incomplete.

16. The Italian contribution in the eighteenth century

In the eighteenth century, Italy was more than ever before the major goal of all educational and artistic journeys. The relevance of Italy to such travellers lay, however, in its being the home of Classical Antiquity and the Renaissance, and hardly at all in contemporary developments. Eighteenth-century Italy undoubtedly lagged behind France and England in general aesthetic and architectural theory, and this has led to an undervaluation and neglect of the Italian contribution. Yet one need recall only a handful of names to be assured of the significance, in European terms, which Italy continued to have in this area even in the eighteenth century, names such as Ferdinando Galli Bibiena, Carlo Lodoli, Giovanni Battista Piranesi and Francesco Milizia. In the eighteenth century, Italy opened itself up to an international debate for which there had seemed little occasion until well into the seventeenth century. An account of Italian architectural theory during the Settecento has, however, not been attempted to date.[1]

Guarini's *Architettura civile* may be regarded as the most important Italian contribution to Baroque architectural theory, with a clear tendency to give priority to problems of geometry and stereometry. Andrea Pozzo's treatise on perspective is devoted exclusively to the perspectival depiction of architecture and therefore cannot count as architectural theory in the narrower sense. At the end of the seventeenth century one may in general observe a shift of interest towards the depiction and optical effect of architecture. Architecture consequently begins to resemble stage decoration, which made sytematic use of such optical effects, and buildings often acquire the appearance of stage-sets; a good example is Filippo Raguzzini's Piazza S. Ignazio in Rome (1725–36).[2]

It is thus indicative that the most important Italian contribution to architectural theory at the turn of the century should have come from a painter and stage-designer. In 1711 Ferdinando Galli Bibiena (1657–1743) published his *Architettura civile*.[3] From the very outset, in his foreword to the reader, Bibiena makes it clear that his main preoccupation will be the laws of perspective. His prime concern is clearly to secure credit for and publicise what he claims as '*mia invenzione*', namely the *scena per angolo*, a construction based on two perspectival axes.[4] However, he expands the book into a general architectural treatise by exploiting existing literature to deal with specific architectural areas. He seeks to 'make it all as easy as possible' ('*redurre il tutto al più facile sia possible*') and gives precedence to practice over theory, so that even 'people of average intelligence' ('*le persone di mediocre ingegno*') may understand him.[5] Being a very busy artist, he takes the liberty of publishing his book unfinished and full of errors.

The five-part works begins with a statement of the rules of geometry, presented by Bibiena as 'instructions'. In the second part he presents a general architectural theory (simply exerpted from Vitruvius) and sets out the Orders in graspable form based on Vignola. Since his main aim is to foster their rapid application to actual buildings, he also shows various possible superpositions of columns in diagrammatic form. The third and fourth parts of the book are concerned with perspective, the depiction of which is divided into 'operations'. It is at this point that Bibiena introduces his instructions on creating the *scena per angolo*.[6] The fifth part deals with mechanics, in particular with hoisting devices.

It is interesting to see how Galli Bibiena quickly disposes of systematic architectural theory by routine use of Vitruvian concepts in order to establish a framework in which to develop optical rules for the designing of stage-sets. He later published an architectural training manual in which he again described his 'operations'.[7]

In 1740 Ferdinando's son, Giuseppe Galli Bibiena (1695–1757), who spent most of his life working as a designer of stage sets and machinery at various German courts, published in Augsburg a book of engravings devoted exclusively to his own designs for stage-sets and festival architecture, the most influential compilation of its kind produced in the eighteenth century.[8] It employs the *scena per angolo* as a matter of course; the method of its construction is no longer described (*Plate 119*). This work served as an important starting-point for Piranesi.

Architectural textbooks, most of them of a Vitruvian-cum-Classical character, were very common in eighteenth-century Italy. They were often adapted to regional requirements or to the teaching programmes of religious schools. Thus in 1764 Girolamo Fonda published a textbook of civil and military architecture, set out in paragraphs, that was intended 'for the use of the Collegio Nazareno' in Rome;[9] in 1768 Mario Gioffredi began publication of a theory of architecture for Neapolitan students,[10] that remains no more than a treatise on the Orders; in 1788 Girolamo Masi published a theory of architecture 'specially for young students of Rome'.[11] Despite the ill-thought-out mixture of Renaissance and eighteenth-century views presented in this book, Masi's concordances of 'doctrines' and measurements, his account of building regulations, his detailed bibliography, and his technical glossary, do give the book some practical value.

A curiosity in the theoretical literature of the eighteenth century is the attempt by Giuseppe Maria Ercolani to trace all architecture back to a single basic module (*'la sesta'*) and to explain all plans, elevations and sections in terms of inscribed circles.[12] Ercolani's influence on similar trends in the nineteenth and twentieth centuries has yet to be investigated.

Many treatises written in the eighteenth century were intended as examination aids for use in schools. Thus in 1765 the Jesuit priest Federico Sanvitali published his *Elementi di architettura civile,*[13] a textbook in question-and-answer form, the answers obviously being intended to be learned by heart. The couching of problems in dialogue form was popular generally, one instance being the dialogues of Ermenegildo Pini on the subjects of dome-construction and fortification.[14]

There was in eighteenth-century Italy an extensive architectural literature, of particularly widespread provincial circulation, in which half-digested views, drained of their original force, were expounded with great self-assurance. Thus the architect Francesco Maria Preti, who was employed in Castelfranco, in all seriousness puts forward the view that architectural *magnificenza* increases in proportion to column diameter![15]

Bernardo Vittone (1705–70), who towards the end of his life published two architectural textbooks (1760, 1766),[16] should also be regarded as belonging to eighteenth-century Vitruvian tradition,[17] which is surprising for an architect who had previously edited Guarini's treatise (1739). This apparent contradiction is indicative of the uncertain position that Vittone's architectural outlook and his executed buildings occupy. Whereas his plans and feeling for space belong to the Guarinian Baroque tradition, there is also a Classicising tendency in his work, exemplified in particular in his statements on ornamentation. He calls, 'firstly for simplicity and naturalness in the origins of objects, in accordance with what they represent; and secondly, for variety and ease in their portrayal.'[18] He rejects ornament used as a 'wanton caprice' ('*licenzioso capriccio*') – by which he means *barochetto* – but seeks to avoid 'too great a simplicity and roughness' ('*troppo grande semplicità, e rustichezza*') through the use of *varietà*.[19] This is perhaps implicit criticism of 'rigorist' positions such as those of Cordemoy, Lodoli and Laugier. Vittone's aesthetic concepts are taken entirely from Vitruvius. His definitions are vague. His exposition of the Orders (*Plate 120*) is reduced to facile structural diagrams based principally on Vignola.

Vittone's later treatise is a rather fortuitous collection of material consisting mainly of his own designs. In contrast to the other eighteenth-century Vitruvians, Vittone shows some appreciation of Gothic, and even publishes two designs of his own (*Plate 121*) '*in stile Gottico*' for the façade of Milan Cathedral 'with the intention of accommodating the parts of the Design to the style of the body of the church'.[20] Vittone is here picking up Guarini's understanding of Gothic; his second design looks like the work of Borromini transposed into the Gothic style.

Vittone's second treatise contains curiously speculative passages such as his reflections on the nature of sound, which relate to theatrical architecture. Returning to the Renaissance idea of an analogy between music and architecture, Vittone endows various musical intervals directly with divine and human qualities (the octave – divinity; the fifth – the unity of divine and human nature, etc.).[21] Both musical intervals and architectural proportions in effect represent degrees of human sinfulness. Moralising passages of this kind are interspersed with down-to-earth sections on statics and the valuation of property.

Vittone's books are scarcely in tune with his times. He conceals his intellectual sources,[22] and only in his use of a few terms such as *semplicità* and *carattere* does he reveal a superficial contact with contemporary architectural discussion. The dedication of his first treatise to God the Father and of his second to the Virgin Mary is a mark of his naïvety.

The architect Luigi Vanvitelli (1700–73) conceived his work on Caserta more as propaganda than architectural theory. His purpose is to show the peoples of Europe that there is no need to fear comparison with the Egyptians, Greeks or Romans.[23] The never executed oval forecourt and *città nuova*, whose gigantic blocks of houses were intended to adopt the proportions of the palace itself, are illustrated, thus disguising the fact that the economically weak Southern Italian monarchy had overreached itself in undertaking such a project.

The debate between the proponents of Late Baroque and Early Neo-classical positions that took place in Italy in the first half of the eighteenth century emerges particularly clearly in the competition for the façade of San Giovanni in Laterano in 1732, in which Vanvitelli took part and which, with the victory of Alessandro Galilei's design, basically marked the end of Baroque and the advent of an International Classicism.[24] It is significant that Galilei had worked for six years (1714–19) in England at the height of Palladianism.[25] In a *Discorso* written in connection with the competition, previously attributed to Galilei although probably the work of Ferdinando Fuga, the author advocates 'a single Order in imitation of the Ancients...without many superfluous embellishments,'[26] clearly a reflection of Pope Clement XII's architectural policy.[27]

The most revolutionary eighteenth-century Italian architectural theoretist was the Franciscan priest Carlo Lodoli (1690–1761). Lodoli left no complete treatise and his theory has come down to us principally in expositions by Francesco Algarotti (1712–64) and Andrea Memmo (1729–92).[28] Lodoli, who came from an aristocratic Venetian family, devoted himself mainly to the study of mathematics and geometry.[29] His most important work was carried out from the monastery of San Francesco della Vigna in Venice, where for several years he ran a private school for the sons of patricians, one of them being Francesco Algarotti. Lodoli developed early on a strong interest in the fine arts and architecture. He built up a private collection of pictures covering the period from the Middle Ages, at that time held in low regard, to the Renaissance, grouping according to local schools in order to demonstrate 'step by step the progress of the art of *disegno*' (*'passo a passo la progressione dell'arte del disegno'*).[30] This method makes Lodoli one of the founders of stylistic art-history. He also collected architectural fragments with the same motivation. Next to the cloister of San Francesco della Vigna he erected his only building, the former hospice for pilgrims to the Holy Land.[31] Lodoli was active in architectural and garden planning and was particularly fond of the English landscape garden. He regarded reason (*'ragione'*) as the central architectural concept, describing rational architecture as 'organic', a term that Memmo, his biographer, expressly states was first coined by him.[32] Reason should dominate, he maintained, right down to the last item of furniture; hence his design for an anatomically correct chair for his own use.

Lodoli started to compose an architectural treatise in couplets, but this has been lost. His ideas are therefore known to us today mainly from Algarotti's and Memmo's presentations, which are based on notes they took from his lectures. However, in his second, posthumously published work, *Elementi d'architettura lodoliana* (1834), Memmo published two handwritten draft synopses by Lodoli for his treatise, and these constitute the most important source of information on Lodoli's thinking.[33] Memmo is therefore the most reliable source on Lodoli. On the other hand, it should be stressed that the above-mentioned presentation of Lodoli's ideas by Algarotti had been available in print since 1757 and had shaped the contemporary image of Lodoli as a 'rigorist'. There had clearly been some kind of split between Lodoli and Algarotti, since the latter does not mention the Franciscan by name in his *Saggio sopra l'architettura*, but merely states in a footnote in the 1756 dedication to Cesare Malvasia that the new philosophical approach to architecture set out in his work is the brainchild of Carlo Lodoli, whom he erroneously describes as already dead.[34] It should not be forgotten that Algarotti's main purpose in presenting Lodoli's theory is to refute it. Algarotti himself holds a more conventional theoretical position.[35] For this reason we shall consider Algarotti's account of Lodoli first.

Algarotti categorises the question of the principles of architecture essentially as a philosophical one. He presents Lodoli as a philosophical purifier of architecture, who proceeds with the 'most rigorous, rational examination' (*'più rigoroso esame della ragione'*) of abuses in architecture; Vitruvian principles are called radically into question.[36] According to Lodoli, it is the task of the architect to shape, to decorate and to show (*'formare, ornare e mostrare'*). But Lodoli's conception of architecture, says Algarotti, amounts to the view that everything that does not have a specific function in a building (*'il proprio suo uffizio'*) must be regarded as a non-integral component and excluded from architecture. Ornament must, accordingly, disappear. Everything besides function is affectation (*'affettazione'*) or falsity (*'falsità'*). Beauty without function is impossible. Architecture may not represent anything not included in its function. Function and its architectural expression are regarded as identical.[37] Algarotti believes Lodoli's concept of function implies 'a too terrible consequence', in that it is reduced to the properties of materials. Why, Algarotti has Lodoli ask, does stone not represent a stone, wood not wood? Why does every material not represent itself and nothing else?[38]

Architectural expression must be determined by the nature of the material; Algarotti actually uses the expression *'natura della materia'* here. Differences in material dictate differences in form. It is absurd to feign one material with another; this is like putting on a mask, a permanent lie. Only material employed everywhere in accordance with its nature produces legitimate harmony and perfect solidity.

Algarotti for his part adheres to the imitative theory of architecture, on which he elaborates at great length. All architecture, he says, is an imitation of the original timber construction – a clear reference to Laugier (1753), although he does not quote him.

In Algarotti's account, Lodoli advocates a rigorist functionalism reduced to mere truth to materials. This is comparable to the analogous functionalist approaches of Frémin (1702) and Cordemoy (1706), though these interpret function (*'usage'*) as a reflection of use. The two positions have similar consequences, but the methodological approach used is different.

Andrea Memmo's account of Lodoli's ideas is less succinct than Algarotti's but not so biased. Large parts are given over to polemical tirades against Algarotti, as when Memmo seeks to prove that Lodoli in no way rejected ornament. If Lodoli's two draft synopses of his proposed treatise reproduced by Memmo are examined, it may be seen that Lodoli envisaged in one case a division into nine books, and in the other a division into six.[39]

Lodoli begins by refuting the familiar architectural systems. In discussing the Orders, he speaks of errors, crimes and contradictions. Architecture, he says, needs a completely new system, freed from the fetters of existing architectural forms and terminology. The aim must be to find 'new forms and new terms'.[40] There then follows the exposition of the theory of truth to materials. In what follows, Lodoli adheres to the idea of proportions, which he terms *'analogia'*, to that of the regularity of stereometric solids, and of symmetry, which he regards as an organic concept.[41] He considers ornament to be an 'arbitrary propriety' (*'proprietà arbitraria'*) which must accord with the character of the building.[42] This approach clearly goes back to Perrault and the contemporary French debate about *caractère*.

Lodoli's second draft is closer to Algarotti's interpretation. The definition of architecture is here subordinated to the concepts of correct function (*'retto funzione'*) and its representation (*'rappresentazione'*). Solidity, proportion, convenience and ornament are all dependent on these.[43] Function and its expression are here considered to be the main task of architecture; they are identical. Ornament is not essential but accessory, and may be used to emphasise correct function and its representation. Here too, function signifies the use of a material in accordance with its properties. Its presentation, combined with geometrical, mathematical and optical rules, is the aesthetic equivalent of function. Lodoli's definition is as follows:

> Representation is the individual and total expression that results from the material used if the latter is disposed according to geometrical, mathematical and optical laws for the desired end.[44]

Memmo prefaced the first edition of his *Elementi* (1786) with an engraving of Antonio Longhi's portrait of Lodoli, bearing the inscription '*Devonsi unir e fabrica e ragione e sia funzion la rapresentazione*' ('Building and reason must unite, and let function be [their] representation'), which according to Memmo went back to Lodoli himself. Reason, function – in the sense of truth to materials and of its expression – are the principles underlying Lodoli's conception of architecture. Given this rigorist position, which his contemporaries regarded as 'visionary',[45] Lodoli may truly be considered the most important forerunner of modern functionalism. Via Algarotti, to a greater extent via Milizia, and to a lesser extent via Memmo, Lodoli's thinking probably influenced theorists as disparate as Durand and Greenough, who must be regarded as the real founders of modern functionalism.

Memmo is keen to portray Lodoli's teaching as not really so rigorist, and he represents him as conceding some variations in architecture, provided structural solidity is maintained. Memmo here mentions Lodoli's friendship with Piranesi, who, he says, sent Lodoli a copy of his *Magnificenza ed architettura de' Romani* (1761) shortly before Lodoli died.[46]

Giovanni Battista Piranesi (1720–78) is known primarily as the foremost engraver of the eighteenth century; he is less well known as an architect, and hardly at all as a theorist.[47] Piranesi's theoretical position was outlined in a now classic essay by Rudolf Wittkower.[48] At the beginning of his career, Piranesi was greatly influenced by Tiepolo, and by the stage designs of Ferdinando and Giuseppe Galli Bibiena. His first book of engravings, the *Prima parte di architetture e prospettive* (1743), clearly reveals the influence of Giuseppe Galli Bibiena's *Architetture e prospettive* (1740). Intellectually, Piranesi seems to have been profoundly influenced by the ideas of Giambattista Vico, whose philosophy of history, in which free will and human licence are elevated to the status of laws of history, is reflected in the extreme freedoms taken by Piranesi's architectural theory.

The engravings produced by Piranesi during the 1750s depict Roman antiquity in a larger-than-life manner corresponding very closely to the ideas on *magnificence* propounded by the students of the French Academy in Rome.[49] Between 1747 and 1761, the engraver of *vedute* Giuseppe Vasi, for whom Piranesi worked for a time, published his ten-volume work *Delle Magnificenze di Roma antica e moderna*. Piranesi's world was an unreservedly Roman one. He considered it a provocation to question the artistic – and historical – priority of Ancient Rome. Such a process was, however, taking place precisely during the 1750s through the work of Winckelmann and also of Allan Ramsay, a friend of Piranesi's, who in his *Dialogue of Taste*, published anonymously in 1755,[50] sought to show that after the conquest of Corinth (146 BC) the Romans had come under Greek influence. The publication of Le Roy's *Ruines des plus beaux monuments de la Grèce* (1758), introducing measured drawings of Greek architecture for the first time, was the last straw for Piranesi's stormy temperament. The result was the dispute between the 'Greeks' and the 'Romans', which was a kind of continuation of the *querelle des anciens et des modernes* that had raged in France since the seventeenth century.[51] The dispute, grounded in history and archaeology, prompted Piranesi to declare his theoretical position. Its consequences for the architectural ideas of the time only gradually emerge.

In 1761 Piranesi published his *Della Magnificenza ed Architettura de' Romani.*[52] This work is a polemical refutation of the theses of Ramsay and above all of Le Roy, with Piranesi making no attempt whatsoever to understand Le Roy's overall theoretical position. Piranesi's main objective is to demonstrate the historical and artistic precedence of the Etruscans over the Greeks, and to portray the Romans as the Etruscans' heirs. He considers that the Etruscans brought 'every kind of art to its ultimate perfection'.[53] He here attributes to the Greeks an addiction to ornament and a 'useless elegance' (*'vana leggiadria'*).[54] He goes so far as to play Vitruvius off against the Greeks, using Vitruvius's observations on the transference of wood construction methods to stone (IV. 2) against the caryatids of the Erektheion, of whom he says it is hardly credible that they would be able to carry so heavy an entablature with such a cheerful expression on their faces.[55] It would, he says, have been more appropriate to use 'satyrs, or sturdy rustics' (*'Silvani, o villani robustissimi'*) for this purpose. He illustrates this passage in his Plate XX by insetting a plate of Le Roy's into his own engraving in the form of a *trompe l'oeil*, in order to contrast the Ionic capital used in the Erektheion with the multiplicity of Roman forms of the Ionic (*Plate 122*). Piranesi uses many of his plates as negative examples 'that bear little relation to the truth'.[56] He finally goes so far as to claim that the Greeks were dependent on the Etruscans,[57] and, basing himself on the Comte de Caylus, traces a link between Egyptian and Etruscan art. Piranesi is here participating in the contemporary revaluation of Etruscan art,[58] which, because it had evolved on Italian soil, could ultimately be claimed as the national art of Italy.

During this period Piranesi also used his archaeological writings to bolster his Etrusco-Roman thesis. This is demonstrated for example in his comments on the Temple of Giove Laziale in Albano, the *magnificenza* of which is copiously illustrated in his *Antichità d'Albano* (1764).[59]

An answer to Piranesi's egregious construction of history was delivered in 1764 by Jean-Pierre Mariette in the form of a letter in the *Gazette Littéraire de l'Europe.* Mariette assumes that the Etruscans were also of Greek origin and that Roman art had its origins in Greece, being exported mainly by Greek slaves.[60] The *'belle et noble simplicité'* and *'bon goût'* of the Greeks had lasted only a short while; under the Romans, art had become *'ridicule & barbare'.*[61] This is the opposite of Piranesi's position in every respect, and Piranesi retorted the following year with a whole book.[62] The polemical tone is a good deal sharper than in the earlier work (*Plate 123*). The very title page is a biting caricature of the pen-pusher Mariette. The picture shows Mariette's hand writing the offending letter and above it the motto *'Aut cum hoc'* ('Either with this'), whilst Piranesi answers as a practitioner supported by history, *'Aut in hoc'* ('Or in this'). He casts the whole book in the form of a feigned supplement to the *Gazette Littéraire de l'Europe.*

Piranesi begins by answering Mariette's letter point by point, rehearsing his old opinions. He ends by taking up Mariette's phrase about the Greeks' *'belle & noble simplicité'* and composes a conversation between a friend, Didascalo, and an opponent, Protopiro, on the subject of new drawings by Piranesi executed in *'une manière ridicule & barbare'*. This *'Parere su l'architettura'*, composed in the form of a Platonic dialogue, forms an integral part of the *'Osservazioni'* and is intended for Mariette's ears; the centrepiece of the book, it is described by Piranesi himself as a playful *'causerie'* (*'cicalata'*).[63]

The tone of the *'Parere'* is ironic and biting, parts of it being pure satire, and this should not be overlooked in assessing its substance. Piranesi has his friend Didascalo state, as a precaution: '...yesterday Piranesi was of one opinion, today of another. So what?'[64] Piranesi clearly intends to be provocative.

Even the vignette on the first page of the *'Parere'*, with its dedication to the Society of Antiquaries in London (of which Piranesi was a member), its 'false' proportions and 'inappropriate' ornamentation, is ambivalent, and is intended to support the claim made by Didascalo at the outset that buildings overloaded with ornament had been popular for centuries (*Plate 124*). Architecture, says Didascalo, is meant to please the public, not the critics.[65] It is custom that fixes the rules, not Vitruvius or Palladio (*'L'uso fa legge'*); rules such as those propounded by the latter have never existed. Didascalo sets himself up as the champion of the 'crazy freedom to work according to one's fancy' (*'pazza libertà di lavorare a capriccio'*)[66] and opposes the *rigoristi*, who keep paring architecture down to basic elements of the primitive hut, until nothing remains – an obvious allusion to Lodoli and Laugier: 'Buildings without walls, without columns, without pilasters, without friezes, without cornices, without vaults, without roofs; piazzas, piazzas, scorched earth.'[67]

A 'rigorist' architecture of this kind, 'as facile as it is simple' (*'tanto più facile quanto più semplice'*), results, says Didascalo, in a monotony that people hate.[68] The system of the Orders is abolished; their individual elements may even be employed irrationally, with *'libertà'*. Nature too has created, not confusion, but a 'delightful arrangement of things' (*'dilettevole disposizione di cose'*).[69]

Four of Piranesi's illustrations bear inscriptions that are intended to support his out-and-out attack on the rules of the past. The first of these illustrations bears a quotation from, of all people, Le Roy: *'Pour ne pas faire de cet art sublime un vil métier où l'on ne feroit que copier sans choix'* ('In order not to make of this sublime art a base craft in which one would do nothing but copy indiscriminately'): the picture illustrates this 'indiscriminate copying', but interpreted in a new way. The second illustration bears a quotation from Ovid's *Metamorphoses* (XV. 252 ff); *'Rerumque novatrix ex alliis alias reddit natura figuras'* ('Nature the renewer of all things creates new forms from old'); the illustration is an accumulation of Antique fragments. The third inscription, taken from Terence's *Eunuch* and incorrectly quoted by Piranesi, translates: 'It is of no consequence to you whether you know or do not know what the ancients did, if the moderns do it'.[70] Not without a hint of irony, Piranesi depicts on one frieze a pair of ancient sandals with a snake slithering through the toes. The fourth inscription is taken from Sallust's *Bellum Iugurthinum* and indicates Piranesi's personal bitterness: *'Novitatem meam contemnunt, ego illorum ignaviam'* ('They despise my novelty, I their timidity'); in the illustration (*Plate 125*) the Orders merge: architraves are covered with friezes, which then zig-zag off in vertical directions. The whole is an inferno of the classical language of the Orders.

In his '*Parere*' Piranesi rejects contemporary architectural theory, which believes that it can find its salvation either in purist rigorism à la Lodoli or Laugier, or in slavish imitation of the Greeks. One can almost feel him being carried away by his anger and scattering the pieces of the game like a sulky child. Didascalo (Piranesi) carries the idea of artistic licence *ad absurdum*. Archaeological fragments become missiles for a slighted revolutionary.

The theses expounded in the '*Parere*' should not be taken too literally, although the underlying notion of artistic freedom is a perfectly serious one. That Piranesi did, in fact, believe during these years that the architecture of Antiquity could be used by the architect to express his own *libertà* is demonstrated in his creation of the Church of the Grand Prior of the Maltese Order and the Piazza dei Cavalieri di Malta on the Aventine[71] during this same period (1764–66). As in the illustrations to the '*Parere*', Antique fragments appear here as *objets trouvés*.

Appended to the '*Parere*' is a text entitled '*Della introduzione e del progresso delle Belle Arti in Europa*', supposedly intended as an introduction to a new book, which, however, was never published. In this text Piranesi repeats his anti-Greek invective.

Piranesi's last theoretical work, *Diversi maniere d'adornare i camini* (1769),[72] moves further in the direction of stylistic eclecticism established in the '*Parere*'. Dedicated to Pope Clement XIII (this Pope was the uncle of Cardinal Giambattista Rezzonico, Piranesi's patron for the work on the Aventine), this work seeks to establish Greek, Egyptian and Etruscan models as equally appropriate for use in contemporary architectural ornament. Piranesi here opens out his rigid interpretation of history to the question of how various historical styles, the relative historical priority of which hardly interest him any longer, may be drawn on as a repertoire for the present.

The *Ragionamento apologetico* in defence of Egyptian and Etruscan architecture appeared in three languages, showing that Piranesi, with the internationalism typical of the eighteenth century, was addressing the whole of educated Europe. Piranesi makes his peace with the Greeks by reasserting his belief in the precedence of Etrusco-Roman art, but by going on to declare that Roman art was a combination of Etruscan and Greek.[73] He dismisses the Neo-classical ideal of simplicity quite simply as a poverty of ideas, contrasting it with the natural principle of ornamental richness.[74] He believes that the use of ornament must vary in accordance with national differences and the character of the building to be erected;[75] for him as a Roman, the affinity with the Egyptians and Etruscans is the deciding factor. It is Piranesi's desire that his own creations that he illustrates in his book should be regarded not as genuine Antique models, but as modern syncretic works. He is particularly proud of his Egyptian-style designs, which made a decisive contribution to late eighteenth-century Egyptomania,[76] the most well-known example being the decoration of the Caffè degli Inglesi on the Piazza di Spagna in Rome (two plates are devoted to this in the *Ragionamento*). Piranesi takes note of the charge of extravagance, that his designs are an attempt to break out of the 'old monotonous style' ('*vecchio monotono stile*') and offer the public something new. Yet he attaches great importance to the fact that his designs have never contravened the laws 'of good design, of proportion, of character ['*carattere*'], of stability'.[77]

Piranesi's designs met with an extremely strong response throughout Europe, particularly in England.[78] With his plea for stylistic pluralism and eclecticism ('*diverse maniere*'), Piranesi pursues the path first trodden by Fischer von Erlach in the *Entwurff einer Historischen Architectur* (1721). Along with Giambattista Vico, Fischer must be regarded as the most important source for Piranesi's thinking, especially in view of the fact that Piranesi made sketches based on Fischer's publication.[79]

Piranesi began by taking up a position in a historical debate. After a phase of almost *Sturm-und-Drang*-like rejection of all authority and the advocacy of a free rein for individual artistic genius, he ultimately arrived at a balanced attitude towards history and towards aesthetic standards, though still refusing to accept these as fixed norms. Piranesi is one of the great pioneers of historicism.

The most influential Italian architectural theorist of the late eighteenth century was Francesco Milizia (1725–98).[80] According to his own engaging description of himself in his autobiography, Milizia was an educated dilettante, an average man with a discriminating eye, keen to learn but not especially profound or reflective.[81] He was closely involved in the circle of Neo-classical artists around Canova, Mengs, Winckelmann and Nicolas de Azara, in sympathy but not identifying completely with their aesthetic views. The common categorisation of Milizia as a Neo-classicist only partially does him justice. His teachings incorporate almost irreconcilable idealist, functionalist, normative and relativist points of view. His work contains every conceivable theoretical position current in the second half of the eighteenth century, presented for the most part in a measured and non-doctrinaire manner. Milizia was fully aware of the disparate roots of his ideas, describing himself as 'a mass of heterogeneousness' ('*un ammasso di eterogeneo*').[82]

As a writer, Milizia was most prolific in the areas of architectural theory and natural history. He had an extensive knowledge of the history of architectural theory and made general use of this without ever identifying his intellectual sources in detail. His writings are permeated by a European Enlightenment, liberal-minded outlook, which together with his simplifying approach contributed to his European impact, his major works being rapidly translated into English, French and German.[83] As late as 1824 Thomas Jefferson could describe Milizia as the most reliable source on architectural aesthetics.[84] His most important works on architectural theory are *Le vite de' più celebri architetti*, better known as the *Memorie degli architetti antichi e moderni* (1768),[85] *Principi di architettura civile* (1781),[86] and *Dizionario delle arti del disegno* (1787).[87] A complete edition of Milizia's writings on aesthetic theory appeared between 1826 and 1828.[88]

Milizia's architectural theory remains largely constant throughout his work, the only difference between the *Principi* (1781) and the *Memorie* (1768) being that the former contains a greater wealth of technical analysis. Space will not here permit comparison of the different editions of his works.

In both the *Memorie* and the *Principi*, Milizia sets out his theory according to the Vitruvian principles of *firmitas, utilitas* and *venustas*, these appearing in reverse order as *bellezza* ('beauty'), *commodità* ('convenience') and *solidità* ('strength'). His works possess an irresistible logic. Milizia reveals himself from the outset, in the introduction to his *Memorie*, as an adherent of the theory of imitation, in particular of Laugier's idea of the primitive hut as the prototype for all architecture. Milizia, however, carries the theory of imitation further than Laugier,[89] recognising two architectural principles, each of which he claims is based on Nature: the Greek principle, being an imitation of the primitive hut, and the Gothic, being an imitation of the forest. In highlighting the existence of a Greek and a Gothic principle, Milizia is following French tradition, in particular Cordemoy (1706), who had sought to demonstrate the equal status of Greek and Gothic architecture using functionalist arguments. He shows his profound ambivalence, however, in leaving open the possibility of deriving Gothic architecture, with its vertical proportions, from Roman murals, which Vitruvius (VII. 5) had rejected as unrealistic.[90] He vacillates too in his assessment of Gothic, whose 'real solidity without its appearing as such', 'extraordinary, technical mastery' and 'sublime invention' ('*solidità reale senze veruna apparenza*', '*scienza transcendente*', '*invenzione tanto sublime*') he acknowledges, but whose 'poor judgement' ('*cattivo giudizio*') he condemns.[91]

In his discussion of the nature of architecture, Milizia reveals himself to be a belated adherent of Bellori's message, according to which man can imitate Nature and improve on it, thereby drawing closer to Ideal Beauty.[92] This view won Milizia the derisive nickname of the 'Don Quixote of Ideal Beauty' amongst his contemporaries.[93] Milizia believes in universally applicable architectural rules but his conceptual definitions are perplexing: he takes *simmetria* to mean proportion in the Vitruvian sense, but goes on to make this vary with the laws of optics as in Perrault,[94] i.e. he does not accept any absolute numerical ratios. He combines the concepts of *varietà*, *unità* and *euritmia*, interpreting the latter very unconventionally as symmetry in the modern sense of the word.[95] *Unità* is unity of impression, which must result from *varietà*, the latter being taken in by the observer in successive stages. The temporal dimension of perception plays an important role in Milizia. Milizia's notion of *convenienza* includes the old idea of *decor*, special importance being attached to consonance between a building and its function. Milizia believes there are two sorts of specifications: those that he regards as naturally-determined constants, and those that he claims are variable factors dependent on climate, human customs, etc.[96] On the question of ornament, Milizia is once again close to Laugier, interpreting the Orders as an integral part of architecture and as 'the framework of a building' ('*ossatura della fabbrica*'), disallowing all ornament not grounded in necessity. Any ornament 'that is made merely as ornament is a vice' ('*che si fa per mero ornamento è vizioso*').[97] Functional necessity dictates the form of each architectural element: 'if it is in appearance, so it must always be in function' ('*quanto è in rappresentazione, deve essere sempre in funzione*').[98] This formulation is a clear paraphrase of Lodoli, but Milizia reinterprets Lodoli's stipulation, which related to truth to materials, to mean Laugier's structural functionalism. The cornerstones of Milizia's position are reason, the naturally-determined architecture of the primitive hut, truth, and plausibility. By morally loading his theory – again a feature traceable to Laugier – Milizia is able to reject models and authorities in the name of reason.[99] Milizia is therefore not a Neo-classicist in the mould of Winckelmann.

Milizia's view of architectural history is close to the 'Greek' position, but seeks also, as already described, to incorporate the Gothic. Of special interest under the heading of *commodità* is Milizia's conception of town-planning. He examines all problems of building types from the point of view of urban development.[100] In accordance with Renaissance tradition, he adheres to geometric lay-outs for new towns, but calls for variety, contrast and even disorder at the heart of old ones. He firmly rejects a uniform townscape, preferring an overall impression made up of an infinite series of attractive elements, all different from one another and creating constant surprise.[101] Very similar ideas had been put forward a few years before in France by Pierre Patte (1765, 1769), and it is to be supposed that Milizia was familiar with these. Descartes' influence on Milizia has also been pointed out.[102]

Milizia considers the town from the point of view of four elements: gates, streets, squares, and individual buildings. He attaches great importance to town gates, which he desires to take the form of triumphal arches *announcing* the town.[103] Milizia is here adopting *architecture parlante*. The width of streets is to be determined by the volume of traffic and the height of buildings. He desires a regular but varied townscape, and in order to ensure this, he demands that every town have an architectural academy whose approval would have to be sought for all building projects. Three storeys is the maximum height he will allow.[104]

In the *Principi*, Milizia takes into account the economy, the labour market, and even tourism, as factors affecting architecture. He concludes, not without irony, that the ruins of Ancient Rome represent modern Rome's major source of support.[105] He regards architecture as an instrument of human happiness. He sees a fundamental link between the general state of a country and its architecture.[106] These are ideas that Milizia could have found in Sulzer, on whose *Theorie der Schönen Künste* (1771–74) he based a work of his own[107] in which he actually relied principally on Lodoli.

Under *solidità* Milizia deals principally with questions relating to building materials. He calls for an appropriate use of materials (*'l'impiego convenevole de' materiali*)[108] in the Lodolian sense, but does not take the logical step, as Lodoli had done, to an architecture expressing the properties of materials.

The major part of the *Memorie* consists of the lives of architects, arranged by period, corresponding to Milizia's view of history. He dismisses the derivation of the Corinthian order from Solomon's Temple, current since the sixteenth century, as a piece of religious fancy.[109] He places the beginning of the decline of Antique architecture in the age of Constantine. The extent to which Milizia was influenced by the norms of Antiquity is revealed in his comments on the Hagia Sophia. He maintains that its capitals are an oddity and have nothing in common with the Greek orders, and he then breaks out into the following lament: 'to such an extent had good architecture degenerated in the very place where it was born, and where it had made its greatest progress.'[110] Milizia classifies the architecture of Late Antiquity up to the tenth century as '*gotico*', the tenth century being regarded as having marked the beginning of '*gotica moderna*', which he sees as based on a principle derived from Nature. His major source of information on the Renaissance is clearly Vasari. He is scathing in his rejection of Baroque, working himself up into frenzied tirades against Borromini, whom he accuses of having failed to understand the nature of architecture, and of having sought to outdo Bernini in breaking every rule and in artistic originality. He regards the church of S. Carlo alle Quattro Fontane as the 'greatest delirium'. He finds the 'undulating and zigzag style' repellant.[111]. Bernini comes off a great deal better, his buildings being judged to display 'nobility' (*'gentilezza'*) and 'elegance' (*'leggiadria'*).[112] As one would expect, Guarini is condemned for his 'Borrominian excesses'.[113]

As far as the eighteenth century is concerned, Milizia complains of a new decline in architecture in Italy. Whenever he has anything positive to say about his contemporaries – for example his friend Temanza – the subject of his praise is a timid and lifeless Neo-classicism. Milizia calls for a regulated course of architectural study as a boost to architecture.[114]

Milizia believes that good architecture is possible in every climate and every country. He praises English Palladianism but rejects the Adam style, in which, he says, you can pay your money and take your choice between the Greek, Gothic, Chinese and French modes.[115]

In the *Principi* Milizia expresses an undisguised aesthetic relativism in accordance with the maxim 'That which pleases is beautiful', but then goes on, in good French tradition, to suggest a method for the acquisition of good taste.[116]

Milizia's typology of buildings is particularly revealing as an indication of his ideas, containing completely heterogeneous currents of thought. Milizia classifies building types according to their *carattere*, thus making literal use of a central concept of French architectural theory. Buildings, above all public buildings, must express their 'character': a circus or theatre must express 'public magnificence', a temple 'the utmost sublimity', etc. Milizia links his concept of character causally to his idea of functionalism: 'The greatest merit of any building consists in its character expressing its true purpose'.[117] Character is reduced to the expression of function. A little uneasy about this all-too-simple explanation, Milizia concedes that there may, at least in the case of artists, be variations in the representation of character. Nonetheless, he maintains that, given the causal connection between function and character, it would be very difficult for a building to change its function.[118]

Milizia's familiarity with designs by French Revolutionary architects is revealed in his readiness to admit a variety of types of plan and in his suggestion that country houses be built in the shape of caves, huts, animals, birds, ships, stars and various other 'bizarreries that would become plausible, and perhaps even reasonable, if they were well arranged and well expressed.'[119] One is immediately reminded of designs by Ledoux and Lequeu. Although character to some extent becomes independent here, as it did with the French, Milizia shortly afterwards states that beauty, function and construction must never be separated.[120]

Milizia's allowance of only three architectural modes in the depiction of character, 'solid, delicate, and between the two' ('*soda, delicata e mezzana*'), and his linking of these to the three Greek Orders,[121] constitute a surprising reversion to the ideas of Roland Fréart de Chambray (1650). Without quoting him, Milizia here adopts one of the tenets of the most uncompromising of French dogmatists, whose basic authoritarian stance he might have been expected to find repugnant. Milizia is an intellectual eclectic, '*un ammasso di eterogeneo*'.

The detail of his typology of buildings is well thought out. He deals proficiently with problems such as the construction of earthquake-proof buildings and protection against fire.[122] He lays down an encyclopaedic professional formation for the architect, and suggests the setting-up of architectural academies, describing their structure and function in detail.[123]

Milizia's *Principi* form the major theoretical basis of Italian Neo-classicism. It is significant that the Milanese architect Giovanni Antolini produced his own annotated edition of the *Principi*, and tried in his notes to 'trim' Milizia and make him into a pure Neo-classicist, stating for example that Milizia's proposals for country houses in the shape of animals, and so on, could never be reconciled with good architectural principles.[124]

Under the influence of Milizia architectural historians, the majority of whom were also architects, attempted in their writings to promote a Neo-classical conception of architecture. Examples of such works are the collection of biographies by Tommaso Temanza (1778)[125] and the measurements of the works of Palladio by Ottavio Bertotti Scamozzi (1776–83),[126] in which the latter attempted to guide his own age back to the 'veri principi della bellezza Architettonica'.

At the end of the eighteenth century Angelo Comolli undertook the production of a critical bibliography of all the literature on architectural theory since Vitruvius.[127] This four-volume work places architectural literature in a very complex context,[128] the first three volumes being concerned with general art theory, biographies and complementary sciences, and only the fourth volume is devoted to architectural theory in the strict sense. Despite its size, Comolli's work is full of gaps. Its value lies mainly in the various judgements Comolli brings together of the theoretical literature of the eighteenth century. Thus his work contains a detailed account of Lodoli's teaching and of contemporary criticism of it.[129] Comolli's work remains to this day the most comprehensive attempt at a bibliography of architectural theory.

17. Eighteenth-century views of Antiquity

Although from the time of the Renaissance onwards architectural theory had been based essentially on Classical models, it was not until the middle of the eighteenth century that Antique monuments were listed and classified. The plan for a complete catalogue of these monuments under the aegis of the sixteenth-century Vitruvian Academy (see Chapter 5) was doomed from the start; Desgodets' *Les édifices de Rome* (1682) remained for a long time a solitary attempt in this direction. From the Renaissance to the early eighteenth century the number of known Classical monuments barely changed, and they all belonged to Roman times. Little was known even about those on Italian territory south of Naples,[1] while Cyriac of Ancona's expeditions to Greece in the fifteenth century, and the sketch-books he produced, were an isolated episode which was brought to an end by the fall of Byzantium.[2] In his *Weltchronik* of 1493, Hartmann Schedel portrayed Athens as a Late Gothic city.[3]

Knowledge of Greece was to a large extent literary, while contemporary links were political and commercial. In the seventeenth and early eighteenth centuries a number of views of the ruins of the eastern Mediterranean cities of Baalbek and Palmyra reached the West, as is evidenced by Jean Marot's prints and the sketch of Palmyra (1711) by the Swede Cornelius Loos, which was used by Fischer von Erlach.[4] It is possible that these may even have had a direct influence on Italian Baroque architecture.[5] Unique are the letters of Leo Allatios (1586/7–1669), a native of Chios, which were published in 1645,[6] and which deal in detail with the architectural principles and the liturgical functions of Byzantine church architecture.

Apart from Desgodets, who took precise measurements with the intention of penetrating the secrets of absolute proportion, these accounts have a haphazard quality and exude a certain self-consciously academic air. The same is true of the account by Jacob Spon and George Wheler of their travels through Greece and along the west coast of Asia Minor in 1675–76.[7] Spon and Wheler were mainly interested in Classical inscriptions but their book also contains a series of illustrations of Greek architecture, some with measurements. The drawings are small and sketchy, nevertheless for two generations they were the main source of information about Greek architecture.

The systematic study of Classical architecture in the eighteenth century received a fresh stimulus through an increasing awareness, since the time of Roland Fréart de Chambray's abstract enthusiasm for Greece (1650), that Greek architecture, both in time and in quality, took precedence over that of Rome. This was a view that remains far from uncontested, giving rise to a classic controversy. From the middle of the eighteenth century, Enlightenment thirst for knowledge, genuine archaeological interest – coupled with the thought of its contemporary application in architecture – and the speculative publication of elaborate volumes of illustrations: all led to the appearance of a rich sequence of folio editions which had a considerable influence on European Neo-classicism. England, which was dominated by Palladian ideals, played a leading part in this.[8] Frequently these works sought to combine the functions of archaeological survey and architectural treatise, which is why they are included here.

Desgodets had carried out his work in Rome on behalf of the Académie Royale d'Architecture, i.e. on behalf of the State. In 1696 the Académie des Inscriptions et Belles-lettres in Paris considered sending students of architecture to Greece, but nothing came of the idea.[9] In England the initiatives came from a different direction, namely from private societies of antiquaries. The oldest of these, the Society of Antiquaries,[10] was founded in 1707; more important was the Society of Dilettanti,[11] founded in 1732 or 1734, originally an association of young gentlemen who had made the Grand Tour of Italy. The Grand Tour was the basis of all the Society's activities, even after its geographical limits had been extended. Only gradually did the Society emerge from the convivial celebration of its members' experiences in Italy to become the sponsor of scholarly archaeological expeditions and publications; and in 1743 Horace Walpole could still write caustically that the 'nominal qualification' of membership was 'having been in Italy, and the real one, having been drunk'.[12]

The first undertaking sponsored by the Society of Dilettanti was an expedition in 1764–65 to Greece and Asia Minor, led by Richard Chandler, with Nicholas Revett and William Pars also in the party. The Society had laid down written instructions for the expedition, and these Chandler subsequently printed as a preface to his account of the journey to Asia Minor.[13] The Society's prime demand was 'that you do procure the exactest plans and measures possible of the buildings you shall find, making accurate drawings of the bas-reliefs and ornaments'.[14]

This expedition produced no fewer than four publications – two folio volumes entitled *Ionian Antiquities* (1769 and 1797),[15] sponsored directly by the Society, and two accounts of Asia Minor and Greece published by Chandler himself.[16] The aim of these publications was not solely scholarly but also to 'promote Taste, and do Honour to the Society.'[17] Entering into the particularities of period and region, Chandler and his fellow-authors speak of the 'elegant, luxuriant, and in some instances fanciful, Architecture of the Asiatic Greeks', contrasting this with the 'more chaste and severe style which prevailed in Greece itself and its European colonies'.[18] They see the Doric as the true Greek style, its simplicity accommodating slight variations 'as occasional convenience and local fashion might chance to require.'[19] The *Ionian Antiquities* consist of picturesque *vedute* with extremely accurate details, drawn to scale, which could be put to immediate use in the architecture of the day.

Before Chandler there had been a number of works by men who travelled at their own expense, and then published accounts of their journeys, upon which they became members of the Society of Dilettanti. One such was Nicholas Revett (1720–1804), who had also accompanied Chandler. From 1748 Revett and James Stuart (1713–88) had been engaged in a survey of the antiquities of Athens and in publishing the results in a number of volumes.[20] As the various prospectuses between 1749 and 1755 show, their primary purpose was from the beginning to make money.[21] The Greek monuments in Attica are extolled as 'the most perfect Models of what is excellent in Sculpture and Architecture',[22] and a three-volume work was planned to contain views, measured drawings on the lines of Desgodets, and finally the publication of sculpture. Their journey lasted from 1751 to 1753, but the ineptitude of their sketching procedures delayed publication of the first volume until 1762, and the fourth and final volume did not appear until 1816. During this time others, who worked more quickly but less accurately, appeared on the scene and satisfied the craving in European countries for archaeological information about Greece and the eastern Mediterranean.

The first of these works, the product of a mere two-week visit in the spring of 1751 by Robert Wood and two companions, consists of two folio volumes dealing with the ruins of the Roman Imperial towns of Palmyra and Baalbek.[23] Wood has to admit to 'slight inaccuracies' in his work, especially as he quotes Desgodets as his model. He gives curiosity – his own and that of the public – as the motivation for his journey and his book. He mentions the local tradition according to which the buildings go back to Solomon and thereby forges a link with the sixteenth and seventeenth centuries, when writers took Solomon's Temple to be the origin of the Classical orders of architecture.

On the other hand Wood is fully aware that the two towns were built in Roman times, and he describes them as 'perhaps the two most surprising remains of antient magnificence which are now left'.[24] The ruins of Palmyra he characterises as having 'a greater sameness...than we observed at Rome, Athens and other great cities',[25] while the ruins of Baalbek he calls 'the remains of the boldest plan we ever saw attempted in architecture'.[26] In a style full of such superlatives Wood publishes his views and measured drawings:

> In the following works we give not only the measures of the architecture, but also the views of the ruins from which they are taken...For as the first gives an idea of the building, when it was entire, so the last shows its present state of decay, and (which is most important) what authority there is for our measures.[27]

His reconstruction of the propylaeum at Baalbek is influenced by Perrault's colonnade on the Louvre, which reveals a remarkable projection into Antiquity of later architectural ideas.[28] Wood knew full well that the monuments he depicted did not correspond to the ideals of Greek Classicism, so, as he put it, he left 'all criticism on the beauties and faults of the architecture...entirely to the reader'.[29] Contemporary reviewers of Wood's work praised it as representing a victory over Chinoiserie and Gothick tendencies in the architecture of the day.[30]

Stuart and Revett broke off their work at the end of 1753. The following spring a Frenchman, Julien-David Le Roy (1724–1803), who was on a scholarship at the French Academy in Rome, arrived in Greece and, using the full resources of diplomatic channels, made a survey of the principal monuments in Athens in less than three months, at the beginning of 1755.[31] Le Roy knew the various 'Proposals' for the work of Stuart and Revett, and he followed these in his own surveys and in the publication of his book, *Les Ruines des plus beaux monuments de la Grèce*,[32] which, hurriedly produced, forestalled his English predecessors and fulfilled the expectations that they themselves had aroused.

Le Roy was at pains to point out that his work followed the principles of the French Académie d'Architecture founded by Louis XIV. He seeks to make a contribution towards, as he puts it, 'the revival of the arts and sciences in Europe', but in the next breath he reveals the chauvinistic desire of the French to occupy first place in matters of the arts, admitting that he was stimulated by 'the desire to carry out a small part of the magnificent plan conceived by our nation during the previous century'.[33] He praises the works of Wood, probably in order to play him off against his rivals Stuart and Revett.

The first part of Le Roy's work is historical, the second theoretical. His starting-point is Vitruvius, whose work he sets out to elucidate. In his *Discours sur l'histoire de l'Architecture civile* he reiterates the evolutionary schema familiar in Paris since the days of François Blondel, but his first-hand experience of Greek architecture compelled him to recognise what he called a '*proportion arbitraire*' in the squat columns of early buildings (columns with a height of less than six times the diameter of their base). According to Le Roy, the idea of making Doric proportions reflect the proportions of the male human figure is of later origin; Ionic proportions, on the other hand, reflect those of the female figure.[34] In the course of his historical survey he asserts the part played in the development of architecture by climate and by national characteristics. This part of his work contains picturesque and highly dramatic views of famous historical sites (*Plate 126*).

The second part of Le Roy's work is headed *Discours sur la nature des Principes de l'Architecture civile.* He defines these principles as of three kinds – those of universal validity, those appertaining to enlightened peoples, and those one might call folkloristic. Le Roy's utterances are typical of French aesthetics at this time – the foundation of architecture is '*solidité*'; all the members must have structural justification, otherwise they are '*bizarre*'.[35] In giving a general definition of the purpose of decoration in art as 'to evoke in our soul thoughts of greatness, nobility, majesty and beauty when we behold it',[36] he is applying the contemporary conception of *caractère* to the architecture of Greece.

Le Roy relativises the rules of Vitruvius and questions whether the Greek orders should be slavishly imitated – in fact, the only models he admits are those of the ages of Pericles and Hadrian, and because of his evolutionary viewpoint, he believes in the 'progress of Architecture',[37] grouping his monuments according to the Orders within which he perceives differing stages of development, and identifying a new '*Ordre Caryatide*', which indirectly returns to the question of a specifically French national Order.

Since he was primarily concerned with architectural principles and not with details, Le Roy applied what he and his age regarded as axioms to his reconstructions of Greek buildings (*Plate 127*). The concept of symmetry, regarded since Perrault as the basis of 'absolute beauty', can be seen particularly clearly in his reconstruction of the Propylaeum of the Acropolis at Athens, which is Antiquity viewed through eighteenth-century spectacles but at the same time is intended to serve as a justification of the architectural theories of the day. In 1762 Le Roy became a teacher of the history and theory of architecture at the Académie Royale d'Architecture in Paris, and exercised a decisive influence on its policies until his death in 1803.

Apparently impressed by Le Roy's success, Stuart, who had assumed sole responsibility for the promotional side of his joint venture with Revett, decided in 1762 to issue the first volume of their *Antiquities of Athens.*[38] The preface makes great claims for the project but lacks any theoretical underpinning. Stuart states his position in the Greek-Roman debate by proposing that Greece should replace Rome as a paragon. Greece he regards as 'the great Mistress of the Arts', Rome as merely her pupil, with the monuments of Imperial Rome as nothing but imitations of Greek originals.[39] It is his aim to make the Greek monuments known, in order to promote 'juster Ideas than have hitherto been obtained, concerning Architecture', and thus to bring a direct and beneficial influence to bear on the art of the day.[40] He saw their publication almost entirely in terms of a collection of models, as 'a valuable addition to the former stock', as 'a material acquisition to the Art'.[41] He makes no lesser claim than having gone to Greece in the expectation that 'the remains we might find there, would excel in True Taste and Elegance everything hitherto published.'[42] The golden age of Greece, as he saw it in artistic terms, stretched from Pericles to the death of Alexander the Great.

Stuart's prime concern was accuracy. He gives accounts, for example, of how the foundations of buildings were uncovered before measurements were taken, and of how adjoining buildings had to be pulled down, as with the Tower of Winds in Athens. Architectural sculpture was measured and copied with equal precision. It is only to be expected that Stuart should have taken a very poor view of Le Roy, who had stolen Stuart's and his colleague's thunder and pursued quite different aims.

The first volume of the *Antiquities of Athens*, which does not deal with the Acropolis or with any buildings of the Classical period, fell far short of fulfilling expectations. The principal subjects of attention are the Tower of Winds, to which nineteen plates, including reconstructions, are devoted, and the Monument of Lysicrates, to which twenty-six plates are given. A letter from Winckelmann to Henry Fuseli in 1764 shows that the work met with a negative reception. Winckelmann was annoyed by what he called 'trivialities' and dubbed the volume a '*monstrum horrendum ingens*'.[43] An indication of Stuart's conception of the exemplary status of his work is seen from his reconstructions of the Tower of Winds, the Monument of Lysicrates, and Hadrian's Arch, in Shugborough Park.[44] Such a naive approach was hardly calculated to raise enthusiasm in the rest of Europe.

The Acropolis is dealt with in the second volume, published after Stuart's death in 1788 (despite the date 1787 on the title page). The engravings of the sculptures in particular show how lifeless, whatever their precision, Revett's drawings have become when interpreted in the spirit of Neo-classicism. The third volume, edited by Willey Reveley, is totally unsystematic. Reveley takes issue with the anti-Greek outbursts of William Chambers, and condemns the use of the Doric order on the Theatre of Marcellus and the Colosseum in Rome as being 'contrary to the apparent rules of solidity'.[45] At the same time he describes the archaic Doric temple at Corinth as 'apparently of great antiquity, and built before architecture had received the improvements it afterwards did in the time of Pericles'.[46] The fourth volume, not published until 1816, is a selection of Stuart's posthumous work, supplemented by material from other sources, such as William Pars's drawings of the sculptures of the Parthenon.

The *Antiquities of Athens* is unsystematic and at the same time pedantic in its attention to detail (*Plate 128*). Its manner is doctrinaire and it paints a lifeless, anaemic picture of Greece which largely prevailed in the nineteenth century and was not replaced by anything better. Like Desgodets, Stuart aimed at providing a definitive theory of architecture but he was quite inadequate to the task.

The works of Wood, Le Roy, Chandler and Stuart and Revett were concerned with public, mostly religious, architecture, whereas there was a palpable and widespread lack of knowledge about private buildings in Classical times. This was a gap that Robert Adam (1728–92) tried partially to fill with his folio volume on the Palace of Diocletian in Spalatro (Split), a volume that was the main product of Adam's Grand Tour between 1754 and 1758.[47] Adam's attraction to Antiquity was greatly enhanced by his friendship with Piranesi and the assistance of Charles-Louis Clérisseau (1721–1820), with whom he spent five weeks in Spalatro in 1757.[48] The Palace of Diocletian was, of course, not entirely unheard of – Palladio had procured drawings of Diocletian's mausoleum,[49] Spon and Wheler had published a schematic representation of the site,[50] and Fischer von Erlach a perspective view[51] – but Adam was the first to give a comprehensive impression of the complex.

Most of the architectural drawings and sketches in Adam's *Ruins of the Palace of the Emperor Diocletian at Spalatro in Dalmatia*, published in 1764 at the author's own expense,[52] are probably the work of Clérisseau, though his name does not appear on the plates. Antiquity was for Adam the absolute, perfect model: 'The buildings of the Ancients are in Architecture, what the works of Nature are with respect to the other arts',[53] and provide 'Models which we should imitate' and 'standards by which we ought to judge'.[54] In his view the descriptions of Classical houses in Vitruvius and Pliny prove the superiority of those of Antiquity over contemporary architecture 'either in grandeur or in elegance'. In order to give the Palace of Diocletian its exemplary character, Adam invents a historical scenario in which Diocletian involves 'the stile and manner of a purer age';[55] by this ruse Adam is able, in his dedication to George III, to compare the King to Diocletian, Pericles, Augustus and the Medici. In the same overweening manner as Wood, he describes his book as containing 'the only full and accurate Designs that have hitherto been published of any private Edifice of the Ancients'.[56] His descriptions, and above all his reconstructions, derive from Vitruvius. As in a modern tourist guide, he opens with a description of the routes through the site, then turns to explanations of the individual plates, which contain charming views, and above all, direct comparisons between the extant ruins and his reconstructions (*Plate 129*). That Adam regarded the Palace of Diocletian as a direct model for contemporary architecture is seen from the Adelphi in London (1768–74; *Plate 130*), where he designed the arched warehouses of the basement facing the Thames to correspond to the waterfront elevation of the Palace at Spalatro, with its crypto-porticus.[57] The views which Adam published of the two façades make the connection clear.[58]

Adam had paid a visit to Herculaneum, but had not realised the possibility of using the remains in order to draw conclusions about the design of Roman houses as described by Vitruvius. In part, no doubt, this was due to the fact that the excavations that had been carried out in the underground galleries had been concerned, not with the houses and the city, but with the frescoes and individual finds. There had been more or less systematic excavations at Herculaneum since 1738, and at Pompeii since 1748,[59] but the early publications generally pay scant attention to the architecture, except in the case of public buildings such as the theatre at Herculaneum and the amphitheatre at Pompeii; the little volume by C.N. Cochin and J.C. Bellicard (1754) remained a lone exception for a long while.[60] Limitations placed on visitors and the monopoly on the publication of the discoveries enjoyed by the Accademia Ercolanense, founded in 1755, created considerable difficulties for those who wished to visit the sites and the finds displayed at Portici.

In 1757 the Academy started to publish the wall paintings, detached portions of the frescoes and individual ornaments being taken out of their architectural context, with no representation of the rooms that they came from.[61] Even illusionistic architectural paintings – *finte architetture* – were published as individual works.[62] The unsatisfactory introduction to the first volume of the lavishly produced *Antichità di Ercolano* makes no effort to deal with the city as a whole or with individual buildings, but is concerned only with the finds displayed at Portici, which are vaguely described as a 'stimolo della nazione'.[63] Since it was never offered for sale, but only presented as a gift by the Neapolitan court, the influence of the work remained slight in the first instance, and only after the pirated versions of the plates had been published in London from 1773 onwards,[64] some of them in reduced format, did the wall-paintings of the two Vesuvian cities begin to have a real effect on interior decoration and on the applied arts in general – considerably later than is often assumed.[65]

Winckelmann's two publications, in 1762 and 1764, deal more comprehensively with the discoveries at Herculaneum and Pompeii,[66] yet Winckelmann too is mainly interested in the individual finds, and specifically opposes the excavation of Herculaneum as an entire city.[67] He pays scant attention to the excavated houses and villas, and fails to recognise the opportunity to compare them with Vitruvius's descriptions. Nor are his books illustrated, which deprived them of half their impact.

One is therefore not surprised to find that in his commentary on Vitruvius (1758)[68] Berardo Galiani, a member of the Accademia Ercolanense, does not illustrate his text with discoveries made in Herculaneum and Pompeii, but addresses himself to the reconstructions of Palladio and Perrault, despite the fact that he had unrestricted access to the excavations.[69]

Karl Philipp Moritz (1756–93), whom we have already mentioned in another context (pp. 190–91), appears to have been the first to see that Herculaneum afforded the opportunity of seeing the Roman house and its decoration as a whole, finding nothing 'more inviting and more attractive than the meaningful ornaments, perfectly matched to the function of the individual rooms, which one frequently encounters there.'[70]

The first to present a Pompeian villa as a unity was Jean-Claude Richard, l'Abbé de Saint-Non (1727–91).[71] In his Voyage pittoresque (1782) he describes, illustrates and reconstructs the so-called Villa of Diomedes, excavated 1771–74; the illustrations are the work of the French architect Louis-Jean Desprez.[72] Its reconstruction of life in the villa before the eruption of Vesuvius in 79 AD was for a long time a formative influence on people's conception of the Roman villa as such.

Desprez's vivid imagination shows itself even more strikingly in his three representations of the Temple of Isis at Pompeii. The first shows the site as it was in his own day, complete with visitors; the second is a reconstruction showing a procession, and the third a reconstruction depicting a scene of a nocturnal sacrifice, both calculated to stimulate the reader's imagination.[73] These illustrations bear witness to the prevailing fashion for things Egyptian both in architecture and in stage design;[74] while the many idyllic illustrations of ruins, etched by Saint-Non from originals by Desprez, Hubert Robert and other leading artists, convey a picture of Antiquity coloured by early Romanticism. What mattered was not primarily the search for Classical models, or taking up a position in the Greek versus Roman debate, but the use of Antique ruins or reconstructions to evoke moods in their own right.[75]

The influence of the newly-discovered cities of Herculaneum and Pompeii was chiefly felt in the fields of interior decoration and the applied arts. The Antichità di Ercolano belong in the last analysis to the category of antiquarian compendia. Since the huge work by Bernard de Montfaucon (1653–1741) had appeared at the beginning of the eighteenth century[76] – a compendium of largely second-hand knowledge about Greek and Roman Antiquity, arranged according to spheres of activity – many such works had been published, which acquired permanent value for collectors but at the same time took their place among the models adopted by craftsmen. Particularly noteworthy is Count Anne-Claude-Philippe Tubières de Caylus's (1692–1765) *Recueil* of his own collections, in seven volumes, divided into sections devoted to Egypt, Etruria, Greece and Rome.[77] Even before Winckelmann, Caylus had attempted to write a general history of the development of the arts in Antiquity, giving supremacy not to the Greeks but to the Egyptians. A much-travelled man, Caylus had propounded his ideas on architecture in an address delivered to the French Académie d'Architecture in 1749, in which he claimed that Egyptian architecture 'had as its sole aim the creation of mighty works conveying grandeur.'[78] Such formulations were welcome to proponents of architectural theory at this time, especially in France, and they led directly to the many pyramidal designs by men such as Boullée and Ledoux, just as Caylus's historiography fuelled the fashion for things Egyptian in the later eighteenth century.[79]

Sir William Hamilton (1730–1803), British ambassador in Naples, published two elaborate works on the collection of antiquities that he had gathered in southern Italy, which went to help form the basis of the collections in the British Museum.[80] He saw his artefacts not as 'merely the objects of fruitless admiration', but also as models for contemporary artists and craftsmen, and it was in this spirit that Josiah Wedgwood produced for the market his black basaltes ware and jasper ware modelled after pieces in Sir William's collection.[81]

The discovery of Herculaneum and Pompeii also left its mark on literature and the theatre. Reproductions *in toto*, such as Friedrich von Gärtner's Pompejanum in Aschaffenburg (1840–48),[82] or the 'Maison pompéienne' in Paris (1854–59),[83] are late and isolated rarities.

The Greek architecture found in Sicily played little part in eighteenth-century discussions of these matters. Jacques-Philippe d'Orville had been to Sicily in 1727, but his drawings were only published posthumously in 1764.[84] For a long time the most important source of knowledge of the Sicilian sites was the two-volume work (1751–52) by the Theatine father Giuseppe Maria Pancrazi,[85] which was also the basis of Winckelmann's knowledge of Sicilian antiquities. In his *Anmerkungen über die Baukunst der alten Tempel zu Girgenti in Sicilien* (1759),[86] Winckelmann calls the Temple of Concordia at Agrigento 'one of the oldest Greek buildings in the world', exuding grandeur and simplicity.[87] The extensive travel literature on Sicily in the eighteenth century yields little as far as Greek antiquities are concerned.[88]

Of particular interest among publications of antiquities are those that deal with the Greek temples at Paestum, built on marshy ground on the Gulf of Salerno. Paestum had attracted occasional visitors since Renaissance times and had not fallen into such complete oblivion as is generally assumed,[89] but around the middle of the eighteenth century a veritable pilgrimage began, the pilgrims finding their varying expectations – Greek, Etruscan, even Roman – invariably confirmed. In a letter from Pietro Summonte to Marcantonio Michiel of 1523 – apparently the first reference to Paestum by a Humanist – the style of the three temples is recognised as Doric, but not that their origin is Greek:

In Paestum or Possidonia, a ruined city, the ancient walls are intact, for the most part with their towers, and inside them are three temples, of Tiburtine stone cut in large blocks.[90]

A memorandum from the Neapolitan architect Ferdinando Sanfelice of 1740 makes it clear that the temples were taken to be Roman, since he suggests ornamenting the royal palace at Capodimonte with the columns from Paestum in order to demonstrate the skill of the ancient Romans:

> May I suggest to Y[our] M[ajesty] that, in order to save time and expense, it would be possible to take stonework from the ancient city of Paestum situated in Capaccio, an ancient Roman settlement, where there is a great quantity of half-ruined buildings, with more than a hundred huge columns, with their capitals, architraves, friezes and entablatures, built of blocks of stone of such proportions as to give one an idea of the power of the ancient Romans...[91]

Uncertainty over the origin of the temples prevailed until the end of the eighteenth century. Most writers realised their Greek origin but even Piranesi, in his series of engravings published in 1778, was still producing tortuous arguments pointing out their Roman features, while in 1784 Paolo Antonio Paoli argued passionately for Etruscan origin. This circumstance, previously overlooked, should encourage rather more caution in interpreting eighteenth-century 'Doricism' as a purely Greek phenomenon.

From the moment when Count Felice Gazzola began having drawings made of the temples around the middle of the century, publications on the subject – often derived from one another – appeared in ever-increasing numbers, and for a few decades Paestum became the focus of attention in discussion of Antique architecture throughout Europe.[92] Between 1764 and 1799 alone, eight works appeared devoted exclusively to the temples,[93] in addition to reports and illustrations in travelogues.[94] The earliest reference and illustration in archaeological literature occurs in Berardo Galiani's edition of Vitruvius (1758), where the temples are referred to in connection with Vitruvius's discussion of the hypaethros (III. 2).[95] Galiani also uses an illustration of the Temple of Athena at Paestum as a vignette (*Plate 131*).[96]

Some of these publications consist of nothing but plates, others also include measured drawings and explanatory texts. Thomas Major, for example, categorically refers in his preface to the *'supériorité des Grecs'*, and calls Greece *'l'école du genre humain'*.[97] The temples at Paestum he sees as Greek architecture in its infancy, a view echoed by Winckelmann.[98] The drawings disguise the squat proportions and the pronounced entasis of the columns which Winckelmann, for one, did not like. All these works also contain interior views which, by leaving out the column placings, give the impression of a spaciousness that does not correspond to the real situation.

It is mainly this technique of presenting the temples from impossible angles that gives Piranesi's late Paestum *vedute* their charm. He dispenses entirely with measured drawings. In the Greek versus Roman debate he was a leading spokesman for the Roman faction, and he makes no reference to the Greek origin of the temples. In his long commentary on Plate X, the view of the second Temple of Hera, he maintains that the 'simple purity' of the temple reflects the Roman spirit, whereas the Greeks had departed from 'the true theory of art' and adopted an architecture 'full of garlands, flowers and other ornaments'.[99] Of the temples at Paestum he is thus able to claim that with their 'grand and majestic architecture' they are 'superior in beauty to those that one can see in Sicily and in Greece'.[100] In contrast to his predecessors, he does not shrink from showing the pronounced entasis of the columns of the first Temple of Hera (the Basilica). For the rest, his *vedute* are from the artistic point of view far superior to all the others, and he presents the temples as examples of the purity of architecture as understood by the Romans.

Paolo Antonio Paoli's work is based on the material left by Count Felice Gazzola at his death in Madrid in 1780, material also used in earlier publications. In his long-winded *Paestanae Dissertationes*, Paoli seeks to prove that both the city and the temples at Paestum were Etruscan.[101] He sees Greek architecture as containing 'marvellous order and proportion, beauty, charm and elegance',[102] whilst Paestum is characterised by 'the character and solidity of the Tuscans'.[103] Linking the base-less columns with the information given in Vitruvius, he declares them to be a specifically Tuscan feature,[104] and designates the first Temple of Hera (the 'Basilica') as an 'Etruscan atrium'.[105] Many of his illustrations are variants of Major's, but they are more complete and more systematic – he even made efforts to reconstruct the entasis of the columns of the 'Basilica'.[106] Shortly afterwards Labrouste produced an entirely different interpretation of this temple.

Sixteen years earlier, in 1768, Paoli had published an elaborate volume on the Classical ruins of Pozzuoli, Cumae and Bajae,[107] for which the leading painters of Naples had supplied the illustrations. His book on Paestum is far inferior, in part, perhaps, because he took over the material that had been prepared for Felice Gazzola.

In 1793 Delagardette undertook a new survey of the temples on a scientific basis, making a systematic comparison of earlier measurements. He put forward a reconstruction of the second Temple of Hera and made a scale comparison of the proportions of the three temples with the Theatre of Marcellus and the Colosseum in Rome, and with the Parthenon and the Hephaisteion in Athens. In appearance Delagardette's work belongs rather to the nineteenth than the eighteenth century, but his stated aim of contributing to the 'progress of the regulation of Architecture in France'[108] sets him in the tradition of the later Enlightenment.

These eighteenth-century publications were the first to provide a knowledge of Greek architecture. At the same time Greek culture was in process of being elevated to a position of absolute greatness, and this view still retains much of its cogency today. Only in Italy, as its cradle, were attempts made to hold on as long as possible to a belief in the historical and artistic superiority of Roman civilisation.

Towards the end of the eighteenth century there appeared a compendious work in seven volumes (1788) which remained the definitive portrayal of Greek civilisation until well into the nineteenth century. Its author was the Abbé Jean-Jacques Barthélémy (1716–95), who had apparently met Le Roy after the latter's return to France, and began his panorama of classical Greece in 1757.[109] Barthélémy weaves his account around a fictitious journey made by a young Scythian, Anacharsis, between 363 and 337 BC. Anacharsis describes the various peoples he meets, their laws and their customs, takes part in theatrical performances, and converses with the great minds of the day. A map in the volume of plates shows the route he followed. The first volume gives a historical summary, and the second describes Anacharsis's visit to the Acropolis, which he views through the eyes of Le Roy, as the accompanying reconstructions show.[110] His visit to a Greek house follows the information given in Vitruvius;[111] later he makes an excursion with Plato and his disciples to Sounion, an event recaptured in a reconstruction of the temple there.[112] Barthélémy sees architecture in terms of its original function. This is in keeping with his historical and cultural panorama; but it also provided a fruitful starting-point for a broader understanding of architecture.

In the course of the nineteenth century the publication of works on Antiquity became increasingly the province of the new, independent science of archaeology, and these works are of less importance for the study of architectural theory.

18. The role of Spain from the sixteenth to the eighteenth century

The Spanish contribution to the theory of art and architecture has hitherto received little attention elsewhere,[1] and even in Spain itself there has been no thorough account of the subject.[2] This is all the more surprising in that a number of theoretical works have come out of Spain, the influence of which has extended to the rest of Europe and to Latin America. Here we shall concentrate on certain stages in this development, in particular on those that have had some resonance in the rest of Europe.

In the sixteenth century Spanish writing on architecture was completely under the spell of the Italians. Vitruvius, Alberti, Serlio and Vignola dominate the scene: 1552 saw a Spanish edition of Books III and IV of Serlio,[3] and 1582 brought complete translations of Vitruvius and Alberti.[4]

The first response to Vitruvius came in a little book that quickly acquired great popularity, being reprinted and translated many times – the *Medidas del Romano* (1526), by a priest called Diego de Sagredo.[5] The only information we have about Sagredo is that he was in Italy – chiefly in Florence and Rome – before 1522, and that after his return to Spain he found his way into the entourage of Alfonso de Fonseca, Archbishop of Toledo, to whom his book is dedicated. It takes the form of a dialogue between Sagredo himself and the painter León Picardo. Sagredo is solely concerned with the theory of proportion and of the Classical orders. He shows his indebtedness to Alberti when he speaks of architecture as a science which rests on the 'secrets and experiences of Nature' and which he wishes to see employed for the general good.[6] He seeks to give definitive measurements for those 'who wish to build in the Antique fashion',[7] but he by no means confines himself to Vitruvius, mentioning in addition Pomponius Gauricus, and he uses Francesco di Giorgio, though without referring to him by name. Basing himself expressly on Vitruvius, he follows Francesco di Giorgio in declaring that all architecture derives its proportions from the human figure,[9] and his illustration of entablatures (*Plate 132*) shows, like Francesco di Giorgio[10] and, later, Bernini and Jacques-François Blondel, a direct transference of the proportions of the human head (*Plates 19, 89*).

Sagredo appears to have been in contact with the Raphael circle in Rome, a conclusion based on the way in which he takes for granted the existence of five Orders (Doric, Ionic, Tuscan, Corinthian and Attic)[11] – a number and classification only recorded at this date in the letter written by Raphael and Baldassare Castiglione to Pope Leo X[12] (Serlio's system of five Orders was only published in 1537).

Particularly interesting is an excursus on 'the design of so-called fantastic columns, candlesticks and balusters',[13] which Sagredo describes as being 'of a different kind' ('*otro genero*'). He gives the baluster virtually the status of an Order in itself, deriving it from the pomegranate tree, and thereby alluding to Granada, where the *reconquista* was completed in 1492.[14] Comparing Sagredo's baluster illustrations with the pilasters

designed a few years earlier by Bartolomé Ordóñez for the tomb of Philip the Fair and
Joanna the Mad, and with those of Felipe Vigarny for the *retablo major* in the Capilla
Real in Granada, one is struck by the similarity. Sagredo specifically acknowledges
Vigarny as his authority in sculpture,[15] and the baluster, with its allusion to Granada
as the symbol of a united Spain, whose reigning monarch, the Emperor Charles V,
dominated Europe at the time, thus acquired the significance of a national Spanish
Order. Sagredo does not say this in so many words, but he does raise the question of
the identity of the *nación* from which Roman architecture came, thus implying the link
between architecture and nationhood. In this he shows himself to be a precursor of
the notion of the 'French Order', which Philibert Delorme tried to introduce a
generation later. By treating the baluster forms inherited from the Plateresque style as
a kind of 'Spanish Order', Sagredo sanctioned a continuation of their use. It is
questionable whether balusters were actually employed in the late sixteenth century
with the significance he envisaged, but it may be worth pointing out that Alonso
Berruguete, who had served his apprenticeship in the school of Bramante, used free-
standing balusters in the form illustrated by Sagredo, for the frame around his alabaster
relief of the Transfiguration in Toledo Cathedral (post-1542). Sagredo deserves our
attention, not only because he was the first Spaniard to write on architectural theory,
but also because of the originality of his ideas.

From this time onwards two main streams can be detected in Iberian writings on
architectural theory: one prescribes Greek, Roman and Italian models, the other seeks
to identify indigenous historical and aesthetic traditions. The same dichotomy can be
observed in the buildings themselves. Charles V's palace in the Alhambra at Granada,
for instance, built by Pedro Machuca, who was trained in Rome, can only be understood
in terms of the Italian Renaissance. Besides this there was an extensive importation of
Italian architectural and sculptural artefacts, most of it from Genoa, whose decorative
Renaissance style was more easily assimilated to the Spanish Plateresque than was the
severer approach developed in Rome. One particularly characteristic case is that of a
palace courtyard transported by ship from Genoa to La Calahorra in the Sierra Nevada.[16]

The trend towards adopting models from Antiquity and the Italian Renaissance
for the arts and architecture of the writer's own country is manifested in the work of
Francisco de Hollanda (1517-84), a Portuguese of Dutch descent, who is chiefly known
for the publication of his conversations with Michelangelo (though these are not
universally regarded as authentic).[17] He was in Italy from 1538 to 1540, and brought
back with him to Portugal an extensive collection of his own drawings, which, however,
he did not publish.[18] These consist of models for sculpture, painting and architecture
(including fortifications) based on Classical and Renaissance sources. The remarkably
squat proportions of his depictions of architecture are unusual. Similarly unpublished
during his lifetime was a treatise, completed in 1571, containing architectural projects
for Lisbon.[19]

The opposite tendency, of turning to the writer's own country for inspiration, is
best represented by the *Ingeniosa comparación entre lo antiquo y lo presente* (1539) by
Cristóbal de Villalón, a Spanish priest who had travelled to France, Italy, Flanders,
Constantinople and Mount Athos.[20] Following the dialogue form found in Sagredo,
Villalón confidently compares the Spanish architecture of his time with the Classical
and Renaissance architecture of Italy, extolling, however, not the Italianate manner of

Machuca but the Plateresque style of León Cathedral, and indeed applying the term
obras de plata, silverware, to architecture, and in a positive sense at that, for the first
time.[21]

A remarkable combination of the Gothic, Northern European tradition of the
masonic lodges with the ideas of the Italian Renaissance emerges in a treatise by Rodrigo
Gil de Hontañón (1500/10–77), who may be regarded as the main representative of a
moderated Plateresque style.[22] Gil's treatise is, however, known only from a revised
version of 1681 by the Salamanca architect Simón García, which means that we need
to undertake the tricky task of distinguishing between medieval tradition, Gil's sixteenth-
century ideas and García's seventeenth-century attitudes.[23] The work has been compared
in importance to Villard de Honnecourt's lodge-book, but Gil's anthropometrical
analogy derived from Vitruvius appears in a different light if one reflects that the model
may well have been Francesco di Giorgio, though he is nowhere mentioned by name,
since he has been shown to be one of Sagredo's principal sources. Gil's citation of
works consulted[24] does, however, contain the name of Cataneo, who made use of
Francesco di Giorgio's anthropometric theory of proportion, and it is hardly credible
that plans of churches should have been derived from the recumbent human form, or
a steeple tower interpreted by analogy with an armless standing figure,[25] unless Francesco
di Giorgio's ideas had been known to the author. Gil thus makes a seamless transition
from the geometric to the anthropometric systems of proportion.

Gil's aesthetic categories and his analogy between architectural proportion and the
theory of musical harmony are largely derived from Alberti, while the system of Orders
propounded in his seventh chapter is based on Serlio, Vignola and Palladio, and may well
be entirely the work of Simón García. Only in some church plans and in the sections
on vaulting is it possible to find traces of the medieval masonic tradition. In his account
of the lines of stress in Gothic rib vaulting Gil uses a human analogy, this time the
fingers of the hand;[26] but only with reservations can one draw conclusions from his
book about the knowledge of statics possessed by masons in the High Middle Ages.

The most comprehensive Spanish sixteenth-century work on sculpture and
architecture is that by Juan de Arfe y Villafañe (1535–1603), a goldsmith of German
descent.[27] Published in two parts in 1585 and 1587,[28] it deals, in four books, with
geometry, human and animal proportions, the Orders, and proportions in ecclesiastical
architecture and goldsmiths' work. Arfe adheres to the Renaissance view that all
proportions are to be derived from the human body, with which he thus deals in some
depth, basing himself chiefly on Dürer's *Four Books on Human Proportion* (1528). In
his third book Arfe even applies his system of proportion to animals. His historiography
establishes a line of descent from Greek and Roman Antiquity through the Italian
Renaissance to the great Spanish sculptors Berruguete and Vigarny.[29]

Arfe's main concern is to give practical instructions. In Book IV he gives an
account of the Orders based on Serlio, albeit with the addition of Plateresque elements
to each individual Order, and adding a sixth, 'Attic' order; this leads on to his work
as a goldsmith, with a precise explanation of the proportional construction of his
monstrances, the most splendid of which is that in Seville Cathedral, with the publication
of which the work ends. This consists of four pyramidally superimposed canopies, each
shorter and narrower than the one below in the ratio of 2:5.[30] With it, Arfe fuses the
Plateresque and the architectural principles of the Renaissance.

Between 1575 and 1591 a remarkable treatise was written by the architect Alonso de Vandelvira, based entirely on the principles of applied geometry. Two reductions of the work, which was not published until 1977, have survived.[31] Vandelvira deals with the geometrical construction of arches, staircases and vaults, then of entire chapels, taking as his starting-point Books III and IV of Philibert Delorme's *L'Architecture* (1567). Both the text and the illustrations make this connection plain, but Vandelvira is also at pains to replace Delorme's French examples with Spanish ones. Surprisingly enough, however, he makes no effort to exploit Delorme's 'French Order' for his own purposes.

Recently a large number of marginal glosses dating from c. 1592–93 in the hand of the painter El Greco were discovered in a copy of Daniele Barbaro's commentary on Vitruvius (1556) in the Biblioteca Nacional in Madrid. These reveal a remarkably anti-Vitruvian attitude[32] and recall, in their rejection of Vitruvius's categories and of his mathematico-geometrical theories, the position taken up by Federico Zuccaro.

At the court of Philip II at this time a complex series of developments was taking place, the consequences of which have not yet been fully explored. The Counter-Reformation, Jesuitism, Mysticism, and the Cabbala were fused in a fascinating synthesis which was felt throughout almost the whole of Europe in the course of the seventeenth and eighteenth centuries. As far as Spain is concerned, the most important names in architectural theory of this period are those of the architect Juan de Herrera and the Jesuit Juan Bautista Villalpando.

Juan de Herrera (c. 1530–97) stands in line of descent from Vignola as an exponent of a cool, cerebral architecture,[33] and is chiefly associated with the Escorial, which was begun by his teacher Juan Bautista de Toledo, and with the cathedral in Valladolid. In 1582 he played an important part in the foundation of the Academy of Mathematics in Madrid, and as the catalogue of his library shows, he also took a deep interest in the occult.[34] In his *Discurso de la Figura Cúbica* he acknowledges his indebtedness to the *Ars generalis* of Ramón Lull (1235–1316), the Catalan mystic, alchemist and encyclopedist.[35] Philip II's entire entourage can probably be reckoned among the disciples of Lull. Herrera's treatise traces all measurements and proportions in Nature back to the cube, and René Taylor has demonstrated the connection between this principle and the planning of the Escorial: in Luca Cambiaso's fresco of the Heavenly Glory in the choir of the church of the Escorial God the Father and Christ have their feet on a cube, while in Pellegrino Tibaldi's frescoes in the library there are also motifs that correspond to Lull's geometric ideas.[36] Philip II was called 'the new Solomon' by his contemporaries, and the Escorial 'the new Temple of Solomon'.[37] It is therefore not surprising that theoretical reconstructions of Solomon's Temple should have been made by members of Philip's entourage, and that the king should have encouraged them. Herrera's library contained a copy of a treatise on Solomon's Temple, so we may assume that he was a party to such ideas,[38] but in his volume of engravings of the Escorial (1589) he makes no mention of them.[39]

This is not the place to enter into a detailed discussion of attempts to reconstruct the appearance of Solomon's Temple,[40] but we must at least concern ourselves with those which were encouraged by the king himself. In 1572 Benito Arias Montano (1527–98), editor of the polyglot Antwerp Bible and subsequently librarian of the Escorial for many years, published a reconstruction which he later reprinted in his *Antiquitatum*

Judaicarum libri IX of 1593.[41] Montano vehemently attacked the as yet unpublished reconstruction by Villalpando and accused the author of heresy, but an Inquisition tribunal appointed by Pope Sixtus V was compelled to pronounce Villalpando innocent.

Juan Bautista Villalpando's (1552–1608) reconstruction of Solomon's Temple forms the core of an extensive commentary on the Book of Ezekiel and has for this reason been largely overlooked in the history of architectural theory, but both the reconstruction and the commentary are among the most interesting products of the turn of the sixteenth century.[42] A native of Cordoba, Villalpando studied mathematics under Juan de Herrera at the time when Herrera was in charge of the building of the Escorial. He evidently also gained experience of architecture under Herrera, for recently he has been identified as the designer of a number of buildings for the Jesuits, whose order he entered in 1575.[43] He was put under the supervision of Jerónimo Prado (1547–95), who had already started a commentary on Ezekiel and now also involved his protégé in the work. However, Villalpando's concern with the reconstruction of Solomon's Temple according to the vision of Ezekiel probably goes back to Herrera himself, or at least received his support, and the above-mentioned manuscript copy of a treatise in Herrera's possession would probably have been a version of Villalpando's reconstruction.

In 1592 the two Jesuits were transferred to Rome, where they continued their work. But differences of opinion developed between them, requiring the intervention, first of Aquaviva, general of the Jesuit order, then of Philip II himself, who, surely under Herrera's influence, decided in Villalpando's favour.[44] When Prado died in 1595, Villalpando was left to complete the commentary on his own, and the three-volume work, dedicated to Philip II, was finally published in Rome between 1596 and 1604.[45] Our concern here is only with the commentary on Ezekiel XL–XLII, in the second volume of the work (1604),[46] which deals with the vision of the Temple and is exclusively the work, both text and illustrations, of Villalpando himself.

According to Villalpando, the importance of Ezekiel's vision of the Temple, which he equates with that of Solomon, rests on the fact that all the numbers and proportions of the building are absolute and perfect,[47] providing us with rules for a perfect architecture which permit no deviation. He quotes his teacher Herrera as saying, when he saw the reconstruction, that no human mind could have thought up such a building, and that it must therefore be the work of God in His infinite wisdom.[48] In probable response to Montano's earlier attacks, Villalpando admits that Ezekiel's vision may have differed in some respects from Solomon's Temple, and then comes to the heart of his argument: that Ezekiel's description was fully compatible with the prescriptions of Vitruvius. He rediscovers the three Classical orders in the elevation of the Holy of Holies, and even makes its massive substructures agree with Vitruvius.[49] This harmonisation of Biblical information about architecture with the Vitruvian tradition is the key to Villalpando's success in Europe. Tentative moves in the same direction by Alberti and Delorme were not worked on down to the last detail like Villalpando's.

Villalpando then enjoins that Christian churches be built on the basis of these combined principles.[50] He even succeeds in reconciling the traditions of the Old Testament, the New Testament, and Antiquity when he identifies the Vitruvian quality of *firmitas* in Solomon's Temple, and interprets it as a shadow which prefigures the 'body that casts the shadow' ('*illius umbrae corpus*'), namely Christ. By manipulating his evidence in this manner, he is able to base himself entirely on Vitruvius in his use of basic architectural concepts, in his views on the qualifications necessary for the professional architect, and in his reconstruction of the Temple.[51] He gives detailed explanations of his fifteen plates, then proceeds to deviate from Vitruvius (*Plates 133–35*). He predicates a 'Salomonic Order',[52] which corresponds in construction with the Corinthian order, but has lilies ornamenting the capitals, and then traces the Vitruvian orders back to this 'Salomonic Order'.[53] This virtually turns the Classical Orders, a basic element in the whole theory of post-Renaissance architecture, into derivatives of the Old Testament!

It is striking that, in his illustration of the 'Salomonic Order', Villalpando describes the capital as 'being made, as it were, with the artistry of a lily' ('*quasi opere lilii fabricata*') but in fact depicts pomegranate seeds and specifically reproduces the *dispositio malorum granatorum* for the soffits of entablature (*Plate 135*). It would hardly be going too far to see in this an echo of Sagredo's Baluster Order, which was regarded as a specifically Spanish feature, and was similarly derived from the pomegranate tree. In this way the 'Salomonic Order' could be identified as a Spanish order, though Villalpando naturally avoids making such a claim. Nonetheless, when Fréart de Chambray took over Villalpando's 'Salomonic Order' in 1650, he replaced the pomegranate motif by the fruits and fronds of palm trees (*Plate 79*).[54]

Villalpando's interpretation of his Temple reconstruction becomes increasingly speculative and 'hermetic' the further his argument advances. For instance, he derives the plan of the Temple from the disposition of the camps of the twelve tribes of Israel around the Ark of the Covenant,[55] merely moving the Holy of Holies slightly to the west; he then links the *castella* of the twelve tribes with the twelve signs of the zodiac, while the seven courtyards are equated with the seven planets. The proportions he bases on the Pythagorean theory of harmony, which he knew from Alberti and from Daniele Barbaro's commentary on Vitruvius.[56] He also draws on anthropometric principles of proportion, by including a standing figure in his description of the Holy of Holies,[57] thereby revealing his indebtedness to Francesco di Giorgio's theory of proportion, which also recurs in Pietro Cataneo. This section of Villalpando's work carries overtones of Cabbalistic ideas,[58] which may have been what led to his arraignment before the Inquisition.

Villalpando's work has a coruscating, highly hermeneutic quality, and was thus able to enjoy a privileged circulation as a Biblical commentary. A comparison of his plan of Solomon's Temple with that of the Escorial shows that he and Herrera have common roots; the plan of Filarete's Ospedale Maggiore in Milan also probably has similar origins.[59] It is therefore no surprise to find that the Escorial, which from the beginning was seen as a latter-day Solomon's Temple, had Villalpando's reconstruction superimposed upon it. Little research has so far been done on the effect of this on the palaces and monasteries built in Europe in the Baroque period.[60]

The importance of the text and plates of Villalpando's work for architectural theory in the Baroque age can hardly be overestimated. As early as 1613 a book on Solomon by a Jesuit priest called Juan de Pineda included an extract from Villalpando's commentary.[61] In Spain itself all seventeenth-century theorists refer to him, and his influence is considerable in almost all the countries of Europe – least so, strangely enough, in Italy, the country in which his work was published, but most so, by contrast, in Protestant countries. In 1680, for instance, a huge wooden model following his reconstruction was begun in Hamburg for a lawyer called Gerhard Schott, which was exhibited in Britain in the eighteenth century, and can still be seen today in the Museum für Hamburgische Geschichte.[62] The principal scholars who concerned themselves with Villalpando in Germany were Goldmann, Sturm and Fischer von Erlach, while in England Christopher Wren, Isaac Newton and John Wood the Elder bear witness to his influence. In France his importance sets in with Fréart de Chambray.[63]

This brief account of Villalpando's work must suffice to show the important role that he played in the history of architectural theory. If one takes account of the Jesuit and Cabbalistic elements in his thinking, one may well be justified in calling him the most significant architectural theorist of the Counter-Reformation.

A number of works dealing with the Escorial and the Hieronymites, to whom the monastery was consigned, gave these ideas wider currency. Fray Juan de San Jerónimo, for example, kept accounts of the building work and was the first chronicler of the monastery;[64] Fray José de Siguenza records that the Escorial was begun in the decisive year of the Council of Trent (1563), and gave permanent form to the Council's conclusions;[65] Fray Francisco de los Santos, in a frequently reprinted volume, hailed the Escorial as a new wonder of the world,[66] while Fray Andrés Ximénez (Jiménez) gave a comprehensive account of all the fitting out of the building.[67] Illustrations of the Escorial, often taken entirely out of context, are to be found in Baroque treatises on architecture throughout Europe.

Probably the most characteristically Spanish architectural treatise of the Baroque period is that by the Augustinian friar and architect Fray Lorenzo de San Nicolás (1595–1679), described by George Kubler as 'the best manual on architecture ever written.'[68] Published in two parts (1633 and 1664), the *Arte y Uso de Architectura* had a considerable influence on buildings executed both in Spain and in Latin America.[69] Always with an eye to practical application, Fray Lorenzo deals in detail with mathematics, geometry and construction. He too sees the Escorial as the eighth wonder of the world. He reveals an academic tendency in his hostility to the predominance of painters and sculptors in architecture, and thereby indirectly counters the view of Serlio, who had assigned them a role of great importance. Fully acquainted with earlier architectural theory, Fray Lorenzo lays special stress on the question of the materials to be used in building, taking his lead from statements found in Scamozzi. He is of the opinion that local materials should be used, whose properties the architect should be well aware of; he was the first, indeed, to employ the concept of truth to materials ('*la propriedad de los materiales*').[70] This may well have laid the foundation for his success in Latin America, where the question of building materials is of vital importance in earthquake areas.

Of less originality and influence were P. Juan Carlos de la Faille's *Tratado de Arquitectura* (1636) which remained in manuscript, and a treatise by the architect Domingo de Andrade, which treats chiefly of military architecture (1695).[72]

Villalpando's new 'Salomonic Order', which had the disadvantage of corresponding too closely to the Corinthian order, was redefined by Fray Juan Ricci (c. 1600–81), a Benedictine of Italian origin, and best known as a painter, who went back for inspiration to the spiral columns of St Peter's in Rome, which were supposed to have had their origin in Solomon's Temple. Until 1662 Ricci lived in Spain, where he wrote his *Tratado de la pintura sabia*, which includes geometry, perspective, architecture and architectural drawing, anatomy and a theory of human proportions. The manuscript of the treatise was only published in 1930.[73] Ricci's architectural theory is based in the main on Serlio and Vignola, but his illustrations make it clear that he also knew Wendel Dietterlin's *Architectura* and probably some of the works of Hans Vredeman de Vries. Ricci took over Serlio's Christianised symbolism of the Classical orders, but adapted it to Spanish taste and increased the number of Orders by proposing an '*orden Rustico*', an '*orden Grutesco*', and various hybrid forms,[74] which can only be explained in terms of Northern European models. His conception of the 'Salomonic Order' (*Plates 136, 137*) consisted of extending the serpentine form of the spiral columns of St Peter's to the base, entablature and other members of the order, so that every member acquired an undulating quality.[75] He formulated corresponding designs for triumphal arches, which could also be adapted to serve as altar retables.[76] Towards the end of the 1650s Guarino Guarini appears to have met Ricci and used his ideas both in a design for the church of Santa Maria della Divina Provvidenza in Lisbon and in his treatise on architecture, although he does not mention Ricci by name.[77] In his theory of human proportions Ricci draws on Dürer, both for his commentary and for his illustrations.

In 1662, before being transferred in 1670 to Monte Cassino, where he was to spend the last years of his life, Ricci went to Rome, where he wrote a short treatise (1663) specifically on his 'Salomonic Order', dedicated to Pope Alexander VII.[78] In this, he goes so far as to propose a new baldachin for St Peter's 'built in the pure Salomonic Order' ('*ex Salomonico Ordine integro constructum*'), together with a choir screen in .the same style.[79] This must be taken as a criticism of Bernini's Baldacchino, which Ricci naturally does not dare to mention. At the end of the treatise there is a proposal for a fountain in front of the Pantheon which sought ingratiatingly to combine the arms of the Chigi family, to which the Pope belonged, with the 'Salomonic Order'.[80]

A criticism of Bernini from a quite different quarter came from Juan Caramuel de Lobkowitz (1606–82), a Spanish Cistercian friar from the entourage of Alexander VII and later Bishop of Vigevano.[81] A versatile cleric, holding philosophical views close to those of Descartes, Caramuel was an amateur architect,[82] as can be seen both from his treatise on architecture and from his façade of the cathedral at Vigevano, his only known architectural design.[83] His *Arquitectura civil recta, y obliqua* (1678)[84] is based on Villalpando and also, possibly, on Ricci, but comes to quite different conclusions. Starting with a '*Tratado proemial*' on Solomon's Temple, and following with seven other 'treatises', Caramuel's work is to a large degree a compilation from earlier literature and has on occasion been subjected to severe criticism.[85] This '*Tratado proemial*' follows Villalpando in text and illustrations but Caramuel makes bold to have his description of the Escorial follow immediately on the reconstructions of Solomon's Temple. In the seven treatises he expounds, in a manner reminiscent of Vincenzo Scamozzi, a completely cerebral conception of architecture. In his first treatise he goes far beyond Vitruvius in the qualifications he requires from the professional architect; treatises 2–4 deal with arithmetic, logarithms and geometry, while treatise 5 contains his theory of architecture proper which he calls '*Arquitectura recta*'. He defines the Vitruvian categories as '*Comodidad*', '*Hermosura*' and '*Perpetuidad*', giving precedence to the first of these.[86] His hierarchy shows obvious French influence. He proceeds from the notion of the primal hut, quoting examples from the West Indian colonies.[87] His theory of the Orders is based on Vignola, but, like Ricci, he increases their number and arrives at a total of eleven, among them an '*orden Gothico*', symptomatic of a positive attitude towards Gothic architecture, which evidently inspired Guarini's '*ordine Gotico*'.[88]

Caramuel's originality lies in the '*Arquitectura obliqua*' discussed in treatise 6. He sees this as a new form of art, an eighth 'liberal art', a tenth Muse, philosophically based on *logica obliqua* and equated with rhetorical devices.[89] '*Arquitectura recta*' is conventional building, according to the rules of straight lines and right angles. *Arquitectura obliqua* is 'to build wrongly, without observing the laws and precepts of art. It is to build walls which match well with other walls with which they create an oblique angle.'[90] He quotes his façade at Vigevano as an example, and sets out the rules of this *arquitectura obliqua*, in effect of Baroque architecture, to show that one can make mistakes in this field just as in *arquitectura recta*. *Arquitectura obliqua* has for him equal validity and represents a God-given principle; he calls God the '*primer Arquitecto*', referring to the 'oblique' ellipsoid paths of the sun and of the signs of the zodiac which God has laid down. In order to arrive at the laws of this 'oblique' architecture, he applies the methods of projection of descriptive geometry (*Plate 138*), regarding the ellipse as a projection of the circle. His crucial step was to attempt to transfer the laws of architectural drawing – the representation of three-dimensional space on a two-dimensional plane – back to space itself. In order to make an elliptical arena appear circular from a central observation point, he proposes making corresponding corrections to the architectural members – the columns become increasingly elongated in section the farther away they are from the observer, i.e. the shaft becomes ellipsoid.[91] Applying this quasi-reversal of the projection process to Bernini's colonnades of St Peter's, he proposes, in an excess of didactic zeal, that the columns should be progressively elongated from the outside to the inside, as regarded from an ideal viewpoint, in order to appear of equal size (*Plate 139*).[92] Measurements taken of the colonnades have shown that Bernini had taken some account of the considerations that Caramuel later expounded.[93]

When it comes to the design of balusters on staircases and other sloping features Caramuel specifies that the gradient be taken into account in their ornamentation – a suggestion adopted by Juvarra and others. He also deals in depth with the problem of entasis, a phenomenon he ultimately seeks to justify from the Bible.[94]

Caramuel regarded architecture as a playground for the laws of optics. Like that of Teofilo Gallaccini, this is a Baroque attitude, but taken to its logical conclusion leads to a deformation of all architectural members and the denial of all absolute proportions. Architects such as Guarino Guarini and Jacques-François Blondel, otherwise so different from one another, were thus united in rejecting Caramuel's ideas. Put in a nutshell, their absurdity lay in the attempt to turn the Baroque conception of an image as space into a conception of space as an image.

Caramuel's work had little impact, although his ideas recur in the fifth volume of a *Compendio Matemático* (1709–15) by Tomás Vicente Tosca (1651–1725), the theologian and mathematician from Valencia.[95] Tosca shares Caramuel's positive assessment of Gothic architecture and gives a pragmatic definition of *arquitectura obliqua* as follows: '*Arquitectura obliqua* erects its structures on sloping sites or in arcades and gateways which run in other than a straight line, or in circular or elliptical temples.'[96] A treatise by Juan García Berruguilla (1747) contains basic information for architects on mathematics, geometry and building construction, and makes the remarkable claim – seventy years after Carmuel – to be the first source to treat of *arquitectura obliqua*.[97] It is only one of many such technical manuals on building.

From the sixteenth century onwards a number of compilations of urban building ordinances were published in Spain which appealed for justification to architectural theory, the best-known being those by Juan de Torija[98] and Teodoro Ardemans (1664–1726).[99] These ordinances remained in force well into the nineteenth century. Ardemans uses the whole gamut of Vitruvian concepts and produces an intellectualised work in the spirit of the Enlightenment. The extremely practical instructions that he gives extend to such questions as rulings on permitted building heights and arrangements for bullfights in the Plaza Mayor.

The most important example of the Enlightenment view of architecture in Spain is a treatise by the Neo-classical architect Diego de Villanueva (1715–74), director of the Academia de S. Fernando (founded in 1752), published in 1766.[100] Villanueva had previously published a Spanish edition of Vignola in 1764. His treatise reflects the argument that had arisen between two Neo-classical factions in his Academy, one led by Ventura Rodríguez, the other by the Villanueva brothers, each group accusing the other of being reactionary and technically incompetent. Villanueva was well read in the modern architectural literature of France, and had a desire to break the dominance of the French.[101] He refers to Laugier, Lodoli and Algarotti, but criticises their excessive dogmatism. By admitting only the validity of the three Greek orders, he returns to the position of Fréart de Chambray (1650), as Robert Morris had done in England in 1728. He is as critical of Baroque and Rococo, in the persons of Borromini and Meissonier, as he is of the *'Retableros de las Provincias'*.[102]

Villanueva advocates a modified functionalism, and his vocabulary – *'conveniencia'*, *'regularidad'*, *'comodidad en una distribución graciosa'*, *'buen gusto'*, etc.[103] – is that of contemporary French architecture. It is pure Neo-classicism when we read of *'grandeza, y simplicidad, que forma su caracter especial'*,[104] and when, in the manner of Lodoli, he urges the imitation of natural principles (*'imitar, y mostrar'*).[105] His treatise contains no original views but is an inconclusive compilation of the ideas of others. By spurning its Spanish background, his work ironically leaves a petty, provincial impression – in fact, his approach is a typical manifestation of Bourbon rule in Spain.

Another work in the Neo-classical tradition is the eighteen-volume travel book of Antonio Ponz, a friend of the Villanueva brothers. Published in successive volumes and often reprinted, Ponz's *Viage de España* is a kind of inventory of Spanish architecture seen through the eyes of a Neo-classicist.[106]

From the eighteenth century onwards Spanish architecture, and the theory relating to it, became increasingly dominated by that of France and Italy, and the great originality it had enjoyed in the sixteenth and seventeenth centuries, with its impact on the rest of Europe, passed into oblivion. Not until the second half of the nineteenth century, and in the twentieth, did Spain rediscover her proud national tradition.

19. Developments in England from the sixteenth to the eighteenth century

Although, strictly speaking, England's contribution to architectural theory dates only from the beginning of the eighteenth century, it immediately acquired a position of virtual dominance in Europe. The needs of the sixteenth and seventeenth centuries were met by translations and adaptations of foreign works, chiefly Italian,[1] although we should not overlook the contribution of English theorists themselves during this period.

A preliminary glance must be devoted to a work devoted to the ideal state, which gave its name to this genre of speculation which was always more: Thomas More's (1478–1535) *Utopia*; for Utopia naturally embraces considerations of architecture and town-planning. Dedicated to More's friend Erasmus,[2] and written and published (1516) before More embarked on his dramatic political career, it is cast in the form of an imaginary voyage around the world by a Portuguese called Raphael Hythloday, grafted onto the historical voyages of Amerigo Vespucci, in the course of which he comes to the island of Utopia, a country easily recognised as England. More's political views do not concern us here, but only the ideas about architecture that emerge from them.

More envisages an overall plan for 54 towns distributed throughout his island of Utopia, all to the same pattern and all looking alike; the capital was to be Amaurotum on the Anydros, i.e. London on the Thames.[3] There is no private ownership of land, and people are constantly moving from the town to farmsteads and vice versa; no private life is permitted, and town dwellings are exchanged by lot every ten years. Amaurotum itself is described as lying on a gentle slope, with an almost square layout. This reminds one of Dürer's work on civil fortifications published ten years later (1527), and since the name of Vespucci occurs in More's story, one may perhaps suspect the influence of the pre-Columbian town plans of Central America,[4] on More as on Dürer. Another possible model is that of the Roman *castrum*.

The streets are wide, protected from the wind and symmetrically laid out with the needs of traffic in mind; the houses, which have three storeys and flat roofs, are grouped in large blocks, the courtyards taking the form of gardens. No house is locked. This design is attributed to Utopos, founder of the state of Utopia, and the architecture is thus seen as an immediate expression of the ideal state. The repetition of a fixed pattern corresponds to the book's conception of a socialist theory. Frontispieces of the early editions – the work is not otherwise illustrated – are adorned with images of late Gothic cities which in no way reflect More's intentions.

The earliest English treatise on architecture in the strict sence is John Shute's *First and Chief Groundes of Architecture,*[5] published in 1563, the year of the author's death. In spite of its title, it amounts to little more than one of the numerous northern European pattern-books dealing with the Classical orders. Shute calls himself a painter and architect. In 1550 he was sent by the Duke of Northumberland to Italy to study the Classical monuments and modern Italian architecture, but his book betrays no first-hand knowledge of that country; in fact, it is an adaptation of Serlio's Book IV and Philander's edition of Vitruvius. A unique feature of the work, however, in its sixteenth-century context, is that Shute takes literally the analogy between the column and the human figure as propounded by Vitruvius and the writers of the Italian quattrocento, and adds a caryatid variant to his illustrations of each of the five Orders. His dedication to Queen Elizabeth I embodies 'organic' conceptions of the state and architecture, but he does not return to this in his text. His derivation of the five Orders from Noah's Ark, and his description of the Tower of Babel as the source of Hebrew and Greek architecture, show his attempt to reconcile a 'pagan' theory of architecture with the tradition of the Bible, as certain circles in the Counter-Reformation were urging at the time, and as Delorme also intended for the planned continuation of his *De l'architecture*.

From the early sixteenth century onwards numerous works on surveying and construction such as *The Art of Measuring* and *The Builders' Manual* were published in England, but these cannot be discussed here.[6]

The philosopher Francis Bacon (1561–1626) introduced extremely interesting ideas into architectural theory by bringing the mind of the scientist to bear on the subject. No. 45 of his *Essays* is called 'Of Building', and it opens with a forthright demand:

> Houses are built to live in, and not to look on; therefore let use be preferred before uniformity, except where both may be had. Leave the goodly fabrics and houses, for beauty alone, to the enchanted palaces of the poets.[7]

The most important consideration in architecture for Bacon is practical use – not for nothing has he been called a 'proto-functionalist'.[8] Aesthetic principles therefore take a back seat and he adopts an empirical position; that is, he rejects rules and the laws of geometric proportions, even daring to call Apelles and Dürer, who were concerned to adduce rules for the proportions of the human body, mere 'triflers'.[9] In his aesthetic relativism Bacon is to some extent a precursor of Claude Perrault with his 'arbitrary beauty'. He describes in detail a royal palace, the appearance and arrangement of which is determined by functional disposition of the rooms, and criticises the Vatican and the Escorial for their lack of usable space.[10]

The fragmentary treatise *The New Atlantis* (published in 1626) is Bacon's answer to More's *Utopia* of a hundred years earlier,[11] and describes an island in the Pacific called Bensalem, which turns out to be a huge research laboratory in which the forces of Nature are harnessed and the evolution of modern civilisation is predicted in detail. Bacon did not reach the stage of describing how the architecture of his society of the future would look, but his allusion to Solomon, and the reference to his lost writings, suggests that he tried to reconcile traditional theories of architecture with his new functionalist ideas. At the end of the treatise he describes a museum devoted to inventions and inventors with fine, spacious halls set round with columns, which reads like an anticipation of the eighteenth century.

Whereas Bacon's functionalist approach has its roots in the natural sciences, the years after 1600 saw a change of direction in English theory and practice, with a turn towards Italy and a first phase of Palladianism, represented by Inigo Jones (1573–1652). Through his two journeys to Italy, in 1601 and 1613–14, the second of them undertaken in the company of Thomas Howard, 2nd Earl of Arundel,[12] an important patron of the arts, Jones acquired an extensive knowledge of Classical and modern architecture which provided the foundation for his own work.[13] Particularly important for him were the works of Palladio and his encounter with the aged Vincenzo Scamozzi. A treatise based on Palladio's *Quattro libri*, which he planned with his pupil John Webb, did not progress beyond preparatory drawings.[14] His strict approach is illustrated by a comment in his Italian sketchbook which expresses a Palladian rejection of the arbitrariness of Mannerist architecture, concluding with the observation that 'in architecture ye outward ornaments oft [ought] to be solid, proporsionable according to the rulles, masculine and unaffected.'[15] This attitude remained fundamental to Jones's own designs, and he even projected it onto prehistoric times, as is shown by his discussion of Stonehenge, published in a version revised by John Webb in 1655.[16] Jones declared Stonehenge to be Roman, and saw in it the harmonious proportions of four superimposed equilateral triangles, which led him to produce a reconstruction corresponding in plan to that of the Antique theatre produced by Palladio for Daniele Barbaro's edition of Vitruvius.[17] Bacon and Inigo Jones thus stand as opposing spokesmen for on the one hand a relativist, on the other a normative aesthetic of architecture.

Between the positions of Bacon and Inigo Jones and acquainted with both of them, stands the diplomat and amateur architect Sir Henry Wotton (1568–1639). Wotton had gained an extensive knowledge of European, and particularly Palladian, architecture in the course of an extensive educational journey through Europe and during his three lengthy periods as English ambassador in Venice. He wrote his treatise *The Elements of Architecture* (1624) as an amateur, to guide potential aristocratic builders in their judgements.[18] It was probably Wotton who arranged for Inigo Jones to acquire a large group of Palladio's drawings, which later came into the possession of Lord Burlington and is now in the possession of the Royal Institute of British Architects.

Wotton's slim volume, without illustrations, is written in a characteristically English style, combining modesty, humour and common sense, and reveals a considerable knowledge of the literature of the subject, which he discusses with critical sympathy. As he sees it, architecture derives from natural principles; in this, as in his view 'that the Place of every part is to be determined by the Use',[19] he shows his instinctive closeness to Bacon. Seeing architecture as an imitation of Nature, he emphasises the need to take climatic, regional and national considerations into account.[20] He betrays the crucial influence of Alberti in regarding ornament as secondary, and also claiming for architecture a 'secret Harmony in the Proportions'.[21] Starting from Renaissance concepts of basic geometric figures, he praises the circle as a 'universall Forme' but then concedes, with characteristic English pragmatism, that the circle 'is in truth a very unprofitable Figure in private Fabriques'.[22] His conception of architecture is organic, and time and again he compares a building to the functions of the human body. After putting forward a number of constructional theorems, he arrives at a rejection of the Gothic pointed arch on account of its 'naturall imbecility'. Indeed, he would ban the Gothic style from architecture altogether,[23] his arguments anticipating in this those of Paolo Frisi in his essay of 1766.

The second part of Wotton's work is devoted to the specific requirements of the English house. He defines the house as a 'Theater of Hospitality' and a 'kinde of private Princedome'.[24] Taking ornament to mean the embellishment of a house, with sculpture and painting, he has brief sections on these. Another form of ornament is for him the garden, which he believes should offer a contrast to the building: 'For as Fabriques should bee regular, so Gardens should be irregular, or at least cast into a very wilde

Regularitie.'[25] As one of the first to insist on the role of the beholder in the considerations governing design of a garden, he is a precursor of the English landscape garden, which was designed to be viewed as a series of pictures.

Finally, Wotton challenges Vitruvius's six fundamental principles of architecture, maintaining that *ordinatio* and *dispositio* are not principles at all but stages of the process of design;[26] for the remaining four concepts (*Eurythmia, Symmetria, Decor, Distributio*) he provides succinct definitions, e.g.: 'Decor is the keeping of a due respect betweene the Inhabitant, and the Habitation'.[27] In his conclusion he touches on national differences in interior decoration – which is what he means by ornament – and describes his own activity as a contribution to 'a kinde of Morall Architecture,'[28] thus paving the way, in his reference to ethics, for views that came to predominate in England in the eighteenth century. Translated into several languages and reprinted a number of times, Wotton's treatise may be regarded as the first original English work on architectural theory. Its quality of moral seriousness tempered by ironical pragmatism also shines through his famous remark, which almost cost him his diplomatic career: 'An ambassador is an honest man sent to lie abroad for the good of his country.'

Few works of any significance appeared in England in the seventeenth century after Wotton. There were belated translations and truncated or misconstrued versions of the great Italian treatises, some of them via French or Dutch editions.[29] One such translation, of Fréart de Chambray's *Parallèle* (1750), was made by the diarist John Evelyn (1620–1706), botanist and secretary of the Royal Society, who appended to his work his own 'Account of Architects and Architecture'.[30] Evelyn had made a tour through France and Italy from 1644 to 1646, which he recorded at length in his diaries.[31] His 'Account' refers repeatedly to Wotton, but Evelyn also contradicts him on occasion. The first edition was dedicated to Charles II, whom Evelyn sought to advise in architectural matters, as Vitruvius had advised the Emperor Octavian. He makes the interesting remark that he regarded building as the 'proper and natural consequent' of his work as a horticulturalist. He also hoped, he said, that through the king's intervention the 'ungouvernable enormities' of the sprawling London suburbs could be got rid of.[32]

Starting with definitions of concepts mostly taken from Vitruvius, Evelyn then appraises other authorities, and finally makes his own observations. He adopts his friend Wotton's reduction in the number of Vitruvius' principles, but defines *decor* in the Vitruvian way, in opposition to Wotton, whom he does not, however, mention by name:

> Decor, which is not only where the Inhabitant, and habitation suite, seeing that is many times accidental; but where a Building, and particularly the Ornaments thereof, become the station, and occasion, as Vitruvius expresly shews in appropriating the several Orders to their natural affections.[33]

Evelyn apparently sensed a danger that the indivisibility of architecture and ornament presupposed by Vitruvius's definition of *decor* might fall apart as it does in Alberti, who may well in his turn have influenced Wotton.

In the first edition of his work Evelyn already referred to 'our busie and Gothic triflings in the Compositions of the Five Orders' which were responsible for 'absurdities in our modern structures'.[34] But only in later editions (1697 and 1707), which are dedicated to Wren, did he add his historical appraisal of the Gothic style – the influence of his discussion with Wren is evident – the 'fantastical and licentious Manner' of which he attributed to the Arabs and the Moors.[35] This is the so-called 'Saracen' theory of the origin of Gothic, which Wren espoused.

Also to be mentioned is an unfinished embryonic treatise, unpublished during the author's lifetime, by Sir Roger Pratt (1620–84), a friend of Evelyn's, with whom he shared lodgings in Rome (in 1644–45).[36] Pratt was an aristocratic amateur architect whose few executed buildings were in the past generally attributed to Inigo Jones. His jottings, not published until 1928, regard architecture from the point of view of the beholder, and show him attempting to systematise the process of perception, i.e. to plot how the observer's eyes roam over the building before him. This inevitably raises the question of how architecture should be 'read'. Almost inevitably he starts from the premise that a building, especially its façade, 'expresses' something which is there to be perceived: 'The fronts of Fabrickes to be chiefly considered, as those which are set to the most to expresse the Noblenesse and Majesty of them (6 February 1672)'.[37] This is an extremely interesting anticipation of the way in which architecture was understood in the eighteenth century, in which the criteria of 'nobility' and 'grandeur' are tied to perception. It is not surprising to find Pratt, in the wake of Bacon, emphasising functional and financial considerations; more remarkable is his insistence that architects should be acquainted with 'the natures, and qualities of all the most usual sort of materials'.[38] Pratt also reveals the beginnings of a comparative historical approach to architecture which anticipates Wren. An important source for him was Villalpando's commentary on Ezekiel, a copy of which he had in his library.[39]

Shortly before Evelyn's translation of Fréart there appeared two treatises by Balthasar Gerbier (1591–1667),[40] a Huguenot painter and architect, who combined an admiration for Inigo Jones with functionalist views based on Bacon and Wotton, and at the same time stated a preference for Gothic flying buttresses over the engaged columns of the Renaissance. But Gerbier's work amounts to little more than a largely unsystematic handbook for conservative would-be builders.

Architectural theory in seventeenth- and early eighteenth-century England suffers from the fact that none of the great architects – neither Inigo Jones, Wren, Vanbrugh nor Hawksmoor – has left more than a few scattered thoughts on the subject. English Baroque architecture, represented above all by Vanbrugh and Hawksmoor, is, like Italian Baroque architecture (with the exception of Guarini's later and rather one-sided *Architettura civile*), devoid of systematic theoretical foundation.

Yet it can hardly be said that Christopher Wren (1632–1723) was uninterested in theoretical matters.[41] The fact that he proceeded from mathematics and the natural sciences to architecture would virtually have predestined him to become the author of a fundamental theory of it, and such written fragments as have survived bear witness to the superior intellect that he did indeed bring to bear on the task. But his writings and letters were only published in the eighteenth century, and were chiefly exploited for biographical ends.[42] His four so-called *Tracts* and his *Discourse on Architecture* may be regarded as preliminary studies for a comprehensive theory of architecture.[43]

The opening sentence of Wren's first Tract shows how much wider his approach is than that of standard handbooks: 'Architecture has its Political Use; publick Buildings being the Ornament of a Country; it establishes a Nation, draws People and Commerce.'[44] He believes in the validity for architecture of the laws of Nature, and in timeless principles of architecture taking over Vitruvius's principles of 'Beauty, Firmness, and Convenience', and adding, like the scientist he was: 'the first two depend upon geometrical Reasons of Opticks and Staticks; the third only makes the Variety.'[45] He is opposed to laying down fixed rules for the proportions of the Classical orders. Following Claude Perrault, whom he may well have met during his visit to Paris in 1665, he distinguishes two kinds of beauty, which he calls 'natural' and 'customary'. 'Natural' beauty, which corresponds to Perrault's 'positive' beauty, derives from geometry, whereas 'customary' beauty – Perrault's 'arbitrary' beauty – is the product of sense perception.[46] One difference from Perrault is that Wren, not quite consistently, assigns proportion to the field of natural beauty, without however saying that it can be applied without further ado to the Orders. He permits the architect a certain latitude in his measurements, but then immediately restricts this by maintaining that 'the true Test is natural or Geometrical Beauty.'[47] With his characteristic flexibility of mind, Wren occupies an intermediate position between Perrault and Blondel.

In his theoretical ideas Wren was strongly influenced by Villalpando's reconstruction of Solomon's Temple (1604), to which he repeatedly refers. Like Villalpando and Caramuel (1678), he adds to the number of the Graeco-Roman Orders by delving further back in history, which leads him to posit a 'Tyrian' order, as an early stage of Doric.[48] Like Fischer von Erlach a little later, he makes attempts at reconstructing the great buildings of Antiquity, such as the Temple of Diana at Ephesus, the Mausoleum at Halicarnassus and the Monument of Porsenna, King of the Etruscans, the last-named of which he designates 'Tyrian Architecture'.[49] He may have thought that his 'Tyrian' order had been applied to Solomon's Temple, but he scorned Villalpando's derivation of the Corinthian order from the Salomonic order used on the Temple as 'meer fancy'.[50]

In his *Discourse on Architecture* Wren gives a historical survey in which his conception of the political aspects of architecture becomes increasingly clear. Thus he rejects an interpretation of the pyramids of Egypt as simply monuments to the fame of the Pharaohs, and suspects 'reasons of state' behind their construction, namely the need to provide employment for large numbers of men 'in that which requir'd no great skill.'[51]

It is only possible to make passing mention of the vital role that Wren played in the reconstruction of London after the Great Fire of 1666.[52] Highly relevant to our subject, however, is his attitude to Gothic architecture, for which, unlike Wotton and his friend John Evelyn, he had great sympathy. This sympathy is especially in evidence in his report of 1713 on the restoration of Westminster Abbey.[53] His view of architecture is based on his understanding of history. Thus he proposed that the concept of the Gothic style that had been so negatively advanced above all by the Italians, be replaced by that of the 'Saracen style', which would be historically more accurate. 'They [i.e. the Saracens] were Zealots in their Religion,' he wrote,

> and where-ever they conquered (which was with amazing Rapidity) erected Mosques and Caravansara's in Haste; which obliged them to fall into another Way of Building; for they built their Mosques round, disliking the Christian Form of a Cross; the old Quarries whence the Ancients took their large Blocks of Marble for whole Columns and Architraves, were neglected, and they thought both impertinent. Their Carriage was by Camels, therefore their Buildings were fitted for small Stones, and Columns of their own Fancy, consisting of many

Pieces; and their Arches were pointed without Keystones, which they thought too heavy. The Reasons were the same in our Northern Climates, abounding in Free-Stone, but wanting Marble.[54]

According to Wren, this 'Saracen' style was spread by the Crusaders to the whole of Europe, especially France – an historically authentic style on which he expresses no critical judgement. For Westminster Abbey he therefore proposes that a tower be built 'according to the original Intention of the Architect', and he puts forward a design 'in the Gothick Form, and of a style with the rest of the Structure, which I would strictly adhere to, throughout the whole Intention; to deviate from the Old Form, would be to run into a disagreeable Mixture, which no Person of a good Taste could relish.'[55] His own designs for Westminster Abbey conform to this principle.[56] Wren adopts here, with unusual clarity, an historical standpoint which also helps to explain the stylistic variations in his designs for St Paul's Cathedral. Here too lie the roots of the historical eclecticism which characterises the finished church – a synthesis of elements taken from Bramante (the drum of the dome), Maderno (articulation of the façade), Perrault (double columns of the façade), Borromini (west towers) and Pietro da Cortona (transept porticos).

These brief remarks will suffice to show that Wren's failure to write his treatise is one of the most lamentable omissions in the history of architectural theory.

To assess the theoretical ideas of Sir John Vanbrugh (1664–1728) and Nicholas Hawksmoor (1661–1736) we have to rely on a handful of memoranda and letters.[57] In 1711 Wren and Vanbrugh submitted parallel memoranda on the construction of the Fifty New Churches of London,[58] which show similar basic attitudes, but with a return on the part of Vanbrugh to Alberti's views on ecclesiastical architecture.[59] Vanbrugh saw not only the religious function of church buildings but also their role as 'Monuments to Posterity', which should be a 'Credit to the Nation',[60] and he demanded that they should have both the 'necessary dispositions in the usefull part of the Fabrick' and 'Grace and Beauty' in their appearance. 'Grace' consisted for him in 'a plain but Just and Noble Stile', whilst a 'Gayety of Ornaments' he considered should be left for other buildings, such as sumptuous palaces.[61]

The rules – derived exclusively from Alberti – which Vanbrugh and Hawskmoor formulate for church architecture, they put into practice in their own buildings in London. Churches should be free-standing – 'insulate' is Vanbrugh's word – so as to emphasise their dignity and ensure them a favourable position in the city as a whole; they should have a portico, both for practical purposes and to add solemn splendour to the building, and bold, tall spires. Bodies should not be buried in the churches themselves but in adjoining architecturally structured cemeteries in which 'Lofty and Noble Mausoleums' should be erected. Vanbrugh's and Hawksmoor's churches, which were also conceived as monuments to the pious Queen Anne, have themselves the character of monuments; on St George's, Bloomsbury, for instance, Hawksmoor turns Wren's reconstruction of the Mausoleum at Halicarnassus[62] into a spire.

Hawksmoor, to a greater extent than Vanbrugh, consciously set himself in the tradition of the Italian Renaissance and Baroque, although he had no more been to Italy than Vanbrugh. This aspiration is revealed by Hawksmoor's proposal for the erection of an obelisk in 1724,[63] where he quotes examples from Rome in support of his project (it was never executed). A letter to the Dean of Westminster (1734–35), which is a kind of continuation of Wren's report of 1713, is an interesting document in the context of the contemporary discussion of Gothic architecture.[64] Like Wren, Hawksmoor sought to give Gothic historical legitimacy but he was sceptical of the 'Saracen theory', which he specifically attributes to Evelyn and Wren. 'What the people call in generall (and without distinction) Gothick',[65] he attempts to differentiate by identifying the various stylistic stages involved, rejecting a concept of Gothic that would subsume the excessive freedom of the contemporary Italians, especially Borromini, and the Islamic architecture of Spain. Interestingly enough, he identifies as a style the Dietterlin 'manner of building' though he ridicules a 'disposition of Antient building into Masquarade'.[66] He shares with Wren the view that, in the interests of inner unity, a building begun in the Gothic style can only be completed in that style, and recounts his own solutions of this task. This principle of stylistic conformity links both Wren and Hawksmoor to the arguments that arose in Italy in the sixteenth century from the competitions for the completion of the façade of S. Petronio in Bologna.[67]

Hawksmoor's dissociation of himself from other concepts of Gothic was directed mainly against the Earl of Shaftesbury (1671–1713), who, in his *Characteristicks* (1711) and the *Letter concerning the Art and Science of Design* (1712), had opened the attack on English Baroque architecture, which he dubbed 'Gothic'. Shaftesbury stood for the doctrine of the superiority of the Greeks, identifying them with the notion of simplicity, which was later to exert such a great influence on Winckelmann.[68] This appeal to the Greeks fell on fertile soil, since at this time the English considered themselves the descendants not only of the Romans and the Venetians but also of the Greeks, and even of the Trojans.[69] Shaftesbury called for a national architecture, the criteria of which emerge from a discussion of Baroque: 'Britain has her models yet to seek, her scale and standards to form with deliberation and good choice.'[70] As Vanbrugh's postulate of a 'plain but Just and Noble Style' for church buildings shows, English Baroque was fully imbued with classical urges, but a more dogmatically-minded generation was subsequently no longer prepared to exercise such historical tolerance and eclectic artistic freedom where earlier styles were concerned.

Shaftesbury's moral philosophy drew attention to the Greeks in general, but little was known at the beginning of the eighteenth century about their architecture. The second generation of Whig aristocratic landowners then channelled this classicising interest in the direction of Palladio, seeing a parallel between their own ideas of a republican oligarchy and the political system in the Republic of Venice, where Palladio had worked. In terms of cultural outlook the rise of Palladianism in the second decade of the eighteenth century can be linked with the rise of freemasonry. The first Grand Lodge was founded in London in 1717. In 1723 James Anderson assembled the principles of masonry in his *Book of Constitutions*, in which the history of the freemasonry is identified with a fictitious history of architecture, stretching from the Tabernacle and the Temple of Jerusalem, through 'Grand Masters' such as Vitruvius, Palladio and Inigo Jones, down to Colen Campbell and Lord Burlington.[71] A number of Palladians were indeed freemasons. As Inigo Jones belongs to the first phase of English Palladianism, so the 'Inigo Jones Revival' became an important factor in the Palladianism of the eighteenth century. For the first time in its history England, as befitted its role as a great power, saw itself as a model for the world in the field of architecture.

In the first instance, therefore, the publications of the Palladians amount to a model compendium of English architecture, and are only secondarily concerned with Palladio himself. John Thorpe and other architects had compiled sketchbooks of English buildings from the sixteenth century onwards,[72] and in 1707 Johannes Kip and Leonard Knyff, two Dutchmen working in England, produced a collection of bird's-eye views of country houses entitled *Britannia Illustrata*,[73] but not until the Palladians did the sense of national destiny become linked to one particular style.

The first and most important publication of the English Palladians is the three-volume *Vitruvius Britannicus* (1715–25)[74] by Colen Campbell (1676–1729). Dedicated to King George I, this is a collection of plates designed to prove that contemporary English architecture was heir to the architecture of Antiquity and the Renaissance. The 'Antiques', according to the manifesto-like introduction, 'are out of the Question', whereas the architects of the Italian Renaissance receive fulsome praise, Palladio being hailed as their foremost figure, and his works as the *ne plus ultra* of architecture.[75] In Campbell's view the Italians lost their 'exquisite Taste of Building' and 'Antique Simplicity' in the course of the seventeenth century, and he rejects the works of Bernini, Fontana and Borromini as 'Gothick' on account of their 'capricious Ornaments'[76] – another example of the pejorative use of the term Gothic rebutted by Wren and Hawksmoor. He raises Inigo Jones to the status of an English Palladio, and declares Inigo's design for the Palace of Whitehall to be beyond compare. Campbell does not give a systematic account of the architectural criteria that he and his fellow-Palladians have adopted, but allows them to emerge from his comments on the individual plates.

Thus he describes Inigo Jones's Banqueting House in Whitehall as representing a union of 'Strength with Politeness, Ornament with Simplicity, Beauty with Majesty', and calls its interior 'without Dispute, the first Room in the World'.[77] His first plates confront St Paul's Cathedral with St Peter's in Rome, which he immediately follows with his own design for a church in Lincoln's Inn Fields, based on the square and the circle, 'the most perfect Figures', and describes as 'most conformable to the Simplicity of the Ancients'.[78] Simplicity, indeed, is Campbell's first and foremost stipulation.

The only contemporary architect regarded by Campbell as outstanding was Vanbrugh – and that rather for political than aesthetic reasons – but Campbell also manages to focus his spotlight on his own designs. Wanstead House in Essex, which was built to his plans, did indeed become one of the prime models for the English Palladian country house. It was commissioned by Sir Richard Child, who was born into a Tory family, but joined the Whigs and signalled his change of allegiance with his commission to Campbell.[79] The latter published all three stages of his design for Wanstead.[80] The first (Wanstead I) consists of a simple block-like structure with a portico, reminiscent of Palladio's Villa Foscari in Malcontenta; the second (Wanstead II) has become a graduated design, the two wings being lower than the centre, with a central cupola over the hall, in the manner of Vanbrugh's Castle Howard (this design, minus the cupola, was executed, but demolished in 1822); the third (Wanstead III) has tower corner projections but no cupola (*Plates 140–42*).[81] The portico is the vital constant of all three designs, and Campbell emphasises the fact that it is 'a just Hexastyle, the first yet practised in this manner in the Kingdom'.[82]

The designs for country houses acquired increasing importance in the *Vitruvius Britannicus*. They exemplified the Palladian style adopted by the landed Whig gentry, and the book served to spread their fame to the continent of Europe. Campbell seeks to go one better than Palladio, either misunderstanding him in the process, consciously or otherwise, or 'improving' on him. In his comments on Houghton Hall, designed for the Whig Prime Minister Robert Walpole, he claims to have set out 'to introduce the Temple Beauties in a private Building',[83] apparently meaning by 'temple beauties' the giant engaged Composite Order of the façade and its adornment with a pediment, but overlooking the fact that Palladio himself had reintroduced temple architecture to domestic architecture. Of his design for Mereworth in Kent he maintains that he had no intention of improving on Palladio's Villa Rotonda,[84] yet the manner in which he lists the functions of each room suggests quite the opposite. He has turned Palladio's circular project into an axial design culminating in the very English Great Gallery, and it is only for aesthetic effect that the porticos of the abandoned transverse axis are retained in the form of balcony-like loggias.

The third volume of *Vitruvius Britannicus* contains a large number of bird's-eye views, together with garden plans, which clearly reflects the Palladian interest in matching architecture with landscape.

The work's remarkable success can be gauged from the rapidity with which the number of subscribers arose – from around 300 for the first volume to around 900 for the third – and later publications tried to capitalise on this success by calling themselves 'continuations' of *Vitruvius Britannicus*. In 1739, for instance, a 'fourth' volume was produced by J. Badeslade and J. Rocque,[85] consisting almost entirely of country houses and large gardens, though not all the buildings illustrated can be called Palladian. Charming as the plates in this volume are, it apparently only reached a very limited public, for today a mere four copies are known to be extant. Contemporaries ignored it, and in 1767 two architects, John Woolfe and James Gandon, published a rival 'fourth' volume of the *Vitruvius Britannicus*,[86] stating it as their conviction 'that architecture was brought to as great a point of perfection in this kingdom in the eighteenth century, as ever was known to be among the Greeks and the Romans', and that 'we far surpassed our contemporaries of every other country.'[87] Without propounding any programme of their own, the authors of this work acknowledge Campbell as their model, and their plates consist entirely of English Palladian or Neo-classical buildings, above all country houses, though without their gardens. The same is true of Woolfe's and Gandon's 'fifth' volume (1771),[88] in which, however, not all the chosen illustrations exemplify a consistent style.[89]

But neither Woolfe and Gandon nor George Richardson, who published two more volumes of a *New Vitruvius Britannicus* between 1802 and 1808,[90] could equal Campbell's success. Richardson gives it as his aim to display 'the taste and science of the English nation in its style of architecture, at the close of the eighteenth century.'[91] Concerned with improvements in the 'elegancies', as he calls them, he concentrates exclusively on the English country house in all its stylistic variations; Campbell's Palladian bias is abandoned.

Vitruvius Britannicus, the publication of which was strung out in this way over almost a century, became the most important source of information about English architecture for the continent of Europe and for America. The Palladianism from which Campbell took his inspiration had the success it did because, at that moment, he was able to raise a style promoted by a small group of fellow-Palladians to the status of an English national style.

It was Campbell who converted one of the great peers of the day to the cause of Palladianism – Richard Boyle, 3rd Earl of Burlington (1694–1753), who became one of Campbell's patrons and also an architect himself.[92] In 1714–15 Burlington made the customary Grand Tour, but developed no particular predilection for Palladio, and only on the publication of the first volume of Campbell's work in 1715 after his return to England did he succumb to the attractions of Palladianism. Embarking on a modest architectural career of his own, initially in Campbell's shadow, Burlington turned to William Kent (1685–1748), at that time a painter in Rome, and made him his protégé – though it quickly became obvious that Kent's abilities far exceeded those of his illustrious patron.[93]

In 1719 Burlington returned to Italy, this time with the aim of studying Palladio's works on the spot. In the course of his stay he discovered in the Villa Maser a large number of Palladio's drawings, which he succeeded in acquiring; he then added these to those of Inigo Jones to compile the largest known collection of Palladio's designs. It was his intention to publish the drawings in his possession but the only ones to appear were those of the Roman baths (1730).[94] In his brief preface, written in Italian, Burlington described his volume as 'a very opportune gift to our age, than which perhaps no other will ever show a greater applicability to costly buildings.'[95] He set out to direct English architecture into Palladian channels. His own buildings, such as Chiswick House and the Assembly Rooms in York, are programmatic embodiments of his sources and ideas, whereas William Kent managed to evolve his own language. At Burlington's behest Kent published Burlington's collection of drawings by Inigo Jones (1727),[96] whom he went so far as to describe as a disciple of Palladio, calling the two 'equal Proofs of the Superiority...to all others;'[97] He establishes the historical filiation by appending illustrations of Palladio's church of S. Giorgio Maggiore in Venice and of a number of Burlington's projects.

Burlington was a close friend of the poet Alexander Pope (1688–1744), who, together with Shaftesbury, promoted the values of a new classicism,[98] both in his writings and in the design of his villa at Twickenham. His *Essay on Criticism* (1711) propounds the classical orientation of his views, while in *The Temple of Fame* (1715) he describes his vision of a temple with four façades – Greek ('somptuous'), Assyro-Persian ('glorious'), Egyptian ('impressive') and Gothic ('o'er-wrought with ornaments of barb'rous Pride'). These characterisations are close to the ideas of *caractère* developed in France a generation later by Jacques-François Blondel. After he moved to Twickenham in 1718, his *villa suburbana*, and above all its garden, exercised a considerable influence. In his *Epistle to Lord Burlington* (1731),[99] prompted by Burlington's *Fabbriche antiche* of the previous year, he assembled his ideas for the design of houses and gardens, issuing a warning against the rigidity produced by an over-zealous adherence to Palladianism.

Apart from a version of Book I by Godfrey Richards in 1663,[100] no complete English translation of Palladio's *Quattro libri* was made, strangely enough, in either the sixteenth or the seventeenth century – and Richards's book was in fact a version of Pierre Le Muet's *Règle de cinq ordres* (1645), which is only partly based on Palladio. The first complete English translation of Palladio was made by Giacomo Leoni (1686–1746), a Venetian who left Italy as a young man, had found his way by 1708 to the Palatine court at Düsseldorf, and was involved in the building of the Palace of Bensberg under Matteo Alberti.[101] A manuscript dated 1708, now in the library of McGill

University in Montreal,[102] in which he discusses Palladio's theory of the Orders and the mathematical knowledge required by engineers, shows that Leoni already concerned himself with such matters in Düsseldorf, while his *Compendious Directions for Builders* (1713), dedicated to Duke Henry of Kent,[103] proves that he must have been in England by this date. He apparently soon joined Colen Campbell's circle, and made Lord Burlington's acquaintance on the latter's return from his first journey to Italy in 1715. With the cooperation of Nicholas Dubois as translator and Bernard Picart as engraver, he quickly set about his edition of Palladio, the first volume of which appeared in 1716[104] – though bearing the date 1715, in order to pretend that it was published in the same year as Campbell's *Vitruvius Britannicus*.

Leoni took five years to complete his undertaking, and fulfilled at the same time a European need by adding to his version both the original Italian text and a French translation. His subtitle announced the future publication of 'Notes and Observations made by Inigo Jones', by which he evidently hoped to put the Inigo Jones revival to his own advantage, but permission was refused,[105] and Inigo's *Notes* did not appear until 1742.[106] Leoni tried to 'improve' Palladio's illustrations to meet contemporary taste; he turned Palladio's planar woodcuts into shaded, spatial engravings, provided frames for windows and doors that formerly had none, added Baroque armorial cartouches to pediments, and varied roof patterns to suit the vogue of the time. The dome of the Villa Rotonda, for instance, he perforated with eight oculi. Contemporaries such as Lord Burlington, committed to Palladianism in its strictest form, could not but regard Leoni's concessions to modern taste as sacrilege. This is also made clear by Isaac Ware in his more faithful edition of Palladio published in 1738, in which he accuses Leoni of having dared 'to alter even the graceful proportions prescribed by this great master' and to 'put in fanciful decorations of his own'.[107]

Yet despite this Leoni's importance in an English context must not be underestimated. In 1726 he published an English translation of Alberti, based, however, not on the Latin original of 1485 but on the Italian translation by Cosimo Bartoli (1550),[108] and this English version of Alberti, often reprinted, is still the standard edition for English readers.

Lord Burlington urged Colen Campbell to undertake a proper version of Palladio, but only the first book ever appeared (1728);[109] Campbell kept closer to Palladio's woodcuts, but in the second edition of 1729 he too added his own designs.[110]

After Campbell's death the publisher Benjamin Cole and the architect Edward Hoppus attempted to profit from the gap in the market by issuing a new edition of *Andrea Palladio's Architecture in Four Books* (1733–35),[111] Book I of which is simply plagiarised from Campbell, and Books II to IV adaptations of Leoni. The work is dedicated, with a certain impertinence, to Lord Burlington. Isaac Ware remarked that it 'is done with so little understanding, and so much negligence, that it cannot but give great offence to the judicious and be of very bad consequence in misleading the unskilful, into whose hands it may happen to fall.'[112]

Ware's own close translation of Palladio finally appeared in 1738,[113] also dedicated to Burlington, who, as Ware emphasised in the dedication, had revised it himself. He attaches great importance to having retained Palladio's measurements and proportions, and his engravings of Palladio's woodcuts are extremely reliable, despite being the wrong way round. Still the authoritative English edition, it was published, however, at a moment when English Palladianism had already passed its peak, and William Kent's vignette at the end of the work, with its Baroque allegory of the Classical orders, hangs like an ironical question-mark over Ware's sober and meticulous work.

Palladianism was the most successful architectural movement in England around the year 1730, but it was far from being the only one. The great Baroque architect Vanbrugh, for example, lived till 1728, Hawksmoor till 1736. James Gibbs (1682–1754) adopted certain Palladian features in his work, but is not to be classified as a Palladian – rather, he occupies an intermediate position between the Wren tradition, Italian Baroque Classicism, and Palladianism. A Tory and a Scot, he was the first architect of the day in England to receive his training in Italy, having worked in Carlo Fontana's office in Rome from 1703 to 1709.[114] His relationship to Campbell and Burlington's circle was strained, and when Campbell called the works of Bernini and Fontana 'affected' and 'licentious' in the introduction to his *Vitruvius Britannicus*,[115] it was probably Gibbs he wished to score off. Gibbs was appointed as one of the 'Surveyors' for the Fifty New Churches in London in 1713; the following year he conceived a plan for a work on architecture, which was not published, however, until 1728. This *Book of Architecture*[116] is one of the most influential pattern-books to have appeared in the eighteenth century, and its influence – based on Gibbs' status as an architect and on the quality of his designs, which are exclusively his own – was also massive in the colonies. A further reason for his success, even among the Whigs, was the undogmatic manner in which he steered a path between the English Baroque tradition and Palladianism, whose 'dictator-ship of taste' he challenges.

Unlike most pattern-books of the time, Gibbs's lavishly-produced folio volume is directed, not towards craftsmen, but at 'such Gentlemen as might be concerned in Building, especially in the remote parts of the Country, where little or no assistance for Designs can be procured.'[117] He assumes that any artisan can understand his designs, and he permits variations from them, but only if undertaken by 'a person of Judgment'. His designs, he says, are 'in the best Taste', following the example of the great Italian masters and in accordance with his own experience after years of study of the works of Antiquity – a cut at the narrow-mindedness of the strict Palladians. At the same time, he establishes a link with Palladianism by making the 'Grace or Beauty and Grandeur' of a building depend on the 'Proportion of the Parts to one another and to the Whole, whether entirely plain, or enriched with a few Ornaments properly disposed.'[118]

In putting forward an alternative, centrally-planned design, derived from Andrea Pozzo, for St Martin-in-the-Fields, and regretting that for financial reasons it could not be executed, Gibbs broke a lance for the late Baroque tradition. He offers a number of designs for steeples (*Plate 143*), accepting their Gothic origin without any value-judgement ('Steeples are indeed of a Gothick Extraction') and maintaining that they can be beautiful 'when their Parts are well dispos'd'.[119] At the same time his designs also stand in the line of Wren and Hawksmoor, as does his executed spire of St Martin's. Gibbs's designs for churches and steeples, modified by alterations such as he was prepared to concede, were also widely copied in New England, by Peter Harrison's King's Chapel in Boston,[120] for example, and by the steeples of the churches of St Michael and St Philip in Charleston, South Carolina.

Gibbs's projects for country mansions can best be described as Palladian, though with traces of earlier traditions, and they too met with great success on the other side of the Atlantic. An advertisement in an issue of the *Maryland Gazette* in 1751 announced that one John Ariss was prepared to construct buildings 'either of the Ancient or Modern Order of Gibbs, Architect',[121] and a number of country houses based on Gibbs's designs were built in Virginia. The White House in Washington, built by the Irishman James Hoban, also follows Gibbs's models.

His designs for garden pavilions, ironwork, chimneypieces, doors, windows, cartouches, tombs and balusters offer a spectrum of styles ranging from Baroque through Palladianism to Rococo, but they are always reserved in their ornamentation, recalling his insistence on restriction to 'a few ornaments properly disposed'.

Gibbs's *Book of Architecture* contains only designs for buildings and parts of buildings, not a system of architecture. In 1732 he sought to remedy this by publishing *Rules for Drawing the Several Parts of Architecture*,[122] a work in the tradition of treatises on the Classical orders. Adopting the proportions of Palladio, he develops a procedure for avoiding complex calculations when seeking individual measurements. This work, too, became a great success. On the other hand, a manuscript with notes from his years in Italy and a brief autobiography, written in a detached, impersonal tone, remain unpublished.[123]

The second quarter of the eighteenth century saw the appearance of a flood of publications which sought in their titles to capitalise on the success of the Palladian *Vitruvius Britannicus*, but their contents were often far from Palladian. For instance, the Scottish architect William Adam (1689–1748) put his own work and that of some fellow-countrymen into a *Vitruvius Scoticus*,[124] but the style that he promoted lies somewhere between Wren, the Palladians and Gibbs.

The word Palladian, in the strict sense of the term, may be used to characterise the works of Robert Castell, James Ralph and Isaac Ware, all of whom belonged to Lord Burlington's circle. In his folio volume *The Villas of the Ancients Illustrated* (1728)[125] Robert Castell assembles the most important Classical texts on the subject of the villa, and appends his reconstructions; he thereby adds an historical, Classical dimension to *Vitruvius Britannicus*, which, in deference to the way of life of the Whig aristocracy, had increasingly concentrated on the building of country houses. Castell's symmetrical reconstructions – his central example being that of the villas of Pliny the Younger – served to confirm the English landed gentry in their Palladianism.

Among those close to the circle of Burlington and Kent was one 'Ralph, Architect', as he is called in a later edition of *A Critical Review of the Publick Buildings, Statues and Ornaments, In, and about London and Westminster* (1734), who is probably to be identified with James Ralph (c.1705–62).[126] This critical guide is dedicated to Burlington, but the author also follows Wren in certain matters, such as symmetry in town planning and the isolation of churches – something that Vanbrugh had also recommended (1711). Palladian 'simplicity' is for Ralph the supreme criterion of judgement, and he shares the Palladians' pejorative use of the word 'Gothick'. He also attaches importance to functionalist considerations of the kind put forward by Bacon and Wotton, and revived by contemporary writers on aesthetics such as George Berkeley and Francis Hutcheson.[127]

The dogmatic tendencies of Palladianism emerge particularly clearly in the writings of Robert Morris (1701–54), a relative of the architect Roger Morris.[128] Robert Morris is the first of the prolific English popularisers, such as William Halfpenny and Batty

Langley, who played an important role in converting Palladianism, which was basically a foreign idiom originally cultivated only by a few members of the aristocracy, into something that could be rgarded as an English national style. His *Essay in Defence of Ancient Architecture* (1728)[129] shows by its title alone its relationship to the *querelle des anciens et des modernes* in France, and the argument of the frontispiece (*Plate 144*) makes it clear that Morris not only takes the side of the *anciens* but adopts the extreme position of Fréart de Chambray (1650): a classically-draped architect has a vision of the three Greek orders – which are all that Morris accepts – labelled '*Tria sunt omnia*' (three are all). Morris attempts to combine an unconditional faith in Antiquity with a belief in scientific progress and philosophical rationalism; this he does by identifying the laws of Nature and reason and proclaiming them to be those of beauty and architecture, with proportion, as understood by the Renaissance, holding the key; 'those unerring rules, those perfect standards of the Law of Reason and Nature, founded upon Beauty and Necessity.'[130] He advances the conventional view of history which sees the Goths and the Vandals – the *modernes* – as responsible for the decline of architecture. Accusing the Goths of 'barbarous Inhumanity',[131] he strikes a highly moralising pose, matched by his rhetorical and long-winded style of writing.

Morris manages to reconcile his dogmatic position with English pragmatism by repeatedly emphasising the functional aspect of architecture ('necessity'), and it is in this spirit that he advances his designs for Palladian villas, but his ideological intolerance shows through when he claims that they were 'composed according to the foregoing Rules, or the Practice of the Ancients.'[132] His position becomes even clearer in a series of lectures he gave between 1730 and 1734 to the 'Society for the Improvement of Knowledge in Arts and Sciences',[133] which he had founded himself. Here he gives unmistakeable precedence to the function of a building over its aesthetic appearance: 'Conveniency must be preferr'd to Beauty.'[134] Nonetheless, architecture as he sees it rests basically on symmetry – which he calls 'regularity' – and on proportions, for which he draws up tables.

In a novel interpretation of the Orders, Morris makes the question of which to choose for a particular house in the country dependent on the character and mood of the surroundings. Thus for a flat, open landscape he prescribes 'the Dorick Order, or something analogous to its simplicity',[135] while the Ionic order is 'most applicable to situations of various kinds.'[136] This shows how crucial landscape had become to English architecture, with the one bringing out the qualities of the other as a 'prospect'. The architecture itself is then made totally subject to geometric proportions. In his *Lectures on Architecture* Morris carries this to the point at which even the façades of his villas are formed from combinations of geometrical figures, particular importance being attached to inscribed circles. Indeed, elevations derived from an accumulation of inscribed circles appear to have been an architectural fancy indulged all over Europe in the second quarter of the eighteenth century, as is shown by the remarkable treatise of Giuseppe Maria Ercolani (1744) referred to in Chapter 16. Morris subsequently published a series of pattern-books for the building of country houses, thus falling in with the most fashionable architectural trend in England in the eighteenth century.[137]

The formal language of Palladianism, though not its intellectual content, was explained to craftsmen in works such as *Palladio Londinensis* by William Salmon, a carpenter.[138] Such books contributed greatly to the standardisation of doors, windows etc. in the building of London houses. The numerous publications of pattern-book type by William Halfpenny (alias Michael Hoare, d.1755), who himself came from the ranks of the artisans,[139] brought a knowledge of Palladian theory to building contractors and craftsmen. Palladio's systematisation of the Orders nearly always formed the basis of collections of designs for architecture. These handbooks were often produced in cheap pocket editions, which enabled them to be easily consulted on the building site: a title like *The Builder's Pocket Companion* (1728) tells its own story.

In 1747, in collaboration with Robert Morris and Thomas Lightoler, Halfpenny produced *The Modern Builder's Assistant.*[140] Like most other authors of the time, Halfpenny remarks on the flood of such publications, but maintains 'that the Subject is so copious that notwithstanding the thousand Authors were to treat ever so largely on each particular Branch of it,'[141] there would still be scope for fresh works. *The Modern Builder's Assistant* starts with an account of the Orders, 'as laid down by the celebrated Palladio', using Palladio's own illustrations as a matter of course. Then, like a distant echo of Vitruvius, Halfpenny quotes 'Conveniency, a fine Prospect and Foundation' as categories – Vitruvius's *'venustas'*, one may observe, being reduced to 'a fine Prospect', i.e. a purely pictorial effect. The second part of the book consists of a collection of model country houses, arranged by cubic content and cost, a procedure reminiscent of Le Muet. The third part contains designs for chimneypieces, windows, staircases and ceilings, in some of which Palladian Classicism has given way to the Rococo; this is pure pattern-book stuff.

Halfpenny's works had considerable influence, which extended to New England. Over and above this he was the first to propagate the current fashion for Chinoiserie in the form of architectural designs:[142] in 1750 appeared his *New Designs for Chinese Temples...*,[143] with three supplements down to 1752, when he issued a second edition with the title *Rural Architecture in the Chinese Taste*. The 'Chinese' features were to be found solely in the decorative forms – the buildings themselves remained largely classical. And that 'Chinese' meant for Halfpenny simply an exotic, non-classical form of decoration, devoid of historical background, is clear from his almost interchangeable use of 'Chinese' and 'Gothick', both here and in the work to which he gave the title *Chinese and Gothic Architecture properly Ornamented* (1752).[144] Starting out as a Palladian, Halfpenny became a typical example of how English Palladianism gradually disintegrated under the pressure of contemporary fashion.

The *Complete Body of Architecture* (1756)[145] by Isaac Ware (d.1766) is a compendium of Palladian thought, which, like Ware's English edition of Palladio, appeared late on the scene but also, like his replica of Palladio's Rotonda at Foots Cray Place in Kent (1754), helped to revive interest in Palladianism. As its rapid succession of reprintings shows, this monumental work became the most influential embodiment of architectural theory in England in the mid-eighteenth century. It was Ware's intention to deal with 'the whole science of architecture, from the first Rudiments to its utmost perfection',[146] and by claiming to include everything worth knowing, he implied that it was superfluous to study earlier works on the subject. He has both the 'practical builder' and his patron in mind. His division of his material into ten books reflects the tradition of Vitruvius and Alberti, although he is considerably more didactic in approach and never loses sight of reality. He does not operate with an apparatus of aesthetic concepts, but there are many passages that make his theoretical position clear.

Ware makes clear in his preface that his view of architecture is that of a functionalist: 'The art of building cannot be more grand than it is useful; nor its dignity a greater praise than its convenience.'[147] And following Perrault, he distinguishes the areas to which rules can be applied from those in which the imagination must be allowed to roam free. He opens his *Complete Body of Architecture* with an index of architectural terms, defined with remarkable precision. He then proceeds to a detailed discussion of building materials and their properties, paying particular attention to those cheaply available in England, above all brick. The materials, however, must be subservient to the design: 'It is the honour of the architect that the form triumph over the materials'[148] – a statement that reveals his desire to combine functionalist and Classical standpoints.

A similar tendency to compromise characterises his account of the Orders, which he regards as 'not essential parts' of architecture since there can be good architecture without them.'[149] What matters above all is proportion. At the same time, by recognising only the three Greek orders, Ware withdraws to the dogmatic position of Fréart de Chambray (1650) (*Plate 145*). Nonetheless, he calls proportions 'arbitrary' – they allow scope for individual variations, as with Perrault, and are not rules demonstrable by reference to Nature. In fact, he maintains, to lay down hard and fast rules is to encourage copying. Ware's position on this question is at odds with that of many of his contemporaries when he writes:

> The origin of the rules of architecture, so far as the orders are concerned, has been just the same: men have found beauties in antient works, and upon those beauties they have founded rules; but they had none who made them.[150]

Ware regards Nature as the model for architecture only in a basic sense. His observations on the Orders follow those of Laugier (1753): columns are imitations of tree-trunks, which are smooth: fluting is therefore an 'early error', which both weakens the column and, from the aesthetic point of view, destroys its 'great simplicity' and is thus 'a false ornament'.[151] His position on the question of ornament is a blend of functionalist, rationalist and Classicist views:

> In the first place let it be considered that there is a nobleness in simplicity which is always broke in upon by ornament; therefore no ornament should be admitted but what is reasonable; and nothing is reasonable in architecture which is not founded on some principle of use.[152]

His aesthetic conclusion is thus: 'The simple and the natural is the proper path to beauty.'[153]

Like Laugier, Ware rejects engaged columns and pillars, and only reluctantly accepts pilasters. In fact, he is not afraid to criticise Classical architecture and also, on occasion, Palladio, as when he condemns the batter of Classical columns and entasis as 'abuse'.[154] By contrast he discusses in detail buildings that do not use the Orders, requiring an architect to be as prepared to design a humble cottage as a splendid palace:

> It is with this reason we have asserted the best architect is not to be above designing the smallest edifice, for nothing is more certain than that he will acquire more reputation from a well-constructed cottage than from a faulty palace.[155]

Ledoux was to adopt a very similar attitude in France a generation later.

In Book III Ware devises case-studies of model country houses for clients of various social degrees, including among them his design for Admiral John Byng's

Wrotham Park in Middlesex, a kind of corrected version of Campbell's Wanstead III.[156]

Ware's functionalist attitude acquires a very modern aspect with his view that there must be a relationship between the embellishment of a façade and the function of a building: it is the rôle of the ornamental features, he says, to express the building's 'intended use'; and, in terms of structure: 'There must not only be strength, but an appearance of strength in all things'[157] – a phrase that recalls Berkeley's 'appearance of use' to connote the source of beauty.[158] Such views were easy to combine with the *architecture parlante* of Boffrand (1745), and Ware refers to the 'character of the edifice'[159] in the same spirit as Boffrand. In a few plates at the end of his work[160] he reaches, by logical progression, a proto-revolutionary position which points forward to Ledoux, who recognised the aesthetic quality of unadorned surfaces. This progressive view emerges in a statement such as: 'Ornaments out of place are no ornaments at all; plainness is always preferable.'[161] Indeed, although from one point of view Ware's treatise is a retrospective survey of Palladianism, it also contains a surprising number of 'modern' features.

His chapters on landscape gardening show Ware fully abreast of his time. For him, architecture and landscape have to be pictorial, for what confronts the observer as he rides along a road or sails down a river is 'a continual moving picture.'[162] He describes the *raison d'être* of a landscape garden with the utmost clarity as an artistic assemblage of the 'beauties of nature' and the creation of a 'universal harmony...that every thing may be free, and nothing savage.'[163] Ware has a sharp eye for the ways in which art can create naturalness:

> Every thing pleasing is thrown open; every thing disgustful is shut out, nor do we perceive the art, while we enjoy its effects: the sunk wall prevents our knowing where the garden terminates; and the very screen from unpleasing objects seems planted only for its natural beauty.[164]

This is a typical example of Ware's succinct style, which sometimes borders on the aphoristic. Today his treatise is strangely underestimated or has sunk into oblivion, perhaps because of its frightening size, but it remains one of the most interesting sources of architectural theory of the eighteenth century.

One of the most unconventional English writers on architecture, a man schooled in the tradition of Palladio but displaying in his writings a remarkable combination of scholarship and fantasy, is John Wood the Elder (1704–53), who is chiefly remembered for his part in the planning of Bath.[165] In 1741 he published a treatise whose title alone shows his opposition to a view of architecture centred on Classical Antiquity: *The Origin of Building: or, the Plagiarism of the Heathens detected in Five Books.*[166] In this he sets out to provide a single, unified programme for the entire history of architecture, in a manner comparable with that of Laugier in his *Essai sur l'architecture* twelve years later. Wood's starting-point was Villalpando's commentary on Ezekiel (1604), which had also been drawn on by Wren, Roger Pratt and other Englishmen; but although he follows Villalpando in close detail, Wood makes no acknowledgement of his source.[167] However, he goes further than Villalpando, for, not content with interpreting Solomon's Temple as the model for Classical architecture, he adopts the Tabernacle erected by Moses in the desert as the basic image for all the principles of architecture – a line of thought already pursued by the freemason James Anderson in his *Book of Constitutions*

(1723). Moses' Tabernacle thus has for Wood a function similar to that of the primitive hut for Laugier.

Wood's descriptions of the details of the Tabernacle are occasionally contradictory, but in the end he even comes to identify in it the preliminary forms of the three Greek orders:

> And therefore, the Pillars of the Tabernacle, by their different situation, being of three different Kinds, furnish'd the various sorts of Building necessary for Man; as the Strong, the Mean, and the Delicate; and which, in Process of Time, were ranked under the Name of Order, with Grecian names; to wit, Dorick, Jonick, and Corinthian.[168]

The terms 'strong', 'mean' and 'delicate' go back to the *'solide'*, *'moyenne'* and *'délicate'* of Fréart de Chambray (1650) who only accepted the legitimacy of the three Greek orders, and was also one of the first to base his work on Villalpando.

Wood was concerned not only, as Delorme and Villalpando had been, to reconcile the evidence of the Bible with Vitruvius, but also to demonstrate 'that the Jewish sacred structures were the Forerunners of the most considerable Works the World ever produced, in 4 different Periods of Time, of about 500 Years in each period.'[169] This is the time-scale within which he accommodates the Tabernacle of Moses and the three Temples of Jerusalem. On the basis of a history of architecture derived from the Old Testament, with direct textual comparisons between Moses and Vitruvius, he adduces psychological criteria as the ultimate occasions of architectural activity, namely: 'Shame, Fear, Pity, Gratitude, and Fidelity'.[170] These categories resemble the *caractères* evolved in France at this same period, but Wood goes further, making them the preconditions of the Vitruvian concepts of *utilitas, firmitas* and *venustas*; concluding 'These produced three Precepts of Building, namely, Convenience, Strength, and Beauty'.[171] This is a *reductio ad absurdum* of Classical theory of architecture.

To Wood all true architecture goes back to the Bible, and Vitruvius is merely derivative. Thus the design of Federico Zuccaro's house in Florence, for example, which he set out by criticising as a 'Caprice', is now traced back to the Bible, whilst Palladio is explained in terms of Vitruvius.[172]

At the end of his final book Wood discusses architecture in England, describing Stonehenge as the work of the Druids and tracing its layout back to Jewish origins.[173] This was a thesis taken over from William Stukeley's work on Stonehenge published a year earlier,[174] which, however, Wood later vehemently attacked.[175] He even attempted to put his 'Salomonic' ideas into practice when he began his restoration of Llandaff Cathedral in 1734; an unpublished manuscript draft for *The Origin of Building* explains the principles behind the operation.[176]

In his little-known *Dissertation upon the Orders of Columns* (1750)[177] Wood proposes a compromise between the Biblical tradition and that of Vitruvius and Palladio. Taking his stand, with Fréart and Robert Morris, as a protagonist of the Greek orders, he proposes the banning of 'all Compositions that have the least Tendency to vitiate the Orders bearing the Grecian Names'.[178] He refines the Vitruvian analogy between tree and column by defining the Doric order as an imitation of dead trees, and the Corinthian, of living trees, and the Ionic as a compromise between the two. But he quickly returns to his old view of the origin of the Orders by crediting Moses with their invention and relating them to the Tabernacle. A comparable historical fancy is his description of the town of Bath,[179] which, he attempts to prove, was the Druids' capital: his own plans for the town stood, as he saw it, in direct line of descent from those of Deinokrates for Mount Athos (Vitruvius, preface to Book II). In the buildings he constructed Wood was a Palladian, and what he hoped to achieve with his fanciful view of history is not clear. One might interpret it as the *idée fixe* of a semi-educated man; on the other hand, its latent Romanticism could be seen as a sign of the inner disintegration of Palladianism.

Outside the framework of Palladianism stands the freemason Batty Langley (1696–1751), who was successively landscape gardener, architect, manufacturer of architectural details and garden figures out of artificial stone, and founder of an academy of drawing for architects.[180] He published numerous pattern-books on architecture and gardening. An early work called *The Builder's Chest-Book* (1727)[181] is in the form of a dialogue between master and pupil, of which he is quick to claim: 'nothing of this kind has been ever yet attempted in the manner here deliver'd.'[182] Palladianism was for him evidently no more than a highly marketable fashion, so in the very first paragraph of his preface he assures his readers that he will acquaint them with 'those beautiful Proportions as were practis'd by that grand Architect Palladio.'[183]

The simple question-and-answer form of the dialogue is probably a fair reflection of the modest theoretical knowledge possessed by most of the practical builders of the time. Langley shows a strikingly functional approach with his demonstration of the practical value of the right angle, on structural grounds by virtue of its strength, on functional grounds for reasons of lighting and the utilisation of space.[184] Polygonal designs belong exclusively, in his view, to military architecture, circular designs to churches and amphitheatres. Structural considerations also play a part in his section on the Orders. Finally, he produces a ready reckoner, with tables, for geometry and measuring and pricing construction work. Everybody, says Langley, can learn about architecture in an entertaining way in his spare time, and this is the purpose of his writings. If one puts on one side his basic rationalism and functionalism, one is left with the view that everything that finds takers is permissible. In *The Builder's Jewel* (1741)[186] he interprets the three Orders in Masonic terms as Wisdom, Strength and Beauty (*Plate 146*). The end result is a somewhat indiscriminate eclecticism in his writings.

Features such as these led to Langley's becoming one of the first representatives of the Gothic Revival, a fashionable interest that arose at about the same time, and for much the same reasons, as the vogue for Chinoiserie.[187] Langley was far from concerned to give a historical interpretation of Gothic, as Wren and Hawksmoor had tried to do, and regarded it rather as a form of decoration, a *dernier cri*. This led to vagaries already mocked in his own day, to be tellingly characterised by Kenneth Clark as 'Rococo Gothic'.[188] The first edition of Langley's book on this subject (1741) bore the remarkable title *Ancient Architecture, Restored and Improved... in the Gothick Mode*, which was changed in the second edition (1742) to the more innocuous *Gothic Architecture, Improved by Rules and Proportions....*[189] That Langley was still a prisoner of Vitruvius and the Antique is made clear by his subjection of Gothic to the discipline of the Orders and proportion, and by his claim that, judged on this basis, Gothic architecture is superior even to that of the Greeks. The theory that the English were the historical heirs of the Greeks provided a kind of justification for this approach, and Langley claimed that his measurements had uncovered the 'Rules by which the Ancient Buildings in this Kingdom were erected.'[190] Gothic thus became in his eyes both a national style and an improvement on Antiquity, as evidenced by the choir of Westminster Abbey, which manifests 'those beautiful proportions and geometric Rules, which were not excelled (if equalled) in any Parts of the Grecian and Roman orders.'[191] By analogy with the five Classical orders Langley produced five 'Gothic' orders – a concept not new in itself, since it is also found in Guarini and others, but new in Langley's assumption of a historical continuum.

The first of his orders is Doric-Gothic, the alternation of metope and triglyph being Gothicised, and the metopes decorated with quatrefoils (*Plate 147*). The Ionic-Gothic order has an ornamental frieze made up of strict geometrical figures, and so on. Even if one concedes that these Gothic orders are the result of an historical reconstruction, the ways they are applied can indeed only be described as 'Rococo-Gothic'; and the doors, windows, chimneypieces and pavilions ('umbrellas') which Langley focuses on are among the most absurd creations the eighteenth century has to offer. His stylistic mélange was soon dubbed the 'Batty Langley Manner' – Horace Walpole called it 'bastard Gothic'.

As in the works of Halfpenny, the terms 'Gothic' and 'Chinese' are used interchangeably for identical kinds of construction. In 1759, for instance, an otherwise unknown architect by the name of Paul Decker published a volume entitled *Gothic Architecture Decorated* ... and another entitled *Chinese Architecture, Civil and Ornamented.*[192] The volumes contain no text but simply illustrations for garden pavilions, hermitages and ironwork; the first contains a few 'Designs of the Gothic Orders' based on Langley; the second conjures up a world of Chinese Rococo. In fact, Decker is concerned neither with Gothic nor with China, but with the profitable propagation of a vogue. However, there were at the same time serious attempts to understand both Gothic and Chinese architecture, albeit motivated by the same desire to exploit them for contemporary purposes.

The question of how the Gothic style has been viewed in England since the seventeenth century has been frequently treated, and all we can do here is to refer to the relevant literature.[193] Space must be found, however, to consider at least briefly the ideas that gave rise to the most famous piece of eighteenth-century neo-Gothic architecture in England – Walpole's villa of Strawberry Hill at Twickenham,[194] which brought a new dimension to the forms of 'ornamented architecture' that had been developed since the 1720s.

Although Horace Walpole (1717–97) dissociated himself from Langley, he may well have found Langley's patriotic tendencies attractive, and the fact that he was a Whig no longer meant that he was tied to Palladianism; he wrote to his friend Horace Mann in 1750, the year work started on Strawberry Hill, that the proper place for the Classical orders was on public buildings. A child of his time, he at first hesitated between 'Chinese' and 'Gothick' for his own house. In the same letter he expresses his pleasure at the asymmetry associated with things Chinese, a quality to which he applied the term 'Sharawadgi',[195] taken over from landscape gardening: 'I am almost as fond of the Sharawadgi, or Chinese want of symmetrie, in buildings, as in grounds or gardens.'[196] His decision to adopt the Gothic style resulted in an overall plan for house and grounds that may have developed organically but was completely asymmetrical, and derived partly from patriotism but also from personal extravagance. He described it[197] as the expression of 'my own taste', intended 'in some degree to realize my own visions'. He talks with delightful irony of his 'small capricious house' and its 'fantastic fabric'.[198] The emotional significance that the Gothic nonetheless had for him emerges from his confession that it was Strawberry Hill that had inspired him to write his 'Gothic' novel *The Castle of Otranto* (1765).

It was only during the long period of construction of his villa that Walpole arrived at conceptions of stylistic unity and purity. Looking back in 1784 he wrote in his *Description of the Villa*...: 'The designs of the inside and outside are strictly ancient',[199] but by 1794 he admitted in a letter that 'every true Goth must perceive that they [the rooms] are more the works of fancy than of imitation.'[200] On the other hand he also concedes the strength of the functionalist arguments of the time: 'In truth, I did not mean to make my house so Gothic as to exclude convenience, and modern refinements in luxury.'[201] This pragmatic attitude enabled him to incorporate fragments, or imitations of fragments, from English cathedrals and chantry chapels for chimneypieces, ceilings, windows, and so on.[202] The ceiling of the Gallery, for example, follows that of Henry VIII's Chapel in Westminstery Abbey; the bookshelves in the library are based on the doors of the rood screen in Old St Paul's, and the chimneypiece in the library is an adaptation of a tomb in Westminster Abbey. Although, or perhaps because, Walpole appointed a 'Committee of Taste' for Strawberry Hill, the result was a remarkably eclectic choice of styles, combined with the use of cheap modern materials such as stucco, which could be made to imitate Gothic forms. Some of these forms, indeed, are not far removed from the detested 'bastard Gothic' of Langley.

Strawberry Hill, the work of a dilettante, already became a place of pilgrimage during its creator's lifetime. His ironical attitude towards his own achievement emerges when, in his *Description of the Villa*..., Walpole adopts Pope's phrase 'a Gothic Vatican of Greece and Rome' to describe the composition and display of his collections.[203] he went beyond the merely fashionable trends of his day, but his attempt to establish a link with the principles of Gothic did not bear fruit until the nineteenth century.

It is interesting to note that the principle of asymmetry employed by Walpole at Strawberry Hill also found the support of painters. William Hogarth, for instance, whose *Analysis of Beauty* (1753) shows him to be a supporter of functionalism in architecture,[204] subordinating the aesthetic categories to the functional principle, queries the appropriateness of symmetry as a basic architectural tenet, and the 'variety' of his serpentine line also becomes a law of architecture.

Sir Joshua Reynolds takes up the question in his *Discourse* of 11 December 1786, emphasising the importance of the element of 'accident' in architecture, and expressing deep-seated objections to uniform patterns, especially in town-planning; Wren's plan for London he calls 'rather unpleasing; the uniformity might have produced weariness, and a slight degree of disgust'.[205] Reynolds's citation of Vanbrugh, in whose work he identified Gothic features, shows how the ideas of Palladianism were gradually losing their influence.[206]

Discussion of the principles behind Chinoiserie, which flourished in England in the 1740s and 1750s, only began in earnest after the vogue had passed its peak. In 1757 there appeared Sir William Chambers's *Designs of Chinese Buildings*. Chambers (1723–

96)[207] made three expeditions to the Far East between 1740 and 1749 in the service of the Swedish East India Company, on the last two of which he spent some considerable time in Canton. His book, was not, however, published immediately after his return, but only after he had studied for a year at the architectural school of Jacques-François Blondel in Paris and then spent five years in Italy (1750–55). His first plan was for a conventional pattern-book, as his *Proposals for Publishing by Subscription, Designs of Villas, &c.* (1757) shows, but this was never published. In that same year he was commissioned by Augusta Princess of Wales to design Kew Gardens, and it is no doubt no coincidence that this was also the year in which his book on China, dedicated to the Prince of Wales, the future George III, appeared.

Chambers's attitude to China is one of reserve. He concedes the artistic originality of the Chinese but has no doubt about the superiority of Graeco-Roman and modern European architecture.[208] He is concerned to put an end to the 'extravagancies that daily appear under the name of Chinese', but at the same time he is anxious to bring to the attention of the public the sketches he made out of curiosity while in Canton. He makes it clear that he does not consider Chinese architecture a suitable model for Europe, since the climatic conditions are quite different and Chinese taste is far inferior to that of Antiquity. In large-scale parks, however, where a 'variety of scenes' would be appropriate, a judicious use of the 'Chinese taste' would be acceptable for minor features.[209] In support of his call for 'variety' he quotes the Emperor Hadrian's Villa at Tivoli, in which 'the manner of the Egyptians and of other nations' was to be found. This is his justification for his exotic designs for Kew; but he is also anxious not to allow his interest in China to discredit his reputation as an architect.

Chambers's justification for publishing his *Designs of Chinese Buildings* is that of a comparative historian of art: 'The architecture of one of the most extraordinary nations in the universe cannot be a matter of indifference to a true lover of the arts.' Hitherto, moreover, there had been no reliable depictions of Chinese architecture. It is not clear, however, whether his own drawings of Chinese houses derive from observation, for in 1756 we find him urgently requesting his brother John to supply him with details about Chinese houses, which suggests that his work is not entirely based on first-hand knowledge.[210]

Chambers's thinking takes a strange turn when he claims to find what he calls 'a remarkable affinity' between Chinese and Classical architecture, though without assuming any historical connection. The link lies, in his view, in a common trend towards a pyramidal massing, and in the use of columns (*Plate 148*). Going on to classify the Chinese columns according to the ratio of diameter to height, he arrives at six types, their height varying between eight and twelve times their diameter.[211] His description of the Chinese house and these illustrations were the first of their kind in Europe, however doubtful their reality may be. His reproductions of furniture and everyday objects, by contrast, are not far removed from the Chinoiseries which he despised.

His section (unillustrated) on Chinese gardens was to prove highly influential. Referring to conversations he had held with the Chinese, and using the aesthetic criteria of his age, he developed a theory of the Chinese garden, which imitated the 'beautiful irregularities' of Nature, as he put it,[212] and thus supported his contemporaries' concept of *sharawadgi*. By making 'variety of scenes' the basic principle of the Chinese garden,[213] by advocating the evocation of the 'pleasing', 'horrid', and 'enchanted', and by raising the question of picturesque ruins, he shows his affinity with Edmund Burke, whose *Philosophical Enquiry into the Origin of our Ideas of the Sublime and Beautiful* had appeared earlier the same year.[214] Chambers's book reads like an indirect plea in support of his design for Kew – which may well have been just what prompted it. But since the fashion for things Chinese was virtually over, it had remarkably little impact, whereas on the Continent its influence was felt into the 1780s.[215] In George Staunton's long account (1797) of an English mission to China in 1792–94,[216] the illustrations by William Alexander still follow the contemporary fashion for the 'picturesque' but this account is a more dependable guide than the work of Chambers or his predecessors.

A few years after his *Designs of Chinese Buildings* Chambers published a folio volume with his designs for Kew Gardens (1763), which contained a variety of garden buildings, not just Chinese but of every kind, testifying to his wide-ranging historical eclecticism.[217] Worried lest *Designs of Chinese Buildings* might 'hurt my reputation as an Architect',[218] Chambers hastened to produce a work containing his actual views on architecture, which appeared in 1759 as the *Treatise on Civil Architecture*,[219] of which he later published two revised editions, the second (1791) being radically amended and more accurately entitled *A Treatise on the Decorative Part of Civil Architecture*, plans for a further volume having come to nothing. The work as we have it amounts to little more than a treatise on the use of the Classical orders. In 1770 he began work on a series of lectures on architecture which he planned to deliver before the Royal Academy, in rivalry with Reynolds's *Discourses on Art*,[220] which had started the previous year, but this plan too failed to materialise.[221]

Yet Chambers's *Treatise* is the most original and, as its frequent reissue in the nineteenth century shows, most influential of English works on architecture. At first sight its programme looks similar to that of Isaac Ware in his *Complete Body of Architecture*, the publication of which only three years earlier must have annoyed Chambers, who gave it as his aim 'to collect in one volume, what lay dispersed in many hundreds, much the greater part of them written in foreign languages.'[222] Apart from differences of generation and attitude, the main distinction between them is that whereas Ware's method is compilatory, Chambers incorporated in his work his own knowledge of the monuments of Antiquity and his practical experience.

Chambers begins by adopting the self-distancing position of the politically concerned observer of architecture in his *Treatise*. In 1757 he had been appointed tutor to the Prince of Wales, later King George III, to whom the third edition is dedicated, and the work was the product of the instruction he gave the prince. Architecture is thus viewed within a national framework – it contributes to the glory of the nation, educates public taste, stimulates craftsmanship and trade, and increases economic profit.[223] Indeed, the king himself can employ architecture to demonstrate his power and the splendour of his rule, and bequeath this glory to future generations.[224]

Like his contemporaries Milizia in Italy, Ledoux in France and Sulzer in Germany, Chambers reflects the rôle played by architecture in society as a whole, though without succumbing to the danger of overestimating his own importance, as Ledoux does. Architecture adds to man's sense of physical and psychological well-being – it can even add to his happiness, and is at the same time a significant source of employment and commerce. Grand public buildings attract tourists. Chambers quotes Rome, where art 'by some extraordinary good management . . . is a treasure never to be exhausted.'[225] The same idea occurs in Milizia. The language of architecture, says Chambers, can be used to sing the praises of the individual or of the nation: 'Materials in architecture are like words in phraseology.'[226] His work is aimed exclusively at 'persons of high rank, and large fortune; the fit encouragers of elegance,'[227] and his own rôle, as he sees it, is that of an arbiter of 'true taste', with the task of setting 'standards of imitation' by disseminating in his designs the virtues of simplicity, order, character and beauty of form.[228] 'Strength and duration' should be combined with 'beauty, convenience, and salubrity…and economy'[229] – criteria based on those adopted in eighteenth-century France, which Chambers had heard discussed in Paris when he sat at the feet of Jacques-François Blondel and his circle there in 1749.

Chambers demanded high standards of the professional architect, requiring the same basic qualities as Vitruvius but adapted to the needs of the day: his vision was of a widely-travelled man, fluent in foreign languages – a man like himself, in fact. Travel stimulated the imagination and encouraged a 'sublime conception'; above all it removed national antipathies and promoted liberality of thought.[230] In sum, Chambers stood for an enlightened cosmopolitanism and liberalism in architecture, without losing sight of his national obligations as an Englishman.

In the section headed 'Of the Origin, and Progress of Building' Chambers unfurls his view of history, using it at the same time to bolster his polemical position in the dispute between the French and Romans over the relative priority of Greece and Rome. He supports Laugier in the key position that he gives to the primitive hut but does not share Laugier's total rejection of pilasters and arcades.[231] Criticising the Vitruvian theory of architectural development, which 'ascribes almost every invention in that art to the Greeks',[232] he points instead to the achievements of the Egyptians, Assyrians and Babylonians, whose architecture revealed great power and wealth, albeit somewhat less skill and taste, since their conception of grandeur was based entirely on sheer size – a point that recalls Burke's 'magnitude in building'.[233] 'Marks of taste and fancy' he finds only in the Egyptians, whom he credits with the invention of columns, bases, capitals and entablatures[234] – in fact, he declares both the religion and the developed architecture of the Greeks to be of Egyptian origin.

These ideas originated in the writings of Count Caylus, which started to appear at the time Chambers was in Rome (1750–55). Chambers turned them against the Greeks, whose originality he challenged in favour both of the Romans and of other peoples,[235] even going so far as to deny the perfection of proportion in Greek architecture. In his view Goujon's caryatid gallery for the Louvre is better proportioned than the porch of the Erechtheum, which he knew from Le Roy and which he called a 'monstrous excess'.[236] In the Greek-Roman debate he struck a defiantly pro-Roman stance.[237] One must recall in this connection that for two years Chambers had lived in the same house as Piranesi in Rome,[238] though he apparently made less obsequious attempts to woo him than his life-long rival Robert Adam.[239] The controversy only broke out after Chambers had returned to England, and he took Piranesi's side, expressly recommending his publications.[240] Piranesi directed his attacks chiefly against Le Roy, who was a friend of Chambers's, whereas Chambers attacked his own compatriots, Stuart and Revett.[241] He could not accept Piranesi's historical premise – later modified – of the precedence of the Etruscans over the Greeks, which is why, with the same aim in view, he adopted the views of Caylus. His explanation for the allegedly inferior quality of architecture among the Greeks – whose supremacy in other fields he does not contest – is a caricature of the Enlightenment position: if their architecture, he argues, was already flawed at the time of Alexander the Great, it must have been even more so a few centuries earlier. Greece was simply too small, too divided and too poor, he concludes, to produce good architecture,[242] and in a manner quite untypical of his normal balanced style, he launches into a veritable hymn of hate in his determination to put an end to the *gusto Greco* in England. By contrast he derives from Roman architecture 'a compleat system of decorative architecture',[243] which, together with the productions of the fifteenth, sixteenth and seventeenth centuries based on the same principles, constituted the 'stock' available to his own day. Over particular points, however, Chambers strikes a critical attitude towards Roman architecture, which corresponds to the generally relativistic nature of his approach.

Chambers' historical views take an unexpected turn when he suddenly sets himself up as a spokesman for the reassessment of Gothic, in which he finds improvements in construction compared with Antiquity. His choice of construction as the means of rehabilitating Gothic shows his dependence on Laugier and Cordemoy. At the same time he recognised the national dimension of this debate by recommending the inception of a project to 'publish to the world the riches of Britain,'[244] in this sphere, for which he himself began to collect material.[245] He does not go so far as to offer Gothic designs of his own, but it is not surprising that a 'Gothicist' like Horace Walpole should have described Chambers's *Treatise* as 'the most sensible book and the most exempt from prejudices that ever was written on that science.'[246]

On the subject of the Orders Chambers takes up a conventional position, following in the main Vignola, to whom he also owes his illustrations. He favours 'variety' in ornament without excess, maintaining that it must be shaped from material, not applied to it.[247]

Yet for all this Chambers did not arrive at a self-contained theoretical system. One can detect the influence of Burke's sensualism,[248] but Chambers was ultimately distrustful of all systems, and retained a pragmatic attitude, that combined Classicising and late Baroque traditions, as in his own self-effacing architecture, which absorbs stimuli from the most varied of sources while still retaining its own personality.

Chambers's somewhat belated intervention in the Greek-Roman debate was directed, as he himself said, against Graecophile taste in England, represented above all by the brothers Robert (1728–92) and James (1730–94) Adam, architects who propagated this *gusto Greco* and prided themselves on having introduced 'a kind of revolution in the whole system'.[249] Since Chambers and Robert Adam met in 1755 at Piranesi's house in Rome there had been bad blood between them, even though both, in their own ways, appealed to Piranesi for support,[250] and James Adam was apparently too deeply involved in the family business to take an independent line over Chambers. Robert Adam's first publication was his sumptuous work on the Palace of Diocletian at Split (1764), which has already been discussed in Chapter 17.[251]

James Adam, who embarked on his Grand Tour of Italy after his elder brother's return from there, began to occupy himself in Rome in 1762 with the creation of a 'British' order of architecture (*Plates 149, 150*) – later used on Carlton House in Pall Mall[252] – and with evolving a theory of architecture[253] which, however, neither of the brothers either finished or even worked out. His basic position, as revealed by the surviving fragment of it, was a rejection of all strict rules, his concern being 'variety of movement', by which he meant, for the exterior of a building, a well disposed variety of high and low projections and recesses, designed to be appreciated from a distance, and for the interior, a variety of vaulting.[254] It is a picturesque approach, and Adam himself compares its principles of composition with those of landscape painting, quoting the example of Blenheim Palace but warning against the excess of breaks in architectural members found in Michelangelo and Borromini. He thus stands for a form of Baroque Classicism which is not so far removed from that of Chambers.

The Adam brothers began publishing their designs in 1773. On the one hand they served as publicity for their firm, on the other they were intended as a contribution to 'the rise and progress of architecture in Great Britain'.[255] The first volume of their *Works of Architecture* repeats almost word for word their theory of 'variety of movement', movement being held to add to 'the picturesque of the composition'.[256] This established a link with one of the favourite aesthetic concepts of the age. In their second volume they provide a historical justification for their style of interior decoration by describing in a somewhat contorted manner their position in the Greek-Roman debate, conceding the priority of Etruscan influence on the Romans but at the same time not denying the influence of the Greeks.[257] The eclecticism of the 'Adam style' is justified by reference to historical connections; and they adduce the example of their decorations for Osterley Park. Their compromise in the Greek-Roman question is made explicit in the frontispiece of their book, which depicts Minerva showing a map to a student of architecture who is being led by Geometry; with her index finger Minerva points to Greece, with her thumb to Italy (*Plate 151*). It was probably this attitude adopted by the Adams that provoked Chambers to indulge in his anti-Greek invective.

The Adam style was promoted not only by the brothers themselves but also in numerous other treatises of the pattern-booke type – though Chambers too had his supporters.[258] Among these publications must be ranked those of James Paine, James Gandon, William Pain, George Richardson and others, who either quote Palladio in the title of their work or describe themselves as continuators of the *Vitruvius Britannicus*. George Richardson, for example, who accompanied James Adam on his Grand Tour as a draughtsman, secretly made drawings for his own purposes during the journey and later used them in his *Treatise of the five orders of architecture* (1787);[259] his *New Vitruvius Britannicus*, as mentioned above, followed in 1802 and 1808.

Attention was drawn, in connection with the earlier discussion of the successors to the original *Vitruvius Britannicus*, to the concentration of interest on the country house, which gave rise to a flood of publications on the subject in the second half of the century. Most of them are little more than pattern-books; what they all share is a scope limited to the requirements of the landed gentry. One work, however, by John Wood the Younger (1728–81), discusses the living conditions of agricultural workers, and subsequently the dwellings of the working class in general. Wood's work, entitled *A Series of Plans for Cottages or Habitations of the Labourer* (1781),[260] is the first study in the history of architectural theory to deal specifically with the provision of workers' housing, and it is a moving social document. In his introduction Wood announces his intention of examining 'the ruinous state of the cottages of this kingdom', observing 'that these habitations of that useful and necessary rank of men, the LABOURERS, were become for the most part offensive both to decency and humanity.'[261] As a result of this state of affairs, he went on, he found it necessary to put himself in the position of these workers and investigate their needs and complaints on the spot, for 'no architect can form a convenient plan, unless he ideally places himself in the situation of the person for whom he designs.'[262] As far as the construction of buildings was concerned, Wood saw simply a gradual linear progression from a humble cottage to a splendid palace, boldly concluding 'that a palace is nothing more than a cottage improved'.[263]

This early observation of a state of social tension has its parallel in France, where Ledoux writes in a similar vein. Listing his precepts for workers' dwellings, Wood produces proposals for houses – detached, semi-detached and terraced – of between one and four rooms, together with assessments of building costs. His houses are simple, practical, completely free of ornamentation, but externally symmetrical. Wood is the first architect to make the design of workers' accommodation a central concern.

The most important transitional figure at the turn of the eighteenth century is Sir John Soane (1753–1837), who, as a protégé of Chambers, journeyed to Italy in 1779–80 before embarking on his extensive career as architect and designer.[264] His writings are comparatively conventional; his *Designs in Architecture* of 1778 are in the tradition of conventional pattern-books,[265] whereas his later publications of his own buildings and projects (1788 and 1793)[266] reveal an independent theoretical standpoint, together with a good deal of information about the author himself. The introduction to his *Plans, Elevations and Sections of Buildings* (1788) opens with a remarkable anthology of statements on architectural theory, but his reflections on ornament finally lead him to define his own position. Ornament, he says, should be simple, regular in form and clear in outline, serving to emphasise the function and character of a building;[267] 'utility in the plans' is more important than elaborate façades, and he aims 'to unite convenience and comfort in the interior distributions, and simplicity and uniformity in the exterior.'[268]

In this work Soane reproduces his projects from purely architectural drawings, whereas his *Sketches in Architecture* of 1793 contain 'pictorial' views in scenic surroundings. And when he states that he has been concerned to work 'on a smaller scale, consisting of cottages for the laborious and industrious parts of the community', and does so along similar lines, he reveals that John Wood's *Series of Plans for Cottages* has also left its mark on the development of his thinking.[269] At the same time he shows his acceptance of the 'picturesque' view of architecture, which had prevailed for decades in landscape gardening and was now about to invade architecture itself.[270] In this context mention must also be made of Charles Thomas Middleton's *Picturesque and Architectural Views for Cottages, Farm Houses and Country Villas*, published in 1793.[271]

In his Royal Academy lectures on architecture delivered between 1809 and 1836, but only published by Arthur Bolton in 1929, Soane shows his aesthetic to be conventional, though with signs of a functionalist approach and a readiness to accept technological innovation.[272] His position may be defined as a combination of Baroque planning, Classical aesthetics, and a belief in technological progress. Among his late writings[273] special reference should be made to his description of his house in Lincoln's Inn Fields in London – a Romantic synthesis of architecture, sculpture and painting, which he bequeathed to the nation as a museum.[274] His theoretical statements are less significant than his achievements as a practical architect, but they help us to understand his own ideas.

20. Concepts of the garden

The literature on the art of gardening, which involves agriculture on the one hand and both architecture and painting on the other, can only be touched on briefly in this book. A garden is an arrangement of Nature; landscape gardening turns Nature into a picture and architecture becomes the staffage of this picture. The stages of this development can be followed in numerous treatises on the art of garden design, the vast majority of them from the eighteenth century, which deal in the main with the theory and practice of the English landscape garden. This chapter will be restricted to giving a sketch of the ideas that emerged in England, France and Germany, paying particular attention to the relationship between garden and architecture.

There had been descriptions, illustrations, and pattern-books of gardens since the sixteenth century.[1] Some, such as that by Jacques Boyceau (1638), show by their vocabulary that gardens were thought of to a large extent as extensions of the interior of the house – terms like room, corridor, enfilade, window, door and cupola are used to describe features of garden design.[2] An autonomous theory of gardening, however, did not emerge until the beginning of the eighteenth century, with the codification of the formal French garden as conceived by André Le Nostre, in Joseph Dezallier d'Argenville's (1680–1765) *La Théorie et la pratique du jardinage* (1709), which, frequently reprinted and translated, became the most influential French work on the subject in the eighteenth century.[3]

Dezallier's principal criteria were derived from the current theory of architecture, and are based on 'a well-planned and well-understood layout, [and] a harmonious relationship between all the parts.'[4] Economy, making the best of, and improving the terrain are the essentials for the 'true grandeur of a fine garden', for which he establishes four basic maxims:

> the first, that Art must yield to Nature; second, not to congest a garden to excess; third, not to expose it all to immediate view; and fourth, always to make it appear larger than it really is.[5]

Dezallier issues a warning against overloading parks with garden buildings, which, if employed at all, must exhibit 'a noble simplicity'.[6] His designs take the main building as their focus, from which the '*conformité*' of the whole can be perceived while points of detail should be characterised by '*variété*'. His complete designs consequently have a schematic quality that renders them greatly inferior to the parks of Le Nostre.

Even after the new English conception of Nature had emerged, France still clung to the idealised view that Nature could only be presented with the help of Art. This was the position taken up by the Abbé Noël-Antoine Pluche (1688–1761) in his treatise *Le spectacle de la nature*: 'A garden is less an imitation of Nature, than Nature herself put before our eyes, and called into play with Art…'. At times, Pluche's phraseology has the tone that one associates with the so-called Revolutionary architects.

The Italian and French garden of the sixteenth and seventeenth centuries was the product of a geometrical arrangement that sought to apply the laws of architecture to the disposition of flower-beds and shrubs, and treat an open-air setting as though it were an interior. Cautious criticism of this conception came from Sir Henry Wotton in his *Elements of Architecture* (1624); he insisted that there be a contrast between the regularity of a building and the irregularity of a garden, and that consideration be given to the role of the spectator.[8] Wotton is a key pioneer of the English landscape garden.

We cannot here go into the way the new feeling towards Nature developed, or how it affected the design of gardens. At all events it was to start with an exclusively English development, in which the 'discovery' of China, or of what was thought to be 'Chinese', played a key role.[9] An important figure in this respect is Sir William Temple (1628–99), who had visited China himself and who, in his essay *Upon the Gardens of Epicurus* (1685),[10] praised the irregular, natural Chinese garden at the expense of the symmetrical Baroque garden cultivated in Europe at the time. 'Among us,' writes Temple,

> the Beauty of Building and Planting is placed chiefly in some certain Proportions, Symmetries, or Uniformities; our Walks and our Trees ranged so, as to answer one another; and at exact Distances. The *Chineses* scorn this Way of Planting, and say a Boy, that can tell an Hundred, may plant Walks of Trees in straight Lines, and over-against one another, and to what Length and Extent he pleases. But their greatest Reach of Imagination is employed in contriving Figures, where the Beauty shall be great, and strike the Eye, but without any Order or Disposition of Parts, that shall be commonly or easily observ'd. And though we have hardly any Notion of this Sort of Beauty, yet they have a particular Word to express it; and, where they find it hit their Eye at first Sight, they say the *Sharawadgi* is fine or is admirable, or any such Expression of Esteem.[11]

The form of the irregular natural garden enshrined in the word Sharawadgi became a central principle in English landscape gardening, and it was easy, in view of the growing trend towards pictorial considerations based upon the spectator's taking up particular positions, to superimpose on Sharawadgi other aesthetic criteria such as that of the Picturesque.[12]

The ideas of Shaftesbury (1671–1713) represent a radical reaction against the formal Baroque garden. To Shaftesbury the gardens of Versailles stood for the spirit of absolutism, set on mutilating the forces of Nature; the 'wilderness' he saw by contrast as an image of human freedom.[13] As a result, ideas of freedom in the design of English landscape gardens became associated with Shaftesbury, although he himself did not express a view in favour of any particular form of garden.

In his influential essay *The Pleasures of the Imagination*, published in Nos 411 *et seq.* of his and Steele's *The Spectator* (1712),[14] Joseph Addison (1672–1797) pleaded for a balance between Nature and Art in garden design. He proposed 'an agreeable Mixture of Garden and Forest' and, by drawing attention to the 'pleasant Prospect' of a cornfield, combined considerations of aesthetics and estate management.[15] He follows Temple in opposing geometrically dissected parks and favouring the irregularity of the Chinese, and his occasional use of the words 'Prospect' and 'Garden' as synonyms reveals his conception of the garden as a picture.[16] Literary associations also play a rôle, as when he compares reading Homer's *Iliad* with a journey through uninhabited territory, and Virgil's *Aeneid* with a stroll through a well-planned garden. In No. 477 of *The Spectator*, in a letter purporting to be written to the editor, he carries his literary analogy to the point of equating types of garden with literary genres: 'Your Makers of Parterres and

Flower Gardens, are Epigrammatists and Sonneteers in this Art, Contrivers of Bowers and Grottos, Treillages and Cascades, are Romance Writers...'[17] He then goes on to describe, in a gently ironical tone, his vision of a garden arranged as a mixture of parterres and kitchen garden, orchard, and flower-beds, which results in 'a Picture of the greatest Variety', with a kitchen garden that is 'a more pleasant Sight than the finest Orangerie'. The 'Sharawadgi' of the Chinese and Shaftesbury's 'wild Nature' become one: 'There is the same Irregularity in my Plantations, which run into as great a wildness as their Natures will permit.'[18] Finally Addison describes the attractions of a winter garden and refers to the rôle of the garden as a substitute for a lost Paradise – on the one hand an allusion to Milton, on the other an anticipation of the numerous parks which were to contain 'Elysian Fields' as part of their design.

The ideas of Lord Burlington's circle about gardens found their clearest expression in Robert Castell's *The Villas of the Ancients Illustrated* (1728),[19] in which the author distinguishes three types of villa and three corresponding types of garden, on the basis of Vitruvius and the descriptions left by Pliny the Younger and Varro. Quoting from Classical sources, Castell describes symmetrical and non-symmetrical gardens, and a combination of the two. His reconstruction of Pliny's Tusculum consists of a totally symmetrical plan for the house, but with a combination of regular and irregular forms for the garden, like Burlington's villa at Chiswick.

The most striking instance of the literary contribution to the image of the garden occurs with Alexander Pope (1688–1744) and the gardens that he laid out around the house in Twickenham where he lived from 1718.[20] Twickenham was the stage on which the characters of an imaginary society acted out their parts; the garden was a mis-en-scène, at its centre the famous Grotto, which was both an image of the world as seen in Newtonian terms and a camera obscura. Pope interpreted it thus:

> When you shut the doors of the Grotto, it becomes on the instant, from a luminous Room, a Camera obscura; on the Walls of which all the Objects of the Rivers, Hills, Woods, and Boats, are forming a moving Picture in their visible radiations; and when you have a mind to light it up, it affords you a very different scene; it is finished with Shells interspersed with Pieces of Looking-glass in angular forms; and in the Ceiling is a Star of the same Material, at which when a Lamp (of an orbicular Figure of thin Alabaster) is hung in the Middle, a thousand pointed Rays glitter and are reflected over the Place.[21]

One is almost certainly entitled to see Pope's grotto as one of the sources for the representation of the cosmos in Boullée's monument to Newton.[22] Pope's starting-point is Addison: Nature and Art are reconciled, but at the same time he is working towards 'a Nature methodiz'd' within a pictorial concept.[23] In characteristically lofty tone he expresses it thus in his *Epistle to Lord Burlington* (1731):

> In all, let Nature never be forgot.
> But treat the Goddess like a modest fair,
> Nor overdress, nor leave her wholly bare;
> Let not each beauty ev'ry where be spy'd,
> Where half the skill is decently to hide.
> He gains all points, who pleasingly confounds,
> Surprizes, varies, and conceals the Bounds.
> Consult the Genius of the Place in all...[24]

The need to 'consult the Genius of the Place' becomes a cardinal principle of all later garden design. Both Pope's poetic entreaty and the religious didacticism of James Thomson's (1700–48) *The Seasons*[25] had a vital influence on the view of Nature that underlay the development of English landscape gardening.

The great innovators in English landscape gardening, such as Charles Bridgeman and William Kent, did not codify their principles as a formal theory of the subject, so that one has to turn to the works of lesser figures to discover what these principles were, figures who were themselves influenced by the philosophical and literary concepts of the time. Such a man was Stephen Switzer, who published a three-volume work, *Ichnographia Rustica, Or, The Nobleman, Gentleman and Gardener's Recreation* (1715–8),[26] which describes the transitional stage between the French and the English garden. Switzer takes the view that the garden must be adapted to suit the site. He appears to be the first theorist to recognise the possibility of enhancing the atmosphere of the locality by erecting ruins, 'since to Noble and Ingenious Natures a Piece of Ruin is more entertaining than the most beautiful Edifice; and the sorrowful Reflections they draw from the Soul ascend to very Heav'ns.'[27] This is the attitude that gave rise to the late eighteenth-century cult of ruins.[28]

Among his architectural pattern-books, Batty Langley (1696–1751) published one called *New Principles of Gardening* (1728),[29] which painted a highly favourable picture of Dezallier and accommodated the principle of irregularity above all in designs for labyrinths. It was Langley's axiom that the parts of a garden 'should be always presenting new Objects, which is continual Entertainment to the Eye',[30] and a particular feature of his 37-point programme is that the principal building in a garden no longer establishes the primary point of departure for the plan but is itself one of the elements of that plan. Yet in spite of his disapproval of 'Mathematical Regularity' and 'Stiffness', Langley is still very close to the concept of the French formal garden.

The 'associative' elements of the landscape garden are especially prominent in the poet William Shenstone's (1714–63) estate The Leasowes and in his posthumously published *Unconnected Thoughts on Gardening*.[31] Shenstone sees a garden as a landscape painting – 'the landskip painter is the gardiner's best designer.'[32] His aesthetic principles are derived from those of Burke, Hutcheson, Gerard, Hogarth and other contemporaries, and he applies the compositional principles of landscape painters by aiming not at symmetry but at 'ballance'. This is the way in which the house itself is built into the picture: 'A building for instance on one side, contrasted by a group of trees, a large oak, or a rising hill on the other.'[33] What matters to him is the associative effect, and he maintains, following Burke, that 'the sublime has generally a deeper effect than the merely beautiful.' Frequently, however, a moralising tendency prevails, emphasised or made explicit by the erection of monuments and the strategic positioning of tablets inscribed with mottos. Thus at The Leasowes he marked all the important viewpoints with benches, or with tablets bearing Greek or Latin inscriptions aimed at evoking the desired associations.

A key concept for Shenstone is 'variety', which, like that of the 'serpentine line', he took from Hogarth. Ruins form part of this 'variety': 'Ruinated structures appear to derive their power of pleasing, from the irregularity of surface, which is variety'.[34] He also adds a historical dimension to this concept by including genuine ruins in his plans.

In the course of a discussion at The Leasowes between Shenstone, William Lyttelton and James Thomson in 1746, the three poets, whilst considering Shenstone's Virgil's Grotto, came to the conclusion that place enhances the poetic spirit, and the poetic spirit enhances the sense of place.[35] The poet thus becomes a landscape painter who is stimulated by his own creation – in this case a work of art that can be entered and enjoyed.

In the second half of the century literary and allegorical interpretation of landscape gardening declined. The aesthetic background of the most successful gardener of the period, Lancelot ('Capability') Brown (1716–83),[36] is that of the theories of Burke and Hogarth, but it is noteworthy that Brown, a true professional, never felt it necessary to provide a theoretical basis for his work.

An intermediate position, based on the philosophical tenet of sensualism, between that of Brown and that of William Chambers (see below) is that adopted by the Scot Henry Home, Lord Kames (1692–1782) in his *Elements of Criticism* (1762),[37] chapter 24 of which is devoted to the art of gardening.[38]

The *Observations on Modern Gardening* (written 1765, published 1770) of Thomas Whately (d.1772) reflects the sensualist theory of gardening and is based on Burke's aesthetics.[39] Whately claims that landscape gardening is superior to landscape painting by virtue of its three-dimensional quality, the constantly changing conditions, such as the play of light, and the fact that the beholder can move around within it. Since Addison there had been an unbroken development towards the concept of the 'ornamental farm', and for Whately the criterion of 'utility' was fully reconcilable with his idyllic view of the landscape garden. His treatise, which, as the numerous editions and translations show, was one of the most influential of the time, also uses Boffrand and Laugier's ideas of '*caractère*' in its proposals for garden buildings.

Similar views are expressed by Horace Walpole (1717–97) in his essay *On Modern Gardening*, written before 1770, though not published until his *Anecdotes on Painting* (volume IV, 1780).[40] Walpole interprets the English garden as a historical phenomenon which owes its existence to William Kent, and sees it as an expression of the British constitution, in contrast to the French garden, the embodiment of absolutism. Previously Walpole had looked favourably on the idea of the 'Chinese' garden but now he rejects it, together with the *jardin anglo-chinois* popular in France, as mere 'caprice' and 'whim'. Both Walpole and Whately had a considerable influence on Continental theories of landscape gardening, such as those of Christian Hirschfeld.

Starting in 1772, William Mason (1725–97), a friend of Walpole's, published a four-part poem, *The English Garden*, to which he appended his own prose commentary.[41] The poem, turgid in style and opaque in meaning, extols English 'simplicity' as the renaissance of Greek freedom, and presents the complete union of garden and architecture; buildings should be disguised so as to merge with the landscape – a farmhouse, for instance, should become a 'Norman castle'. In contrast to Whately, however, Mason returns to the concept of landscape painting as the determining force in landscape gardening, and quotes in his support Claude Lorrain, Poussin, Salvator Rosa and Ruysdael. Although he did not believe that the Romans were acquainted with the art of free garden design, which he attributes to the Greeks, he advocates the construction of 'new Tivolis', a proposal that can only be explained in terms of a pictorial tradition:

> And scenes like these, on Memory's tablet drawn,
> Bring back to Britain; there give local form
> To each Idea; and, if Nature lend
> Materials fit of torrent, rock, and shad,
> Produce new TIVOLIS ... [42]

Mason takes over from Whately the principle that utility can be reconciled with beauty ('Beauty scorns to dwell, where use is exiled'), and maintains that the details in a garden must be made credible by reference to 'plausibility'. This means, for example, that ruins should be Gothic when erected in England, where such ruins would have historical verisimilitude, whereas Greek ruins would fly in the face of the facts.

Walpole and Mason were Whigs, who set out to translate their patriotic and democratic views to the realm of gardening, with the garden as the symbol of English simplicity and freedom. It is worth noting that the concept of the garden had long been associated with ideas of political order and paradise in England,[43] but the whole discussion took a sharply political turn at this moment with the publication in 1772 of *A Dissertation on Oriental Gardening* by the Tory William Chambers (1723–96) and rival publications from the Whiggish Walpole and Mason.[44]

In 1757, in the final section of his *Designs of Chinese Buildings*, Chambers, in the spirit of the Sharawadgi tradition, had praised Chinese gardens for their 'beautiful irregularities' and 'variety of scenes', and introduced 'pleasing, horrid and enchanted' as aesthetic categories. Still making this his point of departure, Chambers now strikes out in a different direction, taking the Chinese garden as merely a pretext for expounding his own ideas. *A Dissertation on Oriental Gardening* is couched in ironic and hyperbolic language and heavily indebted to Whately, yet is more than just a reworking of others' ideas. It opens with an attack on the formal French garden, in which Chambers pokes fun at the false view of architecture it embodied. But he immediately vents his irony also on the kind of English garden that is barely distinguishable from a common field, exhibiting 'little variety' and no artistic sense.[45] A 'resemblance to vulgar Nature' and 'eternal, uniform, undulating lines'[46] he declares unnatural, affected and boring. The target of his attack is Capability Brown, whom, however, he does not mention by name. He then proceeds to lay out his own system, claiming historical support from the observations he purports to have made in China, as well as from various authorities whose works he quotes. In Europe, he says, one finds only 'kitchen gardeners', whereas in China gardening is a 'distinct profession' in which botanists, painters and philosophers are all involved; the Chinese garden imitates the 'beautiful irregularities' of Nature but also corrects Nature's mistakes, and is therefore not averse to the application of the principles of art, for the aim is not only variety 'but also novelty and effect'.[47] At the same time, Chambers goes on, the Chinese are by no means opposed to straight lines and symmetrical geometric figures when they form part of smaller compositions.[48] The landscape gardener is, in fact, a poet: 'The scenery of a garden should differ as much from common nature as an heroic poem doth from a prose relation.'[49]

Chambers then proceeds to describe those features of the English garden of which he approves, calling them 'Chinese' – ha-has, sunk fences and so on. From here on his views become more and more fantastic. He proposes projects governed by the seasons of the year and the time of day, then, quoting the French Jesuit painter Jean-Denis Attiret,[50] refers to the palace-like buildings set in the Emperor's park in Peking, in an attempt to conceal the transition between town and garden. The idea of transferring the principles of town planning to the design of parks, and the patterns of landscape gardening to plans for urban development, figures prominently in eighteenth-century discussions. The garden buildings Chambers proposes for 'autumnal scenes' correspond exactly to those of European garden architecture – hermitages, ruined towers, palaces, temples, derelict religious buildings, and half-buried triumphal arches.[51] This determination of garden buildings by the seasons of the year appears to anticipate Boullée, whose ideas of *caractère* are in part derived directly from the attributes of the seasons.

Chambers then returns to the three modes of park design which he has formerly designated as Chinese, now defining them as 'the pleasing, the terrible and the surprizing',[52] showing a special fascination for 'surprizing, or supernatural scenes', which he describes as being of the 'romantic kind'.[53] Among such features awaiting the visitor are electric shocks, artificial rain and wind, earthquakes and explosions, and animal and human cries,[54] which leave none of his senses unaffected. Chambers had a particular predilection for the use of water, and conceived the possibility of deploying boats, whose movements would offer the spectator 'a thousand momentary varied pictures.'[55] Yet, according to him, every Chinese garden was *sui generis*, and there was no hope that Europeans could ever 'rival Oriental splendor.'[56] In sum, Chambers's work is a statement in extreme form of the sensualist theory of the landscape garden that sees itself as an imitation of Nature in her simplicity.

In his not particularly inspiring *Heroic Epistle* (1773) Mason dismissed Chambers as a Tory. Chambers defended himself in an 'Explanatory Discourse' appended to the second edition of his *Dissertation* (1773), taking issue with what he regarded as a dishonest cult of the idyllic among Whig ideologues, and claiming that a cultivated natural landscape was more 'picturesque' than the average English garden. With only a minimum of human intervention, he maintained, the whole of England could become 'a magnificent garden, bounded only by the sea', and the countryside was 'more picturesque than lawns, the most curiously dotted with clumps.' Chambers' work met with a more favourable reception in France than in England, where it was seen as calling into question the whole concept of the English garden, with its political and national overtones.

From the middle of the century onwards a new concept, already implicit in Shenstone and used by Chambers, came to dominate the discussion of aesthetic principles, especially those governing landscape gardening – the notion of the Picturesque.[57] An important figure in the evolution of this concept was William Gilpin (1724–1804), traveller and connoisseur, who had written in 1748 an anonymous description of the garden at Stowe, in Buckinghamshire, in which he characterised the park as a collection of pictures.[58] Between 1769 and 1777 Gilpin made a number of journeys through England, recording his findings in a series of *Observations* (from 1782), then, in 1792, in *Three Essays: On Picturesque Beauty*.[59] Since these works circulated privately before they were published, we may assume that their contents were known from an earlier date. As Gilpin saw it, 'irregularity' and 'roughness' combined to form the 'Picturesque', which he defines as the 'happy union of simplicity and variety, to which the rough ideas essentially contribute.'[60] Elsewhere he describes the Picturesque as the combination of the Sublime with the Beautiful, and by the end of the century the word, which had initially been used more in the sense of pictorial or painterly, had become a particular term of aesthetic connotation.

The concept of the 'Picturesque' garden may have had a further root in France,[61] for it was first formulated by Claude-Henri Watelet (1718–86), who from 1754 was engaged in making his estate of Moulin-Joli, outside Paris, into what was for a time one of the best-known examples of the 'Picturesque' garden.[62] Watelet recorded his thoughts in his *Essai sur les jardins* (1774)[63] in which elements of Rousseau, Whately and Chambers are to be found. Like Chambers he rejected both the formal French garden and the common English garden. He also advanced the idea of public gardens for townsfolk in need of recreation,[64] and put in a plea, in the French tradition of *utilité*, for the royal parks to be thrown open to the public. Garden design he regarded as an *ars liberalis*. The *ferme ornée*, as he describes it, combines '*utilité*' and '*plaisir*'; and '*simplicité*' ought to be the constant characteristic of garden buildings.[65] He defines his theory thus: 'Use will be the prime consideration of my Art: variety, order, and neatness its ornaments.'[66] Like Chambers, Watelet distinguishes three types of garden – '*le Pittoresque, le Poétique, le Romanesque* [romantic],'[67] the decisive factor in each case being the effect on the spectator. It is difficult to be sure what precisely he owes to his French, and what to his English sources. Following Chambers, he describes his estate of Moulin-Joli as a *jardin chinois*[68] – it combined conventional axial principles with Picturesque elements, which led Horace Walpole to describe it, after his visit in 1775, as a French garden in which no mortal had set foot for a hundred years.

Jean-Jacques Rousseau, whose view of Nature emerges especially clearly from the ideal of the park set out in his epistolary novel *La nouvelle Héloïse* (1761),[69] aimed at the approximation of the park to natural landscape, but in the last analysis his ideas turn out to be intellectualisations. The way in which he psychologises and moralises about the park as a substitute for Nature betrays his dependence on Shaftesbury and the English landscape garden, as does his employment of such criteria as abundance of variety and 'infinite line'. Rousseau's friend René-Louis de Girardin, in a treatise published in 1777,[70] produces a synthesis of ideas taken from Watelet, Whately and Rousseau which treats exclusively of aesthetic criteria, while a similar work, *Théorie des Jardins* (1776), by Jean-Marie Morel, who was employed by Girardin at Ermenonville, anticipates the language, though not the thought content, of so-called 'Revolutionary' architecture.[71] A further work in this context is that of the Abbé de Lille (1782).[72]

Particularly influential was a series of engravings by Georges-Louis Le Rouge, published in twenty-one volumes between 1776 and 1787, of '*jardins à la mode*' or '*jardins anglo-chinois*', which consisted of 492 plates of English, French and German gardens.[73] A French translation of Chambers's *Designs of Chinese Buildings* is incorporated, almost in its entirety, into Le Rouge's work, which combines the traditions of the English garden with Chambers's fanciful image of China and the first reliable views of Chinese gardens themselves.

In the final decade of the eighteenth century the concept of the Picturesque became a key factor in debate on aesthetics in England, and although its application went far beyond the field of landscape gardening, it was in this area that the arguments were at their most heated. Furthermore, one of the most prominent figures in the controversy was the leading landscape gardener of the time, which makes it necessary to summarise the issues that were at stake.

The debate had its origin in Edmund Burke's aesthetic categories of the Sublime and the Beautiful. The Picturesque, with various graduations, was placed somewhere between the two, as Gilpin had tried to establish. The debate took place within a small circle of men who began as friends, publishing their arguments and counter-arguments in a complex and often confusing series of books, poems and pamphlets.[74] The principal names to note are those of Uvedale Price (1747–1829), Richard Payne Knight (1750–1824) and Humphry Repton (1752–1818).[75]

Uvedale Price was a Whig Member of Parliament and owner of an estate at Foxley, which he redesigned according to his own notions. In 1794 he published his *Essay on the Picturesque*, which he revised during the following years and produced in its final form in 1810 in his three-volume work *Essays on the Picturesque*.[76] Like Chambers, he accuses Capability Brown of monotony, and finds his criteria for garden design in landscape painting.[77] Proceeding from Burke and Gilpin, he sets out to establish his concept of the Picturesque as having a validity equal to that of the Sublime and the Beautiful; he also extends the concept to other arts, such as music, and uses it to characterise Gothic architecture.[78] The Sublime was not amenable to human manipulation, but the Picturesque – combined with 'roughness', as Gilpin had put it – could serve as a shaping principle.

The reduction of gardening to the compositional principles of landscape painting, as exemplified by Salvator Rosa above all, was bound to meet with opposition, and this came immediately from Humphry Repton, who published an open letter to Price in 1794,[79] defending, as a professional gardener, his predecessor Brown and declaring that beauty, not picturesqueness, was the true measure of garden design. Without completely denying the relationship between landscape painting and garden design, he lays the emphasis of the latter on practical considerations: 'Propriety and convenience are not less objects of good taste, than picturesque effect.'[80] Repton regards an exclusive appeal to landscape painting as a restricting influence, and therefore plays down the criterion of the Picturesque, insisting that painting and garden design are two different things, as are 'landscape' and 'prospect'.[81]

Price felt that his views had been misunderstood, and expanded his position in an open letter of his own (1795),[82] in which he first rejects Repton's categories of convenience and propriety as non-aesthetic, then declares that the faculty of taste cannot assert itself 'unless the general effect of the picture be good.'[83] It is an extreme view of the garden as a picturesque image, and as such it could not be acceptable to a landscape gardener such as Repton, whose later writings reveal an increasing tendency to stylistic eclecticism,[84] which not unnaturally led to his cooperation with John Nash. This eclecticism issued on the one hand in his so-called 'improvements' – in his *Red Books* it was his habit first to describe the existing situation, then to propose ways of improving it – and on the other hand in his singular development of sylistic correspondences, such as Graeco-Roman = horizontal, Gothic = vertical, Chinese = a combination of the two, a form he denounced as hybrid. The earliest work to be published in this controversy was Richard Payne Knight's didactic poem *The Landscape* (1794).[85] Like Price, Knight opposes Capability Brown and the established rules of garden design:

Nature in all rejects the pedant's chain;
Which binding beauty in its waving line,
Destroys the charm it vainly would define...[86]

Even more rigidly than Price, Knight defines landscape gardening in terms of the imitation of landscape painting, based on the compositional principle of foreground, middle ground and background ('Three points of distance always should unite'). Knight's poem provoked not only Repton's riposte, but also a considerable number of substantial reviews.[87]

In 1805, in *An Analytical Inquiry into the Principles of Taste* – the title itself recalls Burke – Knight set out in a deceptively systematic way to undermine Burke's aesthetic categories,[88] providing an interesting history of the concept of the Picturesque and linking it to Venetian painting of the sixteenth century.[89] But the attraction of the Picturesque lies for him in the excitement of the senses, and is no longer restricted to painting; he sees the essence of the Picturesque in the abandonment of firm outlines, as opposed to the ideal of closed form. Here he anticipates certain points in Wölfflin's *Kunstgeschichtliche Grundbegriffe* (1915). Taking over Hogarth's 'line of beauty', he makes it into the 'line of picturesqueness'. Time and again Knight rejects the idea of regularity, and justifies a combination of different styles by reference to his own Downton Castle, the exterior of which is 'medieval', but the interior 'Roman'. The fact that not only the garden but also architecture itself was judged in terms of the Picturesque shows how blurred the dividing lines between the arts had become by the late eighteenth century.

Another participant in this controversy over the Picturesque was John Claudius Loudon (1783–1843), a Scotsman who, in a massive, encyclopaedic work, set out to establish a new scientific foundation for the art of garden design.[90] In place of the concept of the Picturesque he proposes a new concept, the 'Gardenesque', which he traces back to Repton, whose collected writings he edited in 1840.[91] On the one hand Loudon tries to combine the 'Picturesque' garden with the science of botany; on the other, he returns to the 'geometric' garden and proposes garden buildings in every conceivable style. There is no end to his eclecticism; he is thereby a pioneer of historicism in the field of landscape gardening, an approach already hinted at in Repton's plans for detached gardens in historical styles. His *Encyclopaedia of Gardening* (1822) is the first important comprehensive history of garden design, and *The Gardener's Magazine*, which he edited from 1826, was the first learned journal devoted to the subject.

Also significant is Loudon's contribution to the construction of hothouses, a subject on which he wrote a number of articles from 1805 onwards.[92] His idea was for curvilinear iron structures, of the kind later adopted by his friend Paxton. Loudon took a functionalist view according to which every hothouse should look like what it is, and each part should exhibit its own particular function externally.[93] At the same time he believed that he could combine such ideas with a plurality of architectural styles. Loudon's increasingly scientific approach introduced a new function for the garden which, however, could still accommodate earlier conceptions.

Germany appears comparatively late on the scene in the field of garden design, but when it did, it was with the most comprehensive work that had been seen up to that time.

Sundry plans and descriptions of gardens[94] are found from the seventeenth century onwards but almost without exception they are incorporated in works on architecture. Among the names that come to mind are Furttenbach, Böckler and Decker.[95]

German gardens took their lead first from the formal French garden, then from the English landscape garden.[96] No attempt was made to mirror the local situation. The new feeling for Nature manifested in the literary works of Albrecht von Haller, Ewald von Kleist and Salomon Gessner remained totally without influence on the fashionable gardens of the time, and only in the 1770s did discussions on the theory of the subject begin. In his *Allgemeine Theorie der Schönen Künste* (1771–4), for example, Johann Goerg Sulzer put up a strong case for the basic principles of the English garden,[97] favouring in his somewhat arid Enlightenment manner a garden both large and useful. Sulzer knew Christian Hirschfeld, who makes reference to Sulzer in his work (see below).

How poverty-stricken, however, German adaptations of the English landscape garden were sometimes felt to be emerges from Justus Möser's essay *Das englische Gärtgen* of 1773, in which he mocks not only the Anglomania of the time but the perversion of the very idea of the garden itself. He scornfully describes how a garden with a bleaching-ground and a herb garden is transformed into an 'enchanted island', 'in which one finds everything that one is not expecting, and nothing that one is expecting.' Then there is a Chinese bridge imported from England and, instead of a bleaching-shed, 'a charming little Gothic cathedral.' Möser's final sentence shows how alien the notion of the garden has become: 'when you come, make sure that you bring some white cabbage with you from the town, because we have no room to grow it any longer.'[98]

Möser felt the English garden to be a foreign body, an imposition; the need was for an analysis of what a garden really was, and of whether there was a specifically German form of it. This was the task carried out, with characteristic German painstaking thoroughness, by Christian Cay Lorenz Hirschfeld (1742–92), professor of philosophy in Kiel, whose *Theorie der Gartenkunst* began to appear in 1779, and had swollen to five volumes by 1785.[99] Hirschfeld had already written on the subject in 1773 and 1775,[100] and his *magnum opus* was the most substantial treatment of it in the eighteenth century. Hirschfeld's constant interpolation of fresh personal experiences from his travels and of recent literature on the subject meant that although his work was systematically planned, its execution was far from systematic. Much of his knowledge of European gardens was second-hand – he never visited England, for example – and only his descriptions of certain German gardens are based on personal experience. He propounds his Enlightenment-inspired ideas in a long-winded and moralising manner, without a spark of imagination or humour. Thus, having first translated long passages from Chambers's *Dissertation on Oriental Gardening*, he sets out to justify his doubts as to whether such gardens ever existed.[101] Though far from producing a self-contained, let alone an original, theory of garden design, he makes a number of eclectic points that deserve attention. He conscientiously studied English and French books, but the majority of the lavish volumes of plates of the period were not available to him.[102] The selection of illustrations that he includes in his work is of a random nature and generally of scant relevance to the text – rather, they have the function of taste-forming vignettes.

Hirschfeld is moderate in his judgements. Landscape painting he describes as 'the dearest sister of garden design',[103] and he detects manifestations of national character in the gardens of different countries. He scorns the symmetrical French garden, which he accuses of abusing Nature by forcing it to submit to rules:[104] 'Garden design in their hands was no more than architecture imposed upon the earth.'[105] He expresses distaste and boredom for the gardens of Versailles but observes with a certain satisfaction: 'In our day enlightened ideas about gardening appear to have spread from England to France',[106] then reproduces Watelet's description (1774) of his estate of Moulin-Joli. The English are credited with 'sound taste' and Palladianism is described as 'a noble architecture in the Greek style'.[107] Conjuring up the spirit of the German nation, he finds that Germany 'is perhaps more sensitive to the beauties of Nature than any other nation, and is fonder of the picturesque idyll than any other.'[108] This, however, is hardly adequate as a definition of national character in respect of a specifically German garden, and the only conjecture Hirschfeld can make is: 'A middle way between the two prevailing forms of taste will eventually be found.'[109]

Hirschfeld makes an interesting distinction between architecture and gardening by making kinaesthetic considerations crucial to the latter: 'The aim of the architect is to satisfy the eye instantaneously, to let it seize the whole harmonious arrangement of his structure in one go; the garden designer seeks to maintain interest step by step.' He upholds 'a sweet disorder in the dress', which he translates as *eine gewisse anmuthige Verwickelung* (literally 'a certain charming complexity'), for 'variety of effects', and concludes: 'The garden designer succeeds best when, almost everywhere, he does the opposite of what an architect would do.'[110] In his plea for public parks, on the other hand, he envisages straight avenues and symmetrical designs: 'Straight avenues are here not merely permissible, but to be preferred, in that they facilitate surveillance by the authorities, which is often indispensable in such places.'[111] Just such considerations were then determining the layout of the Prater in Vienna and the cutting back of high hedges in the Tuileries. At the same time Hirschfeld also saw the public park as a place where the different classes could come closer together. Strangely enough, he was prepared to accept garden buildings of all kinds, provided that they were not mere embellishments of a prospect, but harmonised in character and association with their setting.[112]

Both landscapes and parks, in Hirschfeld's view, have an educative function. While the Alps evoke 'a soaring of the human spirit,'[113] a garden enhances 'awareness of God's goodness', and arouses cheerfulness, liveliness and gentleness. For a garden is an intensification of Nature through Art. Hence Hirschfeld's final sentence and summation: 'God created the world; Man embellished it.'[115]

Hirschfeld classifies gardens according to climate, most favourable season and time of day, status of the owner, and 'character of the setting'.[116] For the apprehension of this last he draws both on English sensualism and on the French concept of *caractère*, and offers five categories: 1) pleasing, cheerful, festive gardens; 2) gently melancholy gardens; 3) romantic gardens; 4) solemn gardens; 5) gardens consisting of a combination of these types. The 'romantic' garden evokes surprise, amazement, a pleasant sense of astonishment and a mood of meditation[117] – indeed, it is 'almost wholly a work of Nature'.[118] Garden buildings depend on the ways in which the beholder's feelings respond to the different types of landscape, which it is their function to enhance; thus grottos belong to the 'romantic', hermitages to the 'gently melancholy' garden,[119] while artificial ruins are what he calls 'a fertile source of pleasure and of the sweetest melancholy'.[120]

In many respects Hirschfeld produces a forced synthesis of virtually irreconcilable opposites, and he is sometimes very ungenerous towards his predecessors. He accuses

Decker's designs of 'the most extravagant ornament and excesses, such as only the most vulgar and degenerate taste could invent', and calls the theories of Briseux and Blondel on the design of country villas 'superficial and meagre'.[121] He adopts a critical attitude towards the gardens of his century that he has visited but occasionally finds himself at something of a loss. On Wilhelmshöhe at Kassel, for instance, he writes: 'No more than the imagination can the eye be compelled by laws unknown to Nature', and he also has doubts about the mythological content of the grounds as a whole: 'With all these ideas borrowed from mythology two doubts arise: are they of sufficient interest for the times we live in, and even if they are, is a garden the place for them?'[122]

Rich though it is in information and ideas, Hirschfeld's work does not afford a practical basis for designing parks and gardens, and although it is still today quoted with respect, its influence must not be overestimated. A work such as Grohmann's *Ideenmagazin für Gartenliebhaber*, with its great stock of illustrations, made a far greater impression at the end of the century.

The discussion of the art of garden design spread to other circles at the end of the eighteenth century, and men of letters also became involved.[123] In Weimar, Schiller and Goethe both concerned themselves with the theory of the subject. There is a clear reference to Hirschfeld, for example, in Schiller's review article, *Über den Gartenkalender auf das Jahr 1795*:[124] 'It is thus probable that a good middle way between the rigidity of the French style of garden and the anarchy of the so-called English garden will be found.'[125] Like Möser, Schiller is highly critical of German Anglomania and talks of the 'childish littleness' of the 'English gardens' in Germany. He accepts a 'poetic style of garden', derived from the 'true devotees of feeling' – that is, from the principle of association – but regards the Picturesque garden as a failure, 'because it trespasses beyond its own sphere into that of paintings.'[126] Schiller's own definition of the art of garden design is one 'which uses Nature to exemplify herself, and can only move us insofar as it is absolutely indistinguishable from Nature;'[127] the urge to variety has only resulted in pettiness and arbitrariness. All the more surprising is it, therefore, to find Schiller conclude his review with a highly complimentary description of the park of Hohenheim, near Stuttgart.

An embryonic essay by Goethe and Schiller, *Über den Dilettantismus* (1799),[128] contains the sharpest critical appraisal of the concept of the landscape garden ever made, under the heading '*Gartenkunst*'. Its positive aspects are defined as: 'Making a picture out of the actual, and so in brief, a first step towards Art.'[129] Then following Sulzer and Hirschfeld: 'The social effects of a neat and wholly beautiful environment are always beneficial'.[130] The succeeding critical observations, however, have to be quoted in full.

> Reality is treated as if it were fantasy. The love of gardens tends to break all bounds, because 1) the concept is neither definable nor limitable; and b) its raw materials are random and ever-changing, eternally threatening the Idea with dissolution. The love of gardens pillages the nobler arts in an unworthy fashion, and turns their solid worth into a plaything. Encourages nullity of feeling and imagination. It belittles and dissolves the Sublime in Nature by imitating it. It perpetuates the dominant vice of the age, the desire to fling oneself into the aesthetic without let or rule, and to rhapsodise at will, in that, apparently unlike other arts, it is not susceptible to discipline or correction.[131]

In addition Goethe and Schiller regarded associative buildings as inimical to the true concept of architecture:

> The structures this gives rise to are insubstantial, spindly, made of timber, planks and the like, and destroy the very idea of solid architecture – indeed, they destroy the taste for it. Thatched roofs, clapboard imitations: it all makes for a house of cards.[132]

Though they now virtually rejected the landscape garden, its principles had been Goethe's inspiration for his design of the park in Weimar only a few years earlier.

The Romantics, who talked disparagingly of 'manufacturers of ideal Nature' ('*Verfertiger der schönen Natur*' – Tieck), took a somewhat different line in their vehement criticism of the landscape garden but used similar arguments.[133] They implicitly returned to the concept of the French garden, and Tieck went so far as to the hope 'that in ten years to come many of the so-called natural parks will be converted into such embodiments of artifice.'[134] Hegel then took the logical step in his *Aesthetics* of excluding garden design from the company of the fine arts altogether, and ranging it among the imperfect arts.

When Goethe later returned to the subject of the landscape garden in his novel *Elective Affinities* (1809),[135] he presented the associative principle in an extreme form, making the plan of the garden, and the alterations to it, a direct projection of the spiritual lives of the characters. By 1809 the landscape garden had been written off in literary terms. By drawing an analogy between the planning of the garden and the action of the novel, Goethe was hinting symbolically at the tragic end of the story.

In his design for the gardens of the palace of Nymphenburg outside Munich, Friedrich Ludwig von Sckell (1750–1823) followed the middle way between the English and the French garden proposed by Hirschfeld and Schiller. The most important of all German landscape gardeners, Sckell summed up the results of his practical experience in his *Beiträge zur bildenden Gartenkunst* (1818).[136] Sckell takes up a theoretical position which is thoroughly conventional. He adopts the categories of Vitruvius, whose views he discusses at length in connection with his approval of erecting Classical temples in parks. English and French elements complement each other, and he quotes his sources by name.[137] One is reminded of the language of the French sensualists when he describes gardens as 'images of Nature' and 'Nature in her festive raiment'.[138] He expresses qualified opposition to the geometrical garden, while conceding the value of its majestic avenues and their splendid and imposing vistas for public thoroughfares in cities,[139] and in common with Hirschfeld he supports the idea of public parks because they help to bring about the 'rapprochement of all classes of society ... in the lap of ideal Nature'.[140]

As to his choice of means, Sckell shows himself an eclecticist:

> Hence the garden designer can choose and construct the images that suit the site, regardless of whether they appear large or small. Nature will recognise them as her own, provided that they are shaped by her laws and to her forms, and are brought together in a picturesque image resembling her, without overdoing it.[141]

He accepts all the types of garden buildings developed in the course of the eighteenth century but vents his wrath on what he calls 'formless and tasteless Chinoiseries' ('*form- und geschmacklose chinesische Baukunst*').[142] In his discussion of artificial ruins he calls for the qualities of 'solitude and awesome silence' ('*Einsamkeit und schauerliche Stille*'),[143] showing how firmly set he still was in the tradition of Burke's concept of the Sublime.

Hogarth's 'line of beauty' also has a considerable influence on his thinking: he describes how a landscape designer would mark out his paths by following 'with resolute steps the serpentine line ... which represents his practised eye, and hovers before him as an ideal.'[144] His allegiance to the tradition of the Enlightenment emerges with his constant insistence on the need to combine an appeal to the inspiration of Nature with the demand for Truth; and as with Repton, botanical factors occupy a prominent place in his thinking. Both his formal achievements and his ideas have continued to make themselves felt down to the present day.[145]

Marking the swan-song of the theory of the landscape garden is Prince Hermann von Pückler-Muskau (1785–1871), with his *Andeutungen über Landschaftsgärtnerei* (1834),[146] a work wholly in the English tradition but at the same time demonstrating a full awareness of the dangers of Anglomania. Capability Brown, so often an object of scorn, is for Pückler the 'Shakespeare of the Garden', and elements of the Picturesque garden find themselves natural companions of the ideas of Repton and Loudon. Pückler proceeds from the axiom that a garden must be based on the principle 'of making a concentrated image of natural landscape, creating the poetic ideal of such nature in little.'[147] He sees the garden as a series of pictures – 'for a garden in the grand style is nothing other than a picture gallery.'[148] He is at one with Hirschfeld in insisting that garden buildings should 'stand in rational relationship to their setting, and always have a definable purpose'.[149] Mythology, on the other hand, has no place in his scheme of things.

Pückler gives a great deal of practical advice, based on his experience in designing his park at Muskau, which he describes and illustrates in great detail in the second part of the work, showing how the various 'pictures' of his garden were intended. His appeal to the 'poetic ideal' takes one back to Schiller, but it is at the same time the expression of an escape from reality. The poetic garden is for him a compensation for the social changes that he observes around him, a sanctuary rescued from the past: 'Yours [the *Bürgerlich*] is now the power and the wealth; allow the nobility, which has served its turn, the poetry: the only thing that remains to it.'[150]

In the second half of the nineteenth century and down to the present, discussion of these matters has been determined to a large extent by the aesthetic ideal of the landscape garden. But the theory of garden design has been increasingly absorbed into that of town-planning, which takes its criteria from social and technical concerns, rather than from aesthetic principles.

21. Nineteenth-century France and the Ecole des Beaux-Arts

Since Emil Kaufmann's work on Ledoux and Boullée[1] it has been customary to date the beginnings of modern architecture from the so-called 'Revolutionary architects' of France. As has been pointed out earlier in this book, this is an inaccurate view, for Boullée and Ledoux represent eighteenth-century concepts in their extreme form rather than a radical new beginning, and their influence has been frequently overestimated. Nevertheless, without accepting a historical break – which it suits certain architects' self-image to claim never took place – a change of direction in the generation of Boullée's and Ledoux's pupils may be detected, a turning away from the architect's visionary claims for the importance of his role, an avoidance of the spectacular in favour of more modest, more practicable goals.

In early nineteenth-century France discussion of architectural theory was almost exclusively the prerogative of teachers and graduates of the Ecole des Beaux-Arts and the Ecole Polytechnique in Paris. The outlook of these institutions was given a bad name by adherents of the Modern movement of the twentieth century, despite the fact that the ideas of this period prepared the way for the Modern movement. A distorted historical picture emerged in which the Beaux-Arts tradition was made the cause of all retrogressive tendencies and the vision was created of a Modern style that lay outside history. The rediscovery of the Ecole des Beaux-Arts dates from 1975, when the Museum of Modern Art, New York devoted an exhibition to the hitherto scorned institution, with a major catalogue.[2] Further publications have since appeared,[3] but we are still far from a full assessment of the most influential school of architecture in Europe in the nineteenth century. What follows is a survey of the ideas of the most important figures associated with it.

In 1803 a pupil of Ledoux, Louis-Ambroise Dubut (1760–1846), who in 1797 had won the Grand Prix competition with a design for a public granary,[4] published a work modest in aim and scope, *Architecture civile*.[5] It is clear from the brief text and plates that Dubut worked into his book, which appeared the year before his teacher Ledoux's own *L'Architecture*, his impressions from a visit to Italy undertaken with the first grant awarded by the Ecole des Beaux-Arts after its re-establishment. Dubut's treatise is concerned exclusively with residential buildings, the '*habitation du citadin*'. The link with Ledoux is clear from the plates, but Dubut dispenses with all forms of '*architecture parlante*' and employs the Classical orders and historical styles. His short introduction reveals a deep-seated difference of approach from that of Ledoux; his criteria are '*la disposition, la salubrité et l'économie*',[6] which come together under the heading of '*utilité*': 'Is there anything more pleasurable than a house in which our needs are perfectly satisfied? It brings delight to our lives and helps us to spend our days in happiness.'[7]

For Dubut the exterior decoration of a building ('*décoration*') depended not on considerations of '*décor*' or '*aractère*' but on the arrangement of the plan and the nature of the materials used. This reference to materials harks back to arguments put forward by Scamozzi, Lodoli and others which had been ignored by the Revolutionary architects. Dubut believed that his ideas were already present in Italian palace architecture of the Renaissance, which he sought to imitate and adapt to French needs. His treatise was addressed to both architect and client.

The title-page of Dubut's *Architecture civile* may have influenced Karl Friedrich Schinkel's design for the main staircase of the Altes Museum in Berlin. Eschewing utopian ideas, Dubut based his designs, which have no accompanying text but are merely numbered, on carefully observed Italian models. A remarkable example is his House No. 2, for which he offers designs in two different designs, one 'Gothic', the other 'Italian' (*Plate 152*), with the same plan and spatial arrangement. This reveals an incipient historicism comparable with Schinkel's alternative designs for the Friedrichs-werder Church in Berlin. At the end of the book Dubut shows all the designs he has presented on two plates to the same scale, in order to help a potential client decide on appropriate dimensions.

An even more marked departure from Revolutionary architecture was that of Boullée's pupil Jean-Nicolas-Louis Durand (1760–1834),[8] second prize-winner in the Prix de Rome of 1779 and 1780 with designs for a museum and a college on a triangular site.[9] Durand had studied at the Académie Royale d'Architecture and held a chair of architecture from 1795 to 1830 at the Ecole Polytechnique, the engineering school founded in 1794.[10] His simplifying schematism must be largely attributable to the fact that his students were not architects but engineers. It was a feature of his very first work, *Recueil et parallèle des édifices de tout genre, anciens et modernes* (1800),[11] a typological atlas of architecture, in which he aimed to present in schematic form the most important monuments of all ages and all nations. All the monuments were shown (except on the title-page) in plan, elevation and section only, and to a uniform scale. By treating the different styles as of equal value he made a far greater contribution to historicism than that of Fischer von Erlach (*Plate 153*). Among the perspective views on his title-page is the reconstruction of the Propylaeum of the Acropolis in Athens (*Plate 127*) from *Les Ruines des plus beaux monuments de la Grèce* (1758) by Julien-David Le Roy, a professor of the Académie Royale and head of the Ecole Spéciale d'Architecture (which evolved into the Ecole des Beaux-Arts after his death). Here Durand was still under the influence of Neo-classicism, which his two Grand Prix designs, derived from Marie-Joseph Peyre, also reveal.[12]

Durand's lectures at the Ecole Polytechnique were published from 1802 as *Précis des leçons d'architecture*,[13] the many editions and translations of which made this the most significant treatise on architecture of the first half of the nineteenth century. The author draws particular attention to the increasing divergence of architecture and civil engineering, recognising that the latter will eventually become a discipline in its own right.[14] His general definition of architecture seems to recall Alberti in its emphasis on 'usefulness both public and private, conservation, and the happiness of the individual, the family and society.'[15]

Durand's open break with the Vitruvian tradition, the theory of mimesis and Laugier's theory of the primitive hut leads him to a radical conception of architecture reduced to the two principles of 'propriety' ('*convenance*') and 'economy' ('*économie*'), the former embracing the concepts of '*solidité*', '*salubrité*' and '*commodité*', the latter those of '*symétrie*', '*régularité*' and '*simplicité*'.[16] For him the basic forms of all architecture are the square and the right angle, which he also regards as the basis of town-planning; together with the Neo-classical concept of '*simplicité*', these two ideas are subsumed under the heading of '*économie*' – a profanation of the concepts taught by his teacher Boullée. He formally retains the Classical orders, but by rejecting their derivation from the proportions of the human body[17] he deprives them of their fixed proportional values and opens them to all possibilities.[18]

Durand's overriding concept was that of '*disposition*', which had already dominated discussion of architectural theory in France at the beginning of the eighteenth century. He saw the sole object of architecture as 'the most fitting and the most economic disposition' ('*la disposition la plus convenable et la plus économique*').[19] From this the aesthetic categories of '*grandeur*', '*magnificence*', '*variété*', '*effet*' and '*caractère*' automatically followed.[20] Durand's functionalism was total, and architectural ornament was to him superfluous.

Durand's next step took him along the path of constructive functionalism, in that he now emphasised the dependence of form on properties of material (accepting certain forms evolved by custom, with secondary status). The principle that he put forward, that form is the result of the nature of the materials,[21] probably goes back to Lodoli, whose ideas were popularised by Algarotti; how Durand became acquainted with them is of secondary importance.

Durand's rationalist principles demanded codification into a systematic theory of architectural composition. By postulating their universal validity – 'such are the general principles that at all times and in all places...'[22] – he was also able to project his system back over the entire history of architecture. The result was a grid system of composition which he describes in detail in the second part of his first volume.

For Durand architecture consisted only of horizontals and verticals and combinations of the two, i.e. his starting-point was not that of architectural space but of plan and elevation, whose combination produced a building in terms of volume. Significantly, his *Précis* contains no perspective drawings, and he specifically condemns the use of washes in architectural drawings.[23] This is a matter of considerable consequence, since it makes for an infinite number of combinations of architectural space according to the requirements of '*disposition*', and removes ideas of space and proportion from prime consideration.

As he demonstrates in his grid system (*Plate 154*), Durand sees unlimited possibilities in the combination of architectural features and illustrates such sequences of combinations in individual features and building types. He has reached the theoretical point of standardisation enabling prefabricated construction (*Plate 155*). Durand himself did not envisage this possibility, but Paxton's Crystal Palace, built for the Great Exhibition of 1851, consisted of prefabricated components and was the practical result of Durand's theories; the formal similarity between certain of Durand's sketches and the Crystal Palace is hardly a coincidence.

Durand's rationalist approach to architecture led him to produce soulless designs which Gottfried Semper scornfully dismissed as the work of a 'chess Grand Master of empty ideas' ('*Schachbrettkanzler für mangelnde Ideen*'), but his influence on Romantic Classicists in Germany such as Schinkel, Klenze, Fischer and Weinbrenner was considerable.[24] At many points he anticipated the functionalism of the 1920s, though in including a design by Percier[25] he showed that he was not quite as radical as his *Précis* made him out to be.

Views related to those of Durand, though less radically expressed, were put forward by Jean-Baptiste Rondelet (1734–1829), a friend of Durand's though a generation older, who was one of the founding fathers of the Ecole Polytechnique and taught at the Ecole des Beaux-Arts from 1799, where in 1806 he was appointed to the Chair of Stereotomy and Building Construction.[26] A pupil of Jacques-François Blondel and Boullée, Rondelet travelled through Italy in 1783–84. His five-volume *Traité théorique et pratique de l'art de bâtir* (1802–17)[27] was a practical pendant to Durand's *Précis des leçons*. He summarised his architectural aesthetic in the preface to the first volume, many of the ideas expressed being those of Jacques-François Blondel. Like Durand he stresses the importance of '*distribution*', '*construction*' and '*économie*', but also demands '*magnificence*' and accepts ornament, '*qui doivent être analogues au genre de l'édifice*'.[28]

The main source of Rondelet's importance is the comprehensive theory of materials and building construction given in the second, third and fourth volumes of his work. He was one of the first to undertake systematic analysis of the use of iron and the statics of iron structures, to which he was first drawn while working under Soufflot at the Panthéon in Paris.[29] He examined iron bridges in detail and wrote an analytical study of the famous bridge at Coalbrookdale in Shropshire, built in 1777–81.[30] He was the first to attempt to express the tensile and compressive strength of materials mathematically and in tabular form. He also developed a new method for the precise calculation of building costs, an undertaking considerably favoured by the recent introduction of the metre as a unit of measurement (Durand too used the metric system, the adoption of which had been approved by the French National Assembly in 1795). It is worth mentioning here that there is a relationship between the introduction of the abstract metric system and the simultaneous abandonment of Classical theories of proportion. Ideas of proportion in architecture are derived from anthropometric principles and came to be expressed in measures of anthropometric origin; it is significant that Durand denied any connection between architecture and the human body, and that Rondelet drew attention to the importance of geometry without mentioning the subject of proportion.

In his aesthetic conceptions Rondelet was rooted in eighteenth-century ideas, which enjoyed a new popularity in the Napoleonic age. This is evident, for instance, in his illustration of the Baths of Caracalla in Rome,[31] copied from Marie-Joseph Peyre's book of 1765.[32] The rationalist tendency and proto-functionalism of Dubut, Durand and Rondelet are the roots of decisive developments of the twentieth century. Their ideas made a considerable impact on the debate on architectural theory of their day, but traditionalist thinkers proved more influential and, as a consequence of the political situation, managed to stamp their authority on built architecture.

Napoleon had initially favoured engineer-designed architecture, but as Consul and Emperor he developed a liking for an imperial, prestige style,[33] as practised in particular by the architects Charles Percier (1764–1838) and Pierre-François-Léonard Fontaine (1762–1853), the latter being appointed First Architect in 1807.[34] As with Dubut, the ideas of these two were moulded by their experience of Italy, where they stayed from 1786 to 1792. Their sketches and drawings were published in 1798 as *Palais, Maisons, et autres édifices modernes dessinés à Rome*.[35] Their Rome was that of the High and Late Renaissance, as announced on their title-page bearing medallion portraits of Bramante, Antonio da Sangallo and Peruzzi. The concept of architecture that emerges from their '*Discours préliminaire*' emphasises the link between Antiquity and the Renaissance, but at the same time finding in the latter 'certain aesthetic values' of the contemporary age, such as '*utilité*', '*caractère*', '*bon goût*' and '*économie*'.[36] In Renaissance architecture they find '*raisons d'économie*', and for them the aim of architecture is to achieve 'great effects with the simplest means' ('*beaucoup d'effet avec les moyens les plus simples*').[37] They also represent the view, more effectively formulated by Ledoux, that a simple burgher's house requires as much architectural effort as the most splendid palace.[38] The ambivalence of their attitude to history emerges clearly in this work of 1798 when, instead of requiring that Renaissance buildings be copied exactly, they try to combine 'the direction taken by Italian architects' ('*la marche suivie par les architectes italiens*') with the demands of the French climate, materials and aesthetic preferences.[39] They also devote attention to early Christian basilicas, seeing the Early Church in Renaissance decorative terms.[40]

The immense success of Percier and Fontaine lay in their designs for interior decoration, in which the basic principle was the interaction of architectural structure and decorative forms. Antiquity, which they saw as also embracing Egyptian art, gradually became their sole model, and their *Recueil de décorations intérieures* (1801, 1812)[41] was the most important pattern-book published in the Napoleonic age. In the '*Discours préliminaire*' to this work they apply their view of architecture to interior decoration, rejecting features merely reflective of fashion and demanding that each piece of furniture shall possess 'that quality of utility and convenience which its function demands' ('*cette raison d'utilité, de commodité qu'enseigne son emploi*').[42] They compare the structure of a building to a human skeleton, but 'it must be embellished without being completely concealed' ('*on doit l'embellir sans la masquer entièrement*').[43] A close relationship ('*rapport intime*') exists between construction and decoration, the influence of climate, country and function manifesting itself in the latter. Although Percier and Fontaine did not intend their designs to be taken as models but merely as experiments, their ideas proved to be of considerable subsequent influence.

The clearest statement of their theoretical position comes in their *Résidences de Souverains* (1833),[44] containing their own projects for palaces for Napoleon, most of them never executed, based on buildings from earlier periods. Percier and Fontaine worked on without constraint after Napoleon's fall; their designs convey the spirit of Napoleonic imperialism, their views on architecture being formulated almost incidentally, in the course of their presentation of individual projects. They strongly criticise Perrault's Louvre colonnade as being a mere end in itself, bearing no relationship to the interior plan of the palace.[45] On the subject of the Palazzo Pitti in Florence, they declare their respect for historical solutions – treated with caution in their own designs – and deny the charge of being old-fashioned, appealing to the power of reason and accepting the existence of architectural forms differing from one nation to another and in response to the pressure of customs.[46] They enlarge on the question of the correct use of historical models, on which they had touched in their first work:

> We regard Classical architecture, Renaissance architecture, modern architecture and that of other ages not as types of doctrine which have to be obeyed but as

individual subdivisions which distinguish the products of one and the same art, and work towards the same goal, like scientific discoveries which everyone has exploited according to his own needs and which it is important to study in order to profit from the benefits they convey.[47]

The decisive criteria are those of taste, experience and reason.

Of particular interest is their discussion of the palace of Caserta, which they admire for its grandeur but criticise for its 'complete uniformity': 'everything is grand, everything is magnificent in this rich abode, but everything is also gloomy, monotonous and uncomfortable.'[48] The reason for this, they maintain, lies in the neglect of proportion, a concept to which they do not assign a normative value but which they regard as basic to architecture, providing a criterion of relative scale.[49] They clearly have Durand's grid system in mind:

> When the scale and dimensions of a building are changed, the subdivisions of the whole must be revised on a module of which arithmetical ratios are not the sole foundation. Each part must be given the proportion relative to it, not that prescribed by an arithmetical formula.[50]

As is to be expected, they were also opposed to scale reductions of historical models displayed in parks and gardens. To their rationally controlled conservatism, strict observance of the concept of proportion must have presented the most valid of all arguments. They were conscious defenders of the principle of historical continuity, and evidently sensed the dangers that lurked in their rationalist colleagues' dogmatic, simplistic urge for novelty and change.

Charles-Pierre-Joseph Normand's *Recueil varié* (1815) combined the ideas of Percier and Fontaine and the schematisation of Durand.[51] It is a straightforward pattern-book containing architectural designs in Renaissance tradition, offering designs and 'plans designed and adapted to our purposes',[52] showing a clear link with Durand. Some of these designs border on the absurd, such as that for a triumphal arch with its piers rising out of peripteral temples.[53] Normand is also the author of the much-reprinted *Vignole des ouvriers* (1839), dealing with all types of building.[54]

Unaffected by the debate taking place in his native France, Giuseppe Valadier (1762–1839) settled in Rome, giving a series of lectures at the Accademia di San Luca which reveal a theoretical position firmly in Vitruvian tradition.[55] His survey of Roman monuments measured by him and with explanatory texts by Filippo Aurelio Visconti places him among the later followers of Desgodets.[56] Rome is to him '*la scuola delle Arti*',[57] the source of established norms.

In 1819 the Ecole des Beaux Arts was amalgamated with the schools of the Académie Royale de Peinture et de Sculpture and the Académie Royale d'Architecture.[58] The rapid developments of the Revolution were spanned by the Graeco-Roman Classicism of Julien-David Le Roy (1724–1803), who had been a professor at the Académie.[59] But the principal representative of idealist academic Classicism in the new Ecole des Beaux-Arts was Antoine-Chrysostome Quatremère de Quincy (1755–1849), permanent secretary of the Académie and the Ecole from 1816 to 1839 and also in charge of setting the subjects and awarding the prizes for the Prix de Rome.[60] He set out his view of architecture in a series of works of which only two, the *Dictionnaire d'Architecture* and the *Histoire de la vie et des ouvrages des plus célèbres architectes*, need be mentioned here.[61] Quatremère took a simple, normative view of history according to which the origin, laws, principles, theory and practice of architecture all went back to the Greeks, were then spread by the Romans and became the property of the civilised world as a whole; the Gothic he simply ignored.[62] He applied the same rigid, Classicist view to a number of Baroque architects whose fame he was forced to concede but whose judgement he took to be aberrant. He accused Borromini, for instance, of turning the Greek system upside down, and reproached him for 'the perversity of his taste'.[63] He justified his insistence on the imitation of the Greeks by reference to a general theory of mimesis based on an appeal to Nature.[64] We may note in passing the influential role played by the Grand Prix competitions organised by the Ecole des Beaux-Arts, and the publication of the winning entries.[65]

With *Le Génie du Christianisme* (1802) by François-René Chateaubriand (1768–1848), which had a great impact on its age, architectural ideas took on a religious, romantic hue.[66] To Chateaubriand mood was the decisive factor; French Gothic architecture reminded him of the forests of his homeland, and conveyed to him, despite its 'barbaric proportions...a general sentiment of holiness'.[67] Chateaubriand paved the way for a new view of Gothic which was subsequently to prove reconcilable with rational arguments.

In the Ecole des Beaux-Arts itself the students, in the grip of early Romantic ideas and straining to break the rigid Classicist mould of their educational programmes, were in open revolt. The somewhat incidental and arbitrary issue that triggered off their protests was the argument over architectural polychromy, i.e whether or not buildings had been painted in Antiquity. What began as an archaeological and antiquarian issue became a weapon with which to attack the Classical norms of the Winckelmann tradition, which Quatremère felt bound to uphold. Recent research has shown[68] that those who argued for the existence of polychromy in Antiquity divided into two groups: one set out to incorporate the available evidence into a kind of Romantic Classicism, while the other moved towards a material-based functionalist position which it initially designated '*néo-Grec*'.

It was Quatremère himself, who had been trained as a sculptor and had been collecting evidence since the 1780s that large Greek sculptures had been painted, who opened the argument, publishing his findings in *Jupiter olympien* (1815), which contained hand-coloured plates.[69] Expeditions to Egypt, Greece and southern Italy from the second decade onwards discovered traces of paint on a number of architectural members, but these were quite differently interpreted. This was the case with Franz-Christian Gau (1822) and Jakob Ignaz Hittorff in their publications on Nubia. Johann Martin von Wagner on Aegina (1817) and Otto Magnus van Stackelberg on the Temple of Apollo at Bassae (1826) came to similar conclusions.[70] While these works were primarily contributions to archaeology, they also paved the way for reconstructions of Antique buildings by architects and subsequently for the discussion of the use of colour in contemporary architecture. Hittorff, who had studied with Percier, and Henri Labrouste (1801–75), who had studied at the Ecole des Beaux-Arts, were prominent among those who took the debate from the 1820s onwards to a polemical level.

J. I. Hittorff (1792–1867),[71] like Gau a native of Cologne, first visited Sicily in 1820, returning in 1823 for a longer period in order to make survey drawings. In 1824 he submitted to the Institut de France a paper arguing for architectural polychromy in Antiquity.[72] In 1827 appeared the first fascicle of *Architecture antique de la Sicile*[73] by him and Karl Ludwig Wilhelm von Zanth, which contained tinted drawings and caused a considerable stir. In 1830 he delivered before the Académie des Inscriptions a *Mémoire sur l'Architecture polychrome chez les Grecs* and the following year exhibited his coloured reconstruction of the Temple of Empedocles at Selinunte, which was also the focal point of his work on polychrome architecture (eventually published in 1851).[74] While clearly concerned with archaeological issues, Hittorff was at the same time seeking to examine how far polychromy could be employed in architecture of his own day. He regarded paint as a protective substance, and therefore more appropriate to contemporary Paris than to Classical Athens, and moreover, as a means of emphasising architectural forms, more effective in northern Europe than in the sunny Mediterranean. In such matters Hittorff revealed himself as a moderate rationalist; for the rest his theoretical positions were not far from those of his teacher Percier. His completion of the church of St-Vincent-de-Paul in Paris is a demonstration of the adaptation of polychromy to contemporary use.[75]

Henri Labrouste,[76] a student at the Ecole des Beaux-Arts and winner of the Grand Prix de Rome in 1824 with his design for a Court of Appeal (Tribunal de Cassation),[77] was awarded a grant to study in Rome (1825–29) and southern Italy (1826, 1828), and may already have been acquainted with Hittorff's work. In 1828–29 he made twenty-three drawings of the temples at Paestum with explanatory text; these were exhibited in Rome and Paris but not published until 1877.[78] He also painted for his own private pleasure a watercolour inscribed 'Agrigentum 1828', which shows buildings with Etruscan features covered with peeling layers of brightly-coloured plaster[79] – an evocation of a primitive, pre-Classical world far removed from that represented by Quatremère and the Ecole des Beaux-Arts.

Labrouste's Paestum reconstructions were seen by the Ecole des Beaux-Arts as an act of revolution and architectural heresy by a former pupil. An open quarrel broke out between Quatremère, who accused Labrouste of having made an inaccurate survey of the ruins, and Horace Vernet, Director of the French Academy in Rome, who defended Labrouste's drawings. When Labrouste returned to Paris to open a studio in 1830, he was fêted by student sympathisers as a romantic hero.

The problem of polychromy then took on a wider significance for Labrouste.[80] No longer did he proceed from the 'laws' of a standardised Classical architecture; instead he saw buildings as regional responses to the presence of given local building materials and to the effects of given functional, historical and cultural conditions. This signalled the abolition of Classical norms. Instead of regarding the early buildings at Paestum, with their squat proportions, as a preliminary stage in the evolution of Classical architecture, Labrouste now accorded them complete artistic autonomy. The employment of different kinds of materials in one building, according to local conditions, implied for him that stucco must have been employed from the beginning, while he saw the use of colour as the result of an artistic programme and subject to variation.

Labrouste saw the construction of the buildings at Paestum and their external appearance in purely functional terms. Thus the so-called Basilica (Temple of Hera I) was for him neither a temple nor the oldest of the buildings, but an assembly hall (*portique*) for the populace, designed to provide as large an area as possible at modest cost. In place of pediments, which, on the basis of the function he claimed the building fulfilled, he held to have no justification, he incorporated in his reconstruction a hipped roof.[81] He put the *portique* later than the Temple of Neptune (Temple of Hera II), seeing it as an attempt on the part of the people of Paestum to create a 'new' and 'different' kind of building. Here one realises how far-reaching Labrouste's reconstruction was: he set out to overturn the idea of Classical norms and to envisage a 'new', 'modern' architecture – a step that shook the Beaux-Arts tradition to its roots.

In the historicist context Labrouste's importance lies in the principal distinction he drew between basic structure and exterior decoration, seeing the latter as determined by construction and materials. Significantly, one of the first to assimilate this idea was Gottfried Semper, to whom we shall return later. It will be necessary to survey the complex background of Labrouste's conception of architecture in order to appreciate his technological innovations in the use of iron structures such as may be seen, for example, at the Bibliothèque Ste Geneviève and the Bibliothèque Nationale in Paris, to which recent architectural historians, somewhat one-sidedly, have attached so much importance.[82]

The argument over polychromy went beyond academic bounds, and in the thinking of men like Semper and Owen Jones the subject acquired a whole new dimension. An example of the 'new' architecture is the Thorvaldsen Museum in Copenhagen, by the Danish architect Gottlieb Bindesbøll, begun in 1839, which demonstrates a novel combination of archaising style and polychromy.[83] The spreading ripples of the argument can be seen in Victor Hugo's *Notre-Dame de Paris 1482* (1832) and Franz Kugler's essay *Über die Polychromie der griechischen Architektur und Skulptur und ihre Grenzen* (1835).[84]

The onset of Romanticism, which could be felt in the course of the debate on polychromy conducted in the context of Antiquity, also manifested itself in an interpretation of Gothic which not only extolled it as a French national style (Cordemoy, Laugier and others) but also sought to set it in an evolutionary context. Victor Hugo (1802–85) went considerably further than Chateaubriand by making the third book of the second version of his novel *Notre-Dame de Paris 1482* (1832) [85] a description and historical appreciation of the cathedral itself, the Gothic style and the buildings of Paris, even discussing such practical matters as conservation, and interpreting Gothic as an emblem of national liberty.[86] Jules Michelet (1798–1874), in his *Histoire de France* from 1833, arrived at a mystical and philosophical interpretation of Gothic, applying Aristotelian philosophical scholasticism to the analysis of Gothic architecture and using the phrase 'syllogisms in stone',[87] which anticipates Semper's 'stone scholasticism' and reappears in Panofsky's *Gothic Architecture and Scholasticism* (1951).[88]

The closeness of the link between the literary reappraisal of Gothic and the preservation of national monuments at this time in France was symbolised by the appointment of the writer Prosper Mérimée as 'Inspecteur général des monuments historiques', a post he held from 1835 to 1853.[89] It was Mérimée who created the administrative framework within which his friend Viollet-le-Duc was able to carry out his restoration work.

The scholarly debate on Gothic was opened by Arcisse de Caumont (1801–73), who acquired great influence as founder of the Société Française d'Archéologie and editor of the *Bulletin Monumental*.[90] His subtle analysis of the historical evolution of Gothic began in 1824 with his *Sur l'architecture du moyen-âge* and was further developed in the successive volumes of his *Cours d'antiquités monumentales* (1830–41).[91]

In order to understand the extent and scale of the Gothic debate in France in the middle of the century, it is necessary to appreciate the Classicist attitudes prevalent both in the Ecole des Beaux-Arts and in the Ecole Polytechnique. It is not without significance that following Durand and Rondelet, yet another architectural handbook came from the Ecole Polytechnique, to which the Ecole des Beaux-Arts had no answer. This was the work of Léonce Reynaud (1803–80), who published his lectures at the Ecole Polytechnique under the title *Traité d'architecture* (1850–8).[92] This was a considerably more conventional, not to say reactionary, treatise than those of Durand and Rondelet – an aesthetically simplistic mingling of Vitruvianism and concepts going back to the eighteenth century. In the Vitruvian tradition Reynaud divides architecture into *'commodité'*, *'solidité'* and *'beauté'*, of which the first is the most important,[93] and echoes of the eighteenth-century theory of *caractère* are also to be found. Like Rondelet, Reynaud recognised the possibilities of iron structures and realised that the new material would lead to new forms – he mentions industrial buildings and Labrouste's Bibliothèque Ste Geneviève – and thus influence the future course of architecture. 'Iron,' he maintains, 'like wood, lends itself to all forms – indeed, to an even greater extent than wood.'[94] His illustrations of iron structures therefore, logically enough, show elements that are exclusively Neo-classical in design.

The first volume of Reynaud's work consists of a theory of construction and materials, the second of a typology of buildings with historical examples. His bias towards Neo-classical architecture is plain. In French tradition, he begins with a discussion of *'disposition'*. His aesthetic statements are little more than echoes of eighteenth-century principles, such as: 'The good is the foundation of the beautiful, and form in art must always be true'.[95] His ideas on proportion, setting out as Vitruvian, have a glow about them similar to that of the Revolutionary architects.[96] He introduces the concept of decoration by stating: 'Decoration is to art what pleasure is to life', also declaring that 'man has an inner need for it'.[97] It is banalities such as these, masquerading as a system, that need to be remembered if Viollet-le-Duc's hostility towards Reynaud is to be fully understood.

The Ecole des Beaux-Arts still retained its dogmatic attitudes after Quatremère's resignation. His successor as professor of archaeology, Raoul-Rochette (1790–1854), shifted the emphasis from a Rome-dominated view of Antiquity to a Renaissance-centred approach which is also central to the works of Labrouste and Hittorff. A historicism based on the Renaissance was officially declared to be the style best suited to the nineteenth century. From 1843 controversy grew, both inside and outside the Ecole des Beaux-Arts, between, on the one hand, those who, primarily seeing Gothic in Romantic terms, later became increasingly rationalist in their approach, and on the other, those who stood for a Renaissance-based eclecticism. Common to both factions was an appeal to rationalism. Space will not permit any detailed discussion of the controversy here,[98] but the fundamental point at stake between 'Gothicists' and Classicists was whether the principles of Gothic architecture or those of the Renaissance best met the needs of the nineteenth century. The Gothicists produced considerably more complex arguments, which fundamentally challenged the Classicists' whole understanding of architecture and the theory resulting from it, and hence the bitterness of the debate.

The reform of the Academy in 1863,[99] which had much to do with the government of Napoleon III – together with Viollet-le-Duc's appointment to the chair of history of art and aesthetics in 1864, after two months spent at the Ecole des Beaux-Arts, spelt defeat for the 'Gothicists'. It is against this general political background that one must view the most important systematic architectural theory to come out of France in the nineteenth century, that of Viollet-le-Duc.

Eugène-Emmanuel Viollet-le-Duc (1814–79) has been called 'the last great theorist in the world of architecture', a man the equal of Alberti.[100] But alongside those who see him as responsible for the basic tenets of modern architecture are those who regard him as a positivist of mechanistic leanings, others who see him as a mere neo-Gothicist, and yet others who think of him as a restorer who, on the basis of highly dubious principles, gave a large number of historical monuments an appearance that corresponded to nineteenth-century conceptions of medieval style.[101]

Viollet-le-Duc's republican attitudes, which had a decisive influence on his architectural theory, showed themselves when he mounted the barricades during the revolution of 1830, a gesture that contrasts strangely with the relationship he later developed with Napoleon III. Yet his mind was not dominated from the beginning by the Middle Ages or by the concept of Gothic in the literal sense, as his drawings and letters from his Italian journey in 1836–37 show.[102] He was not a product of the Ecole des Beaux-Arts and he retained an anti-academic bias all his life, though his revolutionary views solidified into a new dogmatism.

The story of Viollet-le-Duc's intellectual development, through his mother's salon, his uncle Etienne Delécluze, the influence of Prosper Mérimée and of the circle of Madame de Staël at Coppet, has often been told. His views began to crystallise after he received, through Mérimée's good offices, a commission to carry out restoration work on the abbey church of Madeleine at Vézelay. In the argument between Gothicists and Classicists, as his articles in the *Annales Archéologiques* from 1844 onwards show, he espoused the Gothic cause with increasing vigour, and by the early 1850s his theoretical system had matured. It is set forth in his two main works, the *Dictionnaire raisonné de l'architecture française du XIe au XVIe siècle* (1854–68) and the *Entretiens sur l'architecture* (1863–72), the former arranged as an alphabetical survey of concepts, the latter as a historical account. Most of his later writings are expositions of his system with reference to individual buildings.[103]

Viollet-le-Duc's view of history was in part the product of Romantic enthusiasm for the Middle Ages. In the context of the history of art it represents a reversal of the principle enunciated by Vasari and thereafter regarded as obligatory, i.e. that Antiquity and the Renaissance were the periods of supreme artistic excellence, whereas the Middle Ages stood for degeneration.[104] For Viollet-le-Duc the summit of artistic achievement was reached with the mid-thirteenth-century Gothic style, the Renaissance being an age of decline, but so different are his terms of reference from those of Vasari and the Classicists that his conclusions are of only limited historical relevance.

Viollet-le-Duc's conception of architecture took account of technical, formal, and above all socio-historical factors. He saw architecture as the direct expression of a given social structure. Sulzer and Milizia had already begun to move in this direction; more important for Viollet-le-Duc was the positivism of Auguste Comte (1798–1857) and the social determinism of Hippolyte Taine (1828–93), who succeeded to the chair of history of art at the Ecole des Beaux-Arts in 1864 after Viollet-le-Duc's stock had fallen.

Viollet-le-Duc announces his standpoint in the preface to the *Dictionnaire*, claiming that French Gothic is to be nationally understood and reflects not only the spirit of the nation but also a 'principle of unity' and a 'straight and logical path' (*'marche régulière et logique'*).[105] His aim is to reveal 'the inner nature of these forms, the principles which have given rise to them, the customs and the ideas in whose midst they were born', and then, against this background, to bring about 'a blessed revolution in architectural studies'.[106] He also emphasises the importance of religious, political, regional and folkloristic premises for architecture. But his concerns are not purely historical, and by presenting Gothic architecture as the rational and perfect expression of a democratic society, he establishes its principles as models for his own day. He is not primarily concerned with imitating the Gothic style, but with abstracting its rational principles as he sees them, a means of procedure that enables him to interpret modern technological progress as virtually a continuation of Gothic. For him art was dependent on the 'instincts of the masses', and this stretched to all areas of creativity down to folk art.[107] Moreover, he invested his conception of Gothic with a moral content, calling it 'the true principle', whereas Greek architecture was 'too foreign to modern civilisation'.[108] This, of course, was a direct challenge to the Ecole des Beaux-Arts.

Viollet-le-Duc gave his account of the evolution of architecture in the article 'Architecture' in his *Dictionnaire*, covering no fewer than 337 pages. The year 1260 marked for him the climax of Gothic, after which he saw a decline in the rational use of materials.[109] The central role that Viollet-le-Duc assigned to the construction process and the use of materials is clearly stated here. For him there was no more complete manifestation of the modern view of architecture than the Gothic cathedral: 'Cathedrals represent the first and greatest application of the modern spirit to architecture, emerging from the midst of an order of ideas quite the opposite of those of Antiquity.'[110]

Functional concepts evolved in the eighteenth century, involving interior layout, building techniques and truth to materials, all come together in Viollet-le-Duc. In his article 'Construction' in the *Dictionnaire* he defines architecture purely and simply as a product of the building process. The same article contains a definition of building based on technological and social principles:

> To build, for the architect, is to use materials according to their properties and their essential nature, with the express intention of fulfilling a purpose by the simplest and strongest means; it is furthermore to give the built structure an aspect of permanence, fitting proportions, subject to certain rules imposed by the human senses, reason and instinct. The methods employed by the builder must therefore vary according to the nature of his materials, the financial means at his disposal, the particular requirements of each kind of building, and the culture into which he has been born.[111]

Viollet-le-Duc puts forward a distinction between constant principles of architecture and variable principles: among the former are the laws governing materials, among the latter are historical and social factors. This makes him a protagonist of national styles of architecture, not a herald of an international language of architecture based solely on technological considerations. The Gothic building he calls 'flexible, free and questing, like the modern spirit', while the Antique building is for him 'absolute in its resources'.[112] His concept of proportion, as might be expected, is a relative one. In rejecting fixed mathematical relationships, he is contradicting Quatremère de Quincy; he sees proportion as derived from statics, and statics as derived from geometry,[113] i.e. proportion is reduced to a peripheral aspect of the building process.

Probably the best-known and most influential part of Viollet-le-Duc's architectural theory is that on restoration, which deliberately set out to put a building into an imaginary ideal state which in reality had never existed. In his article 'Restoration' he laid down: 'To restore a building is not to repair or rebuild it but to re-establish it in a state of entirety which might never have existed at any given moment.'[114] In accordance with his approach to architecture, he took the aim of such restoration to be to reproduce not merely external appearances but also imagined constructional forms.[115] However, for Viollet-le-Duc restoration did not mean reproduction of actual historical conditions but the projection of modern principles onto the past. The consequences of this attitude for the conservation of buildings are well known. Particularly violent were reactions in Britain, where it was realised that restoration often meant destruction, and where a progressive view of restoration showed itself in the 'Anti-scrape' movement.[116]

Viollet-le-Duc's distinction between absolute and relative concepts of style was a further argument in his case for Gothic. The familiar historical styles he called 'relative, absolute style being 'the realisation of an ideal based on a principle',[117] which he found to be the case only in Gothic. This qualitative distinction between 'style' and 'styles' constituted by implication an argument in favour of nineteenth-century neo-Gothic.

Viollet-le-Duc's objective-seeming *Dictionnaire* reveals his characteristic combination of positivist statement and a view of history claiming similar objectivity. The very idea of making medieval French architecture the subject of an encyclopedia, with the rest of architectural history measured against it as a standard, shows the extent of his 'happy revolution'. His understanding of architecture rests on very complex foundations, but so great is his emphasis on technological considerations in individual articles that there is considerable justification in describing him as a rationalistic, mechanistic positivist.

Viollet-le-Duc's *Entretiens* consist of a not wholly systematic combination of architectural history, theory and typology. Their frank and often polemic style makes it understandable that the students of the Ecole des Beaux-Arts should have resented the attempt by Viollet-le-Duc, who had been thrust upon the Ecole in the first place, to overturn the Classicist principles on which it rested. His faith in technological progress had led him to regard Gothic as the rational style *par excellence* but it also made him receptive to new construction methods and the use of new materials. Both Rondelet and Reynaud had been in favour of iron structures, but Viollet-le-Duc went one decisive step further, proposing independent rules and aesthetic for iron structures. He became enthusiastic about machines, which were being violently opposed by some in Britain at the time, and claimed to find in ships, locomotives and so on his ideal of an absolute style, which as far as architecture was concerned he found only in Gothic. 'The locomotive is almost a living being, and its external form is merely the expression of its power. A locomotive thus has style...the true physiognomy of its brute strength.'[118] It is a direct line from this to futurism and Le Corbusier. And in the sixth of his *Entretiens* – composed shortly before he broke off his lectures – he threw down the gauntlet: 'Eclecticism is an evil; for it must necessarily exclude the possibility of style...'[119]

Viollet-le-Duc opened the prospect of a new architecture that would supersede eclecticism, based on functional, national and social premises, but the paradox of his position was that his own solutions constantly harked back to the Gothic forms of the Middle Ages:

> Since an architectural composition must be exclusively derived from 1) the programme laid down and 2) the habits of the culture to which it belongs, it is essential in order to design a building to possess such a programme and also to have a precise understanding of those customs, habits, practices and needs. To repeat: though there may be little basic change in the programmes themselves, the customs and habits of civilised peoples are constantly changing, consequently there must be an infinite variety of forms in architecture.[120]

Viollet-le-Duc's references to the racial theories of Gobineau[121] are not calculated to arouse our admiration today; however, they are only later accretions to his work.[122] After this he returned to the question of materials and the building process, which, as Lodoli and Laugier before him, he links with the question of truth: 'It is necessary to be true to the programme and true to the building process.'[123] He also shows an indebtedness to Descartes.

> First, know the character of the materials that you are going to have to use; secondly, bestow on these materials the function and the strength appropriate to the building purpose, so that the built forms express in the most precise manner possible both this function and this strength; thirdly, introduce a principle of unity and harmony into this expression – that is to say, scale, a system of proportion, an ornamentation in keeping with the building purpose and with its own significance, but also the degree of variety required by the various needs that are to be met.[124]

These demands mean that form is seen as the product of function, function in its turn being seen as dependent not only on programme, material properties and construction but also on the historical complex and social factors that underlie Viollet-le-Duc's conception of architecture: 'The materials employed reveal their function through the form that you give them: the stone must clearly look like stone, iron like iron, wood like wood. And while assuming forms appropriate to their nature, the materials must be in harmony with each other.'[125] This anticipates Sullivan's dictum 'Form follows function', though in the one case as in the other, we need to know exactly what is meant by the term 'function'.

Viollet-le-Duc warns against what he calls second-hand architecture, such as that of the Renaissance, failing to see that his own neo-Gothic is also 'second-hand'. He investigates the tensile and compressive strength of iron and arrives at new combinations by using iron in oblique positions, which brings him close to the Gothic flying buttress (*Plate 156*). While seeing the potential for structures entirely of iron, he realises their disadvantages when subjected to fluctuations of climate, and advocates a combination of masonry and iron: 'It is scarcely possible to find a sound locality, warm in winter, cool in summer and shielded from fluctuations of temperature, which is favourable to iron on its own. Stone walls and vaulting will always have advantages over all other modes.'[126] Hence his preference for a compromise, with the exposed use of iron in an otherwise neo-Gothic context: individual members made of iron take Gothisised forms! Here he betrayed his inner contradiction. For while approving of architecture designed by engineers, he censured architects for 'timidly applying new techniques to old forms',[127] without reflecting that this is just what he himself did.

Going on to discuss at length the practical and economic possibilities of using iron in the construction of private houses, Viollet-le-Duc envisages a limited lease of life for buildings, say one hundred years,[128] making designs for an iron-frame façade.[129] His later work *Habitations modernes* (1875–77) is an illustrated historical compendium.[130] There were few works available in France at this time on the use of iron, and these, such as Joseph Neumann's *Art de construire* (1844),[131] were limited to hothouses and winter gardens, never considering the possibility of using iron for other purposes.

Viollet-le-Duc did not succeed in combining his radical theoretical ideas with new formal concepts. The perspicuity of his thought is highly attractive, though at the same time misleading, in that it leads to a circular argument based on the premise of the absoluteness of the neo-Gothic style, even though he tries to interpret this style merely as the product of technological progress. The few buildings he designed are of scant artistic importance, whilst his restorations, claiming to be based on absolute historical principles, result in a strange a-historical historicism. He evolved his approach to architecture on the basis of his interpretation of a rational and democratic Middle Ages, and fashioned it for the needs of a similarly rational and democratic future, but he was out of tune with his times. He presents the fascinating spectacle of a backward-looking visionary.

It is only a short step from Viollet-le-Duc to Charles Garnier (1825–98), a graduate of the Ecole des Beaux-Arts, who worked for a time in Viollet's office. Most of his writings are devoted to defending his own buildings, chiefly the Paris Opéra.[132] An interesting feature of his *Le Théâtre* (1871) is that he describes the construction of the opera-house from the point of view of the operagoer walking though it.

We must now give brief consideration to the ideas about architecture, and above all town planning, of the French utopian socialists. Foremost among them was Charles Fourier (1772–1837), who, his starting-point the philosophy of Claude-Henri de Saint-Simon (1760–1825), evolved precise ideas about architecture and urban design intended to match the final '*garantiste*' phase of his social model. His theory of history first emerged in his *Théorie des quatre mouvements* (1808) but it is in his later *Théorie de l'unité universelle* (1822)[133] that its consequences for architecture are set out. Fourier envisages a 'unitary architecture' ('*architecture unitaire*') which shall reflect social harmony. His town project for the sixth '*garantiste*' period corresponds to a neo-Renaissance radial plan (*Plate 157*) but is quite different in content, the inner of the three concentric rings being the town proper, the middle ring enclosing inner suburbs and large factories, and the third ring consisting of avenues and outer suburbs;[134] within each ring the architecture was to have a certain uniformity yet merge into that of the other rings, while the streets issuing radially from the centre were to afford picturesque views. Outside the rings were colossal statues and other monuments, including those of elephants, inspired by Napoleon's competition for the Place de la Bastille. The formal result was remarkably close to absolutist concepts of urban design. Fourier rejected Robert Owen's rectangular grid plan. Anticipating future developments, he conceived long covered arcades ('*rues-galeries*') linking the various social facilities.[135] Likewise, his '*phalanstères*', or large-scale community housing blocks, were based on absolutist models like the palace of Versailles and the Escorial.[136] Whether this was a mere anachronism or whether Fourier was taking his revenge on a whole historical epoch is a question that must be left unanswered, but it seems strange that he did not realise the possibilities of designs such as Durand's for his purpose. It was only after Fourier's death that the industrialist Jean-Baptiste-André Godin (1817–88) designed his famous 'familistère'[137] in the little northern French town of Guise (from 1859), embracing domestic housing, communal facilities and factory buildings.

In stark contrast to such social utopias, of very limited circulation, were the realities of population growth, industrial advance and cultural development. The most important practical initiative in France was that for the redesigning of Paris undertaken by Baron Georges Haussmann (1809–91), who gave a detailed account of his scheme in his *Mémoires*.[138] Haussmann's ideas were given a systematic theoretical basis and carried further by Eugène Hénard (1849–1923), who had been at the Ecole des Beaux-Arts. His principles of town-planning were largely governed by the problems raised by traffic, and he produced a typology of traffic to serve as the foundation for planning schemes.[139] His 'towns of the future' exist on various levels, ground-level being done away with as a point of reference.[140] Hénard's theories were among the most important for planners of the first half of the twentieth century, and Le Corbusier's work would be hardly conceivable without him.

Viollet-le-Duc's complex view of history, combined with what was ultimately a Romantic conception of architecture, was carried to greater lengths at the end of the century in a fascinating if simplistic rationalism in the *Histoire de l'architecture* (1899) by Auguste Choisy (1841–1909),[141] an engineer by training, who interpreted the entire history of architecture from prehistoric times to the present in terms of continuous technological development. Like Viollet-le-Duc, he starts from the constants and variables that determine the development of architecture, then proceeds to shift the emphasis arbitrarily onto considerations relating to the building process. He reiterates the importance of matters such as climate, mode of life, social structure and customs, but in the last analysis reduces stylistic evolution in architecture to a reflection of ever-advancing technology; architecture as the expression of technologically conditioned form becomes the rule, the common denominator of the architecture of all ages and all nations. Hence his statement on prehistoric architecture in his first paragraph: 'In all cultures art will confront the same options and obey the same laws: prehistoric art seems to contain within it the seeds of all other art.'[142] Choisy opens each of his historical surveys by stating the premises of materials and construction. He presents his approximately 1700 illustrations in the form of a uniform abstract that combines plan, elevation and section and clearly reveals the constructional framework. Form, as he sees it, is the expression of ideas.

Choisy takes an interesting attitude towards proportion and scale, not seeing proportion as 'that vague sentiment of harmony which one calls taste' but demanding 'firm and methodical planning procedures'.[143] He finds his answer in module systems, which for the Egyptians are to be found in the dimensions of bricks, for the Greeks in the diameter of columns, and since the Gothic era in the dimensions of the human figure. Here is the starting-point for Le Corbusier's 'modulor', which is explicitly based on Choisy, who thus describes the relationship between module and scale: 'It would seem that in a work of architecture certain members must retain dimensions that are virtually invariable, whatever the size of the building. From a purely practical point of view, for example, the height of a door will not differ from the height of the people who pass through it...'[144]

In opposition to the rigid notions of symmetry characteristic of the Ecole des Beaux-Arts, Choisy proposes a concept of the Picturesque derived from landscape gardening.[145] His emphasis on considerations of construction and materials is displayed in his derivation of the volutes of the Corinthian capital from the art of the goldsmith.[146] He joins Viollet-le-Duc in setting a high value on Gothic:

> The new structure is the triumph of logic in art. A building becomes a planned entity, each structural member of which has a form no longer determined by traditional models but by its function, and by its function alone.[147]

The concepts of construction and of organic architecture here become one. That Choisy saw the principle of form as the expression of function most consistently realised in Greek and Gothic architecture is a remarkable parallel to the position adopted by Cordemoy at the beginning of the eighteenth century.

Choisy was of the opinion that plastic decoration may only be an optical adjunct to the construction process, and he saw stylistic development as merely the expression of new methods of construction.[148] He unfolds an all-embracing picture of the history of architecture, drawing also on non-European cultures, but his objectivity suffers through the exaggerated precedence he gives to France since the Middle Ages. His view of the Renaissance is neutral. The French Revolution, on the other hand, represents a break in history: 'A new society has been founded, which desires a new art.'[149] A new spirit demands a new formal language, the basis of which Choisy found in iron architecture; the examples he quotes include Les Halles and the main reading room of the Bibliothèque Nationale in Paris. And the statics of the new material will lead to a new sytem of proportion: 'A new system of proportion has been created, whose harmonic laws will be no other than those of statics'.[150] This establishes a new view of the nature of architecture, which was to prove a potent influence on much of twentieth-century thought, that is, Construction = Form = Harmony.

Choisy's view of the history of architecture reduces it to its logical structures. The appeal of his ideas was felt for a long time. Le Corbusier acquired a copy of the *Histoire* for his library in 1912,[151] but two years earlier he had made a design for a studio villa in La-Chaux-de-Fonds which already clearly reflected Choisy's style of presentation (*Plate 158*).[152] The extent to which *L'Esprit Nouveau*, the journal edited by Le Corbusier and Ozenfant, is indebted to Choisy is an open question.

It was surprisingly not until after the turn of the century that the Ecole des Beaux-Arts produced a synthesis of its own architectural theory. Although in 1867 the librarian Charles Blanc had published his *Grammaire des arts de dessin*,[153] in which stress is laid on *'ordonnance'* as a means of expression, it is only with Julien Guadet's (1834–1908) four-volume *Eléments et théorie de l'Architecture* (1901–04)[154] that we are in possession of a comprehensive survey of the ideas of the Ecole such as had not been attempted in such detail since Jacques-Francois Blondel's *Cours*. Guadet was a pupil of Labrouste; in 1864 he won the Grand Prix with a design for an alpine hospice,[155] returned to the Ecole as a teacher in 1872, and assumed the chair of architectural theory in 1894.

Guadet's work consists of a set of lectures in expanded form devoted mainly to practical building tasks, and does not proceed by theoretical concepts. It was seen by its author as a *'livre élémentaire'*, a student textbook.[156] Its numerous reissues, despite its size, down to the late 1920s prove how successful it was. His Grand Prix hospice design shows the author to be an eclectic, which his work on the Paris Opéra alongside

Garnier confirms; he is neutral in matters of style, and the examples he chooses to exemplify his ideas come from 'all ages and all countries'.[157] His concept of architecture has a functionalist flavour to it, but his theoretical statements are largely random. His programme consists in 'the composition of buildings, in their separate elements and in their ensemble, from the dual point of view of art and of adaptation to specific programmes, to material necessities.'[158]

All that Guadet actually gives is a survey of building components and building types, supported by historical examples. Starting with instructions on what paper and drawing materials to acquire, he familiarises his students with all kinds of problem they are likely to encounter in the course of their studies. It is clear from his inaugural lecture, delivered on 28 November 1894 and printed in full in his book, that he had no consistent architectural theory.[159] His appeal to the French classical tradition and to 'general and immutable principles of art' (*principes généraux et invariables de l'art*)[160] reveals a position between conservatism and certain concepts of Viollet-le-Duc. His principal concern is seen from the emphasis he puts on 'compositional elements' (*éléments de la composition*), 'composition' meaning for him the 'artistic quality' of architecture. His definition runs: 'Composition means assembling, welding and combining the parts of a whole. In their turn, these parts are the elements of the composition.'[161]

Guadet sees proportion as a 'compositional attribute' (*qualité de la composition*),[162] lying within the arena of the architect's free but rational judgement. He rejects binding rules, and discusses the Orders only from practical, constructional and historical points of view. The Platonic expression of his aesthetic – beauty as the reflection of truth – seems artificially superimposed, likewise his definition of the aim of architecture as being 'truth'.

Never before had such stress been laid on the concept of composition in architectural theory, and here Guadet had a considerable influence on the theory of modern design. Guadet was a formalist, and this clearly emerged when, addressing the question of the architect's professional qualifications in his *Eléments*, he simply reprinted a definition that he and Charles Garnier had already given in the *Dictionnaire de l'Académie française*.[163]

Guadet combines his stylistic eclecticism with a rejection of Vitruvius, and just how devoid of content standard architectural concepts became in his hands is shown by the following equations he set down:

disposition = composition

proportion = study

construction = control of study by knowledge[164]

With all his rationalism, it is primarily his lack of intellectual clarity that has made Guadet exemplary for twentieth-century architectural theory.

Intellectually, the works of both Choisy and Guadet exhibit a number of progressive features; stylistically, they tend towards historical eclecticism. Its adherence to this position until well into the twentieth century gave the Ecole des Beaux-Arts a notoriety which was then taken to colour its nineteenth-century history. Gustave Umbdenstock's *Cours d'architecture* (1930), a product of the Ecole Polytechnique, stood firmly in nineteenth-century tradition,[165] paying no regard to modern architecture, while in 1955 Guadet's pupil Albert Ferran published his *Philosophie de la Composition Architecturale*, which displays the same attitudes as his teacher.[166]

22. Germany in the nineteenth century

No systematic account of German nineteenth-century architectural theory has as yet been published. Available histories of architecture[1] barely touch on the theoretical ideas of the architects of the period. Germany was subjected to many and varied influences in the nineteenth century, with practitioners of philosophy and theory of art discussing architecture with a degree of conviction hitherto unknown, which in turn influenced architectural theory itself. It is of course arbitrary to draw a dividing-line between the eighteenth and nineteenth centuries. Goethe has already been discussed in the context of the eighteenth century, and it will also be appropriate to begin the present chapter with a number of names from the eighteenth.

The closest parallel to developments in Germany is provided by France, which to a certain extent determined those developments, though they proceeded in a less centralised and dogmatic manner in Germany, which had no equivalent to the Ecole des Beaux-Arts. Compared with French efforts since the foundation of the Académie Royale d'Architecture in the seventeenth century to arrive at normative architectural theory, the theoretical basis of German Classicism was slight. Attention focused on Winckelmann, who, however, had dealt only in passing with architecture; under his influence Greek Antiquity was made the absolute model for the present, while at almost the same moment the Romantic revolution was directing attention towards the Gothic, which was seen as a national German style. A handful of theorists who sought to combine these two positions became the pioneers of eclecticism and historicism. Particularly striking in Germany was a growing preponderance of historical works distilling the features most relevant for contemporary purposes.

A typical transitional figure, standing between a strict Classicism on the one hand and a functionalist eclecticism on the other, was Christian Ludwig Stieglitz (1756–1836), a Leipzig canon. In his *Geschichte der Baukunst der Alten* (1792)[2] Stieglitz, taking his lead from Winckelmann's preoccupation with cultural history, advocated 'the study of the Ancients' as the only way 'to achieve greatness'[3] (*'um groß zu werden'*) – a direct paraphrase from Winckelmann's *Gedanken über die Nachahmung der Griechen* of 1755. For Stieglitz the architecture of Antiquity had the same exemplary function for the architect as Nature for the artist, and his account of Egyptian and Near Eastern architecture was designed to bring out the greatness of Greece. His application to Greek architecture of terms such as 'noble simplicity, sublimity and grandeur' (*'edle Einfalt, Erhabenheit und Größe'*)[4] shows the language of Winckelmann combining with the French theory of *caractère*; accordingly, Stieglitz describes the effect of the 'gigantic' quality of Egyptian architecture as 'astonishment' (*'Erstaunen'*), whilst the 'splendour and industry [*'Pracht und Fleiß'*] of the Persians and Indians' evoke merely 'admiration' (*'Bewunderung'*).[5] The Classicist view of history that characterises Stieglitz's early work is clear:

> The oldest nations which practised architecture, such as the Egyptians and others, were never able to rise above the mediocre or achieve beauty. The Etruscans came close to true art but their culture was interrupted and they ceased at an early

stage to be a nation. It is only the Greeks who can lay claim to the glory of having taken architecture from its humblest beginnings to the summit of perfection, and of having raised it to the status of true art, leaving rules for this art which have to this day not been superseded and which will retain their value for as long as beauty and good taste are accounted among the essential values of superior architecture.[6]

Roman architecture, for Stieglitz, already marks the onset of decay, though it must also be credited with progress in the fields of decoration and technology;[7] the post-Constantine era, on the other hand, is one of total decline. Stieglitz's work is based exclusively on a study of literary sources – he had no direct experience of the architecture itself. The *Geschichte der Baukunst der Alten* has no illustrations. His *Archaeologie der Baukunst* (1801), however, which expands on the same material, does contain a few modest engravings.[8]

Between 1792 and 1798 Stieglitz published a five-volume *Encyklopädie der bürgerlichen Baukunst*,[9] a work in the tradition of Sulzer and Blankenburg, which is, as admitted in the preface, a compilation. By comparison with the dictionaries of d'Aviler and Roland Le Virloys, and Lukas Vochs' *Allgemeines Baulexikon* of 1781,[10] Stieglitz's claim that his work fulfilled an urgent need appears exaggerated.

Between 1798 and 1800 the house of Voss in Leipzig published a remarkable instalment work under the editorship of Stieglitz, who also contributed an introductory essay in French entitled *Traité abrégé sur le beau dans l'architecture.*[11] According to the publisher, the plates reproduced drawings by the Earl of Findlater and Seafield, engraved by Schwender, each being dedicated to a member of the upper aristocracy of Europe. There is no mention of the fact that the depictions of country houses which make up most of the work are actually anachronistic versions of designs found in *Vitruvius Britannicus*, Briseux's *L'art de bâtir des maisons de campagne*, Jacques-Francois Blondel's *De la Distribution des Maisons de Plaisance* and other sources.[12] Some of them stylistically resemble so-called Revolutionary architecture. There is a certain irony in the fact that it should have been Stieglitz who was commissioned to edit the work. His frontispiece illustration depicts the five Classical Orders arrayed in a ruined setting near the seashore (*Plate 159*); the Doric order, which in his *Archaeologie der Baukunst* he took from the Parthenon,[13] here appears in its Roman form.

In his essay Stieglitz departs from Winckelmann's principles and approaches French theory: 'The form of a piece of architecture is determined by the purpose of the building, and to this purpose it must conform, otherwise it has no function.'[14] Following the doctrine of *caractère*, Stieglitz returns to the categories of 'the majestic, the serious, the magnificent, the terrible, the graceful and the miraculous',[15] including in the last-named both the Gothic and Chinoiserie.[16] But he still locates supreme architectural beauty in the Orders, which he combines with the *caractère* approach.[17] In this work it is difficult to distinguish broad-mindedness from sheer opportunism.

Stieglitz's *Von altdeutscher Baukunst* (1820)[18] was followed in 1827 by *Geschichte der Baukunst vom frühesten Alterthum bis in neuere Zeiten.*[19] In his next work, *Beiträge zur Geschichte der Ausbildung der Baukunst* (1834),[20] he departed from his original view of the architecture of Antiquity as normative. Answering his own question: which style of architecture should now be adopted? – he saw in Classicism merely 'imitation of form, of construction and of decoration...a mere playing with architectural forms, without regard to the character of buildings or their suitability to their purpose'.[21] His verdict on Classicism was now: 'The solemnity of this art permitted only a cold, reflective approach, and the fire that used to pierce the artist's soul was now extinguished.'[22]

Stieglitz now propounded a theory of three styles of equal status – Greek, Byzantine (round arch) and Early German (pointed arch). To these he ascribed the categories, respectively, of Rational, Picturesque and Romantic; in addition he associated the Greek style with horizontalism and the Early German with verticalism, the Byzantine being a combination of the other two.[23] On the question of their suitability for the architecture of his day he writes: 'All three may be adopted, according to which meets the requirements of the building under construction and does not conflict with its character.'[24] Indeed, he no longer recommended Classical models for any purpose, instead proposing the Renaissance – which he called the 'Italian style' and interpreted as a synthesis of Classical and Gothic – as the model for palaces, houses and public buildings. The round-arch style he found best for theatres, city halls, schools, stock-exchanges and the like, and the 'Early German' for churches;[25] here was stylistic pluralism according to a building's purpose.

Surprisingly, Stieglitz concludes his work with an acknowledgement to Durand: the question of style is relegated to the question of decoration, which is subordinated to construction; this thus acquires its own aesthetic quality. 'It is construction alone, the forms of the principal parts and the body of the building as a whole, that leads to beauty in architecture and establishes the basis of that beauty.'[26] Stieglitz now speaks only of 'adornment', which must be in keeping with the whole, not haphazard.

This change in Stieglitz's theoretical position is symptomatic of architectural debate in Germany at the beginning of the nineteenth century. It may well have been occasioned by the publication in 1831 of the German edition of Durand's *Précis des leçons*,[27] though it should be remembered that Clemens Wenzeslaus Coudray (1775–1845), later Oberbaudirektor in Weimar, had studied with Durand in Paris from 1800 to 1804 and assisted in the illustration of the second volume of Durand's lectures.[28] Coudray adopted and modified Durand's ideas when he was in Fulda and later in Weimar, so it may be assumed that they were circulating in Germany before 1831. Furthermore, a former fellow-student of Coudray's in Paris, Carl Friedrich Anton von Conta (1778–1850), who later served in the diplomatic service of the Grand Duchy of Weimar, had already published a German version of Durand's lectures in 1806,[29] so that at least from this date Durand's ideas must have been known in Germany.

Stieglitz's broad-minded approach to architectural history is also characteristic of the work of the engineer and restorer Carl Friedrich von Wiebeking (1762–1842), a man highly esteemed in his time, who in addition to numerous technical publications wrote a substantial work in 1826 entitled *Theoretisch-practische Bürgerliche Baukunde*.[30] A combination of architectural history and practical handbook, this work is addressed to builders, architects and students, and recommends the introduction of a standard pattern of study in architectural schools, even providing suggestions for individual courses.[31] His chief models are Durand and Rondelet, but he is merely a compiler and has no identifiable position of his own. A certain Classicistic rigidity reveals itself in his illustrations, such as his totally symmetrical reconstruction of the Propylaea in Athens, in the tradition of Le Roy.[32]

A distorted reflection of Durand's concept of *économie* is given by Friedrich Oettingen-Wallerstein in his pamphlet *Über die Grundsätze der Bau-Oekonomie* (1835),[33] which demonstrates that in certain cases the principle of durability can be laid aside, and that cheaper buildings with a limited lease of life may prove more economical. Similar considerations occur later in the work of Viollet-le-Duc. This brings us close to the concept of utilitarian architecture, which deals only in terms of profitability and rejects the basic assumptions of all earlier architectural theory.

A different approach to the authority of the architecture of Antiquity was that adopted by the archaeologist Aloys Hirt (1759–1837), a teacher at the Bauakademie in Berlin who had lived in Rome from 1782 to 1796 and met Goethe there. In his *Baukunst nach den Grundsätzen der Alten* (1809)[34] Hirt set out to evolve a 'system' that should embody 'the very ideal of architecture',[35] thinking to find this in Antiquity. His architectural concepts are taken from French eighteenth-century theory, and his opening sentence runs: 'Architecture is the discipline, or the quintessence of such knowledge and skills, by means of which one is enabled to design and construct every type of building in the most effective way'.[36] Hirt's dependence on the French concept of *disposition* emerges clearly in his definition of the principal aim in any work of architecture as being 'a disposition and arrangement corresponding to its purpose', with 'a durable method of construction and beauty being, as it were, merely subsidiary to this principal aim.'[37]

Hirt thinks in functional terms: 'The essence of the beautiful [must] proceed from construction and from 'disposition suited to purpose',[38] while ornament gives 'a pleasing aspect proper to its purpose, both exterior and interior, in the whole and in the parts.'[39] He also evolves a set of six aesthetic criteria reminiscent of, and at times directly alluding to, Vitruvius, but defined in very different ways: 'Proportion [= organic whole]; Symmetry; Harmony [= eurhythmy]; Simplicity of Form; Mass and Materials; Decoration.'[40]

For Hirt architecture is not imitation of Nature; instead he uncovers the inner, 'mechanistic' laws of a process that begins with wooden buildings and is then transferred to stone.[41] Although he proceeds from axioms of this kind, he maintains that by its very nature architecture can be viewed only in historical terms, so it is strange that it should be only in Antiquity that he sees his ideals fulfilled: 'For everything of importance that the art of building requires, be it in wood or in stone, the writings and monuments of the Greeks and Romans provide us with the necessary instructions and models. Thus the man who builds properly inevitably builds in the Greek manner.'[42] And since the Greeks 'have penetrated to the heart of building in all types of material', it follows that their works embody 'the very ideal of architecture itself.'[43] Hirt's architectural theory, founded on historical premises and justifying a functionalist Classicism, turns out to be a historical construct similar in essence to the more complex ideas that led Viollet-le-Duc to his neo-Gothic position.

Hirt's theses were developed further by Carl Boetticher (1806–89), an architect who taught for many years at the Bauakademie in Berlin, in his *Tektonik der Hellenen* (1844).[44] In Greek architecture Boetticher found above all the realisation of the formal principles of construction. He distinguished between 'the form of the work' ('*Werkform*') – by which he understood the structural framework – and 'artistic form' ('*Kunstform*') – the artistic character of the individual members. He saw it as the function of the

Kunstform to serve as an 'explanatory shell' (*'erklärende Hülle'*), which presented the *Werkform* by making the features of the construction visible from without.[45] Form should thus reveal function without becoming identical to it. Certain of Boetticher's ideas derive from the philosophy of idealism, which will be discussed later.

As attested by Goethe and others, Hirt's theory was fiercely attacked. An article by Ben David[46] in Schiller's journal *Die Horen* in 1795 reads almost like a riposte to such a position: 'The comfort of a building seems to have more to do with practical use than with beauty. A farmhouse may be very comfortably furnished without any claim to being beautiful.'[47] David also comments on Sturm's interpretation of the Orders in relation to the classes of society (sovereign, nobility and burghers).[48]

It should be remembered that the doctrine of the Orders in the Vignola tradition still retained its validity even if many architects questioned it. In 1853, for example, L. Bergmann published a two-volume *Schule der Baukunst*, addressed to 'architects, craftsmen, academies and trade schools, builders, etc.'[49] The same author also issued a booklet entitled *Zehn Tafeln Säulen-Ordnungen*, based on Vignola but also taking account of later theory of the Orders and of archaeological discoveries in Greece.

The most important centre for German Classicism was the Bauakademie in Berlin. Here a key figure was David Gilly (1748–1808), who had founded a private architectural school in 1793.[50] Gilly's main interest was in the technicalities of the building process, as is evident from his publications, chief among them his *Handbuch der Land-Bau-Kunst* (1797–1811).[51] The *Sammlung nützlicher Aufsätze* (1797–1806),[52] of which he was first co-editor, then sole editor, contains the programme on the basis of which the Bauakademie was founded in 1799 on the model, not of the department of architecture at the Ecole des Beaux-Arts, but of the Ecole Polytechnique in Paris. Most of the volumes in the series deal with building technology; the few that contain architectural history and theory – by Hirt and others – are conventional. Also in the series are some of the few pieces of writing by Gilly's son Friedrich (1772–1800),[53] among them two descriptions of French country houses and, more importantly, *Einige Gedanken über die Nothwendigkeit, die verschiedenen Theile der Baukunst, in wissenschaftlicher und praktischer Hinsicht, möglichst zu vereinigen* ('Some thoughts on the importance of uniting the different aspects of architecture in both scientific and practical respects').[54] In this piece Friedrich Gilly, who taught optics and perspective at the Bauakademie, opposes a narrow course of architectural training and argues for a survey of the entire range of subjects about which a master builder needs to be informed (*'Abriß des ganzen Bildungsgeschäfts eines Baumeisters'*). The essay reads like a covert attack on the aims of the Bauakademie, which was mainly concerned to train architects to work in Prussian government offices. His reference to the dubious value of a curriculum guided by national considerations (*'nationale Verschiedenheiten'*) shows the boldness of his thinking.

In the same volume as Friedrich Gilly's essay is an exposition of the curriculum of the Bauakademie[55] which shows how closely it was geared to the requirements of the government and how little attention was paid to the issues raised by 'great' architecture. In its early phase the Bauakademie was a training ground for engineers, and it is important to remember this bias towards technology when considering the work of Schinkel, Klenze and others who passed through its doors.

Between 1803 and 1806 Heinrich Gentz (1765–1811), who taught town-planning at the Bauakademie, published *Elementar-Zeichenwerk*,[56] which remained a standard textbook until the appearance in 1821 of the first of the *Vorbilder für Fabrikanten und Handwerker*,[57] edited by Christian Peter Wilhelm Beuth (1781–1853) in collaboration with Schinkel. These publications were not architectural treatises in the narrow sense but rather pattern-books for use in the decorative arts and sets of building instructions for craftsmen.

The need for a standard architectural training curriculum, as well as for textbooks, was evident throughout Germany. The Baden State architect Friedrich Weinbrenner (1766–1826),[58] who had observed the moves being made in this direction in Berlin during his visit there in 1791 but whose real, largely autodidactic training had been in Italy (1792–97), described in his memoirs the profound effect that Roman architecture had had on him,[59] in similar style to accounts by Gentz,[60] Schinkel and other Classicist architects: 'The serious study of architecture that I undertook in Italy could not but bring about a great change in my views on art, and as I came to understand the principles underlying the works of the Ancients, I formed the desire to make these principles the standard for German buildings too.'[61] In Rome Weinbrenner had taken a course on Antique architecture, and he left Italy with the intention, as he put it, 'of contributing to the improvement of German architecture by training young architects and craftsmen.'[62] In Karlsruhe he founded a 'private institute of architecture', and from the same pedagogic impulse wrote his *Architektonisches Lehrbuch*.[63] Like his buildings, this was somewhat academic in approach, but it was by no means confined to a Classicism derived from the architecture of ancient Rome. Rather, it is infused with the functionalist spirit of Durand, with whose work Weinbrenner is known to have been acquainted. Cast in the form of a series of problems and their solutions, the work consists basically of illustrations with brief accompanying instructions. Parts One and Two deal with the principles of geometric and perspective drawing (1810 and 1817), while Part Three (1819) contains the substance of Weinbrenner's ideas about architecture.

Weinbrenner attempts to link Kant's aesthetics to Durand's functionalism: 'Form is to be accounted beautiful when its outlines fully reveal a functional perfection. The functional quality itself is determined by the conception of the form.'[64] He concedes that beauty resides in form, and that colour and materials contribute little to beauty, but a few pages later he writes of 'the complete union of form and functional purpose' and postulates a 'harmonic union of forms and materials' in technical execution.[65] All architectural ornamentation must 'have a meaning in itself which is in harmony with the meaning of that to which it belongs and which serves the purposes of the building.'[66] This leads him to conclude that illusionist landscape painting conflicts with 'the seriousness of art', and that walls should therefore be whitewashed.[67] It is evident that Weinbrenner fails to bridge the gap between form and function.

Weinbrenner's *Ausgeführte und projectirte Gebäude* (1822–35),[68] clearly a response to Schinkel's *Sammlung architektonischer Entwürfe* (1819ff), is a collection of illustrations of the kind that had begun to become obligatory for prominent architects to publish in the nineteenth century, and is almost totally devoid of theoretical substance. The basic distinction between textbooks and publications of architects' own work appears to have begun to be drawn only from the early nineteenth century onwards; up to then writers of treatises had demonstrated principles primarily by means of their own architecture.

It was a pupil of Weinbrenner's, Georg Moller (1784–1852), who published the first large-scale collection of illustrations of Gothic architecture in Germany (*Denkmäler der deutschen Baukunst*, 1815ff).[69] In his executed buildings Moller remained a Classicist, though he also produced neo-Gothic projects;[70] however, he presented the *Denkmäler* in nationalist German and conservationist terms:

> It is the duty of all thinking architects who love their country to do all in their power to ensure that our historic buildings, particularly those of the earliest period, which are becoming ever rarer, be preserved and made known by means of accurate surveys and precise drawings. Animated by this thought, and filled with a desire to save what can still be saved, I addressed myself to this task, as far as time and circumstances allowed, and I offer these pages as a practical contribution to the cultural history of Germany.[71]

Moller – like Goethe in his later comments on the Gothic style – is writing here primarily as an historian. In a letter to Goethe of 24 October 1815 he took issue with what he called the 'Germanomania of the time' and did not speak of Gothic as a suitable model for the present day.[72] Given the intensity of the argument over Gothic in Germany at the beginning of the nineteenth century, it is necessary to distinguish between the documentary historical approach and that which, under the banner of nationalism, was seeking models that could serve the needs of the present. It is impossible to follow the whole debate here, for it extended far beyond architecture and was fuelled above all by works of literature and aesthetics.[73] For present purposes a few specific points must be made.

In 1814, fired by the search begun by his friend Sulpiz Boisserée (1783–1854), Moller succeeded in finding an elevation for Cologne Cathedral in Darmstadt and published it four years later, together with the drawing that Boisserée had rediscovered in Paris.[74] This publication[75] became the focal point of plans to complete the cathedral as a German national monument.[76]

Architectural history, illustrations of monuments and articles in the leading literary journals all addressed themselves to the question of German architecture in the Middle Ages and its relevance for the present. Friedrich Schlegel's periodicals *Europa* (1803–05) and *Deutsches Museum* (1812–13) were particularly influential. Schlegel set out his own views on Gothic architecture in his *Briefe auf einer Reise durch die Niederlande, Rheingegenden, die Schweiz und einen Teil von Frankreich* (1806),[77] in which he conveyed a Romantic, atmospheric image of Gothic, differentiating 'distinct periods of Gothic architecture' but, in a manner characteristic of the time, using 'Gothic' and 'German' interchangeably, claiming this 'national term' ('*Nationalnamen*') to be the true designation 'for the ancient Christian and romantic architecture of the Middle Ages, from Theodoric down to the present day.'[78] 'As one gazes up at the choir vault of the unfinished cathedral in Cologne,' he goes on, 'the heart is filled with wonderment.' Yet a moment later, to our surprise, we find him praising 'the beauty of its proportions, its simplicity, symmetry in delicacy, lightness with grandeur',[79] without realising that he is using the language of Classicism. The third volume of Schlegel's *Deutsches Museum* (1813) contains *Fragmente einer Geschichte der Baukunst im Mittelalter* by Carl Friedrich von Rumohr (1785–1843),[80] in which theories of the evolution of Gothic are expounded without critical evaluation.

Undoubtedly the most important theoretical works on architecture written in Germany in the first half of the nineteenth century are those of Karl Friedrich Schinkel

(1781–1841), despite the fact that he never succeeded in completing his *Architektonisches Lehrbuch* in definitive form.[81] The four posthumous volumes of his writings edited by his son-in-law Alfred von Wolzogen (1862–64)[82] did not arrange his *Lehrbuch* sketches in usable form; the edition was also an unreliable text, certain passages being abridged. The modern edition by Goerd Peschken,[83] however, undertaken as part of Schinkel's collected works, contains a reliable transcription of the notebooks and groups them according to Schinkel's intellectual and artistic development.

Schinkel made his first visit to Italy in the years 1803–05, and his notebooks,[84] while the expression of a young artist eager for experience, are far from showing that he had made up his mind to become an architect. Yet conventional as these jottings often are, they occasionally betray an intense concern with medieval architecture[85] and technical building detail. Other young artists who went to Italy at this time and left similar notebooks include Christian Traugott Weinlig, author of the already-mentioned *Briefe über Rom* (1782–87), Schinkel's Berlin teacher Heinrich Gentz, whose period in Italy (1790–95)[86] overlapped with that of Weinbrenner, and Leo von Klenze.

Considerable space is devoted in Schinkel's notebooks to materials and construction, whilst in his travel sketches architecture is of subsidiary importance, and there are no measured drawings at all. The influence of his teacher David Gilly is seen in the way he looks at buildings, and his aesthetic ideas emerge very clearly from his letters to Gilly.[87] Even before leaving Germany, Schinkel had planned a work devoted to medieval Italian architecture, intending to adopt an eclectic approach.[88] He could be highly critical of what he saw. After being shown round the church of S. Francesco di Paola in Naples by its architect, Pietro Bianchi, on his second journey to Italy in 1824, he wrote:

> Herr Bianchi took me round his new church, where there were a number of good things to see, such as the scaffolding for the dome, light and practical, with a wide opening inside where the materials were hauled up. But overall his design vacillates between ancient and modern, as a result of which much is characterless.[89]

Schinkel had already conceived the idea of an architectural textbook during his first visit to Italy, and he returned to the project time and again until his death. On his way back to Berlin he stayed from November 1804 to January 1805 in Paris, where Durand at the Ecole Polytechnique and his *Précis des leçons* (1802ff) must have been of considerable interest to him, as may be detected in the initial plan for his *Lehrbuch*.

In his edition Peschken plausibly identifies five phases in Schinkel's plan for his *Lehrbuch*: 1) a Romantic phase (1803–05); 2) a national-Romantic phase (1810–15); 3) a Classicist phase (c.1825); 4) a 'technicist' phase (c.1830); 5) a 'legitimist' phase (c.1835).[90]

Phase 1 is governed by the concepts of '*Zweckmäßigkeit*' ('fitness for purpose'), '*Charakter*' and '*Symmetrie*'. These concepts are given similar values by Durand.[91] Under the heading 'The Principle of Art in Architecture' Schinkel evolves a theory of functionalism based entirely on materials, disposition of rooms and construction, from which 'character' and ornamentation ('*Schmuck*') then emerge.[92] In addition to Durand Schinkel appears here also to have had recourse to Dubut's *Architecture civile* (1803): a design for a Venetian palace[93] bears a striking resemblance to one of Dubut's for a Gothic house, which Dubut has set alongside a Renaissance design[94] – a procedure reminiscent of Schinkel's later alternative designs for the Friedrichswerder Church in Berlin.

During his first visit to Italy Schinkel had begun to study the works of the philosopher Johann Gottlieb Fichte. Fichte became professor at the University of Berlin in 1809; the following year Schinkel was appointed as aesthetic adviser to the Prussian building authorities, and became a keen attender at Fichte's lectures. It was Fichte's philosophy, together with Joseph Görres' *Teutsche Volksbücher* (1807), that provided the intellectual background to the national-Romantic Phase 2 of Schinkel's *Lehrbuch*. A further factor was that he found himself in competition with Aloys Hirt, whose lectures he had attended as a student and who in 1809 published his *Baukunst nach den Grundsätzen der Alten*. Schinkel's ideas were in direct opposition to those of Hirt, whom he took to task for a mere mechanical imitation of the Ancients, a failure to consider the ideas that their works expressed, and a misunderstanding of the Middle Ages.[95]

Schinkel's national-Romantic vision of the Middle Ages, based on Fichte's philosophy of nation and state, emerges particularly clearly in his planned section on religious buildings.[96] Here architecture is seen solely as a medium for conveying ideas, with a religious dimension derived from Nature: 'Architecture is the extension of Nature in her constructuve activity,'[97] Schinkel now identifies Antiquity with matter, Gothic with spirit:

> Antiquity, with its higher skills, achieves its effect through physical mass, Gothic, on the other hand, through the spirit, boldly achieving great effects with little physical mass. The work of Antiquity is all vanity, magnificence, because the ornamentation is adventitious; it is an achievement of pure reason, decorated – hence physical life prevails. Gothic spurns meaningless magnificence; everything in it proceeds from one single idea, hence it has the inevitable quality of seriousness, of dignity, of inspiration...[98]

This uncompromisingly Romantic and idealistic interpretation of Gothic marks Schinkel's furthest departure from Classicism. At the same time we must note that it has little to do with the functionalist interpretation of Gothic advanced by Viollet-le-Duc, but is in accordance with the unexecuted Gothic designs that Schinkel made for the mausoleum of Queen Louise of Prussia, the Petrikirche and the memorial church in Berlin at this period.[99]

Phase 3 of Schinkel's plan, the Classicist, is the most fully documented. His rejection of the Romantic revolt took place against the background of the Restoration but he was also influenced by the aesthetics of Karl Wilhelm Ferdinand Solger, who became professor at the University of Berlin in 1811. Nor must we overlook Schinkel's meetings between 1816 and 1824 with Goethe, who had taken the same change of direction from Gothic to Classical as Schinkel was now taking.[100] Unconnected with this are the above-mentioned volumes of *Vorbilder für Fabrikanten und Handwerker* (1821–30), which Schinkel and Beuth began to plan in 1816, and which was quite different in intention from the *Lehrbuch*.

Schinkel now evolved a complex theory of architecture taking into account functional, formal, social and historical factors.[101] He gives both a functional and a Classicist explanation for his rejection of Gothic: 'In the medieval pointed arch proportion is seen as something in process of formation – it grows before our eyes. In the buildings of Antiquity it is presented as something already in existence, something permanent, encompassed by rational laws, thus conveying an agreeable serenity.[102] This leads him to a strange conclusion: 'The pointed arch may have its practical qualities but this does not make it beautiful. It can be put to useful purposes and may therefore be employed in machines and the like...'[103]

A new functionalism now appears in Schinkel's thought: 'The task of architecture is to make something practical, useful and functional into something beautiful', to which he adds the essential relationship between beauty and structure: 'All the essential structural elements of a building must remain visible: as soon as basic parts of the construction are concealed, the entire train of thought is lost. Such concealment leads at once to falsehood...'[104] Ornamentation is subsidiary, and the nature of a building is enhanced 'if each part of it makes its effect freely and without restriction in accordance with the general laws of statics (or appears so to do).'[105] The parenthesis makes it clear that Schinkel does not consider static construction to be automatically beautiful – rather, it must become 'revealed' ('anschaulich'). This is a point that has been developed further in the twentieth century, above all by Pierluigi Nervi.[106] Schinkel made finished drawings of arches and vaulting which show how his ideas about structure developed,[107] while for ornamental features he now fell back on a repertoire from Antiquity. Adopting a dogmatic Classicist stance, and in the spirit of Palladio, he puts together a catalogue of 'faults in architecture', intended less as a piece of historical criticism than as a critique of certain architectural forms and members for future use.

Phase 4 of Schinkel's *Lehrbuch*, called 'technicist' by Peschken, was decisively influenced by the visit made by Schinkel and Beuth to England in 1826. Here he extended a Classicism of the previous phase, taking it in a broader sense and seeking a synthesis between Greek and medieval architecture – 'European architecture synonymous with the extension of Greek architecture', as he put it.[108] He now took the view that the art of the Middle Ages could be adapted to modern purposes 'by being purified in the Greek spirit.'[109] Questions of construction and materials become paramount and dominate his concept of 'Greek', which has little to do with archaeological knowledge. Indeed, he comes remarkably close to his teacher Hirt, who, by similar but less complicated paths, had arrived in 1809 at the conclusion that 'whoever builds correctly must build in the Greek manner.'[110] Schinkel's formulation is as follows:

> For the artist there is only one age of revelation – that of the Greeks. To build in the Greek style is to build correctly, and from this point of view the best products of the Middle Ages are to be called Greek.[111]

Schinkel developed an interest in the whole range of building materials, which led him to coin such phrases as 'artefacts made of dirt'.[112] The breadth of his conception of what constituted 'Classical', a conception based primarily on construction and materials, led to a need for a new stylistic concept. 'Every principal age,' he argued, 'has left the marks of its style on architecture, so why should we not seek to discover a style for our own age?'[113] He envisages a stylistic concept absolute rather than historical, in Nature:

> Style is achieved in architecture if the construction of a complete building 1) takes its visible characteristics in the most practical and beautiful manner from one single material, or 2) takes its visible characteristics from various kinds of material – stone, wood, iron, brick – each in its own peculiar way...[114]

Here, Schinkel's ideas resemble those adopted a little later in France by Viollet-le-Duc, who based his interpretation of Gothic on the distinction between '*le style*' and *'les styles'*, whereas Schinkel, starting from the 'Greek' formal vocabulary, envisages the possibility of an eclectic philosophy:

> Why should we always build in the style of other times? If it is a worthy achievement to apprehend the essence of each style in its purity, so is it an even worthier achievement to arrive at a pure universal style which does not contradict the best that has been achieved in each of the other styles.[115]

Schinkel now no longer believes in the indispensability of symmetry. Criticising the 'empty' symmetry that results from 'a false understanding of the concept of order', he states: 'Symmetry is without doubt the product of sloth and vanity.'[116] His model designs are direct responses to structural problems. On a design for a banqueting hall with an iron roof, for instance, he notes: 'Adequate weight on columns, strength of metal accordingly. Fire-proof roof. Effect of columns. Ceiling without lateral thrust.'[117] There is a close affinity between this design and the interior of the reception hall for his Palace on the Acropolis (1834).[118]

The final phase of the *Lehrbuch*, designated 'legitimist' by Peschken, contains the ideal project for a Royal Residence, included at the request of the Crown Prince Friedrich Wilhelm of Prussia (later King Friedrich Wilhelm IV), himself an amateur architect.[119] Schinkel's work here took on something of the status of an official programme, which imposed unwelcome restrictions on him. It was an effort for him to have to justify the project at the crowning moment of his treatise on the grounds that 'it involved most of the problems facing grand architecture [*'veredelte Architektur'*] at the present time.'[120]

Turning away from the predominantly technological problems that had previously exercised him, Schinkel now accepts 'the higher influence of historical and artistic poetic purposes' on architecture.

> Very early I fell victim to pure abstraction, which led me to evolve the entire concept of a work of architecture from the most immediate trivial purpose and from the construction; the result was a rigid, lifeless design utterly devoid of freedom and lacking two vital elements – the historical and the poetic.[121]

There is a kind of return to Romanticism, or an air of resignation here. Schinkel takes stock of his own position and expresses doubt whether he will ever succeed in transmitting his knowledge and experience to posterity in his projected *Lehrbuch*, since 'trivial concepts' (*'Trivial-Begriffe'*) turn out to be reduced to 'technical artisan's work' (*'wissenschaftliches Handwerk'*), while the essence of architecture lies in the emotions.

> I have now reached the point where the true aesthetic element should take its rightful place in architecture, which in all others respects is, and will remain, a technical craft. And at this point, as throughout the fine arts, it inevitably becomes difficult to produce a teaching method properly speaking, since one is ultimately reduced to educating the emotions.[122]

In the light of sentiments such as these, it was hardly conceivable that Schinkel would ever finish his work. The surviving drafts have the character of reflections of his constantly changing theoretical standpoints, personal and spontaneous in manner, wide-ranging in scope. They also have a symbolic significance in that here the most important German architect of the first half of the nineteenth century attempted to synthesise the theoretical trends of his day, and failed. How widespread the knowledge of Schinkel's ideas was during his lifetime is a question that has yet to be investigated.

In 1819 Schinkel began publication of his own works, both those already executed and those projected for various commissions.[123] This monumental edition in oblong format may have been suggested by the Percier-Fontaine *Recueil de décorations intérieures* (1801, 1812) or by George Richardson's *New Vitruvius Britannicus*, completed in 1808; at all events, it became the prototype of such works in oblong format, with drawings in uniform style – Schinkel made all the preparatory drawings himself – presenting the architectural oeuvre. The great oeuvre publications of the twentieth century, such as those of Le Corbusier and Neutra, continue this tradition. Theoretical conception here takes second place to the presentation of actual works, and aesthetic argument is compressed into a few epigrammatic phrases. On the Friedrichswerder Church in Berlin, for example, Schinkel notes: 'Surrounded on three sides by narrow streets, in which a rich architecture could not be appreciated, the building has been given a very simple exterior...', and on his design for the Bauakademie he confines himself to comments on function, materials and construction.

Schinkel's example was immediately followed by others. In 1822 Friedrich Weinbrenner began the publication of his *Ausgeführte und projectirte Gebäude*, and in 1830 came Klenze's collection with identical title to Schinkel's – *Sammlung architektonischer Entwürfe*.

Seen retrospectively in his historical context, Schinkel has been dubbed 'the man of the future' ('*der kommende Mann*').[124] The single phase in his development dominated by functionalist ideas has been adduced as a precedent for twentieth-century movements such as that associated with Mies van der Rohe; in the Third Reich he was held up as a model of Neo-Classicism,[125] while more recently he has been cited as an example of 'the continuity of history'.[126] Others again have used him as a mirror of their own activity, emphasising his insistence on proceeding by principle.[127] Both in his theoretical and his executed work Schinkel lends himself to all these interpretations, because he broke with historical reference-points to enter territory whose frontiers he could not see.

The changes of direction in Schinkel's thought were brought about in part by the impact of contemporary philosophy, in particular that of German idealist philosophy. Friedrich Wilhelm Joseph von Schelling (1775–1854), for instance, included observations on architecture in his lectures on the philosophy of art delivered in 1802–03.[128] Schelling saw architecture as the representation of organic form in an inorganic context, basing on this conception, firstly the geometric symmetry of architecture, and secondly a view of proportion analogous to that of the human body, so that he supported the Classical orders. Of particular importance for architectural theory in the nineteenth century was his complex concept of the organic,[129] which stimulated renewed discussion of issues that had occupied men's minds since the Renaissance.

In his lectures on aesthetics delivered in Berlin in 1820–21 and published in 1835, Georg Wilhelm Friedrich Hegel (1770–1831) paid considerable attention to architecture, but in contrast to Schelling, he regarded the arts as inferior to religion and philosophy as manifestations of pure spirit. Indebted to Hirt in many respects, Hegel imposed on Hirt's conception of the evolution of architecture a dialectical pattern of three periods in the history of art. The first period he called the 'Symbolic', characterised by the predominance of subject-matter over idea; the second, 'Classical' period established the equality of subject-matter and idea; and the third, Romantic, period represented the supremacy of idea over subject-matter. According to Hegel, the future of art lay in its transposition into the realms of philosophy or religion.

Hegel adopted Schelling's concept of the organic, which he saw manifested above all in the architecture of Antiquity; and he accepted Hirt's view that building in stone was derived from building in wood, together with Hirt's functionalist-structuralist argument. He also drew a basic distinction between 'supporting masses' and 'supported masses', a line of thought carried to extreme limits by Schopenhauer. Hegel saw the column as the basic load-bearing element, the wall as the enclosing element. He explained half-columns in logical terms as 'built-in' or 'walled-up' columns, 'but they remain repugnant, because they represent two purposes standing side by side but in opposition to each other, which merge out of no inner necessity.'[130] This repeats Laugier's view expressed sixty years earlier.

For Hegel 'Romantic' architecture was largely identical with Gothic, and he found in it 'what is peculiarly appropriate to the Christian rite, together with a harmony between the architectural form and the inner spirit of Christianity'.[131] Hegel's interpretation of Gothic architecture, which does not give pride of place to the structural aspect, like Pugin and Ruskin in England, or Viollet-le-Duc in France, but stresses the dissolution of the material, dictated attitudes towards Gothic in Germany until well into the twentieth century.

Hegel's views were developed by Friedrich Theodor Vischer (1807–47) in his *Äesthetik* (1846–58) to take account of the issues of his day.[132] Vischer's opinions coincide at various points with those of Semper, whom he quotes.

The most forthright philosophical statements on architecture at this time come from Arthur Schopenhauer (1788–1860), firstly in the first volume of *Die Welt als Wille und Vorstellung* (1819), and then in greater detail in the second (1844).[133] Schopenhauer posits basic laws of art as 'the objectification of the Will of Nature', and in architecture finds these in the 'single and constant theme' of support and load.[134] The beginnings of a structural functionalism of this kind can be traced back to Alberti, and the concept reaches a high-point with Lodoli in the eighteenth century; it is also to be found in Hirt and Hegel as part of a large-scale historical pattern. But not before Schopenhauer had the idea been raised to so absolute a principle.

Basing his case on Greek architecture – 'Only in a row of columns is the separation complete, the entablature appearing as pure load, the column as pure support' – Schopenhauer explains the Orders in terms of the static relationships between substantial supports and a given load, and rejects the historical derivation of architectural forms and proportions from models found in Nature and the human body:

> Since all the laws of the Orders, and consequently the form and proportions of the column in all its parts and dimensions down to the finest detail, follow from the concept of a generously calculated support for a given load – a concept well understood and consistently put into effect, thus to this extent established as *a priori* – it is clear how mistaken the idea is, so often repeated, that tree trunks, or even the human form – as unfortunately even Vitruvius maintains (IV.i) – could have been the prototype of the column.

Schopenhauer concludes that only the laws of gravity, rigidity and cohesion are valid for architecture, and that the concepts of regular form, proportion and symmetry which had earlier been adopted could not, being merely characteristics of space, become 'the subject of one of the fine arts'. This signifies a complete break with Vitruvian theory. Schopenhauer sees architecture as a demonstration of the laws of gravity, which are best exemplified in monumental buildings:

> In order to achieve aesthetic effect, works of architecture must be of substantial dimensions. They can easily be too small, but never too large. Indeed, other things being equal, the aesthetic effect stands in direct ratio to the dimensions of a building, because only large masses can render the effectiveness of gravity conspicuous and impressive in the highest degree.

This is a line of argument strongly reminiscent of Boullée, as is Schopenhauer's subsequent advocacy of an architecture consisting 'simply of regular shapes composed of straight lines or symmetrical curves, such as those displayed in figures like cubes, parallelepipeds, cylinders, spheres, pyramids and cones...' Schopenhauer sees in this a parallel to organic Nature, and since Greek architecture 'can no longer be surpassed in significant measure...a modern architect cannot depart to any great degree from the rules and models of the Ancients.' Gothic he sees as an arbitrary style, its apparent conquest of gravity an illusion based on nothing other than associations of ideas, and he heaps scorn on neo-Gothic trends and the completion of medieval cathedrals: 'When I see how industriously this pagan age is striving to complete those Gothic churches left unfinished by the pious Middle Ages, it seems to me as if they are trying to embalm the dead body of Christianity.' Schopenhauer's ideas, based on his philosophy of the Will, emerge as an endorsement of Classicism, but they could be made to serve the purposes of any number of modern theories of functionalism.

Such formulations of German Idealist philosophy form the background to architectural history and theory in Germany during this time; through the agency of Transcendentalism they also came to occupy a place of central importance in American architectural theory in the second half of the nineteenth century.[135]

Philosophical reflections on architecture reappear sporadically in early works on art and architectural history in the 1840s, such as those by Carl Schnaase (1798–1875) and Franz Kugler (1808–58), a former student at the Bauakademie and Jacob Burckhardt's teacher.[136] Schnaase, a Hegelian, published a seven-volume *Geschichte der bildenden Künste* between 1843 and 1864,[137] dedicating it to Kugler, whose own *Handbuch der Kunstgeschichte* had appeared in 1842, described by its author as 'the first comprehensive undertaking of its kind'.[138] In the introduction to his work Schnaase quotes mathematical laws and functionality as constituting the essence of architecture, which he assigns to the realm of inorganic Nature.[139] Whilst regarding functionality as a law of Nature, he admits that pure functionality can lead to a 'cold, soulless style', and concludes: 'Beauty in architecture does not reside in functionalism – rather, it begins when art asserts itself over the latter.'[140] His affinity with Schopenhauer shows itself in the regard that he pays to gravity and cohesion in architecture, qualities that he sees as 'necessary aspects' belonging to inorganic Nature.

In an extensive review article on Schnaase's book, Kugler identified 'sub-division, the organic principle in the evolution of the life process', as essential also to architecture.[141] Schnaase responded with a pamphlet *Über das Organische in der Baukunst* (1844),[142] in which he dubbed the fashionable word *organic*, 'the favourite term of the age' and proceeded to point to the closeness of the connection, amounting almost to identity, of the concepts of the organic and the functional:

If one persists in emphasising the 'organic', the purpose and the interrelation of the architectural members – not merely from the point of view of intrinsic meaning but also from that of external appearance – and thus, in a logical development of this line of thought, becomes more and more rigorous in one's rejection of ornamentation, one will ultimately approach the poverty-stricken view of architecture as mere functionalism.[143]

These comments by Schnaase go straight to the heart of a debate which, conducted with imprecise concepts of what constituted the functional and the organic, was to dominate the next hundred years. Schnaase pointed to monotony and a growing internationalism as the palpable dangers facing architecture: 'In practice we shall drift further and further into monotony, not daring to depart from the standard 'organic' model, and taking an increasingly aloof attitude towards the manifold independent creations of the different nations of history.'[144]

In the spirit of the nineteenth century Kugler, in his *Handbuch der Kunstgeschichte*, traced the source of architecture to the 'monument';[145] in his extensive *Geschichte der Baukunst*,[146] on the other hand, which was continued by Jacob Burckhardt and Wilhelm Lübke, he dispensed with evolutionary and axiomatic statements and laid the foundation for all subsequent historiography of architecture, at least in Germany.

An attempt to deal with these complex historical and philosophical issues was made by Leo von Klenze (1784–1864),[147] whose career in Munich was similar in many respects to that of Schinkel in Berlin, only three years his senior. Klenze was the more widely-travelled of the two: he paid repeated visits to Italy after 1806 and was in Greece in 1834. Between 1800 and 1803 he studied with David Gilly in Berlin, also, more intensively, with Aloys Hirt there, and also possibly with Friedrich Gilly. He met Schinkel, and his view of history he owed to Johannes von Müller (1752–1809). His writings show a greater concern than Schinkel's with the literature of archaeology, history and religion, which he attempted to integrate into his systems of thought. Whereas Schinkel showed remarkably little interest in making measured drawings during his travels, Klenze both made and published a number of archaeological drawings, such as those of the Temple of Zeus at Agrigento, dating from the winter of 1823–24. While there, he met Hittorff, whose views on polychromy in the architecture of Antiquity he adopted in the second edition of his work (1827).[148] Klenze's extensive *Architektonische Erwiderungen und Erörterungen über Griechisches und Nichtgriechisches* remained unpublished,[149] but those of his works that were published enable us to assess his position in the history of architectural theory.[150]

A characteristic work of Klenze's is his *Versuch einer Wiederherstellung des toskanischen Tempels nach seinen historischen und technischen Analogien* (1821).[151] Taking as his point of departure Vitruvius's statement on Tuscan temples, on which Hirt had also written at length,[152] Klenze produced a reconstruction of the Tuscan temple based on parallels with Etruscan architecture and with building styles in modern-day Rhaetia in ethnic, religious and even etymological terms. This led him to apply technical features of the modern Tirolean farmhouse, especially in roof construction, to his reconstruction of the Etruscan temple. Invoking the spirit of Antiquity, here as in his view of history, he expresses the opinion that 'Greek architecture is linked by a common chain to the architecture of all ages.'[153]

Klenze's ideas become clearer in his *Anweisung zur Architektur des christlichen*

Cultus (1822),[154] published at public expense and distributed free. Its purpose was restorative: to lay the 'foundation of a general authority and guide for wavering ideas'[155] in the context of Church architecture. This was to be the first in a series of treatises intended to deal also with other kinds of building, 'in so far as they belong to a common type and are amenable to rules of universal validity'.[156] The series, however, never materialised.

Klenze favoured an official architectural policy laid down by the state, 'in order to disseminate the general concept of fixed rules and forms in architecture', and in church architecture he sought to give 'the striving of the time one, and where possible, the same direction'.[157] Even Colbert's Académie Royale d'Architecture, founded under Louis XIV, had never ventured to make such categorical demands as these.

In his preface Klenze distinguishes 'real architecture', defined as 'the servant of religion, of the state and of society, in the superior sense of the word', from 'economic architecture', which he passes over on the grounds that his concern is with 'architectural beauty and form in the higher sense.'[158] 'General architectural norms,' he maintains, in defence of this distinction, 'where they take excessive account of human requirements, the satisfaction of which depends on so many private considerations, circumstances and local conditions, can seldom prove adequate.'[159] Religious architecture, for him, takes pride of place in order to 'restore the shattered columns of the Christian Church and, in full freedom of conscience, re-establish Christianity on firm foundations.'[160] The religions of the world, in Klenze's all-embracing view of history, represent 'a rising evolutionary sequence towards positive Christianity.'[161]

After these ideological preliminaries, Klenze arrives (chapter 3) at what he calls a 'universally valid basic principle of architecture', where the influence of Durand and Hirt is to be detected:

> In the real sense of the word, the ethical sense, architecture is the art of moulding and combining natural materials for the purposes of human society and its needs in such a way that the manner in which the laws of preservation, consistency and function are observed will ensure the highest possible degree of solidity and durability with the least possible outlay of materials and forces.[162]

This is a definition that derives from Durand and is at the same time not far removed from Schinkel's early concepts. Its origins become still clearer in his definition of beauty as 'a quality, in the highest sense of the word, that emerges from the demands of the object, or the purpose of a building, in combination with the laws of statics and economics.'[163] With the exception of the phrase 'in the highest sense of the word', this is a statement that essentially corresponds with the functionalist aesthetics of Durand.

Since Klenze finds the most complete and most perfect fusion of statics, materials and construction in the art of the Greeks – a view adopted from Hirt – he sees no further reason not to regard Greek architecture as 'the architecture of all countries and all ages, and in particular as true, essential and positive in every respect – the architecture, furthermore, of a true, essential and positive Christianity.'[164]

The functions of the Christian Church, however, demand new formal combinations; regional and climatic conditions will also cause local variations in Church architecture, but these Klenze would like to see carried out 'in the strict and beautiful manner of Antiquity'.[165] Klenze's catalogue of desiderata for 'Christian liturgical architecture' anticipates to a remarkable degree the *Thesen über christliche Baukunst* (1824) of

Christian Karl Josias von Bunsen, which was concerned with reviving the building of Protestant churches in Berlin and made its mark on the design for the cathedral there.[166] Klenze's *Anweisung* belongs in the context of the 1820s debate on the Christian basilica, further contributions to this discussion being the *Denkmale der christlichen Religion* (1822–27) by Gutensohn and Knapp[167] and, most important of all, Bunsen's *Die Basiliken des christlichen Roms* (1842–44), to which we shall return.

Klenze was strongly opposed to the current discussion of Gothic, and particularly against 'the still-born idea of its revival'.[168] Yet in his remarkable, 'un-Greek' designs we find the following comment on his project for a Cathedral (*Plate 160*):

> For the exterior we have tried, to the extent that it is possible in Classical architecture, which must almost beware of any kind of excess, to achieve that lightness and transparency which, by virtue of its functional quality, has so often and justifiably been commended in the steeples of the Middle Ages.[169]

Klenze's design is a paraphrase of Saint-Sulpice in Paris, and one is reminded of Abbé de Cordemoy's Greco-Gothic ideas at the beginning of the eighteenth century, which may also have had an influence on Goethe. The designs in his explanatory *Anweisung* show Klenze's concept of 'Greek' to amount to little more than vague imitation of Antique style. The Allerheiligenhofkirche, the only church he built in Munich, turned into a completely un-Classical imitation of St Mark's in Venice, at the express desire of King Ludwig I.[170]

Klenze's concept of 'Greek', rather like Schinkel's, is larely based on technological considerations. The interrelationship between Schinkel and Klenze has yet to be researched but it is significant that Klenze's essay on his Walhalla monument (1842)[171] should consist primarily of explanations of its construction, and conclude: 'The positive side of architectural undertakings needs to be precisely explained – the artistic side can stand for itself.'[172] The interior of the Walhalla, with its iron truss frames, corresponds in large measure to Schinkel's banqueting hall design in his *Lehrbuch* and to the reception hall of his Acropolis project.

In 1830, following the example of Schinkel and Weinbrenner, Klenze began his *Sammlung architektonischer Entwürfe*.[173] He recognised in Greek architecture 'a firm principle for all times'[174] but without raising this to the status of a norm. It would therefore be doing him – and indeed Schinkel – an injustice to categorise him simply as a dogmatic Classicist.

What Klenze set out in his *Anweisung* to do for the architecture of the Roman Catholic Church, Christian Carl Josias von Bunsen (1791–1860), diplomat and theologian, tried to do for the Protestant Church in *Die Basiliken des christlichen Roms* (1842–4),[175] dedicated to Friedrich Wilhelm IV, with whom he was on intimate terms. He had already published his *Thesen über christliche Baukunst* (1824) before his period as Prussian ambassador to the Holy See (1824–38). His view of history was similar to that of Stieglitz: he saw an evolutionary continuity between the architecture of Greece, Rome and the Middle Ages, but brusquely rejected that of the seventeenth and eighteenth centuries. He made a bold attempt to link the architecture of Antiquity with 'the Germanic architecture of the Middle Ages',[176] and regarded Roman basilicas as functional adaptations of Greek buildings, on this basis justifying their re-use in the present. The following passage exemplifies his conception of history:

It is further acknowledged at the present time that there is no chance in our own age of truly restoring the Classical style – a restoration attempted in the fifteenth and sixteenth centuries with inadequate means, and in the seventeenth and eighteenth with lamentable results – as long as thinkers and artists do not have before their eyes a clear and perfect vision of how that style evolved in the Graeco-Roman world. Who does not realise that the Roman basilicas, with impressive earnestness, seek to adapt the ancient elements to the new needs in one of the most important areas of architecture? Indeed, it is recognised that for a vital understanding of the Germanic architecture of the Middle Ages, and for any consequent possibility of reviving it, a knowledge of these old basilicas is of the utmost importance.[177]

Basing his arguments on the Basilica Aemilia and the Basilica Ulpia in Rome, Bunsen reaches a somewhat bizarre conclusion: 'Maybe, in our broad cosmopolitanism and our eclectic Greek-ness, we shall surpass both these buildings. In that case we should, for the time being, have preserved all the decoration of Classical architecture, and at the same time have actually gained a Christian art.'[178]

Using liturgical arguments, Bunsen then seeks to demonstrate the suitability of the early Christian basilicas for Protestant worship, seeing in this revitalised architecture the dawn of a golden age. Early Christian architecture opens up untold possibilities for the present:

[Early] Christian [architecture] presents a truly venerable aspect and shows every prospect of becoming fashionable. But there are many signs that the great slogan of the age is the reconciliation of opposites, to the mockery of all earlier centuries. All would then be satisfied – the old would become joined with the new, the religious with the secular; spirit and flesh, faith and knowledge would become reconciled...[179]

And Bunsen's concluding claim is no less sweeping than Klenze's: 'In view of all this we may regard the basilica as the most universally Christian form and, in the West, almost the only one that will meet our needs.'[180] And for specifically Protestant purposes he proposed a combination of early Christian basilica and medieval ('Germanic') vaulting.

The basilica debate left particularly deep marks on the designs for Berlin Cathedral that were submitted during the reign of King Friedrich Wilhelm IV.[181]

Bunsen's manipulation of history in order to make it serve the needs of the present may be an extreme case, but it is far from being an isolated one in the nineteenth century. The appeal to Greek architecture was general at the time, although the term 'Greek' was used to mask a variety of very different aims. It was therefore something of a sensation when the 'Greek' principle – even as used in a narrowly defined sense – came to be rejected as a model for the present. But this happened in 1828 when Heinrich Hübsch (1795–1863), a pupil of Weinbrenner's, published his essay *In welchem Style sollen wir bauen?*[182]

Hübsch did not reject the architecture of Classical antiquity as such, but merely questioned its claim to precedence, especially in relation to the present day. His approach represents a continuation of Weinbrenner's construction-based ideas and is based on what he calls 'technostatics', i.e. the development of ever wider spans and greater economy of materials. Hübsch distinguished two basic principles of construction – the horizontal and the rounded, or vaulted – which he called 'original styles' ('*Original-*

Style');[183] his concept of style was thus not historical but technological, as in the later phases of Schinkel's *Lehrbuch*. He saw Greek architecture as the expression of the straight-line, horizontal style, unsuited to modern architecture, particularly in Germany, new materials and greater dimensions now having to be reckoned with. For Hübsch this means having recourse to the round or vaulted form:

> The architectural conditions of today are totally different from, even diametrically opposed to, those of Greek times. What greater contrast can there be than between the good quality stone of Antiquity, with its high relative strength, which permitted unbroken horizontal lintels, and the fragile stones of today, which can be used to cover only very short horizontal spans, whereas the vault is a more than adequate substitute? Or between the modest needs of Antiquity, with no great demands for spaciousness, and the huge demands of today, with our insistence on as much spaciousness as possible? Or between the abundance of external columns and one-storey buildings but absence of windows in Antiquity and the rarity of open colonnaded halls but ubiquity of multi-storey buildings and numerous windows of today?[184]

Hübsch sought to take from Greek architecture the principle of simplicity and truth, which he interpreted as the manifestation of structural forces. In this connection he described the applied column as 'the first great lie of conventionality in architecture',[185] and saw Roman architecture as representing simply the 'conflict' between his two 'original' styles. Whilst he saw Greek architecture as antithetical to the needs of the present day, the use of semicircular arches, in his eyes, conformed to those needs and had the aesthetic advantage of coming closer to the ideal of the line of beauty (this is reminiscent of Hogarth).[186] Hübsch was enthusiastic about the cupolas and vaultings of Byzantine and, above all, Romanesque buildings, calling the abbey church of Maria Laach 'the most beautiful I have ever seen.'[187] He rejected stylistic imitation but his 'technostatic' arguments led him to conclusions not far removed from those seen in the Romanesque style:

> If one seeks an existing authority by which to justify the new style, then in recent decades the art of the Middle ages has acquired considerable status ... And a mode of building that from the outset has the same foundation, viz. predominantly that of vaulting, as the architecture of the Middle Ages, and is therefore bound not to be dissimilar to it, will not turn out to be displeasing.[188]

Hübsch goes on to claim that 'in many respects the round-arch style is infused with the same spirit as that found in the Greek style', giving smooth walls and a feeling of 'delicate grandeur and sobriety'.[189] He praises the achievements of Gothic but draws an analogy between semicircular and ogival arches on one hand, and pre-Raphaelite and post-Raphaelite painting on the other, thus establishing a striking link with contemporary taste.[190] The 'new style' he calls an 'objective framework' ('*objektives Skelett*'), and the similarity with the round-arch style 'lies in the nature of the matter and is not the product of the influence of authorities or of personal predilection.'[191] He allows personal imagination free play in ornament, as long as such elements do not 'mask' the rest.[192]

In his case for the round arch Hübsch adopts the same methodological approach as the proponents of the Greek style or, with greater consistency, Viollet-le-Duc in his case for neo-Gothic. All reason along functional and structural lines. It follows from this that their so-called 'rational stylistic evidence' consists merely of pseudo-reasons for their own historical preferences. Hübsch's churches are in a neo-Romanesque style, and his New Pump Room in Baden-Baden (1839–42) has something of the 'delicate grandeur and sobriety' at which he aimed.

Adopting a title similar to Hübsch's, G. Palm published in 1845 the essay *Von welchen Principien soll die Wahl des Baustyls, insbesondere des Kirchenbaustyls geleitet werden ?*[193] Following the eclecticism of Stieglitz, Palm maintains that there must be a relationship between choice of style and the character of a building. For present-day buildings he proposes the use of Graeco-Roman, Gothic and 'modern' styles; the last-named he sees as appropriate for such buildings as polytechnics and railway stations – though he makes no reference to iron – whilst his preferred style for churches is Gothic. Palm demands that architecture display 'truth, purity and characterful organic design' but says nothing about how these aims are to be achieved.[194]

Hübsch was one of the panel of judges in what must be seen as the most remarkable competition to be held in Germany in the nineteenth century, a competition which was to give birth to a totally new architectural style. In 1850 King Maximilian II of Bavaria had the Academy of Arts in Munich organise a competition for an educational establishment to be called the 'Athenaeum'; this eventually led to the Maximilianeum, the Maximilianstraße and the style known as the 'Maximilian Style'.[195] As Crown Prince, Maximilian had already sought the advice of Schinkel and Klenze in such matters. Asked what his 'ideal of architecture' was, Schinkel had replied 'that in every age one's striving after an ideal must necessarily be influenced by the new demands being made.'[196]

The terms of the competition, and in particular the 'Explanatory Comments', are very revealing in the context of this discussion of style.[197] The terms review the various available styles and forms of eclecticism as a preamble to the stated aim of 'wresting from the struggles of the present day a national reshaping of architecture', in which 'the character of the age shall find its natural and unmistakable expression', and in which experience, technological advances and new materials shall be united under the banner of the strictest economy. It is somewhat contradictory to read that the competitors were encouraged to feel entirely free 'to avail themselves of various styles, and their ornamentation, in order to achieve a practicable solution to the problem, so that the design finally chosen is not derived exclusively from any particular one of the known styles'. In effect this would have only seemed to lead to a new eclecticism. And in emphasising the national character of the new style, the document also suggests that 'the principles of Early German, so-called Gothic architecture, together with ornamentation in the form of German flora and fauna, should also, as far as possible, be kept in mind.'[198]

The 'Explanatory Comments' were rather more precise. They called for the new style to be the result of 'deliberate reflection', since the age of 'natural conscious creation, which gave rise to the earlier patterns of building' was now past. The new style was to reflect 'the spirit of the age' and have regard to 'political and social conditions'. The 'character of an architecture truly of its time' was defined as 'practical functionalism, comfort, simplicity and beauty in accordance with the present-day level of technical development, together with the utmost economy of means.' The earlier reference to Gothic was now qualified by a suggestion that entrants to the competition should consider 'combining the simple and restful rectilinear character of Greek architecture with the upward-striving forms of the Gothic style'. It was hoped that on the basis of these premises an 'original and beautiful organic entity' would arise.[199]

As was to be expected, all the entries in the competition were eclectic in character. Delivering his comments in 1852, Klenze stated bluntly that 'none of the entries met all the stated requirements'; the best entry he adjudged to be that by Wilhelm Stier, an architect from Berlin, but Stier's design, he added, 'would probably never be executed because of the immense cost involved.'[200] King Friedrich Wilhelm IV of Prussia also took part, privately, in the competition, meeting the desire for a national German style by the transposition of the 'charming forms' of houses in the Bavarian alps into masonry architecture, adding by way of explanation: 'The new style stands in the same relationship to Bavarian alpine houses as does the final, perfected form of the Greek Classical style to that of the original wooden houses of ancient Greece.'[201]

The judges came to their decision in 1854 and awarded the prize to Stier. But even King Maximilian clearly never seriously intended to have Stier's design executed, for two years earlier he had already started to negotiate with the architect Friedrich Bürklein for an expanded project that should also include the Maximilianstrasse. Maximilian's own observations on this project (1852)[202] show that the Maximilianstrasse as eventually built did in fact conform to his ideas. But the 'Maximilian Style' never acquired the status of a new national style, remaining instead just one more whimsical form of an eclecticism that took its lead from Gothic.

The leading German architectural theorist of the mid-nineteenth century is Gottfried Semper (1803–79),[203] described by his friend Gottfried Keller, the Swiss poet and novelist, as a 'child-like, hypochondriac creature'[204] – a nature which also emerges from his work. Semper was internationally known – as a man, as a writer and as an architect – and quickly exerted an international influence. He began life as a mathematician. His period of study with Friedrich von Gärtner in Munich in 1825 left him dissatisfied, and from 1826 to 1830 he studied in Paris with Franz Christian Gau, who belonged to the school of Durand; it was Gau who introduced Semper to Hittorff, and who provided him with his real architectural training. Hittorff had published his sensational treatise on architectural polychromy in Antiquity in 1824, and this was followed three years later by his and Zanth's work on the Greek ruins in Sicily. Semper may well also have seen Labrouste's reconstructions of Paestum in Paris, the theoretical conclusions of which are often reminiscent of Semper's ideas.

Semper's journeys to Italy, Sicily and Greece between 1830 and 1833 were dominated by the question of architectural polychromy in Antiquity. He spent the winter of 1831–32 in Greece with Jules Goury, who went on to travel through the Near East and southern Spain. From this journey came a three-volume work on the Alhambra in Granada, with plans and elevations in colour.[205]

Semper's first work, *Vorläufige Bemerkungen über bemalte Architektur und Plastik bei den Alten* (1834), dedicated to Gau, deals with the whole question of polychromy.[206] Semper makes it clear in his preface that it was not his intention to write 'a learned antiquarian treatise' but to provide practical hints and 'useful information'.[207] The outlines of his conception of architecture, broad in its theoretical approach yet always practical in application, are already apparent. He vehemently attacks what he calls the 'semi-bankrupt' architecture of the present day together with the schematic procedures of Durand and the imitation of historical styles, and he has Klenze in mind when he refers caustically to the building of 'a Walhalla to look like the Parthenon, a basilica to look like Monreale, a boudoir to look like Pompeii, a palace to look like the Palazzo Pitti.'[208]

In Semper's view architecture is a response to a need, but its organic development can only take place in freedom. He saw from the outset the connection between architecture and social and historical structure. A militant republican, in 1848 he was found on the barricades in Dresden. He never wavered in his conviction that art could only evolve in freedom. 'Mighty patrons of the arts,' he writes, 'may create in the desert a Babylon, a Persepolis, or a Palmyra, where regular patterns of streets, huge squares, magnificent halls and palaces stand waiting for the people in a mournful void...'[209] Architecture must be 'in harmony with the conditions of human society', thus the monuments of Greece are a reflection of 'the higher spiritual laws of the organism of the state'.[210] This context must be remembered if one is to understand correctly Semper's well-known statement on materials, often cited to reduce him to the level of a positivist and functionalist: 'Let materials speak for themselves and appear, undisguised, in whatever form and whatever conditions have been shown by experience and knowledge to be best suited to them. Let brick appear as brick, wood as wood, iron as iron, each according to the structural laws that apply to it.'[211] For a man such as Lodoli a formulation of this kind would have encapsulated his entire philosophy; for Semper it is only a principle that expresses the symbolic value of architecture.

Semper follows Hittorff in seeing painting and applied decoration in terms of protection and durability in the first instance, but he then refers back to prehistoric cultures and interprets the application of colour as symbolising 'obscure religious conceptions'.[212] This deliberate recourse to ethnography is central to his whole approach. He tries to prove, sometimes with forced arguments, that polychromy was a constant in architecture from Antiquity to the early Renaissance, and that 'the novelty of monochromy' only began with Brunelleschi and Michelangelo, leading to 'hybrid creations born of modern tail-coats and Antiquity'.[213] In a direct attack on Classicism he declares: 'It is barbaric that the monuments should have become monochrome.'[214] As he sees it, the question of polychromy in architecture and sculpture is a question of symbolic character; its demands are absolute, which leads him to claim that Greek marble too must have been coloured: 'The painted decorations on Greek monuments are in supreme, most perfect harmony with the plastic decorations on them – indeed, with the monuments as a whole – both in character and in execution.'[215]

Semper seeks directly to influence the taste of his time by explaining the principle of architectural polychromy as a response to and an effect of natural surroundings. 'Colours are less harsh than the dazzling white of our stuccoed walls,' he declares, applying the argument specifically to Northern Europe: 'Are our fields, our forests or our flowers grey and white? Are they not far brighter than in the south?'[216]

Semper is less concerned with proving the case for polychromy on historical grounds than with establishing a principle, and the subject became the basis of his later 'cladding theory', as for Labrouste it was the starting-point for his relativist aesthetics of architecture.

A year after publication of Semper's work (1835) Franz Kugler advanced a scientific case for restricting the unconditional application of Semper's theses:[217]

We may accept as a general principle that, if not others as well, then without doubt all buildings in noble white marble from the Golden Age of Greece – that is, the majority of those in the Attic style – display their stone, in their principal parts, in its original colour, and that only subsidiary details were painted.[218]

Despite the very moderate tone of Kugler's observations, Semper felt himself under attack and reacted with an unpleasant riposte against what, still unrepentant, he called after Kugler's death 'the personification of that widespread and immortal species, the German *Hofrat*.'[219] But there is more to Semper's *Die vier Elemente der Baukunst* (1851), published while he was in exile, than mere polemics.[220] The early chapters continue to put forward arguments in favour of polychromy, and contain a good deal of invective directed at Kugler, but we can also sense that polychromy has come to signify for him an organic artistic expression in the context of a democratic constitution: 'Greek polychromy is no longer seen as a mere isolated phenomenon, it is no figment of the imagination, but reflects the feelings of the masses, the general desire for colour in art, and in the middle of the new movement important voices have been promptly raised in its support.'[221] Polychromy now becomes for Semper a synonym for the artistic expression of a democratic form of government: 'In Greek Antiquity this harmony could result only from a free yet binding alliance between elements with equal rights, a democracy among the arts.'[222] He therefore dismissed contemporary polychromy in Germany as a 'fancy, inflated marchpane style' and 'a blood-red meat style', only masquerading as Greek.[223] Where Labrouste used the polychromy debate to attack Classicist normative aesthetics, Semper – the 'red' Semper, as Kugler called him – made it the basis of a socio-aesthetic ideology.

In chapter 5 of *Die vier Elemente der Baukunst* we find new arguments. Here Semper rejects functionalism, 'which made structure the essence of architecture and thereby bound the latter in iron chains' and insists that 'like Nature, its great teacher, architecture, while selecting and treating its subject-matter according to her laws, must make the form and expression of its creations dependent not on this subject-matter but on the ideas that dwell within it.'[224]

Deriving these ideas from what he calls the 'circumstances of primitive human society', Semper comes to his idea of the four basic elements from which architecture has evolved – hearth, roof, enclosing wall and earthwork (terrace), the last-named being defined, significantly, in terms of the development of mankind as representing 'as it were, man's last creation in mud'.[225] He traces the wall, as textile partition, back to the realm of the decorative arts and adduces the colours in textiles as the final proof of his theory of polychromy in architecture. Etymologically, he points out, the word for wall (German *Wand*) is cognate with *Gewand*, meaning 'garment', 'robe', so that polychromy has its origins in the concept of a 'garment' covering the earliest architecture.[226] For Semper the roots of art and architecture were always to be traced to the applied arts. These ideas appear to show the influence of Boetticher, who also regarded the hearth as the determining element in a house, and compared the walls to woven hangings.[227] The emphasis on materials, tools and climate also occurs in Thomas Hope's *Historical Essay on Architecture* (1835), from which Semper quotes.[228]

In a more idealistic sense than the eighteenth-century 'primitive hut', with its constructional emphasis, Semper desired to use his 'elements' – visual reminders of man in his primitive state – to invoke the image of 'a free people inspired by national sentiment'.[229] Semper was not far at this point from the position of Morris and Ruskin, who believed that the Middle Ages embodied a social structure that was still intact, and drew corresponding conclusions for architecture and the applied arts. Like them, Semper also put his 'elements' to practical use, suggesting that, by remembering that the wall, as partition, evolved from a woven hanging, a wall might be decorated 'by painting a textile on it'.[230]

Semper has often been misunderstood as putting forward an aesthetic solely in terms of materials. But he was not concerned with making construction and materials immediately visible but with illustrating the principle of cladding and the structural aspect of materials. This is made particularly clear in the context of his theory of polychromy:

> In connection with the decorative painting of exposed structural features, such as iron piers and roof trusses, or similar structures in wood, it is important to take account of the structural implications of these materials. For example, for ironwork, which appears more perfect the thinner it is, I would never use bright colours, but black, bronze and a great deal of gold.[231]

These ideas led Semper far away from the proof of his theory of polychromy, and even Kugler noted the 'strange, fanciful cultural thrust' of Semper's thought, with its 'elemental justification' of polychromy.[232] Semper continued his attack on Kugler in his last publication, *Über Baustile* (1869),[233] in which he further developed his conception of the relationship between history and architecture. He now saw the latter as totally dependent on social history, the universally valid, because democratic, model still being the Greek, and the monuments of architectural history he viewed in Darwinian terms, as merely 'the fossil remains of extinct social organisms'.[234]

In 1851 Semper took part in the Great Exhibition in London, an experience that led him to write his essay *Wissenschaft, Industrie und Kunst*. This piece, which makes a bow in the direction of the Communist Manifesto, published in London three years earlier,[235] reveals an increasing concern with the applied arts and with the relationship between 'technical' skills and architectural style. Semper addresses this problem directly in *Entwurf eines Systems der vergleichenden Stillehre* (1853).[236] The idealistic content of his thought now recedes. Working increasingly with the methodology of the natural sciences, he puts forward a classification of works of art – 'props' ('*Krücken*'), as he calls them – in four types, by analogy with Cuvier's classification of the animal kingdom, and arrives at the formula: $Y = F(x, y, z$ etc$)$.[237]

This formula is nothing less than an attempt to express in mathematical terms the relationship between work of art, style and all constituent elements. Y = the work of art, which is determined by constant (F) and variable factors (x, y, z etc). The constants in Semper's scheme are the functions, which he divides into 'types'; the variables are 1) materials; 2) regional, ethnological, climatic, religious and political conditions; 3) personal influences, i.e. exercised by the artist or his patron. The combination of the variables produces the characteristics of 'style'. Materials are given particular attention, but Semper emphasises the need 'to observe the limits imposed by the idea underlying the object.'[238]

'Types' are defined by Semper as 'original forms prescribed by need',[239] which he identifies with his four basic elements. Four basic materials lead to four basic techniques, which lead in their turn to the four basic elements of architecture (Semper's use of terms is not always consistent):

Material:	Clay	Wood	Textile	Stone
	↓	↓	↓	↓
Technique:	Ceramics	Carpentry (Tectonics)	Weaving	Masonry (Stereotomy)
	↓	↓	↓	↓
Basic elements of architecture:	Hearth (Fireplace)	Roof	Enclosure	Substructure (Earthwork, terrace)

Semper does not regard metal as a primary material, because by the time it was discovered, his four types were already established.[240]

This chart, analogous to biological classification, is Semper's point of departure in his principal work, *Der Stil in den technischen und tektonischen Künsten* (two volumes, 1860 and 1863). The biological analogy leads him to adopt a narrower conception of the organism, which, however, still has an ideational quality that takes it beyond matters of statics and construction. Only the Greeks, he still maintains, succeeded in 'breathing organic life into their architectural creations and their industrial products. Greek temples and monuments are organic growths…'[241]

The work remained a torso;[242] a third volume, intended to deal with architecture, was apparently never written.[243] Semper defines his basic attitudes in the prolegomena to the first volume. The present age, he says, is in a state of crisis: 'Practice and industrial speculation, as middlemen between consumption and invention, are handed these latter to exploit as they wish, devoid of any individual style that they could have acquired in the course of a thousand years of common usage.'[244]

For the purposes of architecture Semper divides contemporary leaders of thought into three categories – materialist, historicist and schematic. The first, for whom form is derived exclusively from constructional considerations, are closest to Semper, but he was at pains to distance himself from them: 'Form, idea become object, must not conflict with the material out of which it is made, but it is not absolutely necessary for material as such to become a factor in the art object.'[245] He rejects 'schematic' Gothic on the grounds of its bare functionalism, and neo-Gothic because of the political views of its main representatives. To demonstrate what he sees as the 'lifelessness' of Gothic he asserts: 'Gothic buildings are the stone equivalents of twelfth- and thirteenth-century scholastic philosophy.'[246] Jules Michelet had coined a similar phrase but with a positive connotation.

It is interesting to observe that, having challenged Vitruvius at many points and passed particularly severe judgement on his aesthetic concepts,[247] Semper should have introduced his own aesthetic categories of 'symmetry, proportionality and direction', although he invests them with a scientific quality by drawing a parallel with mineralogy.[248] These categories are, however, of lesser status than those of 'regularity, type and character', which attain the level of 'expression'.[249] In the 'self-contained eurhythmy of crystals and other perfectly regular forms of Nature' lies the justification, as he sees it, for the use of pure geometric forms for architectural monuments, since they are 'symbols of the universe, which knows nothing beyond itself.'[250] By a completely different route Semper here arrives at a result not so far removed from the constructs created by the so-called Revolutionary architects.

Following his earlier conception of four basic elements, Semper devotes volume 1 of *Der Stil* entirely to the art of textiles, expounding his cladding theory in detail.[251]

This 'cladding' ('*Bekleidung*') raises the architectural type to the status of a symbol by the transformation of material, a process that Semper calls 'metabolism'. Although Semper is hostile to Boetticher, he picks up Boetticher's distinction between 'basic' schema ('*Kernschema*') and 'aesthetic' schema ('*Kunstschema*'), describing the latter, which he associates with cladding, the new style, as 'the emancipation of form from the grasp of the material and from brute necessity'.[252] It is the cladding, the symbolic expression of the variable factors that makes up the work of art, that makes style possible.

Semper is sceptical about the possibility of a 'new style' for the present day, 'because nowhere is there any sign of a new concept of world history being consciously and determinedly carried through'; it would, however, be possible to clothe such a conception in 'the appropriate architectural dress'.[253] In his own architecture Semper has recourse to a Neo-Renaissance style as the expression of his cosmopolitanism and liberal political views – an attitude of resignation in the face of the absence of any 'new concept of world history'. Until that time comes, he confesses, 'one must make do as best one can with the old ideas.'[254]

Volume 2 of *Der Stil* deals with ceramics, tectonics (carpentry) and stereotomy (masonry), together with the use of metals. The fact that Semper had earlier not recognised metal as a 'primary' material now leads him to the following conclusions:

> Iron tectonics as such has never become monumental, and the dangerous notion that a new style must needs emerge if one applies construction in iron to monumental architecture has already led many an architect astray – talented architects, but out of tune with real art. The use of iron can, and must, affect style when applied to monumental architecture, but not by its visible presence.[255]

He regards 'experiments in iron Gothic' as utter failures but has words of approval for 'the simple, exposed iron roof-truss designed by engineers for railway-stations and similar shed-like buildings, which bear witness to their provisional nature.'[256] He is very cautious in his opinion of the visible use of iron in 'serious architecture', as his earlier essay on winter gardens shows:[257] an architect ought not to 'have anything to do with this invisible material, so to speak, if it is a question of the effect of mass and not simply trivial detail.'[258] To some degree Semper has here become the victim of his own 'cladding' theory and its connection with the four basic elements; he similarly rejects Labrouste's visible iron roof for the Bibliothèque Nationale in Paris.

It is considerations such as these that make one realise that Semper cannot be seen as a prophet of a modern, material-based aesthetics, although individual statements taken out of context might give that impression. His modern significance lies rather in the vision – which Schinkel also had towards the end of his life – that construction consisting solely of materials in accordance with the laws of structural engineering was in need of being raised to symbolic status. His theory represents the most comprehensive attempt made in Germany in the nineteenth century to understand architecture as the expression of the extremely complex interplay of material and ideational forces. He could not resolve an inherent paradox – that peculiar to the 'seeker of new style' who is also a champion of historicism. Simply to call him an aesthetic materialist does not do justice to his theories, yet assessments of this kind, represented by works such as Alois Riegl's *Stilfragen* (1893) and *Die Spätrömische Kunstindustrie* (1901), have tended to dominate the image presented of him.[259] In fact, in a formal sense the factors at work in Semper's architecture are not so far removed from Riegl's will to form ('*Stilwollen*').

Semper rejected neo-Gothic not only on stylistic grounds but above all on account of the ideology for which it stood. From the early Goethe to Schinkel's Romantic phase the nationalist-Romantic arguments used in favour of Gothic were, while not totally unpolitical, in the main idealistic and emotional in tone. But around the middle of the century the term 'neo-Gothic' became a political slogan adopted by militant supporters of Catholic renewal; one of its exponents mentioned by Semper was Reichensperger. Architectural theory as a concrete investigation into form now became combined with a particular religio-political outlook, militantly proclaimed as holding a monopoly of the truth. Much of the debate was carried on in architectural, political and religious periodicals.[260]

August Reichensperger (1808–95) – lawyer, co-founder and editor of the *Kölner Domblatt*, member of the Frankfurt National Assembly in 1849, a leading figure in the Centre Party in the German Reichstag and a vigorous opponent of the 'Little German' policy that underlay Bismarck's establishment of the Second Reich in 1871[261] – was one of those who used architectural theory as a weapon in his political armoury. His initial enthusiasm for Gothic came from the Romantics; later he acquired more precise knowledge from his extensive travels and from frequent meetings with the leaders of the neo-Gothic movement in France and England – men such as Viollet-le-Duc, Montalembert, Charles Barry, Gilbert Scott and Pugin. Among his numerous writings only the most important can be referred to here.[262]

Reichensperger played a leading role in the movement to mystify the rites of the medieval masonic tradition – a subject that occupied the minds of scholars until quite recently – and was involved in the discovery and publication of the late Gothic lodge-books. His books are couched in a demagogic language which makes them both fascinating and wearisome; typical are phrases such as that the Catholic Church alone could bring about 'a true Restoration within a living organism', for the Church had 'taken the artistic urge of man under her wing' (*Fingerzeige auf dem Gebiete der kirchlichen Kunst*, 1854).[263] The picture of history that he draws is virtually the opposite of Vasari's. Only in the Middle Ages, he declares, and above all in the thirteenth century, was there a true unity of Church, religious feeling and art, 'thus in order to restore and to re-imbibe the laws and traditions of the great art of the Middle Ages, we must make the thirteenth century our point of departure.'[264] Trecento and Renaissance signify a decline, when art was wrenched from its 'organic context' and transferred from the 'life of the people' to the courts of the princes, 'its natural development' thwarted.[265] He rejects Classicism, Romanesque and the basilica, 'for religous art uttered its final, authoritative word in the pointed arch... In the realm of architecture it was the thirteenth century that was able to shout "Eureka!" to the world – and this it did.'[266] Reichensperger reads like Viollet-le-Duc in his arguments for the superiority of Gothic; he speaks of the

> logic and grammar of the Gothic style. Equal to any task, in whatever material, it is a style that has the further advantage of being relatively inexpensive, which will become even more evident once it has been universally adopted in practice...
> Correctness and harmony of proportions cost nothing; and of particular significance

is the fact that, by its very nature, the Gothic style, in relative terms, requires the least mass for enclosing and roofing any given space.[267]

'That objectionable material cast iron', Reichensper comments, is not suited to 'the noble, solemn, healthy style of the thirteenth century',[268] and he repeatedly emphasises its structure of basic geometric forms and ornamentation based on native flora. For him Gothic is both Christian and German, both functional and applicable to all architecture – it is, in fact, the 'Nature-given' ('*naturgemäß*') style of the future. Not for nothing does the frontispiece of Reichensperger's book depict the south porch of the Church of St Victor in Xanten (*Plate 161*), on which he comments: 'The friar and master craftsman are discussing how to preserve the old and how to harmonise the new with it – how to establish the inter-penetration of theology and art.'[269] He defines the spirit of Gothic as 'an organic formative law that will finally restore the proper balance between theory and practice. Speculation and eclecticism will never lead to truly living creations – the search will go on and on but nothing will ever be found.'[270]

This doctrinaire position is an attempt to make architectural theory into an ideological tool. The extent to which the question of style could be turned into a political issue is shown by the arguments that raged round the competition for the Reichstag building in Berlin, in which Reichensperger intervened on a number of occasions on behalf of the Gothic designs. Reichensperger's sophisticated rhetoric may be found distasteful, but it must be admitted that in the field of conservation he took up an intelligent stance by warning against a stylistic egalitarianism and urging the importance of ensuring

> that the traces of the gradual development of an old building, which are almost always evident – its annual rings, so to speak – are not obliterated, and that the various styles, together with those irregularities and accidents that can give even less significant buildings a particular individual charm, are preserved.[271]

Other architects shared Reichensperger's neo-Gothic views to a greater or lesser degree. One such was Friedrich Hoffstadt (1802–46), a lawyer, who in his *Gothisches A-B-C-Buch* (1840–63) provided a textbook for artists and craftsmen containing rules for the construction of neo-Gothic buildings and members on strict geometric principles.[272] Hoffstadt reveals an unusually wide knowledge of Gothic building plans, stonemasons' manuals and major works of stone carving.[273] As he sees it, the root of all form lies in the 'eternal, unchanging laws of geometry,'[274] and pointing to the example of crystals, he also traces the forms of Nature back to geometry: 'Since natural phenomena are subject to the formative laws of geometry, and since these geometrical laws also form the foundation of works in the Gothic style, the affinity is readily explained.'[275] By repeatedly drawing attention to 'the character of our native German plant life', he makes Gothic a national German style, thereby arriving at a succession of equations which is not without its dangers: Geometric = Natural = Christian = Gothic = German.

Hoffstadt's work is a practical manual for craftsmen, with ideological overtones. Opposing a neo-Gothic eclecticism based on the copying of detail, he offers his own designs as 'models of independent production and construction' (*Plate 162*). Of particular interest are his illustrations of 'plant ornaments' with explanatory text;[276] these extend to a geometrically-based alphabet. This attempt to derive ornamentation from geometric and plant forms, and to produce combinations of the two, recalls similar attempts by Ruskin and anticipates the last significant such attempt by Louis Sullivan in his *System of Architectural Ornament* (1924). Hoffstadt concludes his work with a survey of the history of architecture, paying particular attention to 'the restoration and extension of the ogival style.'[277] For him, as for Reichensperger, Gothic represented the summit and goal of architecture, and to consider any other style for the present day was heresy.

Less doctrinaire was the Protestant architect Georg Gottlob Ungewitter (1820–64),[278] who published a number of pattern-books, some of which went through several editions.[279] His pupil Carl Schäfer (1844–1908) was best known as a teacher but was also influential as a writer.[280]

The neo-Gothic movement in Germany owed a considerable debt to English models[281] but developed its own national and political character. An important aspect of this influence was the technological advance associated with the industrial revolution, against which, however, there was also a strong reaction. The Anglo-German relationship is too complex a subject to deal with here,[282] but it may be observed that attempts were being made in Germany to obtain information about architecture and art manufacturers in England long before Hermann Muthesius took up his post at the German embassy in London in 1896, as may be seen from works such as that by Hermann Schwabe on English art manufacturers (1866)[283] and that by Robert Dohme on the English house (1888).[284]

German periodicals at this time were full of articles with the stereotyped title 'In which Style shall we Build?' The answers ranged from eclecticism to one or other of the historical styles. The historicists were unable to provide a comprehensive theoretical justification of their position, while art and architectural history increased its influence on both theory and practice. In an essay *Die Wege und Ziele der gegenwärtigen Kunst* (1867) the art historian Anton Springer (1825–91), an exponent of historicism, wrote:

> First a factory is built, the chimneys begin to smoke, the wheels whirr, miserable workers' cottages are joined by the houses of shopkeepers and well-to-do traders, the inn is joined by a school and a hospital, then comes the town villa of the independent burgher, and finally the palace of the rich factory-owner. It is usually a long while before a monumental church is erected... Today a living architecture depends on secular buildings. It is in this realm that it must prove itself, seeking to banish formlessness and meaninglessness and to bring about an aesthetic transformation.[285]

This reads like a new hierarchy of building types, adapted to the needs of industrial society. But Springer himself indicates the historical impasse, continuing:

> When one looks around in order to decide which of the styles of the past should be adopted, the decision will be determined by whether the chosen model is appropriate for secular buildings or not. There are many indications to suggest that from this point of view the Renaissance style comes closest to our needs...[286]

But here again is Semper's position. Even after Schinkel's death, the stylistic debate, in Berlin, centre of intellectual activity that it was, still moved in a circle.[287] Architecture is dependent on the availability of historical knowledge. This was provided at the time by works such as the *Handbuch der Architektur* and *Grundrißvorbilder von Gebäuden aller Art.* At least an end had been put to a one-sided stylistic doctrine. But in general, German architectural theory and the positivist amassment of historical knowledge cannot disguise this.

The only place where a new line of theoretical thought may be detected, firmly based on historical foundations, is Vienna, where Camillo Sitte (1843–1903),[288] architect and Director of the Imperial College of Arts and Crafts, produced the first German work of any consequence on urban planning theory. *Der Städte-Bau nach seinen künstlerischen Grundsätzen* (1899)[289] is a pioneering work which has gained a new modernity since the functionalist theories of town-planning propounded in the first half of the twentieth century have become obsolete.

Sitte's approach, taking Nature and 'the school of the Ancients' as his points of reference, is thoroughly conventional. He directs his attacks against the over-emphasis of technology at the expense of the experience of history and aesthetic values and analyses a number of historical cities, paying particular attention to public squares and their functions from social and aesthetic points of view. What he witheringly describes as 'the already proverbial boredom that pervades our modern cities'[290] he ascribes to a blue-print mentality dominated by technological functions, which has turned the public piazza into an empty space left over after the network of street intersections and building blocks has been laid out, whereas in historical terms the piazza 'was the centre of the metropolis, a symbol of the *Weltanschauung* of a great nation'.[291] Sitte had no desire to undo modern achievements in the field of technology and hygiene, but he did wish to see streets and piazzas restored to 'public life', instead of being treated merely as traffic arteries and empty spaces. As they have historically evolved, piazzas have almost invariably produced asymmetries and rich displays of monuments and sculptures, and Sitte attached great importance to their formal unity, the integration of public buildings into the scene, not their isolation from it. This unity could be achieved by means of a 'piazza wall' ('*Platzwand*'). The form and dimensions of the piazza, together with the buildings around its perimeter, must all be to the same scale. In an appendix on the origins of the modern concept of symmetry, Sitte rejects the modern concept that would make symmetry 'a panacea for all our ills',[292] arguing instead for natural irregularities and winding streets but being equally well aware that twists and turns that are born on the drawing-board are nothing more than 'formal informalities' ('*erzwungene Ungezwungenheiten*') and no solution to the problem.[293] Linearity and rectangularity are emotionless, monotonous and hostile to one's feeling for Nature, but Sitte does admit the possibility of 'eliciting aesthetically satisfying squares and streets' even from rectangular systems. A city's main squares, he concludes on this subject, should be decked out in 'their Sunday best' and be 'the pride and joy of the citizens, arousing their affection and being a constant source of great and noble emotions in the hearts of generations to come.'[294]

Sitte took a favourable view of Haussmann's plans for the rebuilding of Paris, since he interpreted them as being in the Baroque tradition, of which he approved on the grounds of the theatricality of its visual appeal, although the 'organic' medieval city was closer to his heart. He also expressed himself in favour of the plans for the reconstruction of the Ringstrasse in Vienna, in particular Semper's scheme for the Hofburg and the museums, but also identified certain errors which needed to be rectified: 'The buildings are successful but not the way in which the building plots have been divided up. Fortunately, however, there is so much free space left that this can still be put right.'²⁹⁵

Sitte comments on the area around the Votivkirche in Vienna:

There is here no question of unity of artistic impression. The Votivkirche, the University, the Chemistry Laboratory and various blocks of houses stand there detached and unsupported, without any totality of impression. Instead of skilful positioning and juxtaposition that enhances their effectiveness, each building plays a different tune in a different key, so to speak. When one's eye roams over the Gothic Votivkirche, the noble Renaissance of the University and the various different styles of the apartment blocks, it is as though one were listening to a Bach fugue, the finale from a Mozart opera and a number from Offenbach, all at the same time. Unbearable! Simply unbearable!²⁹⁶

Sitte's own solution for the Votivkirche area was to build up most of the area around it, to integrate the church into the ensemble, and to create stylistic transitions, squares and plazas. The church was to be given a Gothic atrium, which would also serve practical functions; the exterior of the atrium, part of which would contain rented apartments, would be prominent to the view, in the style of the Italian High Renaissance, and it would provide a transition to the University opposite (*Plate 163*). Sitte proposed a similar pattern of buildings of modest scale, with enclosed plazas, for the area between Rathaus and Burgtheater and as far as the Parliament building. He summarised his aims thus:

1) to get rid of the conflict of styles; 2) considerably to enhance the effect of each individual monumental building; 3) to create a group of characteristic plazas; 4) to provide for the erection of a considerable number of statues – some large, some of medium size, some small – in one unified setting.²⁹⁷

Sitte's arguments were in complete conformity with the attitudes of his age, but at the same time he anticipated a number of the problems that were shortly to overtake modern cities, particularly as a result of their size. His solutions to these problems took the form of enclosed areas, designed to an appropriate scale, which would serve as public plazas – an answer to what he called 'our mathematically computed world, in which man himself has become a machine.'²⁹⁸ At times his book reads like a prophetic criticism of the theories of Le Corbusier, who inevitably dismissed Sitte as a man following the 'donkey path'. Sitte has also been criticised for paying one-sided attention to aesthetic questions and ignoring the complexity of the modern city.²⁹⁹ This, however, is not correct, for the aesthetic improvements he proposed do have, from the historical point of view, a functional justification, and are intended to show how we can escape from a conception of town-planning that sees the city merely as a technically efficient machine. This is what makes Sitte's views so thoroughly modern.

In a considerably more militant manner than Sitte, Otto Wagner (1841–1918)³⁰⁰ proposed a new style which would have no truck with historicism, and be felt in every sphere from town-planning to interior decoration. His *Moderne Architektur* (1895), later republished as *Die Baukunst unserer Zeit*,³⁰¹ reads like a declaration inaugurating the architecture of the twentieth century.

Wagner starts with Semper's ideas, which he develops in a narrowly positivistic direction. An unyielding protagonist of a modern architecture, he attacks, in an emotive polemical tone that lies somewhere between Semper and Le Corbusier, what he scornfully calls the 'archaeological' attitudes of the historicists, and propounds a view of architecture as 'the expression of modern life', which creates beautiful forms without finding models for them in Nature. Characteristic is his high-flown claim 'that one must see in architecture the supreme expression of human power – a power, indeed, well-nigh divine.'[302] Le Corbusier takes this conception of the architect as demiurge even further.

Wagner savagely attacks the practice of training architects as though they were engineers, for he is concerned to bring artistic form to the new technologies and not leave them to the tender mercies of the engineering profession. Students of architecture would be well advised, he goes on, to spend some time in Italy, not in order to 'compile a collection of architectural motifs' – this would be 'almost a crime' – but to visit the large cities and 'develop a thorough understanding of the needs of modern man.'[303]

Historicism, to Wagner, represents the height of 'lunacy' ('*Wahnsinnsgebäude*'), for style, in the true sense, is the product of new materials, new technology and social change – 'the absolute and apodictic expression of the ideal of beauty proper to a particular epoch.'[304] Hence: 'The art of our time must offer modern forms that we ourselves have created and that correspond to *our* abilities, to what *we* choose to do or not do.'[305] By adopting Semper's theory of necessity – '*Artis sola domina necessitas*' – Wagner arrives at the conclusion: 'Anything unpractical cannot be beautiful.'[306] Materials and technology are paramount, and everything, including the composition, must serve them: 'The composition must clearly reveal what materials and what techniques have been employed;'[307] if this is done, the 'characteristic and symbolic qualities of the building' will emerge 'of their own accord.'[308] As Wagner sees it, if modern architecture is to express the ethos of the age, it must be simple, practical, even 'military', with an imperative need for symmetry.

Wagner is critical of the 'exotic manner' in which Semper 'evolved a symbolism of construction instead of defining construction itself as the primordial cell of architecture.'[309] He therefore concludes:

Apart from the fact that their form had to correspond to the ideal of beauty sustained by the age in question, these changes came about because the manner of production, the materials, the tools, the available means, needs, aesthetic susceptibilities and the rest, were themselves all different, and acquired different functions in different localities. We may therefore conclude with certainty that new aims and new constructions must needs give birth to new forms.[310]

Although construction is the key factor in the 'artistic form', the two are not identical, for the language of the engineer, based on utilitarian principles, is 'an unsympathetic language for mankind'. The principal new materials are iron and concrete. Wagner makes his peace with social and economic conditions in a different way from Semper, accepting without protest the modern city, the apartment block and economic speculation:

One result of our democratic existence, into which the masses are made to fit, with their cry for cheap and healthy homes, and the enforced frugality of their lives, is the uniformity of our apartment blocks, which will inevitably become prominent in the urban scene of the future … as also will an increase in the number of storeys, rising to seven or eight for housing and office blocks, with skyscrapers in city centres. In every city the number of residential blocks will far exceed that of public buildings, and their juxtaposition in rows will produce a series of uniform, elongated strips alongside the streets. By widening our streets, modern town-planning has turned this uniformity into monumentality... When designing the façade of a modern apartment block, an architect is compelled to accept a flat surface interrupted by a large number of identical windows, with perhaps a protective surrounding cornice and at the most a crowning frieze and a porch...[311]

Wagner does not mention Sitte by name but he implicitly criticises his ideas on a number of occasions, as in the following passage:

The modern eye has lost a feeling for small and intimate scale, and accustomed itself to less varied images, to longer straight lines, to more extensive areas, to larger masses, which suggests that we should exercise greater restraint giving less emphasis to the outlines of such apartment blocks.[312]

Like Le Corbusier after him, Wagner was a proponent of straight lines formed by streets, traffic-ways, elevated and underground railway-lines. He also toyed with the idea of state control of the arts. He gives no aesthetic guidelines, and his answer to the question 'How shall we build?' shows how radically he has restricted the scope for artistic expression:

Our feelings must surely tell us that lines of support, the direct expression of plane surfaces, utmost simplicity of conception and a marked emphasis on construction and materials will dominate the architecture of the future. Modern techniques and the means now at our disposal ensure that this will be so. It goes without saying that the aesthetic quality of this architecture must conform to the condition of modern man and his outlook, and also reveal the individuality of the architect.[313]

One of the few direct aesthetic recommendations that Wagner makes is for the use of porcelain, majolica and mosaic as facing materials, such as he himself had adopted in a number of façades in Vienna. And while expressing himself in favour of national and regional styles, he saw that modern developments would inevitably lead to cosmopolitanism in architecture.

As his *General-Regulierungsplan* for Vienna (1893) and *Die Großstadt* (1911) show, Wagner envisaged the unrestricted growth of cities, dominated by traffic and commercial interests, divided into boroughs and with a gridiron pattern cutting up the area into blocks.[314] In urban planning too he is a significant precursor of Le Corbusier and his *'théorie totale'*, his own projects from 1890 onwards also show this.[315] His immense influence on twentieth-century architecture rests both on his own buildings, which show a development from historicism to a functional Art Nouveau, and on his writings and teaching at the Vienna Academy.[316]

23. England in the nineteenth century

The turn of the eighteenth century did not signify a break in architecture in England, especially as the consequences of the French Revolution and the Napoleonic Wars were felt less strongly there than on the Continent. Although Sir William Chambers and the Adam brothers died in the 1790s, men like Sir John Soane and Payne Knight provided a palpable continuity, as did the final volume of *Vitruvius Britannicus*, which did not appear until 1808. England had made a considerable contribution to the discovery of the architecture of Antiquity, especially Greece, in the eighteenth century, but this had not led to the dominance of Classicism. James Stuart's over-literal replicas of Greek monuments had got no further than the Picturesque, and the same was true of Walpole and the Gothic Revival. It is significant for the situation in England that until the 1820s the principal representatives of the so-called 'Greek Revival' and 'Gothic Revival' were virtually the same,[1] though shortly after the turn of the century the two movements, which had their origins in the eighteenth century, began to go their different ways.

An important figure in the Greek Revival movement was Thomas Hope (1769–1831), a rich amateur architect and son of an English merchant in Amsterdam, whose publications are among the most valuable sources of information about architectural thought of the time.[2] Between 1787 and 1795 he embarked on a remarkably extensive grand tour of Europe that took him to Spain, Italy, France, Germany, Egypt, Syria, Turkey and Greece, in the course of which he acquired a considerable knowledge of architecture. His career as a writer began in 1804 with a privately printed pamphlet criticising the Roman-Doric design of James Wyatt, President of the Royal Academy, for Downing College, Cambridge, demanding instead a pure Greek design.[3] His plea was successful, and an Ionic design by William Wilkins was accepted in place of Wyatt's. His arguments in favour of the purity of Greek architecture were drawn in part, curiously enough, from the contemporary debate on the Picturesque and from the philosophy of sensualism inherited from the previous century, e.g. his claim that Greek Doric, which has no base, stimulates stronger 'vibrations' than Roman Doric.

In the same year, 1804, Hope completed the reconstruction and furnishing of his house in Duchess Street, off Portland Place, originally built by Robert Adam. The house (demolished in 1851) was also intended as a museum for Hope's collections and a model for the decorative arts and for English taste. In 1807 Hope published his designs for the interior of the house (the preparatory drawings for the engravings were his), with a programmatic introduction.[4] His eclecticism took the form of having each room in its own separate style. He intended an aestheticism almost in a secularised religious sense. The ceiling of the Picture Gallery, for example, is supported on four Doric columns like those of the Propylaeum in Athens (*Plate 164*); the organ, its Ionic membering borrowed from the Erechtheum, is intended to create 'the appearance of a sanctuary'.[5] The illustrations, simple outline drawings, follow the example of the Percier-Fontaine *Recueil de décorations intérieures* (from 1801), which Hope greatly admired. His work thus has a similar significance for the Regency period in England to that of Percier and Fontaine for the Empire style in France.

Hope's introduction contains a number of unusually far-sighted observations, such as that in an age of mechanisation 'the powers of mere machinery never can emulate, or supplant the mental faculties of man.'[6] He sees the artistic and economic advantages of a flourishing handicrafts industry, which would give 'new food to the industry of the poor, but new decorum to the expenditure of the rich.'[7] Proceeding from an aristocratic aesthetic viewpoint, Hope reaches similar conclusions about the applied arts to William Morris after him on socialist aesthetic grounds. Hope's 'totally new style of decoration', as he called it, is derived from a combination of intellectual beauty, utility and convenience with an employment of Classical form and ornament adapted to modern needs and habits.[8] His essential Classicism emerges even more clearly from his assertion that it is in the monuments of Antiquity that 'the forms of nature may be most happily adapted to the various exigencies of art.'[9] His attempts, however, to explain the eclecticism of his house – which is ultimately the result of his extensive travels – by reference to Antiquity are sometimes rather forced, as when he traces the Turkish border on his titlepage, consisting of stalactite forms, to Hellenistic architectural ornament. He also commissioned a portrait of himself in Turkish costume from Sir William Beechey, hanging it in the spirit of a manifesto in the entrance hall of his house (the portrait is now in the National Portrait Gallery).

Hope conceived his house primarily as a museum, its design being determined by the exhibits, as shown, for example, by the room, with its iconographic programme, designed specifically around John Flaxman's statue *Aurora and Cephalus*.[10] The furniture, in spite of Hope's intentions, was uncomfortable, as Prince Pückler-Muskau noted after visiting the house.[11] The overall impression was predominantly 'Picturesque', an impression made more strongly by Hope's country house at Deepdene, Dorking, Surrey (from 1807). Not uncharacteristic of the man and his wavering aesthetic position is the fact that an exotic novel, *Anastasius or the Memoirs of a Modern Greek*, which he published anonymously in 1819, was thought in some quarters to be the work of Byron.

Around 1815 Hope was at work on an extensive history of architecture, which was published only after his death.[12] His point of view is that of the later Enlightenment, and he treats the main types of architecture in terms of climate, materials, tools and social conditions. There is a link between this proto-materialist approach and the work of Semper, who made selections from Hope's work.[13] Far from confining himself to Antiquity, Hope paid detailed attention to the Middle Ages, to which the majority of his illustrations are devoted. Romanesque, which he took to have originated in Lombardy, had been spread and internationalised, in his view, by the Freemasons, acting as agents of the Papacy[14] – an eccentric hypothesis which he even tried to apply to Gothic. He justified his predilection for Greek architecture on the grounds of its organic evolution from given climatic conditions, whilst rejecting Renaissance as sham art, and Baroque as an aberration of taste. There is a contradiction in his thought when on the one hand he opposes the imitation of non-European styles – also of Gothic – and then finds his answer to the question of an individual new style not, as hitherto, in the Greek Revival, but in a rationally-based eclecticism:

> No one seems yet to have conceived the smallest wish or idea of only borrowing of every former style of architecture, whatever it might present of useful or ornamental, of scientific or tasteful; of adding thereto whatever other new dispositions or forms might afford conveniences or elegancies not yet possessed;

of making the new discoveries, the new conquests, of natural productions unknown to former ages, the models of new imitations more beautiful and more varied: and thus of composing an architecture which, born in our country, grown in our soil, and in harmony with our climate, institutions, and habits, at once elegant, appropriate, and original, should truly deserve the appellation of 'Our Own'.[15]

Here is a very early statement of a position that has been compared to that expressed in Germany by Heinrich Hübsch in 1828,[16] although in essence it comes closer to the ideas behind the Maximilian competition in Munich in 1850. Hope's development from Classicist to eclecticist is not merely the result of his dilettante status but is significant for the whole nineteenth-century discussion of style in England.

Mention must now be made of a utopist conception that, together with the ideas of Charles Fourier in France, which were formally ambiguous in their consequences, represented the most influential social vision of the nineteenth century. Unlike Fourier, Robert Owen (1771–1858),[17] a man with practical experience of industry, sought to put his ideas into practice. The mill town of New Lanark, in Scotland, which he began to develop in 1800, aroused much interest in Europe.[18] Owen's first exposition of his social ideas came in *A New View of Society* (1813);[19] four years later, in *Report to the Committee of the Association for the Relief of the Manufacturing and Labouring Poor*, he propounded his ideas on urban planning,[20] based on a conception of 'villages of unity', of which he provided a drawing and even a model. These 'villages' were arranged in a rectangular grid, and their design ultimately went back to Thomas More. Particularly important to Owen was the idea of a central community house, which he had already tried to set up in New Lanark.

In 1825 Owen bought the American Protestant settlement of Harmony, Indiana, and with the help of the architect Thomas Stedman Whitwell (c. 1770–1840), a pupil of Soane's, turned it into a model community named 'New Harmony'. Whitwell left a *Description of an Architectural Model* for the settlement (*Plate 165*),[21] and his model (built in 1826) was exhibited several times in the White House. The plan shows an elaborated variant of a 'village of unity'. The stylistic language of the plan is a kind of Gothic: there is a domed 'conservatory' in the centre, with four prominent inwardly projecting cross-ranges on each of the four sides, in which the communal kitchens and dining halls are accommodated. Particularly remarkable are the four fluted towers with spiral bands, which are for lighting and ventilation purposes, but also have a long iconological tradition.[22] Whitwell's comments show how prepared he was to accept the advances of modern technology, especially in lighting and ventilation. Owen eventually abandoned the New Harmony project, but the concept was to have considerable influence on subsequent community projects in the United States of America.[23] His ideas were both more far-reaching than Fourier's backward-looking recourse to Baroque conceptions and more open-minded than William Morris's invocation of the Middle Ages at the end of the nineteenth century.

Forming a background to theoretical discussion in England at this time are a number of architectural manuals and dictionaries, eighteenth-century in type, but highly progressive in their attention to questions of technology. Peter Nicholson (1765–1844) and Joseph Gwilt (1784–1863) are prominent among the authors of such works,[24] the latter's new edition of Chambers's *Civil Architecture* appearing in 1825. Nicholson's numerous works – e.g. his *Architectural Dictionary* (1812–19) and *The Builder and*

Workman's New Director (1824)[25] – have a practical slant and are addressed to architects and to artisans of all trades. The latter is a textbook with sections on geometry, trigonometry, masonry, carpentry, perspective, etc., with the aim of being 'useful in its application to practice'.[26] In an appendix Nicholson describes the Classical orders simply as 'five pillars of specific character supporting a roof',[27] thus showing – as do his plates – that the meaning of the Orders had been lost, and the Orders themselves reduced to the level of associative ornamental features.

The prolific Joseph Gwilt, author of *Rudiments of Architecture* (1826) and *Encyclopedia of Architecture* (1842), among other works, occupies a strange position.[28] In theoretical and historical respects he took his lead from Chambers and Quatremère de Quincy; at the same time he followed the constructive-functionalist line of Durand and Rondelet in his theory of 'fitness' but disapproved of the use of cast iron in architecture. In this, as in his attitude to the question of architectural polychromy, he shows an affinity with Semper. Opposed equally to the Greek Revival and to German Classicism, he proposed a neo-Renaissance solution to the rebuilding of the Houses of Parliament in London.

Hope's *Historical Essay* was representative of the trend of thought that looked to history for answers to the question of style, answers that often resulted in eclecticism, even if the individual historical styles were variously interpreted. Such was the case with Thomas Leverton Donaldson's (1795–1885) *Preliminary Discourse on Architecture* (1842)[29] and Alfred Bartholomew's (1801–45) *Specifications for Practical Architects* (1840).[30] Bartholomew advocated Gothic as a 'rational' style, illustrating its structural principles by somewhat absurd comparisons with the strength of the human body, superimposing sketches of skeletons on flying buttresses and the like. Demanding a return to building conditions as they had been in the Middle Ages, he put forward a scheme for training architects as recommended by freemasonry, starting with 'mason' (*m*) and culminating in 'mathematical master mason' (*mmm*).[31] These ideas were to stimulate Pugin. Strangely enough, however, they led Bartholomew himself not to neo-Gothic but to eclecticism.

A similar path was trodden by Charles Robert Cockerell (1788–1863),[32] archaeologist and successful architect, who in his lectures at the Royal Academy also arrived at an intellectually founded eclecticism, shifting his allegiance between past styles and modernism.[33] The publication of excerpts from Cockerell's lectures in newly-founded architectural journals shows the growing importance of such organs in the mid-nineteenth century,[34] in England as in France. Some of these publications, like John Claudius Loudon's *Architectural Magazine*, were short-lived (1834–39); others, founded in quick succession – *Civil Engineer and Architect's Journal* (founded 1837), *Surveyor, Engineer and Architect* (founded 1840) and in particular the weekly *Builder* (founded 1842) – were in the forefront of contemporary debate on architectural matters.

For several generations the question of the national English roots of Gothic had been raised, but over and above historical interest there had been a growing trend towards considering Gothic as the style for the present (the same trend was observable in France and Germany, though under different circumstances). In his *Attempt to Discriminate the Styles of English Architecture*[35] Thomas Rickman (1776–1841)[36] put forward the now standard terms 'Early English', 'Decorated' and 'Perpendicular' to denote the phases of English Gothic, while at the same time seeking to promote restoration work and provide models for new buildings. Although he also passed favourable judgement on other styles, Rickman's own churches were almost all Gothic, and from his prominent part in designing 'Commissioners' Churches'[37] (built in industrial towns as cheaply as possible following a parliamentary act of 1818), as well as from the evidence of most of the other churches built at this time, it is clear that church architecture, at least, was keenly interested in Gothic in its national English forms.

William Whewell (1794–1866), a friend of Rickman, in *Architectural Notes on German Churches* (1830)[38], put forward stylistic criteria for dating purposes, using a methodology superior to that of Georg Moller in his *Denkmäler der deutschen Baukunst*. The scientist Robert Willis (1800–75) treated Italian Gothic from a similar angle in his *Remarks on the Architecture of the Middle Ages, especially of Italy* (1835),[39] in which he devised a classification of individual architectural members and arrived at a distinction between 'mechanical' and 'decorative' structure. On the assumption that the meaning of Gothic decoration lay in the representation of structure, he concluded that 'this apparent frame is often totally different from the real one.'[40] This distinction between actual and represented structure was an important step forward from the view of Gothic as purely functional.[41] Other works by Willis included an analysis, exemplary in its precision, of medieval vaulting (1842),[42] a dictionary of medieval architectural terms drawn from primary sources (1844),[43] and an English translation (1859) of Villard de Honnecourt's lodge-book.

One of the best-known historical accounts of Gothic architecture was the *Principles of Gothic Architecture* of Matthew Holbeche Bloxham (1805–88), which took Rickman as its starting-point. Between 1829 and 1882 this work ran through no fewer than eleven progressively enlarged editions.[44] It proceeded as a chronology of styles, discussing individual architectural features in an informative manner, but had few illustrations. Of a similar type, but far more lavish, and consisting predominantly of measured drawings, was Raphael and Joshua Arthur Brandon's *An Analysis of Gothick Architecture* (1847),[45] a collection of examples taken from English parish churches, arranged according to function, style and material. There were numerous other publications of a similar kind; the first survey of these works, and still the best, is that given by Charles L. Eastlake (1836–1906) in his *A History of the Gothic Revival* (1872).[46]

The destruction by fire of the Houses of Parliament in 1834 raised again the question of an English national style. The parliamentary committee charged with the rebuilding specified 'Gothic' or 'Elizabethan' when it launched the competition for the new design, but even after Charles Barry's Gothic project had been accepted, the 'battle of the styles' continued to rage.[47]

Augustus Welby Northmore Pugin (1812–52)[48] introduced a new polemical and ideological tone into the Gothic debate. Pugin's first published piece concerned the design for the Houses of Parliament.[49] His father, Augustus Charles Pugin (1762–1832), had already published measured drawings and model-books of Gothic architecture, the best-known being his *Specimens of Gothic Architecture* (1821–28).[50] In 1835 Pugin the Younger became an ardent Roman Catholic, allegedly under the stimulus of his architectural studies, and his religious fanaticism both impelled him to write and determined how and what he wrote. His *Contrasts* (1836),[51] which drew its philosophical content from a variety of sources,[52] represented a point in architectural theory at which non-architectural and non-aesthetic considerations gained the upper hand.

It was axiomatic with Pugin that medieval architecture was superior to post-medieval. This he combined with the functionalist theory, taken from the French, that 'the great test of Architectural beauty is the fitness of the design to the purpose for which it is intended, and that the style of a building should so correspond with its use that the spectator may at once perceive the purpose for which it was erected.'[53]

It was in terms, however, not of use and construction that Pugin demonstrated the functionalist quality of medieval architecture, but in those of the religious purpose that it expressed. He found the immediate expression of Christian revelation in architecture, interpreting vertical lines as 'the emblem of the resurrection'[54] and seeing in the rise and fall of medieval architecture the reflection of the growth and decline of 'true Catholic principles'.[55] He posited a direct link between Reformation, Protestantism, paganisation of thought and architectural decline, and since for him great art could only be rooted in Catholicism, it followed that there must be a return to pure Catholicism before good architecture could reappear. For the 'Commissioners' Churches' he had nothing but scorn.[56]

The illustrations for Contrasts reveal Pugin's demagogic cast of mind. The border on the title page uses late Gothic forms, while the first frontispiece depicts a confection consisting, as he describes it, of 'selections from the works of various celebrated British architects' (Plate 166). In a second frontispiece he shows an advertisement for an 'open competition' for the new church architecture and mocks the 'cheap principles and eclecticism' of the current debate. By juxtaposing illustrations, he contrasts not only architectural forms but the whole concept of an integrated medieval world with the disintegration of modern society: the once glorious Gothic town has become a place of decaying churches, prisons, smoking factory chimneys and tenements. His counterpart to the medieval almshouse is the workhouse, from which the corpses are taken to the anatomical institute.

Pugin's direction becomes clearer in True Principles of Pointed or Christian Architecture (1841),[57] in which the functionalist ideas inadequately explained in Contrasts now come to the fore. His thought rests on two 'great rules': '1st, that there should be no features about a building which are not necessary for convenience, construction, or propriety; 2nd, that all ornament should consist of enrichment of the essential construction of the building.'[58]

This sounds like a summa of French eighteenth-century positions. And when immediately afterwards Pugin raises the subject of materials as a determining factor in construction, the origin of his ideas becomes obvious, although he does not name his sources. These are for him the sole true, immutable principles of architecture, with only climatic and national variations permitted. His central conclusion, to the proof of which his book is devoted, states that 'it is in pointed architecture alone that these great principles have been carried out.'[59] He thus arrives at the equations: True Architectural Principles = Gothic = Christian. In an obvious allusion to Winckelmann's famous dictum – 'The only way for us to become great, indeed, if it be possible, for us to become inimitable, is to imitate the Ancients' – he argues that we should 'strive to revive the glorious works of Christian art in all the ancient and consistent principles',[60] thereby quietly substituting medieval Christianity for Antiquity.

Pugin rejects Greek architecture not only as an expression of pagan superstition but also as an unacceptable transference of wooden architecture to stone architecture which ignores the differences of material. This question of material as the determining factor in construction is central to Pugin's argument. Nor – and here he has in mind the 'enormities' of Strawberry Hill and of an eclectic neo-Gothicism – need this make a building unduly expensive: 'Were the real principles of Gothic architecture restored, the present objection of its extreme costliness would cease to exist.'[61]

Pugin's attitude towards decoration is of particular importance. Decoration he considers with reference to 'propriety', by which he means 'that the external and internal appearance of an edifice should be illustrative of, and in accordance with, the purpose for which it is destined.'[62] Gothic ornament is explained partly in terms of construction, partly in terms of building type. Of proportion he states: 'The human figure is a general standard for scale',[63] but the influence of so-called Revolutionary architecture can be felt in the qualification: 'Without vastness of dimensions it is impossible to produce a grand and imposing effect in architecture.'[64] His emphasis on human scale leads him to contrast the fine detail of Gothic architecture with the massive dimensions of Classical architecture: 'In pointed architecture the different details of the edifice are multiplied with the increased scale of the building: in classic architecture they are only magnified.'[65] This is a complete reversal of the Classicist position represented by Goethe in his essay of 1788: 'Unhappily, all Northern European church decorators sought to make themselves great merely by multiplying details.'[66]

Pugin's *True Principles* also concerns itself with secular architecture and interior decoration. Calling Gothic not a style but a principle, he comes close to Viollet-le-Duc and his designation of Gothic as '*le style*' among '*les styles*' of other ages. For Pugin Gothic now becomes a 'universal style', a concept he expounds in *An Apology for the Revival of Christian Architecture in England* (1843).[67] Strangely enough, he concedes in this work the use of modern machinery and iron construction, while privately branding the Crystal Palace built for the Great Exhibition of 1851 as a 'glass monster' and 'crystal humbug',[68] despite the fact that his own design for the medieval court had been executed at the Exhibition. In the end, however, Pugin, with his religious fanaticism, could not accommodate technological progress within his system as naturally and rationally as did Viollet-le-Duc.

Towards the end of his life Pugin, virtually insane, became intolerant in the extreme. In a treatise on the chancel screen written in 1851 he pronounced anyone who opposed the reintroduction of such screens as an enemy of Roman Catholic tradition.[69] Like Viollet-le-Duc, he sought to give Gothic an absolute status, and his application of functionalist criteria had considerable influence – which his intellectual successors, such as Ruskin and William Morris, put off by his religious fanaticism, could not acknowledge. He has his German counterpart in August Reichensperger, whose study of Pugin was published in 1877.

Pugin's religiously motivated intolerance was by no means unique at this time. In 1839 societies for the study of Gothic architecture were founded in Oxford and Cambridge which pursued aims both scholarly and religious in character. The Oxford Society for Promoting the Study of Gothic Architecture, for example, later rechristened the Oxford Architectural and Historical Society, was primarily scholarly in intention, as was its periodical, the *Transactions of the Oxford Architecture Society*.[70] The Cambridge Camden Society, on the other hand, was an association of religious evangelists which owed its influence to its militant moral appeal.[71] In its early years the Society's Anglican connections were put under strain by a marked trend towards Catholicism, seen, for instance, in an admiration for Pugin. The 'laws' of the Society[72] advocated the reintroduction of parts of the Roman Catholic liturgy into Anglican ritual, adequate conservation and restoration of existing church buildings, and the establishment of Gothic as the style for all new churches. In 1845 the Society changed its name to the Ecclesiological Society, as which it existed until 1868. The term 'ecclesiological' was coined to connote the science of church architecture and church decoration;[73] the members called themselves 'ecclesiologists', and their journal, which appeared five times a year from 1841 to 1868, was called *The Ecclesiologist*.

The co-founders of the Camden Society were John Mason Neale (1818–66) and Benjamin Webb (1819–55). Neale's works have a nationalistic streak by no means typical of all the members: the two most important are *A Few Hints on the Practical Study of Ecclesiastical Antiquities* (1839) and *A Few Words to Church Builders* (1841).[74] Neale took his lead from Pugin but is even more dogmatic, allowing only the Decorated style for new church buildings. A characteristic example of the Society's principles, which looked back to the architectural symbolism of the thirteenth century, is Neale's and Webb's *The Symbolism of Churches and Church Ornaments* (1843), a translation of the first book of William Durandus's *Rationale Divinorum Officiorum*.[75] Neale and Webb wanted a church-building programme to be laid down by the Anglican authorities, in which only Christian architects should be allowed to participate, while these architects, in their turn, should only work for the Anglican Church. Gothic architecture thus came to represent a religious moralism which offended some but in general proved highly successful, with a particular attraction for the Anglican clergy. After the first ten years of its existence the Society became more open-minded and adopted an eclectic line that even admitted non-European styles.

George Edmund Street (1825–81) argued for horizontally banded polychromy in brick buildings, with materials and construction the primary considerations. The key church for this phase of the Ecclesiologists' activities is William Butterfield's All Saints, Margaret Street, London (1848–49),[76] which exhibited a 'constructional polychromy'; the ugliness of the building was regarded as an aesthetic virtue and compared with the later paintings of Millais – 'a deliberate preference of ugliness' was the phrase used.[77]

That the subject of polychromy should suddenly come to the fore is undoubtedly a reflection of developments in France and Germany. Prominent among the intermediaries was Owen Jones, who published a collection of plans and details of the Alhambra (1842–46) and *The Polychromatic Ornament of Italy* (1846).[78] His *Grammar of Ornament* (1856) combines a stylistic eclecticism with the principle of polychrome decoration;[79] in 1858 he provided his own polychrome designs for the decoration of Osler's Gallery in Oxford Street and the Crystal Palace Bazaar. Although he was not a supporter of the Gothic Revival, he exerted a considerable influence on the Ecclesiologists and on the Arts and Crafts movement. His ideas coincide at a number of points with those of Semper.

Such was the missionary zeal of the Ecclesiological Society that its architectural plans were distributed throughout the British Empire – one for Colombo Cathedral consisted of a Gothic design embellished with Buddhist features[80] – as well as America, where an Ecclesiological Society was founded in New York. Nor did the Society's activities cease with churches. Under the banner of a moral rearmament crusade it preached the values of an architecture that should be functional in a Catholic-Gothic sense. Major figures such as William Butterfield and Sir Gilbert Scott can only be understood against this background. When Scott won the competition for the Lutheran Nikolaikirche in Hamburg in 1844, *The Ecclesiologist* criticised the award on the grounds that the winner had worked for 'heretics'.[81] Yet despite its bigotry, the Society was not blind to the possibilities of technological innovation, as can be seen from its reactions to the Crystal Palace or, more strikingly, a design by R. C. Carpenter (published in 1856) for an iron church.[82]

By far the most important protagonist of the Gothic cause in England was John Ruskin (1819–1900), for whom art and architecture formed only a part of a much larger sociological complex.[83] While still a student, he published a series of articles (1837–38) in Loudon's *Architectural Magazine* entitled 'The Poetry of Architecture', which he signed with the pseudonym 'Kata Phusin', i.e. 'According to Nature.'[84] In these, basing his argument on the farmhouse and the villa, he developed the idea of a national architecture derived from living habits, landscape and climate. His ideas about art were considerably influenced by those of Pugin, whom, however, he scorned as a man, and by those of his friend Carlyle, through whom Ruskin found a link with German idealism.[85]

The Seven Lamps of Architecture (1849)[86] already reveals the urgent moral tone that characterises all Ruskin's mature writings on architecture. For him the laws of architecture are identical with those of man's moral life. What in Pugin was religious here becomes ethical.[87] With unmistakable allusions to the Book of Revelation, he evolves a series of principles drawn from the ethic/religious sphere and attempts to reconcile them with his architectural observations and demands. He uses bold type for passages intended as aphoristic statements of the rules of architecture; the illustrations consist of drawings by Ruskin himself. As he states in his introduction, his aim is to produce 'a statement of principles', not an essay on European architecture. His choice of buildings is thus personal ('buildings which I love best'), the fruits of his journeys to Italy and France.

Ruskin does not believe in normative laws derived from the architecture of the past: he accepts only those that have their origin in human nature or are legitimised by materials: 'There is no law, no principle, based on past practice, which may not be overthrown in a moment, by the arising of a new condition, or the invention of a new material.'[88] Here he must have iron in mind, a material he does not like but which he realises has an immense future: 'Abstractedly there appears no reason why iron should not be used as well as wood; and the time is probably near when a new system of architectural laws will be developed, adapted entirely to metallic construction.'[89]

Ruskin's attitude to iron architecture is aesthetically neutral. Reducing railways and railway stations to their practical function, and making little effort to conceal his personal dislike, he arrives at a logical, if impassioned rejection of all ornament where railways are concerned: 'Better bury gold in the embankments, than put it in ornaments on the stations.'[90] At the same time he concedes that railway architecture could, if left entirely to its function, acquire 'a dignity of its own.'

Each of the seven 'lamps' – Sacrifice, Truth, Power, Beauty, Life, Memory and Obedience – has its own chapter; of these only Beauty is a specifically aesthetic concept. Ruskin distinguishes between 'architecture' and 'building', the latter serving a purely functional purpose. Examples he gives of 'building' are a wasps' nest, a mouse-hole and a railway station. 'Architecture' must contain 'certain characters venerable or beautiful, but otherwise unnecessary'[91] – in other words ornament, designed either for the glory of God or in commemoration of man.

The most important chapter is that headed 'Truth'. Here Ruskin warns against three 'architectural deceits':

1st. The suggestion of a mode of structure or support, other than the true one...

2nd. The painting of surfaces to represent some other material than that of which they actually consist (as in the marbling of wood), or the deceptive representation of sculptured ornament upon them.

3rd. The use of cast or machine-made ornaments of any kind.

Ruskin expressly says that the architect is not obliged to expose the structural system, but claims nevertheless, that 'that building will generally be the noblest, which to an intelligent eye discovers the great secrets of its structure, as an animal form does.'[92] Ruskin thus demands the readability of a constructive system, truth to material, and the use of organic and hand-made ornament. 'Forms which are *not* taken from natural objects *must* be ugly,' he maintains.[93] This leads him to be critical of certain ornaments of Greek architecture and the Cinquecento. His own system of ornamentation is arranged according to degrees of abstraction, from basic organic forms to pure geometrical patterns.[94] All ornament, Ruskin maintains, is the expression of its creator's state of mind. We must ask: 'Was it done with enjoyment – was the carver happy while he was about it?'[95] This hints at an intimate relationship between architecture, ornament and the state of society, such as the Enlightenment had envisaged. Moreover, for Ruskin architecture is of necessity national, historical and preservative – hence Ruskin's stand against the restoration of historic buildings, for restoration meant for him destruction. Architecture is only possible under the conditions of the age in which it arose, he maintains: 'the life of the whole, that spirit which is given only by the hand and eye of the workman, never can be recalled. Another spirit may be given by another time, and it is then a new building.'[96]

Ruskin arrives at conclusions diametrically opposed to those of Viollet-le-Duc, who was fully aware of the historical fictions that his restoration work produced. 'We have no right whatever to touch them [i.e. the buildings of the past],' writes Ruskin. 'They are not ours. They belong partly to those who built them, and partly to all the generations of mankind who are to follow us.'[97] His slogan is straightforward: 'Take proper care of your monuments, and you will not need to restore them.'[98]

While much of *The Seven Lamps of Architecture* reads like a moral tract, *The Stones of Venice* (1851–53) reveals Ruskin's commitment to Gothic and his consequent conclusions.[99] The first volume expands on his theory of ornament, which he now defines as 'the expression of man's delight in God's work',[100] with the function of making man happy. The model of every ornament is God's creation. Starting with 'abstract lines, which are most frequent in Nature',[101] he gives a remarkable series of illustrations of abstract lines as models for architecture which almost look like Art Nouveau. Among the models he cites are the elements and the world of flora and fauna, the function of such ornaments being to convey 'the labour of Nature, but not her disturbance'.[102]

In the second volume of *The Stones of Venice*, specifically in the chapter entitled

'The Nature of Gothic', we reach the kernel of Ruskin's ideas about architecture. Postulating the principle of a universal Gothic – what he calls 'Gothicness' – he produces a construct of 'the soul of Gothic' composed of historical, sociological and ethical elements, set out in six remarkable categories: 1) Savageness, 2) Changefulness, 3) Naturalism, 4) Grotesqueness, 5) Rigidity and 6) Redundance. His occasional irrationality and his arbitrary treatment of history are seen, for example, in the section on 'Savageness', where he extends his ideas adumbrated in *The Seven Lamps*, of a relationship between ornament and social structure, involving even the social status of the individual artisan. Here he distinguishes three historically based types of ornament: 1) 'Servile ornament' carried out by slaves degraded to the status of machines; Classical architecture, including that of the Greeks, belongs here. 2) 'Constitutional ornament', by which he means the individualised Christian architecture of the Middle Ages. 3) 'Revolutionary ornament', which has brought about the emancipation of ornament from the building as a whole.

Ruskin has an ideal vision of the northern Gothic artist who, in his quest for truth, fulfils the demands of these categories. The Gothic style conveys his insistence on variety and economy, as well as being aesthetically the best and in rational terms the only style suited to all purposes: 'For in one point of view Gothic is not only the best, but the only rational architecture, as being that which can fit itself most easily to all services, vulgar or noble.'[103]

So we are back with Pugin and Viollet-le-Duc. Yet Ruskin cannot be a full-blooded neo-Gothicist, since for all its universality, Gothic is for him the expression of a particular set of social circumstances. In calling Gothic builders 'naturalists', he is thinking of their dependence on the forms of Nature; starting from this position, he sets out again to ascertain the rules of ornament and finds them in foliate shapes and in 'severely geometrical order and symmetry'.[104] (*Plate 167*) This is the point of departure for Louis Sullivan's theory of architectural ornament.[105]

As Ruskin saw it, good architecture is the expression of a healthy social structure. It is only natural, therefore, that in later years he should have turned his attention to politics and proposed to replace capitalism with a form of agrarian communism (cf. *Fors Clavigera*, from 1871). His own attempts to put his ideas into practice came to nothing, be it the model socialist society of the Saint George's Guild, a road construction project or a wool mill on the Isle of Man. The impact of his ideas, however, continues to be felt in a great variety of spheres to this day, and extends to figures as different as Mahatma Gandhi and Mao Tse-Tung. In architectural theory, which is unsystematic, the evocative power of his language, together with a number of his concepts, have left marks well into the twentieth century – concepts such as the architecture of a healthy society, truth to materials, constructive honesty, organic ornament, the craftsmanship of the individual (as opposed to the output of the machine) and the conservation – not restoration – of the monuments of the past.

In his sociological outlook Ruskin is close to Semper, in his assessment of Gothic to Viollet-le-Duc, while the somewhat diffuse nature of his ideas is compensated for by the directness of his observation of Nature, a quality also manifest in his drawings.[106] His appeal to Nature as the one and only model for architecture sets him in a long and familiar historical tradition, but by adding a moral dimension to the discussion of architecture he brought a new complexity to the subject which was to have a profound influence on future thinking, especially in America, from the Neo-Gothic period to Frank Lloyd Wright.[107]

A man whose modes of thought were very similar to those of Ruskin in a number of respects was James Fergusson (1808–86),[108] a rich indigo merchant who had made his fortune in India, and who was the first in England to set about writing a world history of architecture. His material took him far beyond earlier German attempts in this direction, such as those of Carl Friedrich von Wiebeking – whom he mentions with scorn – Franz Kugler and Carl Schnaase, and contemporaries regarded him as a latter-day Vitruvius. After two early works on Indian architecture Fergusson published in 1849, the same year as Ruskin's *Seven Lamps*, a treatise entitled *An Historical Enquiry in the True Principles of Beauty in Art*[109] – a title reminiscent of Pugin but a work whose resolute liberalism led to totally different conclusions. Fergusson was a thinker who had a system of schemas, categories and tables to hand with which he could absorb any concept. He developed a universal aesthetic and produced a points system by which, by means of three aesthetic categories, the value of a work of art could be judged, rather as Roger de Piles had tried to do for painting in his *Cours de peinture* of 1708. Fergusson drew a distinction between 'technical beauty', at the bottom of the scale, 'sensuous beauty', which had twice the value, and 'phonetic beauty', i.e. intellectual and aesthetic qualities, which was rated three times as high. For the purposes of architecture, however, he rated all three factors equally, devising an 11-point scale with four points to each factor, and arriving at a maximum 24 points by means of the formula $4 + (2 \times 4) + (3 \times 4)$; for literature he arrived at a maximum of 34 points, for rhetoric a maximum of 35 points. The functional aspect is at the bottom of the scale; through 'phoneticisation' it acquires its 'cal-aesthetic' value – one of the fanciful neologisms that Fergusson coined to denote the terms of his system.

In 1855 Fergusson's *Illustrated Handbook of Architecture* appeared, in 1862 *A History of the Modern Styles in Architecture*.[110] The schematic dogmatism of the preface and especially the introduction to the first of these was probably the reason for his success, for like Pugin and Ruskin, he confidently claimed to provide the definitive answers to the questions 'What is architecture?' and 'What are the true principles which ought to guide us in designing or criticising architectural objects?'[111]

Fergusson makes a distinction between 'original' styles (non-European, Classical and Gothic) and 'revival' styles, the former exhibiting a unity of function and ornament. Art is for him the expression of race and social system, and thus cannot be repeated – a rebuke to English Gothic Revival and the Pre-Raphaelites. He takes a similar line to Ruskin in raising the functional requirements of the engineer's work in building to the status of architecture by means of 'ornamental and ornamented construction': the former is for him the 'prose' of building, the latter the 'poetry'. The field of the engineer is to be kept strictly separate from that of the architect, but the two should complement each other. As an example of what he meant, Fergusson designed a façade (*Plate 168*) which could be used for 'a cotton factory, a warehouse, or any very common-place utilitarian building,'[112] and demonstrated the gradual progression from a 'prosaic' form, which he considered automatically bad, to a decorative articulation resulting not from 'the mere application of any amount of ornament' but from the construction itself. In certain historical borderline cases, however, such as Stonehenge and Cistercian monasteries, Fergusson has to concede that 'ornamental construction' can exist without ornament. His justification of ornamentation in terms of construction and function is a return to the eighteenth century. Acknowledging a beauty of form as such, which doubles the 'effect of the disposition' through ornament and its significance,[113] he comes close to the late eighteenth-century concept of *architecture parlante.*

The architectural categories with which Fergusson operates are a strange mixture – section headings read: 'Mass', 'Stability', 'Materials', 'Construction', 'Forms', 'Proportion', 'Ornament', 'Colour' and 'Uniformity'.[114] The dimension of a building is an aesthetic criterion in itself (Mass = Size). The concept of materials involves not only the idea of truth to materials but also setting them in an aesthetic hierarchy according to their physical value. Construction, while important, Fergusson sees as a tool in the hands of the architect – it would be ridiculous to give it precedence: his example is that of the German builders of the Gothic age, of whose status as architects he is sceptical. And as to ornament: 'In true architecture the construction is always subordinate.'[115]

Like Ruskin, Fergusson sees architecture as imitation of Nature, but he adds: 'We ought always to copy the processes, never the forms of Nature.'[116] Then, strangely enough, he returns to the analogy between architecture and the human body which had been obsolete since the time of Durand: 'In short there is no principle involved in the structure of man which may not be taken as the most absolute standard of excellence in architecture.'[117] He rejects historical eclecticism and sees progress as bringing a new style with it: 'a new style must be the inevitable result; and if our civilization is what we believe it to be, that style will not only be perfectly suited to all our wants and desires, but also more beautiful and more perfect than any that has ever existed before.'[118]

This is the view of a Victorian positivist. Like Semper, who was influenced by him and has many affinities with him, Fergusson sees the 'new style' as Neo-Renaissance, which is for him the expression of English public taste; a style based on short-lived edifices such as the Crystal Palace, or on purely engineering principles, he rejected out of hand. His judgements of buildings are sometimes wild and fantastic, sometimes the product of irrelevant considerations. He had neither the penetrating intellect of Viollet-le-Duc, nor the moral intensity of Ruskin, nor the philosophical power of Semper, but his *Handbook* was the standard architectural history of the Victorian age, and remained so until the appearance of Banister Fletcher's *History of Architecture* at the end of the century.[119]

Ruskin's most important follower was William Morris (1834–96).[120] But whereas Ruskin was the utopian theorist and man of letters, Morris was a man of action, while also leaving a substantial body of theoretical and literary work.[121] He was designer, founder of a business, illustrator and printer; he established an architectural conservation society, made political speeches and served on the executive committee of the Socialist League. The only sources for his ideas about art and architecture are a number of lectures and addresses.

During his time in Street's architectural office in 1856 Morris met Philip Webb and as the two men worked together on Morris's Red House at Bexleyheath, Kent, Webb undertaking the architecture and Morris the furnishing and decoration, Morris was able to realise his vision of an all-embracing world of arts and crafts. When he founded his company a few years later, in 1861, it was one of his main intentions that well-known artists should be willing to make designs for the handicrafts industry, and the products of his firm, aesthetically pleasing and of high quality, laid the foundation of the English Arts and Crafts movement.

Morris's concept of architecture was highly complex, since he took the term 'architecture' to embrace the whole human environment as shaped by human hands. In his lecture *The Decorative Arts* (1877),[122] his starting-point was the assumption of the original unity of the 'greater arts' and the 'decorative arts', which led him to the idea, taken as a matter of course since the Enlightenment and familiar to him from Ruskin, of the relationship between art and the social system to which it belongs. He explained the separation of the arts as the result of the division of labour in modern society, and demanded nothing less than a 'new Art', which should lead, on the basis of natural laws – but not mere imitation of Nature – to the creation of a 'decent home,' governed above all by the principle of simplicity: 'Simplicity of life, begetting simplicity of taste, that is, a love for sweet and lofty things, is of all matters most necessary for the birth of the new and better art we crave for; simplicity everywhere, in the palace as well as in the cottage.'[123] He saw the attainment of this aim, however, as only possible in a new society, in which liberty, equality and fraternity would reign. 'I do not want art for a few,' he said, 'any more than education for a few, or freedom for a few.'[124]

Morris's rejection of machines was by no means as categorical as is sometimes made out. His lectures *Art under Plutocracy* (1883)[125] and *Useful Work versus Useless Toil* (1884)[126] maintain that whereas in capitalist society machines reduce the workers to slavery, in his 'true society' they will have the positive function of easing the burden of work. With considerable foresight he viewed manual work as a corrective to mass production.

The clearest statement of Morris's ideas about architecture is given in his essay *The Revival of Architecture* (1888),[127] where he shows himself equally opposed to Classicism and neo-Gothic, while still advocating historical study of the subject. The imitation of earlier styles, in his view, produces merely 'picturesqueness', in the negative sense, whereas as Pugin and Ruskin had already shown, 'a logical organic style evolved as a matter of necessity from the ancient styles of the classical peoples.'[128]

Gothic, too, was the embodiment of 'a living organism' and 'the undying principles of the art'. In medieval society he found a democratic social order comprising 'democratic bodies of actual workmen', with architecture 'the expression of its social life'. Moreover, 'the social life of the Middle Ages allowed the workman freedom of individual expression, which on the other hand our social life forbids him.'[129] Because to Morris architecture is an expression of society, a style cannot be transferred from one set of social circumstances to another. Morris saw Gothic architecture as 'progressive art', but also that a new society was a necessary prerequisite for rejoining the Gothic tradition. Though an opponent of the Gothic Revival in its formal aspects, Morris still believed that 'there is only one style of architecture on which it is possible to found a true living art...and that style is Gothic.'[130] In the nineteenth-century debate on style, he is a prisoner of his age, his thought processes remarkably close to Viollet-le-Duc but leading to totally different conclusions.

The difference is particularly apparent in his attitude to the conservation of historic monuments, where he follows Ruskin in opposing the 'restoration' of bogus historical condition and arguing for the preservation of architectural ensembles in the historical form in which they have developed, bearing the marks of their ageing process and history. His open letter to *The Athenaeum* in March 1877 led to the foundation of the Society for the Protection of Ancient Buildings, popularly known as 'Anti-Scrape', and to a view of restoration diametrically opposed to that of Viollet-le-Duc, as well as to that which prevailed in England at the time.

Morris made no advance on Ruskin's ideas about architecture, but the attention he devoted to artistic design, together with his own practical activity, sets him in a line of development that leads via the Arts and Crafts movement to the Bauhaus. Thus although he did not succeed in finding a new style, there is a certain justice in counting him among the founders of the modern movement.[131]

A synthesis of Morris's thought is to be found in his utopian novel *News from Nowhere* (1890),[132] which creates a socialist image of a new society for London in the twenty-first century, coloured by a vision of the Middle Ages. *News from Nowhere* was stimulated by *Looking Backward* (1888), a highly successful utopian novel by the American social reformer Edward Bellamy (1850–98),[133] who had a vision of a socialist city controlled by machines. Bellamy takes little interest in aesthetic questions; Morris, on the other hand, devotes a great deal of time to describing his idealised medieval environment. His novel stands in a long line of such works; in particular we may recall those of Robert Owen and Charles Fourier – of whose '*phalanstères*' he was highly critical.[134] In 1893 Morris's Kelmscott Press produced a collectors' edition of More's *Utopia*.

In some ways *News from Nowhere*, with its abolition of factories and its image of a society that can dispense with machines and exist on the principle of voluntary labour, is like an inversion of Pugin's *Contrasts*. The buildings that Morris describes are those of the fourteenth century, eclectically embellished. This is how he sees a covered market:

> While above this lower building rose the steep lead-covered roof and the buttresses and higher part of the wall of a great hall, of a splendid and exuberant style of architecture, of which one can say little more than that it seemed to me to embrace the best qualities of the Gothic of northern Europe with those of the Saracenic and Byzantine, though there was no copying of any one of these styles. On the other, the south side, of the road was an octagonal building with a high roof, not unlike the Baptistry at Florence in outline, except that it was surrounded by a lean-to that clearly made an arcade or cloisters to it: it also was most delicately ornamented. This whole mass of architecture which we had come upon so suddenly from amidst the pleasant fields was not only exquisitely beautiful in itself, but it bore upon it the expression of such generosity and abundance of life that I was exhilarated to a pitch that I had never yet reached. I fairly chuckled for pleasure.[135]

Morris here views architecture as the expression of a healthy post-industrial society, but typically employs an entirely medieval vocabulary of forms. The Houses of Parliament, in his novel, are permitted to remain but in the direct democracy of his utopia the building has become redundant and is used only as an occasional market and a manure store. The once busy Trafalgar Square, with St-Martin-in-the-Fields – 'an ugly church at the corner' – and the National Gallery – 'a nondescript ugly cupolaed building' – has been turned into a peaceful plaza with 'whispering trees and odorous blossoms'.[136]

Work and happiness are now synonymous, and in place of factories there are 'banded-workshops; that is, places where people collect who want to work together.'[137] In the German translation 'banded-workshops' was rendered as 'Vereinigte Werkstätten (United Workshops)', from which formulation the Vereinigte Werkstätten founded in Germany in 1898 probably took their name. With his backward-looking Romanticism Morris abolishes all mass production, even replacing iron railway bridges with stone ones. And as work and art are now one, there is no longer any use for the concept of art: '...the production of what used to be called art, but which has no name amongst us now, because it has become a necessary part of the labour of every man who produces.'[138] Art is thus applied art, the shaping of man's environment, of which architecture is an integral part. Here lie also the roots of Russian constructivism, which emerged a generation later, albeit combined with an attempt to link Morris's conception of applied art to the cult of mechanisation.[139]

Morris's ideas had a great influence in Europe, as well as in America,[140] where Oscar Wilde popularised them on a lecture tour in 1882.[141] However, by 'the true and faithful way of building' Wilde had in mind a form of historical eclecticism,[142] for he, no less than Morris himself, could not but remain within the stylistic confines of nineteenth-century England.

Ruskin and Morris were the spiritual progenitors of the Arts and Crafts movement, which combined a commitment to socialism with the integration of art and handicrafts. Following the example of Morris's own company, a number of generally short-lived Guilds sprang up, starting with Ruskin's St George's Guild in 1871.[143] In 1882 Arthur Mackmurdo (1851–1942),[144] an architect who was a friend of Ruskin's and travelled with him to Italy in 1874, founded the Century Guild, which aimed to raise all branches of art from the level of commerce to that of the artist, and to put arts and crafts on a par with painting and sculpture. What Morris did through his company the Century Guild, which survived until 1888, set out to achieve through a cooperative consisting of a voluntary association of artists and craftsmen. Mackmurdo himself was an adherent of Renaissance values and an opponent of the Ruskin-Morris cult of the Middle Ages; in his own architectural projects he aimed at clearly defined structures, and his designs make him a precursor of Art Nouveau. From 1884 he edited *The Hobby Horse*, the first of the literary periodicals largely devoted to art, the most important of these being *The Studio*.

Similar aims were pursued by The Art Workers' Guild, founded in 1884 by William Richard Lethaby (1857–1931),[145] the most interesting writer on architectural theory in England at the turn of the century. Lethaby worked for over ten years in the office of Norman Shaw and met the ageing Morris through the Society for the Protection of Ancient Buildings, but followed his own independent line both as a writer and as a practising architect. His first book, *Architecture, Mysticism and Myth* (1892), expounds a comprehensive theory of architectural symbolism which anticipates many of the results of modern architectural iconology.[146] According to Lethaby, all forms of architecture should be comprehensible as direct imitations of Nature, and all buildings should exhibit a 'cosmical symbolism',[147] examples of which he quotes from the architecture of all cultures and all ages. This symbolism gives constant terms of a very generalised kind, such as 'Pavements like the sea' and 'Ceilings like the sky'. In his introduction Lethaby expounds an involved concept of architecture in which he postulates three basic principles, which are like distant echoes of Vitruvius: 'First, the similar needs and desires of men; secondly, on the side of structure, the necessities imposed by material, and the physical laws of their erection and combination; and thirdly, on the side of style, nature.'[148] Lethaby's book treats only the third principle. The last symbolic scheme of architecture expounded in such missionary spirit had been that of Jean-Louis Viel de Saint-Maux at the end of the eighteenth century, but Lethaby gives no sign of knowing this work. Present-day architecture, he says, requires 'a symbolism, immediately comprehensible by the great majority of spectators',[149] but this symbolism cannot simply be taken from the past, since such a symbolism conveyed 'terror, mystery, splendour'. Basing himself on the insight of sociology, he states: 'The message will still be of nature and man, of order and beauty, but all will be sweetness, simplicity, freedom, confidence, and light.'[150]

Lethaby's insistence on freedom, simplicity and the proper use of materials led him to a logical rejection of all ornament that was not an expression of the material or of contemporary social conditions.[151] His Eagle Insurance Building in Birmingham (1900), which avoids all stylistic reference to the past, has been called 'the quietest revolution in architectural history,'[152] while his church at Brockhampton in Herefordshire (1901–02), with its neo-Gothic touches and remarkable combination of concrete and thatched roof, and still more his orientalising competition design for Liverpool Anglican Cathedral (1902–03), show how bold a technical and formal experimenter he was. At the same time he devoted a great deal of his energy to teaching, first at the London Central School of Arts and Crafts, where he became co-Director with George Frampton in 1896, then, from 1900, at the Royal College of Art. He later wrote a number of works on architectural history.[153] He summarised his conception of art and architecture as embodied in cultural history in the phrase: 'Art is man's thought expressed in his handwork'; of national monuments he says: 'In … great art are crystallised the aspiration and consciousness of an era of national life.'[154]

Lethaby's conception of architecture is based on historical, sociological and technological considerations. He overcame the diffident and hostile attitude of the Arts and Crafts movement towards the use of machines, and proposed measures similar to those of the Deutscher Werkbund, whose activities and discussions he followed closely.[155] This development in his thought emerges especially clearly in *Architecture,*[156] published in 1911, where he writes on the subject of ornament:

> After all, we must remember that beauty may be unadorned, and it is possible that ornamentation, which arises in such arts as tattooing, belongs to the infancy of the world, and it may be that it will disappear from our architecture as it has from our machinery…[157]

The reference to tattooing suggests that he was acquainted with Adolf Loos' essay *Ornament und Verbrechen* (probably 1908),[158] while the idea of an architecture without ornamentation was already to be found in Louis Sullivan's essay of 1892, *Ornament in Architecture.*[159] Lethaby's espousal of a material-based functionalism and a new symbolism of ornamentation gives him an intermediate position between the Chicago School and the debate that was taking place at the time in Vienna. The nature of this position has yet to be investigated.

Lethaby's innovations were not directly taken up by the Arts and Crafts movement; perhaps their significance was grasped too late. The name of the movement derives from an exhibition mounted in 1888 by the Arts and Crafts Exhibition Society, in which the painter and graphic artist Walter Crane (1845–1915) played a leading part.[160] In an article *On the Revival of Design and Handicraft* in one of the Society's publications (1893) Crane defined the movement as 'in some sense a revolt against the hard mechanical conventional life'.[161] The Society's exhibitions attracted considerable attention at home and abroad and were influential in the reception of Arts and Crafts ideas on the Continent.[162] Crane himself left a number of writings on architecture and the applied arts, in which he makes architecture the *fons et origo* of all the arts, taking his examples and concepts chiefly from Ruskin.[163]

It was also in 1888 that the architect Charles Robert Ashbee (1863–1942)[164] founded the Guild and School of Handicraft, which for seven years was linked to a craft school, thus enabling educational workshops and actual production to be combined for the first time – a situation not without interest when one thinks of the Bauhaus. Ashbee went further than anyone else in his attempts to put Morris's ideas into practice, basing his Guild in 1902 in the village of Chipping Campden, in Gloucestershire, as a model socialist community and cooperative. But the experiment failed and five years later the community was disbanded. Ashbee subsequently (1908) wrote an account of the project – a continuation of his book on Ruskin and Morris.[165] A probable influence on his thinking was that of Frank Lloyd Wright, whom he had met in Chicago in December 1900 during one of his many visits to America. Wright was working at that moment on his lecture *The Art and Craft of the Machine*, which he delivered in March 1901. In this lecture Wright attempted to reconcile the views of Morris with an organic-democratic conception of the machine, but although such an attempt was not without its attractions for Ashbee, he was far too radical a socialist to accept capitalist conditions of production.

In 1901, immediately before his Chipping Campden experiment, Ashbee wrote a book on the teachings of Ruskin and Morris.[166] His approach is basically ideological and socio-economic, and like Ruskin and Morris, he sets out from a fixed view of medieval society and medieval craft guilds. He makes a passionate plea for the dismantling of modern cities and industrial mass production, and their replacement by craftsmen's cooperatives in village communities, combined with work on the land. His central demand is for the establishment of standards through hand-made products, whose connection with machine production he could not or would not recognise. When he wrote in 1908: 'To standardize means to make a pattern or type to which any subsequent quantity can be made',[167] the next step would have been to make designs that could be reproduced by machinery. This vital step had been taken by the Deutscher Werkbund in 1907, whereas it was 1911 before Ashbee was ready to admit that 'modern civilization rests on machinery, and no system for the endowment, or the encouragement, or the teaching of art can be sound that does not recognize this.'[168] But by now, in practical terms, it was too late.

The Arts and Crafts movement ultimately foundered on this hesitant or negative attitude towards mechanisation. Occasional voices were to be heard, expressing ideas that seemed to anticipate those of the Deutscher Werkbund, but they could not prevail. The appeal by the engineer James Nasmyth was early as 1835 remains that of a man crying in the wilderness:

I would show the means of combining the most beautiful forms and the most scientific applications of materials employed in the formation of machinery with the greatest economy. In the majority of instances, the most economic disposition of materials coincides with such forms as present the most elegant appearance to the eye.[169]

This is the functionalist aesthetic of mechanisation. Among those within the Arts and Crafts movement whose thinking ran in this direction was the architect John Dando Sedding (1838–91), Crane's successor in the Art Workers' Guild in 1886 and designer of what probably ranks as the movement's most characteristic building, Holy Trinity Church, Sloane Street, London. Sedding envisaged 'a Morris installed in every factory' yet also recognised the opportunities opened up by mechanisation:

> Let us not suppose that machinery will be discontinued. Manufacture cannot be organized on any other basis... Our manufactures must be of good material and make. The designs must be good and well suited to the necessities of modern methods of production. Note, moreover, that it is not enough to get good designs, but the designer should, more or less, superintend their making at the factory. The designer should be part of the working staff of the factory, see his design take shape, and be consulted as required... And the ideal factory is a place where the artist-designer is a handicraftsman and the handicraftsman is an artist in his way.[170]

This is an anticipation of the union of artist, craftsman and industry that was achieved by the Deutscher Werkbund in the early twentieth century.

Another early member of the Art Workers' Guild was the versatile architect and designer Charles F. Annesley Voysey (1857–1941),[171] who in both his designs and his theoretical writings[172] drew a firmer distinction between the present and the past, in stylistic terms, than Morris and most of the other followers of the Arts and Crafts movement. Voysey's houses are characterised by horizontalism, simplicity, flat planes and assymetry, all derived, however, from English tradition. He followed Ruskin in his emphasis on materials: 'We must acquire a complete knowledge of our material, and be thorough masters of the craft to be employed in its production.'[173] He took a critical view of ornament and warned against excessive decoration and lack of simplicity: 'We have a language or ornament and yet nothing to say...'[174] He was also one of those who attached importance to national characteristics and climatic conditions:

> Each country has been given its own characteristics by its Creator and should work out its own salvation... The best architecture of the past has always been native in its own country and has grown out of a thorough knowledge of local requirements and conditions. Requirements include body, mind and spirit. Conditions include Climate and National Character.[175]

Voysey was a religious man who did not share the socialist ideas of others in the Arts and Crafts movement. His own buildings and projects have a functional clarity which point forward into the twentieth century, though in later life he himself disclaimed any such pioneering role.[176]

One of the most successful architects of this period left no record of his theoretical principles: Edwin Lutyens (1869–1944), a rival of Voysey in domestic architecture and apostle of an eclectic Neo-classicism, seen especially in his large-scale projects in India.[177] The same is true of Charles Rennie Mackintosh (1868–1928).[178]

The ideas of the Arts and Crafts movement were studied with interest in America and in Central Europe, and adapted to individual needs, ideological content, however, the product of specifically English circumstances, to a large extent being removed.[179]

Towards the end of the century there appeared a concept of town-planning which differed from such utopian visions as those of men like Robert Owen and William Morris by being grounded in economic reality. *Garden Cities of Tomorrow* (so titled in the 1902 edition; first published in 1898) by Ebenezer Howard (1850–1928) was a book that caused an international stir at the time and has still not entirely lost its influence today.[180] Like Morris's *News from Nowhere*, Howard's work is a reaction to Edward Bellamy's *Looking Backward*, but of a different kind. Eschewing the committed socialism of Bellamy and Morris, which had led the former to the worship of modern technology and the latter to the glorification of the Middle Ages, Howard sought a compromise between the various positions, basing his ideas on exact present-day costings and demanding that land be taken into public ownership, with agricultural and economic development left largely to private initiative. His starting-point was the problem of the overcrowded industrial cities, though while cherishing a clear preference for the country, he did not deny the merits of urban life. Working with an image of the 'magnets' of city and country, he aimed at a compromise that would combine the advantages of both, which he called 'Town-Country'. He gives a precise description of his model, and his missionary tone, enriched with quotations from Ruskin, does not invalidate the realism of his proposals.

Howard envisages garden cities with a population of the order of 32,000 inhabitants, each covering an area of 6,000 acres, one-sixth of which would be given over to housing, the 'garden city' itself. Each is envisaged as having a basically circular layout, adapted to the topography of the site, and at the centre of a radial and concentric street system there will be public buildings and green spaces (*Plate 169*). Surrounding this inner park area will be a concentrically designed 'Crystal Palace', a glass-roofed arcade open to the park, with shops and stalls. In the housing zones will be individually designed detached houses, each with its own garden. Through the centre will run a 'Grand Avenue', on which schools, churches and other buildings will be sited; factories, warehouses, markets and the like will be built round the outer ring, parallel to which will run a circular railway line, joining the main line close to the station. Full use will be made of modern technology, and Howard recommended that all machinery be driven by electricity. He also developed a rather over-lavish programme of public cultural and recreational buildings. To absorb population growth he proposed a 'cluster of cities' arranged in a modified geometric pattern around one central city, which will have a maximum population of 58,000.[181]

In spite of its different geometric form, Howard's garden city concept reminds one of otherwise such different approaches to urban planning as those of Sir Thomas More and Robert Owen. As the examples of Letchworth and Welwyn Garden City show – the former inspired by Howard and begun in 1903, the latter initiated by Howard himself in 1919 – it proved adaptable to various sets of circumstances and became an important force in twentieth-century thinking. Frank Lloyd Wright's Broadacre City stands in this tradition, so too, albeit with a greater emphasis on historical and sociological factors, does the work of the versatile Patrick Geddes (1854–1932), as evidenced by his plan for the town of Dunfermline (1904).[182] Geddes' urge to take account of national, social and historical aspects led him to produce a series of plans for Indian towns and cities under the aegis of Mahatma Gandhi, the most important of which are assembled in his two-volume *Town Planning toward City Development* (1918).[183]

To conclude this survey of nineteenth-century English architectural theory, attention should be drawn to a work which on the one hand stands as a belated justification of the neo-Renaissance style, and on the other provides an analysis of the philosophical and theoretical principles that underlay discussions of art and architecture in the eighteenth and nineteenth centuries. That work is *The Architecture of Humanism* (1914) by Geoffrey Scott (1884–1929),[184] who was at the time librarian and secretary to Bernard Berenson in Florence. Described by the author in the subtitle as a study in the history of taste, this is a highly intelligent and perceptive investigation into the ways in which architecture has been pressed into the service of extra-architectural interests. Scott is strongly influenced by Theodor Lipps's (1851–1914) theory of empathy, and adopts his concepts of mass, space, time and coherence, which he finds represented above all in Antiquity and the Renaissance.

The importance of Scott's book lies less in his own ideas and in his observations on Renaissance architecture than in his revelation of the 'fallacies' in earlier architectural theory. There is an unresolved tension in his work between Lipps's concepts and a historical definition of styles on the basis of the history of taste. As his opening quotation from Vitruvius (in Wotton's formulation) shows, Scott is ultimately concerned to re-establish a normative theory, and his first task is to demonstrate that the Vitruviuan concepts of 'Commodity, Firmness and Delight' each possesses an autonomy which in spite of their interdependence cannot be sacrified to the exclusive advantage of one or the other. This means above all that 'delight' must not be turned into a mere function of 'commodity' and 'firmness' but must contain a value of its own.

The most perceptive part of Scott's book is that which identifies the fallacies underlying architectural theory which uses terms not proper to architecture. The four types of fallacy he distinguishes are the 'Romantic Fallacy', the 'Mechanical Fallacy', the 'Ethical Fallacy' and the 'Biological Fallacy'.

For Scott the 'Romantic' fallacy lies in overlarding attitudes towards architecture with literary associations, as exemplified particularly by the cult of the Middle Ages, with its symbolical religious and political implications:

> The Romantic Movement, in destroying the existing architectural tradition, destroyed simultaneously the interest which was felt in its principles, and replaced it by a misunderstood mediaevalism out of which no principles of value could ever be recovered. The catastrophe for style was equally a catastrophe for thought.[185]

Another element in the Romantic fallacy is the application to architecture of a moralising concept of Nature – a criticism aimed at Ruskin. The replacement of Art by Nature, Scott argues, will lead to chaos and amounts to 'the suicide of taste'.[186]

The second fallacy, the 'mechanical', is the materialist attitude that views architecture as the result of mechanical laws, and defines form as visible construction. Like the later Schinkel, Scott penetrates to the heart of criticism of the functionalist position:

> And not only does this definition, that the beauty of architecture consists in 'good construction truthfully expressed', *not* apply to the Greek and mediaeval architecture, not only does it contradict qualities of these styles which are so

universally enjoyed, but it *does* apply to many an iron railway-station, to a printing press, or to any machine that rightly fulfils its function. Now, although many machines may be beautiful, it would be a *reductio ad absurdum* to be forced to admit that they all are: still more that they are essentially more beautiful than the Greek and Gothic styles of architecture. Yet to this conclusion our definition, as it stands, must lead us.[187]

Without denying that structure makes its own demands, Scott emphasises that 'the optical effect and the structural requirements were distinct,'[188] and taking steel structures as his example, he draws a firm distinction between functional use, perceived by the intelligence, and direct physical experience, seeing no link between them.

The 'ethical' fallacy lies in the projection of political or moral values onto historical styles, which are then accepted or rejected on the basis of these values. This is an attack primarily on Ruskin and Morris; the latter he accuses of 'a picturesque fusion of artistic with democratic propaganda',[189] mocking the idealisation of the Middle Ages typically represented by *News from Nowhere*: 'We may well doubt whether the inspired Gothic craftsmen of that socialist Utopia ever existed in the Middle Ages.'[190]

The final fallacy, which Scott calls 'biological', consists in the application to architecture of evolutionary concepts based on the pattern of growth, maturity and decay. Here his target is not Vasari, whose concept of history rested on a similar analogy, but the positivism of the nineteenth century. The last thing he wanted was to see the individuality of the artist used merely to illustrate a particular phase of evolution:

> But this precisely was the fallacy of evolution. The values of art do not lie in the sequence but in the individual terms. To Brunelleschi there was no Bramante; his architecture was not Bramante's unachieved, but his own fulfilled.[191]

By setting himself in the Vitruvian line, Scott revives the autonomy of architecture as an aesthetic form, challenging the propriety of importing non-architectural criteria and values into the discussion. Not only does his book offer a devastating criticism of virtually all architectural theory of the nineteenth century, it also anticipates many of the charges that have been levelled against that of the Modern Movement. That Scott was not an architect himself, and had no positive solution to offer, does not invalidate his analysis. Authors of later critical works such as Peter Collins (*Changing Ideals in Modern Architecture*, 1965) and Peter Blake (*Form Follows Fiasco*, 1977)[192] are still conceptually guided by Scott's 'fallacies'.

24. The United States: from Thomas Jefferson to the Chicago School

The first treatise on architecture to be published in America appeared in 1775, the year before the Declaration of Independence. However, all such early American publications were, without exception, copies or adaptations of works that had already appeared in England, works of a primarily practical nature.[1] The salient feature of early American architecture is the extensive application to wood of European forms that had been conceived in the context of stone.[2] Relevant here is not this process as such, but the extent to which it enables us to identify a specifically American approach to architecture.

The first to formulate such an approach was Thomas Jefferson (1743–1826), whose ideas and designs were calculated to symbolise the ideals and aspirations of the young democracy. Jefferson's solution was to use a Rome-inspired Classicism for public buildings and the Palladian tradition for private houses.[3] He left no formal treatise but isolated statements in sources such as his autobiography, letters and *Notes on Virginia* (1782), together with his systematic collection of books on architecture,[4] leave no doubt about the nature of his ideas. He had a particular commitment to national buildings, calling on architects such as Charles-Louis Clérisseau and Benjamin Henry Latrobe[5] to assist in these projects and also making his own personal contributions, as evidenced in particular by the designs for the Capitol buildings in Richmond, Virginia and in Washington, DC.[6]

Before he left for Europe in 1784,[7] Jefferson made a bitter attack on the architecture of the State of Virginia:

> There are no other public buildings but churches and court-houses, in which no attempts are made at elegance. Indeed, it would not be easy to execute such an attempt, as a workman could scarcely be found capable of drawing an order. The genius of architecture seems to have shed its maledictions over this land. Buildings are often erected, by individuals, of considerable expense. To give these symmetry and taste, would not increase their cost. It would only change the arrangement of the materials, the form and combination of the members. This would often cost less than the burthen of barbarous ornaments with which these buildings are sometimes charged. But the first principles of the art are unknown, and there exists scarcely a model among us sufficiently chaste to give an idea of them.[8]

Jefferson's was an aesthetic approach.

In France the Maison Carrée at Nîmes struck Jefferson as the right model for the Capitol at Richmond, Virginia, and on 26 January 1786 he wrote:

> There is at Nismes in the South of France a building, called the Maison quarrée, erected in the time of the Caesars, and which is allowed without contradiction to be the most perfect and precious remain of antiquity in existence. Its superiority over anything at Rome, in Greece, at Baalbec or Palmyra is allowed on all hands ... I determined therefore to adopt this model, and to have all its proportions justly observed ...[9]

At the time he wrote this, Jefferson had not yet been to Nîmes, and what he knew of the Maison Carrée came from Clérisseau's book of 1778, which he had acquired from the author himself.[10] Clérisseau was subsequently commissioned to design the Capitol in Richmond,[11] Jefferson intervening to change the original Corinthian Order to Ionic. He later described the episode in his autobiography:

> Thinking it a favorable opportunity of introducing into the State an example of architecture, in the classic style of antiquity, and the Maisson quarrée of Nismes, an ancient temple, being considered as the most perfect model existing of what may be called Cubic architecture, I applied to M. Clerissault, who had published drawings of the Antiquities of Nismes, to have me a model of the building made in stucco, only changing the order from Corinthian to Ionic, on account of the difficulty of the Corinthian capitals.[12]

The term 'cubic architecture' leads to the core of Jefferson's Classicism. He favoured a reduction of architecture to basic geometric forms, which links him to the theories of the French Revolutionary architects whom he encountered during his stay in Paris. The most important product of this approach was his design for the library of the University of Virginia, the Rotunda (1823–25), which the archaeologist Karl Lehmann regarded as superior to its model, the Pantheon in Rome.[13] The most revealing example of his lifelong occupation with architecture is the complicated history of his designs for his villa Monticello, a Roman villa in Palladian style. Jefferson never saw his ideas as constituting an academic doctrine. He was a late protagonist of the Roman cause in the Greek v. Roman debate, but paid scant heed to Vitruvius. What fascinated him about the Greeks was not their architecture but their concept of personal freedom, and his own projects are to a far greater extent the results of studying books on architecture than of observing actual buildings; the notes on architecture that he made on his travels are rather colourless. It was largely because Jefferson, as a Humanist, found his answer to the quest for a symbolic American style in Roman and Palladian models that the country developed a particularly rigorous form of Classicism. The American Palladianism for which Jefferson is intellectually the most significant spokesman later acquired elements of the Adam style through architects such as Charles Bulfinch.[14]

The first book on architecture by an American is *The Country Builder's Assistant* (1797)[15] by Asher Benjamin (1773–1845), an architect who worked chiefly in Boston and who, in his no fewer than seven treatises, frequently revised and reissued in subsequent years,[16] laid the foundations of American writing on the subject. Though making extensive use of English design-books such as those of Gibbs, Chambers and Nicholson, Benjamin strove to eliminate from them what he regarded as superfluous ballast. His works were the American counterparts of the large-format volumes by the English writer William Pain which were reprinted in America in the 1790s.[17]

Benjamin's most important work was *The American Builder's Companion* (1806), which ran through six revised editions by 1827,[18] and which the author claimed, with American timber buildings in mind, to be the work of 'the first who have for a great length of time, published any New System of Architecture.'[19] Two-thirds of European design-books, he asserted, were useless for American needs: 'American-ness' meant making European models simpler and cheaper, especially in the use of the Orders. Even the purity of the Orders did not need to be completely respected: 'We do not conceive it essentially necessary to adhere exactly to any particular order.' He also suggested that in America the Orders could have slimmer proportions than those of their Classical counterparts, at least for private houses, 'to lighten their heavy parts, and thereby lessen the expense both of labour and materials.'[20] In public buildings, on the other hand, the proportions of the Classical canon should be retained.

In *The American Builder's Companion* Benjamin opposes the invention of new orders: 'Attempts which have sometimes been made to compose fancy orders, have only spoiled the works, and no reduction of the expense has been effected.'[21] The reduction of building costs is one of his prime considerations: he proposes, for example, that the absolute dimensions of entablatures should be reduced, thus cutting the cost of materials, and that, as a matter of principle, in all the Orders the length of the shaft should be increased by two diameters. By the time of his *Practice of Architecture* (1833), however, he envisaged a combination of a Greek-Doric capital with a Tuscan base and an Ionic shaft (*Plate 170*), the cost of which would lie 'between that of the Tuscan and Doric orders'.[22]

In the 1827 edition of his *Companion* Benjamin has an appendix in which he gives a detailed description of the architecture of the Greek Revival. For the rest, the book is a handy assemblage of information on structural geometry and the Orders, somewhat sketchy sections on subjects such as 'The Origin of Building', and drawings of his own buildings, all informed by the author's practical approach, exemplified by a statement such as: 'Variety in ornaments should not be carried to an excess. In architecture they are only accessories.'[23] Parts of this 1827 edition are taken over from another book, *The Rudiments of Architecture*, which Benjamin had published in 1814.[24] And in an American declaration of architectural independence he states: 'The style of building in this country differs very considerably from that of Great Britain and other countries of Europe...,' going on to base his case on the differences in materials.[25]

Both Thomas Jefferson and Asher Benjamin, each in his own way and on his own level, came to terms with the models they had inherited from Europe, and used them as means of asserting their self-confidence as Americans. But there was as yet no autonomous American aesthetic of architecture. Its evolution was to be stimulated from far beyond the field of architecture – from the Transcendental movement.[26]

Transcendentalism, which was primarily a literary movement, arose in the 1830s and nurtured an aesthetic of Nature which had its intellectual roots in Protestantism and, to an even greater extent, in German idealism.[27] It remained a powerful source of influence on architectural theory in America until well into the twentieth century. Ralph Waldo Emerson (1803–82) and Henry David Thoreau (1817–62), with their circle in Concord, Massachusetts, evolved an organic-functionalist aesthetic of Nature that could be made relevant to architecture but it did not lead to a systematic theory of the subject. This was to be the achievement of Emerson's friend and fellow alumnus of Harvard, Horatio Greenough (1805–52), a sculptor who spent most of his life in Italy, where he studied with Lorenzo Bartolini.[28] Although commissioned by the Federal Government to undertake a large number of sculptures for the Capitol in Washington, DC, Greenough did not, as an artist, rise above a middle-of-the-road Classicism, but as a theorist he was a figure of considerable significance, as his contemporaries recognised. When he died, Emerson wrote to Carlyle: 'Horatio Greenough, a sculptor, whose tongue was far cunninger in talk, than his chisel to carve, and who inspired great hopes, died two months ago at 47 years.'[29]

Greenough formulated his ideas in an Italian environment. He had already arrived at his basic principles[30] before he met Emerson in Florence in 1833, and the influence passed rather from him to Emerson than vice versa. His starting-point was an opposition to the Greek Revival, and with his essay *American Architecture*, published in the *United States Magazine and Democratic Review* in 1843, he at once made himself the spokesman of the nation.[31]

Greenough saw it as the task of the United States 'to form a new style of architecture.'[32] Modern architecture, he maintained, had abandoned the great principles of the past; the new style would have to be founded on an immediate return to the laws of Nature. The search for 'the great principles of construction' would lead to the observation of 'the skeletons and skins of animals', the variety of which would be apprehended as a source of beauty.[33] The biological analogy leads him to a pronouncement reminiscent of the language of Alberti: 'it [i.e. beauty in Nature] is the consistency and harmony of the parts juxtaposed, the subordination of details to masses, and of masses to the whole.'[34] At the same time he rejected all 'arbitrary laws of proportion' and 'arbitrary laws of taste': only in the system of Nature was 'organic beauty' to be found. In shipbuilding he saw the realisation of the principles of an analogy with Nature: 'Could we carry into our civil architecture the responsibilities that weigh upon our shipbuilding, we should ere long have edifices as superior to the Pantheon.'[35] This foreshadows Le Corbusier's provocative comparison between automobiles and Greek temples in *Vers une architecture* eighty years later.

Rejecting the idea of compressing the functions of buildings into ready-made forms, Greenough proposes starting from the interior lay-out, as the nucleus of a building, and planning outwards. As in the French tradition he proceeds outwards from the disposition of the rooms, which however he gives an absolute significance: 'The most convenient size and arrangement of the rooms that are to constitute the building being fixed, that access of the light that may, of the air that must be wanted, being provided for, we have the skeleton of our building. Nay, we have all excepting the dress.'[36]

The conception of architecture as an organic skeleton covered with a skin became a basic feature of the functionalist theory of architecture. The lay-out and linking of the rooms, which for practical reasons had to stand in a certain relationship to each other, needed, claimed Greenough, to be apparent from the outside: 'they cannot fail to speak of their relation and uses.' The relationship between a building and its site, together with that between interior and exterior, is what gives the building its 'character and expression'.[37] Greenough's aesthetic assessment of his radical functionalism seems like a combination of the eighteenth-century French theory of *caractère* with ideas taken from Durand.

The anatomical relations and proportions, Greenough went on, that have already been achieved in the construction of ships, machines and bridges should be introduced into every construction. The first result of this would be that 'the bank would have the physiognomy of a bank, the church would be recognised as such, nor would the billiard room and the chapel wear the same uniform of columns and pediment.'[38]

An architecture established on these principles could be described as 'organic', i.e. 'formed to meet the wants of their occupants,' or as 'monumental', i.e. expressive of the sympathies, beliefs and taste of the population, and is thus to be understood as the expression of either individual or collective needs. 'Organic' buildings, in Greenough's definition, are machines, 'each individual of which must be formed with reference to the abstract type of its species.'[39] Climate is a primary consideration, and ornamentation must conform to the nature of the expressed function. Greenough developed the concept of function in a later essay *Relative and Independent Beauty*, written shortly before his death,[40] in which he shows his indebtedness to Edward Lacy Garbett's *Rudimentary Treatise on the Principles of Design in Architecture*,[41] published in London in 1850, which in its turn made use of Ruskin's *Seven Lamps of Architecture* (1849). Garbett's insistence on the imitation of Nature and on 'constructive truth' could not but confirm Greenough in his theories. Garbett's conclusion is 'As long as we have no new style in construction, we have none in architecture...a style never grew of itself; it never will. It must be sought, and sought the right way.'[42]

It was Greenough's undisguised aim to create a new national style of architecture that ran parallel to Nature, and to evolve an 'artistic dogma' based on natural science. All his criteria revolve around the concept of function; the aesthetic and moral aspects of architecture become elements of function: 'When I define Beauty as the promise of function; Action as the presence of Function; Character as the record of Function, I arbitrarily divide that which is essentially one.'[43] Indeed, Nature itself is defined as the sum of its functions, which leads Greenough to present his theory in positivist, pseudo-religious terms: 'The many-sided and full and rich harmony of nature is a many-sided response to the call for many functions; not an aesthetical utterance of the Godhead.'[44] This higher union of mathematics, nature and art Greenough calls 'organisation'.

Greenough recognised that his functionalism might lead to architectural 'nakedness' but still defines this as 'the majesty of the essential',[45] which means that the renunciation of decoration becomes a positive value. Here Greenough may have been influenced by Lodoli, Ledoux and Durand, who arrived by similar arguments at the concept of an architecture free of ornament.

Every function, in Greenough's view, is subject to an absolute law, and the degree of a building's conformity to this law defines its 'freedom or obedience to God'; this is reminiscent of Ruskin's *Lamp of Obedience*. In his essay *Structure and Organization* Greenough goes so far as to equate his functional principle with the principle of Divine Creation:

> If there be any principle of structure more plainly inculcated in the works of the Creator than all others, it is the principle of unflinching adaption of forms to functions. I believe that colors also, as far as we have discovered their chemical causes and affinities, are not less organic in relation to the forms they invest than are those forms themselves.[46]

The aesthetic conclusion he draws sounds like a perversion of Alberti:

> ...in art, as in nature, the soul, the purpose of a work will never fail to be proclaimed in that work in proportion to the subordination of the parts to the whole, of the whole to the function.[47]

Therefore every functional improvement is 'an advance in expression, in grace, in beauty, or grandeur, according to the functions of the craft', and beauty becomes identical with the optimalisation of function.

Without going into its implications, Greenough arrives at the concept of standardised solutions for particular functions, for 'God's world has a distinct formula for every function.'[48] The law of economy ('an economical, a cheap style'), already proclaimed by Durand, is raised to the status of a moral precept and can thus be adopted as a national characteristic:

> It is the dearest of all styles! It costs the thought of men, much, very much thought, untiring investigation, ceaseless experiment. Its simplicity is not the simplicity of emptiness or of poverty; its simplicity is that of justness, I had almost said, of justice.[49]

The tone in which Greenough expounds his functionalist views is moralistic and emotional, but in terms of substance he does not go much further than a wide range of European thinkers whom he knew either personally or from their works. We may assume that he was acquainted with the theories of Lodoli and Durand, for example, and he met Labrouste during the latter's stay at the Villa Medici in Rome.[50] In a letter of 1839 to Charles Summers, an American lawyer on a tour of Europe, he enquired after Schinkel:

> If you should have leisure, pray tell me your impression of the works of Shinkel the architect, as regards distribution and adaption, organization in short. That's the germ of future architectures.[51]

Greenough rigorously relates everything to his starting-point.

It was to Emerson above all, who makes constant reference to him in his works, that Greenough owed the propagation of his views.[52] In a letter of 28 December 1851 to Emerson, Greenough summarised his theory thus:

> Here is my theory of structure. A scientific arrangement of spaces and forms to functions and to site – An emphasis of features proportioned to their gradated importance in function – Color and ornament to be decided and arranged and varied by strictly organic laws...I beg you in the interim to reflect that this godlike human body has no ornament...[53]

Emerson was a lifelong friend of W.H. Furness, father of the architect Frank Furness in Philadelphia, in whose studio Louis Sullivan was given his first job. There is thus a direct link between Greenough and the Chicago School, which built on Greenough's theories,[54] and the architecture of an engineer such as William Le Baron Jenney in Chicago could legitimately be regarded as representing the new American style as Greenough envisaged it.

Emerson and Greenough met for the last time in Concord, Massachusetts in 1852, the year of Greenough's death, and the high esteem in which Emerson held his friend can be seen from the characterisation in his book *English Traits*, where he was concerned to demonstrate that Greenough's ideas preceded those of Ruskin. 'At Florence,' wrote Emerson,

> chief among artists I found Horatio Greenough, the American sculptor...His paper on Architecture, published in 1843, announced in advance the leading thoughts of Mr Ruskin on the morality in architecture, notwithstanding the antagonism in their views of the history of art.[55]

Emerson then goes on to quote the central passage of Greenough's letter of 28 December 1851 given above.

The earliest formulation of Emerson's concept of the laws of Nature comes in an essay written in 1836.[56] Here the criterion of 'commodity' plays an important role; only later, under Greenough's influence, does the concept of organic functionality come to the fore, as shown in the following passage from the section on 'Beauty' in his book *The Conduct of Life*:

> Hence our taste in building rejects paint, and all shifts, and shows the original grain of the wood; refuses pilasters and columns that support nothing, and allows the real supporters of the house honestly to show themselves. Every necessary or organic action pleases the beholder.[57]

Like Greenough, Emerson waxes enthusiastic about ship-building, and about animals and the way they move. With his eye on Hogarth he writes: 'Beauty rides on a lion. Beauty rests on necessities. The line of beauty is the result of perfect economy.'[58] As with Greenough, economy of materials is the aesthetic criterion. In his essay *Art and Criticism* Emerson writes: 'In architecture the beauty is increased in the degree in which the material is safely diminished.'[59]

The closest parallel between Emerson and Greenough lies in Emerson's essay *Thoughts on Art*, published in the Transcendalists' journal *The Dial* (1840–41), where we read:

> Fitness is so inseparable an accompaniment of beauty, that it has been taken for it. The most perfect form to answer an end, is so far beautiful...We feel, in seeing a noble building, which rhymes well, as we do in hearing a perfect song, that is spiritually organic, that is, had a necessity in nature, for being, was one of the possible forms in the Divine mind, and is now only discovered and executed by the artist, not arbitrarily composed by him.[60]

A far more radical thinker than either Greenough or Emerson, neither of whom questioned the traditional role of architecture as representing communal values in monumental form, was Thoreau, who in effect confined architecture to house-building and rejected its monumental functions. When Emerson showed him the above-mentioned letter from Greenough, Thoreau reacted sharply and noted in his diary on 11 January 1852:

> R.W.E. showed me yesterday a letter from H. Greenough, the sculptor, on architecture, which he liked very much...But for Greenough, I felt as if it was dilettantism...What of architectural beauty I now see, I know has gradually grown from within outward, out of the character and necessities of the indweller and builder, without even a thought for mere ornament...One of the most beautiful buildings in this country is a logger's hut in the woods, and equally beautiful will be the citizen's suburban box, when the life of the indweller shall be as simple and as agreeable to the imagination.[61]

This is a reflection of the simple life that Thoreau had led in the Massachusetts countryside, where he had built his own log cabin. *Walden* (1854) is a description of his experience there,[62] and the chapter headed 'Economy' closely repeats the above entry in his diary.[63] He calls for a reduction of architecture to the service of primary needs, proposing an American style of the utmost simplicity and, like Greenough and others, drawing a parallel with ship-building. On the subject of modern American houses he writes in his essay *Cape Cod*:

> I call them American, because they are paid for by Americans, and 'put up' by American carpenters; but they are little removed from lumber...Perhaps we have reason to be proud of our naval architecture, and need not go to the Greeks, or the Goths, or the Italians, for the models of our vessels.[64]

Like Greenough and Emerson, Thoreau felt himself called to be an educator of taste. Historical monumental architecture he considered vulgar. 'Consider the beauty of New York architecture,' he wrote in his diary, 'and there is no very material difference between this and Baalbek – a vulgar adornment of what is vulgar.'[65] Architecture should not seek to represent the values of the nation: 'It should not be by their architecture but by their abstract thoughts that a nation should seek to commemorate itself.'[66] For Thoreau, truly American buildings will be concerned with satisfying the needs of the people who live in them.

Alongide personal experiences like Thoreau's in the forests around Walden Pond, experiments in communal living were being made which found an immediate expression in architecture. Many of these had their roots in religious movements or socialist models, and indeed, a larger number of religious sects and utopian groups succeeded in putting their ideas into practice in America in the late eighteenth and early nineteenth century than in Europe.[67] The novelist Nathaniel Hawthorne, for instance, who was a member of the Transcendentalist circle in Concord, Massachusetts, wrote of his experiences in the socialist community of Brook Farm in his novel *The Blithedale Romance* (1852), and mention has already been made of Robert Owen's experiment at New Harmony, Indiana (Chapter 23).

The ideas of these sects and movements often found expression in architecture,[68] most strikingly among the Shakers, descendants of the English Quakers,[69] whose statutes laid down precise instructions for their buildings and objects of everyday use. These instructions were tabulated in the 'Millennial Laws' of 1821.[70] According to Mother Ann Lee, founder of the Shakers, the millennium had already begun, and her communities were regarded as realisations of the New Jerusalem. The Millennial Laws prescribed the right angle as the basis of all planning, even forbidding paths to be laid out in other than rectangular form, or meat and bread to be cut other than at right angles or in cubes. Buildings were planned as the expressions of identified needs, economically and almost without ornament. Art as traditionally understood was regarded as an absurdity. Common needs led to functional design. The celibacy preached by the sect produced a dualistic planning principle which resulted in double doors and staircases and a general insistence on uniformity. Beauty, to the Shakers, derived from simplicity and functionality. The first architectural clauses in Section IX of the Millennial Laws are:

1. Beadings, mouldings and cornices, which are merely for fancy may not be made by Believers.

2. Odd or fanciful styles of architecture, may not be used among Believers, neither should any deviate widely from the common styles of building among Believers, without the union of the Ministry.[71]

There follow precise instructions on the use of colour for the interior and exterior of buildings, while there are rules not only for the use of manufactured goods but also for their production and sale.

Fancy articles of any kind, or articles which are superfluously finished, trimmed or ornamented, are not suitable for Believers...

Believers may not in any case or circumstance, manufacture for sale, any article or articles, which are superfluously wrought, and which would have a tendency to feed the pride and vanity of man, or such as would not be admissible to use among themselves, on account of their superfluity.[72]

The buildings and manufactured products of the Shakers, particularly their furniture, have frequently been interpreted – with some justification – as products of a proto-functionalism.[73] It is hardly a coincidence that their early colonies – Watervliet (founded in 1775) and Mount Lebanon (1779), both in New York State, and Hancock, Massachusetts (1790) – arose in the vicinity of Concord, the centre of Transcendentalism, and for all their differences of doctrine, Shakers and Transcendentalists come remarkably close to each other at times in their ideas on architecture. Other sects, such as the Mormons, remained closer to the American vernacular in their architecture and in the grid plans of their settlements, and did not concern themselves with matters of theory.[74]

Simplicity, economy, functionalism, reduction or total renunciation of ornament: such were the principal features of this phase of architectural theory in America, and these factors, together with the quest for a style to express the ideals and aspirations of the young democracy, were important influences on the theories that emerged in the second half of the nineteenth century. But whatever ideas Greenough and the Transcendentalists may have put forward, and whatever may have been done by sects like the Shakers to make such ideas a practical reality, everyday American architecture remained dominated by European models and designs. Even the efforts of Asher Benjamin, with his adaptations of Classical models to American purposes, had done little to change this.

It was still possible, therefore, for the Philadelphian architect Samuel Sloan (1815–84) to declare as late as 1852: 'American works on architecture are few in number, and no works on American architecture have yet been written.'[75] This sentence comes from the conclusion of *The Model Architect*, one of the most extensive of Sloan's published design-books and a characteristic example of the historicist approach to architecture of the time. It contains views, plans and detail drawings in a variety of styles and for a variety of building types, but with the country house as the focus of attention. The work also contains descriptive material and calculations of cost. But what makes it particularly interesting are its somewhat haphazardly interpolated sections on style, typology, materials and other general questions. Sloan set out to write, as he put it, 'a business like book on cottages and country residences,'[76] but in the course of explaining his projects, he provides the reader – he has his own and other architects' clients in mind – with an introduction to the problems of architectural theory and history.

Sloan presents designs, 'from the humblest cottage to the noblest mansion',[77] in the tradition of Serlio and Le Muet in France, and his principal concern is to educate American taste. His conception of architecture is thoroughly conventional:

> Plans suited to purpose, an appearance in unison with the locality, an adaptation of parts to the whole, and an appropriate use of ornament are all essential to comply with the requisitions of cultivated taste.[78]

The dependence of architecture on landscape is for him a question of national character and a basic criterion of quality.[79]

Sloan demanded that the architect should have extensive practical and technical knowledge, and at the same time 'a thorough appreciation of the wants of society'. Planning proceeds from functions and their technical solution, so that in the end almost all styles are equally good and equally acceptable. He describes the design process thus:

> The arrangements for heating, ventilation, and the admission of light, also create difficulties. After these have been successfully overcome, the next thing is to adopt

a style. In doing this, both the peculiarities of the plan, the locality, and the purpose of the building, have to be taken into consideration.[80]

The choice of style, which in his view can only be an historical style, albeit 'adapted to American tastes and American habits', is determined by national character and by taste, which in their turn are conditioned by geographical factors. If one excepts his recourse to history in the question of style, Sloan can indeed be seen as having developed criteria for the evolution of an autonomous American architecture. His own designs, however, lag behind his ideas in this connection.

It was left to Calvert Vaux (1824–95) a few years later, a native Englishman renowned chiefly as a landscape gardener, to break this link with the styles of the past, in his book *Villas and Cottages* (1857),[81] which constitutes to some extent a continuation of the work of Andrew Jackson Downing (1815–52).[82] The scope of Vaux's work is virtually the same as that of Sloan's, but it was his aim to write a popular and inexpensive book – and in this, as the numerous re-issues show, he was successful. The long introduction starts from premises similar to Sloan's, but Vaux expounds his ideas more clearly and logically. Like all his contemporaries he laments the poor standard of architecture in his country and considers the question of 'Americanism' from various points of view, finding his criteria for this quality in a sense of national identity and a love of landscape and architecture. Observing that his proposals are aimed at providing 'something worth having for the money',[83] he expresses his basic beliefs in these words:

> Indeed a simple, well-planned structure costs less to execute, for the accommodation obtained, than an ill-planned one; and the fact of its being agreeable and effective, or otherwise, does not depend on any ornament that may be superadded to the useful and necessary forms of which it is composed, but on the arrangement of those forms themselves, so that they may balance each other and suggest the pleasant ideas of harmonious proportion, fitness, and agreeable variety to the eye, and through the eye to the mind.[84]

Vaux sees architecture as primarily functional, and this functionalism has its own aesthetic quality. But he attaches greater importance to the social roots of architecture than Sloan:

> The art of building faithfully portrays the social history of the people to whose needs it ministers…We must remember, therefore, that principles of action, perception, convictions, habits of thought, and customs are the directors of all architectural design…Good architecture of some kind must spring up in any society where there is a love of truth and nature.[85]

And in national terms:

> a refined propriety and simple, inexpensive grace ought habitually to be the distinctive marks of every habitation in which a free American dwells.[86]

In his rejection of the adaptation of historical styles for American architecture Vaux calls on the support of Emerson, and in all his ideas one senses the presence of the Transcendentalists – also of Greenough – albeit always against the concrete background of the question of a practical, inexpensive, identifiably American architecture. These are the terms in which he rejects the historical approach in general and the Greek Revival in particular:

> The study of what has been done by other nations, though useful as a help, will never, by itself, lead to much result in America, where the institutions, the needs

of the climate, and the habits of the people, have a distinctive character that requires special consideration; and this remark applies particularly to rural architecture. Thus the Greek mode...is not heartily sympathized with either by the American atmosphere or the spirit of this locomotive age; and, consequently, no architectural effort imitated from the Greek can help being, to a great extent, a mere lifeless parody.[87]

The 39 country houses he presents are all 'comfortably planned, pleasantly designed, and soundly constructed'[88] – a formulation in which an echo of the Vitruvian principles of *firmitas, utilitas* and *venustas* is to be heard. However, Vaux does not view architecture entirely in terms of functionalism, simplicity, economy, etc., but also calls for properties such as 'character and expression'.[89] Vaux draws upon the concepts of *architecture parlante* when he maintains, for example, that a door is not merely an entrance but should also 'express its purpose of shelter', and thus be provided with a porch.[90] His designs are not based on historical styles, like Sloan's, but nor do they have the extreme functional economy of the Shakers' houses; rather, they represent a 'picturesque' vernacular usually called the 'stick style', from the material most commonly used.

Modestly produced and presented, Vaux's *Villas and Cottages* is the most substantial work of its kind dating from the middle of the nineteenth century, but over the decades that followed, it was 'Victorian' pattern-books like Sloan's that dominated the scene, with the difference that they now dispensed almost entirely with explanatory text. Such, for instance, were those of the New York publisher Amos Jackson Bicknell, which contained examples of all conceivable styles, to satisfy all tastes.[91] Bicknell's *The Village Builder* (1870) ran through seven editions, the last of which carried a supplement,[92] and contained practical information for builders who wanted to save themselves the architect's fee, together with specimen contracts between client and building contractor, which even laid down terms for individual manual tasks. Estimated prices were also given. The book was virtually a catalogue from which anyone with the necessary money could order one of the dubious eclectic designs and have it executed. In his introduction Bicknell claims that his book is 'better adapted to the North, South, East and West, than any previous production of similar character'. Here architecture makes buildings universally available as objects of consumer choice and exchange – including courthouses and churches. Pattern-books of 'stick style', 'Queen Anne', 'shingle style', etc. abounded.

Discussion of theoretical issues, which took a new direction under the influence of Ruskin and Viollet-le-Duc, was chiefly carried on in architectural journals, the best survey of which is provided by Vincent J. Scully in his book *The Shingle Style and the Stick Style* (1955).[93] A move away from the development of an autonomous American style showed itself in a pilgrimage of architectural students to Europe, above all to the Ecole des Beaux-Arts in Paris, which exercised a strong influence on recently established schools of architecture in America, and where for several decades Americans were in a majority among overseas students. Richard Morris Hunt enrolled at the Ecole des Beaux-Arts in 1846, to be followed by Henry Hobson Richardson, Charles Follen McKim and many others, including Louis Henry Sullivan.[94] As this relationship grew in the second half of the century,[95] so inner city architecture in America came increasingly under the influence of the Ecole des Beaux-Arts, whilst in the suburbs and in the countryside autonomous developments continued. The most important figure to embody this union of the American tradition with the ideas of the Ecole was Richardson (1838–86), who in his turn had a marked influence on Europe.[96] Richardson's last great work, the Marshall Field Wholesale Store in Chicago (1885–87), the skeleton of which is pure iron, came to be regarded as one of the first works of the Chicago School.

The Chicago School occupies a central position not only in the history of American architecture but also in architectural theory over the last thirty years of the nineteenth century.[97] These architects now followed up the ideas of Greenough and the Transcendentalists, which had never found full or proper expression in executed buildings.

There were two external stimuli for the sudden upsurge in building in Chicago in the 1870s. One was the fire of 1871, which almost completely destroyed the city; the other was the enormous growth in population and in industry and commerce. A key figure in the new building was William Le Baron Jenney (1832–1907), a native of Massachusetts who had studied engineering at the Ecole Centrale des Arts et Manufactures in Paris from 1853 to 1856. He was the first designer of iron-frame structures to make progressive attempts to reveal the structural framework in the exteriors of his buildings.[98] The rationality of his constructions recalls the engineer's aesthetic that prevailed in France at the time. It was in Jenney's office that men such as Sullivan, Holabird and Burnham spent part of their time, men who gave the Chicago School its individuality. His buildings, largely free of ornament, must come close to the style that Greenough had envisaged.

In the theoretical sphere the published work of two men sums up the first phase of the Chicago School, architects whose executed buildings are also among the School's most important achievements – Louis Henry Sullivan and John Wellborn Root.

Only in recent years has the picture of Sullivan (1856–1924)[99] as a precursor of modern functionalism and *neue Sachlichkeit* given way to a more accurate view of him as a man steeped in the American Romantic tradition.[100] His complex and highly personal architectural theory is composed of various strands – American Transcendentalism, German idealism, the theosophy of Swedenborg and the rationalism of the Ecole des Beaux-Arts in Paris, where he studied in 1874/75.[101] The period of his greatest success as an architect, 1883–95, coincided with his partnership with Dankmar Adler, the manager of and the driving force behind the firm, whilst Sullivan confined himself principally to façade design and details of ornamentation.[102]

Sullivan's theoretical writings extend from 1885 to his death in 1924 and form a homogeneous whole, although he was not a systematic thinker.[103] An understanding of his thought is not made easier by his emotional and flowery language, which owes much to Nietzsche. Typical is his *Essay on Inspiration* of 1886,[104] a kind of prose poem which combines ideas from the world of German idealism with the language of Walt Whitman. Sullivan's first contact with German idealism appears to have come through John Edelmann, a German whom he met in Jenney's office and whose 'theory of suppressed functions', as he wrote in his autobiography, had opened his eyes, with the result that 'the world of men began to assume a semblance of form, and of function.'[105] Sullivan, we may recall, had worked briefly in Furness's office in Philadelphia in 1873, and Furness was in direct communication with Emerson, through whom Sullivan could have become acquainted with the ideas of Greenough. However, Sullivan nowhere mentions Greenough in his writings.

Sullivan's autobiography is an important source of information about his conception of architecture, although the lateness of its date (1922–23) means that we must beware of taking it too literally. Looking back on his partnership with Adler, he writes, in a moment of self-characterisation in the third person, that it had been his aim at that time to realise the dream that he had long nourished, namely

> to make an architecture that fitted its functions – a realistic architecture based on well defined utilitarian needs – that all practical demands of utility should be paramount as basis of planning and design...[106]

All architecture must be apprehended plastically; all conventional rigidity must be removed from it, so that it can serve a sensible purpose and not become oppressive. Then comes the important conclusion:

> In this wise the forms under his [i.e. Sullivan's] hand would grow naturally out of the needs and express them frankly, and freshly. This meant...a formula he had evolved, through long contemplation of living things, namely that *form follows function.*[107]

The concept of function is central for Sullivan. He sees all forms of life as expressions of function, and each function creates its own form.[108] Functions in Nature are 'powers' of life. For architecture this means that the function of a building must determine its organisation and form. But this function is defined as the 'application to man's thought and deeds; to his inherent powers and the results of the application of these powers, mental, moral, physical...'[109] This is a law to which there is no exception. In his *Kindergarten Chats* he reiterates this more sharply: '...outward appearances resemble inner purposes...the form, oak-tree, resembles and expresses the purpose or function, oak.'[110] Good architecture must correspond to its function and express it in its appearance, as a whole and in detail – then it will be 'organic'.

Sullivan's concept of function also has its social roots. 'Concerning function and form,' he writes in *Kindergarten Chats*, 'it must be fairly clear to you that the spirit of democracy is a function seeking expression in organized social form.'[111] So to the question of an indigenous American style there is a ready answer: 'that a certain function, aspirant democracy, is seeking a certain form of expression, democratic architecture, and will surely find it.'[112] Hence: 'The form, American architecture, will mean, if it ever succeeds in meaning anything, American life.'[113] Among Sullivan's posthumous papers was found the manuscript of a substantial work on the subject of democracy.[114]

For Sullivan it is natural, social and intellectual factors, the sum of human needs, that constitute the functions which determine the form of a building. The technical, constructional aspect remains in the background and is barely mentioned. Sullivan's concern is to use architectural form to express human functions and needs, not structural laws. It is wrong to interpret his axiom 'Form follows function' in a functionalist, technological sense, for his concept of function is Romantic and thoroughly American.

A year after dissolving his partnership with Adler, Sullivan expanded on his concept of function in an article on that most American of buildings, the skyscraper,[115] where he gives its characteristic as vertical three-part division, lightness, 'power of altitude, glory and pride of exaltation'. The same year Adler replied to Sullivan in an essay *The Influence of Steel Construction and Plate Glass upon Style* (1896),[116] which advocates a material- and structure-based concept of function of the kind to which

Sullivan has often been held to subscribe. Adler's view is that new constructional opportunities produce new styles, a belief expounded with particular vigour by Auguste Choisy in his *Histoire de l'architecture*, published in 1899. Opposing the historicists, but also disagreeing with Sullivan, Adler maintained:

> We are still more blessed in being allowed the privilege of participating in the creation and in witnessing the birth of another epoch of architectural design, the form or style of which will be founded upon the discovery of the steel pillar, the steel beam, the clear sheet of plate glass, electric light and mechanical ventilation, all devoted to the service of functions or wants created by the greater intensity of modern life and by improved means of communication between places and men.[117]

Steel, glass and technology are for Adler the principal factors in a new American style – 'our contribution to the architecture of the new world, the new age of steel, electricity and scientific progress.'[118] Using a technological concept of function, he introduces into the equation the constantly changing historical situation, a factor he calls 'environment', and thus arrives at a reformulation of Sullivan's axiom as 'function and environment determine form.' Adler is a more modern, more pragmatic thinker than Sullivan. It is infillings and the cladding of steel girders that provide, in his view, the proper areas for artistic treatment: 'In these fillings and coverings we obtain media for artistic treatment which may be handled solely with reference to the desire to adapt "form" to "function".'[119] A remark such as this considerably detracts from Sullivan's role in their joint buildings, and this may well be the deeper reason why the two men parted company. After Adler's death in 1900 Sullivan was unable, left on his own, to execute any really significant building, with the exception of the Carson Pirie Scott store in Chicago. While still in partnership with Adler Sullivan had written a short essay in 1891 on the subject of skyscrapers, in which he published precise details, with illustrations, for possible forms of high-rise buildings which are set back,[120] thus anticipating the consequences of the urban zoning laws that were passed from 1916 onwards (*Plate 171*). In the same year Adler and Sullivan published a design for the Fraternity Temple setback skyscraper, but this was never executed. In an essay of 1892 entitled *Light in Tall Office Buildings* Adler himself also pronounced in favour of the setback form.[121]

As stated above, Sullivan's main sphere of activity in his partnership with Adler was ornamentation, and the question of his relationship between building and ornament occupied his mind throughout his life. The importance of ornament, as he wrote in his autobiography, was something that had been a concern of his since childhood; he saw it as standing in a causal relationship to the idea of Nature and its influence, and in it power was manifest. The analogy between biological growth and the development of power is central to Sullivan's thought. He understands architecture as a direct psychologically living language. He speaks of his childhood: 'Buildings had come to speak to Louis Sullivan in their many jargons. Some said vile things, some said prudent things, some said pompous things, but none said noble things.'[122] This sets him in the tradition of psychologising *architecture parlante*, as seen at its extreme in the eighteenth century in Nicolas Le Camus de Mézières.

Sullivan's important essay *Ornament in Architecture* (1892)[123] opens by declaring that a building can make its effect through mass and proportion alone, without ornament: ornament is an intellectual luxury, not a necessity. Hence: 'We should refrain entirely from the use of ornament for a period of years, in order that our thought might concentrate acutely upon the production of buildings well formed and comely in the nude.'[124] This comes close to the 'nakedness' of architecture of which Greenough spoke. These lines were written a year before the Chicago World's Fair of 1893, which spelt for Sullivan the destruction of the Chicago School by the historicism of the Beaux-Arts camp. In his *Autobiography* Sullivan writes bitterly:

> The damage wrought by the World's Fair will last for half a century from its date, if not longer. It has penetrated deep into the constitution of the American mind...There we have now the abounding freedom of Eclecticism, the winning smile of taste, but no architecture. For Architecture, be it known, is dead.[125]

Adolf Loos was also in Chicago for the World's Fair, and his essay *Ornament und Verbrechen* (1908) carries Sullivan's argument to a paradoxical extreme.

It was a vital matter of principle for Sullivan that ornament – 'a garment of poetic imagery', as he called it – was both desirable and important in architecture. It should grow out of the organic principle of function and form, which it should then express. It is the result of a logical process of growth and has to be governed by specific considerations of function, as does the form of the building. It must be individual, never interchangeable or with the appearance of having been superimposed, but looking as though 'it had come forth from the very substance of the material and was there by the same right that a flower appears amid the leaves of its parent plant.'[126]

Sullivan's fullest account of his principles of organic ornament comes in his book *A System of Architectural Ornament According with a Philosophy of Man's Powers* (1924).[127] Taking his stand on Swedenborg's dualistic concept of Nature,[128] he develops a grammar of ornament based on organic (embryonic) and inorganic (geometric) basic forms (*Plate 172*), in which through the overlapping of divisions and expansions, human power shows itself in action 'as applied to a specific form of activity called Architectural Ornament.'[129] This combination of organic and inorganic leads him to phrases such as 'the awakening of the pentagon in action',[130] a phrase in which we can recognise the kinds of ornament found in his buildings. This theory of the origin of ornamental forms has a parallel in Ruskin's ideas about ornament in the section 'The Nature of Gothic' in *The Stones of Venice* (*Plate 167*).

Sullivan's executed ornamentation, which even in his skyscrapers is used over the entire exterior, and in his few later buildings becomes a law unto itself, is far from being as organic in conception as he claimed, for it makes considerable use of models taken from Viollet-le-Duc and from Islamic architecture.[131] This is also the reason why his ornamentation seems today to have a period quality, and why even his contemporaries saw it as belonging to symbolism and Art Nouveau.[132] In fact, he is too closely identified, both as architect and theorist, with nineteenth-century Romantic idealist tradition to be regarded as a real pioneer of the Modern Movement – a role which in any case attracts little admiration today.

Similar to Sullivan both in his aims and in his links with the Transcendentalists was the composer Charles Ives (1874–1954), who was seeking an American style in music and who tried to express what Sullivan had defined in his complex concept of function. Certain passages in Ives' writings read like Sullivan's autobiography, for example his remarks on his Piano Sonata No 2, 'Concord, Mass. 1840–60', composed 1909–15.[133] One might go so far as to compare Ives' musical themes with Sullivan's language of ornamentation.

John Wellborn Root (1850–91),[134] a few years Sullivan's senior, joined in a partnership with Daniel Burnham in 1873 which rivalled that between Adler and Sullivan. Root had a friendship with Sullivan based on common interests in literature and music as well as in architecture, but there also appears to have been a certain jealousy between them, illustrated in Sullivan's observation: 'Architecturally, John Root's mania was to be the first to do this or that or the other.'[135] Root's writings,[136] consisting entirely of essays on the same or similar subjects to Sullivan's, appeared between 1883 and 1891, the year of his death, and thus antedate Sullivan's important later essays by a considerable period. The historical precedence laid claim to by Root may thus well be justified, but the whole question of the relationship between the two men needs further investigation. Root, incidentally, knew German and may well have put this knowledge at Sullivan's disposal. In its issues of 1889 and 1890 the journal *Inland Architect* published excerpts which he had translated from Semper's *Der Stil in den technischen und tektonischen Künsten.*[137]

Root's essay *Architectural Ornamentation* (1885)[138] reads like an advance criticism of Sullivan's views on ornament and takes a position close to that of Adler, whom Root succeeded as President of the Western Association of Architects in 1886. Ornament, says Root, must be subordinate to the construction of a building, and visible construction and decorative elements must not be confused: 'The confusion is greatest in the use of structural features to serve the purpose of decorative, of decorative features to perform the functions of structural...'[139]

Decoration must not conceal construction, nor must it assume any bogus functions. Thus a column, as a primarily structural feature, may be employed only as a load-bearing member and used only for decorative purposes on the smallest of scales, if at all, for 'it is the greatest of architectural crimes to use a great column in a large building for any purpose than primarily to bear loads.'[140] (Root speaks repeatedly of 'crimes' in architecture, and it may well be here that the roots of Adolf Loos's thinking lie.)

> As to the purpose of decoration it is, first, subordinate. It should never be applied so as to conceal the outline and intend of more elementary and essential features. It can never take the place of the vital parts of the structure.[141]

Root defines it as the duty of 'non-essential' ornament, in the service of 'politeness', 'first to avoid offense, and then confer pleasure.' Its form should depend on the beholder to whom it is meant to appeal and on the function of the building; it would be as grotesque to smother office blocks with ornament as to discuss poetry in the middle of the traffic in downtown Chicago. Ornament can give a building certain accents and rhythms, Root maintains, referring specifically to Ruskin, but all construction and decoration must be homogeneous in their expression 'as the organic creations of nature'. This leads him to a distinction between large and small buildings:

> Generally speaking...it will be found that simplest arrangements, not only of the features ornamented, but of the ornament itself, are best suited to great buildings, and more intricate and involved ornament best suited to smaller ones.[142]

He lays emphasis on decorative unity and condemns the use of eclectic set-pieces. On the question of polychromy he reaches similar conclusions, basing his argument on

Nature, where large forms tend to monochromy, smaller forms to polychromy. Caution is therefore to be exercised in the use of colour in large buildings.

Root's comparison of architecture to the processes of Nature – like Sullivan's – seems to be derived from a work hardly known today[143] but to which Root directly refers[144] – *The Nature and Function of Art, More Especially of Architecture* (1881), by Leopold Eidlitz, a native of Prague, working in New York, where we find a sentence such as the following: 'Carved ornament and color decoration have no other purpose than to heighten the expression of mechanical resistance to load and pressure in architectural organisms.'[145]

Root recognises the connection between the concept of ornament and the question of style. For him style signifies expression of construction; historical styles are linked to historical conditions, and there is no justification for using them at the present time. This is another principle that goes back to Ruskin. Moreover, style, which is linked in Root's mind with the concept of function, is the very 'life and existence of the work', and it is the external expression of the function of a house that constitutes its artistic value:

> As far as material conditions permit it to be possible, a building designated for a particular purpose should express that purpose in every part... The force with which that function is expressed measures its value as a work of art.[146]

Root's statements on style show the influence of Semper and also, probably, of Viollet-le-Duc, as his essay *Style* (1887)[147] reveals. Distinguishing historical styles from 'having style', he seeks to characterise the stylistic features of modern buildings in terms of the human qualities of 'Repose, Refinement, Self-containment, Sympathy, Discretion, Knowledge, Urbanity, Modesty', explaining how each of these characteristics in turn can be applied to architecture. On 'Repose', for example, he comes to the following conclusion:

> In large and important buildings, however, especially those built for commercial purposes, simple sky lines, I believe, experience will show to be best, as best conducive to the quality of repose – and more than this, because a very broken sky line is apt to suggest multiplicity of subdivisions or functions, and should, therefore, be coincident with these subdivisions or functions. This in commercial buildings can rarely be the case.[148]

The sequence Function-Ornament-Style leads Root naturally to the understanding of typology as the 'solution of a given problem' in architecture, a question to which he devotes his attention in an article *The Value of Type in Art* (1883),[149] in which he establishes 'Adherence to Type' as a principle of Nature. There is, he maintains, a 'persistence in certain solutions of given problems', with only minimal differences between the various solutions. It is interesting to note that Root later quotes as an example of his typological principle the Parthenon on the Acropolis in Athens, calling it 'perfection as a solution of a given problem'.[150] This formulation recalls that of Greenough, and points forward to Le Corbusier's conclusions on standardisation, which are also based on the example of the Parthenon.

In 1890 Root published an article on skyscrapers, *A Great Architectural Problem*,[151] in which he showed himself closer to Adler than to Sullivan. As an expression of the 'age of steam, of electricity, of gas, of plumbing and sanitation', the skyscraper has to convey the needs of modern life, and to seek to evolve a 'national' style for this purpose is pointless. The exterior should display 'a reasonable appreciation of conditions of our civilization, of our social and business life and of our climatic conditions', a consideration which leads him back to his demand for ornament-free skyscrapers which should express the ideas of modern commercial life through mass and proportion – 'simplicity, stability, breadth, dignity'.[152] A further requirement is extreme economy of material. In fact, Root sees the skyscraper in the functionalist terms often ascribed to Sullivan. His conclusion is as follows:

> So vital has the underlying structure of these buildings become that it must absolutely dictate the general departure of external forms; and so imperative are all the commercial and constructive demands that all architectural detail employed in expressing them must become modified by them.[153]

Root entered into discussions of theory with some of his clients, such as Peter Brooks, who commissioned the Montauk Block (now demolished) in Chicago in 1881 with the stipulation that it be an undecorated brick structure: 'The building throughout is to be for use and not for ornament. Its beauty will be in its all-adaption to its use.'[154] Similarly the Monadnock Block (1889–91) dispenses with all ornament, while in the slightly earlier 'Rookery' (1885–86) ornament has been totally 'subordinated'.

Root was a clearer and more realistic thinker than Sullivan, and had a narrower conception of function, but he did not confine himself to a purist constructional functionalism of the kind preached by Lodoli or by certain twentieth-century writers. In a piece written shortly before his death he blamed himself for having been too ready to adapt, and as such 'to have been to a large extent the victim of his own moods.'[155]

Sullivan and Root are without doubt among the most incisive thinkers on architecture in America at the end of the nineteenth century. But striking though the impact of their thought was on the buildings of the time, it was also shortlived; furthermore, it was confined to the Mid-West. On the East and West Coasts a European-based historicism still prevailed, which after the World's Fair in Chicago extended its dominance to the Mid-West as well. This development came with Root's versatile and business-minded partner Daniel H. Burnham (1846–1912),[156] who was responsible for the lay-out of the World's Fair of 1893 – Root had died two years earlier – and brought in architects of the Beaux-Arts tradition to carry out his plans. Burnham was ready to compromise stylistically. At the same time some of the technologically and formally most advanced skyscrapers, such as the Reliance Building (1894–95) in Chicago, continued to be designed in his office.

Burnham's principal claim to fame, however, is as a town-planner. His plan for Chicago published in 1909 is the first comprehensive American city project.[157] In it Burnham combined the American block gridiron system with the concept of a huge Civic Center, radial and concentric avenues, a rationalised traffic system and a twenty-mile-long green strip along the shore of Lake Michigan. It is clear from the illustrations that Burnham was strongly influenced by Haussmann's plan for Paris. His megalomaniac project, which covered an area of 60-mile radius from the centre of Chicago, set the tone for the 'City Beautiful' movement, which aimed to bring 'dignity' to the cities of America. 'Make no little plans,' said Burnham; 'they have no magic to stir men's blood…Make big plans; aim high in hope and work, remembering that a noble diagram once recorded will never die.'

At the end of the nineteenth century the dream of a national American style of architecture had still not been fulfilled. Historical styles dominated the scene: Richardson had given a fillip to neo-Romanesque; neo-Gothic, encouraged by the considerable influence of Ruskin, retained its importance into the 1920s, its verticalism being regarded as particularly appropriate to skyscraper construction;[158] neo-Renaissance flourished in the buildings of the McKim, Mead and White partnership,[159] where the influence of Richardson and, through him, of the Ecole des Beaux-Arts, asserted itself. In short, the key word was eclecticism,[160] a word that retained its force considerably longer in America than in Europe.

From 1880 onwards the effects of the English Arts and Crafts movement began to show themselves in America, both in architecture and in design.[161] Oscar Wilde made a lecture tour of the country in 1882–83 on behalf of the movement, and in 1896 and 1901 C.R. Ashbee, founder of the Guild and School of Handicraft, was also there, meeting Frank Lloyd Wright during his stay. Gustav Stickley (1857–1942) of Wisconsin, who went to Europe in 1898, on his return in 1901 founded the journal *The Craftsman*, which became a mouthpiece for the ideas of Ruskin and Morris. In 1909 Stickley published a selection of pieces from the journal in his book *Craftsman Homes*, with brief commentaries of his own.[162] His sole concern was with the country house, for which he put forward the criteria of 'simplicity, durability, fitness for the life...harmony with its natural surroundings.'[163] For the exterior of country houses he stipulated 'simplicity of building materials, employment of constructive features as the only decoration, and the recognition of the color element.'[164] As in the Ruskin tradition, Nature is the only criterion of universal validity, and his designs exhibit the simplicity for which he called, largely dispensing with ornament.

Also part of this tradition are the slightly younger architects of the firm of Greene & Greene, and the early work of Frank Lloyd Wright, in whom the ideas of Louis Sullivan and the Arts and Crafts movement come together. The true context of these figures, however, is the twentieth century, not the nineteenth.

25. Germany and its neighbours: 1890s–1945

'International' is one of the catchwords of twentieth-century architecture. From the 1920s onwards, an international architecture emerged which looked everywhere the same, irrespective of climatic, political or economic conditions. Today, however, we know that the 'international style' denotes only one line of development among many, and that attempts to evolve regional and national modes of expression have been going on at the same time – indeed, such attempts have probably predominated most of the time. Gone are the days when writers on architecture, obsessed by a sense of mission, dismissed as anachronistic, irrelevant, chauvinistic, etc. whatever did not conform to the line of 'international architecture'. In fact, national movements, in architecture as in other fields, were hardly less in evidence in the first half of the twentieth century than they had been in the nineteenth, so that it will be appropriate to continue the present survey in basically national terms. At the same time it should be noted that theoretical discussion is often rooted in so many differing traditions that it is impossible to arrive at a single unified 'line of development'.

The last figure discussed in Chapter 22 on nineteenth-century Germany was the Viennese architect Otto Wagner. Of the Viennese architects of the following generation, only Adolf Loos (1870–1933) left a body of writing that amounts to anything approaching a system; contemporaries such as Josef Hoffmann and Joseph Maria Olbrich left nothing to the present purpose. Most of Loos's statements about architecture are of an epigrammatic and often paradoxical nature.[1] His starting-point is the work of Semper, as is made clear in his essay *Das Prinzip der Bekleidung* (1898), in which he summarises Semper's theory of cladding, laying special emphasis on truth to materials:

> Every material has its own formal language, and no material can assume for itself the forms of another material. These forms have emerged from the way in which each material has been produced and employed: they have come into being *with* the material and *through* the material. No material permits interference with its own set of forms.[2]

Where Semper had started from the textile wall-hanging, Loos now wrote: 'The oldest architectural detail is the ceiling', deducing from this that 'cladding is older than structure.'[3] For Loos architecture was not primarily construction, but space with the task of creating effects and 'stimulating human moods ['*Stimmungen*']':

> The challenge facing the architect is thus how to make this mood precise. A room must look comfortable, a house must look habitable. The law courts must appear like a threatening gesture to a secret vice. The bank building must say: Here is your money, safe and sound in the hands of honest folk.[4]

This is a transference to the category of space of eighteenth-century ideas of how to achieve an *architecture parlante* by means of mass and decoration. Loos sees architecture primarily as an arrangement of spaces which becomes consolidated as a '*Raumplan*' ('space plan'), though he did not develop this into a formal theory.[5] The direction of his thought, however, is clear: 'The great revolution in architecture is the solution of a plan in space.'[6] The *Raumplan* leads him to create split levels and room heights in domestic interiors, as with occasional exterior terraces, but his house projects of the 1920s tend to have exteriors characterised by a rigid symmetry, a monumentality and a Neo-classicism which make for an awkward relationship to his idea of the *Raumplan*. The source of the discrepancy may lie in his frequently-declared admiration for the architecture of Antiquity: 'We are able to state that the great architect of the future will be a Classicist – not a man who takes his lead from the works of his predecessors but one who goes back directly to Classical Antiquity.'[7] Only in terms of statements like this is it possible to understand the Greek Doric column design that he entered for the Chicago Tribune Tower competition in 1922.

Loos's rejection of ornament was by no means as total as is often made out. When, in his essay of 1898, he refers to the stimulus that architecture can derive from archaeology–'There are signs that this is already happening in the new ornamentation of the Wagner School' – his tone is one of approval.[8] What he objects to is modern ornament that neither conforms to its materials nor expresses the spirit of the age.

Loos was in America from 1893 to 1896,[9] and his conception of ornament was influenced by Greenough, Sullivan and Root, even down to verbal formulation. In 1843, for example, Greenough had described architectural 'nakedness' as displaying 'the majesty of the essential'; in 1892, in his essay *Ornament in Architecture*, Sullivan had proposed a temporary ban on all architectural ornament, because the organic link between function, form, material and expression had been broken, while Root, in his essay *Architectural Ornamentation* (1885), had called the false and excessive use of ornament an 'architectural crime', and demanded that skyscrapers be kept entirely free of ornament. During his stay in America Loos may also have come into contact with the ornament-free architecture and functionally designed utensils of the Shakers.[10] This American tradition is to be sensed behind some of his statements in the essay *Ornament und Verbrechen* ('Ornament and Crime', 1908). For example:

> Since ornament is no longer organically linked with our civilisation, it is no longer an expression of our civilisation. The ornament being created today is not connected with us, is not connected with anybody, not connected with the order of the world.[11]

He then tries to put this negative situation to positive effect, declaring, in an ironical tone:

> Weep not. For behold, what makes our age great is that it is incapable of producing new ornamentation. For we have conquered ornament, have fought ourselves free of it. Behold, the time is nigh, and fulfilment awaits us. Soon the streets of our cities will shine like white walls, like Zion, the Holy City, the capital of Heaven. Then we shall find fulfilment.[12]

Loos became obsessed with the idea of a continuous cultural development from the tattooed aborigines of Papua down to modern man, who regards tattooing as a crime. Loos thus concludes: 'The evolution of culture is synonymous with the removal of ornament from articles of everyday use.'[13] Such epigrammatic statements are repeated from work to work: 'Not only is ornament produced by criminals but it also commits a crime itself by causing grave injury to human health, to the natural economy and hence to cultural development.'[14] He equates ornaments with 'wasted labour' and 'desecrated material'.

This challenging essay provoked misunderstandings, and was obviously intended to do so. But as his own buildings show, Loos was utterly serious in his demand for freedom from ornament. In *Ornament und Erziehung* (1924) we read: 'Absence of ornament is not absence of charm but is stimulating and acts as a new incentive. It is the mill that does *not* clatter that makes the miller.'[15] Or: 'Form and ornament are the product of the unconscious labour of the people of a whole culture. Everything else is art.'[16] Thus individual ornament, such as the artists and craftsmen of Art Nouveau and the Deutscher Werkbund sought to create, was in Loos's eyes a contradiction in terms, which is why he so brusquely rejected the Werkbund and the Wiener Werkstätte. The beauty of a practical object depended on the degree of its practical value. Ornament was possible only as the collective expression of an age – but not of the present age. Loos is at pains, however, to set the record straight: 'I have never meant, as the purists have carried *ad absurdum*, that ornament must be rigorously and systematically abolished.'[17]

Art, for Loos, is subjective and devoid of purpose; architecture, on the other hand, must serve public needs. So architecture is not art, nor has the craftsman, whose work he values highly, anything to do with the artist:

Am I saying that a house has nothing to do with art, and that architecture is not to be reckoned among the arts? Indeed I am. Only a very small part of architecture belongs to art – tombstones and monuments. Everything else that serves a particular purpose must be excluded from the realms of art.[18]

Loos's ideas are often contradictory. They also run counter to contemporary trends, such as that of the Werkbund, which sought to bring artist and craftsman together. Nor is it always possible to take his high-flown statements seriously. His scattered observations hardly constitute a system – and this may indicate that he pointedly never attempted to produce one.

The same contradiction between interior and exterior runs through Loos's own executed buildings. Indeed, the discrepancy became even greater in his later designs, and continued to characterise the work of his pupils, so that it might even be said that the most fully typical Loos design is not by Loos himself but by his friend, the philosopher Ludwig Wittgenstein, who, together with Loos's pupil Paul Engelmann, built a lavish house in Vienna for his sister, Margarethe Stonborough-Wittgenstein, between 1926 and 1928.[19] The 'logic in the form of a house' ('*hausgewordene Logik*') of this design shows the same uncompromising desire for precision as Wittgenstein's *Tractatus logico-philosophicus* (1921), at the very beginning of which occurs the phrase 'logical space' ('*logischer Raum*').[20] Wittgenstein's sister Hermine wrote in her memoirs of 'the precision that constitutes beauty', and Wittgenstein himself spoke in a letter to a firm of building contractors of 'the precision and propriety necessary for this type of building.'[21]

Through its early receptivity to English ideas, seen in exhibitions devoted to the Arts and Crafts movement and in the foundation of the Werkstätte, Vienna became the first important outpost of new architectural ideas in Central Europe, an importance to which the absorption of American ideas into the work of Loos also contributed.

In the years leading up to the Great War, a remarkable development of a different kind took place in Prague, where a group of artists and architects founded the Skupina Výtvarných Umělců ('Group of Creative Artists'). The group's aim was to apply the new ideas of cubism to all the fine arts, applied arts and architecture.[22] The architects in the group came directly or indirectly from Otto Wagner's school in Vienna, and their spokesman on theoretical matters, Pavel Janák (1882–1956), whose writings are today almost forgotten, embarked on a penetrating critique of the 'materialistic' view of modern architecture. In his articles, most of which were published in the journal *Umělecký měsíčník*, Janák openly challenged the supremacy of function, construction and materials as criteria, emphasising instead artistic expression, which he saw as manifested in plastic forms.[23] He was concerned not to make a break with the past but to establish the continuity of tradition. He defined architecture as the plastic formation of dynamic geometrical masses, to which construction and materials must be made subservient. In his essay *Das Prisma und die Pyramide* (1910) he makes frequent reference to the Baroque, of which a generally negative view was taken at this time, and concludes: 'Such historical movements in architecture arouse our attention by the vivacity of the spirit that has penetrated their material, and by the dramatic nature of the means of expression with whose help their forms have been created.'[24] The most important buildings in this Prague cubist movement are those of Josef Gočár, built around 1911–12, whose formal language points forward to that of the Expressionist architecture of the 1920s and to Art Deco.[25]

In Germany it was above all the ideas of the Arts and Crafts movement that led first to the Deutscher Werkbund and later to the Bauhaus. The first manifestations of the movement in the field of architecture were the activity of Baillie Scott (1897–98) and the Mathildenhöhe Park in Darmstadt (1901). From these examples it is clear that English utopian ideas were recast in Germany in pragmatic economic terms.[26] The most important figure in the transmission of English ideas to Germany was the architect Hermann Muthesius (1861–1927), who was German architectural attaché in London from 1896 to 1903 and published articles in German journals on his experiences in Britain.[27] He also wrote three books on English architecture,[28] the three-volume *Das englische Haus* (1904–05) being the most influential. This is a broad historical survey, although the author concedes that his main focus of attention is the emergence of the architect-designed, middle-class house from around 1860 down to his own day. 'It was not so much my purpose,' he wrote in his introduction, 'to commend the imitation of the English house or its details, as to convey to German readers the cast of mind of those who created it.'[29]

The functionalist sentiments underlying the three epigraphs – from Emerson, Bacon and Viollet-le-Duc – at the beginning of the three volumes are indicative of Muthesius's purpose. He constantly draws attention to the way in which the English house concentrates on necessities and practical considerations. He gives a sympathetic description of the aesthetics of Ruskin and William Morris, failing, however, to mention their socialist background. Morris and Philip Webb's Red House is described as 'the first individual house of the new artistic culture, the first house to be conceived and executed as a whole, interior and exterior, the very first example in the history of the modern house.'[30] Muthesius was particularly attracted to W.R. Lethaby and C.F.A. Voysey: Lethaby's houses he describes as austere, sombre, almost joyless but extraordinarily powerful and self-confident, aesthetically cerebral,[31] while Voysey's 'confine themselves to utter simplicity' and bear 'the stamp of primitivity'.[32] The English house, which cannot, by virtue of the entirely different historical and social conditions from which it emerged, be transferred to Germany, is for him the epitome of simplicity, objectivity and propriety.

The real, decisive value of the English house lies in its utter objectivity. In a word, it is a house in which one desires to live. Money is not spent on prestigious gardens and grounds, there is no fantastic display of ornaments and bits and pieces, no inflation of natural features in achievements of 'art', no pretentiousness, even no 'architecture'. There it stands, without pomp and without affectation, in its natural propriety, a quality that should be so natural but which in our present civilisation has become so rare.[33]

The second volume of Muthesius's book, which is devoted to the functions of the English house, begins and ends with Bacon's maxim: 'Houses are built to live in, not to look at.' The values extolled by Muthesius in the English house are the conquest of historical style, simplicity and 'artistic reticence' ('*künstlerische Enthaltsamkeit*'). His interest is directed entirely to architectural form and 'atmosphere', not to ideological implications.

From 1904 Muthesius combined a career as an architect with a post in the Prussian Ministry of Trade concerned with the reorganisation of Arts and Crafts and Technical Colleges. In response to his experiences in England and the reorganisation of the Arts and Crafts Colleges, he delivered an address at the Handelshochschule in Berlin in the spring of 1907, on the rôle of arts and crafts in contemporary life,[34] which aroused violent protests from official bodies and led later that year to the foundation by Muthesius, the liberal politician Friedrich Naumann and others, of the Deutscher Werkbund in Munich. He contrasted his understanding of the situation in England with the historicism which he characterised as 'the filtering and refiltering of the art of the past.'

If one wishes to take proper account of the conditions of the age, one must first take account of the conditions that govern each individual art object. The initial task of the applied arts today is to become fully aware of the purpose of each individual art object and to develop the form consistent with this purpose. As soon as one turns one's attention away from the superficial imitation of the art of the past, and as soon as the real situation has been grasped, other requirements will present themselves. Every material demands to be treated in its own particular way. Stone requires different dimensions and different forms from wood, wood is different from metal, and among the metals themselves, wrought iron is different from silver. Design according to purpose is thus married to design according to character of material, and considerations of material lead to the construction appropriate to the material. Purpose, material and construction provide the modern craftsman with the only directives he need follow.[35]

As Muthesius saw it, the function of the applied arts was social and educational: 'The goal of the applied arts today is to re-educate our social classes in the paths of uprightness, truthfulness and personal simplicity as citizens.'[36] These principles were also to be applied to public and private architecture, on the reform of which the influence of the applied arts could be brought to bear. Muthesius emphasised the economic necessity of bringing about changes in the applied arts in conjunction with manufacturers and trade, the former having the duty to accept the new style, which would not come about overnight but emerge as 'the sum of all the honest efforts of the age'. Muthesius used the economic argument that 'raising the quality of German workmanship will simultaneously raise the reputation of German products in the markets of the world.'

By combining crafts, industry and commerce, Muthesius sought a way of overcoming the economic collapse of the Arts and Crafts movement. Others, artists and craftsmen, who had also come under the influence of England, had similar ideas, but Muthesius alone, with his insight into the situation and the advantages of his ministerial office, was able to make the problem a national issue. A group calling itself 'The Association for the Preservation of the Economic Interests of the Applied Arts' tried to engineer Muthesius's dismissal but the only result was to accelerate the foundation of the Deutscher Werkbund, the principal ideas of which had already been formulated by Muthesius himself.[37]

For Muthesius, proceeding from English starting-points, as well as for the Werkbund, architecture was a complex concept. In 1908 he wrote of architecture as 'that comprehensive, all-pervasive sense characteristic of the Greeks and also, less consciously, of the Middle Ages.'[38] *Ingenieurbau*, the application of rational engineering principles to building, became not only a new form of construction but a new form of architecture as such, with its own aesthetic. New challenges meant new techniques and new materials – railways, bridges, steamships, machines.[39] 'The form of construction calculated to be the most concise...the most concise form of expression of what is structurally correct...makes a definite impression on the receptive beholder.'[40] *Ingenieurarchitektur* was a response to the 'practical demands of modern life', not only to be understood as an expression of the age but also to be 'enjoyed'. The absence of solid walls in steel-and-glass buildings would lead to the removal of aesthetic conventions, so that we should 'recognise in this material-conquering slimness and transparency a new artistic dimension to which special value will become attached.'[41]

Here Muthesius attempts to integrate the arguments of an engineering-based aesthetic into architecture, but still adheres to the basic principles of architecture, which he finds grounded in 'proportion, logic and rhythm'.[42] It is difficult today to follow his idea that a national architecture 'must be based on unity of expression' ('*Einheitlichkeit des Ausdrucks*') – a phrase that the National Socialists were later to use for their own ends. Twenty years earlier Root had used almost the same argument in Chicago to demonstrate the fallacy of the notion of a national architecture, though he and Muthesius share a conviction of the need to develop discrete, standardised 'types' on the basis of unified forms of expression. One sector of the Werkbund espoused the cause of the codification of design, including that of houses, into types, and almost succeeded in splitting the movement in 1914, when Muthesius put forward his theses on typology at the annual congress. Artists such as Henry van de Velde saw in the theory of types a betrayal of the artist's individuality and a threat of paralysis, which would prevent the emergence of a new style.

The Deutscher Werkbund was a loose association of artists, craftsmen and industrialists which had a considerable influence on industrial design without subscribing to one particular 'style'. Initially architecture did not figure prominently in the Werkbund's activities, and this continued to be the case until the second phase of its existence in the 1920s. The aim of the Werkbund was to combine national, economic and artistic interests, as defined in article 2 of its constitution: 'The aim of the Werkbund is to ennoble the work of the craftsman in the collaboration of arts, crafts and industry, through education, publicity and a united response to relevant questions.'[43] The first yearbooks published by the movement, with essays on subjects such as 'The Spiritualisation of German Labour' (1912), 'Industry and Commerce' (1913) and 'Traffic' (1914), show the directions in which it was heading. Unlike the English Arts and Crafts movement, the Werkbund sought aesthetic reform via industry: its attitude towards machines was basically positive, whereas that of the English movement was ambivalent in this respect. The difference is made clear by Peter Jessen in an article in the nature of a manifesto entitled *Der Werkbund und die Großmächte der deutschen Arbeit* ('The Werkbund and the Great Powers of German Labour'):

> Formerly one looked for salvation to the craftsmen of the medieval school...In today's economy it is the employers who set the tone; if we want to move forwards, we must win them over to our cause and convince them that business and taste need not be enemies.[44]

Here is an obvious turning towards industry.

In the yearbook of the Werkbund for 1913 both Muthesius and Walter Gropius wrote on *Industriebau* and the relationship between industry and architecture. Gropius had a clear-cut view of the relationship between technology, design and aesthetics:

> Not only in the manufacture of everyday articles but also in the construction of machines, vehicles and factory buildings which exist simply to serve a given purpose, does account have to be taken of aesthetic values from the outset in respect of unity of form, colour and overall elegance. It is no longer sufficient today simply to improve the quality of products in order to achieve success in international competition – a product that is technically excellent in every respect must be permeated with intellectual content, with form, if it is to secure a position of precedence among the mass of similar such products. Hence the whole of industry is today faced with the task of devoting itself seriously to artistic questions.[45]

Artistic beauty in factory buildings has a publicity value, says Gropius, pointing to the 'nobility and strength' of Behrens's AEG buildings in Berlin and to the 'unknown majesty' and 'monumental power' of grain silos and factories in America, which he compares with the architecture of ancient Egypt.[46] Such statements explain the formal principles that lie behind Gropius's factory building in Alfeld (1911) and the model factory he contributed to the Werkbund Exhibition in Cologne in 1914.

In an article *Das Form-Problem im Ingenieurbau* (1913) Muthesius restates in essence his position of 1908, adding a warning, based on an instinct educated by historical experience, against regarding purely functional form as possessing aesthetic beauty. The machine occupies an important position in his scheme of things:

> Maybe it was not realised in the past that the simple fulfilment of a purpose does not in itself create visually attractive form but that other forces are also needed, even if they are unconscious. At all events, of all the products of the engineer's hand, it is first and foremost the machine that has developed its own pure style, a style which by the beginning of the present century was so advanced that it became customary to admire the so-called 'beauty of the machine', and to see in this quality the clearest manifestation of a modern style.[47]

The Werkbund applied the same criteria to architecture as to commercial design, although there remained a gap between pure functionalism and creative form which it was the task of the artist and craftsman to bridge. The concept of architecture became all-embracing with the union of civil engineering, mechanical design and the applied arts. The clearest example of the union of artist, architect and designer is Peter Behrens (1868–1940), who worked for the AEG electrical company, where his responsibility extended from architectural planning to design and advertising.[48] Influenced by Nietzsche in his early writings,[49] Behrens was one of the most successful German architects in the early years of the twentieth century, but was not a particularly original thinker. What he had to say, he said in his buildings.[50] Nevertheless his views remain typical of the early phase of the Werkbund's activities, such as those expressed in his article *Der Einfluß von Zeit- und Raumausnutzung auf moderne Formenentwicklung* ('The Influence of Use of Time and Space on the Evolution of Modern Forms') in the Werkbund's yearbook for 1914, where, following Alois Riegl's theory of artistic form ('*Kunstwollen*') he defined architecture as 'the rhythmic embodiment of the Zeitgeist.'[51] Conscious of the increasing speed of modern life, Behrens demanded an architecture 'of surfaces as unified and restful as possible...compact, with no obstructions'.[52] In town-planning he advocated 'long, straight streets', laid out in a manner similar to the 'axial plans of the Baroque age', while the trend towards 'higher buildings' meant that city centres bore in themselves the seeds of new development: 'Cities too strive for substantiality and silhouette, which can be achieved only in the union of compact, vertical masses.'[53] This was an argument in favour of skyscrapers and an aesthetic conception of the skyline. His concept of rhythm led him to judge ships, locomotives and automobiles according to the 'stylishness of their lines'—an idea that anticipates Le Corbusier, who worked in Behrens's studio in 1910.

There were always conflicts of interest in the Werkbund, some of them open, others latent. The tensions between economics and art could never be laid to rest. This was apparent at the Werkbund's first exhibition in the summer of 1914 in Cologne and at the accompanying congress. Carl Rehorst, chief architect to the city of Cologne, described the exhibition as 'a parade of the best forces in German work',[54] thereby striking a nationalistic and economic note by no means consonant with the artistic aspirations of all Werkbund members. And when the outbreak of the Great War brought the exhibition to a premature end, many became all the more convinced that they had become too deeply involved in political and economic matters.

On the whole the 1914 exhibition[55] had considerable artistic tolerance, its buildings displaying features of nationalism, folk-art and Neo-classicism. The outcome, the work of Gropius, van de Velde and Taut excepted, carried little conviction, and many of the participants themselves regarded the exhibition as a failure.

In an address to the congress on the future of the Werkbund, Muthesius gave his reasons for supporting the principle of type in architecture: 'It is characteristic of architecture to press towards standard types. Typology, in its turn, spurns the abnormal and seeks the normal.'[56] This address, together with a public statement of principles by Muthesius on the same question, provoked a passionate argument and induced van de Velde to issue a set of counter-principles. The most far-sighted objections to Muthesius's position, however, came from Karl Ernst Osthaus, who, having examined the relationship between type and standardisation, came to the conclusion: 'Everything is in a state of flux, and to identify today a form of typological codification, let alone to demand it, would be to anticipate history. Apart from that, type has nothing to do with art...'[57]

The Great War brought the first phase of the Werkbund virtually to an end. When the movement restarted in 1919, its development was highly erratic,[58] as may be seen from its journal *Die Form*.[59] In his address to the association in 1919, Hans Poelzig used evocative phrases like 'eternal values' and 'the soul of the people', and demanded the divorce of art and handicrafts from industry and commerce, for 'commerce and industry have in the main merely prostituted art.' Architecture, according to Poelzig, would assert itself as 'the great art which will draw together all the other arts and lead them forward,' and the work of the Werkbund, as 'the conscience of the nation', would have to be 'firmly established on a basis of artistic values and craftsmanship, not of technical and industrial conceptions.'[60]

In the 1920s discussions within the Werkbund became markedly irrational, moralising and political in tone, and often stood in stark contrast to those of its initial years. Programmes were often reduced to hollow slogans, and the centre of interest moved towards urban planning, housing and the construction industry. At the same time its exhibitions, such as *Form ohne Ornament* ('Form without ornament') in Stuttgart in 1924 and *Die Wohnung* ('The House') at the Weißenhofsiedlung in Stuttgart in 1927, attracted considerable attention. The latter, in particular, made a great impact in its championship of the cause of internationalism.[61] But so heterogeneous were the trends within the movement at this time that there is little point in looking for a single coherent theory.

At the exhibition in 1914 there had been a design on display which was difficult to reconcile with the Werkbund's aims. This was the Glass Pavilion (Glashaus) of Bruno Taut (1880–1938). Moving from a utopian Expressionism to Neue Sachlichkeit, then to a Neo-classicism devoid of rational basis, Taut is a characteristic representative of a conception of architecture that vacillated between an exaggerated aestheticism and a commitment to socialism.[62] His numerous writings enable us to trace this development.[63] These writings, especially from the period after the Great War, arose from his enforced inactivity as a practical architect, and are of particular interest as revelations of what was running through the minds of the Expressionists of the time.[64] After his training in Berlin Taut came into contact with the architects, writers and artists of the so-called Chorin Circle, and, by way of the Expressionist journal *Sturm*, met the novelist Paul Scheerbart (1863–1915), whose fantastic works combined socialist ideas with mystic cosmic visions of the future.[65] Conceiving the idea of movable, floating cities, Scheerbart wrote a novel, *Glasarchitektur* (1914), dedicated to Taut, in which he used glass to symbolise the better human race that is to come.[66] The work opens:

> We live most of the time in enclosed rooms. These form the milieu from which our culture grows. Our culture is to a certain extent a product of our architecture. If we wish to raise our culture to a higher level, we are compelled willy-nilly to transform our architecture. And this will become possible only if we remove the closed quality from the rooms in which we live. This we can do only by introducing glass architecture, which admits the light of sun and moon and stars not only through a few windows but through as many walls as possible, walls made of glass, of coloured glass. The new milieu that we thereby create must provide us with a new culture.[67]

For Taut and the other Expressionists of the post-war years who were members of a secret society they called the 'Gläserne Kette' ('Glass Chain'), glass symbolised the purified mankind of the future. And to the age-old symbolism of glass[68] were added the attraction of German mysticism and an interpretation of Gothic by men such as Wilhelm Worringer and Karl Scheffler, which owed much to English tradition.

Taut's Glashaus was the first building in which these ideas were expressed. Its construction was entrusted to glass manufacturers, and it bore an inscription consisting of mottos (*Glashaussprüche*) by Scheerbart, to whom the building was dedicated.[69] Taut's accompanying pamphlet shows the Glashaus on the title-page, with the caption 'The Gothic cathedral is the prelude to glass architecture', and opens with the above-quoted passage from Scheerbart's *Glasarchitektur* (*Plate 173*). Taut then proceeds to launch his programme with the axiom 'The Glashaus has no other purpose than to be beautiful', describing in detail the aesthetic effects he was setting out to achieve, and concluding:'What we urgently need in present-day architecture is to be liberated from the perpetual depressing clichés of monumentalism. The only thing that can bring this about is a flowing quality, a sense of artistic lightness.'[70]

In the years that followed, these ideas came to acquire a life of their own in Taut's mind and no longer had any influence on his actual buildings. In three books, published immediately after the end of the Great War and still largely in Scheerbart's shadow – *Die Stadtkrone* (1919), *Alpine Architektur* (1919) and *Die Auflösung der Städte* (1920)[71] – he propounded the thesis of an architecture that would dominate the world, and transform mountains into buildings, existing for beauty alone and virtually ceasing to serve any useful purpose. In his play *Der Weltbaumeister* (1920) the creative power of the architect is portrayed through the creation and disintegration of colours and forms in the universe; with the addition of music by Hans Pfitzner, the work was intended to provide an experience of synaesthesia.[72] At the centre of the utopian city in his novel *Die Stadtkrone*, in which he quotes architectural examples from all over the world, stands a glass palace; the city itself is planned in a manner both mythological and totalitarian. At the head of *Alpine Architektur* stands the revealing motto '*Aedificare necesse est, vivere non est necesse.*'

Visions of this kind scarcely accord with the commitment to socialism that led Taut to help found the Workers' Council for Art (Arbeitsrat für Kunst) in 1918, an association of artists that grew out of the November Revolution.[73] Typical of his revolutionary attitude is a high-flown pronouncement such as the following:

> A great building plan, so powerful that it will henceforth fill the leisure time of all men and women, the adornment of this planet earth by us, its organs, must be hammered into the minds of the public with all available means.[74]

Taut's pamphlet *Ein Architekturprogramm* (1918) calls for the unity of all the arts under the leadership of architecture: 'There will be no dividing-line between the applied arts and painting or sculpture; all will become one: building.'[75] At the same time the early signs are already there of the architect who was to become one of the great planners of social housing, demanding 'the basic subjection of formal considerations to agricultural and practical interests, with no inhibitions about the simplest of things or about colour.'[76]

A major record of Taut's ideas is the correspondence between him, his brother Max, Hermann Finsterlin, Walter Gropius, Hans Scharoun, the Luckhardt brothers and the other members of the secret society he founded in 1919, the Gläserne Kette.

Parts of this correspondence were published in *Frühlicht*, the journal which Taut edited from 1920 to 1922 and which is one of the principal documents of Expressionist thought on architecture.[77] One of the early numbers contains an illustrated text by Taut entitled *Haus des Himmels* – a combination of the symbolism of mystical numbers, the symbolism of glass and pure aesthetics (*Plate 174*), containing passages like the following:

> A house should be nothing other than beautiful. It should fulfil no other purpose than to be empty, as Master Eckhart, the medieval mystic, put it... The visitor will be filled with the joy of architecture, which will drain all human elements from his soul and make it a receptacle for the divine. Building is the reflection and the greeting of the stars: its plan is stelliform, the holy numbers 3 and 7 combine in it to form a unity... The illumination comes from between the interior and exterior glass shell... If one flies to the house at night in an aeroplane, it shines from afar like a star. And it rings like a bell.[78]

Frühlicht marks the end of the visionary, Expressionist phase of Taut's thought. In 1921 he was appointed city architect in Magdeburg, where he executed house façades reflecting his ideas on coloured buildings.[79] He had taken a close interest in Dutch housing projects of the early 1920s, and a few years later he accepted an appointment as consultant and design architect to the trade union housing organisation Gehag in Berlin, where, using standardised plans and prefabricated units, he built the housing estates in the Berlin suburbs of Zehlendorf, Britz and elsewhere which are his lasting monument. Making domestic dwellings the new focus of his writings, but still referring constantly to Scheerbart, he was now concerned 'predominantly with economic and practical issues, with developing a particular interest in machines, and for the rest confining aesthetic matters to the sidelines.'[80] He goes on: 'Once one has thrown out of one's house, using the strictest and most merciless of criteria, everything – and I mean everything – that is not essential for one's life, then not only will the work of its upkeep become easier but a new beauty will automatically emerge.'[81] He provided contrasting illustrations of rooms before and after his 'purification' (*Plate 175*). Taut's conception of the domestic dwelling was one governed by the technical potentialities of industry. He saw the future of private housing as resting with the techniques of prefabrication, and asked only that, as with the automobile, the parts be assembled 'organically'.[82] This is close to pure functionalism.

Taut showed the same adaptability when, after a disappointing period in Russia, he went to Japan (1933–36) and wrote both on the significance of Western architecture for Japan and on Japanese architecture. The main product of this period is a theoretical work, *Architekturlehre aus der Sicht eines sozialistischen Architekten*, which he completed in Turkey.[83] Here he reverted to a view of architecture as art and rejected the functionalist position. He saw in the functionalist 'trinity of Technique, Construction and Function' a mere aid to building.[84] 'Architecture is the art of proportion,' he now proclaimed.[85] But his conception of proportion remained irrational. His *Architekturlehre* was an attempt to return to the classical tradition of architectural theory, but classical aesthetic concepts seem to have lost their substance. With his shift, first from Expressionism to Functionalism, then back to a call for a new aesthetic rooted in the concept of proportion, Taut's intellectual progress was like that of a pilgrim through all the different stations of the first half of the twentieth century.

Taut's visions in *Die Stadtkrone* and *Alpine Architektur* are translatable into plans and conceivable in structural terms, even though they are not capable of execution. Likewise Hermann Finsterlin (1887–1973), an aesthete of anthropological and biologistic leanings who was active in the Gläserne Kette under the name of 'Prometheus', conceived of an architecture sprouting organically out of the ground, for which he made hundreds of 'designs', not one of which was ever executed.[86] Finsterlin's articles in *Frühlicht*, written in an effuse pseudo-genetic, pseudo-erotic style, conjure up the vision of a new architecture,[87] which he also defines in Darwinian and Freudian terms: 'Human architecture is a biogenetic phenomenon of mankind which lies beyond the foetal.'[88] In an article entitled *Innenarchitektur* he maintains that 'the greater part of mankind prefers to live in the schematic intestines of its cubic, Trojan horse, like its parasites,'[89] whereas living conditions in the future will look very different:

> In the interior of the new house one will feel not only like the occupant of a fairy-tale crystal geode but like an inhabitant of an organism, wandering from organ to organ, the giving and receiving symbiont of a 'gigantic fossilised womb'.[90]

Spinning out the biological metaphor in an Expressionist version of the ideas of the Arts and Crafts movement, he calls in-built fittings and features 'attacks of flatulence': 'A cupboard, for example, with its roots in the wall of a concrete building, can break wind and change into majolica…'[91] The illustrations accompanying the article show a series of amorphous organic forms.

In another essay, *Die Genesis der Weltarchitektur oder die Deszendenz der Dome als Stilspiel* ('The genesis of world architecture, or the evolution of cathedrals as stylistic game'), Finsterlin conceives basic architectural concepts – sphere, cube, cone and pyramid – as crystallisations of the serpentine line ('*Wellenlinie*') in its movement towards other forms, i.e. dome, needle, onion, bell and horn. 'World architecture' originated, he claims, as a play between these forms, and he describes a construction kit of styles, duly patented, with which these forms could be reproduced. The new architecture of the 'organic epoch' to come is based on intuition and will be 'the harmonious union of irregular elements, irregular components… which will yet preserve harmonious proportions in the parts and in the whole complex.'[92] The result of this stylistic game is a series of plastic figures which will herald the coming of 'the truly Romantic age' of architecture. The last figure of the series bears an uncanny resemblance to Jørn Utzon's Sydney Opera House. Finsterlin's is a conceptual confusion which plays with words, whose content is purely associative. Unfortunately – although the fault certainly does not lie only with Finsterlin – linguistic balancing acts of this kind have exerted a fatal attraction for German architects in the twentieth century. In the end Finsterlin was perhaps nothing more than that which he never wanted to be – 'a jester, or the creator of an architectural carnival.'[93]

The influence of theosophy may be present in the spherical forms of Finsterlin's designs. Theosophy attracted many artists and aesthetic thinkers, and one whole movement, in the early twentieth century, the architects among them coming to differing conclusions. Foremost among those who sought to express anthroposophy in architecture was Rudolf Steiner (1861–1925), with his designs for two Goetheanum buildings at Dornach, Switzerland (1913–20 and 1924–28),[94] to which – particularly the first – he devoted a number of lectures.[95] Aroused by his opposition to Semper and Alois Riegl, Steiner set his face against materialism, nationalism and mere functionalism, and envisaged a new architectural style expressive of 'an elemental artistic urge… a particular kind of Weltanschauung,'[96] but also of 'an inner necessity' that issued from 'the spiritual evolution of mankind'.[97] Steiner's concepts are not so far removed from those of other architects but they have a greater consistence by virtue of their anthroposophical roots. Central for Steiner is the concept of the organism, which he interprets in the light of Goethe's theory of metamorphosis, of which, in its turn, he also gives an anthroposophical interpretation. 'In Dornach,' he wrote, referring to the first of the two buildings, 'I attempted to take this living principle to the point at which the purely dynamic, metrical, symmetrical qualities of earlier architectural forms are transferred into the realm of the organic.'[98] This organic quality must not be expressed as imitation of Nature or as allegory or symbol but must proceed from the 'organically creative principle of Nature' and fill the whole, every detail, every ornament, with a sense of inner necessity.[99]

In an analysis of Vitruvius's account of the Callimachus episode (IV.I) giving rise to the origin of the Corinthian capital, Steiner interprets all ornament and all architectural function as reflections of cosmic lines of force, as visible proof of assimilation into 'the organism of the whole world'.[100] The interior of the Goetheanum building is 'created out of the universe': the walls are not meant to enclose but to dissolve in a new transparency of their own:

> The treatment of the walls is what is new in this conception...the artistic principle
> of the walls is that they neutralise themselves, so that inside one can feel that the
> wall does not shut one off, or that the column is not there as a form of barrier
> but that what is expressed in the column and the wall breaks through the wall
> and brings one into a living relationship with the whole universe.[101]

Glass, colour and painted surfaces are essential means of expression, and Steiner's belief that architecture should express its inner functions is remarkably close to that of the Revolutionary architects, although no historical connection can be proved. The concrete boiler-house that he designed in Dornach brings him close to *architecture parlante*, and it was his belief that expression of function and nature of material should coincide. Of his boiler-house he wrote:

> A start had to be made to design a utility building of this kind first in accordance
> with these inner principles, and second, taking the most modern material, concrete,
> into account. Every material makes its own constructional demands, which are
> related to the nature of that material. The constructional principle must express
> both the utility principle and the demands of the material.[102]

Steiner's comments on the Goetheanum lead him to the brink of a symbolic interpretation of it, but this he rejects on principle. The importance that Steiner attaches to the Goetheanum building is made clear by his numerous allusions to Solomon's Temple; at the same time the new 'style' is not to be restricted to the main building but is also to be evident in the utility buildings and the houses of those who have settled in the community – 'an ideal unity...reflecting the inner harmony of those dwelling in the colony.'[103] In the first Goetheanum building Steiner succeeded in creating organic forms with a wooden construction on a concrete base; in the second, built entirely of concrete, each member is to be 'a revelation of the building's inner nature', with buttresses being like 'roots transplanted into architecture'.[104] The result is an expressive use of concrete that gives the entire complex the aspect of a monumental organism.

A number of Dutch artists within the theosophical movement had a considerable influence on their German colleagues at this time, prominent among them Johannes Ludovicus Mathieu Lauweriks (1864–1932), whose importance for architects such as Berlage, Behrens, Adolf Meyer, Gropius and Le Corbusier has yet to be fully assessed.[105] In 1904 Lauweriks was appointed to the Düsseldorf School of Arts and Crafts, of which Behrens had become director the previous year, and taught architectural design according to a programme he had probably developed in Holland in the 1890s. Among his many publications[106] *Ein Beitrag zum Entwerfen auf systematischer Grundlage in der Architektur* ('An essay on systematically based design in architecture'), printed in his periodical *Ring*, must be mentioned.[107] A programmatic article in the opening number of *Ring*, entitled *Leitmotive*, emphasises the central importance of science for the development of art. Starting from a grid system based on the circle and the square, Lauweriks evolves a proportioned 'symbolic geometric original figure' ('...*Entstehungs-figur*') capable of being assembled from system cells in the same way as the subdivided organic cell-structure found in Nature. These system cells are constructed according to Classical mathematical proportions and accumulate their matter in obedience to the needs of the architectural organism. Lauweriks explains the design method through plan and elevation of a church design by his pupil Christian Bayer, making the apodictic demand for architecture using systems cells,

> by which a building is built, by which the architectural organism is formed...the broad rhythmic foundation which must always be present and without which it is impossible to design a building, just as the cell is indispensable to the structure of a natural organism.[108]

Coming to proportion, Lauweriks even refers back to Vitruvius. It is his assumption that the pattern of cosmic order is manifest in architecture, and that behind that cosmic order lies a creative mathematics. Cosmic order, in its turn, then influences the ordering of human society.

Lauweriks anticipates by a few years the theosophical views of M.H.J. Schoenmaekers, which had such a decisive effect on Theo van Doesburg, Piet Mondrian and the De Stijl programme. There is also an interrelationship between Lauweriks and Berlage, whose second design for the Amsterdam Stock Exchange adopted a grid pattern similar to that of Lauweriks. Berlage wrote in 1908:

> At the School of Arts and Crafts in Düsseldorf, under the direction of the Dutchman Lauweriks, all the designs are executed in a similar but highly individual method – and Lauweriks himself carries the method furthest.[109]

In the artists' colony Am Stirnband (1910–14), which Lauweriks created for Karl Ernst Osthaus at Hagen, Westphalia, a uniform system of this kind, based on a 17-centimetre square, was adopted for the overall plan.[110] Le Corbusier happened to be in Hagen at the same time, supervising the construction of some houses nearby on behalf of Behrens, so that Le Corbusier's later 'Modulor' idea may possibly owe its inception to Lauweriks. Around the year 1910 Hagen was something of a melting-pot of artistic and architectural ideas under the impact of Karl Ernst Osthaus, who founded the Folkwang Museum in Essen and was a leading member of the Deutscher Werkbund.[111]

Lauweriks was only one of a number of Dutch architects concerned at this time with evolving a new basis for architectural design. The most important Dutch architect at the turn of the century was Hendrik Petrus Berlage (1856–1934),[112] a man whose writings are considerably more rational than those of Lauweriks and whose starting-points are Semper, Viollet-le-Duc and Sitte.[113] In his essay with the misleading title *Bouwkunst an impressionisme* (1893),[114] Berlage advances the idea of an international method primarily concerned not with architectural form but with its effect. Since the adoption of the styles of the past cannot achieve this, it is necessary to turn to the 'characteristic'.

Berlage's best-known writings are a series of lectures given in Germany. In *Gedanken über Stil in der Baukunst* (1904),[115] delivered in Leipzig, he sets out to provide a more precise definition of a new architecture which was to replace that produced under the capitalist system of the past. The principles he distils from the accepted historical styles are straightforward construction, truth, repose, unity in diversity, and order:

> Our architecture ought therefore to be governed once more by a certain order!
> Would no designing in accordance with a geometric system be a great step
> forward? A method already adopted by many modern Dutch architects.[116]

Berlage's second design for the Amsterdam Stock Exchange (1896) is based on 'Egyptian' triangles (prime ratio 5:4) and a square module system.[117]

In Berlage's view the subjective concept of art, to him the product of capitalism, had to make way for a communal art based on the working-class movement: a rational architecture ('*vernünftige Konstruktion*') is the expression of 'a new feeling towards the world, the social equality of all mankind.'[118] He enlarged on this in his Zürich lectures *Grundlagen und Entwicklung der Architektur* (1908),[119] in which he proclaimed geometry to be the sole basis of any genuine style, a universal law 'to which the entire universe is subject'.[120] Geometry, he maintained, 'is not merely extremely useful for the creation of artistic forms but absolutely essential.'[121] He saw the whole history of architecture in terms of geometric planning, citing the late medieval pinnacle books, neo-Gothic textbooks such as that of Hoffstadt, the masonic mysteries, and the processes of triangulation and quadrature. He made three demands of the architecture of the future:

1) The foundation of an architectural composition shall once again be based on a geometric scheme.

2) The characteristic forms of earlier styles shall not be used.

3) Architectural forms shall be developed in an objective direction ['*nach der sachlichen Seite hin*'].[122]

Ornament too must be governed by geometric laws, for this is the only way in which a new style can develop. One senses the presence of the medieval craft guild and the Arts and Crafts movement in the background: 'Only thus will the architectural work of art not have its own individual character but be the product of the community, of all.'[123]

The idea of a new architecture rooted in socialism, with the individual replaced by the collective, occurs frequently in the nineteenth century, linked with very different sets of intentions. The stylistic consequences of Berlage's position are not so far removed from Lauweriks and the De Stijl movement, but totally different philosophical backgrounds put any rapprochement between the two out of the question.

The Dutch group calling itself De Stijl, after Theo van Doesburg's periodical of that name,[124] had its roots in the theosophical ideas of M.H.J. Schoenmakers, a friend of Doesburg and in particular of Mondrian. As revealed in his books *Het nieuwe wereldbeeld* ('The New World View', 1915) and *Beginselen der beeldende wiskunde* ('Principles of Creative Mathematics', 1916), Schoenmakers' philosophy was that of a neo-Platonic 'positive mysticism' from which emerged a 'plastic mathematics'.

We are now learning to translate the reality that is in our minds into constructs controllable by reason, so that later we can reidentify these same constructs in the natural reality that is around us and thus permeate nature with our creative vision.[125]

Schoenmakers therefore rejects a direct perception of Nature as a hallucination: positive truth resides in 'reducing the relativity of the facts of Nature to the Absolute, so as to reidentify the Absolute in the facts of Nature.'[126]

This exclusion of sensuous reality and the achievement of complete abstraction was the aim of the De Stijl artists, who confined themselves to the use of a handful of basic elements – straight lines, right angles and the primary colours, red, yellow and blue.[127] In his numerous writings the founder and principal theorist of the group, Theo van Doesburg (1883–1931),[128] combined the philosophy of Schoenmakers with Kandinsky's theory of art, which likewise had its origins in theosophy.

The De Stijl movement had its beginning in 1917 and came to an end with Doesburg's death. It set up uniform laws for architecture and the fine arts – a policy reminiscent of the Arts and Crafts movement, to which in all other respects the De Stijl artists stand in stark contrast, especially in their readiness to accept mechanisation and the phenomenon of the metropolis. They aimed at an art of scientific precision, free of subjectivity, emotion and Nature:

It is the spiritual, the utterly abstract, which expresses exactly all that is human, when what relates to the senses does not attain the status of the intellectual and has consequently to be considered as belonging to a lower level of human culture. Art must not move the heart. All emotion, whether it be evoked by pain or by joy, represents a disruption of the harmony and balance between subject (man) and object (the universe). The work of art must create a state of equilibrium between itself and the universe; movements of the emotions create the very opposite.[129]

Architecture was a particular focus of attention for the De Stijl group, and was treated as an applied fine art. Their views often have a ruthless radicalism about them, as in this passage by Mondrian:

The really modern artist regards the city as an embodiment of abstract life. It is closer to him than Nature and is more likely to convey to him a feeling of beauty, for in the city Nature is ordered, regulated by the human mind. The proportions and the rhythm of lines and surfaces mean more to him than do the whims of Nature. In the city beauty expresses itself mathematically; the city is therefore the place from which the mathematical-artistic temperament of the future must be evolved, the place from which the new style must begin its advance.[130]

The challenge, according to Doesburg, was 'to transfer the principles of fine art to architecture.'[131] Architecture was a problem of artistic form: functionalism, construction and materials were subsidiary matters.

The pure expressive means at the disposal of architecture are surface, mass (positive) and space (negative). The architect expresses his aesthetic experience through the relationships of surfaces and masses to interior rooms and space.[132]

Mondrian goes so far as to interpret architecture as a two-dimensional painting, independent of space and time, a carrier of colour like his own compositions:

The new view is not from one particular point but from everywhere and nowhere. Consonant with the theory of relativity, the viewpoint is not bound to time and space; in practice the viewpoint is in front of the surface (the ultimate opportunity for deepening the conception). The new view thus sees architecture as a multiplicity of surfaces, as having the quality of a surface. In an abstract sense this multiplicity unites to form a flat painting...Colour extends over the whole building, all everyday objects, furniture and so on...This gives rise to a conflict with the traditional view of structural purity. The idea that the construction must be revealed is still not dead.[133]

Thus on the one hand architecture claims to penetrate the realms of other arts, on the other it is broken down into a series of images, which gives it a spiritual affinity with Baroque, a style of which the De Stijl artists had a particular abhorrence. Doesburg set out to incorporate concepts such as economy and functionalism into his conception of architecture but his insistence on right angles and straight lines left him little room for manoeuvre. He also made a significant attempt to introduce time into architecture as a formative factor, which led to a certain dynamism of body and surface:

The new architecture is anti-cubic, i.e. instead of seeking to assemble the different functional room-cells in one single enclosed cube, it projects these cells, together with areas such as porches and enclosed balconies, outwards from the centre of the cube, as a result of which height, breadth and depth, plus time, combine to produce a completely new pictorial expression in the open rooms. The building thereby acquires, as far as the structure allows – this is a matter for engineers – a kind of hovering quality which neutralises, to some extent, the force of gravity.[134]

The most striking practical expression of these ideas is Gerrit Rietveld's Schröder House in Utrecht (1924).

The De Stijl movement was launched by Dutchmen but they regarded its relevance as international, and Doesburg in particular tried to absorb related tendencies from other countries. El Lissitzky, for example, worked on the group's journal for a time. Doesburg taught for two not untroubled years at the Bauhaus in Weimar, and his *Grundbegriffe der neuen gestaltenden Kunst* was published under the aegis of the Bauhaus.[135] A postcard of the building which he sent in 1921 has the words 'De Stijl' printed all over it in thick letters.[136]

In spite of the importance that the De Stijl movement ascribed to architecture, a number of the leading architects who had originally been active participants in the group's discussions gradually drifted away, among them J.J.P. Oud and Robert van 't Hoff, the latter having studied in America and been largely responsible for publicising the work of Frank Lloyd Wright in Holland. The movement was so totally indifferent to social questions that Oud, who had been concerned with housing projects and was appointed Rotterdam City Architect in 1918, had to withdraw his support for it, as he made clear in his Bauhaus publication *Holländische Architektur* (1926):

Architecture no longer sets itself the goal of creating the most desirable type of dwelling in an attractive form but has sacrified everything and everybody to a view of beauty which has its origin in a different set of circumstances and has become an obstacle to the unfolding of life. Cause and effect have become confused with each other.[137]

It should be remembered that in contrast to the abstract aesthetic of the De Stijl movement there was in Holland in the 1920s a mass housing programme that was among the most progressive in all Europe.[138]

During the years of the Weimar Republic a number of different groups in Germany were involved in the discussion of architectural problems, many of which used the same vocabulary, differing only in emphases. Pigeonholing by 'styles', such as Expressionism, Neo-classicism, etc. is of only limited value, since many figures defy classification, both in their theory and in their practice.[139] Bruno Taut was one of the few who gave expression to their changes of attitude in theoretical writings; most did not, or, if they did, then with little relevance to their artistic achievement. It is no denigration of the work of men such as Poelzig, Mendelsohn or Scharoun to point to the inadequacies of their theoretical statements.[140]

On the other hand, a less important architect such as Hugo Häring (1882–1958) developed a superficially plausible theory of organic architecture based on a teleological view of history,[141] and Scharoun, whose own buildings were quite different, acknowledged his indebtedness to Häring's ideas.[142] Häring presented a view of history based on genetic evolution from geometric cultures to a pattern of organic building, an evolution that ran parallel to a development from stasis to kinesis, and which he found manifested particularly strikingly in the Mediterranean region. He proposed the following model: Egyptians – square, pyramid; Greeks – rectangle, temple; Romans – circle, dome; Renaissance and Baroque – ellipse. It was the last of these phases that led him to the principle of building from the interior outwards – the 'organic' principle of the time. He characterised the architecture of Northern Europe as exemplifying the change from geometric to organic, applying to the latter the concepts of functional form and expressive form, the products of the architect's creative urge. Functional form originates in an anonymous way; 'organic' form, as he uses the term, means not the imitation of organic form but the application of an organic principle which is at the same time functional. Of the farm buildings he designed for Gut Garkau in 1925 he wrote: 'The design of this building was arrived at by aiming to find the form which met its functional requirements in the simplest and most direct way.'[143]

Häring thus equates the organic with the functional, and when he says that a new life and a new society must penetrate artistic creativity, we hear a faint echo of the concept of function propounded by the Chicago School. But he did not get beyond the sententious use of clichés:

> Geometry demanded an order in space on the basis of geometric laws. An organic culture demands an order in space in order that life may fulfil itself. The former led to the concept of architecture; the latter embodies the whole concept of building, from the earliest moment in history onwards.[144]

By far the most vital force in architecture in Germany in the 1920s was the Bauhaus. On the one hand the Bauhaus idea represents a continuation of the principles of the Deutscher Werkbund, which in its turn represented an adaptation of the English Arts and Crafts movement; on the other hand, in practical terms it was the successor of the Kunstgewerbeschule run by the Belgian Henry van de Velde in Weimar from 1902 to 1915, combining teaching with practical workshop experience.

Quite independently of Muthesius, whom he anticipated in certain respects, Henry van de Velde (1863–1957) acted as a catalyst for English ideas on the Continent, particularly in German-speaking areas. His activities at Weimar make it logical to consider him here as a precursor of the Bauhaus.[145] His general theory of art, which included architecture, was in the tradition of Ruskin and William Morris, from which, however, it differed in certain vital respects, developing in a direction similar to that taken by the Deutscher Werkbund. His numerous writings were aimed at the general public, whom he sought to interest in a new 'style', the principles of which he set out to formulate.[146] His starting-point was the original unity of all the arts, whose sole purpose was that of decoration. Following Ruskin, he blamed the Renaissance for having separated the arts but realised at the same time that a reversion to Gothic was no solution to the problem of style, that modern art had to take account of mechanisation and mass production. A moderate socialist in outlook, he believed it would be possible to influence industry to improve the aesthetic quality of mass-produced articles:

> It is clear that machines will eventually have to make good all the misery they have caused, and atone for the atrocities they have committed ... They produce beautiful things and ugly things indiscriminately. But the mighty power of their iron arms will produce beautiful things as soon as they are governed by beauty.[147]

Van de Velde accepts all new materials and construction methods, and puts engineers and surveyors on the same level as architects. Design is the organic union of function, construction, materials and ornament. To the extent that he visualises usefulness as leading to beauty, he is a functionalist: 'The desire, from the beginning, to create only an object useful in every detail will lead to pure beauty.'[148] The simplicity of architecture, furniture and everyday objects resulting from such an approach is manifested in Van de Velde's Bloemenwerf House in Uccle, in Brussels (1895–96), which is a kind of response to William Morris's Red House. Van de Velde's functionalism, however, does not lead to a rejection of all ornament but only of applied, inorganic ornament. He was much concerned with the question of a new, modern ornament, and wrote in his essay *Was ich will* (1901):

> To whichever of the applied arts any given building may belong, in creating it one has to pay particular attention to ensuring that it and its exterior aspect conform in every respect to its designated purpose and its natural form. Nothing is legitimate that does not form an organism, or a link between the various organisms. No ornament can be permitted that is not organically absorbed.[149]

Van de Velde rejects all symbolic ornament of the past as irrelevant for modern purposes:

> I wish to replace the old symbolic elements, which have lost their effectiveness for us today, with a new, imperishable beauty ... in which ornament has no life of its own but depends on the forms and lines of the object itself, from which it receives its proper organic place.[150]

And elsewhere:

> I see ornament in architecture as having a dual function. On the one hand it offers support to the construction and draws attention to the means it employs; on the other ... it brings life into a uniformly illuminated space by the interplay of light and shade.[151]

There is a pattern of logical laws common to industrial processes and to the art of ornament which leads to the absolute principle that 'any form or ornament which a modern factor cannot easily and repeatedly produce is to be rejected.'[152] This leads him to assert: 'My ideal would be to be able to reproduce my works a thousand times over, albeit under the strictest supervision.' Or, as he put it at the first conference of the Deutscher Werkbund in 1908: 'I would not be a man of my time if I did not endeavour to adapt to modern mechanical and industrial methods of production the ways in which objects used to be produced by craftsmen using only their hands.'[153]

Such was the direction Van de Velde followed in his Kunstgewerbeschule in Weimar, a combination of school and workshop after the model of Ashbee's Guild and School of Handicraft of 1888, but with craft design giving way to machine design. Unlike Muthesius, who was in favour of the standardisation of design, Van de Velde remained faithful to the ideal of individuality. These differences came into the open in the course of the Werkbund congress in Cologne in 1914. Only after the war, under the influence of the progressive Modernist movement 'Neues Bauen', did the adaptable Van de Velde come to accept the concept of a 'universal style' devoid of ornament:

> Today we are witnessing a voluntary renunciation of ornament not only in architecture but also in the furnishing of houses … This renunciation suggests the awakening of a feeling which will discover in a building, in a work of art, in a flower or in the human body an original, in-dwelling ornament which will find its expression in proportions and in volume …[154]

Van de Velde had intended his early theory of a unity composed of functionalism, the organic ornament and industrial design to provide a formula for the new, modern style but in reality it only served as a theoretical foundation for Art Nouveau, to which all his works of this period belonged. It was left to the Bauhaus to carry his ideas further.

The Kunstgewerbeschule in Weimar had no department of architecture, nor did the Bauhaus have one until 1927,[155] which is particularly surprising in view of the fact that, from his earliest negotiations with the civic authorities over his appointment, Walter Gropius (1883–1969)[156] had given architecture pride of place among the subjects on the curriculum. Van de Velde proposed Gropius as his successor in 1915 but the appointment was not made till 1919, when the Kunstgewerbeschule merged with the Sächsische Hochschule für bildende Kunst. From 1908 to 1910 Gropius gained valuable experience in Behrens's office; he designed the Fagus factory in Alfeld, 1910–11, and a model factory for the Werkbund exhibition of 1914 in Cologne. The main focus of interest in his early theoretical writings was the design of standardised housing, for which, following the example of America, he proposed the manufacture of prefabricated parts. 'In this way,' he wrote in 1910, 'art and technology will be brought together in a happy union, and a broad section of the public enabled to come into possession of really good, mature art and reliable, quality products.'[157]

Such ideas corresponded with those of the Werkbund, which Gropius joined that same year. In 1911 he wrote:

> As workplaces we must erect palaces which not only give the factory worker, that slave of modern industrial production, light, air and cleanliness but also convey to him something of the nobility of the great communal idea that drives the whole undertaking.[158]

This sense of social commitment is in marked contrast to his essay *Die Entwicklung moderner Industriebaukunst* in the Werkbund yearbook for 1913, in which he follows the more conventional line adopted by Muthesius.

The foundation of the Bauhaus, which existed from 1919 to 1933, has to be seen against a general background of reform in art education in Germany,[159] although certain basic elements in its constitution are the product of Gropius's own conception of architecture. What particularly fascinated him – like Berlage in Holland – was the concept of the medieval masons' guild, in which he had been interested as early as 1906.[160] It was this, together with a comprehensive view of the arts in their social environment, that lay at the heart of the architectural debate in England from Pugin, Ruskin and Morris to the Arts and Crafts movement. Whereas the Werkbund had sought to breathe new life into architecture and the applied arts in collaboration with industry, Gropius went back to the literal idea of the medieval masons' guild (*Bauhütte*):

> It might be possible to revive that happy corporate activity found in its ideal form in the medieval guilds, in which like-minded artists from related fields – architects, sculptors, craftsmen of all different levels – unassumingly made their own individual contributions to the common enterprise in a spirit of respect for the unity of a collective idea... Through the revival of that proven mode of work, adapted to the modern world, the ways in which the conditions of our modern life express themselves will become more unified, until finally coalescing to form a new style in the days to come.[161]

Gropius's experiences in the Great War were his 'conversion from Saul to Paul', as he put it in a letter of 1919.[162] He flirted with socialism, became a member of the revolutionary Arbeitsrat für Kunst in Berlin and a contributor to the Gläserne Kette. The concept of the medieval guild became tinged with socialist and Expressionist ideas, and found its way in this form into both the name and manifesto of the Bauhaus. The manifesto was published in 1919; on its title-page it carried a woodcut by Feininger (*Plate 177*), and Gropius's text included the following passage:

> Let us form a new guild of craftsmen, without those arrogant class divisions which have insolently erected a wall separating artists from craftsmen. Let us desire, envisage and create together a new guild, the guild of the future, which will be everything in a single form – architecture and sculpture and painting, which will rise aloft from the hands of a million craftsmen as the crystal symbol of a new faith to come.[163]

The Bauhaus sought to establish 'the reunification of all the applied arts', the 'unified work of art' ('*Einheitskunstwerk*'); in the curriculum of the Bauhaus theory was combined with practical experience in the workshops, the members of the school being divided into masters, young masters, journeymen and apprentices, as in medieval times. However, an article written by Gropius for Taut's avant-garde journal *Frühlicht* in 1922, but left unpublished when the journal ceased publication in that year, assigns pride of place to the architect:

> Once the problems of painters and sculptors engage the architect's mind with the same passion as those of his own art, paintings and works of sculpture will again be filled with the spirit of architecture. In the medieval guilds it was from the close emotional commitment of artists of all levels that Gothic cathedrals arose.[164]

Not for nothing did the painter Oskar Schlemmer call the Bauhaus 'the cathedral of socialism'.[165]

Nevertheless, it was not until the Dessau phase of the Bauhaus, 1925–32, that the increased importance of architecture showed itself in the curriculum, with the appointment of Hannes Meyer in 1927 to head the newly founded department of architecture. It was also during this period that the *Bauhausbücher* were published (1925–30), together with the journal *Bauhaus: Zeitschrift für Bau und Gestaltung* (1926–31).[166] From 1926 to 1928 Gropius was also occupied with the construction of a housing estate in the Dessau suburb of Törten, where he put into practice his ideas for standardised housing projects as stated in his 21-point programme *Systematische Vorarbeit für rationellen Wohnungsbau* ('Systematic preparation for rational house-building', 1927), a programme not without totalitarian tendencies:

> Building means shaping the processes of life. Most individuals have similar needs. It is therefore logical, and makes economic sense, to satisfy these similar mass needs in a uniform and similar way.[167]

Like the De Stijl movement in Holland, Gropius stood for an international architecture. In *Internationale Architektur*, the first of the *Bauhausbücher* (1925), technological functionalisation and a unified philosophy are given as prerequisites for an international architecture: 'In modern architecture an objectification of the personal and the national can clearly be detected.'[168] The examples he quotes take account of various international movements, and he makes no attempt to impose a single 'style'. His preface ends with an unqualified vote of confidence in technology:

> The builders represented in this book all take a positive attitude towards the modern world of machines and vehicles and their speed; they are striving for ever bolder means of construction in order to overcome and hover above the sloth of the world in effect and in appearance.[169]

After leaving the Bauhaus, Gropius published a book on the school's buildings in Dessau (1930) in which he again emphasised that it was not the purpose of the institution to create a new 'style'. At the same time he reiterated the paramount principle of standardisation of everyday practical objects:

> Every object is determined by its essence; in order to construct it so that it functions properly, one must ascertain what the essence is, for we must make it serve its purpose perfectly, i.e. fulfil its practical functions and be durable, cheap and 'beautiful'.[170]

Essence now becomes synonymous with function, to which the work of art is also subject:

> The 'work of art' has to 'function', in both the intellectual and material sense, like something produced by an engineer, such as an aeroplane, the obvious purpose of which is to fly.[171]

In effect, however, Gropius does further the emergence of a new 'style', as when pressing for the adoption of flat roofs, which he was sure would become universal in time, and taking aerial perspective into account in planning, like Le Corbusier:

> The introduction of accessible roof-gardens is an effective means of incorporating nature into the concrete desert of the city. The cities of the future, with their gardens on roofs and terraces, will, seen from the air, give the impression of one big garden. The areas of green ground lost through the erection of houses will be reclaimed on the flat roofs.[172]

After emigrating from Germany to England in 1934, Gropius continued to put forward the concept of a standardised, prefabricated architecture collectively designed, as shown by his books *The New Architecture and the Bauhaus* (1935) and the anthology *The Scope of Total Architecture* (1956), and by 'The Architects' Collaborative' (TAC), a cooperative organisation which he set up in America in 1945.[173]

An important contribution to architectural theory was made by László Moholy-Nagy (1895–1946), who ran the introductory course at the Bauhaus from 1923 to 1928 in succession to Johannes Itten.[174] A summary of his teaching appeared in the Bauhaus publication *Von Material zu Architektur* (1929), the last section of which is devoted to the question of space.[175] His first principle of planning is a biological-cum-functionalist concept of space; at the same time he requires a structured 'experience of space as a foundation for the psychological well-being of those who live in it'.[176] He defines architecture as an 'experiential relationship to space' ('*erlebbare Raumbeziehung*'), which he conceives in terms of a relationship between dynamic forces. This leads him to create models for a 'kinetic-constructive system' in which the 'paths of human motion' ('*Bewegungsbahnen*') find a creative correspondence (*Plate 178*). His treatment of space is as a 'focal point of perpetually flowing spatial existences';[177] in his conception of space as a totality, architecture appears as 'the articulation of universal space'.[178] Like Gropius, Moholy-Nagy also sees the aerial view as playing a key role in the new architecture: 'The most important thing for us is the aerial view, a fuller experience of space, because it will change all past ideas.'[179] In 1937 Moholy-Nagy became director of the New Bauhaus in Chicago, which later became the Chicago School of Design.

Hannes Meyer (1889–1954), a Swiss architect who joined the Bauhaus in 1927 and was its director from 1928 to 1930 in succession to Gropius, was both politically and architecturally much more of a radical than his predecessor.[180] In 1926 he published in Switzerland a challenging essay *Die neue Welt* and the following year submitted his celebrated competition design for the new League of Nations building in Geneva. Demanding a complete break with the past, Meyer preached an uncompromising functionalism:

> Building is a technical, not an aesthetic process, and time and again the artistic composition of a house has contradicted its practical function. Planned in ideal and basic terms, our house will become a piece of machinery.[181]

He sees standardisation as 'the index of our community', with the work of art tolerated only as a collective product.[182] Explaining his design for the League of Nations building, he wrote:

> This building makes no attempt to establish an artificial garden-like link with the surrounding park landscape. As a product of the human mind, it offers a justifiable contrast to Nature. It is a building not beautiful and not ugly: it is to be assessed as a structural invention.[183]

Meyer's contributions to the Bauhaus journal are highly provocative in tone, and sometimes even directed against the Bauhaus itself as hitherto constituted. His essay *Bauen* (1928) is a programmatic statement of his internationalist and functionalist position:

> All things in this world are a product of the formula Function times Economy...All art is composition and thus anti-functional...Building is a biological process. Building is not an aesthetic process. In its basic form the house of the future will become not only a machine for living in but a piece of biological apparatus for

spiritual and physical needs…Building is merely organisation – social, technical, economic and psychological organisation.[184]

In *Bauhaus und Gesellschaft* (1919), an essay in the form of a poem, he denied that the Bauhaus pursued artistic aims:

Building and designing are one,

and are a social event.

As an 'academy of design'

the Bauhaus in Dessau is not an artistic

but certainly a social phenomenon.[185]

Meyer's marxist view of art turned discussions within the Bauhaus into arguments over ideology and led to his dismissal in 1930, after only two years as director. On his later visit to Russia he was able to expound the same ideas under the banner of a marxist architecture.[186]

Ludwig Hilberseimer (1885–1967), appointed to the Bauhaus in 1929, was prominent in the field of urban planning during the school's final years. A prolific writer,[187] he propounded in *Großstadtarchitektur* (1927) an organic conception of the city, based on rational principles, which he considered more effective than Le Corbusier's concept of *'urbanisme'* advanced two years earlier.[188] His concept of a two-tier 'vertical' city provided an intense concentration in which offices, shops and traffic-ways were located on a level below that of housing (*Plate 179*). Blocks 600 metres long and 100 metres deep were to contain offices and shops on the lower five storeys, and living apartments on the upper fifteen, the latter being fully equipped so that, as Hilberseimer put it, when people moved house, 'it was only suitcases that needed to be packed, not the removal van.'[189] The blocks were to be separated by streets ten metres wide and linked by bridges at the level of the walkways above the fifth storey. Hilberseimer did not see his grid as an exercise in standardisation but as 'a series of theoretical experiments and a schematic application of the elements out of which a city is built.'[190] To his concept of an 'organic' city strict limits are in fact set. Urban planning is seen as the reduction of architectural form to the most concise, the most essential and the most general, and confinement to cubic forms, which are the basic units of all architecture.'[191] Hilberseimer's vertical city is one of the most comprehensive concepts of town planning that the twentieth century has seen; he developed his ideas further in America after his emigration from Germany in 1938.

Hilberseimer's friend Ludwig Mies van der Rohe (1886–1969), who first met Gropius in Behrens's office in Berlin, completely changed the nature of the Bauhaus during the three years of his directorship (1930–33), turning it into an outright school of architecture.[192] Through the Deutscher Werkbund exhibition in the Weissenhof-Siedlung in Stuttgart in 1927 and the German pavilion at the World Fair in Barcelona in 1929 Mies had made himself the most prominent representative of Neues Bauen. He wrote little, and what he did write is open to misinterpretation.[193] His early writings subscribe to the proposition that form is derived from materials. In his essay *Industrielles Bauen* (1924) he took the implications of mass production much further than Gropius: 'If we succeed in carrying out the process of industrialisation, our social, economic, technological and even artistic problems will be easy to solve.'[194] He then proceeded to make this process of industrialisation depend on the invention of a new building material 'which can be mechanically produced and industrially processed, is hard, weather-resistant, soundproof and with good insulating properties."[195] It is a far cry, however, from the subtle functionalism that he developed during his Bauhaus years to the blunt materialism displayed by Meyer.

A few years later, at the Werkbund conference in Vienna (1930), Mies retreated from an exclusive concentration on materials and laid the emphasis on 'spiritual problems':

> Let us not overestimate questions of mechanisation, standardisation and typing...whether we build high or low, with steel and glass, says nothing about the quality of our work...But it is precisely this question of quality that is decisive. We have to set new standards...For the meaning and the right of every age, including our own, consist in providing the spirit with the conditions necessary for its existence.[196]

It was not until his American period that Mies evolved a theory that bridged the gulf between technology and 'spirit': technology becomes architecture not through freely invented forms but through its union with the expression of the age:

> That is the reason why technology and architecture are so closely related. Our real hope is that they grow together, that some day the one be the expression of the other. Only then will we have an architecture worthy of its name: Architecture is a true symbol of our time.[197]

Nevertheless Mies retained to the end his belief in the objectification of architectural form, writing in 1965:

> I believe today, as I have done for a long while, that architecture has little or nothing to do with the invention of new forms or with personal preferences. True architecture is always objective – the expression of the inner structure of the age out of which it has grown.[198]

It must be remembered that throughout its existence the Bauhaus was receptive to international influences and thoroughly cosmopolitan in its outlook, Dutchmen such as Doesburg, Oud and Stam, and Russians like El Lissitzky and Malevich, held teaching posts there at various times. Most of the staff inclined, to a greater or lesser degree, towards the socialist camp. The political tensions in the Weimar Republic were reflected in their discussions, as in those within the Werkbund.[199] As time went on architects of a more conservative persuasion gained the upper hand and nourished the soil in which the architecture of the Third Reich flourished.

A politically conservative outlook usually went hand in hand with a national architecture that claimed to perpetuate the indigenous traditions of the past. Some of these architects were extremely prolific theorists, and their works paved the way for Nazi cultural ideology. Among them were Paul Schultze-Naumburg (1869–1949), whose nine volumes of *Kulturarbeiten* (1901–17) propagated the values of Germanic culture,[200] and Paul Schmitthenner (1884–1972), whose image of a plain and simple architecture with its roots in popular culture fitted perfectly into the ideology of the Third Reich.[201] Heinrich Tessenow (1876–1950)[202] and Fritz Schumacher (1869–1947),[203] on the other hand, aimed at a balance between traditionalism and modernism, both in their writings and in their buildings, and succeeded in retaining their personal and intellectual integrity throughout the years of the Third Reich. Tessenow, following the line taken by the Werkbund, favoured standardised construction for small houses,[204] based on simplicity, functionalism and objectivity.[205] Moderate in his approach, he was susceptible to the ideas of the New Architecture but did not share its formal purism. His remarks on ornament are typical:

> Ornament or the ornamental is everywhere, but the less we desire it, the more indifferently we treat it, the better it will be...Put it this way: the most that ornament can do is light up a man's labours with an involuntary half-smile...The best aspects of ornament are the abstract, the stupid and the incomprehensible.[206]

Schumacher, chief architect to the city of Hamburg from 1909 to 1933, set his views in a broad historical context.[207] In *Der Geist der Baukunst* (1938) he argues for a synthesis of indigenous traditions, an approach that is 'true to materials, true to function and true to form', and a classical interpretation of proportion, also drawing an analogy between architecture and music.[208] He gives ornament, for example, a rhythmic interpretation: 'The dynamic effects emerge if ornament is combined, not with the surface but with the form, the functional significance of which it can underline and illustrate.'[209] The moderate views of men like Tessenow and Schumacher have received increased attention in recent times, when functionalism has been noticeably shunned.

By citing such figures as Tessenow, Schumacher and Muthesius, Nazi architectural ideologists were able to point to an impeccable pedigree which on the one hand demonstrated the reality of the national historical continuum and on the other could be used to keep the internationalist tendencies of the New Architecture at bay.[210] The vocabulary of the New Architecture, and even Taut's visionary '*Stadtkrone*' ideas, were used in a completely new sense. Typical of this process is a passage from Rudolf Wolters' *Neue deutsche Baukunst* (1943):

> The form of the new buildings, their external design, is the product of their content, their meaning and their purpose. They serve the interests of the people as a whole – public halls, theatres, rooms for receptions and celebrations. All the new buildings belonging to the State and the National Socialist movement will be joined with these to produce grand, all-embracing complexes of ceremonial squares and avenues. Such are to be our new *Stadtkronen*, the centres of our cities of today.[211]

The Nazis had no architectural theory of their own.[212] Like all the arts, architecture was subjected to the processes of *Gleichschaltung*, yet it played an important role in the régime's self-image, as well as in the mind of Hitler, who liked to act the part of an amateur architect.[213] The conservative and nationalistic trends that had persisted through the years of the Weimar Republic found increasing favour, with a new emphasis on exclusivity, and such theoretical utterances as there were had their origin in racial theories and the alleged superiority of Germanic culture. The New Architecture was denounced as a Bolshevik conspiracy, an accusation uttered in particularly virulent tones by the Swiss architect Alexander von Senger in *Krisis der Architektur* (1928).[214]

The Nazi 'philosopher' Alfred Rosenberg, who had had an architectural training, advanced an idea of Greek-cum-Germanic architecture in his influential *Mythus des 20. Jahrhunderts* (1930), attacking neo-Gothic and the historicist position but claiming that the true architecture of the future would emerge from 'the inner will of Gothic and its architectural law'.[215] Rosenberg sought to link the three forces of Greek, Germanic and Gothic to express monumentalism, and so regarded the high-rise building with approval (as evidenced in Hermann Giesler's planning of Munich):

> For its monumental buildings our age must pile one layer of bricks on top of

another; for water towers we need massive, self-contained forms, for corn silos, simple, huge masses. Our factories must straddle the ground like giants, and scattered office buildings will be amalgamated to form colossal workplaces...The Gothic style has been superseded once and for all, but everyone with eyes to see must recognise that the Gothic spirit is fighting to realise itself anew...'[216]

And:

The underlying principles of Greek architecture are at one with Teutonic feeling. The so-called 'Romanesque' cathedral (in reality thoroughly Germanic) and the Gothic cathedral – quite independently of their historical manifestations – have remained faithful to these principles. The form of the basilica, basic to both, expresses the essence of the Northern European concept of space.[217]

A century earlier Bunsen had expressed similar ideas in *Die Basiliken des christlichen Roms* (1842–44). Rosenberg traced the concept of central-plan building back to a Mediterranean matriarchal marsh cult.

The role of expressing the new monumentalism fell to Classicism, as heir to the composite Greek-cum-Germanic-cum-Prussian ideal. In *Der preußische Stil* (1916), reprinted – significantly – in 1931, the nationalist writer Arthur Moeller van den Bruck[218] had advocated a neo-Classicist monumentalism:

Monumentality is a masculine art...Its verses have a heroic ring. Its lines are hieratically superimposed. Its forms have the force of dogmas. It has in itself the march of warriors, the language of lawgivers, scorn of the moment, accountability to eternity...Style only receives its great visibility through monumentality. In a plasma identifiable from afar and immediately recognised, a unity of artists and people comes into being and sets out to impose its will on history; the domination of its forms begins to spread, a domination which is above all a self-domination and which can turn into world-domination. The effect of monumentality is like that of great wars, of popular uprisings, of the foundation of new countries – that is, it liberates, unites, creates and confirms destinies, and orders existence afresh.[219]

Language such as this shows how easily architecture could be manipulated. It is also the language of Hitler's observations on the subject. Art historians like Wilhelm Pinder and Hubert Schrade subsequently provided a 'scholarly' historical background for such utterances in order to prevent them from being dismissed as mere ideological ravings.

Albert Speer (1905–81), a pupil of Tessenow's, claims in his memoirs (1969) to have had a 'theory' of style, and refers elsewhere to having aimed at 'a synthesis of Troost's Classicism and Tessenow's simplicity.'[220] He also maintains that he based his concept of monumentalism on Ledoux and Boullée.[221] But Ledoux's premises were quite different, while Boullée's designs did not become known until after the Second World War. Of Hitler's attitude towards architecture Speer wrote: 'The erection of these monuments was intended as a statement of his determination to rule the world, made long before he dared inform his closest associates of his plans.'[222] Speer's *Ruinenwerttheorie*', suggested by the remains of Roman buildings, that the aesthetic value of ruined structures could somehow be incorporated into the architecture of the Third Reich, has not been without influence.[223] An architectural supplement which he edited for the periodical *Die Kunst im Dritten Reich* (1937 onwards) provides information on the historical models followed at the time but offers no theoretical statement. The link with Classicism is made clear by Wolters, who saw in Schinkel the last great architect with the power 'to stamp his personality on an entire epoch'.[224]

The Nazis aimed at a uniform pattern of architecture based on the values of race, the Fatherland and the German *Volk*, with, however, different styles for different types of building. Monumental Neo-classicism was confined to official and public buildings, housing estates were built in traditional *Heimatstil*, while industrial buildings carried on the international functionalist tradition of the 1920s. The confusd ideological conceptions behind this pattern can be followed in *Das Bauen im Neuen Reich* (1938) by Gerdy Troost, widow of Hitler's architect Paul Ludwig Troost, which contains all the Nazi slogans – 'the primeval forces of the soil', 'blood relationship with the Hellenes', 'loyalty to one's beliefs' and the rest – which it was intended that the buildings of the Nazi community should exemplify.[225] The concept of 'organic growth' is also invoked but only in order to claim that that growth had been interrupted by the pressures of liberalism and industrialisation. 'In the beginning was the farmhouse,' wrote Troost – a building which had a high roof and 'clear functionalism'.[226] Neue Sachlichkeit is branded as cultural bolshevism, whereas the architecture of the future is 'language cast in stone' (in Hitler's phrase), 'National Socialism in built form, the self-portrayal of the most deep-seated cultural forces in an awakened, race-conscious people.'[227] The Nazy party buildings in Munich are to follow the principles of 'Germanic architecture' and exhibit the qualities of moderation and order: 'The design potentialities of modern technology have been exploited to the utmost. Nevertheless nowhere does technology rise above art.'[228]

In the field of industrial building Gerdy Troost twisted the aesthetic arguments of the New Architecture into a typical Nazi demonstration of the 'popular will':

> A number of industrial buildings in our society erected since 1933 have by their existence proven beyond all doubt that fine architectural forms can be developed from a clear sense of technological purpose. The power of a comprehensive *Weltanschauung* can develop appropriate forms from the essence of technology. Buildings exhibiting moderation and order, effective through economy and clarity of line, symbolic of the efficient and accurate work performed in them, have been erected, producing a fine overall effect. Concrete, steel and glass are openly displayed.[229]

This mixing of the language of Neues Bauen with Nazi ideology confused contemporaries and still disturbs us today.

In 1928, in his widely-known *Blaue Bücher* on contemporary German architecture, Walter Müller-Wulckow had praised Gropius's Bauhaus buildings in Dessau in similar terms as perfect examples of 'buildings for communal use',[230] only for the Nazis to banish them as specimens of 'cultural bolshevism'. Standardisation and state control of building also extended to the private sector:

> The government is concerned freely and appropriately to apply the fundamental principles underlying the great works of the community to the great mass of private buildings as well, and thus pave the way for a new architecture which will be universally binding.[231]

Even though the Nazis had no theory of their own, their determination to exploit architecture to the full in the interests of their ideology represents an intervention in architectural affairs unparalleled even in the age of absolutism. Historically speaking, the constituent elements of National Socialist architectural ideology were largely formulated in the nineteenth century and emerged increasingly clearly during the years of the Weimar Republic, prominent among them a conservative, nationalistic trend that acquired a momentum of its own. Thus the years 1933 to 1945 cannot be ignored as though they were not integral to the course of German architecture, any more than all conservative and nationalistically minded architects can be adjudged to have been Nazis. The investment of particular forms (e.g. flat roof and pitched roof) and styles (e.g. Neo-classicism and the New Architecture) with ideological meaning was characteristic not only of the Nazis but also of the protagonists of the New Architecture and of the international style. This association of architectural forms with ideological content was to prove a heavy burden in Germany after the Second World War.

26. France: 1900–1945

At the end of the nineteenth century the architectural debate in France, both inside and outside the Ecole des Beaux-Arts, was characterised by an extreme rationalism, found at its most explicit in the numerous publications of Choisy and Guadet. The latter was the teacher, at the Ecole des Beaux-Arts, of the two men who, though having their beginnings in the tradition of historicism, were to leave this tradition behind and point the way forward for French architecture – Tony Garnier and Auguste Perret.[1]

A native of Lyons, where he spent most of his active life, Tony Garnier (1869–1948)[2] won the Prix de Rome in 1899 (after a number of unsuccessful attempts) with a design for the head office of a bank, with a highly rationalised plan but an exterior in a neo-Renaissance form.[3] While on a scholarship at the Villa Medici in Rome he worked on a reconstruction of the ancient city of Tusculum,[4] which inspired his design for *'une cité industrielle'*. Garnier developed this concept between 1901 and 1917 as a result of his studies of the cities of Antiquity, Howard's concept of the garden city, the regionalist ideas of Patrick Geddes and the utopian vision of Fourier, together with the theories of Sitte and Otto Wagner.[5]

The final, 1917 version of Garnier's *'cité industrielle'* represents the first attempt since Ledoux to design an entire new city, from the overall concept down to the design of individual buildings. A comparable undertaking was Antonio Sant'Elia's *'città nuova'*, but Sant'Elia never completed the project. Even later urban planning concepts like that of Le Corbusier did not go into such detail as Garnier's, which consists of 164 plates, preceded by a brief introduction.[6]

Garnier puts foward an ideal vision, but related specifically to conditions in south-east France (*Plate 180*). Assuming that the cities of the future would be governed entirely by industrial considerations, he first of all laid down that they would have to be sited where raw materials were readily available, where energy could be derived from hydroelectric sources, and where easy communications, including a river, were at hand. He envisaged a site on a hillside, which would take account of solar and wind conditions, and anticipated a town with an initial population of 35,000 but capable of expansion. The town would be strictly zoned: the industrial area would be close to the river and the dam, while the residential area, including public buildings, would occupy a plateau higher up the slope, with hospital buildings above it.

The utopian concept of Garnier's thought emerges in his vision of a form of social progress that would render our present system of laws superfluous. Like Morris and Howard, he builds on the premise that all land will be publicly owned and all basic foodstuffs and medicines provided by the state. And because society will have attained a higher level of morality, buildings such as churches, prisons, law courts and police stations will no longer be necessary. The residential zone will be like a large park, with not more than half the surface area built on, the other half being seen as a kind of communal garden (*Plate 181*). Private fences will not be permitted. Taking his lead from the direction of the prevailing winds, Garnier establishes three criteria for housing:

    1. In each dwelling, the bedrooms must have at least one south-facing window,

large enough to illuminate the entire room and admit an abundance of sunlight.
2. Courtyards and patios, i.e. enclosed areas used for illumination or ventilation,
will be prohibited: every space, however small, must be illuminated and ventilated
from without.

3. In the interior of the dwellings, the walls, floors etc. are to be made of smooth
material, with rounded angles.[7]

Garnier's designs, which are generally for one- or two-storey houses, follow these
criteria. He proposes terrace rows between 30 and 150 metres long, cast in a variety of
forms; the streets thus form a gridiron pattern, roads and avenues being of varying
widths. Public buildings are concentrated in the heart of the residential zone, with a
monumental clock tower and a large assembly hall in the centre. Museums, libraries,
theatres and sports centres are given excessive importance in Garnier's plan, with the
decentralised schools, and the hospital complex above the town, on a similarly large
scale. The only multi-storey buildings – hotels, department stores and apartment
blocks – are clustered round the railway station, so as not to threaten the park-like
character of the rest of the town.

There are a number of Classical references in Garnier's plan. The site he proposes
recalls the Pergamon reconstruction made by Emmanuel Pontremoli in 1900;[8] his sports
stadium descends from the Piazza di Siena in the park of the Villa Borghese in Rome;
one of his atrium buildings incorporates his impressions of Pompeii; and for the
entrance hall of his proposed Art College he goes back to that of the Ecole des Beaux-
Arts.

In his brief commentary to his designs Garnier discusses matters of construction.
All public buildings are to be of reinforced concrete and glass; moulds should be
standardised so as to simplify building operations and reduce costs. The same simplicity
governs the aesthetic aspect:

This simplicity of means leads logically to great simplicity of expression in the
structure. We should also realise that, if our structure is simple, free of ornament,
free of mouldings, absolutely bare, we shall then be able to apply the decorative
arts in all their forms, and that each piece of art-work will retain a greater clarity
and purity of expression in that it will be totally independent of the construction.[9]

For private housing too Garnier prescribes a cubic architecture free of ornament,
though occasionally using a house as a plinth for a piece of monumental sculpture, cf.
his use of the statue of Nike of Samothrace (*Plate 181*). Like Loos, Garnier drew a
sharp distinction between a piece of architecture and a work of art. As he saw it,
simplicity of construction, which expresses itself in horizontals and verticals, conveys
a sense of balance and repose which harmonises with the lines of Nature. This recourse
to Nature shows how firmly rooted Garnier is in traditional architectural theory.

When he returned to Lyons in 1905, Garnier set about putting parts of his utopian
vision into practice,[10] and some of the buildings he erected there, such as an abattoir,
a stadium and a hospital, are integrated into his '*cité industrielle*'. From the aesthetic
point of view his designs, in spite of his acceptance of new forms of construction, are
largely governed by the attitudes that prevailed in the Ecole des Beaux-Arts, as can be
seen from the monumental symmetry of his buildings in Lyons and from the public
buildings designed for the '*cité industrielle*'. His ideas on housing have had a considerable
influence on twentieth-century architecture and town planning, as has his conception

of urban zoning according to function. Le Corbusier, who first visited him in 1907[11] and acquired a copy of *Une cité industrielle* immediately it appeared, owes a direct debt to him on both these counts.

The employment of reinforced concrete in Garnier's '*cité industrielle*' implied a knowledge of the technical and aesthetic properties of the material. This knowledge was provided by engineers such as François Hennebique and, more importantly, Auguste Perret (1874–1954), a graduate, like Garnier, of the Ecole des Beaux-Arts, and later a teacher there until a year before his death.[12] Perret, a personal friend of Guadet's, had studied Viollet-le-Duc in his early years, and his aesthetic ideas, couched only in aphoristic form, show him dominated by the Beaux-Arts tradition.[13] The central problem for architecture, as he saw it, was to reconcile the technological opportunities opened up by the use of concrete with the rationalistic aesthetics of Viollet-le-Duc, Choisy and Guadet.

Perret's argument ran as follows.[14] Construction is the architect's language but architecture is more than just construction – it requires harmony, proportion and scale; construction is for architecture what a skeleton is for an animal; in architecture the laws of Nature take the form of 'permanent' conditions applicable to areas such as structural engineering, properties of materials, durability and optical impression – he refers to the 'universal and eternal meanings of certain lines' – while practical function is to be seen only as a 'temporary' condition. His insistence on symmetry is based on the one hand on a parallel between construction and the skeleton of animals – an idea adapted from Alberti – and on the other hand, on the standardisation and prefabrication of rhythmicised components. A building consists of a structural frame ('*ossature*') and infillings ('*remplissage*'); ornament as decoration is not permitted – the function of ornament is taken over by the structural elements.

Perret is concerned to justify, in terms of his conception of architecture, the use of concrete in both technological and aesthetic respects, the latter leading him, in the tradition of the Classical orders, to create a 'concrete order', which he employed in his buildings but did not elucidate in theoretical terms.[15] Such was his identification with the values of Greek architecture that he never used concrete for exterior arches but only for columns and entablatures.

What Perret claimed as 'the first attempt in the world to make reinforced concrete aesthetic' was his garage building in the Rue de Ponthieu in Paris (1905; demolished in 1970). The façade, a rhythmical span membered in the proportion 3:5:3, is an attempt to transfer the aesthetics of the Ecole des Beaux-Arts to a structure in exposed concrete;[16] indeed, it might even be seen as a modern application of the Gothic triforium and rose window. Perret's concrete church of Notre-Dame in Le Raincy (1922) was regarded as a synthesis of the Greek and Gothic styles made possible by the new material, thus fulfilling a dream that had haunted French architects since the time of Cordemoy.

Perret's conservative aesthetics led in his later buildings to a rigid Neo-classicism. But his importance lies in the fact that he raised the whole question of the aesthetics of concrete, not in any particular solutions he proposed. At the time (1908–09) when Le Corbusier was working in Perret's studio, the garage building in the Rue de Ponthieu had just been completed, and there was as yet no sign of Perret's later found rigidity.

Charles-Edouard Jeanneret, who in 1920 adopted the name Le Corbusier (1887–

1965), was Swiss by birth but is more accurately seen in a French cultural context.[17] The most powerful and eloquent architect of the twentieth century, Le Corbusier wielded an even greater influence through his forceful theories than through his executed designs. He is unusual among architects in that his detailed theory preceded his practice. Intent on presenting a consistent personality, he excluded his early projects from his *Oeuvre complète* and thus obliterated the traces of his long drawn-out and highly complex early spiritual development, which has only recently been researched.[18] He himself supervised the publication (from 1929 onwards) of his *Oeuvre complète*[19] in the landscape format first used by Schinkel in the nineteenth century. His unpublished drawings have since been published under the auspices of the Fondation Le Corbusier.[20]

The Ecole d'Art in La Chaux-de-Fonds, where Le Corbusier was born and studied, made a deep and lasting impression on him.[21] Charles L'Eplattenier, teacher of decorative composition and an adherent of the cult of Nature, encouraged the development of a vernacular style of architecture governed by the nature of the landscape, and urged his students to study the works of Ruskin and Owen Jones' *Grammar of Ornament*. Le Corbusier's earliest buildings, such as the Villa Fallet in La Chaux-de-Fonds (1906–07), are responses to L'Eplattenier's teachings, and a letter written from Paris in 1908, describing his experiences in Perret's studio, shows the strength of his personal link with his teacher.[22]

From the beginning there are in Le Corbusier two strands of thought which appear to be mutually exclusive but which he combined to form a highly personal synthesis: on the one hand his idealistic Swiss Calvinist education, and on the other the rationalist and functionalist influence that came from Viollet-let-Duc, Choisy and Guadet, together with his personal links with Perret and Garnier. He was an avid and attentive reader of works proclaiming that mankind could be made better through art.[23] Many of the ideas he later expressed are to be found, for example, in Henry Provensal's messianic *L'art de demain* (1904), which preaches a doctrine of absolute laws of harmony, a cubic style of architecture and a scale of values based on man. Here, as in Edouard Schuré's *Les grands initiés* (1908),[24] a copy of which L'Eplattenier gave him, Le Corbusier found that Nietzschean tradition of élitism which was to inform his entire outlook, and when he read Ernest Renan's *Life of Jesus* around 1906, he convinced himself with almost wilful determination that he was destined for the role of tragic revolutionary, a martyr come to redeem the world – by architecture.[25] Hence his later formulation 'Architecture or Revolution'.

Through the periods he spent in Paris with Perret (1908–09) and in Berlin with Behrens (1910–11), as well as on his other travels, Le Corbusier acquired a sound knowledge of contemporary trends in architecture from Josef Hoffmann to Loos and Frank Lloyd Wright, which he subsequently absorbed into his own pattern of thought.[26] His first published work, *Etude sur le mouvement d'art décoratif en Allemagne* (1912), discusses the Deutscher Werkbund, the teaching at German schools of arts and crafts and the exhibitions that he had visited during his stay in Germany.[27]

In the autumn of 1911 he wrote an account of a journey to the eastern Mediterranean, not published until 1965, which shows how heterogeneous were the ideas in his mind at this time.[28] He was enthusiastic about straight, asphalt roads, about the 'magic of geometry', about houses built on supports ('*pilotis*'), about the Parthenon, which he called 'a frightful machine' while praising its mathematical symmetry. He summarised his impression of the Acropolis as 'Light! Marble! Monochromy!' These impressions already foreshadow the aesthetic principles manifested in his later buildings and writings.

Le Corbusier's inclination to combine an idealist with a rationalist approach emerges from the very first project (not executed) in his *Oeuvre complète*, a design for artists' studios at La Chaux-de-Fonds (1910; *Plate 182*). There are reminiscences in this cubic design of the Certosa di Galuzzo near Florence, which Le Corbusier had visited in 1907,[29] but in addition he appears to have been influenced – also in the form of his presentation – by a model from Choisy's rationalistic *Histoire de l'architecture* (1899), which he would have come across during his spell in Perret's studio, if not before,[30] i.e. a model of a 'monolithic pagoda' in India (*Plate 158*).[31] Le Corbusier idealised and abstracted his models to the point where they were no longer recognisable as such.

A more striking example of Le Corbusier's idealist-rationalist approach is his Maison Dom-ino of ·1914,[32] a structural framework of prefabricated, standardised reinforced concrete elements, with the pillars set back, so as to establish a contrast with the enclosing, non-load-bearing exterior walls (*Plate 183*). This is a feature also found in the interior of Perret's garage building in the Rue de Ponthieu, but Le Corbusier's aim was to idealise the individual elements and design the absolute independent floorplan, the absolute free façade, the absolute pillar, and so on.[33] The same thought underlies the use of standardised elements – which Garnier had also envisaged for his *'cité industrielle'* – a method of fabrication he justifies on grounds of cost but also uses in order to express order, harmony and perfection. The idealisation of functions leads to their aestheticisation, and not long afterwards he made this a cardinal principle of his doctrine.

In his earliest substantial design, that for the Villa Schwob in La Chaux-de-Fonds (1916), Le Corbusier had not yet succeeded in producing a convincing synthesis of elements taken from buildings by Perret, Garnier and the Mannerists,[34] and he thus omitted it from his *Oeuvre complète*. It was not until 1920 that he achieved this synthesis. His activity as a painter, stimulated by his friendship with Ozenfant, found expression in *Après le Cubisme* (1918), a book written in collaboration with Ozenfant, which supplies a theoretical justification for Purism.[35]

The Left Bank journal *L'Esprit Nouveau*[36] carried the first appearance in print of the pseudonym Le Corbusier, under which name he co-edited the magazine with Ozenfant and the poet Paul Dermée from 1920 to 1925. Here he published excerpts from a book which appeared in 1923 under the title *Vers une architecture*, which brought him rapid fame.[37] At the same time he continued to write on the fine arts under his real name.

Vers une architecture, which Le Corbusier himself saw as a manifesto, is a summary of the long process of his education. In provocative, apodictic language he drills a series of formulae into his readers' minds, casting himself in the eschatalogical role of architect-redeemer. The synthesis of functionalism and idealism is here complete, and Le Corbusier revels in his dual role of saviour and martyr.

Many of the individual ideas that Le Corbusier expresses are also to be found in other architectural writings of the time, but his radical formulations force a reaction from the reader. Such is the effect, for example, of the series of theses at the opening of *Vers une architecture*, which summarise the content of the whole book. He regards architecture as the aesthetic of engineering and as expressive of the laws of economy that bring us into harmony with the laws of the universe. At the same time he maintains that by his arrangement of forms, the pure creation of his intellect, the architect 'gives us the measure of an order which we feel to be in accordance with that of our world...'[38] This is his response to Provensal's book but it also makes us think of Alberti's concept of *concinnitas*.

To Le Corbusier the geometric forms are primary, economic and at the same time beautiful forms which satisfy our minds through mathematics: 'The great problems of modern construction must have a geometrical solution.'[39] In envisaging regulating lines ('*tracés régulateurs*') as a 'condition of order' ('*obligation d'ordre*'), he hints at his future concept of the Modulor. Taking Viollet-le-Duc's position to extremes, he calls the adoption of historical styles a lie and gives his own definition of true style: 'Style is a unity of principle animating all the work of an epoch, the result of a state of mind which has its own special character.'[40] This recalls Riegl's definition of style as the expression of the artistic will, which Le Corbusier may well have come across during his stay in Vienna in 1907–08. The debate on type, which he had followed in Germany – he had attended the Werkbund Exhibition in Cologne in 1914 – is given a further twist when he proposes an apparently logical equation between industrial product, machine, type, house and even historical architecture, bluntly claiming that the problem of the house has not yet really been posed. The concept of standardisation, evolved a long time earlier by Gropius, Muthesius, Tessenow, Garnier and others, now leads Le Corbusier to his famous definition of a house as 'a machine for living in'.[41] Architecture becomes the construction of types, and arguing backwards in time in a manner derived from Choisy, he concludes that the Parthenon too was 'a product of selection applied to a standard.'[42] A conclusion such as this enabled him to compare the basilica at Paestum with a 1907 saloon car, and the Parthenon with a 1921 sports car (*Plate 184*).[43] Yet in the same breath he maintains that architecture is above mere questions of functionalism: it is composed of light, shade, walls and space, and it is the task of the architect – between whom and the 'mere engineer' the former distinction is again drawn – to blend these elements into a single whole.

Vers une architecture preaches the message of the standard house, economical and healthy – also morally healthy, as stated in parenthesis. Industrialised building constitutes a revolution which Le Corbusier links to political revolution by declaring that the various social classes no longer have a proper habitation: the new architecture could give this back to them. Hence his phrase 'Architecture or Revolution'.[44] It is therefore logical that the final sentence of the book should read: 'Revolution can be avoided,'[45] followed by a drawing of a briar pipe as a symbol of reconciliation.

The idea that architecture could have an educative influence on society has often recurred since the Enlightenment, when Ledoux assigned a leading social role to the architect. But by the young Le Corbusier, as by Mies van der Rohe at the same period, this role is vastly overrated, and the architect is turned into a pseudo-religious saviour of mankind who will take his place in the ranks of what Schuré called the 'initiates'. Although he repeatedly tried to resolve the opposition between the virtual certainties of technology and a formal concept of architecture – 'We have demanded health, logic, boldness, harmony and perfection, all in the name of the ocean liner, the aeroplane and the automobile,'[46] – Le Corbusier did not succeed. The ocean liner is frequently illustrated in his book, and he adopted ship motifs in some of his buildings, such as the Villa Savoie at Poissy (1929–31) and the Unité d'Habitation in Marseille (1947–52). It is a tradition of thought that can be traced back to Greenough (1843), but it also led to a whole 'aesthetics of the liner' and to the designing of houses that looked like ships at anchor, devoid of all relationship to their surroundings.[47]

Le Corbusier includes in his book the photographs of American grain silos from Gropius's essay on industrialised building in the 1913 Werkbund annual, but retouches them to eliminate historical elements, commenting, in his characteristically overblown style: 'American engineers are crushing our dying architecture with their calculations.'[48] He then goes on to demand new designs for houses and cities, taking some of his illustrations from Choisy, others from Garnier, and putting forward for the first time the idea of a tower-block city, based on ideas published by Perret.[49] This idea is developed in his 1922 plan for a 'ville contemporaine' and later in his book *Urbanisme* (1925).

The major part of *Vers une architecture* is concerned with matters that lie far beyond mere matters of construction. Not for nothing is his first illustration here that of François Blondel's Porte Saint-Denis in Paris, with an accompanying system of proportion, thus establishing an immediate link with Classical French theory of architecture.

For Le Corbusier the secret of architecture resides in geometry and proportion, the latter being identical in his eyes with the principle of the Golden Section enshrined in Nature. To support his view he quotes a series of historical examples; essentially his position is not far removed from that of Berlage and the De Stijl movement. He returns to the familiar analogy of music, declaring: 'Architectural emotion arises when the work resounds within us, in harmony with a universe whose laws we acknowledge, worship and obey.'[50] At the same time he rationalises his position, making the basic geometric forms into 'truths' of geometry, and geometry into the language of man, who creates order by means of geometry and measurement and brings the work of human hands into harmony with the cosmic order.[51] All his modern examples are taken from his own projects, with his Villa Schwob set in direct opposition to the Petit Trianon in Versailles.

The architect's claim to leadership becomes clear when Le Corbusier describes art as an élitist activity which addresses itself to a privileged minority: 'Art is only an essential pabulum for the chosen few who have need of meditation in order to be able to lead.'[52] Moreover art, in the tradition of French rationalism, is knowledge. Beauty addresses itself to reason and the senses through laws and mensurable order; functionalism, economy, standardisation and the like represent the satisfaction of reason, while the formal creative powers of geometry represent the satisfaction of the senses.[53] All Le Corbusier's stipulations are advanced as laws of Nature, and their high-flown idealism takes them into the realms of the universal and the ethical. In his role as supreme creator, the architect, élitist by destiny, makes the laws of the universe into reality and establishes a harmony with the cosmos, relieving the world of tension and rendering revolution superfluous. This demagogic tone is not without its dangers, as can be seen from the generations of students who have reverentially magnified his positions into axioms for their own thinking and designs.

Le Corbusier is even more radical in his theory of urban planning, the individual elements of which can be traced to Garnier, Perret and also, in all probability, Sant'Elia.[54]

His first exercise in this field was his plan for a *'ville contemporaine'* of three million inhabitants (1922), which he included in his book *Urbanisme* (1925) – his most important work on town planning – and also used in his *Plan Voisin* for Paris of the same year (*Plate 185*).[55] His later works on the subject are less radical but adhere to the same criteria.[56]

Le Corbusier sees urban planning as the product of geometry and functionalism, and *Urbanisme* opens with the challenging statement: 'The town is a tool.'[57] Demanding a break with the past, he condemns the ideas of Sitte: 'Modern urban planning comes to birth with a new architecture. An immense, overwhelming, brutal step in evolution has destroyed the links with the past.'[58] ... 'Winding streets are for donkeys, straight roads are for men...The right angle is the necessary and adequate tool for our purposes.'[59] Following Garnier, Le Corbusier separated the functions of living, working, leisure and communication, the last-named being made, on the basis of statistical information, the foundation of the plan. The construction of high-rise residential blocks was intended to increase the density of population in the city centre, at the same time creating green spaces. Where old towns with narrow streets and historical town-centres were concerned, he demanded that these town-centres be demolished.[60] His *Plan Voisin* for Paris, which had only a few traffic arteries and involved the almost total demolition of the old quarters of the city on the north bank of the Seine, shows what he meant; in their place he proposed a symmetrical gridiron pattern with identical high-rise blocks and interspersed green spaces. He also envisaged a new type of street which would meet the requirements of the street as 'traffic machine'[61] (*Plate 186*), with a traffic network concentrated on several levels in the city centre. The city centre itself would include an airport for air taxis and the central railway station – an idea also found in Sant'Elia's *'Città nuova'* of 1914 (*Plate 188*).

Levelling of the terrain, geometry, mass-production, standardisation – such are the requirements for the new cities. 'The transcendant force of geometry must prevail...The modern city is dying because it is not geometric...Geometry is the very essence of architecture. *Building must be industrialised* if mass-production is to be introduced into urban construction.'[62] The centre of a city of this kind would offer 'a glorious picture of order and power.'[63] The traffic systems and high-rise blocks are intended to act as agents of control 'over a world that has been put in order': '...These skyscrapers contain the City's brains, the brains of the whole country. They stand for the whole process of command and control which governs the activity of the people at large.'[64] It is a concept totalitarian in every respect, and Le Corbusier refers time and again to men such as Richelieu, Colbert, Louis XIV, Napoleon and Haussmann (this also suggsts why he should have been prepared to collaborate with the Vichy government during the Second World War). From the formal point of view the city has become a geometric pattern created by an all-powerful architect enjoying a bird's-eye view of things and set on imposing his own order.

Mass-production and standardisation are for Le Corbusier symbols of that order. Levelling the terrain and geometricising the plan are what he calls 'surgery'.[65] The final illustrations in *Urbanisme* are of human organs, with the caption 'Direct, precise and swift connections between two independent functions',[66] which is aimed at making his urban concept appear 'organic'. *Urbanisme* is one of the most disastrous books on architectural theory ever written, with an influence on town planning that lasted for decades. Elements of his system found their way into the Athens Charter, for the formulation of which he was himself largely responsible, though it represented the views of an international community of architects.

Le Corbusier played an important role in the Congrès Internationaux d'Architecture Moderne (CIAM), which were founded in 1928 in La Sarraz in Switzerland and continued to exist until 1957,[67] even though his dominance of their meetings was not as absolute as is sometimes supposed. Compared with the radicalism of his principles, the resolutions of the CIAM were moderate and objective. The Frankfurt Congress of 1929, for instance, devoted to the theme of 'housing for people living at subsistence level', was dominated by initiatives that came from the Germans. On the other hand the Congress held on board SS *Patris II* in Greece in 1933 on 'The Functional City' was stamped with the personality of Le Corbusier, albeit more in the formulation of its conclusions than in the choice of subjects for discussion.[68] The resolution passed by this Congress was guarded in tone,[69] whereas in his 95-point programme known as the 'Athens Charter' (1943), which was clearly drawn up with the Congress in mind, Le Corbusier returns to the radical demands which could, and probably should, be seen as representing the consensus of opinion in the CIAM at that time. Here he repeats his demand for the erection of high-rise residential blocks in city centres, a demand not included in the Congress resolution, and he is more emphatic in his insistence on zoning. He is only prepared to preserve isolated buildings from the past, replacing the cramped houses in old city centres with green spaces, whereas the Congress resolution did at least call for the preservation of historical quarters 'as expressions of earlier styles of life which are of general interest'.

Since 1904, when he read Provensal's *L'art de demain*, Le Corbusier had been aware of the importance of architectural proportion; the use of regulating networks he learned from Choisy and from architects such as Lauweriks,[70] and *Vers une architecture* employs the principle of the Golden Section. In order to arrive at a new and binding theory of proportion, he had to reconcile the Golden Section with a standard human dimension and make this system of measurement the basis not only of architectural planning but also of the standardisation of pre-fabricated units and of the industrial process in general.

This was the problem to which he addressed himself in the two volumes of his book *Le Modulor* (1948 and 1955),[71] which sets him in the tradition of theorists, going back to Vitruvius, who have sought to combine an anthropometric proportion with geometric and mathematical proportions. In so doing, Le Corbusier adopts the false historical premise that in the Renaissance human beings were measured according to the Golden Section. By combining basic human measurements – he assumed a standard height first of 1.75 metres, later of 1.83 metres – with Fibonacci's Series and the Golden Section, he attempted to arrive at an arithmetical scale which would serve as the basis of all industrial and architectural dimensions (*Plate 187*). The blue and red series are to be seen as constituting a norm of universal validity. He carried the Modulor into practice in his Unité d'Habitation in Marseille, and in later projects. The Modulor is no less dogmatic a system than Le Corbusier's earlier architectural and urban planning theories.

Le Corbusier succeeded in synthesising elements of nineteenth-century rationalism and idealism into a high-flown system which he pronounced axiomatic for the twentieth century. But our necessarily critical view of Le Corbusier the theorist must not be allowed to detract from the achievement of Le Corbusier the creative architect, although the question has to be faced, especially in his housing projects, of the extent to which his buildings are merely demonstrations of his theory. This also makes it difficult to decide where it has been the dogmatic theorist and where the practical architect that has influenced the course of architecture in the twentieth century.

Le Corbusier's writings have dominated the architectural debate far beyond the frontiers of France. How deeply rooted in the French tradition was his establishment of architecture in the world of mathematics, geometry and proportion can be seen from the Socratic dialogue *Eupalinos* (1923) by the poet Paul Valéry, in which geometry, proportion, music and architecture are seen as having originally been one.[72] Valéry sees the effect of architecture as depending on numbers and anthropometry. In the dialogue Phaidros describes a temple as 'the mathematical image of a maid of Corinth whom I loved in happiness',[73] and through the mouth of Socrates Valéry uses architecture to pose the problem of a theory of art that has parted company with reality: 'They construct worlds perfect in themselves, which are sometimes so far removed from our own as to be inconceivable; sometimes, however, they come so close to it as to coincide in part with the real world.'[74] Phaidros's subsequent description of theories as 'weapons for the achievement of practical results' makes one reflect on the relationship between theory and practice in Le Corbusier.

Robert Mallet-Stevens (1886–1945) was only one of the many architects whose theoretical writings remained in Le Corbusier's shadow,[75] while André Lurçat (1894–1970; the chief representative of radical architecture in France) produced a five-volume theory of architecture (1953–57) which reads like a continuation of Guadet.[76] The rationalist tradition is more clearly evident in Lurçat than in Le Corbusier, for Lurçat emphasises 'the need to introduce rational methods into the realm of architectural creation'[77] and is particularly concerned to justify his ideas in historical terms. But in common with Le Corbusier, he sees 'the laws of harmony' as residing in proportion, and even touches on the subject of the Classical orders, for which he can no longer find any use but which can prove helpful when it comes to developing a 'rational aesthetic'.[78] At the same time as Lurçat's work there appeared *La Philosophie de la composition architecturale* (1955) by Guadet's pupil Albert Ferran (1886–1952), which served to emphasise still further the influence that continued to be wielded by the Ecole des Beaux-Arts – where Perret taught until 1953.[79] This influence was considerably greater than mid-century architects and architectural theorists in France were willing to admit.

27. Italy: Futurism and Rationalism

Italy appears to have offered no original contribution to architectural theory in the nineteenth century.[1] The texts we have, like the buildings themselves, are to a large extent no more than reactions to movements taking place in France, England and Germany. Architects such as Camillo Boito, for example, reflect in their views the functionalism of Viollet-le-Duc, while at the turn of the century the so-called Stile Liberty linked up with international trends, in particular with Otto Wagner.[2] The work of Raimondo D'Aronco (1857–1932), signally his contribution to the International Exhibition of Arts and Crafts in Turin in 1902,[3] turned the spotlight on Italy for a moment, but in so far as Italian artists were concerned at all with theoretical matters, their standpoints were conventional in the extreme.[4] Slogans like 'A New Art born of Socialism' were simply echoes of English ideas. Nor did the Jugendstil lead without interruption into modern architecture – rather, the work of the great architects of the Stile Liberty, such as D'Aronco, Ernesto Basile and Giuseppe Sommaruga, was only an episode, and architecture, together with theoretical discussion relevant to it, remained backward-looking right down to the 1920s.[5]

With the arrival of Futurism Italy again assumed a leading role in European art.[6] In architecture, however, Futurism became a force only relatively late in the day and then only in individual projects and a handful of manifestos, leaving the face of building virtually untouched.[7] This is not the place to analyse the all-embracing theory of Futurism as such,[8] but only those basic principles that found their way into the manifesto of Futurist architecture.

The key figure in the foundation and whole development of the Futurist movement is the poet and agitator Filippo Tommaso Marinetti (1876–1944). Marinetti, whose attitudes were decisively influenced by his French education, was a passionate Italian patriot who succeeded in accommodating Futurism, in its second stage, to the ideology of Fascism.[9] The Futurist Manifesto that he published on 20 February 1909 in the Paris *Figaro*[10] was a provocative challenge to history and an intoxicating commitment to the absolute authority of technology. As a preface to the manifesto proper, Marinetti tells a story of a car accident using the vocabulary of an eroticised technology. The manifesto itself is a glorification of technology, speed, aggression, human masses, patriotism, militarism, war ('the only hygiene in the world') and a call for the destruction of museums, libraries and colleges ('Calvaries of crucified dreams').

> We care nothing for the past, we young, strong Futurists!...Seize your pick-axes, your knives and your hammers and tear our venerable cities to pieces, without mercy!...Standing erect on the summit of the world, let us once again hurl our challenge at the stars!

There was no area of life or art left untouched by the provocative manifesto of Marinetti and his friends. The first such document on Futurist architecture appeared at the beginning of 1914, the work of the painter Enrico Prampolini,[11] who claimed architecture to be the expression of a Futurist feeling for life, filled with dynamism, energy, light and air. The only criteria that Prampolini puts forward are those of spatial abstraction and perpetual growth.

The young architect Antonio Sant'Elia (1888–1916) must have joined the Futurists some time before the summer of 1914.[12] His early drawings show him to be following in the wake of Otto Wagner, whose book *Die Großstadt* (1911) he most probably knew from the moment it appeared. His projects for a *'città nuova'* (1913–14), exhibited in the spring of 1914, and his *Messaggio* in the exhibition catalogue, suggest that he was already acquainted with the proclamations of the Futurists.[13]

Sant'Elia's *Messaggio* speaks not of 'Futurist' but of 'modern' architecture, and makes it clear from the beginning that the author's concern is not with a problem of style or form but with the production of rational designs which exploit every technological possibility yet also take account of people's living habits and contemporary attitudes. The conditions of modern life, in Sant'Elia's view, require a break with tradition, with style, with aesthetics and with proportion. His rejection of historical continuity reveals his affinity with the Futurists. The laws governing the new materials steel and concrete require a new ideal of beauty in which the monumental, massive and static values of the past give way to the lightweight structures and practical values of the present. Sant'Elias proposes the demolition of urban slum areas and the erection of grand hotels, railway stations, enormous trunk roads, gigantic docks, etc. to exemplify the new age. The modern city has to be reinvented: Sant'Elia compares it with a huge shipbuilding yard, bustling with energy and dynamic in every detail. Modern houses must resemble giant machines: in place of staircases they are to have elevators which wind their way up the glass and steel façades like snakes. The houses themselves are to be of cement, iron and glass, with no painted or moulded decoration – their beauty will be found in their lines and their plasticity. The house is to be 'remarkably ugly in its mechanical simplicity' (*'straordinariamente brutta nella sua meccanica semplice'*), poised on the edge of a noisy ravine in which, below the houses, multi-level streets, underground railways and escalators are to be found (*Plate 189*). In order to achieve this, monuments, pavements, arcades and stairways all have to be destroyed, streets and squares lowered, and a new level found for the construction of the city, so that the ground plane can be rearranged to meet the needs of the inhabitants.

Sant'Elia condemns the *'architettura di moda'*; of all countries and all styles – ceremonial, Classicist, hieratic, theatrical, decorative, monumental, charming, pleasing and the rest; he also condemns the preservation, reconstruction and reproduction of historical monuments, together with vertical and horizontal lines and cubic and pyramidal forms, which are static, oppressive and thus 'totally outside our modern sensibility' (*'assolutamente fuori della nostra nuovissima sensibilità'*). Instead he demands a cool, calculating architecture of daring simplicity, using reinforced concrete, iron, glass, cardboard, synthetic textiles and all plastic materials and maximum lightness and elasticity. However, architecture is seen not just as a calculated combination of the practical and the useful but an art, i.e. synthesis and expression; applied decoration is absurd, for only the proper employment of rough, bare raw materials in stark colours can produce a decorative quality in truly modern architecture. As the past drew its inspiration from Nature, so the present, its material and intellectual values derived from the artificial, must find its inspiration in the world of machines, the most perfect expression and most complete synthesis of which is embodied in architecture. This rejection of the past, and the associated appeal to technology and dynamism, with architecture as the medium of the message, is very near the Futurist position.

Sant'Elia's *Messaggio* is in part directly linked to his '*città nuova*' projects, though he never produced a complete plan. Our impression of the city and its buildings is based on the considerable number of individual sketches and drawings that he made, but it is not always clear how these relate to his general plan.[14] That the determining factor in the plan is the communications system emerges from the massive multi-level streets and railway lines, spanned by bridges and directly linked to individual buildings. The streets are designed solely with vehicles in mind: nowhere in any drawing is there a tree, an avenue or a pedestrian to be seen. Reflections of Sant'Elia's participation in the competition for the Central Railway Station in Milan (1912) can be seen in his design for a central railway station linked by escalators to an airport and a system of express-ways (*Plate 188*). This centralisation of all means of communication is also a feature of Le Corbusier's plan for a modern city of three million inhabitants (*Plate 186*). In his building designs Sant'Elia shows a predilection for power stations and for tall buildings whose function is not immediately evident but which exemplify the principle of density. In accordance with the theses in his *Messaggio*, these buildings have their elevator shafts on the outside of the walls and the much-criticised verticalism of the time is relieved by setting the storeys back. These designs probably reveal the influence of the argument over the set-back skyscraper which had been going on in the United States since the 1890s and about which Sant'Elia had learned through architectural journals. All his designs are free of ornament but their extensive symmetry gives them a new monumentality. In their external aspect it is hardly possible to distinguish churches from residential blocks, or offices from factories.

Sant'Elia's Futurist manifesto of 14 July 1914, which is accompanied by a number of drawings of the '*città nuova*',[15] is largely identical to the *Messaggio* but has an additional preamble; the words 'modern' and 'new' are replaced by 'Futurist', which, together with a few other alterations, may be due to Marinetti. One new point is the notion of the temporary and transitory nature of Futurist architecture, coupled with the principle that each generation must build its own city: 'The houses will not last as long as we do. Each generation will have to build its own city' ('*Le case dureranno meno di noi. Ogni generazione dovrà fabbricarsi la sua città*'). This experience of the rapid passage of time now leads for the first time to the renunciation of the old principle of durability. Already in the nineteenth century – with Viollet-le-Duc, for instance – economic considerations had led to the idea that buildings might be erected with a limited span of life, but now architecture was not only to become the expression of a life-process but was itself to be absorbed into this process. This idea of a dynamic city occurs as early as 1910 in the urban scenes of Umberto Boccioni ('*La città che sale*' – 'The city that rises'), who also produced a manifesto on Futurist architecture at the beginning of 1914, in which he postulated an 'evolutionary architecture' ('*architettura evolutiva*') based purely on 'necessity'.[16] This 'plastic dynamism' was reduced by Boccioni to the formula 'Necessity = speed'. He saw ships, automobiles and railway stations as expressions of a new aesthetic, and the element of speed even became an important criterion in the architect's choice of material. In an ironic paraphrase of Vitruvius's trinity of *firmitas, utilitas* and *venustas*, Sant'Elia produced the formula '*Economia + utilità + rapidità*'.

Outside Italy Sant'Elia's ideas were taken up most enthusiastically by the De Stijl movement. Compared with Garnier's '*cité industrielle*', however, which put a comparable emphasis on technology, Sant'Elia represents the trend towards all-encompassing architecture that reached its climax with Le Corbusier, but the utopian nature of his designs, and his early death, prevented his ideas from having any influence on architectural practice. Marinetti subsequently described him as a pioneer of Futurist-Fascist architecture. Mario Chiattone (1891–1957), a friend of Sant'Elia, left a number of similar but formally less bold designs, including some for residential housing that anticipate the Italian Rationalist style of the 1920s.

The idea of a 'Futurist reconstruction of the universe' took increasingly fantastic forms as time went on. In the years immediately after the Great War Vincenzo Fani, using the pseudonym VOLT, and Virgilio Marchi (1895–1960) evolved a series of totally unrealistic concepts which bore a formal resemblance to those of the German Expressionists of the same period, such as Taut and Finsterlin. In his manifesto of 1919[17] Fani describes a 'dynamic' architecture with 'flying houses' no longer tied to the ground, which would congregate to form giant cities, then, as one single city, traverse the earth and in alliance with the inhabitants of Venus and Mercury wage war against Mars. Science fiction ideas of this kind have their origins in fairground architecture. Individual houses are described as mere musculature – non-cubic, non-symmetrical, variable. Marchi, in his manifesto of 1920,[18] gives architecture the expressive power of poetry and uses its 'style of movement' as a means of elevating the spirit. Marchi's designs combine a kind of roller-coaster architecture with Expressionist forms and resemble those of Finsterlin, although their basis is quite different.[19] A further logical step led Marchi to envisage architecture based on firework display.

The rapprochement between the so-called Second Futurism and Fascism cannot be explored here, especially as the ideological implications of the architectural debate in the 1920s were not confined to Futurism but involved all movements. As in Germany at this time, there were in Italy many different trends, but whereas in Germany there were irreconcilable ideological differences which were ultimately subjected to the process of *Gleichschaltung* under Hitler, in Italy the various movements all marched under the banner of nationalism and Fascism. Research is still actively being carried out on this subject.[20]

The short-lived neo-Futurist journal *La città futurista* (1928–29), of which only three numbers appeared, contained articles by Luigi Colombo (under the pseudonym Fillia) and Enrico Prampolini, which offered no new material but merely attempted to set Italian architecture in the context of international developments in the 1920s.[21] Other groups had more substantial contributions to make, such as Il Novecento,[22] founded in 1923, which set out to combine national traditions and modernity under the emblem of Italian-ness. The buildings of the Novecento architects are characterised by a Neo-classicism with its roots in Classical Rome and in Italian architecture of the early nineteenth century, but in retrospect they appear as a national variant of international Neo-classicism. The most typical of these architects is Giovanni Muzio (b.1893) of Milan, who in an essay on nineteenth-century Milan architecture published in 1921 reacted against the individualism of the time by advancing a principle of order derived from the Classical tradition, which he proposed to apply to the contemporary situation.[23] Ten years later he openly demanded a return to the models of Italian Classicism both for architecture and for town planning:

The best and most original examples from the past undoubtedly appear to be those of Classical derivation, and particularly in Milan those from the beginning of the nineteenth century. As for urbanism, so for architecture: a return to Classicism is called for, analogous to the way in which this has taken place in literature and the plastic arts.[24]

Terms like 'simplicity' and 'bareness' are used to convey the desire for 'total Italianness' ('*assoluta italianità*'), as found in the buildings of Giuseppe de Finetti (1892–1952), who worked with Loos in Vienna before the Great War and later collaborated with Muzio on a number of projects in Milan.[25] The Neo-classicism, free of ornament, of the Novecento architects also characterises Loos's work of the 1920s, and in 1934 Finetti published in the journal *Casabella* an Italian translation of Loos's essay *Ornament und Verbrechen* ('Ornament and Crime'), thus establishing another point of contact between the Novecento and Rationalists.

It is not yet possible to assess the role of Marcello Piacentini (1881–1960), the most successful Italian architect of the twentieth century. He published numerous articles to accompany his development from the expansive modernity of his youth to the monumental Neo-classical buildings and the excursions into urban planning he undertook at the behest of Mussolini, but his work has not yet been researched in its overall context. The development of his ideas can best be traced in the pages of the journals *Architettura e arti decorative* (1921–31) and *Architettura* (1932–43),[26] which he edited or co-edited, as well as in books such as *Architettura d'oggi* (1930). Piacentini was well acquainted with the various international developments but based his criticism of international architecture on the Italian national tradition and on the particular climatic conditions of the country.[27] Piacentini puts the arguments of functionalism to good account but always regards architecture as existing within a geographical and historical continuum, which puts him in the company of the proponents of *ambientismo*. His attitude towards skyscrapers is revealing: he accepts them, on the basis of the high cost of building land, for hotels and office blocks in American city centres but rejects them completely for Italy: 'No skyscrapers, then, in Italy; economic reasons do not suggest it, nor aesthetic ones permit it.'[28]

In his approach to urban planning Piacentini underwent a remarkable change in the course of his life. In a memorandum of 1916 on the planning of Rome he drew attention to the views of Sitte and pleaded for the total preservation of old town centres, while suggesting new uses for the buildings in order to prevent such towns from becoming museums. Opposing the destruction of town centres, he advocated that expansion be moved to the suburbs,[29] thereby taking up a position contrary to that of 'progressive' town-planners – to be led by Le Corbusier a few years later – who geared everything to the needs of traffic. Then, under Mussolini, it was Piacentini who became responsible for the disembowelling of Italian city centres – a *volte-face* difficult to comprehend, even though it corresponded to the international consensus embodied in the Athens Charter.

The attempt by Futurist architects in Italy to break out of the constraints of history was an interesting episode but it had few practical consequences. It was the Novecentro, conservative, nationalist but by no means reactionary, and with no theory of its own, that was dominant in reality. The Rationalists' attempts to link up with the international trends of the 1920s, on the other hand, have been extensively chronicled.[30]

The Movimento Italiano per l'Architettura Razionale (MIAR) lasted a mere seven years but radically changed its nature during this time. Its activities were concentrated on two exhibitions, in 1928 and 1931, the second of which was accompanied by an increasing politicisation which ultimately destroyed the group's original concern with architecture. Yet even after the various shifts of emphasis have been taken into account, it remains a fact that these Rationalists believed from the outset that they could achieve their aims with the help of Fascism – indeed, that the essence of Rationalism could be identified with Fascism. The position of the Italian Rationalists vis-à-vis the Fascist Party and the Fascist State was thus totally different from that of the modern architectural movement in Germany, such as the Bauhaus, which was largely left-wing in character and thus opposed to the centrist parties and the National Socialists.

If the importance of the Italian Rationalist movement in the 1920s is to be understood, it should be remembered that it was not until the middle of the decade that the so-called international style made any impression in Italy, and that the scene was dominated by the Classicist 'Italian-ness' of the Novecento architects.

The first efforts to draw attention to international modernism in Italy were those of Gaetano Minnucci (1896–1980), who wrote a number of articles on modern Dutch architecture from 1923 onwards.[31] Enthusiastic over the break with tradition, he summarised the new trend as 'cubist, expressionist, romantic and rationalist'.[32] He was also one of the two organisers of the first Rationalist exhibition in 1928.

In 1926 various groups of young architects in Rome, Milan and Turin became so agitated about 'international' architecture, and so insistent on the need for a new conception of architecture, that they banded together to put their programmes before the public. The first and most important of these groups was the Gruppo 7 in Milan, consisting of Ubaldo Castagnoli, Luigi Figini, Guido Frette, Sebastiano Larco, Gino Pollini, Carlo Enrico Rava and Giuseppe Terragni. On 1 December 1926, under the title *Architettura*, this group published in the journal *Rassegna Italiana* the first part of a large-scale manifesto, the later parts of which continued to appear in the same journal up to May 1927.[33] December 1926 must thus be considered the date when the MIAR was born.

The manifesto is the starting-point for any definition of the Rationalist movement in Italian architecture, and contains a statement not only of the Gruppo 7's position but also of how it diverges from that of the related 'international' movement. Compared with Sant'Elia's Futurist manifesto of 1914, it is reserved in tone. It opens with the words 'A new spirit has been born' ('*E nato uno spirito nuovo*') – a clear reference to the journal *Esprit Nouveau*, in which Le Corbusier's *Vers une architecture* had begun to appear in 1920. Le Corbusier is described as one of the most important initiators of a 'rational' architecture – architecture being set in the context of new ideas represented by Picasso and Juan Gris in painting, Cocteau in literature, and Stravinsky in music, together with Le Corbusier, whose artistic ideal, shared by Cocteau, is characterised as one of 'a strict, limpid and crystal-clear logic' ('*logica rigida, limpida, cristallina*').

Opening with a brief survey of the architectural situation in Germany, Austria, Holland and Scandinavia, the manifesto refers to the new directions taken in these countries which are conditioned by national, geographical and climatic factors, and rejects the idea of bringing about a renewal of Italian architecture by simply adopting German practices. Instead it calls for a constructive rationalism that takes full account of landscape and climate, and thus both establishes a link with Piacentini's '*ambientismo*' and, though not in so many words, distances itself from the principle of 'international' architecture. Italy, it is claimed, has a leading role to play in the new architecture by virtue of her historical tradition and of her rise under Mussolini:

It is up to Italy to give the new spirit its fullest development, to take it to its extreme consequences, to the point of dictating a style to other nations, as during its great periods in the past.

Claiming to speak for the young generation, the Gruppo 7 rejected the Futurist revolt, in particular its 'Romantic' denial of the past, and expressed a desire for clarity and order rooted in history and tradition:

So the desire for a new spirit amongst the young is based upon a secure knowledge of the past, it is not founded upon thin air...There is no incompatibility between our past and our present. We do not want to break with tradition...

At the same time the group rejected the traditionalist architecture of the day, which merely tacked historical façades to skeletal frameworks.

This leads to the heart of the theoretical argument in the manifesto, an argument based on a commitment to rationalism, to the 'necessity' of construction, to type, and to a new concept of beauty:

The new architecture, true architecture, must result from a strict adherence to logic, to rationality. A rigid constructivism must dictate the rules. The new architectural forms will have to receive their aesthetic value solely from the nature of their necessity, and only subsequently, by means of selection, will a style be born...we do not claim to create a style...but from the constant employment of rationality, from the perfect correspondence between the building's structure and its intended purpose, the selected style will result. We must succeed in ennobling the indefinable and abstract perfection of pure rhythm; simple constructability alone would not be beauty.

The concept of 'selection' is defined as the necessity of creating a limited number of fundamental types, as stated in Le Corbusier's *Vers une architecture*. But Le Corbusier's concept of the house as a machine is rejected as absurd, and in its place comes a demand that architecture must evolve from the new necessities in its own way, just as machines had done: 'The house will have its own aesthetic, as the aeroplane has its own aesthetic, but the house will not have the aesthetic of the aeroplane.' Moreover, the new, true and original architecture of types can only come about through the renunciation of individuality, the sacrifice of the subjective principle, a concentration on the needs of the present and the strictest application of logic: 'architecture can no longer be individual'. There is also reference, however, to a 'temporary levelling' ('*temporaneo livellamento*'). The spirit of mass-production is set against the elegant eclecticism of the individual. It is not poverty that is the goal but simplicity, and in the perfection of simplicity lies the highest degree of refinement.

As to industrial buildings, typological codification inevitably brings with it a certain internationalisation of form, the uniformity of which may even give an impression of grandeur. In all other kinds of building the emphasis must lie on complete modernity combined with the preservation of national traditions as a kind of classical substratum. The architectural revolution is hailed in high-flown terms as 'a desire for truth, for logic, for order, a clarity redolent of Hellenism'.

The second part of the manifesto of the Gruppo 7 consists of a survey of modern

European architecture and an assessment of its 'rationality'. Le Corbusier is criticised for applying the criteria of pure rationality too rigorously, thereby creating a clinical impression. Concrete offers the opportunity for a new aesthetic, and the rational application of materials will lead to the development of forms which will offer complete solutions to individual problems and be seen as part of an international architectural language, like the Orders or the arch in past eras. The third part of the work deals with the training of architects and calls for more attention to be given to technical problems, so as to create awareness of the possibility of a 'technological aesthetics'. Since architecture expresses the spirit of an age, the current cult of Neo-classicism on the part of the Novecento group is to be rejected.

The fourth and final section of the manifesto deals with the Rationalists' new aesthetic, especially the aesthetics of reinforced concrete, a material which opened up the way to a new Classical monumentality. The new forms, characterised by simplicity of surfaces and by the quiet rhythm of open and closed levels, in which the alternation of geometric shadows creates spatial qualities, are compared with the earliest period of Greek architecture. In the present phase in the development of a new formal language by selection, the argument goes on, all individualism must be renounced: only in this way can a uniform style be created which will lead to a truly 'Italian' architecture, an architecture of 'pure grandeur' ('*pura gradiosità*') and 'serene beauty' ('*bellezza serena*'). The new monumentality will be drawn from history and from the national character. This question of nationalism and internationalism, together with that of the criteria appropriate to the discussion of architectural aesthetics, recurs time and again, and the language of the manifesto was sufficiently vague for polemical passions to be aroused.

With the first *Esposizione Italiana di Architettura Razionale*, held in the Palazzo della Esposizioni in Rome in 1928, the ideas of the Rationalists reached a wider public. The introduction to the catalogue, signed by Gaetano Minnucci and Adelberto Libera, enlarges on the manifesto of 1926–27 and offers for the first time a definition of 'rational' architecture:[34]

> Rational architecture, as we understand it, rediscovers harmonies, rhythms and symmetries in new schemes of construction, in the nature of the materials, and in a perfect response to the requirements for which a building is intended.

This international-sounding definition was given a national slant by the addition of a reference to Roman principles and by the equation of the 'rational' quality of architecture with its 'national' quality, so that, 'in the true Fascist spirit', rational architecture could regain for Italy the glory that it enjoyed under the Romans.[35]

The exhibition itself was arranged according to the regions from which the various groups sent in their designs, and as far as one can judge from the sixty-one plates in the catalogue, the range was considerable. Of the five hundred projects on display, only five were executed (*Plate 190*). The reactions to the exhibits show a high level of theoretical argument, which was as yet barely touched by political considerations. Piacentini's review[36] contains fundamental objections to the Rationalists' whole view of architecture, and demonstrates that, far from being reducible to rationalist terms, the constructional principles of the Romans resulted in aesthetic values that were in fact fundamentally irrational. To the extent that nationalism is concerned with the fulfilment of the functions of a building and with the relationship of interior to exterior, or to the extent that it attacks the practice of stylistic imitation in the architecture of the day, Piacentini is not opposed to it, but he does protest against reducing the essence of architecture to a matter of mere rationality, which he describes as the bread and water of architecture, as 'architectural Franciscanism'. He has trenchant functional criticisms to make of the designs produced by the Rationalists: rows of glass windows are perfectly in order in Northern Europe, he says, but not under an Italian sun; flat roofs, which only expose the upper storeys of buildings to heat and cold, are among the prices of Rationalism; the absence of window shutters removes a source of protection against the midday sun, and so on. He even speaks of new 'architectural drugs' that are being universally used – in churches, schools, market-places, palaces, and so on. Rationalism is for him simply a new style:

> It would not surprise me if tomorrow someone were to commission a building from an architect in the Rational style, just as one might be commissioned in the Renaissance or Gothic style.

Piacentini criticises the inadequate attention paid by the Rationalists in their projects to the pre-existing architectural environment. Moreover, the rejection of historical styles does not mean the rejection of decoration as such. A concentration on reinforced concrete is said to be one-sided, and it is necessary to work with a range of different materials. Piacentini concludes by proposing a new exhibition devoted to thematic design for specific situations.

In an open letter replying to these criticisms on behalf of the Rationalists,[37] Libera accused Piancentini of starting from a false interpretation of the term 'rational': architecture as construction must be concerned in the first instance with technical, utilitarian and rational factors; architecture as art must express the modern spirit and modern sensibility, which, however, must not be allowed to contradict these technical, utilitarian and rational factors, because the atmosphere of the time is governed by them and modern sensibility defined by them. In 1928 Marinetti joined in the debate,[38] believing that he could lead the Rationalists back to the Futurism of Sant'Elia. Marinetti's intervention, which the Rationalists vehemently opposed, has to be seen against the background of the contemporary neo-Futurist movement, which would have dearly liked to absorb the Rationalists into its own ranks.[39]

The discussion that went on between the exhibitions of 1928 and 1931 was marked by a decline in intellectual quality and an increase in political content. *La Casa Bella* (1928–43) was the Rationalists' own journal but many other periodicals also entered the fray. An important figure of this time was Pietro Maria Bardi, gallery-owner, journalist and editor, who embarked on a second career after the Second World War as director of the Museum in São Paulo. Bardi's aim was to produce a total synthesis of the Rationalist theory of architecture and Fascist ideology, to which his essay *Architettura, arte di stato* (1931) and his book *Rapporto sull'architettura per Mussolini* (1931) are devoted.[40] Instead of the basically objective tone of the discussion of 1928 these works of Bardi's are characterised by a distasteful polemicism and an undisguised servility towards Mussolini. Bardi demands that architecture, particularly in Rome, assume a Fascist physiognomy, and calls on the State to assert its authority in this matter, since architecture is the most durable element in any civilisation and will outlive all other products of human hands. Architecture is thus a State art.

These ideas were developed further by Giuseppe Terragni (1904–43), who produced a three-point programme:[41]

1) To declare architecture a State art.

2) To change radically the laws concerning the architectural profession and its relation to building committees.

3) To entrust to architecture, thus renewed, the task of confirming and making eternal the triumph of the Fascist ideal in the world.

In his *Rapporto sull'architettura per Mussolini* Bardi sets out to demonstrate that it is in the work of the Rationalists that the qualities which make up '*latinità*' are to be found; what Fascism needs is a cheerful, brightly coloured, sober, even 'military' architecture 'reflecting the characteristics of robustness and order that are the chief preferences of Mussolini's Italians'. While tracing the roots of Rationalism back to Classical Rome, Bardi also stresses its modernity, adding, with his eye on the Novecento group, which he sought to oust from Mussolini's favour: 'The so-called Rationalist architects are traditionalists'. He concludes with a deferential bow to the Duce:

> ...the young look to Mussolini to control the fate of architecture, which is in such a poor state today. In their petition the youth of today ask Mussolini for a reply. Whatever Mussolini replies will be fine, because Mussolini is always right.

In 1928 the Gruppo 7 became the Movimento per l'Architettura Razionale (MAR),[42] with the Movimento Italiano per l'Architettura Razionale (MIAR) being officially constituted in 1930.[43] Its members took part in conferences of the CIAM (see page 401) and were at pains to strengthen their links with other countries. The MIAR's constitution, as signed by Libera, provided for regional groups but laid down no instructions as to the substance of the movement.[44] The MIAR's most important task lay in preparing for the second exhibition, which opened in March 1931 in Rome and was subsequently shown in Milan and Turin. It was intended that this exhibition should contain 'concrete proposals to put before the Duce'.[45] Mussolini was given a preview of the exhibition and reportedly talked with the architects about their activity, about modern architecture in general, and about 'the works that Fascism expected of them'.[46]

At the opening of the exhibition a manifesto was distributed, the sole purpose of which was to identify Rationalism with Fascism[47] in the spirit of Bardi's *Rapporto*. The general quality of the exhibits was higher than that of the designs in the 1928 show, and the majority followed the international style (*Plate 191*). Many of the designs also displayed the monumentalism that formed part of the Rationalists' programme.

Arguments over the exhibition, which coincided with the construction of the Rome University Building and the highly controversial competition for the design of the central railway station at Florence, reached fever pitch. In the forefront of the discussion was the journalist Ugo Ojetti, who rejected the whole principle of building according to the properties of materials: it was not materials that controlled the architect but the architect who controlled materials, declared Ojetti, who put forward a hierarchy of architectural forms in which 'mechanised architecture' might be appropriate for buildings that served a purely practical function but not for others.[48] Terragni, the most important exponent of the Rationalists' position, took exception to the persistent tendency to equate 'rational' with a solely functionalist architecture, and revived the question of an architectural aesthetic. He saw architecture not merely as construction or the fulfilment of material needs but as something more:

> ...it is strength that directs these constructive and utilitarian achievements towards a goal of higher aesthetic value. When that harmony of proportion which induces

a state of contemplation, or of profound feeling, in the soul of the observer is joined to the constructive scheme, only then will the crowning result be a work of architecture.[49]

In a purely polemical article entitled *Difesa dell'architettura italiana*[50] Piacentini returned to the fray by branding Rationalism, which only pretended to be Fascist, as in fact Bolshevist and internationalist, and going on to attack, like Ojetti, the abandonment of the principle of a hierarchy of buildings, which had resulted in churches becoming indistinguishable from theatres, and schools from houses. At the same time he warned against confusing Fascism with *romanità*, a term widely and crudely taken to imply what was sententious, histrionic and vacuous. To this the Rationalists retorted: 'We in Italy have no need to be Bolshevists in order to be Rationalists.'[51] The MIAR came to a lamentable end after the exhibition of 1931 as a result of the increasingly threadbare quality of the arguments and the disgraceful polemics. The exhibition contained a '*tavola degli orrori*' which mocked the public architecture of the 1920s and was regarded as an attack on the discipline of the Fascist Union of Architects, to which the Rationalists belonged.[52]

The Italian Rationalists produced only an outline of architectural theory. In this context one must note the growing encroachment of Fascist ideology, which was responsible for a number of points of principle, such as the superiority of Italian architecture to that of all other countries, and the cult of a 'military' style. The urge towards *romanità* led Mussolini's totalitarian régime to demand the adoption of an 'imperial' style, such as that exemplified by the Neo-classical monumentalism of Piacentini, but neither Rationalism nor Neo-classicism can be dismissed simply as expressions of Fascism.[53] This does, however, raise the whole complex question of how far architecture can be pressed into service in the name of totalitarianism.[54] The process of *Gleichschaltung* in Germany, for instance, cannot be compared with the situation in Italy, where any theory could be propounded, even though its chances of being put into practice were slight. The Rationalists continued to enjoy Mussolini's goodwill until 1935, and their advice was sought on plans such as those for Rome University and the E 42 trunk road. Certainly a number of them enjoyed political careers that hardly suggest that their ideas needed to be suppressed.[55] The case of Terragni[56] shows how an architect of Fascist persuasion was able to insist on retaining certain forms even though, as with his Casa del Fascio in Como, this involved rejecting on aesthetic grounds various demands made by the Party – such as for a tower and an assembly area ('*arengario*') – for what was, after all, an official Fascist building.[57]

By contrast Edoardo Persico (1900–36), an interior designer[58] who had earlier been an editor of *La Casa Bella*, who increasingly dissociated himself intellectually from the régime, succeeded in sustaining an objective critical position until his early and unexpected death.[59] A similar critical line was taken by the art critic and historian Raffaello Giolli (1889–1945), who worked for the journals *Domus* and *La Casa Bella* and whose work in the resistance led to his being killed by the Fascists.[60] Similarly the architect Giuseppe Pagano (1896–1945), who was an enthusiastic supporter of Mussolini at the time when he took over the editorship of *La Casa Bella* in 1931, became an anti-Fascist and died, like Giolli, in the concentration camp of Mauthausen.[61] Different again is the case of Alberto Sartoris (b.1901), who joined the Futurists in 1920 and later the Rationalists, then embraced the line of international functionalism and devoted numerous works to presenting modern architecture in a broad historical and geographical context.[62]

An accurate assessment of the situation in Italy in the 1930s is made difficult by the fact that it is often scarcely possible to distinguish clearly between the various groups. Thus a successful architect like Angiolo Mazzoni (1894–1979),[63] who worked for Piacentini, joined the neo-Futurists and published, together with Marinetti and Mino Somenzi, an ultimate Futurist manifesto in 1934, while many of his designs adopted the formal language of the Rationalists.[64] The BBPR studio (Gian Luigi Banfi, Ludovico Barbiano di Belgiojoso, Enrico Peressutti and Ernesto Nathan Rogers), founded in 1932, absorbed many different trends, and though close to the Rationalist position, also accepted into its philosophy a number of the ideas associated with *ambientismo*.[65]

The collapse of Fascism did not signify a break either in the development or in the theoretical discussion of architecture, and with the exception of the monumental Neo-classicism of Mussolini's public buildings, the different movements and tendencies all managed to survive. At no time was freedom of discussion destroyed – a fact to be remembered when post-war developments in Italy are compared with those in Germany. In Italy this continuity was to a large extent unaffected by the ideologisation of architectural debate under Fascism, since intellectually every group made its peace with the régime in one way or the other. In Germany, by contrast, a new start had to be made, based on the solution of ideological and moral problems.

28. The Soviet Union

From the Renaissance onwards East European architecture exhibited a dependency on that of Western Europe, in particular of Italy. The high artistic quality of the buildings erected in fifteenth-century Hungary under Matthias Corvinius, during the Jagiellon period in Poland or under Russian Classicism, is not matched by anything in the realm of theory that goes beyond the adaptation of Western sources.[1] The published works by and on the Italo-Russian architect Giacomo Quarenghi (1744–1817) are design collections in the Western tradition, and the reversion to medieval architecture in Russia in the nineteenth century runs parallel to developments that were taking place in Western European countries at the same time. Whereas in painting the last third of the nineteenth century saw fresh initiatives in the search for a modern Russian culture,[2] a comparable movement in architecture only emerged during the years of the First World War, albeit with an intensity that reached its peak with the 1917 Revolution. Here too the lead was given by the fine arts, specifically by Futurism and Cubism, which merged in Russia to form what was called 'Cubofuturism', while Suprematism and Constructivism developed attitudes that covered all the arts, rather like the De Stijl movement in the Netherlands.

In recent years a great deal of source material has come to light on the theory and practice of architecture in the Soviet Union from the Revolution down to the Stalin era.[3] This material is both varied and confusing, on the one hand because artists and architects were convinced that they had a vital contribution to make to society and the new Soviet state, even though their discussions frequently remained in the realm of form and aesthetics, and on the other hand because the state sought to use art and architecture for its own propaganda purposes. There were widely-diverging views over what constituted proletarian culture, views that found their earliest expression in the activities of the organisation known as the 'Proletkult' (1917–21).[4] There was a demand, in the spirit of the Italian Futurists, for a break with the past, even for its total destruction, as in the lurid language of V. T. Kirilov (1890–1943): 'Let us burn Raphael in the name of our tomorrow, let us destroy and stamp on the blossoms of art...We have learnt how to love the power of steam and dynamite, the wailing of the sirens and the rhythmic pounding of pistons and rollers.'[5] Lenin's aim was 'to seize the whole of the culture left by capitalism and use it to build socialism.'[6] Trotsky, on the other hand, denied that there was any connection between the proletariat and a new style of architecture, stating bluntly: 'Not only is there no proletarian culture, but there never will be.'[7]. Hence:

> This means that a new architectural style can never be created apart from the practical task in hand and the constant efforts towards its solution. Attempts to arrive at a style deductively on the basis of the nature of the proletariat, its collectivism, its activity, its atheism and so on are the purest idealism and will lead in practice to nothing but a mass of eccentricities, arbitrary allegories and the same old provincialism and amateurism.[8]

This was the fate that befell Lenin's 'Monumental Propaganda' initiative which, inspired by Tommaso Campanella's utopian vision of a 'City of the Sun' ('*Città del sole*'), set out to use art as a propaganda weapon.[9]

The artistic driving force behind the new architectural movement that now emerged in Russia against the background of Cubofuturism was, significantly, the concept of the *Gesamtkunstwerk*, and the first significant work to embody this synthetic 'union of the arts' was Kruchenykh's Futurist opera *Victory over the Sun* (1913),[10] for which Kazimir Malevich (1878–1935) designed backcloths and costumes. The Suprematist movement founded by Malevich is only of interest in this context by virtue of Malevich's idealised architectural drawings experimenting in the dimension of space, which ultimately led him to postulate a link between his designs and the Communist social system.[11] Malevich's writings and projects of the 1920s,[12] as well as his architectural projects known as *Arkhitektoniki* (from 1922), show the emergence of a new conception (*Plate 192*). The principal sources of his ideas are the treatise *Suprematism I/46* (1923) and the Unovis *Suprematist Manifesto* (1924; 'Unovis' stood for 'Defence of New Forms in Art' and designated both the doctrines of the group centred on Malevich and the group itself).[13] Malevich's starting-point, in common with the Italian Futurists and the German Expressionists, was an aerial view of the earth: 'Hovering *planity* [flying bodies] will determine the new plans of cities and the form of housing for *zemlyanity* [earth-dwellers].[14] The *planity* are incorporeal, 'the new dwellings of the new men are situated in space.' Malevich concedes that 'as yet there are no consumers for the New Art.'[15] His emphasis on the right angle, which suggests links with De Stijl and with Le Corbusier, is made to correspond, by means of highly contrived arguments, to the 'essence of the Communist doctrine', while other forms, such as the triangle, are dismissed as Ancient, pagan or Christian. For him the only form of building appropriate to the new society is one based on the right angle, 'since Communism seeks to distribute power equally to all.'[16] Such statements lie at the extreme of formalism.

Malevich brusquely rejects the formal traditionalism of the Party line which sought to adapt historical forms to new social functions:

> We refuse to turn Classical temples, which were adequate for the purposes both of pagans and Christians, into clubs or 'houses of culture' for the proletariat, even if these temples be named after the leaders of the Revolution and be decorated with their portraits.[17]

Malevich's cubic *Arkhitektoniki*, constructed entirely of right angles, have the appearance rather of sculptures with architectural associations than of designs intended for practical functions, with the exception of a design, with accompanying plan and section, for a workers' club (*Plate 192*). In a piece written on the occasion of the Grand Berlin Art Exhibition in 1927, with the title 'Suprematist Architecture', he refers to a 'pure, absolute architecture' and to architecture as 'a pure art form', proclaiming his Suprematism as marking 'the beginning of a new Classical architecture'.[18] This reduction of architecture to a question of forms, without regard to constructional or functional considerations, was bound to end in failure.

Malevich's Suprematism did, however, provide the artistic starting-point for the Russian Constructivist movement – although the Constructivists eventually arrived at totally different conclusions.[19] An important link between the two movements is provided by El Lissitzky (1890–1941), who was trained as an architect and was active in almost every aspect of design.[20] In 1917 he joined Malevich for a few years as a teacher at the Art Academy in Vitebsk, and as a result of lengthy periods spent in Germany in the 1920s he was able to further the exchange of ideas between Russia and Central Europe. He invented an artistic formula he called 'Proun' (an abbreviation of 'proyekt ustanovleniya/utverzhdeniya novogo' – 'project for the establishment/affirmation of the new'). With his Prouns he sought to supersede the conventional forms of picture, sculpture and architecture,[21] defining Prouns as 'junction-stations where materials change into architecture'. 'Proun changes the productive forms of art,' he continued, envisaging a unified city for all the people of the world, 'to be erected on the Communist foundation of reinforced concrete.'[22]

The most important results of these ideas as far as architecture is concerned were El Lissitzky's high-rise projects which he called 'Cloud Hangers' and with which he intended to revolutionise the appearance of urban Moscow (*Plates 193, 194*).[23] These horizontal structures, each resting on three pillars, were designed to provide a maximum of usable space with a minimum of support, for which El Lissitzky projected technically unrealistic steel constructions. He was highly critical of the new architecture in Western countries, accusing Le Corbusier, for instance, of a 'lyrical pseudo-Functionalism' – an accusation not so far from the truth.[24] In 1930 he wrote the first comprehensive account of modern Russian architecture and the ideas behind it, a valuable source of first-hand material.[25]

The urge to break down the boundaries between the arts is especially evident in the career of the Constructivist Vladimir Tatlin (1885–1953), who began as a painter, then produced reliefs in wire, glass, wood and various other materials, designed the tower for the Third International in Moscow in 1920 (see the interpretation of the project by Nikolay Punin)[26] and eventually became a commercial designer.[27]

A Constructivist manifesto issued in 1922 by Alexey Gan (1889–c.1940)[28] sets out to demonstrate that the movement was essentially Marxist in character, and to lead the government to adopt the Constructivist line. Gan's is an extreme statement of the constructivist position – the abolition of art, Constructivism as the result of the new industrial culture, reversion to the laws of materials as the supreme criterion – laid out in terms of ideological principles. The argument issued in the slogan 'Art belongs to the Factory',[29] which embodied a new definition of the artist as a man who renounces his individuality and takes his lead from the aesthetic quality of manufactured goods. This amounts to a return to the argument over type which had been going on in Western countries since the beginning of the century.

This development led to analytical studies of architectural elements, culminating in the psychotechnical laboratory experiments performed by the Rationalist Nikolay Ladovsky, while discussion of the issues involved dominated Constructivist associations of artists and architects such as Unovis, Inkhuk and OSA, together with art schools such as Vkhutemas and Vkhutein.[30]

In 1924 the architect Moisey Yakovlevich Ginzburg (1892–1946)[31] propounded a comprehensive theory of Constructivism as it applied to architecture, in his work *Style and Epoch* (1924), in which he assessed the challenges facing the age and developed a view of architecture against the background of tradition and of modern theories of art.[32] This book was a response to Le Corbusier's *Vers une Architecture* and may claim comparison with it. Ginzburg had studied at the Ecole des Beaux-Arts in Paris and at the art academies of Toulouse and Milan, gaining his diploma in architecture at Riga in 1917. His thinking bears the marks both of French rationalism and of Italian Futurism; in Milan he had links with the group Nuove Tendenze, to which Sant'Elia and Chiattone belonged. From the point of view of methodology he was strongly influenced by Wölfflin's and Frankl's concepts of style and by Spengler's philosophy of history.

Ginzburg had already attempted in his first book, *Rhythm in Architecture* (1923),[33] to show how the laws of history, given a modern form, could be applied to the needs of the present. He used the concept of rhythm, a universal principle of life, to express the laws of kinetic energy that govern the spirit of an age. The examples he chooses from architecture, like his historical analyses, are largely based on Wölfflin. He defines symmetry as the expression of the law of alternative repetition, quoting Alberti as his authority for regarding symmetry as a given fact of Nature. Symmetry is simple and organic, and the preferred rhythm of spatial, architectural form. Following Renaissance tradition, he proceeds from the basic regular geometric forms and proportions, and claims that the expression of the present lies in the deliberate destruction of Classical proportions and in a new monumentalism. True to the Renaissance tradition he regards Alberti's concept of *concinnitas* as the supreme goal and expresses the desire to see 'the rhythmic pulse beat of the present' embodied in an organic, monumental and harmonious architecture.

Ginzburg's *Style and Epoch*, like Le Corbusier's *Vers une architecture*, begins with an historical argument but then turns to the technological aspects of modern architecture, posing the key question of a new style, 'a grand style for our age', in which the forces of the present shall find expression. His definition of style as 'something that corresponds completely to the needs and concepts of a given place and a given time'[34] again betrays the influence of Wölfflin, and he sees the rise, apogee and decline of an age reflected in the phases of style. There is a structural, utilitarian phase free of ornament, an organic phase in which construction and decoration are perfectly balanced, and a decorative phase, in which ornament makes itself independent of construction. Modern European culture, 'in the final days of its existence',[35] has now reached this final phase of decadence, and contemporary Western architecture is in a corresponding state of decay. The influence of Vasari's theory of the cyclical nature of the development of art, in addition to Spengler's philosophy of history, is evident here.

While rejecting the Italian Futurists' attempt to break with the past, Ginzburg adopts in his search for a new style the same points of departure, dynamism and the machine, but in place of the note of euphoria typical of the Futurists he exhibits a French style of rationalism, defining problems of space as the products of materialised forces of motion.[36] Style, technology and the political system come together, as he sees it, specifically in the area of workers' housing and workplaces, where the machine, the new force in life, finds its collective, synthetic and dynamic expression in constructive logic and through the standardisation of building units.[37]

Ginzburg interprets the concept of 'a free and joyous human labour' in terms of the function of the machine, to which he applies Alberti's definition of beauty (*De re aedificatoria* VI.2), according to which nothing can be added or subtracted from an object without disrupting the whole.[38] The concept of beauty is thus defined by the machine, which here includes the visible use of materials 'at work', together with the exposure of the static and dynamic forces.[39] This assessment of architecture by the same criteria as those applicable to machines brings Ginzburg to his closest rapprochement with Le Corbusier. Since a machine produces a direction of movement which is hardly ever conveyed through symmetrical movements of the machine, asymmetry now becomes the mark of the new style. Ginzburg sees architecture primarily as the product of kinetic energy; his series of stress diagrams illustrates his view that the essence of historical forms of architecture lies in their symmetry (*Plate 195*), where as an example of the dynamism of modern architecture he points to the asymmetrical design of the Vesnin brothers for the Palace of Labour in Moscow (1922–23),[40] in which the tall masts, which project beyond the top of the building, represent pure lines of stress (*Plate 196*). Ginzburg thus espouses the principle of an aesthetics of construction, concluding that the identity of construction and decoration is achieved in visible 'constructivity' and with it the mature, organic phase of the new style.[41] Like Le Corbusier, Ginzburg sees architecture as a new, intensified form of expression derived from the aesthetics of engineering and the analogy of the machine, and the new style as characterised by monumentality and asymmetry as the expression of modern dynamism. Parallel to the concept of 'a free and joyous human labour' runs that of the freedom and joy of 'the mechanised city.'[42] Architecture has an important rôle to play in Ginzburg's scheme as an organising force in the new life, creating a harmonious synthesis derived from a module-based standardisation of constructional units.[43]

The points of contact between Ginzburg and Le Corbusier are evident, although the two men pursued different ideological aims. Ginzburg's Constructivist arguments are more consistent than Le Corbusier's idealistic Rationalism, and his comments on Le Corbusier, together with the correspondence that followed the meeting of the two men in Moscow in 1929–30, show the extent of the differences between them;[44] in particular, Ginzburg recognised the aesthetic formalism of Le Corbusier's concept of functionalism.

In his final book (1934), *Conclusions for Housing from Five years' Work on Housing*, Ginzburg goes so far as to maintain that the industrialised building methods used in the West could really only be exploited as an expression of a socialist society.[45] But as the preface to the book shows, he did not succeed in reconciling his ideas with the official Party line.

Russian Constructivism had its roots in the processes of mass production. A parallel movement was that of a more formalist Rationalism, led by Nikolay Ladovsky (1881–1941). From the few written statements that he left, it emerges that the starting-point for all Ladovsky's ideas was that of space, from which form is created,[46] construction being seen as a secondary consideration; his aim was to determine the laws of architectural form as perceived by the spectator. The rationality of his approach lay in determining the laws of psycho-physiological perception, which would then lead to the production of corresponding architectural forms, and to this end he founded a 'psychotechnical' laboratory in the Vkhutein Institute in Moscow in 1927. His Rationalist architecture is based on the principle of economy, and he distinguishes between a technological rationality and an architectural rationality:

Technological rationality is economy of labour and materials during the construction of a functional building; architectural rationality is economy of psychological energy in the perception of the spatial and functional qualities of the building.[47] Ladovsky's Rationalist aesthetics is thus totally different from that of the French nineteenth-century Rationalists or that of the Italian Rationalists after 1926.

A position close to that of the Rationalists was taken up by Konstantin S. Mel'nikov (1890–1974),[48] a considerable artist whose buildings, such as the Russian Pavilion at the International Exhibition of Decorative Arts in Paris in 1925, commanded great respect, and whose Russakov Club Building (1927) in Moscow, together with his own house there (also 1927), demonstrate the independence of form from materials and function. His few theoretical pronouncements[49] are undoctrinaire and deal with the question of how to produce artistic designs that shall 'leave mankind with monuments that testify to the heroism of our age' (1936).[50]

The idea of the autonomy of architectural form soon began to show itself also in architects who nominally belonged to the Constructivist camp, such as Yakov G. Chernikhov (1889–1951) with his 'architectural fantasies' (1933),[51] and Ivan I. Leonidov (1902–59),[52] author of bold yet highly formalist designs, such as those for a Lenin Institute (1927), a Palace of Culture (1929–30) and the People's Commissariat for Heavy Industry (1934) in Moscow's Red Square which reveal a degree of independent geometric form that recalls the 'Revolutionary architects' of France – although a historical connection can hardly be assumed.[53] The monumentality of these designs forces their assessment in absolute terms. Commenting on his Commissariat design, which would have dominated the centre of Moscow with its three gigantic skyscraper towers, Leonidov wrote:

> It is obvious that the roles of the individual buildings and ensembles in this central complex will change when a grandiose new edifice arises on Red Square. It is my view that the Kremlin building and St Basil's Cathedral will subordinate themselves to the new People's Commissariat, which must occupy a central position in the city. The architecture of Red Square and the Kremlin is a music of sweetness and sublimity. But if one is to introduce into this symphony a vigorous new theme, with its own powerful resonance, then this theme has to become dominant, and its qualities have to outshine those of all the other buildings in the ensemble.[54]

This powerful design of Leonidov's is like a preliminary stage for Le Corbusier's Parliament Building in Chandigarh (1951) and for post-modern American highrise designs of the 1970s.

The urge for formal and theoretical experiment in the Soviet Union in the 1920s had a revolutionary élan which the countries of Western Europe, for all the liveliness of discussion there, could not match. The inability of the Soviet economy and Soviet technology, let alone of the increasingly conservative Party bureaucracy during the Stalin era, to measure up to this challenge becomes particularly evident when one realises how few of these adventurous ideas were actually put into practice, and how poor was the technical quality.

Reports in the Western press about discussions and projects in the Soviet Union, with spectacular individual achievements like Mel'nikov's Pavilion at the Paris Exhibition of 1925 and El Lissitzky's Russian Press Pavilion at the 1928 Cologne *Pressa*,[55] roused the interest of architects in the West, among them a number of Germans whose own position had become precarious by the end of the 1920s, and was to become more so under Hitler. It was therefore no surprise when some of the chief representatives of the New Architecture, among them Taut, May and Hannes Meyer, decided to go to Russia for a time to help build the new socialist state,[16] where they were joined by Mart Stam from the Netherlands and André Lurçat from France. Le Corbusier and Frank Lloyd Wright also visited Russia – the former in 1929–30, the latter in 1937 – but the experience proved a sobering one, coinciding, as it did, with the introduction of 'Soviet Realism' under Stalin,[17] and brought scant reward in the theoretical field. The high hopes that architects worldwide had of the Soviet Union showed themselves in the competition for the Palace of the Soviets (1930–5),[18] but the course and final outcome of the competition marked the end of the mood of optimism.

The main problem in architecture that faced the Soviet Union was how a socialist city should look and what form housing for the new socialist society should take. A mass of different problems – the electrification of the country, industrialisation, the new social structure, on which the emancipation of women had a great influence – had to be included in discussions on urban planning and housing.[19] There had already been a powerful garden-city movement in Russia, based on Ebenezer Howard's ideas, before the Revolution, and Howard's theories continued to dominate the discussion at the beginning of the 1920s. A balance between town and country, together with the idea of decentralisation, seemed an attainable goal through the concept of the garden city. Apart from the question of the form that housing estates should take, there was the problem of the form of the actual dwellings, i.e. the extent to which the concepts of individuality, family and so on should be retained, and whether they should be replaced by collective ideals. The debate centred on the idea of commune housing.

The first urban projects were entirely utopian. In 1921 Anton M. Lavinsky (1893–1968) produced a design for a multi-storeyed 'city on shock absorbers' with revolving houses; Lasar M. Khidekel (b.1904), a pupil of Malevich, designed swaying houses, and Georgy T. Krutikov (1899–1958) a 'flying city' (1928). The Futurist manifestos of Fani and Marchi can be sensed in the background.

Serious discussions of town planning began after the publication in 1929 of the Five-Year Plan which provided for the construction of 2,000 industrial towns and 1,000 market towns. All the planners were united in rejecting the city in its historical form as being the product of capitalism but disagreed over the form that the new cities should take. The Urbanists aimed for a compact, medium-sized town consisting of uniform housing blocks and based on the complete collectivisation of education, catering and other areas of life. The leading exponent of this 'socialist city' (Sotsgorod), with its standardisation of all structural units, was the economist L. M. Sabsovich, who set down his ideas in *The Town of the Future and the Organisation of Socialist Life* (1929).[60] Sabsovich argued for complete collectivisation of all aspects of life, branding any form of individualism as *petit bourgeois*.

The Disurbanists were led by the sociologist M. A. Okhitovich, who regarded the city *per se* as a relic of capitalism, and proposed, using the possibilities afforded by modern means of communication, an anti-urban concept in which manufacturing industry, trade, housing and culture all existed in close proximity to each other, the basic form of such settlements being linear[61] – the Disurbanists' cherished principle. Ginsburg and others produced designs on this basis and developed a plan for Moscow as a 'green city'.[62] As Okhitovich's reference to Henry Ford makes clear, this communications-based linear principle is a socialist version of an anti-metropolitan trend that led Frank Lloyd Wright, at the same period and with similar motives, to his plan for Broadacre City. Okhitovich rejected the idea of the complete regimentation of all aspects of life.

A middle path between these two extremes was struck by Nikolay A. Milyutin (1889–1942), a Communist official and one-time finance minister, in his study *Sotsgorod. The Problem of Socialist Town-Planning* (1930),[63] a realistic investigation which combines socialist principles with economic facts. In an obvious reference to Le Corbusier, a view of whose *Plan Voisin* he reproduces, Milyutin stigmatises the skyscraper, in the first chapter of his work, as an expression of the 'anarchic capitalist system'; disurbanisation, on the other hand, is socialist by nature, and virtually inconceivable in a capitalist society.[64] His starting-point, similar to Garnier's, is that of industrial and agricultural production, and in his fifth chapter he compares the functional and spatial disposition of houses, schools, utilities, offices, lines of communication and so on to the laws governing the operation of a power station (*Plate 197*). He envisages a linear form of settlement with the various functions arranged in a fixed sequence of six zones: railway; industry, departmental stores, schools, etc.; green belt; housing belt, with community services; green zone with sports facilities; and agriculture.[65] Milyutin justifies the order of the zones by referring to the short connecting distances, convenience of development and similar considerations; no deviation from the pattern is allowed but account may be taken of the nature of the terrain. Milyutin also uses the occasion to give a critical review of the various solutions submitted in the competitions for Magnitogorsk and Stalingrad.

For housing Milyutin proposes a similar linear plan, based on the direction from which the sunlight comes. He demands the protection of individual rights and privacy, and allows collectivisation to affect only certain parts of our lives. His programme of 'living units', each with a surface area of 8.4 square metres and a volume of 21.84 cubic metres, calls for a minimum of facilities, such as room to sleep, a table to work on, and room to store linen, clothes, medicines and other personal possessions.[66] For examples of the sort of dwellings he has in mind he refers to Ginzburg's designs and to Gropius's work at the Bauhaus. He attacks Sholtovsky's monumentalism and historical eclecticism and favours the adoption of standardised lightweight constructions, with simple, direct, airy, functional solutions as expressions of the modern age, which is conditioned by the machine, by strict economy, by new materials and by new social relationships.[67] His declaration that a proper solution to a properly formulated problem can also be a source of beauty makes him a supporter of the philosophy of functionalism found in the protagonists of the New Architecture and in Le Corbusier, whose designs Milyutin uses as illustrations in his book.

Milyutin's *Sotsgorod* was an attempt to find a compromise between the two schools of urban planning, and also to adapt to the needs of Soviet Russia the research being carried out in the West on the minimum requirements for housing. In a sense his book is a Communist counterpart to the *Urbanisme* of Le Corbusier, whose *Cité linéaire industrielle* of the 1940s harks back to Russian ideas.[68]

Alongside the various modern trends of the 1920s there emerged in Russia a form of Classicism based on Greek or Renaissance models which, under the name 'Proletarian Classicism', came to dominate Soviet architecture during the Stalin era.[69] Ivan V. Sholtovsky, Ivan A. Fomin, Aleksey Shchusev and a number of others came close to a modern style in various respects, and might be compared with Piacentini in Italy; the dreary monumentalism of Vladimir G. Helfreich and Boris M. Iofan, on the other hand, has a parallel in the work of Speer in Germany. The question of how the spirit of totalitarianism manifested itself in the theory and practice of Stalinist architecture requires to be answered with the same reservations as when the question is asked of the architecture of Nazi Germany.

The critical reappraisal of pre-Stalinist architectural arguments, which has been going on in the Soviet Union since the 1960s,[70] has had an embarrassed reception in Eastern Europe and has suffered in Western countries from a lack of first-hand knowledge or from ideological prejudice. At one time it seemed as if, in a spirit of Euro-Communist euphoria, the West would come into grateful possession of a substantial body of material via Italy. Only in recent years, with works such as Christina Lodder's *Russian Constructivism* (1983) and John Milner's study of Tatlin (1983), have we begun to see a welcome measure of objectivity.

The fact that relationships between Russia and Eastern European countries in the 1920s were so close continues to make it difficult, in many cases, to resolve the question of intellectual priority. It is at any rate clear that the theoretical discussions on architecture which took place in Russia between 1917 and 1930 represent an important international contribution to the subject, to be neither underestimated on ideological grounds nor shrouded in mystery. The activity of Berthold Lubetkin in England[71] has shown that an architecture derived from Soviet principles of the 1920s can also be successful in Western Europe.

29. The United States in the first half of the twentieth century

Ever since Jefferson a basic theme in American architectural theory has been the quest for a vernacular American style. Those who came closest to reaching this goal were the Chicago School, both in theory and in practice. But their success was merely a regional episode, and architecture in general was governed by a commercialised eclecticism which dominated the urban scene considerably longer than in Europe.[1] The skyscraper type became more and more the symbol of national identity, and the earlier question of form and style disappeared from sight in the advancing flood of eclecticism.[2] The search for an American style led, if it led anywhere, to debate about the form of skyscrapers. Francisco Mujica, for instance, in his *History of the Skyscraper* (1929), proposed high-rise buildings in the 'Neo-American style' (*Plate 198*), taking his lead from pre-Columbian architecture and adapting forms from Mexican temples to produce set-back skyscrapers.[3] A trivialisation of historical models went hand in hand with technological development, which led to so-called 'cathedrals of commerce', of which one of the most successful was Cass Gilbert's Woolworth Building in New York (1911–13).[·] These buildings have no real foundation in architectural theory but exist on the basis of associations, like verticality in Gothic; and because of their verticality, skyscrapers attracted a preference for Gothic Revival. Ruskin's writings, influential in America, played a part in this development.[4]

Efforts to arrive at a characteristically American architecture in the twentieth century met with considerably more success in the field of the family house than of the large-scale commercial building. This consideration must be kept in mind for an appreciation of the work, theoretical and practical, of the greatest American architect of the first half of the twentieth century – Frank Lloyd Wright (1867–1959). Wright's career is a steady expansion from the designing of family houses to the planning of cities. Yet for all his fame he was an outsider, and the first large-scale attempts to assess his achievements were made in Europe where, at least until around 1910, his impact was greater than in his native country.[5]

Wright came to architecture as an engineering draughtsman.[6] A great deal has recently been written about the stimulus he received in his kindergarten days from the educational games developed by the educationalist Froebel,[7] but his later studies of Viollet-le-Duc,[8] Ruskin and the Arts and Crafts movement must have been equally important.[9] The greatest influence on the development of his ideas, however, was the six years, 1887–93, that he spent in the Chicago office of Louis Sullivan, whose posthumous designs he published in 1949.[10]

Wright's theoreteical writings on architecture, consisting of numerous books and hundreds of articles, are directly related to the buildings on which he was engaged at the time,[11] and the outcome is a rare harmony of theory and practice. At the same time there is much repetition in them, and since he was constantly revising his theoretical position, sometimes even retracting earlier statements, his continually expanding conception of architecture never found its ultimate form.

In 1900, immediately before his Chipping Campden venture, C.R. Ashbee visited Wright in Chicago, and the following year Wright delivered an address, *The Art and Craft of the Machine*, in which he gave his views on the Arts and Crafts movement.[12] In 1910 he visited Ashbee in Chipping Campden, and in 1911 Ashbee added an introduction to Wright's *Ausgeführte Bauten*, published that year in Berlin. Wright was thus fully acquainted with the architectural debate taking place in Britain at this time,[13] which makes his own independent views all the more valuable. He differs from William Morris, for example, in welcoming the advent of machines, calling them 'the precursors of democracy', the liberators of human self-expression, and speaking of their 'organic nature,' the machine, the motor and the battleship being 'the art works of the century'. The tall office building with steel skeletal frame he describes as 'a machine pure and simple', and his fusing of Viollet-le-Duc's Rationalism with Sullivan's concepts emerges from the following passage:

The steel skeletal frame has become recognised as the basis for a simple, honest clothing in a workable material; this material spiritualises the function of the steel frame without any structural pretence.[14]

Wright did not share the English Arts and Crafts movement's criticism of society but, like the Deutscher Werkbund later, spoke out in favour of cooperation between artists and industry, seeing in the machine, as a paradigm of organic growth from which man can learn, the way to a new simplicity.

Remember, I say, to reflect that the texture of the city, this great Machine, is the warp upon which will be woven the woof and pattern of the Democracy we pray for. Realize that it has been deposited here, particle by particle, in blind obedience to law – law no less organic as far as we are concerned than the laws of the great solar universe. That universe too, in a sense, is but an obedient machine.[15]

Already at this stage in his career Wright was clearly prepared to accept advances in technology, though the overall conception of his prairie houses was still strongly influenced by the Arts and Crafts movement.

These prairie houses, erected between 1893 and 1910, follow a programme drawn up in 1894 and published in 1908 in the first of many articles to which he gave the title *In the Cause of Architecture*.[16] Based on Nature and on his experience of Japanese art – he first visited Japan in 1905 and published a book on Japanese woodcuts in 1912[17] – his programme comprises six principles: 1) simplicity and repose – terms evidently drawn from the vocabulary of John Wellborn Root, to whom he refers; 2) there should be as many kinds (styles) of house as there are kinds (styles) of people and individuals; 3) a house should appear to grow easily from its site and be shaped to harmonise with its surroundings; the prairie house should share the horizontality of the landscape, with gently sloping roofs, low proportions, quiet sky lines, suppressed, heavy-set chimneys and sheltering overhangs; 4) its colours should conform to those of Nature; 5) the nature of the materials should be brought out; 6) a house of character will become more valuable with age.

The house is made to mirror the personality of its occupants – hence Wright's preoccupation with the personality of his clients.[18] At the same time the aim of architecture is the expression of democracy, which leads to the formula: 'Variety in

Unity'. Ornament emerges from the structure of the material: he accepted machine-made ornaments, and later demanded specific ornamental forms for prefabricated concrete units, even executing some of his own. This opened a wide gap between him and the ornament-free style being adopted by modern architects in Europe.

The concept of 'organic architecture', so important for Wright, belongs to the tradition of Greenough and Sullivan. For the prairie house it signifies primarily a design that flows between the interior and the exterior. Wright defined it thus: 'By organic architecture I mean an architecture that develops from within outward in harmony with the conditions of its being, as distinguished from one that is applied from without.'[19] It is a long way from this to the far more complicated form of the concept that Wright expounded in 1939 in his series of lectures *An Organic Architecture*. In his Kahn Lectures at Princeton in 1930, entitled *Modern Architecture*,[20] he gave a clearer summary of the ideas behind his prairie houses, setting out in a nine-point programme the principles of the unbroken transition from interior to exterior, the open plan and what he called 'the destruction of the box'.[21]

The events of Wright's life, his practical activity and the development of his theories go hand in hand.[22] From the 1920s onwards he increasingly devoted his energy to the problems of the American city, giving his mind over to the question of how to create an architecture that would view the individual in his relationship to society and to the state. His thoughts found expression in a number of publications on urban planning and on the problem of low cost housing. The text of his three books on town-planning – *The Disappearing City* (1932), *When Democracy Builds* (1945) and *The Living City* (1958) is identical over long stretches.[23] In them he develops a vision of a utopian state he calls 'Usonia', i.e. the United States, in which, as in so many such utopias, the role of architecture is given special importance.[24] Numerous received ideas found their way into his plan, some of whose sources he names, others not. Four key-words characterise Wright's thought – *organic, decentralisation, integration, democracy*. On the basis of an historical construct, he declares that it was the cave-dweller, *qua* type, who created the modern city, and that this type tends to absolutism and Communism. The nomad type, on the other hand, produces a decentralised, organic, democratic architecture. Wright equates 'organic' with 'democratic' architecture. The capitalist metropolis he brands as the root of all evil, envisaging in its place a form of natural economic order which he does not define, but which can be assumed to correspond to the ideas of Henry Ford.

Wright's call for urban decentralisation has as its background the wide open spaces of the United States, where he found the roots of the national culture. Every citizen, he says, should be given one acre of land, and the new settlements would take the form of his Broadacre City, a large-scale model of which he submitted in 1935 (*Plate 199*). The illustrations of this model and the two later versions of *The Disappearing City* complement each other.

Wright sees the feasibility of this decentralisation as resting on two technological achievements – electrification and the development of communications – and on an organic architecture that is at one with the natural landscape and with the available materials.

With organic architecture his resource, man is a noble feature worthy of his own ground; integral there, as trees, streams or the rock ribs that are the hills...Architects of democratic spirit are here, demanding deeper organic foundations for an organic society. Everywhere this new American architecture is demanding more organic foundations for economic, ethical, social, aesthetic daily life; insists all future planning now begin at the beginning. Planned revolution by evolution is now organic.[25]

Broadacre City was to create a synthesis of mechanical design, prefabrication and decentralisation, while retaining 'the desirable features of the city' and the freedom of the 'Good Ground', as he calls it, rid of 'petty partitions of property and wilful deformations of natural beauty.'[26] He saw Broadacre City as democracy demonstrated in architectural terms.

Wright's thought moved in national channels, and he had strong reservations about trends towards an 'international' style. He regarded style as an expression of national character, and perpetuated the tradition of the eighteenth-century French concept of *caractère*, of which he may have learned through his study of Viollet-le-Duc. 'This new American concept of architecture,' he wrote, 'has style as the expression of character.'[27] Finally Wright puts foward a typology of buildings, each planned in detail in accordance with his model, and with particular attention paid to matters such as convenience of vehicular access. Industrial production would be decentralised. He describes the position of a community centre: 'The civic center would always be an attractive automobile objective – perhaps situated just off some major highway in interesting landscape – noble and inspiring.'[28] Thoughts of this kind are analogous to those being expressed in the Soviet Union at the same time.

Wright assumed a highly-developed technology but one that should be made to serve human needs; *The Living City* contains a series of science-fiction type illustrations of new kinds of public transportation, which reveal his enthusiasm for technological inventions (*Plate 200*). The high-rise blocks in Broadacre City are free-standing, surrounded by green spaces.

Wright had a vague vision of a direct form of democracy, in which a new architectural environment would improve mankind and make police, prisons and the like redundant – a conception reminiscent of Garnier's *Cité industrielle*, and an overestimation of the architect's influence comparable to Le Corbusier's: 'In his own home thus the Broadacre citizen would be not only impregnable. He would be inviolate. This nation indestructible!... He is the country.'[29] Wright anticipates certain of the criticisms of urban development that were to be heard in the 1960s and 1970s but one must remember that he had an unshakeable faith in technology, and that he did not raise issues such as ecology and conservation of energy resources. His theories belong to the American context and are an expression of an American attitude towards life.

The Broadacre City concept led naturally to the question of low-cost housing. Wright's prairie houses, like his houses of the 1920s, were for the most part commissioned by well-to-do clients; now a solution had to be found for the provision of family houses on freehold sites at an affordable price. That this was entirely possible he proved in 1937 with a 'Usonian' house built for the journalist Herbert Jacobs near Madison, Wisconsin.[30] The theories underlying this type of house emerged in a series of articles that Wright wrote from 1936 onwards and collected in the book *The Natural House* (1954).[31] The term 'Usonian', according to Wright, goes back to Samuel Butler's utopian novel *Erewhon* (1872), though the word itself does not occur there.[32] At all events it serves to denote Wright's conception of the new American low-cost house. The primary architectural problem of the age he stated at the opening of the chapter headed 'The Usonian House I' to be this: 'The house of moderate cost is not only America's major architectural problem but the problem most difficult for her major architects.'[33]

The root of the problem, as Wright saw it, was that the American people did not really know how they ought to live. Starting with practical considerations, and assuming the extensive use of prefabricated units, he first produced a list of nine conventional features he proposed to do away with, including visible roofs, garages, cellars, interior decoration, radiators (he proposed underfloor heating), almost all furniture (he advocated inbuilt closets), rendering and guttering.[34] He then stated his own requirements – a large living room 'with as much vista and garden coming in as we can afford'; an adequate kitchen-cum-dining room, which can form a unit with the living room; two bedrooms; and a studio. It is a simple house, horizontal in lay-out, 'a companion to the horizon', and the architect should also make himself responsible for the design of the garden. Thus the house, its built-in furniture and the garden are united in an integral design which echoes the idea of the *Gesamtkunstwerk* – even the inevitable automobile becomes an integral part of the house. The natural use of building materials, a precise pattern of prefabricated concrete slabs, and the visual merging of the house and garden combine to make the Usonian house the American house of the future:

> Where does the garden leave off and the house begin? Where the garden begins and the house leaves off. Withal, this Usonian dwelling seems a thing loving the ground with the new sense of space, light and freedom – to which our USA is entitled.[35]

This does not imply, however, a standardised form of house. Wright offers a variety of possible solutions, but they all conform to the 'grammar', which enables the 'Usonian Automatic System' to use pre-fabricated units.

Judged in the context of Wright's own highly American demands, the Usonian house is one of the most significant attempts to solve the twentieth-century problem of low-cost housing and has been unjustly overshadowed by spectacular but isolated projects like his Fallingwater design (1936).[36] In his oeuvre as a whole the Usonian house must be accorded a similar status to that of his prairie houses of around 1900.

In his later years Wright tended to become dogmatic and long-winded in his writings, witness his semi-autobiographical *A Testament* (1957),[37] and *An Organic Architecture*, the text of four lectures delivered in London in 1939.[38] Nevertheless these lectures do provide a synthesis of his 'message', and were later incorporated in his book *The Future of Architecture* (1953).[39] The 'organic' here is an all-embracing principle, like the concept of function for Sullivan. Before there can be an 'organic' architecture, there must be an 'organic' economic system and an 'organic' society. This brings Wright close to the position adopted by Ruskin, Morris and Semper, but he does not share their argument for the necessity of a socialist revolution; rather, he saw architecture as being itself an element in social reform, which sets him in the company of Le Corbusier and his slogan 'Architecture or Revolution'. The character of the terrain, local industrial conditions, the nature of the materials and the function of the building in question were to Wright the factors that determine the form and character of all good architecture.

For Wright organic architecture meant the unity of form and function. He thus took Sullivan's phrase 'Form follows Function' one stage further and turned it into 'Form and Function are one.' His concept of form was a strange blend of Plato, for whom form was pre-existent, and Lao Tse, to whose concept of space Wright repeatedly alluded. This led to statements such as 'No organic building may ever be finished', or 'The complete goal is never reached.' Architecture grows like Nature, he said, and he compared his buildings, his teaching activity and his planning work in the two Taliesin studios with the growth of a tree that sends out branches and foliage. Restating his theories of Broadacre City and the Usonian house, he presented organic architecture as 'the enlarged scale of living, the swift, clean beauty of speed, of the richness of broadened community contacts,' a new sense of spaciousness and the removal of the borders between interior and exterior. Buildings become elements in the landscape. With missionary zeal he declared: 'Standing here as I do again today, I am really an emissary of the ground, preaching the salt and savor of new and fresh life.'[40]

Wright's anti-metropolitan attitudes are directed in *An Organic Architecture* against London, whose future he envisaged in terms that recall Morris's *News from Nowhere*: all the slums are to be demolished, and in their place green spaces are to be laid out to surround important historical monuments, so that what was formerly a city would be turned into a park for the benefit of future generations. Transferring his American vision to England, he urges that 'the people, having learned how to build, go further afield, and all the countryside of England becomes one beautiful modern city, in the new sense, wherein the country was the more beautiful because of the buildings, yes, even the factories.'[41] Such a declaration represents a combination of William Morris, the specifically American qualities of Broadacre City, and the Athens Charter.

Wright had the gift of intuitively absorbing into his thinking the most varied of stimuli and reproducing them as integral parts of his own system. This makes it difficult to assess his philosophy of architecture since it constantly underwent 'organic' development and never attained a final form. Both as architect and theorist, he had a basic inner strength which overcame any apparent logical contradictions. Even his central concept of 'organic architecture' was never defined once and for all but only adumbrated, and the definition produced by Twombly is both complicated and unsatisfactory:

> If a building is organic, it is harmonious in all its parts, a coherent expression and unification of its environment, its inhabitants, materials, construction methods, site, purpose, cultural setting, and of the ideas which called it into being, each being a consequence of the others. An organic structure defines and prophesies life, grows along with those who use it, assumes its own 'essential reality' or 'internal nature', and, by including everything necessary and nothing unnecessary for solving the immediate architectural problem, is as unified and as economical as nature itself.[42]

Wright's theory of architecture was a vision that became increasingly broad and at the same time increasingly blurred. His conception of the architect as the designer of a new order who would improve mankind bears a certain resemblance to the totalitarian claims made by Le Corbusier but the significance of his own theory, and of a large percentage of his executed buildings, lies in the fact that his recourse to technology was always tempered by a reference to what was natural, organic and humane. In spite of the enthusiastic reception given to his ideas, especially in Europe, he left behind him no 'school' – he was too American for that. Yet even in his native country he remained an outsider in his struggle, first against an eclecticism dominated by European models, then against an internationalism also imported by Europeans.

Yet he was not a completely isolated figure. The values of the prairie house and related projects were shared by others – the most helpful survey of the subject is to be derived from the pages of architectural journals such as *The Architectural Record, The House Beautiful* and *The Inland Architect*. In Chicago George Grant Elmslie followed Wright's lead,[43] while in California the Greene Brothers, Charles Sumner Greene and Henry Mather Greene (Greene & Greene),[44] like Irving Gill, who had worked with the firm of Sullivan & Adler at the same time as Wright, developed similar house designs; likewise their few statements on theoretical matters show their total dependence on Wright's inspiration.

The 1920s are almost a vacuum as far as architectural theory in America is concerned. Current views on architecture received a public airing at the time of the competition for the Chicago Tribune Building in 1922,[45] the aim of which was nothing less than to produce a design for 'the most beautiful office building in the world'.[46] The neo-Gothic design by John Mead Howells (1868–1959) and Raymond M. Hood (1881–1934), which won first prize and was executed and that by the Finn Eliel Saarinen, which came second, are landmarks in the history of the American skyscraper. Hood's buildings and public statements are pragmatic to the point of opportunism,[47] and the logic of his career from his time as a student at the Ecole des Beaux-Arts in Paris to the Chicago Tribune Tower, the Daily News Building (1930) and the McGraw-Hill Building in New York (1931), down to his designs for the Rockefeller Center, is difficult to grasp. In 1932 his work was exhibited at the prestigious international exhibition of modern architecture in the Museum of Modern Art, New York.

Saarinen's design for the Chicago Tribune Tower, which was highly praised by Sullivan,[48] had a decisive influence on skyscraper building in the 1920s, particularly on Art Deco buildings in New York.[49] In general, of course, these years were marked by uncertainty and economic depression.[50] In 1932 came a turning-point with the exhibition *Modern Architecture* in New York, arranged by Philip Johnson and Henry-Russell Hitchcock.[51] The trend of the exhibition was towards the 'international style' as exemplified by European figures such as Gropius, Le Corbusier, Oud and Mies van der Rohe, together with the work of Americans like Frank Lloyd Wright, Hood, Howe & Lescaze, Neutra and the Bowman Brothers. There was also a section, presided over by Lewis Mumford, that concerned itself specifically with questions of housing. In his introduction to the catalogue Alfred H. Barr distinguishes between the 'international style' and a 'modernistic or half-modern decorative style',[52] with Frank Lloyd Wright given a special position. A short historical survey by Johnson and Hitchcock, based on their book *The International Style* (1932),[53] puts forward a number of aesthetic principles which can be subsumed under three headings: 1) volume and space instead of mass and solidity; 2) regularity instead of axial symmetry; 3) exposure of materials instead of applied ornament. The pragmatic approach of Johnson and Hitchock leads to a certain simplification of the situation in Europe, but it is interesting to observe that they retain their belief in aesthetic categories vis-à-vis such extreme functionalists as Hannes Meyer, to whom they frequently refer. They reaffirm, for instance, their faith in proportion; 'Proportions, which according to the theories of the extreme functionalists are but a relic of the nineteenth century, are still the aesthetic touchstone of the best modern design.'[54]

Apart from a handful of American examples, Johnson and Hitchcock include in their book only European buildings in the international style, though their interpretation of that term is stylistically narrower, vis-à-vis functionalism and the New Architecture, than that of Gropius in his *Internationale Architektur* of 1925. While still acknowledging aesthetic considerations, their book, together with the exhibition and its catalogue, equated modernity with functionalism (defined in aesthetic terms), which they then recommended as the appropriate style for American architecture. This paved the way in America for Mies van der Rohe, Gropius, the New Bauhaus and others from Europe.

One of the most important of these immigrants from Europe was Richard J. Neutra (1892–1970),[55] who became an American citizen in 1932. A native of Vienna, like his schoolfriend and sometime partner Rudolph Schindler (1887–1953),[56] Neutra settled in California and helped to secure the acceptance of European functionalism in the 1920s. Schindler, a pupil of Otto Wagner's, arrived in America in 1914 and worked for a few years for Frank Lloyd Wright. His principal concern was to develop the concept of space, a subject on which he wrote a number of articles under the title *Space Architecture* (1934–35).[57] Neutra was already familiar with Frank Lloyd Wright's work before he left for America in 1923, where he first worked in the studio of Holabird & Roche in Chicago. He visited Louis Sullivan before his death and was present at Sullivan's funeral in 1924, where he met Wright for the first time, a man who was to exert a considerable influence on him.

Neutra's earliest books were devoted to describing his American experiences for the benefit of European readers. *Wie baut Amerika?* (1927), for example, gives an account of the construction of the Palmer House in Chicago, in which he had himself been involved during his time with Holabird & Roche,[58] while his second book, *Amerika: Die Stilbildung des Neuen Bauens in den Vereingten Staaten* (1930),[59] was written during the time when, in cooperation with Schindler, he was building the Lovell House in Los Angeles, the project which made him famous overnight.[60] In this book he promoted Schindler's work and the Californian architecture of Irving Gill, which was almost unknown in Europe at the time. These works of Neutra's made a great impact on Europe – even on Japan – and did more to promote an understanding of American architecture than, for example, Erich Mendelsohn's *Amerika: Bilderbuch eines Architekten* (1926).

Neutra's knowledge of Europe, his preoccupation with extending the ideas of Wright, and his architectural experience in California came together in his most important theoretical work, *Survival Through Design*, begun in the 1940s, published in 1954 and dedicated to Wright.[61] In this highly complicated work Neutra sets out to complement Wright's concept of the organic with knowledge drawn from the natural sciences. Proceeding from the 'biorealistic' principle that man's biological needs are more important than questions of building technique, function and arbitrary concepts of beauty, he considered from all angles the physical and psychological effects on man of materials, colours and forms, and ultimately proposed that the knowledge gained from this interplay be made the foundation of all design. He recognised the danger that this might lead to the replacement of art and design by science and technology – a development he rejected – but he nevertheless believed that scientific discoveries must find an immediate application to the world of design.[62]

The arguments that Neutra deploys are both historical and scientific and testify to his immense learning, though his unsystematic approach makes the book repetitive and hard to read. Every design, he claims, must have its 'biological fitness', on which the future existence of mankind depends:

> If design production and construction cannot be channeled to serve survival, if we fabricate an environment – of which, after all, we seem an inseperate [sic] part – but cannot make it an organically possible extension of ourselves, then the end of the race may well appear in sight. It becomes improbable that a species like ours, wildly experimenting with its vital surroundings, could persist.[63]

This appears to be a position of great far-sightedness, with its interrelationship of design concept and ecological demands, but Neutra offers little by way of specific proposals. The question of the physiological perception of forms leads him to suggest that aesthetic form may on occasion take priority over function, that 'function may itself be a follower of form.'[64] Such a formulation is both a reversal of the functionalist credo 'Form follows function' and a response to Wright's dictum 'Form and function are one.' There remains, however, a contradiction between Neutra's 'biorealistic' concept and his adherence to basic aesthetic principles such as proportion and form. The significance of his work lies in the fact that his conception of architecture as a social force opens up a physical and psychological dimension which helped to overcome the limitations of functionalism as it had hitherto been understood. This represents an exaggerated view of the social role of architecture which he shares with Wright, Le Corbusier, Mies van der Rohe and others. He believed that 'the steady improvement of man-made environment in the direction of an enhancement of all, even the finest biological values', would lead to our creation of 'a safe stairway leading to more wholesome and more spacious levels of man-conditioned existence.'[65]

The account of his intellectual development that Neutra gives in his autobiography (1962), written in German, is an interesting source of critical information on trends in architecture during his lifetime.[66]

From the 1920s onwards Neutra worked on an urban project which he called 'Rush City'. Based on a strict gridiron plan and traffic system, this goes back to the projects of Le Corbusier and Hilberseimer. A European model claiming to be American, it is diametrically opposed to Frank Lloyd Wright's Broadacre City.[67] Broadacre City, in the version in *The Disappearing City* (1932), was evidently the starting-point for the fundamentally new theory of town planning developed by another European, the Finn Eliel Saarinen (1873–1950)[68] in his book *The City* (1943),[69] although he does not refer to Wright by name. Saarinen emigrated to America in 1923, the year after the Chicago Tribune Tower competition, and became Director of the Cranbrook Academy of Art in Michigan in 1925. Whereas Wright's utopian project assumed a new social structure and involved the dismantling of existing cities, Saarinen's plan was more realistic and put forward concrete proposals to be introduced step by step after the end of the Second World War. He was not opposed to towns and cities as such but wanted to eliminate their negative features, coining for this purpose the term 'organic decentralisation'.

Founding his case on the basic biological concept of the organic, Saarinen compares urban structures to cell tissues and advances proposals for the renewal of 'sick' urban areas. He sees a close interaction between the form of a city and its social order, and thus starts, logically enough, with the problem of housing. Like many others, he developed pedagogical tendencies as his work proceeded, but to a more moderate degree than some of his colleagues, who thought that they could solve the problems of mankind through architecture and urban planning. Saarinen described architecture in his book as 'the supreme educator of the people: toward better physical living, toward better spiritual living, toward better standards of taste, and toward deeper cultural aims.'[70] The total decentralisation proposed by Wright was not what Saarinen sought, for many opportunities for cultural advancement are only available in cities: 'The basic reason for cultural concentration in the city is to offer everyone the opportunity to make contact with cultural achievements, strifes and intellectual activities of one kind or another.'[71]

Saarinen derives his basic principles of planning from analyses of towns of the past, above all those of the Middle Ages. His ideas come close to those of Sitte, whom he discusses at length, and his formula 'Formal v. Informal' brought him into direct conflict with contemporary views of town planning. Vehemently attacking a two-dimensional view of town planning geared to practical and technological considerations, he puts foward a three-dimensional conception which takes account of physical, social, cultural and aesthetic factors, and demonstrates in detail his concept of 'organic decentralisation' with reference to New York. His book contains numerous schematic diagrams which illustrate not only the decentralisation principle in the abstract but also how existing cities could be decentralised. It was a work that raised an early voice of warning against building cities according to purely technological principles – a voice that has unfortunately too often gone unheard since the end of the Second World War.[72]

It was the work of men such as Neutra and Schindler, coupled with the 1932 exhibition in New York, that paved the way for the great figures from Europe who were to change the face of architecture in America. Gropius, Mies van der Rohe, Hilberseimer, Moholy-Nagy and others arrived as émigrés in the second half of the 1930s and revolutionised American views on architecture both through their buildings and through their teaching. Their architectural language and their thought, already discussed in Chapter 25 above, had been forged by their European experience, which they were now called upon to apply to new contexts.

30. Since 1945

Preceding chapters on the first half of the twentieth century omitted certain countries which should receive at least brief mention here.

In Spain Ildefonso Cerdá made a significant contribution to the theory of urban planning in the mid-nineteenth century with his plan for Barcelona of 1859 and his two-volume theoretical work of 1867.[1] Antonio Gaudí, on the other hand, left no formal statement of his highly original style.[2] From the late nineteenth century to the time of Franco the principal subject of discussion in Spain was the creation of a sense of national tradition and the attempt by a group of architects during the Second Republic (1931–39) to associate themselves with international modernism remained an isolated episode to which few were able to relate.[3] José Luis Sert, a disciple of Le Corbusier, spent most of his life in America, and his theories have ill-defined relevance to the situation in Spain.

The omission of Great Britain from earlier chapters, after the point of Geoffrey Scott's *The Architecture of Humanism* (1914) had been reached and following Britain's dominant international role in architecture theory in the eighteenth and nineteenth centuries, might appear even more open to question. Yet perhaps the omission is not as questionable as it at first seems, for in the twentieth century architectural theory in Britain has been virtually replaced by architectural history,[4] and trends such as neo-Classicism, represented above all by Sir Edwin Lutyens, and the later revival of the Picturesque,[5] stand in the shadow of historical research. After the Second World War architects such as Alison and Peter Smithson expounded the theories underlying their work,[6] but in general the British contribution to architectural theory remained reserved.

It was not until the twentieth century that Scandinavia began to make its presence felt. The leading figure here is Alvar Aalto (1898–1976), a Finnish architect who took his lead from landscape and natural materials but who left only a few statements of theory.[7] Equally sparse is the theoretical background of Swedish Neo-classicism, whose chief representative was Gunnar Asplund (1885–1940).[8]

It is not uncommon for parts of the world with little tradition in architectural theory to contribute to architectural history before producing a comparable body of theory. This is true not only of Scandinavia but also of Latin America, where, for instance, Oscar Niemeyer in Brazil and Carlos Raúl Villanueva in Venezuela joined the highest ranks of international architects but left little theoretical material that was much more than an explanation of their own work.[9]

The first emergence of original ideas in Japan came after the Second World War with attempts to combine European thought with the native historical tradition.[10] Kunio Maekawa (b.1905), who had worked with Le Corbusier, conveyed the principles of European modernism to his colleague Kenzo Tange (b.1913), who set out to combine these principles with the Japanese tradition of wooden buildings, and who was the first to achieve an influence in the West with a Japanese architecture that drew much of its substance from European sources.[11]

The most important contribution by Japan to contemporary architectural theory, however, is without doubt what is known as Metabolism, a doctrine proclaimed in 1960 in a manifesto published by Kisho Kurokawa (b.1934) and others.[12] Metabolism goes further than European functionalism by applying biological symbols to the evolution of human society; it fuses the Buddhist tradition with that of European individualism and demands an architecture in which man, machine and space combine to form an organic body.[13] The central idea is that of the individual capsule, a movable, prefabricated unit with a theoretical status similar to that of the primitive hut in the eighteenth century (*Plate 201*). The best-known realisation of this idea is Kurokawa's Nakagin Capsule Tower (1972) in Tokyo, in which the 144 units, attached to two fixed nuclei, are intended to be seen as expressing the personality of their occupants. The question of the relationship between prefabrication and individuality is not raised. Kurokawa even claimed that his high technology 'meta-architecture', with its notions of organic life-cycles, introduced an ecological system into architecture.[14] His large-scale structures are very similar to the 'Mesa City' which Soleri was developing in the United States at almost the same time.

Immediately after 1945, when attention in Europe was focused on rebuilding the cities destroyed in the war, there was little published by way of architectural theory.[15] For the German rebuilding programme the theories of functionalism, particularly of the New Architecture, were considered adequate, especially as it was felt that these architects were entitled to some patronage after the Neo-classicism of the Nazi period, with the ideological overtones that had so often been laid upon it. From their vantage-point in the United States the main representatives of the New Architecture determined to a large extent the nature of the buildings erected in the 1950s and 1960s but they offered no fresh theory. Their view received support from Sigfried Giedion's historical work *Space, Time and Architecture*, which from the moment of its publication in 1941 defined for a generation or more what constituted 'modern architecture'. Rival interpretations such as that given by Bruno Zevi in *Towards an Organic Architecture* (1950) made a much lesser impact.

In Germany, where the primary need was to get rid of the ideological ballast that had burdened the subject since the 1920s, it was believed that a new starting-point could be found in the expression of the country's new political consciousness. Such a view was expressed by Adolf Arndt in his address *Demokratie als Bauherr* in 1961,[16] which however gives the feeling that attention is somehow being diverted from the realities of the situation of architecture. Compared with the developments in the rest of the world, German architecture of the first post-war decade, together with theoretical works on the subject, seems provincial[17] – a judgement that is not invalidated by the work of a few outstanding figures such as Hans Scharoun. The *Versuch einer Standortsbestimmung der Gegenwartsarchitektur* (1956) by the Swiss architect Justus Dahinden[18] is not concerned with coming to terms with past ideologies but presents a survey of theoretical and historical material from Vitruvius to Wölfflin, and culminates in speculations on the cycles of history. Dahinden gives pride of place to the problem of form, for which he adduces criteria such as the relationship between support and load, simplicity, and the purity of primitive crystalline forms, combining motifs from aesthetics and the psychology of perception to produce a schema at the centre of which is the concept of the creative will. There is no place here for the functional and technological aspects of architecture.

The lack of conceptual clarity in Dahinden's work is typical of most theoretical writing in German after the Second World War. In Germany itself the discussion of theoretical issues had all but dried up during the Nazi years, so that the sense of historical continuity was under threat. The writings of Egon Eiermann (1904–70), for example, an important figure in post-war development, are honest and down-to-earth in their practical intent but they hardly amount to a theoretical system.[19] Only with the decline in building activity in the 1970s did interest in theory begin to grow again, and with it the realisation that contemporary architectural theory was in fact lacking, a lack that had to be made good by improvised statements and reactions. And since contact had been lost with the values and concepts of the past, these statements could hardly conceal their inadequacy. This sense of insecurity in theoretical matters, coupled with the absence of a practical sense of direction, emerged clearly from a series of interviews with German architects edited by Heinrich Klotz and published in 1977 under the title *Architektur in der Bundesrepublik.*[20]

Of particular note is the work of Frei Otto (b.1925), who aimed at a new conception of architecture in the commentary with which he accompanied his pneumatic and tent constructions and his experiments with lightweight structures. The keywords in his vocabulary are 'natural' and 'biological'. His essays show him to be a critical observer of architectural trends, while in his books he deals with technical problems, but without losing sight of his overall conception.[21] In his 'bionic theory' he goes beyond earlier biologistic speculations, like those of Neutra, by translating the laws of Nature into immediate construction. For lightweight construction he coined the term '*Bic*', defined as 'the ratio of the mass of an object to the product of the force transmitted and the distance over which it is transmitted.'[22] The principle of lightweight construction is more important than the question of functionalism, since it provides the link to the aesthetic dimension. Otto does not, however, hold the view of the constructive functionalists 'that objects which are functional or lightweight are automatically aesthetic', but, striving to accommodate the historically determined concepts of structural honesty, type and individuality, arrives at his own definition of the aesthetics of lightweight structures:

> They become aesthetic at the moment when, without becoming any more unfunctional, they reveal their ideal, 'perfect', 'true' countenance to the receptive, unprejudiced observer, and when they reflect not only the typical form of all fully perfect, economically functional structures of the same kind but also their common and individual quality, including the variations, i.e. imperfections, typical of individuals.[23]

According to Otto's theory of biological architecture, as applied to lightweight constructions, it is not that an architectural design seeks a technical solution but that the 'form-finding processes' are governed by the laws of lightweight construction. As he writes in his critique (1958) of Hugh Stubbins' Kongresshalle in Berlin: 'One cannot design such buildings – one can only help them to acquire their ultimate form by constant searching.'[24] His demand for the primacy of his 'scientific form-finding process' is expressed with great vigour in an article on the roof for the Olympic stadium in Munich (for which he himself supplied calculations), designed by the firm of Günter Behnisch and Partners, whom he accuses of artistic manipulation, concluding: 'The desire for a prominent design contradicts the search for the underlying form, a form as yet unknown, but subject to the laws of Nature.'[25] Logically enough, this led Otto to investigate the whole question of ecological building.

Otto's statement of his position is an exception in the post-war German context, while the urge felt by architects who have become successful draughtsmen to express themselves in print has led to little more than semi-critical descriptions of the contemporary scene, satisfying the need to justify their own work. *Die Verantwortung des Architekten* (1982) by Meinhard von Gerkan is one such work.[26]

A particular contribution to the subject of housing came from Holland in the post-war years. J.H. Van den Broek (1898–1978) and Jaap B. Bakema (1914–81), two architects who broke away from the tradition of functionalism, recommended an architecture that found its starting-point in landscape and in basic concepts such as Space, Nature and Energy, and acknowledged the primary importance of aesthetic form.[27] This led to 'Structuralism'[28] (related to but not reduceable to Structuralism in the literary/anthropological sense) and the Nieuwes Bowen movement, in which Aldo van Eyck (b.1918) and Herman Hertzberger (b.1932) have played leading roles. Taking his lead from Gerrit Rietveld, Van Eyck worked towards a new relationships between interior and exterior in architecture and a formal wealth of interior structuring, quoting Alberti's formula of the house as a town and the town as a house.[29] Working with the structural categories of Cubism, he advocated the use of bold colours, especially as found in the spectrum of the rainbow. His ideas have been put into practice both in new housing estates and in historical quarters in Holland, and have attracted international attention.

The most important influences since 1945 have come from the United States, where architectural theory has generally been discussed in a more pragmatic and liberal spirit than that which prevailed in Europe during the first half of the century, which provided the subject-matter for American post-war debate. Much of the development in America, following the lines of discussion in pre-war Europe, has consisted of a formal assessment of, followed by a gradual movement away from, the positions adopted by the great figures who emigrated from Europe in the 1920s and 1930s, but the theoretical substance has generally been of subsidiary importance compared with actual buildings erected. Indeed, the most successful American architectural firms, which have constructed buildings combining technology and form in the manner of Gropius and Mies van der Rohe, have paid scant attention to theory. Such is the case, for example, with Skidmore, Owings & Merill, a firm which continues to attach prime importance to functionalism and technology, cautiously adapting the aesthetic appearance of their buildings to the trend of the moment.[30] The only poetic content to be found is in the designs and occasional essays of Gordon Bunshaft. Eero Saarinen (1910–61), following in his father Eliel's footsteps, has produced expressive formal solutions using concrete, but without developing any new theory.[31]

Published collections of interviews with architects offer a wealth of material on the complex spectrum of architectural discussion in the United States since 1945.[32] One of the most instructive cases is that of Philip Johnson (b. 1906), who came to architecture by way of art history. He was one of the organisers of the exhibition *Modern Architecture* in New York in 1932 and a co-editor of the book *The International Style*, published the same year; he then fell under the spell of Mies van der Rohe, on whom he wrote a monograph in 1947, and from whose influence he gradually freed himself in the 1950s.[33] His swing from one extreme to another, on which he has himself wittily and perceptively commented, has taken him to a deliberately eclectic 'romantic Classicism' and made him one of the spiritual fathers of so-called Post-Modernism. He has himself stated that reading Geoffrey Scott's *The Architecture of Humanism* in the 1940s left a profound impression on him,[34] and it may well also have accelerated his turning to Neo-classicism. In his lecture *The Seven Crutches of Modern Architecture* (1954)[35] – the title, besides the reference to Ruskin, is an ironic play on Scott's 'fallacies' – he challenges in a highly provocative way the design principles adopted at American schools of architecture. His main target is the concept of utility: he denies outright that there is any connection between functionalism and aesthetic quality in architecture, and calling Nietzsche as his witness, sets the principle of form before questions of morality, function, materials, structure and all the other nineteenth- and twentith-century criteria that Scott had already dismissed as irrelevant to the subject of quality. Here Johnson lays the foundation for his later view of architecture, which makes free play with historical forms as mere forms, and concerns itself only with the aesthetic result, heedless of the political and social context and of who his client might be.[36] His interest is now devoted entirely to the achievement of form – an attitude that recalls Le Corbusier, who, however, based his approach on a different set of premises. Johnson regards himself as being in the opposing camp to Frank Lloyd Wright, whom he ironically calls 'the greatest architect of the nineteenth century'.[37]

In contrast to Johnson's striking repudiation of functionalism and formalism, Louis J. Kahn (1901–74) adopted an intermediate position between functionalism, which he by no means rejected, and a new expressive language.[38] In his theory, which he never systematised, Kahn set out to combine conceptions of Nature, order, geometry and module, moving beyond functionalism, as a force directed towards the satisfaction of needs, to a view of architecture as the expression of human desires. These desires are determined not by individuality but by the 'form of life' of a particular age, and their realisation in architecture has the quality of truth. Kahn's experience of the past – such as his intensive study of the architecture of Classical Rome – found its way into his own style: his observations of Hadrian's Villa in Tivoli, for instance, left their mark on his buildings in India and Bangladesh, though not, as with Johnson, as an eclectic whim. In respect of materials Kahn – who described the use of brick and concrete as 'a celebration of the moment when two materials meet'[39] – adopted a position close to that of Wright. Architecture meant for him in the first instance the experience of space.

With Richard Buckminster Fuller (1895–1983), on the other hand, we find all conventional concepts of architecture scattered to the winds.[40] Fuller saw architecture as applied technology – an arrangement of universal laws expressed in terms of energy, mathematics, rationality, etc. His models sprang from his experience in shipbuilding and aircraft construction. The decisive moment in his career came in 1927 with his designs for ten-storey lightweight apartment houses which could be lowered into place by an airship, and for a mass-produced family house which he called the 'Dymaxion House' (*Plate 202*). The word 'Dymaxion', a conflation of 'dynamic' and 'maximum', was meant to signify maximum benefit for minimum energy input. Fuller envisaged that such houses would be built all over the world. The Dymaxion House, which he developed further in 1945–46 into the prototype of the 'Wichita House',[41] exhibited every mechanical refinement in lighting, air conditioning and labour-saving devices, and its forms, such as the hexagonal plan, followed a fixed structural pattern. Fuller's vision was of an all-embracing project designed to extend from the harnessing of the world's energy resources to a total control of climatic conditions. His lightweight constructions, which generally consisted of a combination of sphere and tetrahedron, acquired ever larger dimensions, culminating in structures to enclose whole towns or sections of towns in 'geodesic' hemispherical domes with their own controlled climatic conditions. His most spectacular project of this kind was for a two-mile hemispherical dome to encase the entire city of New York City (*Plate 203*).

Fuller's lightweight constructions serve a function as large temporary buildings for exhibitions and similar purposes but they cannot be considered as architecture, nor should the principles behind them be considered as relevant to architecture. Moreover, the dangers inherent in such structures showed themselves in 1976, when Fuller's pavilion for the Olympic Games in Montreal went up in flames in the course of the welding work.

The opposition to the functionalist and technological view of architecture in the United States took a variety of forms. Attention may be drawn to the work of two men, Bruce Goff (1904–82) and Paolo Soleri (b.1919), who, without being direct disciples of Frank Lloyd Wright, were decisively influenced by him, and whose activity lies outside the mainstreams of development.

Goff's work is highly individual and subjective, and includes bizarre, dream-like solutions which look as though they had emerged from the realm of the subconscious.[42] Soleri, on the other hand, who went to America from Italy, looked for a fundamentally new concept of architecture based on what he called 'arcology', i.e. architecture + ecology, an aesthetic, spiritualised, ecological concept to which technology is made subject.[43] In the tradition of urban utopias, Soleri designed a new 'transtechnological' *Civitas Dei* which was to improve the conditions of man's social existence and even shape his genetic structure.[44] Soleri's remarkable solution was the three-dimensional 'Mesa City', a huge, vertical mega-metropolis up to 800 metres high (*Plate 204*), in which lines of communication are shortened, vehicular traffic eliminated, Nature preserved and human relationships thus made more meaningful. He sees architecture as contributing to 'neo-nature' and as being 'dependent on the wholeness of nature'.[45] His domination by aesthetic considerations is reflected in his reversal of Sullivan's axiom 'form follows function' to read 'function follows form',[46] and his solar 'city of the future' of Arcosanti, near Cordes Junction, Arizona, on the realisation of which he has been working since 1970, demonstrates the union of his utopian vision with Frank Lloyd Wright's concept of craftsmanship. Soleri's own view of architecture extends from the earth house at one extreme to the mega-structure at the other, and he aims to express, as he puts it, 'the human quality which we are trying to build into the universe.'[47] Here is a conception as complex as that of Buckminster Fuller. Both men speak in terms of environment and ecological issues, and the totality of their demands leads far beyond any conventional conception of architecture.

Dissatisfaction with functionalist attitudes, indeed with planned architecture of any kind, showed itself in the interest that was aroused by an exhibition mounted by the Museum of Modern Art in New York in 1964 under the title *Architecture without Architects*.[48] A travelling exhibited devoted to earth houses, which has been shown in Europe, America and various Third World countries since 1982, follows a similar line.[49] Interest in America in anonymous architecture, often based on natural forms and materials, led to isolated realisations of an 'alternative architecture' as a counterweight to official trends, but such works are only on the fringes of our subject.

A profound criticism of the functionalist position was put forward by the German philosopher Ernst Bloch (1885–1977) in his work *Das Prinzip Hoffnung*, written between 1938 and 1947 during his exile in the United States.[50] Bloch writes from the standpoint of an independent, 'dissident' Marxist; his book contains a devastating attack on functionalist architecture, which he calls the product of the 'ice-cold world of robots, created by the consumer society' (*'die eiskalte Automatenwelt der Warengesellschaft'*).[51] Emphasising how functionalism spelt death for symbolism, he concluded:

> For over a generation this steel-furniture, concrete-cube, flat-roof creature has stood there, bereft of history, the ultimate in modernity, boring, apparently daring but in reality trivial, claiming to be full of hatred for the cliché in every ornament yet more trapped in stereotypes than any stylistic copy ever was in the bad old nineteenth century.[52]

Bloch demanded a return to 'organic ornament', derived not from historical models but from the conditions that govern a new society. Central to his position was the need to overcome functionalism, which he interpreted as the product of capitalism, and a new view of architecture as 'an attempt at production in the real human environment,' with room for 'organic ornament'.[53]

This is not to say that Bloch can be credited with having initiated the anti-functionalist discussion in the United States. He did, however, provide a remarkably far-sighted panorama of the twentieth-century scene, of which later architectural theory seems to be little more than variation and appendix. This applies, for instance, to the writings of Robert Venturi (b.1925), some of them produced in collaboration with his wife Denise Scott Brown (b.1931), which have received extraordinary acclaim. His book *Complexity and Contradiction in Architecture* (1966) was described by Vincent Scully as 'probably the most important writing on the making of architecture since Le Corbusier's *Vers une Architecture* of 1923.'[54] This is a considerable overestimation yet in its return to the values of the past and to the essential symbolic nature of architecture, it is a work that has had a signal influence.

The target of Venturi's attack is Mies van der Rohe's formula 'less is more', a phrase coined to denote a form of aestheticised functionalism. Venturi's response, illustrated by historical examples, is 'More is not less', or, in a particularly aggressive formulation, 'Less is a bore.'[55] Venturi sets out to put his experience of Mannerism and Baroque to the service of a new concept of architecture by returning to the complexity, in form and substance, of these two styles; at the same time his experience of contemporary Pop Art turns his thoughts to the everyday world of the consumer society, whose simple commercial and symbolic language he seeks to employ in architecture and urban planning.[56] 'Main Street is almost all right,' meaning that the business districts of modern cities, with their automobiles, their stores and their places of entertainment, give us optical signals which are comparable in their significance to those we receive from the architecture of the past.[57] He has been led to concentrate on the 'commercial strip', which he analyses in *Learning from Las Vegas* (1972),[58] significantly subtitled in its revised version 'The Forgotten Symbolism of Architectural Form'. Venturi's theories are considerably more clearly expressed here than in his earlier book, with its subjective, bombastic style and superficial use of historical material.

Learning from Las Vegas contains many flashes of insight and brilliant aperçus, but its conclusions are highly questionable. On the one hand it contains striking observations such as the following: 'Recent Modern architecture has achieved formalism while rejecting form, promoted expressionism while ignoring ornament, and deified space while rejecting symbols.'[59] But Venturi's own quest for a new architectural symbolism takes the form of an affirmation and aesthetic overvaluation of the everyday world around us, the banal symbols of which he equates with the symbolism of past ages, seriously comparing the night-lit Strip in Las Vegas with the mosaic interior of the Norman church of La Martorana in Palermo and the Amalienburg Palace in Munich,[60] concluding:

> The Strip shows the value of symbolism and allusion in an architecture of vast space and speed and proves that people, even architects, have fun with architecture that reminds them of something else, perhaps of harems or the Wild West in Las Vegas, perhaps of the nation's New England forbears in New Jersey. Allusion and comment, on the past or present or our great commonplaces or old clichés, and inclusion of the everyday in the environment, sacred and profane – these are what is lacking in present-day Modern architecture.[61]

'Fun' is here a more or less serious architectural criterion, and Venturi gives an analysis of the fairground eclecticism of Caesar's Palace in Las Vegas to justify his position (*Plate 205*).[62] His critique of functionalism leads to a plea for any kind of eclecticism, formal or historical, which returns to ornament. Architecture becomes a 'decorated shed', and ornament is 'ugly and ordinary'[63] but at the same time aesthetically assured, as he illustrates by comparing Paul Rudolph's Crawford Manor in New Haven with the Venturi and Rauch Guild House in Philadelphia. From behind a mask of wit and irony he provides a theoretical justification for making totally free use of historical forms such as the 'primitive vernacular'. This is the only way in which it is possible to understand how he can decorate the surface of a coffee service tray with the pattern of the paving-stones of the Capitol in Rome.[64] When the high quality of Venturi's own buildings is considered, it can only be assumed that he did not really want his theory to be applied so rigidly. However, this is the meaning he conveys, and his book has the status of a kind of manifesto that ushers in the era of so-called Post-Modernism.

The ideas of Charles Moore (b.1925) have often been compared with those of Venturi, but to Moore himself the parallels are very limited.[65] They both share a belief that architecture works in the first instance symbolically, although the basis for its symbolic quality is seen entirely differently by each. Moore states his position in *Body, Memory and Architecture* (1977),[66] written in collaboration with the sculptor Kent C. Bloomer and based on a series of introductory university lectures on basic problems in architecture. Moore develops a consistent anthropological conception of architecture; architecture is measured by the way it is experienced by the human body in space. Starting from the basic elements as objects of human perception – space, site, walls, roof, etc., with the significant reintroduction of the Orders – he comes very close to Renaissance theory.[67] In a historical digression on functionalist theory 'The Mechanization of Architecture' he presents the eighteenth century's 'scientific' conception of architecture as leading away from fundamentals, and bases his own approach on empathy and the principles of Gestalt psychology. For Moore architecture is physical and psychological taking possession of a place by a building's inhabitant who finds

confirmation of his own identity in the symbols of individual and historical memory.
We require a measure of possession and surrounding to feel the impact and the beauty of the building. The feeling of buildings and our sense of dwelling within them are more fundamental to our architectural experience than the information they give us.[68]
This is a long way from Venturi.

Moore sees architecture as the projection of human experience, as valid for the city as for the house (*Plate 206*). The basic task of architecture is the reproduction of 'the inner landscape of human beings', as realised in such buildings as the Acropolis in Athens, the Wieskirche in Bavaria, Frank Lloyd Wright's Winslow House, and Moore's own works. Moore's incorporation of the everyday world and of models from the past proceeds, so to speak, from within, whereas Venturi starts from the external symbolic form.

Moore's attitude to the past has varied in the course of time. *The Place of Houses* (1974; with Gerald Allen and Donlyn Lyndon)[69] is a model-book in the nineteenth-century tradition and puts his own house designs into a historical context. His human-based programme is expressed in the formulation: 'Rooms to live in, machines that serve life, and the inhabitants' dreams made manifest.'[70] A more whimsical attitude towards historical models emerges from his *Dimensions. Space, Shape and Scale in Architecture* (1976; with Gerald Allen), in which the basic elements of architecture are interpreted in a manner similar to that in *Body, Memory and Architecture*;[71] a section here on the Villa Hadriana reads like a preliminary description of his Piazza d'Italia in New Orleans of 1977–78.

In the last analysis Moore's use of historical models is as arbitrary as Venturi's. Since it forms part of man's memory and man's identity, the architecture of the past can be made to serve the needs of the present. But instead of replicating a particular historical style, Moore makes ironical, discordant references to it in a new, changed context. For the realisation of his Piazza d'Italia, for instance, he employs the techniques of Pop Art: he introduces the five Classical orders and a fanciful 'American' order, which creates an effect of alienation by using modern materials and attaching neon strip-lights to the columns.[72] Yet he takes it for granted that the associative power of the picture-postcard world he has created in his Piazza d'Italia, with Sicily at its centre, will provide a place with which the Italo-Sicilian community of New Orleans can identify. This seems to question Moore's considerable achievements, in the fields of housing and campus buildings. The human-centred aims he sets out in his books cannot be achieved through exercises in historical irony. His Piazza d'Italia is a piece of three-dimensional Pop Art masquerading as architecture.

Each in his own way, Moore and Venturi set out to use the architecture of the past as a set of visual signs as seen through the eyes of the twentieth century. The inner meaning of that architecture, however, cannot be transported in this way. The result is a façade architecture laid round a functional shell, laying claim to durability but having an air of impermanence about it. Such fair-booth architecture cannot be a true alternative to functionalism, however justified the opposition to functionalism may be. History and the models of the past are here treated casually and superficially, which is one of the fundamental objections to so-called Post-Modernist architecture, with its use of ironical, eclectic gestures in place of substance and symbol.

The mid-1970s saw an increasing number of works devoted to analysing the reasons for the failure of modern functionalism, among them Brent C. Brolin's *The Failure of Modern Architecture* (1976) and especially Peter Blake's *Form Follows Fiasco. Why Modern Architecture hasn't Worked* (1977).[73] Blake, once a disciple of modern architecture, here becomes its most violent critic, calling up the 'fallacies' in Geoffrey Scott's *The Architecture of Humanism* and setting alongside them what he calls the 'fantasies' of modern architecture, thereby putting into question such of its basic principles as function, open plan, purity, technology, highrise buildings and so on. The weakness of these two works is that they offer no suggestions as to where alternatives might be found. Likewise Wolfgang Pehnt, surveying what he took to be the demise of Post-Modernism in his *Das Ende der Zuversicht* (1983), was unable to reach any firm conclusion.[74]

The idea of a 'Post-Modern' architecture (variously dubbed Post-Functionalist, Symbolic, Anthropological, etc.) is present in the work of architects otherwise as different from each other as Philip Johnson, Moore and Venturi, though without the term as such being used. It established itself as a stylistic concept with Charles A. Jencks' *The Language of Post-Modern Architecture*,[75] which appeared in the same year (1977) as Blake's *Form Follows Fiasco* and was followed by a series of works in which Jencks' ideas became more and more frivolous. The term 'Post-Modern' has since become a catchword for anything and everything genuinely or allegedly anti-functionalist, embracing the most heterogeneous of trends, and is applied indiscriminately to Neo-Rationalists such as Aldo Rossi as well as to others like the 'New York Five'.[76] It implies the discovery of a new 'style', whereas it originally denoted simply a reaction against Modernism – a meaning that no longer corresponds to present-day usage – and has now acquired the sense: 'All is permitted.'

Alongside the tendency to revert to historicist models there arose in the United States a concern with the fundamental nature of architecture and an attempt to interpret every design process as an expression of the entire complex of human existence. Thus Christopher Alexander (b.1936), who came to California from Vienna, made a passionate plea in his first book, *Notes on the Synthesis of Form* (1964), for 'an entirely new attitude to architecture and planning...an alternative which will, we hope, gradually replace current ideas and practices.'[77] Alexander postulates a design process which shall take account of a mass of independent factors, substantiating his demand with numerous diagrams and mathematical formulae.[78] In fact his approach is not so far from the comprehensive concept of functionalism characteristic of the tradition of Louis Sullivan.

Alexander's *The Timeless Way of Building* (1979), rhetorical in style, opens with a set of maxims in a manner that recalls Le Corbusier's *Vers une architecture*, and proceeds with formulaic repetitions and such techniques as the use of a different typeface for the expression of eternal verities, all of which creates an atmosphere of religiosity to which one can either submit or turn away from in scepticism. Alexander develops an associative theory of correspondences between 'pattern languages' in architecture – which he sees as 'part of nature' – and 'patterns of events,' which leads to 'the quality without a name' in which his 'timeless way of building' achieves fulfilment. With a dazzling display of conceptual and linguistic virtuosity he produces statements on architecture which, by virtue of their very generality, have a certain validity but which can scarcely be turned to practical account.

In contrast to the high-flown nature of his theories, Alexander's own designs, such as his wooden Linz Café (1981), are unassuming, though by no means devoid of charm. Conceived merely as a temporary structure, this 'alternative design', which was published in the manner of a manifesto,[79] shows a broad discrepancy between idea and reality. However, it is quite conceivable that Alexander's ideas will turn out to be a vital stimulus to the emergence of a new conception of architecture, though they are far from typical of the arguments at present heard in the United States.

No clear line of development can be detected in America, although the ideas of Johnson, Venturi and Moore have had such a widespread effect that hardly a building is constructed today that avoids eclecticism or historical associations of one kind or another. The different paths taken by the individual members of the 'New York Five' (Peter Eisenman, Michael Graves, Richard Gwathmey, John Hejduk and Richard Meier), who all started from the formalism of Le Corbusier, are revealing. Graves (b.1934), whose buildings have a highly pictorial quality, shows particularly clearly the move towards an eclecticism of quotations, as in his Public Service Building for Portland, Oregon, which deliberately harks back to American Art Deco; he himself has also made clear his indebtedness to historical, anthropomorphic theories of architecture.[80] Meier (b.1934), on the other hand, has kept to a form of aestheticsed functionalism which he sees as belonging to a great historical tradition, and he rejects the use of ornament on the basis of arguments almost identical to those heard in the 1920s.[81]

Thomas Gordon Smith and Stanley Tigerman put forward a case for the totally free use of historical architectural forms based on a collage of traditional ideas that can be described, according to one's taste, as whimsical, ironic or just silly.[82] Tigerman's aim of destroying the Giedion-Pevsner view of the development of twentieth-century architecture was shown in his imaginary second competition (1980) for the Chicago Tribune Tower, which presented a view of the entries for the actual competition of 1922 totally different from that generally accepted.[83] Here was a strange attempt to escape from history by inventing alternative history.

The theoretical basis of fashionable high technology architecture, be it fanciful, bombastic or vulgar (e.g. Helmut Jahn or John C. Portman), is sketchy, but in all cases particular regard is paid to the needs and habits of the user. The extent to which this historicist 'Romantic' tendency has made its mark on the general public can be seen from the competition for the Southwest Center in Houston (1983), the designs submitted – the winner was Jahn – owing their *raison d'être* to the Gothic Revival or Art Deco.[84]

Discussion of architectural theory in the United States continues to follow a more liberal and pragmatic course than in Europe, though European developments are closely followed. Whereas in America architecture is treated primarily as a matter of technology and form, in most European countries ideological and social questions predominate.

In Europe the liveliest discussion of architectural theory since the end of the Second World War has taken place in Italy,[85] where almost all theoretical statements have been characterised by a keen awareness of history. Many historians of art and architecture – Bruno Zevi, Leonardo Benevolo, Manfredo Tafuri, Giulio Carlo Argan – have influenced the course of the debate; conversely, architects have also been active in the historiography of their subject – Paolo Portoghesi, for instance. Probably the most significant architect in this connection has been Carlo Scarpa (1906–78),[86] who combined his knowledge of Venice with the influence of Frank Lloyd Wright and with a study of the historical setting, using concrete to achieve solutions that approached the poetic. However, he left no account of the theoretical basis of his work.

In contrast to Germany, activity in Italy resumed after 1945 with little interruption, especially in Milan, where a studio like that of the BBPR could survive political change.[87] This is also true, though in a different way, of Pier Luigi Nervi (1891–1979), an engineer working mainly in Rome, who concerned himself with the aesthetic questions related to his structures.[88] Nervi came to the conclusion that scientific calculations were inadequate to demonstrate the functional qualities of a building and that functions and forces need to be made explicit in the design.[89] This realisation, coming from an engineer, spelt the end of a merely structural functionalism, both in theory and in practice.

Developments in Italy since the Second World War have taken many different directions. A constant concern with historical cities has led to a particular emphasis on town planning and local history, two subjects that invariably go hand in hand. Two influential works have been *L'urbanistica e l'avvenire della città* (1959) by Giuseppe Samonà and *Origine e sviluppo della città moderna* (1964) by Carlo Aymonino.[90]

The most important contribution to the theory of urban planning is *L'architettura della città* (1966) by Aldo Rossi (b.1931),[91] who strongly opposes the application of purely functionalist criteria and argues for a return to aesthetic and monumental categories under the banner of socialism. Rossi is a key figure in modern Italian architecture.[92] His early experiences of Stalinist architecture in Moscow and East Berlin have left their marks, both ideologically and formally, while in his numerous writings, as well as in his designs, he has expressed his reactions to the work of theorists old and new – the Revolutionary architects, Milizia, Loos, the Surrealists, Italian Rationalism, Le Corbusier, etc.[93]

The manifesto *Architettura Razionale*, which Rossi issued on the occasion of the 15th Milan Triennale in 1973, gave birth to a movement that was quickly joined by architects from all over Europe, among them Vittorio Gregotti, Giorgio Grassi, Carlo Aymonino, Leon and Rob Krier, James Stirling, Oswald Matthias Ungers and Josef Paul Kleihues (*Plate 207*).[94] Their designs are characterised by a suggestive pictorial quality or by a precision of presentation that goes back to Durand. The influence of this architecture is exercised more by drawings and designs than by completed buildings; indeed, such drawings are often ends in themselves, as they were with Boullée, whose treatise on architecture Rossi translated into Italian.[95] Architectural drawing becomes compensation for a reality found inadequate, and liberties are taken which would have no meaning if the plan were to be realised. Architects like Massimo Scolari and Rob Krier are primarily draughtsmen who occasionally publish architectural programmes which contain little by way of formally presented theory.[96]

The increasing imprecision of the term 'Rationalism' became clear when attempts were made to link the European movement with America – with Venturi, for example – where the theoretical situation was quite different. The only common ground was the concept of a new symbolism in architecture based on a reversion to the past. It was only logical, therefore, that the vague concept of 'Post-Modernist' should subsume the 'Neo-Rationalist' movement, even though these 'Rationalists' generally object to such a tendency.[97] Yet the modern trend, as revealed in exhibitions and their corresponding catalogues, has been to try and make the alliance between Post-Modernism and

Rationalism a fact, heedless of what is actually built. This trend can be clearly seen in the activities of the Deutsches Architekturmuseum in Frankfurt[98] and the International Bauausstellung (IBA) exhibitions in Berlin in 1987.[99] Germany, together with America and Italy, is a centre for architectural experiments in how to build within the historical framework of pre-existing urban structures, and the outcome of the IBA in Berlin, where, under Hardt-Waltherr Hämer and Josef Paul Kleihues, a cautious programme of urban renewal has been carried out, shows the feasibility of these ideas.

Mention should also be made in this connection of the often fundamental influence on architectural theory of psychology and sociology. The return to the symbolic quality of architecture is due on the one hand to historical studies in architectural iconography, on the other to the semiotics of sociologists such as Gillo Dorfles and Umberto Eco.[100] In his book *Intentions in Architecture* (1963) Christian Norberg-Schulz has incorporated the findings of investigations in these fields into a new synthesis of criteria for architectural judgement.[101] New ideas in urban planning have come from Jane Jacobs, with her *Death and Life of Great American Cities* (1961) and from Alexander Mitscherlich's *Die Unwirtlichkeit unserer Städte* (1965),[102] while Rudolf Arnheim, working from the viewpoint of perceptual psychology, has produced a logical refutation of functionalism.[103]

There has been no dearth of attempts to bring these and other areas of thought to bear on architectural theory. Niels Luning Prak, for example, using a questionable methodology in his *Language of Architecture* (1968), makes architectural aesthetics dependent on social history.[104] An attractive plea for a pluralistic view, accompanied by gently ironical judgements on the dogmas of the past, is contained in Bruce Allsopp's *A Modern Theory of Architecture* (1977),[105] which – in its remarks on the nature of architectural decoration, for instance – gives a positive slant to the negative conclusions in the books by Brolin and Blake mentioned above, and encourages the treatment of architectural theory in a cautious, undoctrinaire spirit.

In the current theoretical writings of architects there seems no way out of the dilemma of a purely negative reaction to functionalist Modernism. 'Post-Modernism' signifies nothing more than a series of heterogeneous attempts to break loose from the functionalist grip. Neo-Historicism, one of the most prominent of these attempts, lacks firm intellectual foundation and, like any primitive historicist tendency, can only lead back to a new form of functionalism. A characteristic recent example of this superficial, ill-considered play with a collective historical memory would seem the monumental housing estates designed by Ricardo Bofill (b.1939), who uses poetic allusions – to Kafka's *The Castle*, *Walden*, *Abraxas*, etc. – to demonstrate his mastery of large-scale Baroque forms and eclectic stylistic quotation;[106] but his theory is refuted by reality.

If architecture and its theoretical reflection are consciously to rejoin a historical continuum, there must be a thorough, unprejudiced appraisal of the situation. The break with the past which is alleged to have taken place in the first half of the twentieth century has in fact severed vital links with tradition in the late twentieth-century mind which cannot easily be restored. An alternative to functionalism is not to be found in a return to indigenous styles or to a formalistic Neo-classicism, or in any other forms of historical eclecticism. The study of architectural history and theory can only reveal what practical steps might be taken in an age whose aesthetics, technological faith and ecology have been shaken to their foundations.

Notes

Introduction

[1] *'Der Gedanke, daß theoretisch-kritische Erwägungen das künstlerische Schaffen beeinflussen, ist unhaltbar. Dieses entspringt gegebenen Empfindungen, einer bestimmtn Veranlagung, den gesamten geistigen Voraussetzungen der betreffenden Epoche und noch manchen anderen Faktoren, aber nie und nimmer zeitgenössischer Reflexion. Diese wurzelt vielmehr ebenso in ihrer Zeit wie das künstlerische Schaffen, ist ebenso bedingt wie dieses, ebenso unfrei... Die Kunsttheorie selbst ist nichts anderes als ein* Ausdruck des Zeitempfindens und ihre Bedeutung beruht nicht darin, daß sie in ihrer eigenen Gegenwart die Wege weist, sondern darin, daß sie als Denkmal vergangener Geistigkeit den Nachgeborenen dient.' Emil Kaufmann, 'Die Architekturtheorie der französischen Klassik und des Klassizimus', *Repertorium für Kunstwissenschaft* 44, 1924, p. 235.

[2] Paul Valéry, *Eupalinous ou l'Architecte, précédé de l'Ame et la Danse*, Paris 1923.

1. Vitruvius and architectural theory in Antiquity

[1] Cf. Friedrich Wilhelm Schlikker, *Hellenistische Vorstellungen von der Schönheit des Bauwerks nach Vitruv*, Berlin 1940, pp. 10ff.

[2] See esp. Hugh Plommer, *Vitruvius and Later Roman Building Manuals*, Cambridge 1973 (with Faventinus's text).

[3] On Vitruvius, see esp. J.A. Jolles, *Vitruvs Ästhetik*, diss., Freiburg 1906; Ludwig Sontheimer, *Vitruv und seine Zeit*, diss., Tübingen 1908; Auguste Choisy, *Vitruve*, Paris 1909; Adalbert Birnbaum, *Vitruvius und die griechische Architektur*, Vienna 1914; Achille Pellizzari, *I trattati attorno le arti figurative in Italia e nella Peninsula Iberica*, vol. I, Naples 1915, pp. 90ff.; W. Sackur, *Vitruv und die Poliorketiker*, Berlin 1925; Erik Wistrand, *Vitruvstudier*, diss., Götenburg 1933; F. Pellati, *Vitruvio*, Rome 1938; E. Stuerzenacker, *Vitruvius über die Baukunst*, Essen 1938; Friedrich W. Schlikker, *Hellenistische Vorstellungen von der Schönheit des Bauwerks nach Vitruv*, Berlin 1940; C. J. Moe, *Numeri di Vitruvio*, Milan 1945; Paul Thielscher, *Vitruvius Mamurra (Real Encyclopädie der Altertumswissenschaft, 2. Reihe, 17. Halbband)*, 1961, cols 427–89; Roland Martin, 'Vitruvius', *Enciclopedia Universale dell'Arte*, XIV, 1966, cols 832–37; Hugh Plommer, *Vitruvius and Later Roman Building Manuals*, Cambridge 1973; Pierre Gros, Vitruve: l'architecture et sa théorie, à la lumière des études récentes', in: Hildegard Temporini and Wolfgang Haase (eds), *Aufstieg und Niedergang der römischen Welt*, 30.1: *Principat*, Berlin–New York 1982, pp. 659–95; *Bauplanung und Bautheorie der Antike (Diskussionen zur archäologischen Bauforschung 4*, Berlin 1983; Heiner Knell and Burkhardt Wesenberg (eds), *Vitruv-Kolloquium des Deutschen Archäologen-Verbandes*, Darmstadt 1984; Heiner Knell, *Vitruvs Architekturtheorie. Versuch einer Interpretation*, Darmstadt 1985.

[4] Thielscher, 1961, pp. 427ff. Faventinus is the first to give 'Polio' as *praenomen* or *cognomen* of Vitruvius (Plommer, 1973, pp. 40, 87); but this, even if correct, throws no light on the identity of Vitruvius.

[5] Thielscher, 1961, cols 431f. Roland Martin, 1966, col. 832, dates publication to between 27 and 23 BC.

[6] Vitruvius, *De architectura* ... II. preface. 1–4. *De architectura* ..., Latin-English ed., tr. and ed. Frank Granger, London–Cambridge 1931 (Loeb Classical Library – cited henceforth as Loeb), vol. I, pp. 72–75.

[7] *'per auxilia scientiae scriptaque, ut spero, perveniam ad commendationem.' De architectura*, II. preface. 4 (Loeb, vol. I, p. 74).

[8] *'[quod] animadverti multa te aedificavisse et nunc aedificare, reliquo quoque tempore et publicorum et privatorum aedificiorum, pro amplitudine rerum gestarum ut posteris*

*memoriae traderentur, curam habiturum.
Conscripsi praescriptiones terminatas, ut eas
adtendens et ante facta et futura qualia sint
opera, per te posses nota habere. Namque
his voluminibus aperui omnes disciplinae
rationes.'* Ibid., I. preface. 3 (Loeb, vol. I,
p. 4).

⁹ Ibid., VI. preface.

¹⁰ *'Quas ob res corpus architecturae rationesque
eius putavi diligentissime conscribendas,
opinans in munus omnibus gentibus non
ingratum futurum.'* Ibid., VI. preface. 7
(Loeb, vol. II. p. 8).

¹¹ *'De artis vero potestate quaeque insunt in
ea ratiocinationes polliceor, uti spero, his
voluminibus non modo aedificantibus sed
etiam omnibus sapientibus cum maxima
auctoritate me sine dubio praestaturum.'*
Ibid., I.i.18 (Loeb, vol. I, pp. 22–24).

¹² Ibid, VII. preface, 11–4 (Loeb, vol. II. pp.
70–75).

¹³ *'homines imitabili docilique natura…'* Ibid.,
II.i.3. (Loeb, vol. I, p. 78).

¹⁴ Ibid., II.i.6 (Loeb, vol. I, p. 84).

¹⁵ *'deinde observationibus studiorum e vagan-
tibus induciis et incertis ad certas symmetriarum perduxerunt rationes.'* Ibid., II.i.7
(Loeb, vol. I, p. 84).

¹⁶ Ibid., IX.i.2 (Loeb, vol. II, p. 213–13).

¹⁷ Cf. Joachim Gaus, 'Weltbaumeister und
Architekt', in: Günter Binding (ed.), *Beiträge über Bauführung und Baufinanzierung
im Mittelalter*, Cologne 1974, pp. 38–67.

¹⁸ *De architectura*, I.i.1 (Loeb, vol. I, p. 6);
IX.vi.2 (Loeb, vol. II, pp. 244–46). On
Vitruvius's ideal of the architect's education,
see Frank E. Brown, 'Vitruvius and the
Liberal Art of Architecture', *Bucknell
Review* II, 4, 1963, pp. 99–107.

¹⁹ *'uti commentariis memoriam firmiorem
efficere possit.'* Ibid., I.i.4 (Loeb, vol. I, p. 8).

²⁰ Ibid, I.i.11 (Loeb, vol. I, p. 16).

²¹ *Haec autem ita fieri debent, ut habeatur
ratio firmitatis, utilitatis, venustatis. Firmitatis erit habita ratio, cum fuerit fundamentorum ad solidum depressio, quaque e
materia, copiarum sine avaritia diligens
electio; utilitatis autem [cum fuerit] emen-
data et sine impeditione usus locorum dispositio et ad regiones sui cuiusque generis apta
et commoda distributio; venustatis vero,
cum fuerit operis species grata et elegans
membrorumque commensus isutas habeat
symmetriarum ratiocinationes.'* Ibid., I.iii.2
(Loeb, vol. I, p. 34).

²² Cf. also Miloutine Borissavliévitch, *Les théories de l'architecture*, Paris 1951, pp. 51ff.
This author deals in particular with Vitruvian concepts as understood by Claude Perrault.

²³ *'Ordinatio est modica membrorum operis
commoditas separatim universeque pro-
portionis ad symmetriam comparatio. Haec
conponitur ex quantitate, quae graece
posotes dicitur. Quantitas autem est modu-
lorum ex ipsius operis sumptio e singulisque
membrorum partibus universi operis conveniens effectus.'* De architectura, I.ii.2 (Loeb,
vol. I, p. 24).

²⁴ *'Dispositio autem est rerum apta conlocatio
elegansque conpositionibus effectus operis
cum qualitate. Species dispositionis, quae
graece dicuntur* ideae, *sunt hae: ichnographia, orthographia, scaenographia. Ichnographia est circini regulaeque modice continens
usus, e qua capiuntur formarum in solis
arearum descriptiones. Orthographia
autem est erecta frontis imago modiceque
picta rationibus operis futuri figura. Item
scaenographia est frontis et laterum absce-
dentium adumbratio ad circinique centrum
omnium linearum responsus. Hae nascuntur
ex cogitatione et inventione. Cogitatio est
cura studii plena et industriae vigilantiaeque
effectus proposti cum voluptate. Inventio
autem est quaestionum obscurarum explica-
tio ratioque novae rei vigore mobili reperta.
Hae sunt terminationes dispositionum.'* Ibid,
I.ii.2 (Loeb, vol. I, pp. 24–25).

²⁵ *'Eurythmia est venusta species commodusque
in conpositionibus membrorum aspectus.
Haec efficitur, cum membra operis convenientia sunt altitudinis ad latitudinem, latitudinis ad longitudinem, et ad summam omnia
respondent suae symmetriae.'* Ibid, I.ii.3
(Loeb, vol. I, p. 26).

²⁶ *'Item symmetria est ex ipsius operis membris
conveniens consensus ex partibusque separatis ad universae figurae speciem ratae
partis responsus. Uti in hominis corpore e
cubito, pede, palmo, digito ceterisque parti-
culis symmetros est eurythmiae qualitas, sic
est in operum perfectionibus. Et primum in
aedibus sacris aut e columnarum crassitudi-
nibus aut triglypho aut etiam embaterre…
invenitur symmetriarum ratiocinatio.'* Ibid,
I.ii.4 (Loeb, vol. I, p. 26).

²⁷ *'Decor autem est emendatus operis aspectus
probatis rebus conpositi cum auctoritate. Is
perficitur statione, quod graece* thematismo

dicitur, seu consuetudine aut natura. Statione, cum Iovi Fulguri et Caelo et Soli et Lunae aedificia sub divo hypaethraque constituentur; horum enim deorum et species et effectus in aperto mundo atque lucenti praesentes vidimus. Minervae et Marti et Herculi aedes doricae fient; his enim diis propter virtutem sine deliciis aedificia constitui decet. Veneri, Florae, Proserpinae, Fonti Lumphis corinthio genere constitutae aptas videbuntur habere proprietates, quod his diis propter teneritatem graciliora et florida foliisque et volutis ornata opera facta augere videbuntur iustum decorem. Iunoni, Dianae, Libero Patri ceterisque diis qui eadem sunt similitudine, si aedes ionicae construentur, habita erit ratio mediocritatis, quod et ab severo more doricorum et ab teneritate corinthiorum temperabitur eorum institutio proprietatis.' Ibid, I.ii.5 (Loeb, vol. I, pp. 26–28).

On Vitruvius's concept of *decor*, see the excellent analysis by Alste Horn-Oncken, *Über das Schickliche. Studien zur Geschichte der Architekturtheorie* I (*Abhandlungen der Akademie der Wiss. in Göttingen. Philol.-hist. Kl.*, Ser. 3, No. 70), Göttingen 1967.

28 *'Distributio autem est copiarum locique commoda dispensatio parcaque in operibus sumptus ratione temperatio. Alter gradus erit distributionis, cum ad usum patrum familiarum et ad pecuniae copiam aut ad eloquentiae dignitatem aedificia alte disponentur. Namque aliter urbanas domos oportere constitui videtur, aliter quibus ex possessionibus rusticis influunt fructus; non idem feneratoribus, aliter beatis et delicatis; potentibus vero, quorum cogitationibus respublica gubernatur, ad usum conlocabuntur; et omnino faciendae sunt aptae omnibus personis aedificiorum distributiones.'* Ibid, I.ii.8–9 (Loeb, vol. I, pp. 30–32).

29 Cf. the chapter 'Vitruvius and the theory of proportion' in: Peter Hugh Scholfield, *The Theory of Proportion in Architecture*, Cambridge 1958, pp. 16–32.

30 *'Aedium compositio constat ex symmetria, cuius ratinem diligentissime architecti tenere debent. Ea autem paritur a proportione, quae graece analogia dicitur. Proportio est ratae partis membrorum in omni opere totiusque commodulatio, ex qua ratio efficitur symmetriarum. Namque non potest aedis ulla sine symmetria atque proportione rationem habere compositionis, nisi uti ad hominis bene figurati membrorum habuerit*

exactem rationem.' De architectura, III.i.1 (Loeb, vol. I, p. 158).

31 This proportional canon goes back to that of Polyclitus, now lost. On its recovery and Vitruvius's use of it, see Hans von Steuben, *Der Kanon des Polyklet*, Tübingen 1973, pp. 68ff.; Richard Tobin, 'The Canon of Polykleitos', *American Journal of Archaeology* 79, 1975, pp. 307–21. On the anthropometric tradition in systems of proportion, see esp. Erwin Panofsky, 'Die Entwicklung der Proportionslehre als Abbild der Stilentwicklung', *Monatshefte für Kunstwissenschaft* XIV, 1921, pp. 188–219 (reprinted in: E. Panofsky, *Aufsätze zu Grundfragen der Kunstwissenschaft*, Berlin 1964, pp. 169–204); see also the appropriate essays in *Der 'vermessene' Mensch. Anthropometrie in Kunst und Wissenschaft*, Munich 1973.

32 *'Similiter vero sacrarum aedium membra ad universam totius magnitudinis summam ex partibus singulis convenientissimam debent habere commensus responsum.'* De architectura, III.i.3 (Loeb, vol. I, p. 160).

33 *'Item corporis centrum medium naturaliter est umbilicus. Nampque si homo conlocatus fuerit supinus manibus et pedibus pansis circinique conlocatum centrum in umbilico eius, circumagendo rotundationem utrarumque manuum et pedum digiti linea tangentur. Non minus quemadmodum schema rotundationis in corpore efficitur, item quadrata designatio in eo invenietur. Nam si a pedibus imis ad summum caput mensum erit eaque mensura relata fuerit ad manus pansas, invenietur eadem latitudo uti altitudo, quemadmodum areae quae ad normam sunt quadratae.'* Ibid.

34 *'Ergo si convenit ex articulis hominis numerum inventum esse et ex membris separatis ad universam corporis speciem ratae partis commensus fieri responsum, relinquitur, ut suscipiamus eos, qui etiam aedes deorum immortalium constituentes ita membra operum ordinaverunt, ut proportionibus et symmetriis separatae atque universae convenientesque efficerentur eorum distributiones.'* Ibid, III.i.9 (Loeb, vol. I, pp. 164–66).

35 Ibid, IV.i.5–8 (Loeb, vol. I, p. 206). The theory of *'genera'* is given a good deal less emphasis in Vitruvius than in architectural treatises from the Renaissance onwards. Vitruvius recognises only the three *'genera'* of Corinthian, Doric and Ionic. Thus he

does not recognise a Tuscan order *per se*, but speaks of '*tuscanae dispositiones*' in the Tuscan temple (IV.vii).

[36] Cf. Christof Thoenes, 'Gli ordini architettonici – Rinascità o invenzione?' in the proceedings of the symposium *Roma e l'antico nell'arte e nella cultura del Cinquecento (Rome 1982)*, Rome 1985; Hubertus Guenther, *Deutsche Architekturtheorie zwischen Gotik und Renaissance*, Darmstadt 1988, pp. 89–98.

[37] '*Cum ergo constituta symmetriarum ratio fuerit et commensus ratiocinationibus explicati, tum etiam acuminis est proprium providere ad naturam loci aut usum aut*

speciem, adiectionibus temperaturas efficere, cum de symmetria sit detractum aut adiectum, uti id videatur recte esse formatum in aspectuque nihil desideretur.' De architectura, VI.ii.1 (Loeb, vol. II, p. 20).

[38] *Vitruve, De Architectura. Concordance. Documentation bibliographique, lexicale et grammaticale*, ed. L. Callebat, P. Bouet, Ph. Fleury, M. Zuinghedau, 2 vols, Hildesheim –Zürich–New York 1984; the most recent Italian edition of Vitruvius, *Vitruvio Pollione, Dell'architettura, interpretazione*, ed Giovanni Florian, Pisa 1978, has a commentary restricted to historical statements.

2. The Vitruvian tradition and architectural theory in the Middle Ages

[1] Cf. Herbert Koch, *Vom Nachleben des Vitruv*, Baden-Baden 1951, p. 9.

[2] Cf. ibid., pp. 11ff.

[3] On the dissemination of Vitruvius, see besides Koch, esp.: Francesco Pellati, 'Vitruvio nel Medioevo e nel Rinascimento', *Bollettino del Reale Istituto di Archeologia e Storia dell'Arte* V, 1932, pp. 111–32; Félix Peeters, 'Le *Codex Bruxellensis* 5253 (b) de Vitruve et la tradition manuscrite du *De Architectura*', *Mélanges dédiés à la mémoire de Félix Grat* II, Paris 1949, pp. 119–43; Lucia A. Ciapponi, 'Il *De Architectura* di Vitruvio nel primo umanesimo (dal ms. Bodl. Auct. F. 5.7)', *Italia medioevale e umanistica* III, 1960, pp. 59–99; Karl-August Wirth, 'Bemerkungen zum Nachleben Vitruvs im 9. und 10. Jahrhundert und zu dem Schlettstädter Vitruv-Codex', *Kunstchronik* 20, 1967, pp. 281–91; Carol Herselle Krinsky, 'Seventy-Eight Vitruvius Manuscripts', *Journal of the Warburg & Courtauld Institutes* XXX, 1967, pp. 36–70; Carol Heitz, 'Vitruve et l'architecture du haut moyen-âge', *Settimane di Studio del Centro Italiano di Studi sull'Alto Medioevo* XXII, 1974, pp. 725–57; Giangiacomo Martines, 'Hygino Gromatico: Fonti iconografiche antiche per la ricostruzione rinascimentale della città vitruviana', in: *Ricerche di Storia dell'Arte* 1–2, 1976, pp. 277–85; Manfredo Tafuri in: *Scritti Rinascimentali di Architettura*, Milan 1978, 389ff.

[4] Koch (1951), p. 10.

[5] Pellati (1932), pp. 111f.

[6] '*Aedificiorum partes sunt tres: dispositio, constructio, venustas*'. *Isidori Hispalensis*

Episcopi Etymologiarum sive Originum Libri XX, ed. W. M. Lindsay, Oxford 1911 (several subsequent printings), XIX.ix.

[7] *Dispositio est areae vel solii et fundamentorum descriptio.*' Ibid., XIX.ix.

[8] '*Venustas est quidquid illud ornamenti et decoris causa aedificiis additur…*' Ibid., XIX.xi.

[9] '*Columnae pro longitudine et rotunditudine vocatae, in quibus totius fabricae pondus erigitur. Antiqua ratio erat columnarum altitudinis tertia pars latitudinum. Genera rotundarum quattuor: Doricae, Ionicae, Tuscanicae, Corinthiae, mensura crassitudinis et altitudinis inter se distantes. Quintum genus est earum quae vocantur Atticae, quaternis angulis aut amplius, paribus laterum intervallis.*' Ibid., XV.viii.14.

[10] Cf. Krinsky (1967), p. 36 n. 4.

[11] Cf. Julius von Schlosser, *Schriftquellen zur Geschichte der karolingischen Kunst*, Vienna 1892, pp. 6f. no. 16.

[12] Cf. Wirth (1967), pp. 282f.

[13] Cf. Heitz (1974), pp. 747f.

[14] Krinsky (1967), pp. 36ff. The most important manuscript is in the British Museum, Harleian mss. 2767 (cf. Krinsky, p. 51).

[15] Sélestat, Bibl. munic., ms. 1153 bis.

[16] See esp. Wirth (1967), pp. 283ff. (pls. 1–4); the illustrations in the Sélestat Codex were first published in V. Mortet, *La mesure et les proportions des colonnes antiques*, Mélanges d'archéologie, 1ᵉ série, Paris 1914, pp. 49–65, pls I, II. See also: Krinsky (1967), pp. 41f., 47. The wind diagram appears several times as an example of Vitruvian

manuscript illustration; cf. Krinsky, p. 41.

[17] Wirth (1967), p. 289.

[18] Cf. Wirth, p. 286 (pl. 3).

[19] Koch (1951), pp. 15f. (n. 22).

[20] Cf. Gustina Scaglia, 'A Translation of Vitruvius and Copies of Late Antique Drawings in Buonaccorso Ghiberti's Zibaldone', Transactions of the American Philosophical Society 69, part I, 1979, pp. 11ff. The author dates the original drawings to 750–800 AD. The linking of these with Aachen is made credible by analogy with copies by Buonaccorso Ghiberti of very similar illustrations of Vitruvius.

[21] Scaglia (1969), p. 13.

[22] Hartwig Beseler and Hans Roggenkamp, Die Michaeliskirche in Hildeseim, Berlin 1954, pp. 112ff., 147ff.; Heitz (1974), pp. 749f.

[23] British Museum, Harleian mss. 2726.

[24] See esps. Beseler and Roggenkamp, pp. 147ff.; see also Konrad Algermissen (ed.), Bernward und Godehard von Hildesheim. Ihr Leben und ihr Wirken, Hildesheim 1960, esp. pp. 112ff.

[25] On the place of St Michael in Ottonian architecture, cf. esp. Hans Jantzen, Ottonische Kunst (1947), Hamburg ²1959, pp. 15ff. A direct adaptation of Antique models in the plastic arts may be seen in the Bernwardsäule in Hildesheim: cf. Rudolf Wesenberg, Bernwardinische Plastik, Berlin 1955, pp. 125f., pls 256ff.

[26] On architectural descriptions in Classical literature, cf. Paul Friedländer, Johannes von Gaza, Paulus Silentiarius. Kunstbeschreibungen justinianischer Zeit, Berlin–Leipzig 1912 (repr. Hildesheim–New York 1969), pp. 41ff. For a survey of medieval architectural descriptions, see Gerhard Goebel, Poeta Faber, Heidelberg 1971, pp. 23ff. and the literature cited.

[27] Glanville Downey, 'Ekphrasis', in: Reallexikon für Antike und Christentum IV, 1959, vols 921–44.

[28] The most important collections of source material on the history of Byzantine art are: Friedrich Wilhelm Unger, Quellen zur byzantinischen Kunstgeschichte, Vienna 1878; Jean Paul Richter, Quellen der byzantinischen Kunstgeschichte, Vienna 1897; Cyril Mango, The Art of the Byzantine Empire 312–1453, Englewood Cliffs, N.J. 1972. The compilations by Unger and Richter are exclusively devoted to the architecture of Constantinople; Unger's is further restricted to secular architecture.

[29] See esp. an excellent appreciation in Richard Krautheimer, Early Christian and Byzantine Architecture (The Pelican History of Art), Harmondsworth 1965, pp. 153ff.; and a survey and comprehensive bibliography in: Wolfgang Müller-Wiener, Bildlexikon zur Topographie Istanbuls, Tübingen 1977, pp. 84ff.

[30] Procopii Caesariensis Opera III, 2, ed. J. Haury, Leipzig 1913; Procopius (Loeb Classical Library), vol. VII, Greek-English ed. H. B. Dewing and Glanville Downey, London–Cambridge, Mass. 1940.

[31] Procopius (Loeb), vol. VII, pp. 2ff.

[32] Procopius (Loeb), vol. VII, pp. 10–32.

[33] 'Θέαμα τοίνυν ἡ ἐκκλησία κεκαλλιστευμένον γεγένηται, τοῖς μὲν ὁρῶσιν ὑπερφυές, τοῖς δὲ ἀκούουσι παντελῶς ἄπιστον· ἐπῆρται μὲν γὰρ ἐς ὕψος οὐράνιον ὅσον, καὶ ὥσπερ τῶν ἄλλων οἰκοδομημάτων ἀποσαλεύουσα ἐπινένευκεν ὑπερκειμένη τῇ ἄλλῃ πόλει, κοσμοῦσα μὲν αὐτήν, ὅτι αὐτῆς ἐστιν, ὡραϊζομένη δέ, ὅτι αὐτῆς οὖσα καὶ ἐπεμβαίνουσα τοσοῦτον ἀνέχει ὥστε δὴ ἐνθένδε ἡ πόλις ἐκ περιωπῆς ἀποσκοπεῖται.' Procopius, Περι κτισματων (On Buildings), I.i.27 (Loeb, Procopius, vol. VII, p. 12).

[34] Procopius (Loeb), vol. VII ('ἁρμονία τοῦ μέτρου, οὔτε τι ὑπεράγαν οὔτε τι ἐνδεὺς ἐχουσα').

[35] 'ταῦτα δὲ πάντα ἐς ἀλλήλά τε παρὰ δόξαν ἐν μεταρσίῳ ἐναρμοσθέντα, ἔκ τε ἀλλήλων ᾐωρημένα καὶ μόνοις ἐναπερειδόμενα τοῖς ἄγχιστα οὖσι, μίαν μὲν ἁρμονίαν ἐκπρεπεστάτην τοῦ ἔργου ποιοῦνται, οὐ παρέχονται δὲ τοῖς θεωμένοις αὐτων τινι ἐμφιλοχωρεῖν ἐπὶ πολὺ τὴν ὄψιν, ἀλλὰ μεθέλκει τὸν ὀφθαλμὸν ἕκαστον, καὶ μεταβιβάζει ῥᾷστα ἐφ' ἑαυτό.' Procopius, Περι κτισ. (On Buildings), I.i.47 (Loeb, vol. VII, p. 20).

[36] Friedländer (1912), with annotated Greek text; an extract in English translation in: Mango (1972), pp. 80–91.

[37] Cf. the extract in English translation in: Mango, pp. 96–102.

[38] Hans Sedlmayr, Das erste mittelalterliche Architektursystem, Kunstwissenschaftliche Forschungen II, 1933, pp. 25–62; repr. in:

Sedlmayr, *Epochen und Werke*, vol. I, Vienna
and Munich 1959, pp. 80–193; Krautheimer
(1965), pp. 149ff.

[39] Cf. Georg Scheja, *Hagia Sophia und Templum Salomonis (Istanbuler Mitteilungen 12)*, 1962, pp. 44–58, 47f.

[40] Scheja, pp. 53ff.

[41] Cf. Richard Krautheimer, 'Introduction to an "Iconography of Medieval Architecture",' *Journal of the Warburg & Courtauld Institutes* 5, 1942, pp. 1ff. On Solomon's Temple cf. Günter Bandmann in: *Lexikon der christlichen Ikonographie*, vol. 4, cols 255ff.

[42] The most important systematic collections of source material are: for the tenth century, Otto Lehmann-Brockhaus, *Die Kunst des X. Jahrhunderts im Lichte der Schriftquellen*, Strasbourg 1935; on France (eleventh–thirteenth centuries), Victor Mortet, *Recueil de textes relatifs à l'histoire de l'architecture et à la condition des architectes en France au moyen âge*, 2 vols, Paris 1911 and 1929; on Germany and Italy, Otto Lehmann-Brockhaus, *Schriftquellen zur Kunstgeschichte des 11. und 12. Jahrhunderts für Deutschland, Lothringen und Italien*, 2 vols, Berlin 1938 (source material on architecture, pp. 1–535); on England, Otto Lehmann-Brockhaus, *Lateinische Schriftquellen zur Kunst in England, Wales und Schottland vom Jahre 901 bis zum Jahre 1307*, 5 vols, Munich 1955–60.

[43] *Chronica monasterii Cassinensis (Monumenta Germaniae Historica*, SS VII, pp. 551–844; new ed. by Hartmut Hoffmann, in: *MGH, Scriptores* 34, Hanover 1980); extracts in: Julius von Schlosser, *Quellenbuch zur Kunstgeschichte des abendländischen Mittelalters*, Vienna 1896, pp. 192–217; Lehmann-Brockhaus (1938), pp. 476ff., 681f.; in English trans. in: Elizabeth Gilmore Holt, *A Documentary History of Art* vol. I, Garden City, NY, 1957, pp. 8–17.

[44] Schlosser (1896), p. 203.

[45] On Suger see esp. Erwin Panofsky, *Abbot Suger. On the Abbey and Church of St.-Denis and its Art Treasures*, Princeton 1946 (²1979, ed. Gerda Panofsky-Soergel) (with text and English trans. of selected passages from Suger's writings). See also Paul Frankl, *The Gothic. Literary Sources and Interpretations through Eight Centuries*, Princeton 1960, pp. 3–24. Suger's writings are: *Ordinationes* (1140/41), *Libellus alter de consecratione ecclesiae Sancti Dionysii* (1144–1146/47), and *Liber de rebus in administratione sua gestis* (1144–49).

[46] Suger (*Libellus alter de consecratione*), ed. Panofsky, p. 90. A description of the Carolingian basilica of Saint-Denis, dating from 799, with astonishingly exact figures and measurements, has been published: Bernhard Bischoff, 'Eine Beschreibung der Basilika von Saint-Denis aus dem Jahre 799', *Kunstchronik* 34, 1981, pp. 97–103).

[47] See esp. Krautheimer (1942), pp. 10f.

[48] Suger (*Liber de rebus in administratione*), ed. Panofsky, pp. 62ff.

[49] Cf. Schlosser (1896), p. xviii.

[50] William Stubbs, *The Historical Works of Gervase of Canterbury*, 2 vols, London 1879–80 (text vol. II, pp. 325–414); Schlosser (1896), pp. 252–65; Frankl (1960), pp. 24–35; Teresa G. Frisch, *Gothic Art 1140–c.1450*, Englewood Cliffs, NJ 1971, pp. 14–23 (English trans.).

[51] Carl Schnaase, *Geschichte der bildenden Künste im Mittelalter*, vol. III, Düsseldorf 1856, p.242.

[52] On the building of the choir of Canterbury Cathedral, see Geoffrey Webb, *Architecture in Britain. The Middle Ages (Pelican History of Art)*, Harmondsworth 1956, pp. 72ff.; Peter Draper, 'William of Sens and the original design of the choir termination of Canterbury Cathedral 1175–1179', *Journal of Architectural Historians* XLII, 1983, pp. 238–48.

[53] '*Nunc autem quae sit operis utriusque differentia dicendum est. Pilariorum igitur tam veterum quam novorum una forma est, una et grossitudo, sed longitudo dissimilis. Elongati sunt enim pilarii novi longitudine pedum fere duodecim. In capitellis veteribus opus erat planum, in novis sculptur subtilis...*

Ibi murus super pilarios directus cruces a choro sequestrabat, hic vero nullo intersticio cruces a choro divisae in unam clavem quae in medio fornicis, magnae consistit, quae quatuor pilariis principalibus innititur, convenire videntur...' Schlosser (1896), p. 264.

[54] For this possibility see Schnaase (1856), p. 245.

[55] The works of Hildegard von Bingen are included in entirety in: J.-P. Migne, *Patrologiae cursus completus, ser. lat.* CXCVII, Paris 1882 (*Liber divinorum operum*, cols.

739ff.); Ildefons Herwegen (Ein mittelalterlicher Kanon des menschlichen Körpers',
Repertorium für Kunstwissenschaft XXXII,
1909, pp. 445f.) first drew attention to
Hildegard's theory of proportion, but
without being able to indicate any connection with earlier proportional systems.
[56] *'Nam longitudo staturae hominis latitu-
doque ipsius, brachiis et manibus aequaliter
a pectore extensis, aequales sunt…'* Liber
divinorum operum, col. 815.
[57] *'quemadmodum etiam firmamentum aequa-
lem longitudinem et latitudinem habet…'*
Ibid.
[58] Ibid., col. 815.
[59] Lucca, Bibl. Governativa, Codex 1942, fol.
9r and 27v. Cf. Herbert von Einem, *Der
Mainzer Kopf mit der Binde (Arbeitsgemeinschaft für Forschung des Landes Nordrhein-
Westfalen, Geisteswiss.*, vol 37), Cologne
and Opladen 1955, pp. 25f., pls 26, 27.
[60] Rheims, Bibl. Municipale, ms 672, fol. I.
Einem, p. 25, pl. 28.
[61] *Liber divinorum operum*, cols 845f.: *'Sed et
in spatio quod est inter finem gutteris et
umbilicum aer designatur, qui de nubibus
usque ad terram descendit… Anima enim
ab altitudine coeli ad terrene descendens,
hominem quem vivificat, sed a Deo creatum
esse intellegere facit, ipsaque aeri, qui inter
coelum et terram medius videtur, assimila-
tur…'*.
[62] Einem (1955) and Günter Bandmann, 'Zur
Deutung des Mainzer Kopfes mit der Binde',
Zeitschrift für Kunstwissenschaft X, 1956,
pp. 153–74.
[63] Kenneth J. Conant, 'The after-life of Vitruvius in the Middle Ages', *Journal of the
Society of Architectural Historians* XXVII,
1968, pp. 33–8; Heitz (1974), p. 751.
[64] *Sicardi Cremonensis episcopi mitrale, sive
de officiis ecclesiasticis summa* (J.-P. Migne,
Patrologiae ser. lat. ccxiii, 1855; see esp.
Book 1 'De ecclesiae aedificatione, ornatu
et utensilibus', cols 13ff.); on Sicardus see
Paul Gerhard Ficker, *Der Mitralis des
Sicardus nach seiner Bedeutung für die Ikonographie des Mittelalters*, Leipzig 1889.
[65] From the extensive literature on the subject
the following should be singled out: Josef
Sauer, *Symbolik des Kirchengebäudes und
seiner Ausstattung in der Auffassung des
Mittelalters*, Freiburg ²1924; Günter Band-
mann, *Mittelalterliche Architektur als
Bedeutungsträger*, Berlin 1951.

[66] On the problem of architectural iconology,
see esp. Günter Bandmann, 'Ikonologie der
Architektur', *Jahrbuch für Ästhetik und
Allgemeine Kunstwissenschaft*, 1951, pp. 67–
109 (reprinted in book form with the same
title, Darmstadt 1969).
[67] Erwin Panofsky, *Gothic Architecture and
Scholasticism* (1951), Cleveland–New York
⁶1963; Otto von Simson, *The Gothic
Cathedral. Origins of Gothic Architecture
and the Medieval Concept of Order*, New
York 1956 (German ed. Darmstadt 1968;
this ed. cited hereafter).
[68] Cf. von Simson, p. 38.
[69] Aurelius Augustinus, *De libero arbitrio*,
in: J.-P. Migne, *Patrologiae, ser. lat.* xxxii,
1877, col. 1263 (this volume also includes
St Augustine's key aesthetic works *De
musica* and *De ordine*).
[70] Cf. von Simson, p. 44.
[71] Cf. ibid., pp. 45ff.
[72] Alanus ab Insulis, *Liber de Planctu Naturae*, in J.-P. Migne, *Patrologiae, ser. lat.*
ccx, 1855, *col.* 453. The importance of
mathematics, esp. geometry, in early Cistercian architecture was established by Hanno
Hahn in his work on the Abbey of Eber-
bach, c.1145–86 (*Die frühe Kirchenbaukunst der Zisterzienser*, Berlin 1957, pp.
66ff., 73ff.).
[73] Cf. von Simson, p. 56; Joachim Gaus,
'Weltbaumeister und Architekt', in: Günter
Binding (ed.), *Beiträge über Bauführung und
Baufinanzierung im Mittelalter*, Cologne
1974, pp. 38–67.
[74] Cf. von Simson, p. 56.
[75] The classification of subject-matter in the
Speculum majus was taken over by Emile
Mâle in the arrangement of his substantial
work *L'art religieux du XIIIᵉ siècle en
France*, Paris, ⁶1924 (English ed. used: *The
Gothic Image. Religious Art in France of the
Thirteenth Century*, New York 1958).
[76] See esp. Achille Pellizzari, *I trattati attorno
le arti figurative*, vol. I, Naples 1915, pp.
371ff.; and on p. 435 see contents list of
Book XI of the *Speculum doctrinale*, with
quotations from it going back to Vitruvius.
[77] St Thomas Aquinas, for example, appears
not to have had direct knowledge of Vitruvius's text; in *De regimine principum* he
mistakenly calls him Vegetius; cf. W. A.
Eden, 'St Thomas Aquinas and Vitruvius',
Mediaeval and Renaissance Studies (Warburg Institute) II, 1950, pp. 183–5.

[78] Especially by Paul Frankl (1960), p. 103; 'If then one asks about the book on the aesthetics of architecture in Gothic times the paradoxical answer must be: Vitruvius.'

[79] The prime edition is still that of Hans R. Hahnloser, *Villard de Honnecourt. Kritische Gesamtausgabe des Bauhüttenbuches ms. fr. 19093 der Pariser Nationalbibliothek*, Vienna 1935 (2nd enlarged ed. Graz 1972); J. B. A. Lassus, *Album de Villard de Honnecourt*, Paris 1968; Theodore Bowie, *The Sketchbook of Villard de Honnecourt*, New York 1959, ²1962 (with English trans. of texts). From the extensive literature on Villard the following should be mentioned: Frankl (1960), pp. 35–54; R. W. Scheller, *A Survey of Medieval Model Books*, Haarlem 1963, pp. 88–94; François Bucher, *Architector. The Lodge Books and Sketchbooks of Medieval Architects*, vol. I, New York 1979, pp. 15ff. (this volume contains a complete edition of the drawings with comments on individual pages, and attempts a biography and bibliography); Cord Meckseper, 'Über die Fünfeckkonstruktion bei Villard de Honnecourt und im späten Mittelalter', *Architectura* 13, 1983, pp. 31–40; Carl F. Barnes, Jr., *Villard de Honnecourt. The Artist and His Drawings. A Critical Bibliography*, Boston, Mass. 1982; *Proceedings of the symposium 'Abbot Suger and St Denis'* (Metropolitan Museum of Art 1981), New York 1986.

[80] Hahnloser (1935), p. 241.

[81] 'Wilars de Honecort vous salue, et sie proie a tos ceus qui ces engiens ouvrront con trovera en cest livre quil por s'arme et quil lor soviegne de lui. Car en cest livre puet on trover gran consel de la grant force de maçonerie et des engiens de carpenterie et si troverez le force de le portraiture, les trais ensi comme li ars de iometrie le commans et enseigne.' *Album de Villard de Honnecourt*, ed. J. Lassus, Paris 1968, p. 61.

[82] Hahnloser (1935), p. 241.

[83] Thus Frankl (1960), p. 37.

[84] Hahnloser, p. 257; Carl Lachmann, *Gromatici Veteres*, Berlin 1848; on the medieval tradition of the '*Gromatici veteres*', see Giangiacomo Martines, 'Gromatici Veteres tra antichità e medioevo', in: *Ricerche di Storia dell'Arte* 3, 1976, pp. 3–23.

[85] '*Ci comence li force des trais de portraiture si con li ars de iometrie les enseigne por legierement ovrer...*' *Album de Villard de Honnecourt*, p. 139.

[86] Cf. Erwin Panofsky, 'Die Entwicklung der Proportionslehre als Abbild der Stilentwicklung', *Monatshefte für Kunstwissenschaft* XIV, 1921, pp. 188–219; repr. in: Panofsky, *Aufsätze zu Grundfragen der Kunstwissenschaft*, Berlin 1964, esp. pp. 183f.

On the question of proportion in Villard see also Nikolaus Speich, 'Die Proportionslehre des menschlichen Körpers', diss., Zürich 1957, pp. 121ff.

[87] Panofsky (1964), pp. 184, pls 48, 49.

[88] '*Vesci une glise desquarie ki fu esgardee a faire en lordene di Cistiaux.*' *Album de Villard de Honnecourt*, p. 113.

[89] But Walter Ueberwasser ('Nach rechtem Maß,' *Jahrbuch der Preussischen Kunstsammlungen* 56, 1935, pp. 259ff.) shows it to be probable that plans were made by the addition of squares, as he demonstrates with Villard's drawing of the plan of a tower of Laon Cathedral.

[90] See esp. Carl Heideloff, *Die Bauhütte des Mittelalters in Deutschland*, Nuremberg 1844; Ferdinand Janner, *Die Bauhütten des deutschen Mittelalters*, Leipzig 1876; Pierre Du Colombier, *Les chantiers des cathédrales*, Paris 1953, (²1973); Frankl (1960), pp. 110ff.

[91] See esp. Paul Frankl, 'The Secret of Mediaeval Masons', *The Art Bulletin* 27, 1945, pp. 46ff.; Frankl, pp. 48ff.

[92] For critical discussion of this problem, very heatedly treated in older literature, see esp. Ueberwasser (1935), pp. 250–72; id., 'Beiträge zur Wiedererkenntnis gotischer Bau-Gesetzmäßigkeiten', *Zeitschrift für Kunstgeschichte* 8, 1939, pp. 303–09; particularly persuasive is an article by James S. Ackerman based on the discussions in the Milan Cathedral lodge, 'Ars sine scientia nihil est'. Gothic Theory of Architecture at the Cathedral of Milan', *The Art Bulletin* 31, 1949, pp. 84–111; a comprehensive treatment is Konrad Hecht, 'Maß und Zahl in der gotischen Baukunst', *Abhandlungen der braunschweigischen Wissenschaftlichen Gesellschaft* XXI, 1969, pp. 215–326; XXII, 1970, pp. 105–263; XXIII, 1971, pp. 25–263 (published in book form, Hildesheim–New York 1979).

[93] See esp. Ueberwasser (1935); Ackerman (1949); Hecht (1969 and esp. 1970, pp. 137ff.).

[94] For a résumé of the knowledge on these stonemasons' books, cf. Paul Booz, *Der Baumeister der Gotik*, Munich 1956; Frankl (1960), pp. 144ff.; Elke Weber, 'Steinmetzbücher-Architekturmusterbücher', in: Günter Binding and Norbert Nussbaum (eds.), *Der mittelalterliche Baubetrieb nördlich der Alpen in zeitgenössischen Darstellungen*, Darmstadt 1978, pp. 22–42; Anneliese Seeliger-Zeiss, 'Studien zum Steinmetzbuch des Lorenz Lochler von 1516', *Architectura* 12, 1982, pp. 125–50; Hubertus Günther (ed.), *Deutsche Architekturtheorie zwischen Gotik und Renaissance*, Darmstadt 1988, pp. 31ff; Ulrich Coenen, *Die spätgotischen Werkmeisterbücher in Deutschland als Beitrag zur mittelalterlichen Architekturtheorie*, diss., Aachen 1989.

[95] There is still only the overview by Kurt Rathe, 'Eine Architektur-Musterbuch des Spätgotik mit graphischen Einklebungen', *Festschrift der Nationalbibliothek Wien*, Vienna 1926, pp. 667–92; but see esp. Frankl (1960), pp. 145ff.; for a later dating ('from the end of the fifteenth century at the earliest'), see Elke Weber (1978), p. 25.

[96] Published in: Heideloff (1844), pp. 95–9; cf. Frankl, pp. 147f.

[97] Matthäus Roriczer, *Das Büchlein von der Fialen Gerechtigkeit* and *Die Geometria Deutsch*, facs. ed. by Ferdinand Geldner, Wiesbaden 1965; text with commentary and English trans. by Lou R. Shelby, *Gothic Design Techniques. The Fifteenth-Century Design Booklets of Mathes Roriczer and Hanns Schmuttermayer*, London–Amsterdam 1977 (and see the review by Werner Müller in: *Architectura* 8, 1978, pp. 190–3).

[98] Facs. text ed. Geldner (1965); text with commentary and English trans. in: Shelby (1977).

[99] Text with commentary and English trans. in: Shelby (1977).

[100] Published in: August Reichensperger, *Vermischte Schriften über christliche Kunst*, Leipzig 1856, pp. 133–55; cf. Lou R. Shelby and Robert Mark, 'Late Gothic Structural Design in the "Instructions" of Lorenz Lecher', *Architectura* 9, 1979, pp. 113–31; Anneliese Seeliger-Zeiss, 'Studien zum Steinmetzbuch des Lorenz Lechler von 1516', *Architectura* 12, 1982, pp. 125–50. On Lechler's architectural work see

Anneliese Seeliger-Zeiss, *Lorenz Lechler von Heidelberg und sein Umkreis*, Heidelberg 1967.

[101] Quoted from Reichensperger (1856), p. 133.

[102] François Bucher, *Architector. The Lodge Books and Sketchbooks of Medieval Architects*, vol. I, new York 1979, pp. 375ff.

[103] See also the recently published stonemasons' book of the master W. G. (1572) in the Städelsches Kunstinstitut, Frankfurt; this has no text and consists only of sections and drawings. Most of the 222 designs are of Late Gothic vaulting, clearly based on late fifteenth-century models. Cf. Elke Weber (1978), pp. 26ff; Elke Pauken (-Weber), *Das Steinmetzbuch WG 1972 im Städelschen Kunstinstitut zu Frankfurt am Main* (15. Veröffentlichung der Abt. Architektur des Kunsthistorischen Instituts der Universität Köln), Cologne 1979; François Bucher (1979), pp. 195ff.

[104] Ueberwasser (1935).

[105] Oxford, Bodleian Library, Auct. F. 5. 7; cf. Lucia A Ciapponi, 'Il "De Architectura" di Vitruvio nel primo umanesimo (dal ms. Bodl. Auct. F. 5. 7)', *Italia medioevale e umanistica* III, 1960, pp. 73ff.; Krinsky (1967), pp. 52f.

[106] Cf. Ciapponi, pp. 83ff.

[107] Cennino Cennini, *Il libro dell'arte*, ed. Licisco Magagnato, Vicenza 1971, pp. 81f.; Nikolaus Speich, 'Die Proportionen des menschlichen Körpers', diss., Zürich 1957, pp. 130ff. relates Cennini to the medieval tradition of Villard de Honnecourt.

[108] Filippo Villani, *De origine civitatis Florentiae*; for a critical view of Villani's knowledge of Vitruvius, see Carl Frey, *Il Codice Magliabechiano*, cl. XVII 17, Berlin 1892, xxxiiif.

[109] Herbert Koch, *Vom Nachleben Vitruv*, Baden-Baden 1951, p. 15 n. 18; Ciapponi (1960), p. 98.

[110] See catalogue of manuscript copies in: Krinsky (1967) and Manfredo Tafuri in: *Scritti rinascimentali di architettura*, Milan 1978, p. 393.

[111] Cf. Hanno-Walter Kruft and Magne Malmanger, 'Der Triumphbogen Alfonsos in Neapel. Das Monument und seine politische Bedeutung', *Acta ad Archaeologiam et Artium Historiam Pertinentia* VI, 1974, p. 262.

[112] Pius II (Enea Silvio Piccolomini), *I commen-*

tarii, Italian trans. Giuseppe Benetti, vol. III (*I Classici Cristiani* no. 222), Siena 1973, p. 227.

[113] Cf. *Lorenzo Ghiberti's Denkwürdigkeiten*, ed. Julius von Schlosser, 2 vols, Berlin 1912; Richard and Trude Krautheimer, *Lorenzo Ghiberti* (1956), Princeton [2]1970, esp. pp. 306ff.

[114] Lorenzo Ghiberti writes at the end of the second book of his *Commentarii*; '*Faremo un trattato d'architettura e tratteremo d'essa materia.*' Cf. exh. cat. *Lorenzo Ghiberti. Materia e ragionamenti*, Museo dell' Accademia e Museo di San Marco, Florence 1978, pp. 452ff.

[115] Cf. Gustina Scaglia, 'A Translation of Vitruvius and Copies of Late Antique Drawings in Buonaccorso Ghiberti's Zibaldone', *Transactions of the American Philosophical Society* 69 Part I, 1979.

[116] This translation forms a part of Buonaccorso Ghiberti's 'Zibaldone' (Florence, Bibl. Naz., Codex Banco Rari 228). The text is now published in: Scaglia (1979), pp. 19–30.

[117] Cf. Piero Morselli, 'The Proportions of Ghiberti's Saint Stephen: Vitruvius's *De architectura* and Alberti's *De statua*', *The Art Bulletin* LX, 1978, pp. 235–41.

[118] For depictions of architecture as an *ars mechanica* (e.g. on Laon Cathedral), see Jochen Kronjäger, *Berühmte Griechen und Römer als Begleiter der Musen und der Artes Liberales in Bildzyklen des 2. bis 14. Jahrhunderts*, diss., Marburg 1973, pp. 27ff., 35ff.

3. Leone Battista Alberti

[1] The most important biography of Alberti is still: Girolamo Mancini, *Vita di Leon Battista Alberti*, Rome 1911 (fac. repr. Rome 1971); what was hitherto described as an anonymous biography is now considered to be by Alberti himself: Riccardo Fubini and Anna Menci Gallorini, 'L'autobiografia di Leon Battista Alberti: studio e edizione', *Rinascimento* XII, 1972, pp. 21–78. For new presentations of his work see Joan Gadol, *Leon Battista Alberti. Universal Man of the Early Renaissance*, Chicago-London 1969 ([2]1973); Franco Borsi, *Leon Battista Alberti*, Milan 1975.

[2] For dating see esp. Cecil Grayson, 'The composition of L. B. Alberti's "Decem libri de re aedificatoria"', *Münchner Jahrbuch der bildenden Kunst*, 3rd series XI, 1960, pp. 152–61.

[3] Cf. e.g. Irene Behn, *Leone Battista Alberti als Kunstphilosoph*, Strassburg 1911; Willi Flemming, *Die Begründung der modernen Ästhetik und Kunstwissenschaft durch Leon Battista Alberti*, Leipzig–Berlin 1916 (a pseudo-neo-Kantianism here gives a wholly distorted view of Alberti); P. H. Michel, *La pensée de L. B. Alberti*, Paris 1930; Maria Luisa Gengaro, *L. B. Alberti teorico e architetto*, Milan 1939; Günter Hellmann, 'Studien zur Terminologie der kunsttheoretischen Schriften Leone Battista Albertis', diss. ms, Cologne 1955; Jan Białostocki, 'The Power of Beauty. A Utopian Idea of Leone Battista Alberti', *Studien zur toskanischen Kunst. Festschrift Ludwig H. Heydenreich*, Munich 1964, pp. 13–19; John Onians, 'Alberti and Filarete', *Journal of the Warburg and Courtauld Institutes* XXXIV, 1971, pp. 96ff.; Eugenio Battisti, 'Il metodo progettuale secondo il "De Re Aedificatoria" di Leon Battista Alberti, in: *Il Sant' Andrea di Mantova e Leon Battista Alberti, Atti del convegno di studi...*, Mantua 1972 [1974], pp. 131–56; Rozsa Feuer-Tóth, 'The "apertionum ornamenta" of Alberti and the Architecture of Brunelleschi', *Acta Historiae Artium Academiae Scientiarum Hungaricae* XXIV, 1978, pp. 147–52; Richard Tobin, 'Leon Battista Alberti: Ancient Sources and Structure in the Treatises on Art', diss., Bryn Mawr College 1979 (important links with Classical rhetoric).

[4] For a compendium of Greek and Latin authors cited by Alberti, cf. Mancini (1911), pp. 355f.

[5] Alberti's 'theory' takes on near-dogmatic character for Rudolf Wittkower (*Architectural Principles in the Age of Humanism*, London 1949, [3]1962); Hellmut Lorenz ('Studien zum architektonischen und architekturtheoretischen Werk L. B. Albertis', diss., ms, Vienna 1971) stresses the undogmatic character of Alberti's treatise (pp. 197ff.); Heinrich Klotz also argues against Wittkower's dogmatism, 'L. B. Albertis "De re aedificatoria" in Theorie und Praxis', *Zeitschrift für Kunstgeschichte* 32, 1969, pp. 93–103. Françoise Choay

(*La règle et le modèle. Sur la théorie de l'architecture et de l'urbanisme*, Paris 1980) sets out to interpret Alberti wholly in the light of rule-making; her application of modern linguistic and semiotic concepts to Alberti is methodologically questionable. Heiner Mühlmann (*Ästhetische Theorie der Renaissance. Leon Battista Alberti*, Bonn 1981) employs a post-Enlightenment conceptual apparatus in his consideration of Alberti's treatise in the context of Renaissance aesthetic theory.

[6] Lorenz (1971), p. 8.

[7] Cf. esp. Richard Krautheimer, 'Alberti and Vitruvius', in: *Studies in Western Art*, II, Princeton, NJ 1963, pp. 42–52; repr. in: Richard Krautheimer, *Studies in Early Christian, Medieval, and Renaissance Art*, New York–London 1969, p. 323–32.

[8] Alberti, *The Ten Books on Architecture*, VI. 1; tr. James Leoni, ed. Joseph Rykwert, London 1955, p. 112. '*Nihil usquam erat antiquorum operum, in quo aliqua laus elucesceret, quin ilico ex eo pervestigarem, siquid possem perdiscere. Ergo rimari omnia, considerare, metiri, lineamentis picturae colligere nusquam intermittebam, quoad funditus, quid quisque attulisset ingenii aut artis, prehenderem atque pernoscerem; eoque pacto scribendi laborem levabam discendi cupiditate atque voluptate.*' *De re aedificatoria*, ed. Giovanni Orlandi, 2 vols, Milan 1969, vol. II, p. 443.

[9] Ibid., ed. Rykwert, p. 111. '*Namque dolebam quidem tam multa tamque praeclarissima scriptorum monumenta interisse temporum hominumque iniuria, ut vix unum ex tanto naufragio Vitruvium superstitem haberemus, scriptorem procul dubio instructissimum, sed ita affectum tempestate atque lacerum, ut multis locis multa desint et multis plurima desideres. Accedebat quod ista tradidisset non culta: sic enim loquebatur, ut Latini Graecum videri voluisse, Graeci locutum Latine vaticinentur; res autem ipsa in sese porrigenda neque Latinum neque Graecum fuisse testetur, ut par sit non scripsisse hunc nobis, qui ita scripserit, ut non intelligamus.*' Ed. Orlandi, vol. II, p. 441.

[10] Ibid., Preface, p. ix; ed. Rykwert. '*Quales autem hae sint ates, non est ut prosequar: in promptu enim sunt; verum si repetas, ex omni maximarum artium numero nullam penitus invenies, quae non spretis reliquis*

suos quosdam et proprios fines petat et contempletur. Aut si tandem comperias ullam, quae, cum huiusmodi sit; ut ea carere nullo pacto possis, tum et de se utilitatem voluptati dignitatique coniunctam praestet, meo iudicio ab earum numero excludendam esse non duces architecturam: nanque ea quidem, siquid rem diligentius pensitaris, et publice et privatim commodissima et vehementer gratissima generi hominum est dignitateque inter primas non postrema.' Ed. Orlandi, vol. I, p. 7.

[11] Ibid.; ed. Rykwert, Preface, pp. ix. '*Non enim tignarium adducam fabrum, quem tu summis caeterarum disciplinis viris compares: fabri enim manus architecto pro instrumento est. Architectum ego hunc fore constituam, qui certa admirabilique ratione et via tum mente animoque diffinire tum et opere absolvere didicerit, quaecunque ex ponderum motu corporumque compactione et coagmentatione dignissimis hominum usibus bellissime commodentur.*' Ed. Orlandi, ibid.

[12] Ibid., ed. Rykwert, Preface, p. 10. '*Demum hoc sit ad rem, stabilitatem dignitatem decusque rei publicae plurimum debere architecto, qui quidem efficiat, ut in ocio cum amoenitate festivitate salubritate, in negocio cum emolumento rerumque incremento, in utrisque sine periculo et cum dignitate versemur.*' Ed. Orlandi, vol. I, p. 13.

[13] Ibid.

[14] Cf. Krautheimer (1963) for a comparison of expositional structure between Vitruvius and Alberti.

[15] Cf. Krautheimer, op. cit. (1963).

[16] Alberti, I, 1; ed. Rykwert, p. 2. '*Haec cum ita sint, erit ergo lineamentum certa constansque perscriptio concepta animo, facta lineis et angulis perfectaque animo et ingenio erudito*'. Ed. Orlandi, vol. I, p. 21.

[17] Alberti, I, 2.

[18] The attempt by Edward Robert De Zurko ('Alberti's Theory of Form and Function', *The Art Bulletin* XXXIX, 1957, pp. 142–45) to see Alberti as a functionalist must be viewed with circumspection; De Zurko was working from James Leoni's English translation of 1715, which treats Alberti from an Enlightenment point of view (which should be borne in mind when reading the extracts from it reproduced here).

[19] Alberti, I.9; ed. Rykwert, p. 13. 'ac veluti in animante membra membris, ita in aedificio partes partibus respondeant condecet.' Ed. Orlandi, vol. I, p. 65.

[20] Ibid; ed. Rykwert, ibid. 'Erit ergo eiusmodi, ut membrorum in ea nihilo plus desideretur, quam quod adsit, et nihil, quod adsit, ulla ex parte improbetur.' Ed. Orlandi, vol. I, p. 67.

[21] Ibid.; ed. Rykwert, p. 14. 'ne in id vitium incidas, ut fecisse monstrum imparibus aut humeris aut lateribus videare.' Ed. Orlandi, vol. I, p. 69.

[22] On the concept of Varietas cf. Martin Gosebruch, '"Varietas" bei Alberti und der wissenschaftliche Renaissancebegriff', Zeitschrift für Kunstgeschichte XX, 1957, pp. 229–38.

[23] Alberti, I.9; ed. Rykwert, p. 13. 'Et cedant ea quidem inter se membra mutuo oportet ad communem totius operis laudem et gratiam...' Ed. Orlandi, vol. I, p. 67. The key sentence for an understanding of Alberti's position here reads in the original: 'Condimentum quidem gratiae est omni in re varietas, si compacta et conformata sit mutua inter se distantium rerum parilitate' (ed. Orlandi, p. 69).

[24] Ibid.; ed. Rykwert, p. 14. 'sed quo inde admoniti novis nos proferendis inventis contendamus parem illis maioremve, si queat, fructum laudis assequi.' Ed. Orlandi, vol. I, p. 69.

[25] Ibid., I.10, ed. Rykwert, p. 15. 'dicendum sit, quando ipsi ordines columnarum haud aliud sunt quam pluribus in locis perfixus adapertusque paries.' Ed. Orlandi, vol. I, p. 70.

[26] Alberti (I.10; ed. Orlandi, p. 73) speaks of 'columnae quadrangulae', i.e. pillars, which proves that a systematic separation of column and pillar is only to a certain extent possible. But in VI.6 Alberti stresses the separateness of column and pillar. Such contradictions may be attributed to the unfinalised state of his text.

[27] Wittkower (ed. 1962), pp. 34ff.

[28] Klotz (1969), pp. 99ff.

[29] Alberti, III. 6 (Orlandi, pp. 194ff.); cf. esp. Feuer-Tóth (1978), p. 148f.

[30] Alberti, VI. 13 (Orlandi, pp. 502f.).

[31] Alberti, IV. 1.

[32] Ibid.; ed. Rykwert, p. 65. 'Sed cum aedificiorum circumspicimus copiam et varietatem, facile intelligimus non tantum hos esse ad usus omnia, neque horum tantum aut illorum gratia comparata, sed pro hominum varietate in primis fieri, ut habeamus opera varia et multiplicia. Quod si aedificiorum genera et generum ipsorum partes satis, uti instituimus, annotasse voluerimus, omnis investigandi ratio nobis hinc captanda sit atque inchoanda, ut homines, quorum causa constent aedificia, et quorum ex usu varientur, accuratius consideremus quid inter se differant, quo inde singula clarius recognita distinctius pertractentur.' Ed. Orlandi, vol. I, p. 265.

[33] Cf. De Zurko's (1957) exaggeratedly functionalist interpretation of Alberti (see n. 18 above).

[34] On Alberti's dependence on Cicero (De officiis) in these concepts, cf. Onians (1971), pp. 101ff.

[35] Alberti, IX. 5; ed. Rykwert, p. 194. 'Nunc, quod dicturos polliciti sumus, ad ea venio, ex quibus universa pulchritudinis ornamentorumque genera existent, vel quae potius expressa ex omni pulchritudinis ratione emanarint. Difficilis nimirum pervestigatio. Nam, quicquid unum illud, quod ex universo partium numero et natura exprimendum seligendumque sit aut singulis impartiundum ratione certa et coaequabili aut ita habendum, ut unam in congeriem et corpus plura iungat contineatque recta et stabili cohesione atque consensu, cui nos hic persimile quippiam quaerimus, profecto ipsum id eorum omnium vim et quasi succum sapiat necesse est, quibus aut coherescat aut immisceatur; alioquin discordia discidiisque pugnarent atque dissiparentur.' Ed. Orlandi, vol. II, p. 811.

[36] Ibid.; ed. Rykwert, p. 195.

[37] Ibid. 'Ut vero de pulchritudine iudices, non opinio, verum animis innata quaedam ratio efficiet.' Ed. Orlandi, vol. II, p. 813.

[38] Ibid.; ed. Rykwert, pp. 195–96. 'Nanque ex numero quidem ipso primum intellexere alium esse parem, alium imparem. Ambobus usi sunt; sed paribus alibi, imparibus item alibi. Ossa enim aedificii, naturam secuti, hoc est columnas et angulos et eiusmodi, numero nusquam posuere impari. Nullum enim dabis animal, quod pedibus aut stet aut moveatur imparibus. Tum et contra nusquam pari apertiones numero posuere; quod ipsum naturam observasse in promptu est, quando animantibus hinc atque hinc aures oculos nares compares quidem, sed

medio loco unum et propatulum apposuit os.' Ed. Orlandi, vol. II, p. 819.

[39] The rôle of number and mathematics in Alberti's thinking shows a kinship with the philosophy of Nicholas of Cusa, with whom he was on terms of friendship, as well as with that of the mathematician Toscanelli. Number is the crucial instrument in Nicholas's theory of knowledge. His use of number is in the tradition of the Early Church Fathers and the Scholastics (sources that he names himself). Such a statement as: 'If number is taken away, then all distinction, order, relationship (*proportio*), harmony, and diversity in existing things ceases' (*De docta ignorantia*, 1440) corresponds with Alberti's point of view. But Alberti makes no reference to Nicholas of Cusa in his treatise. The occurrence of identical series of numbers (e.g. $1 + 2 + 3 + 4 = 10$) in Alberti (IX.5) and Nicholas of Cusa (*De conjecturis*, c. 1441–44; I.5) may be attributable to commonly used sources. In the case of Alberti's architectural treatise the question as to dependence on Nicholas of Cusa may be settled in the negative. On the relationship between the two, cf. Leonardo Olschki, *Geschichte der neusprachlichen wissenschaftlichen Literatur*, vol. I, Leipzig 1919, pp. 79ff.; Ernst Cassirer, *Individuum und Kosmos in der Philosophie der Renaissance*, Leipzig und Berlin 1927, pp. 54ff.; Franco Borsi, *Leon Battista Alberti*, Milan 1975, p. 339; Dorothy Koenigsberger, *Renaissance Man and Creative Thinking*, Hassocks, Sussex 1979, pp. 100ff.

[40] Alberti, IX.5; ed. Rykwert, p. 196. '*Finitio quidem apud nos est correspondentia quaedam linearum inter se, quibus quantitates dimetiantur. Earum una est longitudinis, altera latitudinis, tertia altitudinis.*' Ed. Orlandi, vol. II, p. 821.

[41] Ibid.

[42] After setting out the laws of musical harmony (IX.5), Alberti states: 'It is most fitting that architects use all these numbers.' On the relationship between architectural theory and its foundations in musical theory in Alberti, cf. esp. Paul von Naredi-Rainer, 'Musikalische Proportionen, Zahlenästhetik und Zahlensymbolik im architektonischen Werk L. B. Albertis', *Jahrbuch des kunsthistorischen Institutes der Universität Graz* XII, 1977, pp. 86ff.

[43] Alberti, IX.7; ed. Rykwert, p. 201. '*tam ex natura est, ut dextera sinistris omni parilitate correspondeant.*' Ed. Orlandi, vol. II, p. 839.

[44] Ibid., IX.5; ed. Rykwert, p. 195; ed. Orlandi, vol. II, p. 817. Alberti's definition of beauty (VI.2) as 'the exact and correct agreement of all parts, such that nothing may be added or subtracted or altered without making it less pleasing' would appear to go back to Vitruvius, VI.2, where Vitruvius speaks of subtraction and addition in dimensions in order to make allowances for optical conditions.

[45] Ibid.; ed. Rykwert, ibid. '*Quicquid enim in medium proferat natura, id omne ex concinnitatis lege moderatur.*' Ed. Orlandi, vol. II, p. 815.

[46] On the concept of *concinnitas* which Alberti clearly borrows from Cicero, cf. Luigi Vagnetti, 'Concinnitas: riflessione sul significato di un termine albertiano', in: *Studi e documenti d'architettura*, n. 2, 1973, pp. 139–61. This author's equation of *concinnitas* with the Italian concept of *organicità* (p. 156) seems to me to be unfortunate, overlaid as the latter term has come to be with later functionalist and organic ideas of architecture.

[47] Alberti, IX.5; ed. Rykwert, p. 195. '*spectantesque aedificium ab aedificio, uti superioribus transegimus libris, fine et officio plurimum differre, aeque re haberi varium oportere.*

'*Natura idcirco moniti tris et ipsi adinvenere figuras aedis exornandae, et nomina imposuere ducta ab his, qui alteris aut aliis delectarent, aut forte, uti ferunt, invenerint. Unum fuit eorum plenius ad laboremque perennitatemque aptius: hoc doricum nuncuparunt; alterum gracile lepidissimum: hoc dixere corinthium; medium vero, quod quasi ex utriusque componerent, ionicum appellarunt. Itaque integrum circa corpus talia excogitarunt.*' Ed. Orlandi, II, p. 817.

[48] Alberti, VI.2; ed. Rykwert. '*At pulchritudo etiam ab infestis hostibus impetrabit, ut iras temperent atque inviolatam se esse patiantur; ut hoc audeam dicere: nulla re tutum aeque ab hominum iniuria atque illesum futurum opus, quam formae dignitate ac venustate.*' Orlandi, vol. II, p. 447. The working up of Platonic and Ciceronic ideas in this passage has been analysed by Białostocki (1964), pp. 13ff. Vagnetti (1973,

pp. 156f.) goes so far as to equate Alberti's concepts of beauty and of truth. In the present writer's opinion this step is an anachronistic projection of Enlightenment ideas (Lodoli, etc.) onto Alberti.

[49] Alberti, VII.6; Alberti indeed refers (I.10) to a 'tuscanica partitio', but must here mean his 'Italian', i.e. Composite, order. On Alberti's limited interest in the Orders, cf. Erik Forssman, Dorisch, jonisch, korinthisch. Studien über den Gebrauch der Säulenordnungen in der Architektur des 16.–18. Jahrhunderts, Stockholm 1961, pp. 17f. On Alberti's treatment of the Orders, see esp. Christof Thoenes, 'Gli ordini architettonici – Rinascità o invenzione?', in the proceedings of the symposium Roma & l'antico nell'arte e nella cultura del Cinquecento (Rome 1982), Rome 1985.

[50] Published as the work of Alberti by Hubert Janitschek, Leone Battista Alberti's kleinere kunsttheoretische Schriften, Vienna 1877, pp. 207–25 (Italian text with German trans.). The first doubt was cast on Janitschek's ascription by Paul Hoffmann, Studien zu Leon Battista Albertis zehn Büchern De Re Aedificatoria, diss., Frankenberg i.S. 1883, pp. 51ff. A close analysis of the text with consideration of all the arguments by Franco Borsi, 'I cinque ordini architettonici e L. B. Alberti', in: Studi e documenti di architettura, n. 1, 1972, pp. 57–130 (with the text). Borsi's investigation finally rules out the ascription to Alberti.

[51] Alberti, VI.2; ed. Rykwert, p. 113. 'Id si ita persuadetur, erit quidem ornamentum quasi subsidiaria quaedam lux pulchritudinis atque veluti complementum. Ex his patere arbitror, pulchritudinem quasi suum atque innatum toto esse perfusum corpore, quod pulchrum sit; ornamentum autem affecti et compacti naturam sapere magis quam innati.' Ed. Orlandi, vol. II, p. 449.

[52] A similar assessment of Alberti's concept of ornament in Onians (1971), pp. 103f.

[53] Cf. Lücke, Alberti-Index I, 1975, pp. 319ff. (decor, decus); II, 1976, pp. 944 ff. (ornamentum).

[54] Alberti, IX.1.

[55] Ibid. IX.2; ed. Rykwert, p. 188. 'Inter aedes urbanas et villam, praeter illa quae superioribus libris diximus, hoc interest: quod urbanarum ornamenta prae illis multo sapere gravitatem oportet, villis autem omnes festivitatis amoenitatisque illecebrae concedentur.' Ed. Orlandi, vol. II, p. 789.

[56] This is directed against Vitruvius I.1.

[57] Alberti, IX.9; ed. Rykwert, p. 205. 'Magna est res architectura, neque est omnium tantam rem aggredi. Summo sit ingenio, acerrimo studio, optima doctrina maximoque usu praeditus necesse est, atque in primis gravi sinceroque iudicio et consilio, qui se architectum audeat profiteri. De re aedificatoria laus omnium prima est iudicare bene quid deceat. Nam aedificasse quidem necessitatis est; commode aedificasse, cum a necessitate id quidem, tum et ab utilitate ductum est; verum ita aedificasse, ut lauti approbent, frugi non respuant, nonnisi a peritia docti et bene consulti et valde considerati artificis proficiscetur.' Ed. Orlandi, vol. II, p. 855.

[58] By about 1438 Alberti had already completed a work entitled Villa, which has only recently come to light, in which he offers practical guidance on land purchase and agricultural management but says nothing about the architectural appearance of the villa. Cf. Cecil Grayson, 'Villa: un opuscolo sconosciuto', Rinascimento 4, 1953, pp. 45–83; reprinted in: Leon Battista Alberti, Opere volgari, ed. Cecil Grayson, vol. I, Bari 1960, pp. 357–63.

[59] Wittkower (1949); Joan Gadol (1969) also follows this line.

[60] Lorenz (1971), esp. pp. 199ff.; id., 'Zur Architektur L. B. Albertis: Die Kirchenfassaden', Wiener Jahrbuch für Kunstgeschichte XXIX, 1976, pp. 65–100.

[61] Lorenz (1971), p. 199: 'Therefore, Alberti's treatise must be seen primarily as the work of a Humanist historian seeking to identify the principles of architecture in the course of reflection about history, and not as the self-expression of an artist and his ideas.'

[62] Lorenz (1971), p. 221.

[63] Ibid., p. 220.

[64] v. Naredi-Rainer (1977), esp. pp. 164ff.; cf. also Gerda Soergel, 'Untersuchungen über den theoretischen Architekturentwurf von 1450–1550 in Italien', diss., Cologne 1958, pp. 8ff.

[65] Richard Krautheimer, 'Alberti's Templum Etruscum', Münchner Jahrbuch der bildenden Kunst, 3. F., XII, 1961, pp. 65–72; reprinted in: Krautheimer, Studies in Early Christian, Medieval, and Renaissance Art, New York–London 1969, pp. 333–44.

[66] Cited in Krautheimer (1961), p. 71.

[67] Bartoli's Italian translation of 1550 was the first to be illustrated.

4. Quattrocento theory after Alberti

[1] '*narrare modi e misure dello edificare...*', '*quelli che più periti e più in lettere intendenti sarrano...*'. Antonio Averlino detto il Filarete, *Trattato di architettura*, 2 vols, ed. Anna Maria Finoli and Liliana Grassi, Milan 1972, p. 11.

[2] The most important literature on Filarete: M. Lazzaroni and A. Muñoz, *Filarete, scultore e architetto del secolo XV*, Rome 1908; on his architectural treatise: Howard Saalman, 'Early Renaissance Architectural Theory and Practice in Antonio Filarete's *Trattato di Architettura*', *The Art Bulletin* XLI, 1959, pp. 89–106; Peter Tigler, *Die Architekturtheorie des Filarete*, Berlin 1963; Hermann Bauer, *Kunst und Utopie. Studien über das Kunst- und Staatsdenken in der Renaissance*, Berlin 1965, pp. 70–83; Gerhard Goebel, *Poeta Faber. Erdichtete Architektur in der italienischen, spanischen und französischen Literatur der Renaissance und des Barock*, Heidelberg 1971, pp. 35ff.; John Onians, 'Alberti and Filarete. A Study of their sources', *Journal of the Warburg and Courtauld Institutes* XXXIV, 1971, pp. 96–114; S. Lang, 'Sforzinda, Filarete and Filelfo', ibid. XXXV, 1972, pp. 391–97; papers read at a conference on Filarete that took place in 1972 in: *Arte Lombarda* 18, 1973 (especially important on the treatise: John Onians, 'Filarete and the "qualità": architectural and social', pp. 116–28); Giorgio Muratore, *La città rinascimentale. Tipi e modelli attraverso i trattati*, Milan 1975, pp. 175–94; Alessandro Rovetta, 'Le fonti monumentali milanesi delle chiese a pianta centrale del Trattato d'Architettura del Filarete', *Arte Lombarda* 60, 1981, pp. 24–32; Ralph Quadflieg, *Filaretes Ospedale Maggiore in Mailand. Zur Rezeption islamischen Hospitalwesens in der italienischen Frührenaissance*, Cologne 1981.

[3] Tigler (1963), pp. 7f.

[4] Ibid., pp. 5f. Marcel Restle ('Bauplanung und Baugesinnung unter Mehmet II. Fâtih. Filarete in Konstantinopel', *Pantheon* XXXIX, 1981, pp. 361–67) attempts to show the probability of a visit by Filarete to Constantinople after 1465. The author goes so far as to ascribe the planning of the madrassahs attached to the Fâtih Camii to Filarete, but is unable to prove that Filarete actually did visit Constantinople. However, he shows it to be probable that Italian systems of measurement were used in some buildings. Analogies between Filarete's Ospedale Maggiore in Milan, Villalpando's reconstruction of Solomon's Temple (1604), and the shape of the ground-plan of the Mehmediy Foundation in Constantinople are hypothetical.

[5] Goebel (1971), p. 35.

[6] Tigler (1963), pp. 8ff.

[7] Ibid., pp. 13ff.

[8] On the treatise as a whole, cf. the thoroughgoing analysis by Tigler (1963).

[9] Onians (1971), p. 104ff.

[10] Filelfo was the foremost Greek scholar at the court of Milan. On his work on Plato and his mediating function with Filarete, cf. ibid., pp. 106ff.

[11] Cf. Cod. Magl. II, I, 140 fol. 47r. (the Cathedral of Sforzinda) and fol. 119v. (the Cathedral of Plusiapolis).

[12] Filarete, ed. Finoli-Grassi (1972), p. 12.

[13] Ibid., p. 14.

[14] Filarete, Cod. Magl. II, I, 140 fol. 4v., 5r., 5v. Extraordinarily, Joseph Rykwert (*On Adam's House in Paradise*, New York 1972) does not discuss Filarete's illustrations of the primal hut; he shows only that of Adam seeking shelter (p. 117); on Filarete's conception of the primal hut, cf. also Joachim Gaus, 'Die Urhütte. Über ein Modell in der Baukunst und ein Motiv in der bildenden Kunst', *Wallraf-Richartz-Jahrbuch* XXXIII, 1971, pp. 10ff., 16f.

[15] Filarete (ed. 1972), p. 211.

[16] Filarete, Cod. Magl. II, I, 140 fol. 54v.

[17] '*lo edificio si è dirivato da l'uomo, cioè dalla forma e membri e misura.*' Filarete (ed. 1972), p. 28.

[18] '*le qualità, secondo posso comprendere, delle misure de l'uomo sono cinque.*' Ibid., p. 15.

[19] The identity of *testa* and *capitello* is explicitly stated in Book VIII, ibid., p. 216.

[20] Ibid., p. 17.

[21] Ibid., p. 18.

[22] '*gli altri più infimi sono a utilità e necessità e servitudine del signore.*' Ibid., p. 218. On the *qualità* of the Orders, cf. Onians (1973) pp. 116ff.

[23] Cod. Magl. II, I, 140 fol. 57v.

[24] '*E come loro comunamente le [le chiese] facevano basse, e noi per l'opposito le facciamo alte...*' Filarete (ed. 1972), p. 187.

[25] On Filarete's relationship to Gothic building geometry, cf. Tigler (1963), pp. 58ff.

[26] '... *quello che sia, el circolo, tondo, el quadro e ogni altra misura è dirivata da l'uomo.*' Filarete (ed. 1972), p. 21.

[27] '*Tu non vedesti mai niuno dificio, o vuoi dire casa o abitazione, che totalmente fusse l'una come l'altra, né in similitudine, né in forma, né in bellezza...*' Ibid., p. 26.

[28] '*l'uomo, se volesse, potrebbe fare molte case che si asomigliassero tutte in una forma e in una similitudine, in modo che saria l'una come l'altra.*' Ibid., p. 27.

[29] '*Io ti mostrerrò l'edificio essere proprio uno uomo vivo, e vedrai che così bisogna a lui mangiare per vivere, come fa proprio l'uomo: e così s'amala e muore, e così an(che) nello amalare guarisce molte volte per lo buono medico... Tu potresti dire: lo edificio non si amala e non muore come l'uomo. Io ti dico che così fa proprio l'edificio: lui s'amala quando non mangia, cioè quando non è mantenuto, e viene scadendo a poco a poco, come fa proprio l'uomo quando sta sanza cibo, poi si casca morto. Così fa proprio l'edificio e se ha il medico quando s'amala, cioè il maestro che lo racconcia e guarisca, sta un buon tempo in buono stato...*'. Ibid., p. 29.

[30] '*nove e sette mesi fantasticare e pensare...*' Ibid., p. 40.

[31] Ibid., pp. 51f.

[32] '*perchè non v'entra troppa spesa, neanche magistero.*' Ibid., p. 52; on page 331 Filarete summarises his proposals for a poor man's house in the curt phrase: 'do what you can' ('*fa' come tu puoi*').

[33] Cf. Tigler (1963), p. 115ff. Filarete (ed. 1972, pp. 427ff.) goes back to Vitruvius in his conception of the architect's training.

[34] Filarete (ed. 1972), p. 53.

[35] Cf. Helen Rosenau, *The Ideal City. Its architectural evolution* (1959), London ²1974, p. 51.

[36] Cod. Magl. II, I, 140 fol. 11v., 13v., 43r.

[37] See esp. Filarete (ed. 1972), pp. 63f., 165ff.

[38] Ibid., pp. 147ff.

[39] Ibid., pp. 161f.; Illustration Cod. Magl. II, I, 140 fol. 41v.

[40] Muratore (1975), pp. 175ff.

[41] Filarete (ed. 1972), pp. 632ff.; Cod. Magl. II, I, 140 fol. 172r. On this monument cf. John Spencer, 'Il progetto per il cavallo di bronzo per Francesco Sforza', *Arte Lombarda* 18, 1973, pp. 23–35.

[42] Filarete (ed. 1972), pp. 531ff.; Cod. Magl. II, I, 140 fols. 105ff. Cf. also Bauer (1965), pp. 80f.

[43] Cf. Liliana Grassi (introduction in ed. 1972), p. LXVI.

[44] On his medieval sources, see esp. S. Lang (1972), pp. 391ff.

[45] On the division of labour, cf. Filarete (ed. 1972), pp. 94ff.

[46] Thus Onians (1971), pp. 111ff., projecting the Greek versus Roman argument back into the Early Renaissance.

[47] See esp. Allen S. Weller, *Francesco di Giorgio 1439–1501*, Chicago 1943; Roberto Papini, *Francesco di Giorgio Architetto*, 3 vols, Florence 1946; Günter P. Fehring, *Studien über die Kirchenbauten des Francesco di Giorgio*, diss. ms, Würzburg 1956; Carlo Del Bravo, *Scultura senese del Quattrocento*, Florence 1977, pp. 100ff.; Max Seidel, 'Die Fresken des Francesco di Giorgio in S. Agostino in Sienna', *Mitteilungen des Kunsthistorischen Institutes in Florenz* XXIII, 1970, pp. 1–108.

[48] See besides the edition by Corrado Maltese (1967), esp. Alessandro Parronchi, 'Di un manoscritto attribuito a Francesco di Giorgio Martini', *Atti e memorie dell'Accademia Toscana di Scienze, Lettere ed Arti 'La Columbaria'* XXXI, 1966, pp. 164–213; id., 'Sulla composizione dei Trattati attribuiti a Francesco di Giorgio Martini', ibid., XXXVI, 1971, pp. 165–230; J. Eisler, 'Remarks on Some Aspects of Francesco di Giorgio's Trattato', *Acta Historiae Artium* XVIII, 1972, pp. 193–231; Richard Johnson Betts, 'The Architectural Theories of Francesco di Giorgio', PhD. diss., Princeton University, ms 1971; id., 'On the Chronology of Francesco di Giorgio's Treatises: New Evidence from an Unpublished Manuscript', *Journal of the Society of Architectural Historians* XXXVI, 1977, pp. 3–14; Gustina Scaglia, 'The *Opera de Architectura* of Francesco di Giorgio Martini for Alfonso Duke of Calabria', *Napoli Nobilissima* 15, 1976, pp. 133–61 (with transcription of the treatise *Opera de architectura* in the Spencer Collection, New York Public Library). And finally, on the question of the manuscripts of the Council of Europe exhibition, cf. 'Firenze e la Toscana dei Medici nell'Europa del Cinquecento' in the part-volume *La rinascita della Scienza*, Florence 1980, pp. 154ff.; Alessandro Parronchi (ed.), [Baldassarre Peruzzi] *Trattato di architettura militare*, Florence 1982, introduction; Lawrence Lowic, 'Francesco di Giorgio on the Design of Churches: The Use and Significance of

Mathematics in the Trattato', *Architectura*
12, 1982, pp. 151–63; id., 'The Meaning and
Significance of the Human Analogy in
Francesco di Giorgio's Trattato', *Journal of
the Society of Architectural Historians* XLII,
1983, pp. 360–70.
49 Carlo Promis und Cesare Saluzzo (eds),
*Trattato di Architettura civile e militare di
Francesco di Giorgio Martini*, 2 vols, Turin
1841.
50 Gustina Scaglia (ed.), *Il 'Vitruvio Magliabechiano' di Francesco di Giorgio Martini*
(*Documenti inediti di cultura toscana*, VI),
Florence 1985.
51 Ed. Maltese (1967), vol. I. A variant of this
manuscript is the Codex Ashburnham 361
in the Biblioteca Laurenziana, Florence,
which has marginalia by Leonardo da Vinci.
The variants in this text are discussed in
Maltese's edition. See also the partial edition
by Gino Arrighi, *Francesco di Giorgio Martini. La praticha di geometria dal Codice
Ashburnham 361 della Biblioteca Medicea
Laurenziana di Firenze*, Florence 1970.
52 Ed. Maltese (1967), vol. I, p. 3, pl. 1.
53 Ibid., pl. 8; on proportional figures of the
Quattrocento, cf. Bernhard Degenhart and
Annegrit Schmitt, *Corpus der italienischen
Zeichnungen 1300–1450*, Part II, vol. 4:
Mariano Taccola, Berlin 1982, pp. 121ff.
54 Ed. Maltese (1967), vol. I, pp. 36f.
55 Ibid., p. 39.
56 *Ed avendo le basiliche misura e forma del
corpo umano, siccome el capo dell'omo è
principal membro d'esso, così la maggiore
cappella formar si debba come principale
membro e capo del tempio*56.' Ibid., p. 45.
57 Ibid., pls 18, 19.
58 Ibid., p. 62.
59 '*aceso desiderio di volere quelle innovare…*
' Ibid., p. 275, pl. 129.
60 Ibid., pls 151, 152.
61 Ibid., pl. 155.
62 Cf. Earl Rosenthal, 'The Antecedents of
Bramante's Tempietto', *Journal of the Society of Architectural Historians* XXIII, 1964,
pp. 55–79.
63 Cod. Magl. II.I.141. Ed. Maltese (1967),
vol. II. Betts (1971, pp. 254ff.) sees the
manuscript S.IV.4 in the Biblioteca Com-
munale, Siena as an intermediary stage and
dates it to the 1480s. Parronchi (1966, 1982)
does not consider it to be Francesco di
Giorgio's work at all, dating it to the 1530s.
64 Ed. Maltese (1967), vol. II, p. 296.
65 Ibid., p. 295.

66 Ibid., p. 297.
67 Ibid., p. 299. On Francesco di Giorgio's
sources, cf. Betts (1971), pp. 238ff.
68 Ed. Maltese (1967), vol. II, pp. 342ff.
69 Ibid., p. 343.
70 Cf. ibid., vol. I, introduction, p. xxi.
71 '*l'uomo, chiamato piccolo mondo, in se tutte
le generale perfezioni del mondo totale
contiene.*' Ibid., vol. II, p. 361. In the
foreword to Book V (p. 414) man is
described as the image of God. In his
treatment of proportion Francesco also
uses medieval building methods such as
quadrature, as has been proved by Günter
Hellmann ('Proportionsverfahren des Francesco di Giorgio Martini', *Miscellanea Bibliothecae Hertzianae*, Munich 1961), pp.
157–66.
72 '*le colonne espressamente quasi tutte le proporzioni hanno dell'uomo.*' Ed. Maltese
(1967), vol. II, p. 361.
73 Ibid., p. 372.
74 Ibid., pp. 373ff.
75 Ibid., pp. 376ff.
76 Ibid., p. 390, pl. 227.
77 On the building of this church and on its
proportions, cf. esp. Fehring (1956), pp.
109ff.
78 Henry Millon, 'The Architectural Theory
of Francesco di Giorgio', *The Art Bulletin*
40, 1958, pp. 257–61; repr. in: Creighton
Gilbert (ed.), *Renaissance Art*, New York
1973, pp. 133–47.
79 Millon (1958), p. 258; Hellmann (1961), p.
162.
80 Ed. Maltese (1967), vol. II, p. 425. Here
mention should also be made of the considerable number of drawings of artillery
and fortifications to which no text refers
(included in Cod. Magl. II, 1, 141); cf. F.
Paolo Fiore, *Città e macchine del '400 nei
disegni di Francesco di Giorgio Martini*,
Florence 1978.
81 Ed. Maltese (1967), vol. II, p. 483f.
82 Ibid., p. 489.
83 '*non puo senza il disegno esprimere e dichia-
rare el concetto suo.*' Ibid., p. 506.
84 Cf. also Gerda Soergel, *Untersuchungen
über den theoretischen Architekturentwurf
von 1450–1550 in Italien*, diss., Cologne
1958, pp. 32ff., 65ff.; Paul von Naredi-
Rainer, 'Raster und Modul in der Architektur der italienischen Renaissance', *Jahrbuch
für Ästhetik und allgemeine Kunstwissenschaft* XXIII/2, 1978, pp. 147f.
85 Accademia di Belle Arti, Florence, ms.

E.2.1.28. Alessandro Parronchi (ed.) [Baldassare Peruzzi] *Trattato di architettura militare* (*Documenti inediti di cultura toscana*, V), Florence 1982. Parronchi makes it credible (pp. 23ff.) that this manuscript is in the hand of Lorenzo di Girolamo Donati. Whether or not it is a copy of a lost treatise by Peruzzi, as Parronchi supposes, and if so, whether this treatise is itself the basis of the treatise Magl. II.I.141 hitherto ascribed to Francesco di Giorgio, which he considers to be a later compilation, remains unproven. That Peruzzi possessed drawings by Francesco and in certain cases reworked them himself has been demonstrated by Pietro C. Marani ('A Reworking by Baldassare Peruzzi of Francesco di Giorgio's Plan of a Villa', *Journal of the Society of Architectural Historians* XLI, 1982, pp. 181–88).

[86] From the extensive literature cf. esp. Jean Paul Richter (ed.), *The Notebooks of Leonardo da Vinci* (1883), vol. II (fac. repr. New York 1970; and cf. note 93 below for source of text cited in the present volume), pp. 25ff.; Ludwig H. Heydenreich, *Die Sakralbau-Studien Leonardo da Vinci's* (1929), Munich 1971; Luigi Firpo (ed.), *Leonardo architetto e urbanista*, Turin 1971; Arnaldo Bruschi et al., *Scritti rinascimentali di architettura*, Milan, 1978, pp. 277ff.; Carlo Pedretti, *Leonardo architetto*, Milan 1978.

[87] This is evident from the list of books in the Madrid Codices of Leonardo. Cf. Leonardo da Vinci, *Codices Madrid*, vol. III: Commentary by Ladislao Reti, Frankfurt 1974, p. 101 no. 19.

[88] The marginalia in the Cod. Ashb. 361 of the Bibl. Laurenziana in Florence are collected in Pedretti (1978), p. 196ff.; cf. further the excerpts from Francesco di Giorgio in the second Madrid Codex, fol. 86–98 (ed. Reti, 1974), which were made in 1504.

[89] Cf. p. 66 of the present volume.

[90] Heydenreich (1929, 1971), pp. 77–84.

[91] Cf. esp. Pedretti (1978), p. 196.

[92] Cf. Firpo (1971), pp. 63ff.; Pedretti (1978), pp. 55f.

[93] '—Le strade · m · sono · piv · alte · che le strade · p · s · braccia 6 ·, e ciascuna strada . de' essere larga braccia 20, e avere ½ braccio di calo dalle stremità al mezzo, e in esso mezzo sia a ogni braccio uno braccio di fessura, largo uno dito, dove l'acqua che pioue debba scolare nelle cave fatte al medesimo piano di p · s ·, e da ogni stremità della larghezza di detta strada · sia . uno · portico di larghezza di braccia 6 ĩ sulle colonne, e sappi che, chi volesse andare per tutta la terra per le strade alte, potrà a suo acconcio usarle, e chi volesse andare per le basse, ancora il simile; per le strade alte non devono andare carri, nè altre simili cose, anzi siano solamēte per li gièteli omini; per le basse deono andare i carri e altre some al uso e commodità del popolo ·; l'una casa de' volgiere le schiene all' altra ·, lasciādo la strada bassa in mezzo, ed agli usci · n si mettano le vettovaglie, come legnie, vino e simili cose; per le vie sotterrane si de' votare destri, stalle e simili cose fetide dall' uno arco all' altro de' essere braccia 300, cioè ciascuna via che ricieve il lume dalle fessure delle strade di sopra, e a ogni arco de' essere una scala a lumaca tōda, perchè ne' cātoni delle quadre si piscia, e larga, e nella prima uolta sia vn uscio ch'entri ĩ destri e pisciatoi comuni, e per detta scala si disciēda dalla · strada alta · alla bassa, e le strade alte si comūcino fori delle porte, e givnte a esse porte abbia no conposto l'altezza di braccia 6; Fia fatta detta terra o presso a mare o altro fiume grosso, acciocchè le brutture della città, menate dall' acqua, sieno portate · via.' Paris, Institut de France, Leonardo, Ms B, fol. 16. Citation from *The Literary Works of Leonardo da Vinci*, ed. J. P. Richter, London 1970, vol. II, pp. 27f.

[94] Cf. e.g. Eugenio Garin, *Scienza e vita civile nel Rinascimento italiano*, Bari 1965, pp. 33ff.; Corrado Maltese (in Bruschi et al., 1978, p. 283) speaks precisely of the '*città come espressione di uno Stato oligarchico*'. Firpo (1971, pp. 78ff) takes the contrary view that Leonardo is distinguishing merely functional, not social, relationships.

[95] Cod. Atlant., fol. 175 v. (1494); cited in Firpo (1961), p. 65.

[96] Paris, Bibl. Nat., Cod. Ashb. 2037 (completion of Cod. B), fol. 5; illus. in: Firpo (1971), p. 60; Bruschi (1978), pl. XLIV.

[97] Cod. B, fol. 36r. Cited in Bruschi (1978), p. 311.

[98] Cod. B., fol. 39v. Cited in Bruschi (1978), p. 311.

[99] Francesco Colonna, *Hypnerotomachia Poliphili, ubi humana omnia non nisi somnium*

esse docet, Venice 1499 (numerous modern reprints).

[100] The major monograph is M. T. Casella and G. Pozzi, *Francesco Colonna. Biografia e opere*, 2 vols, Padua 1959; the arguments in favour of Francesco Colonna as author of the *Hypnerotomachia* are brought together in Pozzi–Ciapponi, vol. II (1964), pp. 3f.; Maurizio Calvesi ('Identificato l'autore del "Polifilo",' *L'Europa letteraria* 6, 1965, No. 35, pp. 9–20) seeks to identify the author with a member of the Colonna family of Palestrina; Emanuela Kretzlesco Quaranta has suggested in succession the Humanist Pico della Mirandola as author, Lorenzo de' Medici (il Magnifico) as protagonist, and even Alberti as part-author ('L'itinerario spirituale di 'Polifilo'. Uno studio necessario per determinare la paternità dell'opera', *Atti della Acc. Naz. dei Lincei, ser. 8. Rendiconti, cl. di scienze mor., stor. e filol.* 22, 1967, pp. 269–83; 'L'itinerario archaeologico di Polifilo. Leon Battista Alberti come teorico della Magna Porta', *ibid.*, 25, 1970, pp. 175–201; *Les jardins du songe. Poliphile et la mystique de la Renaissance*, Rome–Paris 1976). None of these suggestions is conclusive; they all assume a close knowledge of Rome and Palestrina on the part of the author of the *Hypnerotomachia*, which in no way emerges from the text, and take the date of 1467 given at the end of the work literally, whereas it is surely fictional. Maurizio Calvesi has argued in an extensive study (*Il sogno di Polifilo prenestino*, Rome 1980) that topographical references in the novel fit Palestrina, but falls entirely short of conclusive proof.

[101] On his chronology cf. esp. Casella-Pozzi (1959), vol. I, pp. 103ff.

[102] See esp. the literary analysis by Goebel (1971), pp. 38–68. A second dream narrative, the *Delphili somnium*, has been published in recent times (in: Casella-Pozzi (ed.), 1959, vol. II, pp. 159ff.).

[103] Julius Schlosser *Magnino, La letteratura artistica*, Florence–Vienna ³1964, p. 135.

[104] Detailed summary in Goebel (1971), p. 41f.

[105] Hermann Bauer, *Kunst und Utopie*, Berlin 1965, p. 88ff.

[106] Goebel (1971), p. 39.

[107] Abridged translation prepared by Antonio Bonfini for Matthias Corvinius, acquired by the friary of SS. Giovanni e Paolo in 1492; now in the Bibl. Naz. di San Marco, Venice,

Ms 2796. Cf. Csaba Csapodi and Klára Csapodi-Cárdonyi, *Bibliotheca Corviniana. Die Bibliothek des Königs Matthias Corvinus von Ungarn*, Munich–Berlin 1969, pp. 63, 262ff.

[108] Cf. Pozzi-Ciapponi (1964), vol. II, pp. 5ff., 15f.

[109] Cf. ibid., p. 40. The question of who executed the woodcuts need not be discussed here. Cf. also Alessandro Parronchi, 'Lo xilografo della Hypnerotomachia Poliphili: Pietro Paolo Agabiti ?', *Prospettiva* 33–36, 1983–84, pp. 101–11.

[110] Copy in the Bayerische Staatsbibliothek, Munich; cf. G. Leidinger in: *Sitzungsberichte der Bayerischen Akademie der Wissenschaften*, 1929, fasc. 3.

[111] French translations appeared in 1546 and 1554; cf. a survey of editions of the *Hypnerotomachia* in: Casella-Pozzi (1959), vol. I, pp. XVIIf. On the tradition in France, cf. esp. Anthony Blunt, 'The Hypnerotomachia Poliphili in 17th Century France', *Journal of the Warburg and Courtauld Institutes* I, 1937/38, pp. 117–37.

[112] Cf. esp. the systematic analysis by Dorothea Schmidt, *Untersuchungen zu den Architekturekphrasen in der Hypnerotomachia Poliphili. Die Beschreibung des Venus-Tempels*, Frankfurt 1978.

[113] *Colonna*, ed. Pozzi-Ciapponi (1964), vol. I, pp. 14ff.

[114] Cf. ibid., vol. II, p. 58.

[115] Ibid., vol. I, pp. 27ff.

[116] William S. Heckscher, 'Bernini's Elephant and Obelisk', *The Art Bulletin* 29, 1947, pp. 155–82. Eugenio Battista (*L'antirinascimento*, Milan 1962, pp. 123ff.) links the *Hypnorotomachia* with the park at Bomarzo (c. 1552). The large elephant and castle at Bomarzo is a possible link between the woodcut in the *Hypnerotomachia* and the Bernini monument.

[117] Colonna, ed. Pozzi-Ciapponi (1964), vol. I, pp. 34ff.

[118] Cf. ibid., vol. II, p. 69ff. with a reconstruction of the portal.

[119] '*La principale regula peculiare al'architecto è quadratura... la sua admiranda compositione...*' Ibid., vol. I, p. 39.

[120] Ibid., vol. I, pp. 191ff.

[121] Ibid., vol. II, pp. 156ff.

[122] On the historical derivations and matters of detail regarding this description, cf. Dorothea Schmidt (1978).

[123] 'digno monumento delle cose magne alla posteritate.' Colonna, ed. Pozzi-Ciapponi (1964), vol. I, pp. 229f.

[124] Cf. Bauer (1965), pp. 92f.

[125] Colonna, ed. Pozzi-Ciapponi (1964), vol. I, pp. 286f.

[126] Plato, Kritias 113d.

[127] Cf. esp. Ernst Robert Curtius, *Europäische Literatur und lateinisches Mittelalter* (1948), Bern–Munich 1965, p. 204.

[128] Colonna, ed. Pozzi-Ciapponi (1964), vol. I, pp. 233f.

[129] The chief source (A. F. Doni, *Libraria seconda*, Venice 1544, p. 44) is the authority for supposing the existence of three treatises by Bramante, *Pratica, Architettura* (on the Orders), and *Modo di fortificare*. Schlosser (1964) points to the unreliability of Doni, a known literary forger. Gian Paolo Lomazzo, in his *Idea del Tempio della pittura* (1590), refers to a work by Bramante on the '*ordini e le misure delle antichità di Roma*', but may here be dependent on Doni; see the edition: Gian Paolo Lomazzo, *Scritti sulle arti*, ed. Roberto Paolo Ciardi, vol. I, Florence 1973, pp. xxvii, 257f.; cf. esp. Pedretti, *Leonardo architetto*, Milan 1978, pp. 120f.

[130] Cf. esp. Franz Graf Wolff Metternich, 'Der Kupferstich Bernardos de Prevedari aus Mailand von 1481. Gedanken zu den Anfängen der Kunst Bramantes', *Römisches Jahrbuch für Kunstgeschichte* 11, 1967/68, pp. 7–108; Otto H. Förster, *Bramante*, Vienna–Munich 1956, pp. 86ff.; Arnaldo Bruschi, *Bramante architetto*, Bari 1969, pp. 150ff.

[131] Cf. the reconstruction in: Bruschi (1969), figs 94, 95.

[132] Guglielmo De Angelis D'Ossat, 'Preludio romano del Bramante', *Palladio*, n.s., XVI, 1966, pp. 92–94; Doris D. Fienga, 'Bramante autore delle "Antiquarie prospettiche Romane", poemetto dedicato a Leonardo da Vinci', in: *Studi Bramanteschi*, Rome 1974, pp. 417–26; Carlo Pedretti, 'Newly Discovered Evidence of Leonardo's Association with Bramante', *Journal of the Society of Architectural Historians* XXVII, 1973, pp. 223–27; id., *Leonardo architetto* (1978), pp. 116–20.

[133] Pedretti (1973), p. 225; (1978), p. 116. Cf. Werner Gramberg, *Die Düsseldorfer Skizzenbücher des Guglielmo della Porta*, Berlin 1964, text volume, p. 123: '*Bramante*

Architetto affermava ch'a tutti coloro che vengono mastri a Roma in questa professione, era necessario spogliarsi à guisa de i serpi di tutto ciò c'havevano altrove imparato…'

[134] '*ch'ei suscitasse la buona Architettura, che da gli antichi sino a quel tempo era stata sepolta.*' Sebastiano Serlio, *Tutte l'opere d'architettura*, Book III, ed. Venice 1619, fol. 64v.

[135] Ed. of all reports, with commentary, Bruschi et al., *Scrittori rinascimentali di architettura* (1978), pp. 321ff.

[136] Ibid., p. 367.

[137] On Pacioli cf. Schlosser (1964), pp. 141ff.; Eugenio Battisti, 'Bramante, Piero e Pacioli ad Urbino', in: *Studi Bramanteschi*, Rome 1974, pp. 267–82; Byrna Rackusin, 'The Architectural Theory of Luca Pacioli: De Divina Proportione', ch. 54 in: *Bibliothèque d'Humanisme et Renaissance* XXXIX, 1977, pp. 479–502; Arnaldo Bruschi et al., *Scritti rinascimentali di architettura*, Milan 1978, pp. 23ff. (bibl. p. 51).

[138] Luca Pacioli, *Divina Proportione, opera a tutti glingegni perspicaci e curiosi necessaria que ciascun studioso di Philosophia, Prospectiva, Pictura, Sculptura, Architectura, Muscia e altre Mathematice suavissima, sottile e admirabile doctrina conseguirà… de secretissima scientia*, Venice 1509; facs. ed. Urbino 1969.

[139] On the relationship between Pacioli and Piero della Francesca, see esp. Margaret Daly Davis, *Piero della Francesca's Mathematical Treatises*, Ravenna 1977, pp. 98ff.

[140] For qualifications to this, cf. Winterberg (1889), p. 4.

[141] Pacioli, Part II, introduction, ed. Bruschi (1978), pp. 93f.

[142] Ibid., ch. 1, p. 97.

[143] Ibid., pp. 98f.; cf. Villard de Honnecourt, pl. XXXVI.

[144] Ibid., p. 100.

[145] Ibid., ch. 7, p. 118.

[146] Ibid., preface, p. 85.

[147] Francesco Mario Grapaldi, *De partibus aedium. Addita modo verborum explicatione*, Parma 1494 (numerous editions up to: Dordrecht 1618); cf. Angelo Comolli, *Bibliografia storico-critica dell'Architettura civile*, vol. I, Rome 1788, pp. 81ff.

[148] Paolo Cortesi, *De Cardinalatu*, Città Cortesiana 1510; cf. Kathleen Weil-Garris and John D'Amico, 'The Renaissance Cardinal's

Ideal Palace: A Chapter from Cortesi's *De Cardinalatu*', *Memoirs of the American Academy in Rome* XXXV, 1980 (= *Studies in Italian Art and Architecture 15th through 18th Centuries*, ed. A. Millon), pp. 45–123 (pp. 69ff. Latin–English ed. of Book II, ch. 2).

[149] Cortesi (1510); Weil-Garris and D'Amico (1980), pp. 86f.

[150] Christoph Luitpold Frommel, *Der römische Palastbau der Hochrenaissance*, vol. I, Tübingen 1973, pp. 53ff.

[151] Ms ital. fol. 473. Vladimir Juřen, 'Un traité inédit sur les ordres d'architecture et le problème des sources du Libro IV de Serlio', *Monuments et Mémoires publiés par L'Académie des Inscriptions et Belles-Lettres*, 64, 1981, pp. 195–239.

[152] 'Nota che puoi pigliare secondo il tuo comodo la grosezza della colonna, e quella partirai in 6 parte che così è la sua misura.' Juřen (1981), p. 205.

[153] On the Renaissance rules for the Orders, cf. Christof Thoenes and Hubertus Günther, 'Gli ordini architettonici: rinascita o invenzione?', in: *Roma e l'antico nell' arte e nella cultura del Cinquecento*, ed. Marcello Fagiolo, Rome 1985, pp. 261–310.

5. Vitruvian tradition in the Renaissance

[1] See p. 39 of the present volume.

[2] Manuscripts in the Biblioteca Nazionale, Florence, Cod. Magliabechiano II.I.141 and Biblioteca Comunale, Siena, ms. S.IV. 4; cf. Corrado Maltese (ed.), *Francesco di Giorgio Martini, Trattati*, Milan 1967, pp. XXVIIIf. The manuscript in Florence published: Gustina Scaglia (ed.), *Il 'Vitruvio magliabechiano' di Francesco di Giorgio Martini*, Florence 1985.

[3] E.g. by Silvano Morosini, Battista da Sangallo, Francesco Alighieri, Bernardino Donati; cf. Luigi Vagnetti and Laura Marcucci, 'Per una coscienza Vitruviana. Regesto cronologico e critico', *Studi e documenti di architettura*, n. 8, 1978, p. 28 n. 35.

[4] Corrado Maltese (ed.), *Francesco di Giorgio* (1967), p. 20. Vitruvian man, pl. 8.

[5] Cf. ibid., p. XXXVII.

[6] Transcription of the text with English trans. in: Jean Paul Richter (ed.), *The Notebooks of Leonardo da Vinci*, I, London 1883 (facs. repr. New York 1970), p. 182; on this drawing cf. Günter Hellmann, 'Die Zeichnung Leonardos zu Vitruv', *Mouseion. Studien zur Kunst und Geschichte für Otto H. Förster*, Cologne 1960, pp. 96–98; Carlo Pedretti, *Leonardo architetto*, Milan 1978, pp. 149f. (the drawing is here dated to 1490). See the related drawing in Codex Huygens, fol. 7; Erwin Panofsky, *The Codex Huygens and Leonardo da Vinci's Art Theory*, London 1940, pl. 5.

[7] Cf. esp. the two surveys of editions of Vitruvius: Bodo Ebhardt, *Vitruvius. Die Zehn Bücher der Architektur des Vitruv und ihre Herausgeber*, Berlin 1918 (facs. repr. New York 1962), pp. 67ff.; Vagnetti and Marcucci (1978), pp. 29ff. Ebhardt's survey appears to have been unknown to these authors. On Renaissance attitudes to Vitruvius, cf. Fritz Burger, 'Vitruv und die Renaissance', *Repertorium für Kunstwissenschaft* XXXII, 1909, pp. 199–218; Francesco Pellati, 'Vitruvio nel Medio Evo e nel Rinascimento', *Bollettino del Reale Istituto di Archeologia e Storia dell'Arte* V, 1932, pp. 15–36; Paolo Fontana, 'Osservazioni intorno ai rapporti di Vitruvio colla teoria dell'Architettura del Rinascimento', *Miscellanea di Storia dell'Arte in onore di Igino Benvenuto Supino*, Florence 1933, pp. 305–22; Erik Forssman, *Säule und Ornament*, Stockholm 1956; Vassili Pavlovitch Zoubov, *Vitruve et ses commentateurs du XVIᵉ siècle*, Colloque international de Royaumont (1957), Paris 1960, pp. 67–90; Erik Forssman, *Dorisch, Jonisch, Korinthisch*, Stockholm 1961; Sabine Weyrauch, *Die Basilika des Vitruv. Studien zu illustrierten Vitruvausgaben seit der Renaissance mit besonderer Berücksichtigung der Rekonstruktion der Basilika von Fano*, diss., Tübingen 1976; Manfredo Tafuri, 'Cesare Cesariano e gli studi vitruviani nel Quattrocento', in: Franco Borsi (ed.), *Scritti rinascimentali di architettura*, Milan 1978, pp. 387ff.; Pamela Olivia Long, 'The Vitruvian Commentary Tradition and Rational Architecture in the Sixteenth Century: A Study in the History of Ideas', PhD thesis, University of Maryland, 1979; Alessandro Rovetta, 'Cultura e codici vitruviani nel primo umanesimo milanese', *Arte lombarda* 60, 1981, pp. 9–14.

[8] This edition is without a title-page. On

Giovanni Sulpicio's edition, cf. Laura Marcucci, 'Giovanni Sulpicio e la prima edizione
del De Architecture di Vitruvio', *Studi e
documenti di architettura*, n. 8. 1978, pp.
185–95.

⁹ Vagnetti und Marcucci (1978), p. 31. Battista
da Sangallo (1496–1552) still used Sulpico's
text for his illustrations in the Bibl. Corsiana
(2093. 43. G. 8); cf. Marcucci (1978), pp.
193f.

¹⁰ Vagnetti and Marcucci (1978), pp. 31f.

¹¹ *M. Vitruvius per Iocundum solito castigatur
factus cum Figuris et tabula ut iam legi et
intellegi possit*, Venice 1511. Cf. Lucia A.
Ciapponi, 'Fra Giocondo da Verona and
his Edition of Vitruvius', *Journal of the
Warburg and Courtauld Institutes* XLVI,
1983, pp. 72–90.

¹² *'non modo nostri aevi principes, sed et
superioris quoque et numero et magnificentia
superasti'*. Giocondo, 1511, dedication.

¹³ In the case of two illustrations of siege
machines in Book X, the use of models
from Byzantine manuscripts has recently
been proved (cf. Giocondo, 1511, fol. 106v
with Cod. Parisinus gr. 2442, fol. 63;
Giocondo, 1511, fol. 105v with Cod.
Vaticanus gr. 1164, fol. 114v); Pier Nicola
Pagliara, 'Una fonte di illustrazioni del
Vitruvio di Fra Giocondo', in: *Ricerche di
Storia dell'Arte* 6, 1977, pp. 113–20.

¹⁴ Giocondo, 1511, fol. 2r and 2v.

¹⁵ Ibid., fols 4r and 4v.

¹⁶ Ibid., fols 22r and 22v. Hellmann (1960), p.
97 assumes that Fra Giocondo could have
used the Leonardo drawing in Venice. But
if that were to have been the case, Giocondo
would scarcely have omitted the brilliant
superimposition of the two diagrams. Furthermore, Leonardo states that the triangle
formed by the legs in the *homo ad quadratum* should be equilateral. These specifications in Leonardo's drawings, which are
not from Vitruvius, are not followed by
Giocondo.

¹⁷ Giocondo, 1511, fol. 46v.

¹⁸ Cf. Sabine Weyrauch (1976).

¹⁹ *Vitruvius iterum et Frontinus a Iocundo
revisi repurgatique quantum ex collatione
licuit*, Florence 1513.

²⁰ Giocondo, 1513, fol. 34.

²¹ Cf. Raphael's letter of 15 August 1514 to
Fabio Calvo, acknowledging receipt of a
copy of '*Vetruvio vulgare per parte vostra*',
and promising: '*quando arò tempo (e per le

molte mia occupazioni tempo non serà cosi
tosto come ho desidero) ve designerò ne'bianchi le figure che v'hanno a essere e ve farò
el fróntespizio de ordine dorico con un arco
e le figure drento de la virtù con varie altre
invenzioni che me nascono per la fantasia,
che forsi ve piaceranno.*' Cited from Paola
Barocchi (ed.), *Scritti d'arte del Cinquecento*,
III, Milan–Naples 1977, p. 2969.

²² The translation of Vitruvius prepared by
Fabio Calvo '*in Roma in casa di Raphael-
lo...et a sua instantia*' is now available in
a critical edition: Vincenzo Fontana and
Paolo Morachiello, *Vitruvio e Raffaello. Il
'De Architectura' di Vitruvio nella tradu-
zione inedita di Fabio Calvo ravennate*,
Rome 1975.

²³ Cf. Fontana-Morachiello (1975), pp. 32f.

²⁴ Probably written in 1519. Cf. two recent
editions of this letter in: Paola Barocchi
(ed.), *Scritti d'arte del Cinquecento*, III, 1977,
pp. 2971ff. and by Renato Bonelli in:
Arnaldo Bruschi (ed.), *Scritti rinascimentali
di architettura*, Milan 1978, pp. 469ff.

²⁵ *Di Lucio Vitruvio Pollione de Architectura
libri decem traducti de Latino in Vulgare
affigurati, commentati* etc., Como 1521; a
facs. repr. with an introduction by Carol
Herselle Krinsky, Munich 1969; another
facs. repr., Milan 1981. On Cesariano cf.
esp. Carol Herselle Krinsky, 'Cesare Cesariano and the Como Vitruvius Edition of
1521', PhD thesis ms, New York 1965; ead.,
'Cesariano and the Renaissance without
Rome', *Arte Lombarda* XVI, 1971, pp.
211–18; Francesco Paolo Fiore, 'Cultura
settentrionale e influssi albertiani nelle architetture vitruviane di Cesare Cesariano',
Arte Lombarda 64, 1983, I, pp. 43–52.
Extracts from Cesariano with commentary in: Paola Barocchi, *Scritti d'arte del
Cinquecento*, III, 1977, pp. 2986ff.; Manfredo Tafuri in: Arnaldo Bruschi (ed.),
Scritti rinascimentali di architettura, 1978,
pp. 439ff.

²⁶ Carol Herselle Krinsky (1971), p. 214.

²⁷ Cesariano, 1521, fols VI, VII.

²⁸ Ibid., fols XIII, XV, XVI.

²⁹ *'Et questa e quasi como la regula che usato
hano li Germanici Architecti in la Sacra
Aede Baricephala de Milano.*' Ibid., fol.
XIIIv.

³⁰ Ibid., fol. XLIv.

³¹ Ibid., fol. XLVIIIff.

³² In the present writer's opinion, the possi-

bility is too strongly stated by Rudolf Wittkower, *Architectural Principles in the Age of Humanism* (1949), ed. London 1962, p. 15 and by Hellmann (1960), pp. 96ff. Cesariano, in his commentary on Vitruvius, III.i (fol. XLVIIIv), mentions many contemporary artists who observed Vitruvian rules of proportion, but Leonardo is not amongst them.

[33] Cf. p. 35 of the present volume.

[34] *'Et in la supra data figura del corpo humano: per li quali symmetriati membri si po ut diximus sapere commensurare tute le cose che sono nel mundo.'* Ibid., vol. Lv.

[35] Ibid., fol. LXIII.

[36] Ibid., fol. LXXIIII.

[37] Cf. Wittkower (1962), p. 92, figs 32a, 32c; the designs for S. Celso attributed to Cesariano are reproduced in: Borsi (1978), pls LXX, LXXI.

[38] *'In questa lectione Vitruvio dopoi ne ha dato il modo di sapere construre tuti li supra dicti aedificii* [i.e. basilicas].' Cesariano, 1521, fol. LXXIIIIv.

[39] M. Vitruvio, *De Architectura libri decem, summa diligentia recogniti, atque excusi. Cum nonnullis figuris sub hoc signo* positis nunquam antea impressis...*, (Lyons) 1523.

[40] Giocondo, 1523, fols 12ff.

[41] Ibid., fols 39v, 46, 46v, 98.

[42] Ibid., fol. 60.

[43] *M. L. Vitruvio Pollione de Architectura traducto di Latino in Vulgare... da niuno altro fin al presente facto ad immensa utilitate di ciascuno studioso*, Venice 1524.

[44] Diego de Sagredo, *Medidas del Romano: necessarias a los officiales que quieren seguir las formaciones de las basas coluñas capiteles y otras pieças de los edificios antiguos*, Toledo 1526; Nigel Llewellyn, 'Two notes on Diego da Sagredo', *Journal of the Warburg and Courtauld Institutes* XL, 1977, pp. 292–300.

[45] Cf. esp. Vagnetti-Marcucci (1978), passim.

[46] *Architettura con il suo commento et figure, Vetruvio in volgar lingua raportato per M. Gianbatista Caporali di Perugia*, Perugia 1536 (facs. repr. Perugia 1985).

[47] Modern editions of this text (exact transcription in: Fontana (1933), p. 315ff.) in: Gustavo Giovannoni, *Antonio da Sangallo il Giovane*, I, Rome 1959, pp. 394–97; Paola Barocchi (ed.), *Scritti d'arte del Cinquecento*, III, 1977, pp. 3028–31.

[48] Printed in: Paola Barocchi (ed.), *Scritti*

d'arte del Cinquecento, III, 1977, pp. 3037–46; annotated text by Sandro Benedetti and Tommaso Scalesse, in: *Pietro Cataneo – Giacomo Barozzi da Vignola, Trattati*, ed. Elena Bassi et al., Milan 1985, pp. 31–61.

[49] *Guglielmi Philandri Castilioni Galli Civis Ro. in Decem Libros M. Vitruvii Pollionis De Architectura Annotationes..*, Rome 1544 (numerous editions).

[50] *Architecture ou Art de bien bastir, de Marc Vitruve Pollion... par Jan Martin Secretaire de Monseigneur le Cardinal de Lenoncourt*, Paris 1547 (facs. repr. Gregg 1964).

[51] The sources of the illustrations are identified in: Pierre du Colombier, 'Jean Goujon et le Vitruve de 1547', *Gazette des Beaux-Arts* V, 1931, pp. 155–78.

[52] Martin (1547), fols 75v, 77v, 78v.

[53] Ibid., fols 2v, 3v.

[54] Knowledge of the engraving by Marcantonio Raimondi, which shows a façade with caryatids, may be supposed to lie behind not only Goujon's caryatids at the Louvre of 1550/51, but also his illustrations to Vitruvius of 1547.

[55] Cf. Pierre du Colombier, *Jean Goujon*, Paris 1949, pp. 87ff.; Christiane Aulanier, *La salle des Caryatides (Histoire du Palais et du Musée du Louvre)*, Paris 1957, pp. 11ff.

[56] Thus du Colombier (1949), pp. 96f.; Christiane Aulanier (1957), p. 17.

[57] Martin (1547), fols 28, 28v.

[58] Ibid., fol. 35.

[59] Ibid., fols 37v, 38.

[60] Ibid., appendix to index (no folio).

[61] *Vitruvius Teutsch... erstmals verteutscht, und in Truck verordnet durch D. Gualtherum H. Rivium Medi. & Math. vormals in Teutsche sprach zu transferiren noch von niemand sonst understanden sonder fur unmüglichen geachtet worden*, Nuremberg 1548; repr. with introduction by Erik Forssman, Hildesheim–New York 1973.

[62] *M. Vitruvii, viri suae professioinis peritissimi de Architectura libri decem... per Gualtherium H. Ryff Argentinum medicum*, Strassburg 1543.

[63] *Vitruvius Teutsch* 1548, foreword.

[64] *'alle künstliche Handwercker, Werckmeister, Steinmetzen, Baumeister, Zeug- und Büxenmeister, Brunnenleytere, Berckwercker, Maler, Bildhauer, Goltschmide, Schreiner und alle die welche sich des Zirckels und Richtscheids künstlichen gebrauchen'* ...'*durch das wortlin Architectur eine solche kunst ver-*

standen werden, die mit vilfeltigen anderen Kunsten dermassen geziert ist, das der, so diser kunst erfaren ist,…, alles das, was uns zu zeitlicher und leiblicher unterhaltung zur noturfft, lust und nutzbarkeit reichen mag, füglichen und aus gutem Verstand in das Werck zu ordnen und bauen.'

[65] Cf. Heinrich Röttinger, *Die Holzschnitte zur Architektur und zum Vitruvius Teutsch des Walther Rivius*, Strassburg 1914; Röttinger names as illustrators Virgil Solis, Jörg Pencz, Hans Brosamer and Hans Springinklee. On the contribution of Virgil Solis cf. Ilse O'Dell-Franke, *Kupferstiche und Radierungen aus der Werkstatt des Virgil Solis*, Wiesbaden 1977, pp. 50, 60.

[66] Rivius (1548), fol. LXXXIIIIv.

[67] Ibid., fols CCIXff.

[68] Ibid., fol. LXIIv.

[69] Giovanni Battista Bertani, *Gli oscuri e difficili passi dell'opera jonica di Vitruvio*, Mantua 1558; cf. Francesco Pellati, 'Giovanni Battista Bertani. Architetto, pittore, commentatore di Vitruvio', *Scritti in onore*

di Mario Salmi, Rome 1963, III, p. 31–38; Vagnetti-Marcucci (1978), pp. 63f.

[70] Illus. in Pellati (1963), p. 33, fig. 1.

[71] Francesco Salviati, *Regola di far perfettamente col compasso la voluta del capitello ionico e d'ogn'altra sorte*, Venice 1552.

[72] Giovanantonio Rusconi, *Della architettura…con Centosessanta Figure…secondo i Precetti di Vitruvio…libri dieci*, Venice 1590 (facs. repr. 1968).

[73] On Rusconi cf. Vincenzo Fontana, '"Arte" e "Isperienza" nei Trattati d'architettura Veneziani del Cinquecento', *Architectura* 8, 1978, pp. 60ff.; Vagnetti-Marcucci (1978), pp. 72f.; exhib. cat. *Architettura e Utopia nella Venezia del Cinquecento*, Milan 1980, p. 181, cat. no. 182; p. 208, cat. no. 249; Giancarlo Cataldi, 'Le origini, dell'architettura nella trattatistica classica', *Studi e documenti di architettura* II, 1983, pp. 39–54; Anna Bedon, 'Il 'Vitruvio' di Giovan Antonio Rusconi', *Ricerche di Storia dell'Arte* 19, 1983, pp. 84–90.

[74] Rusconi (1590), pp. 24ff.

6. Sixteenth-century codification

[1] Sebastiano Serlio, *Tutte l'opere d'architettura et prospettiva…diviso in sette libri*, Venice 1619 (Gregg Reprint 1964), Book IV, foreword to the reader, fol. 126.

[2] Ibid., introduction to Book II, fol. 18.

[3] The most important literature on Serlio: Giulio Carlo Argan, 'Sebastiano Serlio' (first in: *L'Arte* XXXV, 1932, pp. 183–99) and: 'Il "Libro Extraordinario" di Sebastiano Serlio' (1933), in: Argan, *Studi e note dal Bramante a Canova*, Rome 1970, pp. 45–70; Ludwig H. Heydenreich, 'Sebastiano Serlio', in: Thieme-Becker, *Allgemeines Lexikon der bildenden Künstler* 30, 1936, pp. 513–15; William Bell Dinsmoor, 'The Literary Remains of Sebastiano Serlio', *The Art Bulletin* XXIV, 1942, pp. 55ff., 115ff.; Erik Forssman, *Säule und Ornament*, Stockholm 1956, pp. 62ff.; Julius von Schlosser, *La letteratura artistica* (1924), Florence–Vienna, ³1964, pp. 406ff., 418ff.; various articles by Stanislaw Wilinski in: *Bollettino del Centro Internazionale di Studi di Architettura "Andrea Palladio"*, 1964ff.; Marco Rosci, *Il trattato di architettura di Sebastiano Serlio*, Milan. n.d. (1967; together with facsimile of Serlio's "Sesto Libro"); Paolo Marconi, 'Un progetto di

città militare. L'VIII libro inedito di Sebastiano Serlio', *Controspazio* I, 1969, n. 1, pp. 51–9; n. 3, pp. 53–9; Myra Nan Rosenfeld, 'Sebastiano Serlio's Drawings in the Nationalbibliothek in Vienna for the Seventh Book on Architecture', *The Art Bulletin* LVI, 1974, pp. 400–09; ead., *Sebastiano Serlio on Domestic Architecture*, New York 1978; also cf. Bibliography by Ciro Luigi Anzivino, *Jacopo Barozzi il Vignola e gli architetti italiani del Cinquecento*, Vignola 1974, pp. 192–6; Hubertus Günther, 'Studien zum venezianischen Aufenthalt des Sebastiano Serlio', *Münchner Jahrbuch der bildenden Kunst*, 3rd ser., XXXII, 1981, pp. 42–94; Hubertus Günther, 'Porticus Pompeji. Zur archäologischen Erforschung eines antiken Bauwerks in der Renaissance und seine Rekonstruktion im dritten Buch des Sebastiano Serlio', *Zeitschrift für Kunstgeschichte* 44, 1981, pp. 358–98; Christof Thoenes (ed.), *Sebastiano Serlio*, Milan 1989; Mario Carpo, *La maschera e il modello. Teoria architettonica ed evangelismo nell' Extraordinario Libro di Sebastiano Serlio (1551)*, Milan 1993.

[4] Serlio (1619), introduction to Book IV, fol. 126.

[5] On their order of publication, cf. Dinsmoor (1942), Rosci (1967), Rosenfeld (1978).

[6] On Book VII cf. esp. Rosenfeld (1974).

[7] On these translations, see esp. Schlosser (1964), pp. 418f.

[8] Sebastiano Serlio, *Libro primo d'architettura* etc., Venice 1566, dedication by Francesco de'Franceschini to Daniele Barbaro. In this edition the illustrations are reduced in size.

[9] Sebastiano Serlio, *Von der Architectur Fünff Bucher...*, Basel 1608.

[10] '& più necessario de gli altri per la cognitione delle differenti maniere de gli edificij, & de' loro ornamenti.' Serlio (1619), foreword to Book IV, fol. 126.

[11] It should be remembered that Vitruvius (IV.i) speaks only of three *'genera'*, Doric, Ionic and Corinthian, not accepting the Tuscan order as a *'genus'* and referring only to *'tuscanae dispositiones'* (IV.vii). Alberti (VII.vi) had been the first to recognise the Composite as a distinct Order, which he called the 'Italian'. On the ascription of *I cinque ordini architettonici* to Alberti, see Chapter 3, note 50. Raphael, in his well-known letter to Leo X, speaks of the five Orders (*'cinque ordini che usavano li antiqui'*) as if they were well established. (Paola Barocchi, *Scritti d'arte del Cinquecento*, vol. III, Milan–Naples 1977, p. 2983). On Serlio's conception of the Tuscan order, cf. James S. Ackerman, 'The Tuscan/Rustic Order: A Study in the Metaphorical Language of Architecture', *Journal of the Society of Architectural Historians* XLII, 1983, pp. 15–34; on the Orders, cf. also Erik Forssman, *Dorisch, Jonisch, Korinthisch*, Stockholm 1961. An important source on Serlio is the recently published ms. ital. 473 in the Bibliothèque Nationale, Paris; cf. Vladimir Juřen, 'Un traité inédit sur les ordres d'architecture et le problème des sources du Libro IV de Serlio', *Monuments et Mémoires publiés par l'Académie des Inscriptions et Belles-Lettres* 64, 1981, pp. 195–239.

[12] Serlio (1619), foreword to Book IV, fol. 126.

[13] 'darò a gli huomini, secondo lo stato, & le professioni loro.' Ibid., fol. 126v.

[14] 'una quasi quinta maniera'...'il quale non ha potuto abbracciar il tutto.' Ibid., fol. 183.

[15] Serlio, ibid., fol. 133v.

[16] In this connection Serlio (ibid., fol. 133 v) significantly refers to Giulio Romano's Palazzo del Tè in Mantua.

[17] Serlio, ibid., fol. 147v.

[18] 'la maggior parte de gli huomini appetiscono il più delle volte cose nuove.' Ibid., *Il Sesto libro (Libro Extraordinario)*, fol. 2.

[19] Serlio, ibid., Book IV, fols 153v. ff.

[20] Cf. Serlio, ibid., fols 161v.ff. Serlio's attitude to Vitruvius is especially clear in the *Libro Extraordinario* (fol. 2): 'Ma o voi Architettori fondati sopra la dottrina di Vitruvio (la quale sommamente io lodo, & dalla quale io non intendo allontanarmi molto...'. *Sesto libro*, 1619, fol. 2.

[21] 'alcuni luoghi nell'Architettura, a i quali posson essere date quasi certe regole'. Ibid., Book IV, fol. 187.

[22] Ibid., fols 191v.ff.

[23] Ibid., Book III, introduction, fol. 30.

[24] Ibid., Book III, fol. 64v.

[25] 'bench'ella non si fece in opera, laquale andava accordata con l'opera vecchia'. Ibid., fol. 67.

[26] Ibid., fols 121ff.

[27] Ibid., fols 93f.

[28] 'cose ·de i Greci'...'forse che supereriano le cose de i Romani'...'maravigliosissime cose dell'Egitto'...'sogni & chimere'. Ibid., fol. 123v.

[29] Ibid., Book II, preface, fol. 18v.

[30] Ibid., fols 44ff.

[31] Cf. eg. Hans Heinrich Borchardt, *Das europäische Theater im Mittelalter und in der Renaissance* (1935), Reinbek 1969, pp. 113ff.

[32] 'perchè la forma tonda è la più perfetta di tutte le altre.' Serlio (1619), Book V, fol. 202.

[33] 'tanti ornamenti..., di tanti cartocci, volute & di tanti superflui'. Ibid., *Il Sesto libro (Libro Extraordinario)*, fol. 2.

[34] Ibid., Book VII, p. 70.

[35] Ibid., pp. 156f., 168–71.

[36] 'cosa che è molto contraria alla buona Architettura'. Ibid., p. 156.

[37] On the relationship between these manuscripts, cf. Rosci (1967) and Rosenfeld (1978).

[38] Cf. esp. his stated aim: 'io intendo di accompagnare la commodità francese al costume ed ornamento italiano', Serlio, Book VI, ed. Rosenfeld (1978), text to pl. II.

[39] 'più cose licensiose che regolari segondo la dotrina di Vitruvio'. Serlio, Book VI, ed. Rosci 1967), fol. 74.

[40] Cod. Icon. 190. See esp. Marconi (1969); Heinrich Wischermann, 'Castrametatio und Städtebau im 16. Jahrhundert: Sebasti-

ano Serlio', *Bonner Jahrbücher des Rheinischen Landesmuseums in Bonn* 175, 1975, pp. 171–86; Rosenfeld (1978), pp. 35ff.; exhib. cat. *Architettura e Utopia nella Venezia del Cinquecento*, Palazzo Ducale, Milan 1980, pp. 173ff., n. 173; June Gwendolyn Johnson, 'Sebastiano Serlio's Treatise on Military Architecture' (Bayerische Staatsbibliothek, Munich, Codex Icon. 190), PhD thesis, University of California, Los Angeles 1984.

[41] Rosenfeld (1978) has commented on the Dürer connection (pp. 35ff).

[42] On Serlio's historical judgment, cf. Rosci (1967), ch. 1.

[43] For a modern view of Serlio, cf. Argan (1932).

[44] See eg. the examination of Serlio's influence on Polish Mannerist and Baroque architecture by Jerzy Kowalczyk, *Sebastiano Serlio a sztuka Polska* (with Italian résumé), Wroclaw 1973.

[45] Antonio Labacco, *Libro appartenente al'architettura nel qual si figurano alcune notabili antiquità di Roma*, Rome 1552 (the present writer has used the edition Rome 1567).

[46] Labacco (1567), pls 26–8. Labacco comments on pl. 26: '*La pianta qui sotto dimostrata è moderna, di nostra inventione, insieme col suo dirito qual si dimostra nella seguente carta: et benche l'intentione nostra fusse di trattar solo di cose antiche, nondimeno ci è parso notarlo con l'altre cose, per util'e piacere di ciascuno studioso di quest'arte.*' Wolfgang Lotz ('Die ovalen Kirchenräume des Cinquecento', *Römisches Jahrbuch für Kunstgeschichte* 7, 1955, p. 22) has demonstrated that Labacco's design is plagiarised from Antonio da Sangallo the Younger's design for S. Giovanni dei Fiorentini in Rome.

[47] Paola Barocchi, *Scritti d'arte del Cinquecento*, vol. III, Milan–Naples 1977, pp. 3555f. (with bibliography). Cf. a new critical ed.: Pietro Cataneo, *L'architettura* (1567), ed. Elena Bassi and Paola Marini, in: *Pietro Cataneo – Giacomo Barozzi da Vignola, Trattati*, ed. Elena Bassi et al., Milan 1985, pp. 163–498.

[48] '*La più bella parte dell'Architettura certamente serà quella, che tratta delle città.*' Pietro Cataneo, I quattro primi libri di architettura, Venice 1554, dedication.

[49] Ibid., fols. 6ff.

[50] Ibid., fol. 17. It is clear that Cataneo made use of his compatriot Francesco di Giorgio's treatises; cf. the latter's plans in: F. di Giorgio Martini, *Trattati*, ed. Corrado Maltese, vol. I, Milan 1967, pl. 10. The plan of the army camp is only included in Cataneo's second ed. (1567).

[51] Cf. esp. the relevant contributions in: *Atti del XV Congresso di Storia dell'Architettura. L'architettura a Malta dalla preistoria all'Ottocento* (1967), Rome 1970; J. Quentin Hughes, *The Building of Malta* (1956) and *Fortress, Architecture and Military History in Malta* (1969).

[52] Cataneo (1554), fol. 35v.

[53] Cf. Anthony Blunt, *Artistic Theory in Italy 1450–1600* (1940), Oxford 1962, p. 130; Paola Barocchi, *Trattati d'arte del Cinquecento*, vol. III, Bari 1962, pp. 383f.

[54] '*Avvenga che nessun corpo humano da quello di Giesu Cristo in poi oltre alla sua divina bontà, non fusse mai di proportione di persona perfetta.*' Cataneo (1554), fol. 36.

[55] Cataneo (1567), pp. 65 ff.

[56] Ibid., pp. 108ff.

[57] Cataneo (1554), fol. 1.

[58] Ibid., fol. 1v.

[59] From extensive literature on Vignola, cf. esp.: Maria Walcher Casotti, *Il Vignola*, 2 vols, Trieste 1960; the anthology *La vita e le opere di Jacopo Barozzi da Vignola*, Vignola 1974; cf. further the bibliography by Ciro Luigi Anzivino, *Jacopo Barozzi il Vignola e gli architetti italiani del Cinquecento*, Vignola 1974.

[60] Jacomo Barozzi da Vignola, *Le due regole della prospettiva pratica*, Rome 1583 (facs. repr. with introduction by Maria Walcher Casotti, Vignola 1974); cf. esp. the contribution by Maria Walcher Casotti in: *La vita e le opere* etc. (1974), pp. 191ff.; Luigi Vagnetti, 'De naturali et artificiali perspectiva', *Studi e documenti di architettura* 9–10, 1979, pp. 321ff.

[61] On the *Regola delli cinque ordini* and its various editions, cf. esp. A.G. Spinelli, 'Bio-Bibliografia dei due Vignola', in: *Memorie e studi intorno a Jacopo Barozzi*, Vignola 1908, pp. 15ff.; Christof Thoenes in: *La vita e le opere di Jacopo Barozzi da Vignola* (1974), pp. 179–89; id., 'Vignolas "Regola delli cinque ordini"', *Römisches Jahrbuch für Kunstgeschichte* 20, 1983, pp. 345–76; a

new critical edition of the *Regola* (with a bibliography of editions) by Maria Walcher Casotti in: *Pietro Cataneo – Giacomo Barozzi da Vignola, Trattati*, ed. Elena Bassi et al., Milan 1985, pp. 499–577.

[62] '*Come è detto il mio intento è stato di essere inteso solamente da quelli che habbino qualche introduttione nell'arte, et per questo non haveva scritto il nome a niuno de'membri particolari di questi cinque ordini presuponendoli per noti.*' Vignola (1976), pl. III.

[63] '*al giudicio comune appaiono più belli*'. Ibid.

[64] Ibid.

[65] '*breve regola facile, et spedita*'…'*ogni mediocre ingegno…in un' occhiata sola senza gran fastidio*'. Ibid.

[66] See esp. the analysis by Thoenes (1983), pp. 352ff.

[67] Cf. ibid., pp. 360 ff.

[68] Vignola, pl. XXXI; on Salomonic columns, cf. Hans-Wolfgang Schmidt, *Die gewundene Säule in der Architekturtheorie von 1500 bis 1800*, Stuttgart 1978, esp. pp. 74ff.

[69] See for example a five-language edition, Amsterdam 1642, with an extensive appendix including illustrations of works by Michelangelo; at the end are ten plates showing designs of chimneypieces, and above each chimneypiece is displayed a biblical scene in which fire plays a central part – a somewhat dubious application of the resolutions of the Council of Trent.

7. Palladio and the North Italian Humanists

[1] From the very extensive literature on Palladio, the following selective listing of publications is of those that aim to establish links between Palladio's activity as an architect and his theoretical ideas: Rudolf Wittkower, *Architectural Principles in the Age of Humanism* (1949), London 1962 (German: Munich 1969); Erik Forssman, *Palladios Lehrgebäude. Studien über den Zusammenhang von Architektur und Architekturtheorie bei Andrea Palladio*, Stockholm 1965; James S. Ackerman, *Palladio*, Harmondsworth 1966; Lionello Puppi, *Andrea Palladio*, Venice 1973 (German: Stuttgart 1977); Ursel Berger, *Palladios Frühwerk. Bauten und Zeichnungen*, Cologne–Vienna 1978; Lionello Puppi (ed.), *Palladio e Venezia*, Florence 1982; *Vierhundert Jahre Andrea Palladio*. Colloquium, Gesamthochschule Wuppertal, Heidelberg 1982; various articles in *Bollettino del Centro Internazionale di Studi d'Architettura* (henceforward cited as *Bollettino CISA*), *Andrea Palladio*, Vicenza 1959ff.

[2] On Trissino cf. esp. Bernardo Morsolin, *Giangiorgio Trissino*, Vicenza 1878 (Florence ²1894); Guido Piovene, 'Trissino e Palladio nell'umanesimo vicentino', *Bollettino CISA* V, 1963, pp. 13–23; Wittkower (1969), pp. 51ff.; Lionello Puppi, 'Un letterato in Villa: Giangiorgio Trissino a Cricoli', *Arte Veneta* XXV, 1971, pp. 72–91; Ursel Berger (1978), pp. 9ff.; Franco Barbieri, 'Giangiorgio Trissino e Andrea Palladio', in: Neri Pozza (ed.), *Convegno di Studi su Giangiorgio Trissino*, Vicenza 1980, pp. 191–211.

[3] Andrea Palladio, *I quattro libri dell'architettura*, Venice 1570, Book I, p. 5.

[4] '*E quel cortile e circondato intorno Di larghe logge, con colonne tonde Che son tant'alte, quanto a la larghezza Del pavimento, e sono grosse ancora L'ottava parte, e piu di quella altezza. Et han sovr'esse capitei d'argento Tant'alti, quanto la colonna e grossa; E sotto han spire di metal, che sono Per la meta del capitello in alto.*' Trissino, *Italia liberata dai Goti*, Book V. Quoted by Wittkower (1969), p. 52.

[5] Wittkower (1969), p. 52.

[6] Cf. S. Rumor, 'Villa Cricoli', *Archivio Veneto Tridentino*, 1926, I, pp. 202–16; A.M. Dalla Pozza, *Andrea Palladio*, Vicenza 1943, p. 51; Puppi (1971); on Serlio's relationship with Trissino regarding the villa, cf. Hubertus Günther, 'Studien zum venezianischen Aufenthalt des Sebastiano Serlio', *Münchner Jahrbuch der bildenden Kunst*, 3rd ser., XXXII, 1981, pp. 47ff.

[7] Wittkower (1969), p. 53. Ursel Berger (1978, p. 10) has shown that the villa's pedagogic function did not begin until after Trissino's death. On the possibility of its use as an 'academy', cf. Ottavio Bertotti Scamozzi, *Il Forestiere istruito…della Città di Vicenza*, Vicenza 1761, p. 107.

[8] Serlio (1619; see Chapter 6, note 1 above), Book III, fol. 121v.; cf. Forssman (1965), pp. 14f.; Puppi (1971, pp. 83ff.) attributes the loggia to Trissino and Serlio on the

ground of its close connection with Serlio's woodcut.

[9] First published in: Nozze Pesaro-Bertolini: G.G. Trissino, Dell'Architettura. Frammento, Vicenza 1878; repr. in: G.G. Trissino, Scritti scelti, ed. A. Scarpa, Vicenza 1950; new ed. in: Lionello Puppi, Scrittori vicentini d'architettura del secolo XVI, Vicenza 1973, pp. 79ff. (text pp. 82ff.), on dating p. 81. Also in: Paola Barocchi (ed.), Scritti d'arte del Cinquecento, vol. III, Milan–Naples, 1977, pp. 3032–6; critical ed. by Camillo Semenzato in: Pietro Cataneo-Giacomo Barozzi da Vignola, Trattati, ed. Elena Bassi et al., Milan 1985, pp. 19–29.

[10] 'La architettura è un artificio circa lo habitare de li homini, che prepara in esso utilità e dilettazioni'. Trissino, cited by Puppi (1973), p. 82.

[11] Ibid., p. 83.

[12] On Cornaro cf. esp. Giuseppe Fiocco, Alvise Cornaro. Il suo tempo e le sue opere, Vicenza 1965; with texts of Cornaro's writings and letters. Cf. also Fritz-Eugen Keller, 'Alvise Cornaro zitiert die Villa des Marcus Terentius Varro in Cassino', L'Arte 14, 1971, pp. 29–53; exhib. cat. Alvise Cornaro e il suo tempo, Padua 1980.

[13] On Falconetto, cf. Erik Forssman, 'Falconetto e Palladio', Bollettino CISA VIII, 2, 1966, pp. 52–67 and esp. Gunter Schweikhart, 'Studien zum Werk des Giovanni Maria Falconetto', Bollettino del Museo Civico do Padova LVII, 1968 (special number 1969).

[14] Schweikhart (1969), pp. 20ff.

[15] 'Gentil huomo di eccellente giudizio, come si conosce dalla bellissima loggia, & dalle ornatissime stanze fabricate da lui per la sua habitatione in Padova.' Palladio (1570), Book I, p. 61.

[16] Fiocco (1965), pp. 156ff., 162ff.; Barocchi (ed.), Scritti d'arte del Cinquecento vol. III, 1977, pp. 3134–61; Paolo Carpeggiani (ed.), Alvise Cornaro. Scritti sull'architettura, Padua 1980.

[17] Cf. Paolo Carpeggiani in the exhib. cat. Alvise Cornaro e il suo tempo (1980), p. 29.

[18] Fiocco (1965), p. 156.

[19] 'et oltre a ciò une fabrica può ben esser bella, et commoda, et non esser nè Dorica nè di alcuno de tali ordini…' Ibid.

[20] 'io lauderò sempre più la fabrica honestamente bella, ma perfettamente commoda, che la bellissima et incommoda…' Ibid.

[21] Ibid., p. 162.

[22] 'mi servirò di quei nomi, che gli artefici hoggidi communamente usano.' Palladio (1570), Book I, p. 6.

[23] See the proof in Fiocco (1965), p. 77.

[24] Ibid., p. 156.

[25] Ibid., p. 187.

[26] On Barbaro cf. Wittkower (1969), pp. 57ff.; Vassili Pavlovitch Zoubov, 'Vitruve et ses commentateurs du XVIᵉ siècle', Colloque international de Royaumont 1957, Paris 1960, pp. 71ff. (esp. on Barbaro's sources); Erik Forssman, 'Palladio und Daniele Barbaro', Bollettino CISA VIII/2), 1966, pp. 68–81; Manfredo Tafuri, Venezia e il Rinascimento, Turin 1985, pp. 185ff.; Vincenzo Fontana, 'Il "Vitruvio" del 1556: Barbaro, Palladio, Marcolini', in: Trattati scientifici nel Veneto fra il XV e XVI secolo, Saggi e Studi, ed. Enzo Riondato, Vicenza 1985, pp. 39–72.

[27] But not all. Barbaro (1556; see Editions), p. 40 writes: 'ne i dissegni de le figure importanti ho usato l'opera di M. Andrea Palladio Vicentino Architetto.' Cf. Forssman (1966), pp. 68f. The preparatory MSS in the Bibl. Marciana, Venice shows various hands in the figurative drawings: cf. exhib. cat. Architettura e Utopia nella Venezia del Cinquecento, Milan 1980, p. 178, n. 177.

[28] Comparison of the editions by Forssman (1966), pp. 69f. Further to Forssman's observations, it should be added that one woodcut from the 1556 ed. is reused in the rather larger format Latin ed. of 1567 (p. 37). The illustrations of Vitruvian man (p. 89) and a view of Venice (p. 204) are retained only in the Latin ed. of 1567.

[29] Barbaro (1567; see Editions), p. 4.

[30] 'il principio dell'arte, che è lo intelletto humano, ha gran simiglianza col principio, che muove la natura, che è una intelligenza.' Ibid., p. 37.

[31] Ibid., pp. 96ff.

[32] Ibid., p. 11.

[33] Ibid., p. 14.

[34] Ibid., p. 4.

[35] In the present writer's opinion, the significance of Neoplatonism in Barbaro is overstressed by Vincenzo Fontana, '"Arte" e "Isperienza" nei Trattati d'Architettura Veneziani del Cinquecento', Architectura 8, 1978, pp. 49ff.

[36] Palladio would not seem to have approved of the execution of all the woodcuts in

Barbaro's edition of Vitruvius; thus in the third book of *Quattro libri* (1570), pp. 38ff. he reproduces two drawings of a reconstruction of Vitruvius's basilica of Fano with the comment: '*io ne porrei qui i disegni, se dal Reverendissimo Barbaro nel suo Vitruvio non fossero stati fatti con somma diligenza.*'

[37] '*vaghi disegni delle piante, di gli alzati, & dei profili, come ne lo esequire e far molti e superbi Edificij ne la patria sua, & altrove che contendono con gli antichi, danno lume a moderni, e daran meraviglia a quelli che verranno.*' Barbaro (1556), p. 40.

[38] For a discussion of the dating, cf. Puppi, *Andrea Palladio*, London 1975, pp. 314ff.

[39] Cf. the analysis by Wittkower (1969), pp. 109f.; on the possible participation of the Barbaro brothers in the villa's design, cf. Norbert Huse, 'Palladio und die Villa Barbaro' in: 'Maser: Bemerkungen zum Problem der Autorschaft,' *Arte Veneta* XXVIII, 1974, pp. 106–22. See also Donata Battilotti, 'Villa Barbaro a Maser: un difficile cantiere', *Storia dell'arte* 53, 1985, pp. 33–48; Inge Jackson Reist, 'Renaissance Harmony: The Villa Barbaro at Maser', PhD thesis, Columbia University, New York 1985.

[40] Daniele Barbaro, *La pratica della perspettiva... opera molto utile a Pittori, Scultori, e ad Architetti*, Venice 1568/69.

[41] Cf. Wittkower (1969), pp. 83ff.; Manfredo Tafuri, *Jacopo Sansovino e l'architettura del '500 a Venezia*, Padua 1969 (1972), pp. 24ff.; Antonio Foscari and Manfredo Tafuri, *L'armonia e i conflitti. La chiesa di San Francesco della Vigna nella Venezia del '500*, Turin 1983; critical ed. by Licisco Magagnato in: Pietro Cataneo-Giacomo Barozzi da Vignola, *Trattati*, ed. Elena Bassi et al., Milan 1985, pp. 1–17.

[42] Francesco Giorgi, *De Harmonia Mundi totius cantica tria*, Venice 1525.

[43] Francesco Giorgi (memorandum for S. Francesco della Vigna, 1535) in: Giannantonio Moschini, *Guida per la Città di Venezia*, vol. I, Venice 1815, pp. 55–61: Foscari-Tafuri (1983), pp. 208ff.

[44] Cf. Ludwig Schudt, *Le Guide di Roma*, Vienna–Augsburg 1930, p. 136f.

[45] On Palladio's preparatory drafts, and the whole project, cf. esp. Giangiorgio Zorzi, *I disegni delle antichità di Andrea Palladio*, Venice 1959, pp. 145ff. (pp. 161ff. reproduce Palladio's fragmentary drafts); Heinz Spiel-

mann, *Andrea Palladio und die Antike*, Munich 1966, pp. 26ff., 51ff.

[46] '*Io dunque tratterò prima delle case private, & verrò poi a publici edificij: e brevemente tratterò delle strade, dei ponti, delle piazze, delle prigioni, delle Basiliche, cioè luoghi del giudizio, dei Xisti, e delle Palestre, ch'erano luoghi, ove gli huomini si esercitavano; dei Tempij, dei Theatri, & degli Anfitheatri, degli Archi, delle Terme, degli Acquedotti, e finalmente del modo di fortificar le Città, & dei Porti.*' Palladio (1570), Book I, p. 6.

[47] Spielmann (1966), pp. 51f.

[48] Only Palladio's drawings of Roman baths were published: Richard Boyle, Earl of Burlington, *Fabbriche antiche disegnate da Andrea Palladio vicentino*, London 1730 (facs. repr. 1969).

[49] On the dissemination and translations of the *Quattro libri*, cf. Deborah Howard, 'Four Centuries of Literature on Palladio', *Journal of the Society of Architectural Historians*, XXXIX, 1980, pp. 226ff.; cf. also the conflation of editions in the critical ed. by Licisco Magagnato and Paola Marini, Milan 1980, pp. lxixff.

[50] Goethe, *Tagebücher und Briefe Goethes aus Italien an Frau von Stein und Herder (Schriften der Goethe-Gesellschaft,* vol. 2), Weimar 1886, p. 128.

[51] '*Mi posi anco all'impresa di scriver gli avertimenti necessarij, che si devono osservare da tutti i belli ingegni, che sono desiderosi di edificar bene, & leggiadramente... ardisco di dire, d'haver forse dato tanto di lume alle cose di Architettura in questa parte, che coloro, che dopo me verranno, potranno con l'esempio mio, esercitanto l'acutezza dei lor chiari ingegni.*' Palladio (1570), Book I, p. 3 (dedication to Giacomo Angarano).

[52] Ibid., p. 5.

[53] Ibid., p. 6.

[54] '*corrispondenza del tutto alle parti, delle parti fra loro, e di quelle al tutto*'. Ibid., p. 6.

[55] Ibid., p. 51.

[56] Ibid., p. 52.

[57] On the relationship between Palladio and Vignola, cf. Magagnato-Marini in their edition of Palladio (1980), p. 422.

[58] Palladio (1570), Book I, p. 22.

[59] '*E perche commoda si deverà dire quella casa, la quale sarà conveniente alla qualità di chi l'haverà ad habitare e le sue parti*

corrispoderanno al tutto, e fra se stesse.'
Ibid., Book II, p. 3.

[60] *'Ma spesse volte fa bisogno all'Architetto accommodarsi più alla volontà di coloro, che spendono, che a quello, che si devrebbe osservare.'* Ibid.

[61] Cod. Cicogna 3617, fol. 14v. (Venice, Museo Correr): *'Ma prima ch'io venga a i disegni [delle fabbriche] è conveniente ch'io faccia una giusta escusatione mia appresso i lettori, la quale à che in molte delle seguenti fabriche mi è stato bisogno obedire non tanto alla natura de i siti, quanto alla volontà de i padroni, i quali, parte per conservare le fabbriche vecchie in piedi, parte per altri rispetti e voglie loro, hanno fatto ch'io mi sia partito in qualche parte da quello ch'io ho avvertito che si debba osservare e che havrei fatto, benché mi sia sforzato sempre appressarmeli più che habbi possuto.'* Cited in Palladio, ed. Magagnato-Marini, 1980, p. xxxi.

[62] Ibid., p. 4.

[63] Ibid., pp. 8ff.

[64] *'Il sito è degli ameni, e dilettevoli che si possono ritrovare: perche è sopra un monticello di ascesa facilissima, & è da una parte bagnato dal Bacchiglione fiume navigabile, e dall'altra è circondato da altri amenissimi colli, che rendono l'aspetto di un molto grande Theatro, e sono tutti coltivati, & abondanti di frutti eccellentissimo, & di buonissime viti: Onde perche gode da ogni parte di bellissime viste, delle quali alcune sono terminate, alcune piu' lontane, & altre, che terminano con l'Orizonte; vi sono state fatte le loggie in tutte quattro le faccie...'* Palladio (1570), Book II, p. 18.

[65] Ibid., p. 69.

[66] Ibid., Book III, p. 5.

[67] Ibid.

[68] Ibid., pp. 38ff.

[69] *'Queste Basiliche de'nostri tempi sono in questo dall'antiche differenti; che l'antiche erano in tirreno, ò vogliam dire à pie piano: e queste nostre sono sopra i volti; ne'quali poi si ordinano le botteghe per diverse*

arti...' Ibid., p. 42.

[70] Ibid., p. 42.

[71] *'semplice, uniforme, eguale, forte e capace...'* *...'Unità, la infinita Essenza, la Uniformità, & la Giustitia di Dio'.* Ibid., Book IV, p. 6.

[72] Ibid., p. 7.

[73] *'se si dipingeranno, non vi staranno bene quelle pitture, che con il significato loro alienino l'animo dalla contemplatione delle cose Divine; percioche non si dobbiamo nei Tempij partire dalla gravità...'* Ibid., p. 7.

[74] Even though Palladio is supposed to have been influenced by Protestant reformism through the Thiene family, these observations would still be comprehensible; cf. Guglielmo De Angelis D'Osaat, 'Palladio e l'antichità', *Bollettino CISA* XV, 1973, pp. 39ff.

[75] *'Bramante sia stato il primo à metter in luce la buona, e bella Architettura, che da gli Antichi fin'a quel tempo era stata nascosta.'* Palladio (1570), Book IV, p. 64.

[76] Palladio's conception of proportion, which has been set out systematically above all by Wittkower (1969), has been further analysed by Deborah Howard and Malcolm Longair, 'Harmonic Proportion and Palladio's Quattro Libri', *Journal of the Society of Architectural Historians* XLI, 1982, pp. 116–43.

[77] Aesthetic and theoretical inferences from the extant material are most clearly drawn by Spielmann (1966), pp. 97ff.; cf. also Ursel Berger, 'Palladio publiziert seine eigenen Bauten. Zur Problematik des "Secondo Libro",' *Architectura* 14, 1984, pp. 20–40.

[78] Cf. esp. J.R. Hale, 'Andrea Palladio, Polybius and Julius Caesar', *Journal of the Warburg and Courtauld Institutes* XL, 1977, pp. 240–55; the commentary on Polybius, recently discovered in London, was exhibited for the first time in Venice in 1980; cf. exhib. cat. *Architettura e Utopia nella Venezia del Cinquecento*, Milan 1980, p. 184, n. 188.

[79] *'tutti i siti delle Città, de'Monti, e de' Fiumi'.* Introduction to the commentary on Polybius; quoted by Hale (1977), p. 254.

8. The Counter-Reformation, Baroque and Neo-classicism

[1] Cf. esp. the debate between Werner Weisbach, *Der Barock als Kunst der Gegenreformation*, Berlin 1921; and Nikolaus Pevsner, 'Gegenreformation und Manieris-

mus', *Repertorium für Kunstwissenschaft*, 46, 1925, pp. 243–62.

[2] Charles Dejob, *De l'influence du Concile de Trente sur la littérature et les Beaux*

Arts chez les peuples catholiques, Paris 1884; Anthony Blunt, *Artistic Theory in Italy 1450–1600* (1940), Oxford 1962, pp. 103ff.; all the important treatise texts are published in: Paola Barocchi, *Trattati d'arte del Cinquecento fra Manierismo e Controriforma*, 3 vols, Bari 1960–62.

[3] On the Council of Trent, cf. Hubert Jedin, *Geschichte des Konzils von Trient*, 4 vols, Freiburg-Basel-Vienna 1951–75; on the decree on the worship of saints, relics and images, cf. esp. vol. IV, 2, 1975, pp. 183f.; and cf. Hubert Jedin, 'Entstehung und Tragweite des Trienter Dekrets über die Bilderverehrung', *Tübinger Theologische Quartalsschrift* 116, 1936, pp. 143–88, 404–29; id. 'Das Tridentinum und die bildenden Künste', *Zeitschrift für Kirchengeschichte* 74, 1963, pp. 321–39.

[4] '*nihil falsum, nihil profanum, nihil inhonestum, nihil praepostere, nihil non recte atque ordine*'. Quoted by Barocchi (1962), vol. III, p. 441.

[5] Published in: Barocchi (1961), vol. II.

[6] Published in: ibid., vol. III, pp. 117ff.

[7] '*dolentissimo, di essere stato in mia vita instrumento di tali statue*'. Giovanni Gaye, *Carteggio inedito d'artisti dei secoli XIV, XV, XVI*, vol. III, Florence 1840, pp. 578f.

[8] On the role of Carlo Borromeo, cf. Ludwig von Pastor, *Geschichte der Päpste*, vol. VII (*Pius IV*), Freiburg 1923, pp. 340ff., 580f.; Jedin, vol. IV, 2 (1975). Borromeo's *Instructiones* were strangely overlooked by Dejob (1884), who gave a detailed account of the Cardinal's other activities; Dejob (pp. 264ff.) thus arrived at the false conclusion that the resolutions of the Council of Trent had no influence on architecture.

[9] Crit. ed. in: Paola Barocchi, vol. III (1962), pp. 1–113; Evelyn Carole Voelker, 'Charles Borromeo's Instructiones Fabricae...A Translation with Commentary and Analysis' (PhD thesis: Syracuse University 1977), Ann Arbor and London 1979. On the authorship, interpretation and impact of Borromeo's treatise, cf. Susanne Mayer-Himmelheber, *Bischöfliche Kunstpolitik nach dem Tridentinum. Der Secunda-Roma-Anspruch Carlo Borromeos und die mailändischen Verordnungen zu Bau und Ausstattung von Kirchen*, Munich 1984.

[10] On the application of the *Instructiones* by Carlo Borromeo in Milan and the role of the architect Pellegrino Tibaldi, cf. Aurora Scotti, 'Architettura e riforma cattolica nella Milano di Carlo Borromeo', *L'Arte* 19/20, 1972, pp. 54–90. Cf. also Blunt (1962), pp. 127ff.

[11] Borromeo, *Instructiones*, ed. Barocchi, vol. III (1962), pp. 7f.

[12] Ibid., p. 9. Floor space is estimated at $1\frac{2}{3}$ cubits per worshipper ('*mensura unius cubiti et unciarum octo*').

[13] Ibid., pp. 9ff. His comment on the circular form reads: '*Illa porro aedificii rotundi species olim idolorum templis in usu fuit, sed minus usitata in populo christiano*' (p. 10).

[14] Ibid., p. 11.

[15] Ibid., p. 12.

[16] Ibid., p. 17.

[17] '*Fabrica ornatuque nihil operis, qualequale sit, statuatur, fiat, inscribatur, effingatur exprimaturve quod a christiana pietate et religione remotum, aut quod profanum, quod deforme, quod voluptarium, quod turpe vel obscenum sit.*' Ibid., p. 112.

[18] Ibid., p. 113.

[19] Cf. in Rudolf Wittkower and Irma B. Jaffe (eds), *Baroque Art: The Jesuit Contribution*, New York, 1972, esp. Wittkower (pp. 1ff.) and James Ackerman (pp. 15ff.)

[20] Pellegrino Tibaldi, 'Discorso dell'Architettura' (ms in Biblioteca Ambrosiana, Milan, ms P 246 sup.); Pellegrino Tibaldi, 'Regole di architettura' (ms in Bibl. Nat., Paris). Cf. Julius von Schlosser, *La lett. art.* (1964), p. 722; Adriano Peroni, 'Il "discorso di architettura" di Pellegrino Tibaldi', in: *Omaggio alle Lettere, Quaderni del Collegio Borromeo*, Pavia 1960, pp. 3–12. The manuscript in the Biblioteca Ambrosiana, which I have examined, with a title-page stating it to be a copy made by Giovanni Battista Guida Bonbarda in 1610, consists of two parts. It in fact consists only of notes for a treatise, based largely on excerpts from Alberti. What Tibaldi says of particular types of building is second-hand and conventional. No 'architectural theory of the Counter-Reformation' could possibly be extracted from this material, and only occasional comments reveal a knowledge of Borromeo's *Instructiones*.

The manuscript in Paris has recently been published: Pellegrino Pellegrini, *L'ar-*

chitettura, ed. Giorgio Panitte, Milan 1990.

21 Cf. esp. Erwin Panofsky, *Idea. Ein Beitrag zur Begriffsgeschichte der älteren Kunsttheorie* (1924), Berlin ²1960, pp. 39ff.; Blunt (1962), pp. 86ff.

22 Cf. Wolfgang Kemp, 'Disegno. Beiträge zur Gechichte der Begriffs zwischen 1547 und 1607', *Marburger Jahrbuch für Kunstwissenschaft* 19, 1974, pp. 219–40.

23 Giorgio Vasari, *Le vite de'più eccellenti pittori, scultori e architettori* (1568). The most important critical editions are those of Gaetano Milanesi, 1878–85, the Club del Libro, Milan 1962–66, and Paola Barocchi. The Club del Libro edition, vol. I is cited hereafter.

On Vasari's aesthetic theory cf. various papers in the proceedings of the conference *Il Vasari storiografo e artista* (1974), Florence 1976; cf. also T. S. R. Boase, *Giorgio Vasari. The Man and the Book*, Princeton 1979. On Vasari's attitude to the Counter-Reformation cf. Giorgio Spini, introduction to *Architettura e politica da Cosimo I a Ferdinando I*, Florence 1976, pp. 25ff.; exhib. cat. (Regione Toscana, Arezzo) *Giorgio Vasari. Principi, letterati e artisti nelle carte di Giorgio Vasari*, Florence 1981.

24 Vasari (1962), vol. I, p. 47.

25 In the Proemio of the *Vite* (p. 43), Vasari calls architecture '*la più universale e più necessaria et utile agli uomini.*'

26 Vasari, vol. I (1962), p. 83.

27 Ibid.

28 Ibid., p. 84. On Vasari's *maniera tedesca*, cf. esp. Boase (1979), pp. 93ff.

29 Vasari, vol. I (1962), p. 90.

30 Ibid., p. 91.

31 On the 'Accademia del Disegno', cf. Sergio Rossi, *Dalle botteghe alle accademie. Realtà sociale e teorie artistiche a Firenze dal XIV al XVI secolo*, Milan, 1980, pp. 146ff. On the Academy's cultural function at large, cf. Spini (1976), pp. 62ff, 75ff. Cf. also the detailed study by Zygmunt Wazbinski, *L'Accademia Medicea del Disegno a Firenze nel Cinquecento*, 2 vols, Florence 1987.

32 Cf. esp. Spini (1976), introduction.

33 Benvenuto Cellini, 'Della architettura', in: *Cellini, La Vita, i trattati, i discorsi*, Rome 1967, pp. 565–70.

34 Giovanni Antonio Dosio, *Roma antica e i disegni di architettura agli Uffizi*, ed. Franco Borsi et al., Rome 1976, esp. pp. 109ff.

35 Pirro Ligorio, 'Il libro delle antichità di Roma' (mss in Naples, Oxford, Paris, Turin); cf. Erna Mandowski and Charles Mitchell, *Pirro Ligorio's Roman Antiquities*, London 1963.

36 Gherardo Spini, *'I tre primi libri sopra l'istituzioni de'Greci et latini architettori intorno agl'ornamenti che convengono a tutte le fabbriche che l'architettura compone'*, ed. Cristina Acidini, in: Franco Borsi et al., *Il disegno interrotto. Trattati medicei d'architettura*, 2 vols, Florence 1980, vol. I, pp. 11–201. Cf. esp. Wazbinski (1987), pp. 215ff.

37 Spini (1980), p. 33.

38 Roland Fréart de Chambray, *Parallèle de l'architecture antique et de la moderne*, Paris 1650.

39 Spini (1980), pp. 34, 58.

40 Ibid., p. 60.

41 Ibid., p. 73: '...*senz'il quale [decoro] ogni cosa dov'egli non si ritruova si rassomiglia ad un furruscito della sua patria che nell'altrui contrade con poca dignità dimori...*'

42 Ammannati's draft material is published in: Bartolomeo Ammannati, *La Città. Appunti per un trattato*, ed. Mazzino Fossi, Rome 1970.

43 Cf. *Giorgio Vasari il Giovane, La Città ideale. Piante di Chiese (palazzi e ville) di Toscana e d'Italia*, ed. Virginia Stefanelli, introduction by Franco Borsi, Rome 1970. Cf. also: Loredana Olivato, 'Giorgio Vasari il Giovane. Il funzionario del "Principe"', *L'Arte* 14, 1971, pp. 5–28; 'Giorgio Vasari il Giovane, Porte e finestre di Firenze e Roma', ed. Franco Borsi, in: Borsi et al. (eds), (1980), vol. I, pp. 293–321.

44 *Vasari il Giovane* (1970), p. 58.

45 Ibid., pp. 61ff.

46 Ibid., pp. 136f.

47 Gian Paolo Lomazzo, *Trattato dell'arte della pittura*, Milan 1584 (facs. repr. Hildesheim 1968); id., *Idea del tempio della pittura*, Milan 1590 (facs. repr. Hildesheim 1965). Cf. the critical ed. *Gian Paolo Lomazzo, Scritti sulle arti*, ed. Roberto Paolo Ciardi, 2 vols, Florence 1973, 1974.

On Lomazzo's theory of art, cf. esp. Panofsky (1960), pp. 53ff.; Gerald M. Ackerman, 'Lomazzo's Treatise on Painting', *The Art Bulletin* XLIX, 1967, pp. 317–26.

48 Lomazzo, *Trattato* (1584), ed. Ciardi, II, p. 21.

49 Ibid., pp. 71f.

[50] Ibid.

[51] Ibid., p. 91.

[52] The statues and minutes of the 'Accademia del Disegno' were published by the secretary of the Academy, Romano Alberti, under the title *Origine, et progresso dell' Academia del Disegno*, Pavia 1604 (facs. repr. Bologna 1978).

Federico Zuccaro's *L'idea de'pittori, scultori et architetti* was published in 1607 in Turin. The writings of Federico Zuccaro are now available in: Detlef Heikamp (ed.), *Scritti d'arte di Federico Zuccari*, Florence 1961.

On Zuccaro's theory of art, cf. esp. Panofsky (1960), pp. 47ff.; Blunt (1962), pp. 137ff.; Denis Mahon, *Studies in Seicento Art and Theory* (1947), repr. Westport, Conn. 1971, pp. 160ff.; Claudio Massimo Strinati, 'Studio sulla teorica d'arte primoseicentesca tra Manierismo e Barocco', *Storia dell'arte* 14, 1972, pp. 69ff.

[53] 'disegno interno, forma, idea, ordine, regola, termine, & oggetto dell'intelletto, in cui sono espresse le cose intese.' Federico Zuccaro, *L'idea* (1607), ed. Heikamp, 1961, p. 153.

[54] Ibid., p. 222.

[55] Ibid., pp. 249ff.

[56] Federico Zuccaro–Romano Alberti, *Origine* (1604), ed. Heikamp, 1971, pp. 46ff.

[57] Tommaso Campanella, *La Città del Sole* (1602), in: *Scritti scelti di Giordano Bruno e Tommaso Campanella*, ed. Luigi Firpo, Turin ²1968, pp. 405–63.

On Campanella, cf. Gisela Bock, *Thomas Campanella. Politisches Interesse und philosophische Spekulation*, Tübingen 1974 (with bibliography).

[58] Cf. on Ludovico Agostini and the relationship between his ideas and those of Campanella: Luigi Firpo, *Lo Stato ideale della Controriforma*, Bari 1957.

[59] Cf. Gisela Bock (1974), pp. 160ff.

[60] 'Sopra l'altare non v'ha che due globi, dei quali il più grande porta dipinto tutto il cielo, il secondo la terra. Nell'area poi della volta principale stanno dipinte le stelle del cielo, dalla prima alla sesta grandezza, segnata ciascuna col proprio nome; e tre sottoposti versetti appalesano quale influenza ogni stella eserciti su le vicende terrestri.' Campanella, *La Città del Sole*, 1602.

[61] Ibid.

[62] 'V'ha maestri che spiegano questi dipinti, ed avvezzano i fanciulli ad imparare senza

fatica, e quasi a modo di divertimento, tutte le scienze, pero con metodo istorico, avanti il decimo anno.' Ibid.

[63] Cf. Hans-Jürgen Drengenberg, *Die sowjetische Politik auf dem Gebiet der bildenden Kunst von 1917 bis 1934 (Forschungen zur osteuropäischen Geschichte)*, Berlin 1972, p. 186.

[64] On Scamozzi, see esp. Richard Kurt Donin, *Vincenzo Scamozzi und der Einfluß Venedigs auf die Salzburger Architektur*, Innsbruck 1948; Franco Barbieri, *Vincenzo Scamozzi*, Vicenza 1952; Giangiorgio Zorzi, 'La giovinezza di Vincenzo Scamozzi secondo nuovi documenti I', *Arte Veneta* X, 1956, pp. 119–32; Vincenzo Scamozzi, *Taccuino di viaggio da Parigi a Venezia (14 marzo–11 maggio 1600)*, ed. Franco Barbieri, Venice–Rome 1959; Carmine Jannaco, 'Barocco e razionalismo nel trattato d'architettura di Vincenzo Scamozzi (1615)', *Studi Seicenteschi*, 1961, pp. 47–60; Lionello Puppi, 'Vincenzo Scamozzi trattatista nell'ambito della problematica del manierismo', *Bollettino del Centro Internazionale di Studi d'Architettura (CISA)* IX, 1967, pp. 310–29. Cf. bibliography in: Ciro Luigi Anzivino, *Jacopo Barozzi il Vignola e gli architetti italiani del Cinquecento. Repertorio Bibliografico*, Vignola 1974, pp. 185ff.

[65] Vincenzo Scamozzi, *L'idea della architettura universale*, Venice 1615 (facs. repr. Ridgewood, NJ 1964; Bologna 1982), Proemio to Part I, Book I, p. 4. On Paolo Gualdo's introduction to Scamozzi's *Idea*, which did not ultimately appear with the book, cf. Lionello Puppi, 'Sulle relazioni culturali di Vincenzo Scamozzi', *Ateneo Veneto*, N.S., 1969, pp. 49–66; Gualdo's text is published as an appendix to this article, and also in: Puppi, *Scrittori vicentini d'architettura del secolo XVI*, Vicenza 1973, pp. 108ff. On later editions of Scamozzi's *Idea*, cf. exhib. cats. *Theorie der Architektur* (Stiftsbibliothek) Göttweig 1975, p. 33, and *Architettura e Utopia nella Venezia del Cinquecento*, Milan 1980, p. 182, cat. no. 184.

[66] The authorship of the *Indice copiosissimo* and of the *Discorso* is in dispute as between Gian Domenico and Vincenzo Scamozzi. For a summary of the arguments, cf. Lionello Puppi, *Scrittori vicentini* (1973), pp. 97ff. (with the text of the *Discorso*).

It is probable that Gian Domenico had written the *Discorso* and begun preparation of the index by the time of his death, and that his son Vincenzo finished the index; this would appear to be the case, at any rate, from the headings over the index and the *Discorso*; cf. Sebastiano Serlio, *Tutte l'opere d'architettura*, Venice 1619 (facs. repr. 1964), index and *Discorso* (unpaginated).

[67] Scamozzi (1615), *Proemio*, Part I, Book I, p. 4.

[68] Ibid.

[69] Ibid., Part I, Book I, pp. 5f.

[70] Ibid., p. 8.

[71] Ibid., p. 10.

[72] Ibid., p. 17.

[73] Ibid., p. 18.

[74] Ibid., Part I, Book III, pp. 266ff.; Pliny the Younger describes the Laurentinum (II.17) and the Tuscium (V.6) in his letters.

[75] On the reconstructions of Pliny's villas, cf. Helen H. Tanzer, *The Villas of Pliny the Younger*, New York 1924; Marianne Fischer, *Die frühen Rekonstruktionen der Landhäuser Plinius' des Jüngeren*, diss., Berlin 1962.

[76] 'e perciò si vede quanta Giometria ha in se il corpo humano.' Scamozzi (1615), Book I, Part I, p. 38.

[77] Ibid., p. 41.

[78] Ibid., p. 42. Scamozzi's definition of the idea reads (p. 47): 'Il pensiero nella Idea dell' Architetto... non è altro che un desiderio, & una cura di studio, piena d'industria, e vigilantia, & uno effetto proposto nella mente, accompagnato con grandissimo desiderio di ritrovarne la certezza.'

[79] Ibid., p. 46.

[80] Ibid., Part I, Book II, p. 100.

[81] Ibid., p. 105.

[82] Cf. Horst de la Croix, 'Palmanova. A study in sixteenth century urbanism', in: *Saggi e memorie di storia dell'arte*, vol. 5, 1967, pp. 23–41.

[83] Scamozzi (1615), Part I, Book II, pp. 164ff.

[84] Cf. the radial system in Girolamo Maggi and Giacomo Castriotto, *Della fortificatione libri tre*, Venice 1564, fol. 52v. Scamozzi's direct specifications for Palmanova (1615), pp. 206ff.

[85] Scamozzi (1615), Part I, Book III, pp. 226ff.; Palladio, *Quattro libri* (1570), Book II, pp. 43f.

[86] Scamozzi (1615), Part II, Book VI, p. 1.

[87] Ibid., pp. 15ff.

[88] Ibid., p. 4.

[89] A German translation of excerpts from Books III and VI appeared under the title *Grundregeln der Bau-Kunst oder klärliche Beschreibung der fünf Säulen-Ordnungen und der gantzen Architektur*, Nuremberg 1678 (thus on the frontispiece, but on the title-page the date of publication is given as 1697).

[90] Vincenzo Scamozzi, *Les cinq ordres d'architecture... Tirez du sixième Livre de son Idée générale d'architecture*, ed. Charles-Augustin d'Aviler, Paris 1685.

[91] Scamozzi (1615), Part II, Book VII, p. 174.

[92] 'Non è molto lodevole cosa, che l'Architetto tenti di far come violenza alla materia: in modo che egli pensi di ridur sempre à voler suo le cose create dalla Natura, per volerle dare quelle forme, che egli vole...' Ibid.

[93] Scamozzi (1615), Part II, Book VII, p. 176.

[94] Cf. Scamozzi, ed. Barbieri (1959).

[95] Cf. ibid. Cf. Rudolf Wittkower, *Gothic versus Classic*, New York 1974, pp. 85ff.

[96] Scamozzi, ed. Barbieri (1959), p. 41.

[97] Scamozzi (1615), Part I, *Proemio*, p. 1.

[98] Cf. esp. Denis Mahon, *Studies in Seicento Art and Theory* (1947), repr. Westport, CT 1971.

[99] Giovanni Pietro Bellori, *Le vite de'pittori, scultori e architetti moderni*, Rome 1672 (ed. Eugenio Battisti, in: *Quaderni dell'Istituto di Storia dell'arte della Università di Genova*, N. 4, Genoa 1967; crit. ed. Evelina Borea, Turin 1976). On Bellori see esp. Panofsky (1960), pp. 59ff.; Ferruccio Ulivi, *Galleria di scrittori d'arte*, Florence 1953, pp. 165ff.; Anna Pallucchini, 'Per una situazione storica di Giovan Pietro Bellori', *Storia dell'arte* 12, 1971, pp. 285–95.

[100] 'Quel sommo, ed eterno intelletto autore della natura nel fabbricare l'opere sue maravigliose altamente in se stesso riguardando, costituì le prime forme chiamate idee; in modo che ciascuna specie espressa fù da quella prima idea, formandosene il mirabile contesto delle cose create. Ma li celesti corpi sopra la luna non sottoposti a cangiamento, restarono per sempre belli, & ordinati, qualmente dalle misurate sfere, e dallo splendore de gli aspetto loro veniamo a conoscerli perpetuamente giustissimi, e vaghissimi. Al contrario avviene de'corpi sublunari soggetti alle alterazioni, & alla brutezza...' Bellori (1672), ed. Battisti (1967), p. 19.

[101] Ibid., p. 26.

[102] 'Quanto l'Architettura, diciamo che l'Architetto deve concepire una nobile Idea, e stabiliarsi una mente, che gli serva di legge e di ragione, consistento le sue inventioni nell'ordine, nella dispositione, e nella misura, ed euritimia del tutto e delle parti. Ma rispetto la decoratione, & ornamenti de gli ordini sia certo trovarsi l'Idea stabilita, e confermata sù gli essempi de gli Antichi, che con successo di lungo studio, diedero modo à quest'arte; quando li Greci le costituirono termini, e proportioni le migliori, le quali confermate da i più dotti secoli, e dal consenso, e successione de'Sapienti, divvennero leggi di una meravigliosa Idea, e bellezza ultima, che essendo una sola in ciascuna specie, non si può alterare, senza distruggerla.' Ibid., p. 29.

[103] 'Tanto che deformando gli edifici, e le città istesse, e le memorie, freneticano angoli, spezzature, e distorcimenti di linee, scompongono basi, capitelli e colonne, con frottole di stucchi, tritumi, e sproportioni; e pure Vitruvio condanna simil novità...' Ibid., p. 30.

[104] Ibid., p. 21.

[105] Cf. Panofsky (1960), p. 62.

[106] Vincenzo Giustiniani, Discorsi sulle arti e sui mestieri, ed. Anna Banti, Florence 1981, pp. 47–62 (first published in: Giov. Gaet. Bottari, Raccolta di lettere sulla Pittura, Scultura ed Architettura... dei secoli XV, XVI e XVII, 7 vols, Rome 1754–73; ed. Stef. Ticozzi, 8 vols, Milan 1822–25.

[107] Giustiniani (ed. 1981), p. 55.

[108] Ibid., p. 59.

[109] Teofilo Gallaccini, Trattato sopra gli errori degli architetti, with a biographical introduction by Giovanni Antonio Pecci, Venice 1767 (facs. repr. 1970); the manuscript of the treatise is in the British Library; for the differences between manuscript and printed form, and an assessment of Gallaccini's theoretical position, cf. Eugenio Battisti, ' "Sopra gli errori degli architetti" di Teofilo Gallaccini al British Museum di Londra', Bollettino del Centro di Studi per la Storia dell'Architettura 14, 1959, pp. 28–38; for the publication of a travel sketch-book dating from 1610, cf. Giuseppe M. Della Fina, 'Un taccuino di viaggio di Teofilo Gallaccini (1610)', Prospettiva 24, January 1981, pp. 41–51.

[110] Gallaccini (1767), p. 3.

[111] Ibid., p. 22.

[112] Ibid., p. 32.

[113] Ibid., p. 53.

[114] 'poichè dove non si osserva ordine, quivi è confusione, e dove è confusione, ivi è deformità, ed ove questa si vede, non regna perfezione alcuna.' Ibid., p. 56.

[115] Cf. the comparisons with the originals by Battisti (1959).

[116] Antonio Visentini, Osservazioni, che servono di continuazione al trattato di Teofilo Gallaccini sopra gli errori degli architetti, Venice 1771 (facs. ed. 1970). Visentini was primarily an architectural draughtsman. His drawings reached England through Consul Joseph Smith; cf. John McAndrew, Catalogue of the Drawings Collection of the Royal Institute of British Architects: Antonio Visentini, Farnborough 1974, pp. 7ff.

[117] Visentini (1771), pp. 137ff.

[118] Pietro Antonio Barca, Avvertimenti e regole cira l'architettura civile, Scultura, Pittura, Prospettiva e Architettura militare, Milan 1620.

Gioseffe Viola Zanini, Della architettura libri due, Padua 1629 (1677, 1698).

Giovanni Branca, Manuale d'Architettura, breve, e risoluta Pratica, diviso in sei libri, Ascoli 1629 (Rome 1718, 1757, 1772, 1781, 1783, 1784, 1786).

Carlo Cesaro Osio, Architettura civile dimostrativamente proporzionata e accresciuta..., Milan 1641 (1661, 1686).

Costanzo Amichevoli, Architettura civil ridotta a metodo facile e breve, Turin 1675.

Alessandro Capra, La nuova Architettura civile e militare, Bologna 1678 (Cremona 1717).

[119] Giov. Branca (1629), cited from ed. of 1772, p. XXIII.

[120] Capra (1678), cited from ed. of 1717, Al Lettore.

[121] Giovanni Domenico Ottonelli and Pietro Berrettini, Trattato della pittura, e scultura, uso, et abuso loro..., Florence 1652; ed. Vittorio Casale, Treviso 1973; Vittorio Casale, 'Trattato della pittura e scultura "opera stampata ad instanza del S. r Pietro da Cortona", Paragone 313, 1976, pp. 67–99 (with documentation of Jesuit censorship of the work).

[122] Cf. Karl Noehles, La Chiesa dei SS. Luca e Martina nell'opera di Pietro da Cortona, Rome 1970.

[123] 'et que l'architecture consistait en proposition tirèe du corps de l'homme; que c'est la raison pourquoi les sculpteurs et les peintres réuississent plutôt en architecture que d'autres, d'autant que ceux-là étudient incessamment après la figure de l'homme.' M. de Chantelou, *Journal du voyage du Cav. Bernini en France*, German ed. Munich 1919, p. 36. On Bernini's architectural ideas, cf. Rudolf Wittkower, 'A counter-project to Bernini's "Piazza di San Pietro", *Journal of the Warburg and Courtauld Institutes* III, 1939–40, pp. 88–106; Georg Charles Bauer, 'Gian Lorenzo Bernini: The Development of an Architectural Iconography', PhD thesis, Princeton 1974 (ms); Hanno-Walter Kruft, 'The Origin of the Oval in Bernini's Piazza S. Pietro', *The Burlington Magazine* CXXI, 1979, pp. 796–801.

[124] Francesco Borromini, *La Chiesa e Fabrica della Sapienza di Roma*, ed. Sebastiano Giannini, Rome 1720 (facs. repr.: ed. Alessandro Martini, n.p., n.d.); Francesco Borromini, *Opus Architectonicum (Opera... cavata da' suoi originali cioè L'Oratorio, e Fabrica per l'Abitazione De PP. dell'Oratorio di S. Filippo Neri di Roma...*, Rome 1725 (ed. Paolo Portoghesi, Rome 1964). On the *Opus Architectonicum*, cf. introduction by Portoghesi entitled 'L'Opus Architectonicum del Borromini' in: *Essays in the History of Architecture Presented to Rudolf Wittkower*, London 1967, pp. 128–133.

[125] Borromini, *Opus Architectonicum*, ed. Portoghesi (1964), dedication, p. 24.

[126] Ibid., p. 38.

[127] Ibid.

[128] Almost all Giovanni Battista Montano's publications were posthumous. They are collected in: *Le cinque libri di architettura*, Rome 1691.

On Montano, cf. esp. Giuseppe Zander, 'Le invenzioni architettoniche di Giovanni Battista Montano Milanese (1534–1621)', *Quaderni dell'Istituto di Storia dell'Architettura* 30, 1958, pp. 1–21 (pp. 18f. n. 1 lists all Montano's publications), 49–50, 1962, pp. 1–32. On the relationship with Borromini, cf. Zander (1962), pp. 26ff.; Anthony Blunt in: *Studies in Western Art. Acts of the Twentieth International Congress of the History of Art*, vol. III, Princeton 1963, pp. 7ff.; id., *Borromini*, London 1979, pp. 41ff.

[129] Blunt (1979), p. 44 shows that Montano's approach in his reconstruction of an

Antique Roman building is still in the manner of an inverted telescope, while Borromini is the first to exploit the gain in depth of the optical field for perspective effect in the colonnade of the Palazzo Spada.

[130] Cf. esp. Paolo Portoghesi, *Guarino Guarini*, Milan 1956; Rudolf Wittkower, *Art and Architecture in Italy 1600 to 1750*, Harmondsworth ([1]1958), [2]1965, pp. 268ff.; Werner Hager, 'Guarini. Zur Kennzeichnung seiner Architektur', *Miscellanea Bibliothecae Hertziane*, Munich 1961, pp. 418–28; congress proceedings *Guarino Guarini e l'internazionalità del Barocco*, 2 vols, Turin 1970; Claudia Müller, *Unendlichkeit und Transzendenz in der Sakralarchitektur Guarinis*, Hildesheim–Zürich–New York 1986; H.A. Meek, *Guarino Guarini and his architecture*, New Haven–London 1988.

[131] Guarino Guarini, *Trattato di fortificazione che hora si usa in Fiandra, Francia, e Italia...*, Turin 1676; cf. Gianni Carlo Sciolla in: congress proceedings *Guarini* (1970), vol. I, pp. 513–29.

[132] Dissegni d'architettura civile et ecclesiastica inventati, e delineati dal padre D. Guarino Garini modenese..., Turin 1686 (printed as an appendix in: Bernardi Ferrero, *I 'Disegni d'architettura civile et ecclesiastica' di Guarino Guarini*, Turin 1966).

[133] Juan Caramuel de Lobkowitz, *Architectura civil recta, y obliqua, considerada y dibuxada en el Templo de Jerusalem...*, 3 vols, Vigevano 1678; on the Caramuel-Guarini relationship, cf. Daria De Bernardi Ferrero (1966), pp. 37ff.; Werner Oechslin, 'Bemerkungen zu Guarino Guarini und Juan Caramuel de Lobkowitz', *Raggi* 8, Heft 1, 1968, pp. 91–109.

[134] Guarini, ed. Nino Carboneri and Bianca Tavassi La Greca, Milan 1968, p. 10.

[135] Roland Fréart de Chambray, *Parallèle de l'architecture antique et de la moderne*, Paris 1650, p. 7. This similarity is not perceived by Carboneri-Tavassi La Greca (1968), p. 10 n. 2.

[136] Guarini, ed. Carboneri–Tavassi La Greca (1968), p. 8.

[137] Ibid., p. 9.

[138] Ibid., p. 11.

[139] Ibid., p. 15f.

[140] Ibid., p. 17ff.

[141] 'Onde vediamo ancora che i pittori e gli scultori fanno le immagini e le statue rozze de lantono, e solamente quasi sbozzate,

apparendo meglio cosi imperfette, che total-mente finite.' Ibid., p. 18.

[142] Ibid., pp. 21ff.

[143] Cf. Werner Müller, 'The Authenticity of Guarini's Stereotomy in his "Architettura Civile", *Journal of the Society of Architectural Historians* XXVII, 1968, pp. 202–08.

[144] Guarini, ed. Carboneri–Tavassi La Greca (1968), p. 102.

[145] Ibid., p. 110.

[146] Ibid., p. 127.

[147] Ibid., pp. 207ff.

[148] Ibid., p. 208.

[149] Ibid., pp. 208f. On the relationship of Guarini's work to Gothic and Islamic architecture in Spain, cf. Wittkower (1965), p. 274.

[150] Guarini, ed. Carboneri–Tavassi La Greca (1968), p. 207.

[151] Ibid., p. 209.

[152] On Guarini's role in the understanding of Gothic, cf. esp. Rudolf Wittkower, *Gothic versus Classic*, New York 1974, p. 92; Georg Germann, *Neugotik*, Stuttgart 1974, pp. 15f.

[153] Guarini, ed. Carboneri–Tavassi La Greca (1968), pp. 216f.

[154] Ibid., pp. 175f.

[155] On this link cf. the masterly article by Juan Antonio Ramirez, 'Guarino Guarini, Fray Juan Ricci and the "Complete Salomonic Order", *Art History* 4, 1981, pp. 175–85.

[156] Guarini (1968); cf. appendix by Bianca Tavassi La Greca, pp. 439ff.

[157] Andrea Pozzo, *Perspectiva Pictorum et Architectorum*, Rome 1693, 1698; Latin-German ed., *Perspectivae pictorumque atque architectorum*, Part I, ed. Johann Boxbarth, Augsburg 1708; Part II, ed. Georg Conrad Bodeneer, Augsburg 1711; a survey of editions and translations of Pozzo, Luigi Vagnetti, 'De naturali et artificiali perspectiva', *Studie e documenti di architettura* 9–10, 1979, pp. 416f.; ed. used, vol. I, Rome 1717; vol. II, Rome 1700.

On Pozzo see esp. Nino Carboneri, *Andrea Pozzo Architetto*, Trento 1961; Bernhard Kerber, *Andrea Pozzo*, Berlin–New York 1971; Vittorio de Feo, 'L'Architettura immaginata di Andrea Pozzo gesuita', *Rassegna di Architettura e Urbanistica* XVI, April 1980, pp. 79–109.

[158] Pozzo, vol. I (ed. 1717), *Avvisi a principianti*.

[159] Pozzo, vol. II (ed. 1700), pp. 63ff.

[160] Domenico de' Rossi, *Studio d'architettura civile...*, 3 vols, Rome 1708, 1711, 1721 (also: *Disegni di vari altari e cappelle nelle Chiese di Roma...*, Rome n.d., probably 1713); facs. repr. of all vols with introduction by Anthony Blunt, 1972.

9. The theory of fortification

[1] On the history and theory of military architecture cf. Max Jähns, *Geschichte der Kriegswissenschaften, vornehmlich in Deutschland*, 3 vols, Munich and Leipzig 1889–91; Enrico Rocchi, *Le fonti storiche dell'architettura militare*, Rome 1908; H. Delbrück, *Geschichte der Kriegskunst*, Berlin 1920; L. A. Maggiorotti, *Architetti e architettura militare*, Rome 1935; Sidney Toy, *A History of Fortification from 3000 B.C. to A.D. 1700*, London 1955 ('1966); Horst De la Croix, 'Military Architecture and the Radial City Plan in Sixteenth Century Italy', *The Art Bulletin* XLII, 1960, pp. 263–90; id., 'The Literature on Fortification in Renaissance Italy', *Technology and Culture* IV, 1, 1963, pp. 30–50; id., *Military Considerations in City Planning: Fortifications*, New York 1972; Paolo Marconi et al., *La città come forma simbolica. Studi sulla teoria dell'architettura nel Rinascimento*, Rome 1973; Quentin Hughes, *Military Architecture*, London 1974; J.R. Hale, *Renaissance Fortification. Art or Engineering?*, London 1977; Rudolf Huber and Renate Rieth (eds), *Festungen. Der Wehrbau nach Einführung der Feuerwaffen* (*Glossarium Artis*, vol. 7), Tübingen 1979 (containing explanations of terminology and a good bibliography, pp. 215ff.).

[2] Cf. Jähns (1889).

[3] Cf. esp. the works by De la Croix, Marconi and Hale.

[4] Flavius Vegetius Renatus, *Epitoma rei militaris* (c.400), ed. C. Lang, ²1885 (facs. ed. 1967). On the content and diffusion of this work, cf. Jähns, vol. I (1889), pp. 109ff.

[5] Roberto Valturio, *De re militari libri XII*, Verona 1472 (numerous editions and translations in the fifteenth and sixteenth centuries); cf. Jähns, vol. I (1889), pp. 358ff.

[6] Cf. note 49 to Chapter 4 of the present volume.

[7] Vgl. Jähns, vol. I (1889), pp. 278f.; the

Florence Ms. Pal. 766 is available in facs. repr. ed. J. H. Beck, *Mariano di Jacopo detto il Taccola. Liber tertius de Ingeneis ac Edificiis non usitatis*, Milan 1969 (with transcription of the Latin text); on the same ms., cf. Frank D. Prager and Gustina Scaglia, *Mariano Taccola and his Book 'De Ingeneis'*, Cambridge, Mass.-London 1972; the Munich Cod. lat. 28800 is available in facs. ed. Gustina Scaglia: Mariano Taccola, *De Machinis. The Engineering Treatise of 1449*, 2 vols, Wiesbaden 1971; an ed. of Cod. lat. Mon. 197, ed. Gustina Scaglia and Ulrich Montag, is announced; for a reconstruction of the original sequence of the manuscripts, cf. esp. Bernhard Degenhart and Annegrit Schmitt, *Corpus der italienischen Zeichnungen 1300–1450*, Part II, vol. 4; *Mariano Taccola*, Berlin 1982.
[8] Giovan Battista della Valle di Venafro, *Vallo. Libro continente appartenentie ad Capitanij: retenere et fortificare una Cita con Bastioni, artificj de fuoco...*, Naples 1521; cf. Jähns, vol. I (1889), pp. 776ff.
[9] Niccolò Machiavelli, *Dell'arte della guerra*, Florence 1521; cf. ed. Sergio Bertelli, Niccolò Machiavelli, *Arte della guerra e scritti politici minori*, Milan 1961.
[10] Cf. A. Burd, *The Literary Sources of Machiavelli's 'Arte della guerra'*, Oxford 1891.
[11] Albrecht Dürer, *Etliche underricht, zu befestigung der Stett, Schloß, und flecken*, Nuremberg 1527 (facs. repr., Unterschneidheim 1969). Lat. ed. Paris 1535.
On Dürer's preparatory material, cf. Hans Rupprich, *Dürers schriftlicher Nachlaß*, vol. III, Berlin 1969, pp. 371ff.
Cf. also Jähns, vol. I (1889), pp. 783ff.; Wilhelm Waetzoldt, *Dürers Befestigungslehre*, Berlin 1916; Alexander von Reitzenstein, 'Etliche underricht... Albrecht Dürers Befestigungslehre', in: *Albrecht Dürers Umwelt. Festschrift zum 500. Geburtstag Albrecht Dürers am 21. Mai 1971* (= *Nürnberger Forschungen*, 15), Nuremberg 1971, pp. 178–92; id. in exhib. cat. (Germanisches Nationalmuseum, Nuremberg) *Albrecht Dürer 1471–1971*, Munich 1971, pp. 355ff.
[12] Dürer (1527), fol. D.
[13] Ibid., fol. Dv.
[14] '*Der König sol nicht unnütze leut in disem schloß wonen lassen, sunder geschickte, frumme, weyse, manliche, erfarne, kunstreyche menner, gut handwercks leut di zum*

schloß düglich sind, püchsengiesser und gute schützen.' Ibid., fol. D II v.
[15] Ibid., fol. A II v.
[16] Cf. Myra Nan Rosenfeld, *Sebastiano Serlio on Domestic Architecture*, New York 1978, pp. 35ff.
[17] Hernando Cortés, *Praeclara de Nova maris Oceani Hyspania Narratio*, Nuremberg 1524; cf. E. W. Palm, 'Tenochtitlan y la Ciudad ideal de Dürer', *Journal de la Société des Américanistes*, n.s. XL, 1951, pp. 59–66.
[18] Paul Zucker, *Town and Square* (1959), Cambridge, Mass.-London 1970, pp. 120ff.; Hermann Bauer, *Kunst und Utopie*, Berlin 1965, p. 100; contradicted by Reitzenstein (1971), p. 186.
There is a striking parallel between Dürer's ideal city and south American town plans as definitively set down in the *Leyes de las Indias* (1573); cf. Wolfgang W. Wurster, 'Kolonialer Städtebau in Iberoamerika – Eine Zusammenfassung', *Architectura* 12, 1982, pp. 1–19, esp. pp. 4ff.
[19] On the design of Freudenstadt, cf. the account by Schickhardt himself in: Wilhelm Heyd, *Handschriften und Handzeichnungen des herzoglich württembergischen Baumeisters Heinrich Schickhardt*, Stuttgart 1902, pp. 346f.; cf. also Julius Baum, *Heinrich Schickhardt*, Strassburg 1916, pp. 17ff. (the connection with Dürer goes unnoticed by Baum); cf. also the volume on 'Herzog Friedrichs Freudenstadt im ersten Jahrhundert seiner Geschichte', *Freudenstädter Beiträge* 6, 1987; Hanno-Walter Kruft, *Städte in Utopia*, Munich 1989, pp. 68ff.
[20] Cf. John Archer, 'Puritan Town Planning in New Haven', *Journal of the Society of Architectural Historians* XXXIV, 1975, pp. 140–49.
[21] Nicolo Tartaglia, *La Nova Scientia*, Venice 1537 (repr. by the author, Venice 1550); id., *Quesiti et inventioni diverse*, Venice 1538 (repr. by the author, Venice 1554); cf. Jähns, vol. I (1889), pp. 596ff.
[22] The name is variously spelt as Bellucci, Beluzzi, Belici, etc. Cf. esp. Horst De la Croix (1960), p. 274; Daniela Lamberini (ed.), 'Giovanni Battista Belluzzi, Il Trattato delle fortificazioni di terra', in: Franco Borsi et al., *Il Disegno interrotto. Trattati medicei d'architettura*, Florence 1980, pp. 373ff.
[23] Giovan Battista Belici, *Nuova inventione di*

fabricar fortezze, di varie forme..., Venice 1598.

24 Giovanni Battista Belluzzi, *Diario autobiografico (1535–1541)*, ed. Pietro Egidi, Naples 1907 (facs. repr. Bologna 1975).

25 Ed. Daniela Lamberini (1980), pp. 421ff.

26 Bellucci, ed. Lamberini (1980), p. 422.

27 Ibid., p. 421.

28 Bellucci (Belici) (1598), Kap. I.

29 Ibid., Kap. XXIII.

30 Giovanni Battista Zanchi, *Del modo di fortificar le città*, Venice 1554.

31 François de la Treille, *La manière de fortifier villes, Chasteaux, et faire autres lieux fortz*, Lyons 1556.

32 Robert Corneweyle, *The Maner of Fortificacion of Cities, Townes, Castelles and Other Places* (1559; ms., British Library, Additional M.S. 28030), ed. Martin Biddle, Richmond, Surrey 1972.

33 Cf. Chapter 6 of the present volume.

34 Cf. Luigi Marini (ed.), 'Francesco de Marchi', *Architettura militare*, Rome 1810, vol. I, pp. 1ff.; Carlo Promis, 'Gl'ingegneri e gli scrittori militari bolognesi del XV e XVI secolo', *Miscellanea di Storia Italiana* IV, 1863, pp. 56–92; Jähns, vol. I (1889), pp. 803ff.; De la Croix (1960), pp. 278, 285ff.

35 Francesco de Marchi, *Della Architettura militare libri tre*, Brescia 1599, fol. 44v, 256.

36 Cf. note 35 above. This edition is comparatively rare (I have used that in the Hessische Landesbibliothek Darmstadt, gr. Fol. 1/169). A lavish reissue: Luigi Marini (ed.), Francesco de' Marchi, *Architettura militare*, 6 vols, Rome 1810; the plates in this edition have been reworked by Marini and are of limited value.

37 Bologna, Bibl. Comun. dell Archiginnasio Ms. B. 1566; de Marchi's copy dates from 1555; cf. Daniela Lamberini (1980), pp. 406ff.

38 De Marchi (1599), 'A'lettori', fol. 1.

39 Ibid., fol. 5v.

40 'Però li valenti, & ingeniosi Soldati, & Architetti, potranno in simil sito far cose inespugnabili, & belle, per la commodità del sito, che ubidirà all' arte, posta in essecutione da valent' huomo ingenioso.' Ibid., fol. 6v.

41 Ibid.

42 'Però anchora senza lettere, con un'amore e dilettatione e longa esperienza si può scrivere di buone cose e sinceramente senza sofisticatione come ho fatto io.' Ibid., fol. 29.

43 Ibid., fol. 252ff. (*pianta CL*). This plan has hitherto been left out of consideration in the study of the history of Valletta. Cf. esp. Quentin Hughes, *The Building in Malta during the period of the Knights of St. John of Jerusalem 1530–1795* (1956), London ²1967, pp. 20ff.; id., *Fortress. Architecture and Military History in Malta*, London 1969, pp. 51ff.; *Atti del XV Congresso di Storia dell'Architettura. L'architettura a Malta dalla preistoria all'Ottocento* (1967), Rome 1970; Alison Hoppen, *The Fortification of Malta by the Order of St John 1530–1798*, Edinburgh 1979. In the edition of de Marchi's treatise available to me, Plan LXXVIII was replaced by a detailed map of the Turkish siege of Malta in 1565. Cf. also Hanno-Walter Kruft, 'Reflexe auf die Türkenbelagerung Maltas (1565) in der Festungsliteratur', *Architectura* 12, 1982, pp. 34–40; id., *Städte in Utopia*, Munich 1989, pp. 52ff.

44 De Marchi (1599), pp. 133ff.

45 Ibid., fol. 44v.

46 Girolamo Maggi and Jacomo Castriotto, *Della Fortificatione della Citta... libri tre*, Venice 1564.

47 Cf. De la Croix (1960), pp. 278f.

48 Castriotto describes Bellucci as '*già mio amicissimo*' (Maggi and Castriotto, 1564, fol. 138v).

49 Ibid., fol. 7v.

50 Ibid., fol. 22v, 73f.

51 Ibid., fol. 18ff.

52 Ibid., 51vff.

53 Ibid., fol. 76.

54 Ibid., fol. 92vff.

55 Francesco Montemellino on the fortification of the Borgo in Rome; Giocchino da Coniano on battle formations; Castriotto on fortifications in France, etc.

56 Cf. esp. Jähns, vol. I (1889); De la Croix (1963), pp. 48ff (bibliography).

57 Galasso Alghisi, *Delle fortificazione... libri tre*, Venice 1570.

58 'Perche tutte le fabbriche non sono altro, che dissegno con Architettura, Arithmetica, Geometria & Perspettiva composte.' Ibid., p. 36.

59 (Galeazzo Alessi), 'Libro di Fortificatione in modo di Compendio...', Ms., Modena, Biblioteca Estense, Fondo Campori (γ.L.11.1); cf. Gianni Baldini, 'Un ignoto manoscritto d'architettura militare autografo di Galeazzo Alessi', *Mitteilungen des*

Kunsthistorischen Instituts in Florenz XXV, 1981, pp. 253–78.

[60] Cf. esp. De la Croix (1960), pp. 275ff.

[61] Bonaiuto Lorini, *Della fortificationi libri cinque*, Venice 1592; thus the date of the first edition according to Jähns, vol. I (1889), p. 845. De la Croix gives both 1596 and 1597 for the date of the first edition. The edition here used is *Le fortificationi ... nuovamente ristampate ... con l'aggiunta del sesto libro*, Venice 1609, pp. 52ff.

[62] On Palmanova, see esp. Horst De la Croix, 'Palmanova: A Study in Sixteenth Century Urbanism', in: *Saggi e memorie di Storia dell'Arte* 5, 1967, pp. 25–41; Piero Damiani et al., Palmanova, 3 vols, Istituto Italiano dei Castelli. Sez. Friuli Venezia Giulia, 1982; on the participation of Vincenzo Scamozzi, cf. my conjecture offered on page 100.

[63] Pietro Sardi, *La corona imperiale dell'architettura militare*, Venice 1618; I have used the edition: *Corno Dogale Della Architettura Militare*, Venice 1639, p. 1.

[64] E.g. in Francesco Tensini, *La fortificazione, guardia difesa et espugnazione delle fortezze esperimentata in diverse guerre*, Venice 1624.

[65] Cf. Jähns, vol. I (1889).

[66] Jähns, vol. I (1889), pp. 822ff.

[67] Daniel Speckle, *Architectura von Vestungen, wie die zu unsern zeiten mögen erbawen werden, an Stätten Schlößern, und Clussen zu Wasser, Land*, etc., Strassburg 1589 (facs. repr.: Unterschneidheim 1971; Portland, OR 1972; a new edition, with posthumous material and a rhymed biography added by his brother-in-law, the publisher Lazarus Zetzner, appeared in Strassburg in 1599 (reprinted Strassburg 1608, the edition used here); further editions: Dresden 1705, 1712, 1736.

[68] Speckle (1608), fol. III.

[69] Ibid., fol. IIv.

[70] Ibid., fol. IVr and v.

[71] Ibid., fol. 57vff.

[72] Ibid., fol. 59.

[73] Ibid., fol. 61.

[74] 'Wohmüglichen sollen alle Häuser von puren Steinen und zum wenigsten die undern Gemach und zimmer, auch die Keller alle Gewölbt, und alle Häuser in gleicher schnur ebne, auch hohe und alle Dächer von Ziglen und nicht von Holtz bedeckt. Die undern Fenster alle vergettert, mit starcken thüren versehen, und alle Gassen gepflästert sein, auff das, da ein Feind eine solche Vestung schon einneme, man sich auß allen Häusern mit schiessen und werffen wehren könne.' Ibid., fol. 59.

[75] Ibid., fol. 82vff. Speckle's description has hitherto been neglected in studies of the rebuilding of Valletta. On this subject, cf. esp. *Atti del XV Congresso di Storia dell' Architettura. L'architettura a Malta dalla preistoria all'Ottocento* (1967), Rome 1970; Kruft (1982, 1989).

[76] Speckle (1608), fols 87vff.; engraving no. 4 within the plate is signed by Matthäus Greuter.

[77] Ibid., fol. 89.

[78] Cf. Jähns, vol. I (1889), pp. 831ff.

[79] Jean Errard (de Bar-le-Duc), *La Fortification reduicte en art et demonstrée*, Paris 1600 (further eds: 1604, 1620; German trans: Frankfurt 1604); cf. Jähns, vol. I (1889), pp. 832ff.

[80] Claude Flamand, *Le guide des Fortifications et conduite militaire pour bien se difendre*, Montbéliard (Mömpelgard) 1597 (2nd ed. 1611; German trans. Basel 1612); cf. Jähns, vol. I (1889), pp. 835ff.

[81] Jacques Perret, *Des fortifications et artifices d'architecture et perspective*, Paris 1601 (according to other accounts, 1594 or 1597; the dedication to the king is dated 1 July 1601; facs. repr. of this ed., Unterschneidheim 1971); German eds: Frankfurt 1602; Oppenheim 1613; Frankfurt 1621. The illustrations in the German ed. of 1602 are reversed in comparison with the 1601 ed.

[82] The 1601 ed. lacks page numbers and the plans are unnumbered. In the German ed. of 1602 the projects are designated by capital letters, this particular plan being D.

[83] Perret (1602), Project E.

[84] Perret (1602), Projects Y, Z.

[85] Cf. Jähns, vol. II (1890), pp. 1335ff.

[86] Ibid., pp. 1403ff.

[87] Ibid., pp. 1440ff.; cf. also Reginald Blomfield, *Sébastien le Prestre de Vauban 1633–1707* (1938), New York–London 1971.

10. France in the sixteenth century

[1] Cf. esp. Louis Hautecoeur, *Histoire de l'Architecture classique en France*, vol. I, Paris 1943, pp. 192ff.; Antonio Hernandez, *Grundzüge einer Ideengeschichte der franzö-*

sischen Architekturtheorie von *1560–1800*, Basel 1972, pp. 6ff.

[2] Anthony Blunt, *Art and Architecture in France 1500 to 1700*, Harmondsworth 1953, pp. 3ff.; Hanno-Walter Kruft, 'Genuesische Skulpturen der Renaissance in Frankreich', *Actes du XXIIe Congrès International d'Histoire de l'Art* (1969), Budapest 1972, pp. 697–703; Wolfram Prinz and Ronald G. Kecks, *Das französische Schloß der Renaissance. Form und Bedeutung der Architektur, ihre geschichtlichen und gesellschaftlichen Grundlagen*, Berlin 1985.

[3] Hautecoeur (1943), p. 196.

[4] Cf. the account of Martin, ibid., pp. 205ff.

[5] Heinrich von Geymüller, *Les Du Cerceau*, Paris–London 1887; Hautecoeur (1943), pp. 215ff.; on J. A. du Cerceau's date of birth, cf. Blunt (1953), p. 106 n. 22; Hernandez (1972), pp. 8ff.

[6] Jacques Androuet du Cerceau, *XXX Exempla Arcuum, partim ab ipso inventa, partim ex veterum sumpta monumenta*, Orléans 1549.

[7] Id., *De Architectura...Opus quo descriptae sunt aedificiorum quinquaginta...*, Paris 1559; simultaneous edition in French, *Livre d'architecture...contenant les plans & dessaigns de cinquante bastiments tous differencs: pour instruire ceux qui desirent bastir, soient de petit, moyen, ou grand estat...*, Paris 1559 (facs. repr. together with Books II and III, Ridgewood, NJ 1965).

[8] Id., *Second Livre d'architecture...contenant plusieurs et diverses ordonnances de cheminees, lucarnes, portes, fonteines...*, Paris 1561.

[9] Id., *Livre d'architecture...auquel sont contenues diverses ordonnances de plans et élévations de bastiments de Seigneurs... qui voudront bastir aux champs*, Paris 1582.

[10] Id., *Le premier volume des plus excellents Bastiments de France*, Paris 1577; *Le second volume des plus excellents Bastiments de France*, Paris 1577 (facs. reprs of both parts, 1972).

[11] On Bullant cf. esp. Hautecoeur (1943), pp. 233ff.; Blunt (1953), pp. 91ff.; Volker Hoffmann, *Das Schloß von Ecouen*, Berlin 1970, pp. 7ff.; Volker Hoffmann, 'Artisti francesi a Roma: Philbert Delorme e Jean Bullant', *Colloqui del Sodalizio*, 2. ser., n. 4, 1973–74, esp. pp. 63ff.

[12] Jean Bullant, *Reigle géneralle d'architecture des cinque manières de colonnes, à scavoir toscane, dorique, ionique, corinthe et composite et enrichi de plusieurs autres à l'exemple de l'antique suivant les reigles et doctrine de Vitruve...*, Paris 1564.

[13] On Philibert Delorme, see esp.: Hautecoeur (1943), pp. 219ff.; Anthony Blunt, *Philibert De L'Orme*, London 1958; Hernandez (1972), pp. 15ff.; Hoffmann (1973–74), pp. 55ff., Françoise Boudon and Jean Blécon, *Philibert Delorme et le château royal de Saint-Léger-en-Yvelines*, Paris 1985; Jean-Marie Pérouse de Montclos, 'Horoscope de Philibert de l'Orme', *Revue de l'Art* 72, 1986, pp. 16–18.

[14] Philibert Delorme, *Le premier tome de l'architecture*, Paris ¹1567, ²1558, ³1626, ⁴1648 (facs. reprs of the 1648 ed., 1894, 1964, 1981).

[15] 'vrais Architectes'...'plusiers qui s'en attribuent le nom, doibuent plustost estre appellez maistres maçons...' Delorme (1568), fol. 1 v. On the rôle of the architect, Hautecoeur (1943), pp. 241ff.

[16] Id., fol. 65.

[17] Id., fols 65vff.

[18] Cf. Bernard Palissy, *Recepte Véritable* (1563), in: Bernard Palissy, *Les Oeuvres*, ed. Anatole France, Paris 1880, pp. 65f. Palissy has hitherto been paid scant regard in the history of architectural theory, although a figure of some originality. In the *Recepte véritable*, for example, observation of stone formations and certain characteristics of animal behaviour leads him to the conception of a spirally planned city (ed. Anatole France, 1880, pp. 144ff.).

[19] Delorme (1568), fol. 217v. On formal models for the tree-columns, cf. Blunt (1958), p. 118; on Delorme's attitude to the Gothic, cf. Michael Hesse, *Von der Nachgotik zur Neugotik*, Frankfurt–Bern–New York 1984, pp. 33ff.

[20] Cf. Blunt (1958), pp. 120f.

[21] Cf. Nigel Llewellyn, 'Two notes in Diego da Sagredo', *Journal of the Warburg and Courtauld Institutes* XL, 1972, pp. 292ff.

[22] Cf. Jean-Marie Pérouse de Montclos, 'Le Sixième Ordre d'Architecture, ou la Pratique des Ordres Suivant les Nations', *Journal of the Society of Architectural Historians* XXXVI, 1977, pp. 223–40.

[23] Delorme (1568), fol. 235; cf. Hautecoeur (1943), p. 229.

[24] Delorme (1568), fol. 4.

[25] Alberti, *De re aedificatoria* IX. 7.

[26] Rudolf Wittkower, *Architectural Principles*

in the Age of Humanism, London ³1962, pp. 102ff., 155ff.

²⁷ Delorme (1568), fols 28off.

²⁸ François Rabelais, Oeuvres complètes, ed. Jacques Boulenger (Bibl. de la Pléiade, 15), Paris 1955, pp. 149ff. (Gargantua and Pantagruel, translated by J. M. Cohen, Penguin Classics, Harmondsworth 1970). On the abbey of Thélème, cf. esp. Charles Lenormant, Rabelais et l'architecture de la Renaissance. Restitution de l'Abbaye de Thélème, Paris 1840; Blunt, Philibert de l'Orme (1958), pp. 7ff.; Hernandez (1972), pp. 27ff.; Gerhard Goebel, Poeta Faber, Heidelberg 1971, pp. 146ff. (with further literature).

²⁹ Bartolommeo Marliani, Topographia antique Romae, Lyons 1534. On the editions of Marliani, cf. Ludwig Schudt, Le Guide di Roma, Vienna–Augsburg 1930, pp. 370ff.

³⁰ Rabelais, Gargantua, ch. LVII.

³¹ 'gens liberes, bien nez, bien instruictz, conversans en compaignies honnestes, ont par nature un instinct et aguillon, qui tousjours les poulse à faictz vertueux...' Ibid., original text cited from Rabelais, Gargantua, ed. Pierre Michel, Paris 1965, p. 423.

³² Baldassar Castiglione, Il libro del Cortegiano, Venice 1528 (The Book of the Courtier, trans. Sir T. Hoby, 2nd rev. ed., Everyman's Library, London 1974).

³³ 'Feut ordonné que là ne seroient repcues sinon les belles, bien formées et bien naturées, et les beaulx, bien formez et bien naturez.' Rabelais, Gargantua, ch. LII (1965), p. 395.

³⁴ 'Tant noblement estoient apprins qu'il n'estoit entre eulx celluy ne celle qui ne sceust lire, escripre, chanter, jouer d'instrumens harmonieux, parler de cinq et six langaiges, et en iceulx composer tant en carme, que en oraison solue.' Ibid., ch. LVII, p. 425.

³⁵ Ibid., ch. LIII. On the form of the superlative comparison, cf. Goebel (1971), p. 148.

³⁶ 'belles grandes galleries, toutes pinctes des antiques prouesses, histoires et descriptions de la terre.' Ibid., ch. LIII, pp. 401/3.

³⁷ Blunt (1958), pp. 12f. Serlio's Book III, in which the illustration appears, was first published in 1537, but Rabelais could have seen the reconstruction in some other form.

³⁸ Cf. Walter Pabst, 'Die Pforte von Thélème und Dantes Höllentor', Wissenschaftliche Zeitschrift der Friedrich-Schiller-Universität Jena 3, 1955/6, pp. 325–28; Goebel (1971), p. 149.

³⁹ Cf. esp. Helen Rosenau, The Ideal City. Its architectural evolution (1959); London ²1974.

II. The Classical synthesis in seventeenth-century France

¹ Cf. Louis Hautecoeur, Histoire de l'architecture classique en France, vol. I, Paris 1943, pp. 508ff.; Anthony Blunt, Art and Architecture in France 1500–1700, Harmondsworth 1953, p. 119; Antonio Hernandez, Grundzüge einer Ideengeschichte der französischen Architekturtheorie von 1560–1800, Basel 1972, p. 34f.

² Pierre Le Muet, Règles des cinque ordres d'architecture de Vignole revues, augmentées et réduites du grand au petit en octavo, Paris 1632. This octavo volume appeared in various editions, and in a German translation.

Pierre Le Muet, Règles des cinque ordres d'architecture dont se sont servi les anciens, traduites de Palladio, Paris 1645.

³ A second ed., to which the Augmentations de nouveaux bastimens faits en France par les ordres & desseins du Sieur le Muet is added as a second part, Paris 1647. A facs. repr. of the 1647 text, ed. Anthony Blunt, Richmond, Surrey 1972 (with '1664' erroneously on the title-page). A somewhat expanded new ed. of the Manière de bien bastir and the Augmentations, Paris 1681.

⁴ Le Muet (1647), dedication.

⁵ 'de travailler de plus en plus à l'utilité publique en ce qui regarde mon employ et ma profession.' Ibid., 'Au lecteur'.

⁶ Ibid., pp. 2f.

⁷ 'simmétrie, qui doit estre poisée selon la largeur ou hauteur'. Ibid., p. 4.

⁸ Alessandro Francini, Livre d'architecture contenant plusieurs portiques, Paris 1631 (facs. repr. 1966).

⁹ Antoine Le Pautre, Les oeuvres d'architecture, Paris 1652 (facs. repr. Farnborough 1966).

¹⁰ Louis Savot, L'Architecture françoise des bastiments particuliers, Paris 1624 (further eds 1632; with commentary by François Blondel, 1673, 1685; facs. repr. of latter, Geneva 1973).

[11] Savot (ed. 1685), pp. 338ff.

[12] Cf. Wilhelm Fraenger, *Die Bildanalysen des Roland Fréart de Chambray. Der Versuch einer Rationalisierung der Kunstkritik in der französischen Kunstlehre des 17. Jahrhunderts*, diss., Heidelberg 1917; Hernandez (1972), pp. 36ff.; François Fichet, *La théorie architecturale à l'âge classique*, Brussels 1979, pp. 101ff.

[13] On Poussin's view of art, cf. Anthony Blunt, *Nicolas Poussin*, New York 1967, vol. I, pp. 219ff.; Nicolas Poussin, *Lettres et propos sur l'art*, ed. Anthony Blunt, Paris 1964.

[14] Andrea Palladio, *Les quatre livres de l'architecture. Traduction intégrale de Roland Fréart de Chambray*, Paris 1650 (facs. ed. François Hébert-Sevens, Paris 1980).

[15] Roland Fréart de Chambray, *Parallèle de l'architecture antique et de la moderne, avec un recueil des dix principaux autheurs qui ont écrit des cinq Ordres...*, Paris 1650 ([2]1702); English trans. by John Evelyn, London 1664, entitled 'A Parallel of the Antient Architecture with the Modern' (with English trans. of Alberti's *De statua* in appendix); facs. repr. of the latter, 1970.

[16] Roland Fréart de Chambray, *Idée de la perfection de la peinture demonstrée par ses principes de l'art...*, Le Mans 1662 (facs. ed. Anthony Blunt, 1968).

[17] Fréart de Chambray (1650), dedication.

[18] Ibid., p. 2.

[19] '*l'union et le concours générale de toute ensemble, laquelle vient à former comme une harmonie visible*'. Ibid., p. 3.

[20] '*Car l'excellence & la perfection d'un art ne consiste pas en la multiplité de ses principes; au contraire les plus simples & en moindre quantité le doivent rendre plus admirable: ce que nous voyons en ceux de la Géometrie, qui est cependant la base & le magazin général de tous les arts, d'ou celui-cy aesté tiré, & sans l'aide de laquelle il est impossible qu'il subsiste.*' Ibid., p. 7.

[21] J. J. Winckelmann, *Gedanken über die Nachahmung der griechischen Werke in der Malerei und Bildhauerkunst* (1755), in: J. J. Winckelmann, *Kleine Schriften, Vorreden, Entwürfe*, ed. W. Rehm and H. Sichtermann, Berlin 1968, p. 29.

[22] Hernandez (1972), p. 39.

[23] Fréart de Chambray (1650), p. 4.

[24] Ibid., p. 4.

[25] Ibid., p. 70; Jerónimo Prado and Juan Bautista Villalpando, *In Ezechielem Explanationes*, Rome 1596–1604.

[26] Hans Rose (ed.), *Tagebuch des Herrn von Chantelou über die Reise des Cavaliere Bernini nach Frankreich*, Munich 1919, pp. 100f.

[27] On Abraham Bosse see esp. the compilation of texts *Abraham Bosse, le peintre converti*, ed. Roger-Armand Weigert, Paris 1964.

12. The foundation of the French Academy of Architecture and the subsequent challenge to it

[1] Cf. Nikolaus Pevsner, *Academies of Art Past and Present* (1940), New York [2]1973, pp. 39ff.

[2] Cf. Henry Lemonnier (ed.), *Procès-Verbaux de l'Académie Royale d'Architecture 1671–1793*, vol. I, Paris 1911, pp. VIIff.; Louis Hautecoeur, *Histoire de l'architecture classique en France*, vol. II, Paris 1948, pp. 462ff.; Donald Drew Egbert, *The Beaux-Arts Tradition in French Architecture*, Princeton 1980, pp. 11ff.

[3] Cf. Hautecoeur (1948), pp. 414ff.

[4] '*L'Académie règne sur les architectes, sur les étudiants, sur les entrepreneurs, sur les bâtiments du Roi, des provinces, des villes. Elle est un instrument puissant au service du pouvoir central.*' Hautecoeur (1948), p. 467.

[5] Henry Lemonnier (ed.), *Procès-Verbaux de l'Académie Royale d'Architecture 1671–1793*, 10 vols, Paris 1911–29.

[6] 1671: Blondel (director), Félibien (secretary), Bruand, Gittard, Le Pautre, Le Vau, Mignard, d'Orbay.

[7] Lemonnier, vol. I (1911), pp. XVIIIf.

[8] Ibid., p. XXVIII; Jean-Marie Pérouse de Montcos ('Le Sixième Ordre d'Architecture, ou la Pratique des Ordres Suivant les Nations', *Journal of the Society of Architectural Historians* XXXVI, 1977, pp. 223–40) sees no connection between the Académie d'architecture and the 'French order'.

[9] Cf. Hautecoeur (1948), pp. 468f.

[10] Cf. ibid. On the *querelle des anciens et des modernes*, cf. Hubert Gillot, *La querelle des anciens et des modernes en France. De*

la Défense et illustration de la langue française, Nancy 1914 (facs. repr. Geneva 1968); Hans Kortum, *Charles Perrault und Nicolas Boileau, Der Antike-Streit im Zeitalter der klassischen französischen Literatur*, Berlin 1966.

11 *'Ce qu'on ne voyait plus que dans les ruines d'l'ancienne Rome et de la vieille Grèce, devenu moderne éclate dans nos portiques et dans nos péristyles. De même on ne saurait en écrivant rencontrer le parfait, et, s'il se peut, surpasser les anciens que par leur imitation.'* La Bruyère, *Les Caractères*, chapter 'Ouvrages de l'esprit'.

12 Cf. Hautecoeur, vol. II (1948), p. 412.

13 Ibid., p. 352ff.; Georges Wildenstein, 'Note sur un projet d'ordre français', *Gazette des Beaux-Arts* LXIII, 1964, pp. 257–60; Johannes Langner, 'Zum Entwurf der französischen Ordnung von Le Brun', in: *Kunstgeschichtliche Studien für Kurt Bauch zum 70. Geburtstag*, Munich–Berlin 1967, pp. 233–40; Joseph Rykwert, *On Adam's House in Paradise*, New York 1972, pp. 77ff.; Jean Marie Pérouse de Montclos, 'Le Sixième Ordre de'Architecture, ou la Pratique des Ordres Suivant les Nations', *Journal of the Society of Architectural Historians* XXXVI, 1977, pp. 223–40.

14 François Blondel, *Cours d'architecture*, Parts 2 and 3, Paris 1683, pp. 249ff.

15 Lemonnier, vol. I (1911), p. 3.

16 Ibid., p. 4.

17 Ibid.

18 Antonio Hernandez, *Grundzüge einer Ideengeschichte der französischen Architekturtheorie von 1560–1800*, Basel 1972, p. 48.

19 Lemonnier, vol. I (1911), pp. XXIIff.; Mauclair and Vigoureux, *Nicolas-François de Blondel*, Laon c. 1936; Hautecoeur (1948), pp. 468ff.

20 Cf. a bibliography for Blondel in: Françoise Fichet, *La théorie architecturale à l'âge classique*, Brussels 1979, p. 173.

21 François Blondel, *Cours d'architecture enseigné dans l'Académie Royale d'Architecture*, Part I, Paris 1675; Parts II–V, Paris 1683 (facs. of 2nd ed. 1698: Hildesheim–New York 1982).

22 *'enseigner publiquement les règles de cet art tirées de la doctrine des plus grands Maîtres et des exemples des plus beaux Edifices qui nous restent de l'antiquité.'* Ibid. (1675), dedication.

23 Ibid., p. 2.

24 Ibid., p. 9.

25 Ibid., Part II (1683), p. 2.

26 Ibid., p. 3.

27 Ibid., p. 4.

28 Ibid., pp. 11ff.

29 Ibid., Part III (1683), p. 250.

30 Ibid., Part I (1675), p. 10.

31 *'L'Architecture est l'art de bien bâtir. L'on appelle un bon bâtiment, celuy qui est solide, commode, sain & agréable.'* Ibid., p. 1.

32 Ibid., Part IV (1683), p. 618.

33 Ibid., p. 622; cf. an analysis by A. E. Brinckmann, *Die Baukunst des 17. und 18. Jahrhunderts in den romanischen Ländern*, Berlin–Neubabelsberg 1915, p. 230, fig. 252.

34 Blondel, Part V (1683), p. 727.

35 Ibid.

36 Ibid., pp. 730ff.

37 Ibid., pp. 748ff.

38 Ibid., p. 755.

39 René Ouvrard, *Architecture Harmonique, ou Application de la doctrine des proportions de la musique à l'architecture*, Paris 1679; excerpts in: Françoise Fichet (1979), pp. 176ff.

40 Ouvrard (1679); cited from Fichet (1979), p. 180.

41 Blondel, Part V (1683), p. 765.

42 Ibid., p. 767.

43 Ibid., p. 768.

44 Ibid., pp. 774ff.

45 *'On y trouvera un grand nombre des mêmes proportions qui sans doute en font la beauté, & sont cause du plaisir que l'on ressent quand on les regard.'* Ibid., p. 778. On Blondel's changing attitudes towards the Gothic, cf. also Michael Hesse, *Von der Nachgotik zur Neugotik*, Frankfurt–Bern–New York 1984, pp. 55ff.

46 On Claude Perrault, cf. Wolfgang Herrmann, *The Theory of Claude Perrault*, London 1973.

The literature on the Blondel-Perrault dispute has grown significantly in recent years. The very different arguments that have been put forward seem to me either peripheral to the main discussion (e.g. Brönner 1972) or governed by anachronistic polemic (Kambartel 1972). Especially to be mentioned is: Tonis Kask, *Symmetrie und Regelmäßigkeit – französische Architektur im Grand Siècle*, Basel–Stuttgart 1971; but see also: Hernandez (1972), pp. 54ff.; Walter Kambartel, *Symmetrie und Schönheit. Über mögliche Voraussetzungen des neueren Kunstbewußtseins in der Architekturtheorie Claude Perraults*, Munich 1972 (cf. the review of this by Wolfgang Herrmann in: *Architectura* 6, 1976, pp. 75–78); Wolfgang Dieter Brönner, *Blondel-Perrault. Zur Architekturtheorie des 17. Jahrhunders in Frankreich*, diss., Bonn 1972 (with overemphasis of the optical presuppositions of Blondel and Perrault); Joseph Rykwert, *The First Moderns. The Architects of the Eighteenth Century*, Cambridge, MA–London 1980, pp. 23ff.

[47] On the empirical psychology of perception in Perrault, cf. esp. Brönner (1972).

[48] Herrmann (1973), p. 17.

[49] Claude Perrault, *Les dix livres d'Architecture de Vitruve corrigez et traduits nouvellement en François, avec des Notes & des Figures*, Paris 1673 (repr. ed. André Dalmas, 1979, but unsatisfactory); a second edition of this translation, revised and enlarged by Perrault, appeared under the same title, Paris 1684 (facs. repr. Brussels 1979). The 1684 edition is cited hereafter.

[50] The Académie began the reading of Vitruvius in 1673 in Jean Martin's translation, but then decided to await Perrault's new translation (cf. Lemonnier (1911), p. 21.

[51] Claude Perrault, *Ordonnance des cinq espèces de colonnes selon la methode des anciens*, Paris 1683.

[52] Lemonnier, vol. I (1911), pp. 77ff.

[53] Ibid., p. 87.

[54] Hernandez (1972), p. 56.

[55] Herrmann (1973) and esp. his review of Kambartel in: *Architectura* 6, 1976, pp. 75–78.

[56] On the triumphal arch, cf. Hautecoeur, vol. II (1948), p. 455; Runar Strandberg, *Pierre Bullet et J.-B. Chamblain à la lumière des dessins de la Collection Tessin-Hårlemann du Musée National de Stockholm*, Stockholm 1971, pp. XLIIIf., figs 10, 11; Michael Petzet, 'Das Triumphbogenmonument für Ludwig XIV. auf der Place du Trône', *Zeitschrift für Kunstgeschichte* 45, 1982, pp. 145–94.

[57] Perrault, *Ordonnance* (1683), p. I.

[58] Perrault, *Les dix livres* (1684), p. 105 n. 7.

[59] 'Toute l'Architecture est fondée sur deux principes, dont l'un est positif & l'autre arbitraire. Le fondement positif est l'usage & la fin utile & nécessaire pour laquelle un Edifice est fait, telle qu'est la Solidité, la Salubrité & la Commodité. Le fondement que j'apelle arbitraire, est la Beauté qui dépend de l'Autorité & de l'Acoûtumance: Car bienque la Beauté soit aussi en quelche façon établie sur un fondement positif, qui est la convenance raisonnable & l'aptitude que chaque partie a pour l'usage auquel elle est destinée...' Perrault, *Les dix livres* (1684), p. 12 n. 13.

[60] In his first edition of Vitruvius (1673) Perrault had emphasised the part played by the artist's imagination: 'Car la beauté n'ayant guère d'autre fondement que la fantaisie...' This passage of the foreword does not appear in the second edition.

[61] 'l'usage auquel chaque chose est destinée selon sa nature, doit estre une des principales raisons sur lesquelles la beauté de l'Edifice doit estre fondée.' Perrault, *Les dix livres* (1684), p. 214 n. 6.

[62] 'on entend autre chose par le mot de Symmetrie en François; car il signifie le rapport que les parties droites ont avec les gauches, & celuy que les hautes ont avec les basses, & celles de devant avec celles de derrières, en grandeur, en figure, en hauteur, en couleur, en nombre, en situation; & généralement en tout ce qui les peut rendre semblables les une aux autres; & il est assez étrange que Vitruve n'ait point parlé de cette sorte de Symmetrie qui fait une grande partie de la beauté des Edifices.' Ibid., p. 11 n. 9.

[63] Cf. Herrmann in: *Architectura* 6, 1976, pp. 75f.

[64] Cf. Kask (1971), Kambartel (1972); similarly Herrmann in: *Architectura* 6, 1976, pp. 75ff.

[65] 'la grâce de la forme qui n'est rien autre chose que son agréable modification sur laquelle une beauté parfaite et excellente peut estre fondée...' Perrault, *Ordonnance* (1683), p. I.

[66] Ibid., p. II.

[67] Ibid., p. XII.

[68] Ibid., p. 96.

[69] 'Le goust de nostre siècle, ou du moins de nostre nation, est différent de celuy des Anciens, & peut-estre qu'en cela il tient un peu du Gothique: car nous avons l'air, le jour & les dégagemens. Cela nous a fait inventer une sixième manière de disposer ces colonnes, qui est de les accoupler & de les joindre deux à deux.' Perrault, *Les deux livres* (1684), p. 79 n. Here Perrault is explicitly referring to the critique expounded by Blondel in his lectures.

[70] Cf. also Perrault's recently identified illustrations to Louis Compiègne de Veils' translation of Maimonides (1678): Wolfgang Herrmann, 'Unknown Designs for the "Temple of Jerusalem" by Claude Perrault', *Essays in the History of Architecture Presented to Rudolf Wittkower*, London ²1969, pp. 143–58.

[71] Perrault, *Les dix livres* (1684), p. 33 pl. V; Giovanantonio Rusconi, *Della Architettura*, Venice 1590, pp. 27f.

[72] Perrault, *Les dix livres* (1684), p. 217 pl. LVI; cf. Palladio's illustration in Daniele Barbaro's Latin ed. of Vitruvius (1567, p. 227) and Andrea Palladio, *I quattro libri dell'architettura*, Venice 1570, Book II, p. 44.

[73] Cf. Kambartel (1972), Herrmann (1973 and 1976).

[74] Lemonnier, vol. I (1911), p. 5.

[75] Cf. Hernandez (1972), p. 68.

[76] Charles Perrault, *Paralèlle des Anciens et des Modernes, en ce qui regarde les arts et les sciences*, Paris 1688–97 (facs. repr. in: *Theorie und Geschichte der Literatur und der Schönen Künste*, vol. 2, with contributions by H. R. Jauss and Max Imdahl, Munich 1964).

[77] Cf. Kambartel (1972). p. 105.

[78] On Desgodets, cf. the substantial article by Wolfgang Herrmann, 'Antoine Desgodets and the Académie Royale d'Architecture', *The Art Bulletin* XL, 1958, pp. 23–53.

[79] On Desgodets' relationship with the Académie, esp. his strained relations with Blondel, cf. Herrmann (1958), pp. 25ff.

[80] Antoine Desgodets, *Les édifices antiques de Rome*, Paris 1682 (²1695); a 2-vol. English-French ed. by George Marshall, London 1771, 1795 (facs. repr. of 1682 ed., Portland, OR 1972).

[81] Desgodets (1682), dedication.

[82] Ibid., Préface.

[83] Desgodets does not mention Blondel in his treatise by name, but in his foreword he is unmistakably referring to Blondel in speaking of *'tant de doctrine'* that would not be concerned with exact details; cf. Herrmann (1958), pp. 26ff.

[84] Desgodets (1682), Préface.

[85] Ibid.

[86] Cf. Herrmann (1958), pp. 26f., 31.

[87] Antoine Desgodets, 'Traité des Ordres d'Architecture' (ms., Paris, Bibl. des Institut de France, ms. 1031); 'Cours d'Architecture' (ms. Paris, Bibl. Nat., Cabinet des Estampes Ha 23, 23a; Paris, Bibl. de l'Arsenal, ms. 2545; London, library of the Royal Institute of British Architects, ms. 72). On the evaluation of these manuscripts, cf. Herrmann (1958), pp. 33ff.

[88] Cf. ibid., pp. 47f.

[89] Cf. Herrmann (1958), pp. 39ff.

[90] Cf. the bibliography for Félibien, in: Françoise Fichet (1979), pp. 136ff.

[91] André Félibien, *Des Principes de l'architecture, de la Sculpture, de la Peinture*, Paris 1676 (²1690, ³1699); facs. repr. of 1699 ed., 1966.

[92] *'Il faut toujours en bastissant se proposer la solidité, la Commodité & la Beauté; & pour ce qui regarde les Ornemens on s'en sert comme on le juge à propos, suivant la disposition des lieux & la dépense qu'on veut faire.'* Félibien (³1699), p. 32.

[93] Ibid., p. 520.

[94] Jean-François Félibien, *Recueil Historique de la vie et des ouvrages des plus célèbres architectes*, Paris 1687 (and later German eds, Hamburg 1711 [facs. repr. Leipzig 1975], Berlin 1828).

[95] Antoine-Nicolas Dézallier d'Argenville, *Vies des fameux architectes depuis la Renaissance des arts*, Paris 1787 (facs. repr. Geneva 1972).

[96] Philippe de la Hire, 'Architecture civile', ms. (London, library of the Royal Institute of British Architects, ms. 725); cf. Herrmann (1958), p. 33.

[97] *'ce qui fait que ces bastiments ne sont pas propres à l'usage de France, où l'on préfère souvent la commodité du dedans à la décoration du dehors; sur quoy la Compagnie a jugé qu'il ne faut pas apporter moins de soin dans l'architecture à bien distribuer les logemens qu'à bien décorer des façades.'* Lemonnier, *Procès-Verbaux*, vol. III (1913), p. 93.

[98] Augustin-Charles d'Aviler, *Cours d'architecture qui comprend les ordres de Vignole...*, Paris 1691 (²1696).

[99] 1735, 1738, 1756, 1760.

[100] D'Aviler (²1696), p. 302.

[101] Ibid., pp. 306ff.

[102] Augustin-Charles d'Aviler, *Dictionnaire d'Architecture ou explication de tous les termes*, Paris 1693.

[103] *'c'est le rapport de parité, soit de hauteur,*

de largeur ou de longueur de parties, pour composer un beau tout... Et Simmetrie respective, celle dont les côtez opposez sont pareils entr'eux.' D'Aviler, Dictionnaire (1693), p. 229.

[104] 'c'est la justesse des membres de chaque partie d'un Bâtiment, & la relation des parties au tout ensemble.' Ibid., p. 212.

[105] C. F. Roland Le Virloys, Dictionnaire d'architecture, civile, militaire et navale... dont tous Les Termes sont exprimés, en François, Latin, Italien, Espagnol, Anglois et Allemand, 3 vols, Paris 1770–71.

[106] Pierre Bullet, L'architecture pratique, qui comprend le détail du toise, & du devis des ouvrages..., Paris 1691 (facs. repr. Geneva 1973); cf. Eric Langenskiöld, Pierre Bullet. The Royal Architect, Stockholm 1959, p. 19; Runar Strandberg, Pierre Bullet et J. B. de Chamblain, Stockholm 1971, p. IX.

[107] 'La théorie de l'Architecture est un amas de plusieurs principes qui établissent, par exemple, les règles de l'analogie, ou la science des proportions, pour composer cette harmonie qui touche si agréablement la vue.' Bullet (1691), Avant-Propos.

[108] 'caractère convenable au sujet que l'on s'est proposé.' Ibid.

[109] Michel de Frémin, Mémoires critiques d'architecture contenans l'idée de la vraye & de la fausse Architecture, Paris 1702 (facs. repr. 1967). On Frémin, cf. Dorothea Nyberg, 'Michel de Frémin, Mémoires critiques d'Architecture. A Clue to the Architectural Taste of Eighteenth Century France', PhD thesis, New York 1962 : ead., 'The Mémoires Critiques d'architecture by Michel de Frémin', Journal of the Society of Architectural Historians XXII, 1693, pp. 217–24; Françoise Fichet (1979), pp. 257ff.

[110] Frémin (1702), Avertissement.

[111] Ibid., p. 11.

[112] Ibid., p. 22.

[113] 'L'architecture est un Art de bâtir selon l'objet, selon le sujet, et selon le lieu.' Ibid.

[114] Ibid., p. 23.

[115] Ibid.

[116] Ibid., p. 25.

[117] Ibid., pp. 26ff.

[118] 'rapport naturel & convenable à l'usage propre (observez bien mes termes) pour lequel le Bâtiment est ordonné.' Ibid., p. 58.

13. Relativist architectural aesthetics, the Enlightenment and Revolutionary architecture

[1] Jean-Louis de Cordemoy, Nouveau Traité de toute l'Architecture ou l'art de bastir, Paris 1706 (2nd enlarged ed. with replies to the attacks of Amédée-François Frézier and the Dissertation sur la manierè dont les églises doivent être bâties, Paris 1714 (facs. repr. 1966).

[2] On Cordemoy, see esp. R. D. Middleton, 'The Abbé de Cordemoy and the Graeco-Gothic Ideal: A Prelude to Romantic Classicism', Journal of the Warburg and Courtauld Institutes 25, 1962, pp. 278–320; 26, 1963, pp. 90–123; Dorothea Nyberg, 'La sainte Antiquité. Focus of an Eighteenth-century Architectural Debate', Essays in the History of Architecture Presented to Rudolf Wittkower, London ²1969, pp. 159–69; Françoise Fichet, La théorie architecturale à l'âge classique, Brussels 1979, pp. 182ff.; Michael Hesse, Von der Nachgotik zur Neugotik, Frankfurt–Bern–New York 1984, esp. pp. 96ff.

[3] 'L'Ordonnance est ce qui donne à toutes les parties d'un Bâtiment la juste grandeur qui

leur est propre par rapport à leur usage.' Cordemoy (²1714), p. 3.

[4] 'l'arrangement convenable de ces mêmes parties.' Ibid.

[5] 'Et la Bienséance est ce qui fait que cette Disposition est telle qu'on n'y puisse rien trouver qui soit contraire à la nature, à l'accoutumance, ou à l'usage des choses.' Ibid.

[6] Ibid., p. 87.

[7] Ibid., p. 98.

[8] Cf. Middleton (1962), p. 307; cf. Wend Graf Kalnein and Michael Levey, Art and Architecture of the Eighteenth Century in France, Harmondsworth 1972, p. 211. (pl. 204).

[9] Cf. Middleton (1962), pp. 305ff.

[10] Cf. eg. Antonio Hernandez, Grundzüge einer Ideengeschichte der französischen Architekturtheorie von 1560–1800, Basel 1972, p. 166 n. 261.

[11] On this dispute, cf. Middleton (1962), pp. 287ff. and esp. Dorothea Nyberg (1969), pp. 159ff. On Frézier, cf. Pierre du Colombier,

'Amédée-François Frézier. Ingénieur Ordinaire en Chef du Roy à Landau', *Festschrift für Karl Lohmeyer*, Saarbrücken 1954, pp. 159–66; Fichet (1979), pp. 333ff.

[12] Amédée-François Frézier, *La Théorie et la pratique de la coupe des pierres et des bois pour la construction des voûtes et autres parties des bâtiments civils et militaires, ou Traité de Stéréometrie, à l'usage de l'architecture* (Appendix: 'Dissertation historique et critique sur les ordres d'architecture', 1738), Strassburg 1737–39 (facs. repr. Nogent-Le-Roi 1980).

[13] Cf. the excerpts from Frézier in: Fichet (1979), pp. 334ff.

[14] Sébastien Le Clerc, *Traité d'architecture, avec des remarques et des observations très-utiles pour les jeuns gens qui veulent s'appliquer à ce bel art*, Paris 1714 (translated into English, 1732; Dutch, n.d.; and German, 1759, 1797).

[15] Cf. Hernandez (1972), pp. 76ff.

[16] Le Clerc (1714), preface.

[17] Ibid., p. 3.

[18] '*Par proportion, on n'entend pas ici un rapport de raisons à la manière des geomètres; mais une convenance de parties, fondée sur le bon goût de l'architecte.*' Ibid., p. 39.

[19] Ibid., p. 16.

[20] Ibid., pp. 193ff., pls 173ff.

[21] Gilles-Marie Oppenordt, *Livre de fragments d'architecture recueillis et dessinés à Rome d'après les plus beaux monuments*, Paris, c. 1715 (Marianne Fischer, in exhib. cat. (Kunstbibliothek Berlin) *Architektur in Darstellung und Theorie*, Berlin 1969, p. 36, dates this work, without foundation, after 1742).

[22] On Oppenordt, cf. Louis Hautecoeur, *Histoire de l'architecture classique en France*, vol. III, Paris 1950, pp. 250ff.; Fiske Kimball, *The Creation of the Rococo* (1943), New York 1964; id., *Le style Louis XV. Origine et évolution du Rococo*, Paris 1949.

[23] '*bon goust en architecture consiste en ce qui a un rapport plus simple dans toutes les parties et qui, se faisant connoître plus aisément à l'âme, la satisfoit davantage.*' Henry Lemonnier (ed.), Procès-Verbaux de l'Académie Royale d'Architecture 1671–1793, vol. IV, Paris 1915, p. 10.

[24] Ibid.

[25] Ibid., vol. V, 1918, p. 134.

[26] '*Le bon goust consiste dans l'harmonie ou l'accord du tous et de ses parties. L'harmonie*

qui donne aux ouvrages la qualité d'être de bon goust dépend de trois conditions qui sont l'ordonnance, la proportion et la convenance.

'*L'ordonnance est la distribution des parties tant extérieures qu'intérieures. Elle doit dépendre de la grandeur de l'édifice et de l'usage auquel il est destiné.*

'*La proportion est la règle des mesures convenables qu'il faut donner au tout et aux parties suivant leur usage et leur places. Elle est presque toujours fondée sur la belle nature dont elle nous fait imiter la sagesse.*

'*La convenance est un assujettissement aux usages établis et reçus. Elle donne des règles pour mettre chaque chose à sa place.*' Ibid., pp. 142f.

[27] Ibid., p. 144.

[28] Germain Boffrand, *Livre d'architecture contenant les principes generaux de cet art*, Paris 1745 (facs. repr. with *La figure equestre de Louis XIV* [1743], 1969).

[29] Cf. Hautecoeur, vol. III (1950), pp. 124ff; Kalnein and Levey (1972), pp. 206ff.; on Boffrand's architectural theory, cf. Emil Kaufmann, 'Three Revolutionary Architects, Boullée, Ledoux, and Lequeu', *Transactions of the American Philosophical Society*, N.S., 42, 1952, pp. 446ff.; Hernandez (1972), pp. 83ff. On Boffrand's built architecture, cf. Michel Gallet and Jörg Garms, *Germain Boffrand 1667–1754. L'aventure d'un architecte indépendant*, Paris 1986.

[30] Boffrand (1745), p. 1.

[31] Ibid., p. 3.

[32] Ibid., p. 4.

[33] Ibid.

[34] Ibid., p. 6.

[35] Ibid., pp. 12ff.

[36] '*chaque partie relativement au tout doit avoir une proportion et une forme convenable à son usage.*' Ibid., p. 10.

[37] Ibid., p. 8.

[38] Ibid., p. 15.

[39] Ibid., p. 8.

[40] Ibid., pp. 11ff.

[41] '*Les différents Edifices par leur disposition, par leur structure, par la manière dont ils sont décorés, doivent annoncer au spectateur leur destination.*' Ibid., p. 16.

[42] Ibid., pp. 45f.; Kalnein-Levey (1972), pp. 211ff.

[43] Yves André, *Essai sur le beau, ou l'on examine en quoi consiste précisément le beau dans le physique, dans le moral, dans les ouvrages d'esprit et dans la musique*, Paris

1741 (later eds 1759, 1763, 1824, 1827, 1856). On Père André, cf. Françoise Fichet (1979), pp. 323ff.

[44] Père André (1741); Françoise Fichet (1979), p. 330.

[45] Cf. Hautecoeur, vol. III (1950); Hernandez (1972), pp. 90ff.; Françoise Fichet (1979), pp. 347ff.

[46] Charles-Etienne Briseux, L'Architecture moderne, ou l'Art de bien bâtir pour toutes sortes des personnes, 2 vols, Paris 1728. The work appeared anonymously. On 28 June 1728 it was examined by the Académie d'architecture and passed for publication; Lemonnier, vol. V (1918), p. 29 – even here Briseux is not given as author: Lemonnier (p. 29) records its traditional ascription to Briseux.

[47] Briseux eventually published Jean Courtonne's designs for the Hôtel Matignon and the Hôtel de Noirmoutier in Paris (Distribution 57, 58), and Courtonnes' design for a 'Pyramid' (Distribution 60).

[48] Charles-Etienne Briseux, l'Art de bâtir des maisons de campagne, ou l'on traite de leur distribution, de leur construction, & de leur décoration, 2 vols, Paris 1743 ('1761; facs. repr. 1966).

[49] 'Cette Décoration doit offrir une beauté naturelle, aussi noble que simple, qui contente la vue par la seule symmetrie...' ...'avec convenance & sans confusion...' Briseux ('1761), vol. II, pp. 115f.

[50] Charles-Etienne Briseux, Traité du Beau Essentiel dans les arts appliqué particulièrement à l'Architecture..., Paris 1752 (facs. repr. Geneva 1974).

[51] 'Il n'a donc pas été possible d'en constater de fixes [proportions] mais tous les auteurs sont d'accord sur la nécessité d'en observer.' Ibid (1752), pp. 4f.

[52] Ibid., p. 2.

[53] 'un principe commun, qui les rendit agréables, ou désagréables, et que l'Ame, qui est le Juge de toutes les sensations, reçevoit dans chaque sens les impressions d'agrément, ou de désagrément d'une manière uniforme...' Ibid., p. 35.

[54] Ibid., p. 47.

[55] Hernandez (1972), p. 98.

[56] Briseux (1752), pp. 103f.

[57] Ibid., p. 103.

[58] 'Si l'âme n'a pas reçu d'instruction, elle se contente de goûter le plaisir par simple sensation; mais si elle a été éclairée par des préceptes, elle apprécie aussi ce plaisir par examen et par discussion.' Ibid., p. 7.

[59] 'Les objets, dont on veut orner une façade, doivent être non seulement rélatifs à son caractère, mais y paroitre utiles, nécessaires, et y mériter leur place...' Ibid., p. 71.

[60] On Blondel's built architecture, cf. Hautecoeur, vol. III (1950), pp. 598ff.; on his theory, ibid., pp. 466ff.; Emil Kaufmann (1952), p. 436; id., Architecture in the Age of Reason (1955), New York 1968, pp. 131ff.; Hernandez (1972), pp. 110ff.

[61] Cf. the bibliography in: Françoise Fichet (1979), pp. 460f.

[62] Jacques-François Blondel, De la Distribution des Maisons de Plaisance, et de la Décoration des édifices en general, 2 vols, Paris 1737-38 (facs. repr. 1967).

[63] Ibid., vol. II (1738), p. 26.

[64] Ibid., vol. I (1737), dedication to Monseigneur Turgot.

[65] Ibid., vol. II, pp. 65ff.

[66] Jacques-François Blondel, Architecture françoise, ou Recueil des plans, élévations, coupes et profils des églises, maisons royales, palais, hôtels et édifices les plus considérables de Paris, 4 vols, Paris 1752-56 (new ed. Paris 1904).

[67] Jacques-François Blondel, Cours d'architecture, 6 vols of text and 3 of plates, Paris 1771-77 (vols 5 and 6 are by Pierre Patte).

[68] Blondel, vol. I (1771), pp. Vff.

[69] Ibid., pp. XVII.

[70] Cf. Hautecoeur, vol. III (1950), p. 468.

[71] Blondel, vol. III (1772), p. 8.

[72] Blondel, vol. I (1771), pp. 260ff.

[73] Francesco di Giorgio Martini, Trattati, ed. Corrado Maltese, vol. II, Milan 1967, p. 390, pl. 227.

[74] Blondel, vol. I (1771), p. 390.

[75] Ibid., p. 380.

[76] Ibid., p. 373.

[77] Ibid., vol. III (1772), p. LXXVIII.

[78] 'dans toutes les parties le style qui lui est propre, sans aucune espèce de mêlange; celle qui présente un caractère décidé, qui met chaque membre à sa place, qui n'appelle que les ornements qui lui sont nécessaires pour l'embellir.' Ibid., vol. I (1771), p. 391.

[79] 'l'Architecture Egyptienne étoit plus étonnante que belle; l'Architecture Grecque, plus régulière qu'ingénieuse; l'Architecture Romaine plus savante qu'admirable; la Gothique, plus solide que satisfaisante; notre Architecture Françoise enfin, est peut-être

plus commode que véritablement intéres-sante.' Ibid., p. 377.

[80] Ibid., pp. 448ff.

[81] Ibid., p. 450.

[82] Ibid., vol. V (1777), foreword.

[83] Ibid., vol. II (1771), pp. 253ff.

[84] Jacques-François Blondel, *Discours sur la nécessité de l'étude de l'architecture*, Paris 1754 (facs. repr. Geneva 1973), Avertisse-ment.

[85] Ibid. (1754), p. 28.

[86] Ibid., p. 29.

[87] Ibid., p. 41.

[88] Ibid., p. 44.

[89] Ibid., pp. 71ff.

[90] Ibid., pp. 83ff.

[91] Cf. Kevin Harrington, *Changing Ideas on Architecture in the 'Encyclopédie', 1750–1776*, Ann Arbor, MI 1985.

[92] On Patte, cf. Reginald Blomfield, *A History of French Architecture* (1921), New York 1973, vol. IV, pp. 155ff.; Hautecoeur, vol. IV (1952); Françoise Fichet (1979), pp. 387ff.

[93] Cf. the bibliography in: Françoise Fichet (1979), pp. 406f. His most important works are: *Discours sur l'architecture*, Paris 1754; *Mémoires sur les objets les plus importants de l'architecture*, Paris 1769 (facs. repr. Geneva 1973). On Patte cf. esp.: Mahé Mathieu, *Pierre Patte, sa vie, son oeuvre*, Paris 1940; Françoise Choay, *La règle et le modèle. Sur la théorie de l'architecture et de l'urbanisme*, Paris 1980, pp. 261ff.

[94] Pierre Patte, *Monuments érigés en France à la gloire de Louis XV*, Paris 1765.

[95] Ibid., pp. 71–117.

[96] Ibid., pp. 187ff.

[97] Ibid., p. 213n.

[98] *'Il n'est pas nécessaire, pour la beauté d'une ville, qu'elle soit percée avec la froide symme-trie des villes du Japon & de la Chine, & que ce soit toujours un assemblage de maisons disposées bien régulièrement dans des quarrés ou dans des parallélogrammes...'* Ibid., p. 222.

[99] Ibid.

[100] Cf. his plans (1765), pp. 233ff.

[101] *'Jamais le vrai goût de l'architecture antique n'a été aussi général...Les maisons des simples particuliers sont aujourd'hui décorées avec une noblesse, que n'avoient pas toujours autrefois les palais des grands.'* Ibid., p. 4.

[102] Patte, *Mémoires* (1769), pp. 5ff.

[103] Ibid., p. 8.

[104] Ibid., p. 14.

[105] Ibid., p. 17.

[106] Ibid., p. 81.

[107] Ibid., pp. 19ff.

[108] Charles-Antoine Jombert, *Architecture moderne ou l'art de bien bâtir*, 2 vols, Paris (¹1728) ²1764.

[109] On Laugier, see esp. Wolfgang Herrmann, *Laugier and Eighteenth Century French Theory*, London 1962; on his theory, cf. also Hernandez (1972), pp. 100ff.

[110] Cf. the bibliography in: Herrmann (1962), pp. 256ff.

[111] Anon. (Marc-Antoine Laugier), *Essai sur l'Architecture*, Paris 1753; 2nd enlarged ed., Paris 1765 (facs. repr. 1966).

Marc-Antoine Laugier, *Observations sur l'Architecture*, Paris 1765 (facs. repr. 1966).

A serviceable new ed. of both works: Marc-Antoine Laugier, *Essai sur l'Architec-ture. Observations sur l'Architecture*, ed. Geert Bekaert, Brussels 1979.

[112] Laugier, *Essai* (1765), Préface.

[113] Notably La Font de Saint-Yenne, *Examen d'un essai sur l'architecture*, Paris 1753 (facs. ed. Geneva 1973), who even charges Laugier with being dangerous.

[114] Laugier, *Essai* (1765), p. XXXV.

[115] Ibid., pp. 8ff.

[116] On the primitive hut, see esp. Joachim Gaus, 'Die Urhütte. Über ein Modell in der Baukunst und ein Motiv in der bildenden Kunst', *Wallraf-Richartz-Jahrbuch* XXXIII, 1971, pp. 7–70; Joseph Rykwert, *On Adam's House in Paradise. The Idea of the Primitive Hut in Architectural History*, New York 1972.

[117] Laugier, *Essai* (1765), p. 9.

[118] Ibid., p. XVII.

[119] On Laugier's concept of proportion, cf. his *Essai* (1765), p. 107 and *Observations* (1765), pp. 5ff.

[120] Laugier, *Observations* (1765), p. 4.

[121] *'& qu'étant regardés comme la Nation qui a l'ésprit le plus délicat & les moeurs les plus légères, l'ordre françois soit le plus léger des ordres.'* Ibid., p. 276.

[122] Laugier, *Essai* (1765), p. 206.

[123] Laugier, *Observations* (1765), pp. 188ff.

[124] Cf. Edward Robert de Zurko, *Origins of Functionalist Theory*, New York 1957.

[125] Laugier, *Essai* (1765), pp. 222f.; *Observa-tions* (1765), pp. 312ff.

[126] *'Il y a plus art & de génie dans ce seul morceau, que dans tout ce que nous voyons*

ailleurs de plus merveilleux.' Laugier, *Essai* (1765), p. 201.

[127] Jacques-François Blondel, *Discours sur la nécessité de l'étude de l'architecture*, Paris 1754, p. 88; *L'homme du monde éclairé par les arts*, vol. II, Amsterdam 1774, p. 13.

[128] Cf. Ernst Beutler in his ed. of Goethe's *Von deutscher Baukunst*, Munich 1943, p. 31. But Beutler gives the date of the first German ed. of the *Essai* as 1768.

[129] Goethe, ed. Beutler (1943), p. 10.

[130] Goethe, *Italienische Reise*, 19 September 1786.

[131] On this subject, cf. Bruno Reudenbach, *G. B. Piranesi. Architektur als Bild. Der Wandel der Architekturauffassung des 18. Jahrhunderts*, Munich 1979.

[132] Kaufmann (1952), pp. 450ff.; John Harris, 'Le Geay, Piranesi and International Neoclassicism in Rome 1740–1750', *Essays in the History of Architecture Presented to Rudolf Wittkower*, London ²1969, pp. 189–96; Gilbert Erouart, 'Jean-Laurent Legeay, Recherches', in: *Piranèse et les Français* (conference proceedings 1976), Rome 1978, pp. 199–208; Reudenbach (1979), p. 86; Johannes Erichsen, *Antique und Grec*, diss. (1975), Cologne 1980, pp. 243–80; Gilbert Erouart, *Architettura come pittura. Jean-Laurent Legeay, un piranesiano francese nell'Europa dei Lumi*, Milan 1982.

[133] Harris (1969), p. 191.

[134] On Peyre, cf. Hautecoeur, vol. IV (1952), pp. 225ff.; Hernandez (1972), pp. 117ff.; Monika Steinhauser and Daniel Rabeau, 'Le théâtre de l'Odéon de Charles de Wailly et Marie-Joseph Peyre', *Revue de l'Art* 19, 1973, pp. 8–49; exhib. cat. *Piranèse et les Français 1740–1790*, Rome 1976, pp. 266ff.

[135] Marie-Joseph Peyre, *Oeuvres d'Architecture*, Paris 1765 (facs. repr. 1967); *Oeuvres d'Architecture. Supplément, composé d'un Discours sur les monuments des anciens*, Paris 1795.

[136] On Charles De Wailly, cf. exhib. cat. *Charles De Wailly. Peintre architecte dans l'Europe des lumières*, Paris 1979.

[137] Peyre (1765), p. 27, pls 18, 19.

[138] Ibid., Avertissement.

[139] Ibid.

[140] Ibid., p. 9, pls 3, 4.

[141] Ibid., p. 6.

[142] Ibid., p. 11, pl. 6.

[143] Ibid., p. 19, pls 13, 14.

[144] Cf. Paolo Marconi, Angela Cipriani, Enrico Valeriani, *I disegni di architettura dell'*

Archivio storico di San Luca, Rome 1974, vol. I, p. 19 (figs 495–508). The prizes in the Concorso of 1754 went to Filippo Marchionni, Pietro Camporese and Bernardo Liegeon.

[145] Peyre (1765), p. 23, pl. 16.

[146] Ibid., p. 8.

[147] E.g. his design for a round church: ibid., p. 17, pl. 12.

[148] Ibid., p. 3, Avertissement.

[149] Jean-François de Neufforge, *Recueil élémentaire d'architecture*, 10 vols, Paris 1757–1780; on Neufforge, cf. esp. Kaufmann (1968), pp. 151ff.; Johannes Erichsen, *Antique und Grec*, diss. (1975), Cologne 1980, pp. 386–91.

[150] Cf. Kaufmann (1969), pp. 149ff.; Remy G. Saisselin, 'Architecture and language: The sensationalism of Le Camus de Mézières', *British Journal of Aesthetics* 15, 1975, pp. 239–53.
The most important works of Nicolas Le Camus de Mézières are: *La génie de l'architecture ou l'analogie de cet art avec nos sensations*, Paris 1780 (facs. repr. Geneva 1972); *Le guide de ceux qui veulent bâtir*, Paris 1781 (Paris ²1786; facs. rpr. of this ed. Geneva 1972).

[151] Le Camus de Mézières (1780), p. 2.

[152] Ibid., p. 3. Cf. Charles Le Brun, *Méthode pur apprendre à dessiner les Passions proposée dans une conférence sur l'expression générale et particulière*, Amsterdam–Paris 1698 (numerous editions).

[153] Le Camus de Mézières (1780), p. 3.

[154] Ibid., pp. 10ff.

[155] Ibid., pp. 56ff.

[156] 'Le genre terrible est l'effet de la grandeur combinée avec la force. On peut comparer la terreur qu'inspire une scène de la nature à celle qui naît d'une scène dramatique.' Ibid., p. 59.

[157] Ibid., p. 64.

[158] Ribart de Chamoust, *L'ordre François trouvé dans la nature présenté au roi, le 21 septembre 1776*, Paris 1783 (facs. repr. 1967); cf. Jean-Marie Pérouse de Montclos, 'Le Sixième Ordre d'Architecture, ou la Pratique des Ordres Suivant les Nations', *Journal of the Society of Architectural Historians* XXXVI, 1977, pp. 233ff.

[159] Ribart de Chamoust (1783), p. 8.

[160] Ibid., p. 49.

[161] Jean-Louis Viel de Saint-Maux, *Lettres sur l'architecture des anciens et celle des*

modernes, dans lesquelles se trouve développé le génie symbolique qui présida aux Monuments de l'Antiquité, Paris 1787 (facs. repr. Geneva 1974). This treatise was formerly considered to be the work of Charles-François Viel (1745–1819), who was confused with Jean-Louis Viel de Saint-Maux. The two were identified as separate individuals by Jean-Marie Pérouse de Montclos, 'Charles-François Viel, architecte de l'Hôpital général et Jean-Louis Viel de Saint-Maux, architecte, peintre et avocat au Parlement de Paris', *Bulletin de la Société d'histoire de l'art français*, 1966, pp. 257–69; Françoise Fichet (1979), pp. 491f.

[162] Viel de Saint-Maux (1787), Introduction, pp. IXf.

[163] Ibid., letter I, p. 14.

[164] Ibid., letter II, pp. 8ff.

[165] Ibid., p. 14.

[166] Ibid., letter IV, p. 19.

[167] Ibid., Introduction, p. IX; letter I, p. 17.

[168] Ibid., letter II, p. 9.

[169] Cf. note 161 above; on Charles-François Viel's changing outlook, cf. Kaufmann (1952), pp. 457f.; cf. esp. Pérouse de Montclos, op. cit (1966), p. 257ff.

[170] Charles-François Viel, *Décadence de l'architecture à la fin du dix-huitième siècle*, Paris 1800.

Viel makes frequent reference to a further, self-published work, *Principes de l'Ordonnance*, which was not available to me (further published works are listed by Fichet (1979), p. 491). Viel made frequent contributions to the debate about Sufflot's design for Sainte-Geneviève in Paris, the last being *Moyens pour la restauration des piliers du dome du Panthéon François*, Paris 1797 (cf. Michael Petzet, *Soufflots Sainte-Geneviève und der französische Kirchenbau des 18. Jahrhunderts*, Berlin 1961; this work of Viel's was not known to the author).

[171] Charles-François Viel, *Projet d'une Monument consacré à l'histoire naturelle*. Paris 1797.

[172] Ibid., p. 2.

[173] Ibid.

[174] Ibid., p. 4.

[175] Ibid., p. 7.

[176] The most important of Emile Kaufmann's writings are: *Von Ledoux zu Corbusier. Ursprung und Entwicklung der autonomen Architektur*, Vienna 1933; 'Three Revolutionary Architects, Boullée, Ledoux and

Lequeu', *Transactions of the American Philosophical Society*, N.S., 42, 1952, pp. 429–564; *Architecture in the Age of Reason* (1955), New York 1968.

As the title of the first-mentioned work indicates, Kaufmann takes modern architecture to begin with Ledoux. In his later works he sees the Revolutionary architects more markedly in their historical context.

[177] They were first exhibited in November 1964 at the Bibliothèque Nationale, Paris, after some had been published by Kaufmann (1952). There have since been exhibitions of 'Revolutionary architecture' in several European countries and in the USA.

[178] Cf. Adolf Max Vogt, *Russische und französische Revolutions-Architektur 1917–1789*, Cologne 1974.

[179] Cf. esp. Jean-Marie Pérouse de Montclos, *Etienne-Louis Boullée (1728–1799). De l'architecture classique à l'architecture révolutionnaire*, Paris 1969.

[180] Helen Rosenau (ed.), *Boullée's Treatise on Architecture*, London 1953; Jean-Marie Pérouse de Montclos (ed.), *Etienne-Louis Boullée. Architecture. Essai sur l'art*, Paris 1968 (with further writings of Boullée); Helen Rosenau, *Boullée and Visionary Architecture*, London 1976 (with French–English text of the *Essai*).

[181] These are in the Uffizi; they belonged to the estate of the architect Giuseppe Martelli, who acquired them in 1818/19 from Boullée's heirs (cf. the catalogue *La Firenze di Giuseppe Martelli (1792–1876)*, Florence 1980, pp. 130f.). The drawings have been published by Klaus Lankheit: *Der Tempel der Vernunft. Unveröffentlichte Zeichnungen von E. L. Boullée*, Basel–Stuttgart 1968 ([2]1973).

[182] Besides Kaufmann, Helen Rosenau, Pérouse de Montclos and Lankheit above-cited, cf. esp. Adolf Max Vogt, *Boullées Newton-Denkmal. Sakralbau und Kugelidee*, Basel-Stuttgart 1969; Jacques de Caso, 'Remarques sur Boullée et l'architecture funéraire à l'âge des lumières', *Revue de l'art* 32, 1976, pp. 15ff.; Monika Steinhauser, 'Etienne-Louis Boullée's 'Essai sur l'art'. Zur theoretischen Begründung einer autonomen Architektur', *Idea. Jahrbuch der Hamburger Kunsthalle* II, 1983, pp. 7–47; Philippe Madec, *Boullée*, Paris 1986. Aldo Rossi's presentation of and preface to an Italian translation

of the *Essai* (Etienne-Louis Boullée, *Architettura. Saggio sull'arte*, ed. Aldo Rossi, Padua 1967, ²1977) is an indication of present-day architects' strong interest in Boullée.

[183] Claude-Nicolas Ledoux, *L'Architecture considérée sous le rapport de l'art...*, Paris 1804 (new ed. 1961), p. 113. On the whole question of the links between painting and architecture, cf. Bruno Reudenbach, *G. B. Piranesi. Architektur als Bild*, Munich 1979, esp. pp. 122ff.

[184] Boullée (ed. Pérouse de Montclos, 1968, p. 35 ('Considérations sur l'importance et l'utilité de l'architecture').

[185] Boullée, 'Considérations' (1968), p. 40.

[186] Boullée, *Essai* (1968), p. 47.

[187] '*Oui, je le crois, nos édifices, surtout les édifices publics, devraient être, en quelque façon, des poèmes. Les images qu'ils offrent à nos sens, devraient exciter en nous des sentiments analogues à l'usage auquel ces édifices sont consacrés.*' Ibid., pp. 47f.

[188] Ibid., p. 48.

[189] Ibid., p. 41.

[190] Ibid., p. 49.

[191] Ibid., p. 63.

[192] Ibid.

[193] Ibid.

[194] Ibid.

[195] Ibid., p. 64.

[196] Ibid., p. 67.

[197] Ibid., p. 65.

[198] Ibid., p. 73.

[199] Ibid., p. 74.

[200] Boullée, 'Considérations' (1968), p. 34: '*L'architecture étant le seul art par lequel puisse mettre la nature en oeuvre...*'

[201] Boullée, *Essai* (1968), pp. 69ff.

[202] Ibid., p. 82.

[203] Ibid., p. 85.

[204] Ibid., p. 133.

[205] Ibid.

[206] Ibid., p. 137.

[207] Ibid., p. 140.

[208] Cf. Vogt (1969), p. 268.

[209] Cf. Lankheit (1968, ²1973).

[210] On Boullée's deep involvement in the Académie's affairs (for example, he was present at the last session before its dissolution in 1793), cf. Lemonnier (ed.), vols IX and X. On the influence of Boullée, cf. Pérouse de Montclos (1969), pp. 209ff.; on Boullée's collaborative designs in the field of domestic architecture, cf. Werner Szambien, 'Notes

sur le recueil d'architecture privée de Boullée (1792–1796)', *Gazette des Beaux-Arts* 123, 1981, pp. 111–24.

[211] Besides the works on Revolutionary architecture to which reference has already been made, the following from the extensive literature on Ledoux should be cited: Wolfgang Herrmann, 'The Problem of Chronology in Claude-Nicolas Ledoux's Engraved Work', *The Art Bulletin* XLII, 1960, pp. 191–210; Johannes Langner, 'Ledoux' Redaktion der eigenen Werke für die Veröffentlichung', *Zeitschrift für Kunstgeschichte* 23, 1960, pp. 136–66; Yvan Christ, *Projets et divagations de Claude-Nicolas Ledoux*, Paris 1961; Johannes Langner, 'Ledoux und die "Fabriques". Voraussetzungen der Revolutionsarchitektur im Landschaftsgarten', *Zeitschrift für Kunstgeschichte* 26, 1963, pp. 1–36; Helen Rosenau, 'Boullée and Ledoux as Town-planners. A Re-Assessment', *Gazette des Beaux-Arts* LXIII, 1964, pp. 173–88; Helen Rosenau, *Social Purpose in Architecture. Paris and London Compared, 1760–1800*, London 1970; Serge Conard, 'De l'architecture de Claude-Nicolas Ledoux, considérée dans ses rapports avec Piranèse', conference proceedings *Piranèse et les Français*, Rome 1978, pp. 161–75; exhib. cat. *Ledoux et Paris* (*Cahiers de la Rotonde*, 3), Paris 1979 (with detailed bibliography); Michel Gallet, *Claude-Nicolas Ledoux 1736–1806*, Paris 1980; Bernard Stoloff, *L'affaire Claude-Nicolas Ledoux, Autopsie d'un mythe*, Brussels–Liège 1977; Anthony Vidler, *Claude-Nicolas Ledoux: Architecture and social reform at the end of the Ancien Régime*, Cambridge, Mass. 1990.

[212] Sebastien Mercier in *Tableau de Paris* (1781–88); cited from exhib. cat. (Staatliche Kunsthalle) *Revolutionsarchitektur: Boullée, Ledoux, Lequeu*, Baden-Baden 1970, p. 108.

[213] Kaufmann (1952), p. 499.

[214] Claude-Nicolas Ledoux, *L'architecture considérée sous le rapport de l'art, des moeurs et de la législation*, Paris 1804; a second edition, with posthumous material added, appeared in 1847, ed. Daniel Ramée (facs. repr. Paris 1961); facs. of 1804 edition with new plates of 1847 edition, 2 vols, Nördlingen 1981, 1984; facs. of 1847 edition with introduction by Anthony Vidler, Princeton 1983; for an account of the genesis

and composition of the work, cf. Gallet (1980), pp. 222ff.

[215] '*j'ai placé tous les genres d'édifices que réclame l'ordre social.*' Ledoux (1804), p. 1.

[216] '*La maison du pauvre, par son extérieur modeste, rehaussera la splendeur de l'hôtel du riche...*' Ibid.

[217] Ibid., p. 17.

[218] '*l'homme de métier est l'automate du Créateur; l'homme de génie est le Créateur lui-même.*' Ibid., p. 175.

[219] Ibid., p. 2.

[220] '*L'artiste ne peut pas toujours offrir aux yeux ces proportions gigantesques qui en imposent; mais s'il est véritablement Architecte, il ne cessera pas de l'être, en construisant la maison du bûcheron...*' Ibid., p. 198.

[221] '*Si la societé est fondée sur un besoin mutuel qui commande une affection réciproque, pourquoi ne réuniroit-on pas, dans des maisons particulières, cette analogie des sentiments et de goûts qui honorent l'homme?...Le caractère des monuments, comme leur nature, sert à la propagation et à l'épuration des moeurs.*' Ibid., p. 3.

[222] Ibid., p. 2.

[223] Ibid., pls 103, 104.

[224] '*L'unité type du beau, "omnis porro pulchritudinis unitas est", consiste dans le rapport des masses avec les détails ou les ornements, dans la non-interruption des lignes qui ne permettent pas que l'oeil soit distrait par des accessoires nuisibles.*' Ibid., p. 10.

[225] Ibid.

[226] Cf. Helen Rosenau, *Social Purpose in Architecture*, London 1970, pp. 14f.

[227] '*Pour la première fois on verra sur la même échelle la magnificence de la guingette et du palais...*' Ledoux (1804), p. 18.

[228] Ibid.

[229] '*ce vaste univers qui vous étonne, c'est la maison du pauvre, c'est la maison du riche que l'on a dépouillé.*' Ibid., p. 104, pl. 33.

[230] Cf. esp. Langner (1960), pp. 151ff.

[231] Ledoux (1804), pl. 88.

[232] Ibid., pl. 6.

[233] Ibid., pls 99, 100.

[234] Ledoux (1847), pls 313–16; cf. Gallet (1980), pp. 34ff.

[235] Hans Sedlmayr, *Verlust der Mitte*, Salzburg 1948, pp. 96f.

[236] Exhib. cat. *Revolutionsarchitektur* (1970), pp. 248f.

[237] Kaufmann (1952), pp. 538ff., places Lequeu among the Revolutionary architects. Cf. also Günter Metken, 'Jean-Jacques Lequeu ou l'architecture rêvée', *Gazette des Beaux-Arts* LXV, 1965, pp. 213–30; Jacques Guillerme, 'Lequeu et l'invention du mauvais goût', *Gazette des Beaux-Arts* LXVI, 1965, pp. 153–66; catalogue *Revolutionsarchitektur* (1970), pp. 165ff. Cf. also Philippe Duboy, *Lequeu: An Architectural Enigma*, London 1986, of unsound sensational thesis but with abundant source-material.

14. Germany and the Netherlands in the sixteenth century

[1] Cf. pages 110ff. of the present volume.

[2] Cf. the pioneering study by Erik Forssman, *Säule und Ornament. Studien zum Problem des Manierismus in den nordischen Säulenbüchern und Vorlageblättern des 16. und 17. Jahrhunderts*, Stockholm 1956.

[3] Pieter Coecke van Aelst, *Die inventie der colommen met haren coronementen ende maten*, Antwerp 1539 (facs. text in: Rudi Rolf, *Pietr Coecke van Aelst en zijn architektuuruitgaves van 1539*, Amsterdam 1978).

[4] Cf. Rolf (1978), pp. 21ff.

[5] Pieter Coecke van Aelst, *Generale reglen der architecturen*, Antwerp 1539 (further eds: Antwerp 1549, Amsterdam 1606, Basel 1608); facs. text of 1539 ed. in: Rolf (1978).

[6] Heinrich Vogtherr, *Ein frembds und wunderbars Kunstbüchlin allen Molern, Bildschnitzern, Goldschmiden, Steyn-metzen, Schreynern, Platnern, Waffen- und Messerschmiden hochnutzlich zu gebrauchen...*, Strassburg 1537, foreword (further eds 1538, 1572, 1608; facs. of 1572 ed., Zwickau 1913). On Vogtherr, cf. Forssman (1956), pp. 51f.

[7] Cf. p. 78; Rivius, cf. Josef Benzing, 'Walther H. Ryff und sein literarisches Werk. Eine Bibliographie', *Philobiblon* 2, 1958, pp. 126–54, 203–26.

[8] Walther Rivius, *Der furnembsten, notwendigsten, der gantzen Architectur angehörigen Mathematischen und Mechanischen künst, eygentlicher bericht...*, Nuremberg 1547 (facs. repr. Hildesheim 1981).

[9] Rivius (1547), dedication to the Bürgermeister and Council of Nuremberg. He mentions *inter alia* Pacioli, Cesare Cesariano, Philander, Serlio and Tartaglia. Julius von

Schlosser (*La letteratura artistica*, Florence-Vienna ³1964, p. 277) also cites Francesco Colonna's *Hypnerotomachia* and Valturio as sources. Schlosser's evaluation of Rivius's rambling, clumsy work as '*la vera Bibbia del tardo Rinascimento tedesco*' (p. 277) seems to me highly questionable. On Rivius, cf. also Wilhelm Lübke, *Geschichte der Renaissance in Deutschland*, vol. I, Stuttgart ²1882, pp. 152ff.

¹⁰ To this subject Rivius's treatise *Der fünff maniren der Colonen...*, Nuremberg 1547 (cf. Benzing, 1958, p. 219 no. 184) is devoted.

¹¹ Cf. p. 125.

¹² Rivius (1547), 'Von der befestigung', etc., fol. VI.

¹³ Ibid., dedication.

¹⁴ Albrecht Dürer, *Underweysung der Messung mit dem Zirckel und Richtscheyt*, Nuremberg 1525; 2nd enlarged ed., Nuremberg 1538; cf. bibliography by Luigi Vagnetti, 'De naturali et artificiali perspectiva', *Studi e documenti di architettura* 9–10, 1979, pp. 315ff.

¹⁵ Hieronymus Rodler, *Eyn schön nützlich büchlin und underweisung der kunst des Messens mit dem Zirckel, Richtscheidt oder Lineal*, Simmern 1531 (new ed. with introduction by Trude Adrian, Graz 1970).

¹⁶ Cf. Michael Prechtl in exhib. cat. *Wenzel Jamnitzer, Hans Lencker und Lorenz Stöer, drei Nürnberger Konstruktivisten des 16. Jahrhunderts*, Nuremberg 1969.

¹⁷ Lorenz Stöer, *Geometria et perspectiva. Hier Inn Etliche Zerbrochne Gebew den Schreinern in eingelegter Arbeit dienstlich...*, Augsburg 1567 (facs. repr. Frankfurt 1972).

¹⁸ Johannes Lencker, *Perspectiva literaria*, Nuremberg 1567 (facs. repr. Frankfurt 1972); *Perspectiva hierinnen auffs kützte beschrieben...*, Nuremberg 1591 (²1617).

¹⁹ Wenzel Jamnitzer, *Perspectiva Corporum Regularium*, Nuremberg 1568 (facs. repr. Frankfurt 1972).

²⁰ Cf. esp. Carsten-Peter Warncke, *Die ornamentale Groteske in Deutschland 1500–1650*, 2 vols, Berlin 1979.

²¹ Cf. esp. Ernst von May, *Hans Blum von Lohr am Main. Ein Bautheoretiker der deutschen Renaissance*, Strassburg 1910.

²² May (1910), pp. 27ff.

²³ Hans Blum, *Quinque columnarum exacta descriptio*, Zürich 1550; Hans Blum, *Von den fünff Sülen, Grundtlicher Bericht...*, Zürich 1555.

²⁴ Cf. survey by May (1910), pp. 76ff.; Rudolf Wittkower, 'La letteratura palladiana in Inghilterra', *Bollettino del Centro Internazionale di Studi di Architettura 'Andrea Palladio'*, VII, 1965, Part II, p. 132, speaks of 29 editions and translations. An English translation: Hans Bloome, entitled *A Description of the Five Orders of... Architecture*, London 1678 (facs. repr. 1967) is enhanced by plates by Wendel Dietterlin (1598) at the end.

²⁵ Cf. esp. Forssman (1956), pp. 75ff.

²⁶ Cf. May (1910), pp. 36ff.; Forssman (1956), p. 77.

²⁷ For a comparison, cf. esp. Christof Thoenes, 'Vignolas "*Regola delle cinque ordini*", *Römisches Jahrbuch für Kunstgeschichte* 20, 1983, pp. 347ff.

²⁸ Hans Blum, *Architectura antiqua, das ist Wahrhafte und eigentliche Contrafacturen ettlich alter und schönen Gebeuwen...*, Zürich 1561; cf. May (1910) pp. 61ff., 83ff.; Forssman (1956), p. 78.

²⁹ Forssman (1956), p. 78 concludes from this that the study of Serlio evidently spared Blum the necessity of visiting Italy. But as Blum is recorded as having been in Rome (according to Bertolotti, *Artisti svizzeri in Roma*, p. IX and 29), all one is entitled to conclude is that Blum made no use of drawings of Antique buildings of his own.

³⁰ Forssman (1956), p. 77.

³¹ Cf. esp. Forssman (1956), pp. 86ff., 156ff.; Eugeniusz Iwanoyko, *Gdański okres hansa Vredemana de Vries*, Poznań 1963; cat. of the engravings in: *Hans Mielke, Hans Vredeman de Vries*, diss., Berlin 1967; on the architectural paintings cf. Jean Ehrmann, 'Hans Vredeman de Vries (1527–1606)', *Gazette des Beaux-Arts* XCIII, 121, 1979, pp. 13–26.

³² Hans Vredeman de Vries, *Architectura der Bauung der Antiquen auss dem Vitruvius...*, Antwerp 1577, 1581 (facs. of 1581 ed., Hildesheim–New York 1973). His sources are given in the introduction to *Dorica*.

³³ '*...aber in dissen Niderlanden hatt man ain andren condition, zuvvissen in Stoetten vonn grosser negotsen, da die ortt khlein und theur sein so meuss es man allss inn die hoeche suechen umb fuil geriffs zuh iben, mitt ful liechts zu suechen inn der hoeche.*' Vredeman de Vries, *Architectura* (1581), introduction to *Dorica*.

34 'ingenium der Architectur wissen zu accommodieren nach der gelegenhayt dess landts artt und gebrauch...' Ibid.

35 'Denn es schickt sich nicht ubel, wenn man das alte mit dem newen maeßiglich schmucket'. Hans Vredeman de Vries, das ander Buech gemacht auff die zway Colonnen Corinthia und Composita, Antwerp ('1565) 1578; cited from Forssman (1956), p. 89.

36 'der Griff des Nordländers um den kalten Marmorschaft, die Eroberung der Materie ohne klassizistische Bedenken.' Forssman (1956), p. 89.

37 Cf. Forssman (1956), pp. 156ff.

38 Hans Vredeman de Vries, Perspective, Latin ed., Leiden 1604–05 (facs. repr. New York 1968); German ed. also Leiden 1604–05.

39 Hans and Paul Vredeman de Vries, Architectura, die köstliche und weitberumbte Khunst..., 1606.

40 These plates first appeared in Variae Architecturae Formae, ed. Hans and Paul Vredeman de Vries, Antwerp 1601.

41 Hans Vredeman de Vries, Hortorum Viridariorumque elegantes et multiplices formae..., Antwerp 1583.

42 Wendel Dietterlin, Architectura von Außtheilung, Symmetria und Proportion der Fünff Seulen und aller darauß volgender Kunst Arbeit von Fenstern, Caminen, Thurgerichten, Portalen, Bronnen und Epitaphien, Nuremberg 1598 (published in parts from 1593; facs. repr. with introduction by Hans Gerhard Evers, Darmstadt 1965; with introduction by Adolf K. Placzek, New York 1968).

43 Margot Pirr, Die Architectura des Wendel Dietterlin, diss. (Berlin 1940), Gräfenhainichen n.d.; on his painting, cf. Kurt Martin, 'Der Maler Wendel Dietterlin' in: Festschrift für Karl Lohmeyer, Saarbrücken 1954, pp. 14–29.

44 Cf. esp. the analyses by Forssman (1956), pp. 160ff.

45 Dietterlin (1598), fol. 3.

46 Ibid., fol. 5.

47 Such an attempt has been made by Forssman (1956), p. 167.

48 Forssman (1956), p. 168 points to a colour woodcut by Andrea Andreani dated 1588 as a model for this engraving.

49 The title-page of the 1598 edition states the print quantity to have been only 200 copies. The only reprint is dated 1655. On Dietter-

lin's influence, cf. Margot Pirr (1940), pp. 138ff.

50 Daniel Meyer, Architectura oder Verzeichnuß allerhand Eynfassungen an Thüren Fenstern und Decken etc. sehr nützlich unnd dienlich allen Mahlern, Bildhawern, Steinmetzen, Schreinern und anderen Liebhabern dieser Kunst, Frankfurt 1609.

51 'daß erstlich Wendel Dietterlins Werck nit also beschaffen, daß es jeder meniglich dienlich seyn könte, dieweil die Inventiones etwas schwer, mühsam unnd voller Arbeit, welche nicht einem jeden annemblichen, auch nicht ein jeder solche ad usum transferieren oder gebrauchen kann. Zum andern, so ist das Werck an ihm selber groß und hoch am Tax, derohalben nicht eines jeden gelegenheit, diß bey sich zu haben. Und zum dritten, dieweil die Welt allezeit nach newer Manier trachtet, so werden die nunmehr für bekannt und alt geachtet. Diese Werck aber im gegentheyl ist mehrens theyls componirt und zusammen gesetzt von etlichen leichtfertigen, geringschätzigen und doch zierlichen Innfassungen, so bißhero zuwegen zubringen gewesen, und doch zierlichen anzusehen sind, beneben auch mehrern theyls auff die jetzige Welt gerichtet.' Ibid., fol. 3.

52 Ibid.

53 Cf. Forssman (1956), pp. 172ff.

54 Gabriel Krammer, Architectura Von den funf Seulen sambt ihren Ornamenten und Zierden..., Cologne 1600; Prague 1606 (1606 ed. used).

55 Georg Caspar Erasmus (title-page anonymous; the author's name appears in the foreword), Seulen-Buch Oder Gründlicher Bericht Von den Fünf Ordnungen der Architectur-Kunst...durch Einen Liebhaber der Edlen Architectur-Kunst an den Tag gegeben, Nuremberg 1672; 1688 (foreword dated 1666).

56 Wilhelm Heyd (ed.), Handschriften und Handzeichnungen des herzoglich württembergischen Baumeisters Heinrich Schickhardt, Stuttgart 1902, pp. 15ff.

57 Heinrich Schickhardt, Beschreibung einer Reiß...in Italiam, Mömpelgard (Monbérliard) 1602; repr. Tübingen 1603; text in: Heyd (1902), pp. 65ff. Cf. Ludwig Schudt, Italienreisen im 17. und 18. Jahrhundert, 1959, pp. 52ff.

58 'Dise Biechlein sol man nach meinem Absterben in hohem Werdt halten und von meindt wegen auffheben.' Heinrich Schick-

hardt, *Etliche Gebey, die ich...zu Itallien verzaichnet hab, die ir lieb send* (in: Heyd 1902, pp. 303ff.); Gunter Schweikhart, 'Zur Wirkung Palladios in Mitteleuropa', *Actes du XXII ͤ Congrès International d'Histoire de l'Art* (1969), Budapest 1972, vol. I, pp. 677ff.
[59] Cf. Heyd (1902), pp. 335ff.
[60] 'besahe zu Venedig alles wohl und wunderlich Sachen, die mir zu meinem Bau-Werk ferner wohl erspriesslich waren.' Christian Meyer (ed.), *Die Selbstbiographie des Elias Holl*, Augsburg 1873, p. 22; Christian Meyer (ed.), *Die Hauschronik der Familie Holl (1487–1646)*, Munich 1910, p. 42.
[61] Elias Holl's manuscript is in the Graphische Sammlung of the Augsburg Museum (Inv. No. 11216); cf. Hanno-Walter Kruft and Andres-René Lepik, 'Das Geometrie- und Meßbuch von Elias Holl', *Architectura* 15, 1985, pp. 1–12.

15. The German-speaking regions in the seventeenth and eighteenth centuries

[1] Cf. esp. Curt Habicht, 'Die deutschen Architekturtheoretiker des 17. und 18. Jahrhunderts', *Zeitschrift für Architektur und Ingenieurwesen*, new series, 21, 1916, cols 1–30, 261–88; 22, 1917, cols 209–44; 23, 1918, cols 157–184, 201–30; Erik Forssman, *Säule und Ornament*, Stockholm 1956; Ulrich Schütte, *'Ordnung' und 'Verzierung'. Untersuchungen zur deutschsprachigen Architekturtheorie des 18. Jahrhunders*, diss., Heidelberg 1979. Schütte has an excellent bibliography and extensive material on the history of individual concepts; however, since the relationship between German and Italian, French and English architectural theory is treated only sporadically, the question of the originality of German theory is not addressed (Schütte's work is available in shortened form as a book with the same title, Brunswick–Wiesbaden 1986); Mario-Andreas von Lüttichau, *Die deutsche Ornamentkritik im 18. Jahrhundert*, Hildesheim–Zürich–New York 1983.
[2] Cf. Habicht (1916), cols 5ff.; Margot Berthold, *Joseph Furttenbach (1591–1667). Architekturtheoretiker und Stadtbaumeister in Ulm. Ein Beitrag zur Theater- und Kunstgeschichte*, diss. (typescript), Munich 1951; Wilhelm Reinking, *Die sechs Theaterprojekte des Architekten Joseph Furttenbach 1591–1667*, Frankfurt 1984.
[3] Joseph Furttenbach, *Newes Itinerarium Italiae in welchem der Reisende nicht allein gründtlichen Bericht...*, Ulm 1627 (facs. with foreword by Hans Foramitti, Hildesheim–New York 1971).
[4] Furttenbach (1627), pp. 182ff.
[5] Ibid., p. 193, pls 10, 11.
[6] Peter Paul Rubens, Palazzi di Genova, 1622; cf. ed. with introduction by Hildebrand Gurlitt, Berlin 1924 (on the eds of Rubens's work, cf. Gurlitt, p. V); with Furttenbach's illustrations, cf. esp. Rubens (ed. 1924), pl. 39. On *Palazzi di Genova*, cf. Ida Maria Botto, 'P. P. Rubens e il volume i "Palazzi di Genova",' in: exh. cat. *Rubens a Genova*, Genoa 1978, pp. 59–84; cf. also Anthony Blunt, 'Rubens and Architecture', *The Burlington Magazine* CXIX, 1977, pp. 609–21.
[7] 'Die Privatarchitektur aber, die ja in ihrer Gesamtheit den Stadtkörper ausmacht, sollte man nicht vernachlässigen, zumal die Bequemlichkeit der Gebäude fast immer mit ihrer Schönheit und guten Form übereinstimmt.' Cited from Gurlitt (trans., 1924), p. IV.
[8] Cf. Margot Berthold (1951), bibliography, pp. 230–32.
[9] Cf. Forssman (1956), pp. 196ff.
[10] Joseph Furttenbach, *Architectura civilis, das ist, Eigentlich Beschreibung wie man nach bester form und gerechter Regul fürs Erste Palläst...erbawen soll...*, Ulm 1628 (facs. text in: Hans Foramitti, ed., *Joseph Furttenbach, Architectura civilis...*, Hildesheim–New York 1971).
[11] Joseph Furttenbach, *Architectura universalis, das ist von Kriegs-, Statt- und Wasser Gebäwen...*, Ulm 1635.
[12] Joseph Furttenbach, *Architectura recreationis, das ist von Allerhand Nutzlich und Erfrewlichen Civilischen Gebäwen...*, Augsburg 1640 (facs. text in: Foramitti, ed., 1971).
[13] Joseph Furttenbach, *Architectura privata, das ist gründtliche Beschreibung neben conterfetischer Vorstellung, inn was Form und Manier ein gar Irregular, Burgerliches Wohn-Hauß...*, Augsburg 1641 (facs. text in: Foramitti, ed., 1971).
[14] 'Sintemablen es ja Weltkündig, das in Italia die allerköstlichste, Kunstreicheste, Würlich-

ste und Stärckeste Gebäw alß irgend anderstwo in gantz Europa zu sehen, gefunden werden.' Furttenbach, *Architectura civilis* (1628), 'Vorrede.'

[15] Ibid., p. 48.

[16] '*wol angelegt, künstlich eingethailt, dero Zimmer nach gebührender notturfft zum geschäfft und zur ruhe accomodirt und gerichtet sein sollen.'* Ibid., 'Vorrede.'

[17] '*Sondern mein intent geht dahin, den fürnemmen Zweck nach der Symmetrischen völligern Bestellung wie nemblich inwenaig an dem Baw-Corpore die Zimmer zuordnen (waran auch am maisten gelegen und wardurch der rechte finis der operation erarnet wird) auß richtigem fundament anzuzeigen und zu demonstrirn.'* Ibid.

[18] Ibid.

[19] '*der Liebhaber dergleichen zieraden nach wolgefallen studiren und erlernen kann.'* Ibid., p. 15.

[20] Ibid., pp. 1ff.

[21] Furttenbach, *Architectura universalis* (1635), p. 79.

[22] Ibid., Part II, pp. 44ff.

[23] Ibid., pp. 54ff., pl. 21.

[24] '*mit geringster impens... das Hauss mit wol accomodirten Zimmern zu renoviren bedacht.'* Furttenbach, *Architectura recreationis* (1640), p. 21.

[25] Furttenbach, *Architectura privata* (1641), pp. 19ff.

[26] Margot Berthold (1951), p. 214; Forssman (1956), pp. 196f. Notable amongst these joint works is the volume of plates *Feriae Architectonicae* (1649), edited by Joseph Furttenbach the Younger, which contains designs by Furttenbach the Elder, from various sources along with plates by his son.

[27] Cf. Habicht (1916), cols 261ff.

[28] Daniel Hartmann, *Burgerliche Wohnungs Baw-Kunst...*, Basel 1673 ('1688; this ed. used).

[29] '*gegenwärtige Riß entweder für sich selbsten oder nach des Bawherren Belieben zu veränderen und eitele Kram-läden, Bawrenhäuser, Scheuren oder Stallungen darauff zu machen....* Hartmann (1688), p. 40.

[30] Johann Wilhelm, *Architectura Civilis, Beschreib- oder Vorreissung der fürnembsten Fachwerck...*, Frankfurt 1649 ('1654); slightly revised ed., Nuremberg 1668 ('1702); facs. of 1668 ed., Hanover 1977.

On Wilhelm, cf. Werner Oechslin in exh. cat. *Vorarlberger Barockbaumeister*, Einsiedeln 1973, pp. 56ff.

[31] Oechslin (1973), p. 57 speaks of a dedication to Ludwig, Landgrave of Hesse. It is possible that the self-published book contained two different dedications. But the copy I have used, in the Hessische Landesbibliothek, Darmstadt (Sig. 31A 123), which originally belonged to the library of the Grand Duke of Hesse, does not contain such a dedication.

[32] Fame was clearly important to Wilhelm; his dedication declares that 'the begetting of children and the building of houses makes one's name immortal' ('*daß nehmlich Kinderzeugen und Häuserbauen den Namen unsterblich mache*').

[33] '*daß bey dieser letzten Römischen Monarchi der Griechen Architectur gleichsam in ihrer Würde auff die obersten Stueffen kommen.'* Wilhelm (1649), p. 2.

[34] *Architecturae Civilis Pars II*, ed. by the publisher, Paul Fürst, Nuremberg, n.d. (facs. in appendix of ed. Hanover 1977). In his foreword the publisher describes the book as his own work.

[35] Joachim von Sandrart, *L'Academia Todesca della Architectura Scultura et Pictura: Oder Teutsche Academia...*, Nuremberg 1675; *Der Teutschen Academie Zweyter und letzter Haupt-Teil*, Nuremberg 1679 (Latin ed., Nuremberg 1683). Sandrart's complete writings, ed. Johann Jacob Volkmann under the title *Teutsche Akademie der Bau-, Bildhauer- und Maler-Kunst* in 3 parts and 8 vols, Nuremberg 1768–75.

Excerpts ed. A. R. Peltzer, *Joachim von Sandrarts Academie der Bau, Bild- und Mahlerey-Künste von 1675*, Munich 1925.

[36] Cf. the analysis of Sandrart's sources in Jean Louis Sponsel, *Sandrarts Teutsche Academie kritisch gesichtet*, Dresden 1896.

[37] '*Sandrarts Absicht war, die besten Muster der alten und neuen Baukunst in Kupfern vorzustellen, und von derselben einige Nachrichten zu geben. Die Theorie oder die Regeln der Kunst hat er nur als eine Nebenabsicht betrachtet.'* Sandrart, ed. Volkmann, vol. I, 2 (1769), p. 6.

[38] Published by Victor Fleischer, *Fürst Karl Eusebius von Liechtenstein als Bauherr und Kunstsammler (1611–1684)*, Vienna–Leipzig 1910, pp. 87–209.

[39] '*ohne Zierdt mit glatter Mauer ist für ihn*

in allen zu schenden und zu verachten und gantz nichts zu schatzen und keiner Gedechtnus wierdig, und nur ein ordinari Werk, dehren die gantze Weldt mit ordinari Heusern vol ist...' Fleischer (1910), p. 96.

[40] Heinrich von Sachsen, *Fürstliche Bau-Lust, nach dero eigenen hohen Disposition...*, Glücksburg 1698.

[41] On Böckler, cf. Bernd Vollmar, *Die deutsche Palladio-Ausgabe des Georg Andreas Böckler, Nürnberg 1698. Ein Beitrag zur Architekturtheorie des 17. Jahrhunderts* (diss., Erlangen–Nuremberg), Ansbach 1983 (*Mittelfränkische Studien*, vol. III), with appendix containing a catalogue of Böckler's works and their editions.

[42] Georg Andreas Böckler, *Compendium Architecturae Civilis*, Frankfurt 1648.

[43] Georg Andreas Böckler, *Architectura civilis, nova & antiqua, das ist: Von den Fünff Säulen...*, Frankfurt 1663 (reprint bearing description as first ed., Frankfurt 1684).

[44] Georg Andreas Böckler, *Die Baumeisterin Pallas, oder der in Teutschland erstandene Palladius, das ist: Des vortrefflich-Italiänischen Baumeisters Andreae Palladii Zwey Bücher von der Bau-Kunst...*, Nuremberg 1698; (facs. repr. with introduction by Bernd Vollmar: Nördlingen 1988); cf. Gunter Schweikhart, 'L'edizione tedesca del trattato palladiano', *Bollettino del Centro Internazionale di Studi d'Architettura 'Andrea Palladio'* XII, 1970, pp. 273–91; Vollmar (1983).

[45] Georg Andreas Böckler, *Manuale Architecturae Militaris oder Hand-Büchlein über die Fortification...*, Frankfurt 1645; id., *Schola Militaris Moderna...* Frankfurt 1668 (²1685, ³1706).

[46] Georg Andreas Böckler, *Architectura curiosa nova. Das ist: Neue Ergötzliche Sinn- und Kunstreiche auch Nützliche Bau- und Wasser-Kunst...*, Nuremberg 1664 (facs. repr. with introduction by Renate Wagner-Rieger, Graz 1968).

[47] '*viel zierliche und künstliche Brönnen, welche hin und wieder in Italien, Franckreich, Engelland und Teutschland anjetzo befindlich, mit Fleiß abgerissen und verzeichnet, sambt Beyfügung eines jeden kurtzer Beschreibung.*' Böckler (1664), p. 2.

[48] On the original designs cf. Wagner-Rieger (1968), pp. 2ff. The connection with Charles Le Brun's *Livre de Fontaines...gravé à l'Eau-forte...* (cf. 1686) and the considerably earlier designs has yet to be studied, cf.

Gerold Weber, 'Charles Le Bruns „Recueil de divers desseins de fontaines",' *Münchner Jahrbuch der bildenden Kunst*, 3rd series, XXXII, 1981, pp. 151–81; Gerold Weber, *Brunnen und Wasserkünste in Frankreich im Zeitalter von Ludwig XIV*, Worms 1985, pp. 77ff.

[49] '*Was die Architectur oder Baukunst sey, und worinn dieselbe bestehe, ist eigentlich unser Vorhaben nicht hierinn zu tractiren, insonderheit weilen solches zuvor bey den alten und dann auch jetzo den neuen hocherfahrnen Scribenten und Baumeistern umständig und aus-führlich zu befinden.*' Böckler (1664), Part 4, 'Vorrede', p. 1.

[50] Latin translation by L. Chr. Sturm, 1664 and 1701; 2nd ed. of the German work, 1702–04.

[51] Salomon de Bray, *Architectura Moderna ofte Bouwinge van onsen tyt...*, Amsterdam 1631 (facs. repr. with introduction by E. Taverne, Soest 1971); cf. esp. Forssman (1956), pp. 204ff.

[52] Cf. p. 137.

[53] Jerónimo Prado and Juan Bautista Villalpando, *In Ezechielem Explanationes*, Rome 1596–1604; cf. Forssman (1956), pp. 208ff.; in the present volume, pp. 223ff.

[54] On Nicolaus Goldmann, cf. esp. Max Semrau, 'Zu Nicolaus Goldmanns Leben und Schriften', *Monatshefte für Kunstwissenschaft* IX, 1916, pp. 349–61, 463–73; Habicht (1917), cols 209ff.

[55] On Leonhard Christoph Sturm, cf. Isolde Küster, 'Leonhard Christoph Sturm. Leben und Leistung auf dem Gebiet der Zivilbaukunst in Theorie und Praxis', diss. (typescript), Berlin 1942; cf. also a monograph on the son by Fritz von Osterhausen, *Georg Christoph Sturm. Leben und Werk des Braunschweiger Hofbaumeisters*, Munich–Berlin 1978.

[56] E.g. Nicolaus Goldmann, *Tractatus de usu proportionatorii*, Leyden 1656; on his other works, cf. Semrau (1916), pp. 463ff.

[57] Cf. Semrau (1916), pp. 357ff.

[58] Nicolaus Goldmann, *Vollständige Anweisung zu der Civil-Bau-Kunst...vermehret von Leonhard Christoph Sturm*, Wolfenbüttel 1696 (facs. Baden-Baden–Strasbourg 1962); 2nd enlarged ed. with the addition of *Erste Ausübung der Vortrefflichen und Vollständigen Anweisung zu der Civil-Bau-Kunst Nicolai Goldmanns...herausgeben von Leonhard Christoph Sturm,*

Brunswick 1699 (this ed. here cited); 3rd ed., Leipzig 1708.

[59] 'vernünfftige Bau-Arth'...'ihren Uhrsprung von dem Tempel Salomonis nicht läugnen kan.' Goldmann-Sturm (1699), 'Dedicatio.'

[60] 'Dieser hat seine Bau-Kunst von dem Tempel Salomonis, als dem rechten Uhrquell abgezogen und zugleich die Ströhme der Alt-Römischen Weisheit damit vereiniget.' Ibid.

[61] Leonhard Christoph Sturm, De Sciagraphia templi Hierosolymitani, Leipzig 1694.

[62] 'Viel herrliche Gebäude werden geführet, da fast weder Seulen noch Bogen-Stellungen gebraucht werden.' Goldmann-Sturm (1699), 'Vorrede'.

[63] 'die Leichtigkeit des Vignola, das Ansehen des Palladio, und die genaue Außmessung samt der schönen Eintheilung des Scamozzi gleichsam mit einander zu vermählen.' Ibid.

[64] 'Dann die großen Baumeister scheinen von dieser Sache mit rechter Sorgfalt geschwiegen zu haben.' Ibid.

[65] 'mit allzuvielen und unnützen ausszieren der Bau-Kunst Ansehen verderben.' Ibid., p. 2.

[66] Ibid.

[67] 'daß er unsere Schrifften zu keinem Abgotte mache'. Ibid., p. 8.

[68] Ibid., p. 24.

[69] 'das Gemüthe gleichsam bestürtzen und verursachen, daß man sich darüber verwundern muß'. Ibid., p. 28.

[70] 'Dann unangesehen, daß ein Garten oder Lust-Wald, welcher also von Natur verwildert ist, lustig außsiehet, so ist doch gewiß, daß wann die Bäume in gleichen Weiten nach der Schnur gesetzet werden und gleiche Höhe haben, solches die Natur noch annehmlicher mache'. Ibid.

[71] Ibid., p. 32.

[72] Ibid., pp. 77ff.

[73] Ibid., 'Vorrede'.

[74] 'meistentheils altväterische Erfindungen... die der ißo gewöhnlichen Bau-Art ganz nicht gemäß...' Ibid., 'Vorrede' to the 'Erste Ausübung'.

[75] 'was ein Gebäude schön machen kan'. Ibid.

[76] Ibid., 'Erste Ausübung', pp. 13ff.

[77] On other attempts at a German Order, and also Silesian and Brandenburg orders, cf. Schütte (1979), pp. 141ff.

[78] Cf. Küster (1942), bibliography, pp. 201ff.; Schütte (1979), pp. 437ff.

[79] Leonhard Christoph Sturm, Vademecum Architectonicum bestehend in neu ausgerech-

neten Tabellen zu der Civil- und Militar-Baukunst..., Amsterdam 1700.

[80] Leonhard Christoph Sturm, Prodromus Architecturae Goldmannianae, Augsburg 1714.

[81] Leonhard Christoph Sturm, Architectonisches Bedencken von der protestantischen kleinen Kirchen Figur und Einrichtung, 1712; Vollständige Anweisung aller Art von Kirchen wohl anzugehen, 1718.

[82] Carl Philipp Dieussart, Theatrum Architecturae Civilis, in drey Bücher getheilet, Güstrow 1682; Bamberg 1697.

[83] Nikolaus Person, Novum Architecturae Speculum, Mainz n.d. (published between 1699 – the date on pl. 51 – and 1710, the year of Person's death); reissue, ed. Fritz Arens, (Beiträge zur Geschichte der Stadt Mainz, vol. 23), Mainz 1977.

On Person, cf. esp. Habicht (1916), pp. 276ff. (with erroneous evaluation of Person's originality as a designer); contributions by Elisabeth Geck and Reinhard Schneider in: Arens, 1977).

[84] On Person's sources, cf. Schneider (1977), pp. 5ff.

[85] Person (ed. 1977), pls 11, 12.

[86] On the 'Auer Lehrgänge', see esp. Norbert Lieb and Franz Dieth, Die Vorarlberger Barockbaumeister, Munich–Zürich 1960, pp. 14ff. (Munich ³1976); Werner Oechslin in exh. cat. Die Vorarlberger Barockbaumeister, Einsiedeln 1973, pp. 62ff.

[87] Johann Georg Bergmüller, Nachbericht zu der Erklärung des geometrischen Maasstabes der Säulenordnungen, Augsburg 1752.

[88] Paulus Decker, Fürstlicher Baumeister oder: Architectura Civilis, wie Grosser Fürsten und Herren Palläste...nach heutiger Art auszuzieren; zusamt den Grund-Rissen und Durchschnitten, auch vornehmsten Gemächern und Säälen eines ordentlichen Fürstlichen Pallastes, Augsburg 1711; Deß Fürstlichen Baumeisters Anhang zum Ersten Theil..., Augsberg 1713; Deß Fürstlichen Baumeisters oder Architecturae Civilis Anderer Theil, welcher Eines Königlichen Pallastes General-Prospect...vorstellet, Augsburg 1716.

On Paul Decker, cf. esp. Habicht (1918), cols 157ff.

On the relationship between Decker and Sturm, cf. ibid. (1917), cols 219f. and Isolde Küster (1942), pp. 161ff.

[89] Paulus Decker, Ausführliche Anleitung zur Civilbau-Kunst, 3 parts, Nuremberg n.d.

Published by Christoph Weigel, Nuremberg, it would appear, in 1719/20; for this little known and rare work is found bound together with Johann Jacob Schübler's *Perspectiva Pes picturae* in some copies of the latter issued by the same publisher; cf. eg. the copy in the Stiftsbibliothek, Göttweig, with which all three parts of Decker's work are bound together (cf. Gregor Martin Lechner in exh. cat. *Theorie der Architektur*, Göttweig 1975, pp. 62f.) The copy of Schübler's *Perspectiva* in the Kunsthistorisches Institut der Technischen Hochschule Darmstadt contains only Part 3 of Decker's work. As far as I am aware, only the first two parts have hitherto been known, insofar as the work has been known at all.

[90] At the end of this work are a number of plates illustrating church-building, rustication of façades, floor design, and timber construction. Some plates are signed by Daniel Heumann (1691–1759), which indicates that at least the third part is a posthumously published compilation by the publisher.

[91] *Damit der Geneigte Leser meine Gedancken von dem Titul-Kupffer, so dem gantzen Werck oran stehet und am ersten in die Augen fället, nur ein wenig wissen möge, so stellet sich hier die Gottheit für mit einer Flamme auf dem Haupt und in Wolcken durch eine Glorie, sich hernieder lassend; in der einen Hand Hält sie den Scepter als Regentin der Welt benebenst einer Tafel, auf welcher die Abzeichnung eines Gebäudes zu sehen ist; mit der andern Hand überreicht Sie der Ihr zu Seiten stehenden Architectur einen Circul und Winckel-Maaß, anzudeuten, Sie pflanze Ihr hiermit den gehörigen Verstand und Weißheit ein, allerley Sachen schicklich und zierlich auszuarbeiten. Die Architectur begleitet ein Genius, tragende eine Wasser-Waage in der Hand und haltende eine andere Tafel in der Hand, worauff der Grund-Riß eines Gebäudes stehet; der Genius selbst sieht mit seinen Augen auf einen zu seinen Füssen liegenden Quadranten. Die Mahlerey als der Architectur getreue Gehülffin, welche die angelegten Wercke und Gebäude ansehnlich schmücket und zieret, kniet neben der Architectur, und um sie herum liegen ihre bekandte und gewöhnliche Werck-Zeuge. Der Drey-Fuß, auf welchem besagte Künste der Gottheit ein wolriechendes Opffer bringen, zielet dahin, daß diese edle Künste sich Gott widmen und Ihm zu*

Ehren allerhand Gebäude, z. E. Tempel, Schulen Altäre u.s.f. auffrichten. Neben dem Drey-Fuß findet sich ein alter Mann mit einem Spiegel in der Hand, welcher die kluge Anweisung, durch die man zu den Künsten gelangen muß, vorstellig macht. Hart an ihm kommt die Bildhauer-Kunst hastig herzu gelauffen und herzo geeilet und hält in ihren Armen ein Modell von einer Statua, zu bemercken, daß schöne Gebäude durch die Statuen am besten ausgeschmückt und lebendig gemacht werden. Zunächst der Gottheit zeigen sich zwey Engel in einer Glorie und tragen eine Sternen-Crone, anzudeuten, die wahren Virtuosen erlangten nicht allein in ihrem Leben allbereit grosse Ehr und Estime; sondern ihr Ruhm bleibe nach ihrem Tod unsterblich. Noch mehr oben folget ein anderer Engel in einer Glorie und trägt in einer Hand ein Cornu Copiae mit verschiedenen Früchten; in der anderen aber hält er eine guldene Kette, daran kostbahre Medaillen hangen, und geht seine Absicht dahin, daß wahre Virtuosen durch ihre Geschicklichkeit grosser Herren Gnade erlangen und nicht selten Reichthum und Vergnügen sich erwerben. In der ferne ist auf der einen Seiten der Tempel der Ehren, auf der andern ein Lust-Gebäude entworfen.' Decker (1711), 'Erklärung des Titul-Kupffers'.

[92] Ibid., 'Vorrede'.

[93] *Lust-Häuser, Gärten, Orangerien, Grotten und Grotten-Häuser'* ... *'Risse von Kirchen und Capellen...'* *'Rath-Häuser, Schulen, Spittäle, Boursen, Zeug-Häuser...'* Ibid.

[94] Andrea Pozzo, *Perspectiva pictorum et architectorum*, 2 parts, Rome 1693–98.

[95] Curt Habicht, 'Die Herkunft der Kenntnisse Balthasar Neumanns auf dem Gebiet der „Civilbaukunst",' *Monatshefte für Kunstwissenschaft* IX, 1916, pp. 46–61.

[96] Cf. Schütte (1979), bibliography, pp. 434ff. (omitting the *Perspectiva*). A volume of Schübler's designs for interiors and furniture was edited by Albert Ilg (*Intérieurs und Mobiliar des XVIII. Jahrhunderts nach Erfindung des Johann Jacob Schübler*, Vienna 1885); on Schübler, cf. esp. Heinrich Gürsching, 'Johann Jacob Schübler. Ein Nürnberger Baumeister des Barockzeitalters', *Mitteilungen des Vereins für die Geschichte der Stadt Nürnberg* 35, 1937, pp. 17–57; Hans Reuther, 'Johann Jacob Schübler und Balthasar Neumann', *Mainfränkisches*

Jahrbuch für Geschichte und Kunst 7, 1955, pp. 345–52.

[97] Johann Jacob Schübler, *Perspectiva, Pes Picturae. Das ist: Kurtze und leichte Verfaßung der practicabelsten Regul zur Perspectivischen Zeichnungs-Kunst*, parts 2, Nuremberg 1719–20; Part I, '*Vorrede*': '*Wer sich die Regeln des Pozzo in seinem zweyten Theil bereits bekand gemacht, und darinnen weiter fortzufahren gedencket, der wird verhoffentlich, seine Begierde in gegenwärtigen Wercke, nach und nach befriedigen können.*'

[98] '*daß alles dasjenige, was in der Mahlerey und Zeichnungs-Kunst, wieder die Principia der Mathematik streitet, und durch dieselbe nicht zu demonstriren ist, mit grösten Recht zu verwerffen*'. Ibid.

[99] '*daß ohne die Perspectiv nicht das geringste sichtbare Object ohne Fehler vorgestellt werden kan*'. Ibid.

[100] '*Perspectiv, mit aller ihrer Accuratesse, die Fehler der Antiquen und modernen Architectur niemal verbergen kan; sondern vielmehr vor jedermanns Augen entdecket und offenbahr machet. Drum muß in solcher Verhältnüß, vor allem die Symmetria in jedem Stück der Invention wol beachtet werden...*' Ibid.

[101] Ibid., p. 29.

[102] '*die edle Kunst der Mahlerey als eine Tochter der Vernunfft*'. Schübler (1720), Part II, p. 3.

[103] Ibid., pp. 53ff. (pls 23, 24).

[104] '*Je länger man nun diese Betrachtung continuiret, je mehr Zufriedenheit überkommet das Gemüthe.*' Ibid., p. 54.

[105] '*die Optische Wissenschafft sey mit unter die subtilesten Kunst-Griffe der menschlichen Belustigung zu rechnen.*' Ibid., p. 53.

[106] Johann Bernhard Fischer von Erlach, *Entwurff einer Historischen Architectur*, Vienna 1721 (with German and French text; facs. repr. in much reduced format with afterword by Harald Keller, Dortmund 1978); 2nd ed., Leipzig 1725 (in separate vols with German and French text; this German ed. is here cited from a copy in the Hess. Landesbibliothek Darmstadt gr. Fol. 4/178; facs. of 1725 French text, 1964, with text of the first English trans. of 1730 in appendix); further eds, Leipzig 1742 (French text), London 1730, 1737 (English text).

On the *Entwurff einer Historischen Architektur*, cf. esp. Artur Schneider, 'Johann

Bernhard Fischer von Erlachs Handzeichnungen für den "Entwurf einer historischen Architektur",' *Zeitschrift für Kunstgeschichte* 1, 1932, pp. 249–70; Justus Schmidt, 'Die Architekturbücher der beiden Fischer von Erlach', *Wiener Jahrbuch für Kunstgeschichte* 9, 1934, pp. 147–56; George Kunoth, *Die Historische Architektur Fischers von Erlach* (Bonner Beitr. zur Kunstwiss., vol. 5), Düsseldorf 1956; Joseph Rykwert, *The First Moderns*, Cambridge, MA–London 1980, pp. 67ff.

[107] On the life and work of Fischer von Erlach, cf. esp. Hans Sedlmayr, *Johann Bernhard Fischer von Erlach*, Vienna–Munich 1956, revised 1976.

[108] Fischer von Erlach (1725), '*Vorrede*'.

[109] On the preparatory drawings, preserved in Zagreb, cf. Schneider (1932); clearly, Fischer originally intended his own work to feature more prominently. The plate with the depiction of Persepolis, engraved for the manuscript edition, was excluded from the published book (cf. Kunoth, 1956, fig. 102).

[110] Kunoth (1956), p. 24.

[111] '*das Auge der Liebhaber ergötzen und denen Künstlern zu Erfindungen Anlaß geben.*' Fischer von Erlach (1725), '*Vorrede*'.

[112] '*zu Beförderung sowohl der Wissenschaften als der Künste dienen*'. Ibid.

[113] '*wo man einem jeden Volke sein Gutdunken so wenig abstreiten kan als den Geschmack*'. Ibid.

[114] '*gewissen allgemeinen Grund-Sätzen fest, welche ohne offenbahren Ubelstand nicht können gergessen werden. Dergleichen sind die Symmetrie...*' Ibid.

[115] '*Corinthische Ordnung zu erst nach dem Salomonischen Bau durch die Phoenicier und Griechen entlehnet.*' Fischer von Erlach (1725), explanation to pls I and II.

[116] Fischer's sources have been thoroughly investigated by Kunoth (1956).

[117] For the most basic comparison, cf. Kunoth (1956).

[118] Stockholm, Nationalmuseum; reproduced by Kunoth (1956), fig. 70.

[119] Fischer von Erlach (1725), '*Vorrede*'.

[120] Jan Nieuhof, *Het Gezantschap Der Neerlandtsche Ost-Indische Compagnie...*, Amsterdam 1670; cf. Hugh Honour, *Chinoiserie. The Vision of Cathay* (1961), New York 1973, pp. 19ff.; exh. cat. *China und Europa*, Berlin 1973, p. 158 (No. E 12a);

Madeleine Jarry, *China und Europa*, Stuttgart 1981, pp. 20ff.

[121] Cf. Kunoth (1956), pp. 222ff.

[122] Salomon Kleiner, *Representation naturelle... de la Favorite...*, Augsburg 1726; *Representation au naturel des chateaux de Weissenstein au dessus de Pommersfeld, et de celui de Geibach...*, Augsburg 1728; *Representation exacte du chateau... Marquardsbourg ou Seehof...*, Augsburg 1731; cf. Karl Lohmeyer (ed.), *Schönbornschlösser. Die Stichwerke Salomon Kleiners...*, Leipzig 1927; a very reduced-size reprint of all three editions with afterword by Harald Keller, Salomon Kleiner, *Schönbornschlösser*, Dortmund 1980.

[123] François Cuvilliés, *Morceaux des caprices à divers usages*, Munich–Paris 1738, 1745, 1756 (continued up to 1799 by his son). Known copies differ in details of arrangement and sequence. Select facs., ed. Norbert Leib, Munich 1981.

[124] Johann Friedrich Penther, *Erster Theil einer ausführlichen Anleitung zur Bürgerlichen Bau-Kunst enthaltend ein Lexicon Architectonicum*, Augsburg 1744 (Part 2, 1745; Part 3, 1746; Part 4, 1748).

Albert Daniel Mercklein (*Mathematischer Anfangsgründe fünffter Theil Darinnen Die Architectura Civilis Oder Die Civil-Baukunst...*, Frankfurt–Leipzig 1737) had already set out practical rules for bourgeois building within the compass of a Vitruvius-based survey of architecture.

[125] Lorenz Johann Daniel Suckow (Succov), *Erste Gründe der bürgerlichen Baukunst im Zusammenhange entworfen*, Jena 1751 (²1763, ³1781, ⁴1798; facs. of 4th ed., Leipzig 1979), 1798 ed. used.

[126] Ibid., 'Vorrede'.

[127] '*verzierte Stützen, die als Stützen eine Last vor dem Falle sicher stellen sollen*'. Ibid.

[128] '*wenigstens zugleich in die Augen fallende... eine symmetrische Lage haben.*' Ibid., p. 14.

[129] Johann David Steingruber, *Practische bürgerliche Baukunst*, Nuremberg 1773.

[130] Johann Baptist Izzo, *Anfangsgründe der Bürgerlichen Baukunst*, Vienna n.d. (1773; German ed. used); *Elementa architecturae civilis*, Vienna 1784.

[131] '*Bequem ist ein Gebäude nach dem 3 §, wenn das Ganze und die einzelnen Theile also angeordnet sind, daß man die Geschäfte, zu welchen es vom Bauherrn bestimmet*

ist, gemächlich, Hinderniß, und Eckel darinn verrichten könne. Wird aber ein Gebäude wohl alles dieses leisten, in welchem man immer mit Unpäßlichkeiten kämpfen, oder immer wegen seiner Gesundheit in Sorgen stehen muß? in welchem man das Licht, das bey den meisten Handlungen des menschlichen Lebens so unentbehrlich ist, vermisset? in welchem man wegen der ungeschickten Anordnung der Theile von schädlicher Witterung, Müdigkeit, üblem Geruche und andern Unbequemlichkeiten belästiget wird? in welchem man endlich von einem Theile zum andern nur durch lange Umschweife kommen kann? Izzo (1773), p. 73.

[132] Ibid., pp. 82f.

[133] Ibid., p. 116.

[134] '*Diese Anordnung der Theile und des Ganzen wird desto schöner seyn, und in dem Gemüthe der Ansehenden ein desto grössers Vergnügen erwecken, je leichter sie das Aug wird bemerken und unterscheiden können; indem nur jenes für schön gehalten wird, was in die Sinne fällt und gefällt.*' Ibid., p. 113.

[135] Ibid., pp. 114ff.

[136] Johann Baptist Izzo (the author's identity emerges only from the preface), *Anleitung zur bürgerlichen Baukunst. Zum Gebrauch der deutschen Schulen in den kaiserl. königl. Staaten*, Vienna 1777.

[137] Franz Ludwig von Cancrin, *Grundlehren der Bürgerlichen Baukunst nach Theorie und Erfahrung vorgetragen*, Gotha 1792.

[138] Cancrin (1792), p. 269, para. 309.

[139] Johann Joachim Winckelmann, *Geschichte der Kunst des Altertums*, Dresden 1764 (facs. repr. Baden-Baden–Strasbourg 1966; cited from Wilhelm Senff (ed.), Weimar 1964).

[140] On Winckelmann and the theoretical background to his thought, cf. esp. Carl Justi, *Winckelmann und seine Zeitgenossen* (1866–72), 3 vols, Cologne ⁴1956; Gottfried Baumecker, *Winckelmann in seinen Dresdner Schriften*, Berlin 1933; Ingrid Kreuzer, *Studien zu Winckelmanns Ästhetik. Normativität und historisches Bewußtsein*, Berlin 1959; on Winckelmann's excerpts from the literature of artistic theory, cf. esp. André Tibal, *Inventaire des manuscrits de Winckelmann déposés à la Bibliothèque Nationale*, Paris 1911, pp. 104ff. (except from Blondel, p. 109).

For Winckelmann's collected writings, Johann Winckelmann, *Sämtliche Werke*, 12 vols, ed. Joseph Eiselein, Donaueschingen 1825–29 is still not superseded.

141 Winckelmann (1764, ed. 1964), p. 114.

142 Ibid., p. 121.

143 Johann Joachim Winckelmann, *Gedancken über die Nachahmung der Griechischen Wercke in der Mahlerey und Bildhauer-Kunst* (1755); cited from the critical ed. of Walther Rehm and Hellmut Sichtermann, J. J. Winckelmann, *Kleine Schriften, Vorreden, Entwürfe*, Berlin 1968, p. 43.

144 Cf. esp. the critical ed. of Rehm-Sichtermann (1968), pp. 342f.; on the derivation of '*noble simplicité*', cf. Martin Fontius, 'Winckelmann and die französische Aufklärung', *Sitzungsberichte der Deutschen Akademie der Wiss. zu Berlin. Kl. für Sprachen, Lit. und Kunst*, 1968, 1, p. 12; Johannes Erichsen, *Antique und Grec*, diss. (1975), Cologne 1980, pp. 41–90.

145 '*ein anderer muß durch allgemeine Anmerkungen und Regeln lehren*'. Johann Joachim Winckelmann, *Anmerkungen über die Baukunst der alten Tempel zur Girgenti in Sicilien* (1759), in: Rehm-Sichtermann (1968), p. 185.

146 '*In der Baukunst ist das Schöne mehr allgemein, weil es vornehmlich in der Proportion besteht; denn ein Gebäude kann durch dieselbe allein, ohne Zierrathen, schön werden und seyn.*' Johann Joachim Winckelmann, *Abhandlung von der Fähigkeit der Empfindung des Schönen in der Kunst* (1763), in: Rehm-Sichtermann (1968), p. 226.

147 Johann Joachim Winckelmann, *Anmerkungen über die Baukunst der Alten*, Dresden 1762 (facs. repr. Baden-Baden–Strasbourg 1964).

148 Friedrich August Krubsacius, *Betrachtungen über den Geschmack der Alten in der Baukunst*, *Neuer Büchersaal der schönen Wissenschaften und freyen Künste*, vol. IV, 1747, pp. 411–28. The significance of Krubsacius for Winckelmann has been indicated by Justi (1956), vol. I, pp. 308f. On Krubsacius cf. also Eberhard Hempel, *Geschichte der deutschen Baukunst*, Munich 1949, pp. 502f.

149 Cf. also Justi (1956), vol. II, pp. 425ff.

150 '*Das Wesentliche begreift in sich, vornehmlich theils die Materialien, und die Art zu bauen, theils die Form der Gebäude und die nöthigen Teile derselben.*' Winckelmann (1762), p. 1.

151 '*Ein Gebäude ohne Zierde ist wie die Gesundheit in Dürftigkeit… und wenn die*

Zierde in der Baukunst sich mit Einfalt gesellet, entsteht Schönheit: denn eine Sache ist gut und schön, wenn sie ist, was sie seyn soll. Es sollen daher Zierrathen eines Gebäudes ihrem allgemeinen so wohl, als besonderem Endzwecke gemäß bleiben… und je größer ein Gebäude von Alage ist, desto weniger erfordert es Zierrathen…' Ibid., p. 50.

152 Ibid., p. 21.

153 Cf. Dora Wiebenson, *Sources of Greek Revival Architecture*, London 1969, pp. 50f.

154 Johann Georg Sulzer, *Allgemeine Theorie der Schönen Künste*, 2 vols, Leipzig 1771–74 (pirate eds, Leipzig 1773/74, Biel 1777, the latter here cited; further pirate eds, Leipzig 1777/78 and 1778/79); an ed. with the addition of extensive bibliographies ('*Literarische Zusätze*') by Friedrich von Blankenburg, 4 vols, Leipzig 1786/87, 5-vol. ed. with Blankenburg's *Literarische Zusätze*, Leipzig 1792/94 (facs. repr. Hildesheim 1967–70); a complete ed. of Blankenburg's '*Literarische Zusätze*' without Sulzer's text, 3 vols, Leipzig 1796/98 (facs. repr. Frankfurt 1972).

On Sulzer's aesthetic theory, cf. esp. a detailed study by Johannes Dobai, *Die bildenden Künste in Johann Georg Sulzers Ästhetik*, Winterthur 1978. On Sulzer's contributions to the *Encyclopédie*, cf. Kevin Harrington, *Changing Ideas on Architecture in the 'Encyclopédie', 1750–1776*, Ann Arbor, MI 1985.

155 Sulzer (1777), vol. I, p. VI.

156 '*Aus einem öfters widerholten Genuß des Vergnügens an dem Schönen und Guten, erwächst die Begierde nach demselben, und aus dem widrigen Eindruck, den das Häßliche und Böse auf uns macht, entsteht der Widerwillen gegen alles, was der sittlichen Ordnung entgegen ist.*' Ibid.

157 '*völlige Bewürkung der menschlichen Glückseligkeit*'. Ibid.

158 Ibid., p. VIII.

159 In the *Frankfurter gelehrte Anzeigen* of 1772; cf. *Frankfurter Gelehrte Anzeigen 1772. Auswahl*, Leipzig 1971, pp. 50ff., 344ff. Merck's comment on Sulzer's work is apt: '*Es enthält dieses Buch Nachrichten eines Mannes, der in das Land der Kunst gereist ist; allein er ist nicht in dem Lande geboren und erzogen, hat nie darin gelebt, nie darin gelitten und genossen*' (op. cit., 1971, p. 50). ('This book contains reports from a man

who has travelled in the land of Art; but he was not born or brought up there, nor has he ever lived there, nor known suffering and joy there'.)

[160] Sulzer (1777), vol. I, pp. 169–77.

[161] 'Bewundrung, Ehrfurcht, Andacht, feyerliche Rührung… dieses sind Würkungen des durch Geschmak geleiteten Genies…' Ibid.

[162] 'Jeder organisierte Körper ist ein Gebäude; jeder innere Theil ist vollkommen zu dem Gebrauch, wozu er bestimmt ist, tüchtig; alle zusammen aber sind in der bequemsten und engesten Verbindung; das Ganze hat zugleich in seiner Art die beste äußerliche Form, und ist durch gute Verhältnisse, durch genaue Uebereinstimmung der Theile, durch Glanz und Farbe angenehm.' Ibid, p. 171.

[163] 'sich in den wahren Geschmack des Alterthums zu setzen'. Ibid., p. 175.

[164] 'Wenn man fragt, welche Bauart die beste sey; so könnte man antworten; für Tempel, Triumphbogen und große Monumente sey die alte Bauart die beste; für Palläste die italiänische, aber mit der griechischen Genauigkeit verbunden; zu Wohnhäusern aber die französische'. Ibid., p. 169.

[165] Ibid., pp. 317ff. ('Denkmal').

[166] Ibid., p. 655 ('Gothisch').

[167] Dobai (1978) in my opinion overemphasises the significance of Sulzer's English sources.

[168] Cf. note 154 above.

[169] On Sulzer's influence, cf. Dobai (1978), pp. 221ff.

[170] Christian Traugott Weinlig, Briefe über Rom verschiedenen die Werke der Kunst, der öffentlichen Feste, Gebräuche und Sitten betreffenden Innhalts, 3 vols, Dresden 1782–87.

On Weinlig, cf. esp. Paul Klopfer, Christian Traugott Weinlig und die Anfänge des Klassizismus in Sachsen, Berlin 1905; Schütte (1979), pp. 65ff.

[171] Klopfer (1905), pp. 30ff.

[172] 'Vielleicht trugen aber auch die systematischen Werke eines Vignola, Scamozzi, Branca und Andrer zu diesem Verfall der Baukunst nicht wenig bey'. Weinlig, vol. II (1784), p. 2.

[173] Karl Philipp Mortiz, Vorbegriffe zu einer Theorie der Ornamente, Berlin 1793 (facs. repr. with introduction by Hanno-Walter Kruft, Nördlingen 1986). For further analysis of this work, cf. Ruth Ghisler, "Vorbegriffe zu einer Theorie der Ornamente' von

Karl Philipp Moritz', Jahrbuch des Freien Deutschen Hochstifts, 1970, pp. 32–58.

[174] 'Das schönste Säulenkapitäl trägt und stützt nicht besser als der stumpfe Schafft – Das kostbarste Gesimse deckt und wärmt nicht besser, als die platte Wand.' Moritz (1793), p. 4.

[175] 'durch das Auge die Seele ergötzen und unmerklich auf die Verfeinerung des Geschmacks und Bildung des Geistes wirken'. Ibid.

[176] 'das Wesen der Sache, woran sie befindlich ist, auf alle Weise anzudeuten und zu bezeichnen, damit wir in der Zierrath die Sache gleichsam wieder erkennen und wieder finden.' Ibid., p. 18.

[177] Ibid., p. 19.

[178] Ibid., p. 20.

[179] Ibid., pp. 67f.

[180] Ibid., pp. 73ff.

[181] 'Ein Gebäude soll durch seine edle Zweckmäßigkeit, durch das schöne Ebenmaß seiner Theile, je länger man es betrachtet, den Blick immer wieder an sich fesseln, und durch das Auge der nachdenkenden Vernunft Beschäftigung geben.' Ibid., pp. 76ff.

[182] 'Untersuchungen über den Charakter der Gebäude; über die Verbindung der Baukunst mit den Schönen Künsten und über die Wirkungen, welche durch dieselbe hervorgebracht werden sollen,' Dessau 1785 (2nd ed. Leipzig 1788; facs. repr. of 1788 ed. with introduction by Hanno Walter Kruft, Nördlingen 1986); on this work, cf. Hanno-Walter Kruft, 'Revolutionsarchitektur für Deutschland?', Jahrbuch des Zentralinstituts für Kunstgeschichte 3, 1987, pp. 277–89.

[183] Untersuchungen (1788), p. 10.

[184] 'Ein prächtiges Haus stellt uns allemal einen glücklichen Menschen vor.' Ibid., p. 23.

[185] Ibid., pp. 38ff, 109.

[186] Ibid., pp. 87ff.: 'Die Verzierungen der Säulen haben in dem Character der Gebäude weiter keinen Einfluß, als daß sie die Mannigkfaltigkeit befördern' (p. 88). ('The ornamentation of the Orders has no further effect, in the character of a building, than that of contributing variety.')

[187] 'Je reicher die Colonnade ist, desto mehr zieht sie unsere Aufmerksamkeit von dem Geist des Gebäudes ab. Sie frappiert, aber sie rührt nicht. Sanfte Charaktere also, überhaupt alle, die Bewunderung und stilles Nachdenken erwecken sollen, vertragen keine zahlreichen Säulenstellungen. Vielmehr

sind diese dem lebhaften, prächtigen und heroischen Character eigen.' Ibid., p. 93.

188 Ibid., pp. 178f.

189 The preface (p. 6) is dated January 1784 (Berlin).

190 Johann Wolfgang von Goethe, *Von deutscher Baukunst*, Darmstadt 1772 (1773); included by Herder in the anthology *Von Deutscher Art und Kunst* (Hamburg 1773); cf. esp. the critical ed. *Von deutscher Baukunst. Goethes Hymnus auf Erwin von Steinbach*, ed. Ernst Beutler, Munich 1943. On Goethe's changing attitude to the Gothic, cf. esp. W. D. Robson-Scott, *The Literary Background of the Gothic Revival in Germany*, Oxford 1965; Harald Keller, *Goethes Hymnus auf das Straßburger Münster und die Wiedererweckung der Gotik im 18. Jahrhundert (Bayer. Ak. d. Wiss., Philol.-Hist. Kl., Sitzungsberichte 1974*, Heft 4); on the theoretical background to the work, cf. Norbert Knopp, 'Zu Goethes Hymnus "Von Deutscher Baukunst",' *Deutsche Vierteljahrsschrift für Literaturwissenschaft und Geistesgeschichte* 53, 1979, pp. 617–50; Hanno-Walter Kruft, 'Goethe und der Architektur', *Pantheon* XL, 1982, pp. 282–89.

191 Cited from Goethe (Berliner Ausgabe), vol. 19 (*Schriften zur bildenden Kunst*, 1), Berlin–Weimar 1973, p. 33.

192 Paolo Frisi, *Saggio sopra l'architettura gotica*, Livorno 1776.

193 Cf. new ed. of *Von deutscher Art und Kunst*, ed. Dietrich Irmscher, Stuttgart 1968, pp. 105ff.

194 '*Aus Wahrheit und Lüge ein Drittes bildet, dessen erborgtes Dasein uns bezaubert*'. Goethe, *Italienische Reise*, 19 September 1786. On Goethe's attitude to Palladio, cf. Herbert von Einem, *Beiträge zu Goethes Kunstauffassung*, Hamburg 1956, pp. 179ff.; Günther Martin, 'Goethe und Palladio – Fiktion klassischer Architektur', *Jahrbuch des Freien Deutschen Hochstifts*, 1977, pp. 61–82.

195 '*Denn wie die Jahrhunderte sich aus dem Ernsten in das Gefällige bilden, so bilden sie den Menschen mit, ja sie erzeugen ihn so. Nun sind unsere Augen und durch sie unser ganzes inneres Wesen an schlankere Baukunst hinangetrieben und entschieden bestimmt, so daß uns diese stumpfen, kegelförmigen, enggedrängten Säulenmassen lästig, ja furchtbar erschienen.*' Goethe, *Italienische Reise*, 23 March 1787.

196 '*die letzte und, fast möcht' ich sagen, herrlichste Idee, die ich nun nordwärts vollständig mitnehme, erscheint.*' Ibid., 17 May 1787. On the whole question cf. Walther Rehm, *Griechentum und Goethezeit*, Leipzig ²1938, Humphrey Trevelyan, *Goethe and the Greeks*, London 1941.

197 '*Leider suchten alle nordischen Kirchenverzierer ihre Größe nur in der multiplizierten Kleinheit.*' Goethe, 'Baukunst' (1788), in: Goethe (Berliner Ausgabe), vol. 18 (*Schriften zur bildenden Kunst*, 1), 1973, p. 75.

198 Goethe, 'Baukunst' (1795), in: Goethe (Berlinger Ausgabe), vol. 19 (*Schriften zur bildenden Kunst*, 1), 1973, p. 108. Cf. Alste Horn-Oncken, *Über das Schickliche. Studien zur Geschichte der Architekturtheorie* I, Göttingen 1967, pp. 9ff.

199 '*Solange man nur den nächsten Zweck vor Augen hatte und sich von dem Material mehr beherrschen ließ, als daß man es beherrschte, war an keine Kunst zu denken...*' Ibid., p. 109.

200 '*die auch in der Baukunst gern alles zu Prosa machen möchten*'. Ibid., p. 111.

201 '*Es ist eigentlich der poetische Teil, die Fiktion, wodurch ein Gebäude wirklich zum Kunstwerk wird.*' Ibid., p. 119.

202 '*Das Äußere der Gebäude sprach ihre Bestimmung unzweideutig aus, sie waren würdig und stattlich, weniger prächtig als schön. Den edlern und ernsteren in Mitte der Stadt schlossen sich die heitern gefällig an, bis zuletzt zierliche Vorstädte anmutigen Stils gegen das Feld sich hinzogen, und endlich als Gartenwohnungen zerstreuten.*' Goethe, *Wilhelm Meisters Wanderjahre* (1821), Book II, chapter 8.

203 '*Bildende Künstler müssen wohnen wie Könige und Götter, wie wollten sie denn sonst für Könige und Götter bauen und verzieren?*' Ibid.

204 See esp. Herrmann Wirth, 'Clemens Wenzeslaus Coudray (1775–1845). Architekturtheoretische Anschauungen', *Wissenschaftliche Zeitschrift der Hochschule für Architektur und Bauwesen Weimar* 22, 1975, pp. 473–83, Anita Bach et al., *Clemens Wenzeslaus Coudray. Baumeister der späten Goethezeit*, Weimar 1983.

205 Goethe (Berliner Ausgabe), vol. 19 (*Schriften zur bildenden Kunst*, 1), 1973, pp. 121ff.

206 Hans Ruppert, *Goethes Bibliothek*, cat., Weimar 1958, pp. 339ff.

207 '*das Geschichtliche dieser ganzen Angele-*

genheit'. Goethe (Berliner Ausgabe), vol. 20 (*Schriften zur bildenden Kunst*, 2), 1974, p. 357; cf. Robson-Scott (1965, pp. 213ff. and exhib. cat. *Der Kölner Dom im Jahrhundert seiner Vollendung*, vol. 2, Cologne 1980, esp. pp. 171f.

[208] 'So beschauen wir mit Vergnügen einige Massen jener gotischen Gebäude, deren Schönheit aus Symmetrie und Proportion des Ganzen zu den Teilen und der Teile *untereinander entsprungen erscheint und bemerklich ist, ungeachtet der häßlichen Zierraten, womit sie verdeckt sind...*' Goethe (1974), p. 336.

[209] 'Eines der vorzüglichsten Kennzeichen des Verfalls der Kunst ist die Vermischung der verschiedenen Arten derselben.' Goethe, introduction to *Propyläen*, vol. I, 1798, p. XXIV (facs. repr. with introduction by Wolfgang von Löhneysen, Darmstadt 1965).

16. The Italian contribution in the eighteenth century

[1] Although a start has been made by the following: Emil Kaufmann, *Architecture in the Age of Reason* (1955), New York 1968, pp. 89ff.; Carroll L. V. Meeks, *Italian Architecture 1750–1914*, New Haven–London 1966, pp. 3ff.; Luciano Patetta, *L'Architettura dell'eclettismo. Fonti, teorie, modelli 1750–1900*, Milan 1975; Alessandro Gambuti, *Il dibattito sull' architettura nel Settecento europeo*, Florence 1975.

[2] On the history of its design, cf. Dorothy Metzger Habel, 'Piazza S. Ignazio, Rome, in the 17th and 18th Centuries', *Architectura* 11, 1981, pp. 31–65.

[3] Ferdinando Galli Bibiena, *L'Architettura civile preparata su la geometria, e ridotta alle prospettive, considerazioni pratiche...*, Parma 1711 (facs. ed. Diana M. Kelder, New York 1971).

On Ferdinando Galli Bibiena cf. Franz Hadamowsky, *Die Familie Galli Bibiena in Wien*, Vienna 1962 (publishing part of a working sketchbook of the family Galli Bibiena); exh. cat. ed. Maria Teresa Muraro and Elena Povoledo, *Disegni teatrali dei Bibiena*, Venice 1970; exh. cat. *Architettura, Scenografia, Pittura di paesaggio (L'Arte del Settecento emiliano)*, Bologna 1980, pp. 263f.

[4] Galli Bibiena (1711), 'A'Lettori'. Cf. also Deanna Lenzi, 'La "veduta per angolo" nella scenografia', exh. cat. *Architettura, scenografia*, etc. (1980), pp. 147ff.

[5] Galli Bibiena (1711), 'A'Lettori'.

[6] Ibid., pp. 130ff.

[7] Ferdinando Galli Bibiena, *Direzioni a' giovani studenti nel disegno dell'architettura civile...*, Bologna 1725 (1731, 1745, 1753, 1777).

[8] Giuseppe Galli Bibiena, *Architetture, e Prospettive*, Augsburg 1740 (facs. repr. with intro. by A. Hyatt Mayor under the title *Architectural and Perspective Designs*, New York 1964).

[9] Girolamo Fondo, *Elementi di architettura civile, e militari ad uso del Collegio Nazareno*, Rome 1764.

[10] Mario Gioffredi, *Dell'architettura. Parte prima nella quale si tratta degli Ordini del Architettura de' Greci, e degl' Italiani, e si danno le regole più spedite per designarli*, Naples 1768 (all that was published).

[11] Girolamo Masi, *Teoria e pratica di architettura per istruzione della gioventù specialmente Romana*, Rome 1788.

[12] Giuseppe Maria Ercolani (described as 'opera di Neralco P.A.'), *I tre ordini d'architettura dorico, jonico, e corintio, presi dalle Fabbriche più celebri dell' Antica Roma, esposti in uso con un nuovo esattissimo metodo*, Rome 1744.

[13] Federico Sanvitali, *Elementi di Architettura civile*, Brescia 1765.

[14] Ermenegildo Pini, *Dell'Architettura. Dialogi*, Milan 1770.

[15] Francesco Maria Preti, *Elementi di Architettura*, Venice 1780, p. 47.

[16] Bernardo Antonio Vittone, *Istruzioni Elementari per indirizzo de'giovani allo studio dell'Architettura Civile divise in libri tre...*, 2 vols, Lugano 1760.

Bernardo Antonio Vittone, *Istruzioni diverse concernenti l'officio dell'Architetto Civile... ad aumento alle Istruzioni Elementari... Della misura delle Fabbriche, del Moto, Misura delle acque correnti, estimo de'beni...*, 2 vols, Lugano 1766.

[17] On Vittone see esp. Carlo Perogalli, 'Nota sull'architettura di Bernardo Vittone', *Arte in Europa. Scritti di Storia dell'arte in onore di Edoardo Arslan*, vol. I, 1966, pp. 875–90; Paolo Portoghesi, *Bernardo Vittone. Un Architetto tra Illuminismo e Rococò*, Rome 1966, pp. 23ff.; *Bernardo Vittone e la disputa*

fra classicismo e barocco nel Settecento, Atti del convegno internationale (1970), 2 vols, Turin 1972–74 (see esp. Augusto Cavallari Murat, 'Aggiornamento tecnico e critico nei trattati vittoniani', vol. I, pp. 457–554); Werner Oechslin, *Bildungsgut und Antikenrezeption im frühen Settecento in Rom. Studien zum römischen Aufenthalt Bernardo Antonio Vittones*, Zürich 1972.

[18] '*primo la semplicità, e naturalezza dell'origine degli oggetti in ordine a quel che rappresentano; secondo la varietà, e lo scherzo delle loro figure.*' Vittone (1760), vol. I, p. 412.

[19] Ibid.

[20] '*con riflesso d'uniformarsi nel Disegno di tale di lei parte allo stile, di cui è formato il corpo della chiesa.*' Vittone (1766), vol. I, p. 174; vol. II, pls 46, 47. Cf. also Karl Noehles, 'I progtti del Vanvitelli e del Vittone per la facciata del Duomo di Milano', *Arte in Europa. Scritti di Storia dell'arte in onore di Edoardo Arslan*, vol. I, 1966, pp. 869–74; Nino Carboneri, 'Il dibattito sul gotico', in: *Atti (Vittone)* (1972), vol. I, pp. 111–38.

[21] Vittone (1766), vol. I, p. 322.

[22] This is shown by a catalogue of Vittone's library; cf. Portoghesi (1966), pp. 12ff.

[23] Luigi Vanvitelli, *Dichiarazione dei Disegni del Reale Palazzo di Caserta*, Naples 1756, dedication to the king.

[24] The most informative contributions to the extensive literature on this competition are the following: Adriano Prandi, 'Antonio Deriset e il Concorso per la facciata di S. Giovanni in Laterano', *Roma* 22, 1944, pp. 23–31 esp. on the jury's attitude; Vincenzo Golzio, 'La facciata di S. Giovanni in Laterano e l'architettura del Settecento', in: *Miscellanea Bibliothecae Hertzianae*, Munich 1961, pp. 450–63; Hellmuth Hager et al., *Architectural Fantasy and Reality*, exh. cat., University Park, Penn. 1982, pp. 43ff.; Elisabeth Kieven, *Alessandro Galilei*, London (in preparation).

[25] Cf. Ilaria Toesca, 'Alessandro Galilei in Inghilterra', *English Miscellany* III, 1952, pp. 189–220.

[26] '*un sol Ordine ad imitazione degli antici... senza tanti superflui abbellimenti...*' *Discorso*; Golzio (1961), p. 462. I am indebted to Elisabeth Kieven for the oral information that the *Discorso* cannot be by

Galilei, but is very probably the work of Fuga (cf. Kieven, note 24 above).

[27] Cf. Ludwig von Pastor, *Geschichte der Päpste*, vol. 15, Freiburg 1930, pp. 750ff.

[28] Francesco Algarotti, *Saggio sopra l'architettura* (1756); first published in: Francesco Algarotti, *Opere varie*, Venice 1757; citations hereafter from Francesco Algarotti, *Opere*, 17 vols, Venice 1791–94 (vol. III, 1791, p. 352). Modern edition: Francesco Algarotti, *Saggi*, ed. Giovanni da Pozzo, Bari 1963, pp. 29–52. Literature on the *Saggio* frequently cites an erroneous publication date of 1753.

Andrea Memmo, *Elementi dell'architettura lodoliana*, Rome 1786; Andrea Memmo, *Elementi d'Architettura lodoliana... libri tre*, 2 vols, Zara 1833–34 (facs. repr. Milan 1973, cited hereafter).

The most important literature on Lodoli: Emil Kaufmann, 'Piranesi, Algarotti and Lodoli', *Gazette des Beaux-Arts* XLVI, 1955, pp. 21–28; Kaufmann, *Architecture in the Age of Reason* (1955, ed. 1968), pp. 95ff.; Edgar Kaufmann jr, 'Memmo's Lodoli', *The Art Bulletin* XLVI, 1964, pp. 159–75; Augusto Cavallari-Murat, 'Congetture sul trattato d'architettura progettato dal Lodoli', *Atti e rassegna tecnica della Società Ingegneri e Architetti in Torino*, new series, 20, 1966, pp. 271–80; Ennio Concina, 'Architettura militare e scienza: prospettive e indagine sulla formazione veneziana e sull' "entourage" familiare di Padre Carlo Lodoli', *Storia Architettura* II, 3, 1975, pp. 19–22; Ennio Concina, 'Per padre Carlo Lodoli – Giovanbattista Lodoli ingegnere militare', *Arte Veneta* XXX, 1976, p. 240; Joseph Rykwert, 'Lodoli on function and representation', *Architectural Review* CLX, 1976, 2, pp. 21–26; Joseph Rykwert, '*The First Moderns*', Cambridge, MA–London 1980, pp. 288f.

[29] On Lodoli's life, cf. esp. Memmo (1833), vol. I, pp. 39ff.

[30] Ibid., p. 79.

[31] Rykwert (1976), pp. 21f. (fig. 2).

[32] Memmo (1833), vol. I, p. 84.

[33] Ibid. (1834), vol. II, pp. 51–62; text of these synopses with English trans. in Kaufmann Jr (1964).

[34] Algarotti (1791), vol. III, p. 5.

[35] For an assessment of Algarotti, cf. Francis Haskell, *Patrons and Painters. A Study in the Relations Between Italian Art and Society*

in the Age of the Baroque, London 1963, pp. 347ff.
Further writings on architecture by Algarotti are his *Lettere sopra l'architettura*, 1742–63 in: Algarotti, *Opere*, vol. VIII, 1794, pp. 209ff.

[36] Algarotti, *Saggio* (1791), vol. III, p. 11.
[37] Ibid., p. 11ff.
[38] Ibid., p. 17.
[39] Memmo (1973), vol. II, pp. 51ff.
[40] Ibid., p. 52.
[41] Ibid., p. 56.
[42] Ibid., p. 57.
[43] Ibid., p. 59.
[44] *'Rappresentatione è l'individua e totale espressione che risulta dalla materia qualor essa venga disposta secondo le geometrico-aritmetico-ottiche ragioni al proposto fine.'* Ibid., p. 60.
[45] Ibid., vol. I, p. 4.
[46] Ibid., vol. III, p. 139.
[47] On Piranesi, cf. esp. Henri Focillon, *Giovanni Battista Piranesi*, Paris 1918 (²1963); Jonathan Scott, *Piranesi*, London and New York 1975; John Wilton-Ely, *The Mind and Art of Giovanni Battista Piranesi*, London 1978; Norbert Miller, *Archäologie des Traums. Versuch über Giovanni Battista Piranesi*, Munich 1978. Among catalogues of numerous Piranesi exhibitions in recent years the following are the most important: *Piranesi*, ed. Alessandro Bettagno, Venice 1978; *Piranèse et les Français 1740–1790*, Rome 1976; and conference proceedings under the same title, ed. Georges Brunel, Rome 1978; also conference proceedings *Piranesi tra Venezia e l'Europa*, ed. Alessandro Bettagno (1978), Florence 1983.
[48] Rudolf Wittkower, 'Piranesi's "Parere su l'architettura",' *Journal of the Warburg and Courtauld Institutes* II, 1938/39, pp. 147–58; repr. in: Wittkower, *Studies in the Italian Baroque*, London 1975, pp. 235–46. Cf. further Maria Grazia Messina, 'Teoria dell'architettura in Giovanbattista Piranesi', *Controspazio* II/8–9, 1970, pp. 6–13; *Controspazio* III/6, 1971, pp. 20–28.
[49] On this subject, cf. Bruno Reudenbach, *G. B. Piranesi. Architektur als Bild. Der Wandel in der Architekturauffassung des achtzehnten Jahrhunderts*, Munich 1979; also exh. cat. *Piranesi nei luoghi di Piranesi*, Rome 1979; Joseph Rykwert. *The First Moderns*. Cambridge, MA–London 1980, pp. 338ff.

[50] Allan Ramsay, 'A Dialogue of Taste', *The Investigator*, No. 332, London 1755; on Ramsay cf. Johannes Dobai, *Die Kunstliteratur des Klassizismus und der Romantik in England*, vol. II: *1750–1790*, Bern 1975, pp. 866ff.
[51] Cf. Dora Wiebenson, *Sources of Greek Revival Architecture*, London 1969, pp. 47ff.
[52] Giovanni Battista Piranesi, *Della Magnificenza ed Architettura, de'Romani*, Rome 1761; facs. text ed. John Wilton-Ely, in: Giovani Battista Piranesi, *The Polemical Works*, Farnborough, Hants 1972.
[53] Piranesi (1761), fol. XIX.
[54] Ibid., fol. XCIX v.
[55] Ibid., fol. CVII v.
[56] Ibid.
[57] Ibid., fol. CLXVII.
[58] Cf. Wittkower (1975), p. 238. Wittkower comments on the Etruscological work of A. F. Gori, G. B. Passeri and M. Guarnacci.
[59] Giambattista Piranesi, *Antichità d'Albano e di Castel Gandolfo descritte ed incise...*, Rome 1764, p. 3.
[60] Piranesi reprinted Mariette's letter with a point-by-point riposte in: Giovanni Battista Piranesi, *Osservazioni di Giov. Battista Piranesi sopra la Lettre de Monsieur Mariette aux Auteurs de la Gazette Littéraire de l'Europe*, Rome 1765, pp. 1–8 (facs. text ed. Wilton-Ely, 1972).
[61] Mariette as quoted by Piranesi (1765), p. 7.
[62] Piranesi (1765); cf. n. 60.
[63] Ibid., p. 16.
[64] Ibid., p. 12.
[65] Ibid., p. 9.
[66] Ibid., p. 10.
[67] *'Edifizj senza pareti, senza colonne, senza pilastri, senza fregj, senza cornici, senza volte, senza tetti; piazza, piazza, campagna rasa.'* Ibid., p. 11.
[68] Ibid., p. 12.
[69] Ibid., p. 15.
[70] *'A[e]quum est vas [vos] cognoscere atque ignoscere quae veteres factitarunt si faciunt novi.'*
[71] On Piranesi as an architect, cf. esp. Werner Körte, 'Giovanni Battista Piranesi als praktischer Architekt', *Zeitschrift für Kunstgeschichte* 2, 1933, pp. 16–33; Wittkower (1975), pp. 247–58; Manfredo Tafuri, 'Il complesso di S. Maria del Priorato sull'Aventino', exh. cat. *Piranesi* (1978), pp. 78–87.
[72] Giovanni Battista Piranesi, *Diverse maniere*

d'adornare i cammini ed ogni altra parte degli edifizj desunte dall'architettura egizia, etrusca, greca e romana, Rome 1769 (facs. text ed. Wilton-Ely, 1972).

[73] Piranesi (1769), p. 15.

[74] Ibid., pp. 4f.

[75] Ibid., p. 8.

[76] Cf. Nikolaus Pevsner and Suzanne Lang, 'The Egyptian Revival' (first published in: *The Architectural Review* CXIX, 1956), in: Pevsner, *Studies in Art, Architecture and Design*, vol. I, London 1968, pp. 213–35; Rudolf Wittkower, 'Piranesi e il gusto egiziano', in: *Sensibilità e razionalità nel Settecento*, Florence 1967, vol. II, pp. 659ff. and in: *Studies in the Italian Baroque* (1975), pp. 259–73.

[77] Piranesi (1769), p. 35.

[78] For the best presentation of Piranesi's designs, cf. Wilton-Ely (1978), pp. 102ff.

[79] Cf. Felice Stampfle, *Giovanni Battista Piranesi. Drawings in the Pierpont Morgan Library*, New York 1978, p. XI, figs 17, 18.

[80] On Milizia, see esp. Giuseppina Fontanesi, *Francesco Milizia scrittore e studioso d'arte*, Bologna 1932; Ferruccio Ulivi, 'Francesco Milizia scrittore', *Paragone* III, 1952, pp. 3–18; id. in: *Galleria di scrittori d'arte*, Florence 1953, pp. 207–44; William B., O'Neal, 'Francesco Milizia. 1725–1798', *Journal of the Society of Architectural Historians* XIII, 1954, n. 3, pp. 12–15; Kaufmann (1955, ed. 1968), pp. 100ff.; Eva Brües, 'Die Schriften des Francesco Milizia (1725–1798)', *Jahrbuch für Ästhetik und allgemeine Kunstwissenschaft* 6, 1961, pp. 69–113; Michael Gollwitzer, *Francesco Milizia: Del Teatro. Ein Beitrag zur Ästhetik und Kulturgeschichte Italiens zwischen 1750 und 1790*, diss. Cologne 1969; Italo Prozzillo, *Francesco Milizia. Teorico e storico dell'architettura*, Naples 1971.

[81] Francesco Milizia, *Notizie di Francesco Milizia scritte da lui medesimo*, Venice 1804; repr. in: *Milizia, Principi* (ed. 1804), vol. I, p. VIII.

[82] Milizia, *Notizie* (1804); *Principi* (ed. 1804), vol. I, p. IX.

[83] For the most comprehensive bibliography of eds and trans. of Milizia, cf. O'Neal (1954), pp. 13ff.

[84] Ibid., p. 12.

[85] Francesco Milizia, *Le vite de'più celebri architetti*, Rome 1768. From the 2nd ed. with the title *Memorie degli architetti antichi e moderni*, 2 vols, Rome 1768; Parma ³1781; Bassano ⁴1785 (facs. repr. in 2 vols, Bologna 1978); French trans. Paris 1771 (and 1819); English trans. London 1826.

[86] Francesco Milizia, *Principi di Architettura civile*, 3 vols, Finale 1781 (Bassano 1785; Bassano 1804; with illus. by Giov. Battista Cipriani; Bassano 1813; Bassano 1825); ed. Giovanni Antolini, Milan 1832 (²1847; facs. repr. Milan 1972).

[87] Francesco Milizia, *Dizionario delle arti del disegno*, 2 vols, Bassano 1787 (²1797); Milan 1802, 1804.

[88] Francesco Milizia, *Opere complete... risguardanti le belle arti*, 9 vols, Bologna 1826–28.

[89] On Milizia's position in primitive hut theory, cf. Joachim Gaus, 'Die Urhütte', *Wallraf-Richartz-Jahrbuch* XXXIII, 1971, p. 25; Joseph Rykwert, *On Adam's House in Paradise*, New York 1972, pp. 67ff.

[90] Milizia, *Principi* (ed. 1847), pp. 105.

[91] Ibid., pp. 105f.

[92] Milizia, *Memorie* (ed. 1785), p. XXVI.

[93] Milizia, *Opere complete*, vol. I (1826), p. VII.

[94] Milizia, *Memorie* (ed. 1785), vol. I, pp. XLIff.

[95] Ibid., pp. XLIXf. and *Principi* (ed. 1847), p. 126.

[96] Milizia, *Memorie* (ed. 1785), vol. I, pp. LIf.

[97] Ibid., p. XXVII.

[98] Ibid.

[99] Ibid., p. XXVIII.

[100] For a historical view of Milizia's theory of town planning, cf. Mario Zocca, 'Francesco Milizia e l'urbanistica del Settecento', *Atti del VIII Congresso Nazionale di Storia dell'Architettura*, Rome 1956, pp. 220–38.

[101] Milizia, *Memorie* (ed. 1785), vol. I, pp. LXIIIf.; *Principi* (ed. 1847), pp. 204ff.

[102] Zocca (1956), p. 224.

[103] As note 101.

[104] Milizia, *Memorie* (ed. 1785), vol. I, pp. LXIVf.

[105] Milizia, *Principi* (ed. 1847), p. 2.

[106] Ibid.

[107] Francesco Milizia, *Dell'arte di vedere nelle belle arti del disegno secondo i principii di Sulzer e di Mengs*, Venice 1781 (facs. repr. Bologna 1983): (German trans. Halle 1785; French trans. Paris 1798; Spanish trans. Madrid 1827).

[108] Milizia, *Memorie* (ed. 1785), vol. I, p. LXXIV.

[109] Ibid., p. 5.

[110] 'Tanto la buona Architettura aveva degenerato vicino dove era nata, e dove aveva fatto i suoi gran progressi.' Ibid., p. 82.

[111] Ibid., vol. II, pp. 157ff.

[112] Ibid., p. 185.

[113] Ibid., p. 198.

[114] Ibid., p. 213.

[115] Ibid., p. 311.

[116] Milizia, Principi (ed. 1847), pp. 177ff.

[117] 'Il principalissimo pregio di qualunque edifizio consiste nel suo carattere esprimente il suo proprio destino.' Ibid., p. 216.

[118] Ibid.

[119] 'bizzarrie che diverrebbero plausibili, e forse anche ragionevoli, quando fossero ben collocate e ben espresse.' Ibid., p. 200.

[120] Ibid., p. 202.

[121] Ibid., p. 215.

[122] Ibid., pp. 497ff.

[123] Ibid., pp. 554ff., 576ff.

[124] Ibid. (ed. 1832), p. 234 (n.); (1847), p. 200 (n.).

[125] Tommaso Temanza, Vite dei più celebri Architetti, e Scultori Veneziani..., Venice 1778 (facs ed. Liliana Grassi, Milan 1966).

[126] Ottavio Bertotti Scamozzi, Le fabbriche e i disegni di Andrea Palladio, 4 vols, Vicenza 1776–83 (Vicenza ²1796; facs. ed. J. Quentin Hughes, Venice–London 1968). On Bertotti Scamozzi see esp. Loredana Olivato, Ottavio Bertotti Scamozzi studioso di Andrea Palladio, Vicenza 1975; Christine Kamm-Kyburz, Der Architekt Ottavio Bertotti Scamozzi 1719–1790, Bern 1983.

[127] Angelo Comolli, Bibliografia storico-critica dell'Architettura civile, 4 vols, Rome 1788–92.

[128] Comolli (1788), vol. I, pp. 7ff. sets out the principles of his classification of architectural literature in a 'Lettera dell'autore ad un amico in cui si dà un'idea di tutta l'opera'.

[129] Comolli (1792), vol. IV, pp. 50ff.

17. Eighteenth-century views of antiquity

[1] Cf. esp. the two sections 'The Antiquities of Italy' in Roberto Weiss, The Renaissance Discovery of Classical Antiquity, Oxford 1969, pp. 105ff.

[2] On the history of expeditions to Greece in the Middle Ages and the Renaissance, cf. esp. Léon de Laborde, Athènes aux XVe, XVIe et XVIIe siècles, Paris 1854; Henri Omont, Athènes au XVIIe siècle, Paris 1898; Max Wegner, Land der Griechen, Berlin 1943 (good bibl. pp. 305ff); J. Morton Paton, Chapters in Mediaeval and Renaissance Visitors to Greek Lands, Princeton 1951; Roberto Weiss, 'The Discovery of the Greek World', in: op. cit. (1969), pp. 131ff.; id., Medieval und Humanist Greek, Padua 1977.

On Cyriac of Ancona, cf. esp. B. Ashmole, 'Cyriac of Ancona', Proceedings of the British Academy XLV, 1959, pp. 25–41; E. W. Bodnar, Cyriacus of Ancona and Athens, Brussels–Berchem 1960; Roberto Weiss (1977), pp. 284ff.

On the transformation of Greek models in Renaissance conceptions based on Roman Antiquity, cf. Beverly Louise Brown and Diana E.E. Kleiner, 'Giuliano da Sangallo's Drawings after Ciriaco d'Ancona: Transformations of Greek and Roman Antiquities in Athens', Journal of the Society of Architectural Historians XLII, 1983, pp. 321–35.

[3] Hartmann Schedel, Weltchronik, Nuremberg 1493, fol. XXVII v.

[4] Cf. Anthony Blunt, The Burlington Magazine CXVIII, 1976, p. 323. The Grand Marot, published in the 1660s, contained 17 views of Baalbek.

On Cornelius Loos's sketch of Palmyra, cf. Georg Kunoth, Die historische Architektur Fischers von Erlach, Düsseldorf 1956, pp. 88ff. (fig. 70).

[5] Cf. Margaret Lyttelton, Baroque Architecture in Classical Antiquity, London 1974; Blunt (1976).

[6] Leo Allatios, De Templis Graecorum recentioribus, and: De narthece ecclesiae veteris, Paris–Cologne 1645 (crit. ed. in English trans. by Anthony Cutler: Leo Allatios, The Newer Temples of the Greeks, University Park–London 1969).

[7] Jacob Spon and George Wheler, Voyage d'Italie, de Dalmatie, de Grèce, et du Levant, fait aux années 1675 & 1676, 2 vols, Lyons 1678, Amsterdam 1679 (cited here), London 1682.

[8] Cf. esp. Nikolaus Pevsner and Suzanne Lang, 'The Doric Revival' (first published in: The Architectural Review CIV, 1948), in: Pevsner, Studies in Art, Architecture and

Design, vol. 1, London 1968, pp. 197–211; Dora Wiebenson, *Sources of Greek Revival Architecture*, London 1969; J. Mordaunt Crook, *The Greek Revival. Neo-Classical Attitudes in British Architecture 1760–1870*, London 1972; Michael McCarthy, 'Documents on the Greek Revival in Architecture', *Burlington Magazine* CXIV, 1972, pp. 760–69; Johannes Dobai, *Die Kunstliteratur des Klassizismus und der Romantik in England*, vol. II, Bern 1975, pp. 476ff.; Johannes Erichsen, *Antique und Grec. Studien zur Funktion der Antike in der Architektur und Kunsttheorie des Frühklassizismus*, diss. (1975), Cologne 1980; Joseph Rykwert, *The First Moderns*, Cambridge, MA–London 1980, pp. 262ff.

⁹ Wiebenson (1969), p. 20 (with detailed sources).

¹⁰ Cf. Johannes Dobai, *Die Kunstliteratur des Klassizismus und der Romantik in England*, vol. 1, Bern 1974, pp. 798ff.

¹¹ Cf. William Richard Hamilton, *Historical Notes of the Society of Dilettanti*, London 1855; Lionel Cust and Sidney Colvin, *History of the Society of Dilettanti*, London 1898 (²1914); Cecil Harcourt-Smith, *The Society of Dilettanti: Its Regalia and Pictures*, London 1932; Wiebenson (1969), pp. 25ff.; an excellent bibl. of the publications of the Society and its circle is contained in the bookseller's cat. *The Society of Dilettanti*, No. 25, Weinreb & Breman, London 1968.

¹² Horace Walpole to H. Mann, 14 April 1743; W. S. Lewis (ed.), *Horace Walpole's Correspondence*, XVIII, 2, New Haven 1954, p. 211.

¹³ Richard Chandler, *Travels in Asia Minor: or: an account of a tour made at the expense of the Society of Dilettanti*, Dublin 1775; modern edition by Edith Clay as: Richard Chandler, *Travels in Asia Minor 1764–1765*, London 1971 (the 'instructions' on pp. 5ff.).

¹⁴ Chandler (1775; ed. 1971), p. 6.

¹⁵ Richard Chandler, Nicholas Revett, William Pars, *Ionian Antiquities*, published with permission of the Society of Dilettanti, London 1769; *Antiquities of Jonia*, published by the Society of Dilettanti, London 1797.

¹⁶ Richard Chandler (1775); and *Travels in Greece: or an account of a tour made at the*

expense of the Society of Dilettanti, Oxford 1776.

¹⁷ Chandler, Revett, Pars (1769), p. ii.

¹⁸ Chandler, Revett, Pars (1797), p. i.

¹⁹ Ibid.

²⁰ On Stuart and Revett, cf. esp. Leslie Lawrence, 'Stuart and Revett: Their Literary and Architectural Careers', *Journal of the Warburg and Courtauld Institutes* 2, 1938/39, pp. 128–46; Wiebenson (1969), pp. 1ff.; on Stuart, cf. a concise monograph by David Watkin, *Athenian Stuart. Pioneer of the Greek Revival*, London 1982.

²¹ Repr. in: Wiebenson (1969), pp. 75ff.

²² Proposal of 1751 (Wiebenson (1969), p. 77).

²³ Robert Wood, *The Ruins of Palmyra, otherwise Tedmor, in the Desert*, London 1753 (simult. French ed.: *Les ruines de Palmyre, autrement dite Tedmor, au désert*, London 1753); *The Ruins of Balbec otherwise Heliopolis in Coelosyria*, London 1757; later eds of both works: Robert Wood, *The Ruins of Palmyra and Balbec*, London 1827.

²⁴ Wood (1753), p. 1.

²⁵ Ibid., p. 15.

²⁶ Wood (ed. 1827), p. 58.

²⁷ Wood (1753), p. 35.

²⁸ Wood (ed. 1827), pl. V. Perrault was possibly influenced in turn by Marot's engravings of Baalbek; cf. Wiebenson (1969), p. 37.

²⁹ Wood (ed. 1827), p. 53.

³⁰ Wiebenson (1969), p. 38 (Documents nos 41 and 44, pp. 98f.).

³¹ On Le Roy, cf. esp. Louis Hautecoeur, *Histoire de l'Architecture classique en France*, vol. IV, Paris 1952, pp. 18ff.; vol. V, Paris 1953, pp. 263ff.; Wiebenson (1969), pp. 11f., 14, 33 ff.; Richard Chafee, 'The Teaching of Architecture at the Ecole des Beaux-Arts', in: Arthur Drexler (ed.), *The Architecture of the Ecole des Beaux-Arts*, London 1977, pp. 70ff.; Donald Drew Egbert, *The Beaux-Arts Tradition in French Architecture*, Princeton 1980, pp. 37ff.

³² Julien-David Le Roy, *Les Ruines des plus beaux monuments de la Grèce*, Paris 1758 (²1770; English ed. London 1759); 1758 ed. cited hereafter.

³³ Ibid., p. V, *Préface*.

³⁴ Ibid., p. XI.

³⁵ Ibid., Part II, p. IV.

³⁶ 'pour produire dans notre âme, à leur aspect, les idées de grandeur, de noblesse, de majesté & de beauté...' Ibid., p. II.

[37] Ibid., pp. Vf.

[38] James Stuart and Nicholas Revett, *The Antiquities of Athens*, vol. I, London 1762; vol. II, London 1787 (completed by William Newton and published after Stuart's death in 1788); vol. III, London 1794 (edited by Willey Reveley); vol. IV, London 1816 (consisting of posthumous material by Stuart, edited by Josuah Taylor and Joseph Wood). Later eds: London 1825–30; 1837; 1849; 1881; French ed. Paris 1818; German eds Darmstadt 1829–33, Leipzig 1829–33.

[39] Stuart and Revett (1762), vol. I, p. I.

[40] Ibid.

[41] Stuart and Revett (1762), vol. I, p. II.

[42] Ibid.

[43] Johann Joachim Winckelmann, *Briefe*, ed. Hans Diepolder and Walther Rehm, vol. III, Berlin 1956, p. 57 (to Füssli, 22 Sep. 1764).

[44] Cf. Lawrence (1938/39), p. 141 (with illus.).

[45] Stuart and Revett (1794), vol. III, p. XV.

[46] Stuart and Revett (1794), vol. III, p. 41.

[47] On Adam's Grand Tour, cf. esp. John Fleming, *Robert Adam and His Circle in Edinburgh & Rome*, Cambridge, MA 1962.

[48] On Adam's relationship with Piranesi, cf. Damie Stillman, 'Robert Adam and Piranesi', in: *Essays in the History of Architecture Presented to Rudolf Wittkower* ([1]1967), London [2]1969, pp. 197–206.
On Clérisseau cf. Thomas J. McCormick, 'Charles-Louis Clérisseau and the Roman Revival', diss., Princeton 1971 (microfilm); id., 'Piranesi and Clérisseau's Vision of Classical Antiquity', in: *Piranèse et les Français*, conference proceedings (1976), Rome 1978, pp. 303–10; id., *Charles-Louis Clérisseau and the Genesis of Neo-Classicism*, Cambridge, Mass.–London 1990.

[49] Giangiorgio Zorzi, *I disegni delle Antichità di Andrea Palladio*, Venice 1959, p. 106, figs 266, 267.

[50] Spon and Wheler (1679), vol. I, pp. 74ff. (folding plate after p. 78).

[51] Johann Bernhard Fischer von Erlach, *Entwurff einer Historischen Architectur* (1721), Leipzig 1725, pl. x; on Fischer's source, cf. Georg Kunoth, *Die Historische Architektur Fischers von Erlach*, Düsseldorf 1956, pp. 79ff.

[52] Robert Adam, *Ruins of the Palace of the Emperor Diocletian at Spalatro in Dalmatia*, London 1764.

[53] Adam (1764), p. 1.

[54] Ibid.

[55] Ibid., p. 2.

[56] Ibid., p. 4.

[57] This connction was observed by Boris Lossky, 'Les ruines de Spalatro, Palladio et le néoclassicisme', in: *Urbanisme et architecture. Etudes écrites et publiées en l'honneur de Pierre Lavedan*, Paris 1954, p. 249.

[58] Adam (1764), pl. VII; *The Works in Architecture of Robert and James Adam*, vol. III, London 1822, pl. I (ed. Roberto Oresko, London–New York 1975, p. 146).

[59] For recent surveys of the history of the excavations at Pompeii and Herculaneum, cf. Peter Werner, *Pompeji und die Wandmalerei der Goethezeit*, Munich 1970, p. 24ff.; Fausto Zevi, 'Gli scavi di Ercolano', in: exh. cat. *Civiltà del '700 a Napoli*, vol. II, Florence 1980, pp. 58ff.; exh. cat. *Pompei e gli architetti francesi dell'Ottocento*, Naples 1981.

[60] Ch. N. Cochin and J. Ch. Bellicard, *Observations sur les antiquités d'Herculanum*, Paris 1754 ([2]1755).

[61] *Le Antichità di Ercolano esposte*, vols 1–5: *Le pitture antiche d'Ercolano e contorni incise con qualche spiegazione*, Naples 1757–69; *De Bronzi di Ercolano e contorni*, vol. I: *Busti*, Naples 1767; vol. II: *Statue*, Naples 1771; *Le lucerne ed i candelabri d'Ercolano e contorni*, Naples 1792.

[62] Cf. esp. vol. I (1757), pp. 209ff.

[63] Vol. I (1757), *Prefazione*.

[64] Cf. esp. Mario Praz, *On Neoclassicism* (1940), London 1972, pp. 74f.; id., 'Le antichità di Ercolano', in: exh. cat. *Civiltà del '700 a Napoli*, vol. I, Florence 1979, pp. 35ff.; and cf. F. and P. Piranesi, *Antiquités d'Herculanum (gravées par Th. Piroli)*, 6 vols, Paris 1804–06.

[65] On the influence of the wall-paintings at Pompeii and Herculaneum in the German-speaking regions, cf. esp. Werner (1970).

[66] Johann Joachim Winckelmann, *Sendschreiben von den Herculanischen Entdeckungen*, Dresden 1762; *Nachrichten von den neuesten Herculanischen Entdeckungen*, Dresden 1764 (facs. of both, Baden-Baden–Strasbourg 1964).

[67] Winckelmann (1762), p. 21.

[68] Berardo Galiani, *L'architettura di M. Vitruvio Pollione* (Latin–Italian ed.), Naples 1758.

[69] Even Aloisio Marinio, in his monumental

four-volume edition of Vitruvius (Rome 1836), still relied on Palladio for illustrations of the Roman house, despite plentiful new excavations of houses.

[70] 'einladender und reizender, als die bedeutungsvollen, der Bestimmung der einzelnen Zimmer ganz angemessenen Verzierungen, welche man dort häufig findet.' Karl Philipp Moritz, Vorbegriffe zu einer Theorie der Ornamente, Berlin 1793, p. 83.

[71] Jean-Claude Richard de Saint-Non, Voyage pittoresque ou description des Royaumes de Naples et de Sicile, vol. II, Paris 1782, pp. 125ff. And see esp. Neil MacGregor, 'Le Voyage Pittoresque de Naples et de Sicile', The Connoisseur 196, 1977, pp. 130–38.

[72] Cf. Nils G. Wollin, Desprez en Italie, Malmö 1935.

[73] Saint-Non (1782), vol. II, pp. 115ff., pls 74, 75, 75 bis.

[74] Cf. also Nikolaus Pevsner and Suzanne Lang, 'The Egyptian Revival' (first published in: The Architectural Review CXIX, 1956), in: Pevsner, Studies in Art, Architecture and Design, vol. I, London 1968, pp. 213–35.

[75] Cf. Robert Rosenblum, Transformations in Late Eighteenth Century Art (1967), Princeton 1970, pp. 107ff.

[76] Bernard de Montfaucon, L'Antiquité expliquée et représentée en figures, Paris 1719ff.

[77] Anne-Claude-Philippe de Tubières, Comte de Caylus, Recueil d'Antiquités égyptiennes, étrusques, grecques et romaines, 7 vols, Paris 1752–67.

On Caylus, see esp. Carl Justi, Winckelmann und seine Zeitgenossen, ed. Walther Rehm, vol. III, Cologne ⁵1956, pp. 104ff.

On Caylus's literary work and his ethical and aesthetic ideas, cf. Franz Josef Hausmann, 'Eine vergessene Berühmtheit des 18. Jahrhunderts: Der Graf Caylus, Gelehrter und Literat', Deutsche Vierteljahrsschrift für Literaturwissenschaft und Geistesgeschichte 53, 1979, pp. 191–209.

[78] Anne-Claude-Philippe de Tubières, Comte de Caylus, Von der Baukunst der Alten (1749), German trans. in: Caylus, Abhandlungen zur Geschichte und zur Kunst, 2 vols, Altenburg 1768, 1769; vol. I, p. 307.

[79] Cf. Lang and Pevsner (1968), pp. 230ff.

[80] William Hamilton (ed. P. F. H. d'Hancarville), Collection of Etruscan, Greek, and Roman antiquities..., 4 vols, Naples 1766–67. William Hamilton (ed. Wilhelm Tischbein), Collection of engravings from ancient vases mostly of pure Greek workmanship..., 3 vols, Naples 1791–95. On Hamilton, cf. esp. Brian Fothergill, Sir William Hamilton. Envoy Extraordinary, London 1969.

[81] Fothergill (1969), pp. 67f.

[82] Cf. Werner (1970), pp. 95ff.; Erich Bachmann, Schloß Aschaffenburg und Pompejanum, Munich ³1973, pp. 46ff.

[83] Cf. Louis Hautecoeur, Histoire de l'Architecture classique en France, vol. VII, Paris 1957, pp. 124f.; id., Paris, vol. 2: de 1715 à nos jours, Paris 1972, pp. 526f.; Donald David Schneider, The Works and Doctrine of Jacques Ignace Hittorf (1792–1867), diss., Princeton 1970 (printed Ann Arbor–London 1981), pp. 596ff.

[84] Jacques-Philippe D'Orville, Sicula, quibus Siciliae Veteris Rudera, 2 vols, Amsterdam 1764.

[85] Giuseppe Maria Pancrazi, Antichità Siciliane spiegate, 2 vols, Naples 1751–52.

[86] In: Johann Joachim Winckelmann, Kleine Schriften, Vorreden, Entwürfe, ed. Walther Rehm and Hellmut Sichtermann, Berlin 1968, pp. 174–85.

[87] Winckelmann (1968), pp. 175, 179; cf. also C. Andrea Pigonati, Stato presente degli antichi monumenti siciliani, Naples 1767.

[88] Cf. the survey by Hélène Tuzet, La Sicile au XVIIIe siècle vue par les voyageurs étrangers, Strasbourg 1955. Among the well-illustrated travel accounts the following are noteworthy: Jean Houel, Voyage pittoresque des isles de Sicile, de Lipari et de Malte, 4 vols, Paris 1782–87; Richard de Saint-Non, Voyage pittorsque ou description des Royaumes de Naples et de Sicile, vol. IV (2 parts), Paris 1785–86.

[89] On the early visits to Paestum; cf. esp. Domenico Mustilli, 'Prime memorie delle rovine di Paestum', in: Studi in onore di Riccardo Filangieri, vol. III, Naples 1959, pp. 105–21; Pietro Laveglia, Paestum dalla decadenza alla riscoperta fino al 1860, Naples 1971; Joselita Raspi Serra (ed.), Paestum and the Doric Revival 1750–1830, New York–Florence 1986.

[90] 'In Pesto overo Possidonia, città rovinata, le mure antique sono intiere, per una gran parte con le torri, e dentro sono tre templi, di opera dorica, di pietra viva e tiburtina in quadroni grandi.' Fausto Nicolini, L'arte napoletana del Rinascimento e la lettera di Pietro Summonte a Marcantonio Michiel, Naples 1925, p. 174. This reference escapes Mustilli (1959), but is taken up by Roberto

Weiss (1969), p. 130 and Laveglia (1971), p. 18.

[91] *'Pertanto rappresenta alla M. V. che per avanzare il tempo e la spesa si potrebbe prendere le pietre che sono nell'antica Città di Pesto, situato nel territorio di Capaccio, che fu antica Colonia de Romani, dove vi sono tante quantità d'edificij mezzi diruti, essendovi più di cento colonne di dismusurata grandezza con i loro capitelli, architravi, freggi, e cornicioni di pezzi cosi grandi che fan conoscere la potenza degl'antichi Romani...'* Mustilli (1959), p. 120; Laveglia (1971), p. 72.

[92] Cf. the authoritative study of the literature on Paestum by Suzanne Lang, 'The Early Publications of the Temples at Paestum', *Journal of the Warburg and Courtauld Institutes* 13, 1950, pp. 48–64.

[93] G. P. M. Dumont, *Suite de plans, coupes, profils... de Pesto... mesurés et dessinés par J. G. Soufflot architecte du roy en 1750*, Paris 1764. Filippo Morghen, *Sei vedute delle rovine di Pesto*, 1766. Anon. (John Berkenhout?), *The Ruins of Poestum or Posidonia, a City of Magna Graecia...*, London 1767. Thomas Major, *The Ruins of Paestum, otherwise Posidonia in Magna Graecia*, London 1768 (French: *Les Ruines de Paestum...*, London 1768; facs. repr. 1969). G. P. M. Dumont, *Les Ruines de Paestum... Traduction libre de l'anglois imprimé à Londres en 1767...*, London–Paris 1769. Giambattista Piranesi, *Differentes vues de quelques restes de trois grands édifices qui subsistent encore dans le milieu de l'ancienne ville de Pesto autrement Posidonia, qui est située dans la Lucanie*, Rome 1778 (facs. repr. Unterschneidheim 1973). Paolo Antonio Paoli, *Paesti quod Posidoniam etiam dixere rudera*, Rome 1784. C. M. Delagardette, *Les Ruines de Paestum ou Poseidonia*, Paris VII (1799).

And cf. a survey of the discoveries at and the literature on Paestum, including a discussion of Delagardette's work, by August Rode, 'Über die Monumente von Pästum', in: *Sammlung nützlicher Aufsätze und Nachrichten*, ed. David Gilly, vol. IV, 1800, Part II, pp. 48–67.

[94] Cf. esp. Richard de Saint-Non, *Voyage pittoresque, ou description des Royaumes de Naples et de Sicile*, vol. III, Paris 1783, pp. 153ff.

[95] Berardo Galiani, *L'architettura di M. Vitruvio Pollione...*, Naples 1758, p. 102. n. 3: *'Presso l'antica città di Pesti esistono ancora in piedi alcuni tempj, quasi interi, uno de'quali Pseudodiptero ha nove colonne alle fronti...'*

[96] Galiani (1758), p. 124. The very rough engraving shows seven front columns.

[97] Cited from the London-published French ed. (1768) of Major, p. VII.

[98] Johann Joachim Winckelmann, *Anmerkungen über die Baukunst der alten Tempel zu Girgenti in Sicilien* (1759), in: J. J. Winckelmann, *Kleine Schriften, Vorreden, Entwürfe*, ed. Walther Rehm and Hellmut Sichtermann, Berlin 1968, p. 179.

[99] Piranesi (1778), pl. X. On this, cf. esp. Roberto Pane, *Paestum nelle acqueforti di Piranesi*, Milan 1980.

[100] Piranesi (1778), title-page.

[101] Paoli (1784), pp. 43f., 79, 103, 111ff.

[102] *'ordine e proporzione maravigliosa, leggiadria, vaghezza, eleganza'*. Ibid., p. 43.

[103] *'l'indole e la sodezza de' Toscani'*. Ibid.

[104] Ibid., p. 103.

[105] Ibid., pp. 131ff.

[106] Ibid., pl. XLI.

[107] Paolo Antonio Paoli, *Antichità di Pozzuoli (Avanzi delle Antichità esistenti a Pozzuoli, Cuma e Baja)*, Naples 1768.

[108] Delagardette (1799), p. 5.

[109] Jean-Jacques Barthélémy, *Voyage du jeune Anacharsis en Grèce, dans le milieu du quatrième siècle avant l'ère vulgaire*, 7 vols, Paris 1788 (also *Recueil de cartes géographiques, plans, vues et médailles de l'ancienne Grèce relatifs au voyage du jeune Anacharsis*, Paris 1788), 2nd ed., Paris 1788 used. This work was reprinted some thirty times up to the middle of the nineteenth century, and appeared in various translated editions.

[110] Barthélémy (1789), vol. II, pp. 242ff. (*Recueil*, 1789, pls 9, 10).

[111] Ibid., pp. 500ff.

[112] Ibid., vol. V, p. 46 (*Recueil*, pl. 24).

18. The role of Spain from the sixteenth to the eighteenth century

[1] Cf. the brief mention in Julius von Schlosser, *La letteratura artistica*, Florence–Vienna 1964, pp. 505ff.

[2] The most comprehensive survey of the Spanish literature of art is offered by F. J. Sáchez-Cantón, *Fuentes literarias para la*

Historia del Arte Español, 5 vols, Madrid 1923–41 (but the selection of excerpts from architectural treatises in this anthology is not representative). The best survey of the Spanish literature of architecture (written from a Neo-classical viewpoint) is offered by Eugenio Llaguno y Amirola and Juan Agustín Ceán-Bermúdez, Noticias de los arquitectos y arquitectura de España desde su restauracion, 4 vols, Madrid 1829 (facs. repr. Madrid 1977); Marcelino Menéndez y Pelayo, Historia de la ideas estéticas en España, 9 vols, Madrid 1883ff. (several editions), vol. III (³1920) covering the 17th and 18th centuries, vol. IV (³1923) aesthetic theory from the 16th to the 18th century; indispensable is the bibliography by Florentino Zamora Lucas and Eduardo Ponce de León, Bibliografía española de arquitectura (1526–1850), Madrid 1947; cf. also Ramón Gutiérrez, Notas para una bibliografía hispanoamericana de arquitectura (1526–1875), Universidad del Nordeste (Argentina) n.d. (c. 1972; esp. on the impact of Spanish architectural literature in Latin America); Antonio Bonet Correa (ed.), Bibliografía de arquitectura, ingenieria y urbanismo en España (1498–1880), 2 vols, Madrid–Vaduz 1980. On 16th–18th century architecture, cf. esp. Fernando Chueca Goitia, 'Arquitectura del siglo XVI' (Ars Hispaniae XI), Madrid 1953; George Kubler, 'Arquitectura de los siglos XVII y XVIII' (Ars Hispaniae XIV), Madrid 1957; George Kubler and Martin Soria, Art and Architecture in Spain and Portugal and Their American Dominions 1500 to 1800, Harmondsworth 1959.

³ Sebastiano Serlio, Tercero y quarto libro de Architectura, ed. Francisco Villalpando, Toledo 1552 (facs. repr. ed. George Kubler, Valencia 1977).

⁴ Vitruvius, De Architectura, trans. Miguel de Urrea and Juan Gracian, Alcala de Henares 1582 (facs. repr. ed. Luis Moya, Valencia 1978). Leon Battista Alberti, Los diez libros de architectura, Madrid 1582 (facs. repr. ed. José María de Azcárate, Valencia 1977).

⁵ Diego de Sagredo, Medidas del Romano, Toledo 1526 (Madrid 1946; ed. Luis Cervera Vera, Valencia 1976).

On Diego de Sagredo and the various editions of his treatise, see esp. Llaguno y Amirola and Ceán-Bermúdez (1829), vol. I, pp. 175ff.; José Maria Maroñón, 'Las ediciones de la "Medidas del Romano", in: Zamora Lucas and Ponce de León (1947), pp. 9–34; Laura Marcucci, 'Regesto cronologico e critico', in: 2000 anni di Vitruvio, Studi e documenti di architettura, n. 8, Florence 1978, pp. 43ff.

⁶ Sagredo (1526), fol. A j v.

⁷ Ibid., jjjj v.

⁸ Cf. Nigel Llewellyn, 'Two Notes on Diego da Sagredo', Journal of the Warburg and Courtauld Institutes XL, 1977, pp. 292–300 (I was unable to consult his unpublished diss., 'Diego da Sagredo's "Medidas del Romano" and the Vitruvian tradition', London 1975).

⁹ Sagredo (1526), fol. A jjjj v ff.

¹⁰ Cf. Francesco di Giorgio Martini, Trattati, ed. Corrado Maltese, 2 vols, Milan 1967; vol. I, pl. 37; vol. II, pl. 227.

¹¹ Sagredo (1526), fol. B jjj.

¹² Cf. Paola Barocchi, Scritti d'arte del Cinquecento, vol. III, Milan–Naples 1977, p. 2983.

¹³ Sagredo (1526), fol. B vjjj v ff.

¹⁴ On this subject cf. Llewellyn (1977), pp. 297ff.; also an enlargement upon this by Paul Davies and David Hemsoll, 'Renaissance balusters and the antique', Architectural History 26, 1983, pp. 1–23.

¹⁵ Sagredo (1526), fol. A v (referring to him as 'Phelipe de Borgoña').

¹⁶ On this subject cf. Carl Justi, Miscellaneen aus drei Jahrhunderten spanischen Kunstlebens, vol. I, Berlin 1908; A. de Bosque, Artisti italiani in Spagna dal XIV° secolo ai Re Cattolici, Settimo Milanese (Milan) 1968; Hanno-Walter Kruft, 'Un cortile rinascimentale italiano nella Sierra Nevada: La Calahorra', Antichità viva VIII/2, 1969, pp. 35–51; id., 'Ancora sulla la Calahorra: Documenti', Antichità viva XI/1, 1972, pp. 35–45; id., 'Concerning the date of the Codex Escurialensis', The Burlington Magazine CXII, 1970, pp. 44–47; id., 'Pace Gagini and the Sepulchres of the Ribera in Seville', Actas del XXIII Congreso Internacional de Historia del Arte, vol. II, Granada 1977, pp. 327–38.

¹⁷ Cf. Jorge Segurado, Francisco D'Ollanda, Lisbon 1970; Sylvie Deswarte, 'Contribution à la connaissance de Francisco de Hollanda', Arquivos do Centro Cultural Português VII, 1974, pp. 421–29; J. B. Bury, Two Notes on Francisco de Hollanda, London 1981.

¹⁸ The 'Desenhos das Antigualhas que vio

Francisco d'Ollanda', extant in the Escorial, have been published in two editions: Achille Pellizzari (ed.), *Opere di Francisco de Hollanda*, vol. II, Naples 1915; Elias Tormo (ed.), *Os Desenhos das Antigualhas que vio Francisco D'Ollanda*, Madrid 1940 (with extensive commentary).

[19] Francisco de Hollanda, *Da Fabrica que falece ha Cidade de Lysboa* (1571), ed. Joaquim de Vasconcellos, Oporto 1879; ed. Seguardo, in: op. cit. (1970).

[20] Cristóbal de Villalón, *Ingeniosa comparación entre lo antiquo y lo presente*, Valladolid 1539; cf. Sáchez-Cantón, vol. I (1923), p. xvi, pp. 21ff., excerpts pp. 25–33. On Villalón's architectural descriptions cf. Gerhard Goebel, *Poeta Faber*, Heidelberg 1971, pp. 113ff.

[21] Sánchez-Cantón, vol. I (1923), p. 31.

[22] On Rodrigo Gil de Hontañon cf. esp. Llaguno y Amirola and Cean-Bermudez (1829), vol. I, pp. 212ff., 315ff.; Chueca Goitia (1953), pp. 329ff.; Kubler (1959), pp. 8ff.; John Hoag, 'Rodrigo Gil de Hontañón, His Work and Writings', diss., Yale Univ. 1958; Antonio Casaseca Casaseca, *Rodrigo Gil de Hontañon*, Salamanca 1988.

[23] On Simón García's manuscript extant in the National Library in Madrid (n. 8884), 'Compendio de Architectura y simetria de los Templos conforme a la medida del cuerpo humano...Año de 1681', cf. José Camón, 'La intervención de Rodrigo Gil de Hontañon en el manuscrito de Simón García', *Archivo español de arte* XIV, 1940/41, pp. 300–305; id., *Compendio de architectura y simetria de los templos por Simón García año de 1681*, Salamanca 1941; George Kubler, 'A Late Medieval Computation of Gothic Rib-Vault Thrusts', *Gazette de Beaux-Arts* XXVI, 1944, pp. 135–48; Sergio Luis Sanabria, 'The Mechanization of Design in the 16th Century: The Structural Formulae of Rodrigo Gil de Hontañón', *Journal of the Society of Architectural Historians* XLI, 1982, pp. 281–93.

[24] Camón (1941), p. 19.

[25] Camón (1941), p. 37: '*la torre significa un cuerpo entero sin brazos, los brazos la yglesia, o templo*' (fig. 14).

[26] Camón (1941), p. 66, fig. 29; cf. esp. Kubler's analysis (1944), pp. 138ff.

[27] On Juan de Arfe cf. Llaguno y Amirola and Cean-Bermudez (1829), vol. III, pp. 98ff. and esp. Carl Justi, 'Die Goldschmiedefami-

lie der Arphe' (first published, *Zeitschrift für christliche Kunst*, 1894) in: Justi, *Miscelaneen* (1908), vol. I, pp. 269–90, esp. pp. 284ff.; Francisco Javier Sánchez-Cantón, *Los Arfes, escultores de plata y oro (1501–1603)*, Madrid 1920.

[28] Juan de Arfe y Villafañe, *De varia commensuración para la Esculptura y Architectura*, Seville 1585 (Books III and IV: 1587); further editions 1675, 1736, 1763, 1773, 1795, 1806; facs. of 1585 edition: ed. Antonio Bonet Correa, Madrid 1974 (contains only Books I and II); ed. Francisco Iñiguez, Valencia 1979 (also contains Books III and IV).

[29] Arfe (1585), Libro segundo, fol. 1 v ff.

[30] Arfe (1587), Book IV, fol. 39; cf. Justi (1908), p. 288.

[31] Geneviève Barbé-Coquelin de Lisle (ed.), *El tratado de arquitectura de Alonso de Vandelvira*, 2 vols, Albacete 1977 (vol. I: edition of the texts; vol. II: facs. of the ms. in the Biblioteca de la Escuela de Madrid, Ms. R 10).

[32] Fernando Marías and Agustín Bustamante García, 'El Greco et sa théorie de l'architecture', *Revue de l'Art* 46, 1979, pp. 31–39; id., *Las ideas artísticas de El Greco*, Madrid 1981 (transcription of El Greco's marginalia, pp. 225ff).

[33] On Herrera cf. esp. Llaguno y Amirola and Cean-Bermudez (1829), vol. II, pp. 117ff.; Augustín Ruiz de Arcaute, *Juan de Herrera*, Madrid 1936.

[34] Cf. Francisco Javier Sáchez-Cantón, *La Librería de Herrera*, Madrid 1941; for the most thorough study of his ideas, cf. René Taylor, 'Architecture and Magic. Considerations on the Idea of the Escorial', in: *Essays in the History of Architecture Presented to Rudolf Wittkower*, London ²1969, pp. 81–109.

[35] Juan de Herrera, *Discurso de la Figura Cúbica*, ed. Julio Rey Pastor, Madrid 1935; ed. Edison Simons and Roberto Goday, Madrid 1976.
On Lull cf. esp. Frances Yates, 'The Art of Ramón Lull', *Journal of the Warburg and Courtauld Institutes* XVII, 1954; on his influence on Herrera, cf. Taylor (1969), pp. 81ff.

[36] Taylor (1969).

[37] The complex subject of the Escorial cannot be explored here; cf. the comprehensive study by Cornelia von der Osten Sacken,

San Lorenzo el Real de el Escorial. Studien zur Baugeschichte und Ikonologie, Mittenwald-Munich 1979; George Kubler, Building the Escorial, Princeton 1982.

[38] In his library catalogue a 'Copia del tratado que se hizo del templo de salomon manoescripto' is included; cited from Simons-Goday (1976), p. 443.

[39] Juan de Herrera, Sumario y breve declaración de los diseños y estampas de la fábrica de San Lorenzo el Real del Escurial, Madrid 1589; ed. Luis Cervera Vera, Las estampas y el Sumario de el Escorial por Juan de Herrera, Madrid 1954.

[40] Cf. esp. Wolfgang Herrmann, 'Unknown Designs for the "Temple of Jerusalem" by Claude Perrault', in: Essays in the History of Architecture Presented to Rudolf Wittkower, London 1969, pp. 143–58 (pp. 154ff. chronological bibliography on Solomon's Temple); Helen Rosenau, Vision of the Temple. The Image of the Temple of Jerusalem in Judaism and Christianity, London 1979.

[41] Benito Arias Montano, Antiquitatum Judaicarum libri IX, Leyden 1583.

[42] On Villalpando cf. the fundamental René Taylor, 'El Padre Villalpando (1552–1608) y sus ideas esteticas', in: Academia, Anales y Boletin de la Real Academia de Bellas Artes de San Fernando, 3rd ser., vol. I, 1951, pp. 409–73; id. (1969); id., 'Hermetism and Mystical Architecture in the Society of Jesus', in: Rudolf Wittkower and Irma B. Jaffe (ed.), Baroque Art: The Jesuit Contribution, New York 1972, pp. 63–97.

[43] On Villalpando as Architect cf. Taylor (1972), pp. 69ff.

[44] Cf. Taylor (1972), p. 74.

[45] Jerónimo Prado and Juan Bautista Villalpando, In Ezechielem, Explanationes et Apparatus Urbis, ac Templi Hierosolymitani Commentariis et imaginibus illustratus, 3 vols, Rome 1596, 1604, 1604.

There is a manuscript of Prado entitled 'Compendio de la segunda parte de los comentarios sobre el propheta Ezechiel...' in the William H. Schab Collection, New York (cf. Juan Antonio Ramírez, Art History 4, 1981, p. 182, n. 1).

[46] This volume, the publication date of which is 1604, has a dedication to Philip III dated March 1605.

[47] Villalpando, vol. II (1604), pp. 16ff. On p. 17 the Temple is described as 'aedificium, omnibus numeris absolutum, atque perfectum, cuius singula membra incredibili artificio, ac proportione secum ipsa, & cum aedificio universo mirificè responderent...'

[48] Villalpando, vol. II (1604), p. 18, citing Juan de Herrera: 'ab humano ingenio excogitatum non fuisse eiusmodi aedificium, sed à Deo ipso infinita sapientia architectatum...'

[49] Villalpando, vol. II (1604), pp. 22, 80.

[50] Villalpando, vol. II (1604), pp. 25ff. ch. X.

[51] Villalpando, vol. II (1604), pp. 41ff.

[52] Ibid., pp. 414ff.

[53] Ibid., pp. 436ff. In ch. XIII (p. 436) it is concluded that 'omnes Basilicae construendae leges ex hac una Salomonis mutuatus est Vitruvius.'

[54] Roland Fréart de Chambray, Parallèle de l'architecture antique avec la moderne, Paris 1650, p. 71.

[55] Villalpando, vol. II (1604), pp. 466ff., Ill. p. 467.

[56] Cf. Taylor (1951), pp. 423ff.

[57] Villalpando, vol. II (1604), pp. 471f.

[58] Cf. François Secret, 'Les Jésuites et le kabbalisme chrétien', Bibliothèque d'Humanisme et Renaissance 20, 1958, p. 552.

[59] Cf. Marcel Restle, 'Bauplanung und Baugesinnung unter Mehmet II. Fâtih. Filarete in Konstantinopel', Pantheon XXXIX, 1981, pp. 361–67.

[60] Cf. the important Gregor Martin Lechner OSB, 'Villalpandos Tempelrekonstruktion in Beziehung zu barocker Klosterarchitektur', Festschrift Wolfgang Braunfels, Tübingen 1977, pp. 223–37.

[61] Juan de Pineda, De rebus Salomonis regis libri octo, Mainz 1613; cf. Taylor (1951), p. 455.

[62] Cf. Hans Reuther, 'Das Modell des Salomonischen Tempels im Museum für Hamburgische Geschichte', Niederdeutsche Beiträge zur Kunstgeschichte 19, 1980, pp. 161–98.

[63] For the most detailed studies of Villalpando's influence cf. Taylor (1951), pp. 455ff.; Helen Rosenau (1979) passim; and the relevant writings covered in the present chapter.

[64] Fray Juan de San Jerónimo, 'Memorias desde Monasterio de Sant Lorencio el Real (1563–1591)', in: Colección de documentos inéditos para la Historia de España VII, Madrid 1845; excerpts in: Sánchez-Cantón, vol. I (1923), pp. 229–60.

[65] Fray José de Siguenza, Historia de la Orden

de San Gerónimo, libro tercero y cuarto: La Fundación del Monasterio de San Lorenzo el Real, Madrid 1605 (modern edition in: *Nueva Bibliotheca de autores españoles*, vol. II, Madrid 1909); excerpts in: Sánchez-Cantón, vol. I (1923), pp. 327–448.

[66] Fray Francisco de los Santos, *Descripción breve del Monasterio de San Lorenzo el Real del Escorial, unica maravilla de mundo…*, Madrid 1657 (1667, 1671, 1681, 1698, 1760; English ed. London 1671); excerpts in: Sánchez-Cantón, vol. II (1933), pp. 225–88.

[67] Fray Andrés Jiménez, *Descripción del Real Monasterio de San Lorenzo del Escorial…*, Madrid 1764; Zamora Lucas and Ponce de León (1947), p. 65 Nr. 49 also mention a folio edition of 1654, said to consist of plates only. Excerpts in: Sánchez-Cantón, vol. V (1941), pp. 61–104.

[68] On Fray Lorenzo de San Nicolás cf. esp. Llaguno y Amirola and Ceán-Bermúdez (1829), vol. IV, pp. 20ff.; Sánchez-Cantón, vol. III (1934), pp. 1ff.; Kubler (1957), pp. 79ff. (p. 80 'el mejor libro sobre instrucción arquitectónica escrito jamás').

[69] Fray Lorenzo de San Nicolas, *Arte y Uso de Architectura*, Part I, Madrid 1633; Part II: Madrid 1664; repr. of Part I: Madrid 1667; both Parts: Madrid 1736 (1796); the 1796 edition was used.

[70] Fray Lorenzo de San Nicolás (1796), p. 215.

[71] Cf. Sánchez-Cantón, vol. V (1941), pp. 275ff.

[72] Domingo de Andrade, *Excelencias antiguedad, y nobleza de la Arquitectura…*, Santiago 1695.

[73] Elías Tormo Monzó and Enrique Lafuente Ferrari, *La vida y la obra de Fray Juan Ricci*, 2 vols, Madrid 1930; vol. I, pp. 109ff. On Ricci cf. esp. Kubler (1957), p. 82; fundamental is Juan Antonio Ramirez, 'Guarino Guarini, Fray Juan Ricci and the "Complete Salomonic Order", *Art History* 4, 1981, pp. 175–185.

[74] Ricci (1930), fol. 20ff., pls XVIIIff.

[75] Ibid., fol. 36ff., pls XXXVIIff.

[76] Ibid., pls XL, LXIII; cf. Ramon Otero Tuñez, 'Las primeras columnas salomonicas de España', *Boletin de la Universidad Compostelana* 63, 1955, pp. 335–44. On the subject of twisted columns, cf. Hans Wolfgang Schmidt, *Die gewundene Säule in der Architekturtheorie von 1500 bis 1800*, Stuttgart 1978; on Ricci pp. 79f. Comments on Villalpando's 'Salomonic

order' by Pablo de Céspedes are to be found in his *Discurso sobre el templo de Salomón* (1604; published by Cean-Bermúdez in: *Diccionario histórico de los más ilustres profesores de las Bellas Artes en España*, vol. V, Madrid 1800, p. 316f.).

[77] On the possibility of Ricci and Guarini meeting, and the time and place, cf. Ramirez (1981), p. 179.
Guarino Guarini, *Architettura civile*, Turin 1737; plate on the Corinthian Order among work illustrations, pl. 18.

[78] The manuscript, extant at Montecassino (V-590), was published in an appendix of the edition of 1930, pls CLX–CLXVIII: *Epitome arquitecturae de ordine salomonico integro* (1663).

[79] Ricci (1930), pl. CLXVI.

[80] Ibid., pl. CLXVIII.

[81] On Caramuel cf. esp. Daria De Bernardi Ferrero, 'Il Conte Juan Caramuel di Lobkowitz, vescovo di Vigevano, architetto e teorico dell'architettura', *Palladio*, new series, XV, 1965, pp. 91–110; Werner Oechslin, 'Bemerkungen zu Guarino Guarini und Juan Carmuel de Lobkowitz', *Raggi* 8, n. 1, 1968, pp. 91–109; Angela Guidoni Marino, 'Il Colonnato di Piazza S. Pietro: dall'architettura obliqua di Caramuel al 'classicismo' Berniniano', *Palladio*, new series, XXIII, 1973, pp. 81–120.

[82] On his philosophical outlook cf. Angela Guidoni Marino (1973).

[83] On Vigevano's Piazza Ducale, cf. Wolfgang Lotz, 'La Piazza Ducale de Vigevano. Un foro principesco del tardo Quattrocento', in: *Studi Bramanteschi. Atti del Congresso internazionale*, 1970, pp. 205–21; on Caramuel's façade cf. Daria De Bernardi Ferrero (1965), pp. 108ff.

[84] Juan Caramuel de Lobkowitz, *Architectura civil recta, y obliqua, considerada y dibuxada en el Templo de Ierusalem… promivada a suma perfecion en el Templo y Palacio de S. Lorenco cerca del Escurial*, 3 vols, Vigevano 1678.

[85] E.g. by Leopoldo Cicognara (*Catalogo ragionato dei libri d'arte e d'antichità posseduti dal Conte Cicognara*, vol. 1, Pisa 1821): 'un magazino indigesto di tutte le cognizioni riguardanti l'Architettura'.

[86] Caramuel (1678), Tratado V, pp. 5ff.

[87] Caramuel (1678), Tratado V, pls XI ff.

[88] Caramuel (1678), Tratado V, p. 74; cf. Oechslin (1968), pp. 100ff.

[89] Caramuel (1678), Tratado VI, pp. 1f.; cf. Angela Guidoni Marino (1973), pp. 86ff.

[90] *'edificar mal, edificar sin guardar las leyes y preceptos del Arte. Y edificare obliqua, es edificar muros, que con otros, con quienzes hazen angulo obliquo, tengan buena correspondencia.'* Caramuel (1678), Tratado VI, p. 2.

[91] Ibid., p. 11, pl. XXIII.

[92] Ibid., p. 12, pl. XXIV.

[93] Angela Guidoni Marino (1973), p. 105; the author cites an eighth treatise by Caramuel, not contained in the edition I have used (Bibl. Apost. Vatic., Cicognara VII/463); here Caramuel's entire criticism of Bernini is summarised as five points (text reprinted in Guidoni Marino (1973), p. 117, n. 36).

[94] Caramuel (1678), Tratado VI, p. 33.

[95] Cf. Francisco José León Tello, 'Introducción a la teoría de la arquitectura del P. Tosca (1651–1735)', *Revista de ideas estéticas* 35, 1977, pp. 287–98; the author does not notice the connection with Caramuel.

[96] *'La arquitectura obliqua edifica sus fábricas sobre suelos inclanados o en pasadizos y puertas que corren en viaje o en templos redondos o elípticos'.* Cited from ibid., p. 298.

[97] Juan García Berruguilla, *Verdadera practica de las resoluciones de la geometria, sobre las tres dimensiones para un perfecto architecto,* Madrid 1747 (facs. repr., ed. Santiago Garma Pons, Murcia 1979).

[98] Juan de Torija, *Tratado breve, sobre las Ordenanzas de la Villa de Madrid...,* Madrid 1661 (1664, 1728, 1754, 1760).

[99] Teodoro Ardemans, *Ordenanzas de Madrid y otras diferentes...,* Madrid 1720 (1754, 1760, 1765, 1791, 1796, 1798, 1820, 1844, 1848). I have used the 1791 edition.

[100] Diego de Villanueva, *Colección de diferentes papeles críticos sobre todas las partes de la Arquitectura...,* Valencia 1766 (facs. repr. with summaries by Luis Moya, Valencia 1979). On Diego de Villanueva cf. esp. Llaguno y Amirola and Ceán-Bermúdez (1829), vol. IV, 269ff.; Fernando Chueca Goitia and Carlos de Miguel, *La Vida y las Obras del Arquitecto Juan de Villanueva,* Madrid 1949; Kubler (1957), pp. 242ff.; Kubler (1959), pp. 49ff.

[101] Villanueva, p. 17.

[102] Ibid., p. 37.

[103] Ibid., pp. 35ff.

[104] Ibid., p. 56.

[105] Ibid., p. 100.

[106] Antonio Ponz, *Viage (Viaje) de España...,* 18 vols, Madrid 1772–94.

19. Developments in England from the sixteenth to the eighteenth century

[1] Cf. the following general studies and bibliographies: H. M. Colvin, *A Biographical Dictionary of English architects 1660–1840,* London 1954 ('1978); John Harris, 'Sources of Architectural History in England', *Journal of the Society of Architectural Historians* XXIV, 1965, pp. 297–300; Rudolf Wittkower, 'La letteratura palladiana in Inghilterra', *Bollettino del Centro Internazionale di Studi di Architettura 'Andrea Palladio'* VII, 1965, Part 2, pp. 126–52; id., 'English Literature on Architecture', in: Wittkower, *Palladio and English Palladianism,* London 1974, pp. 93ff.; Wittkower (1974, p. 100) has the trenchant comment: 'No other British architect before Colen Campbell's Vitruvius Britannicus of 1715 contemplated, wrote or published a work on architecture. The theory was supplied by foreigners, mainly by the Italians'. For the most thorough and comprehensive appraisal of English architectural theory, cf. Johannes Dobai, *Die Kunstliteratur des Klassizismus und der Romantik in England,* vol. I: 1700–1750, Bern 1974; vol. II: 1750–90, Bern 1975; vol. III: 1790–1840, Bern 1977; vol. IV: index vol., Bern 1984; Christian Ferdinand Wolsdorff, *Untersuchungen zu englischen Veröffentlichungen des 17. und 18. Jahrhunderts, die Probleme der Architektur und des Bauens behandeln* (diss. 1978), Bonn 1982 is esp. informative on the English book market. For a good description of individual publications, cf. *Katalog der Architektur- und Ornamentstichsammlung der Kunstbibliothek Berlin,* Part I: 'Baukunst England', ed. Marianne Fischer, Berlin 1977.

On English architectural history, cf. esp. John Summerson, *Architecture in Britain 1530–1830* (The Pelican History of Art), Harmondsworth 1953, '1970; Emil Kaufmann, *Architecture in the Age of Reason* (1955), New York 1968; on the changing role of the architect, cf. Frank Jenkins, *Architect and Patron. A Survey of Pro-*

fessional Relations and Practice in England from the Sixteenth Century to the Present Day, London 1961; and cf. *Catalogue of the Drawings Collections of the R.I.B.A.*, Farnborough 1968ff. On English Palladianism cf. also the exhib. cat. *Palladio. La sua eredità nel mondo*, Venice 1980, pp. 31ff.; John Harris, *The Palladians*, London 1981.

² Thomas More, *De Optimo Reipublicae Statu, deque nova Insula Utopia... (1515)*, Löwen 1516, Paris 1517, Basel 1518; numerous editions and translations – cf. trans. with an introduction by Klaus J. Heinisch in: *Der utopische Staat*, Hamburg 1960 (several editions); on More's innovative impact on architectural theory, cf. Françoise Choay, *La règle et le modèle. Sur la théorie de l'architecture et de l'urbanisme*, Paris 1980, p. 46ff.

³ More, ed. Heinisch, pp. 48ff.

⁴ Cf. the general study by Jorge Hardoy, *Urban Planning in Pre-Columbian America*, New York 1968.

⁵ John Shute, *The First and Chief Groundes of Architecture*, London 1563 (facs. repr. 1912 and 1964); several editions 1579, 1584, 1587. On Shute cf. Summerson (ed. 1970), pp. 46f., 54f.; Wittkower (1974), p. 100; Dobai, vol. I (1974), pp. 357f.

⁶ Cf. esp. Wittkower (1965), pp. 128f.; Wittkower (1974), pp. 96ff.; Wolsdorff (1982), pp. 33ff.

⁷ Francis Bacon, Essays (1597), cited from Bacon, *Works*, ed. J. Spedding, R. L. Ellis and D. D. Heath (14 vols, London 1857–1874; facs. repr.: Stuttgart 1959ff.), vol. 6, 1963, p. 481.

⁸ Cf. Dobai, vol. I (1974), pp. 365f.; cf. esp.: Edward Robert De Zurko, *Origins of Functionalist Theory*, New York 1957, pp. 62ff.

⁹ In Essay XLIII ('On Beauty'), op. cit (1963), p. 478.

¹⁰ Bacon (1963), p. 482.

¹¹ Francis Bacon, *Nova Atlantis*, ed. William Rawley, London 1638 (numerous editions and translations).

¹² Cf. Francis C. Springell, *Connoisseur and Diplomat. The Earl of Arundel's Embassy to Germany in 1636...*, London 1963.

¹³ On Jones cf. esp. James Lees-Milne, *The Age of Inigo Jones*, London 1953; Summerson (ed. 1970), pp. 111ff.; John Summerson, *Inigo Jones*, Harmondsworth 1966; cat. 'The King's Arcadia: Inigo Jones and the Stuart

Court', London 1973; Wittkower in: *Palladio and English Palladianism* (1974), pp. 51ff.; John Harris, *Catalogue of the Drawings Collection of the R.I.B.A.: Inigo Jones & John Webb*, Farnborough 1972. The literature of English journeys up to the end of the 17th century is sparse; cf. R. S. Pine-Coffin, *Bibliography of British and American Travel in Italy to 1860*, Florence 1974.

Thomas Coryate, in *Crudities Hastily gobled etc*, dated 1608 (London 1611), describes Vicenza in detail without mentioning the name of Palladio. Inigo Jones was unable to relate his interests to any existing tradition.

¹⁴ Cf. Wittkower (1974), p. 76.

¹⁵ Note of 20 January 1615; cited Summerson (ed. 1970), p. 118.

¹⁶ John Webb, *The Most Notable Antiquity of Great Britain, vulgarly called Stone-Heng, on Salisbury Plain, Restored*, London 1655.

¹⁷ Cf. Wittkower (1974), p. 63.

¹⁸ Henry Wotton, *The Elements of Architecture*, London 1624 (facs. repr. with introduction by Fredrick Hard, Charlottesville 1968; Farnborough 1969); several editions and translations, cf. Dobai, vol. I (1974), pp. 367ff. 458.

¹⁹ Wotton (1624), p. 7.

²⁰ Ibid., p. 9f.

²¹ Ibid., pp. 10f.

²² Ibid., p. 17.

²³ Ibid., p. 47ff.

²⁴ Ibid., p. 82.

²⁵ Ibid., p. 109.

²⁶ Ibid., p. 118.

²⁷ Ibid., p. 121.

²⁸ Ibid., p. 122.

²⁹ Cf. Wittkower (1965), pp. 130ff.; also Dobai, vol. I (1974), pp. 310ff.; Wolsdorff (1982), pp. 15ff.

³⁰ John Evelyn, *A Parallel of the Antient Architecture with the Modern... written in French by Roland Fréart, Sieur de Chambray*, London 1664 (facs. repr. 1970); further editions 1680, 1697, 1707, 1723, 1733.

On Evelyn's trans. cf. Hard in his introduction to Wotton (1968), pp. lxixff.; Dobai, vol. I (1974), pp. 376ff., 419.

³¹ John Evelyn, *The Diary of John Evelyn*, ed. E. S. Beer, 6 vols, Oxford 1955 (journey to Italy in vol. II); for an appraisal of his diary notes cf. Ludwig Schudt, *Italienreisen im 17. und 18. Jahrhundert*, Vienna–Munich 1959, pp. 61ff.; Kerry Downes, 'John Evelyn

and Architecture: A First Inquiry', *Concerning Architecture. Essays on Architectural Writers...* presented to Nikolaus Pevsner, ed. John Summerson, London 1968, pp. 28–39.

32 Evelyn (1664), dedication.

33 Evelyn (1664), p. 122.

34 Evelyn (1664), dedication.

35 Evelyn (ed. 1707), p. 9. On these additions cf. Paul Frankl, *The Gothic. Literary Sources and Interpretations through Eight Centuries*, Princeton 1960, pp. 359f.

36 R. T. Gunter, *The Architecture of Sir Roger Pratt. Charles II's Commissioner for the Rebuilding of London after the Great Fire Now Printed for the First Time from his Note-Books*, Oxford 1928; Summerson (ed. 1970), pp. 149ff.; on his literary fragments cf. Dobai, vol. I (1974), pp. 412ff.

37 Gunter (1928), p. 34.

38 Gunter (1928), p. 83 (7 December 1665).

39 Gunter (1928), p. 286 (the model of the Temple), p. 304 (catalogue of the library).

40 Balthasar Gerbier, *A Brief Discourse, Concerning the Three Chief Principles of Magnificent Building...*, London 1662; id., *Counsel and Advise to all Builders...*, London 1663 (facs. repr. [together with: Thomas Wilsford, *Architectonicae, or the Art of Building*, London 1659] 1969). On Gerbier cf. Dobai, repr. vol. I (1974), pp. 378ff.

41 From extensive literature on Wren: Eduard Sekler, *Wren and His Place in European Architecture*, London 1956; Victor Fuerst, *The Architecture of Sir Christopher Wren*, London 1956; the 20 vols published by the Wren Society (Oxford 1924–43) remain the most important reference on Wren.

42 Stephen Wren, *Parentalia: or, Memoirs of the Family of the Wren*, London 1750 (facs. repr. of the 'Heirloom Copy' at the R.I.B.A.: Farnborough 1965); for a detailed survey of Wren's writings, cf. Dobai, vol. I (1974), pp. 380ff. (bibliography, pp. 459ff.).

43 *Tracts* I–IV, first published in Stephen Wren, *Parentalia* (1750); here cited from the edition with introduction by Arthur T. Bolton in: *Wren Society* 19, 1942, pp. 121ff., with (pp. 140ff.) the 'Discourse', after Wren's ms (in the 'Heirloom Copy').

44 Wren, *Tract* I (*Wren Society* 19, 1942, p. 126).

45 Ibid.

46 Wren speaks in *Tract II* of 'arbitrary'

proportions (*Wren Society* 19, 1942, p. 128).

47 Wren, *Tract* I (*Wren Society* 19, 1942, p. 126).

48 Wren, *Tract* III (*Wren Society* 19, 1942, p. 133).

49 Wren, 'Discourse on Architecture' (*Wren Society* 19, 1942, p. 143).

50 Ibid., p. 142.

51 Ibid., p. 141.

52 For a general study, cf. Summerson (ed. 1970), pp. 203ff.

53 Published in Stephen Wren, *Parentalia* (1750), here cited from *Wren Society* 11, 1934, pp. 15–20.

54 Wren, *Report*, 1713; *Wren Society* 11, 1934, p. 16.

55 Ibid., p. 20.

56 *Wren Society* 11, 1934, pls II–V.

57 Cf. Suzanne Lang, 'Vanbrugh's Theory and Hawksmoor's Buildings', *Journal of the Society of Architectural Historians* XXIV, 1965, pp. 125–51; Dobai, vol. I (1974), pp. 420ff., 462ff.; cf. the monographs (with most of the texts of the writings) by Kerry Downes, *Hawksmoor*, London 1959 (²1979), *Vanbrugh*, London 1977.

58 Wren's 'Memorandum' in Stephen Wren, *Parentalia* (1750) and *Wren Society* IX, pp. 15–18; Vanbrugh's Memorandum published in Downes (1977), pp. 257f.; cf. Howard M. Colvin, 'Fifty New Churches', *The Architectural Review* 107, 1950, pp. 189–96.

59 For a detailed comparison with Alberti, cf. Suzanne Lang (1965), pp. 126ff.

60 Cited from Downes (1977), p. 257.

61 Ibid.

62 Suzanne Lang (1965), p. 133; Dobai, vol. I (1974), p. 421.

63 Hawksmoor, 'The Explanation of the Obelisk', in: Downes (1959), pp. 262ff.

64 Downes (1959), pp. 255f. (No. 147).

65 Ibid., p. 257.

66 Ibid.

67 Cf. esp. Erwin Panofsky, 'Das erste Blatt aus dem "Libro" Giorgio Vasaris. Eine Studie über die Beurteilung der Gotik in der italienischen Renaissance', *Städel-Jahrbuch* VI, 1930, pp. 25–72 (in: Panofsky, *Meaning in the Visual Arts*, Garden City, NY 1955, pp. 169–235); Rudolf Wittkower, *Gothic versus Classic. Architectural Projects in Seventeenth-Century Italy*, New York 1974, pp. 65ff.; Suzanne Lang (1965), pp. 135ff.

68 Cf. Suzanne Lang (1965), pp. 140ff.; for a

detailed study of Shaftesbury's doctrine, cf. Dobai, vol. I (1974), pp. 47ff.

[69] Cf. G. S. Gordon, 'The Trojans in Britain', *Essays and Studies by Members of the English Association* IX, 1924.

[70] Shaftesbury, 'A Letter Concerning Design' (1712), in: B. Rand (ed.), *Second Characters or the Language of Forms (1914)*, New York 1969, pp. 23f.

[71] James Anderson, *The Constitutions of the Freemasons. Containing the History, Charges, Regulations...*, London 1723 (²1738); cf. also Eugen Lennhoff and Oskar Posner, *Internationales Freimaurerlexikon*, Vienna 1932 (repr. Vienna–Munich 1980), pp. 31ff.
Adrian von Buttlar, 'Moral Architecture. Zum englischen Palladianismus des 18. Jahrhunderts', in: *Neue Zürcher Zeitung* 4./5. April 1980 and in his book *Der englische Landsitz*, Mittenwald 1982, pp. 115ff., 133ff. gives a thorough account of these links. On the rôle played by freemasonry in English architecture, cf. Joseph Rykwert, *The First Moderns*, Cambridge MA–London 1980, pp. 159ff.

[72] Cf. John Summerson, 'The Book of Architecture of John Thorpe in Sir John Soane's Museum', *Walpole Society* XL, 1964–66; Mark Girouard, *Robert Smythson and the Architecture of the Elisabethan Era*, London 1966, pp. 25ff.

[73] Johannes Kip and Leonard Knyff, *Britannia Illustrata, or Views of Noblemen's and Gentlemen's Seats, Cathedrals and Collegiate Churches...*, London 1707 (facs. repr. ed. John Harris, Farnborough 1970; cf. also John Harris, *Die Häuser der Lords und Gentlemen*, Dortmund 1982).

[74] Colen Campbell, *Vitruvius Britannicus, or the British Architect*, vol. I, London 1715; vol. II, London 1717; vol. III, London 1725 (facs. repr. ed. with introduction by John Harris, New York 1967). On Campbell cf. esp. Howard E. Stutchbury, *The Architecture of Colen Campbell*, Manchester 1967; John Harris, *Catalogue of the Drawings Collection of the R.I.B.A.: Colen Campbell*, Farnborough 1973; on *Vitruvius Britannicus* cf. Dobai vol. I (1974), pp. 264ff.; on the genesis of *Vitruvius Britannicus*, cf. Eileen Harris, '*Vitruvius Britannicus* before Colen Campbell', *The Burlington Magazine* CXXVIII, 1985, pp. 340–46.

[75] Campbell, vol. I (1715), Introduction.

[76] Ibid., Introduction.

[77] Ibid., p. 3.

[78] Ibid., pls 8, 9.

[79] Cf. Stutchbury (1967), pp. 27ff.

[80] Campbell, vol. I (1715), pl. 21–27; vol. III (1725), pls 39, 40.

[81] On the designs for Wanstead; cf. also Summerson (ed. 1970), pp. 320ff.

[82] Campbell, vol. I (1715), p. 4.

[83] Campbell, vol. II (1717), p. 4, pls 83–4.

[84] Campbell, vol. III (1725), p. 8, pls 35–8.

[85] J. Badeslade and J. Rocque, *Vitruvius Britannicus, Volume the Fourth...*, London 1739 (facs. text in ed. by John Harris, New York 1967).

[86] John Woolfe and James Gandon, *Vitruvius Britannicus, or the British Architect...*, vol. IV, London 1767 (facs. text in ed. by John Harris, New York 1967). On Gandon cf. Edward McPartland, *James Gandon: Vitruvius Hibernicus*, London 1985.

[87] Woolfe and Gandon (1767), Introduction.

[88] Woolfe and Gandon, *Vitruvius Britannicus...*, vol. V, London 1771.

[89] With the possible exception of the sixteenth-century Longford Castle (Woolfe and Gandon, vol. V, 1771, pl. 94ff.).

[90] George Richardson, *The New Vitruvius Britannicus*, 2 vols, London 1802 and 1808 (facs. repr. New York 1970 and 1978).

[91] Richardson, vol. I (1802), Introduction.

[92] On Lord Burlington cf. esp. the essays by Wittkower in: Wittkower, *Palladio and English Palladianism* (1974), pp. 113ff.; James Lees-Milne, *Earls of Creation: Five Patrons of Eighteenth-Century Art* (1962), London 1986, pp. 85–151.

[93] On Kent cf. Margaret Jourdain, *The Work of William Kent*, London and New York 1948.

[94] Richard Lord Burlington, *Fabbriche Antiche disegnate da Andrea Palladio Vicentino*, London 1730 (facs. repr. 1969).

[95] 'opportunissimo Presente all'Età nostra, di cui niun' altra forse dimostrò mai maggiore disposizione a dispendiose Fabbriche...' Burlington (1730), 'All'intendente Lettore.'

[96] William Kent, *The Designs of Inigo Jones...*, 2 vols, London 1727 (facs. repr. 1967); further editions: 1735, 1770, 1825.

[97] Kent, vol. I (1727), Advertisement.

[98] On Pope cf. esp. Dobai, vol. I (1974), pp. 170ff., 211ff. (bibliography); Morris R. Brownell, *Alexander Pope & the Arts of Georgian England*, Oxford 1978.

[99] Alexander Pope, *An Epistle to the Right Honourable Earl of Burlington...*, London 1731.

[100] Godfrey Richards, *The First Book of Architecture by Andrea Palladio*, London 1663 (repr. frequently up to 1733). On English translations of Palladio cf. esp. Rudolf Wittkower, Giacomo Leoni's Edition of Palladio's 'Quattro libri dell'architettura', *Arte Veneta* VIII, 1954, pp. 310–316; id., 'Le edizione inglesi del Palladio', *Bollettino del Centro Internazionale di Studi d'Architettura 'Andrea Palladio'* XII, 1970, pp. 292–306; id., 'English Neo-classicism and the Vicissitudes of Palladio's *Quattro Libri*', in: Wittkower, *Palladio and English Palladianism* (1974), pp. 71ff.; Dobai, vol. I (1974), pp. 287ff., 308f.; Wolfsdorff (1982), pp. 137ff.

[101] Cf. Wittkower's essays; also Jörg Gamer, *Matteo Alberti. Oberbaudirektor des Kurfürsten Johann Wilhelm von der Pfalz*, Düsseldorf 1978, p. 42 and passim.

[102] Reference by Wittkower (1970), p. 295; (1974), p. 79, fig. 108 (title-page of the ms.).

[103] Cf. note 102. Ms in the library of Lady Lucas and Dingwall, Woodgates Manor, Wiltshire.

[104] Giacomo Leoni, *The Architecture of A. Palladio; In Four Books*, London 1716 (1715)–1719 (or 1720).

[105] Cf. Wittkower (1954), p. 313.

[106] Cf. Grant Keith in: *Journal of the Royal Institute of British Architects* 1925, pp. 102f. Inigo Jones's notes are also published in Leoni's edition of Palladio of 1742.

[107] Isaac Ware, *The Four Books of Andrea Palladio's Architecture*, London 1738 (repr. with introduction by Adolf K. Placzek, New York 1965), Advertisement.

[108] Giacomo Leoni, *Ten Books on Architecture by Leone Battista Alberti*, London 1726, ³1755 (facs. repr. ed. Joseph Rykwert, London 1955, ²1965).

[109] Colen Campbell, *Andrea Palladio's Five Orders of Architecture...*, London 1728 (²1729).

[110] On the use of Campbell's engravings acquired by the publisher Robert Sayer in William and John Halfpenny, Robert Morris and Thomas Lightoler, *The Modern Builder's Assistant; Or, a concise Epitome of the whole System of Architecture*, London 1742 (²1757), cf. Wittkower (1974), pp. 87f.

[111] Benjamin Cole and Edward Hoppus,

[—] *Andrea Palladio's Architecture in Four Books...*, London 1733–35 (1736).

[112] Ware (1738), Advertisement.

[113] Ware (1738).

[114] On Gibbs cf. esp. B. Little, *The Life and Works of James Gibbs*, London 1955; Summerson (ed. 1970), pp. 347ff.; Kaufmann (1955), pp. 6ff.; Dobai, vol. I (1974), pp. 444, 469ff.; Terry Friedmann, *James Gibbs*, New Haven–London 1984.

[115] Campbell, *Vitruvius Britannicus* vol. I, 1715, Introduction.

[116] James Gibbs, *A Book of Architecture containing Designs of Buildings and Ornaments*, London 1728 (facs. repr.: New York 1968); London ²1739.

[117] Gibbs (1728), p. i.

[118] Ibid., pp. iif.

[119] Ibid., p. viii.

[120] John Coolidge (Peter Harrison's First Design for King's Chapel, Boston', *De Artibus Opuscula* vol. XL. *Essays in Honor of Erwin Panofsky*, New York 1961, pp. 64–75) describes John Halfpenny's unexecuted design for Holy Trinity, Leeds (published in: Halfpenny, *The Art of Sound Building*, 1825) as the chief model for King's Chapel, Boston. The model for the existing interior of King's Chapel, however, is seen as Gibbs' St Martin-in-the-Fields, 1721–26 (with doubling of supporting columns).

[121] Summerson (ed. 1970), p. 543.

[122] James Gibbs, *Rules for Drawing the Several Parts of Architecture...*, London 1732 (facs. repr. Farnborough 1968); London ²1738, ³1753.

[123] James Gibbs, 'Cursury Remarks' and 'A Short Accompt of Mr James Gibbs Architect And of several things he built in England & affter his returne from Italy', ms., Sir John Soane's Museum, London; cf. John Holloway, 'A James Gibbs Autobiography', *The Burlington Magazine* XCVII, 1955, pp. 147–51.

[124] William Adam's project originating in 1726 was finally published c. 1810 by John Adam, *Vitruvius Scoticus: Being a Collection of Plans, Elevations, and Sections of Public Buildings, Noblemen's, Gentlemen's Houses in Scotland: Principally from the Designs of the late William Adam*, Edinburgh, n.d. (facs. repr. 1980). Cf. John Fleming, *Robert Adam and His Circle in Edinburgh and Rome*, Cambridge, MA 1962, pp. 33ff.

[125] Robert Castell, *The Villas of the Ancients*

Illustrated, London 1728 (facs. repr. New York–London 1982); cf. Marianne Fischer, *Die frühen Rekonstruktionen der Landhäuser Plinius' des Jüngeren*, diss., Berlin 1962, ch. III; Dobai, vol. I (1974), pp. 277ff.

[126] James Ralph, *A Critical Review of the Publick Buildings, Statues and Ornaments, In, and about London and Westminster*, London 1734 (facs. repr. Farnborough 1970); 2nd ed., *A New Critical Review...*, London 1736, ³1763, ⁴1783 (with the announcement: 'Originally written by Ralph, Architect'). On Ralph, cf. *Dictionary of National Biography*, vol. XVI, 1909, pp. 164ff.; cf. however Dobai, vol. I (1974), pp. 281ff.

[127] Cf. Edward De Zurko, *Origins of Functionalist Theory*, New York 1957, pp. 75ff.; Dobai, vol. I (1974), pp. 125ff.

[128] On Robert Morris cf. esp. Kaufmann (1955), pp. 22ff.; Dobai, vol. I (1974), pp. 318ff.; David Leatherbarrow, 'Architecture and Situation: A Study of the Architectural Writings of Robert Morris', *Journal of the Society of Architectural Historians* XLIV, 1985, pp. 48–59.

[129] Robert Morris, *An Essay In Defence of Ancient Architecture; Or, a Parallel of the Ancient Buildings with the Modern...*, London 1728 (facs. repr. Farnborough 1971).

[130] Morris (1728), p. xviii.

[131] Ibid., p. 20.

[132] Ibid., p. 84.

[133] Robert Morris, *Lectures on Architecture, Consisting of Rules Founded upon Harmonick and Arithmetical Proportions in Building*, London 1734–1736; ²1759 (facs. repr. Farnborough 1971).

[134] Morris, *Lectures* (ed. 1759), p. 65.

[135] Ibid., p. 67.

[136] Ibid., p. 69.

[137] Cf. Dobai, vol. I (1974), pp. 489ff., 504.

[138] William Salmon, *Palladio Londinensis, or the London Art of Building*, London 1734 (facs. repr. Farnborough 1969); eight editions up to 1733; cf. Dobai, vol. I (1974), pp. 339f.

[139] Cf. Colvin (1954), pp. 260f.; Dobai, vol. I (1974), pp. 474ff., 501f.

[140] William and John Halfpenny, Robert Morris and Thomas Lightoler, *The Modern Builder's Assistant*, London 1747 (facs. repr. Farnborough 1971).

[141] Halfpenny, Morris, Lightoler (1747), Preface.

[142] The most important literature on Chinoiserie: Hugh Honour, *Chinoiserie. The Vision of Cathey (1961)*, New York 1973; cat. *China und Europa. Chinaverständnis und Chinamode im 17. und 18. Jahrhundert*, Berlin 1973; Luciano Patetta, *L'architettura dell'eclettismo. Fonti, teorie, modelli 1750–1900*, Milan 1975, pp. 9ff.; Oliver Impey, *Chinoiserie. The Impact of Oriental Styles on Western Art and Decoration*, New York 1977; Madeleine Jarry, *China und Europa*, Stuttgart 1981.

[143] William Halfpenny, *New Designs for Chinese Temples, Triumphal Arches, Garden Seats...*, London 1750; parts II–IV (in collaboration with John Halfpenny) 1751–1752; 2nd ed. entitled *Rural Architecture in the Chinese Taste...*, London 1752 (³1755).

[144] William and John Halfpenny, *Chinese and Gothic Architecture properly Ornamented...*, London 1752.

[145] Isaac Ware, *A Complete Body of Architecture*, London 1756; ²1757; ³c.1758–60, ⁴1768 (facs. repr. Farnborough 1971); on Ware's work and other writings, cf. Colvin (1954), pp. 649ff.; Wolsdorff (1982), pp. 181ff.

[146] Ware (ed. 1768), Preface.

[147] Ibid., Preface.

[148] Ibid., p. 40.

[149] Ibid., pp. 94, 127, 297ff.

[150] Ibid., p. 133.

[151] Ibid., p. 136.

[152] Ibid.

[153] Ware (ed. 1768), p. 137.

[154] Ibid., pp. 138, 143.

[155] Ibid., p. 345.

[156] Ibid., pls. 52, 53; cf. Summerson (ed. 1970), p. 374.

[157] Ware (ed. 1768), pp. 621f.

[158] George Berkeley, *Alciphron, or the Minute Philosopher*, London 1732; cf. De Zurko (1957), p. 85.

[159] Ware (ed. 1768), p. 636.

[160] In pls 120, 121 illustrating perspective architectural representations.

[161] Ware (ed. 1768), p. 137.

[162] Ibid., p. 96.

[163] Ibid., p. 637.

[164] Ibid.

[165] On John Wood cf. esp. John Summerson, 'John Wood and the English Town-Planning Tradition', in: Summerson, *Heavenly Mansions and other essays on architecture (1948)*, New York 1963, pp. 87–110; Summerson (ed. 1970), pp. 386ff.; Rudolf

Wittkower, 'Federico Zucari and John Wood of Bath', *Journal of the Warburg and Courtauld Institutes* 6, 1943, pp. 220–22; Dobai vol. I (1974), pp. 445f.

[166] John Wood, *The Origin of Building: or the Plagiarism of the Heathens detected in Five Books*, Bath 1741 (facs. repr.: Farnborough 1968).

[167] One reason for this might have been Wood's supposed freemasonry; cf. Adrian von Buttlar, *Der englische Landsitz 1715–1760*, Mittenwald 1982, pp. 118f.

[168] Wood (1741), pp. 70f.

[169] Ibid., p. 180.

[170] Ibid., p. 39.

[171] Ibid.

[172] Wood (1741), p. 67; cf. Wittkower (1943).

[173] Wood (1741), p. 221.

[174] William Stukeley, *Stonehenge: a Temple Restaur'd to the British Druids*, London 1740; cf. A. L. Owen, *The Famous Druids*, Oxford 1962; Dobai, vol. I (1974), pp. 449f., 816ff.

[175] John Wood published his debate with Stukeley under the title *Choir Gaure, Vulgarly called Stonehenge...*, Oxford 1747.

[176] Cf. Christine Stevenson, 'Salomon, Engothicked: The Elder John Wood's Restoration of Llandaff Cathedral', *Art History* 6, 1983, pp. 301–314.

[177] John Wood, *A Dissertation upon the Orders of Columns, And Their Appendages...*, London 1750.

[178] Wood (1750), p. 13.

[179] John Wood, *An Essay towards a Description of Bath...*, London 1742; ²1749, 1769 (facs. repr. Bath 1969, Farnborough 1970).

[180] Colvin (1954), pp. 354f.; Dobai, vol. I (1974), pp. 480ff., 502ff.

[181] Batty Langley, *The Builder's Chest-Book; or a Complete Key to the Five Orders of Columns in Architecture...*, London 1727 (facs. repr. Farnborough 1971).

[182] Langley (1727), Dedication.

[183] Ibid., p. i.

[184] Ibid., pp. 2f.

[185] Cf. Dobai, vol. I (1974), p. 483.

[186] Batty Langley, *The Builder's Jewel*, London 1741 (numerous further editions); cf. Eileen Harris, 'Batty Langley: A Tutor to Freemasons', *The Burlington Magazine* CXIX, 1977, pp. 327–35.

[187] Cf. Kenneth Clark, *The Gothic Revival. An Essay in the History of Taste* (1928), ed. 1974, pp. 46ff.

[188] Clark (ed. 1974), p. 56.

[189] Batty and Thomas Langley, *Ancient Architecture, Restored and Improved by a Great Variety of Grand and Useful Designs, entirely new, in the Gothick Mode, for the Ornamenting of Building and Gardens*, London 1741; 2nd ed., *Gothic Architecture, Improved by Rules and Proportions...* (with 'Historical Dissertation on Gothic Architecture'), London 1742; 3rd ed., London 1747 (without 'Historical Dissertation'); facs. repr. of 1747 ed., Farnborough 1967.
Cf. esp. Clark (ed. 1974), pp. 51ff.; Dobai, vol. I (1974), pp. 485ff.

[190] Langley (ed. 1742), *Historical Dissertation*.

[191] Ibid.

[192] Paul Decker, *Gothic Architecture Decorated, consisting of a Large Collection...*, London 1759 (facs. repr. Farnborough 1968); Paul Decker, *Chinese Architecture, Civil and Ornamental, Being a Large Collection...*, London 1759 (facs. repr. Farnborough 1968).

[193] Cf. esp. Kenneth Clark, *The Gothic Revival. An Essay in the History of Taste* (1928), ed. 1974; Paul Frankl, *The Gothic. Literary Sources and Interpretations through Eight Centuries*, Princeton 1960; Suzanne Lang, 'The Principles of Gothic Revival in England', *Journal of the Society of Architectural Historians* XXV, 1966, pp. 240–67; Georg Germann, *Gothic Revival in Europe and Britain*, London 1972; James Macauly, *The Gothic Revival 1745–1845*, Glasgow–London 1975 (especially on Scotland).

[194] The most important works from extensive literature: Paget Toynbee, *Strawberry Hill Accounts...*, Oxford 1937; Wilmarth Sheldon Lewis, 'The Genesis of Strawberry Hill', *Metropolitan Museum Studies* V, 1934, pp. 57–92; R. W. Ketton-Cremer, *Horace Walpole, A Biography*, London 1940 (New York 1966); Wilmarth Sheldon Lewis, *Horace Walpole*, New York 1961, pp. 97ff.; Suzanne Lang (1966), p. 251ff.; Germann (ed. 1974), p. 51ff.; Nikolaus Pevsner, *Some Architectural Writers of the Nineteenth Century*, Oxford 1972, pp. 1ff.; Dobai, vol. II (1975), pp. 253ff. (with bibliography).

[195] Cf. esp. Nikolaus Pevsner and Suzanne Lang, 'A Note on Sharawaggi' (first published in: *The Architectural Review* 106, 1949) in: Pevsner, 'Studies in Art', *Architecture and Design*, vol. I, London 1968, pp. 103–06.

[196] Walpole to Horace Mann (25. II. 1750).

[197] Horace Walpole, *A Description of the Villa ...at Strawberry Hill near Twickenham, Middlesex*, Strawberry Hill 1774; ²1784 (with additions: facs. repr. London 1964).

[198] Walpole (ed. 1784), p. iv.

[199] Walpole (ed. 1784), p. iii.

[200] Walpole to Mary Berry (17. 10. 1794).

[201] Walpole (ed. 1784), p. iii.

[202] Ibid., p. i.

[203] Ibid., p. iii.

[204] William Hogarth, *The Analysis of Beauty*, London 1753 (numerous reprs), cf. esp. chch. 1–8; for a summary of Hogarth, cf. Dobai, vol. II (1975), pp. 639ff.

[205] Joshua Reynolds, *Discourses on Art*, ed. Robert R. Wark, London 1966, p. 213.

[206] On Vanbrugh's special rôle in the matter of asymmetric plans, cf. Nikolaus Pevsner, Richard Payne Knight (first published in: *The Art Bulletin* XXXI, 1949), in: Pevsner, *Studies in Art, Architecture and Design*, vol. I, London 1968, pp. 110ff.

[207] William Chambers, *Designs of Chinese Buildings, Furniture, Dresses, Machines, and Utensils...*, London 1757 (facs. repr. Farnborough 1970; New York 1980). On Chambers cf. esp. John Harris, *Sir William Chambers. Knight of the Polar Star*, London 1970 (including Eileen Harris on the 'Designs', pp. 144ff.); Dobai, vol. II (1975), pp. 527ff.

[208] Chambers (1757), Preface.

[209] Ibid.

[210] Cf. Harris (1970), pp. 144ff., establishing Chambers' use of earlier literature on Chinese houses.

[211] Chambers (1757), pp. 11f.

[212] Ibid., p. 15.

[213] Ibid.

[214] Edmund Burke, *A Philosophical Enquiry into the Origin of our Ideas of the Sublime and Beautiful*, London 1757; on the Burke-Chambers relationship, cf. Eileen Harris, 'Burke and Chambers on the Sublime and Beautiful', *Essays in the History of Architecture Presented to Rudolf Wittkower*, London ²1969, pp. 207ff.

[215] Cf. Harris (1970), pp. 147f.

[216] George Staunton, *An authentic account of an embassy from the King of Great Britain to the emperor of China...*, 3 vols, London 1797.

[217] William Chambers, *Plans, Elevations, Sections, and Perspective Views of the Gardens and Buildings of Kew in Surrey*, London 1763 (facs. repr. Farnborough 1966).

[218] Chambers (1757), Preface.

[219] William Chambers, *A Treatise on Civil Architecture...*, London 1759; London ²1768. The 3rd ed. appeared under the title *A Treatise on the Decorative Part of Civil Architecture*, London 1791 (facs. repr. with introduction by John Harris, New York 1968; Farnborough 1969); a number of further editions, some of them annotated, appeared in the 19th century; cf. Harris (1970), p. 143; Dobai, vol. II (1975), pp. 553f.

[220] Joshua Reynolds, *Discourses on Art* (1797), ed. Robert W. Wark (1959), London ⁴1969. Reynolds' treatise, with its important aesthetic distinctions, cannot here be discussed; cf. Magne Malmanger, 'Sir Joshua Reynolds' Discourses: attitude and ideas', *Acta ad Archaeologiam et Artium Historiam Pertinentia*, vol. IV, 1969, pp. 159–211.

[221] The mss are in the library of the R.I.B.A., London.

[222] Chambers (1791), p. iv.

[223] Ibid., Dedication.

[224] Ibid.

[225] Ibid., p. ii.

[226] Ibid., p. iii.

[227] Ibid., p. iv.

[228] Ibid., p. iv f.

[229] Ibid., p. 7.

[230] Ibid., p. 15.

[231] Ibid., pp. 64ff.

[232] Ibid., p. 17.

[233] Burke (ed. 1759), p. 136 ('Magnitude in Building').

[234] Chambers (ed. 1791), p. 18.

[235] Ibid., pp. 18f.: 'it must candidly be confessed, that the Grecians have been far excelled by other nations, not only in the magnitude and grandeur of their structures, but likewise in point of fancy, ingenuity, variety, and elegant selection.'

[236] Chambers (1791), p. 71.

[237] Cf. pp. 224ff.

[238] Harris (1970), p. 6.

[239] On the Rome circle, cf. John Fleming, *Robert Adam and His Circle in Edinburgh & Rome*, Cambridge, MA 1962, pp. 164ff.

[240] Chambers (1791), p. 19. Chambers mentions no particular work, but he evidently means Piranesi's *Della Magnificenza* (1761) and *Osservazioni* (1765).

[241] Cf. Dora Wiebenson, *Sources of Greek*

Revival Architecture, London 1969, pp. 47ff. (and Appendix III, pp. 126ff. with excerpts from Chambers' notes on this question.).

[242] Chambers (1791), p. 19.

[243] Ibid., pp. 22f.

[244] Ibid., p. 24.

[245] The mss. at the R.I.B.A. include 'Materials for a History of Gothic Architecture in England and its Origins'; cf. Harris (1970), p. 128 n. 2.

[246] Horace Walpole, *Anecdotes of Painting in England*, ed. Ralph N. Wornum, London 1888, p. xiv.

[247] Chambers (1791), pp. 30f.

[248] Cf. esp. Eileen Harris (1969), pp. 207ff.

[249] Robert and James Adam, *The Works in Architecture*, vol. I, London 1773, Preface. On the brothers Adam cf. esp. Arthur T. Bolton, *The Architecture of Robert & James Adam*, 2 vols, London 1922; Geoffrey Beard, *The Work of Robert Adam*, Edinburgh 1978; Dobai, vol. II (1975), pp. 578ff., 105f.

[250] Cf. esp. John Fleming, *Robert Adam and His Circle in Edinburgh & Rome*, Cambridge, MA 1962; Damie Stillman, 'Robert Adam and Piranesi', *Essays in the History of Architecture Presented to Rudolf Wittkower*, London ²1969, pp. 197–206.

[251] Cf. pp. 238f.

[252] Varied somewhat; cf. Robert and James Adam, *The Works of Architecture*, vol. I, no. V, 1778, pl. II (design by James Adam dated 1762).

[253] Fleming (1962), pp. 303ff.; James Adam's manuscript dated 27 November 1762 published in: Fleming, pp. 315–19.

[254] Fleming (1962), p. 315.

[255] Robert and James Adam, *The Works of Architecture*, vol. I, London 1773–78; vol. II, 1779; vol. III, 1822 (new editions 1902, 1931, 1959, 1975, 1981). Edition by Robert Oresko, London–New York 1975, here used; quotation from the introduction to vol. I.

[256] Robert and James Adam, ed. Oresko (1975), p. 46.

[257] Ibid., pp. 58f.

[258] Cf. detailed coverage by Dobai, vol. II (1975), pp. 556ff.

[259] George Richardson, *A Treatise on the five orders of architecture*, London 1787 (facs. repr. 1969).

[260] John Wood, *A Series of Plans for Cottages or Habitations of the Labourer...*, London 1781 (²1792; ³1806; facs. repr. of 1806 ed.

1972; cf. Dobai, vol. II (1975), pp. 460ff.

[261] Wood (ed. 1806), p. 3.

[262] Ibid.

[263] Ibid.

[264] Cf. esp. Arthur T. Bolton, *The Works of Sir John Soane*, London 1924; John Summerson, *Sir John Soane*, London 1952; Dorothy Stroud, *The Architecture of Sir John Soane*, London 1961; Pierre de la Ruffinière du Prey, *John Soane's Architectural Education 1753–80*, diss. (Princeton 1972), Ann Arbor–London 1981; id., *John Soane: The Making of an Architect*, Chicago 1982; *Architectural Monographs: John Soane* (including essays by John Summerson and others), London–New York 1983; Dorothy Stroud, *Sir John Soane, Architect*, Boston–London 1984.

[265] John Soane, *Designs in Architecture consisting of Plans, Elevations and Sections for Temples, Baths, Cassines, Pavillons, Garden-Seats, Obelisks, and Other Buildings...*, London 1778.

[266] John Soane, *Plans, Elevations and Sections of Buildings, Executed in the Counties of Norfolk, Suffolk etc.*, London 1788 (facs. repr. 1971); id., *Sketches in Architecture Containing Plans and Elevations of Cottages, Villas and Other Useful Buildings...*, London 1793 (facs. repr. 1971); cf. Dobai, vol. II (1975), pp. 624ff.

[267] Soane (1788), p. 8.

[268] Ibid., p. 11.

[269] Soane (1793), Introduction.

[270] Cf. Christopher Hussey, *The Picturesque. Studies in a Point of View*, London 1927 (²1967); Nikolaus Pevsner's essays in: Pevsner, *Studies in Art, Architecture and Design*, vol. I, 1968, pp. 79ff.; W. J. Hipple, *The Beautiful, The Sublime, and The Picturesque in Eighteenth-Century British Aesthetic Theory*, Carbondale 1957; David Watkin, *The English Vision: The Picturesque in Architecture, Landscape and Garden Design*, London 1982.

[271] Charles Thomas Middleton, *Picturesque and Architectural Views for Cottages, Farm Houses and Country Villas*, London 1793 (facs. repr. 1970); cf. Dobai, vol. III (1977), pp. 666ff.

[272] Arthur T. Bolton (ed.), *Lectures on Architecture, by Sir John Soane...*, London 1929; for a detailed study of these lectures, cf. Dobai, vol. III (1977), pp. 752ff.

[273] Cf. Dobai, vol. III (1977), pp. 782ff.

[274] John Soane, *Description of the House and Museum on the North Side of Lincoln's Inn Fields*, London 1830 (further eds 1832, 1835, 1893; new ed., A. T. Bolton 1930; cf.

Susan G. Feinberg, 'The Genesis of Sir John Soane's Museum Idea: 1801–1810', *Journal of the Society of Architectural Historians* XLIII, 1984, pp. 225–37.

20. Concepts of the garden

[1] Cf. F. Hamilton Hazlehurst, *Jacques Boyceau and the French Formal Garden*, Athens 1966; for surveys of garden literature, cf. Dieter Hennebo and Alfred Hoffmann, *Geschichte der deutschen Gartenkunst*, vol. II: *Der architektonische Garten. Renaissance und Barock*, Hamburg 1965, pp. 301ff.; Ursula Erichsen-Firle, *Geometrische Kompositionsprinzipien in den Theorien der Gartenkunst des 16. bis 18. Jahrhunderts*, diss., Cologne 1971, pp. 226ff.

[2] Jacques Boyceau, *Traité du jardinage selon les raisons de la nature et de l'art*, Paris 1638, Book III, ch. VI, p. 74; cf. Erichsen-Firle (1971), p. 10.

On the early formal garden in France, see esp. Sten Karling, 'The Importance of André Mollet and His Family for the Development of the French Formal Garden', in: Elisabeth B. Macdougall and F. Hamilton Hazlehurst (ed.), *The French Formal Garden*, Washington, DC 1974, pp. 3–25; for a general survey of the formal garden, cf. also Wilfried Hansmann, *Gartenkunst der Renaissance und des Barock*, Cologne. 1983.

On the application of interior architectural concepts to the garden, cf. A. Rommel, *Die Entstehung des klassischen französischen Gartens im Spiegel der Sprache*, Berlin 1954.

[3] Antoine Joseph Dezallier d'Argenville, *La Théorie et la pratique du jardinage...*, Paris 1709 (1713, 1722, 1732, 1747, 1760); facs. repr. of ed. of 1760, ed. Hans Foramitti, Hildesheim–New York 1972. English trans., London 1712, 1728, 1743; German trans., Augsburg 1731, 1764.

On Dezallier d'Argenville cf. esp. Ingrid Dennerlein, *Die Gartenkunst der Régence und des Rokoko in Frankreich (1972)*, Worms 1981.

[4] 'disposition bien entendue & bien raisonnée, une belle proportion de toutes les parties.' Dezallier d'Argenville (ed. 1760), p. 15.

[5] 'vraie grandeur d'un beau Jardin... On peut distinguer quatre maximes fondamentales, pour bien disposer un Jardin: la première, de faire céder l'Art à la Nature; la seconde,

de ne point trop offusquer un Jardin; la troisième, de ne le point trop découvrir; & la quatrième, de le faire toujours paroître plus grand qu'il ne l'est effectivement...'; Ibid., p. 18.

[6] Ibid., p. 19.

[7] 'Un jardin est moins une imitation de la nature, que la nature même rapprochée sous nos yeux, et mise en oeuvre avec art...' Noël Antoine Pluche, *Le Spectacle de la Nature, ou entretiens sur les particularités de l'histoire naturelle...*, 8 parts, 9 vols, Paris 1732 ff. (gardens treated in vol. II, 1733, chch. II–V). On the significance of Pluche's work, cf. Ingrid Dennerlein (1981), pp. 28f.

[8] Henry Wotton, *The Elements of Architecture*, London 1624, p. 109.

[9] On this topic cf. esp. Arthur O. Lovejoy, 'The Chinese Origin of a Romanticism' (first published in: *The Journal of English and Germanic Philology*, Jan. 1933), in: Lovejoy, *Essays in the History of Ideas (1948)*, Baltimore–London ³1970, pp. 99–135; Eleanor von Erdberg, *Chinese Influence on European Garden Structures*, Cambridge, MA 1936; H. F. Clark, 'Eighteenth Century Elysiums. The Role of 'Association' in the Landscape Movement', *Journal of the Warburg and Courtauld Institutes* 6, 1943, pp. 165–89; Nikolaus Pevsner, 'The Genesis of the Picturesque' (first published in: *The Architectural Review* XCVI, 1944); Nikolaus Pevsner and Suzanne Lang, 'A Note on Sharawaggi' (first published in: *The Architectural Review* CVI, 1949), both essays repr. in: Pevsner, *Studies in Art, Architecture and Design*, vol. I, London 1968, pp. 78–107; Rudolf Wittkower, 'English Neo-Palladianism, The Landscape Garden, China and the Enlightenment' (first published in: *L'Arte* 6, 1969), in: Wittkower, *Palladio and English Palladianism*, London 1974, pp. 177–90; Suzanne Lang, 'The Genesis of the English Landscape Garden', in: Nikolaus Pevsner (ed.), *The Picturesque Garden and Its Influence Outside the British Isles*, Washington, DC

1974, pp. 1–29; Johannes Dobai, *Die Kunstliteratur des Klassizismus und der Romantik in England*, vol. I: 1700–1750, Bern 1974, p. 529 (a good general coverage of English ideas of the garden); John Dixon Hunt and Peter Willis (eds), *The Genius of the Place. The English Landscape Garden 1620–1820*, London 1975 (a useful anthology of source material).

10 William Temple, 'Upon the Gardens of Epicurus' (1685); first published in: *Miscellanea*, London 1690; excerpts in: Hunt-Willis (1975), pp. 96ff.

11 Temple (1685); cited from Hunt-Willis (1975), p. 99.

12 Cf. esp. Christopher Hussey, *The Picturesque. Studies in a Point of View*, London 1927 (²1967); Walter John Hipple Jr, *The Beautiful, The Sublime & The Picturesque in Eighteenth-Century British Aesthetic Theory*, Carbondale 1957; David Watkin, *The English Vision: The Picturesque in Architecture, Landscape and Garden Design*, London 1982.

13 Cf. Dobai, vol. I (1974), pp. 87ff., 552f.

14 Joseph Addison and Richard Steele (ed.), *The Spectator* 1712 (available in Everyman's Library, 4 vols, New York–London 1907, several impressions). In no. 414 Addison distinguishes his viewpoint from Shaftesbury's: 'If the Products of Nature rise in Value, according as they more or less resemble those of Art, we may be sure that artificial Works receive a greater Advantage from their Resemblance of such as are natural.'

15 *The Spectator* No. 414 (25.6.1712).

16 *The Spectator* No. 417 (28.6.1712).

17 *The Spectator* No. 47 (6.9.1712).

18 Ibid.

19 Robert Castell, *The Villas of the Ancients Illustrated*, London 1728 (facs. repr. ed. John Dixon Hunt, New York–London, 1982); cf. Dobai, vol. I (1974), pp. 277ff., 561f.

20 For a contemporary description, cf. esp. J. Serle (Searle), *A Plan of Mr. Pope's Garden as it was left at his Death, with a Plan and a perspective View of the grotto...*, London 1745 (facs. repr. New York 1982), and Morris R. Brownell, *Alexander Pope and the Arts of Georgian England*, Oxford 1978, esp. pp. 118ff.; also Dobai, vol. I (1974), pp. 564ff.; Adrian von Buttlar, *Der Landschaftsgarten*, Munich 1980, pp. 28ff.

21 Pope to Edward Blount, 2 June 1725; cited from Dobai, vol. I (1974), p. 565; for an interpretation of Pope's grotto and garden, cf. Maynard Mack, *The Garden and the City. Retirement and Politics in the Later Poetry of Pope 1731–1743*, Toronto–Buffalo–London 1969.

22 On the relationship of Pope to Boullée, cf. esp. Adolf Max Vogt, *Boullées Newton-Denkmal*, Basel–Stuttgart 1969, pp. 303ff.; but Vogt does not see the link with Pope's grotto.

23 Pope, *Essay on Criticism* (1711).

24 Alexander Pope, 'Epistle IV to Richard Boyle, Earl of Burlington' (1731), in: *Alexander Pope, Epistles to Several Persons*, ed. F. W. Bateson, London–New-Haven (1951) ²1961, p. 142.

25 James Thomson, *The Seasons* (1726–1746), ed. James Sambrook, Oxford 1981 (crit. ed.).

26 Stephen Switzer, *Ichnographia Rustica: Or, The Nobleman, Gentleman and Gardener's Recreation...*, 3 vols, London 1715–1718 (²1741/42).

27 Switzer, vol. III (1718); cited from Dobai, vol. I (1974), p. 560.

28 Cf. Dobai, vol. I (1974), p. 560; Günter Hartmann, *Die Ruine im Landschaftsgarten*, Worms 1981.

29 Batty Langley, *New Principles of Gardening: Or, The Laying out and Planning Parterres...*, London 1728 (facs. repr. Farnborough 1970).

30 Langley (1728), cited from Hunt-Willis (1975), p. 178.

31 William Shenstone, 'Unconnected Thoughts on Gardening', in: *Works in Prose and Verse of William Shenstone*, vol. II, London 1764, pp. 125–48 (excerpts in: Hunt-Willis 1975, pp. 289ff.). On Shenstone cf. esp. Clark (1943); Dobai, vol. I (1974), pp. 573ff.; von Buttlar (1980), pp. 57ff.

32 Shenstone (1764), cited from Hunt-Willis (1975), p. 291.

33 Ibid., p. 292.

34 Ibid., p. 291.

35 Shenstone, 'Account of an Interview between Shenstone and Thomson (1746)', *Edinburgh Magazine*, 1800, Hunt-Willis (1975), pp. 244ff.

36 Cf. esp. Dorothy Stroud, *Capability Brown*, London 1950 (²1957; ³1975).

37 Henry Home (Lord Kames), *Elements of Criticism*, 3 vols, Edinburgh 1762 (on the

publishing history of this work, cf. Dobai, vol. II, 1975, p. 193); on Kames cf. Dobai, vol. II (1975), pp. 114ff.; Maria Grazia Messina, 'Psicologia associazionistica ed architettura: il contributo di Lord Kames', *Ricerche di Storia dell'Arte* 22, 1984, pp. 37–42.

[38] Cf. Dobai, vol. II (1975), pp. 131ff., 1061; on the significance of Kames's work, cf. also Wolfgang Schepers, *Hirschfelds Theorie der Gartenkunst*, Worms 1980, pp. 139ff.

[39] Thomas Whately, *Observations on modern Gardening, illustrated by Descriptions*, London 1770 ([2]1770; [3]1771; [4]1777; [5]1801); facs. repr. of 1801 ed., Farnborough 1970; French ed., Paris 1771; German ed., Leipzig 1771.

[40] Horace Walpole, *On Modern Gardening* (1770), first published in vol. IV of Walpole's *Anecdotes of Painting*, 1771 (under the title *History of the Modern Taste in Gardening*). Critical editions (with textural variants): I. W. U. Chase, *Horace Walpole: Gardenist. An Edition of Walpole's The History of Modern Taste in Gardening*, Princeton 1943. German ed. by A. W. Schlegel in: *Historische, Litterarische und unterhaltende Schriften von Horatio Walpole*, Leipzig 1800, pp. 384–446; cf. Dobai, vol. II (1975), pp. 285ff.

[41] William Mason, *The English Garden*, London 1772–81 (together: York–London 1781, Dublin 1782, York 1783; facs. repr. of this ed., Farnborough 1971); cf. Dobai, vol. II (1975), pp. 1067ff.

[42] Mason (1783), p. 4.

[43] On this subject, cf. Thomas Finkenstaedt, 'Der Garten des Königs', in: *Probleme der Kunstwissenschaft*, vol. II; *Wandlungen des Paradiesischen und Utopischen*, Berlin 1966, pp. 183–209.

[44] William Chambers, *A Dissertation on Oriental Gardening*, London 1772; enlarged ed. with *An Explanatory Discourse...*, London 1773 (French ed. London 1772; German ed., Gotha 1775). Responses by William Mason, *An Heroic Epistle to Sir William Chambers.* (1773) and *An Heroic Postscript to the Public* (1774); facs. repr. of these texts with introduction by John Harris (Chambers. 1772; Mason, ed. 1777 and 1774), 1972. Cf. esp. John Harris, *Sir William Chambers. Knight of the Polar Star*, London 1970, pp. 153ff.

[45] Chambers (1772), Preface, p. V.

[46] Ibid., pp. 94 and 50.

[47] Ibid., p. 14.

[48] Ibid., p. 15.

[49] Ibid., p. 19.

[50] J. D. Attiret (English trans.), *A Particular of the Emperor of China's Gardens near Pekin*, London 1752.

[51] Chambers (1772), p. 34.

[52] Ibid., p. 35.

[53] Ibid., p. 38.

[54] Ibid., p. 39.

[55] Ibid., p. 64.

[56] Ibid., p. 93.

[57] Cf. esp. Hussey (1927, [2]1967) and Hipple Jr (1957); Dobai, vol. II (1975), pp. 296ff.; Watkin (1982).

[58] William Gilpin, *A Dialogue upon the Gardens of the Right Honourable the Lord Viscount Cobham at Stow...*, London 1748 (excerpts in: Hunt-Willis 1975, pp. 254ff.).

[59] William Gilpin, *Observations...*, London 1782ff.; *Three Essays: On the Picturesque Beauty...*, London 1792; on the publishing history of Gilpin's work, cf. Dobai, vol. II (1975), pp. 327ff.

[60] Gilpin, *The Three Essays* (ed. [2]1794), vol. I, p. 28; cf. Hipple (1957), pp. 196ff.

[61] Cf. Dora Wiebenson, *The Picturesque Garden in France*, Princeton 1978. On the Picturesque garden outside England, cf. also Nikolaus Pevsner (ed.), *The Picturesque Garden and its Influence Outside the British Isles*, Washington, DC 1974; on the French garden in the second half of the 18th century, cf. the detailed cat. *Jardins en France 1760–1820. Pays d'illusion. Terre d'expériences*, Paris 1977.

[62] Cf. Wiebenson (1978), pp. 15ff.

[63] Claude-Henri Watelet, *Essai sur les jardins*, Paris 1774 (facs. repr. Geneva 1972); on Moulin-Joli pp. 125–37. On the *Essai* cf. esp. Wiebenson (1978), pp. 64ff.

[64] Watelet (1774), pp. 5ff.

[65] Ibid., pp. 22.

[66] Ibid., pp. 53.

[67] Ibid., pp. 55ff.

[68] Ibid., pp. 125ff.

[69] Cf. Sieghild Bogumil, 'Die Parkkonzeption bei Rousseau oder die Natur als Lenkung und Ablenkung', in: *Park und Garten im 18. Jahrhundert*, Gesamthochschule Wuppertal (1976), Heidelberg 1978, pp. 100ff.

[70] René-Louis de Girardin, *De la composition des paysages ou des moyens d'embellir la nature...*, Paris 1777 (ed. Michel H. Conan, Paris 1979).

[71] Jean-Marie Morel, *Théorie des jardins*, Paris 1776.

[72] J. De Lille, *Les jardins, ou l'art d'embellir les paysages: poème*, Paris 1782.

[73] Georges Louis Le Rouge, *Détails des nouveaux jardins à la mode; Jardins anglo-chinois à la mode*, 21 nos, Paris 1776–87; facs. repr. with introduction by Daniel Jacomet, Paris 1978.

[74] Following pioneering research by Hussey (1927, ²1967), cf. esp. Hipple (1957), pp. 202ff., clarifying the chronological sequence of these publications. Cf. also Dobai, vol. III (1977), pp. 15ff., 1241ff.

[75] Besides the above-cited Hussey, Hipple, Dobai and Watkin, cf. esp. the essays by Nikolaus Pevsner in his *Studies in Art, Architecture and Design*, vol. I, London 1968, pp. 108ff.

On Price, cf. Mareia Allentuck, 'Sir Uvedale Price and the Picturesque Garden: the Evidence of the Coleorton Papers', in: Nikolaus Pevsner (ed.), *The Picturesque Garden etc.* (1974), pp. 57–76.

On Knight cf. Suzanne Lang, 'Richard Payne Knight and the Idea of Modernity', in: *Concerning Architecture. Essays on Architectural Writers... presented to Nikolaus Pevsner*, ed. John Summerson, London 1968, pp. 85–97; exhib. cat. *The Arrogant Connoisseur: Richard Payne Knight 1751–1824*, d. Michael Clarke and Nicholas Penny, Manchester 1982.

On Repton cf. Dorothy Stroud, *Humphry Repton*, London 1962.

[76] Uvedale Price, *An Essay on the Picturesque, as Compared with the Sublime and Beautiful, and, on the Use of Studying Pictures, for the Purpose of Improving Real Landscape*, London 1794 (on the publishing history of this work, cf. Dobai, vol. III, 1977, pp. 63f.). Uvedale Price, *Essays on the Picturesque...*, 3 vols, London 1810 (facs. repr. Farnborough 1971). Here the 1810 edition is cited.

[77] Price, vol. I (1810), pp. 2f.

[78] Ibid., pp. 52f.

[79] Humphry Repton, *A Letter to Sir Uvedale Price Esq.*, London 1794 (also reprinted in Price's *Essays*, vol. III, 1810, pp. 3–22).

[80] Repton (1794); cited from Price, vol. III (1810), p. 6.

[81] Repton (1794); cited from Price, vol. III (1810), p. 18.

[82] Uvedale Price, *A Letter to Humphry Repton Esq.*, London 1795 (cited from Price, vol. III, 1810), pp. 25–180).

[83] Price (1795); cited from ed. 1810, vol. III, pp. 49f.

[84] Humphry Repton's major writings are the following: *Sketches and Hints on Landscape Gardening*, London 1795; *Observations on the Theory and Practice of Landscape Gardening, including some Remarks on Grecian and Gothic Architecture...*, London 1803 (²1805); *An Inquiry into the Changes of Taste in Landscape Gardening...*, London 1806; (with John Aday), *Fragments on the Theory and Practice of Landscape Gardening...*, London 1816; edition of Repton's writings under the title *The Landscape Gardening and Landscape Architecture of the Late Humphry Repton, Esq.*, ed. J. C. Loudon, London 1840 (facs. repr. Farnborough 1969).

[85] Richard Payne Knight, *The Landscape, A Didactic Poem, in Three Books*, London 1794 (²1795; facs. repr. of this ed.: Farnborough 1972).

[86] Knight (1794), pp. 140ff.

[87] Cf. Dobai, vol. III (1977), p. 42.

[88] Richard Payne Knight, *An Analytical Inquiry into the Principles of Taste*, London 1805 (²1805; ³1806; ⁴1808; facs. repr. of 1808 ed. Farnborough 1972).

[89] Knight (ed. 1808), pp. 150f.

[90] For a general account and bibliography, cf. Dobai, vol. III (1977), pp. 1280ff.; Elisabeth B. Macdougall (ed.), *John Claudius Loudon and the Early Nineteenth Century in Great Britain*, Washington, DC 1980. The major writings of John Claudius Loudon: *A Treatise on forming, improving, and managing Country Residences...*, 2 vols, London 1806; *An Encyclopaedia of Gardening...*, London 1822 (numerous editions; German trans. *Eine Encyclopaedia des Gartenwesens...*, 3 vols, Weimar 1823–1826); *An Encyclopaedia of Cottage, Farm and Villa Architecture and Furniture...*, London 1833 (several new editions).

[91] John Claudius Loudon, *The Landscape Gardening and Landscape Architecture of the Late Humphry Repton*, London 1840 (facs. repr. Farnborough 1969), p. viii.

[92] John Claudius Loudon, *A Short Treatise on Several Improvements, recently made in Hot-Houses...*, Edinburgh 1805; *Remarks on the Construction of Hothouses...*, London 1817; *Sketches of Curvilinear Hot-*

houses..., London 1818; *The Green House Companion*..., London 1824 (²1832).

[93] On Loudon's importance in the history of the hothouse, cf. Stefan Koppelkamm, *Gewächshäuser und Wintergärten im neunzehnten Jahrhundert*, Stuttgart 1981, pp. 19ff.

[94] For example, for a description of the Schloss garden at Heidelberg, cf. Salomon de Caus, *Hortus Palatinus* Frankfurt 1620 (facs. repr. Worms 1980).

[95] Cf. esp. Dieter Hennebo-Alfred Hoffmann, *Geschichte der deutschen Gartenkunst*, vol. II, Hamburg 1965, pp. 96ff., 304ff.

[96] On the landscape garden in Germany, cf. Franz Hallbaum, *Der Landschaftsgarten. Sein Entstehen und seine Einführung in Deutschland durch Friedrich Ludwig von Sckell*, Munich 1927; Erich Bachmann, 'Anfänge des Landschaftsgartens in Deutschland', *Zeitschrift für Kunstwissenschaft*, vol. V, 1951, pp. 203–28; Alfred Hoffmann, *Der Landschaftsgarten* (vol. III of: Hennebo-Hoffmann, *Geschichte der deutschen Gartenkunst*), Hamburg 1963; on literary expression of the debate, cf. Siegmar Gerndt, *Idealisierte Natur. Die literarische Kontroverse um den Landschaftsgarten des 18. und frühen 19. Jahrhunderts in Deutschland*, Stuttgart 1981; Adrian von Buttlar, 'Englische Gärten in Deutschland. Bemerkungen zu Modifikationen ihrer Ikonologie', in: *Sind Briten hier?*, Munich 1981, pp. 97ff.

[97] Johann Georg Sulzer, *Allgemeine Theorie der Schönen Künste*, 2 vols, Leipzig 1771–1774 (several partly enlarged editions; facs. repr. of 1792–94, ed. Hildesheim 1967–70); under head-word 'Gartenkunst'. On Sulzer cf. esp. Johannes Dobai, *Die bildenden Künste in Johann Georg Sulzers Ästhetik*, Winterthur 1978, esp. pp. 152ff.

On knowledge of garden literature in Germany at the end of the 18th century, cf. Friedrich von Blankenburg, *Literarische Zusätze zu Johann Georg Sulzers allgemeiner Theorie der schönen Künste* (1786–87), Leipzig 1796–98 (facs. repr.: Frankfurt 1972), vol. I, pp. 598ff.

[98] 'Wenn Sie aber kommen, so bringen Sie uns doch etwas weißen Kohl aus der Stadt mit, denn wir haben hier keinen Platz mehr dafür.' Justus Möser, *Das englische Gärtgen* (first published in: *Wöchentliche Osnabrückische Anzeigen*, 1773; then in Part II of Möser's *Patriotische Phantasien*, Berlin 1775, No. 86, pp. 465–67; here cited from Justus Möser, *Anwalt des Vaterlandes (Ausgewählte Werke)*, Leipzig–Berlin 1978, pp. 234–36; text also in: Gerndt (1981), pp. 82f.

[99] Christian Cay Lorenz Hirschfeld, *Theorie der Gartenkunst*, 5 vols, Leipzig 1779–85 (facs. repr. with introduction by Hans Foramitti, 2 vols, Hildesheim–New York 1973); simultaneous French ed. *Théorie de l'Art des Jardins*, Leipzig 1779–1785 (facs. repr. Geneva 1973).

On the origins of the garden and historical classification, cf. Wolfgang Schepers, *Hirschfelds Theorie der Gartenkunst*, Worms 1980.

[100] Christian Cay Lorenz Hirschfeld, *Anmerkungen über die Landhäuser und die Gartenkunst*, Frankfurt–Leipzig 1773 (²1779). Christian Cay Lorenz Hirschfeld, *Theorie der Gartenkunst*, Frankfurt–Leipzig 1775 (²1777).

[101] Hirschfeld, vol. I (1779), pp. 81ff.

[102] In his foreword to the last volume (V, 1785, p. 2) Hirschfeld comments somewhat bitterly: 'Ich habe an meinem Wohnort nichts gehabt, was zur Beförderung dieses Werks hätte beytragen können; alles mußte ich erst aus der Ferne suchen.' ('I had no material to hand which could have provided a basis for this work; I had to search for everything abroad.') On Hirschfeld's sources cf. Schepers (1980); besides the authors quoted in his text, his pictorial sources listed at the end of each volume give a good idea of the material that was available to him.

[103] 'vertrauteste Schwester der Gartenkunst...' Hirschfeld, vol. I (1779), p. xiii.

[104] Ibid., p. 37.

[105] 'Die Gartenkunst war unter ihren Händen nichts anderes, als Architektur auf die Erdfläche angewandt.' Ibid., p. 120.

[106] 'In unseren Tagen scheint die Aufklärung über die Gartenkunst sich aus England nach Frankreich verbreitet zu haben...' Ibid., p. 38.

[107] 'gesunden Geschmack...' ...'edle Architektur im griechischen Geschmack.' Ibid., pp. 53f.

[108] 'vielleicht mehr als eine andere gegen die Schönheiten der Natur empfindlich ist, mehr als eine andere die malerische Idylle liebt.' Ibid., p. 72.

[109] '*Es wird sich in der Folge zwischen beyden Arten des herrschenden Geschmacks ein Mittelweg ergeben...*' Ibid., p. 144.

[110] '*Der Architekt will auf einmal das Auge befriedigen, es auf einmal die ganze harmonische Einrichtung seines Werks umfassen lassen; der Gartenkünstler will nach und nach mit einer allmählichen Fortschreitung unterhalten*'...'*einen gewissen anmuthigen Verwickelung*'...'*Verschiedenheit der Wirkungen*'...'*Der Gartenkünstler arbeitet am glücklichsten, wenn er fast überall as Gegentheil von dem thut, was der Baumeister beobachtet.*' Ibid., p. 138.

[111] '*Gerade Alleen sind hier nicht allein zuläßig, sondern verdienen selbst den Vorzug, indem sie die Aufsicht der Polizey, die an solchen Plätzen oft unentbehrlich ist, erleichtert.*' Hirschfeld, vol. 5 (1785), pp. 68ff.

[112] Hirschfeld, vol. I (1779), p. 142.

[113] Ibid., p. 187.

[113] Ibid., p. 187. Hirschfeld is influenced by Haller's *Alpen* (1729), from which he repeatedly quotes.

[114] Hirschfeld, vol. I (1779), p. 158.

[115] '*Gott schuf die Welt, und der Mensch verschönert sie.*'

[116] '*...Charakter der Gegend.*' Hirschfeld, vol. IV (1782), p. 27.

[117] Hirschfeld, vol. I (1771), p. 214.

[118] '*fast ganz ein Werk der Natur.*' Hirschfeld, vol. IV (1782), p. 90.

[119] Hirschfeld, vol. III (1780), p. 97.

[120] '*eine reiche Quelle des Vergnügens und der süßesten Melancholie.*' Ibid., p. 111; on this topic cf. Günter Hartmann, *Die Ruine im Landschaftsgarten*, Worms 1981.

[121] '*die äußersten Überladungen und Verzierungen, die nur der Üppigste und ausschweifendste Geschmack ausfinden kann...*'...'*flüchtig und mager.*' Ibid., pp. 6f.

[122] '*Das Auge läßt sich so wenig als die Einbildungskraft Gesetze aufdringen, welche die Natur nicht kennt.*'...'*Bey allen aus der Mythologie entlehnten Vorstellungen entstehen zwey Fragen: ob sie für unser Zeitalter noch interessant genug sind, und sodann, ob sie sich in Gartenanlagen schicken?*' Hirschfeld, vol. V (1785), p. 233.

[123] Cf. esp. Berndt (1981).

[124] Friedrich von Schiller, *Über den Gartenkalender auf das Jahr 1795*; quoted from Schiller, *Sämtliche Werke*, vol. 12, Stuttgart-Tübingen 1847, pp. 342–50.

[125] '*Es wird sich alsdann wahrscheinlicher Weise ein ganz guter Mittelweg zwischen der Steifigkeit des französischen Gartengeschmacks und der gesetzlosen Freiheit des sogenannten englischen finden.*' Ibid., p. 346.

[126] '*poetischen Gartengeschmack*'...'*richtigen Factum der Gefühle*'...'*weil er aus seinen Gränzen trat und die Gartenkunst in die Malerei hinüberführte.*' Ibid., p. 345.

[127] '*welche die Natur durch sich selbst repräsentirt und nur insofern rühren kann, als man sie absolut mit der Natur verwechselt...*' Ibid.

[128] Goethe, Schiller and Heinrich Meyer, *Über den Dilettantismus* (1799); quoted from Goethe, *Berliner Ausgabe*, vol. 19, Berlin-Weimar 1973, pp. 309–333 (discussion of gardens, pp. 322ff.).

[129] '*Ein Bild aus der Wirklichkeit zu machen, kurz, erster Eintritt in die Kunst.*'

[130] '*eine reinliche und vollends schöne Umgebung wirkt immer wohltätig auf die Gesellschaft.*'

[131] '*Reales wird als ein Phantasiewerk behandelt. Die Gartenliebhaberei geht auf etwas Endloses hinaus: 1) weil sie in der Idee nicht bestimmt und begrenzt ist; 2) weil das Materiale als ewig zufällig sich immer verändert und der Idee ewig entgegenstrebt. Die Gartenliebhaberei läßt sich die edlern Künste auf eine unwürdige Art dienen und macht ein Spielwerk aus ihrer soliden Bestimmung. Befördert die sentimentale und phantastische Nullität. Sie verkleinert das Erhabene in der Natur und hebt es auf, indem sie es nachahmt. Sie verewigt die herrschende Unart der Zeit, im Ästhetischen unbedingt und gesetzlos sein zu wollen und willkürlich zu phantasieren, indem sie sich nicht wie wohl andere Künste korrigieren und in der Zucht halten läßt.*'

[132] '*Die dabei vorkommenden Gebäude werden leicht, spindelartig, hölzern, brettern pp. aufgeführt und zerstören den Begriff solider Baukunst. Ja sie heben das Gefühl für sie auf. Die Strohdächer, bretterne Blendungen, alles macht eine Neigung zu Kartenhaus-Architektur.*'

[133] Cf. Berndt (1981), pp. 169ff.

[134] '*daß man in Zukunft manche der natürlichen Parks wieder in dergleichen künstliche Anlagen umarbeiten möchte.*' Ludwig Tieck, *Phantasus*, quoted from Berndt (1981), p. 174.

[135] Cf. esp. Berndt (1981), pp. 145ff.; Berndt

attempts (p. 146) a plan of Goethe's description of the garden.

[136] Friedrich Ludwig von Sckell, *Beiträge zur bildenden Gartenkunst für angehende Gartenkünstler und Gartenliebhaber*, Munich 1818 ('1825), facs. repr. of 1825 ed. with an afterword by Wolfgang Schepers, Worms 1982. Cf. Carl August Sckell's introduction to the 2nd ed. of the *Beiträge* and Hallbaum, op. cit. (1927).

[137] Sckell (1825), pp. 5, 14, 17.

[138] *'Bilder der Natur'…'Natur in ihrem festlichem Gewande…'* Ibid., p. 1.

[139] *'imposanten Anblick von hoher Pracht…'* Ibid., p. 2.

[140] *'Annäherung aller Stände…im Schoße der schönen Natur.'* Sckell (1825), pp. 2f. and 197ff. On Sckell's achievement at Munich, cf. the essays by Adrian von Buttlar: 'Der Garten als Bild–das Bild des Gartens. Zum Englischen Garten in München', in exhib. cat. *Münchner Landschaftsmalerei 1800–1850*, Munich 1979, pp. 160ff.; 'Vom Englischen Garten zum Glaspalast, Englisches in München 1789–1854', in *Englische Architekturzeichnungen des Klassizismus 1760–1830*, Galerie Carroll, Munich 1979, pp. 28ff.; op. cit. (1980), pp. 173ff.; 'Englische Gärten in Deutschland', in *Sind Briten hier? Relations between English and Continental Art 1680–1880*, Munich 1981, pp. 97ff.

[141] *'Daher kann auch der Gartenkünstler nach Gefallen jene Bilder wählen und aufstellen, die zu seinem Locale passen, unbekümmert, ob solche groß oder klein erscheinen. Die Natur wird sie anerkennen, sind sie nur*

nach ihren Formen und Gesetzen gestaltet, ausgeführt und in einem malerischen Bilde, ihr ähnlich und nicht überladen, aufgestellt worden.' Sckell (1825), p. 7.

[142] Ibid., p. 21.

[143] Ibid., pp. 36ff.

[144] *'mit starken Schritten der schönen Wellen-Linie'…'die ihm seine geübte Einbildungskraft vorbildet, und gleichsam vor ihm herschweben läßt.'* Ibid. p. 76 (pl. I).

[145] Cf. Günter Grzimek, *Gedanken zur Stadt- und Landschaftsarchitektur seit Friedrich Ludwig von Sckell (Reihe der Bayer. Akademie der Schönen Künste)*, Munich 1973; Schepers, afterword to Sckell (1982).

[146] Hermann von Pückler-Muskau, *Andeutungen über Landschaftsgärtnerei*, Stuttgart 1834 (new ed. 1933; a further edition with introduction by Albrecht Kruse-Rodenacher, Stuttgart 1977; last ed. here cited.

On Pückler-Muskau cf. esp. Hermann von Arnim, *Ein Fürst unter den Gärtnern. Pückler als Landschaftskünstler und der Muskauer Park*, Frankfurt–Berlin–Vienna 1981.

[147] *'aus dem Ganzen der landschaftlichen Natur ein concentriertes Bild, eine solche Natur im Kleinen als poetisches Ideal zu schaffen…'* Pückler-Muskau (1834; ed. 1977), p. 18 n.

[148] *'denn ein Garten im großen Style ist eben nur eine Bildergallerie…'* Ibid., p. 26.

[149] *'mit ihrer Umgebung in sinniger Berührung stehen und immer einen bestimmten Zweck haben.'* Ibid., p. 28.

[150] *'Euer ist jetzt das Geld und die Macht, laßt dem ausgedienten Adel die Poesie, das einzige, was ihm übrig bleibt.'*

21. Nineteenth-century France and the Ecole des Beaux-Arts

[1] Cf. Emil Kaufmann, *Von Ledoux bis Le Corbusier. Ursprung und Entstehung der autonomen Architektur*, Leipzig–Vienna 1933; 'Three Revolutionary Architects, Boullée, Ledoux, and Lequeu', *Transactions of the American Philosophical Society*, N.S., 42/3, 1952, pp. 431–564; *Architecture in the Age of Reason* (1955), New York 1969.

[2] Arthur Drexler (ed.), *The Architecture of the Ecole des Beaux-Arts*, London–New York 1977.

[3] Donald Drew Egbert, *The Beaux-Arts Tradition in French Architecture, Illustrated by the Grands Prix de Rome*, Princeton 1980; Robin Middleton (ed.), *The Beaux-Arts and*

Nineteenth-Century French Architecture, London 1982.

[4] Louis-Ambroise Dubut, *Architecture Civile. Maisons de ville et de campagne de toutes formes et de tous genres…*, Paris 1803 ('1837), facs. repr. of 1803 ed., Unterschneidheim 1974.

On Dubut cf. esp. Kaufmann (1933; Italian ed., *Da Ledoux a Le Corbusier*, Milan 1973, pp. 120ff.); id. (1952), pp. 534ff.; id. (1955), pp. 208ff.

[5] For a complete list of prize-winning designs with publication details, cf. Egbert (1980), pp. 168ff.; Dubut's design is illustrated in colour in: Drexler (1977), pp. 126ff.

[6] Dubut (1803), Introduction.

[7] '*Est-il rien de plus agréable qu'une Maison où nos besoins sont parfaitement satisfaits? elle fait le charme de notre vie, et contribue à nous faire passer des jours heureux.*' Dubut (1803), Introduction.

[8] On Durand, cf. Louis Hautecoeur, *Histoire de l'Architecture classique en France*, vol. V, Paris 1953, pp. 259ff.; Kaufmann (1955), pp. 210ff.; Edward Robert De Zurko, *Origins of Functionalist Theory*, New York 1957, pp. 168ff.; Henry-Russell Hitchcock, *Architecture: Nineteenth and Twentieth Century* (1958), Harmondsworth 1971, pp. 47ff.; Antonio Hernandez, 'Jean-Nicolas-Louis Durand und die Anfänge der funktionalistischen Architekturtheorie', in: *Architekturtheorie. Internationaler Kongreß an der TH Berlin*, 1967, pp. 135–51 (English trans. in: *Perspecta* XII, 1969, pp. 153–60); Drexler (1977), pp. 72f.; Egbert (1980), pp. 48f.; Werner Szambien, 'Durand and the continuity of tradition', in: Middleton (1982), pp. 18–33; Werner Szambien, *Jean-Nicolas-Louis Durand 1760–1834*, Paris 1984.

[9] Illus., Szambien (1982), p. 18; Drexler (1977), p. 117.

[10] On the precursors and function of the Ecole Polytechnique, cf. Egbert (1980), pp. 46ff.

[11] Jean-Nicolas-Louis Durand, *Recueil et parallèle des édifices de tout genre, anciens et modernes*, Paris 1800; considerably enlarged ed.: *Raccolta e parallelo delle fabriche classiche di tutti i tempi...*, ed. J. G. Legrand, Venice, 1833, Lüttich 1842; J. G. Legrand, *Essai sur l'histoire générale de l'architecture pour servir de texte explicatif au recueil et parallèle des édifices par J. N. L. Durand*, Lüttich 1842 (both last-mentioned together, facs. ed. Nördlingen 1986).

[12] On Durand's sources, cf. Szambien (1982), pp. 19ff.

[13] Jean-Nicolas-Louis Durand, *Précis des leçons d'architecture données à l'Ecole Polytechnique*, 2 vols, Paris 1802–05 (rev. ed. Paris 1817–19); *Partie graphique des Cours d'Architecture*, Paris 1821; facs. reprs of 1817, 1819 and 1821 eds, Unterschneidheim 1975.
A German summary of Durand's lectures: Carl Friedrich Anton von Conta, *Grundlinien der bürgerlichen Baukunst Nach Herrn Durand*, Halle 1806; a complete trans. entitled *Abriß der Vorlesungen über*

Baukunst, 2 vols, Karlsruhe and Freiburg 1831.

[14] Durand (1819), vol. I, p. 5.

[15] '*utilité publique et particulière, la conservation, le bonheur des individus, des familles et de la société.*' Ibid., p. 6.

[16] Ibid., pp. 6ff.

[17] Ibid., p. 14.

[18] Ibid., p. 55.

[19] Ibid., p. 21.

[20] Ibid., p. 19.

[21] Ibid., pp. 37 and 53.

[22] Ibid., p. 8.

[23] Ibid., p. 34.

[24] Cf. Hitchcock (1971), pp. 49ff., showing *inter alia* the influence of Durand's gallery designs on Klenze's Glyptothek in Munich.

[25] Cf. Szambien (1982), p. 21.

[26] On Rondelet, cf. Richard Chafee in: Drexler (1977), p. 77 and Egbert (1980), pp. 47ff.

[27] Jean-Baptiste Rondelet, *Traité théorique et pratique de l'art de bâtir*, 5 vols, Paris 1802–17 and vol. of plates; numerous eds (⁸1838).

[28] Rondelet, vol. I (1802), p. 8.

[29] Ibid., vol. IV (1817), pp. 491ff.

[30] Ibid., pp. 537ff., pl. CLXXV.

[31] Ibid., vol. of plates, pl. LXXXIII.

[32] Marie-Joseph Peyre, *Oeuvres d'architecture*, Paris 1765, pl. 19.

[33] On Napoleon's approach to art and architecture, Hautecoeur, vol. V (1953), pp. 150ff.; Paul Wescher, *Kunstraub unter Napoleon*, Berlin 1976.

[34] On Percier and Fontaine, cf. esp. Maurice Fouché, *Percier et Fontaine*, Paris 1905; Jeanne Duportal, *Charles Percier, Reproductions de dessins conservés à la Bibliothèque de l'Institut*, Paris 1931; Hautecoeur, vol. V (1953), pp. 156ff., 252ff.; Marie-Louise Biver, *Pierre-François-Léonard Fontaine. Premier architecte de l'Empereur*, Paris 1964; Hans Ottomeyer, *Das frühe Oeuvre Charles Perciers (1782–1800). Zu den Anfängen des Historismus in Frankreich*, diss. (Munich 1976), Altendorf 1981; Hans-Joachim Haasengier, *Das Palais du Roi de Rome auf dem Hügel von Chaillot. Percier-Fontaine-Napoleon*, Frankfurt–Bern 1983; and the recently published journals of Fontaine, Pierre-François-Léonard Fontaine, *Journal 1799–1853*, 2 vols, Paris 1987.

[35] Charles Percier and Pierre-François-Léonard Fontaine, *Palais, Maisons, et autres édifices*

modernes dessinés à Rome, Paris 1798 (facs. repr. with intro. by Hans Foramitti, Hildesheim–New York 1980).

[36] Ibid. (1798), pp. 5ff.

[37] Ibid., p. 6.

[38] Ibid., p. 4f.

[39] Ibid., p. 8.

[40] Ibid., Pl. 92, and commentary on p. 27.

[41] Charles Percier and Pierre-François-Léonard Fontaine, Recueil de décorations intérieures, comprenant tout ce qui a rapport à l'ameublement..., Paris 1801 (enlarged ed., Paris 1812); on editions of this work, cf. Ottomeyer (1981), pp. 195ff.

[42] Ibid. (1812), p. 10.

[43] Ibid., p. 15.

[44] Charles Percier and Pierre-François-Léonard Fontaine, Résidences de Souverains. Parallèle entre plusieurs Résidences de Souverains de France, d'Allemagne, de Suède, de Russie, d'Espagne, et d'Italie, Paris 1833 (facs. repr. with intro. by Hans Foramitti, Hildesheim–New York 1973).

[45] Ibid. (1833), p. 39.

[46] Ibid., pp. 266f.

[47] 'nous considérons l'architecture antique, celle de la renaissance des arts, celle des temps modernes et autres, non comme des types de doctrine auxquels il faut se conformer, mais comme des subdivisions particulières qui distinguent les productions d'un même art et tendent au même but, comme des découvertes de sciences que chacun a pu exploiter selon besoins, et qu'il est important d'étudier pour mettre à profit les avantages qu'elles comportent.' Ibid., p. 271.

[48] 'Tout est grand, tout est somptueux dans cette riche demeure, mais tout y est triste, monotone et peu commode.' Ibid., p. 288.

[49] Ibid., pp. 288ff.

[50] 'Il faut, en changeant l'échelle et l'étendue d'un édifice, que les subdivisions de l'ensemble soient refaites sur un module dont les rapports mathématiques ne doivent pas être l'unique base. Il faut que chaque partie reçoive la proportion qui lui est relative, et non celle qui serait prescrite par un formulaire de chiffres.' Ibid., p. 289.

[51] Charles-Pierre-Joseph Normand, Recueil varié de plans et de façades de maisons de ville et de campagne..., Paris 1815.

[52] Ibid., Blatt 2.

[53] Ibid., Pl. 51, centre.

[54] Charles-Pierre-Joseph Normand, Le Vignole des ouvriers. Ou la méthode facile pour tracer les cinque ordres d'architecture, 4 parts, 2 vols, 7th ed., Paris 1839.

[55] Giuseppe Valadier, L'architettura pratica dettata nella scuola e cattedra dell'insegne Accademia di San Luca, 5 vols, Rome 1828–38.

On Valadier, cf. esp. Elfriede Schulze-Battmann, Giuseppe Valadier, ein klassizistischer Architekt Roms 1762–1839, Dresden 1939; Paolo Marconi, Giuseppe Valadier, Rome 1964; Elisa Debenedetti, Valadier diario architettonico, Rome 1979; exh. cat. Valadier. Segno e architettura, ed. Elisa Debenedetti, Rome 1985.

[56] Giuseppe Valadier and Filippo Aurelio Visconti, Raccolta delle più insegni fabbriche de Roma antica, 7 fascicles, Rome 1810–26.

[57] Valadier and Visconti, vol. I (1810), p. 1.

[58] Cf. esp. Richard Chafee, 'The Teaching of Architecture at the Ecole des Beaux-Arts', in: Drexler (1977), pp. 61ff.; Egbert (1980), pp. 36ff.

[59] Cf. Chafee in: Drexler (1977), pp. 70ff.; Ottomeyer (1981), pp. 29ff.

[60] On Quatremère de Quincy, cf. René-Gabriel Schneider, L'estétique classique chez Quatremère de Quincy (1805–1835), diss., Paris 1910; id., Quatremère de Quincy et son intervention dans les arts (1788–1830), Paris 1910; Hautecoeur, vol. V (1953), pp. 246ff.; Chafee in: Drexler (1977), pp. 67ff.; Egbert (1980), pp. 42ff.

[61] Antoine-Chrysostome Quatremère de Quincy, Dictionnaire d'Architecture, vol. I, Paris 1789, vol. II, 1832; Histoire de la vie et des ouvrages des plus célèbres architectes, 2 vols, Paris 1830 (facs. repr., New York 1970).

[62] Quatremère de Quincy (1830), vol. I, p. VII.

[63] Ibid., vol. II, pp. 194f.

[64] Antoine-Chrysostome Quatremère de Quincy, Essai sur la nature, le but et les moyens de l'imitation dans les Beaux-Arts, Paris 1823 (facs. repr. with intro. by Leon Krier and Demetri Porphyrios, Brussels 1980).

[65] Cf. Helen Rosenau, 'The Engravings of the Grands Prix of the French Academy of Architecture', Architectural History III, 1960, pp. 17–173; Wanda Bouleau-Rabaud, 'L'Académie d'Architecture à la fin du XVIIIe siècle', Gazette des Beaux-Arts LXVIII, 1966, pp. 355–64; and esp. Egbert (1980), pp. 163ff. (with designs and bibliog.).

[66] François-René Chateaubriand, *Génie du Christianisme ou beauté de la religion chrétienne* (1802), in: *Bibliothèque de la Pléiade*, Paris 1978, pp. 457ff.

[67] 'proportions barbares... un sentiment vague de la divinité.' Chateaubriand (1802), Part III, Book I, chapter 8, ed. 1978, p. 801.

[68] On the debate on polychromy, cf. esp. the following: Karl Hammer, *Jakob Ignaz Hittorff. Ein Pariser Baumeister 1792–1867*, Stuttgart 1968, pp. 101ff.; David Van Zanten, 'The Architectural Polychromy of the 1830s' (PhD thesis, Harvard Univ. 1970), New York–London 1977; Neil Levine, 'The Romantic Idea of Architectural Legibility: Henri Labrouste and the Neo-Grec', in: Drexler (1977), pp. 325ff.; R. D. Middleton, 'Hittorff's polychrome campaign', in: Middleton (ed.) (1982), pp. 175–95; David Van Zanten, 'Architectural polychromy: life in architecture', in: Middleton (ed.) (1982), pp. 197–215; Marie-Françoise Billot, 'Recherches aux XVIIIe et XIXe siècles sur la polychromie de l'architecture grecque', in: exh. cat., *Paris–Rome–Athènes*, Paris 1982, pp. 61–125.

[69] Antoine-Chrysostome Quatremère de Quincy, *Jupiter olympien: l'art de la sculpture antique considerée sous un nouveau point de vue*, Paris 1815. Cf. esp. Van Zanten (1977), pp. 9ff. (intro.), pp. 3ff.

[70] Cf. Van Zanten (1977), pp. 19ff. The most important writings of this period in support of the use of architectural polychromy in Antiquity are: Franz-Christian Gau, *Les Antiquités de Nubie*, Paris 1822 (German: Stuttgart 1823). Johann Martin von Wagner, *Bericht über die Aeginetischen Bildwerke im Besitz des Kronprinzen von Bayern*, Stuttgart 1817. Otto Magnus von Stakkelberg, *Der Apollotempel zu Bassae in Arcadien und die daselbst ausgegrabenen Bildwerke*, Rome 1826. Leo von Klenze, *Der Tempel des olympischen Jupier von Agrigent*, Munich 1827.

[71] On Hittorff, cf. Hautecoeur, vol. VI (1955), pp. 228ff.; Erich Schild, *Der Nachlaß des Architekten Hittorff*, diss., Aachen 1956; Karl Hammer, *Jakob Ignaz Hittorff. Ein Pariser Baumeister 1792–1867*, Stuttgart 1968; Donald David Schneider, 'The Works and Doctrine of Jacques Ignace Hittorff (1792–1867): Structural Innovation and Formal Expression in French Architecture, 1810–1867', PhD thesis (Princeton Univ.

1970), 2 vols, Ann Arbor–London 1981.

[72] Jakob Ignaz Hittorff, 'Mémoires sur mon voyage en Sicile, lu à l'Académie des Beaux-Arts de l'Institut avec l'extrait du procès-verbal de la séance du 24 juillet 1824' (Paris, Institut de France, Ms 4641); cf. Hammer (1968), pp. 101f.

[73] Jakob Ignaz Hittorff and Karl Ludwig Wilhelm von Zanth, *Architecture antique de la Sicile ou Recueil des plus intéressants monuments d'architecture des villes et des lieux, les plus remarquables de la Sicile ancienne, mesurés et dessinés...*, Paris 1828.

[74] Jakob Ignaz Hittorff, *Restitution du Temple d'Empédocle à Sélinonte ou l'Architecture polychrome chez les Grecs*, Paris 1851.

[75] Cf. esp. Middleton in: Middleton (ed.) (1982), pp. 188ff.

[76] On Labrouste, cf. Hautecoeur, vol. VI (1955), pp. 241ff.; Levine (1977), pp. 325–416; Pierre Saddy, exh. cat. *Henri Labrouste architecte 1801–1825*, Paris 1977; Van Zanten (1977), pp. 36ff.

[77] Illus. in Drexler (ed.) (1977), pp. 156ff.

[78] Henri Labrouste, *Temples de Paestum par Labrouste. Restaurations des monuments antiques par les architectes pensionnaires de France à Rome*, Paris 1877.

[79] Cf. Van Zanten in: Middleton (ed.) (1982), p. 199, col. pl. II.

[80] Cf. the analysis by Levine (1977), pp. 366ff.

[81] Illus. in Drexler (ed.) (1977), pp. 361ff.; exh. cat., *Paris-Rome-Athènes* (1982), pp. 132ff.

[82] See esp. Levine (1977), pp. 325ff.

[83] Cf. Siegfried Gohr, 'Thorvaldsens Museum', in: exh. cat., *Bertel Thorvaldsen*, Cologne, 1977, pp. 89ff.

[84] Franz Kugler, *Über die Polychromie der griechischen Architektur und Sculptur und ihre Grenzen*, Berlin 1835 (with additions in: Kugler, *Kleine Schriften und Studien zur Kunstgeschichte*, Part I, Stuttgart 1853, pp. 265ff.).

[85] Victor Hugo, *Notre-Dame de Paris 1482* (1832), here cited in ed. Bibl. de la Pléiade, Paris 1975, pp. 106ff.

[86] See esp. Lucien Refort, 'L'art gothique vu par Victor Hugo et Michelet', *Revue d'Histoire Littéraire de la France* 33, 1926, pp. 390–94; Paul Frankl, *The Gothic. Literary Sources and Interpretations through Eight Centuries*, Princeton 1960, pp. 483ff.; exh. cat. *Le 'gothique' retrouvé avant Viollet-le-Duc*, Paris 1979, pp. 63ff.

[87] Cf, Frankl (1960), p. 487; Eric Fauquet, 'J. Michelet et l'histoire de l'architecture républicaine', *Gazette des Beaux-Arts* 126, 1984, pp. 71–79; cf. crit. ed., Jules Michelet, 'Histoire de France', ed. Robert Casanova, in: Jules Michelet, *Oeuvres complètes*, vols IV–VIII, Paris 1974–80.

[88] Erwin Panofsky, *Gothic Architecture and Scholasticism* (1951), Cleveland–New York [6]1963.

[89] Cf. Hautecoeur, vol. VI (1955), pp. 292ff.; Mérimée's letters to Viollet-le-Duc in: *Oeuvres complètes de Prosper Mérimée*, vol. II. *Lettres à Viollet-le-Duc*, ed. Pierre Trahard, Paris 1927; exh. cat., *Prosper Mérimée, Inspecteur général des Monuments historiques (Les Monuments historiques de la France)*, 1970, n. 3; on editions of the works and letters of Mérimée, cf. Louise Dupley Dickenson, 'A Half-Century of Mérmimée Studies: An Annotated Bibliography of Criticism in French and English 1928–1976', PhD thesis (Vanderbilt Univ., Nashville, Tenn. 1976), Ann Arbor, MI 1976, pp. 303ff.

[90] On Caumont, cf. Frankl (1960), pp. 519ff.; Nikolaus Pevsner, *Some Architectural Writers of the Nineteenth Century*, Oxford 1972, pp. 36ff.

[91] Arcisse de Caumont, 'Sur l'architecture du moyen-âge particulièrement en Normandie', *Mémoires de la Société des Antiquaires de Normandie* I, 1824, Part 2; id., *Cours d'antiquités monumentales*, Paris 1830–41.

[92] Léonce Reynaud, *Traité d'architecture contenant des notions générales sur les principes de la construction et sur l'histoire de l'art*, 2 vols text and 2 vols pls, Paris 1850–58.

On Reynaud cf. F. de Dartein, *Léonce Reynaud, sa vie, ses oeuvres*, Paris 1885; Nikolas Pevsner (1972), pp. 203ff.

[93] Reynaud, vol. I (1850), pp. 1ff.

[94] '*Or le fer, comme le bois, et même mieux que lui, se prête à toutes les formes.*' Ibid., p. 446.

[95] '*Le bon est le fondement du beau, et les formes de l'art doivent être toujours vraies.*' Ibid., vol. II (1858), p. 20.

[96] Ibid., pp. 28ff.

[97] '*La décoration est dans l'art que le plaisir est dans la vie...besoin inné chez l'homme.*' Ibid., p. 66.

[98] On the argument between Gothicists and Classicists and the Ecole's attempts at reform, cf. Hautecoeur, vol. VI (1955), pp.

332ff.; Pevsner (1972), pp. 198ff.; Chafee in: Drexler (ed.) (1977), pp. 97ff.; Egbert (1980), pp. 58ff.; Italian trans. of the most important polemical works, Luciano Patetta, *La polemica fra i Goticisti e i Classicisti dell'Académie des Beaux-Arts Francia 1846–47*, Milan 1974.

[99] Richard A. Moore, 'Academic Dessin Theory in France after Reorganization of 1863', *Journal of the Society of Architectural Historians* XXXVI, 1977, pp. 145–74.

[100] John Summerson, 'Viollet-le-Duc and the Rational Point of View', in: Summerson, *Heavenly Mansions and other essays on architecture* (1948), New York 1963, p. 135.

[101] The literature on Viollet-le-Duc is extensive. Cf. esp.: Pol Abraham, *Viollet-le-Duc et le rationalisme médiéval*, Paris 1934; Summerson (1948; ed. 1963), pp. 135–58; Maurice Besset, 'Viollet-le-Duc. Seine Stellung zur Geschichte', in: Ludwig Grote (ed.), *Historismus und bildende Kunst*, Munich 1965, pp. 43–58; Renato De Fusco, *L'idea di architettura. Storia della critica da Viollet-le-Duc a Persico* (1968), Milan 1977, pp. 4ff.; Nikolaus Pevsner, *Ruskin and Viollet-le-Duc*, London 1969; id., 'Viollet-le-Duc and Reynaud', in: Pevsner (1972), pp. 194–216; Robin Middleton, 'Viollet-le-Duc's Academic Ventures and the Entretiens sur l'Architecture', in: *Gottfried Semper und die Mitte des 19. Jahrhunderts*, Basel–Stuttgart 1976, pp. 239–54; Ivo Tagliaventi, *Viollet-le-Duc e la cultura architettonica dei revivals*, Bologna 1976; Pierre-Marie Auzas, 'Eugène Viollet-le-Duc 1814–1879', Paris 1979, Gert Bekaert (ed.), *A la recherche de Viollet-le-Duc* (collection of essays), Brussels 1980; Architectural Design Profile, *Viollet-le-Duc*, London 1980; Robin D. Middleton, 'Viollet-le-Duc's Influence in Nineteenth-Century England', *Art History* 4, 1981, pp. 203–19; *Actes du Colloque International Viollet-le-Duc* (1980), Paris 1982.

Important catalogues: *Viollet-le-Duc. Centenaire de la mort à Lausanne*, Lausanne 1979; *Viollet-le-Duc*, Paris 1980; *Le voyage d'Italie d'Eugène Viollet-le-Duc 1836–1837*, Florence 1980; *Viollet-le-Duc e il restauro degli edifici in Francia*, Milan 1981.

[102] Geneviève Viollet-le-Duc (ed.), *E. Viollet-le-Duc. Lettres d'Italie 1836/37 adressées à sa famille*, Paris 1971; exh. cat., *Le voyage d'Italie d'Eugène Viollet-le-Duc 1836–1837*, Florence 1980.

[103] Eugène Emmanuel Viollet-le-Duc, *Dictionnaire raisonné de l'architecture française du XIe au XVIe siècle*, 10 vols, Paris 1854–68 (facs. repr. Paris 1967); cf. select eds: Viollet-le-Duc, *L'architecture raisonnée. Extraits du Dictionnaire de l'architecture française*, ed. Hubert Damisch, Paris 1964; Philippe Boudon and Philippe Deshayes, *Viollet-le-Duc. Le Dictionnaire d'architecture. Relevés et observations*, Brussels 1979.
Eugène Emmanuel Viollet-le-Duc, *Entretiens sur l'architecture*, 2 vols, Paris 1863–72 (facs. repr. Brussels 1977); English trans. Boston 1875–81; London 1877–82.
A bibliog. of writings by Viollet-le-Duc in exh. cat. *Viollet-le-Duc* (Paris 1980), pp. 397ff. (most published in facs. repr. by Mardaga, Brussels).

[104] Cf. esp. Besset (1965), pp. 43ff.

[105] Viollet-le-Duc, *Dictionnaire*, vol. I (1854), p. III.

[106] '*les raisons d'être de ces formes, les principes qui les ont fait admettre, les moeurs et les idées au milieu desquelles elles ont pris naissance...*' '*une heureuse révolution dans les études de l'architecture...*' Ibid., pp. II, IV.

[107] Ibid., p. XII.

[108] '*trop étranger à la civilisation moderne.*' Ibid., pp. xivf.

[109] Ibid., p. 154.

[110] '*Les cathédrales sont le premier et le plus grand effort du génie moderne appliqué à l'architecture, elles s'élèvent au centre d'un ordre d'idées opposé à l'ordre antique.*' Ibid., vol. II (1854), p. 385.

[111] '*Construire, pour l'architecte, c'est employer les matériaux, en raison de leurs qualités et de leur nature propre, avec l'idée préconçue de satisfaire à un besoin par les moyens les plus simples et les plus solides; de donner à la chose contruite l'apparence de la durée, des proportions convenables soumises à certaines règles imposées par les sens, le raisonnement et l'instinct humains. Les méthodes du constructeur doivent donc varier en raison de la nature des matériaux, des moyens dont il dispose, des besoins auxquels il doit satisfaire et de la civilisation au milieu de laquelle il naît.*' Ibid., vol. IV (1859), p. 1.

[112] '*souple, libre et chercheuse comme l'esprit moderne...*' '*absolue dans ses moyens.*' Ibid., p. 58.

[113] Ibid., vol. VII (1864), p. 534.

[114] '*Restaurer un édifice, ce n'est pas l'entretenir, le réparer ou le refaire, c'est le rétablir dans un 'état complet qui peut n'avoir jamais existé à un moment donné.*' Ibid., vol. VIII (1866), p. 14.

[115] Ibid., p. 23.

[116] Cf. Middleton (1981), p. 207.

[117] '*la manifestation d'un idéal établi sur un principe.*' Viollet-le-Duc, vol. VIII (1866), p. 478.

[118] '*La locomotive est presque un être, et sa forme extérieure n'est que l'expression de sa puissance. Une locomotive donc a du style...la physionomie vraie de sa brutale énergie...*' Viollet-le-Duc, *Entretiens*, vol. I (1863), p. 186.

[119] '*l'eclecticisme est un mal; car, dans ce cas, il exclut nécessairement le style...*' Ibid., p. 191.

[120] '*La composition architectonique devant dériver absolument: 1) du programme imposé, 2) des habitudes de la civilisation au milieu de laquelle on vit, il est essentiel, pour composer, de posséder un programme et d'avoir le sentiment exact de ces habitudes, de ces usages, de ces besoins. Encore un fois, si les programmes changent peu quant au fond, les habitudes des peuples civilisés, les moeurs se modifient sans cesse; par suite, les formes de l'architecture doivent varier à l'infini.*' Ibid., p. 330.

[121] Arthur de Gobineau, *Essai sur l'inégalité des races humaines*, Paris 1855.

[122] This argument is convincingly put by Besset (1965), p. 54.

[123] '*Il faut être vrai selon le programme, vrai selon les procédés de construction*'. Viollet-le-Duc, *Entretiens*, vol. I (1863), p. 451.

[124] '*1) Connaître d'abord la nature des matériaux que nous devons employer; 2) donner à ces matériaux la fonction et la puissance relatives à l'objet, les formes exprimant le plus exactement et cette fonction et cette puissance; 3) admettre un principe d'unité et d'harmonie dans cette expression, c'est-à-dire l'échelle, un système de proportion, un ornementation en rapport avec la destination et qui ait une signification, mais aussi la variété indiquée par la nature diverse des besoins à satisfaire.*' Ibid., p. 465.

[125] '*ces matériaux mis en oeuvre indiquent leur fonction par la forme que vous leur donnez; que la pierre paraisse bien être de la pierre; le fer, du fer; le bois, du bois; que ces matières, tout en prenant les formes qui*

conviennent à leur nature, aient un accord entre elles.' Ibid., p. 472.

[126] 'Il n'est guère possible d'obtenir un local sain, chaud en hiver, frais en été, soustrait aux variations de la température, à l'aide du fer seulement. Les murs, les voûtes en maçonnerie présenteront toujours des avantages supérieurs à tout autre mode.' Ibid., vol. II (1872), p. 64.

[127] 'appliquer timidement les nouveaux moyens à de vieilles formes.' Ibid., p. 90.

[128] Ibid., p. 307.

[129] Ibid., pl. XXXVI.

[130] Eugène Emmanuel Viollet-le-Duc, Habitations modernes, 2 vols, Paris 1875–77 (facs. repr. Brussels 1979).

[131] Joseph Neumann, Art de construire et de gouverner les serres, Paris 1844 (facs. repr. with introduction by Michel Vernes, Neuilly-sur-Seine 1980).

[132] Charles Garnier, Le Théâtre, Paris 1981; id., Le nouvel Opéra de Paris, 4 vols, Paris 1878–81. See esp. Monika Steinhauser, Die Architektur der Pariser Oper, Munich 1969; esp. pp. 161ff. Cf. also Charles Garnier, A travers les arts, ed. François Loyer, Paris 1985.

[133] Charles Fourier, Oeuvres complètes, 12 vols, Paris 1841 ff. (facs. repr., ed. S. Debout Oleszkiewicz, Paris 1979ff.).

On Fourier, cf. August Bebel, Charles Fourier, Stuttgart 1907; Mechtild Schumpp, Stadtbau-Utopien und Gesellschaft, Gütersloh 1972; Franziska Bollerey, Architekturkonzeption der utopischen Sozialisten, Munich 1977, pp. 94ff.; Barbara Goodwin, Social Science and Utopia. Nineteenth-Century Models of Social Harmony, Sussex 1978.

[134] Fourier, Théorie de l'unité universelle (1822), in: Oeuvres complètes, vol. 4, 1841 (1971), pp. 300ff.

[135] Ibid., p. 305.

[136] Ibid., p. 455ff.

[137] Cf. Bollerey (1977), pp. 150ff. On Godin, cf. exh. cat. Jean-Baptiste André Godin 1817–1888. La Familistère de Guise ou les équivalents de la richesse, Brussels 1980.

[138] Georges Haussmann, Mémoires, 3 vols, Paris 1890–93.

[139] Eugène Hénard, Etudes sur les transformations de Paris, 8 fascicles, Paris 1903–09; an anthology of his writings in Italian trans. in: Eugène Hénard. Alle origini dell'urbanistica. La costruzione della metropoli, ed. Donatella Calabi and Marino Folin (1972),

Padua ²1976; Eugène Hénard, Etudes sur les transformations de Paris. Et autres écrits sur l'urbanisme, ed. Jean Louis Cohen, Paris 1982.

[140] Eugène Hénard, 'The Cities of the Future', in: Transactions: Town Planning Conference, London 10–15 October 1910, London 1911, pp. 357–67; Calabi and Folin (1976), pp. 183ff.

[141] Auguste Choisy, Histoire de l'architecture, 2 vols, Paris 1899; several editions (facs. repr. of 1889 ed., Geneva–Paris 1982). On Choisy, cf. esp. Reyner Banham, Theory and Design in the First Machine Age, London 1960.

[142] 'Chez tous les peuples, l'art passera par les mêmes alternatives, obéira aux mêmes lois: l'art préhistorique semble contenir tous les autres en leur germe.' Choisy (1899), vol. I, p. 1.

[143] 'ce vague sentiment de l'harmonie qu'on nomme le goût'...'procédés de tracé définis et méthodiques'. Ibid., p. 51.

[144] 'Il semble que, dans une oeuvre d'architecture, certains membres doivent conserver, quelle que soit la grandeur de l'édifice, une dimension à peu près invariable: à prendre les choses par le côté purement utilitaire, la hauteur d'une porte n'aurait d'autre mesure que la hauteur de l'homme auquel elle donnera passage...' Ibid., p. 401.

[145] Ibid., p. 419: 'Chaque motif d'architecture pris à part est symétrique, mais chaque groupe est traité comme un paysage ou les masses seules se pondèrent.' ('Each architectural element taken separately is symmetrical, but each ensemble is treated as a landscape in which there is balance between masses only.')

[146] Ibid., p. 371.

[147] 'La structure nouvelle est le triomphe de la logique dans l'art; l'édifice devient un être organisé où chaque partie constitue un membre, ayant sa forme réglée non plus sur des modèles traditionnels mais sur sa fonction, et seulement sur sa fonction.' Ibid., p. 141.

[148] Ibid., vol. II, p. 339: 'Le style ne change pas suivant les caprices d'une mode plus ou moins arbitraire, ses variations ne sont autres que celles des procédés: l'ornement, dans ses moindres détails, ressort de la bâtisse elle-même, et la logique des méthodes implique la chronologie des styles.' ('Style does not change according to the whim of any single more or less arbitrary fashion, its variations are purely and simply those of the building

process: ornament, down to the most minute detail, derives from the building itself, and it is the logic of building methods that dictates stylistic chronology.')

[149] 'Une société nouvelle s'est constituée, qui veut un art nouveau.' Ibid., vol. II, p. 762.

[150] 'désormais un système nouveau de proportions s'est fait jour; où les lois harmoniques ne seront autres que celles de la stabilité...' Ibid., p. 764.

[151] Cf. Paul Venable Turner, The Education of le Corbusier, New York–London 1977, p. 234.

[152] Le Corbusier and later literature emphasise a connection with his visits to the Certosa di Galuzzo in Florence in 1907 and 1910, but in my opinion a connection may also be seen in Choisy's illustration of a pagoda (Choisy, (1899), vol. I, p. 173).

[153] Charles Blanc, Grammaire des arts de dessin: Architecture, sculpture, peinture, Paris 1867.

[154] Julien Guadet, Eléments et théorie de l'Architecture. Cours professé à l'Ecole Nationale et Spéciale des Beaux-Arts, 4 vols, Paris 1901–04, [6]1929–30.

[155] On Guadet, cf. Banham (1964), pp. 7ff.; Drexler (1977), pp. 255ff. (Grand Prix design, 1864); Egbert (1980), pp. 65f.

[156] Guadet, vol. I (ed. 1929), p. 4.

[157] Ibid., p. 2.

[158] 'composition des édifices, dans leur éléments et dans leur ensembles, au double point de vue de l'art et de l'adaptation à des programmes définis, à des nécessités matérielles.' Ibid., p. 2.

[159] Ibid., pp. 76ff.

[160] Ibid., p. 87.

[161] 'Composition – C'est mettre ensemble, souder et combiner les parties d'un tout. A leur tour, ces parties, ce sont les éléments de la composition.' Ibid., vol. II (1929), p. 4.

[162] Ibid., vol. I, p. 139.

[163] Ibid., vol. IV (1930), pp. 504ff.

[164] 'disposition = la composition; proportions = l'étude; construction = contrôle de l'étude par la science.' Ibid., vol. I, p. 100.

[165] Gustave Umbdenstock, Cours d'architecture (Ecole Polytechnique), 2 vols, Paris 1930.

[166] Albert Ferran, Philosophie de la Composition Architecturale, Paris 1955.

22. Germany in the nineteenth century

[1] For general coverage cf. Cornelius Gurlitt, Die deutsche Kunst des Neunzehnten Jahrhunderts, Berlin [2]1900, [3]1907 (the sections on architecture repr. in: Cornelius Gurlitt, Zur Befreiung der Baukunst. Ziele und Taten deutscher Architekten im 19. Jahrhundert, ed. Werner Kallmorgen, Bauwelt Fundamente 22, Gütersloh–Berlin 1969); Hermann Beenken, Das neunzehnte Jahrhundert in der deutschen Kunst, Munich 1944. On architecture: Sigfried Giedion, Spätbarocker und romantischer Klassizismus, Munich 1922; Wolfgang Herrmann, Deutsche Architektur des 19. und 20. Jahrhunderts. 1. Teil: von 1770–1840, Breslau 1932 (together with 2. Teil: Von 1840 bis zur Gegenwart which was to have appeared in 1933 but was suppressed: Basel and Stuttgart 1977); Hermann Beenken, Schöpferische Bauideen der deutschen Romantik, Mainz 1952; Kurt Milde, Neorenaissance in der deutschen Architektur des 19. Jahrhunderts, Dresden 1981; Tilman Mellinghoff and David Watkin, German Architecture and the classical ideal 1740–1840, London 1987; texts with commentary in 3-vol. Kunsttheorie und Kunstgeschichte des 19. Jahrhunderts in Deutschland, vol. II: Architektur, ed. Harold Hammer-Schenk, Stuttgart 1985. For a clarification of the stylistic debate in Germany, cf. Klaus Döhmer, 'In welchem Style sollen wir bauen?' Architekturtheorie zwischen Klassizismus und Jugendstil, Munich 1976.

[2] Christian Ludwig Stieglitz, Geschichte der Baukunst der Alten, Leipzig 1792.

[3] Stieglitz (1792), p. vii.

[4] Ibid.

[5] Ibid.

[6] 'Die ältesten Völker, welche die Baukunst ausübten, wie die Aegypter und andere, konnten sich nie über das Mittelmäßige erheben und nie zur Schönheit gelangen; die Etrusker aber nahten sich zwar der schönen Kunst, allein sie wurden in ihrer Cultur gestört, und hörten frühzeitig auf eine Nation zu seyn. Die Griechen allein können auf den Ruhm Anspruch machen, die Baukunst von der niedrigsten Stufe an bis zu der höchsten Vollkommenheit geführt, sie zu einer Kunst erhoben und solche Regeln in dieser Kunst hinterlassen zu haben, die

noch bis jetzt von keinen andern verdrängt wurden, und die ihren Werth so lange behalten werden, als man Schönheit und guten Geschmack zu dem Wesentlichen der höhern Baukunst rechnen wird.' Stieglitz (1792), p. 173.

[7] Ibid., p. 368.

[8] Christian Ludwig Stieglitz, *Archaeologie der Baukunst der Griechen und Römer*, Weimar 1801.

[9] Christian Ludwig Stieglitz, *Encyklopädie der bürgerlichen Baukunst*, 5 vols, Leipzig 1792–98.

[10] Lukas Vochs, *Allgemeines Baulexicon oder Erklärung der deutschen und französischen Kunstwörter...*, Augsburg and Leipzig 1781.

[11] Christian Ludwig Stieglitz, *Plans et dessins tirés de la belle architecture... accompagné d'un traité abrégé sur le beau dans l'architecture*, Leipzig 1800.

[12] Cf. eg. Stieglitz (1800), pls 4, 5 with Holkham (Woolfe and Gandon, *Vitruvius Britannicus*, vol. V, London 1771, pls 66–69).

[13] Stieglitz (1801), fig. 2.

[14] *'La forme dans les productions de l'architecture est déterminée par le but de l'oeuvre, au quel il fait nécessairement qu'elle corresponde, sans quoi elle seroit sans utilité.'* Stieglitz (1800), p. 2.

[15] *'le majestueux, le sérieux, le magnifique, le terrible, le gracieux et le merveilleux...'* Ibid., p. 6.

[16] Ibid., p. 7.

[17] Ibid., p. 10.

[18] Christian Ludwig Stieglitz, *Von altdeutscher Baukunst*, Leipzig 1820.

[19] Christian Ludwig Stieglitz, *Geschichte der Baukunst vom frühesten Alterthum bis in neuere Zeiten*, Nuremberg 1827.

[20] Christian Ludwig Stieglitz, *Beiträge zur Geschichte der Ausbildung der Baukunst*, 2 vols, Leipzig 1834.

[21] *'...Nachahmung der Form, der Construction, der Zierde...Spiel mit architektonischen Formen, ohne die Zweckmäßigkeit zu beachten, ohne die Bestimmung und den Charakter de Gebäude vor dem Auge zu haben.'* Stieglitz, vol. II (1834), p. 178.

[22] *'Das Ernste dieser Kunst erlaubte nur kalt und bedachtsam aufzutreten, das Feuer war erloschen, das sonst den Künstler durchdrang.'* Ibid.

[23] Stieglitz, vol. II (1834), p. 179.

[24] *'Sie können alle drei befolgt werden, nachdem dieses oder jenes den Forderungen des anzulegenden Bauwerkes genügt und seinem Charakter nicht widersprechend ist.'* Ibid.

[25] Ibid., pp. 180ff.

[26] *'Die Construktion allein, die Formen der Hauptteile, der Körper des ganzen Bauwerks führt schon zur architektonischen Schönheit und legt den Grund zu ihr.'* Ibid., pp. 189ff.

[27] Jean-Nicolas-Louis Durand, *Abriß der Vorlesungen über Baukunst...*, 2 vols, Karlsruhe and Freiburg 1831.

[28] On Coudray cf. Walther Schneemann, C. W. Coudray, *Goethes Baumeister*, Weimar 1943 (on Coudray's collaboration with Durand, see the autobiographical notes, pp. 83ff.); Alfred Jericke and Dieter Dolgner, *Der Klassizismus in der Baugeschichte Weimars*, Weimar 1975, pp. 227ff.; Hermann Wirth, 'Clemens Wenzeslaus Coudray (1775–1845). Architekturtheoretische Anschauungen', *Wissenschaftliche Zeitschrift für Architektur und Bauwesen*, Weimar 22, 1975, pp. 473–83; Anita Bach a.o., *Clemens Wenzeslaus Coudray. Baumeister der späten Goethezeit*, Weimar 1983.

[29] Carl Friedrich Anton von Conta, *Grundlinien der bürgerlichen Baukunst nach Herrn Durand...*, Halle 1806.

[30] Carl Friedrich von Wiebeking, *Theoretisch-practische Bürgerliche Baukunde durch Geschichte und Beschreibung der merkwürdigsten Baudenkmahle und ihre genauen Abbildungen bereichert*, 4 vols., Munich 1826 (enlarged French ed., Munich 1827ff.).

[31] Wiebeking, vol. I (French ed. 1827), pp. 22ff.

[32] Wiebeking, vol. II (French ed. 1828), pl. XXIII.

[33] Friedrich Oettingen-Wallerstein, *Ueber die Grundsätze der Bau-Oekonomie*, Prague 1835.

[34] Aloys Hirt, *Die Baukunst nach den Grundsätzen der Alten*, Berlin 1809; later ed. entitled *Die Geschichte der Baukunst bei den Alten* in 3 vols, Berlin 1821–27. On Hirt cf. Adolf Heinrich Borbein, 'Klassische Archäologie in Berlin vom 18. bis zum 20. Jahrhundert', in: *Berlin und die Antike. Aufsätze*, Berlin 1979, pp. 106ff.

[35] Hirt (1809), p. IV.

[36] *'Die Baukunst ist die Lehre, oder der Inbegriff derjenigen Kenntnisse und Fertigkeiten, durch welche man in Stand gesetzt wird, jede Art von Bau zweckmäßig zu entwerfen und auszuführen.'* Hirt (1809), p. 1.

37 '... eine der Bestimmung entsprechende Anordnung und Einrichtung... dauerhafte Constructionsweise und die Schönheit gleichsam nur [als] begleitende Zwecke dieses Hauptzweckes'. Hirt (1809), p. 11.

38 '... das Wesen des Schönen aus der Construction und einer zweckmäßigen Anordnung hervorgehen...' Ibid., p. 13.

39 '... Verschönerung [wird] ein ihrer Bestimmung entsprechendes, gefälliges Ansehen von Außen und Innen, im Ganzen und in den Theilen'. Ibid., p. 12.

40 'Verhältnismaß... Gleichmaß... Wohlgereimtheit... Einfachheit der Formen, Material und Massen, Verzierung'. Ibid., pp. 13ff.

41 Ibid., pp. 27ff.

42 'Für alles, was die Construction, sey es in Holz, sey es in Stein, wesentlich erheischt, liefern uns theils die Schriften, theils die Denkmäler der Griechen und Römer die erforderlichen Vorschriften und Muster. Wer demnach richtig construirt, bauet eben dadurch griechisch.' Ibid., p. 38.

43 '... Wesen einer richtigen Construction in jeder Art von Material erschöpft... das Ideal der Baukunst selbst'. Ibid.

44 Carl Boetticher, Die Tektonik der Hellenen, 2 vols, Potsdam 1844–52. On Boetticher cf. esp. Eva Börsch-Supan, Berliner Baumeister nach Schinkel 1840–1880, Munich 1977, pp. 556ff.

45 Carl Boetticher, 'Das Prinzp der Hellenischen und germanischen Bauweise hinsichtlich der Übertragung in die Bauweise unserer Tage', Allgemeine Bauzeitung 11, 1846, pp. 111–25 (quotation p. 123).

46 Ben David, 'Ueber griechische und gothische Baukunst', in: Die Horen, vol. III, 8. Stück, 1795, pp. 87–102.

47 'Ich weiß nicht, ob dieses so ganz richtig ist. Bequemlichkeit des Gebäudes scheint mehr die Brauchbarkeit als die Schönheit desselben zu betreffen: ein Bauernhaus kann sehr bequem eingerichtet seyn, ohne sich es je beykommen zu lassen, auf Schönheit Ansprüche zu machen.' David (1795), p. 89.

48 David (1795), pp. 101f.

49 L. Bergmann, Die Schule der Baukunst. Handbuch, 2 vols, Leipzig 1853; id., Zehn Tafeln Säulen-Ordnungen nebst Construktion der architectonischen Glieder, Leipzig n.d. (1853).

50 Marlies Lammert, David Gilly. Ein Baumeister des deutschen Klassizismus, Berlin 1964 (facs. repr. Berlin 1982), pp. 22ff.

51 David Gilly, Handbuch der Land-BauKunst vorzüglich in Rüksicht auf die Construction der Wohn- und Wirtschaftsgebäude für angehende Cameral-Baumeister und Oeconomen, parts I and II, Berlin 1797–98; Brunswick ²1800; part III, Halle 1811; ⁵1831; Leipzig and Halle ⁶1836.

52 Sammlung nützlicher Aufsätze und Nachrichten, die Baukunst betreffend. Für angehende Baumeister und Freunde der Architektur, vols. 1–6, 1797–1806.

53 Cf. Alste Oncken, Friedrich Gilly 1772–1800, Berlin 1935 (²1981); Alfred Rietdorf, Gilly. Wiedergeburt der Architektur, Berlin 1940 (pp. 152ff. for texts by Friedrich Gilly); cat. Friedrich Gilly 1772–1800 und die Privatgesellschaft junger Architekten, Berlin 1984.

54 In: Sammlung nützlicher Aufsätze, vol. III, 1799, part II, pp. 3–12 (Rietdorf, 1940, pp. 170ff.). Friedrich Gilly is not here named as the author of these pieces, unlike the authors of the other contributions.

55 The review is by the director of planning, Eytelwein, who taught statics, hydrostatics, hydraulics, etc. at the Bauakademie (Sammlung nützlicher Aufsätze, vol. III, 1799, vol. II, pp. 28–40: 'Nachricht von der Errichtung der Königlichen Bauakademie zu Berlin').

56 Heinrich Gentz (ed.), Elementar-Zeichenwerk zum Gebrauch der Kunst- und Gewerbe-Schulen der Preußischen Staaten, Berlin 1803–1806. On the authorship of this work cf. Adolph Doebber, Heinrich Gentz, ein Berliner Baumeister um 1800, Berlin 1916, p. 75.

57 Peter Beuth (ed.), Vorbilder für Fabrikanten und Handwerker, Berlin 1821–37; Berlin ²1863; cf. esp. Goerd Peschken, Das architektonische Lehrbuch (Schinkel. Lebenswerk), Munich–Berlin 1979, pp. 41ff.; Barbara Mundt, 'Ein Institut für den technischen Fortschritt fördert den klassizistischen Stil im Kunstgewerbe', in vol. of essay supplementary to cat. Berlin und die Antike, Berlin 1979, pp. 455ff.; cat. Karl Friedrich Schinkel (1980), pp. 258ff.

58 On Weinbrenner cf. esp. Arthur Valdenaire, Friedrich Weinbrenner. Sein Leben und seine Bauten, Karlsruhe 1919, ²1926, ³1976; Stefan Sinos, 'Eintwurfsgrundlagen im Werk Friedrich Weinbrenners', Jahrbuch der Staatlichen Kunstsammlungen Baden-Württemberg 13, 1971, pp. 195–216; cat. Friedrich

Weinbrenner 1766–1826, Karlsruhe 1977, ²1982; Klaus Lankheit, *Friedrich Weinbrenner und der Denkmalskult um 1800*, Basel and Stuttgart 1979.

[59] Friedrich Weinbrenner, *Denkwürdigkeiten aus seinem Leben*, ed. Aloys Schreiber, Heidelberg 1829; ed. Kurt K. Eberlein, Potsdam 1920 (this ed. cited); ed. Arthur von Schneider, Karlsruhe 1958.

[60] Cf. Adolph Doebber, *Heinrich Gentz. Eine Berliner Baumeister um 1800*, Berlin 1916, pp. 18ff.; selections from the italian diary repr. in: *Neue Deutsche Monatsschrift* (ed. Fr. Gentz), vol. III, 1795, pp. 314–45.

[61] '*Mein ernstes Studium der Baukunst in Italien mußte meine Begriffe von der Kunst sehr verändern, und indem ich auf die Grundsätze der alten Architektur einging, wollte ich dieselbe später auch bei Gebäuden in Deutschland zum Maßstabe nehmen.*' Weinbrenner, *Denkwürdigkeiten* (ed. 1920), p. 230.

[62] '*…besonders auf die Verbesserung der deutschen Baukunst durch Bildung junger Architekten und Handwerker zu wirken…*' Ibid., pp. 211, 231.

[63] Friedrich Weinbrenner, *Architektonisches Lehrbuch*, Tübingen 1810–19.

[64] '*Schön ist demnach eine Gestalt, in deren Umrissen sich durchaus eine zweckmäßige Vollendung zeigt. Die Zweckmäßigkeit selbst wird durch den Begriff der Gestalt bestimmt.*' Weinbrenner, *Architektonisches Lehrbuch*, Teil III, Heft 1, 1819, p. 6. Weinbrenner has the footnote: '*Kant: Schönheit sei die Form der Zweckmäßigkeit eines Gegenstandes.*'

[65] '*…vollkommene Übereinstimmung der Form mit dem Zweck der Erfordernisse… harmonische Übereinstimmung der Formen mit dem Material*'. Ibid., Heft 5, pars 3, 5.

[66] '*…eine Bedeutung in sich haben, die mit der Bedeutung des angehörigen Gegenstandes zusammen stimmt und dem Zweck des Bauwerks entspricht.*' Ibid., Heft 2, par 11.

[67] Ibid., Heft 2, par. 18.

[68] Friedrich Weinbrenner, *Ausgeführte und projectirte Gebäude* (instalment work), Karlsruhe 1822–35; ed. of Hefte 1–3 and 7 by Wulf Schirmer, Karlsruhe 1978.

[69] Georg Moller, *Denkmäler der deutschen Baukunst*, 3 vols, Darmstadt 1815–49. On Moller cf. esp. Marie Frölich and Hans-Günther Sperlich, *Georg Moller. Baumeister der Romantik*, Darmstadt 1959, pp. 74ff.;

cat. *Darmstadt in der Zeit des Klassizismus und der Romantik*, Darmstadt 1978, pp. 71ff.

[70] Cf. Frölich-Sperlich (1959), pp. 348ff.

[71] '*Allen denkenden und ihr Vaterland liebenden Baukünstlern ist es daher Pflicht, nach Kräften dahin zu wirken, daß unsere alten, und namentlich die immer seltner werdenden Bauwerke der ersten Perioden durch treue Messungen und deutliche Zeichnungen erhalten und bekannt gemacht werden. Durchdrungen von diesem Gedanken, und erfüllt von dem Wunsche zu retten was noch zu retten ist, habe ich, soviel mir Zeit und Umstände erlaubten, Hand an das Werk gelegt und übergebe diese Blätter als einen Beitrag zu den Materialien der Bildungs-Geschichte Deutschlands.*' Moller (1821), introduction.

[72] He writes explicitly in his foreword to the *Denkmäler* (1815): '*Die Kunst, welche das Straßburger Münster, den Dom zu Cöln und andere Meisterstücke hervorbrachten, ist herrlich und erhaben, aber sie war das Resultat ihrer Zeit… Wir können diese Werke bewundern und nachahmen, aber nicht schaffen; weil die äußeren Verhältnisse, unter welchen jene Kunst entstand, in keiner Hinsicht mehr dieselben sind… Mit der Baukunst der Griechen, welche wir noch täglich anwenden, ist der Fall verschieden. Wie bei der deutschen Baukunst Phantasie und Religion einen vorzüglichen Antheil haben, so scheint die griechische Baukunst als Frucht des klaren Verstandes und eines richtigen Schönheitssinnes. Sie beschränkt sich strenge auf das Nothwendigste, dem sie die schönsten Formen zu geben sucht, und deswegen wird diese Kunst nie aufhören, anwendbar zu seyn.*'

[73] On this problem cf. esp. Paul Frankl, *The Gothic, Literary Sources and Interpretations through Eight Centuries*, Princeton 1960; W. D. Robson-Scott, *The Literary Background of the Gothic Revival in Germany*, Oxford 1965; Georg Germann, *Gothic Revival in Europe and Britain: Sources, Influences and Ideas*, London 1972; Christian Baur, *Neugotik*, Munich 1981.

[74] Georg Moller, *Bemerkungen über die aufgefundenen Originalzeichnungen des Domes zu Köln*, Darmstadt 1818 (Leipzig–Darmstadt ²1837). For an account of this discovery, cf. Frölich-Sperlich (1959), pp. 5ff.

[75] Sulpiz Boisserée, *Ansichten, Risse und ein-*

zelne *Theile des Domes von Köln...*, Stuttgart 1821; *Geschichte und Beschreibung des Domes von Köln...*, Stuttgart 1823 (Munich ²1842); facs. repr. of 1821 and 1842 eds, Cologne 1979. On Boisserée cf. esp. Mathilde Boisserée (ed.), *Sulpiz Boisserée*, 2 vols, Stuttgart 1862 (Göttingen 1970); Eduard Firmenich-Richartz, *Die Brüder Boisserée*, vol. I (no further vols), Jena 1916.

⁷⁶ Cf. esp. the vol. of essays accompanying the exhib. *Der Kölner Dom im Jahrhundert seiner Vollendung*, Cologne 1980.

⁷⁷ Friedrich Schlegel, 'Briefe auf einer Reise durch die Niederlande, Rheingegenden, die Schweiz und einen Teil von Frankreich', in: *Poetisches Tagebuch für das Jahr 1806*, ed. Friedrich Schlegel, Berlin 1806, pp. 257–390; in critical ed. of the works of Friedrich Schlegel, vol. IV, section 1, ed. Hans Eichner: 'Ansichten und Ideen von der christlichen Kunst', Paderborn–Munich–Vienna 1959, pp. 153–204.

⁷⁸ '...*für die altchristliche und romantische Bauart des Mittelalters, von Theoderich bis auf die moderne Zeit'.* Schlegel (1806), ed. 1959, pp. 161, 180.

⁷⁹ '...*erfüllt der Blick in die Höhe des Chorgewölbes jede Brust mit Bewunderung... die Schönheit der Verhältnisse, die Einfalt, das Ebenmaß bei der Zierlichkeit, die Leichtigkeit bei der Größe...'* Schlegel (1806), ed. 1959, p. 177.

⁸⁰ Carl Friedrich von Rumohr, 'Fragmente einer Geschichte der Baukunst im Mittelalter', in: Friedrich Schlegel (ed.), *Deutsches Museum*, vol. III, Vienna 1813, pp. 224–46, 361–85, 468–502.

⁸¹ On Schinkel cf. esp. the volumes of the *Lebenswerk* that have appeared since 1939. The most important monographs: August Grisebach, *Carl Friedrich Schinkel, Architekt, Städtebauer, Maler*, Leipzig 1924 (new ed., Munich–Zürich 1981); Paul Ortwin Rave, *Karl Friedrich Schinkel*, Munich 1953 (ed. Eva Börsch–Supan, Munich 1981); Hermann G. Pundt, *Schinkel's Berlin. A Study in Environmental Planning*, Cambridge, Mass. 1972; Erik Forssman, *Karl Friedrich Schinkel. Bauwerke und Baugedanken*, Munich–Zürich 1981. The most important exhibition catalogues: *Karl Friedrich Schinkel 1781–1841*, Berlin (East) 1980; *Karl Friedrich Schinkel. Architektur, Malerei, Kunstgewerbe*, Berlin (West) 1981;

Zeitschrift des Deutschen Vereins für Kunstwissenschaft, vol. XXXV, 1981 (Schinkel anniversary issue).

⁸² Alfred von Wolzogen (ed.), *Aus Schinkel's Nachlaß. Reisetagebücher, Briefe und Aphorismen*, 4 vols, Berlin 1862–64 (facs. repr., Mittenwald 1981). Friedrich Schinkel, *Reise nach England, Schottland und Paris*, ed. Karl Gottfried Riemann, Berlin and Munich 1986; id., *Die Reise nach Frankreich und England im Jahre 1826*, ed. Reinhard Wegner, Munich-Berlin 1990.

⁸³ Goerd Peschken, *Das Architektonische Lehrbuch (Karl Friedrich Schinkel. Lebenswerk)*, Munich–Berlin 1979.

⁸⁴ Karl Friedrich Schinkel, *Reisen nach Italien. Tagebücher, Briefe, Zewichnungen*, ed. Gottfried Riemann, Berlin 1979.

⁸⁵ Cf. Georg Friedrich Koch, 'Karl Friedrich Schinkel und die Architektur des Mittelalters. Die Studien auf der ersten Italienreise und ihre Auswirkungen', *Zeitschrift für Kunstgeschichte 1966*, pp. 177–222.

⁸⁶ Adolph Doebber, *Heinrich Gentz. Ein Berliner Baumeister um 1800*, Berlin 1916 (pp. 18ff. 'Teile aus dem Reisetagebuch'); Heinrich Gentz, 'Briefe über Sizilien', *Neue Deutsche Monatsschrift*, ed. Friedr. Gentz, vol. III, Berlin 1795, pp. 314–45.

⁸⁷ Cf. Schinkel, *Reisen nach Italien*, ed. Riemann (1979), pp. 117ff.

⁸⁸ Letter to the publisher Johann Friedrich Unger, in: Schinkel, *Reisen nach Italien*, ed. Riemann (1979), pp. 115ff. Because of Unger's death in 1904 this volume was not published. Schinkel's drawings were used in: Ernst Friedrich Bußler (ed.), *Verzierungen aus dem Alterthume*, 21 Hefte, Potsdam and Berlin 1806ff.

⁸⁹ '*Herr Bianchi führte mich in seinem neuen Kirchenbau umher, wo es manche schöne Konstruktion gab; leicht und sinnreich ist das Kuppelgerüst mit einer weiten innern Öffnung gebaut, in welcher die Materialien in die Höhe gezogen werden. Übrigens hat er sich beim Entwurf immer zwischen antik und modern gehalten, wodurch vieles charakterlos geworden ist.'* Schinkel, *Reisen nach Italien*, ed. Riemann (1979), p. 192.

⁹⁰ For a critical assessment of this classification, cf. Norbert Knopp's review of Peschken's edition of the *Lehrbuch* in: *Kunstchronik 36*, 1983, p. 363.

⁹¹ German ed.: Carl Friedrich Anton von Conta (ed.), *Grundlinien der bürgerlichen*

Baukunst Nach Herrn Durand..., Halle 1806.

92 Schinkel, *Das Architektonische Lehrbuch*, ed. Peschken (1979), pp. 21f.

93 Ibid., p. 18. ill. 14.

94 Louis-Ambroise Dubut, *Architecture Civile*, Paris 1803, pl. III.

95 Schinkel, *Das Architektonische Lehrbuch*, ed. Peschken (1979), pp. 28–30.

96 Ibid., pp. 30ff.

97 '*Die Architectur ist die Fortsetzung der Natur in ihrer constructiven Thätigkeit.*' Ibid., p. 35.

98 '*Das Antike wirkt in seiner größeren Kunstfertigkeit in den Materiellen Massen, das Gothische durch den Geist. Daher ist es kühn mit wenig materieller Masse viel bewirkt. Das Antike ist Eitel, Prunkvoll, weil die Verzierung daran ein Zufälliges ist, es ist das reine Verstandeswerk ausgeziert daher das phisische Leben mehr vorwiegend. Das Gothische verschmäht den bedeutungslosen Prunk, alles in ihm geht aus der einen Idee hervor und deßhalb hat es den Character der Nothwendigkeit des Ernstes der Würde und Erhebung...*' Ibid., p. 36.

99 Cf. esp. Georg Friedrich Koch, 'Schinkels architektonische Entwürfe im gotischen Stil 1810–1815', *Zeitschrift für Kunstgeschichte* 1969, pp. 262–316.

100 On Goethe's relationship with Schinkel cf. Peschken (1979), pp. 39, 72.

101 Schinkel, *Das Architektonische Lehrbuch*, ed. Peschken (1979), p. 45.

102 '*In der Mittelalter Spitzbogen Baukunst ist das Verhältnis als ein Werdendes betrachtet es entsteht noch vor uns. Im Antiken Bau ist es als ein bestehendes in Vernunftgesetzen Haltbares Ausdauerndes hingestellt und wirkt so mit wohlthuender Ruhe.*' Ibid., p. 45.

103 '*Der Spitzbogen kann etwas Gebrauchsfähiges haben aber deshalb ist er noch nicht schön. Er kann zum Nützlichen verwendet werden u deshalb mag er bei Maschinen pp Anwendung finden...*' Ibid., p. 71.

104 '*Ein gebrauchsfähiges Nützliches Zweckmäßiges schön zu machen ist Aufgabe der Architectur.*' ...'*Von der Konstruktion des Bauwerkes muß alles Wesentliche sichtbar bleiben. Man schneidet sich die Gedankenreihe ab, sobald man wesentliche Theile der Konstruction verdeckt; das überdeckende Mittel führt sogleich auf Lüge...*' Ibid., p. 58.

105 '*... wenn jeder Theil eines Bauwerkes frei u ungebunden nach den allgemeinen Gesetzen der Statik wirkt (oder zu wirken scheint).*' Ibid.

106 Cf. Grötzebach, *Der Wandel der Kriterien bei der Wertung des Zusammenhanges von Konstruktion und Form in den letzten 100 Jahren*, diss. TU Berlin, Berlin 1965, pp. 36f.

107 Schinkel, *Das Architektonische Lehrbuch*, ed. Peschken (1979), pp. 59ff., illus. 35ff.

108 '*Europäische Baukunst gleichbedeutend mit Griechischer Baukunst in ihrer Fortsetzung...*' Ibid., p. 114.

109 '*... durch Läuterung im griechischen Geiste uns zu fortbestehender forthin anwendbarer Kunst werden.*' Ibid.

110 '*Wer demnach richtig construirt, bauet eben dadurch griechisch.*' Aloys Hirt, *Die Baukunst nach den Grundsätzen der Alten*, Berlin 1809, p. 38.

111 '*Für den Künstler giebt es nur eine Periode der Offenbarung die der Griechen. – Griechisch bauen ist recht bauen und aus diesem Gesichtspunkt sind die besten Erscheinungen des Mittelalters griechisch zu nennen*'. Schinkel, *Das Architektonische Lehrbuch*, ed. Peschken (1979), p. 148.

112 Ibid., p. 117.

113 '*Jede Hauptzeit hat ihren Styl hinterlassen in der Baukunst – warum wollen wir nicht versuchen ob sich nicht auch für die unsrige ein Styl auffinden läßt?*' Ibid., p. 146.

114 '*Styl in der Architektur wird gewonnen wenn die Construction eines ganzen Bauwerks: 1) auf die zweckmäßigste u schönste Art aus einem einzigen Material sichtbar characterisiert wird, 2) wenn die Construction aus mehreren Arten von Material, Stein, Holz, Eisen, Backsteine, jedes auf die ihm eigenthümliche Art sichtbar characterisiert wird...*' Ibid., p. 117.

115 '*Warum sollen wir immer nur nach dem Styl einer anderen Zeit bauen? – Ist das ein Verdienst die Reinheit jedes Styls aufzufassen – So ist es noch ein größeres einen reinen Styl im allgemeinen zu erdenken, der dem Besten was in jedem andern geleistet ist nicht widerspricht.*' Ibid., p. 146. On this subject, cf. Norbert Knopp, 'Schinkels Idee einer Stilsynthese', in: Werner Hager and Norbert Knopp (eds), *Beiträge zum Problem des Stilpluralismus*, Munich 1977, pp. 245–54.

116 '*Die Symetrie ist ohne Zweifel durch die*

Faulheit und durch die Eitelkeit entstanden.'
Ibid., p. 119.

[117] *'Hinlängliches Gewicht auf der Säule, darnach Stärke des Metalls. Feuersichere Überdeckung. Säulenwirkung. Decke ohne Seitenschub'.* Ibid., p. 124, illus. 167. Peschken dates this 1820; in my opinion 1830 is more likely.

[118] Cf. cat. *Karl Friedrich Schinkel* (1980), cat. Nr. 640 (col. pl.), Karl Friedrich Schinkel, *Werke der höheren Baukunst. Für die Ausführung erfunden und dargestellt. 1: Entwurf zu einem Königspalast auf der Akropolis zu Athen*, Potsdam 1840–42.

[119] Cf. esp. Ludwig Dehio, *Friedrich Wilhelm IV. von Preußen. Ein Baukünstler der Romantik*, Munich–Berlin 1961.

[120] *'...weil daran die meisten Aufgaben der neueren Zeit für veredelte Architektur vorkommen.'* Schinkel, *Das Architektonische Lehrbuch*, ed. Peschken (1979), p. 148.

[121] *'...höheren Einwirkungen von Geschichtlichen und artistischen poetischen Zwecken...Sehr bald gerieth ich in den Fehler der rein radicalen Abstraction, wo ich die ganze Conception für ein bestimmtes Werk der Baukunst aus seinem nächsten trivialen Zweck allein und aus der Konstruction entwikkelte, in diesem Falle entstand etwas Trockenes, Starres das der Freiheit ermangelte und zwei wesentliche Elemente: das Historische und das Poetische ganz ausschloß.'* Ibid., p. 150.

[122] *'...anschaulich, daß ich auf dem Punct in der Baukunst angekommen sei wo das eigentlich artistische Element seinen Platz in dieser Kunst einnähme, die in allem übrigen ein wissnschafliches Handwerk sei und bleibe; daß auf diesem Punkte, wie überall in der schönen Kunst, das Wesen einer wirklichen Lehre schwer seyn müsse und sich am Ende auf die Bildung des Gefühls reducire.'* Ibid.

[123] Karl Friedrich Schinkel, *Sammlung architektonischer Entwürfe enthaltend theils Werke welche ausgeführt sind, theils Gegenstände deren Ausführung beabsichtigt wurde*, 28 Hefte, Berlin 1819–40; Potsdam 1841–43; 1843–47; 1852; 1857–58; 1866; (facs. repr. Berlin 1973, 1980).

[124] For this phrase cf. Fritz Stahl, *Schinkel*, Berlin 1912, p. 3.

[125] Cf. Peschken's attempt to characterise one group of Schinkel's buildings as *'faschistoid'*: Goerd Peschken, 'Klassik ohne Maß.

Eine Episode in Schinkels Klassizismus', in: *Aufsatzband 'Berlin und die Antike'* (1979), pp. 495–507.

[126] Oswald Matthias Ungers, 'Fünf Lehren aus Schinkels Werk', in: cat. *Karl Friedrich Schinkel. Werke und Wirkungen* (1981), pp. 245–49.

[127] Giorgio Grassi, *Schinkel als Meister*, Hanover 1983.

[128] Friedrich Wilhelm Joseph von Schelling, *Werke*, ed. Manfred Schröter, 3rd supplementary vol., Munich 1959, pp. 223ff.; on Schelling's philosophy of art cf. Dieter Jähnig, *Schelling. Die Kunst in der Philosophie*, 2 vols, Pfullingen 1966–69.

[129] Cf. Oskar Walzel, *Deutsche Romantik.* vol. I: *Welt- und Kunstanschauung*, Leipzig and Berlin ⁴1918, pp. 39ff.

[130] *'...dennoch sind Halbsäulen schlechthin widerlich, weil dadurch zweierlei entgegengesetzte Zwecke ohne innere Notwendigkeit nebeneinander stehen und sich miteinander vermischen.'* Georg Wilhelm Friedrich Hegel, *Vorlesungen über die Ästhetik*, III. 1. 2, 2b.

[131] *'...das eigentümlich Zweckmäßige für den christlichen Kultus sowie das Zusammenstimmen der architektonischen Gestaltung mit dem inneren Geist des Christentums.'* Ibid., III. 1.3.

[132] Friedrich Theodor Vischer, *Ästhetik oder Wissenschaft des Schönen* (1846–1858), 6 vols, Munich 1922–23 (facs. repr. Hildesheim–New York 1975). On architecture: part III (ed. 1922), pp. 206–395.

[133] Arthur Schopenhauer, *Die Welt als Wille und Vorstellung*, Leipzig 1819 (²1844; ³1859); vol. I, par. 43.

[134] Schopenhauer (1844), vol. II, *Ergänzungen zum dritten Buch*, ch. 35 (from which the following passages are cited):
'In der Säulenreihe allein ist die Sonderung vollständig, indem hier das Gebälk als reine Last, die Säule als reine Stütze auftritt.'
'Weil nun also aus dem wohlverstandenen und konsequent durchgeführten Begriff der reichlich angemessenen Stütze zu einer gegebenen Last alle Gesetze der Säulenordnung, mithin auch die Form und Proportion der Säule, in allen ihren Teilen und Dimensionen bis ins einzelne herab folgt, also insofern a priori bestimmt ist, so erhellt die Verkehrtheit des so oft wiederholten Gedankens, daß Baumstämme oder gar (was leider selbst Vitruvius, IV, 1, vorträgt) die mensch-

*liche Gestalt das Vorbild der Säule gewesen
sei.'*

*'Vielmehr müssen die Werke der Architek-
tur, um ästhetisch zu wirken, durchaus eine
beträchtliche Größe haben, ja sie können nie
zu groß, aber leicht zu klein sein. Sogar steht,
ceteris paribus, die ästhetische Wirkung im
geraden Verhältnis der Größe der Gebäude,
weil nur große Massen die Wirksamkeit der
Schwerkraft in hohem Grad augenfällig und
eindringlich machen.'*

*'... lauter regelmäßigen Figuren aus ger-
aden Linien oder gesetzmäßigen Kurven,
imgleichen die aus solchen hervorgehenden
Körper wie Würfel, Parallelopipeden, Zyl-
inder, Kugeln, Pyramiden und Kegel...'*

*'... keiner bedeutenden Bereicherung mehr
fähig ist... kann der moderne Architekt sich
von den Regeln und Vorbildern der Alten
nicht merklich entfernen.'*

*'Wenn ich nun sehe, wie dieses ungläubige
Zeitalter die vom gläubigen Mittelalter
unvollendet gelassenen gotischen Kirchen so
emsig ausbaut, kommt es mir vor, als wolle
man das dahingeschiedene Christentum ein-
balsamieren.'*

135 Cf. Donald Drew Egbert, 'The Idea of
Organic Expression and American Architecture', in: Stow Persons (ed.), *Revolutionary Thought in America*, New Haven 1950,
pp. 336–96, esp. pp. 376ff.

136 On Schnaase and Kugler cf. esp. Wilhelm
Waetzoldt, *Deutsche Kunsthistoriker*, vol.
II, Leipzig 1924, pp. 70ff., 143ff.

137 Carl Schnaase, *Geschichte der bildenden
Künste*, 7 vols, Düsseldorf 1843–64.

138 Franz Kugler, *Handbuch der Kunstgeschichte* (1842), ed. Wilhelm Lübke, 2 vols,
Stuttgart 1872; vol. I, p. V.

139 Schnaase, vol. I (1843), pp. 52ff.

140 *'Die Schönheit aber beruht auch in der
Architektur nicht auf der Zweckmäßigkeit,
sie fängt vielmehr erst da an, wo die Kunst
sich über dieselbe erhebt.'* Ibid., pp. 53f.

141 *'... Gliederung, Organismus zur Entwicklung des Lebensprocesses...'* Franz Kugler,
in: *Kunstblatt* 1844; no. 17ff.; here cited
from Franz Kugler, *Kleine Schriften und
Studien zur Kunstgeschichte*, vol. II,
Stuttgart 1854, pp. 436ff.

142 Carl Schnaase, 'Ueber das Organische in
der Baukunst. Sendschreiben an Professor
Dr. Kugler', *Kunstblatt* no. 58, 18 July 1844,
pp. 245–47.

143 *'Denn wenn man überall nur auf das*

*'Organische', auf die Zweckbestimmung und
den Zusammenhang der Glieder (nicht blos
durch den innern Gedanken, sondern in
äußerer Erscheinung) dringt, und in conse-
quenter Entwicklung dieser Ansicht gegen
das Ornament immer strenger wird, so wird
man zuletzt von der dürftigen Auffassung
der Architektur unter dem Gesichtspunkte
der Zweckmäßigkeit nicht gar weit entfernt
sein.'* Schnaase (1844), p. 247.

144 *'In der Praxis wird man immer mehr in
eine Monotonie gerathen, welche nicht wagt,
sich von dem angenommen Typus des Organischen zu entfernen, in der Geschichte immer
spröder gegen die mannigfaltigen individuellen Gestaltungen vieler Völker werden.'*
Ibid., p. 247.

145 Kugler (1842), ed. Lübke, vol. I (1872), p. 1.

146 Franz Kugler, *Geschichte der Baukunst*,
Stuttgart 1856ff.

147 On Klenze cf. Oswald Hederer, *Leo von
Klenze. Persönlichkeit und Werk*, Munich
1964 (²1981); exhib. cat. *Leo von Klenze als
Maler und Zeichner 1784–1864*, Munich
1977; Norbert Lieb and Florian Hufnagl,
Leo von Klenze. Gemälde und Zeichnungen,
Munich 1979; exhib. cat. *Ein griechischer
Traum. Leo von Klenze. Der Archäologe*,
Munich 1985.

148 Leo von Klenze, *Der Tempel des olym-
pischen Jupiter von Agrigent*, Stuttgart and
Tübingen ¹1821 (²1827); cf. David Van
Zanten, *The Architectural Polychromy of the
1830s*, (diss., Harvard Univ. 1970), New
York–London 1977, pp. 23ff.

149 MS in MSS department ('Klenzeana'), Bayerische Staatsbibliothek, Munich; cf. the
listing of Klenze's unpublished writings in:
Hederer (²1981), pp. 394ff.

150 For a listing of Klenze's publications, cf.
ibid., p. 147.

151 Leo von Klenze, 'Versuch einer Wiederherstellung des toskanischen Tempels nach
seinen technischen und historischen Analogien', in: *Denkschriften der Königlichen
Akademie der Wissenschaften zu München
für die Jahre 1821 und 1822*, vol. VIII,
Munich 1824, pp. 1–86.

152 Aloys Hirt, 'Über die Toscanische Bauart
nach Vitruv', in: *Sammlung nützlicher Aufsätze und Nachrichten, die Baukunst
betreffend*, vol. III, part I (1799), pp. 1–23;
cf. also August Rode, 'Sendschreiben betreffend die Abhandlung des Herrn Hofrath
Hirt, über die Toskanische Baukunst

nach Vitruv', ibid., vol. III, part 2 (1799), pp. 12–20 and Hirt's reply (pp. 20–27).

[153] '… *Geist antiker Kunst… auch die griechische Architektur an einer gemeinschaftlichen Kette mit den Bauarten aller Zeiten hängt.*' Klenze (1824), p. 8.

[154] Leo von Klenze, *Anweisung zur Architectur des christlichen Cultus*, Munich 1822 (²1834); facs. repr. of 1822 ed. with introduction by Adrian von Buttlar, Nördlingen 1987. Cf. Marina Sczesny, *Leo von Klenzes 'Anweisung zur Architectur des Christlichen Cultus'*, diss. (Munich 1967), Hamburg 1974.

[155] '… *Grundstein zu einem allgemeinen Stützpunkte der schwankenden Ideen*'. Klenze (1822), p. iv.

[156] '… *insofern sie sich nämlich auf einen gewissen Typus und allgemein gültige Regeln zurückführen lassen.*' Ibid.

[157] '… *den allemeinen festen Begriff architektonischer Regel und Form auszubreiten… dem Streben der Zeit eine und wo möglich dieselbe Richtung*'. Ibid., p. ii.

[158] '… *eigentliche Architektur… Dienerin der Religion, des Staatswesens und der Gesellschaft im höheren Sinne des Wortes… ökonomische Baukunst… architektonische Schönheit und Form im höheren Sinne*'. Ibid.

[159] '… *allgemeine architectonische Normen, wenn sie zu sehr ins Einzelne der menschlichen Bedürfnisse eingehen wollen, deren Befriedigung von so vielen Privatrücksichten, Umständen und örtlichen Verhältnissen abhängt selten genügend…*' Ibid., p. iii.

[160] '… *erschütterten Säulen der christlichen Kirche wieder zu festigen, und bei voller Freiheit des Gewissens den Cultus wieder auf sichere Grundlagen herzustellen.*' Ibid.

[161] '… *eine Stufenfolge der Entwicklung zum positiven Christenthume.*' Ibid., p. 2.

[162] '*Vom allgemein gültigen Grundsatze der Architektur… Architektur im eigentlichen Sinne des Wortes… Architektur im ethischen Sinne ist die Kunst, Naturstoffe zu Zwecken der menschlichen Gesellschaft und ihrer Bedürfnisse so zu formen und zu vereinigen, daß die Art, wie die Gesetze der Erhaltung, Stetigkeit und Zweckmäßigkeit bey dieser Vereinigung befolgt werden, ihren Hervorbringungen die möglichste Festigkeit und Dauer, bey dem geringsten Aufwande von Stoffen und Kräften gewährt.*' Ibid., pp. 6f.

[163] '… *aus den Erfordernissen des Gegenstandes, oder der Bestimmung eines Gebäudes, und den Gesetzen der Statik und Oeconomie im höheren Sinne des Wortes entwickelte Charakteristik.*' Ibid.

[164] '… *kein Grund mehr vorhanden, sie* [die griechische Architektur] *nicht als Architektur aller Zeiten und Länder, besonders aber als durchaus wahr, wesentlich und positiv, auch als die Architektur des wahren, wesentlichen und positiven Christenthums anzuerkennen.*' Ibid., p. 7.

[165] '… *im strengen und schönen Sinne der Antike*'. Ibid., p. 21.

[166] Cf. Marina Sczesny (1974), pp. 48ff.; on Bunsen's unpublished programme and its impact on the planning of Berlin Cathedral, cf. Carl Wolfgang Schümann, *Der Berliner Dom im 19. Jahrhundert*, Berlin 1980, pp. 22ff.

[167] J. G. Gutensohn and J. M. Knapp, *Denkmale der christlichen Religion, oder Sammlung der ältesten christlichen Kirchen oder Basiliken Roms vom 4ten bis zum 13ten Jahrhundert*, Tübingen–Stuttgart 1822–27.

[168] Klenze (1822), pp. 11ff.

[169] '*Am Aeußern haben wir gesucht, die an den Thürmen des Mittelalters so oft, und zwar wegen ihrer Zweckmäßigkeit mit Recht gerühmte Leichtigkeit und Durchsichtigkeit in so weit zu erreichen, als es der klassischen Architektur, welche sich immer vor jedem Zuviel hüthen muß, erlaubt ist.*' Ibid., p. 32 (on pl. XXIV).

[170] In the second edition of the *Anweisung* (1834), p. 13, Klenze sets out to justify the Allerheiligenhofkirche by making it appear that its Byzantine style can promote an architectural regeneration ('*architektonische Palingenesie*'). On Ludwig I's attitude to the Middle Ages, cf. Gottlieb Leinz, 'Ludwig I. von Bayern und die Gotik', *Zeitschrift für Kunstgeschichte* 44, 1981, pp. 399–444.

[171] Leo von Klenze, *Walhalla in artistischer und technischer Beziehung*, Munich 1842.

[172] '*Das Positive architektonischer Unternehmungen muß genau erläutert werden, das Artistische sich selbst erklären und vertreten.*' Klenze (1842), p. 8.

[173] Leo von Klenze, *Sammlung architectonischer Entwürfe welche ausgeführt, oder für die Ausführung entworfen wurden*, Munich 1830ff.; 2nd edition 1850ff. (facs. repr. of 1st edition, ed. Florian Hufnagl, Worms 1983).

[174] Klenze (1824), p. 7.

175 Christian Carl Josias von Bunsen, *Die Basiliken des christlichen Roms nach ihrem Zusammenhange mit Idee und Geschichte der Kirchenbaukunst*, 2 vols, Munich 1842–44.

176 Bunsen (1842), p. vi.

177 *'Es ist ferner in unserer Zeit anerkannt, daß an die wahre Wiederherstellung des klassischen Baustyls, welche im 15ten und 16ten Jahrhundert mit unzureichenden. Mitteln angestellt wurde, im 17ten und 18ten aber entschieden mißglückte, in unserer Zeit nicht gedacht werden kann, so lange Künstler und Denker die Entwicklung jenes Baustyls in der griechisch-römischen Welt nicht rein und vollständig vor sich haben. Und wer sieht nicht, daß die römischen Basiliken die alten Elemente mit achtungswerthem Sinne und Ernste, in einem der bedeutendsten Theile der Baukunst, den neuen Bedürfnissen anzupassen streben? Ja, endlich für ein lebendiges Verständniß der germanischen Baukunst des Mittelalters und für die daran geknüpfte Möglichkeit ihrer fruchtbaren Neubelebung ist eine solche Kenntniß der alten Basiliken anerkanntermaßen von der größten Bedeutung.'* Ibid.

178 *'Wir werden nun, in unserer kosmopolitschen Allgemeinheit und kritisch-eklektischen Griechheit beide vielleicht noch übertreffen. So hätten wir uns also vorerst allen Schmuck der klassischen Baukunst gesichert, und erhielten zugleich in Wahrheit eine christliche Kunst.'* Ibid., p. 7.

179 *'Das Christliche giebt ein überaus ehrwürdiges Ansehen, und verspricht entschieden Mode zu werden. Die Vereinigung des Widersprechenden ist aber, nach manchen Zeichen, vielleicht das große Losungswort der Zeit, zum Spotte aller früheren Jahrhunderte. So wäre alles befriedigt; Altes und Neues, Kirchliches und Weltliches wäre vereinigt; der Geist und das Fleisch, Glaube und Wissen versöhnten sich...'* Ibid.

180 *'Nach allem diesem dürfen wir die Basilikenform als die allgemeinste christliche, und, im Abendlande, als die fast ausschließlich gebräuchliche ansehen.'* Ibid., p. 37.

181 Cf. esp. Carl-Wolfgang Schümann, *Der Berliner Dom im 19. Jahrhundert*, Berlin 1980.

182 Heinrich Hübsch, *In Welchem Style sollen wir bauen?*, Karlsruhe 1828 (facs. with afterword by Wulf Schirmer: Karlsruhe 1984). On Hübsch cf. esp. Joachim Göricke,

Die Kirchenbauten des Architekten Heinrich Hübsch, diss., Karlsruhe 1974 (p. 174 for a listing of Hübsch's writings); cf. also Nikolaus Pevsner, *Some Architectural Writers of the Nineteenth Century*, Oxford 1972, pp. 64f.; Dagmar Waskönig, 'Konstruktionen eines zeitgemäßen Stils zu Beginn der Industrialisierung in Deutschland, Historisches Denken in H. Hübschs Theorie des Rundbogenstils (1828)', in: *'Geschichte allein ist zeitgemäß'. Historismus in Deutschland*, Giessen 1978, pp. 93–105; Barry Bergdoll, 'Archaeology vs. History: Heinrich Hübsch's Critique of Neoclassicism and the Beginnings of Historicism in German Architectural Theory', in: *Oxford Art Journal* 5, 1982, H. 2, pp. 3–12; cat. *Heinrich Hübsch 1795–1863. Der große badische Baumeister der Romantik*, Karlsruhe 1983. Unhelpful is Klaus Döhmer, *In welchem Style sollen wir bauen?*, Munich 1976, which merely borrows Hübsch's title. Hübsch's later work *Die Architektur und ihr Verhältnis zur heutigen Malerei und Skulptur* (Stuttgart–Tübingen, 1847), ed. Jürgen Eckhardt and Helmut Geisert, Berlin 1985.

183 Hübsch (1828), p. 8.

184 *'Die heutigen Gestaltungsmomente sind demnach von jenen des griechischen Styls durchaus verschieden, ja geradezu entgegengesetzt. Denn was kann... entgegengesetzter sein, als dort gute Steine, welche sehr viele relative Festigkeit besitzen und durchgängige Horizontal-Überdeckung gestatten – hier gebrechliche Steine, welche nur bei ganz kleinen Spannungen Horizontal-Überdeckung zulassen, wofür indessen das Gewölbe reichlichen Ersatz leistet; dort ganz kleine Bedürfnisse und dabei wenig Anforderung an Geräumigkeit – hier sehr große Bedürfnisse, wobei die möglichste Geräumigkeit verlangt wird; dort äußerlich reichliche Säulenstellungen, keine Fenster und nur ein Stokwerk – hier selten äußere Hallen, sehr viele Fenster und mehrere Stokwerke.'* Ibid., p. 17.

185 *'... die erste große Conventionalitäts-Lüge in der Architektur...'*; Ibid., p. 20.

186 Ibid., p. 28.

187 Ibid., p. 39.

188 *'Um auch die zu Gebot stehende Autorität für den neuen Styl zu vindiciren, so ist seit den letzten Jahrzehnten die mittelalterliche Kunst in ziemlich allgemeinen Credit gekom-*

men... Nun kann aber eine Bauart, welche vorerst schon die Basis – nämlich vorherrschende Gewölb-Construction, mit der mittelalterlichen gemein hat, und ihr also in keinem Falle sehr unähnlich werden wird, nicht leicht häßlich ausfallen.' Ibid., p. 29.

[189] '... in mancher Beziehung in dem Rundbogen-Style derselbe Geist, welcher den griechischen Styl belebt'. Ibid., p. 38.

[190] Ibid., p. 42.

[191] '... Rundbogen Style... ergibt sich aus der Natur der Sache, und wurde nicht durch den Einfluß von Autoritäten oder individueller Vorliebe herbeigeführt.' Ibid., p. 51.

[192] Ibid., pp. 4, 20, 52.

[193] G. Palm, Von welchem Principien soll die Wahl des Baustyls, insbesondere des Kirchenbaustyls geleitet werden?, Hamburg 1845. On Palm cf. Pevsner, Some Architectural Writers (1972), pp. 257f.

[194] '... Wahrheit, Reinheit und charaktervolle organische Gestaltung.' Palm (1845), p. 92.

[195] Cf. esp. August Hahn, 'Der Maximilianstil', in: Heinz Gollwitzer (ed.), 100 Jahr Maximilianeum, Munich 1953, pp. 77–167 (revised in book form: Munich 1982); Gerhard Hojer, 'München–Maximilianstraße und Maximilianstil', in: Ludwig Grote (ed.), Die deutsche Stadt im 19. Jahrhundert, Munich 1974, pp. 33–65); Eberhard Drüeke, Der Maximilianstil. Zum Stilbegriff der Architektur im 19. Jahrhundert, Mittenwald 1981.

[196] '... daß das Streben nach dem Ideal in jeder Zeit sich nach den neu eintretenden Anforderungen modificiren wird.' Alfred von Wolzogen, Aus Schinkel's Nachlaß, vol. III, Berlin 1863, p. 334 (letter c. 1834).

[197] Repr. in: Drüeke (1981), pp. 97ff.; Hahn (ed. 1982), pp. 19ff.

[198] '... Ringen der Gegenwart nach einer nationalen Neugestaltung der Architektur... der Character der Zeit so recht unverkennbar seinen verständlichen Ausdruck...' '... in voller Freiheit der verschiedenen Baustyle und ihrer Ornamentik zur zweckmäßigen Lösung der vorliegenden Aufgabe bedienen, damit die zu erwählende Bauart keinem der bekannten Baustyle ausschließlich und speziell angehöre?. '... das Formenprinzip der altdeutschen sogenannten gothischen Architectur, und beim Ornament die Anwendung deutscher Thier- und Pflanzenform, wo möglich, nicht ganz aus den Augen zu lassen.' Drüeke

(1981), pp. 97f.

[199] '... selbstbewußten Reflexion... Zeit des bewußten, naturnothwendigen Schaffens, durch welches früher die Bauordnungen entstanden...' '... Geist der Zeit... politischen und sozialen Verhältnisse'. '... Character einer zeitgemäßen Architectur... praktische Zweckmäßigkeit, Comfort des Lebens, Einfachheit und Schönheit nach der gegenwärtigen Ausbildung der Technik, verbunden mit dem möglichsten Haushalte in den Mitteln.'
'... eine Verbindung des einfachen und ruhigen Charakters der geradlinigen griechischen Form mit dem in die Höhe strebenden Momente des gothischen Baustyls der Beachtung werth.' '... originelles, schönes, organisches Ganzes'. Ibid., pp. 9ff.

[200] Hahn (1982), pp. 25f.

[201] '... lieblichen Bauweise...' '... der neue Stil verhält sich zum Stil der bayerischen Hochlandshäuser wie der vollendete griechischklassische Stil zu dem des ursprünglichen Holzbaues der altgriechischen Wohnhäuser.' Ibid. (ed. 1982), p. 25.

[202] Drüeke (1981), p. 104.

[203] On Gottfried Semper cf. esp. Leopold D. Ettlinger, Gottfried Semper und die Antike. Beiträge zur Kunstanschauung des deutschen Klassizismus, Halle 1937; Heinz Quitzsch, Die ästhetischen Anschauungen Gottfried Sempers, Berlin 1962 (revised as Gottfried Semper – Praktische Ästhetik und politischer Kampf, Brunswick–Wiesbaden 1981); Martin Fröhlich, Gottfried Semper. Zeichnerischer Nachlaß an der ETH Zürich, Basel–Stuttgart 1974; symposium Gottfried Semper und die Mitte des 19. Jahrhunderts, Basel–Stuttgart 1976; Wolfgang Herrmann, Gottfried Semper im Exil, Basel–Stuttgart 1978; cat. Gottfried Semper 1803–1879. Baumeister zwischen Revolution und Historismus, Dresden 1979 (= Munich 1980); Wolfgang Herrmann, Gottfried Semper. Theoretischer Nachlaß in der ETH Zürich. Katalog und Kommentare, Basel–Boston–Stuttgart 1981; Wolfgang Herrmann, Gottfried Semper. In Search of Architecture, Cambridge, Mass.–London 1984. Cf. the following editions of Semper's writings: Gottfried Semper, Kleine Schriften, ed. Hans and Manfred Semper, Berlin and Stuttgart 1884 (facs. repr. Mittenwald 1979); Gottfried Semper, Wissenschaft, Industrie und Kunst und andere Schriften,

ed. Hans M. Wingler (*Neue Bauhausbücher*), Mainz and Berlin 1966; for the best survey of Semper's writings, cf. cat. (1979), pp. 340f.

[204] Gottfried Keller, 17 November 1857 to Hermann Hettner, cf. Jakob Baechtold, *Gottfried Sempers Leben. Seine Briefe und Tagebücher*, vol. II, Berlin 1894, p. 404.

[205] Owen Jones and Jules Goury, *Plans, Elevations, Sections and Details of the Alhambra*, 3 vols, London 1836–45.

[206] Gottfried Semper, *Vorläufige Bemerkungen über bemalte Architektur und Plastik bei den Alten*, Hamburg-Altona 1834; repr. in: Semper, *Kleine Schriften* (1884), pp. 215–58. Cf. Rudolf Zeitler in: symposium *Gottfried Semper und die Mitte des 19. Jahrhunderts* (1976), pp. 12ff.

[207] '...eine rein antiquarische, gelehrte Abhandlung zu liefern... unmittelbaren Nutzen schaffen'. Semper (1834), ed. 1884, pp. 215f.

[208] '...Bestellung einer Walhalla à la Parthenon, einer Basilika à la Monreale, eines Boudoir à la Pompeji, eines Palastes à la Pitti'. Ibid., p. 217.

[209] '*Mächtige Kunstbeschützer* [können] *ein Babylon, ein Persepolis, ein Palmyra aus der Sandwüste erheben, wo regelmäßige Straßen, meilenweite Plätze, prunkhafte Hallen und Paläste in trauriger Leere auf die Bevölkerung harren...*' Ibid.

[210] '...*Einklang mit dem Zustande der menschlichen Gesellschaft... die höheren geistigen Gesetze des Staatsorganismus*'. Ibid., p. 221f.

[211] '*Es spreche das Material für sich und trete auf, unverhüllt, in der Gestalt, in den Verhältnissen, die als die zweckmäßigsten für dasselbe durch Erfahrungen und Wissenschaften erprobt sind. Backstein erscheine als Backstein, Holz als Holz, Eisen als Eisen, ein jedes nach den ihm eigenen Gesetzen der Statik*.' Ibid., p. 219.

[212] Ibid., p. 226.

[213] '...*monochrome Neuertum... Bastardgeburten des modernen Fracks mit der Antike*.' Ibid., p. 223.

[214] '...*die Monumente sind durch Barbarei monochrom geworden*'. Ibid., p. 236.

[215] '...*daß die gemalten Verzierungen an griechischen Monumenten mit den plastisch auf ihnen dargestellten und überhaupt mit dem Ganzen im höchsten, vollkommensten Einklang des Charakters und der Ausführung stehen*.' Ibid., p. 235. Cf. Semper's coloured

reconstruction of a corner of a pediment of the Parthenon: Fröhlich (1974), p. 215.

[216] '*Farben sind minder schreiend als das blendende Weiß unserer Stuckwände... Sind unsere Wiesen, unser Wälder, unsere Blumen grau und weiß? Sind sie nicht viel bunter als im Süden?*' Semper (1834, ed. 1884), p. 253.

[217] Franz Kugler, *Über die Polychromie der griechischen Architektur und Sculptur und ihre Grenzen*, Berlin 1835; repr. in: Kugler, *Kleine Schriften und Studien zur Kunstgeschichte*, part I, Stuttgart 1853, pp. 265–327.

[218] '*Im Allgemeinen leitet uns hierbei der oben dargelegte Grundsatz: daß, wenn nicht durch andere, so doch bestimmt die aus edlem weissem Marmor aufgeführten Gebäude der Blüthezeit Griechenlands (d. h. eben die Mehrzahl der attischen) in ihren Haupttheilen den Stein in seiner eigenthümlichen Farbe gezeigt haben; daß also die Bemalung nur auf untergeordnete Details zu beziehen ist*.' Kugler (1835), ed. 1853, p. 302.

[219] Gottfried Semper, *Der Stil in den technischen und tektonischen Künsten*, vol. I, Frankfurt 1860, p. 514, n. 1.

[220] Gottfried Semper, *Die vier Elemente der Baukunst. Ein Beitrag zur vergleichenden Baukunde*, Brunswick 1851 (facs. repr. in: Quitzsch (1981), appendix).

[221] '*Griechische Polychromie steht nicht mehr da als isolirte Erscheinung, sie ist kein Hirngespinst mehr, sondern entspricht dem Gefühle der Masse, dem allgemein angeregten Verlangen nach Farbe in der Kunst, und mitten in der neuen Bewegung macht sie sich rechtzeitig durch gewichtige Stimmen geltend, die sich dafür erheben*.' Semper (1851), p. 12.

[222] '*Bei den Griechen konnte diese Harmonie nur durch ein freies und doch gebundenes Zusammenwirken gleichberechtigter Elemente geschehen, durch eine Demokratie in den Künsten*.' Ibid., p. 8.

[223] '...*zierlich verblasenen Marzipanstyl... blutrothen Fleischstyl*'. Ibid., p. 129.

[224] '...*die Construction als das Wesen der Baukunst erkannte und letztere somit in eiserne Fesseln schmiedete... die Baukunst gleich der Natur, ihrer großen Lehrerin, zwar ihrem Stoff nach den durch sie bedungenen Gesetzen wählen und verwenden, aber Form und Ausdruck ihrer Gebilde nicht vom ihm, sondern von den Ideen abhängig machen, welche in ihnen wohnen*.' Ibid., p. 54.

[225] '...*Urzuständen der menschlichen Gesell-*

schaft…Erdaufwurf…gleichsam letzte Schlammschöpfung'. Ibid., p. 55.

226 '…Bekleidungswesen der ältesten Baukunst'. pp. 57ff.

227 Cf. Herrmann (1981), pp. 26ff. It is possible that Semper had Boetticher's *Tektonik der Hellenen* to hand before 1852, the year of issue at the British Museum established by Herrmann.

228 Herrmann (1981), pp. 27, 54.

229 Semper (1851), p. 93.

230 '…Malerei des Teppichs.' Ibid., p. 100.

231 '…endlich muß bei der künstlerischen Behandlung des Anstriches sichtbarer constructiver Theile, z.B. eiserner Säulen, eiserner Dachconstructionen oder dergleichen von Holz, auf die diesen Stoffen eigenthümlichen statischen Verhältnisse Rücksicht genommen werden. So würde ich z.b. bei Eisenwerk, das, je dünner, desto vollkommener erscheint, niemals helle Farben anwenden, sondern Schwarz, Bronzefarbe und viele Vergoldung.' Ibid., p. 101.

232 '…eigenthümliche, culturgeschichtlich poetische Interesse…urthümliche Begründung.' Franz Kugler, 'Antike Polychromie. Nachträge 1851', in: Kugler, *Kleine Schriften* vol. I (1853), p. 354.

233 In Semper, *Kleine Schriften* (1884), pp. 395ff.

234 '…die fossilen Gehäuse ausgestorbener Gesellschaftsorganismen.' Ibid., p. 401.

235 Gottfried Semper, 'Wissenschaft, Industrie und Kunst. Vorschläge zur Anregung nationalen Kunstgefühles', Brunswick 1852 (repr. in: Semper, ed. Wingler (1966), pp. 27–71). Semper took the distinction between 'technical' and 'phonetic' qualities (p. 41) from James Fergusson's 'Historical Enquiry into the True Principles…' (1849); cf. Dobai, vol. III (1977), p. 460. On Semper's assessment of Fergusson cf. Herrmann (1981), p. 27.

236 In: Semper, *Kleine Schriften* (1884), pp. 259ff.

237 Semper (1884), pp. 267ff.

238 '…die Grenzen zu beobachten, welche die dem Gegenstande zu Grunde liegende Idee bedingt.; Ibid., p. 280.

239 '…ursprüngliche von dem Bedürfnis vorgeschriebene Formen'. Ibid., p. 282.

240 Ibid., p. 284.

241 '…ihren architektonischen Bildungen und ihren industriellen Erzeugnissen organisches Leben zu verleihen. Die griechischen Tempel und Monumente, sie sind gewachsen…' Ibid., p. 278.

242 Gottfried Semper, *Der Stil in den technischen und tektonischen Künsten oder praktische Aesthetik. Ein Handbuch für Techniker, Künstler und Kunstfreunde*, 2 vols, Frankfurt 1860, Munich 1863 (facs. repr. with introduction by Adrian von Buttlar, Mittenwald 1977); Munich ²1878–79. For an account of the writing of this work, cf. Herrmann (1978), pp. 95ff.

243 A draft opening to a third volume is published in: Herrmann (1981), pp. 250ff.

244 'Die Praxis und die industrielle Spekulation, als Mittlerinnen zwischen der Konsumtion und der Erfindung, erhalten diese zu beliebiger Verwerthung ausgeliefert, ohne daß durch tausendjährigen Volksgebrauch sich vorher ein eigener Stil für sie ausbilden konnte.' Semper (1860), p. xii.

245 'Die Form, die zur Erscheinung gewordene Idee, darf dem Stoffe aus dem sie gemacht ist nicht widersprechen, allein es ist nicht absolut nothwendig daß der Stoff als solcher zu der Kunsterscheinung als Faktor hinzutrete.' Ibid., p. xv.

246 'Eben so war der gothische Bau die lapidarische Uebertragung der scholastischen Philosophie des 12. und 13. Jahrhunderts.' Ibid., p. xix.

247 Gottfried Semper, 'Bemerkungen zu des M. Vitruvius Pollio zehn Büchern der Baukunst' (1856), in: Semper, *Kleine Schriften* (1884), pp. 191ff.

248 Semper (1860), pp. xxivff.

249 Ibid., p. xlii.

250 Ibid., p. xliii.

251 '…eurhythmische Abgeschlossenheit der Kristalle und anderer vollkommen regelmäßiger Formen der Natur…als Symbole des Alls das nichts außer sich kennt'. Ibid., pp. 217ff.

252 '…Emanzipation der Form von dem Stofflichen und dem nackten Bedürfnis, ist die Tendenz des neuen Stils.' Ibid., p. 445.

253 '…sich nirgend eine neue welthistorische mit Kraft und Bewußtsein verfolgte Idee kundgibt…das geeignete architektonische Kleid zu verleihen.' Semper, 'Über Baustile' (1869), in: Semper, *Kleine Schriften* (1884), p. 426.

254 '…welthistorischen Idee: Bis es dahin kommt, muß man sich, so gut es gehen will, in das Alte schicken.' Ibid.

255 'Die Eisenzimmerei ward als solche niemals

monumental. *Die gefährliche Idee, aus der Eisenkonstruktion, angewandt auf Monumentalbau, müsse für uns ein neuer Baustil hervorgehen, hat schon manchen talentvollen, aber der hohen Kunst entfremdeten Architekten auf Abwege geführt. Wohl kann und muß sogar ihre Anwendung auf Monumentalbau auf den Stil der Baukunst einwirken, aber nicht... durch ihr sichtbares Hervortreten.'* Semper (1863), p. 550. On Semper's view of iron as a building material, cf. Herrmann (1981), pp. 61ff.

256 '*... Versuche in eiserner Gotik... den sichtbaren einfachen eisernen Dachstuhl des Eisenbahn-Ingenieurs bei Einsteighallen und sonstigen Schuppen als Wahrzeichen ihres Provisoriums'.* Semper (1863), p. 551.

257 Semper, 'Über Wintergärten' (1849), in: Semper, *Kleine Schriften* (1884), pp. 484ff.

258 '*... mit diesem gleichsam unsichtbaren Stoffe nicht einlassen, wenn es sich um Massenwirkungen und nicht bloß um leichtes Beiwerk handelt.'* Semper (1884), p. 485.

259 Alois Riegl, *Stilfragen*, Berlin 1893, pp. viff.; id., *Spätrömische Kunstindustrie* (1901), Vienna ²1927, pp. 8f.

260 Cf. *Bibliographie zur Architektur im 19. Jahrhundert. Die Aufsätze in den deutschsprachigen Architekturzeitschriften 1789–1918* by Stephan Waetzoldt (edited by Verena Haas), 8 vols, Nendeln 1977.

261 On Reichensperger cf. esp. Ludwig Pastor, *August Reichensperger 1808–1895*, 2 vols, Freiburg 1899; Johann Wilhelm Koch, 'August Reichenspergers künstlerische Bestrebungen', in: *Der Kölner Dom. Festschrift zur Siebenhundertjahrfeier 1248–1948*, Cologne 1948, pp. 268–96; Georg Germann, *Neugotik*, Stuttgart 1974, pp. 93ff., 139ff.

262 August Reichensperger, *Die christlich-germanische Baukunst und ihr Verhältniß zur Gegenwart*, Trier 1845 (²1852); id., *Fingerzeige auf dem Gebiete der kirchlichen Kunst*, Leipzig 1854; id., *Vermischte Schriften*, Leipzig 1856.

263 '*... wahrhafte Restauration* [in einem] *lebenvollen Organismus... den kunstbildenden Trieb im Menchen unter ihre Obhut genommen.'* Reichensperger (1854), pp. 2, 10.

264 '*... die Gesetze und Traditionen der großen mittelalterlichen Kunst wieder zu unserem Bewußtsein zu bringen und zu verkörpern, indem man das 13. Jahrhundert als Ausgangspunkt nimmt.'* Ibid., p. 26.

265 '*... organischen Zusammenhang... naturgemäßen Entwicklung... Leben des Volkes...'* Ibid., pp. 2ff.

266 '*... Spitzbogenstyle spricht die kirchliche Kunst dem Principe nach ihr letztes Wort... Das dreizehnte Jahrhundert konnte in Bezug auf die Architektur das εύρηκα in die Welt hineinrufen, und hat dies denn auch wirklich gethan.'* Ibid., pp. 22ff.

267 '*... Logik und Grammatik des gothischen Stils: Jeder Aufgabe in jedwedem Materiale gewachsen, bietet dieser Styl auch noch den Vortheil relativ größerer Wohlfeilheit dar, zumal wenn er einmal allgemein zu praktischer Geltung gekommen sein wird... Die Richtigkeit und Harmonie der Verhältnisse kosten nichts;... von entscheidendem Gewichte in dieser Hinsicht ist, daß der gothische Styl, seinem Wesen nach, verhältnismäßig am wenigsten Masse zur Einschließung und Überdeckung einer gegebenen Räumlichkeit erfordert.'* Ibid., p. 23.

268 '*... verwerfliche Gußeisen... edlen, ernsten, kerngesunden Styl des dreizehnten Jahrhunderts.'* Ibid., pp. 24, 31.

269 '*Der Mönch und der Werkmeister berathen, wie das Alte zu erhalten und das Neue damit in Einklang zu bringen, wie die wechselseitige Durchdringung von Gottesgelehrsamkeit und Kunst herzustellen sein möchte.'* Ibid., p. 136.

270 '*... Geist... organisches Bildungsgesetz, daß endlich auch die Theorie wieder in das rechte Verhältniß zur Praxis tritt. Auf dem Wege der Speculation und des Eklektizismus wird man nimmer zu wahrhaft lebendigen Bildungen gelangen; man wird stets suchen und niemals finden.'* Ibid., p. 138.

271 '*... daß die bei einem alten Bauwerk fast stets vorhandenen Spuren seines allmählichen Anwachsens, gleichsam seine Jahresringe nicht verwischt, daß die verschiedenen Style, sowie jene Unregelmäßigkeiten und Zufälligkeiten, welche auch dem sonst minder bedeutenden Gebäude einen eigenthümlich-individuellen Reiz verleihen, erhalten bleiben.'* Ibid., p. 32.

272 Friedrich Hoffstadt, *Gothisches A-B-C-Buch, das ist: Grundregeln des gothischen Styls für Künstler und Werkleute*, Frankfurt 1840–63.

273 Hoffstadt, pp. 65ff.

274 '*... in den ewigen und unveränderlichen Gesetzen der Geometrie'.* Ibid., p. vi.

275 '*Da nun den Naturbildungen geometrische*

Bildungsgesetze zu Grunde liegen, und dieselben geometrischen Gesetze auch bei den Schöpfungen des gothischen Styles untergelegt sind, so ist die Verwandtschaft in den Resultaten beider erklärlich.' Ibid., p. ix.

276 '...*Charakter der vaterländischen Vegetation...Vorlegeblätter einer selbständigen Produktion und...vegetabilischen Verzierungen*'. Ibid., pp. 202ff., pls XVII, XVIII.

277 '...*mit besonderer Beziehung auf die Wiederherstellung und Fortbildung des Spitzbogenstyls.*' Ibid., pp. 247ff.

278 On Ungewitter cf. esp. August Reichensperger, *G. G. Ungewitter und sein Wirken als Baumeister*, Leipzig 1866; Jutta Schuchard, *Carl Schäfer 1844–1908. Leben und Werk des Architekten der Neugotik*, Munich 1979, pp. 44ff.

279 Cf. the bibliography in: Jutta Schuchard (1979), p. 325. The most important publications: Georg Gottlob Ungewitter, *Entwürfe zu gothischen Ornamenten, zunächst für Decken und Wände*, Leipzig 1854; id., *Lehrbuch der gothischen Constructionen*, Leipzig 1859–64 ('1875; ed. K. Mohrmann '1901–03); id., *Sammlung mittelalterlicher Ornamentik in geschichtlicher und systematischer Anordnung*, Leipzig 1863–65.

280 On Schäfer's published works, cf. esp. Jutta Schuchard (1979), pp. 316ff. Among them are: Carl Schäfer, *Die Bauhütte. Entwürfe im Stile des Mittelalters, angefertigt von Studirenden unter Leitung von Carl Schäfer*, 3 vols, Berlin 1893–95; id., *Von deutscher Kunst. Gesammelte Aufsätze und nachgelassene Schriften*, Berlin 1910.

281 Cf. Stefan Muthesius, *Das englische Vorbild. Eine Studie zu den deutschen Reformbewegungen in Architektur, Wohnbau und Kunstgewerbe im späten 19. Jahrhundert*, Munich 1974; Georg Germann, *Neugotik*, Stuttgart 1974; Jutta Schuchard (1979), pp. 30ff.

282 On the historical background to this subject, cf. esp. Percy Ernst Schramm, 'Deutschlands Verhältnis zur englischen Kultur nach der Begründung des Neuen Reiches', in: *Schicksalswege deutscher Vergangenheit. Festschrift Siegfried A. Kaehler*, Düsseldorf 1950, pp. 289–319; id., 'Englands Verhältnis zur deutschen Kultur zwischen Reichsgründung und der Jahrhundertwende', in: *Deutschland und Europa. Festschrift Hans Rothfels*, Düsseldorf 1951, pp. 135–75.

283 Hermann Schwabe, *Der Stand der Kunstindustrie in England und der Stand dieser Frage in Deutschland*, Berlin 1866.

284 Robert Dohme, *Das englische Haus. Eine kultur- und baugeschichtliche Studie*, Brunswick 1888.

285 'Zuerst erhebt sich eine industrielle Anlage, es dampfen die Schlote, es schnurren die Räder, an dürftige Arbeiterwohnungen schließen sich allmählich die Häuser der Krämer, der wohlhabenden Händler an, zum Wirthshause gesellt sich die Schule, das Hospital, es bleibt das stattliche Haus des unabhängigen Bürgers nicht aus, es folgt der Palast des reichen Fabrikherrn. Ehe aber eine monumentale Kirche in die Höhe steigt, vergeht gewöhnlich eine lange Zeit...Eine lebendige Architektur muß vorzugsweise den Profanbau im Auge behalten, im Kreise des letzteren sich bewähren, aus diesem das Formleere und Formwidrige verbannen, eine künstlerische Verklärung desselben versuchen.' Anton Springer, 'Die Wege und Ziele der gegenwärtigen Kunst', in: A. Springer, *Bilder aus der neueren Kunstgeschichte*, Bonn 1867, p. 375.

286 'Und hält man dann Umschau, an welchen der vergangenen Stile man sich anlehnen, an welchen anknüpfen soll, so wird die Rücksicht entscheiden, ob sich das Vorbild im Profanbau verwerthen lasse oder nicht. Mannigfache Anzeichen lassen darauf schließen, daß der Renaissancestil uns in dieser Hinsicht am nächsten steht...' Ibid.

287 Cf. esp. Eva Börsch-Supan, *Berliner Baukunst nach Schinkel 1840–1870*, Munich 1977, pp. 185ff.; Mohamed Scharabi, *Einfluß der Pariser Ecole des Beaux-Arts auf die Berliner Architektur in der 2. Hälfte des 19. Jahrhunderts*, diss., Berlin 1968.

288 On Camillo Sitte cf. esp. George R. and C. C. Collins, *Camillo Sitte and the Birth of Modern City Planning*, New York 1955; D. Wieszorek, *Camillo Sitte et les débuts de l'urbanisme moderne*, Paris 1982.

289 Camillo Sitte, *Der Städte-Bau nach seinen künstlerischen Grundsätzen*, Vienna 1889 ('1901 – this ed. cited hereafter, '1909 [repr. of this ed., Brunswick–Wiesbaden 1983]). French ed., *L'art de bâtir les villes*, Geneva–Paris 1902 (1918); English ed., *City Planning According to Artistic Principles*, New York 1965.

290 '...bereits sprichwörtliche Langweiligkeit moderner Stadtanlagen...' Sitte (1901), p. 2.

291 '...in Wahrheit der Mittelpunkt einer bedeutenden Stadt, die Versinnlichung der Weltanschauung eines großen Volkes.' Ibid., p. 11.

192 Ibid., pp. 59ff.

293 Ibid., p. 119.

294 '...künstlerisch vollendete Plätze und Straßen abgerungen werden... Sonntagskleid... zum Stolz... und zur Freude der Bewohner, zur Erweckung des Heimatgefühles, zur steten Heranbildung großer edler Empfindungen bei der heranwachsenden Jugend dienen.' Ibid., p. 98.

295 'Gelungen sind die Bauten, nicht gelungen die Parcellierung. Glücklicherweise ist aber so viel leerer Raum vorhanden, daß die Schäden der letzteren noch behoben werden können.' Ibid., p. 156.

296 'Von der Geschlossenheit eines künstlerischen Eindruckes kann da keine Rede sein. Votivkirche, Universität, Chemisches Laboratorium und die verschiedenen Häuserblöcke stehen da einzeln und haltlos herum ohne jede Gesammtwirkung. Statt sich gegenseitig durch geschickte Aufstellung und auch Zusammenstimmung im Effecte zu heben, spielt jedes Bauwerk gleichsam eine andere Melodie in anderer Tonart. Wenn man die gothische Votivkirche, die im edelsten Renaissance-Styl erbaute Universität und die den verschiedensten Geschmacksrichtungen huldigenden Miethhäuser zugleich überschaut, ist es nicht anders, als ob man eine Fuge con S. Bach, ein großes Finale aus einer Mozart'schen Oper und ein Couplet von Offenbach zu gleicher Zeit anhören sollte. Unerträglich! Geradezu unerträglich!' Ibid., p. 158.

297 '... Style italienischer Hochrenaissance... 1.) die Beseitigung des Stylconflictes; 2.) eine wesentlich gesteigerte Wirkung jedes einzelnen Monumentalbaues; 3.) eine Gruppe charakteristischer Plätze; 4.) die Möglichkeit, eine Menge größter, mittlerer und kleiner Denkmäler hier vereinigt aufzustellen.' Ibid., p. 173.

298 '...Riesendimensionen... unser mathematisch abgezirkeltes modernes Leben, in dem der Mensch förmlich selbst zur Maschine wird.' Ibid., p. 113.

299 E.g. Françoise Choay, The Modern City: Planning in the 19th Century, New York 1969, p. 106.

300 On Otto Wagner cf. Heinz Geretsegger and Max Peintner, Otto Wagner 1841–1918, Salzburg–Vienna 1964 (³1978, ⁴1983); Adri-

ana Giusti Baculo, Otto Wagner. Dall'architettura di stile allo stile utile, Naples 1970; Otto Antonia Graf, Otto Wagner. Das Werk des Architekten, 2 vols, Vienna–Cologne–Graz 1985.

301 Otto Wagner, Moderne Architektur. Seinen Schülern ein Führer auf diesem Kunstgebiete, Vienna 1895 (²1899; ³1902); 4th ed. entitled Die Baukunst unserer Zeit. Dem Baukunstjünger ein Führer auf diesem Kunstgebiete, Vienna 1914 (repr. Vienna 1979). Of the translations, cf. the Italian ed. Giuseppe Samonà: Otto Wagner, Architettura moderna e altri scritti, Bologna 1980.

302 '...Ausdruck des modernen Lebens... ohne das Vorbild in der Natur zu finden... daß in der Baukunst der höchste Ausdruck menschlichen, an das Göttliche streifenden Könnens erblickt werden muß.' Wagner (1914), p. 14.

303 '...um eine Sammlung von Architekturmotiven anzulegen... fast ein Verbrechen Bedürfnisse der modernen Menschheit gründlich einzuüben.' Ibid., p. 27.

304 '...der ganz apodiktische Ausdruck des Schönheitsideals einer bestimmten Zeitperiode.' Ibid., p. 31.

305 'Die Kunst unserer Zeit muß uns moderne, von uns geschaffene Formen bieten, die unserem Können, unserem Tun und Lassen entsprechen.' Ibid., p. 33.

306 'Etwas Unpraktisches kann nicht schön sein.' Ibid., p. 44.

307 'Die Komposition muß also schon ganz deutlich das Ausführungsmaterial und die angewandte Technik erkennen lassen.' Ibid., p. 45.

308 '... Charakteristik und Symbolik des Werkes wie von selbst'. Ibid., p. 46.

309 '...exotische Weise... mit einer Symbolik der Konstruktion beholfen... statt die Konstruktion selbst als die Urzelle der Baukunst zu bezeichnen.' Ibid., p. 61.

310 'Diese Veränderungen sind, abgesehen davon, daß die Form dem Schönheitsideale der jeweiligen Epoche entsprechen mußte, dadurch entstanden, daß die Art der Herstellung, das Material, die Werkzeuge, die verfügbaren Mittel, das Bedürfnis, das Kunstempfinden etc. verschieden waren und ihnen überdies in verschiedenen Gegenden auch verschiedene Zweckerfüllungen zukamen. Es kann daher mit Sicherheit gefolgert werden, daß neue Zwecke und neue Konstruktionen neue Formen gebären müssen.' Ibid., p. 60.

[311] 'Unser demokratisches Sein, in welches die Allgemeinheit mit dem Schrei nach billigen und gesunden Wohnungen und mit der erzwungenen Ökonomie der Lebensweise eingepaßt wird, hat die Uniformität unserer Wohnhäuser zur Folge. Deshalb wird auch diese im künftigen Stadtbilde stark zum Ausdruck kommen... ist die Mehrung der Stockwerke, bei Wohn- und Geschäftshäusern bis zu 7 oder 8 Geschossen, ja bis zum Wolkenkratzer im Stadtzentrum naturgemäß. Die Zahl der Wohnhäuser wird in jeder Großstadt die Anzahl der öffentlichen Bauten weit überwiegen; aus ihrer Zusammenlagerung entstehen daher lange und gleiche Straßeneinfassungsflächen. Die Kunst unserer Zeit hat durch diese Erbreiterung unserer Straßen diese Uniformität zur Monumentalität erhoben... Die Baukunst ist bei der Durchbildung der Façade des modernen Miethauses auf eine glatte, durch viele gleichwertige Fenster unterbrochene Fläche angewiesen, wozu sich das schützende Hauptgesims und allenfalls noch ein krönender Fries und ein Portal etc. gesellen.' Ibid., pp. 77, 87.

[312] 'Auch hat das moderne Auge, wie erwähnt, den kleinen intimen Maßstab verloren, es hat sich an weniger abwechslungsreiche Bilder, an längere gerade Linien, an ausgedehntere Flächen, an größere Massen gewöhnt, weshalb ein stärkeres Maßhalten, eine weniger reiche Silhouettierung solcher Mietobjekte gewiß angezeigt erscheint.' Ibid., p. 87.

[313] '... Wie sollen wir bauen?... Unser Gefühl muß uns aber heute schon sagen, daß die tragende und stützende Linie, die tafelförmige Durchbildung der Fläche, die größte Einfachheit der Konzeption und ein energisches Vortreten von Konstruktion und Material bei der künftigen neuerstehenden Kunstform stark dominieren werden; die moderne Technik und die uns zu Gebote stehenden Mittel bedingen dies. Selbstredend hat der schönheitliche Ausdruck, welchem die Kunst den Werken unserer Zeit geben wird, mit den Anschauungen und der Erscheinung moderner Menschen zu stimmen und die Invidualität des Künstlers zu zeigen.' Ibid., p. 136.

[314] Otto Wagner, Die Großstadt. Eine Studie über diese, Vienna 1911.

[315] Otto Wagner, Einige Skizzen, Projekte und ausgeführte Bauwerke, vol. I, Vienna 1890; vol. II, Vienna 1897; vol. III, Vienna 1906; vol. IV, Vienna 1922; repr. of original 4 vols, Tübingen 1987.

[316] Cf. Otto Antonia Graf, Die vergessene Wagnerschule, Vienna 1969; Marco Pozzetto, La scuola di Wagner, Trieste 1979 (German ed. Die Schule Otto Wagners, Vienna–Munich 1980).

23. England in the nineteenth century

[1] Cf. John Summerson, Architecture in Britain 1530 to 1830 (1953), Harmondsworth [5]1970, p. 497ff. Besides Summerson, the major literature on architecture and architectural theory of the first half of the century is as follows: Howard Colvin, A Biographical Dictionary of British Architects 1600–1840, London 1954 ([2]1978); Henry-Russell Hitchcock, Early Victorian Architecture in Britain, 2 vols, New Haven 1954 (New York [2]1972); James Macaulay, The Gothic Revival 1745–1845, London 1975; J. Mordaunt Crook, The Greek Revival. Neo-Classical Attitudes in British Architecture 1760–1870, London 1972; Johannes Dobai, Die Kunstliteratur des Klassizismus und der Romantik in England, vol. III: 1790–1840, Bern 1977; David B. Brownlee, 'The First High Victorians: British Architectural Theory in the 1840s', Architectura 15, 1985, pp. 33–46.

[2] On Thomas Hope cf. David Watkin, Thomas Hope 1769–1831 and the Neo-Classical Idea, London 1968; Nikolaus Pevsner, Some Architectural Writers of the Nineteenth Century, Oxford 1972, pp. 62ff.; J. Mordaunt Crook (1972); Dobai (1977), pp. 189ff.

[3] Thomas Hope, Observations on the Plans and Elevations designed by James Wyatt, Architect, for Downing College, Cambridge, in a letter to Francis Annesley, esq., M.P., London 1804.

[4] Thomas Hope, Household Furniture and Interior Decoration executed from Designs by Thomas Hope, London 1807 (facs. reprs: London 1937 (without texts); London 1947 (without texts); with introduction by Clifford Musgrave, London 1970; with introduction by David Watkin, New York 1971).

[5] Hope (1807), pl. II with commentary.

[6] Ibid., p. 5.
[7] Ibid., p. 6.
[8] Ibid., p. 7.
[9] Ibid., p. 17.
[10] Ibid., pl. VII with commentary. Partial reconstruction 1972, London, in exhib. *The Age of Neo-classicism.*
[11] Hermann von Pückler-Muskau, *Briefe eines Verstorbenen* (1830), vol. I, Stuttgart ²1836, pp. 170f.
[12] Thomas Hope, *An Historical Essay on Architecture by the late Thomas Hope, illustrated by drawings made by him in Italy and Germany,* 2 vols, London 1835 (⁴1843); French ed.: Paris–Brussels 1839 (²1852); Italian ed. 1840.
[13] Wolfgang Herrmann, *Gottfried Semper. Theoretischer Nachlaß an der ETH Zürich. Katalog und Kommentare,* Basel–Boston– Stuttgart 1981, pp. 27, 54.
[14] Hope (1835), pp. 224ff., 525.
[15] Ibid., p. 561.
[16] Pevsner (1972), pp. 62ff.
[17] On Robert Owen cf. esp. the autobiography: Robert Owen, *The Life of Robert Owen,* 2 vols, London 1857–58 (repr. New York 1967). For an overall view of Owen and related ideas, cf. Sidney Pollard and John Salt (ed.), *Robert Owen. Prophet of the Poor,* London 1971; on the place of Owen in urban utopias, cf. Mechtild Schumpp, *Stadtbau-Utopien und Gesellschaft,* Gütersloh 1972, pp. 52ff.; Franziska Bollerey, *Architekturkonzeption der utopischen Sozialisten,* Munich 1977, pp. 28ff.
[18] Good documentation in: Bollerey (1977) pp. 49ff.
[19] Robert Owen, *A New View of Society,* London 1813, ²1816 (ed. G. D. H. Cole, London 1927; ed. John Saville, Clifton, NJ 1972).
[20] Robert Owen, 'Report to the Committee of the Association for the Relief of the Manufacturing, and Labouring Poor' (March 1817), in: Owen, *The Life,* vol. I A (1858), Appendix C.
[21] Thomas Stedman Whitwell, *Description of an Architectural Model from a Design by Stedman Whitwell Esq. for a Community upon a principle of united interests, as advocated by Robert Owen Esq.,* London 1830; repr. in: Bollerey (1977), pp. 216ff.
[22] Cf. the derivation given by Bollerey (1977), pp. 216ff.
[23] Cf. Arthur Eugene Bestor, *Backwoods Utopias: The Sectarian and Owenite Phases of Communitarian Socialism in America 1663–1829,* London–Philadelphia 1950 (²1970).
[24] For a survey cf. Dobai, vol. III (1977), pp. 402ff.
[25] Peter Nicholson, *An Architectural Dictionary, containing a correct Nomenclature...,* 2 vols, London 1812–19 (new ed. E. Lomax and T. Gunyon entitled *Encyclopaedia of Architecture...,* 2 vols, London 1852; 1857– 62). Peter Nicholson, *The Builder & Workman's New Director...,* London 1824 (²1834). For a bibliography of Nicholson cf. Dobai, vol. III (1977), pp. 466, 586f.
[26] Nicholson (1824), Preface.
[27] Ibid., p. xxxviii.
[28] Joseph Gwilt, *Rudiments of Architecture, Practical and Theoretical,* London 1826 (²1835; ³1839; ⁴1899); *An Encyclopaedia of Architecture, Historical, Theoretical and Practical,* London 1842 (1845, 1854, 1859; ed. Wyatt Papworth: 1867, 1876, 1899); facs. of 1867 ed. with introduction by Michael Mostoller, New York 1982. On Gwilt cf. Dobai, vol. III (1977), pp. 404ff., 466f.; Colvin (ed. 1978), pp. 371f.
[29] Thomas Leverton Donaldson, *Preliminary Discourse on Architecture,* London 1842. On Donaldson cf. esp. Pevsner (1972), pp. 8ff.; Dobai, vol. III (1977), pp. 445f., 632ff., 659f.
[30] Alfred Bartholomew, *Specifications for Practical Architecture, Preceded by an Essay on the Decline of Excellence in the Structure and in the Science of Modern English Buildings: with the Proposal for Remedies for these Defects,* London 1840 (²1846). On Bartholomew cf. Pevsner (1972), pp. 86ff.; Dobai, vol. III (1977), pp. 446ff.
[31] Cf. Pevsner (1972), p. 92.
[32] Cf. esp. David Watkin, *The Life and Work of C. R. Cockerell,* London 1974; Colvin (ed. 1978), pp. 221ff.; Dobai, vol. III (1977), pp. 603ff., 656ff.
[33] Charles Robert Cockerell (Royal Academy Lectures 1841–1856), excerpts in: *The Builder,* vol. I, 13. 2. 1843ff.; further excerpts in *The Athenaeum* and *Civil Engineer and Architect's Journal.*
[34] On English architectural journals cf. esp. Frank Jenkins, 'Nineteenth-Century Architectural Periodicals', in: John Summerson (ed.), *Concerning Architecture. Essays on Architectural Writers and Writing presented*

to *Nikolaus Pevsner*, London 1968, pp. 153–60; Pevsner (1972), pp. 76ff.

[35] Thomas Rickman, 'An Attempt to Discriminate the Styles of English Architecture, From the Conquest to the Reformation…' (first in: *Panorama of Science and Art*, ed. James Smith, Liverpool 1815), London 1819 (six further editions up to 1881).

[36] On Rickman cf. Colvin (ed. 1978), pp. 688ff.; Pevsner (1972), pp. 28ff.; Dobai, vol. III (1977), pp. 1413ff.

[37] Cf. Pevsner (1972), pp. 32ff.

[38] William Whewell, *Architectural Notes on German Churches*, Cambridge and London 1830 (1st ed. anon. ²1835; ³1842). On Whewell cf. J. Todhunter, *William Whewell*, 2 vols, London 1876; Pevsner (1972), pp. 45ff.; Dobai, vol. III (1977), pp. 1432ff.

[39] Robert Willis, *Remarks on the Architecture of the Middle Ages, especially of Italy*, Cambridge 1835. On Willis cf. Pevsner (1972), pp. 52ff.; Dobai, vol. III (1977), pp. 1437ff.

[40] Willis (1835), pp. 15f.

[41] Cf. Dietmar Grötzebach, *Der Wandel der Kriterien bei der Wertung des Zusammenhanges von Konstruktion und Form in den letzten 100 Jahren*, diss., TU, Berlin 1965 (Willis is not discussed here).

[42] Robert Willis, *On the Construction of Vaults in the Middle Ages*, Royal Institute of British Architects, London 1842.

[43] Robert Willis, *The Architectural Nomenclature of the Middle Ages*, London 1844.

[44] Matthew Holbeche Blox(h)am, *The Principles of Gothic Architecture Elucidated by Question and Answer*, London 1829 (eleven editions constantly enlarged up to 1882, later ones entitled *The Principles of Gothic Ecclesiastical Architecture*; for a summary, cf. foreword to 11th ed. (vol. I, 1882), pp. iiif.); German trans. Leipzig 1847. On Bloxham cf. Dobai, vol. III (1977), pp. 1426ff.

[45] Raphael and Joshua Arthur Brandon, *An Analysis of Gothick Architecture: Illustrated by a Series of Upwards of Seven Hundred Examples of Doorways, Windows etc.*, 2 vols, London 1847.

[46] Charles L. Eastlake, *A History of the Gothic Revival*, London 1872 (facs. repr. ed. J. Mordaunt Crook, Leicester–New York 1970; ed. Alan Gowans, Watkins Glen, N.Y. ¹1975, ²1979); cf. further Dobai, vol. III (1977), pp. 1480ff.

[47] On contemporary discussion of the competition, cf. Eastlake (1872), pp. 170–77; Dobai, vol. III (1977), pp. 521ff., 569f.; cf. also Michael H. Port (ed.), *The Houses of Parliament*, New Haven–London 1976.

[48] On Pugin cf. Benjamin Ferrey, *Recollections of A. N. Welby Pugin, and His Father Augustus Pugin…*, London 1861; (facs. repr. with introduction by Clive and Jane Wainwright, London 1978); August Reichensperger, *August Welby Pugin, der Neubegründer der christlichen Kunst in England*, Freiburg 1877; Phoebe Stanton, *Pugin*, London 1971; Pevsner (1972), pp. 103ff.; Dobai, vol. III (1977), pp. 796ff.; Alexandra Wedgwood, *A. W. N. Pugin and the Pugin Family (Catalogue of Architectural Drawings in the Victoria and Albert Museum)*, London 1985; Margaret Belcher, *A. W. N. Pugin, An Annotated Critical Bibliography*, London–New York 1987.

[49] Augustus Welby Northmore Pugin, *A Letter to A. W. Hakewill, Architect, in Answer to his 'Reflections on the Style for Rebuilding the House of Parliament'*, Salisbury 1835.

[50] Augustus Charles Pugin (and E. J. Willson, text), *Specimens of Gothic Architecture; Selected from Various Ancient Edifices in England and France…*, 2 vols, London 1821–28 (²1838–39).

[51] Augustus Welby Northmore Pugin, *Contrasts: or, A Parallel between the Noble Edifices of the Fourteenth and Fifteenth Centuries and Similar Buildings of the Present Day; Shewing the Present Decay of Taste*, Salisbury 1836 (London ²1841; facs. repr. ed. H. R. Hitchcock, Leicester and New York 1969).

[52] Cf. Phoebe Stanton, 'The Sources of Pugin's "Contrasts"', in: *Concerning Architecture. Essays on Architectural Writers and Writing presented to Nikolaus Pevsner*, ed. John Summerson, London 1968, pp. 120–39; Ashby Bland Crowder, 'Pugin's Contrasts: Sources for its Technique', *Architectura* 13, 1983, pp. 57–63.

[53] Pugin (ed. 1841), p. 1.

[54] Ibid., p. 3.

[55] Ibid., p. 7.

[56] Ibid., p. 49.

[57] Augustus Welby Northmore Pugin, *The True Principles of Pointed or Christian Architecture*, London 1841 (²1853); repr. of 1841 ed.: London–New York 1973; repr. of 1853 ed.: Oxford 1969.

[58] Pugin (1841), p. 1.

[59] Ibid.

[60] Ibid., p. 76.

[61] Ibid., p. 47.

[62] Ibid., p. 50.

[63] Ibid., p. 74.

[64] Ibid., p. 72.

[65] Ibid.

[66] Goethe, *Berliner Ausgabe*, vol. 19, Berlin and Weimar 1973, p. 75.

[67] Augustus Welby Northmore Pugin, *An Apology for the Revival of Christian Architecture in England*, London 1843 (facs. repr. Oxford 1969).

[68] Cf. Pevsner (1972), p. 115.

[69] Augustus Welby Northmore Pugin, *A Treatise on Chancel Screens and Rood Lofts*, London 1851, p. 13.

[70] On the 'Oxford Movement' cf. esp. S. L. Ollard, 'The Oxford Architectural and Historical Society and the Oxford Movement', *Oxoniensia* V, 1940; Dobai, vol. III (1977), pp. 833f.

[71] On the Cambridge Camden Society cf. Kenneth Clark, *The Gothic Revival* (1928), London 1974, pp. 150ff.; James F. White, *The Cambridge Movement. The Ecclesiologists and the Gothic Revival*, Cambridge 1962 (²1979); Phoebe B. Stanton, *The Gothic Revival and American Church Architecture 1840–1856*, Baltimore 1968; Pevsner (1972), pp. 123ff.; Georg Germann, *Gothic Revival in Europe and Britain*, London 1972; Stefan Muthesius, *The High Victorian Movement in Architecture 1850–1870*, London–Boston 1972; George L. Hersey, *High Victorian Gothic. A Study in Associatism*, Baltimore–London 1972, pp. 61ff.; Dobai, vol. III (1977), pp. 834ff.

[72] Laws of the Cambridge Camden Society, Cambridge 1839 (repr. in: White, ed. 1979, pp. 225ff.).

[73] White (ed. 1979), p. xi.

[74] John Mason Neale (and John F. Russell), *A Few Hints on the Practical Study of Ecclesiastical Antiquities for the Use of the Cambridge Camden Society*, Cambridge 1839 (²1840, ³1842, ⁴1843).

John Mason Neale, *A Few Words to Church Builders*, Cambridge 1841 (new eds up to 1844).

[75] John Mason Neale and Benjamin Webb, *The Symbolism of Churches and Church Ornaments: A Translation of the First Book of the Rationale Divinorum...*, Leeds 1843.

[76] On All Saints cf. Paul Thompson, *William Butterfield. Victorian Architect*, Cambridge, MA 1971; Hersey (1972), pp. 104ff.; Muthesius (1972), pp. 59ff.

[77] Cf. Dobai, vol. III (1977), p. 845.

[78] Owen Jones, *Plans, Elevations, Sections and Details of the Alhambra*, London 1842–46. Owen Jones, *The Polychromatic Ornament of Italy*, London 1846.

[79] Owen Jones, *Grammar of Ornament*, London 1856 (¹⁰1986); cf. Pevsner (1972), pp. 163ff.

[80] Cf. esp. Hersey (1972), pp. 78ff.

[81] Dobai, vol. III (1877), p. 846.

[82] On R. C. Carpenter cf. Dobai, vol. III (1977), p. 846.

[83] Cf. *John Ruskin, The Works*, ed. E. T. Cook and A. Wedderburn, 39 vols, London 1903–12 (= Library Edition = L.E.); a useful selection arranged by subject: Kenneth Clark, *Ruskin Today*, London 1964 (Harmondsworth 1967); Joan Evans and John Howard Whitehouse (ed.), *The Diaries of John Ruskin*, 3 vols, Oxford 1956–69.

Amongst the vast recent literature on Ruskin, the following are the most important monographs and studies of his architectural ideas: E. T. Cook, *The Life of John Ruskin*, 2 vols, London 1911 (²1912); John D. Rosenberg, *The Darkening Glass. A Portrait of Ruskin's Genius*, New York–London 1961 (²1962); Nikolaus Pevsner, *Ruskin and Viollet-le-Duc*, London 1969; Pevsner (1972), pp. 139ff.; Jürgen Paul, 'Die Kunstanschauung John Ruskins', in: *Beiträge zur Theorie der Künste im 19. Jahrhundert*, ed. H. Koopmann and J. A. Schmoll-Eisenwerth, vol. I, 1971; George P. Landow, *The Aesthetic and Critical Theories of John Ruskin*, Princeton 1971; Kristine Ottesen Garrigan, *Ruskin on Architecture*, Madison, Wisc. 1973; Robert Hewison, *John Ruskin. The argument of the eye*, Princeton 1976; John Dixon Hunt, *The Wider Sea. A Life of John Ruskin*, London–Melbourne–Toronto 1982; id. and F. M. Holland (ed.), *The Ruskin Polygon. Essays on the Imagination of John Ruskin*, Manchester 1982; Wolfgang Kemp, *John Ruskin 1819–1900. Leben und Werk*, Munich–Vienna 1983.

[84] John Ruskin, 'The Poetry of Architecture' (1837/38), in: *L. E.* vol. I.

[85] Cf. eg. Patrick R. M. Conner, 'Pugin and Ruskin', *Journal of the Warburg and Cour-*

tauld Institutes XLI, 1978, pp. 344–50; Peter Krahé, *Thomas Carlyle, John Ruskin, Matthew Arnold. Die weltanschauliche Krise und ihre literarische Verarbeitung*, Bonn 1978; George Allan Cate (ed.), *The Correspondence of Thomas Carlyle and John Ruskin*, Stanford, CA, 1982.

[86] John Ruskin, *The Seven Lamps of Architecture* (1849), L. E. VIII.

[87] On this subject cf. the problematic work by David Watkin, *Morality and Architecture. The Development of a Theme in Architectural History and Theory from the Gothic Revival to the Modern Movement*, Oxford 1977.

[88] Ruskin, *The Seven Lamps*, Introductory.

[89] Ibid., ch. II par. 9.

[90] Ibid., ch. IV par. 21.

[91] Ibid., ch. I par. 1.

[92] Ibid., ch. II par 7.

[93] Ibid., ch. IV par. 3.

[94] Ibid., ch. IV par. 40.

[95] Ibid., ch. V par. 24.

[96] Ibid., ch. VI par. 18.

[97] Ibid., ch. VI par. 20.

[98] Ibid., ch VI par. 19.

[99] *The Stones of Venice*, (1851–1853), L. E. IX–XI.

[100] *The Stones of Venice*, vol. I, ch. 20, p. 3.

[101] Ibid., vol. I, ch. XX, p. 17.

[102] Ibid., vol. I, ch. XX, p. 22.

[103] Ibid., vol. II, ch. VI, p. 38.

[104] Ibid., vol. II, ch. VI, p. 97.

[105] Louis H. Sullivan, *A System of Architectural Ornament* (1924), New York 1966.

[106] On Ruskin's drawings cf. Paul H. Walton, *The Drawings of John Ruskin*, Oxford 1972; Robert Hewison, *Ruskin and Venice*, London 1978.

[107] Cf. Henry-Russell Hitchock, 'Ruskin and American Architecture, or Regeneration Long Delayed', in: John Summerson (ed.), *Concerning Architecture. Essays... presented to Nikolaus Pevsner*, London 1968, pp. 166–208; Roger B. Stein, *John Ruskin and Aesthetic Thought in America 1840–1900*, Cambridge, MA 1967; R. B. Harmon, *The Impact of John Ruskin on Architecture: A Selected Bibliography*, Monticello, VA 1982.

[108] On Fergusson cf. Maurice Craig, 'James Fergusson', in: John Summerson (ed.), *Concerning Architecture. Essays... presented to Nikolaus Pevsner*, London 1968, pp. 140–52; Pevsner (1972), pp. 238ff.; Dobai, vol.

III (1977), pp. 459ff., 470; David Watkin, *The Rise of Architectural History*, London 1980, pp. 82ff.

[109] James Fergusson, *An Historical Enquiry in the True Principles of Beauty in Art, more especially with Reference to Architecture*, London 1849.

[110] James Fergusson, *The Illustrated Handbook of Architecture being a concise popular account of the different styles of architecture prevailing in all ages and countries*, 2 vols, London 1855. James Fergusson, *A History of Modern Styles in Architecture*, London 1862. A summary of both works in: *A History of Architecture* 4 vols, London 1865–76.

[111] Fergusson (1855), vol. I, p. xxv.

[112] Ibid., vol. I, p. xxvii.

[113] Ibid., vol. I, p. xxix.

[114] Ibid., vol. I, pp. xxxff.

[115] Ibid., vol. I, p. xliii.

[116] Ibid., vol. I, p. li.

[117] Ibid.

[118] Ibid., vol. I, p. lv.

[119] Banister Fletcher, *History of Architecture on the Comparative Method for the Student, Craftsman, and Amateur*, London 1896 (numerous enlarged editions; [19]1987).

[120] Cf. esp. the bibliography by J. W. Mackail, *The Life of William Morris*, 2 vols, London 1899 (new ed. Sidney Cockerell, London 1950); May Morris, *William Morris, Artist, Writer, Socialist*, 2 vols, Oxford 1936 (facs. repr. New York 1966); Edward P. Thompson, *William Morris. Romantic to Revolutionary*, London 1955 (New York [2]1976); Philip Henderson, *William Morris. His Life, Works and Friends*, London 1967 (paperback 1973); Jack Lindsay, *William Morris. His Life and Work*, London 1975 (New York [2]1979).

For a classification of Morris' social utopia, cf. esp. Paul Meier, *La pensée utopique de William Morris*, Paris 1972. For interpretation of Morris cf. Mario Manieri Elia, *William Morris e l'ideologia dell' architettura moderna*, Rome–Bari 1976 and: Edmund Goldzamt, *William Morris und die sozialen Ursprünge der modernen Architektur*, Dresden 1976.

On Morris's architectural ideas, cf. esp. Nikolas Pevsner, 'William Morris and Architecture' (first published in: *Journal of the Royal Institute of British Architects*, 3rd.

ser., LXIV 1957), in: Pevsner, *Studies in Art, Architecture and Design. Victorian and After*, London 1968 (²1982), pp. 109ff.; Pevsner, *Some Architectural Writers* (1972), pp. 269ff.

[121] William Morris, *The Collected Works*, ed. May Morris, 24 vols, London 1910–15 (facs. repr. New York 1966); Philip Henderson (ed.), *The Letters of William Morris to his family and his friends*, London 1950; Eugene Dennis Le Mire, *The Unpublished Lectures of William Morris*, diss. (Wayne State Univ., 1962), Ann Arbor, MI 1962.
Useful selections of texts: Asa Briggs (ed.), *William Morris. Selected Writings and Designs*, Harmondsworth 1962 (repr.); A. L. Morton (ed.), *Political Writings of William Morris*, London 1973.

[122] William Morris, 'The Decorative Arts', published under the title 'The Lesser Arts' (1878), in: *Collected Works* vol. XXII, pp. 3ff.; Briggs, *Selected Writings* (1962), pp. 84ff.; Morton, *Political Writings* (1973), pp. 31ff.

[123] Morris (1877); cited from Briggs (1962), p. 102.

[124] Ibid.

[125] Morris, 'Art under Plutocracy' (1883), in: *Collected Works*, vol. XXIII, pp. 164ff.; Morton, *Political Writings* (1973), pp. 57ff.

[126] Morris, 'Useful Work Versus Useless Toil' (1884), in: *Collected Works*, vol. XXIII, pp. 98ff.; Morton, *Political Writings* (1973), pp. 86ff.

[127] Morris, 'The Revival of Architecture', *Fortnightly Review*, May 1888; repr. in: Pevsner (1972), pp. 315ff.

[128] Morris, *The Revival* (1888); cited from Pevsner (1972), p. 316.

[129] Ibid., p. 319.

[130] May Morris, vol. I, 1936, p. 266.

[131] Morris's rôle here is exaggerated in Nikolaus Pevsner, *Pioneers of Modern Design. From William Morris to Walter Gropius*, London 1936 (New York ²1949).

[132] William Morris, *News from Nowhere or an epoch of rest* (first published in *The Commonweal* 1890), Boston 1890 (London 1891); ed. James Redmond, London 1970 (²1972).

[133] Edward Bellamy, *Looking backward 2000–1887* (1888), London 1889; ed. Frederic R. White, New York 1956.
On Bellamy cf. esp. Arthur E. Morgan,

Edward Bellamy, New York 1944; on his connection with Morris cf. esp. Paul Meier (1972), pp. 114fff.

[134] Morris, *News from Nowhere*, ed. Redmond (1970), p. 55.

[135] Ibid., pp. 19f.

[136] Ibid., p. 35.

[137] Ibid., p. 38.

[138] Ibid., p. 114.

[139] Cf. Christina Lodder, *Russian Constructivism*, New Haven–London 1983, p. 74.

[140] Cf. Manieri Elia (1976); Kirsch (1983), pp. 252ff.; Robert Judson Clark (ed.), *The Arts and Crafts Movement in America*, Princeton, NJ, 1972; id. (ed.), 'Aspects of the Arts and Crafts Movement in America', *Record of the Art Museum Princeton University* 34, 2, 1975.

[141] Oscar Wilde's lectures of 1882 are published in the vol. entitled *Miscellanea* in: *First Collected Edition of the Works of Oscar Wilde*, ed. Robert Ross, London 1908 (facs. repr. London 1969), pp. 241ff.

[142] Wilde (1908), p. 303.

[143] On the Arts and Crafts movement and the guilds cf. esp. Nikolaus Pevsner, 'William Morris, C. R. Ashbee und das zwanzigste Jahrhundert', *Deutsche Vierteljahrsschrift für Literaturwissenschaft und Geistesgeschichte* 14, 1936, pp. 536–62; Pevsner, *Pioneers of Modern Design* (1936); Julius Posener, *Anfänge des Funktionalismus. Von Arts and Crafts zum Deutschen Werkbund (Bauwelt Fundamente, 11)*, Berlin etc. 1964; Robert Macleod, *Style and Society. Architectural Ideology in Britain 1835–1914*, London 1971; Gillian Naylor, *The Arts and Crafts Movement*, London 1971; Peter Davey, *Arts and Crafts Architecture: The Search for Earthly Paradise*, London 1980.

[144] Cf. esp. Pevsner, 'Arthur H. Mackmurdo' (first published in: *The Architectural Review* LXXXIII, 1938), *Studies in Art, Architecture etc.* (vol. II, 1968; ²1982), pp. 133ff.

[145] On Lethaby, cf. Posener (1964), pp. 27ff. (with German trans. of selected texts); P. Ferriday, 'W. R. Lethaby,' in: John Summerson (ed.), *Concerning Architecture. Essays... presented to Nikolaus Pevsner*, London 1968, pp. 161–65; Macleod (1971), pp. 55ff.; Davey (1980), p. 56ff.; Godfrey Rubens, *William Richard Lethaby, his Life and Work 1857–1931*, London 1986.

[146] William Richard Lethaby, *Architecture,*

Mysticism and Myth, London 1892 (facs. repr. with introduction by Godfrey Rubens, London 1974); rev. version entitled *Architecture, Nature and Magic* (in *The Builder*, 1928), London 1956.

[147] Lethaby (1892), p. 5.

[148] Ibid., p. 3.

[149] Ibid., p. 7.

[150] Ibid., p. 8.

[151] Cf. esp. Macleod (1971), pp. 58ff.

[152] Ibid., p. 59, ill. 4, 3.

[153] Cf. esp. William Richard Lethaby, *The Church of Sancta Sophia, Constantinople: a study of Byzantine Building*, London 1894; id., *Mediaeval Art*, London 1904 (²1940); id., *Westminster Abbey and the King's Craftsmen: A Study of Mediaeval Building*, London 1906; id., *Philip Webb and His Work* (1925), London 1935 (facs. repr. London 1979).

[154] Lethaby (1904), p. 1; on his conception of history cf. David Watkin, *The Rise of Architectural History*, London 1980, p. 87ff.

[155] Cf. his essay in *The Imprint*, 1913; Posener (1964), pp. 37ff.

[156] William Richard Lethaby, *Architecture*, London 1911 (²1929; ³1955).

[157] Lethaby (1911), p. 240.

[158] First published in 1913, but in Loos' collection *Trotzdem* (1931) dated 1908.

[159] Louis Sullivan, 'Ornament in Architecture' (first published in: *Engineering Magazine*, August 1892), in: *Sullivan, Kindergarten Chats and other writings* (1918), New York 1947, pp. 187ff.

[160] Cf. Isobel Spencer, *Walter Crane*, New York 1975; Gianna Piantoni, 'Il linguaggio della linea nella teoria di W. Crane', in: *Ricerche di Storia dell'Arte* 5, 1977, pp. 47–66.

[161] *Arts and Crafts Essays, by members of the Arts and Crafts Exhibition Society*, London 1893, p. 12.

[162] On the work of Ashbee and Baillie Scott in Germany and Switzerland, cf. James D. Kornwolf, *M. H. Baillie Scott and the Arts and Crafts Movement*, Baltimore–London 1972; Katharina Medici-Mall, *Das Landhaus Waldbühl von M. H. Baillie Scott. Ein Gesamtkunstwerk zwischen Neugotik und Jugendstil*, Bern 1979; Hanno-Walter Kruft, 'Die Arts-and-Crafts-Bewegung und der deutsche Jugendstil', in: Gerhard Bott (ed.), *Von Morris zum Bauhaus. Eine Kunst*

gegründet auf Einfachheit, Hanau 1977, pp. 25ff.

[163] Walter Crane, *The Claims of Decorative Art*, London 1892; id., *The Bases of Design*, London 1898; id., *Line and Form*, London 1900.

[164] On Ashbee cf. Posener (1964), pp. 95ff.; Naylor (1971), pp. 166f.; Davey (1980), pp. 139ff.; Fiona MacCarthy, *The Simple Life. C. R. Ashbee in the Cotswolds*, London 1981; Alan Crawford, *C. R. Ashbee. Architect, Designer & Romantic Socialist*, New Haven–London 1985.

[165] Charles Robert Ashbee, *Craftsmanship in Competitive Industry*, Campden 1908 (facs. repr. New York–London 1977).

[166] Charles Robert Ashbee, *An Endeavour Towards the Teaching of John Ruskin and William Morris*, Campden 1901 (facs. repr. New York 1977).

[167] Ashbee (1908), p. 91.

[168] Charles Robert Ashbee, *Should we Stop Teaching Art?*, London 1911 (facs. repr.: New York 1977).

[169] Cited from Naylor (1971), p. 147.

[170] John Dando Sedding, *Art and Handicraft*, London 1893 (facs. repr. New York 1977), p. 129.

[171] On Voysey cf. Nikolaus Pevsner, 'C. F. A. Voysey' (first published in: *Elseviers Maandschrift*, May 1940), in: Pevsner, *Studies in Art, Architecture etc.*, vol. II (1968, ²1982), pp. 141ff.; David Gebhard, *Charles F. A. Voysey*, Los Angeles 1975; Joanna Symonds, *Catalogue of Drawings by C. F. A. Voysey in the Drawings Collection of the Royal Institute of British Architects*, Farnborough 1976; John Brandon-Jones a.o., *C. F. A. Voysey: architect and designer 1857–1941* (cat.), London 1978; Duncan Simpson, *C. F. A. Voysey. An architect of individuality*, London 1979.

[172] Charles F. Annesley Voysey, *Reason as a basis of art*, London 1906; id., *Individuality*, London 1915.

[173] 'An Interview with Mr. Charles F. Annesley Voysey, architect and designer', *The Studio* I, 1893, p. 234.

[174] Ibid.

[175] Charles F. A. Voysey, 'Patriotism in architecture', in: *Architectural Association Journal* XXVIII, 1912, pp. 21–25.

[176] Cf. Pevsner (1968, ²1982), p. 151.

[177] From the extensive literature on Lutyens, cf. on his houses Peter Inskip, *Edwin*

Lutyens (*Architectural Monographs* 6) London 1979; on his work in India cf. Robert Grant Irving, *Indian Summer. Lutyens, Baker, and Imperial Delhi*, New Haven–London 1981.

[178] On Mackintosh cf. Thomas Howarth, *Charles Rennie Mackintosh and the Modern Movement* (1952), London ²1977; Robert Macleod, *Charles Rennie Mackintosh. Architect and Artist*, London 1983.

[179] Cf. Davey (1980), pp. 183ff.; Naylor (1971), pp. 172ff.; Kruft (1977), pp. 27ff.

[180] Ebenezer Howard, *Tomorrow: a Peaceful Path to Real Reform*, London 1898; entitled *Garden Cities of Tomorrow*, London 1902; ed. F. J. Osborn, Cambridge, MA–London 1965 (several reprs).

See the introductions to Osborn (1965) and Posener (1968); Dugald Macfadyen, *Sir Ebenezer Howard and the town planning movement*, Cambridge, MA 1970; also Julius Posener, 'Ebenezer Howard' (1972), in: Posener, *Aufsätze und Vorträge 1931–1980*, Brunswick–Wiesbaden 1981, pp. 230–243.

On the German garden city movement cf. Kristiana Hartmann, *Deutsche Gartenstadtbewegung. Kulturpolitik und Gesellschaftsreform*, Munich 1976.

[181] Howard (ed. Osborn, ³1970), pp. 142f.

[182] Patrick Geddes, *City Development. A Study of Parks, Gardens, and Culture-Institutes. A Report to the Carnegie Dunfermline Trust*, Edinburgh–Birmingham 1904 (facs. repr. Shannon 1973; New Brunswick, NJ 1973).

On Geddes cf. Philip Boardman, *The World of Patrick Geddes. Biologist, Town planner, Re-educator, Peace-warrior*, London–Henley–Boston 1978.

[183] Patrick Geddes, *Town Planning toward City Development: A Report to the Durbar of Indore*, 2 vols, Indore 1918.

[184] Geoffrey Scott, *The Architecture of Humanism. A Study in the History of Taste* (¹1914, ²1924), ed. Henry Hope Reed, New York 1974.

On Scott cf. David Watkin, *The Rise of Architectural History*, London 1980, pp. 116ff. Oddly enough, Watkin, in *Morality and Architecture* (Oxford 1977), while showing a sympathetic understanding of Scott, makes little reference to his work.

[185] Scott (ed. 1974), p. 49.

[186] Ibid., p. 78.

[187] Ibid., p. 85.

[188] Ibid., p. 89.

[189] Ibid., p. 110.

[190] Ibid., p. 111.

[191] Ibid., p. 134.

[192] Peter Blake, *Form Follows Fiasco. Why Modern Architecture Hasn't Worked*, Boston–Toronto 1977.

24. The United States: from Thomas Jefferson to the Chicago School

[1] The major bibliographies on early American architecture and architectural literature are: Frank J. Roos, *Writings on American Architecture* (¹1943), 2nd ed. entitled *Bibliography of Early American Architecture. Writings on Architecture Constructed Before 1860 in Eastern and Central United States*, Chicago–London 1968; Henry-Russell Hitchcock, *American Architectural Books. A List of Books, Portfolios, and Pamphlets on Architecture and Related Subjects Published in America before 1895* (¹1946), Minneapolis ²1962 (facs. repr. New York 1976 with a useful 'Chronological Short-Title List' as an appendix).

The first architectural treatise published in America is Abraham Swan, *The British Architect: or, The builder's treasury of staircases...* (first published London 1745; ²1750; ³1758; facs. repr. of 1758 ed., New York 1967), Philadelphia 1775.

[2] On early American architecture cf. esp. Talbot Hamlin, *Greek Revival Architecture in America* (¹1944), New York–London ²1964; among numerous accounts of American architectural history, cf. the short but informative study by James Marston Fitch, *American Building. The Historical Forces That Shaped It* (¹1947), New York ²1973; Henry-Russell Hitchcock, *Architecture: Nineteenth and Twentieth Centuries*, Harmondsworth 1958 (several reprints).

Useful anthologies of American architectural theory, containing selected 19th-century source-material: Lewis Mumford (ed.) *Roots of Contemporary American Architecture* (¹1952), New York 1972; Don Gifford (ed.), *The Literature of American Architecture*, New York 1966; Leland M. Roth (ed.), *America Builds. Source Documents in American Architecture and Planning*, New York 1983.

3 On Thomas Jefferson, as architect cf. esp. Fiske Kimball, *Thomas Jefferson Architect. Original Designs in the Collection of Thomas Jefferson Coolidge, Jr.*, Boston 1916 (facs. repr. New York 1968); Karl Lehmann, *Thomas Jefferson. American Humanist* (¹1947), Chicago–London 1965 (facs. repr. 1973); Buford Pickens, 'Mr. Jefferson as Revolutionary Architect', *Journal of the Society of Architectural Historians* XXXIV, 1975, pp. 257–70; Felix Aeppli, *Thomas Jefferson: The Urban Critic of the City*, Zürich 1975; Fredrick Doveton and Ralph E. Griswold, *Thomas Jefferson. Landscape Architect*, Charlottesville, VA 1978; Mary N. Woods, 'Thomas Jefferson and the University of Virginia: Planning the Academic Village', *Journal of the Society of Architectural Historians* XLIV, 1985, pp. 266–83; William B. O'Neal, 'An Intelligent Interest in Architecture. A Bibliography of Publications about Thomas Jefferson as an Architect…', *The American Association of Architectural Bibliographers, Papers*, VI, 1969.

4 On Jefferson's library cf. esp. Kimball (1916), pp. 90ff.; William Bainter O'Neal, *Jefferson's Fine Arts Library. His Selections for the University of Virginia Together with His Own Architectural Books*, Charlottesville, VA 1976.

5 Cf. esp. Paul F. Norton, *Latrobe, Jefferson and the National Capitol*, diss. (Princeton 1952), New York–London 1977.

6 Cf. Norton (1977); Henry-Russell Hitchcock and William Seale, *Temples of Democracy: The State Capitols of the USA*, New York–London 1976.

7 On Jefferson's travels cf. Edward Dumbauld, *Thomas Jefferson. American Tourist* (¹1946), Oklahoma City ²1976.

8 Thomas Jefferson, *Notes on the State of Virginia* (1782); cited from Saul K. Padover (ed.), *The Complete Jefferson*, Freeport, NY 1943 (²1969), p. 671.

9 William Buchanan and James Hay; Julian P. Boyd (ed.), *The Papers of Thomas Jefferson*, vol. 9, Princeton 1954, p. 220.

10 Charles-Louis Clérisseau, *Antiquités de la France*, part I, Paris 1788; cf. O'Neal (1976), pp. 71ff. (no. 29).

11 Cf. Boyd (ed.), op. cit., vol. 9 (1954), pp. 602ff.

12 Thomas Jefferson, 'Autobiography' (1821), in: Padover (ed.), *The Complete Jefferson* (1943), p. 1147.

13 Lehmann (ed. 1973), p. xi.

14 On Palladianism in America cf. cat. *Palladio in Amerika*, Milan 1976; Margherita Azzi Visentini, *Il Palladianesimo in America e l'architettura della villa*, Milan 1976. On Bulfinch cf. Harold Kirker, *The Architecture of Charles Bulfinch*, Cambridge MA 1969.

15 Asher Benjamin, *The Country Builder's Assistant: containing a collection of new designs of carpentry and architecture…*, Greenfield 1797 (²1798; ³1800; ⁴1805); repr. of first ed. in: *The Works* (1972).

16 For the best general account of the writings and editions of Asher Benjamin, cf. Hitchcock (ed. 1976), pp. 9ff. For a concise study of his work and thought, cf. Jack Quinan, 'Asher Benjamin and American Architecture', *Journal of the Society of Architectural Historians* XXXVIII, 1979, pp. 244–56. Facs. repr. of all first eds: Asher Benjamin, *The Works of A. B. From the First Editions*, ed. Everard M. Upjohn, 7 vols, New York 1972.

17 Cf. Hitchcock (ed. 1976), pp. 74f.

18 Asher Benjamin, *The American Builder's Companion: or, a New System of Architecture particularly adapted to the present style of building in the United States of America*, Boston 1806 (²1811; ³1816; ⁴1820; ⁵1826; ⁶1827); repr. of first ed. in: *The Works* (1972); repr. of 1827 ed., ed. William Morgan: New York 1969.

19 Benjamin (1806), p. viii.

20 Ibid., p. vi.

21 Ibid., p. vii.

22 Asher Benjamin, *Practice of Architecture, Containing the five orders of architecture and an additional column and entablature…*, New York 1833 (²1835; ³1836; ⁴1840; ⁵1847; ⁷1851), pl. vii, Preface and p. 34; facs. repr. of 1st ed. in: *The Works* (1972).

23 Benjamin, *The American Builder's Companion* (ed. 1829), p. 28.

24 Asher Benjamin, *The Rudiments of Architecture: Being a Treatise on Practical Geometry, on Grecian and Roman Mouldings…*, Boston 1814 (²1820); facs. repr. of 1st ed. in: *The Works* (1972).

25 Benjamin, *The American Builder's Companion* (ed. 1806), p. v.

26 Amongst extensive literature on American

Transcendentalism, cf. esp.: F. O. Matthiessen, American Renaissance, *Art and Expression in the Age of Emerson and Whitman*, London–Toronto–New York 1941 (³1946); Perry Miller, *The Transcendentalists. An Anthology*, Cambridge, MA 1950 (⁵1971); Paul F. Boller, Jr, *American Transcendentalism 1830–1860*, New York 1974.

On Transcendentalist aesthetics and architectural theory, cf. esp. Charles R. Metzger, *Emerson and Greenough. Transcendental Pioneers of an American Esthetic* (¹1954), Westport, CT 1970; *Thoreau and Whitman. A Study of their Esthetics* (¹1961), Washington 1968.

²⁷ On German influence on Transcendentalist aesthetics, cf. Donald Drew Egbert, 'The Idea of Organic Expression and American Architecture', in: Stow Persons (ed.), *Revolutionary Thought in America*, New Haven 1950, pp. 336–96; esp. Stanley M. Vogel, 'German Literary Influences on the American Transcendentalists', *Yale Studies in English*, vol. 127, New Haven 1955 (facs. repr. 1970).

²⁸ On Greenough cf. esp. Henry T. Tuckerman, *A Memorial of Horatio Greenough*, New York 1853; Thomas Brumbaugh, 'Horatio and Richard Greenough: A Critical Study with a Catalogue of their Sculpture', diss., Ohio State Univ. 1955; Nathalia Wright, *Horatio Greenough. The First American Sculptor*, Philadelphia 1963; Nikolaus Pevsner, *Some Architectural Writers of the Nineteenth Century*, Oxford 1972, pp. 188ff.; Nathalia Wright (ed.), *Letters of Horatio Greenough. American Sculptor*, Madison, WI 1972.

²⁹ Letter of 19.4.1853; Joseph Slater (ed.), *The Correspondence of Emerson and Carlyle*, New York–London 1964, p. 486.

³⁰ The outlines of Greenough's architectural theory are to be found in a letter of October 1831 to Washington Allston; cf. Wright (ed.), *Letters of Horatio Greenough* (1972), pp. 86ff.

³¹ Horatio Greenough, 'American Architecture' (first published in: *United States Magazine and Democratic Review* 13, 1843, pp. 206–210), in: *Horatio Greenough, Form and Function. Remarks on Art, Design and Architecture*, ed. Harold A. Small, Berkeley–Los Angeles–London 1947 (⁶1969), pp. 51ff.;

abridged text in: Lewis Mumford (ed.), *Roots of Contemporary American Architecture* (1952), New York 1972, pp. 32ff. Greenough himself published the volume *The Travels, Observations and Experience of a Yankee Stonecutter* under the pseudonym Horace Bender (New York 1852); Tuckerman (1853) contains an enlarged selection of Greenough's writings, which forms the basis for the edition by Small (1947).

³² Greenough, *American Architecture* (ed. 1947), p. 51.

³³ Ibid., pp. 57f.

³⁴ Ibid., p. 58.

³⁵ Ibid., p. 61.

³⁶ Ibid., p. 62.

³⁷ Ibid.

³⁸ Ibid., p. 63.

³⁹ Ibid., p. 65.

⁴⁰ Horatio Greenough, 'Relative and Independent Beauty', in: Greenough, *Form and Function* (ed. 1947), pp. 69ff.

⁴¹ Edward Lacy Garbett, *Rudimentary Treatise on the Principles of Design in Architecture as Deducible from Nature and Exemplified in the Works of the Greek and Gothic Architects*, London 1850.

On Garbett cf. R. W. Winter, 'Fergusson and Garbett in American Architectural Theory', *Journal of the Society of Architectural Historians* XVII, December 1958, pp. 25–30; Pevsner (1972), pp. 189ff.

⁴² Garbett (1850); cited from Pevsner (1972), p. 192.

⁴³ Greenough (ed. 1947), p. 71.

⁴⁴ Ibid., p. 74.

⁴⁵ Ibid., p. 75.

⁴⁶ Ibid., p. 118.

⁴⁷ Ibid., p. 121.

⁴⁸ Ibid., p. 123.

⁴⁹ Ibid., p. 128.

⁵⁰ Cf. Nathalia Wright (1963), p. 188.

⁵¹ *Letters of Horatio Greenough*, ed. Nathalia Wright (1972), p. 268.

⁵² Cf. Metzger (1954, ed. 1970), pp. 67ff.

⁵³ *Letters of Horatio Greenough*, ed. Nathalia Wright (1972), pp. 400f.

⁵⁴ Cf. Carl W. Condit, *The Chicago School of Architecture* (1964), Chicago–London 1973, pp. 10ff.

⁵⁵ Ralph Waldo Emerson, *English Traits*; cited from *The Complete Works of Ralph Waldo Emerson*, vol. V, Boston–New York 1903 (facs. repr. New York 1968), pp. 5f.

On Emerson's organic-functionalist theory cf. esp. Robert B. Shaffer, 'Emerson and His Circle: Advocates of Functionalism', *Journal of the Society of Architectural Historians* VII, 1948, Nrs 3–4, pp. 17–20; Richard P. Adams, 'Emerson and the Organic Metaphor', in: *Publications of the Modern Language Association of America* LXIX, 1954, pp. 117–30.

56 Ralph Waldo Emerson, 'Nature' (1836); in: *The Complete Works of R. W. E.*, vol. I, Boston–New York 1903, New York 1968), pp. 1ff.

57 Ralph Waldo Emerson, 'The Conduct of Life'; in: *The Complete Works of R. W. E.*, vol. 6, Boston–New York 1904 (repr.: New York 1968), p. 291.

58 Emerson, 'The Conduct of Life'; cited from *Complete Works*, vol. VI, 1904, p. 294.

59 Emerson, 'Art and Criticism'; in: *The Complete Works of R. W. E.*, vol. 12, Boston and New York 1904 (facs. repr. New York 1968), p. 291.

60 Ralph Waldo Emerson, 'Thoughts on Art', in: *The Dial*, vol. I, 1840/41, p. 375.

61 Henry David Thoreau, *Journal*, vol. III, ed. Bradford Torrey (1906), New York 1968, pp. 181ff.

62 Henry David Thoreau, 'Walden' (1854), in: *The Writings of Henry David Thoreau*, vol. II (1906), New York 1968; illus. ed. with introduction by J. Lyndon Shanley: Henry D. Thoreau, *The Illustrated Walden*, Princeton 1973.

63 Thoreau, *Walden* (ed. 1973), pp. 46f.

64 Henry David Thoreau, 'Cape Cod', in: *The Writings of H. D. Th.*, vol. IV (1906), New York 1968, p. 29.

65 Thoreau, *Journal*, vol. IV (1906), 1968, p. 153.

66 Ibid., 1968, p. 152.

67 Cf. Arthur Eugene Bestor, *Backwoods Utopias: The Sectarian Origins and the Owenite Phase of Communitarian Socialism in America, 1663–1829*, Philadelphia ¹1950, ²1970; for a good general account of the 19th century, cf. Dolores Hayden, *Seven American Utopias. The Architecture of Communitarian Socialism, 1790–1975*, Cambridge, MA–London ¹1976, ²1977.

68 Cf. esp. Dolores Hayden (¹1976, ²1977).

69 From the extensive literature on the Shakers, cf. Edward Deming Andrews, *The People Called Shakers: A Search for the Perfect Society*, New York 1954 (²1963); Edward Deming Andrews and Faith Andrews, *Work and Worship: The Economic Order of the Shakers*, Greenwich, CT 1974 (facs. repr. entitled *Work and Worship Among the Shakers. Their Craftsmanship and Economic Order*, New York 1982); exhib. cat. *Die Shaker. Leben und Produktion einer Commune in der Pionierzeit Amerikas*, Munich 1974; Dolores Hayden (²1977), pp. 65ff.; Herbert Schiffer, *Shaker Architecture*, Exton, PA 1979.

For an early account of Shaker ideas cf. Calvin Green and Seth Y. Wells (eds), *A Summary View of the Millennial Church or United Society of Believers Commonly Called Shakers* (¹1823), Albany ²1848 (facs. repr. New York 1973); for a substantial selection of Shaker verse and song, cf. Daniel W. Patterson (ed.), *The Shaker Spiritual*, Princeton 1979.

70 *The Millennial Laws* of 1821 were first published in: Andrews (1954, ²1963).

71 *Millennial Laws* (1821); cited from Andrews (1953), p. 285.

72 Ibid., p. 282.

73 Edward Deming Andrews and Faith Andrews, *Shaker Furniture: The Craftsmanship of an American Communal Sect*, New Haven, Conn. 1937 (facs. repr. New York 1950, 1964); Juni Sprigg, *By Shaker Hands*, New York ¹1975, ³1981.

74 For a general account cf. Dolores Hayden (¹1976, ²1977).

75 Samuel Sloan, *The Model Architect. A series of original designs for cottages, villas, suburban residences...*, 2 vols, Philadelphia 1852; vol. II, p. 99; further eds of this work: 1860, 1865, 1868, 1873; facs. repr. of 1852 ed. under the title *Sloan's Victorian Buildings*, ed. Harold N. Cooledge, Jr, New York 1980.

On Sloan's writings cf. Hitchcock, *American Architectural Books* (ed. 1976), pp. 98f.

76 Sloan (1852), vol. I, p. 7; vol. II, p. 99.

77 Sloan (1852), vol. I, p. 7.

78 Ibid., p. 9.

79 Ibid., pp. 11, 26.

80 Ibid., pp. 34f.

81 Calvert Vaux, *Villas and Cottages. A Series of Designs Prepared for Execution in the United States*, New York 1857 (²1864; ³1867; ⁴1869; ⁵1872; ⁶1874); facs. repr. of 1864 ed., New York 1970.

On editions of this work cf. Hitchcock, *American Architectural Books* (ed. 1976), pp. 108f.

[82] On Downing's writings, cf. Hitchcock, *American Architectural Books* (ed. 1976), pp. 31ff.; for a detailed study of Downing cf. Vincent J. Scully, *The Shingle Style and the Stick Style. Architectural Theory and Design from Richardson to the Origins of Wright*, New Haven–London ([1]1955), [2]1971, pp. xxviiiff.

[83] Vaux (ed. 1864), pp. ixf.

[84] Ibid., p. 27.

[85] Ibid., pp. 32f.

[86] Ibid., p. 48.

[87] Ibid., p. 45.

[88] Ibid., p. 53.

[89] Ibid., p. 82.

[90] Ibid., p. 83.

[91] For a survey of Bicknell's writings, cf. Hitchcock, *American Architectural Books* (ed.), pp. 14ff.

[92] Amos Jackson Bicknell (ed.), *Bicknell's Village Builder. Elevations and plans for cottages, villas, suburban residences, farm houses...*, New York 1870 ([1]1886); *Supplement to Bicknell's Village Builder, containing eighteen modern designs for country and suburban houses of moderate cost...*, New York c. 1871; (facs. repr. of ed. with supplement, New York 1878): New York 1979.

[93] Scully ([1]1955, [2]1971).

[94] Cf. Arthur Drexler (ed.), *The Architecture of the Ecole des Beaux-Arts*, London 1977, pp. 464ff.; on Richardson cf. Richard Chafee, 'Richardson's Record at the Ecole des Beaux-Arts', *Journal of the Society of Architectural Historians* XXXVI, 1977, pp. 175–88; a vivid account of American architectural training around the year 1900 is given by Harold Bush-Brown, *Beaux-Arts to Bauhaus and Beyond*, New York 1976.

[95] Cf. the essays by Henry-Russell Hitchcock and Robert Judson Clark in: *The Shaping of Art and Architecture in Nineteenth-Century America*, New York (The Metropolitan Museum of Art) 1972.

[96] On Richardson, cf. esp. Marina Griswold Van Rensselaer, *Henry Hobson Richardson and His Works*, Boston–New York 1888 (facs. repr. New York 1969); Henry-Russell Hitchcock, *The Architecture of H. H. Rich-*

ardson and His Times ([1]1936, [2]1961), Cambridge, MA [3]1966; James F. O'Gorman, *H. H. Richardson and His Office*, Cambridge, MA 1974; Jeffrey Karl Ochsner, *H. H. Richardson: Complete Architectural Works*, Cambridge, MA [1]1982, [2]1983.

On Richardson's use of architectural literature, cf. the listing of the contents of his library in: James F. O'Gorman, 'An 1886 Inventory of H. H. Richardson's Library, and Other Gleanings from Probate', *Journal of the Society of Architectural Historians* XLI, 1982, pp. 150–55.

[97] On the Chicago School cf. esp. W. Condit, *The Chicago School of Architecture. A History of Commercial and Public Building in the Chicago Area, 1875–1925*, Chicago–London ([1]1964) [2]1973; Harold M. Mayer and Richard C. Wade, *Chicago: Growth of a Metropolis*, Chicago and London 1969; cat. *100 Jahre Architektur in Chicago. Kontinuität von Struktur und Form*, Munich 1973; exhib. cat. *Chicago. 150 ans d'architecture 1833–1983*, Paris 1983; exhib.cat. *Chicago Architectur 1872–1922*, ed. John Zukowsky, Munich 1987 (English ed. *Chicago Architecture, 1872–1922: Birth of a Metropolis*, Munich–Chicago 1987).

[98] For an account of Jenney's work cf. Condit (ed. 1973), pp. 28ff., 79f., 83ff.; on Jenney cf. Theodore Turak, *William Le Baron Jenney: A Pioneer of Modern Architecture*, Ann Arbor, MI 1986.

[99] The most important literature on Sullivan: Hugh Morrison, *Louis Sullivan. Prophet of Modern Architecture* (1935), New York 1962; John Scarkowsky, *The Idea of Louis Sullivan*, Minneapolis 1956; Willard Connely, *Louis Sullivan. The Shaping of American Architecture*, New York 1960; Sherman Paul, *Louis Sullivan. An Architect in American Thought*, Englewood Cliffs, NY 1962; Hugh Dalziel Duncan, *Culture and Democracy. The Struggle for Form in Society and Architecture in Chicago and the Middle West During the Life and Times of Louis H. Sullivan*, Totowa, NJ 1965; Paul E. Sprague, *The Drawings of Louis Henry Sullivan*, Princeton 1979; Narciso G. Menocal, *Architecture as Nature. The Transcendentalist Idea of Louis H. Sullivan*, Madison, WI and London 1981; David S. Andrew, *Louis Sullivan and the Polemics of Modern Architecture*, Chicago 1985; Robert

Twombly, *Louis Sullivan. His Life and Work*, New York 1986; Wim De Wit (ed.), *Louis Sullivan. The Function of Ornament*, New York–London 1986.

100 The functionalist interpretation of Sullivan originated largely with European writers, of whom Sigfried Giedion (*Space, Time and Architecture*, 1941) was one of the most influential; for a new assessment of Sullivan, cf. esp. Menocal (1981), pp. 149ff.

101 Menocal (1981) gives the best account of the sources of Sullivan's theory, although in the present writer's opinion he overestimates the influence of German idealism at the expense of American Transcendentalism.

102 For the most convincing acount of the relationship between Sullivan and Adler, cf. Menocal (1981), pp. 43ff.

103 For the most thorough survey of Sullivan's writings, cf. Menocal (1981), pp. 203ff. The most important are: Louis H. Sullivan, 'Kindergarten Chats' (first published in: *Interstate Architect & Builder* 1901/02); revised 1918; ed. Claude F. Bragdon, Lawrence 1934); ed. Isabella Athey *Kindergarten Chats and Other Writings*, New York 1947 (several reprs). Louis H. Sullivan, *Democracy: A Man-Search* (final version 1908), ed. Elaine Hedges, Detroit 1961. Louis H. Sullivan, *The Autobiography of an Idea* (first published in: *Journal of the American Institute of Architects* 10/11, 1922/23), New York 1924; ed. Ralph Marlow Line, New York 1956 (several reprs). Louis H. Sullivan, *A System of Architectural Ornament According with a Philosophy of Man's Powers*, New York 1924; ed. Ada Louise Huxtable, New York 1967.

104 Louis H. Sullivan, 'Essay on Inspiration', *Inland Architect*, 8 December 1886, pp. 61–64 (facs. repr. Chicago 1964); repr. in: Menocal (1981), pp. 155ff. On a French version of this essay (1893) and its significance, cf. Lauren S. Weingarden, 'Louis H. Sullivan: Investigations of a Second French Connection', *Journal of the Society of Architectural Historians* XXXIX, 1980, pp. 297–303.

105 Sullivan, *The Autobiography* (ed. 1956), p. 207.

106 Ibid., p. 257.

107 Ibid., p. 258.

108 On the concept of function cf. esp. Sullivan, *Kindergarten Chats* (ed. 1947), pp. 42ff. and: *The Autobiography* (ed. 1956), p. 290.

109 Ibid., p. 290.

110 Sullivan, *Kindergarten Chats* (ed. 1947), p. 43.

111 Ibid., p. 99.

112 Ibid.

113 Sullivan, *Kindergarten Chats* (ed. 1947), p. 44.

114 Sullivan, *Democracy: A Man-Search* (Ms. 1908), ed. Elaine Hedges, Detroit 1961; cf. esp. Duncan (1965), pp. 427ff.; Menocal (1981), pp. 95ff.

115 Louis Sullivan, 'The Tall Office Building Artistically Considered', *Lippincott's Magazine* 57, March 1896, pp. 403–09; *Inland Architect* 27, May 1896, pp. 32–34; repr. in: Sullivan, *Kindergarten Chats* (ed. 1947), pp. 202ff.

116 Dankmar Adler, 'The Influence of Steel Construction and Plate Glass Upon Style', in: *The Proceedings of the Thirtieth Annual Convention of the American Institute of Architects*, 1896, pp. 58–64; repr. in: Mumford (ed.), *Roots of Contemporary American Architecture* (ed. 1972), pp. 243–50. A listing of writings by Dankmar Adler in: Menocal (1981), pp. 206f.

117 Adler (1896); cited from Mumford (ed.) (1972), pp. 244f.

118 Ibid., p. 248.

119 Ibid., p. 250.

120 Louis H. Sullivan, 'The High-Building Question', *The Graphic* V, 19 December 1891, p. 405; repr. in: Donald Hoffmann, 'The Setback Skyscraper City of 1891; An Unknown Essay by Louis H. Sullivan', *Journal of the Society of Architectural Historians* XXIX, 1970 (pp. 181–87), pp. 186f.

121 Dankmar Adler, 'Light in Tall Office Buildings', *Engineering Magazine* 4, 3 September 1892, pp. 171–86.

122 Sullivan, *The Autobiography* (ed. 1956), p. 117; cf. Lauren S. Weingarden, 'Louis H. Sullivans Ornament und die Poetik der Architektur', in cat. *Chicago Architektur 1872–1922* (1987), pp. 231–51.

123 Louis H. Sullivan, 'Ornament in Architecture' (first published in: *The Engineering Magazine* 3, August 1892, pp. 633–44), in: *Kindergarten Chats* (ed. 1947), pp. 187ff.

124 Sullivan (1892); cited from Sullivan, *Kindergarten Chats* (ed. 1947), p. 187.

[125] Sullivan, *The Autobiography* (ed. 1956), p. 325.

[126] Sullivan (1892); cited from Sullivan, *Kindergarten Chats* (ed. 1947), p. 189.

[127] Sullivan, *A System of Architectural Ornament* (1924); here cited from the 1967 ed.

[128] In this connection cf. Menocal (1981), pp. 25ff.

[129] Sullivan, *A System of Architectural Ornament* (ed. 1967), Interlude.

[130] Ibid., pl. 4.

[131] Cf. Menocal (1981), pp. 24ff.

[132] Cr. esp. Weingarden (1980).

[133] For a comparison of Ives with Sullivan cf. Rosalie Sandra Perry, *Charles Ives and the American Mind*, Kent, OH ('1974) ²1976, esp. pp. 33ff.
On the Concord Sonata cf. esp. Charles Ives, *Essays before a Sonata* (first published 1920), ed. Howard Boatwright, New York 1961; cf. the analysis of the sonata by Hermann Conen, 'All the wrong notes are right.' On Charles Ives's Sonata No. 2, 'Concord, MA 1840–60', in: *Neuland. Ansätze zur Musik der Gegenwart*, vol. I, ed. Herbert Henck, Cologne 1980, pp. 28–42.

[134] On Root cf. esp. Harriet Monroe, *John Wellborn Root*, Boston and New York 1896; Donald Hoffmann, *The Architecture of John Wellborn Root*, Baltimore–London 1973; a fair assessment in: Condit, *The Chicago School* (ed. 1973), pp. 44ff.

[135] Sullivan, *The Autobiography* (ed. 1956), p. 287.

[136] There seems no complete bibliography of Root's writings. Some unpublished writings are included in: Harriet Monroe (1896). The only sizeable volume of texts is Donald Hoffmann (ed.), *The Meanings of Architecture. Buildings and Writings by John Wellborn Root*, New York 1967; two of the texts published in Harriet Monroe (1896) are reprinted in: Mumford, *Roots of Contemporary America Architecture* (ed. 1972), pp. 269ff.

[137] Under the title 'Development of Architectural Style', *Inland Architect* 14, December 1889, pp. 76–78; 15 February 1890, pp. 5f.

[138] John Wellborn Root, 'Architectural Ornamentation', (first published in: *Inland Architect and Builder* V, special number, April 1885, pp. 54f.), in: Hoffmann (ed.) (1967), pp. 16–21.

[139] Root (1885); cited after Hoffmann (ed.) (1967), p. 17.

[140] Ibid.

[141] Ibid.

[142] Root (1885); cited after Hoffmann (ed.) (1967), p. 18.

[143] Leopold Eidlitz, *The Nature and Function of Art, More Especially of Architecture*, New York 1881; excerpts repr. in: Leland M. Roth (ed.), *America Builds*, New York 1983, pp. 274ff.

[144] Hoffmann (ed.), op. cit. (1967), p. 27; on the possible influence of Eidlitz on Sullivan, cf. Menocal (1981), pp. 64f.

[145] Eidlitz (1881); cited after Roth (ed.) (1983), p. 284.

[146] John Wellborn Root, *Broad Art Criticism*, first published in: *Inland Architect and News Record* XI, February 1988, pp. 3–5); cited after Hoffmann (ed.) (1967), p. 28.

[147] John Wellborn Root, 'Style' (first published in: *Inland Architect and Builder* VIII, January 1887, pp. 99–101); in: Hoffmann (ed.) (1967), pp. 159–68.

[148] Root (1887); cited after Hoffmann (ed.) (1967), p. 162.

[149] John Wellborn Root, 'The Value of Type in Art' (first published in: *Inland Architect and Builder* II, November 1883, p. 132); in: Hoffmann (ed.) (1967), pp. 169–71.

[150] Root (1887); cited after Hoffmann (ed.) (1967), p. 164.

[151] John Wellborn Root, 'A Great Architectural Problem' (first published in: *Inland Architect and News Record* XV, June 1890, pp. 67–71); in: Hoffmann (ed.) (1967), pp. 130–42.

[152] Root (1890); cited after Hoffmann (ed.) (1967), p. 141.

[153] Root (1890); cited after Hoffmann (ed.) (1967), p. 142.

[154] Letter of 15 March 1881; cited after Condit (ed. 1973), p. 52.

[155] John Wellborn Root, 'Architects of Chicago' (first published in: *America* V, 11 December 1890; *Inland Architect and News Record* XVI, 8 January 1891, pp. 91f.); cited after Hoffmann (ed.) (1967), p. 236.

[156] On Burnham, cf. Charles Moore, *Daniel H. Burnham, Architect, Planner of Cities*, 2 vols, Boston–New York 1921 (facs. repr. New York 1968); Thomas S. Hines, *Burnham of Chicago. Architect and Planner*, New York 1974.

[157] On early American city planning concepts, cf. Albert Fein, 'The American City: The Idea and the Real', in: Edgar Kaufmann, Jr. (ed.), *The Rise of an American Architecture*, New York–London 1970, pp. 51ff. Daniel H. Burnham and Edward Bennett, *The Plan of Chicago*, Chicago 1909 (facs. repr. New York 1970); cf. cat. *The Plan of Chicago: 1909–1979*, Chicago 1979; on the history of the plan for Chicago, cf. Hines (1974), pp. 312ff.

[158] On American neo-Gothic cf. Calder Loth and Julius Trousdale Sadler, Jr, *The Only Proper Style, Gothic Architecture in America*, Boston 1975.

[159] On McKim, Mead & White cf. esp. *A Monograph of the Works of McKim, Mead & White, 1879–1915*, 4 vols, New York 1915–20 (facs. repr. in one vol. with a foreword by Leland Roth, New York 1973;

1977); Charles Herbert Reilly, *McKim, Mead & White*, London 1924 (facs. repr. New York 1973); Leland Roth, *The Architecture of McKim, Mead & White, 1870–1920: A Building List*, New York 1978; Richard Guy Wilson, *McKim, Mead & White. Architects*, New York 1983.

[160] Cf. Walter C. Kidney, *The Architecture of Choice: Eclecticism in America 1880–1930*, New York 1974.

[161] On the Arts and Crafts movement in America cf. Robert Judson Clark (ed.), *The Arts and Crafts Movement in America 1876–1916*, Princeton 1972; Peter Davey, *Architecture of the Arts and Crafts Movement*, London–New York 1980, pp. 183ff.

[162] Gustav Stickley, *Craftsman Homes*, New York 1909 (facs. repr. New York 1979).

[163] Stickley (1909), p. 9.

[164] Ibid., pp. 10f.

25. Germany and its neighbours: 1890s–1945

[1] Most of Adolf Loos's newspaper and periodical articles are collected in the two volumes: Adolf Loos, *Ins Leere gesprochen 1897–1900*, Paris–Zürich 1921 (Innsbruck ²1931/32); id. *Trotzdem 1900–1930*, Innsbruck 1931. These two collections are published in: Adolf Loos, *Sämtliche Schriften*, vol. 1, ed. Franz Glück, Vienna–Munich 1963 (vol. 2 has not appeared). Cf. the collected 3-vol. ed. of Loos's writings, ed. Adolf Opel: Adolf Loos, *Ins Leere gesprochen*, Vienna 1981; *Trotzdem*, Vienna 1982; *Die Potemkin'sche Stadt. Verschollene Schriften 1897–1933*, Vienna 1983. On Loos cf. esp. Heinrich Kulka, *Adolf Loos*, Vienna 1931; Ludwig Münz and Gustav Künstler, *Der Architekt Adolf Loos*, Vienna–Munich 1964; Burkhard Rukschcio and Roland Schachel, *Adolf Loos. Leben und Werk*, Salzburg–Vienna 1982; Benedetto Gravagnuolo, *Adolf Loos. Theory and Works*, Milan 1982; exhib. cat. *Adolf Loos 1870–1933. Raumplan-Wohnungsbau*, Berlin 1983; anthology, ed. Österreichisches Kulturinstitut in Paris, *Adolf Loos 1870–1933*, Brussels 1983; Hildegard Amanshauser, *Untersuchungen zu den Schriften von Adolf Loos*, Vienna 1985.

[2] '*Ein jedes material hat seine eigene formensprache, und kein material kann die formen eines anderen materials für sich in anspruch nehmen. Denn die formen haben sich aus*

der verwendbarkeit und herstellungsweise eines jeden materials gebildet, sie sind mit dem material und durch das material geworden. Kein material gestattet einen eingriff in seinen formenkreis.' Adolf Loos, 'Das Prinzip der Bekleidung' (1898), in: id., *Ins Leere gesprochen* (ed. 1981), p. 140.

[3] '*Die decke ist das älteste architekturdetail … die bekleidung älter als die konstruktion.*' Ibid., pp. 139, 141.

[4] '*… Stimmungen im Menschen erwecken soll: Die aufgabe des architekten ist es daher, diese stimmung zu präzisieren. Das zimmer muß gemütlich, das haus wohnlich aussehen. Das justizgebäude muß dem heimlichen laster wie eine drohende gebärde erscheinen. Das bankhaus muß sagen: hier ist dein geld bei ehrlichen leuten fest und gut verwahrt.*' Id., 'Architektur' (1909), in: Loos, *Trotzdem* (ed. 1982), pp. 102f.

[5] On the *Raumplan* cf. esp. Dietrich Worbs, 'Der Raumplan im Wohnungsbau von Adolf Loos', in: exhib. cat. (1983), pp. 64ff.

[6] '*Denn das ist die große revolution in der architektur: das lösen eines grundrisses im Raum.*' Adolf Loos, 'Josef Veillich' (1929), in: id., *Trotzdem* (ed. 1982), p. 215.

[7] '*Wir können daher behaupten: Der zukünftige große Architekt wird ein Classiker sein. Einer, der nicht an die Werke seiner Vorgänger, sondern direct an das classische Alterthum anknüpft.*' Id., 'Die alte und die*

neue Richtung in der Baukunst' (1898), in: id., *Die Potemkin'sche Stadt* (1983), p. 66.

[8]'*Ansätze dazu zeigen sich auch schon in der neuen Ornamentik der Wagner-Schule.*' Ibid.

[9]On Loos's years in America, cf. the graphic account by Richard Neutra, *Auftrag für morgen*, Hamburg 1962, pp. 178ff.

[10] Cf. Adolf Opel in foreword to: Loos, *Die Potemkin'sche Stadt* (1983), p. 9.

[11] '*Da das ornament nicht mehr organisch mit unserer kultur zusammenhängt, ist es auch nicht mehr ausdruck unserer kultur. Das ornament, das heute geschaffen wird, hat keinen zusammenhang mit uns, hat überhaupt keine menschlichen zusammenhänge, keinen zusammenhang mit der weltordnung.*' Adolf Loos, 'Ornament und Verbrechen' (1908), in: id., *Trotzdem* (ed. 1982), p. 84.

[12] '*Weinet nicht. Seht, das macht ja die größe unserer zeit aus, daß sie nicht imstande ist, ein neues ornament hervorzubringen. Wir haben das ornament überwunden, wir haben uns zur ornamentlosigkeit durchgerungen. Seht, die zeit ist nahe, die erfüllung wartet unser. Bald werden die straßen der städte wie weiße mauern glänzen! Wie Zion, die heilige stadt, die hauptstadt des himmels. Dann ist die erfüllung da.*' Ibid., p. 80.

[13] '*evolution der kultur is gleichbedeutend mit dem entfernen des ornamentes aus dem gebrauchsgegenstande.*' Ibid., p. 79.

[14] '*denn das ornament wird nicht nur von verbrechern erzeugt, es begeht ein verbrechen dadurch, daß es den menschen schwer an der gesundheit, am nationalvermögen und also an seiner kulturellen entwicklung schädigt.*' Ibid., p. 82.

[15] '*vergeudeter Arbeitskraft und geschändetem Material.*' '*Ornamentlosigkeit ist nicht reizlosigkeit, sondern wirkt als neuer reiz, belebt. Die mühle, die nicht klappert, weckt den müller.*' Ibid., p. 175.

[16] '*Form und ornament sind das resultat unbewußter gesamtarbeit der menschen eines ganzen kulturkreises. Alles andere ist kunst.*' Ibid.

[17] '*Ich habe aber damit niemals gemeint, was die puristen ad absurdum getrieben haben, daß das ornament systematisch und konsequent abzuschaffen sei.*' Ibid., p. 177.

[18] '*So hätte also das haus nichts mit kunst zu tun und wäre die architektur nicht unter die künste einzureihen? Es ist so. Nur ein ganz kleiner Teil der Architektur gehört der kunst an: das grabmal und das denkmal. Alles andere, was einem Zweck dient, ist aus dem reiche der kunst auszuschließen.*' Id., 'Architektur' (1909), in: id., *Trotzdem* (ed. 1982), p. 101.

[19] Cf. Allan Janik and Stephan Toulmin, *Wittgenstein's Vienna*, New York 1973, p. 207; Bernhard Leitner, *The Architecture of Ludwig Wittgenstein. A Documentation*, New York 1976; Hartley Slater, 'Wittgenstein's Aesthetics', *The British Journal of Aesthetics* 23, 1, 1983, pp. 34–37.

[20] Ludwig Wittgenstein, 'Tractatus logicophilosophicus' (1921), in: Wittgenstein, *Schriften*, Frankfurt 1960, p. 11: '*Die Tatsachen im logischen Raum sind die Welt.*'

[21] '*dieser Bauart notwendigen Praezision & Sachgemaeßheit.*' Cited from Leitner (1976), pp. 29 and 122ff.

[22] Cf. esp. Ivan Margolius, *Cubism in Architecture and the Applied Arts. Bohemia and France 1910–1914*, London 1979.

[23] Cf. Margolius (1979), pp. 34f., 40ff.

[24] '*Diese historischen Architekturrichtungen erregen unsere Aufmerksamkeit durch die Lebendigkeit des Geistes, welcher in die Materie eingedrungen ist, sowie durch die Dramatisierung der Ausdrucksmittel, mit deren Hilfe ihre Formen geschaffen worden sind.*' Pavel Janák, 'Das Prisma und die Pyramide' (Czech text in: *Umelêcký Měsičnik* vol. II, 1911/12, pp. 162–70); in German trans. in: Marco Pozzetto, *Die Schule Otto Wagners 1894–1912*, Vienna–Munich 1980, pp. 163–68, quotation from p. 165.

[25] Cf. illus. in: Margolius (1979), pp. 53ff.

[26] On Darmstadt and German adoption of English ideas, cf. esp. *Ein Dokument Deutscher Kunst*, ed. Alexander Koch (Darmstadt 1901; facs. repr. Darmstadt 1979); Hanno-Walter Kruft, 'Die Arts-and-Crafts-Bewegung und der deutsche Jugendstil', in: Gerhard Bott (ed.), *Von Morris zum Bauhaus. Eine Kunst gegründet auf Einfachheit*, Hanau 1977, pp. 27–39.

[27] There is no monograph on Muthesius. Cf. the cat. *Hermann Muthesius 1861–1927*, Berlin 1978; among a number of articles on Muthesius by Julius Posener is 'Muthesius als Architect' in: *Werkbundarchiv* 1, 1972, pp. 55–79 (repr. in: Posener, *Berlin auf dem Wege zu einer neuen Architektur*, Munich 1979, pp. 127ff.). A listing of Muthesius's published writings in: Hans-Joachim

Hubrich, *Hermann Muthesius. Die Schriften zu Architektur, Kunstgewerbe, Industrie in der 'Neuen Bewegung'*, Berlin 1981, pp. 317ff.; a selection of Muthesius's writings in: Julius Posener (ed.), *Anfänge des Funktionalismus*, Frankfurt–Vienna 1964, pp. 109ff.

[28] Hermann Muthesius, *Die englische Baukunst der Gegenwart. Beispiele neuer englischer Profanbauten, mit Grundrissen, Textabbildungen und erläuterndem Text*, 4 vols, Leipzig–Berlin 1900–03; id., *Die neue kirchliche Baukunst in England. Entwicklung, Bedingungen und Grundzüge des Kirchenbaues der englischen Staatskirche und der Secten*, Berlin 1901; id., *Das englische Haus. Entwicklung, Bedingungen, Anlage, Aufbau, Einrichtung und Innenraum*, 3 vols, Berlin ¹1904–05 (²1908–11).

[29] 'Es kam mir nicht sowohl darauf an, eine Nachahmung des englischen Hauses oder seiner Einzelheiten zu empfehlen, als die Gesinnung, die diesem zugrunde liegt, dem deutschen Leser zu erschließen.' Muthesius, *Das englische Haus*, vol. I (²1908), p. iv.

[30] 'Es ist das erste individuelle Haus der neuen künstlerischen Kultur, das erste Haus, das innen und außen als Ganzes gedacht und ausgeführt war, das erste Beispiel in der Geschichte des modernen Hauses überhaupt.' Ibid., p. 106.

[31] Ibid., pp. 150f.

[32] Ibid., p. 162.

[33] 'Was aber am englischen Hause von eigentlichem, ausschlaggebenden Werte ist, ist seine völlige Sachlichkeit. Es ist schlecht und recht ein Haus, in dem man wohnen will. Da ist kein Aufwand an Repräsentationsanlagen, kein Phantasieerguß an Ornament und Formenkram, kein Aufblähen das Natürlichen und Zurechtmachen zum Künstlerischen, keine Prätension, selbst keine 'Architektur'. Es steht da ohne Prunk und Zier, in jener selbstverständlichen Anständigkeit, die, so natürlich sie sein sollte, in unserer heutigen Kultur so selten geworden ist.' Ibid., p. 237.

[34] Hermann Muthesius, 'Die Bedeutung des Kunstgewerbes', *Dekorative Kunst* X, 1907, pp. 177–92; abridged in: Posener (1964), pp. 176ff. and in cat. *Zwischen Kunst und Industrie. Der Deutsche Werkbund*, Munich 1975, pp. 39ff.

[35] 'Will man also den Bedingungen der Zeit gerecht werden, so ist es zunächst nötig,

den Einzelbedingungen jedes Gegenstandes gerecht zu werden. Und so bildete es von vornherein den Hauptinhalt des modernen Kunstgewerbes, sich den Zweck eines jeden Gegenstandes zunächst einmal recht deutlich klarzumachen und die Form logisch aus dem Zweck zu entwickeln. Sobald aber der Sinn nur einmal von der äußerlichen Nachahmung der alten Kunst abgelenkt war, sobald die Realität erfaßt war, gesellten sich sogleich noch andere notwendige Forderungen hinzu. Jedes Material stellt für die Bearbeitung seine besonderen Bedingungen. Stein erfordert andere Dimensionen und andere Formen als Holz, Holz wieder andere als Metall, und von den Metallen Schmiedeeisen andere als Silber. Zu der Gestaltung nach dem Zweck kam also die Gestaltung nach dem Charakter des Materials und mit der Rücksicht auf das Material war gleichzeitig die Rücksicht auf die dem Material entsprechende Konstruktion gegeben. Zweck, Material und Fügung geben dem modernen Kunstwerbler die einzigen Direktiven, die er befolgt.' Muthesius (1907); Posener (1964), pp. 178ff.; exhib. cat. (1975), p. 42.

[36] 'Das Kunstgewerbe hat das Ziel, die heutigen Gesellschaftsklassen zur Gediegenheit, Wahrhaftigkeit und bürgerlichen Einfachheit zurückzuziehen.' Muthesius (1907); exhib. cat. (1975), p. 44.

[37] The ideas of the Deutscher Werkbund are most clearly expressed in the *Jahrbuch des Deutschen Werkbundes* which appeared from 1912 onwards.

On the Werkbund cf. esp.: Theodor Heuss, *Was ist Qualität? Zur Geschichte und zur Aufgabe des Deutschen Werkbundes*, Stuttgart 1951; *50 Jahre Deutscher Werkbund*, ed. Hans Eckstein, Berlin 1958; exhib. cat. *Zwischen Kunst und Industrie. Der Deutsche Werkbund*, Munich 1975; Joan Campbell, *The German Werkbund. The Politics of Reform in the Applied Arts*, Princeton 1978 (German ed., Stuttgart 1981); Lucius Burckhardt (ed.), *Der Werkbund in Deutschland, Österreich und der Schweiz*, Stuttgart 1978; Kurt Junghanns, *Der Deutsche Werkbund. Sein erstes Jahrzehnt*, Berlin 1982.

[38] 'in jenem allumfassenden, unser ganzes Leben durchdringenden Sinne, der dem Begriffe bei den Griechen eigen war und den auch das Mittelalter, wenngleich weniger bewußt, teilte.' Hermann Muthesius, *Die*

Einheit der Architektur. Betrachtungen über Baukunst, Ingenieurbau und Kunstgewerbe, Berlin 1908, p. 46.

[39] Muthesius (1908), p. 20.

[40] *'rechnerisch gefundene knappste Konstruktionsform … als knappste Ausdrucksform des konstruktiv Richtigen … einen bestimmten Eindruck auf den empfänglichen Beschauer.'* Ibid., pp. 30f.

[41] *'gerade in dieser, die Materie überwindenden Schlankheit und Durchsichtigkeit ein neues künstlerisches Moment erkennen, dem man einen besondern Wert beimessen wird.'* Ibid., pp. 32f.

[42] Ibid., p. 5.

[43] *'Der Zweck des Bundes ist die Veredlung der gewerblichen Arbeit im Zusammenwirken von Kunst, Industrie und Handwerk durch Erziehung, Propaganda und geschlossene Stellungnahme zu einschlägigen Fragen.'* The constitution of the Werkbund is printed as an appendix to the *Jahrbücher* of 1912 and 1913.

[44] *'Man erwartete das Heil von dem Kunsthandwerker mittelalterlichen Schlages … In der heutigen Wirtschaft gibt der Unternehmer den Ausschlag; wollen wir vorwärts, so müssen wir ihn für uns gewinnen, ihn überzeugen, daß Geschäft und Geschmack nicht Feinde zu sein brauchen.'* *Jahrbuch des Deutschen Werkbundes 1912,* p. 3.

[45] *'Nicht nur bei der Fabrikation von Gebrauchsartikeln, auch beim Bau von Maschinen, Fahrzeugen und Fabrikgebäuden, die dem nackten Zwecke dienen, kommen ästhetische Gesichtspunkte in bezug auf Geschlossenheit der Form, auf Farbe und auf Eleganz des ganzen Eindrucks von vornherein zur Geltung. Augenscheinlich genügt nicht mehr die materielle Steigerung der Produkte allein, um im internationalen Wettstreite Siege erringen zu können. Das technisch überall gleichvorzügliche Ding muß mit geistiger Idee, mit Form durchtränkt werden, damit ihm die Bevorzugung unter der Menge gleichartiger Erzeugnisse gesichert bleibt. Deshalb ist die gesamte Industrie heute vor die Aufgabe gestellt, sich mit künstlerischen Fragen ernsthaft zu befassen.'* Walter Gropius, 'Die Entwicklung moderner Industriebaukunst', in: *Jahrbuch des Deutschen Werkbundes 1913,* p. 17.

[46] Gropius (1913), pp. 20f.

[47] *'Vielleicht ahnte man damals noch nicht, daß die Erfüllung des reinen Zweckes an und für*

sich noch keine das Auge befriedigende Form schafft, vielmehr hierzu noch andere Kräfte, sei es auch unbewußt, mitwirken müssen. Jedenfalls entwickelte sich von allen Werken des Ingenieurs am ehesten die Maschine zu einem reinen Stil, der am Beginn des laufenden Jahrhunderts so gut durchgebildet dastand, daß es üblich wurde, die sogenannte Schönheit der Maschine zu bewundern und in ihr gewissermaßen die ausgeprägteste Erscheinung einer modernen Stilbildung zu erblicken.' Hermann Muthesius, 'Das Form-Problem im Ingenieurbau', *Jahrbuch des Deutschen Werkbundes 1913,* p. 25.

[48] On Peter Behrens and the AEG cf. esp. Tilmann Buddensieg a.o., *Industriearchitektur. Peter Behrens und die AEG 1907–1914,* Berlin 1979.
On the Darmstadt exhibition cf. esp. the festschrift: Peter Behrens, *Ein Dokument deutscher Kunst. Die Ausstellung der Künstlerkolonie in Darmstadt 1901,* Munich 1901.
On Nietzsche's influence on Behrens's Darmstadt house, cf. Tilmann Buddensieg, 'Das Wohnhaus als Kultbau. Zum Darmstädter Haus von Peter Behrens', in exhib. cat. *Peter Behrens and Nürnberg,* Munich 1980, pp. 37–47.

[50] On Behrens cf. Fritz Hoeber, *Peter Behrens,* Munich 1913 (pp. 223ff.: bibliography of Peter Behrens up to 1912); Stanford Owen Anderson, *Peter Behrens and the New Architecture of Germany,* 1900–1917 (diss. Columbia Univ. 1968), Ann Arbor, MI 1983 (pp. 486ff. bibliography of Behrens' writings, incomplete); Hans-Joachim Kadatz, *Peter Behrens,* Leipzig 1977; Tilmann Buddensieg a.o., *Industriekultur. Peter Behrens und die AEG 1907–1914,* Berlin 1979; Guglielmo Bilancioni, *Il primo Behrens, Origini del moderno in architettura,* Florence 1981; Alan Windsor, *Peter Behrens, Architect and Designer,* New York 1981.

[51] Motto in: Hoeber (1913).

[52] *'möglichst geschlossenen, ruhigen Flächen …, die durch ihre Bündigkeit keine Hindernisse'.* Peter Behrens, 'Einfluß von Zeit- und Raumausnutzung auf moderne Formentwicklung', *Jahrbuch des Deutschen Werkbundes 1914,* pp. 7–10, here p. 8.

[53] *'weithin geführten geraden Straßen … axialen Anlagen des Barockzeitalters … Höhenentwicklung … Auch die Stadtanlage verlangt nach Körperlichkeit und*

Silhouette, die nur in der Zufügung von kompakten, vertikalen Massen gefunden werden kann.' Behrens (1914), p. 9.

[54] Carl Rehorst, 'Die Deutsche Werkbund-Austellung', Cologne 1914, in: *Jahrbuch des Deutschen Werkbundes 1913*, p. 88.

[55] On the Cologne exhib. of the Werkbund cf. esp. cat. *Deutsche Werkbund-Ausstellung Cöln 1914*, Cologne 1914 (facs. repr. Cologne 1981; forming part of *Frühe Kölner Kunstausstellungen*; cf. in the vol. of commentary, Wolfram Hagspiel, pp. 37ff.); *Jahrbuch des Deutschen Werkbundes 1915* entitled *Deutsche Form im Kriegsjahr. Die Ausstellung Köln 1914*; Fritz Stahl, 'Die Architektur der Werkbund-Ausstellung', *Wasmuths Monnatshefte für Baukunst 1914/1915*, pp. 153ff.; exhib. cat. *Der Westdeutsche Impuls*, Cologne 1984.

[56] 'Es ist das Eigentümliche der Architektur, daß sie zum Typischen drängt. Die Typisierung aber verschmäht das Außerordentliche und sucht das Ordentliche' Hermann Muthesius, 'Die Werkbundarbeit der Zukunft,' in: Friedrich Naumann, *Werkbund und die Weltwirtschaft. Der Werkbund-Gedanke in den germanischen Ländern*, Jena 1914; cf. Posener (1964), pp. 199ff.; exhib. cat. (1975), pp. 85ff.

[57] 'Alles ist im Werden, und es wäre infolgedessen ein Vorgriff in die Zukunft, schon heute eine Typisierung zu konstatieren oder auch nur zu verlangen. Dazu kommt, daß Typisierung mit Kunst überhaupt nichts zu tun hat...' Posener (1964), p. 211.

[58] On this phase of the Werkbund cf. esp. Joan Campbell (1978; 1981); cf. also 'Die zwanziger Jahre des Deutschen Werkbunds', *Werkbund-Archiv* 10, 1982.

[59] *Die Form* appeared in 1922 and from 1925 to 1934. A selection in: Felix Schwarz and Frank Gloor (ed.), *Die Form: Stimme des Deutschen Werkbundes 1925–1934* (*Bauwelt Fundamente* 24), Gütersloh 1969.

[60] 'als große, alle anderen Künste sammelnde und leitende Kunst...' 'streng auf handwerklichkünstlerischem Boden, nicht auf technisch-industriellem ruhen.' Text of Poelzig's address in cat. (1975), pp. 161ff.

[61] Cf. exhib. cat. *Die Wohnung*, Stuttgart 1927.

[62] On Bruno Taut cf. Kurt Junghanns, *Bruno Taut 1880–1938*, Berlin ('1970, ²1983; exhib. cat. *Bruno Taut 1880–1938*, Berlin 1980; Jain Boyd Whyte, *Bruno Taut. Baumeister einer neuen Welt. Architektur und Aktivismus 1914–1920*, Stuttgart 1981 (English ed. London 1982); Giacomo Ricci, *La Cattedrale del futuro. Bruno Taut 1914–1921*, Rome 1982.

[63] For a bibliography of Taut's writings cf. Junghanns (1983), pp. 268ff.

[64] On Expressionism in architecture and its intellectual background, cf. Wolfgang Pehnt, *Die Architektur die Expressionismus*, Stuttgart 1973.

[65] On Scheerbart cf. esp. Rosemarie Haag Bletter, 'Paul Scheerbart's Architectural Fantasies', *Journal of the Society of Architectural Historians* XXXIV, 1975, pp. 83–97 (in German trans. in cat. (1980), pp. 86ff.).

[66] Paul Scheerbart, *Glasarchitektur*, Berlin 1914; new edition ed. Wolfgang Pehnt, Munich 1971.

[67] 'Wir leben zumeist in geschlossenen Räumen. Diese bilden das Milieu, aus dem unsere Kultur herauswächst. Unsere Kultur ist gewissermaßen ein Produkt unserer Architektur. Wollen wir unsere Kultur auf ein höheres Niveau bringen, so sind wir wohl oder übel gezwungen, unsere Architektur umzuwandeln. Und dieses wird uns nur dann möglich sein, wenn wir den Räumen, in denen wir leben, das Geschlossene nehmen. Das aber können wir nur durch Einführung der Glasarchitektur, die das Sonnenlicht und das Licht des Mondes und der Sterne nicht nur durch ein paar Fenster in die Räume läßt – sondern gleich durch möglichst viele Wände, die ganz aus Glas sind – aus farbigen Gläsern. Das neue Milieu, das wir uns dadurch schaffen, muß uns eine neue Kultur bringen.' Scheerbart (1914; ed. 1971), p. 25.

[68] Cf. esp. Rosemarie Haag Bletter, 'The Interpretation of the Glass Dream – Expressionist Architecture and the History of the Crystal Metaphor', *Journal of the Society of Architectural Historians* XL, 1981, pp. 20–43; the speculative essay by Marcello Fagiolo, 'La cattedrale di cristallo. L'architettura dell'Expressionismo e la "tradizione" esoterica', in: Giulio Carlo Argan (ed.), *Il Revival*, Milan 1974, pp. 225–88.

[69] The best illustrations in: *Jahrbuch des Deutschen Werkbundes 1915*, pls 77ff.

[70] 'Das Glashaus hat keinen anderen Zweck, als schön zu sein... Wir brauchen in dem heutigen Bauen dringend die Befreiung von der traurig machenden unentwegten Klischee-Monumentalität. Das Fließende, künstlerisch Leichte kann sie allein bringen.'

Bruno Taut, *Glashaus. Werkbund-Ausstellung Cöln 1914*, Berlin 1914 (repr. in the vol. of commentary *Frühe Kölner Kunstausstellungen*, Cologne 1981, pp. 287ff.).

[71] Bruno Taut, *Die Stadtkrone. Mit Beiträgen von Paul Scheerbart und anderen*, Jena 1919; id., *Alpine Architektur*, Hagen 1919; id., *Die Auflösung der Städte oder Die Erde eine gute Wohnung oder Der Weg zur Alpinen Architektur*, Hagen 1920.

[72] Bruno Taut, *Der Weltbaumeister. Architekturschauspiel für symphonische Musik. Dem Geiste Paul Scheerbarts gewidmet*, Hagen 1920 (texts repr. in exhib. cat. *Arbeitsrat für Kunst Berlin 1918–1921*, Berlin 1980, p. 79); cf. Pehnt (1973), p. 73.

[73] Cf. Helga Kliemann, *Die Novembergruppe*, Berlin 1969; cat. *Arbeitsrat für Kunst Berlin 1918–1921*, Berlin 1980 (in which publications of the Workers' Council for Art repr.).

[74] 'Ein großer Baugedanke, so gewaltig, daß die Mußezeit aller immerfort damit erfüllt ist, Schmuck des Sterns Erde durch uns, seine Organe, ist der Allgemeinheit mit allen Mitteln einzuhämmern.' Bruno Taut, in: *Ja! Stimmen des Arbeitsrates für Kunst in Berlin*, Berlin 1919; cited from cat. (1980), p. 70.

[75] 'Dann gibt es keine Grenze zwischen Kunstgewerbe und Plastik oder Malerei, alles ist eins: Bauen.' Bruno Taut, *Ein Architektur-Programm* (*Flugschriften des Arbeitsrates für Kunst* Berlin I), Berlin ¹1918, ²1919; cited from cat. (1980), p. 86.

[76] 'Zurücktreten des Formalen grundsätzlich hinter das Landwirtschaftliche und Praktische, keine Scheu vor dem Allereinfachsten, auch nicht vor der – Farbe.' Ibid.

[77] Bruno Taut (ed.), *Frühlicht*, 1920 as supplement to *Stadtbaukunst in alter und neuer Zeit*, 1921/22 in separate vols; repr. of a selection: Bruno Taut, *Frühlicht 1920–1922. Eine Folge für die Verwirklichung des neuen Baugedankens* (*Bauwelt Fundamente* 8), Berlin–Frankfurt–Vienna 1963. The letters of the Gläserne Ketter are available in an English edition: Iain Boyd Whyte (ed.), *The Crystal Chain Letters. Architectural Fantasies by Bruno Taut and His Circle*, Cambridge, MA 1985.

[78] 'Ein Haus, des nichts anderes als schön sein soll. Keinen anderen Zweck soll es erfüllen, als leer sein nach dem Spruch von Meister Eckhart…Das Glück der Baukunst wird den Besucher erfüllen, seine Seele leer machen vom Menschlichen und zu einem Gefäß für das Göttliche. Der Bau ist Abbild und Gruß der Sterne. Sternförmig ist sein Grundriß, die heiligen Zahlen 7 und 3 verbinden sich in ihm zur Einheit… Zwischen der äußern und innern Glashaut sitzt die Beleuchtung… Fährt man nachts im Flugzeug zum Hause hin, so leuchtet es von weitem wie ein Stern. Und es klingt wie eine Glocke.' Bruno Taut, 'Haus des Himmels,' in: Taut (ed.), *Frühlicht* (1920), cited from ed. (1963), p. 33.

[79] Bruno Taut, 'Der Regenbogen. Aufruf zum farbigen Bauen; Farbe im äußeren Raum', in: Taut (ed.), *Frühlicht* (1921); ed. (1963), pp. 97ff.

[80] 'in erster Linie an das Wirtschaftliche und Praktische denken, für die Maschine ein besonderes Interesse haben und im übrigen das Ästhetische ganz als Nebensache ansehen.' Bruno Taut, *Die Neue Wohnung*, Leipzig 1924.

[81] 'Wenn aus einer Wohnung nach strengster und rücksichtsloser Auswahl alles, aber auch alles, was nicht direkt zum Leben notwendig ist, herausfliegt, so wird nicht bloß ihre Arbeit erleichtert, sondern es stellt sich von selbst eine neue Schönheit ein.' Taut (1924), p. 31.

[82] Ibid., p. 101.

[83] Bruno Taut, *Architekturlehre aus der Sicht eines sozialistischen Architekten* (Turkish ed., Istanbul 1938), ed. Tilmann Heinisch and Goerd Peschken, Hamburg–Berlin 1977.

[84] Taut (1977), p. 29.

[85] Ibid., p. 37.

[86] On Finsterlin cf. Franco Borsi (ed.), *Hermann Finsterlin: Idea dell'architettura*, Florence 1969; Pehnt (1973), pp. 95ff.; exhib. cat. *Hermann Finsterlin*, Stuttgart 1973 (English ed. New York 1985).

[87] 'der Schöpfung siebenten Tag weitertragen um eine Welle in der Brandungskette, die liebend tändelt mit Unendlichkeit.' Hermann Finsterlin, 'Der achte Tag', in: Taut (ed.), *Frühlicht* (1920); ed. (1963), pp. 52–59, here p. 52.

[88] 'Die menschliche Architektur ist ein biogenetisches Phänomen des Menschenwesens, das jenseits des Fötalen liegt.' Finsterlin (1920); ed. (1963), p. 54.

[89] 'der Menschheit Großteil gern in den schemat-

isierten Eingeweiden seiner kubischen, tro-
janischen Rosse haust gleich seinen Parasi-
ten...' Hermann Finsterlin, 'Innenarchitektur', in: Taut (ed.), *Frühlicht* (Winter
1921/22); ed. (1963), pp. 105–109, here, p.
105.

⁹⁰'*Im Innenraum des neuen Hauses wird man
sich nicht nur als Insasse einer märchen-
haften Kristalldrüse fühlen, sondern als
interner Bewohner eines Organismus, wan-
dernd von Organ zu Organ, ein gebender
und empfangender Symbiote eines "fossilen
Riesenmutterleibes.*" Finsterlin (1921/22);
ed. (1963), p. 107.

⁹¹'*So kann sich z.B. ein Schrank mit seiner
Wurzel aus der Wand eines Betonbaues
herausblähen, übergehend in Majolika...*'
Ibid., p. 108.

⁹²'*harmonische Verbindung unregelmäßiger
Teile, unregelmäßiger Bauelemente...unter
Wahrung der harmonischen Proportion in
den Teilen und im Gesamtkomplex.*' Hermann Finsterlin, 'Die Genesis der Weltarchitektur, oder die Deszendenz der Dome als
Stilspiel,' in: Taut (ed.), *Frühlicht* (1923) ed.
(1963), pp. 149–58, here p. 154.

⁹³ Finsterlin (1921/22); ed. (1963), p. 109.

⁹⁴ On the Goetheanum and the architectural
ideas of Rudolf Steiner cf. Felix Kayser
(ed.), *Architektonisches Gestalten*, Stuttgart
1933 (esp. on secular architecture); Carl
Kemper, *Der Bau. Studien zur Architektur
und Plastik der ersten Goetheanums*,
Stuttgart 1966; Rex Raab a.o., *Sprechender
Beton. Wie Rudolf Steiner den Stahlbeton
verwendete*, Dornach 1972; Hagen Biesantz
and Arne Klingborg, *Das Goetheanum. Der
Bau-Impuls Rudolf Steiners*, Dornach 1978;
Mike Schuyt and Joost Elffers (eds), *Rudolf
Steiner und seine Architektur*, Cologne 1980;
Wolfgang Bachmann, *Die Architekturvor-
stellungen der Anthroposophen*, Cologne–
Vienna 1981; Walther Roggenkamp, *Das
Goetheanum als Gesamtkunstwerk. Rudolf
Steiner, Der Baugedanke des Goetheanum.
Bildband*, Dornach 1986.

⁹⁵ Rudolf Steiner's most important statements
on architecture and the Goetheanum are
contained in his lectures from 1911 onwards,
available in the following editions: Rudolf
Steiner, *Wege zu einem neuen Baustil 'und
der Bau wird Mensch'*, Dornach 1926,
Suttgart ²1957, Dornach ³1982; *Architektur,
Plastik und Malerei des Ersten Goetheanum*,
Dornach ¹1972 (²1982); *Der Baugedanke*

des Goetheanum, Dornach ¹1932, Stuttgart
²1958.

⁹⁶'*elementarisch künstlerischen Schöpfung...
besondere Art der Weltanschauungssprache
...*' Steiner (1932), p. 19.

⁹⁷'*innerer Notwendigkeit...geistigen Entwick-
lungsgang der Menschheit...*' Steiner
(1926, ³1982), p. 30.

⁹⁸'*In Dornach ist der Versuch gemacht, dieses
Lebendige so weit zu treiben, daß man wirklich das bloße Dynamische Metrische, Symmetrische früherer Bauformen übergeführt
hat in das Organische*' Steiner (1932), p. 21.

⁹⁹ Ibid.

¹⁰⁰ Steiner (1926, ³1982), p. 50.

¹⁰¹ '*Das ist das Neue der Wandbehandlung bei
diesem Baugedanken...Diese Wände sind so
in ihrem künstlerischen Prinzip, daß sie sich
selber aufheben, so daß man drinnen das
Gefühl haben kann: die Wand schließt einen
nicht ab, die Säule steht nicht da, um
irgendeine Grenze zu bilden, sondern dasjenige, was in der Säule ausgedrückt ist,
was auf der Wand ausgedrückt ist, das
durchbricht die Wand und läßt einen in
lebendige Beziehung kommen mit dem
ganzen Weltenall.*' Steiner (¹1972, ²1982), p.
36.

¹⁰² '*Es mußte aber ein Anfang gemacht werden,
erstens einen solchen Utilitätsbau einmal zu
gestalten nach solchen inneren Schaffens-
prinzipien, zweitens mit Rücksicht auf das
modernste Material, den Beton. Jedes
Material fordert seine bestimmten Bauprin-
zipien, die mit der Natur des Materials
zusammenhängen, bauen. Der Baugedanke
muß ebenso die Utilitätsgedanken zum Aus-
drucke bringen, wie auch die Anforderungen
des Materials.*' Ibid., p. 40.

¹⁰³ '*ideelle Einheit...ein Abdruck...der inneren
Harmonie der Kolonie Wohnenden.*'
Steiner (1926, ³1982), p. 41.

¹⁰⁴ '*jedes Glied...eine Offenbarung des inneren
Wesens sein...wie ins Architektonische
umgesetzte·Wurzeln.*' Steiner, lecture of 1
January 1924; cited from: Steiner (³1982),
p. 117 and Biesantz-Klingborg (1978), p. 76.

¹⁰⁵ On Lauweriks, cf. esp. Nic. Tummers, *Der
Hagener Impuls. Das Werk von J. L. M.
Lauweriks und sein Einfluß auf Architektur
und Formgebung um 1910*, Hagen 1972;
Peter Stressig in: *Karl Ernst Osthaus. Leben
und Werk*, Recklinghausen 1971, pp. 423ff.
Nic. Tummers in: exhib. cat. *Der westdeut-
sche Impuls 1900–1914*, vol.: *Die Folk-*

[106] *wang-Idee des Karl Ernst Osthaus*, Hagen 1984, pp. 149ff.; Gerda Breuer a.o., *J. L. M. Lauweriks*, Krefeld 1987.
[106] Lauwericks' writings listed in cat. *Niederländische Architektur 1893–1918. Architectura*, Düsseldorf 1977, pp. 65f.
[107] Johannes Ludovicus Mathieu Lauweriks, 'Einen Beitrag zum Entwerfen auf systematischer Grundlage in der Architectur,' in: Ring I, Heft 4, 1909, pp. 25–34; repr. in: Tummers (1972), pp. 22ff.
[108] *'Systemzellen, worauf das Gebäude wird aufgebaut, woraus sich der architektonische Organismus bildet...die allgemeine rhythmische Basis, die immer vorhanden sein muß, und ohne welche das Entwerfen eines Gebäudes unmöglich ist, ebenso wie in einem natürlichen Organismus die Zelle unentbehrlich ist für dessen Aufbau.'* J. L. M. Lauwericks, 'Leitmotive', in: Ring I, Heft 1, 1909, pp. 5–9; repr. in: Tummers (1972), pp. 11ff.
[109] *'An der Kunstgewerbeschule zu Düsseldorf z.B. werden unter der Leitung des holländischen Lehrers Lauweriks alle Entwürfe nach einer ähnlichen, aber sehr speziellen Methode ausgeführt. Er geht allerdings darin am weitesten.'* H. P. Berlage, *Grundlagen und Entwicklung der Architektur*, Berlin 1908, p. 56.
[110] Cf. Stressig (1971), pp. 429ff.; Tummers (1972) pp. 35ff.
[111] On Osthaus cf. esp.: Herta Hesse-Frielinghaus a.o., *Karl Ernst Osthaus. Leben und Werk*, Recklinghausen 1971; a bibliography of writings, pp. 542ff.; exhib. cat. (1984).
[112] On Berlage cf. esp. Pieter Singelenberg, *H. P. Berlage. Idea and Style. The Quest for Modern Architecture*, Utrecht 1972; *Berlage 1856–1934* (Stichting Architectur Museum, Amsterdam) ¹1975, ²1979; Manfred Bock, *Anfänge einer neuen Architektur. Berlages Beitrag zur architektonischen Kultur der Niederlande im ausgehenden 19. Jahrhundert*, 's-Gravenhage and Wiesbaden 1983; Sergio Polano a.o. (ed.), *Hendrik Petrus Berlage. Complete Works*, New York 1988.
[113] bibliography of Berlage in: Bock (1983) pp. 406f.
[114] Hendrik Petrus Berlage, 'Bouwkunst an impressionisme,' in: *Architectura* 2, 1884, pp. 93–95, 98–100, 105f., 109f. (repr. in: Bock (1983), pp. 383–90); a close reading of this article in: Bock (1983), pp. 113ff., 229ff.

[115] Hendrick Petrus Berlage, *Gedanken über Stil in der Baukunst*, Leipzig 1905.
[116] *'Unsere Architektur sollte daher auch wieder nach einer gewissen Ordnung bestimmt werden! Wäre das Entwerfen nach einem geometrischen System nicht ein großer Schritt vorwärts? Eine Methode, nach der viele der modernen niederländischen Architekten schon arbeiten.'* Berlage (1905), p. 33.
[117] Cf. Bock (1983), pp. 64ff.
[118] Berlage (1905), p. 47.
[119] Hendrik Petrus Berlage, *Grundlagen und Entwicklung der Architektur. Vier Vorträge, gehalten im Kunstgewerbemuseum zu Zürich*, Berlin 1908.
[120] Berlage (1908), p. 4.
[121] *'für die Bildung künstlerischer Formen nicht nur von großem Nutzen, sondern sogar von absoluter Notwendigkeit...'* Ibid., p. 1.
[122] *'Erstens: Die Grundlage einer architektonischen Komposition soll wiederum nach einem geometrischen Schema bestimmt werden.*

'Zweitens: Die charakteristischen Formen früherer Stile sollen nicht verwendet werden.

'Drittens: Die architektonischen Formen sollen nach der sachlichen Seite hin sich entwickeln.' Ibid., p. 100.
[123] *'Dann wird aber auch das architektonische Kunstwerk nicht einen spezifisch individuellen Charakter haben, sondern das Resultat der Gemeinschaft, in diesem Sinne, aller, sein.'* Ibid., p. 117.
[124] On De Stijl cf. esp. Hans L. C. Jaffé, *De Stijl 1917–1931. The Dutch Contribution to Modern Art*, Amsterdam 1956 (German ed.: *De Stijl 1917–1931. Der niederländische Beitrag zur modernen Kunst*, Frankfurt–Vienna 1965); the anthology *Die Stijl: 1917–1931. Visions of Utopia*, New York 1982. The journal *De Stijl* (1917–1932), ed. Theo van Doesburg, the main source for the group's aesthetics, is available in a 2-vol. edition, Amsterdam 1968; for a selection in German trans. cf. H. L. C. Jaffé (ed.), *Mondrian und De Stijl*, Cologne 1967; Giovanni Fanelli, *De Stijl*, Rome–Bari 1983 (German ed.: *Stijl-Architektur. Der niederländische Beitrag zur frühen Moderne*, Stuttgart 1985); Yve-Alain Bois a.o., *De Stijl et l'architecture en France*, Lüttich–Brussels 1985.
[125] *'plastischen Mathematik...Jetzt lernen wir die Wirklichkeit in unserer Vorstellung in*

Konstruktionen zu übersetzen, die mit der Vernunft kontrollierbar sind, damit wir diese gleichen Konstruktionen später in der vorhandenen natürlichen Wirklichkeit wiederfinden, um so die Natur mit der gestaltenden Sicht zu durchdringen.' Cited from Jaffé (1965), p. 67.

126 'die Relativität der natürlichen Tatsachen auf das Absolute zu reduzieren, um das Absolute in natürlichen Tatsachen wiederzufinden.' Schoenmakers; cited from Jaffé (1965), p. 67.

127 On van Doesburg, cf. Joost Baljeu, Theo van Doesburg, New York 1974; Michael Schumacher, Avantgarde und Öffentlichkeit. Zur Soziologie der Künstlerzeitschrift am Beispiel von 'De Stijl', diss., Aachen 1979; Hannah L. Hedrick, Theo Van Doesburg. Propagandist and Practitioner of the Avant-Garde, 1909–1923, Ann Arbor, MI 1980; also the edited papers Theo van Doesburg 1883–1931, 's-Gravenhage 1983.

128 For a bibliography of van Doesburg's writings, cf. Baljeu (1974), pp. 205ff. (containing a selection of texts in English trans.); more detailed is the bibliography in: Sergio Polano (ed.), Theo van Doesburg. Scritti di arte e di architettura, Rome 1979, pp. 548ff. (this volume contains a wide-ranging selection of texts).

129 'C'est le spirituel, l'abstrait complet qui exprime précisément ce qui est humain, alors que ce qui est sensitif n'atteint pas encore la hauteur de ce qui est intellectuel et par conséquent doit être considéré comme appartenant à un degré inférieur de la culture humaine. L'art ne doit pas émouvoir le coeur. Toute émotion, qu'elle appartienne accidentellement à la douleur ou à la joie, signifie une rupture de l'harmonie, de l'équilibre entre le sujet (l'homme) et l'objet (l'univers). L'oeuvre d'art doit créer un état d'équilibre entre elle et l'univers; des émotions du sentiment créent précisément l'état contraire.' Theo van Doesburg in: De Stijl V, 1922, p. 185.

130 'Der wahrhaft moderne Künstler betrachtet die Großstadt als eine Verkörperung abstrakten Lebens. Sie ist ihm näher als die Natur; sie wird ihm eher ein Gefühl der Schönheit vermitteln. Denn in der Großstadt erscheint die Natur schon geordnet und durch den menschlichen Geist reguliert. Die Proportionen und der Rhythmus von Linien und Flächen bedeuten ihm mehr als die Launen der Natur. In der Metropole drückt sich die Schönheit mathematisch aus. Daher ist sie der Ort, von woher man das zukünftige mathematisch-künstlerische Temperament entwickeln muß, der Ort, von wo aus der neue Stil vorwärtsdringen muß.' Piet Mondrian in: De Stijl I, 1917, p. 132 (in Dutch); in German trans. in: Jaffé (1965), p. 83.

131 Theo van Doesburg in: De Stijl VII, memorial issue 1927, p. 39.

132 'Das reine Ausdrucksmittel der Baukunst ist Fläche, Masse (positiv) und Raum (negativ). Der Architekt drückt seine ästhetische Erfahrung durch Verhältnisse von Flächen und Massen zu Innenräumen und zum Raum aus.' Theo van Doesburg, Grundbegriffe der neuen gestaltenden Kunst (Bauhausbücher, 1925), ed. Hans M. Wingler, Mainz–Berlin 1966, p. 15.

133 'Die neue Sicht erfolgt nicht von einem bestimmten Punkt aus: ihr zufolge ist der Blickpunkt von überall und nirgends her bestimmt. Sie begreift ihn nicht an Raum und Zeit gebunden (in Übereinstimmung mit der Relativitätstheorie). In der Praxis legt sie ihn vor die Fläche (die extremste Möglichkeit der Gestaltungsvertiefung). So sieht sie die Architektur als eine Vielfalt von Flächen: also wiederum flächenhaft. Dies Vielfalt fügt sich daher (abstrakt) zu einem flächigen Bild...Die Farbe erstreckt sich über die gesamte Architektur, Gebrauchsgegenstände (Möbel) usw... So kommt es auch zum Konflikt mit der traditionellen Auffassung von konstruktiver Reinheit. Die Idee, derzufolge die Konstruktion gezeigt werden müsse, ist noch immer nicht tot...' Piet Mondrian in: De Stijl V, 1922, pp. 68f. (in Dutch); in German trans.: Jaffé (1967), pp. 161f.

134 'Die neue Architektur ist antikubisch, d.h. sie strebt nicht danach, die verschiedenen funktionellen Raumzellen in einem einzigen geschlossenen Kubus zusammenzufassen, sondern sie projiziert die funktionellen Raumzellen (wie auch Schutzdachflächen, Balkon-Volumen usw.) aus dem Mittelpunkt des Kubus nach draußen, wodurch Höhe, Breite und Tiefe plus Zeit zu einem völlig neuen bildnerischen Ausdruck in den offenen Räumen kommen. Dadurch erhält die Architektur (soweit es konstruktiv möglich ist – Aufgabe der Ingenieure) einen mehr oder weniger schwebenden Aspekt, der gewissermaßen die natürliche Schwerkraft aufhebt.'

Theo van Doesburg in: *De Stijl* VI/VII, 1924, p. 81 (in Dutch); in German trans. in: Jaffé (1967), p. 191.

[135] Theo van Doesburg, *Grundbegriffe der neuen gestaltenden Kunst (Bauhausbücher 1925)*, ed. Hans M. Wingler, Mainz–Berlin 1966.

[136] Illus. of this postcard in: *Theo van Doesburg* (1983), p. 101.

[137] '*Es stellt sich der Baukunst nicht mehr das Ziel, die wünschenwerteste Art des Beherbergens in schöner Form zu verkörpern, sie opfert dagegen alles und alle einer von vornherein festgestellten Schönheitsanschauung, welche aus anderen Umständen hervorgegangen, ein Hindernis für Lebensentfaltung geworden ist. Ursache und Wirkung sind verwechselt.*' Jacobus Johannes Pieter Oud, *Holländische Architektur (Bauhausbücher, 1926)*, ed. Hans M. Wingler, Mainz–Berlin 1976, p. 64.

[138] For a good general account cf. *Funzione e senso. Architettura-Casa-Città. Olanda 1870–1940*, Munich 1979.

[139] On German architecture in the 1920s, cf. Norbert Huse, *Neues Bauen 1918 bis 1933*, Munich 1975; Wolfgang Pehnt in: Erich Steingräber (ed.), *Deutsche Kunst der 20er und 30er Jahre*, Munich 1979, pp. 13–114.

[140] Cf. Hans Poelzig, *Gesammelte Schriften und Werke*, ed. Julius Posener, Berlin 1970; Mendelsohn's writings listed in: Bruno Zevi, *Erich Mendelsohn. Opera completa*, Milan 1970, pp. lxxix; Peter Pfankuch (ed.), *Hans Scharoun. Bauten, Entwürfe, Texte*, Berlin, 1974.

[141] Cf. Hugo Häring, *Schriften, Entwürfe, Bauten*, ed. Jürgen Joedicke, Stuttgart 1965; Jürgen Joedicke (ed.), *Das andere Bauen. Gedanken und Zeichnungen von Hugo Häring*, Stuttgart 1982; id., 'Geometrie und Organik als Prinzipien des Bauens. Zum 100. Geburtstag von Hugo Häring', *Pantheon* XL, 1982, pp. 195–200; Sabine Kremer, *Hugo Häring (1882–1958): Wohnungsbau. Theorie und Praxis*, Stuttgart 1984.

[142] Cf. Eckehard Janofske, *Die Architekturauffassung Hans Scharouns. Ihr gedanklicher Ansatz und dessen praktische Umsetzung*, diss., Darmstadt 1982; id., *Architektur-Räume. Idee und Gestalt bei Hans Scharoun*, Brunswick–Wiesbaden 1984.

[143] '*Die gestalt dieses baues ist also gewonnen worden, indem das ziel gesetzt wurde, die form zu finden, welche den ansprüchen an die leistungserfüllungen des bauwerkes am einfachsten und unmittelbarsten entsprach*'. Häring (first published in: *Die Form*, October 1925) (1965), p. 17.

[144] '*Die geometrie forderte eine ordnung im raume auf grund geometrischer gesetze. Eine organhafte kultur fordert eine ordnung im raume zum zwecke einer lebenserfüllung. Das eine führte zu dem begriff der architektur, das andere is der begriff des bauens schlechthin und von uranfang an.*' Häring (first published in: *Deutsche Bauzeitung*, July 1934) (1965), p. 35.

[145] On Henry van de Velde, cf. in this connection Clemens Rességuier, 'Die Schriften Henry van de Veldes, Zürich' (diss., New York 1955); Karl-Heinz Hüter, *Henry van de Velde. Sein Werk bis zum Ende seiner Tätigkeit in Deutschland*, Berlin 1967.

[146] The most important editions of van de Velde's writings are: Henry van de Velde, *Die Renaissance im modernen Kunstgewerbe*, Berlin 1901; id., *Kunstgewerbliche Laienpredigten*, Leipzig 1902; id., *Vom Neuen Stil*, Leipzig 1907; id., *Essays*, Leipzig 1910; id., *Geschichte meines Lebens*, ed. Hans Curjel, Munich 1962 (new ed. with foreword by Klaus-Jürgen Sembach: Munich–Zürich 1986). The best recent selection of texts: *Henry van de Velde. Zum Neuen Stil. Aus seinen Schriften ausgewählt und eingeleitet von Hans Curjel*, Munich 1955 (bibliography of van de Velde, pp. 252ff.).

[147] '*Denn die Maschinen – das ist klar – werden später einmal all das Elend wieder gut machen, das sie angerichtet, und die Schandtaten sühnen, die sie verbrochen haben… Wahllos lassen sie Schönes und Häßliches entstehen. Durch das mächtige Spiel ihrer Eisenarme werden sie Schönes erzeugen, sobald die Schönheit sie leitet.*' Henry van de Velde, 'Säuberung der Kunst' (1894), in: *Zum Neuen Stil* (1955), p. 34.

[148] '*Wer zu Anfang nur ein in allen Einzelheiten nützliches Ding schaffen wollte, gelangt zur reinen Schönheit.*' Id., 'Ein Kapitel über Entwurf und Bau moderner Möbel' (first published in: *Pan*, 1897), in: *Zum Neuen Stil* (1955), p. 58.

[149] '*Welchem Zweige des Kunstgewerbes ein Gegenstand auch angehören mag, bei der Darstellung eines jeden hat man vor allem darauf zu sehen, daß der Bau und die äußere*

Gestalt seinem eigentlichen Zweck und seiner naturgemäßen Form vollkommen angemessen seien. Nichts ist berechtigt, was nicht ein Organ bildet oder ein Bindeglied der verschiedenen Organe untereinander; kein Ornament darf Geltung finden, das nicht organisch sich anfügt.' Id., 'Was ich will' (first published in: *Die Zeit,* 9 March 1901), in: *Zum Neuen Stil* (1955), p. 81.

150 *'An die Stelle der alten symbolischen Elemente, denen wir heute keine Wirksamkeit mehr zuerkennen, will ich eine neue und ebenso unvergängliche Schönheit setzen... daß das Ornament kein eigenes Leben für sich hat, sondern von dem Gegenstande selbst, seinen Formen und Linien abhängt und von ihnen den organischen und richtigen Platz erhält.'* Ibid., pp. 83f.

151 *'Die Aufgabe des Ornamentes in der Architektur scheint mir eine doppelte. Sie besteht teils darin, die Konstruktion zu unterstützen und ihre Mittel anzudeuten, teils... durch das Spiel von Licht und Schatten, Leben in einen sonst gleichmäßig erhellten Raum zu bringen.'* Id., 'Kunstgewerbliche Laienpredigten' (1902), in: *Zum neuen Stil (1955),* p. 129.

152 *'... ausnahmelos durchgeführten Grundsatz jede Form und jedes Ornament zu verwerfen, die ein moderner Maschinenbetrieb nicht leicht herstellen und wiederholen kann'... 'Mein Ideal wäre eine tausendfache Vervielfältigung meiner Schöpfungen, allerdings unter strengster Überwachung.'* Id., 'Ein Kapitel über den Entwurf und Bau moderner Möbel' (first published in: *Pan,* 1897), in: *Zum Neuen Stijl* (1955), pp. 64f.

153 *'Ich müßte kein moderner Mensch sein, wenn ich nicht die Herstellung der Gegenstände, die früher durch Menschenhand entstanden und von Kunsthandwerkern gefertigt wurden, der neuen maschinellen und industriellen Herstellungsart anzupassen suchte.'* 'Kunst und Industrie' (1908), in: *Zum Neuen Stil* (1955), p. 211.

154 *'Heute beobachten wir nun den freiwilligen Verzicht auf das Ornament nicht nur in der Architektur, sondern auch in der Innenausstattung der Häuser... Dieser Verzicht deutet auf das Erwachen einer Empfindung, die in einem Bau, an einem Gegenstand, an einer Blume oder am menschlichen Körper ein ursprüngliches (souveränes) Ornament entdecken wird, das sich in Proportionen und Volumen verwirklicht...'* Id., 'Das

Neue: Weshalb immer Neues?' (1929), in: *Zum Neuen Stil* (1955), p. 231.

155 On Bauhaus cf. esp. Hans M. Wingler, *Das Bauhaus 1919–1933 Weimar Dessau Berlin und die Nachfolge in Chicago seit 1937,* Bramsche (¹1962, ²1968) ³1975; Karl-Heinz Hüter, *Das Bauhaus in Weimar,* Berlin ²1976; on the Dessau phase cf. *50 Jahre Bauhaus Dessau,* Wissenschaftliche Zeitschrift der Hochschule für Architektur und Bauwesen Weimar 23, 1976, Heft 5/6; Fritz Hesse, *Von der Residenz zur Bauhausstadt. Erinnerungen an Dessau,* privately published, Bad Pyrmont 1964, esp. pp. 195ff.

156 On Gropius cf. Sigfried Giedion, *Walter Gropius. Work and Teamwork,* London 1954; Giulio Carlo Argan, *Gropius e la Bauhaus,* Turin 1951 (German: *Gropius und das Bauhaus,* Reinbek 1962); Reginald R. Isaacs, *Walter Gropius. Der Mensch und sein Werk,* 2 vols, Berlin 1983, 1984; Karin Wilhelm, *Walter Gropius. Industriearchitekt,* Brunswick–Wiesbaden 1983; Winfried Nerdinger, *Walter Gropius,* Berlin 1985; Horst Claussen, *Walter Gropius. Grundzüge seines Denkens,* Hildesheim 1986; Hartmut Probst and Christian Schädlich, *Walter Gropius,* 3 vols, Berlin 1968, 1987, 1988.

157 *'Damit wird Kunst und Technik zu einer glücklichen Vereinigung gebracht und einem breiten Publikum die Möglichkeit geboten werden, in den Besitz wirklich reifer, guter Kunst und solider, gediegener Ware zu gelangen.'* Walter Gropius, 'Programm und Gründung einer allgemeinen Hausbaugesellschaft auf künstlerisch einheitlicher Grundlage' (1910); in Wingler (³1975), p. 26; cf. Isaacs (1983), pp. 93ff.

158 *'Der Arbeit müssen Paläste errichtet werden, die dem Fabrikarbeiter, dem Sklaven der modernen Industriearbeit, nicht nur Licht, Luft und Reinlichkeit geben, sondern ihn noch etwas spüren lassen von der Würde der gemeinsamen großen Idee, die das ganze treibt.'* Walter Gropius, *Monumentale Kunst und Industriebau* (ms., 1911); cited from Isaacs (1983), p. 106.

159 Cf. Hans M. Wingler (ed.), *Kunstschulreform 1900–1933,* Berlin 1977.

160 Cf. Isaacs (1983), p. 76.

161 *'... könnte eine ähnlich glückliche Arbeitsgemeinschaft wiedererstehen, wie sie vorbildlich die mittelalterlichen 'Hütten' besaßen, in denen sich zahlreiche artverwandte Werkkünstler – Architekten, Bildhauer und*

Handwerker aller Grade – zusammenfanden
und aus einem gleichgearteten Geist heraus
den ihnen zufallenden gemeinsamen Aufgaben ihr selbständiges Teilwerk bescheiden
einzufügen verstanden aus Ehrfurcht vor der
Einheit einer gemeinsamen Idee ... Mit der
Wiederbelebung jener erprobten Arbeits-
weise, die sich der neuen Welt entspre-
chend anpassen wird, muß das Ausdrucksbild
unserer modernen Lebensäußerungen an
Einheitlichkeit gewinnen, um sich schließlich
wieder in kommenden Tagen zu einem neuen
Stile zu verdichten.' Gropius (1916); cited
from Wingler (^{3}1975), p. 30.
162 Isaacs (1983), p. 196.
163 'Bilden wir also eine neue Zunft der
Handwerker ohne die klassentrennende
Anmaßung, die eine hochmütige Mauer
zwischen Handwerkern und Künstlern
errichten wollte! Wollen, erdenken, erschaf-
fen wir gemeinsam den neuen Bau der
Zukunft, der alles in einer Gestalt sein wird:
Architektur und Plastik und Malerei, der
aus Millionen Händen der Handwerker einst
gen Himmel steigen wird als kristallenes
Sinnbild eines neuen kommenden Glaubens.'
Walter Gropius, Programm des Staatlichen
Bauhauses in Weimar, Weimar 1919;
Wingler (^{3}1975), p. 39.
164 'Wenn die Probleme der Maler und Bildhauer
erst seinen Geist wieder so leidenschaftlich
berühren wie die eigenen der Baukunst, so
müssen sich auch die Werke dieser wieder
mit architektonischem Geiste füllen. In den
Bauhütten des Mittelalters, in enger persön-
licher Fühlung der Künstler aller Grade
entstanden die gotischen Dome.' Walter Gropius (probably), Der freie Volksstaat und
die Kunst (ms., 1922); cited from Isaacs
(1983), p. 289.
165 Oskar Schlemmer, 'Das Staatliche Bauhaus
in Weimar' (1923), in: Wingler (^{3}1975), p.
79.
166 The Bauhausbücher are available as facs.
reprs Neue Bauhausbücher, ed. Hans H.
Wingler; the journal Bauhaus. Zeitschrift
für Bau und Gestaltung, Dessay 1926–31 is
also available as a facs. repr. (Nendeln,
Liechtenstein).
167 'Bauen bedeutet Gestaltung von Lebensvor-
gängen. Die Mehrzahl der Individuen hat
gleichartige Lebensbedürfnisse. Es ist daher
logisch und im Sinne eines wirtschaftlichen
Vorgehens, diese gleichgearteten Massenbe-
dürfnisse einheitlich und gleichartig zu befrie-

digen.' Walter Gropius, Systematische Vorarbeit für rationellen Wohnungsbau (in:
Bauhaus 1, No. 2, 1927); cited from Wingler
(^{3}1975), p. 136.
168 'In der modernen Baukunst ist die Objekti-
vierung von Persönlichem und Nationalem
deutlich erkennbar.' Walter Gropius, Internationale Architektur, Munich 1925 (^{2}1927;
facs. repr. of 1927 ed., Mainz 1981), p. 7.
169 'Die Baumeister dieses Buches bejahen die
heutige Welt der Maschinen und Fahrzeuge
und ihr Tempo, sie streben nach immer
kühneren Gestaltungsmitteln, um die Erden-
trägheit in Wirkung und Erscheinung
schwebend zu überwinden.' Gropius (1925),
p. 8.
170 'Standardisierung der praktischen Lebens-
vorgänge ... Jedes Ding ist bestimmt durch
sein Wesen, um es so zu gestalten, daß es
richtig funktioniert, muß sein Wesen erforscht
werden; es soll seinem Zweck vollendet
dienen, d.h. seine Funktionen praktisch
erfüllen, dauerhaft, billig und, "schön" sein.'
Walter Gropius, Bauhausbauten Dessau,
Fulda 1930 (facs. repr., Mainz–Berlin 1974),
p. 8.
171 'Das 'Kunstwerk' hat im geistigen wie im
materiellen Sinne genau so zu 'functionieren'
wie das Erzeugnis des Ingenieurs, wie z.B.
ein Flugzeug, dessen selbstverständliche
Bestimmung es ist zu fliegen.' Gropius
(1930), p. 9.
172 'Die Anwendung begehbarer, mit Pflanzen
bestandener Dachgärten ist ein wirksames
Mittel, die Natur in die Steinwüste der
Großstädte einzubeziehen. Die Städte der
Zukunft werden mit ihren Gärten auf
Terassen und Dächern – vom Luftweg aus
gesehen – den Eindruck eines großen Gartens
geben. Der durch den Bau der Häuser verlor-
ene begrünbare Boden wird auf den flachen
Dächern wiedergewonnen.' Ibid., p. 55.
173 Walter Gropius, The New Architecture and
the Bauhaus, London 1935; id., The Scope
of Total Architecture, New York 1955; id.
a.o., The Architects Collaborative 1945–
1965, Teufen 1966.
174 Cf. esp. Sibyl Moholy-Nagy, Laszlo Moholy-Nagy, ein Totalexperiment (American
ed., New York 1950, 1969), Mainz–Berlin
1972.
175 László Moholy-Nagy, Von Material zu
Architektur, Munich 1929 (facs. ed., Mainz–
Berlin 1968).
176 'Raumerlebnis als Grundlage für das psych-

ologische Wohlbefinden der Einwohner.' Moholy-Nagy (1929), p. 198.

177 *'Knotenpunkt ewig flutender räumlicher Existenzen.'* Ibid., p. 211. Experience of space through movement is also the basis for the idea of Frederick Kiesler's (1890–1965) idea of the 'endless house' which he developed from 1934 onwards; cf. Frederick Kiesler, 'Kiesler's Pursuit of an Idea,' *Progressive Architecture*, July 1961, pp. 104–16; exhib. cat. *Frederick Kiesler. Architekt 1890–1965*, Vienna n.d.

178 *'Architektur als Gliederung des universellen Raumes…'* Ibid., p. 199.

179 *'Aber das wesentlichste ist für uns die Flugzeugsicht, das vollere Raumerlebnis, weil es alle gestrige Architekturvorstellung verändert.'* Ibid., p. 222.

180 On Hannes Meyer cf. C. Schnaidt, *Hannes Meyer: Buildings, Projects and Writings*, London 1965; *Hannes Meyer, Bauen und Gesellschaft. Schriften, Briefe, Projekte*, Dresden 1980; cat. *Hannes Meyer 1889–1954*, Berlin 1989.

181 *'Bauen ist ein technischer, kein ästhetischer Prozeß, und der zweckmäßigen Funktion eines Hauses widerspricht je und je die künstlerische Komposition. Idealerweise und elementar gestaltet, wird unser Wohnhaus eine Maschinerie.'* Hannes Meyer, *Die Neue Welt* (in: *Das Werk* 13, 1926); cited from Meyer (1980), p. 29.

182 Meyer, ibid., p. 341.

183 *'Dieses Gebäude sucht keinen künstlichen gartenkünstlerischen Anschluß an die Parklandschaft seiner Umgebung. Als erdachtes Menschenwerk steht es in berechtigtem Gegensatz zur Natur. Dieses Gebäude ist nicht schön und nicht häßlich. Es will als konstruktive Erfindung gewertet sein.'* Hannes Mayer, *Ein Völkerbundgebäude für Genf* (in: *Bauhaus* I, 1927, Heft 4); cited from Meyer (1980), p. 34.

184 *'Alle Dinge dieser Welt sind ein Produkt der Formel: (Funktion mal Ökonomie)…Alle Kunst ist Komposition und Prozeß. Elementar gestaltet wird das neue Wohnhaus nicht nur eine Wohnmaschinerie, sondern ein biologischer Apparat für seelische und körperliche Bedürfnisse…Bauen ist nur Organisation: soziale, technische, ökonomische, psychische Organisation.'* Hannes Meyer, 'Bauen' (in: *Bauhaus* 2, 1928, H. 4); in: Wingler (³1975), pp. 160f.; Meyer (1980), pp. 47ff.

185 *'Bauen und gestalten sind eins, und sie sind ein gesellschaftliches Geschehnis. Als eine "hohe Schule der Gestaltung" ist das Bauhaus Dessau kein künstlerisches, wohl aber ein soziales Phänomen.'* Hannes Meyer, *Bauhaus und Gesellschaft* (in: *Bauhaus* 3, 1929, H. 1); Meyer (1980), p. 50.

186 Cf. Meyer (1980), pp. 92ff.

187 Cf. David Spaeth, *Ludwig Karl Hilberseimer. An Annotated Bibliography and Chronology*, New York–London 1981 (with some later mss repr. in appendix).

188 Ludwig Hilberseimer, *Großstadtarchitektur*, Stuttgart 1927 (²1978).

189 Hilberseimer (1927), p. 19.

190 *'theoretische Untersuchungen und eine schematische Anwendung der Elemente, aus denen eine Stadt sich aufbaut.'* Ibid., p. 20.

191 *'Reduktion der architektonischen Form auf das Knappste, Notwendigste, Allgemeinste, eine Beschränkung auf die geometrisch kubischen Formen: die Grundelemente aller Architektur.* Ibid., p. 103.

192 On Mies van der Rohe cf. Philip Johnson, *Mies van der Rohe* (New York ¹1947), Boston ³1978; Ludwig Hilberseimer, *Mies van der Rohe*, Chicago 1956; Arthur Drexler, *Ludwig Mies van der Rohe*, New York 1960; Peter Blake, *The Master Builders*, New York–London 1960 (²1976); Werner Blaser, *Mies van der Rohe*, London 1965; Wolfgang Frieg, *Ludwig Mies van der Rohe. Das europäische Werk (1907–1937)*, diss., Bonn 1976; Wolf Tegethoff, *Die Villen und Landhausprojekte von Mies van der Rohe*, 2 vols, Krefeld 1981; Franz Schulze, *Mies van der Rohe. A Critical Biography*, Chicago–London 1985.

193 David A. Spaeth, *Ludwig Mies van der Rohe. An Annotated Bibliography and Chronology*, New York–London 1979; some texts by Mies in: Ulrich Conrads (ed.), *Programme und Manifeste zur Architektur des 20. Jahrhunderts (Bauwelt Fundamente* 1), (¹1964), Gütersloh–Berlin–Munich ²1971, pp. 76f., 114, 146; some texts in English trans. in: Johnson (1947; ³1978), pp. 186ff. Mies's complete writings in: Fritz Neumeyer, *Mies van der Rohe. Das kunstlose Wort. Gedanken zur Baukunst*, Berlin 1986.

194 *'Gelingt es uns, diese Industrialisierung durchzuführen, dann werden sich die sozialen, wirtschaftlichen, technischen und auch*

künstlerischen Fragen leicht lösen lassen.'
Ludwig Mies van der Rohe, 'Industrielles
Bauen', in: *G*, No. 3, June 1924, pp. 8–13;
cited from Conrads (ed.), op. cit. (1971), p.
76.

[195] '*das sich technisch herstellen und industriell
verarbeiten läßt, das fest, wetterbeständig,
schall- und wärmesicher ist.*' Mies van der
Rohe (1924); cited from Conrads (ed.),
(1971), p. 77.

[196] '*Auch die Frage der Mechanisierung, der
Typisierung und Normung wollen wir nicht
überschätzen…ob wir hoch oder flach
bauen, mit Glas und Stahl bauen, besagt
nichts über den Wert dieses Bauens…Aber
gerade die Frage nach dem Wert ist entschei-
dend. Wir haben neue Werte zu setzen…Denn Sinn und Recht jeder Zeit, also
auch der neuen liegt einzig und allein darin,
daß sie dem Geist die Voraussetzung, die
Existenzmöglichkeit bietet.*' Ludwig Mies
van der Rohe, 'Die Neue Zeit', in: *Die
Form* 5, 1930, H. 15, p. 406; Conrads (ed.)
(1971), p. 114.

[197] Ludwig Mies van der Rohe, 'Address of
Illinois Institute of Technology' (1950); in:
Johnson ([3]1978), p. 204.

[198] '*Heute, wie seit langem, glaube ich, daß
Baukunst wenig oder nichts zu tun hat mit
der Erfindung interessanter Formen noch mit
persönlichen Neigungen. Wahre Baukunst ist
immer objektiv und ist Ausdruck der inneren
Struktur der Epoche, aus der sie wächst.*'
Ludwig Mies van der Rohe, *The Art of
Structure*, introduction in Blaser (1965);
cited from German trans. (1972), p. 5.

[199] Cf. Joan Campbell, *The German Werkbund*,
Princeton 1978.

[200] Paul Schultze-Naumburg, *Kulturarbeiten*,
9 vols, Munich 1901–17 ([2]1922ff.). Paul
Schultze-Naumburg, *Kunst und Rasse*,
Munich 1927.

[201] Paul Schmitthenner, *Die Baukunst im
Neuen Reich*, Munich 1934.

[202] On Heinrich Tessenow cf. Gerda Wangerin
and Gerhard Weiss, *Heinrich Tessenow. Ein
Baumeister 1876–1950*, Essen 1976 (pp.
157ff. his writings listed); a selection of his
writings, Heinrich Tessenow, 'Geschriebenes. Gedancken eines Baumeisters', ed.
Otto Kindt, *Bauwelt Fundamente 61*, Brunswick–Wiesbaden 1982.

[203] On Fritz Schumacher cf. esp. his autobiography: Fritz Schumacher, *Stufen des Lebens*.

Erinnerungen eines Baumeisters, Stuttgart
1935 ([2]1949).

[204] Heinrich Tessenow, *Der Wohnungsbau*,
Munich 1909.

[205] Cf. esp. Heinrich Tessenow, *Hausbau und
dergleichen*, Berlin 1916 (numerous eds, the
latest Munich 1984).

[206] '*Das Ornament oder das Ornamentale ist
überall; aber es ist um so besser, je weniger
wir es wollen, je gleichgültiger wir es behandeln…Sozusagen: Das Ornament über-
strahlt im besten Fall ein männliches
Arbeiten mit einem unwillkürlichen halben
Lachen…Das beste am Ornament ist das
Abstrakte, das Dumme und das Unbegreif-
liche.*' Tessenow, *Hausbau und dergleichen*; cited from Tessenow (1982), pp. 41f.

[207] Cf. e.g. Fritz Schumacher, *Strömungen in
deutscher Baukunst seit 1800* ([2]1935), Cologne [2]1955.

[208] Fritz Schumacher, *Der Geist der Baukunst*,
Stuttgart 1938 (repr. Stuttgart 1983), pp.
214ff.

[209] '*Die dynamischen Wirkungen treten hervor,
wenn das Ornament sich nicht mit der
Fläche, sondern mit der Form verbindet,
deren funktionelle Bedeutung es zu unterstrei-
chen und zu illustrieren vermag.*' Schumacher (1938), p. 241.

[210] Rudolf Wolters, *Neue Deutsche Baukunst*,
Prague 1943, p. 8.

[211] '*Die Form, die äußere Gestalt der neuen
Bauten geht aus ihrem Inhalt, ihrem Sinn
und Zweck hervor. Diese Bauten dienen
dem Volksganzen: Saalbauten, Theater- und
Feierräume. Alle übrigen neuen Gebäude des
Staates und der Bewegung werden mit diesen
zusammengefaßt in geschlossener Wirkung zu
großen repräsentativen Straßen- und Platzräu-
men. Diese solle unsere neuen Stadtkronen,
die Mittelpunkte unserer heutigen Städte
sein.*' Wolters (1943), p. 10.

[212] On the architecture of the Third Reich, cf.
Anna Teut, *Die Architektur im Dritten
Reich 1933–1945*, Berlin–Frankfurt–
Vienna 1967; Barbara Miller Lane, *Architec-
ture and Politics in Germany, 1918–1945*,
Cambridge, MA 1968; Robert R. Taylor,
*The Word in Stone. The Role of Architecture
in the National Socialist Ideology*, Berkeley–
Los Angeles–London 1974; Joachim Petsch,
*Baukunst und Stadtplanung im Dritten
Reich*, Munich 1976.

[213] Cf. esp. Jochen Thies, *Architekt der Welt-*

herrschaft. Die 'Endziele' Hitlers, Düsseldorf 1976.

[214] Alexander von Senger, *Krisis der Architektur*, Zürich 1928; on Senger cf. Miller Lane (1968), pp. 140ff. and Edi Müller in exhib. cat. *Dreißiger Jahre Schweiz. Ein Jahrzehnt im Widerspruch*, Zürich 1981, p. 142.

[215] Alfred Rosenberg, *Der Mythus des 20. Jahrhunderts. Eine Wertung der seelischgeistigen Gestaltenkämpfe unserer Zeit* (1930), Munich 1941, p. 381.

[216] *'Für Monumentalbauten muß unsere Zeit Bauklötze auf Bauklötze türmen, für Wassertürme braucht sie gewaltige geschlossene Formen, für Kornsilos einfache, gigantische Massen. Wuchtig müssen unsere Fabriken daliegen; zerstreute Geschäftsgebäude werden zu Riesenhäusern der Arbeit zusammengefaßt ... Die gotische Form erweist sich als für immer überwunden, die gotische Seele ringt aber bereits für jeden Nichtblinden sichtbar um eine neue Verwirklichung...'* Rosenberg (1930; ed. 1941), pp. 379f.

[217] *'Die Ausbildung und der Grundgedanke griechischer Baukunst sind also eines Wesens mit germanischem Gefühl. Diesem Gedanken – unabhängig von der zeitlich gebundenen Form – sind auch der 'romanische' (in Wirklichkeit durchaus germanische) und gotische Dom treu geblieben. Das basilikale Prinzip, welches beiden Formen zugrunde liegt, bedeutet das Wesen nordischer Raumauffassung.'* Ibid., p. 383.

[218] Arthur Moeller van den Bruck, *Der preußische Stil* (1916), Breslau ³1931.

[219] *'Monumentalität ist die männliche Kunst... Ihre Strophen tönen heroisch. Ihre Linien stufen sich hieratisch. Ihre Körper wirken wie Dogmen. In ihr oder der Schritt von Kriegern, die Sprache von Gesetzgebern, die Verachtung des Augenblicks, die Rechenschaft vor der Ewigkeit ... Durch Monumentalität bekommt Stil erst seine große Sichtbarkeit: in einem weithin erkennbaren und alsbald bekannten Plasma baut sich die Einheit von Künstlern und Volk auf, die sich in der Geschichte durchsetzen will, und eine Herrschaft seiner Formen breitet sich aus, die vor allem eine Selbstherrschaft ist und die zu einer Weltbeherrschung werden kann. So wirkt Monumentalität wie große Kriege, wie Völkererhebungen, wie Staatengründungen zu wirken pflegen: befreiend, zusammenfassend, Schicksal schaffend wie bestäti-*gend, und von neuem das Dasein ordnend...' Ibid., p. 147.

[220] Albert Speer, *Erinnerungen*, Berlin 1969, pp. 174f., 75.

[221] Speer (1969), p. 169; cf. also Albert Speer, *Architektur. Arbeiten 1933–1942*, Berlin 1978, pp. 7ff.

[222] *'Die Errichtung dieser Monumente sollte dazu dienen, einen Anspruch auf Weltherrschaft anzumelden, lange bevor er ihn seiner engsten Umgebung mitzuteilen wagte.'* Speer (1969), p. 83; cf. esp. Thies (1976).

[223] Speer (1969), pp. 69 and 532f.

[224] Rudolf Wolters, *Neue Deutsche Baukunst*, Prague 1943, p. 7.

[225] Gerdy Troost, *Das Bauen im Neuen Reich*, Bayreuth 1938, pp. 5ff.

[226] Troost (1938), p. 6.

[227] *'das Wort aus Stein ... gebauter Nationalsozialismus ... Selbstdarstellung der ureigensten Kulturkräfte eines erwachten, rassebewußten Volkes.'* Ibid., p. 10.

[228] *'Die Gestaltungsmöglichkeiten der modernen Technik sind bis zum äußersten ausgenützt. Trotzdem erhebt sich die Technik nirgends über die Kunst.'* Ibid., pp. 15, 20.

[229] *'Eine Reihe von technischen Bauten der Gemeinschaft, die seit 1933 errichtet wurden, haben durch die Tat den eindeutigen Beweis erbracht, daß aus der klaren, technischen Zweckbestimmung schöne Bauformen entwickelt werden können. Aus dem Wesen der Technik kann die Kraft einer einordnenden Weltanschauung sinngemäße Formen entwickeln. Bauten von Maß und Ordnung, wirksam durch sparsame und klare Linien, Sinnbild der präzisen sauberen Arbeit, die in ihnen geleistet wird, sind hier gestaltet worden. Sie ergeben eine schöne Gesamtwirkung. Beton, Stahl und Glas treten offen hervor.'* Ibid., p. 73.

[230] Walter Müller-Wulckow, *Deutsche Baukunst der Gegenwart. Bauten der Gemeinschaft*, Königstein 1928, p. 8, ills 84–86. Walter Müller-Wulckow's *Blaue Bücher* are reprinted in the text of their latest editions under the title *Architektur der Zwanziger Jahre in Deutschland*, ed. Reyner Banham, Königstein 1975.

[231] *'Diese Führung erstrebt, die wesentlichen Grundgedanken der großen Gemeinschaftswerke in freier sinngemäßer Anwendung auch die große Masse privater Bauten zu übertragen und so einer allgemein verpflichtenden neuen Baukultur Bahn zu brechen.'* Troost p. 16.

26. France: 1900–1945

[1] For a general account cf. Reyner Banham, *Theory and Design in the First Machine Age*, London 1960.

[2] On Garnier cf. the monograph by Christophe Pawlowski, *Tony Garnier et les débuts de l'urbanisme fonctionnel en France*, Paris 1967 (Italian ed., Faenza 1976); cat. *Tony Garnier*, Lyons 1970; Maria Rovigatti and Tony Garnier, *Architetture per la città industriella*, Rome 1985.

[3] Cf. Arthur Drexler (ed.), *The Architecture of the Ecole des Beaux-Arts*, London 1977, pp. 309ff.

[4] Cf. Pawlowski (ed. 1976), pp. 57ff.

[5] Tony Garnier, *Une cité industrielle. Etude pour la construction des villes*, Paris 1917 ([2]1932).
Cf. Pawlowski (ed. 1976), pp. 67ff.; Dora Wiebenson, 'Utopian Aspects of Tony Garnier's Cité Industrielle', *Journal of the Society of Architectural Historians* XIX, 1960, pp. 16–24; ead., *Tony Garnier: The Cité Industrielle*, New York 1969.

[6] Garnier (1917); in English trans. in: Wiebenson (1969), pp. 107ff.

[7] '*1. Pour l'habitation, les chambres à lit doivent avoir au moins une fenêtre au sud, assez grande pour donner de la lumière dans toute la pièce et laisser entrer largement les rayons du soleil.*
'*2. Les cours et courettes, c'est-à-dire les espaces clos de murs servant pour éclairer ou pour aérer, sont prohibés. – Tout espace, si petit soit-il, doit être éclairé et ventilé par l'extérieur.*
'*3. A l'intérieur des habitations, les murs, les sols, etc., sont de matière lisse, avec leurs angles de rencontre arrondis.*' Garnier (1917).

[8] Cf. Wiebenson (1969), p. 26.

[9] '*Cette simplicité de moyens conduit logiquement à une grande simplicité d'expression dans la structure. Notons d'ailleurs que, si notre structure reste simple, sans ornement, sans moulure, nue partout, nous pouvons ensuite disposer les arts décoratifs sous toutes leurs formes, et que chaque objet d'art conservera son expression d'autant plus nette et pure qu'il sera totalement indépendant de la construction.*' Garnier (1917).

[10] Cf. Tony Garnier, *Les Grands Travaux de la Ville de Lyon*, Paris 1920; Pawlowski (ed. 1976), pp. 121ff.

[11] Cf. Wiebenson (1969), p. 98.

[12] On the history of the use of concrete and Perret's approach to this material, cf. esp. Peter Collins, *Concrete. The Vision of a New Architecture. A Study of Auguste Perret and his precursors*, London 1959.
On Perret cf. Paul Jamot, *A. et G. Perret et l'architecture du béton armé*, Paris–Brussels 1927; Ernesto N. Rogers, *Auguste Perret*, Milan 1955; Marcel Zahar, *D'une doctrine d'architecture. Auguste Perret*, Paris 1959 (with a selection of Perret's writings); cat. *A. et G. Perret. Architectes français*, Paris 1976. Two essays on Perret by Max Raphael are published in: Max Raphael, *Für eine demokratische Architektur. Kunstsoziologische Schriften*, ed. Jutta Held, Frankfurt 1976, pp. 33ff., 45ff.

[13] Cf. esp. Auguste Perret, *Contributions à une théorie de l'architecture*, Paris 1952.

[14] Cf. Raphael (1976), pp. 33ff.; Collins (1959), pp. 194ff.

[15] On Perret's conception of the Orders cf. Collins (1959), pp. 200ff.

[16] '... *première tentative [au monde] de béton armé esthétique.*' Banham (1964), p. 35.

[17] Cf. the following general monographs: Peter Blake, *The Master Buildings* ([1]1960), New York [2]1976; Maurice Besset, *Wer war Le Corbusier?*, Geneva 1968; Stanislaus von Moos, *Le Corbusier. Elemente einer Synthese*, Frauenfeld–Stuttgart 1968; Charles Jencks, *Le Corbusier and the Tragic View of Architecture*, London 1973; Norbert Huse, *Le Corbusier*, Reinbek 1976. Cf. major studies by Colin Rowe and Robert Slutzky, *Transparenz*, Le Corbusier Studien, vol. I, Basel and Stuttgart 1968; Colin Rowe, *The Mathematics of the Ideal Villa and Other Essays*, Cambridge, MA–London 1976 ([5]1980); also two essay collections: Peter Serenyi (ed.), *Le Corbusier in Perspective*, Englewood Cliffs, NJ 1975; Russell Walden (ed.), *The Open Hand. Essays on Le Corbusier*, Cambridge, MA–London 1977; exhib. cat. *Le Corbusier. Synthèse des arts. Aspekte des Spätwerks*, Karlsruhe 1986; catalogues and other publications in commemoration of the centenary of Le Corbusier's birth in 1987 are too numerous to list.

[18] Cf. esp. Paul Venable Turner, *The Education of Le Corbusier* (diss. Harvard Univ. 1971), New York–London 1977; Mary Patricia May Sekler, *The Early Drawings of Charles-*

Edouard Jeaneret (Le Corbusier) 1902–1908
(diss. Harvard Univ. 1973), New York–
London 1977.

¹⁹ Willy Boesiger (ed.), *Le Corbusier. Oeuvre
complète*, 8 vols, Zürich 1929–70 (several
reprs). On his own view of his work, cf. Le
Corbusier, *My Work*, Stuttgart 1960.

²⁰ Cf. Le Corbusier Sketchbooks, 4 vols, Cam-
bridge, MA 1981–82 (text by Françoise de
Franclieu). H. Allan Brooks (ed.), *The Le
Corbusier Archive*, 32 vols, New York–
London 1982ff.

²¹ On the Ecole d'Art and on L'Eplattenier
cf. Sekler (1977), pp. 1ff.; Turner (1977),
pp. 4ff; cf. also the journal *Archithèse* 1983,
no. 2, which is devoted to La Chaux-de-
Fonds.

²² Letter of 22 November 1908 published in *La
Gazette Littéraire*, Lausanne 4/5 September
1965; repr. in Italian trans. in: Charles-
Edouard Jeanneret (Le Corbusier), *Il Viaggio d'Oriente*, Faenza 1974, pp. 197ff.

²³ On Le Corbusier's early reading cf. Turner
(1977), pp. 8ff.

²⁴ Trans. into German by Marie Steiner with
an introduction by Rudolf Steiner: Edouard
Schuré, *Die großen Eingeweihten* (Leipzig
1925).

²⁵ Cf. Turner (1977), pp. 61ff.

²⁶ On Wright's early influence on Le Corbusier
cf. Paul Venable Turner, 'Frank Lloyd
Wright and the Young le Corbusier', *Journal
of the Society of Architectural Historians*
XLII, 1983, pp. 350–59.

²⁷ Charles-Edouard Jeanneret (Le Corbusier),
*Etude sur le mouvement d'art décoratif en
Allemagne*, La Chaux-de-Fonds 1912 (facs.
repr. New York 1968).

²⁸ Charles-Edouard Jeanneret (Le Corbusier),
Le voyage d'Orient (1911), Paris 1965 (Italian
ed. *Il viaggio d'oriente*, Faenza 1974).

²⁹ Le Corbusier and Pierre Jeanneret, *Oeuvre
complète 1910–1929*, Zürich 1967, p. 22.
Cf. e.g. von Moos (1968), p. 26, 34; Turner
(1977), pp. 70ff.

³⁰ The book was in Le Corbusier's library in
1913.

³¹ Auguste Choisy, *Histoire de l'architecture*,
vol. I, Paris 1899, p. 173.

³² Le Corbusier and Pierre Jeanneret, *Oeuvre
complète 1910–1929*, (ed. 1967), p. 23.

³³ Cf. Turner (1977), pp. 122f.

³⁴ Cf. Rowe (1976: ⁵1980), pp. 30ff. The villa
was, however, published in an extensive
article by Julien Caron (*Une villa du Le
Corbusier 1916*) in the journal coedited by

Le Corbusier, *L'Esprit Nouveau* (no. VI, pp.
679–704).

³⁵ Charles-Edouard Jeanneret and Amedée
Ozenfant, *Après le Cubisme*, Paris 1918
(facs. repr. Turin 1975).

³⁶ *L'Esprit Nouveau. Revue Internationale
Illustrée de l'Activité Contemporaine*, 28 nos,
Paris 1920–25; facs. repr. in 8 vols New
York 1968; cf. Robert Gabetti and Carlo
Olmo, *Le Corbusier & 'L'Esprit Nouveau'*,
Turin ²1975.

³⁷ Le Corbusier-Saugnier, *Vers une architecture*, Paris 1923 (³1928). Passages here quoted
in translation are from *Towards a New
Architecture*, trans. Frederick Etchells, London 1927.

³⁸ '*nous donne la mesure d'une ordre qu'on
sent en accord avec celui du monde…*' Le
Corbusier (1923; ed. 1928), p. xvii.

³⁹ '*Les grands problèmes de la construction
moderne seront réalisés sur la géométrie.*'
Ibid., p. xviii.

⁴⁰ '*Le style, c'est une unité de principe qui anime
toutes les oeuvres d'une époque et qui résulte
d'un état d'esprit caractérisé.*' Ibid., p. xix.

⁴¹ '*une machine à habiter.*' Ibid.

⁴² '*un produit de sélection appliquée à un
standart [sic].*' Ibid.

⁴³ Ibid., pp. 106f.

⁴⁴ Ibid., p. xxi.

⁴⁵ Ibid., p. 243.

⁴⁶ '*Nous avons réclamé, au nom du paquebot,
de l'avion et de l'auto, la santé, la logique,
la hardiesse, l'harmonie, la perfection.*' Ibid.,
p. 9.

⁴⁷ On the ship analogy, cf. Gert Kähler,
*Architektur als Symbolverfall. Das
Dampfermotiv in der Baukunst*, Brunswick–
Wiesbaden 1981.

⁴⁸ '*Les ingénieurs américains écrasent de leurs
calculs l'architecture agonisante.*' Le
Corbusier (1923; ed. 1928), p. 20.

⁴⁹ Perret's 'Ville-tour' in: *L'Illustration* 1922.

⁵⁰ '*L'émotion architecturale, c'est quand
l'oeuvre sonne en vous au diapason d'un
univers dont nous subissons, reconnaissons
et admirons les lois.*' Le Corbusier (1923;
ed. 1928), p. 9.

⁵¹ Ibid., pp. 54ff.

⁵² '*L'art n'est un aliment nécessaire que pour
les élites qui ont à se recueiller pour pouvoir
conduire.*' Ibid., p. 79.

⁵³ Ibid., pp. 113f.

⁵⁴ Cf. Anthony Sutcliffe and Robert Fishman,
in: Walden (ed.) (1977), pp. 215ff.; Theo
Hilpert, *Die funktionelle Stadt. Le Corbusiers*

Stadtvision – Bedingungen, Motive, Hintergründe, Brunswick 1978.

[55] Le Corbusier, *Urbanisme*, Paris 1925. Passages here quoted in translation are from *The City of Tomorrow and its Planning*, trans. from 8th French ed. by Frederick Etchells, London 1929.

[56] Cf. esp. Le Corbusier, *La ville radieuse*, Paris 1935 (new ed. Paris 1965); *Précisions sur un état présent de l'architecture et de l'urbanisme*, Paris 1929 ('1960); *La Charte d'Athènes*, Paris 1943; *Propos d'urbanisme*, Paris 1946.

[57] '*La ville est un outil de travail.*' Le Corbusier (1925), p. i.

[58] *L'Urbanisme moderne naît avec une nouvelle architecture. Une évolution immense, foudroyante, brutale, a coupé les ponts avec le passé.*' Ibid., p. iv.

[59] '*Le rue courbe est le chemin des ânes, la rue droite le chemin des hommes... L'angle droit est l'outil nécessaire et suffisant pour agir.*' Ibid., pp. 10 and 13.

[60] Ibid., pp. 92–96.

[61] '*une machine à circuler*'. Ibid., p. 126.

[62] '*La géométrie transcendante doit régner...La ville actuelle se meurt d'être non géométrique...La géométrie est l'essence même de l'Architecture. Pour introduire la série dans la construction de la ville, il faut industrialiser le bâtiment.*' Ibid., p. 166.

[63] '...*jouissant d'un spectacle d'ordre et d'intensité.*' Ibid., p. 165.

[64] '...*ces gratte-ciel recèlent le cerveau de la Ville, le cerveau de tout le pays. Ils représentent le travail d'élaboration et de commandement sur lequel se règle l'activité générale.*' Ibid., p. 177.

[65] '*chirurgie*'. Ibid., p. 241.

[66] '*Rapports directs et précis, rapides, entre deux fonctions indépendantes...*' Ibid., p. 292.

[67] On the first phase of the CIAM cf. Martin Steinmann (ed.), *CIAM. Dokumente 1928–1939*, Basel–Stuttgart 1979.

[68] Cf. Steinmann (ed.) (1979), pp. 111ff.

[69] Text in: Steinmann (ed.) (1979), pp. 160ff.

[70] In connection with the Modulor Le Corbusier specifically refers to Choisy and Thorn-Prikker (*Der Modulor*, Stuttgart ³1978, p. 26f.).

[71] Le Corbusier, *Le Modulor*, Boulogne-sur-Seine 1948 (German ed. Stuttgart 1953, ³1978); *Modulor 2*, Boulogne-sur-Seine 1955 (German ed. Stuttgart 1958, ²1979). Cf. also Le Corbusier, *Oeuvre complète 1946–52* (1953; ed. 1970), pp. 178ff.

On the Modulor cf. Peter Collins, 'Modulor', *Architectural Review* 116, 1954, pp. 5–8; Rudolf Wittkower, 'Le Corbusier's Modulor', in: *Four Great Makers of Modern Architecture* (1963), New York 1970; pp. 196–204 (both essays repr. in: Serenyi (ed.), op. cit. (1975), pp. 79ff.).

[72] Paul Valéry, *Eupalinos ou l'Architecte*, précédé de *l'Ame et la Danse*, Paris 1923.

[73] Valéry (1923; 1973), p. 79 (English trans. from German trans. by Rainer Maria Rilke, Leipzig 1927; facs. repr., Frankfurt 1973).

[74] Ibid., p. 145.

[75] Cf. Robert Mallet-Stevens, *Une cité moderne*, ed. Frantz Jourdain, Paris 1922.

On the writings of Mallet-Stevens cf. bibliography in: *Rob Mallet-Stevens. Architecte*, Brussels 1980, p. 390.

[76] André Lurçat, *Formes, Composition et lois d'Harmonie. Eléments d'une science de l'ésthétique architecturale*, 5 vols, Paris 1953–57.

On Lurçat cf. the two essays by Max Raphael, *Für eine demokratische Architektur*, ed. Jutta Held, Frankfurt 1976, pp. 7ff., 27ff.; Bruno Cassetti, 'André Lurçat in URSS: il recupero dell'architettura come istituzione', in: *Socialismo, città, architettura URSS 1917–1937. Il Contributo degli architetti europei* ('1971), Rome ³1976, pp. 197ff.

[77] '*la nécessité d'introduire dans le domaine de la création architecturale des méthodes rationelles...*' Lurçat, vol. I (1953), Préface.

[78] Lurçat, vol. V (1957), p. 330.

[79] On this period of the Ecole des Beaux-Arts, cf. Donald Drew Egbert, *The Beaux-Arts Tradition in French Architecture*, Princeton 1980, pp. 74ff.

27. Italy: Futurism and Rationalism

[1] On Italian architecture in the 19th century cf. Carroll I. Meeks, *Italian Architecture 1750–1914*, New Haven–London 1966; Luciano Patetta, *L'architettura dell' Eclettismo. Fonti, teorie, modelli 1750–1900*, Milan 1975, pp. 260ff; Renato de Fusco, *L'architettura dell' Ottocento*, Turin 1981; Amerigo Restucci, 'Città e architettura dell'Ottocento', in: *Storia dell'arte italiana*, vol. II, ed. Federico Zeri, Turin 1982, pp. 725–90.

[2] On Italian Stile Liberty architecture, cf.

Manfredi Nicoletti, *L'architettura liberty in Italia*, Rome–Bari 1978.

[3] On D'Aronco cf. Manfredi Nicoletti, *D'Aronco e l'architettura liberty*, Rome–Bari 1982; also *Atti del Congresso Internazionale di Studi su Raimondo D'Aronco e il suo tempo*, Udine 1982.

[4] Cf. Nicoletti (1978), pp. 107ff.; on D'Aronco's theoretical position cf. Eleonora Bairati in: *Atti* (1982), pp. 227ff.

[5] Besides Nicoletti (1978, 1982) cf. the general account by Cesare De Seta, *L'architettura del Novecento*, Turin 1981.

[6] On Futurism cf. Christa Baumgarth, *Geschichte des Futurismus*, Reinbek 1966 (with German trans. of the most important manifestos) Maurizio Calvesi, *Il futurismo*, 3 vols, Milan 1967 (*L'arte moderna* 13–15; with an anthology of texts). The manifestos of Futurism are collected in: L. Caruso, *Manifesti futuristi 1909–1944*, 4 vols, Florence 1980; a shorter anthology: Luigi Scrivo, *Sintesi del futurismo. Storia e documenti*, Rome 1968.

[7] On Futurist architecture cf. Ezio Godoli, *Il futurismo*, Rome–Bari 1983 (with texts of all important architectural manifestos).

[8] Besides the above-cited literature, cf. Marianne W. Martin, *Futurist Art and Theory 1909–1915*, Oxford [1]1968, [2]1978; Anna Maria Brescia, *The Aesthetic Theories of Futurism*, diss. (Columbia Univ. 1971), Ann Arbor 1974.

[9] All Marinetti's Futurist writings in: F. T. Marinetti, *Teoria e invenzione futurista*, ed. Luciano De Maria, Milan [1]1968, [2]1983; cf. also Giovanni Lista (ed.), *Marinetti et le futurisme*, Lausanne 1977.

[10] Marinetti ([2]1983), pp. 7ff.

[11] Enrico Prampolini, *L'atmosferastruttura' basi per un'architettura futurista* (first published in 1914 and 1918); text in: Godoli (1983), pp. 181f.

[12] On Sant'Elia cf. Giulio Carlo Argan, 'Il pensiero critico di Antonio Sant'Elia', *L'Arte* XXXII, 1930, pp. 491–98; Umbro Apollonio, *Antonio Sant'Elia*, Milan 1958; cat., ed. Luciano Caramel and Alberto Longatti, *Antonio Sant'Elia*, Como 1962; J. P. Schmidt-Thomsen, *Floreale und futuristische Architektur. Das Werk von Antonio Sant'Elia*, diss., TU Berlin 1967; Nicoletti (1978), pp. 351ff.; Godoli (1983), pp. 221ff.; Giulio Carlo Argan a.o., *Dopo Sant'Elia*, Milan 1935 (facs. repr. ed. Luciano Caruso,

Livorno 1986); Luciano Caramel and Alberto Longatti (ed.), *Antonio Sant' Elia. The Complete Works*, New York 1988.

[13] Antonio Sant'Elia, *Messaggio* (published with no title), in cat. *Prima Esposizione d'arte del gruppo 'Nuove Tendenze' alla Famiglia Artistica di Milano* (20 May–10 June 1914); text in: Caramel-Longatti (ed.) (1962), pp. 121ff.; Godoli (1983), pp. 182f.

[14] On the '*città nuova*' cf. Caramel-Longatti (1962); Nicoletti (1978), pp. 371ff.; Godoli (1983), pp. 121ff.

[15] Antonio Sant'Elia, 'L'Architettura Futurista. Manifesto, Flugblatt', Milan 1914; repr. in: *Lacerba* vol. II, n. 15, August 1914, pp. 228–31 (facs. repr. Milan 1980); manifesto repr. in: Caramel-Longatti (1962), pp. 125–29; Scrivo (1968), pp. 105f.; Godoli (1983), pp. 183–85.

[16] Umberto Boccioni, 'Architettura futurista. Manifesto'; published in: Umberto Boccione, *Altri inediti e apparati critici*, ed. Z. Birolli, Milan 1972; repr. in: Godoli (1983), pp. 185–87.

[17] Vicenzo Fani, 'Manifesto della Architettura Futurista' (1919) (first published in: G. Scriboni, *Tra Nazionalismo e Futurismo. Testimonianze inedite di Volt*, Padua 1980), in: Godoli (1983), pp. 188f.

[18] Virgilio Marchi, 'Manifesto dell'architettura futurista dinamica, stato d'animo, drammatica' (first published in: *Roma Futurista* III, n. 72, 29 February 1920), in: Godoli (1983), pp. 189f. Cf. Also Virgilio Marchi, *Architettura futurista*, Foligno 1924.

[19] Cf. Godoli (1983), pp. 44ff., 129ff. (with references to further literature).

[20] On Italian architecture and architectural discussion in the 1920s and '30s, cf. Cesare De Seta, *La cultura architettonica in Italia tra le due guerre*, Bari [1]1972, Rome–Bari [2]1983 and id., *Architettura e città durante il fascismo*, Bari 1971; for a good general account of individual groups of architects with an extensive selection of texts, cf. Luciano Patetta, *L'Architettura in Italia 1919–1943. Le polemiche*, Milan 1972. The major catalogues are the following: Silvia Danesi and Luciano Patetta (ed.), *Il Razionalismo e l'architettura in Italia durante il Fascismo*, Venice 1976; *Annitrenta. Arte e Cultura in Italia*, Milan 1982. cf. also Margrit Estermann-Juchler, *Faschistische Staatsbaukunst. Zur ideologischen Funktion der öffentlichen Architektur im faschistischen*

Italien, Cologne–Vienna 1982; Giorgio Ciucci, 'Il dibattito sull'architettura e la città fasciste', in: *Storia dell'arte italiana*, part II, vol. 3, ed. Federico Zeri, Turin 1982, pp. 263–378; id., *Il destino dell'architettura. Persico Giolli Pagano*, Rome–Bari 1985.

²¹ Fillia, 'Futurismo e fascismo' (*La città futurista*, April 1929), in: Patetta (1972), pp. 257ff.; Enrico Prampolini, 'Architettura Futurista' (*La città futurista*, February 1928), in: Godoli (1983), pp. 190–92.

²² Cf. the comprehensive anthology: Paola Barocchi (ed.), *Testimonianze e polemiche figurative in Italia. Dal Divisionismo al Novecento*, Messina–Florence 1974.

²³ Giovanni Muzio, *L'architettura a Milano intorno all'Ottocento* (in: *Emporium*, n. 317, May 1921); repr. in: Giuseppe Gambirasio and Bruno Minardi, *Giovanni Muzio. Opere e scritti*, Milan 1982, pp. 224–33.

²⁴ 'Gli esempi più buoni ed originali del passato apparvero con sicurezza quelli di derivazione classica e particolarmente a Milano quelli del primo Ottocento…Come per l'urbanistica anche per l'architettura s'impose un ritorno al classicismo in modo analogo a quanto avveniva nelle arti plastiche e nella letteratura'. Giovanni Muzio, 'Alcuni architetti d'oggi in Lombardia' (in: *Dedalo* XV, 1931), in: Gambirasio-Minardi (ed.) (1982), p. 255; also in: Patetta (1972), p. 80.

²⁵ On Finetti cf. Giovanni Cislaghi a.o. (ed.), *Giuseppe de Finetti. Milano, costruzione di una città*, Milan 1969; Giovanni Cislaghi a.o. (ed.), *Giuseppe d Finetti. Progetti 1920–1951*, Milan (XVI Triennale di Milano) 1982.

²⁶ On his architectural writings, cf. Patetta in cat. Danesi-Patetta (1976), pp. 43ff., 196ff.

²⁷ Marcello Piacentini, *Architettura d'oggi*, Rome 1930; excerpts in: Patetta (1972), pp. 75ff.

²⁸ 'Niente grattacieli, dunque, in Italia: né le ragioni economiche le suggeriscono, né quelle estetiche le permettono'. Marcello Piacentini, 'In tema di grattacieli', *Architettura e Arti Decorative* II, 1922/23, pp. 311–13; repr. in Barocchi (ed.) (1974), pp. 438f.

²⁹ Marcello Piacentini, *Sulla conservazione della Bellezza di Roma e sullo sviluppo della città moderna*, Rome 1916.

³⁰ On the Italian Rationalists cf., further to the surveys and catalogues cited below, esp. Michele Cennamo (ed.), *Materiali per l'analisi dell'architettura moderna. La prima*

Esposizione Italiana di Architettura Razionale, Naples 1973; id. (ed.), *Materiali per l'analisi dell'architettura moderna. Il M.I.A.R.*, Naples 1976; a concise essay which grew out of new discussion of Rationalism: Hanno-Walter Kruft, 'Rationalismus in der Architektur – eine Begriffsklärung,' *Architectura* 9, 1979, pp. 45–57 (repr. in: *Der Architekt*, April 1981, p. 176–81).

³¹ Gaetano Minnucci in: *Architettura e arti decorative*, pp. 1923ff.; cf. Cennamo (1973), pp. 25ff. (bibliog. of Minnucci's writings pp. 254f.).

³² Minnuci (1923); Cennamo (1973), p. 27.

³³ Gruppo 7, *Architettura* I–IV, in: *Rassegna Italiana*, December 1926–May 1927; repr. in: Cennamo (1973), pp. 37ff., from which the following passages are cited:

'Stà all'Italia di dare allo spirito nuovo il massimo sviluppo, di portarlo alle sue consequenze estreme, fino a dettare alle altre nazioni uno stile, come nei grandi periodi del passato.'

'Il desiderio dunque di uno spirito nuovo nei giovani è basato su una sicura conoscenza del passato, non è fondato sul vuoto…Tra il passato nostro e il nostro presente non esiste incompatibilità. Noi non vogliamo rompere con la tradizione…'

'La nuova architettura, la vera architettura deve risultare da una stretta aderenza alla logica, alla razionalità. Un rigido costruttivismo deve dettare le regole. Le nuove forme dell'architettura dovranno ricevere il valore estetico dal solo carattere di necessità, e solo in seguito, per via di selezione, nascerà lo stile. Poiche, noi non pretendiamo affatto creare uno stile…; ma dall' uso costante della razionalità, dalla perfetta rispondenza della struttura dell'edificio agli scopi che si propone, risultará per selezione lo stile. Occore riuscire a questo: nobilitare l'indefinibile e astratta perfezione del puro ritmo, la semplice construttività che da sola non sarebbe bellezza.'

'La casa avrà una sua nuova estetica, come l'aeroplano ha una sua estetica, ma la casa non avrà quella dell'aeroplano.'

'…l'architettura non può più essere individuale.'

'…un desiderio di verità, di logica, di ordine, una lucidità che sa di ellenismo…'

³⁴ 1ª Esposizione Italiana di Architettura Razionale, Rome 1928, p. 6; Cennamo (1973), p. 105, from which the following passages are cited:

'*L'architettura razionale – come noi la intendiamo –* ritrova le armonie, i ritmi, le simmetrie nei nuovi schemi costruttivi, nei caratteri dei materiali e nella rispondenza perfetta alle esigenze cui l'edificio è destinato.'

'*Non mi meraviglierei che domani si ordinasse ad un architetto un edificio in stile razionale, così come lo si potrebbe ordinare in stile rinascenza o gotico.*'

[35] Cat. (1928), p. 8; Cennamo (1973), pp. 105f.

[36] Marcello Piacentini in: *Architettura e Arti Decorative*, August 1928; Cennamo (1973), pp. 127ff.

[37] Adalberto Libera in: *Rassegna italiana*, May 1929; Cennamo (1973), pp. 137ff.

[38] Filippo Tommaso Marinetti, 'Sant'Elia ed i razionalisti', in: *La Fiera Letteraria*, 8 April 1928; Cennamo (1973), pp. 165ff.

[39] Cf. Luciano Patetta, 'Neo-futurismo, Novecento e Razionalismo. Termini di una polemica nel periodo fascista', *Controspazio*, 4–5 April–May 1971, pp. 87–96.

[40] Pietro Maria Bardi, 'Architettura, arte di stato', in: *L'Ambrosiano*, 31 January 1931; Cennamo (1976), pp. 37ff.; Pietro Maria Bardi, *Rapporto sull'architettura per Mussolini*, Rome 1931; Cennamo (1976), pp. 120–59.

[41] Giuseppe Terragni, 'Architettura di Stato?' in: *L'Ambrosiano*, 11 December 1931; repr. in: Enrico Mantero, *Giuseppe Terragni e la città del razionalismo italiano*, 1969, pp. 157ff.; Cennamo (1976), pp. 43ff. from which the following passages are cited:

'*1) diachiarare l'architettura Arte di Stato;*

2) modificare radicalmente le leggi che riguardano la professione dell'architetto nei confronti delle commissioni edilizie;

3) affidare all'architettura così rinnovati il compito di eternare e suggellare il trionfo dell'idea fascista nel mondo.'

'*... rispecchiante i caratteri di robustezza e d'ordine che sono le preferenze precipue degli Italiani di Mussolini...*'

'*Gli architetti cosiddetti razionalisti sono dei tradizionali.... i giovani si rivolgono a Mussolini, perchè regoli le sorti dell'architettura, oggi male in arnese. Nella loro petizione i giovani chiedono a Mussolini una risposta. Quello che risponderà Mussolini i andrà bene. Perchè Mussolini ha sempre ragione.*'

[42] Cf. Cennamo (1976), p. 77.

[43] Ibid., pp. 84ff.

[44] Ibid., pp. 86f.

[45] Press release, 26 January 1931; Cennamo (1976), p. 98.

[46] Cennamo (1976), p. 103, n. 10.

[47] Ibid., pp. 103f.

[48] Ugo Ojetti, 'Spirito e forma della moderna architettura italiana', *La Tribuna*, 3 March 1931; in: Cennamo (1976), pp. 227ff.

[49] '*è la forza che disciplina queste doti costruttive ed utilitarie ad un fine di valore estetico più alto. Quando si sarà raggiunta quella armonia di proporzioni che, induca l'animo dell'osservatore a sostare in una contemplazione, o in una commozione, solo allora, allo schema costruttivo, si sarà sovrapposto un'opera d'architettura*'. Giuseppe Terragni, 'Per un'architettura italiana moderna', *La Tribuna*, 23 March 1931; in: Cennamo (1976), pp. 242ff.

[50] Marcello Piacentini, 'Difesa dell'architettura italiana', *Il Giornale d'Italia*, 2 May 1931; in: Cennamo (1976), pp. 285ff.

[51] '*Noi, in Italia, non abbiamo bisogno d'essere bolscevichi per essere razionalisti*'. Gruppo Romano Architetti Razionalisti, 'Difesa del Razionalismo', *Giornale d'Italia*, 8 May 1931; Cennamo (1976), pp. 292ff.

[52] Cf. Cennamo (1976), pp. 425ff.

[53] Cf. Margrit Estermann-Juchler, *Faschistische Staatsbaukunst*, Cologne–Vienna 1982.

[54] Cf. Hanno-Walter Kruft, 'Nationalsozialismus – Faschismus – Falange. Rechte Diktaturen in ihrem Verhältnis zur Architektur', in: *Der Architekt*, April 1983, pp. 181–83.

[55] Cf. esp. Diane Yvonne Ghirardo, 'Italian Architects and Fascist Politics: An Evaluation of the Rationalist's Role in Regime Building', *Journal of the Society of Architectural Historians* XXXIX, 1980, pp. 109–27.

[56] On Terragni cf. Enrico Mantero, *Giuseppe Terragni e la città del razionalismo italiano*, n.p. 1969; Bruno Zevi, *Giuseppe Terragni*, Bologna 1980; cat. *Giuseppe Terragni 1904–1943*, ed. Mario Fosso and Enrico Mantero, Como 1982; Thomas L. Schumacher, *Terragni e il Danteum*, 1938, Rome ²1983.

[57] Cf. Diane Ghirardo, 'Politics of a Masterpiece: The Vicenda of the Decoration of the Facade of the Casa del Fascio, Como 1936–39,' *The Art Bulletin* LXII, 1980, pp. 466–78.

[58] On Persico cf. cat. *Edoardo Persico 1900–1936. Autografi, scritti e disegni dal 1926 al 1936*, ed. Maurizio di Pudo, Rome 1978.

[59] Edoardo Persico, *Scritti d'architettura (1927/1935)*, ed. Giulia Veronesi, Florence 1968; Edoardo Persico, *Oltre l'architettura.*

Scritti scelti e lettere, ed. Riccardo Mariani, Milan 1977.
[60] Cf. Raffaello Giolli, *L'architettura razionale*, ed. Cesare de Seta, Bari 1972 (anthology of Giolli's writings).
[61] Cf. Giuseppe Pagano, *Architettura e città durante il facismo*, ed. Cesare de Seta, Bari 1976 (anthology of Pagano's writings); Antonio Saggio, *L'opera di Giuseppe Pagano tra politica e architettura*, Bari 1984.
[62] On Sartoris cf. cat *Alberto Sartoris*, ed. J. Gubler, Zürich 1978; A. Cuomo, *Alberto Sartoris, l'architettura italiana tra tragedia e forma*, Rome 1978.
The most important of these works: Alberto Sartoris, *Gli elementi dell'architettura funzionale*, Milan 1932. Alberto Sar-

toris, *Enclyclopédie de l'architecture nouvelle*, 3 vols, Milan 1948–56.
[63] On Mazzoni cf. Alfredo Forti, *Angiolo Mazzoni. Architetto fra fascismo e libertà*, Florence 1978; Godoli (1983), pp. 107ff., 169ff., 218f. (bibliography); cat. *Angiolo Mazzoni (1894–1979). Architetto nell'Italia*, Bologna 1985.
[64] Filippo Tommaso Marinetti-Angiolo Mazzoni-Mino Somenzi, 'Manifesto Futurista dell'architettura aerea', in: *Sant'Elia* vol. II, n. 3, 1 February 1934; in: Godoli (1983), pp. 195f.
[65] CF. Ezio Bonfanti and Marco Porta, *Città Museo e architettura. Il Gruppo BBPR nella cultura architettonica italiana 1932–1970*, Florence 1973, p. A 137ff. (bibliography).

28. The Soviet Union

[1] On the Renaissance in Eastern Europe, cf. Jan Białostocki, *The Art of the Renaissance in Eastern Europe. Hungary–Bohemia–Poland*, Oxford 1976; Jolán Balogh, *Die Anfänge der Renaissance in Ungarn. Matthias Corvinus und die Kunst*, Graz 1975, pp. 27ff.; Oskar Wulff, *Die neurussische Kunst im Rahmen der Kulturentwicklung Rußlands von Peter dem Großen bis zur Revolution*, 2 vols, Augsburg 1932. In his account of Polish architectural theory from the 16th to the 19th century Adam Malkiewicz (*Teoria architektury w nowożytnym piśmiennictwie polskim*, Cracow 1976, p. 128) speaks of the 'secondariness of Polish writings about architecture'.
On the first architectural theory in Russia, cf. a.o. Alice Biró, *Russische Baufachsprache des 18. Jahrhunderts. Dolžnost 'architekturnoj éspedicii (Slavica Helvetica*, vol. 20), Bern–Frankfurt 1982, esp. pp. 29ff.
[2] Cf. esp. Camilla Gray, *The Russian Experiment in Art 1863–1922*, London 1962.
[3] The following references are limited to works of translations in Western languages. Cf. esp. Anatole Senkevitch, Jr, *Soviet Architecture 1917–1962. A Bibliographical Guide to Source Material*, Charlottesville, VA 1974. For a general account of architectural-theoretical discussion at the beginning of the 1920s, cf. V. E. Chazanova, 'La teoria dell'architettura all'inizio degli anni' 20', in: *Rassegna sovietica*, vol. XXIV, 1973, 2, pp. 85–124.
Major anthologies of source-material: John E. Bowlt (ed.), *Russian Art of the*

Avant-Garde. Theory and Criticism 1902–1934, New York 1976; Hubertus Gaßner and Eckhart Gillen, *Zwischen Revolutionskunst und sozialistischem Realismus. Dokumente und Kommentare. Kunstdebatten in der Sowjetunion von 1917 bis 1934*, Cologne 1979; Anatole Kopp, *Architecture et mode de vie*, Grenoble 1979.
General accounts of architecture: Vittorio De Feo, *URSS. Architettura 1917–1936*, Rome 1963; Anatole Kopp, *Ville et Révolution. Architecture et urbanisme soviétiques des années vingt*, Paris 1967 (Engl. trans. New York 1970; Ital. trans.: Milan 1972, ²1977); K. N. Afanasjew, *Ideen-Projekte-Bauen. Sowjetische Architektur 1917 bis 1932*, Dresden 1973; the most comprehensive account is offered by Selim O. Chan-Magomedow, *Pioniere der sowjetischen Architektur. Der Weg zur neuen sowjetischen Architektur in den zwanziger und zu Beginn der dreißiger Jahre*, Vienna–Berlin 1983.
Cf. also the following exhibition catalogues: *Art in Revolution. Soviet Art and Design since 1917*, London 1971; *Tendenzen der Zwanziger Jahre*, Berlin 1977; *L'Espace urbain en URSS, 1917–1978*, Paris 1978; and the supplementary volume by Jean-Louis Cohen a.o., *URSS 1917–1978: La ville, l'architecture* (French–Italian), Rome 1979; *Paris–Moscou 1900–1930*, Paris 1979; *Architettura nel paese dei Soviet 1917–1933. Arte di propaganda e costruzione della città*, Milan 1982.
[4] Richard Lorenz (ed.), *Proletarische Kulturre-*

volution in Sowjetrußland (1917–1921).
Dokumente des 'Proletkult', Munich 1969.
[5] Cited from Lorenz (ed.) (1969), p. 78.
[6] Ibid., p. 15.
[7] Leo Trotsky, *Literature and Revolution* (Russian, 1924), German ed. *Literatur und Revolution*, Berlin 1968; Munich 1972, p. 156.
[8] Trotsky (1924, German ed. 1972), p. 113.
[9] Cf. the account by Anatoly Lunacharsky, 'Lenin und die Kunst' (1924), in: *Lunatscharski, Vom Proletkult zum sozialistischen Realismus. Aufsätze zur Kunst der Zeit*, Berlin 1982, pp. 142–47; on the Monumental Propaganda initiative, cf. Hans-Jürgen Drengenberg, *Die Sowjetische Politik auf dem Gebiet der bildenden Kunst von 1917 bis 1934*, Berlin 1972, esp. pp. 181ff.
[10] Cf. exhib. cat. *Sieg über die Sonne. Aspekte russischer Kunst zu Beginn des 20 Jahrhunderts*, Berlin 1983.
[11] On Malevich cf. Larissa A. Shadova, *Malewitsch*, Munich 1982 (English ed. London 1983).

Cf. further an anthology published by the Galerie Gmurzynska, *Kasimir Malewitsch zum 100. Geburtstag*, Cologne 1978.
[12] The major editions of Malevich's writings are the following: Kasimir Malewitsch, *Die gegenstandslose Welt (Bauhausbücher)*, Munich 1927), facs. repr. with introduction by Stephan von Wiese, Mainz–Berlin 1980. Kasimir Malewitsch, *Suprematismus. Die gegenstandslose Welt*, ed. Werner Haftmann, Cologne 1962. Kasimir Malewitsch (Malevich), *Essays on Art and Unpublished Writings*, ed. Troels Andersen, 4 vols, Copenhagen 1968–78.
[13] Both texts in: Malewitsch (1962), pp. 225ff., 283ff.
[14] Malevich, 'Suprematismus I/46', in: op. cit. (1962), p. 274.
[15] Malevich, 'Suprematistisches Manifest Unowis', in: op. cit. (1962), pp. 283ff.
[16] Malevich, 'Suprematismus I/46', in: op. cit. (1962), pp. 280f.
[17] Malevich, 'Suprematistisches Manifest Unowis', in: op. cit. (1962), p. 286.
[18] Kasimir Malevich, 'Suprematistische Architektur', in: *Wasmuths Monatshefte für Baukunst* vol. XI, 1927, pp. 412–14; cf. Eberhard Steneberg, *Russische Kunst Berlin 1919–1932*, Berlin 1969, esp. pp. 38ff.
[19] On Constructivism cf. Christina Lodder, *Russian Constructivism*, New Haven–Lon-

don 1983. On Constructivist architecture cf. Vieri Quilici, *L'architettura del costruttivismo*, Bari 1969 (Rome–Bari ²1978; with extensive anthology of texts in Italian trans.).
[20] Cf. Sophie Lissitzky-Küppers, *El Lissitzky – Maler, Architekt, Typograf, Fotograf*, Dresden 1967 (English ed. London ¹1968; ²1980); exhib. cat. *El Lissitzky*, Cologne 1976; the major edition of El Lissitzky's writings is: *El Lissitzky, Proun und Wolkenbügel. Schriften, Briefe, Dokumente*, ed. Sophie Lissitzky-Küppers and Jan Lissitzky, Dresden 1977.
[21] Cf. esp. Lissitzky's lecture of 1921, 'Proun', in: op. cit. (1977), pp. 21ff.; exhib. cat. (1976), pp. 60ff.
[22] Lissitzky, 'Proun' (1921), in: op. cit. (1977), p. 33.
[23] Cf. Lissitzky's project 'Eine Serie von Hochhäusern für Moskau' (1923–25), in: op. cit. (1977), pp. 80–84.
[24] El Lissitzky, 'Idole und Idolverehrer' (in: *Bauindustrie* 11/12, 1928), in: Lissitzky (1977), pp. 41–54.
[25] El Lissitzky, *Rußland. Die Rekonstruktion der Architektur in der Sowjetunion*, Vienna 1930; new ed. entitled *Rußland: Architektur für eine Weltrevolution (Bauwelt Fundamente 14)*, Berlin–Frankfurt–Vienna 1965.
[26] Some texts by Tatlin are included in exhib. cat. Stockholm 1968; Nikolay Punin, *Monument tret'ego internatsionala*, Petrograd 1920; cf. Milner (1983), pp. 151ff.
[27] On Tatlin, cf. exhib. cat. *Vladimir Tatlin*, Stockholm 1968; John Milner, *Vladimir Tatlin and the Russian Avant-Garde*, New Haven–London 1983; Larissa Alekseevna Zhadova (ed.), *Tatlin*, London 1988.
[28] Alexej Gan, *Konstruktivizm*, Moscow 1922; in Italian trans. in: Quilici (ed. 1978), pp. 122ff.; on Gan cf. Lodder (1983), pp. 98ff.
[29] Cf. exhib. cats *Kunst aus der Revolution* and *Kunst in die Produktion*, Berlin 1977.
[30] Cf. Gaßner-Gillen (1979); Lodder (1983); Chan-Magomedow (1983); S. Frederick Starr, 'OSA: The Union of Contemporary Architects', in: George Gibian and H. W. Tjalsma (ed.), *Russian Modernism. Culture and the Avant-Garde, 1900–1930*, Ithaca, NY–London 1976, pp. 188–208.
[31] On Ginzburg cf. Selim O. Chan-Magomedow, *M. Ia. Ginzburg*, Moscow 1972 (Italian trans. Milan 1975).
[32] Moisey Yakovlevich Ginzburg, *Stil' i epokka*, Moscow 1924; Italian trans. in:

Moisej Ja. Ginzburg, *Saggi sull'architettura costruttivista*, ed. Emilio Battisti, Milan 1977 (this edition here cited); English trans.: Moisei Ginzburg, *Style and Epoch*, with introduction by Anatole Senkevitsch, Jr, Cambridge, MA–London 1982.

[33] Moisey Jakovlevich Ginzburg, *Ritm v arkhitekture*, Moscow 1923; in Italian trans. in: Ginzburg (1977).

[34] Ginzburg (1924; Italian ed. 1977), p. 76.

[35] Ibid., p. 134.

[36] Ibid., p. 107.

[37] Ibid., pp. 113ff.

[38] Ibid., p. 119.

[39] Ibid., pp. 121ff.

[40] Ibid., pp. 127f.

[41] Ibid., p. 136.

[42] Ibid., p. 140.

[43] Ibid., pp. 142ff.

[44] The correspondence is published in: *Sovremennaya arkhitektura* 1–2, 1930; in Italian trans. in: Paolo Ceccarelli (ed.), *La costruzione della città sovietica*, Padua (¹1970) ³1977, pp. 64ff.

[45] Moisey Jakovlevich Ginzburg, *Zhilishchiy opyt pyatiletney raboty nad problemoy zhilishcha*, Moscow 1934; in Italian trans. in: Ginzburg (1977), p. 181.

[46] On Ladovsky cf. Chan-Magomedow (1983), pp. 106ff., 543ff. (texts); cf. also Chan-Magomedow in: *Lotus International*, no. 20, Venice 1978.

[47] Ladovsky, cited from Chan-Magomedow (1983), p. 544; a longer excerpt from this essay in Italian trans. in: Quilici (1978), pp. 246–51.

[48] On Mel'nikov cf. S. Frederick Starr, *Melnikov. Solo Architect in a Mass Society*, Princeton 1978 (¹1981).

[49] Cf. Chan-Magomedow (1983), pp. 551f.; cf. Starr (1981), pp. 240ff.

[50] Mel'nikov (1936); cited from Chan-Magomedow (1983), p. 552.

[51] Jakov G. Chernikov, *Konstruktsiya arkhitekturnykh i mashinal'nykh form*, Leningrad 1931; excerpts in English trans. in: Bowlt (1976), pp. 254ff.; id., *Arkhitekturnyye fantazii*, Leningrad 1933.

[52] On Leonidov cf. P. A. Alexandrow and S. O. Chan-Magomedow, *Ivan Leonidov* (Ital.), Milan 1975; Chan-Magomedow (1983), pp. 234f., 552ff. (including texts).

[53] One was attempted by Adolf Max Vogt, *Russische und französische Revolutionsarchitektur 1917–1989. Zur Einwirkung des*

Marxismus und des Newtonismus auf die Bauweise, Cologne 1974 (on Leonidov esp. pp. 93ff.).

[54] Leonidov (1934); cited from German trans. in: Chan-Magomedow (1983), p. 555.

[55] Cf. Wulf Herzogenrath (ed.), *Frühe Kölner Kunstausstellungen*, Cologne 1981, pp. 202ff. with facs. repr. of the exhibition catalogue designed by El Lissitzky (1928).

[56] Cf. Kurt Junghanns, 'Die Beziehungen zwischen deutschen und sowjetischen Architekten in den Jahren 1917 bis 1933', in: *Wissenschaftliche Zeitschrift der Humboldt-Universität zu Berlin* XVI, 1967, Heft 3; Alberto Asor Rosa a.o., *Socialismo, città, architettura URSS 1917–1937. Il contributo degli architetti europei*, Rome 1971 (³1976); Christian Borngräber, 'Ausländische Architekten in der UdSSR: Bruno Taut, die Brigaden Ernst May, Hannes Meyer und Hans Schmidt', in: exhib. cat. *Wem gehört die Welt – Kunst und Gesellschaft in der Weimarer Republik*, Berlin 1977, pp. 109–42.

[57] Cf. Anatole Kopp, *L'architecture de la période stalinienne*, Grenoble 1978.

[58] On this competition, cf. Max Raphael, *Für eine demokratische Architektur*, ed. Jutta Held, Frankfurt 1976, pp. 53ff.; Alberto Samonà (ed.), *Il Palazzo dei Soviet 1931–1933*, Rome 1976; Kopp (1978), pp. 239ff; cat. *Naum Gabo und der Wettbewerb zum Palast der Sowjets Moskau 1931–1933*, Berlin 1992.

[59] Cf. Kopp (1967; Ital. ed. ²1977); Marco de Michelis and Ernesto Pasini, *La città sovietica 1925–1937*, Venice 1976; James H. Bater, *The Soviet City*, London 1980; Paul M. White, *Soviet Urban and Regional Planning. A Bibliography with Abstracts*, London 1980; Chan-Magomedow (1983), pp. 273ff.

For major anthologies of texts on town planning, cf. Paolo Ceccarelli (ed.), *La costruzione della città sovietica 1929–31*, Padua 1970 (³1977), and Anatole Kopp, *Architecture et mode de vie. Textes des années vingt en U.R.S.S.*, Grenoble 1979.

[60] Leonid M. Sabsovich, *Gorod budushchego i organizatsiya sozialischeskogo uklada zhyzni*, Moscow 1929; in Italian trans. in: Ceccarelli (³1977), pp. 3–28; an excerpt in French trans. in: Kopp (1979), pp. 224ff.

[61] Cf. Okhitovich in: *Sovremmennaya arkhitektura*, no. 4, 1929 (in French trans. in: Kopp 1979, pp. 237ff.).

[62] Cf. Mikhail O. Barch and Moysey Ginzburg, 'Zelyonyy gorod. Sotsialisticheskaya perestroyka Moskvy', in: *Sovremmennaya arkhitektura*, nos 1–2, 1930 (in Italian trans. in: Ceccareli [3]1977, pp. 189–208).

[63] Nikolay A. Milyutin, *Sotsgorod. Problema sotsialisticheskogo planirovaniya gorodov*, Moscow 1930; Italian trans., ed. Vieri Quilici, Milan 1971; English trans. ed. Arthur Sprague, Cambridge, MA–London 1974.

[64] Milyutin (1930; ed. 1974), p. 54.

[65] Ibid., p. 66.

[66] Ibid., p. 81ff.

[67] Ibid., p. 106.

[68] Cf. Le Corbusier, *Oeuvre complète 1938–1946*, ed. Willy Boesiger, Zürich 1946 ([6]1971), pp. 72ff.

[69] Cf. esp. Kopp (1978), pp. 193ff.

[70] Cf. S. Frederick Starr, 'Writings from the 1960s on the Modern Movement in Russia', *Journal of the Society of Architectural Historians* XXX, 1971, pp. 170–78; for an interesting discussion of forms of housing in communist Eastern Europe, cf. G. A. Gradow, *Stadt und Lebensweise*, (East) Berlin 1971; an unresolved relationship with the discussion of the 1920s continues in Russia even in the Materialist works of Chan-Magomedow, e.g. in his survey of 1983.

[71] Cf. exhib. cat. *Berthold Lubetkin. Un moderne en Angleterre*, ed. Peter Coe and Malcolm Reading, Lüttich 1981; John Allan, *Lubetkin: Architecture and the Tradition of Progress*, London 1992.

29. The United States in the first half of the twentieth century

[1] Cf. on this question Walter C. Kidney, *The Architecture of Choice: Eclecticism in America 1880–1930*, New York 1974.

[2] On the history of the skyscraper, cf. Winston Weisman, 'A New View of Skyscraper History', in: Edgar Kaufmann, Jr, (ed.), *The Rise of an American Architecture*, New York and London 1970, pp. 115ff.; Paul Goldberger, *The Skyscraper*, New York 1981.

[3] Francisco Mujica, *History of the Skyscraper*, Paris and New York 1929 (facs. repr. New York 1977).

[4] Cf. Henry-Russell Hitchcock, 'Ruskin and American Architecture, or Regeneration Long Delayed', in: John Summerson (ed.), *Concerning Architecture. Essays... presented to Nikolaus Pevsner*, London 1968, pp. 166–208; Roger B. Stein, *John Ruskin and Aesthetic Thought in America 1840–1900*, Cambridge, Mass. 1967.

[5] Cf. Frank Lloyd Wright, *Ausgewählte Bauten und Entwürfe*, Berlin 1910 ([2]1924); Frank Lloyd Wright, *Ausgeführte Bauten, Einführung von Charles Robert Ashbee*, Berlin 1911 (facs. repr. with introduction by Grant Carpenter Manson; New York 1982); H. Th. Wijdeveld (ed.), *The Life Work of the American Architect Frank Lloyd Wright* (the so-called Wendingen Edition), Santport 1925 (facs. repr.: New York 1965); Heidi Kief-Niederwöhrmeier, *Frank Lloyd Wright und Europa*, Stuttgart [1]1978, [2]1983.

[6] Cf. R. L. Sweeney, *Frank Lloyd Wright. An Annotated Bibliography*, Los Angeles 1978; Patrick J. Meehan, *Frank Lloyd Wright. A Research Guide to Archival Sources*, New York and London 1983.

Of numerous monographs the most important seem to the present author to be the following: Henry-Russell Hitchcock, *In the Nature of Materials. The Buildings of Frank Lloyd Wright 1887–1941*, New York 1942 (new ed. New York 1973; several reprs); Grant Carpenter Mason, *Frank Lloyd Wright to 1910. The First Golden Age*, New York 1958; H. Allan Brooks, *The Prairie School. Frank Lloyd Wright and His Midwest Contemporaries*, University of Toronto Press 1972 (paperback ed. New York 1976); Robert C. Twombly, *Frank Lloyd Wright. An Interpretative Biography*, New York 1973 (several reprs); H. Allan Brooks (ed.), *Writings on Wright*, Cambridge, Mass. 1981 ([2]1983).

[7] On the significance for Wright of Froebel's educational games, cf. besides Manson (1958): Stuart Wilson, 'The Gifts of Friedrich Froebel', *Journal of the Society of Architectural Historians* XXVI, December 1967; Richard MacCormac, 'The Anatomy of Wright's Aesthetic', *Architectural Review* CXLIII, February 1968, pp. 143–46; Richard MacCormac, 'Froebel's kindergarten gifts and the early work of Frank Lloyd Wright', *Environment and Planning* B, 1, 1974, p. 29–50; Edgar Kaufmann, Jr 'Form Became Feeling, a New View of Froebel and

Wright', *Journal of the Society of Architectural Historians* XL, 1981, pp. 130–37; Edgar Kaufmann, Jr, 'Frank Lloyd Wright's Mementos of Childhood', *Journal of the Society of Architectural Historians* XLI, 1982, pp. 232–37.

[8] Cf. esp. Donald Hoffmann, 'Frank Lloyd Wright and Viollet-le-Duc', *Journal of the Society of Architectural Historians* XXVIII, 1969, pp. 173–83.

[9] Cf. David A. Hanks, *The Decorative Designs of Frank Lloyd Wright*, New York 1979.

[10] Frank Lloyd Wright, *Genius and the Mobocracy*, New York 1949 (enlarged ed. New York 1971); cf. Paul E. Sprague, *The Drawings of Louis Henry Sullivan. A Catalogue of the Frank Lloyd Wright Collection at the Avery Architectural Library*, Princeton 1979.

[11] A complete bibliography in: Sweeney (1978); a more practical arrangement by Twombly (1973, ed. 1974), pp. 345ff. The most important anthologies in German trans.: Frank Lloyd Wright, *Schriften und Bauten*, Munich–Vienna 1963; Frank Lloyd Wright, *Humane Architektur*, ed. Wolfgang Braatz (*Bauwelt Fundamente* 25), Gütersloh–Berlin 1969.

[12] Incorporated, slightly revised, in the Kahn Lectures given by Wright at Princeton in 1930: Frank Lloyd Wright, *Modern Architecture. Being the Kahn Lectures for 1930*, Princeton 1931, pp. 7–23 (variously repr., eg in: Lewis Mumford (ed.), *Roots of Contemporary American Architecture* (1952), New York 1972, pp. 169–85; Leland M. Roth (ed.) *America Builds. Source Documents in American Architecture and Planning*, New York 1983, pp. 36ff.); in German trans. in: Wright, *Schriften und Bauten* (1963), pp. 52ff. (in the original version); Wright, *Humane Architektur* (1969), pp. 21ff.

[13] Cf. Gillian Naylor, *The Arts and Crafts Movement*, London 1971, pp. 172ff.; Peter Davey, *Architecture of the Arts and Crafts Movement*, London and New York 1980, pp. 188ff.

[14] Wright, *Schriften und Bauten* (1963), p. 60.

[15] Wright, 'The Art and Craft of the Machine', in: Wright, *Modern Architecture*, Princeton, NJ 1931, p. 14.

[16] Frank Lloyd Wright, 'In the Cause of Architecture', *Architectural Record* XXIII, 1908, pp. 155–221 (repr. with all later essays with the same title: Frank Lloyd Wright, *In the Cause of Architecture*, ed. Fredrick Gutheim,

New York 1975; and in Wendingen Edition, ed. Wijdeveld, 1925 and 1965, pp. 8ff.).

[17] Frank Lloyd Wright, *The Japanese Print. An Interpretation*, Chicago 1912 (new ed. New York 1967).

[18] On this and other points, cf. Leonard K. Eaton, *Two Chicago Architects and Their Clients: Frank Lloyd Wright and Howard Van Doren Shaw*, Cambridge, Mass. and London 1969; Paul R. and Jean S. Hanna, *Frank Lloyd Wright's Hanna House. The Clients' Report*, Cambridge, Mass. and London 1981 ([2]1982).

[19] Frank Lloyd Wright, 'In the Cause of Architecture, Second Paper', *Architectural Record* XXXV, 1914, pp. 405–413 (cf. ed. Gutheim, 1975; Wendingen Edition, ed. Wijdeveld, 1925 and 1965, p. 25).

[20] Frank Lloyd Wright, *Modern Architecture. Being the Kahn Lectures for 1930*, Princeton 1931 (the parts on the prairie house in German trans. in: Wright, *Schriften und Bauten*, 1963, pp. 45ff.).

[21] Cf. H. Allan Brooks, 'Frank Lloyd Wright and the Destruction of the Box', *Journal of the Society of Architectural Historians* XXXVIII, 1979, pp. 7–14.

[22] Despite reviews, Twombly's (1973) still seems to the present author the most instructive monograph on the subject.

[23] Frank Lloyd Wright, *The Disappearing City*, New York 1932 (new ed. entitled *The Industrial Revolution Runs Away*, New York 1969); *When Democracy Builds*, Chicago 1945; *The Living City*, New York 1958 (facs. repr. New York 1970).

[24] On Wright's urban planning ideas, cf. George R. Collins, 'Broadacre City: Wright's Utopia Reconsidered', in: *Four Great Makers of Modern Architecture* (Symposion 1961), New York 1970, pp. 55–75; Robert Fishman, *Urban Utopias in the 20th Century. Ebenezer Howard, Frank Lloyd Wright and Le Corbusier*, New York 1977; Lionel March, 'An Architect in Search of Democracy: Broadacre City', in: Brooks (ed.), *Writings on Wright* ([2]1983), pp. 195ff.

[25] Wright, *The Living City* (1958, ed. 1970), p. 66.

[26] Ibid., p. 74.

[27] Ibid., p. 97.

[28] Ibid., p. 193.

[29] Ibid., p. 233.

[30] For a concise account of the Usonian house, cf. John Sergeant, *Frank Lloyd Wright's*

Usonian Houses. The Case for Organic Architecture, New York 1976 (³1978).

[31] Frank Lloyd Wright, *The Natural House*, New York 1954 (New York 1970; London 1972).

[32] Cf. Sergeant (³1978), p. 16.

[33] Wright, *The Natural House* (1954, ed. 1970), p. 68.

[34] Wright, *The Natural House* (1954, ed. 1970), pp. 73ff.

[35] Wright, *The Natural House* (1954, ed. 1970), p. 81.

[36] On Fallingwater cf. Donald Hoffmann, *Frank Lloyd Wright's Fallingwater*, New York 1978.

[37] Frank Lloyd Wright, *A Testament*, New York 1957 (London 1959).

[38] Frank Lloyd Wright, *An Organic Architecture. The Architecture of Democracy. The Sir George Watson Lectures of the Sulgrave Manor Board for 1939*, London 1939 (facs. repr. 1941, 1970).

[39] Frank Lloyd Wright, *The Future of Architecture*, New York 1953 (London 1955, New York 1970).

[40] Ibid., p. 262.

[41] Ibid., p. 266.

[42] Twombly (1973, ed. 1974), pp. 235f.

[43] Cf. Brooks, *The Prairie School* (1972; 1976).

[44] Cf. Randell L. Makinson, *Greene & Greene. Architecture as a Fine Art*, Salt Lake City and Santa Barbara 1977 (³1980).

[45] Cf. esp. the volume published by the Chicago Tribune, *The International Competition for a New Administration Building for the Chicago Tribune MCMXXII*, Chicago 1923 (facs. repr. New York 1980; cf. also the companion vol., ed. Stanley Tigerman *Late Entries to the Chicago Tribune Tower Competition*, New York 1980).
On the theoretical background to this competition, cf. Hanno-Walter Kruft, '"Das schönste Bürohaus der Welt"'. Der internationale Wettbewerb für den Chicago Tribune Tower' (1922), *Pantheon* XXXIX, 1981, pp. 76–89.

[46] *The International Competition* (1923), p. 31.

[47] On Hood cf. Walter H. Kilham, Jr, *Raymond Hood, Architect, Form Through Function in the American Skyscraper*, New York 1973 (bibliography of Hood's writings, p. 194); cat. Raymond Hood, New York 1982.

[48] Louis H. Sullivan, 'The Chicago Tribune Tower Competition', *The Architectural Record* 53, 1923, pp. 151–57.

[49] Cf. Cervin Robinson and Rosemarie Haag Bletter, *Skyscraper Style. Art Deco New York*, New York 1975.

[50] Cf. a general appraisal by Giorgio Ciucci a.o., *La città americana dalla guerra civile al New Deal*, Rome–Bari 1973 (English ed. Cambridge, MA 1979, London 1980); on the situation in Chicago cf. Carl W. Condit, *Chicago 1910–29. Building, Planning, and Urban Technology*, Chicago and London 1973.

[51] *Modern Architecture. International Exhibition*, Museum of Modern Art, New York 1932 (facs. repr.: New York 1969).

[52] *Modern Architecture* (1932), p. 15.

[53] Henry-Russell Hitchcock and Philip Johnson, *The International Style: Architecture Since 1922*, New York 1932 (new ed. with foreword and appendix by Hitchcock: New York 1966).

[54] Hitchcock-Johnson (1932, ed. 1966), p. 62.

[55] On Neutra cf. W. Boesiger (ed.), *Richard J. Neutra: Bauten und Projekte*, 3 vols, Zürich 1951–66; Thomas S. Hines, *Richard Neutra and the Search for Modern Architecture. A Biography and History*, New York and Oxford 1983.

[56] Cf. David Gebhard, *Schindler*, London 1971.

[57] Bibliography of Schindler in: Gebhard (1971), pp. 205f.; *Space Architecture* (first in: *Dune Forum*, Feb. 1934, pp. 44–46) repr. in: Gebhard (1971), pp. 193ff.

[58] Richard J. Neutra, *Wie Baut Amerika?*, Stuttgart 1927.

[59] Richard Neutra, *Amerika. Die Stilbildung das Neuen Bauens in den Vereinigten Staaten*, Vienna 1930.

[60] On the building history of Lovell House cf. Hines (1983), pp. 75ff., 303ff.

[61] Richard Neutra, *Survival Through Design*, New York and London 1954 (paperback ed.: London–New York 1969; several reprs); German trans. under the title *Wenn wir weiterleben wollen…Erfahrungen und Forderungen eines Architekten*, Hamburg ²1956 (an 'edited version' appeared under the title *Gestaltete Umwelt. Erfahrungen und Forderungen eines Architekten*, Dresden 1968, ²1976).

[62] Neutra (1954, ed. 1969), pp. 381ff.

[63] Ibid., p. 21.

[64] Ibid., pp. 111ff.

[65] Ibid., pp. 325, 336.

[66] Richard Neutra, *Auftrag für morgen*, Hamburg 1962.

[67] Cf. Hines (1983), pp. 60ff.

[68] On Eliel Saarinen cf. the monograph by Albert Christ-Janer, *Eliel Saarinen*, Chicago 1948 (Chicago–London ²1979).

[69] Eliel Saarinen, *The City. Its Growth, its Decay, its Future*, New York 1943 (paperback ed.: Cambridge, Mass. ³1971).

[70] Saarinen (1943, ed. 1971), p. 350.

[71] Ibid., p. 197.

[72] Saarinen expressed his ideas in a wider context in a further book, *The Search for Form in Art and Architecture*, New York 1948 (facs. repr., New York 1985).

30. Since 1945

[1] Ildefonso Cerdá, *Teoria general de la Urbanización y aplicación de sus principios y doctrinas a la Reforma y Ensanche de Barcelona*, 2 vols, Madrid 1867 (facs. repr. Barcelona 1968).

[2] Cf. Antoni Gaudí, *La seva vida. Les seves obres. La seva mort*, Barcelona 1926; on Gaudí's theory cf. esp. César Martinell, *Gaudí. His Life – His Theories – His Work*, Barcelona 1975.

[3] On Spain cf. Juan Antonio Nuño, *Arte del siglo XX* (Ars Hispaniae, vol. XXII), Madrid 1977; Oriol Bohigas, *Arquitectura española de la Segunda Republica*, Barcelona 1970 (²1973); Gabriel Ureña, *Arquitectura y Urbanistica Civil y Militar en el Periodo de la Autarquía (1936–1945)*, Madrid 1979.

[4] Cf. esp. David Watkin, *The Rise of Architectural History*, London 1980; id. 'Architectural Writing in the Thirties', in: *Architectural Design Magazine* 24: *Britain in the Thirties*, London n.d., pp. 84–89.

[5] Cf. Reyner Banham, 'Revenge of the Picturesque: English Architectural Polemics, 1945–1965', in: John Summerson (ed.), *Concerning Architecture. Essays on Architectural Writers and Writing presented to Nikolaus Pevsner*, London 1968, pp. 265–73.

[6] Cf. Alison & Peter Smithson, *Ordinariness and Light: Urban Theories 1952–1960 and their application in a building project 1963–1970*, London 1970; *Without Rhetoric: An Architectural Aesthetic 1955–1972*, London 1973.

[7] Aalto's theoretical writings collected in: Göran Schildt (ed.), *Alvar Aalto: Sketches*, Cambridge, Mass.–London 1978; cf. Göran Schildt, *Det vite bordet*, Helsingfors 1983.

[8] Cf. Gunnar Asplund a.o., *Acceptera-Manifesto*, Stockholm 1931.

[9] Cf. Carlos Raúl Villanueva, *La Caracas de ayer y de hoy*, Caracas 1943; on Villanueva cf. esp. Sibyl Moholy-Nagy, *Carlos Raúl Villanueva und die Architektur Venezuelas*, Stuttgart 1964.

Oscar Niemeyer, *Minha Esperiencia em Brasilia*, Rio de Janeiro 1961; on Niemeyer cf. Stamo Papadaki, *Oscar Niemeyer*, Ravensburg 1962; Christian Hornig, *Oscar Niemeyer. Bauten und Projekte*. Munich 1981; Alexander Fils (ed.), *Oscar Niemeyer. Selbstdarstellung. Kritiken. Oeuvre*, Münsterschwarzach n.d.

[10] On modern Japanese architecture cf. Udo Kultermann, *Contemporary Architecture of Japan*, New York 1960; Manfred Speidel (ed.), *Japanische Architektur. Geschichte und Gegenwart*, Düsseldorf–Stuttgart 1983 (with German trans. of numerous theoretical texts).

[11] Cf. Kenzo Tange a.o., *Katsura – Tradition and Creation in Japanese Architecture*, Tokyo and New Haven 1960. On Tange cf. esp. Udo Kultermann (ed.), *Kenzo Tange 1946–69: Architecture and Urban Design*, London–New York 1972.

[12] For a study of Metabolism and a selection of its most important texts, cf. Kisho Kurokawa, *Metabolism in Architecture*, Boulder, Col. 1977; on its philosophical basis cf. Chuan-Wen Sun, *Der Einfluß des chinesischen Konzeptes auf die moderne Architektur*, diss., Stuttgart 1982, 126ff.

[13] Kurokawa (1977), pp. 75ff.; cf. Speidel (ed.) (1983), p. 97.

[14] Kurokawa (1977), pp. 86ff.

[15] For a good overall survey cf. Warren Sanderson (ed.), *International Handbook of Contemporary Developments in Architecture*, Westport, Conn.–London 1981; subjective in judgement are Adolf Max Vogt, a.o., *Architektur 1940–1980*, Frankfurt–Vienna–Berlin 1980 and Wolfgang Pehnt, *Das Ende der Zuversicht. Architektur in diesem Jahrhundert. Ideen–Bauten–Dokumente*, Berlin 1983.

[16] Adolf Arndt, *Demokratie als Bauherr*,

Akademie der Künste Berlin (Anmerkungen zur Zeit, 6), Berlin 1961.

[17] Cf. the translation by Wolfgang Pehnt, *German Architecture 1960–1970*, New York–Washington 1970; Paola Nestler and Peter M. Bode, *Deutsche Kunst seit 1960. Architektur*, Munich 1976.

[18] Justus Dahinden, *Versuch einer Standortsbestimmung der Gegenwartsarchitektur*, Zürich 1956.

[19] Cf. Wulf Schirmer (ed.), *Egon Eiermann. Bauten und Projekte*, Stuttgart 1984; Immo Boyken, 'Egon Eiermann, 1904–1970. Kritische Gedanken zu seiner Architektur', *Architectura* 14, 1984, pp. 67–82.

[20] Heinrich Klotz, *Architektur in der Bundesrepublik*, Frankfurt–Berlin–Vienna 1977.

[21] Frei Otto, *Das hängende Dach. Gestalt und Struktur*, diss., Berlin 1954; Frei Otto a.o., *Zugbeanspruchte Konstruktionen. Gestalt, Struktur und Berechnung von Bauten aus Seilen, Netzen und Membranen*, 2 vols, Berlin 1962–64; Frei Otto a.o., *Natürliche Konstruktionen*, Stuttgart 1982; Frei Otto, *Schriften und Reden 1951–1983*, ed. Berthold Burckhardt, Brunswick–Wiesbaden 1984.

[22] '...das Verhältnis der Masse eines Gegenstandes zum Produkt aus der übertragenen Kraft und der übertragungsstrecke dieser Kraft'. Frei Otto, 'Biologie und Bauen' (1972), in: Frei Otto, *Schriften und Reden* (1984), p. 179.

[23] 'Sie werden erst ästhetisch, wenn sie – ohne dabei zugleich etwas unfunktioneller zu werden – ideal geformt, 'vollendet' ihre 'wahre' Gestalt, dem unvoreingenommenen (aber aufgeschlossenen) Beobachter 'zeigen', wenn sie sowohl die typische Form aller vollendet optimierten – ökonomisch – funktionellen Objekte der gleichen Art als auch das Gemeinsame und Individuelle spiegeln, also durchaus mit den für Individuen typischen Abweichungen (Imperfektionen)'. Frei Otto, 'Das Ästhetische' (1979), in: Frei Otto, *Schriften und Reden* (1984), p. 208.

[24] 'Solche Bauten kann man nicht entwerfen, man kann ihnen nur durch ständiges Suchen beistehen, die endgültige Gestalt anzunehmen'. Frei Otto, 'Die Kongreßhallen-Debatte' (1958), in: Frei Otto, *Schriften und Reden* (1984), p. 46.

[25] 'Der Wille zur betonten Gestaltung steht im Gegensatz mit der Suche nach der noch unbekannten, aber den Naturgesetzen unterliegenden Form.' Frei Otto, 'Das Zeltdach. Subjektive Anmerkungen zum Olympiadach' (1972), in: Frei Otto, *Schriften und Bauten* (1984), p. 101.

[26] Meinhard von Gerkan, *Die Verantwortung des Architekten. Bedingungen für die gebaute Umwelt*, Stuttgart 1982.

[27] Cf. Jürgen Joedicke (ed.), *Architektur und Städtebau. Das Werk der Architekten van den Broek und Bakema*, Stuttgart 1963; J. B. Bakema, *Thoughts about architecture*, ed. Marianne Gray, London–New York 1981.

[28] Cf. Arnulf Lüchinger, *Structuralism in Architecture and Urban Planning*, Stuttgart 1980.

[29] Cf. esp. Hermann Hertzberger a.o., *Aldo van Eyck*, Amsterdam 1982.

[30] Cf. the work surveys: Henry-Russell Hitchcock, *Architektur von Skidmore, Owings & Merrill, 1950–1962*, Stuttgart 1962; Arthur Drexler, *Architektur von Skidmore, Owings & Merrill, 1963–1973*, Stutgart 1974; Albert Bush-Brown, *Skidmore, Owings & Merrill. Architektur und Städtebau 1973–1983*, Stuttgart 1983.

[31] Cf. Allan Temko, *Eero Saarinen*, New York 1962. The following composite volumes should be mentioned: Paul Heyer, *Architects on Architecture. New Directions in America*, New York 1966; Heinrich Klotz and John W. Crook, *Conversations with Architects*, New York 1973; Barbaralee Diamonstein, *American Architecture Now*, New York 1980; Barbaralee Diamonstein, *American Architecture Now* vol. II, New York 1985.

[33] Philip Johnson, *Writings*, New York 1979; on Johnson's most recent ideas, cf. Philip Johnson and John Burgee, *Architecture, 1979–1985*, New York 1985.

[34] Johnson, afterword in: *Writings* (1979), p. 270.

[35] First published in *Perspecta* 3, 1955, pp. 40–4; in: Johnson, *Writings* (1979), pp. 137ff.

[36] Cf. the particularly crass statements in the interview with Klotz-Crook (1973).

[37] Johnson (1955; 1979), p. 140.

[38] On Louis J. Kahn cf. a bibliography of his writings and secondary literature by Jack Perry Brown in: *The American Association of Architectural Bibliographers. Papers XII*, 1977, pp. 3ff.

The major monographs: Vincent Scully Jr, *Louis J. Kahn*, New York 1962; Heinz Ronner, Sharad Jhaveri and Alessandro

Vasella, *Louis J. Kahn. Complete Works 1935–1974*, Stuttgart–Basel–Boulder, Col., 1977; cf. interview in Klotz and Crook (1973); Alexandra Tyng, *Beginnings: Louis I. Kahn's philosophy of architecture*, 1984.
39 Klotz-Crook (1973).
40 Cf. John McHale, *R. Buckminster Fuller*, New York 1962. The major edition of his writings: R. Buckminster Fuller, *No More Second-hand God and Other Writings*, Carbondale 1963.
41 Cf. McHale (1964), pp. 18f.
42 Cf. Jeffrey Cook, *The Architecture of Bruce Goff*, New York–San Francisco–London 1978; P. J. Meehan, *Bruce Goff, Architect: Writings 1918–1978*, Monticello, Ill. 1979.
43 Cf. esp. Paolo Soleri, *Arcology: The City in the Image of Man*, Cambridge, Mass. 1969. Paolo Soleri, *The Bridge Between Matter and Spirit Is Matter Becoming Spirit. The Arcology of Paolo Soleri*, Garden City, NY 1973.
44 Cf. Soleri (1973), pp. 66, 247.
45 Soleri (1973), p. 46.
46 Ibid., p. 60ff.
47 Cited from Heyer, *Architects on Architecture* (1966), p. 80.
48 Cat. by Bernard Rudofsky, *Architecture Without Architects. A Short Introduction to Non-Pedigreed Architecture*, Garden City, NY 1964.
49 Jean Dethier (ed.), *Lehmarchitektur. Die Zukunft einer vergessenen Bautradition*, Munich 1982.
50 Ernst Bloch, *Das Prinzip Hoffnung*, 3 vols (1954–59), Frankfurt 1973, pp. 819ff.
51 Bloch (1973), p. 869.
52 '*Seit über einer Generation stehen darum dieses Stahlmöbel-, Betonkuben-, Flachdach-Wesen geschichtslos dar, hochmodern und langweilig, scheinbar kühn und echt trivial, voll Haß gegen die Floskel angeblich jedes Ornaments und doch mehr im Schema festgerannt als je eine Stilkopie im schlimmen 19.Jahrhundert.*' Ibid., p. 860.
53 '*...Produktionversuch menschlicher Heimat*'. '*...organisches Ornament*'. Ibid., pp. 871f. Theodor W. Adorno's lecture *Funktionalismus heute* delivered at the 1965 Berlin conference of the Deutscher Werkbund narrows the discussion to shadow-boxing with Loos's positions and is far behind Bloch's conclusions; repr. in: *Neue Rundschau 1966*, Heft 4; Theodor W. Adorno,

Ohne Leitbild. Parva Aesthetica (1967), Frankfurt 6 1979, pp. 104–127.
54 Robert Venturi, *Complexity and Contradiction in Architecture*, introduction by Vincent Scully, New York 1966, p. 11; cf. Stanislaus von Moos, *Venturi, Rauch & Scott Brown*, Fribourg 1987.
55 Venturi (1966), pp. 23ff.
56 Ibid., pp. 52, 103.
57 Cf. Venturi's statements in the interview with Klotz-Crook (1973).
58 Robert Venturi, Denise Scott Brown, Steven Izenour, *Learning From Las Vegas*, Cambridge, Mass.–London 1972; rev. ed. 1978 (several reprs).
59 Venturi-Scott Brown-Izenour (1972, ed. 1978), p. 148.
60 Ibid., p. 116.
61 Ibid., p. 53.
62 Ibid., p. 51.
63 Ibid., pp. 87ff.
64 Cf. the vol. of the '*Officina Alessi*': *Tea & Coffee Piazza. 11 Servizi da the e caffè disegnati da Michael Graves...*, Crusinallo 1983, p. 71.
65 Cf. Klotz-Crook (1973); Gerald Allen, *Charles Moore. Ein Architekt baut für den 'einprägsamen' Ort*, Stuttgart 1981; David Littlejohn, *Architect. The Life and Work of Charles W. Moore*, New York 1984.
66 Kent C. Bloomer and Charles W. Moore, *Body, Memory and Architecture*, New Haven and London 1977 (several reprs).
67 Bloomer-Moore (1977), pp. 5f.
68 Ibid., p. 36.
69 Charles Moore, Gerald Allen, Donlyn Lyndon, *The place of houses*, New York 1974.
70 Moore-Allen-Lyndon (1974), p. ix.
71 Charles Moore and Gerald Allen, *Dimensions. Space, Shape & Scale in Architecture*, New York 1976.
72 On the Piazza d'Italia cf. Moore's statements in: Diamonstein, *American Architecture Now*, New York 1980, pp. 128f.
73 Brent C. Brolin, *The Failure of Modern Architecture*, New York–London 1976; Peter Blake, *Form Follows Fiasco. Why Modern Architecture Hasn't Worked*, Boston–Toronto 1977.
74 Wolfgang Pehnt, *Das Ende der Zuversicht. Architektur in diesem Jahrhundert*, Berlin 1983.
75 Charles A. Jencks, *The Language of Post-Modern Architecture*, London 1977; for a general study of the concepts and ideology

of Post-Modernism, cf. Jacob Kaufman, *'Post-Modern Architecture'*: *An ideology*, diss., Univ. of California, Los Angeles 1982.

[76] The following seem to me to be particularly rewarding treatments of the increasing dissipation of the concept of Post-Modernism: cat. of the Venice Architectural Biennale, 1980, *La presenza del passato*; Paolo Portoghesi, *Dopo l'architettura moderna*, Rome–Bari 1980; Paolo Portoghesi, *Postmodern. The Architecture of the Postindustrial Society*, New York 1982; Heinrich Klotz, *Moderne und Postmoderne. Architektur der Gegenwart 1960–1980*, Brunswick–Wiesbaden 1984; Heinrich Klotz (ed.), cat. *Revision der Moderne. Postmoderne Architektur 1960–1980*, Munich 1984.

[77] Christopher Alexander's programme as printed opposite the title-page of *The Timeless Way of Building*, New York 1979. On Alexander's theoretical development and the development of his ideas cf. a somewhat uncritical study by Stephen Grabow, *Christopher Alexander. The Search for a New Paradigm in Architecture*, Boston–Henley–London 1983 (pp. 229ff. bibliography of Alexander's writings).

[78] Christopher Alexander, *Notes on the Synthesis of Form* (1964), Cambridge, Mass.–London 1971 (frequently repr.).

[79] Christopher Alexander, *The Linz Café*, Oxford–Vienna 1981.

[80] Cf. the statements by Michael Graves in: Barbaralee Diamonstein, *American Architecture Now*, New York 1980, pp. 47ff. Cf. also the vol. on Michael Graves in the series *Architectural Monographs* (vol. 5, London 1979).

[81] Cf. the statements by Richard Meier in: Diamonstein (1980), pp. 103ff.

[82] Cf. Stanley Tigerman, *Versus An American Architect's Alternatives*, New York 1982.

[83] Cf. Stanley Tigerman, *Late Entries to the Chicago Tribune Tower Competition*, New York 1980.

[84] Peter Arnell and Ted Bickford (ed.), *Southwest Center. The Houston Competition*, New York 1983.

[85] The best account is given in: Cina Conforto a.o., *Il dibattito architettectonico in Italia 1945–1975* (thematically organised and with a detailed bibliography of Italian writing on architecture); cf. also Cesare De Seta, *L'architettura del Novecento (Storia dell'arte in Italia)*, Turin 1981; Amedeo

Belluzzi and Claudia Conforti, *Architettura italiana 1944–1984*, Rome–Bari 1985.

[86] On Scarpa cf. esp. Francesco Dal Co and Giuseppe Mazzariol, *Carlo Scarpa. L'opera completa*, Milan 1984.

[87] Cf. Ezio Bonfanti and Marco Porta, *Città, Museo e architettura. Il gruppo BBPR nella cultura architettonica italiana 1932–1970*, Florence 1973.

[88] Pier Luigi Nervi, *Scienza o arte del costruire*, Rome 1945. Pier Luigi Nervi, *Aesthetics and Technology in Building*, Cambridge, Mass.–London 1965. On Nervi cf. Giulio Carlo Argan, *Pier Luigi Nervi*, Milan 1955; Alda Louisa Huxtable, *Pier Luigi Nervi*, New York 1960; Paolo Desideri a.o., *Pier Luigi Nervi*, Bologna 1979.

[89] In this connection cf. Dietmar Grötzebach, *Der Wandel der Kriterien bei der Wertung des Zusammenhanges von Konstruktion und Form in den letzten 100 Jahren*, diss., Berlin 1965.

[90] Giuseppe Samonà, *L'urbanistica e l'avvenire della città negli stati europei*, Bari 1959 (²1960); paperback ed. Rome–Bari 1967 (variously reprinted). Carlo Aymonino, *Origine e sviluppo della città moderna*, Padua 1964.

[91] Aldo Rossi, *L'Architettura della Città*, Padua 1966.

[92] On Aldo Rosso cf. Vittorio Savi, *L'architettura di Aldo Rossi*, Milan 1976 (²1977); Gianni Braghieri, *Aldo Rossi*, Bologna 1981.

[93] Cf. anthology: Aldo Rossi, *Scritti scelti sull'architettura e la città 1956–1972*, Milan 1975; Aldo Rossi, *A Scientific Autobiography*, Cambridge, Mass. 1982.

[94] Aldo Rossi a.o., *Architettura Razionale (XV Triennale di Milano. Sezione Internazionale di Architettura)*, Milan, 1973. Cf. Hanno-Walter Kruft, 'Rationalismus in der Architektur – eine Begriffsklärung', *Architectura* 9, 1979, pp. 45–57 (facs. repr. in: *Der Architekt*, April 1981, pp. 176–81).

[95] Etienne-Louis Boullée, *Architettura. Saggio sull'arte*, ed. Aldo Rossi, Padua 1967 (²1977).

[96] Cf. e.g. Rob Krier, '10 Theses on Architecture', in: Rob Krier, *On Architecture*, London–New York 1982, p. 5.

[97] Cf. literature listed in note 76 above.

[98] Cf. cat. *Revision der Moderne. Postmoderne Architektur 1960–1980*, ed. Heinrich Klotz, Munich 1984.

[99] Cf. cats *Idee, Prozeß, Ergebnis. Die Reparatur und die Rekonstruktion der Stadt*, Berlin

1984; *Das Abenteuer der Ideen. Architektur und Philosophie seit der industriellen Revolution*, Berlin 1984.

[100] Cf. e.g. Gillo Dorfles, *Simbolo, Comunicazione, Consumo*, Turin 1962; Umberto Eco, *La struttura assente*, Bologna 1968; cf. also *Architektur als Zeichensprache*, ed. Alessandro Carlini and Bernhard Schneider (*Konzept* 1), Tübingen 1971.

[101] Christian Norberg-Schulz, *Intentions in Architecture*, Oslo 1963.

[102] Jane Jacobs, *The Death and Life of Great American Cities*, New York 1961; Alexander Mitscherlich, *Die Unwirtlichkeit unserer Städte. Anstiftung zum Unfrieden*, Frankfurt 1965.

[103] Rudolf Arnheim, *Toward a Psychology of Art*, Berkeley–Los Angeles 1966; *Art and Visual Perception* ([1]1954): the new version, Berkeley–Los Angeles 1974; *The Dynamics of Architectural Form*, Berkeley–Los Angeles–London 1977.

[104] Niels Luning Prak, *The language of architecture. A contribution to architectural theory*, The Hague–Paris 1968.

[105] Bruce Allsopp, *A Modern Theory of Architecture*, London–Henley–Boston 1977.

[106] On Bofill cf. Ricardo Bofill a.o. (*Taller de arquitectura), La cité: Histoire et Technologie. Projets Français 1978/81*, Milan 1981; Ricardo Bofill, *Taller de arquitectura. Los espacios de Abraxas. El palacio, el teatro, el arco*, ed. Annabella d'Huart, Milan 1981.

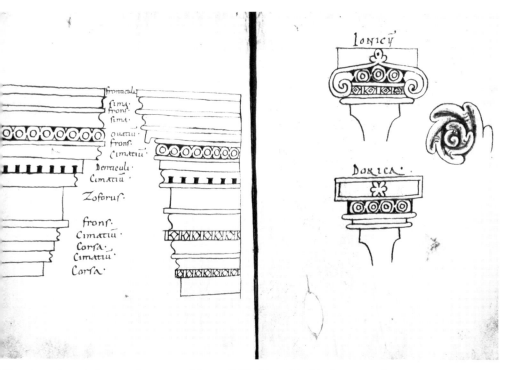

Vitruvius codex, ninth or tenth century; Sélestat, Bibliothèque Municipale, ms. 1153 bis.
Sketch of Doric and Ionic orders

Hildegard von Bingen, *Liber divinorum operum*, thirteenth century; Lucca, Biblioteca Governativa, ms. 1942, fol. 9r. Representation of the macrocosm

3. *Liber pontificalis*, twelfth century; Rheims, Bibliothèque Municipale, ms. 672, fol. 1 v.
Representation of the *aer* (lower air)

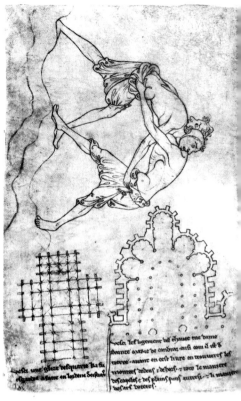

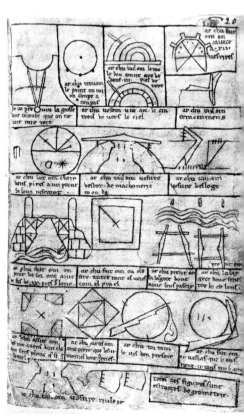

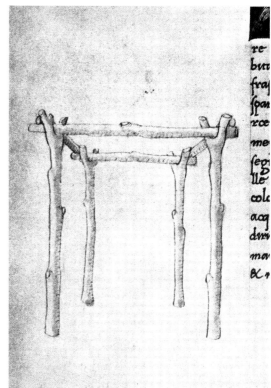

Construction of the primal hut; Filarete, fol. 5v

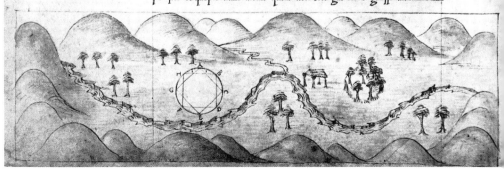

A

B

C

V

P

C

Q

10. Doric, Corinthian and Ionic orders; Filarete,
fol. 57v

Opposite, above
12. Plan of Sforzinda; Filarete, fol. 43f

Opposite, below, left
13. Citadel tower of Sforzinda; Filarete, fol. 41r.

Opposite, below, right
14. Section of House of Vice and Virtue; Filarete,
fol. 144r.

11. Siting of Sforzinda; Filarete, fol. 11v

Ilfiume sforzindo
Lauualle inda:

375 braccia :

375

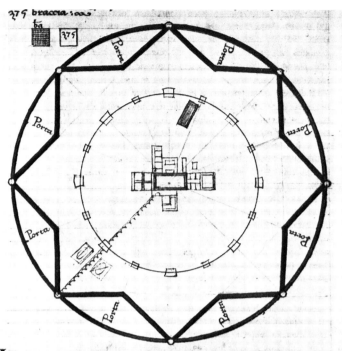

I nella testa doriente Io fo lachiesa maggiore & inquella doccidente fo

Lulye

sommita & onde altr aeque duplo bisogno &
gli luoghi sovenutri come sono comue & onde
oppa terra nate quelle compartione che erano
o lolen compartione più hordinate Caneora
comparire conquesti modi & me che acquelle
tro quanto disiano Cr fare nate questa m
come era hordinato & merlati nati ntorn
questa altrzza dello trenta braccia infino
o imin checchorgoli delle torn quanto qu
dve fino ontopesto & merla sopra dicchefoch
nenti braccia alto sldometro solo di dodin bn
folamente illoro muro & cosi haueuano dispo
& dentro inquesti romani andaua lafcala
llalten & nella sommita una cupoletta acua
lla colla una bandiera conffia doisi & cosi f
leondstote & come leuatoio & pundchene K
lofnere) fate magieluoghi dentro dipma a
che ame) pnue disiare alcuno cose fusi fo
primo latove dmezzo delle soprenti braxc
lo secondo che era determinato & comparite
freno stanto molnuduer conquesti dhome qu
latove fu dan lordine urnalo & fanto lasca
fvor conquesti modi & fontiqumion dalu
rreto Io fese uno spore didue braccia comu
alla torre questo indate & più come a donu
faciam fu finestre daquatro braccia dimano
tro braccia danato dalma allatra dplnfpn
freco infsen & nfa anconu uno plastn di
dspatno & din braccia quaresdta & ddte qun
mue qhesti plastn puer derogthma lnqual u
& puppoftabi a cons fen grossi & sostenen qun
fnlem daponre andaue ntorno disuon smod
ingrado di cremna braccia nnterna braccia
stre fono tanto quante braccia elle alta cor
Vedendo questa torre nquella forma diff
re tanto finghre & ande dento danolo quelle nan
& affarcatn aor noto facen & pn adoka t
pdsho fate nante finghre fo pue ckopa dola
trecento fosanta omgi braccia Io lo uolua fa
do de come larmo e'nne di cosi.o fuoso tant
cosi como uedoto sono mezze fenere & mez
ro formo chola date lo gueno date pdse con
Qua dallato fara disogmata latove aln g

163.

t porn
tto n
o didie
ra una
andua
. cosi ao
pno mo
ogna

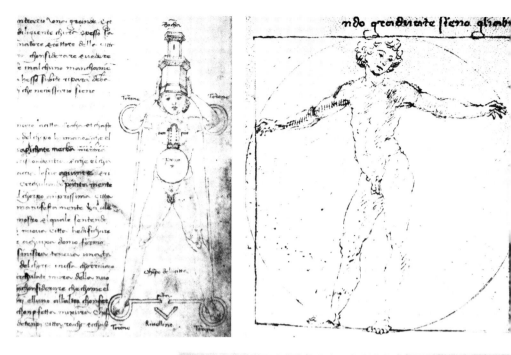

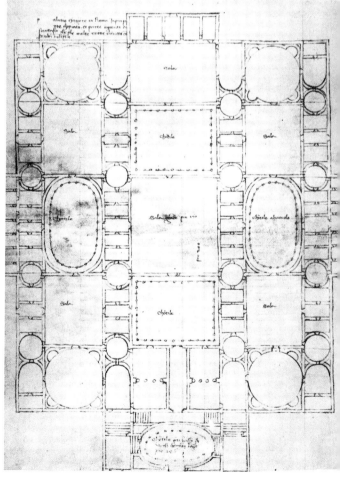

Top, left
15. Francesco di Giorgio
Martini, *Architettura, ingegneria
e arte militare*, late fifteenth
century; Turin, Codex
Saluzzianus 148, fol. 3. The
'body of the town', with fortress

Top, right
16. Francesco di Giorgio
Martini, illustration of Vitruvius,
III.i.3; Florence, Ashburnham
Codex 361, fol. 5v

Right
17. Francesco di Giorgio
Martini, reconstruction of the
Palatine; Codex Saluzzianus 148,
fol. 82v.

right
. Francesco di Giorgio
artini, rotundas; Codex
aluzzianus 148, fol. 84

low, left
. Francesco di Giorgio
artini, anthropometric
tablature; Florence, Biblioteca
azionale, Cod. Magl. II, i, 141,
l. 37

low, right
. Francesco di Giorgio
artini, anthropometric façade
 S. Maria delle Grazie al
alcinaio, Cortona; Cod. Magl.
 i, 141, fol. 38v

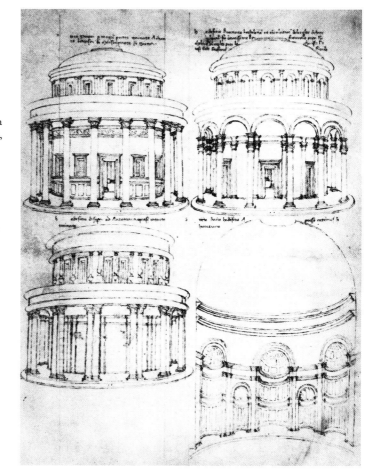

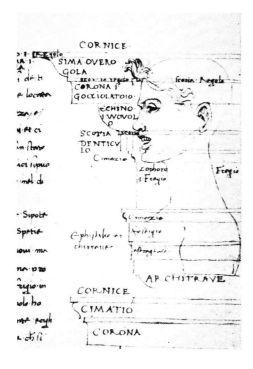

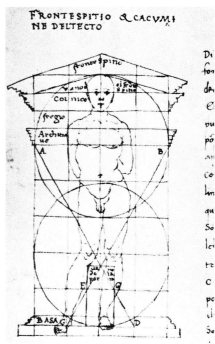

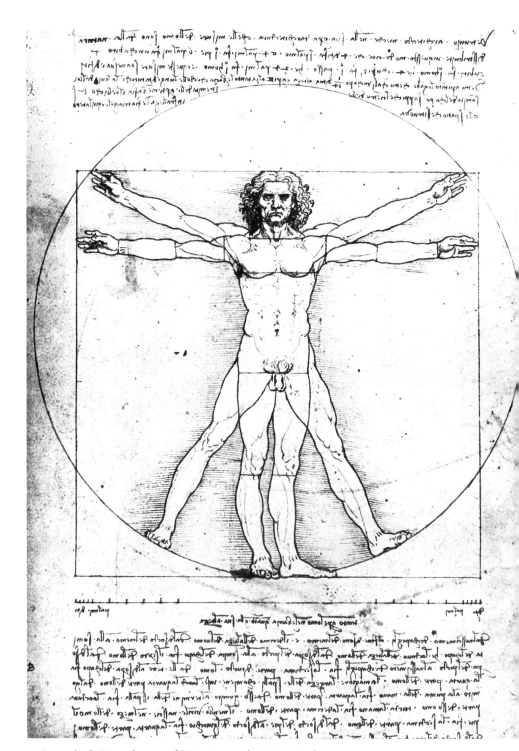

21. Leonardo da Vinci, drawing of 'Vitruvian man'; Venice, Academy

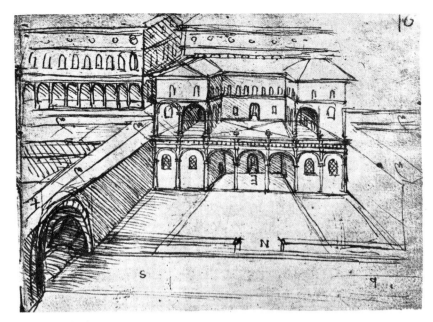

22. Leonardo da Vinci, illustration of street crossing; Paris, Institut de France, Codex B, fol. 16

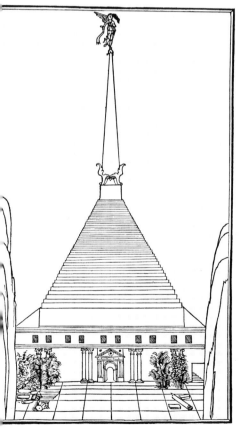

Francesco Colonna, *Hypnerotomachia Poliphili*,
99. Pyramid with obelisk

24. Francesco Colonna, *Hypnerotomachia Poliphili*.
Temple of Venus Physizoa

25. Francesco Colonna, *Hypnerotomachia Poliphili*. Polyandrion

26. Bramante (?), *Prospectivo Melanese, Depictore, Antiquarie Prospettiche Romane*, c. 1500. Title-page

a domus
regia
b secretus
portus
c fons

d fanum
ueneris

e portus

f forum

g mauso
leum

h platea

i fanum
Mercurii

LIBER   PRIMVS

IDEA GEOMETRICAE ARCHITECTONICAE AB ICHNOGRAPHIA SVMPTA · VT PERAMVSSINEAS POSSINT
PER ORTHOGRAPHIAM AC SCAENOGRAPHIAM PERDVCERE OMNES QVASCVNQVAE LINEAS · NON
SOLVM AD CIRCINI CENTRVM · SED QVAE A TRIGONO ET QVADRATO AVT ALIO QVOVISMODO
PERVENIVNT POSSINT SVVM HABERE RESPONSVM · TVM PER EVRYTHMIAM PROPOR-
TIONATAM QVANTVM ETIAM P SYMMETRIAE QVANTITATEM ORDINARIAM AC PER
OPERIS · DECORATIONEM OSTENDERE · VTI ETIAM HEC QVAE A GERMANICO MORE PERVE-
NIVNT DISTRIBVENTVR PENE QVEMADMODVM SACRA CATHEDRALIS AEDES MEDIOLANI
PATET · ELC^A   P·M·C·A·A·P·VL·Q5·C·AC AF·D·

Top, left
27. Fra Giocondo, edition of
Vitruvius, Venice, 1511.
Illustration of 'Vitruvian
man' (III.i)

Top, right
28. A cheaper edition of
Vitruvius, Florence, 1513.
Depiction of mausoleum of
Halicarnassus (II.8)

Left
29. Cesare Cesariano, edition
of Vitruvius, 1521.
Illustration of *orthographia*
using the example of Milan
Cathedral

30. Cesare Cesariano, depiction of
Halicarnassus, 1521

31. Cesare Cesariano, depiction of the
three Orders (Vitruvius IV.i), 1521

7. Cesare Cesariano, reconstruction of
Vitruvius's basilica at Fano (V.i), 1521

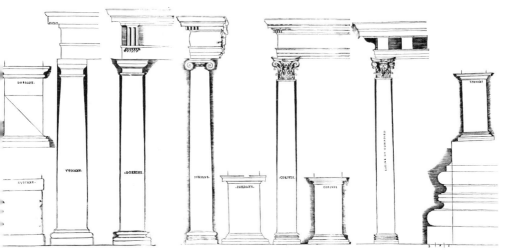

8. Plate by Jean Goujon illustrating Jean Martin's translation of Vitruvius, 1547. The five Orders

Figur des gantzen Gebews/vom König Mausolo zu
Halicarnasso auffgericht/vnd vnder die Sie-
ben Wunderwerck.

praponendoui loto, et facendo i tetti pendenti, diedero la caduta all'acque,
& si asicurarono maggiormente, del modo che uediamo espresso qui sotto.

F A mentione Vitruuio, che in Francia, in Ispagna, in Portogallo, & in
Guascogna si faceuano de gl'edificij così rozzi, coperti di tauole segate di
Rouere, ouero con paglie, & strame; come appare nelle due seguenti figure,
& potrassi aggiungere, che sino al dì d'hoggi per la Germania si ueggono
gran parte delle case coperte di tauolette di Pino, & che per la Polonia, &
per la Moscouia poche case si trouano, che non siano conteste di legnami,
anco nelle Città più nominate, & più celebri.

34. Rivius, translation of Vitruvius, Strassburg, 1548.
Depiction of Halicarnassus

35. Giovanantonio Rusconi, *Della architettura*, 1590.
Representation of types of house

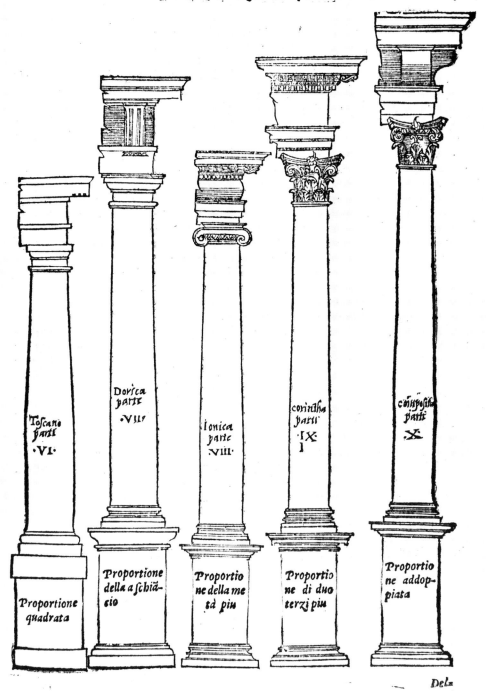

Toscano
parti
·VI·

Proportione
quadrata

Dorica
parte
·VIII·

Proportione
della a schia-
cio

ionica
parte
·VIII·

Proportio
ne della me
tá piu

corintha
parti
·IX·
I

Proportio
ne di duo
terzi piu

composit
parti
·X·

Proportio
ne addop-
piata

Del

6. Sebastiano Serlio, *Regole generali di architettura* (Book IV of *L'architettura*), 1537 (1566 ed.). The five Orders

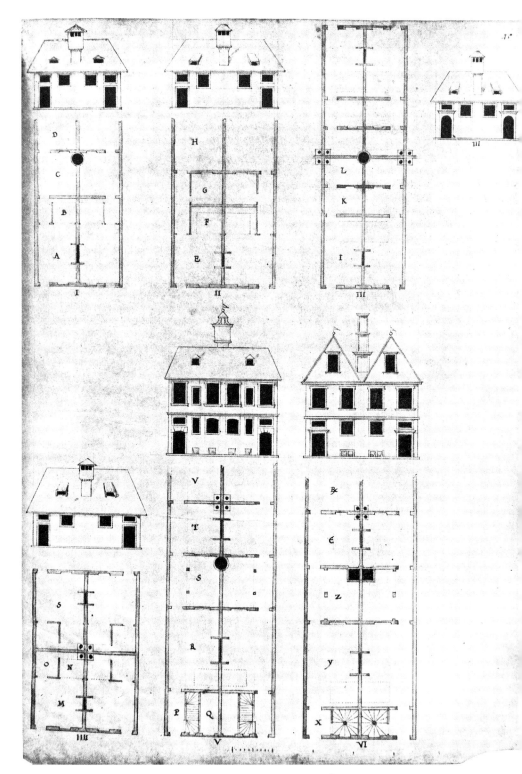

37. Sebastiano Serlio, 'Delle habitationi di tutti li gradi degli homini' ('Book VI of *L'architettura*, unpublished until 1967/78); Munich, Bayerische Staatsbibliothek, Cod. Icon. 189, fol. 45. Plans and elevations of private houses

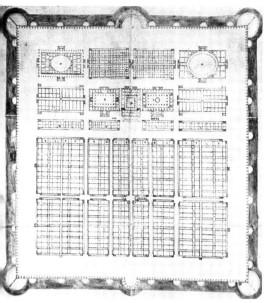

38. Sebastiano Serlio, 'Della castrametatio di Polibio' (unpublished Book VIII of *L'architettura*); Munich, Bayerische Staatsbibliothek, Cod. Icon. 190, fol. 1. Reconstruction of a Roman town

39. Pietro Cataneo, *L'architettura*, 1567. Anthropometric church plan

40, 41. Vignola, *Regola delli cinque ordini d'architettura*, 1562. Proportions of the Tuscan order

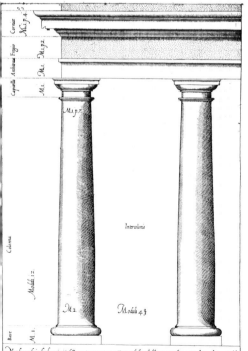

42. Title-page of Vignola's *Regola*, 1562

43. Title-page of Daniele Barbaro's edition of Vitruvius, 1556, with illustrations based on drawings by Palladio

44. Daniele Barbaro, Latin edition of
Vitruvius, 1567. Plan of Greek house

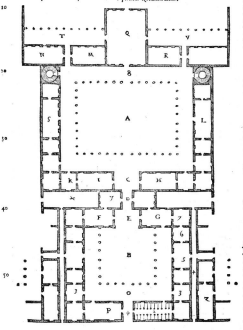

Græcorum ædes earumq; partium dispositiones.

A. *peristylium amplum.* E. *peristylium primum.* C. *aditus amplus.* D. *aditus ab uno ad aliud peristylium.* E. *prostas ubi erant duæ antæ.* F. G. *Antithalamus.* H. I. *gynæconitides.* K. *cubicula muliebria.* L. S. *oeci, & bibliotecæ, & ubi sunt pictores.* M. R. *pinacotheca.* N. *cyzicena triclinia.* O. *porticus ad septentrionem.* P. *cella hostiaria.* Q. *oeci quadrati.* T. V. *porticus ad triclinia cyzicena.* X. *hypæthra loca.* Y. *oeci magni ubi matres familiariæ cum lanificijs habent sessiones.* Z. *hostiaria.* 1. *thirorium.* 2. *Equilia.* 3. *cubicula.* 4. *mesaulæ & androne.* 5. *triclinia quotidiana.* 6. *posthalamus.* 7. *thalamus.* 8. *porticus Rhodiaca altior.*

diversas ædificandi consuetudines Græcorum, & Italorum ostendat. Atrijs Græci quia non utebantur, necesse erat, cùm apud Romanos essent prope ianuas, ut eorum loco aliquid esset apud Græcos. Quare statim ab ianua

QVESTA E VNA PARTE DELLA FACCIATA DELLA CASA PRIVATA.

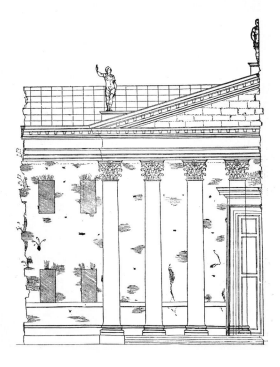

45. Daniele Barbaro, edition of Vitruvius,
1556. Façade of private house of Antiquity

46. Andrea Palladio, *I quattro libri dell'architettura*, 1570. Title-page

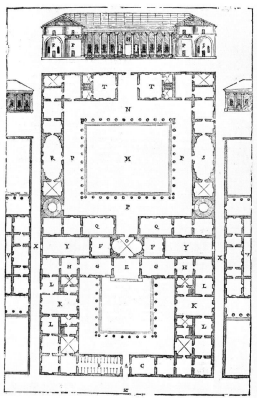

47. Andrea Palladio, plan and section of Greek house; *I quattro libri*

48. Andrea Palladio, Villa Rotonda;
I quattro libri

49. Andrea Palladio, unpublished illustrated
commentary on Polybius; London, British
Library 293.g.20. Depiction of Hannibal's
siege of Taranto

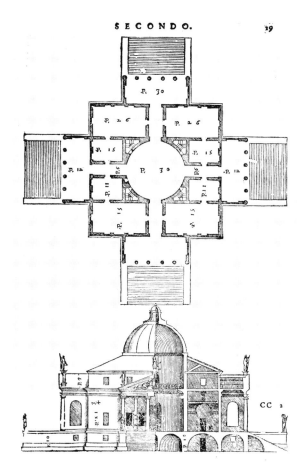

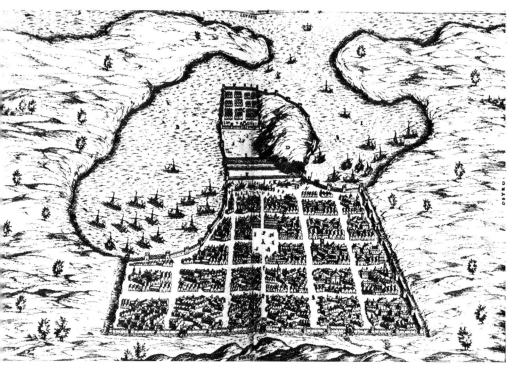

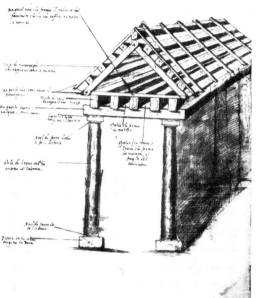

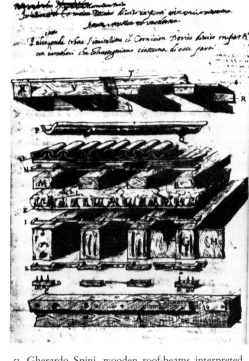

50. Gherardo Spini, 'I tre primi libri', 1568/69;
Venice, Biblioteca Marciana, ms. It. IV, 38 c. 37r.
Design for the primal hut

51. Gherardo Spini, wooden roof-beams interpreted
as prototype of Doric entablature; 'I tre primi libri',
112v.

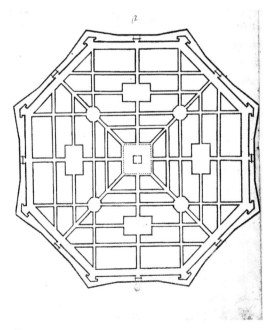

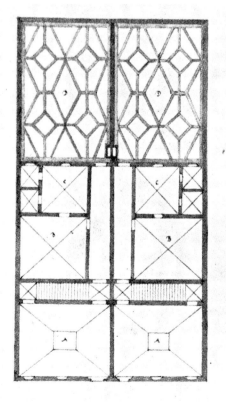

Above
52. Giorgio Vasari il Giovane, plan of an ideal city;
from an unpublished treatise dated 1598

Right
53. Giorgio Vasari il Giovane, plan for semi-detached
houses for manual workers, 1598

4. Vincenzo Scamozzi, *L'idea della architettura universale*, 1615. Title-page

55. Vincenzo Scamozzi, diagram of 'Vitruvian man'; *L'idea della architettura universale*

56. Vincenzo Scamozzi, design for an ideal city (Palmanova); *L'idea della architettura universale*

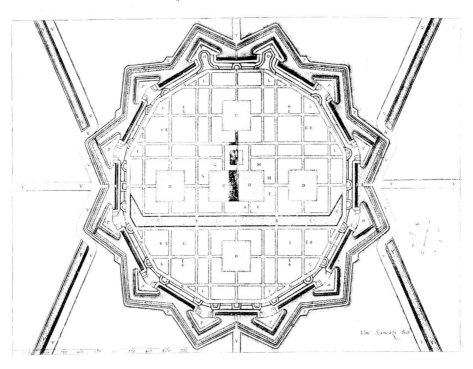

7. Vincenzo Scamozzi, representation of the five Orders; *L'idea della architettura universale*

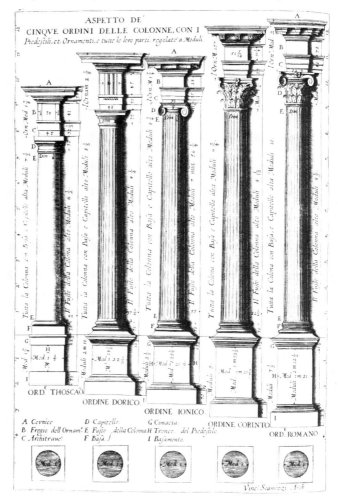

8. Teofilo Gallaccini, *Trattato sopra gli errori degli architetti*, 1625 (published 1767). Correction of optical foreshortening

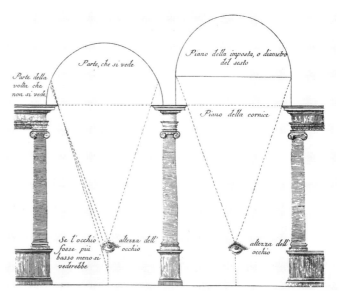

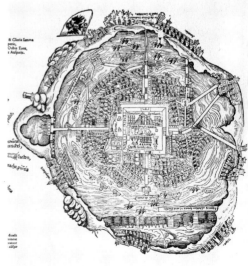

59. Guarino Guarini, *Architettura civile*, 1737 (posthumously published). Representation of the 'Gothic' order

60. Guarino Guarini, representation of the 'Salomonic' order; *Architettura civile*

61. Albrecht Dürer, *Etliche underricht*, 1527. Plan for a utopian city

62. Depiction of the Aztec capital Tenochtitlan in an edition of the first of Hernando Cortès's letters to the Emperor Charles V, Nuremberg, 1524

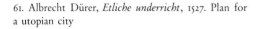

63. Nicolò Tartaglia, *Nova scientia*, 1550. Frontispiece

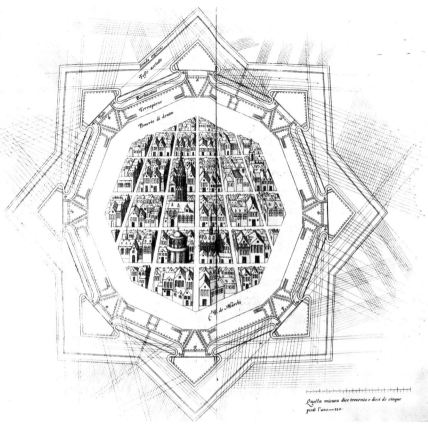

Della Fortif. delle Città

che così grande spatio di terreno fusse stato chiuso dentro alle mura per custodir-
ui e nutrirui bestiami, ò uero per seminarui quando il luogo fusse assediato, tenen-
do e'cittadini la rocca picciola fortificata dalla natura.

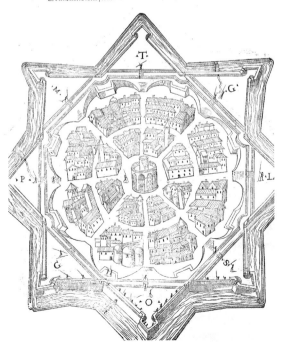

64. Francesco de Marchi, *Della
architettura militare*, 1599. Plan of a
fortified town

65. Girolamo Maggi and Jacomo
Fusto Castriotto, *Delle fortificationi*,
1564. Plan of a utopian fortified city

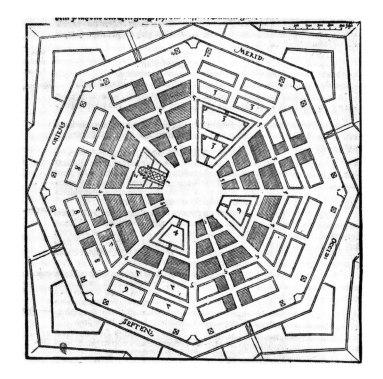

Daniel Speckle,
Architectura von Vestungen,
. Plan of a utopian city

Engraving by Matthäus
 uter depicting a
* nderbarlich Hauss*'; in
  iel Speckle, *Architettura*
  Vestungen

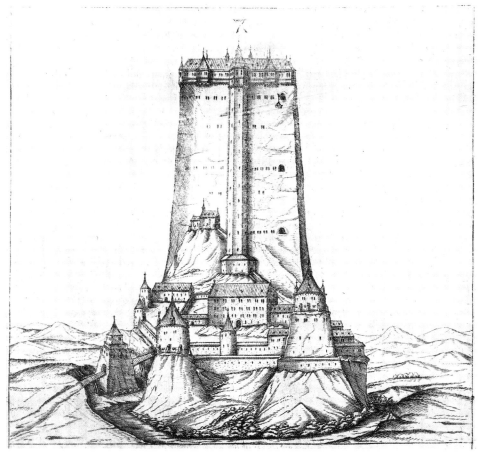

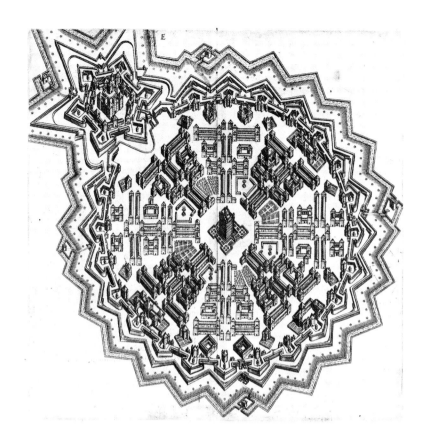

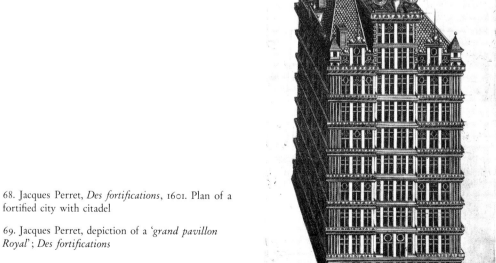

68. Jacques Perret, *Des fortifications*, 1601. Plan of a
fortified city with citadel

69. Jacques Perret, depiction of a *'grand pavillon
Royal'*; *Des fortifications*

SECVNDA ICHNOGRAPHIA SECVNDÆ CONTIONATIONIS

PRIMA ICHNOGRAPHIA PRIMÆ CONTIONATIONIS

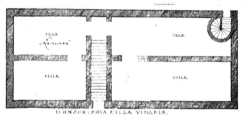

ICHNOGRAPHIA CELLÆ VINARIÆ

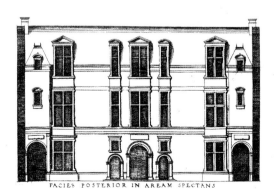

FACIES ANTERIOR IN VIAM SPECTANS

LITERA NOTATA B

FACIES POSTERIOR IN AREAM SPECTANS

70, 71. Jacques Androuet du Cerceau, *De architectura*, 1559. Plans and elevations for house I

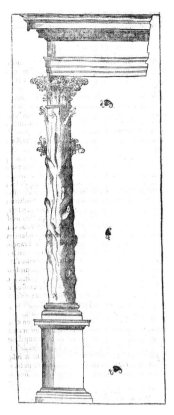

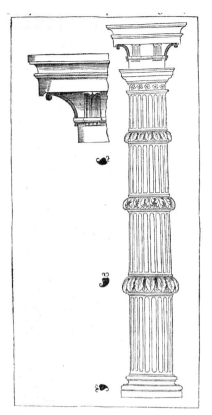

72. Philibert Delorme, *Le premier tome de l'architecture*, 1567. Column composed of a tree trunk

73. Philibert Delorme, representation of the 'French' order; *Le premier tome de l'architecture*

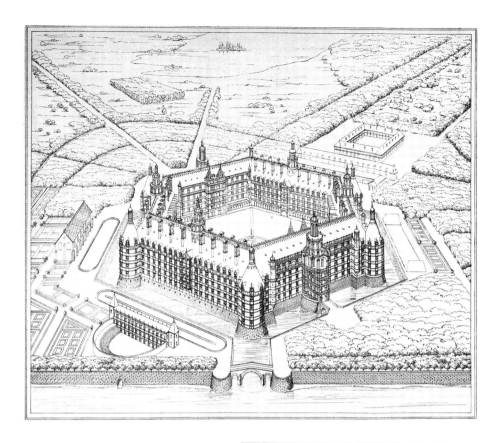

76. Depiction of the Abbey of Thelema in Rabelais' *Gargantua*; after Charles Lenormant, 1840

77. Pierre Le Muet, *Manière de bien bastir pour toutes sortes de personnes*, 1681. Plans, elevation and section detail for private house

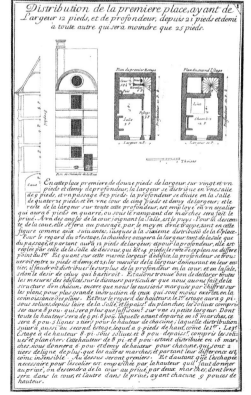

75. Philibert Delorme, allegories of the [ba]d and the good architect; *Le premier [volu]me de l'architecture*

78. Second volume of Pierre Le Muet's *Manière de bien bastir*, 1681. Title-page

MANIERE DE BIEN BASTIR
POUR
TOUTES SORTES DE PERSONNES
Contenant plusieurs figures Plans et Elevations desplus
beaux bastimens et Edifices de France
SECONDE PARTIE

79. Roland Fréart de Chambray, *Parallèle de l'architecture antique avec la moderne*, 1650. Representation of the 'Salomonic' order

Abraham Bosse, *Traité des manières de dessiner les ordres de l'architecture*, 1664.
Frontispiece

L'Origine des Chapiteaux des Colonnes.

81. François Blondel, *Cours d'architecture*,
1675–83. Depiction of the origin of the Orders

82. Frontispiece of François Blondel's *Cours
d'architecture*, showing the Porte Saint-Denis

On the book in the image: "EN DIX LIVRES / D'ARCHITECTVRE / DE / VITRVVE"

Signatures: G. Scotin Sculp.

ontispiece of Claude Perrault's commentary on Vitruvius, 1684

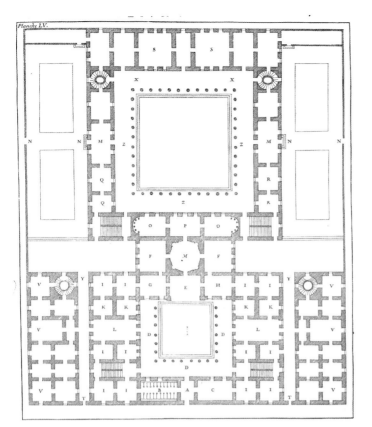

84. Plan of Greek house in Claude Perrault's commentary on Vitruvius

85. Augustin-Charles d'Aviler, *Cours d'architecture*, 1696.
'*Colonnes extraordinaires et symboliques*'

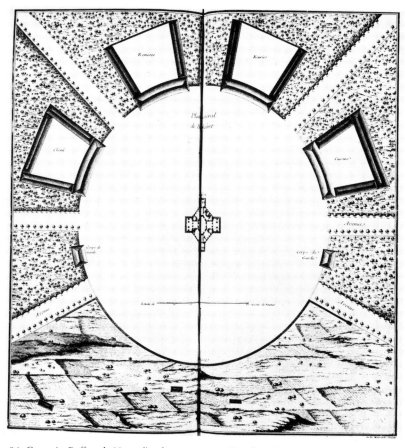

86. Germain Boffrand, *Livre d'architecture*, 1745. Plan for a hunting lodge at Bouchefort

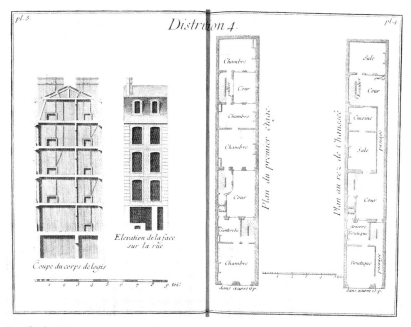

87. Charles-Etienne Briseux, *L'architecture moderne*, 1728. Section, elevation and plan for a private house in Paris ('*Distribution 4*')

TEMPLE DE L'ARCHITECTURE

Briseux *inven̄it*   *Moreau Sculpsit*

Right
90. Pierre Patte, *Monuments érigé[s]
France à la gloire de Louis XV*, 1
Plan of Paris showing locations c
monuments to Louis XV

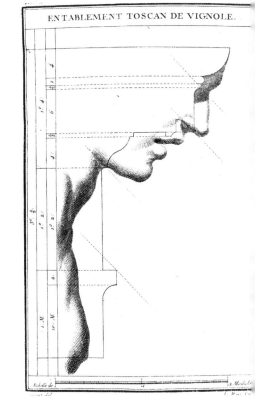

88. Charles-Etienne Briseux, *L'Art de bâtir des
maisons de campagne*, 1761. Frontispiece

89. Jacques-François Blondel, *Cours d'architecture*,
1771. Entablature with proportions after Vignola

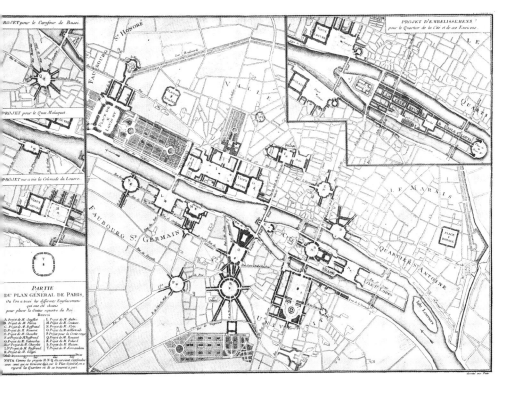

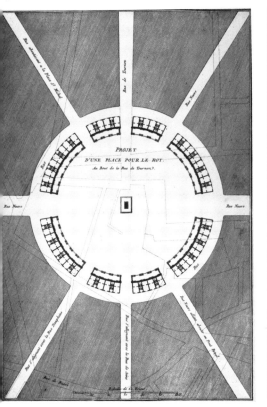

91. Pierre Patte, *Monuments érigés en France*. Plan of a square with a monument to Louis XV

92. Marc-Antoine Laugier, *Essai sur l'architecture*, 1755. Frontispiece

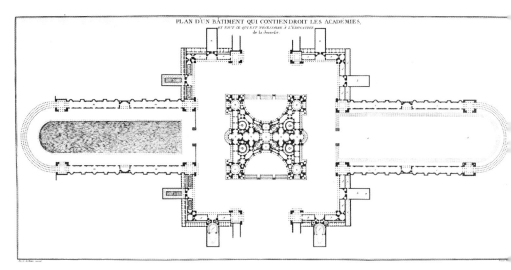

93, 94. Marie-Joseph Peyre, *Oeuvres d'architecture*, 1765. Academy project

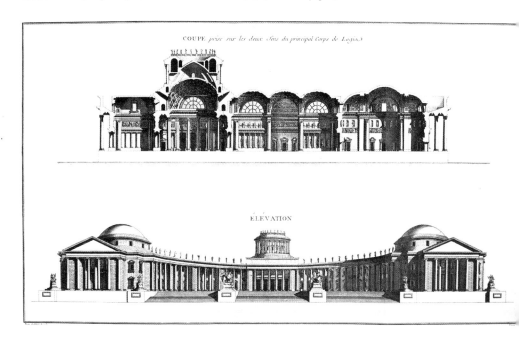

TYPE DE L'ORDRE FRANÇOIS.

L'ORDRE FRANÇOIS DÉVELOPPÉ.

Left
95. Marie-Joseph Peyre, *Oeuvres d'architecture.*
Project for a cathedral

96. Ribart de Chamoust, *L'Ordre François trouvé dans la nature*, 1783. Representation of 'French order'

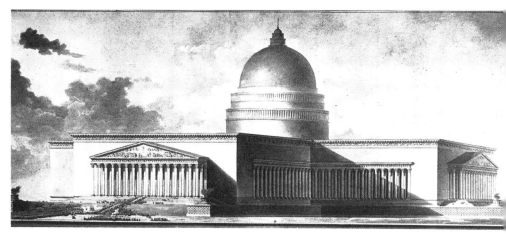

97. Etienne-Louis Boullée, *Essai sur l'art*, written and executed 1781–93.
Design for a cathedral

98. Etienne-Louis Boullée, *Essai sur l'art*. Monument to Newton; at night

Vue perspective de la Ville de Chaux

9. Claude-Nicolas Ledoux, *L'architecture*, 1804. View of Chaux

L'ABRI DU PAUVRE

10. Claude-Nicolas Ledoux, *L'architecture*. 'L'abri du pauvre'

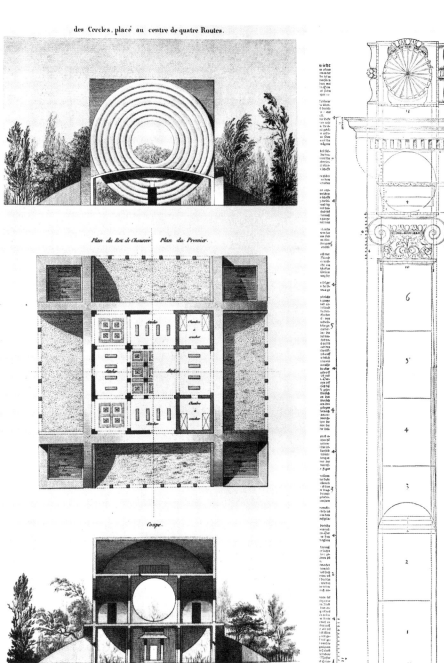

des Cercles, placé au centre de quatre Routes.

Plan du Rez de Chaussée   Plan du Premier.

Coupe.

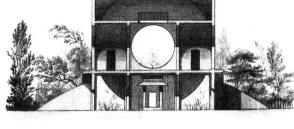

Echelle de

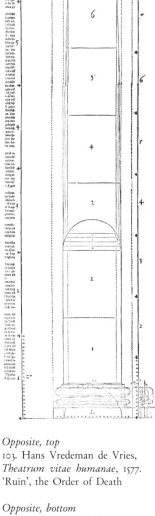

Above
101. Claude-Nicolas Ledoux, *L'architecture*. 'House of a Hoopmaker'

Right
102. Hans Blum, design for the Ionic order in his *Säulenbuch*, edition of 1596

Opposite, top
103. Hans Vredeman de Vries, *Theatrum vitae humanae*, 1577. 'Ruin', the Order of Death

Opposite, bottom
104. Hans and Paul Vredeman de Vries, *Architectura*, 1606. The Sense of Touch represented by the Composite order

Deniq, quicquid erit, Deus aut Natura quoad uſſum,
Principium ſub ſolo aedit, mortale neceſſe eſt,

RVYNE.
6.

Paulatim accreſcit, paulatim labitur, atq,
Tempore commutat Vitam cũ morte ſueſla, ↄ.

Donc pour concluſion, comme tout Baſtiment
Eſt deſtruit, ſoit par Feu par Eau, Téps qui tout mine
Ainſi l'homme à ſon Tems, cours & deñnement
Eſtant ſubiect à Mort qui ſur Mortels domine
Et a la Fin ſemblable a ſon Commancement.

105. Wendel Dietterlin, *Architectura*, 1598. Representation of the Ionic order

106. Wendel Dietterlin, *Architectura*. The victory of Death

107. Daniel Meyer, *Architectura*, 1609.
Treatment of the Orders

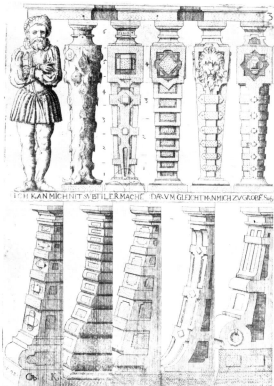

108. Gabriel Krammer, *Architectura Von
den funf Seulen...*, edition of 1606.
Treatment of the Tuscan order

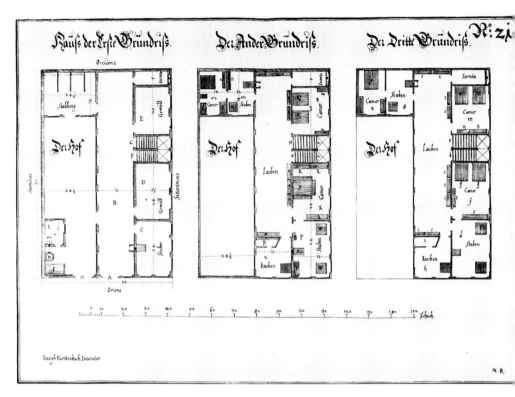

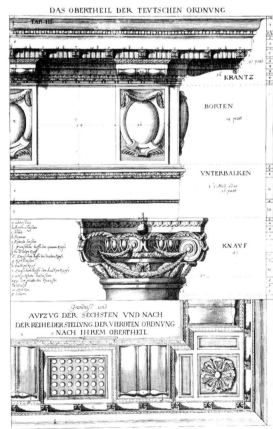

109. Joseph Furttenbach, *Architectura universalis*, 1635. Plans of a three-storey 'burgher's house'

110. Leonhard Christoph Sturm, *Erste Ausübung der Vortrefflichen und Vollständigen Anweisung*, 1699. Upper part of a 'German' order

11. Frontispiece of Leonhard Christoph Sturm's *Erste Ausübung*, depicting a building using the 'German' order

12. Paul Decker, *Ausführliche Anleitung zur Civilbaukunst*, c. 1719/20. Elevation, section and plan of burgher's house

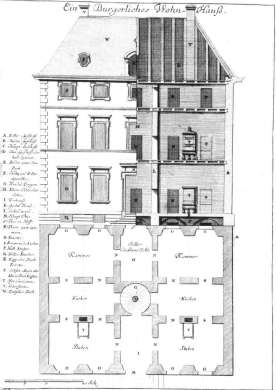

113. Paul Decker, *Fürstlicher Baumeister*, 1711. Frontispiece

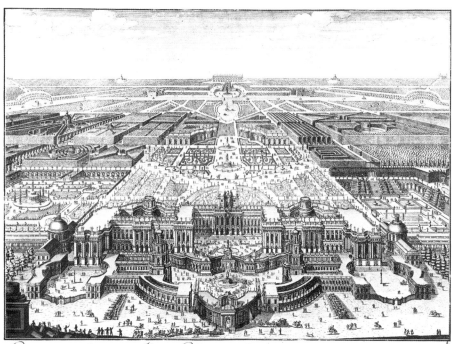

Perspectivischer Auffzug des Königl. Pallasts mit allen seiten Gebäuden, und einem theil des Gartens.

114. Second part of Paul Decker's *Fürstlicher Baumeister*, 1716.
Design for a 'royal palace'

Optica Longimetrica.
Invenit Johann Jacob Schübler.

Michael Rentz et F. d'à Montolgnes fc.

115. Johann Jacob Schübler, *Perspectiva, pes picturae*, part II, 1720.
View in 'longimetric perspective'

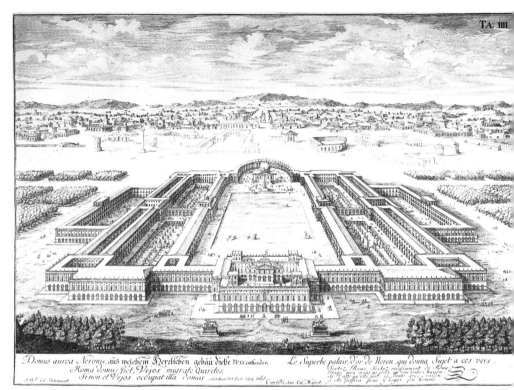

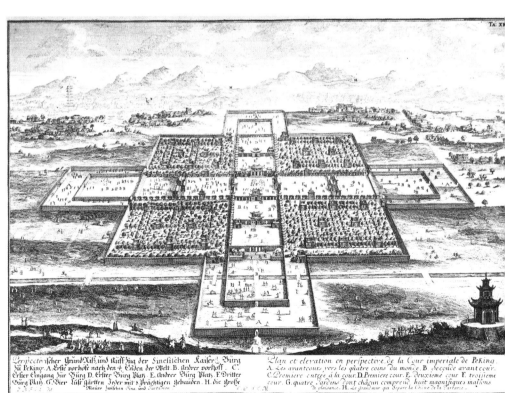

117. Johann Bernhard Fischer von Erlach, *Entwurf einer Historischen Architektur*.
Plan of the imperial palace, Peking

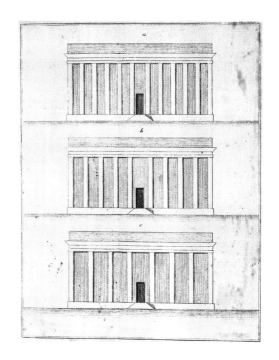

Left
116. Johann Bernhard Fischer von Erlach,
Entwurf einer Historischen Architektur, edition of
1725. Reconstruction of Nero's Domus Aurea

118. Anon., *Untersuchungen über den Charakter der Gebäude*, 1785. Depiction of a colonnade with varying intercolumniation

119. Giuseppe Galli Bibiena, *Architetture, e prospettive*, 1740. 'Scena per angolo'

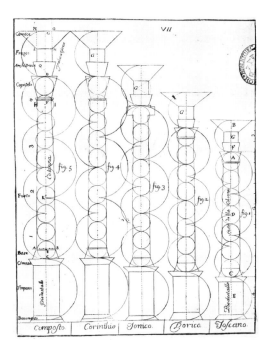

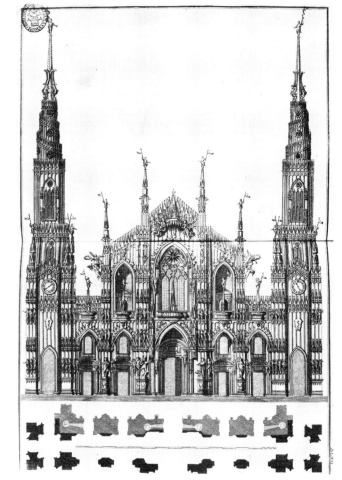

120. Bernardo Vittone, *Istruzioni elementari*, 1760. Exposition of the Orders

121. Bernardo Vittone, *Istruzioni diverse*, 1766. Design for façade of Milan Cathedral

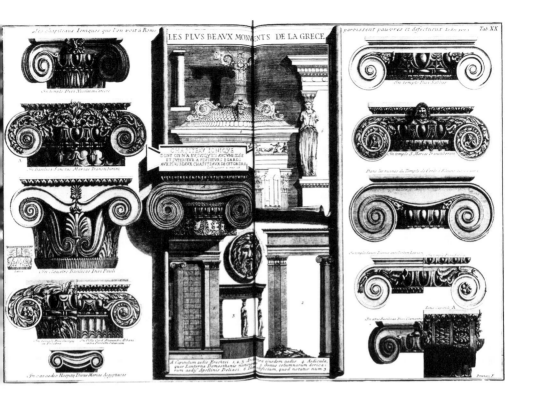

122. Giovanni Battista Piranesi, *Della Magnificenza ed Architettura de' Romani*, 1761. Designs for Roman Ionic capitals

123. Giovanni Battista Piranesi, *Osservazioni*, 1765. Title-page

124. Giovanni Battista Piranesi, *Parere su l'architettura*, 1765.
Vignette on first page

125. Giovanni Battista Piranesi, *Parere su l'architettura*.
Representation of architectural liberty

26. Julien-David Le Roy, *Les Ruines des plus beaux monuments de la Grèce*, 1758.
View of Dromos, Sparta

27. Julien-David Le Roy, *Les Ruines*.
Reconstruction of the Propylaeum on the Acropolis of Athens

128. James Stuart and Nicholas Revett, *Antiquities of Athens*, volume II, 1788.
Façade of the Parthenon

View of the Crypto Porticus or Front towards the Harbour

129. Robert Adam, *Ruins of the Palace of the Emperor Diocletian at Spalatro in Dalmatia*, 1764.
Façade

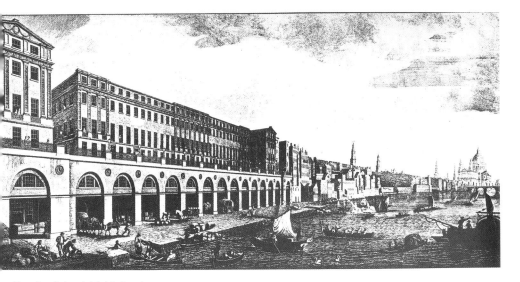

30. Façade of the Adelphi, London;
from *The Works of Robert and James Adam*, 1779

31. Berardo Galiani, edition of Vitruvius, 1758.
Depiction of the temple of Athena at Paestum

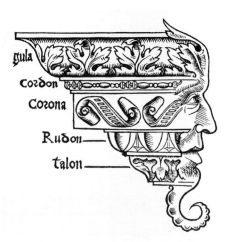

gula

cordon

corona

Rudon

talon

132. Diego de Sagredo, *Medidas del Romano*, 1526. Anthropometric entablature

133. Juan Bautista Villalpando, *In Ezechielem explanationes*, volume II, 1604. Reconstructed plan of Solomon's Temple

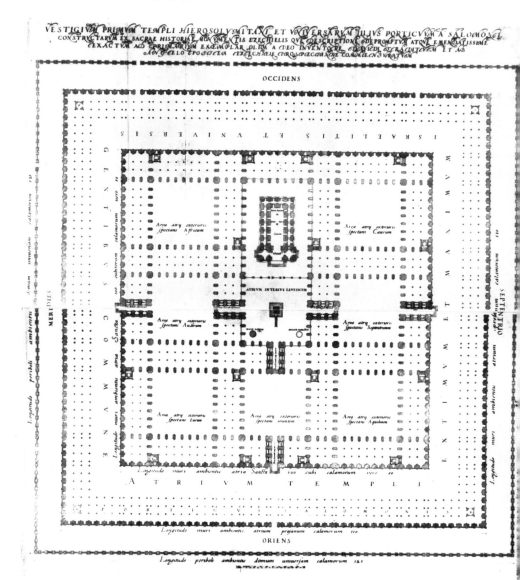

NTALIS FACIES SVBSTRVCTIONIS AB IMIS VALLIBVS CVBITOS TRECENTOS ERECTAE AD SVSTINENDOS AGGERES QVIBVS ATRICH TEMPLI AREAM SALOMON LAXANDAM CVRAVIT NECNON PERIBVLI ACMETA BICVMQVA ADHEBRAOS SVAQVE AD GENTILES PERTINEBANT

SVB MINIMA CVBITORVM MENSVRA QVA ETIAM VNIVERSALIA VESTIGIA DIMETIVNTVR

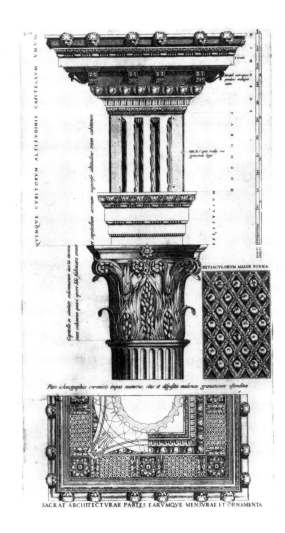

Juan Bautista Villalpando, *In Ezechielem Explanationes*, volume II. Reconstruction of Solomon's Temple

Juan Bautista Villalpando, *In Ezechielem Explanationes*, volume II. Design for a 'Solomonic' order

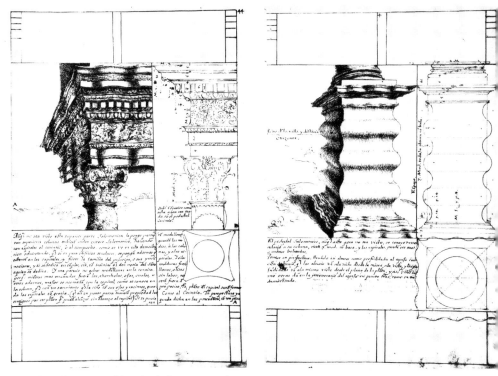

136, 137. Fray Juan Ricci, *Tratado de la pintura sabia*, written in 1662. Drawings of a 'Salomonic' order

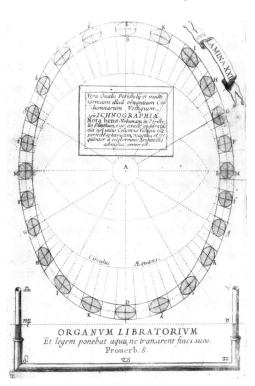

138. Juan Caramuel de Lobkowitz, *Arquitectura civil recta, y obliqua*, 1678. Elliptical plan

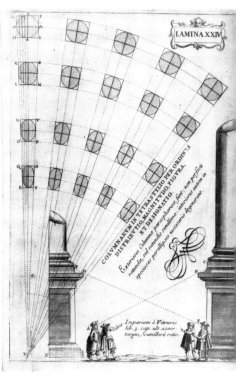

139. Juan Caramuel de Lobkowitz, *Arquitectura.* Proposals for the construction of the colonnades of St Peter's

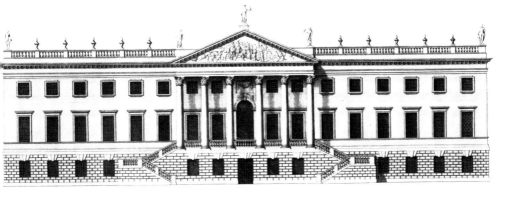

10. Colen Campbell, *Vitruvius Britannicus*, 1715–25. Wanstead I

11. Colen Campbell, *Vitruvius Britannicus*. Wanstead II

12. Colen Campbell, *Vitruvius Britannicus*. Wanstead III

P. 20.

143. James Gibbs, *A Book of Architecture*, 1728. Designs for the tower of St Martin-in-the-Fields

144. Robert Morris, *An Essay in Defence of Ancient Architecture*, 1728. Frontispiece

145. Isaac Ware, *A Complete Body of Architecture*, 1768. Frontispiece

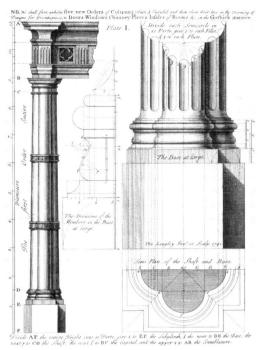

. Batty Langley, *The Builder's Jewel*, 1741.
erpretation of the Orders in Masonic terms:
sdom, Strength and Beauty

147. Batty Langley, *Gothic Architecture, Improved by
Rules and Proportions*, 1747. Representation of the
Doric-Gothic order

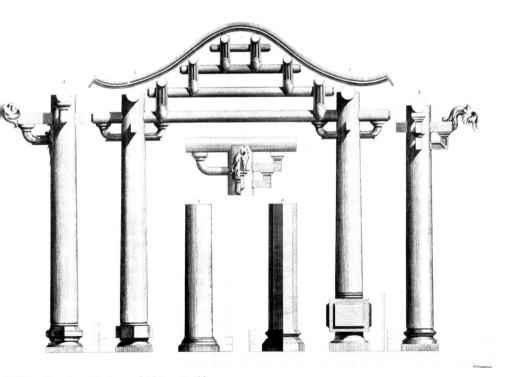

William Chambers, *Designs of Chinese Buildings*, 1757.
inese' orders

149. James Adam, representation of a 'British Order', 1762; New York, Columbia University, Avery Architectural Library

150. Robert and James Adam, *The Works of Architecture*, 1778. Representation of a 'Britannic Order'

151. Robert and James Adam, *The Works of Architecture*, 1778. Frontispiece

Louis-Ambroise Dubut,
Architecture civile, 1803. Designs for
[Ho]use No. 2, 'in two different
[styl]es'

Jean-Nicolas-Louis Durand,
*[Rec]ueil et parallèle des édifices de
[tout] genre, anciens et modernes*,
[180]o. Title-page

Coupe

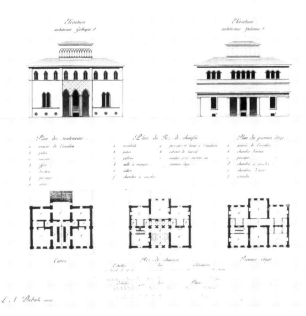

L. A. Dubut inv.

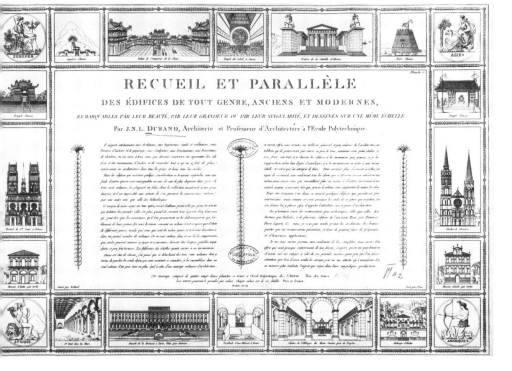

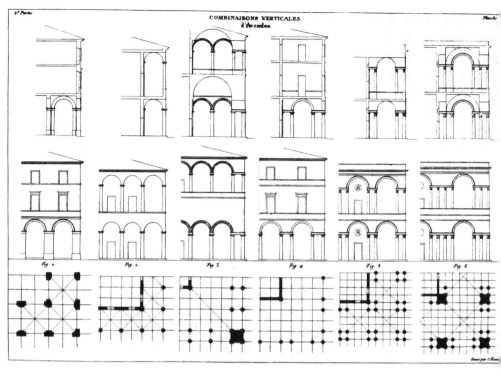

154. Jean-Nicolas-Louis Durand, *Précis des leçons d'architecture*, volume II, 1819.
Designs for arcades, using grid system

155. Jean-Nicolas-Louis Durand, *Précis*, volume II.
Combinations of horizontals and verticals

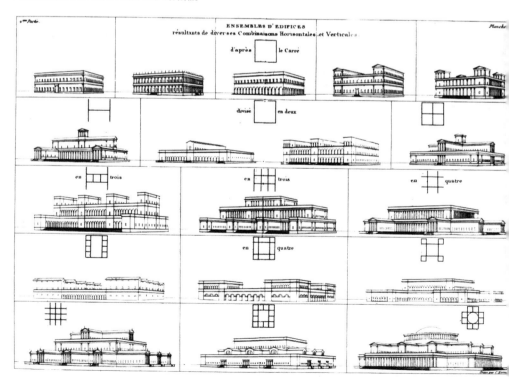

Eugène-Emmanuel Viollet-le-Duc, *Entretiens l'architecture*, volume II, 1872. Vaulted hall of ...al and brick construction

. View of Charles Fourier's '*garantiste*' town

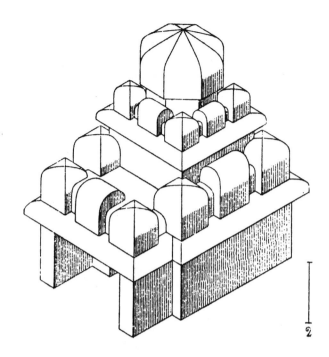

159. Christian Ludwig Stieglitz, *Plans et dessins tirés de la belle architecture*, 1800.
Frontispiece

160. Leo von Klenze, *Anweisung zur Architektur des christlichen Cultus*, 1822.
Project for a cathedral

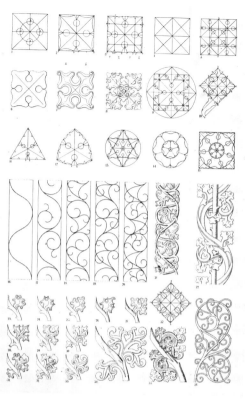

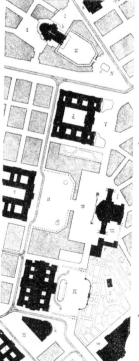

161. August Reichensperger, *Fingerzeige auf dem Gebiete der kirchlichen Kunst*, 1854. Frontispiece

162. Friedrich Hoffstadt, *Gothisches A-B-C-Buch*, 1840. Geometric ornamental motifs

163. Camillo Sitte, *Der Städtebau und seine künstlerischen Grundsätze*, 1901. Plan for reconstruction of the Ringstrasse, Vienna

4. Thomas Hope, *Household Furniture*, 1807. 'Picture Gallery'

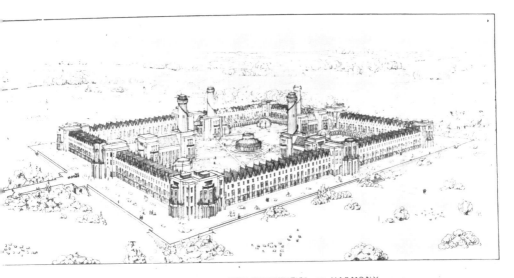

A BIRD'S EYE VIEW OF ONE OF THE NEW COMMUNITIES AT HARMONY.
IN THE STATE OF INDIANA NORTH AMERICA.
AN ASSOCIATION OF TWO THOUSAND PERSONS FORMED UPON THE PRINCIPLES ADVOCATED BY

ROBERT OWEN

STEDMAN WHITWELL ARCHITECT

65. Thomas Stedman Whitwell, *Description of an Architectural Model*, 1830.
Design for New Harmony

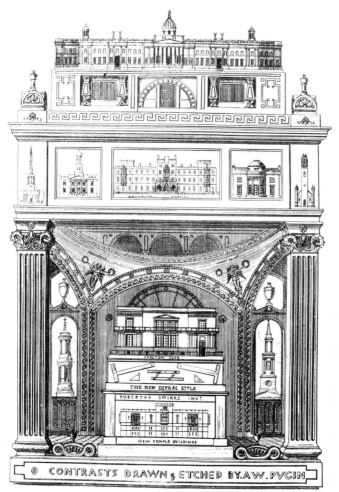

166. Augustus Welby Northmore Pugin, *Contrasts*, 1841.
Frontispiece

167. John Ruskin, *The Stones of Venice*, 1851–53. Symmetrical
geometric ornamental motifs

Fig. 18

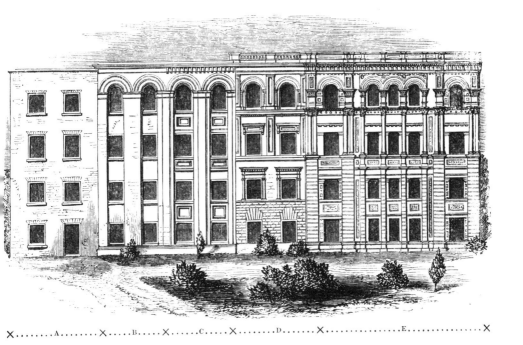

X........A........X....B.....X......C.....X........D......X.................E.............X

58. James Fergusson, *The Illustrated Handbook of Architecture*, 1855.
orms of façade decoration with variations

59. Ebenezer Howard, *Garden Cities of Tomorrow*, 1902. Plan of a garden city

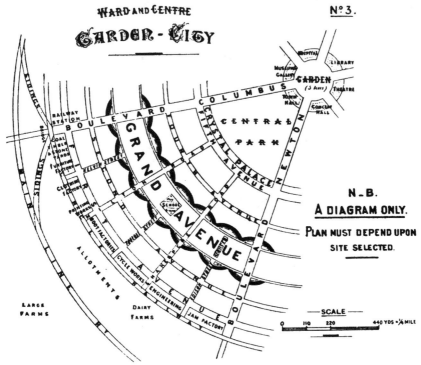

WARD AND CENTRE OF GARDEN CITY

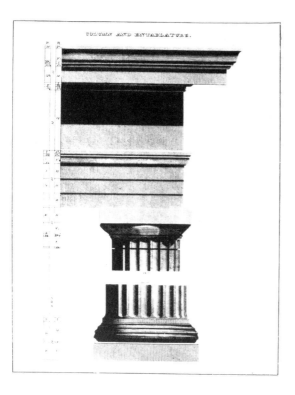

170. Asher Benjamin, *The Practice of Architecture*, 1833. Design for a new Order

171. Louis H. Sullivan, *Setback Skyscraper City Concept*, 1891. Project for setback skyscrapers

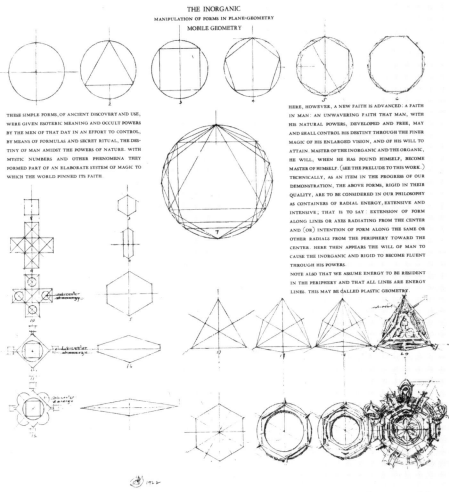

THESE SIMPLE FORMS, OF ANCIENT DISCOVERY AND USE, WERE GIVEN ESOTERIC MEANING AND OCCULT POWERS BY THE MEN OF THAT DAY IN AN EFFORT TO CONTROL, BY MEANS OF FORMULAS AND SECRET RITUAL, THE DESTINY OF MAN AMIDST THE POWERS OF NATURE. WITH MYSTIC NUMBERS AND OTHER PHENOMENA THEY FORMED PART OF AN ELABORATE SYSTEM OF MAGIC TO WHICH THE WORLD PINNED ITS FAITH.

HERE, HOWEVER, A NEW FAITH IS ADVANCED: A FAITH IN MAN: AN UNWAVERING FAITH THAT MAN, WITH HIS NATURAL POWERS, DEVELOPED AND FREE, MAY AND SHALL CONTROL HIS DESTINY THROUGH THE FINER MAGIC OF HIS ENLARGED VISION, AND OF HIS WILL TO ATTAIN. MASTER OF THE INORGANIC AND THE ORGANIC, HE WILL, WHEN HE HAS FOUND HIMSELF, BECOME MASTER OF HIMSELF. (SEE THE PRELUDE TO THIS WORK.) TECHNICALLY, AS AN ITEM IN THE PROGRESS OF OUR DEMONSTRATION, THE ABOVE FORMS, RIGID IN THEIR QUALITY, ARE TO BE CONSIDERED IN OUR PHILOSOPHY AS CONTAINERS OF RADIAL ENERGY, EXTENSIVE AND INTENSIVE; THAT IS TO SAY: EXTENSION OF FORM ALONG LINES OR AXES RADIATING FROM THE CENTER AND (OR) INTENTION OF FORM ALONG THE SAME OR OTHER RADIALS FROM THE PERIPHERY TOWARD THE CENTER. HERE THEN APPEARS THE WILL OF MAN TO CAUSE THE INORGANIC AND RIGID TO BECOME FLUENT THROUGH HIS POWERS.

NOTE ALSO THAT WE ASSUME ENERGY TO BE RESIDENT IN THE PERIPHERY AND THAT ALL LINES ARE ENERGY LINES. THIS MAY BE CALLED PLASTIC GEOMETRY.

172. Louis H. Sullivan, *A System of Architectural Ornament*, 1924. Development of ornamental forms from basic geometric shapes

173. Bruno Taut's pamphlet *Das Glashaus*, 1914. Title-page

174. Text illustration by Bruno Taut, *Haus des Himmels*, 1920

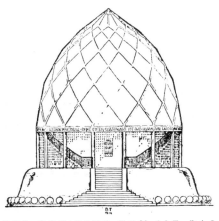

DER GOTISCHE DOM IST DAS
PRALUDIUM DER GLASARCHITEKTUR

175. Bruno Taut, *Die neue Wohnung*, 1924.
Redecoration of a manual worker's room

176. Hermann Finsterlin, *Der Genius der Weltarchitektur*,
1923. Stylistic motifs

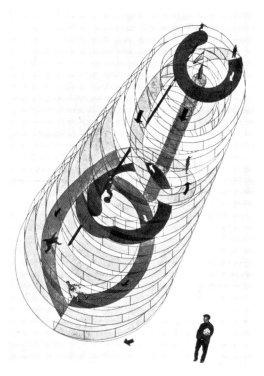

177. Lyonel Feininger, woodcut for title-page of
Walter Gropius's *Manifest und Programm des
Staatlichen Bauhauses in Weimar*, 1919

178. László Moholy-Nagy, *Von Material zu Architektur*,
1929. Kinetic-Constructive system

9. Ludwig Hilberseimer, *Großstadt Architektur*, 1927.
heme for a skyscraper city

o. Tony Garnier, *Une cité industrielle*, 1917. Design of city centre

181. Tony Garnier, *Une cité industrielle*. Residential quarter

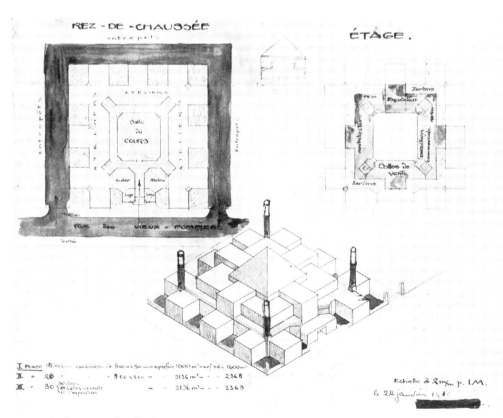

182. Le Corbusier, *Atelier d'artistes*, 1910.
Project for La Chaux-de-Fonds

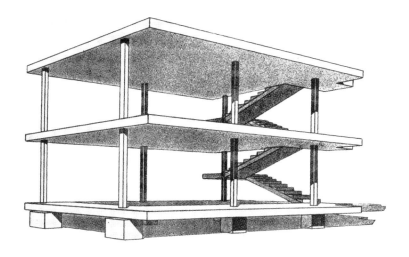

VERS UNE ARCHITECTURE

PAESTUM, de 600 à 550 av. J.-C.

Le Parthénon est un produit de sélection appliquée à un
standart établi. Depuis un siècle déjà, le temple grec était organisé
dans tous ses éléments.

Lorsqu'un standart est établi, le jeu de la concurrence immé-
diate et violente s'exerce. C'est le match; pour gagner, il faut

4. Le Corbusier, *Vers
ie architecture*, 1923.
ustration of the
oblem of type

Cliché de *La Vie Automobile*.

HUMBERT, 1907.

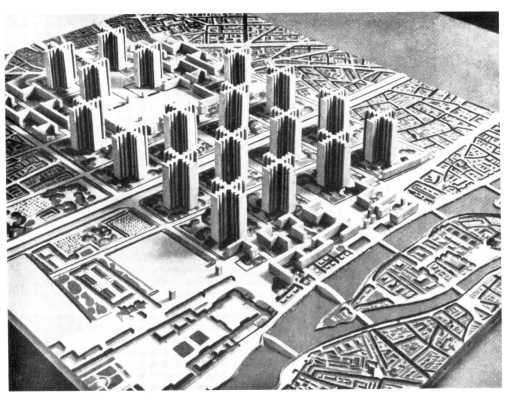

185. Le Corbusier, *Plan Voisin* for Paris, 1925

186. Le Corbusier, *Urbanisme*, 1925. Impression of capital city centre

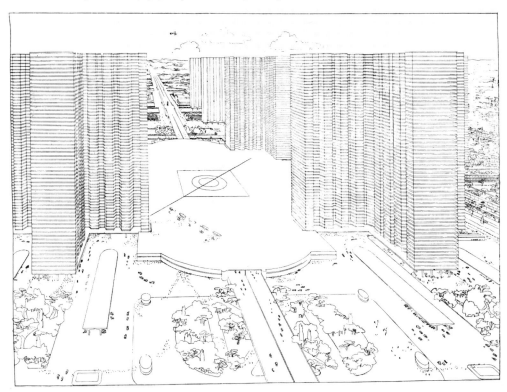

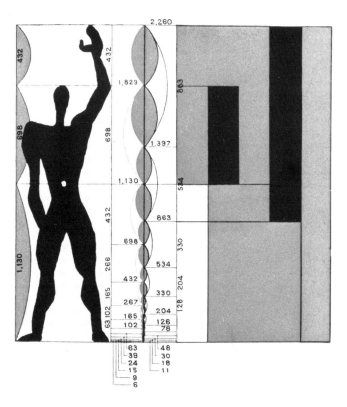

187. Le Corbusier, Modulor

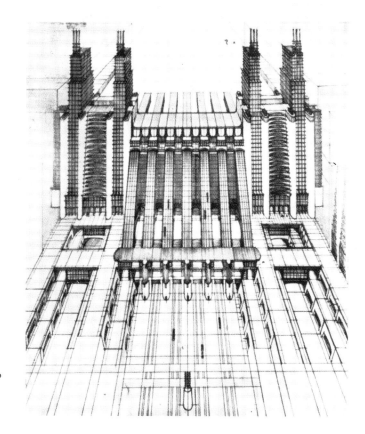

188. Antonio Sant'Elia, main railway station of the 'città nuova', 1914; Como, Villa Olmo

189. Antonio Sant'Elia, illustration of houses with escalators and walks to
trafficways for the '*città nuova*', 1914; Como, Villa Olmo

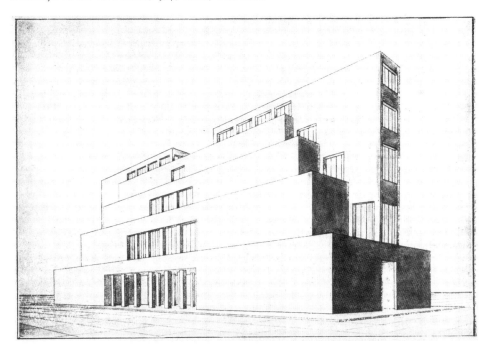

190. Giorgio Rosi, design for an art exhibition building; shown at the 'Esposizione
Italiana di Architettura Razionale', 1928

Right
91. Alberto Sartoris, project for a
cathedral in Fribourg; exhibited
1931

Below left
92. Kazimir Malevich,
Arkhitektonik, 1924–26

Below, right
93. El Lissitzky, plan for Moscow,
1923–26

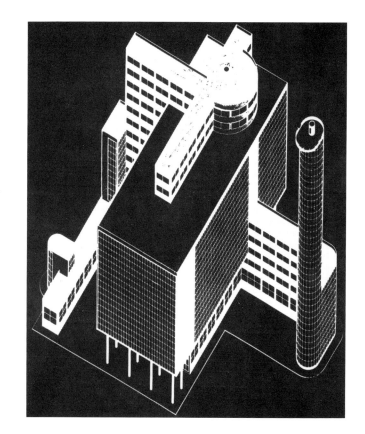

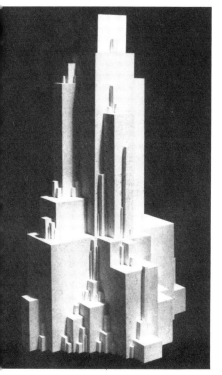

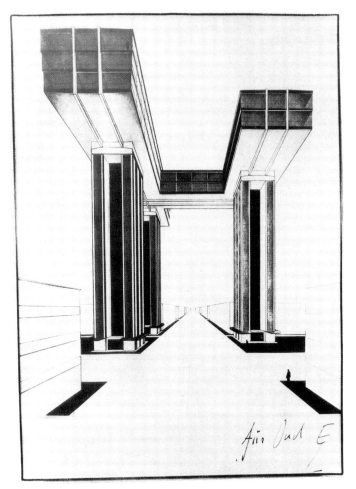

194. El Lissitzky, 'Cloud Hangers', 1924

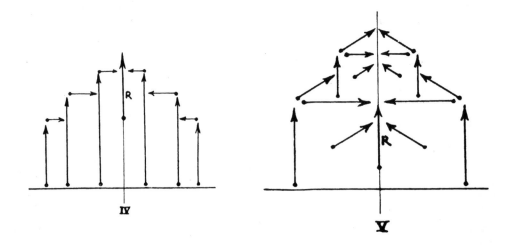

195. Moisey Yaklovlevich Ginzburg, *Style and Epoch*, 1924. Stress diagram for a Gothic and a Baroque building

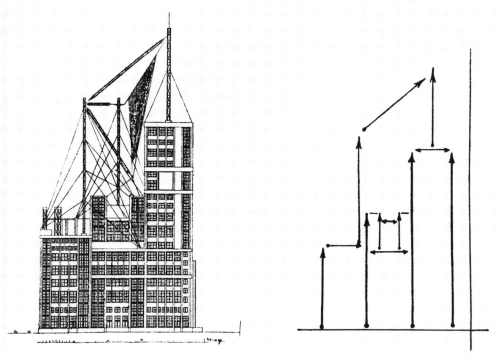

Бр. Весниы—Дворец труда

96. Moisey Yakovlevich Ginzburg, *Style and Epoch*, Stress diagram for the Vesnin
Brothers' design for the Palace of Labour, Moscow, 1922/23

97. Nikolay A. Milyutin, *Sotsgorod*, 1930. General plan for the town of Magnitogorsk

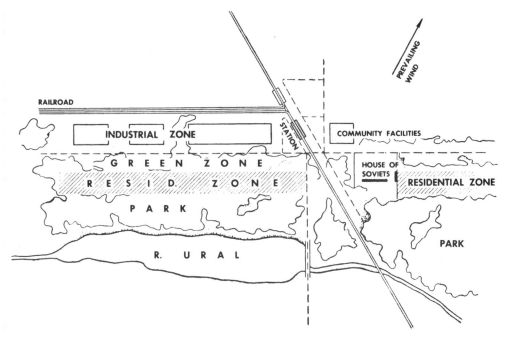

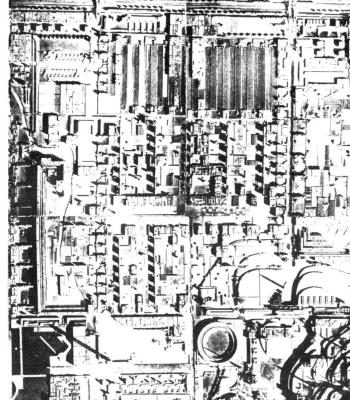

198. Francisco Mujica, *History of the Skyscraper*, 1929. 'Neo-American style' skyscrapers

199. Frank Lloyd Wright, model for Broadacre City, 1934

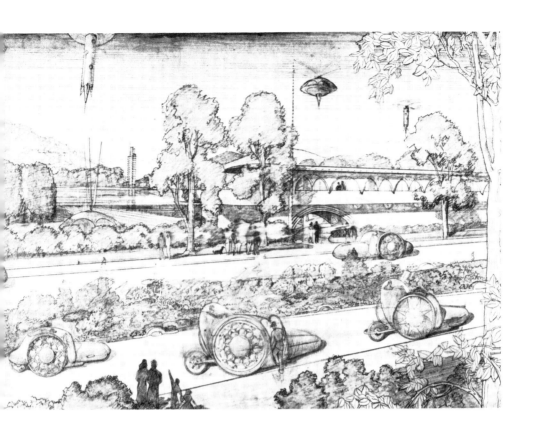

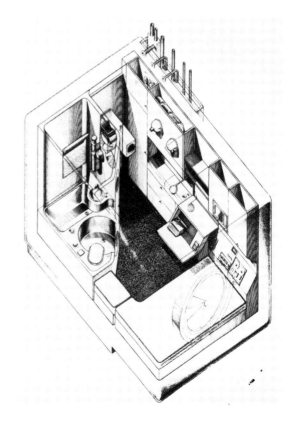

o. Frank Lloyd Wright, depiction of
roadacre City, 1958

1. Kisho Kurokawa, isometric representation
a capsule for living

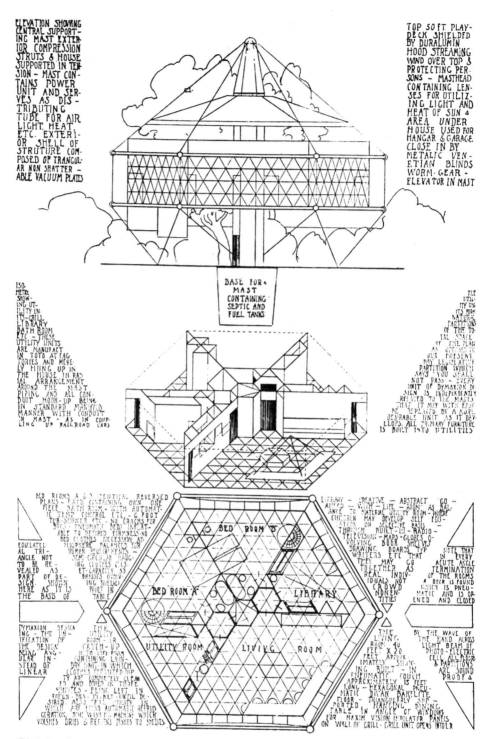

202. Richard Buckminster Fuller, the Dymaxion House

203. Richard Buckminster Fuller, project for a two-mile dome to encase the centre of New York City

204. Paolo Soleri, model for Mesa City, 1969

205. Robert Venturi, Denise Scott Brown and Steven Izenour, 'Caesar's Palace sign'; *Learning from Las Vegas*, 1972

206. Charles Moore, 'The experience of architecture';
Body, Memory and Architecture, 1977

ARCHITETTURA RAZIONALE

**XV Triennale di Milano
Sezione Internazionale di Architettura**

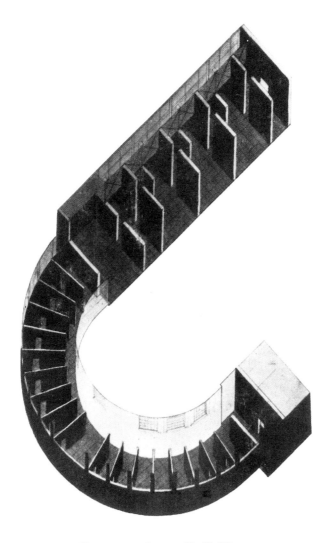

Franco Angeli Editore

207. Manifesto *Architettura Razionale* issued by
Aldo Rossi (XV Triennale, Milan 1973)

Bibliography

This bibliography is confined to general works and a list of sources. For more specialised material and monographs on individual figures, see Notes. English-language translations of sources, of all periods, are listed on pages 681–84.

I. Secondary literature

1. General works on art and architectural theory

BAUER, Hermann, *Kunst und Utopie. Studien über das Kunst- und Staatsdenken in der Renaissance*, Berlin 1965

BORINSKI, Karl, *Die Antike in Poetik und Kunsttheorie*, 2 vols, Leipzig 1914–24 (Darmstadt 1965)

BORISSAVLIEVITCH, Miloutine, *Les théories de l'architecture*, Paris 1926

CHOAY, Françoise, *La règle et le modèle. Sur la théorie de l'architecture et de l'urbanisme*, Paris 1980

CICOGNARA, Leopoldo, *Catalogo ragionato dei libri d'arte e d'antichità posseduti dal Conte Cicorgnara*, 2 vols, Pisa 1821 (facs. repr. Bologna 1979)

DEJOB, Charles, *De l'influence du Concile de Trente sur la littérature et les Beaux-Arts chez les peuples catholiques*, Paris 1884 (facs. repr. Bologna 1975)

DRESDNER, Albert, *Die Entstehung der Kunstkritik*, Munich 1915 (²1968)

FAGIOLO, Marcello, *Natura e artificio. L'ordine rustico, le fontane, gli automi nella cultura del Manierismo europeo*, Rome 1979

FALKE, Rita, 'Versuch einer Bibliographie der Utopien', *Romantistisches Jahrbuch VI*, 1953/54, pp. 92–109

GAMBUTI, Alessandro, *Il dibattito sull'architettura nel Settecento europeo*, Florence 1975

GERMANN, Georg, *Einführung in die Geschichte der Architekturtheorie*, Darmstadt 1980 (³1993)

GOEBEL, Gerhard, *Poeta Faber. Erdichtete Architektur in der italienischen, spanischen und französischen Literatur der Renaissance und des Barock*, Heidelberg 1971

GRASSI, Luigi, *Teorici e storia della critica d'arte*, 3 vols, Rome 1970–79

HAUSER, Arnold, *Sozialgeschichte der Kunst und Literatur*, Munich 1953 (special ed. 1967)

——, *Soziologie der Kunst*, Munich 1974

cat. *Architekt und Ingenieur. Baumeister in Krieg und Frieden*, Wolfenbüttel 1984

KAUFMANN, Emil, *Architecture in the Age of Reason. Baroque and Post-Baroque in England, Italy, and France* (1955), New York 1968

MUMFORD, Lewis, *The City in History. Its Origins, its transformations, and its prospects* (1961), Harmondsworth 1975

OLSCHKI, Leonardo, *Geschichte der neusprachlichen wissenschaftlichen Literatur*, 2 vols, Leipzig 1919–22

PANOFSKY, Erwin, *Idea. Ein Beitrag zur Begriffsgeschichte der älteren Kunsttheorie* (1924), Berlin ²1960

PATETTA, Luciano, *L'architettura dell'eclettismo. Fonti, teorie, modelli 1750–1900*, Milan 1975

——, *Storia dell'Architettura. Antologia critica.* Milan 1975

PELLIZZARI, Achille, *I trattati attorno le arti figurative in Italia e nella Peninsola Iberica*, 2 vols, Naples 1915, Genoa 1942

PÉREZ-GÓMEZ, Alberto, *Architecture and the Crisis of Modern Science*, Cambridge, Mass.–London 1983

PEVSNER, Nikolaus, *Studies in Art, Architecture and Design*, 2 vols, London 1968

ROSENAU, Helen, *The Ideal City. Its Architectural Evolution* (1959), London ²1974

——, *Social Purpose in Architecture. Paris and London Compared, 1760–1800*, London 1970

——, *Vision of the Temple. The Image of the Temple of Jerusalem in Judaism and Christianity*, London 1979

RYKWERT, Joseph, *On Adam's House in Paradise. The Idea of the Primitive Hut in Architectural History*, New York 1972

——, *The First Moderns. The Architects of the Eighteenth Century*, Cambridge, Mass–London 1980

SCHLOSSER (MAGNINO), Julius von, *Die Kunstliteratur*, Vienna 1924; Italian ed., revised by Otto Kurz: *La letteratura artistica*, Florence–Vienna ³1964

SCHMIDT, Hans-Wolfgang, *Die gewundene Säule in der Architekturtheorie von 1500 bis 1800*, Stuttgart 1978

SUMMERSON, John, *Heavenly Mansions and other essays on architecture* (1948), New York 1973

TAFURI, Manfredo, *Teorie e storia dell'architettura* (1968), Rome–Bari ⁴1976

VAGNETTI, Luigi, *De naturali et artificiali perspectiva, Studi e documenti di architettura*, 9–10, 1979

——, *L'architetto nella storia di occidente*, Padua 1980

VENTURI, Lionello, *Storia della critica d'arte* (1936), Turin 1964

WIEBENSON, Dora (ed.), *Architectural Theory and Practice from Alberti to Ledoux*, cat., Chicago 1982

ZUCKER, Paul, *Town and Square. From the Agora to the Village Green* (1959), Cambridge, Mass.–London 1970

2. Individual periods

a. The Middle Ages

ACKERMAN, James S., '"Ars sine scientia nihil est." Gothic Theory of Architecture at the Cathedral of Milan', *Art Bulletin* 31, 1949, pp. 84–111

BANDMANN, Günter, *Mittelalterliche Architektur als Bedeutungsträger*, Berlin 1951 (several eds)

——, 'Ikonologie der Architektur', *Jahrbuch für Ästhetik und allgemeine Kunstwissenschaft*, 1951, pp. 67–109 (reprinted in vol. form Darmstadt 1969)

BOOZ, Paul, *Der Baumeister der Gotik*, Munich 1956

Du Colombier, Pierre, *Les Chantiers des Cathédrales*, Paris 1953 (²1973)

Frankl, Paul, *The Gothic. Literary Sources and Interpretations Through Eight Centuries*, Princeton 1960

Friedländer, Paul, *Johannes von Gaza, Paulus Silentiarius. Kunstbeschreibungen justinianischer Zeit*, Berlin–Leipzig 1912 (facs. repr. Hildesheim–New York 1969)

Gaus, Joachim, 'Weltbaumeister und Architekt', in: Günther Binding (ed.), *Beiträge über Bauführung und Baufinanzierung im Mittelalter*, Cologne 1974, pp. 38–67

Hecht, Konrad, 'Maß und Zahl in der gotischen Baukunst', *Abhandlungen der Braunschweigischen Wissenschaftlichen Gesellschaft* XXI, 1969, pp. 215–326; XXII, 1970, pp. 105–263; XXIII, 1971, pp. 25–263 (vol. pub. Hildesheim–New York 1979)

Heideloff, Carl, *Die Bauhütte des Mittelalters in Deutschland*, Nuremberg 1844

Janner, Ferdinand, *Die Bauhütten des deutschen Mittelalters*, Leipzig 1876

Male, Emile, *L'art religieux du XIIIe siècle en France*, Paris ⁶1924

Panofsky, Erwin, *Gothic Architecture and Scholasticism* (1951), Cleveland–New York ⁶1963

Pauken (-Weber), Elke, *Das Steinmetzbuch WG 1572 im Städelschen Kunstinstitut zu Frankfurt am Main*, Cologne 1979

Rathe, Kurt, *Ein Architektur-Musterbuch der Spätgotik mit graphischen Einklebungen*, Festschrift der Nationalbibliothek Wien, Vienna 1926, pp. 667–92

Reichensperger, August, *Vermischte Schriften über christliche Kunst*, Leipzig 1856, pp. 133 ff.

Saufer, Josef, *Symbolik des Kirchengebäudes und seiner Ausstattung in der Auffassung des Mittelalters*, Freiburg ²1924

Scheller, R. W., *A Survey of Medieval Model Books*, Haarlem 1963

Shelby, Lou R., and Mark, Robert, 'Late Gothic Structural Design in the "Instructions" of Lorenz Lechler', *Architectura* 9, 1979, pp. 113–31

Simpson, Otto von, *The Gothic Cathedral. Origins of Gothic Architecture and the Medieval Concept of Order*, New York 1956

Ueberwasser, Walter, 'Nach rechtem Maß,' *Jahrbuch der Preußischen Kunstsammlungen* 56, 1935, pp. 250–72

——, 'Beiträge zur Wiedererkenntnis gotischer Bau-Gesetzmäßigkeiten', *Zeitschrift für Kunstgeschichte* 8, 1939, pp. 303–9

Warnke, Martin, *Bau und Überbau. Soziologie der mittelalterlichen Architektur nach den Schriftquellen*, Frankfurt 1976

Weber, Elke, 'Steinmetzbücher – Architekturmusterbücher', in: Günther Binding and Norbert Nussbaum (ed.), *Der mittelalterliche Baubetrieb nördlich der Alpen in zeitgenössischen Darstellungen*, Darmstadt 1978, pp. 22–42

b. Italy: fifteenth to eighteenth century

Blunt, Anthony, *Artistic Theory in Italy 1450–1600* (1940), Oxford 1962

Cassirer, Ernst, *Individuum und Kosmos in der Philosophie der Renaissance*, Leipzig–Berlin 1927

Cantone, Gaetana, *La città di marmo. Da Alberti a Serlio. La Storia tra progettazione e restauro*, Rome 1978

Contardi, Bruno, *La retorica e l'architettura barocca*, Rome 1978

FIRPO, Luigi, *Lo Stato ideale della Controriforma. Ludovico Agostini*, Bari 1957

HAGER, Hellmut, *Architectural Fantasy and Reality. Drawings from the Accademia Nazionale di San Luca in Rome. Concorsi Clementini 1700–1750*, cat., University Park, Penn. 1982

HERSEY, George L., *Pythagorean Palaces, Magic and Architecture in the Italian Renaissance*, London ¹1976, ²1980

KEMP, Wolfgang, 'Disegno. Beiträge zur Geschichte des Begriffs zwischen 1547 und 1607', *Marburger Jahrbuch für Kunstwissenschaft* 19, 1974, pp. 219–40

KOENIGSBERGER, Dorothy, *Renaissance Man and Creative Thinking. A History of Concepts of Harmony 1400–1700*, Hassocks, Sussex 1979

MAHON, Denis, *Studies in Seicento Art and Theory*, London 1967 (facs. repr. Westport, Conn. 1971)

MEEKS, Carroll L. V., *Italian Architecture 1750–1914*, New Haven–London 1966

MURATORE, Giorgio, *La città rinascimentale. Tipi e modelli attraverso i trattati*, Milan 1975

OECHSLIN, Werner, *Bildungsgut und Antikenrezeption des frühen Settecento in Rom. Studien zum römischen Aufenthalt Bernardo Antonio Vittones*, Zürich 1972

PORTOGHESI, Paolo, *L'angelo della storia. Teorie e linguaggi dell'architettura*, Rome–Bari 1982

ROSSI, Sergio, *Dalle botteghe alle accademie. Realtà sociale e teorie artistiche a Firenze dal XIV al XVI secolo*, Milan 1980

SIMONCINI, Giorgio, *Città e società nel Rinascimento*, 2 vols, Turin 1974

STRINATI, Claudio Massimo, 'Studio sulla teorica d'arte primoseicentesca tra Manierismo e Barocco', *Storia dell'arte* 14, 1972, pp. 67–82

TAFURI, Manfredo, *L'architettura del Manierismo*, Rome 1966

——, 'L'idea di architettura nella letteratura teorica del manierismo,' *Bollettino del Centro Internazionale di Studi d'Architettura 'A. Palladio'* IX, 1967, pp. 369–84

ULIVI, Ferruccio, *Galleria di scrittori d'arte*, Florence 1953

WITTKOWER, Rudolf, *Architectural Principles in the Age of Humanism* (1949), London ³1962 (several reprs)

——, *Gothic Versus Classic. Architectural Projects in Seventeenth Century Italy*, New York 1974

ZAREBSKA, Teresa, *Teoria urbanistyki wloskiej XV i XVI wieku*, Warsaw 1971 (French summary)

c. France: sixteenth to eighteenth century

BLOMFIELD, Reginald, *A History of French Architecture from the Reign of Charles VIII till the Death of Mazarin, 1494–1661*, 4 vols, London 1921 (facs. repr. New York 1973)

BLUNT, Anthony, *Art and Architecture in France 1500 to 1700*, Harmondsworth 1953

EGBERT, Donald Drew, *Beaux-Arts Tradition in French Architecture. Illustrated by the Grands Prix de Rome*, Princeton, NJ 1980

HAUTECOEUR, Louis, *Histoire de l'architecture classique en France*, Paris 1943 ff.

HERNANDEZ, Antonio, *Gründzüge einer Ideengeschichte der französischen Architektur-theorie von 1560–1800*, Basel 1972

HESSE, Michael, *Von der Nachgotik zur Neugotik. Die Auseinandersetzung mit der Gotik in der französischen Sakralarchitektur des 16ten, 17ten und 18ten Jahrhunderts* (Bochumer Schriften zur Kunstgeschichte, vol. 3), Frankfurt–Bern–New York 1984

KALNEIN, Wend Graf and LEVEY, Michael, *Art and Architecture of the Eighteenth Century in France*, Harmondsworth 1972

KASK, Tonis, *Symmetrie und Regelmäßigkeit – französische Architektur im Grand Siècle*, Basel–Stuttgart 1971

KAUFMANN, Emil, 'Die Architekturtheoretiker der französischen Klassik und des Klassizismus', *Repertorium für Kunstwissenschaft*, 44, 1924, pp. 197–237

——, 'Three Revolutionary Architects, Boullée, Ledoux, and Lequeu', *Transactions of the American Philosophical Society, N.S.*, 42, 1952, pp. 429–564

KIMBALL, Fiske, *The Creation of the Rococo* (1943), New York 1964

——, *Le Style Louis XV. Origine et évolution du Rococo*. Paris 1949

KNABE, Peter-Eckhard, *Schlüsselbegriffe des kunsttheoretischen Denkens in Frankreich von der Spätklassik bis zum Ende der Aufklärung*, Düsseldorf 1972

LEMONNIER, Henry (ed.), *Procès-Verbaux de l'Académie Royale d'Architecture 1671–1793*, 10 vols, Paris 1911–29

PEROUSE DE MONTCLOS, Jean-Marie, 'Le Sixième Ordre d'Architecture, ou la Pratique des Ordres Suivant les Nations', *Journal of the Society of Architectural Historians* XXXVI, 1977, pp. 223–40

——, *L'architecture à la française XVIe, XVIIe, XVIIIe siècles*, Paris 1982

——, (ed.), *'Le prix de Rome'. Concours de l'Académie royale d'architecture au XVIIIe siècle*, Paris 1984

d. Spain: sixteenth to eighteenth century

BONET CORREA, Antonio (ed.), *Bibliografia de arquitectura, ingenieria y urbanismo en España (1498–1880)*, 2 vols, Madrid–Vaduz 1980

CHUECA GOITIA, Fernando, 'Arquitectura del siglo XVI' (*Ars Hispaniae* XI), Madrid 1953

GUTIERREZ, Ramón, *Notas para una bibliografia hispanoamericana de arquitectura (1526–1875)*, Universidad de Nordeste (Argentina), n.d. (c. 1972)

KUBLER, George, 'Arquitectura de los siglos XVII y XVIII' (*Ars Hispaniae* XIV), Madrid 1957

——, and SORIA, Martin, *Art and Architecture in Spain and Portugal and their American Dominions 1500 to 1800*, Harmondsworth 1959

LLAGUNO Y AMIROLA, Eugenio and CEAN-BERMUDEZ, Juan Agustin, *Noticias de los arquitectos y arquitectura de España desde su restauración*, 4 vols, Madrid 1829 (facs. repr. Madrid 1977)

MENENDEZ Y PELAYO, Marcelino, *Historia de la ideas estéticas en España*, 9 vols, Madrid 1883 ff.

ZAMORA LUCAS, Florentino and PONCE DE LEON, Eduardo, *Bibliografia española de arquitectura (1526–1850)*, Madrid 1947 *e.* Germany and its neighbours: sixteenth to eighteenth century

Cat. *Architekt und Ingenieur. Baumeister in Krieg und Frieden*, Wolfenbüttel 1984

FORSSMAN, Erik, *Säule und Ornament. Studien zum Problem des Manierismus in den nordischen Säulenbüchern und Vorlageblättern des 16. und 17. Jahrhunderts*, Stockholm 1956

HABICHT, Curt, 'Die deutschen Architekturtheoretiker des 17. und 18. Jahrhunderts', *Zeitschrift für Architektur und Ingenieurwesen*, N.F., 21, 1916, cols. 1–30, 261–88; 22, 1917, cols. 209–44; 23, 1918, cols. 157–84, 201–30

HITCHCOCK, Henry-Russell, *German Renaissance Architecture*, Princeton, NJ 1981

LÜBKE, Wilhelm, *Geschichte der Renaissance in Deutschland*, 2 vols, Stuttgart ²1882

SCHÜTTE, Ulrich, *'Ordnung' und 'Verzierung'. Untersuchungen zur deutschsprachigen Architekturtheorie des 18. Jahrhunderts*, diss., Heidelberg 1979

WARNCKE, Carsten-Peter, *Die ornamentale Groteske in Deutschland 1500–1650*, 2 vols, Berlin 1979

f. England: sixteenth to eighteenth century

BROWNELL, Morris R., *Alexander Pope & the Arts of Georgian England*, Oxford 1978

CERUTTI FUSCO, Annarosa, *Inigo Jones. Vitruvius Britannicus*, Rimini 1985

COLVIN, Howard, *A Biographical Dictionary of English Architects 1660–1840*, London 1954 (²1978)

DOBAI, Johannes, *Die Kunstliteratur des Klassizismus und der Romantik in England*, vol. I: 1700–1750, Bern 1974; vol. II: 1750–1790, Bern 1975; vol. III: 1790–1840, Bern 1977; vol. IV: index vol., Bern 1984

FISCHER, Marianne, *Katalog der Architektur- und Ornamentstichsammlung. Kunstbibliothek Berlin*, part I: *Baukunst England*, Berlin 1977

HARRIS, John, 'Sources of Architectural History in England', *Journal of the Society of Architectural Historians* XXIV, 1965, pp. 297–300

——, *The Palladians*, London 1981

HIPPLE, W.J., *The Beautiful, The Sublime, and The Picturesque in Eighteenth–Century British Aesthetic Theory*, Carbondale 1957

HUSSEY, Christopher, *The Picturesque. Studies in a Point of View*, London 1927 (²1967)

JENKINS, Frank, *Architecture and Patron. A Survey of Professional Relations and Practice in England from the Sixteenth Century to the Present Day*, London 1961

LANG, Suzanne, 'The Principles of Gothic Revival in England', *Journal of the Society of Architectural Historians* XXV, 1966, pp. 240–67

SUMMERSON, John, *Architecture in Britain 1530–1830*, Harmondsworth 1953, ⁵1970

WATKIN, David, *The English Vision: The Picturesque in Architecture, Landscape and Garden Design*, London 1982

WITTKOWER, Rudolf, 'La letteratura palladiana in Inghilterra', *Bollettino del Centro Internazionale di Studi di Architettura 'A. Palladio'* VII, 1965, part 2, pp. 126–52

——, *Palladio and English Palladianism*, London 1974 (²1984)

WOLSDORFF, Christian Ferdinand, *Untersuchungen zu englischen Veröffentlichungen des 17. und 18. Jahrhunderts, die Probleme der Architektur und des Bauens behandeln* (diss. 1978), Bonn 1982

g. Nineteenth and twentieth centuries: general

BANDMANN, Günter, 'Der Wandel der Materialbewertung in der Kunsttheorie des 19. Jahrhunderts', in: Helmut Koopmann and J. Adolf Schmoll (Eisenwerth) (ed.), *Beiträge zur Theorie der Künste im 19. Jahrhundert*, vol. I, Frankfurt 1971, pp. 129–57

BANHAM, Reyner, *Theory and Design in the First Machine Age*, London 1960

BENEVOLO, Leonardo, *Storia dell'architettura moderna* (1960), Rome–Bari 1977

BOLLEREY, Franziska, *Architekturkonzeption der utopischen Sozialisten*, Munich 1977

CHOAY, Françoise, *The Modern City: Planning in the 19th Century*, New York 1969

COLLINS, Peter, *Changing Ideals in Modern Architecture 1750–1950* (1965), London 1967

DE FUSCO, Renato, *L'idea di architettura. Storia della critica da Viollet-le-Duc a Persico* (1968), Milan 1977

FRAMPTON, Kenneth, *Modern Architecture. A Critical History*, London 1980

GIEDION, Sigfried, *Space, Time and Architecture. The growth of a new tradition* (1941), Cambridge, Mass.–London ⁵1967

GRÖTZEBACH, Dietmar, *Der Wandel der Kriterien bei der Wertung des Zusammenhanges von Konstruktion und Form in den letzten 100 Jahren*, diss., TU Berlin, Berlin 1965

HITCHCOCK, Henry-Russell, *Architecture: Nineteenth and Twentieth Century* (1958), Harmondsworth 1971

KÄHLER, Gert, *Architektur als Symbolverfall. Das Dampfermotiv in der Baukunst*, Brunswick–Wiesbaden 1981

MIGNOT, Claude, *L'Architecture au XIXᵉ siècle*, Fribourg 1983

PEVSNER, Nikolaus, *Pioneers of Modern Design. From William Morris to Walter Gropius*, London 1936 (New York ²1949)

——, *Some Architectural Writers of the Nineteenth Century*, Oxford 1972

RAPHAEL, Max, *Für eine demokratische Architektur? Kunstsoziologische Schriften*, ed. Jutta Held, Frankfurt 1976

SARTORIS, Alberto, *Encyclopédie de l'architecture nouvelle*, 3 vols, Milan 1948–56

SCHILD, Erich, *Zwischen Glaspalast und Palais des Illusions*, Frankfurt–Vienna 1967

SCHUMPP, Mechthild, *Stadtbau-Utopien und Gesellschaft*, Gütersloh 1972

SHARP, Dennis, *Sources of Modern Architecture. A Critical Bibliography* (1967), London ²1981

STEINMANN, Martin (ed.), *CIAM. Dokumente 1928–1939*, Basel–Stuttgart 1979

WATKIN, David, *Morality and Architecture. The Development of a Theme in Architectural History and Theory from the Gothic Revival to the Modern Movement*, Oxford 1977

h. France: nineteenth century

Cat. *Paris–Rome–Athènes*, Paris 1982

Cat. *Roma Antiqua. 'Envois' degli architetti francesi (1788–1924). L'area archeologica centrale*, Rome–Paris 1985

DREXLER, Arthur (ed.), *The Architecture of the Ecole des Beaux-Arts*, London–New York 1977

EGBERT, Donald Drew, *The Beaux-Arts Tradition in French Architecture, illustrated by the Grands Prix de Rome*, Princeton 1980

HAUTECOEUR, Louis, *Histoire de l'architecture classique en France*, vols. V–VII, Paris 1953–57

MIDDLETON, Robin (ed.), *The Beaux-Arts and nineteenth-century French architecture*, London 1982

MOORE, Richard A., 'Academic Dessin Theory in France after Reorganization of 1863', *Journal of the Society of Architectural Historians* XXXVI, 1977, pp. 145–74

PATETTA, Luciano, *La polemica fra i Goticisti e i Classicisti dell'Académie des Beaux-Arts Francia 1846–47*, Milan 1974

ROSENAU, Helen, 'The Engravings of the Grands Prix of the French Academy of Architecture', *Architectural History* III, 1960, pp. 17–173

VAN ZANTEN, David, *The Architectural Polychromy of the 1830's* (PhD thesis, Harvard Univ. 1970), New York–London 1977

i. Germany: nineteenth century

BEENKEN, Hermann, *Das neunzehnte Jahrhundert in der deutschen Kunst*, Munich 1944
——, *Schöpferische Bauideen der deutschen Romantik*, Mainz 1952

BÖRSCH-SUPAN, Eva, *Berliner Baukunst nach Schinkel 1840–1880*, Munich 1977

BRIX, Michael and STEINHAUSER, Monika (ed.), 'Geschichte allein ist zeitgemäß', *Historismus in Deutschland*, Giessen 1978

DÖHMER, Klaus, *'In welchem Style sollen wir bauen?' Architekturtheorie zwischen Klassizismus und Jugendstil*, Munich 1976

GIEDION, Sigfried, *Spätbarocker und romantischer Klassizismus*, Munich 1922

GURLITT, Cornelius, *Die deutsche Kunst des Neunzehnten Jahrhunderts*, Berlin ²1900, ³1907 (see also excerpts in: Cornelius Gurlitt, *Zur Befreiung der Baukunst. Ziele und Taten deutscher Architekten im 19. Jahrhundert*, ed. Werner Kallmorgen, Bauwelt Fundamente 22, Gütersloh–Berlin 1969)

HERRMANN, Wolfgang, *Deutsche Baukunst des 19. und 20. Jahrhunderts*, part 1: *Von 1770–1840*, Breslau 1932; part 2: *Von 1840 bis zur Gegenwart* (originally planned to appear in 1933), Basel–Stuttgart 1977

MILDE, Kurt, *Neorenaissance in der deutschen Architektur des 19. Jahrhunderts*, Dresden 1981

MUTHESIUS, Stefan, *Das englische Vorbild. Eine Studie zu den deutschen Reformbewegungen in Architektur, Wohnbau und Kunstgewerbe im späteren 19. Jahrhundert*, Munich 1974

j. England: nineteenth century

CROOK, J. Mordaunt, *The Greek Revival. Neo-Classical Attitudes in British Architecture 1760–1870*, London 1972

DAVEY, Peter, *Arts and Crafts Architecture: The Search for Earthly Paradise*, London–New York 1980

DOBAI, Johannes, *Die Kunstliteratur des Klassizismus und der Romantik in England*, vol. III: 1790–1840, Bern 1977

HERSEY, George L., *High Victorian Gothic. A Study in Associatism*, Baltimore–London 1972

HITCHCOCK, Henry-Russell, *Early Victorian Architecture in Britain*, 2 vols, New Haven, Conn. 1954 (New York ²1972)

JENKINS, Frank, 'Nineteenth-Century Architectural Periodicals', in: John Summerson (ed.), *Concerning Architecture. Essays on Architectural Writers and Writing presented to Nikolaus Pevsner*, London 1968, pp. 153–60

MACAULAY, James, *The Gothic Revival 1745–1845*, London 1975

MACLEOD, Robert, *Style and Society. Architectural Ideology in Britain 1835–1914*, London 1971

MUTHESIUS, Stefan, *The High Victorian Movement in Architecture 1850–1870*, London–Boston 1972

NAYLOR, Gillian, *The Arts and Crafts Movement*, London 1971

OLLARD, S. L., 'The Oxford Architectural and Historical Society and the Oxford Movement', in: *Oxoniensia V*, 1940

PEVSNER, Nikolaus, 'William Morris, C. R. Ashbee und das zwanzigste Jahrhundert', *Deutsche Vierteljahrsschrift für Literaturwissenschaft und Geistesgeschichte*, 14, 1936, pp. 536–62

——, *Some Architectural Writers of the Nineteenth Century*, Oxford 1972

——, *Studies in Art, Architecture and Design. Victorian and After*, London 1968 (²1982)

POSENER, Julius, *Anfänge des Funktionalismus. Von Arts and Crafts zum Deutschen Werkbund* (*Bauwelt Fundamente* 11), Berlin 1964

WATKIN, David, *The Rise of Architectural History*, London 1980

WHITE, James F., *The Cambridge Movement. The Ecclesiologists and the Gothic Revival*, Cambridge 1962 (²1979)

k. United States: nineteenth century

ANDREWS, Wayne, *American Gothic. Its Origins, Its Trials, Its Triumphs*, New York 1975

AZZI VISENTINI, Margherita, *Il Palladianesimo in America e l'architettura della villa*, Milan 1976

BESTOR, Arthur Eugene, *Backwoods Utopias: The Sectarian Origins and the Owenite Phase of Communitarian Socialism in America, 1663–1829*, Philadelphia ¹1950, ²1970

CONDIT, Carl W., *The Chicago School of Architecture. A History of Commercial and Public Buildings in the Chicago Area, 1875–1925* (¹1964), Chicago–London 1973

EGBERT, Donald Drew, 'The Idea of Organic Expression and American Architecture', in: Stow Persons (ed.), *Revolutionary Thought in America*, New Haven, Conn. 1950, pp. 336–96

FITCH, James Marston, *American Building. The Historical Forces That Shaped It* (¹1947), New York ²1973

GIFFORD, Don, *The Literature of American Architecture*, New York 1966

HAYDEN, Dolores, *Seven American Utopias. The Architecture of Communitarian Socialism, 1790–1975*, Cambridge, Mass.–London ¹1976, ²1977

HITCHCOCK, Henry-Russell, *American Architectural Books. A List of Books, Portfolios, and Pamphlets on Architecture and Related Subjects Published in America before 1895* (¹1946), Minneapolis ²1962 (facs. repr. New York 1976)

———, and SCALE, William, *Temples of Democracy: The State Capitols of the U.S.A.*, New York–London 1976

KAUFMANN, Jr, Edgar (ed.), *The Rise of an American Architecture*, New York–London 1970

KIDNEY, Walter C., *The Architecture of Choice: Eclecticism in America 1880–1930*, New York 1974

MUMFORD, Lewis, *Sticks and Stones. A Study of American Architecture and Civilization* (1924), New York 1955

———, (ed.), *Roots of Contemporary American Architecture* (¹1952), New York 1972

ROOS, Frank J., 'Writings on American Architecture' (¹1943); in 2nd ed. entitled *Bibliography of Early American Architecture. Writings on Architecture Constructed Before 1860 in Eastern and Central United States*, Chicago–London 1968

ROTH, Leland M., *America Builds. Source Documents in American Architecture and Planning*, New York 1983

SADLER, Jr, Julius Trousdale, *The Only Proper Style. Gothic Architecture in America*, Boston, Mass. 1975

SCHUYLER, Montgomery, *American Architecture and Other Writings*, 2 vols, Cambridge, Mass. 1961

SCULLY, Vincent J., *The Shingle Style and the Stick Style. Architectural Theory and Design from Richardson to the Origins of Wright*, New Haven, Conn.–London ¹1955, ²1971

SKY, Alison and STONE, Michelle, *Unbuilt America. Forgotten Architecture in the United States from Thomas Jefferson to the Space Age*, New York 1976

STANTON, Phoebe B., *The Gothic Revival and American Church Architecture 1840–1856*, Baltimore, Maryland 1968

The Shaping of Art and Architecture in Nineteenth-Century America, Metropolitan Museum of Art, New York 1972

l. Germany and its neighbours: 1900–1945

BOTT, Gerhard (ed.), *Von Morris zum Bauhaus. Eine Kunst gegründet auf Einfachheit*, Hanau 1977

BURCKHARDT, Lucius (ed.), *Der Werkbund in Deutschland, Österreich und der Schweiz*, Stuttgart 1978

CAMPBELL, Joan, *The German Werkbund. The Politics of Reform in the Applied Arts*, Princeton, NJ 1978

Cat. *Zwischen Kunst und Industrie. Der Deutsche Werkbund*, Munich 1975

Cat. 'Funzione e Senso. Architettura – Casa – Città. Olanda 1870–1940', Milan 1979

Cat. *Arbeitrat für Kunst Berlin 1918–1921*, Berlin 1980

Cat. *De Stijl: 1917–1931. Visions of Utopia*, New York 1982

ECKSTEIN, Hans (revised), *50 Jahre Deutscher Werkbund*, Berlin 1958

HÜTER, Karl-Heinz, *Das Bauhaus in Weimar*, Berlin ²1976

HUSE, Norbert, *'Neues Bauen' 1918 bis 1933*, Munich 1975

JAFFÉ, Hans L. C., *De Stijl 1917–1931. The Dutch Contribution to Modern Art*, Amsterdam 1956

JUNGHANNS, Kurt, *Der Deutsche Werkbund. Sein erstes Jahrzehnt*, Berlin 1982

Margolius, Ivan, *Cubism in Architecture and the Applied Arts. Bohemia and France 1910–1914*, London 1979

Miller Lane, Barbara, *Architecture and Politics in Germany, 1918–1945*, Cambridge, Mass. 1968

Müller-Wulckow, Walter, *Deutsche Baukunst der Gegenwart*, 4 vols, Königstein 1925–1932 (in one vol. under the title *Architektur der zwanziger Jahre in Deutschland*, ed. Reyner Banham, Königstein 1975)

Petsch, Joachim, *Baukunst und Stadtplanung im Dritten Reich*, Munich 1976

Pozzetto, Marco, *Die Schule Otto Wagners 1894–1912*, Vienna–Munich 1980

Steingräber, Erich (ed.), *Deutsche Kunst der 20er und 30er Jahre*, Munich 1979

Taylor, Robert R., *The Word in Stone. The Role of Architecture in the National Socialist Ideology*, Berkeley–Los Angeles–London 1974

Teut, Anna, *Die Architektur im Dritten Reich 1933–1945*, Berlin–Frankfurt–Vienna 1967

Wingler, Hans M., *Das Bauhaus 1919–1933 Weimar, Dessau, Berlin und die Nachfolge in Chicago seit 1937*, Bramsche ¹1962, ²1968, ³1975

——, (ed.), *Kunstschulreform 1900–1933*, Berlin 1977

m. Italy: 1900–1945

Baumgarth, Christa, *Geschichte des Futurismus*, Reinbek 1966

Calvesi, Maurizio, *Il futurismo*, 3 vols, Milan 1967 (*L'arte moderna* 13–15)

Cat. *Il Razionalismo e l'architettura in Italia durante il Fascismo* ed. Silvia Danesi and Luciano Patetta, Venice 1976

Cat. '*Annitrenta. Arte e Cultura in Italia*', Milan 1982

Cennamo, Michele (ed.), *Materiali per l'analisi dell'architettura moderna. La prima Esposizione Italiana di Architettura Razionale*, Naples 1973

——, *Materiali per l'analisi dell'architettura moderna. Il M.I.A.R.*, Naples 1976

Ciucci, Giorgio, 'Il dibattito sull'architettura e la città fasciste, in: *Storia dell'arte italiana*, part II, vol. 3, ed. Federico Zeri, Turin 1982, pp. 263–378

De Seta, Cesare, *Architettura e città durante il fascismo*, Bari 1971

——, *La cultura architettonica in Italia tre le due guerre*, Bari ¹1972, Rome–Bari ²1983

——, *L'architettura del Novecento*, Turin 1981

Estermann-Juchler, Margrit, *Faschistische Staatsbaukunst. Zur ideologischen Funktion der öffentlichen Architektur im faschistischen Italien*, Cologne–Vienna 1982

Godoli, Ezio, *Il futurismo*, Rome–Bari 1983

Kruft, Hanno-Walter, 'Rationalismus in der Architektur–eine Begriffsklärung', *Architectura* 9, 1979, pp. 45–57 (repr. in: *Der Architekt*, April 1981, p. 176–81)

Mariani, Riccardo, *Fascismo e 'città nuove'*, Milan 1976

Martin, Marianne W., *Futurist Art and Theory 1909–1915*, Oxford ¹1968, ²1978

Nicoletti, Manfredi, *L'architettura liberty in Italia*, Rome–Bari 1978

Patetta, Luciano, 'Neo-futurismo, Novecento e Razionalismo. Termini di una polemica nel periodo fascista', *Controspazio*, 4–5, April–May 1971, pp. 87–96

n. Soviet Union: 1900–1945

Afanasjew, K. N., *Ideen – Projekte – Bauten. Sowjetische Architektur 1917 bis 1932*, Dresden 1973

BATER, James H., *The Soviet City*, London 1980

BORNGRÄBER, Christian, 'Ausländische Architekten in der UdSSR: Bruno Taut, die Brigaden Ernst May, Hannes Meyer und Hans Schmidt', in cat. *Wem gehört die Welt–Kunst und Gesellschaft in der Weimarer Republik*, Berlin 1977, pp. 109–42

Cat. *Art in Revolution. Soviet Art and Design Since 1917*, London 1971

Cat. *Tendenzen der Zwanziger Jahre*, Berlin 1977

Cat. *L'Espace urbain en URSS, 1917–1978*, Paris 1978

Cat. *Paris-Moscou 1917–1930*, Paris 1979

Cat. *Architettura nel paese dei Soviet 1917–1933. Arte di propaganda e costruzione della città*, Milan 1982

CHAN-MAGOMEDOW, Selim O., *Pioniere der sowjetischen Architektur. Der Weg zur neuen sowjetischen Architektur in den zwanziger und zu Beginn der dreißiger Jahre*, Vienna–Berlin 1983

CHAZANOVA, V. E., 'La teoria dell'architettura all'inizio degli anni '20', in: *Rassegna sovietica* XXIV, 1973, 2, pp. 85–124

COHEN, Jean Louis a.o., *URSS 1917–1978: La ville, l'architecture* (French–Ital.), Rome 1979

DE FEO, Vittorio, *URSS. Architettura 1917–1936*, Rome 1963

DE MICHELIS, Marco and PASINI, Ernesto, *La città sovietica 1925–1937*, Venice 1976

DRENGENBERG, Hans-Jürgen, *Die sowjetische Politik auf dem Gebiet der bildenden Kunst von 1917 bis 1934*, Berlin 1972

GRADOW, G. A., *Stadt und Lebensweise*, Berlin 1971

GRAY, Camilla, *The Russian Experiment in Art 1863–1922*, London 1962

JUNGHANNS, Kurt, 'Die Beziehungen zwischen deutschen und sowjetischen Architekten in den Jahren 1917 bis 1933', *Wissenschaftliche Zeitschrift der Humboldt-Universität zu Berlin* XVI, 1967, Heft 3

KOPP, Anatole, *Ville et Révolution. Architecture et urbanisme soviétiques des années vingt*, Paris 1967 (Engl. ed. New York 1970; Ital. 1972, ²1977)

——, *L'architecture de la période stalinienne*, Grenoble 1978

LISSITZKY, El, *Die Rekonstruktion der Architektur in der Sowjetunion*, Vienna 1930; new ed. entitled *Rußland: Architektur für eine Weltrevolution* (*Bauwelt Fundamente* 14), Berlin–Frankfurt–Vienna 1965

LODDER, Christina, *Russian Constructivism*, New Haven, Conn.–London 1983

QUILICI, Vieri, *L'architettura del costruttivismo*, Bari 1969, Rome–Bari ²1978

ROSA, Alberto Asor a.o., *Socialismo, città, architettura URSS 1917–1937. Il contributo degli architetti europei*, Rome 1971, ³1976

SENKEVITCH, Jr, Anatole, *Soviet Architecture 1917–1962. A Bibliographical Guide to Source Material*, Charlottesville, Va. 1974

SHIDKOVSKY, O. A., *Building in the USSR 1917–1932*, London 1971

STARR, S. Frederick, 'Writings from the 1960s on the Modern Movement in Russia', *Journal of the Society of Architectural Historians* XXX, 1971, pp. 170–78

——, 'OSA: The Union of Contemporary Architects', in: George Gibian and H. W. Tjalsma (ed.), *Russian Modernism. Culture and the Avant-Garde, 1900–1930*, Ithaca–London 1976, pp. 188–208

STENEBERG, Eberhard, *Russische Kunst Berlin 1919–1932*, Berlin 1969

VOGT, Adolf Max, *Russische und französische Revolutionsarchitektur 1917–1978. Zur Einwirkung des Marxismus und des Newtonismus auf die Bauweise*, Cologne 1974

WHITE, Paul M., *Soviet Urban and Regional Planning. A Bibliography with Abstracts*, London 1980

ZELINSKY, Bodo (ed.), *Russische Avantgarde 1907–1921. Vom Primitivismus zum Kunststruktivismus*, Bonn 1983

o. United States: 1900–1945

BROOKS, H. Allen, *The Prairie School. Frank Lloyd Wright and His Midwest Contemporaries*, Toronto 1972

CIUCCI, Giorgio a.o., *La città americana dalla guerra civile al New Deal*, Rome–Bari 1973 (Engl. ed. Cambridge, Mass. 1979–London 1980)

CONDIT, Carl W., *The Chicago School of Architecture*, Chicago–London 1964 (²1973)

——, *Chicago 1910–29. Building, Planning and Urban Technology*, Chicago–London 1973

GOLDBERGER, Paul, *The Skyscraper*, New York 1981

HITCHCOCK, Henry-Russell and JOHNSON, Philip, *The International Style: Architecture Since 1922*, New York 1932 (new ed. New York 1966)

KAUFMANN, Jr, Edgar (ed.), *The Rise of an American Architecture*, New York–London 1970

KIDNEY, Walter C., *The Architecture of Choice: Eclecticism in America 1880–1930*, New York 1974

Modern Architecture. International Exhibition, Museum of Modern Art, New York 1932 (facs. repr. New York 1969)

MUJICA, Francisco, *History of the Skyscraper*, Paris–New York 1929 (facs. repr. New York 1977)

ROBINSON, Cervin and HAAG BLETTER, Rosemarie, *Skyscraper Style. Art Deco New York*, New York 1975

p. Since 1945

BANHAM, Reyner, 'Revenge of the Picturesque: English Architectural Polemics, 1945–1965,' in: John Summerson (ed.), *Concerning Architecture. Essays on Architectural Writers and Writing presented to Nikolaus Pevsner*, London 1968, pp. 265–73

BLAKE, Peter, *Form Follows Fiasco. Why Modern Architecture Hasn't Worked*, Boston–Toronto 1977

BROLIN, Brent C., *The Failure of Modern Architecture*, New York–London 1976

Cat. *La presenza del passato*, Venice 1980

Cat. *Revision der Moderne. Postmoderne Architektur 1960–1980*, ed. Heinrich Klotz, Munich 1984

Cat. *Idee, Prozeß, Ergebnis. Die Reparatur und Rekonstruktion der Stadt*, Berlin 1984

CONFORTO, Cina a.o., *Il dibattito architettonico in Italia 1945–1975*, Rome 1977

DIAMONSTEIN, Barbaralee, American Architecture Now, New York 1980

HEYER, Paul, *Architects on Architecture. New Directions in America*, New York 1966

JENCKS, Charles A., *The Language of Post-Modern Architecture*, London 1977 (numerous eds and trans.)

KLOTZ, Heinrich, *Architektur in der Bundesrepublik*, Frankfurt–Berlin–Vienna 1977

——, *Moderne und Postmoderne. Architektur der Gegenwart 1960–1980*, Brunswick-Wiesbaden 1984

——, and CROOK, John W., *Conversations with Architects*, New York 1973

KULTERMANN, Udo, *Contemporary Architecture of Japan*, New York 1960

LÜCHINGER, Arnulf, *Structuralism in Architecture and Urban Planning*, Stuttgart 1980

NESTLER, Paolo and BODE, Peter M., *Deutsche Kunst seit 1960. Architektur*, Munich 1976

PEHNT, Wolfgang, *German Architecture 1960–1970*, New York–Washington, DC 1970

——, *Das Ende der Zuversicht. Architektur in diesem Jahrhundert. Ideen–Bauten–Dokumente*, Berlin 1983

PORTOGHESI, Paolo, *Dopo l'architettura moderna*, Rome–Bari 1980

——, *Postmodern. The Architecture of the Postindustrial Society*, New York 1982

SANDERSON, Warren (ed.), *International Handbook of Contemporary Developments in Architecture*, Westport, Conn.–London 1981

SPEIDEL, Manfred (ed.), *Japanische Architektur. Geschichte und Gegenwart*, Düsseldorf–Stuttgart 1983

SUN, Chuan-Wen, *Der Einfluß des chinesischen Konzeptes auf die moderne Architektur*, diss., Stuttgart 1982

VOGT, Adolf Max a.o., *Architektur 1940–1980*, Frankfurt–Vienna–Berlin 1980

3. Historical topics

a. Theory of the Orders

ACKERMAN, James S., 'The Tuscan/Rustic Order: A Study in the Metaphorical Language of Architecture', *Journal of the Society of Architectural Historians* XLII, 1983, pp. 15–34

BORSI, Franco, 'I cinque ordini architettonici di L. B. Alberti', in: *Studi e documenti di architettura*, n. 1. 1972, pp. 57–130

FORSSMAN, Erik, *Dorisch, jonisch, korinthisch. Studien über den Gebrauch der Säulenordnungen in der Architektur des 16.–18. Jahrhunderts*, Stockholm 1961

JUŘEN, Vladimir, 'Un Traité inédit sur les ordres d'architecture et le problème des sources du Libro IV de Serlio', *Monuments et Mémoires publiés par l'Académie des Inscriptions et Belles-Lettres* 64, 1981, pp. 195–239

SCHÜTTE, Ulrich, '"Als wenn eine ganze Ordnung da stünde...". Anmerkungen zum System der Säulenordnungen und seiner Auflösung im späten 18. Jahrhundert', *Zeitschrift für Kunstgeschichte* 44, 1981, pp. 15–37

THOENES, Christof and GÜNTHER, Hubertus, 'Gli ordini architettonici – Rinascità o invenzione?' in: congress proceedings *Roma & l'antico nell'arte a nella cultura del Cinquecento* (Rome 1982), Rome 1985, pp. 261–310 *b*. Vitruvian tradition in the Renaissance

BROWN, Frank E., 'Vitruvius and the Liberal Art of Architecture', *Bucknell Review* II, 4, 1963, pp. 99–107

BURGER, Fritz, 'Vitruv und die Renaissance', *Repertorium für Kunstwissenschaft* XXXII, 1909, pp. 199–218

CIAPPONI, Lucia A., 'Il "De Architectura" di Vitruvio nel primo umanesimo' (ms. Bodl. Auct. F. 5.7), *Italia medioevale e umanistica* III, 1960, pp. 59–99

CONANT, Kenneth J., 'The After-Life of Vitruvius in the Middle Ages', *Journal of the Society of Architectural Historians* XXVII, 1968, pp. 33–38

EBHARDT, Bodo, *Vitruvius. Die zehn Bücher der Architektur des Vitruv und ihre Herausgeber*, Berlin 1918 (facs. repr. New York 1962)

FONTANA, Paolo, 'Osservazioni intorno ai rapporti di Vitruvio colla teorica dell'architettura del Rinascimento', *Miscellanea di Storia dell'Arte in onore di Igino Benvenuto Supino*', Florence 1933, pp. 303–22

HAMBERG, Per Gustaf, 'Vitruvius, Fra Giocondo and the City Plan of Naples', *Acta Archaeologica* 36, 1965, pp. 105–125

HEITZ, Carol, 'Vitruve et l'architecture du haut moyen âge', *Settimane di Studio del Centro Italiano di Studi sull' Alto Medioevo* XXII, 2, 1974, pp. 725–57

HERSELLE KRINSKY, Carol, 'Seventy-Eight Vitruvius Manuscripts', *Journal of the Warburg and Courtauld Institutes* XXX, 1967, pp. 36–70

HORN-ONCKEN, Alste, *Über das Schickliche. Studien zur Geschichte der Architekturtheorie*, I, Göttingen 1967

KOCH, Herbert, *Vom Nachleben des Vitruv*, Baden-Baden 1951

MARÍAS, Fernando and BUSTAMANTE, Augustín, *Las ideas artísticas de El Greco*, Madrid 1981 (El Greco's marginalia to Barbaro's ed. of Vitruvius of 1556)

MARTINES, Giangiacomo, 'Hygino Gromatico: Fonti iconografiche antiche per la ricostruzione rinascimentale della città vitruviana', *Ricerche di Storia dell'Arte* 1–2, 1976, pp. 277–85

MORTET, V., *La mesure et les proportions des colonnes antiques*, Mélanges d'archéologie, 1st series, Paris 1914, pp. 49–65

PEETERS, Félix, 'Le "Codex Bruxellensis" 5253 (b) de Vitruve et la tradition manuscrite du "De Architectura"', *Mélanges dédiés à la mémoire de Félix Grat*, vol. II, Paris 1949, pp. 119–43

PELLATI, Francesco, 'Vitruvio nel Medioevo e nel Rinascimento', *Bollettino del Reale Istituto di Archeologia e Storia dell'Arte* V, 1932, pp. 15–36

ROVETTA, Alessandro, 'Cultura e codici vitruviani nel primo umanesimo milanese', *Arte Lombarda* 60, 1981, pp. 9–14

SCAGLIA, Gustina, 'A Translation of Vitruvius and Copies of Late Antique Drawings In Buonaccorso Ghiberti's Zibaldone', *Transactions of the American Philosophical Society*, vol. 69, part I, 1979, pp. 3–30

VAGNETTI, Luigi and MARCUCCI, Laura, 'Per una coscienza vitruviana. Regesto cronologico e critico delle edizioni…', *Studi e documenti di architettura* 8, 1978, pp. 11–195

WEYRAUCH, Sabine, *Die Basilika des Vitruv. Studien zu illustrierten Vitruvausgaben seit der Renaissance mit besonderer Berücksichtigung der Rekonstruktion der Basilika von Fano*, diss., Tübingen 1976

WIRTH, Karl-August, 'Bemerkungen zum Nachleben Vitruvs im 9. und 10. Jahrhundert und zu dem Schlettstädter Vitruv-Codex', *Kunstchronik* 20, 1967, pp. 281–91

ZOUBOV, Vassili Pavlovitch, 'Vitruve et ses commentateurs du XVI ᵉ siècle', *Colloque international de Royaumont 1957*, Paris 1960, pp. 67–90

c. Theory of proportion

Der 'vermessene' Mensch. Anthropometrie in Kunst und Wissenschaft, Munich 1973

GRAF, Hermann, *Bibliographie zum Problem der Proportionen. Literatur über Proportionen, Maß und Zahl in Architektur, bildender Kunst und Natur*, part I: *von 1800 bis zur Gegenwart*, Speyer 1958

NAREDI-RAINER, Paul von, 'Raster und Modul in der Architektur der italienischen Renaissance', *Jahrbuch für Ästhetik und allgemeine Kunstwissenschaft* XXIII, 2, 1978, pp. 139–62

———, *Architektur und Harmonie. Zahl, Maß und Proportion in der abendländischen Baukunst*, Cologne 1982

PANOFSKY, Erwin, 'Die Entwicklung der Proportionslehre als Abbild der Stilentwicklung', *Monatshefte für Kunstwissenschaft* XIV, 1921, pp. 188–219 (repr. in: Panofsky, *Aufsätze zu Grundfragen der Kunstwissenschaft*, Berlin 1964, pp. 169–204)

SPEICH, Nikolaus, *Die Proportionslehre des menschlichen Körpers. Antike, Mittelalter, Renaissance*, Andelfingen 1957

SCHOLFIELD, Peter Hugh, *The Theory of Proportion in Architecture*, Cambridge 1958

STEUBEN, Hans von, *Der Kanon des Polyklet*, Tübingen 1973

d. Theory of fortification in Europe: fifteenth to seventeenth century

DE LA CROIX, Horst, 'Military Architecture and the Radial City Plan in Sixteenth Century Italy', *Art Bulletin* XLII, 1960, pp. 263–90

———, 'The Literature on Fortifications in Renaissance Italy', *Technology and Culture* IV, 1963, pp. 30–50

———, *Military Considerations in City Planning: Fortifications*, New York 1972

DELBRÜCK, H., *Geschichte der Kriegskunst*, Berlin 1920

HALE, J. R., *Renaissance Fortification. Art or Engineering?*, London 1977

HUBER, Rudolf and RIETH, Renate (ed.), 'Festungen. Der Wehrbau nach Einführung der Feuerwaffen', *Glossarium Artis*, vol. 7, Tübingen 1979

HUGHES, Quentin, *Military Architecture*, London 1974

JÄHNS, Max, *Geschichte der Kriegswissenschaften, vornehmlich in Deutschland*, 3 vols, Munich–Leipzig 1889–91

MAGGIOROTTI, Leone A., *Architetti e architetture militari*, 3 vols, Rome 1935

MARCONI, Paolo a.o., *La città come forma simbolica. Studi sulla teoria dell'architettura nel Rinascimento*, Rome 1973

ROCCHI, Enrico, *Le fonti storiche dell'architettura militare*, Rome 1908

TOY, Sidney, *A History of Fortification from 3000 BC to AD 1700*, London 1955 (²1966)

e. Gothic Revival

BAUR, Christian, *Neugotik*, Munich 1981

Cat., *Le 'gothique' retrouvé avant Viollet-le-Duc*, Paris 1979

CLARK, Kenneth, *The Gothic Revival. An Essay in the History of Taste* (1928), 1974

EASTLAKE, Charles L., *A History of the Gothic Revival*, London 1872 (repr., ed. J. Mordaunt Crook, Leicester and New York 1970; ed. Alan Gowans, Watkins Glen, N.Y. ¹1975, ²1979)

FRANKL, Paul, *The Gothic. Literary Sources and Interpretations Through Eight Centuries*, Princeton 1960

GERMANN, Georg, *Gothic Revival in Europe and Britain*, London 1972

HESSE, Michael, *Von der Nachgotik zur Neugotik. Die Auseinandersetzung mit der Gotik in der französischen Sakralarchitektur des 16ten, 17ten und 18ten Jahrhunderts* (*Bochumer Schriften zur Kunstgeschichte*, vol. 3), Frankfurt–Bern–New York 1984

MACAULEY, James, *The Gothic Revival 1745–1845*, Glasgow–London 1975

PANOFSKY, Erwin, 'Das erste Blatt aus dem "Libro" Giorgio Vasaris; eine Studie über die Beurteilung der Gotik in der italienischen Renaissance mit einem Exkurs über zwei Fassadenprojekte Domenico Beccafumis', *Städel-Jahrbuch* VI, 1930, pp. 25–72 (Engl. trans. in: Panofsky, *Meaning in the Visual Arts*, Garden City, NY 1955, pp. 169ff.)

ROBSON-SCOTT, W. D., *The Literary Background of the Gothic Revival in Germany*, Oxford 1965

WITTKOWER, Rudolf, *Gothic versus Classic. Architectural Projects in Seventeenth Century Italy*, New York 1974

f. Rediscovery of Classical antiquity

Cat., *The Society of Dilettanti*, Weinreb & Breman, London 1968

Cat., *Civiltà del '700 a Napoli*, 2 vols, Florence 1979/80 (cf. esp. contributions by Mario Praz and Fausto Zevi)

Cat., *Pompei e gli architetti francesi dell'Ottocento*, Naples 1981

Cat. *Paris–Rome–Athènes. Le voyage en Grèce des architectes français aux XIXᵉ et XXᵉ siècles*, Paris 1982

CROOK, J. Mordaunt, *The Greek Revival. Neo-Classical Attitudes in British Architecture 1760–1870*, London 1972

ERICHSON, Johannes, *Antique und Grec. Studien zur Funktion der Antike in der Architektur und Kunsttheorie des Frühklassizismus*, diss. (1975), Cologne 1980

LABORDE, Léon de, *Athènes aux XVᵉ, XVIᵉ et XVIIᵉ siècles*, Paris 1854

McCARTHY, Michael, 'Documents on the Greek Revival in Architecture', *Burlington Magazine* CXIV, 1972, pp. 760–69

OMONT, Henri, *Athènes au XVIIᵉsiècle*, Paris 1898

PATON, J. Morton, *Chapters in Mediaeval and Renaissance Visitors to Greek Lands*, Princeton, NJ 1951

PEVSNER, Nikolaus and LANG, Suzanne, 'The Doric Revival' (first in: *The Architectural Review* CIV, 1948), in: Pevsner, *Studies in Art, Architecture and Design*, vol. I, London 1968, pp. 197–211

ROSENBLUM, Robert, *Transformations in Late Eighteenth Century Art* (1967), Princeton, NJ 1970

TUZET, Hélène, *La Sicile au XVIIIᵉ siècle vue par les voyageurs étrangers*, Strasbourg 1955

WEGNER, Max, *Land der Griechen*, Berlin 1943
WEISS, Roberto, *The Renaissance Discovery of Classical Antiquity*, Oxford 1969
——, *Medieval and Humanist Greek*, Padua 1977
WERNER, Peter, *Pompeji und die Wanddekoration der Goethezeit*, Munich 1970

g. Concepts of the garden

BACHMANN, Erich, 'Anfänge des Landschaftsgartens in Deutschland', *Zeitschrift für Kunstwissenschaft* V, 1951, pp. 203–28
BROWNELL, Morris R., *Alexander Pope and the Arts of Georgian England*, Oxford 1978
BUTTLAR, Adrian von, *Der Landschaftsgarten*, Munich 1980 (²1989)
——, *Der englische Landsitz 1715–1760. Symbol eines liberalen Weltentwurfs*, Mittenwald 1982
Cat. *Jardins en France 1760–1820. Pays d'illusion, Terre d'expériences*, Paris 1977
CLARK, H. F., 'Eighteenth Century Elysiums. The Role of "Association" in the Landscape Movement', *Journal of the Warburg and Courtauld Institutes* 6, 1943, pp. 165–89
ERDBERG, Eleanor von, *Chinese Influence on European Garden Structures*, Cambridge, Mass. 1936
ERICHSEN-FIRLE, Ursula, *Geometrische Kompositionsprinzipien in den Theorien der Gartenkunst des 16. bis 18. Jahrhunderts*, diss., Cologne 1971
FINKENSTAEDT, Thomas, 'Der Garten des Königs', in: *Probleme der Kunstwissenschaft*, vol. II, Berlin 1966, pp. 183–209
GERNDT, Siegmar, *Idealisierte Natur. Die literarische Kontroverse um den Landschaftsgarten des 18. und frühen 19. Jahrhunderts in Deutschland*, Stuttgart 1981
HALLBAUM, Franz, *Der Landschaftsgarten. Sein Entstehen und seine Einführung in Deutschland durch Friedrich Ludwig von Sckell*, Munich 1927
HARTMANN, Günter, *Die Ruine im Landschaftsgarten. Ihre Bedeutung für den frühen Historismus und die Landschaftsmalerei der Romantik*, Worms 1981
HAZLEHURST, F. Hamilton, *Jacques Boyceau and the French Formal Garden*, Athens 1966
HENNEBO, Dieter and HOFFMANN, Alfred, *Geschichte der deutschen Gartenkunst*, 3 vols, Hamburg 1962–1965 (facs. repr. 1981)
HIPPLE, Jr, Walter John, *The Beautiful, The Sublime, and The Picturesque in Eighteenth-Century Aesthetic Theory*, Carbondale 1957
HUNT, John Dixon and WILLIS, Peter (eds), *The Genius of the Place. The English Landscape Garden 1620–1820*, London 1975
HUSSEY, Christopher, *The Picturesque. Studies in a Point of View*, London 1927 (²1967)
LOVEJOY, Arthur O., 'The Chinese Origin of Romanticism' (first in: *Journal of English and Germanic Philology*, January 1933) in: *Lovejoy, Essays in the History of Ideas* (1948), Baltimore, MA–London ⁵1970, pp. 99–135
MACDOUGALL, Elisabeth B., 'John Claudius Loudon and the Early Nineteenth Century in Great Britain' (*Dumbarton Oaks Colloquium on the History of Landscape Architecture*, VI), Washington, DC 1980
—— and HAZLEHURST, F. Hamilton (ed.), *The French Formal Garden*, Washington DC 1974

PEVSNER, Nikolaus (ed.), *The Picturesque Garden and Its Influence Outside the British Isles*, Washington, DC 1974

ROMMEL, A., *Die Entstehung des klassischen französischen Gartens im Spiegel der Sprache*, Berlin 1954

WIEBENSON, Dora, *The Picturesque Garden in France*, Princeton, NJ 1978

WITTKOWER, Rudolf, 'English Neo-Palladianism, The Landscape Garden, China and the Enlightenment' (first in: *L'arte* 6, 1969), in: Wittkower, *Palladio and English Palladianism*, London 1974 (²1984), pp. 177–90

II. Sources

1. Anthologies: Middle Ages

BUCHER, François, Architector, *The Lodge Books and Sketchbooks of Medieval Architects*, vol. I, New York 1979

FRIEDLÄNDER, Paul, *Johannes von Gaza, Paulus Silentiarius. Kunstbeschreibungen justinianischer Zeit*, Berlin–Leipzig 1912 (repr. Hildesheim–New York 1969)

FRISCH, Teresa, G., *Gothic Art 1140–c. 1450*, Englewood Cliffs, NY 1971

LEHMANN-BROCKHAUS, Otto, *Die Kunst des 10. Jahrhunderts im Lichte der Schriftquellen*, Strasbourg 1935

——, *Schriftquellen zur Kunstgeschichte des 11. und 12. Jahrhunderts für Deutschland, Lothringen und Italien*, 2 vols, Berlin 1938

——, *Lateinische Schriftquellen zur Kunst in England, Wales und Schottland vom Jahre 901 bis zum Jahre 1307*, 5 vols, Munich 1955–60

MANGO, Cyril, *The Art of the Byzantine Empire 312–1453*, Englewood Cliffs, NY 1972

MIGNE, J.-P., *Patrologiae cursus completus, Series latina*, 4 vols. Paris 1844–64

MORTET, Victor, *Recueil de textes relatifs à l'histoire de l'architecture et à la condition des architectes en France au moyen âge*, 2 vols, Paris 1911–29

RICHTER, Jean Paul, *Quellen zur byzantinischen Kunstgeschichte*, Vienna 1897

SCHLOSSER, Julius von, *Schriftquellen zur Geschichte der karolingischen Kunst*, Vienna 1892

SHELBY, Lon R., *Gothic Design Techniques. The Fifteenth-Century Design Booklets of Mathes Roriczer and Hanns Schmuttermayer*, London–Carbondale, Ill. 1977

UNGER, Friedrich Wilhelm, *Quellen zur byzantinischen Kunstgeschichte*, Vienna 1878

VALENTINI, Roberto and ZUCCHETTI, Giuseppe, *Codice Topografico della Città di Roma*, 4 vols, Rome 1940–53

2. Anthologies: fifteenth to eighteenth century

BAROCCHI, Paola (ed.), *Trattati d'arte del Cinquecento*, 3 vols, Bari 1960–62

——, *Scritti d'arte del Cinquecento*, 3 vols, Milan–Naples 1971–77

BORSI, Franco a.o., *Il disegno interrotto. Trattati medicei d'architettura*, 2 vols, Florence 1980

BOTTARI, Giovanni Gaetano, *Raccolta di Lettere sulla Pittura, Scultura ed Architettura... dei secoli XV, XVI e XVII*, 7 vols, Rome 1754–73; ed. Stefano Ticozzi, 8 vols, Milan 1822–25 (repr. of 1822–25 ed. Hildesheim–New York 1976)

BRUSCHI, Arnaldo (ed.), *Scritti rinascimentali di architettura*, Milan 1978

DE FUSCO, Renato, *Il Codice dell'Architettura, Antologia di trattatisti*, Naples 1968

FICHET, Françoise (ed.), *La théorie architecturale à l'âge classique. Essai d'anthologie critique*, Brussels 1979

GAYE, Giovanni (ed.), *Carteggio inedito d'artisti dei secoli XIV, XV, XVI*, 3 vols, Florence 1839–40 (facs. repr. Turin 1961)

LEMONNIER, Henry, *Procès-Verbaux de l'Académie Royale d'Architecture*, 10 vols, Paris 1911–29

PUPPI, Lionello, *Scrittori vicentini d'architettura del secolo XVI*, Vicenza 1973

SÁNCHEZ-CANTÓN, F. J., *Fuentes literarias para la Historia del Arte Español*, 5 vols, Madrid 1923–41

3. Anthologies: nineteenth and twentieth centuries

BAROCCHI, Paola (ed.), *Testimonianze e polemiche figurative in Italia. Dal Divisionismo al Novecento*, Messina–Florence 1974

BOWLT, John (ed.), *Russian Art of the Avant-Garde. Theory and Criticism 1902–1934*, New York 1976

CARUSO, L. (ed.), *Manifesti futuristi 1909–1944*, 4 vols, Florence 1980

CECCARELLI, Paolo (ed.), *La costruzione della città sovietica*, Padua ¹1970, ³1977

CONRADS, Ulrich (ed.), 'Programme und Manifeste zur Architektur des 20. Jahrhunderts' (*Bauwelt Fundamente* I), Gütersloh–Berlin–Munich ¹1964, ²1971

DAL CO, Francesco, *Teorie del moderno. Architettura Germania 1880–1920*, Rome–Bari 1982

GASSNER, Hubertus and GILLEN, Eckhardt, *Zwischen Revolutionskunst und sozialistischem Realismus. Dokumente und Kommentare. Kunstdebatten in der Sowjetunion von 1917 bis 1934*, Cologne 1979

GIFFORD, Don (ed.), *The Literature of American Architecture*, New York 1966

KOPP, Anatole, *Architecture et mode de vie. Textes des années vingt en U.R.S.S.*, Grenoble 1979

MUMFORD, Lewis (ed.), *Roots of Contemporary American Architecture* (1952), New York 1972

PATETTA, Luciano, *L'architettura in Italia 1919–1943. Le polemiche*, Milan 1972

POSENER, Julius (ed.), *Anfänge des Funktionalismus. Von Arts und Crafts zum Deutschen Werkbund* (*Bauwelt Fundamente* II), Berlin–Frankfurt–Vienna 1964

ROTH, Leyland M. (ed.), *America Builds. Source Documents in American Architecture and Planning*, New York 1983

SCRIVO, Luigi, *Sintesi del futurismo. Storia e documenti*, Rome 1968

4. Sources by author to 1945

ADAM, John, *Vitruvius Scoticus: Being a Collection of Plans and Sections of Public Buildings, Noblemen's, Gentlemen's Houses in Scotland: Principally from the Design of the late William Adam*, Edinburgh n.d. (facs. repr. of 1812 ed. Edinburgh 1980)

ADAM, Robert, *Ruins of the Palace of the Emperor Diocletian at Spalatro in Dalmatia*, London 1764

ADAM, Robert and James, *The Works of Architecture*, London 1773–78; vol. II, 1799; vol. III, 1822 (repr. 1902, 1931, 1959, 1975, 1981)

ADDISON, Joseph and STEELE, Richard (ed.), *The Spectator* (1711–14)

ADLER, Dankmar, 'Light in Tall Office Buildings', *Engineering Magazine* 4, 3 September 1892, pp. 171–86

——, 'The Influence of Steel Construction and Plate Glass Upon Style' in: *The Proceedings of the Thirtieth Annual Convention of the American Institute of Architects*, 1896, pp. 58–64

ALBERTI, Leon Battista, *Opere volgari*, ed. Cecil Grayson, 3 vols, Bari 1960–73

——, *Kleinere kunsttheoretische Schriften*, ed. Hubert Janitschek, Vienna 1877 (facs. repr. Osnabrück 1970)

——, 'Descriptio Urbis Romae', published in: R. Valentini and G. Zucchetti, *Codice Topografico della Città di Roma*, vol. IV, Rome 1953, pp. 209–22; L. Vagnetti, 'La "Descriptio Urbis Romae",' in *Quaderno* n. I, Università degli Studi di Genova. Facoltà di Architettura, 1968, pp. 25–88

——, *De Re Aedificatoria*, Florence 1485 (facs. repr. Munich 1975; cf. Hans-Karl Lück (revised), '*Alberti-Index*': *Index Verborum*, 3 vols, Munich 1975ff.). First Ital. ed. Cosimo Bartoli, Florence 1550. Critical ed. L. B. Alberti, *L'architettura* (Lat.-Ital.), ed. Giovanni Orlandi, 2 vols, Milan 1966

ALBERTI, Romano, *Origine, et progresso dell'Academia del Dissegno*, Pavia 1604 (facs. repr. Bologna 1978)

ALESSI, Galeazzo, *Il Libro dei Misteri. Progetto di pianificazione urbanistica, architettonica e figurativa del Sacro Monte di Varallo in Valsesia (1565–1569)*, ed. Stefania Stefani Perrone, 2 vols, Bologna 1974

——, *Libro di Fortificatione in modo di compendio...*, Ms., Modena, Biblioteca Estense, Fondo Campori (γ.L.11.1.), c. 1564–70

ALGAROTTI, Francesco, 'Saggio sopra l'architettura' (1756), first in: Francesco Algarotti, *Opere varie*, Venice 1757; Algarotti, *Opere* (17 vols, Venice 1791–94), III, 1791, pp. 3–52; Francesco Algarotti, *Saggi*, ed. Giovanni da Pozzo, Bari 1963, pp. 29–52

——, 'Lettere sopra l'architettura' (1742–1763), in: Algarotti, *Opere*, vol. VIII, 1794, pp. 209ff.

ALGHISI, Galasso, *Della fortificazioni... libre tre*, Venice 1570

ALLATIOS, Leo, *De Templis Graecorum recentioribus* and *De narthece ecclesiae veteris*, Paris–Cologne 1645

AMICHEVOLI, Costanzo, *Architettura civile ridotta a metodo facile e breve*, Turin 1675

AMMANNATI, Bartolomeo, *La Città. Appunti per un trattato*, ed. Mazzino Fossi, Rome 1970

ANDRADE, Domingo de, *Excelencias antiguedad, y nobleza de la Arquitectura...*, Santiago 1695

ANDRÉ, Yves (Père), *Essai sur le beau, ou l'on examine en quoi consiste précisément le beau dans le physique, dans le moral, dans les ouvrages d'esprit et dans la musique*, Paris 1741 (1759, 1763, 1824, 1827, 1856)

(anon.), 'Dimostrazioni fatte a penna e Regole manoscritte per formar bene de Cinque Ordini d'Architettura' (Paris, Bibl. Nat., ms. ital. 473); Vladimir Juřen, 'Un traité inédit sur les ordres d'architecture et le problème des sources du Libro IV de

Serlio', *Monuments et Mémoires publiés par l'Académie des Inscriptions et Belles-Lettres* 64, 1981, pp. 195–239

ARDEMANS, Teodoro, *Ordenanza de Madrid y otras diferentes…*, Madrid 1720 (1754, 1760, 1765, 1791, 1796, 1798, 1820, 1830, 1844, 1848)

ARFE Y VILLAFAÑE, Juan de, *De varia commensuración para la Esculptura y Architectura*, Seville 1585 (books III and IV: 1587); further eds. 1675, 1736, 1763, 1773, 1795, 1806; facs. reprs. of 1585 ed., ed. Antonio Bonet Correa, Madrid 1974 (contains only Books I and II); ed. Francisco Iñiguez, Valencia 1979 (also contains Books III and IV)

ARGENVILLE, Antoine-Joseph Dézallier d', *La théorie et la pratique du jardinage…*, Paris 1709 (1713, 1722, 1732, 1747, 1760); facs. repr. of 1760 ed., ed. Hans Foramitti, Hildesheim–New York 1972

ARGENVILLE, Antoine-Nicolas Dézallier d', *Vies des fameux architectes depuis la Renaissance des arts*, Paris 1787 (facs. repr. Geneva 1972)

ASHBEE, Charles Robert, *An Endeavour Towards the Teaching of John Ruskin and William Morris*, Campden 1901 (facs. repr. New York 1977)

———, *Craftmanship in Competitive Industry*, Campden 1908 (facs. repr. New York–London 1977)

———, *Should we Stop Teaching Art?*, London 1911 (facs. repr. New York 1977)

ASPLUND, Gunnar a.o., *Acceptura-Manifesto*, Stockolm 1931

ATTIRET, Jean-Denis, *A Particular of the Emperor of China's Gardens near Pekin*, London 1752

BACHAUMONT, L.-Petit de, *Essai sur la peinture, la sculpture, et l'architecture*, Paris 1751 (²1752); facs. repr. of 1752 ed. Geneva 1971

BACON, Francis, *Essays* (first 1597); cf. Bacon's works, ed. J. Spedding, R. L. Ellis and D. D. Heath, 14 vols, London 1857–74 (facs. repr. 1959ff.), vol. 6, 1963

———, *Nova Atlantis*, ed. William Rawley, London 1638 (numerous eds)

BADESLADE, J. and ROCQUE, J., *Vitruvius Britannicus. Volume the Fourth…*, London 1739 (facs. repr., ed. John Harris, New York 1967)

BARBARO, Daniele, *I dieci libri dell'architettura di M. Vitruvio tradutti e commentati da Monsignor Barbaro, eletto patriarca d'Aquileggia*, Venice 1556; enlarged ed., Venice 1567; Latin ed. *M. Vitruvii Pollionis De Architectura Libri Decem, cum commentariis Danielis Barbari*, Venice 1567

———, *La pratica della perspettiva… opera molto utile a Pittori, Scultori e ad Architetti*, Venice 1568/69 (facs. repr. Bologna 1980)

BARCA, Pietro Antonio, *Avvertimenti e regole circa l'architettura civile, Scultura, Pittura, Prospettiva e Architettura militare*, Milan 1620

BARDI, Pietro Maria, *Rapporto sull'architettura per Mussolini*, Rome 1931

BARTHÉLÉMY, Jean-Jacques, *Voyage du jeune Anacharsis en Grèce, dans le milieu du quatrième siècle avant l'ère vulgaire*, 7 vols, Paris 1788 (also *Recueil de cartes géographiques, plans, vues et médailles de l'ancienne Grèce relatifs au voyage du jeune Anacharsis*, Paris 1788); Paris ²1789; some 30 eds and trans. up to the mid-19th century

BARTHOLOMEW, Alfred, *Specifications for Practical Architecture, Preceded by an Essay on the Decline of Excellence in the Structure and in the Science of Modern English Buildings: With the Proposal for Remedies for these Defects*, London 1840

(^{2}1846)

BEHRENS, Peter, *Ein Dokument deutscher Kunst. Die Ausstellung der Künsterkolonie in Darmstadt 1901*, Munich 1901

——, 'Einfluß der Zeit- und Raumausnutzung auf moderne Formentwicklung', in: *Jahrbuch des Deutschen Werkbundes* 1914, pp. 7–10

BÉLIDOR, Bernard Forest de, *Architecture Hydraulique, ou l'art de conduire, d'élever, et de menager les eaux*, 4 vols, Paris 1737–53

BELLAMY, Edward, *Looking backward 2000–1887*, London 1889; ed. Frederic R. White, New York 1956

BELLICARD, J. Ch. see COCHIN, Ch. N.

BELLORI, Giovanni Pietro, *Le vite de'pittori, scultori e architetti moderni*, Rome 1672 (preceded by *L'idea del pittore, dello scultore, e dell'architetto scelta dalla bellezze naturali superiore alla Natura*, 1664); ed. Eugenio Battisti, Genoa 1967; ed. Evelina Borea, Turin 1976

BELLUZZI (Bellucci, Belici), Giovanni Battista, 'Il Trattato delle fortificazioni di terra', ed. Daniela Lamberini, in: Franco Borsi, *Il disegno interrotto. Trattati medicei d'architettura*, Florence 1980, pp. 373 ff.

——, *Nuova inventione di fabricar fortezze, di varie forme...*, Venice 1598

——, *Diario autobiografico* (1535–1541), ed. Pietro Egidi, Naples 1907 (facs. repr. Bologna 1975)

BENJAMIN, Asher, *The Works of Asher Benjamin From the First Editions*, ed. Everard M. Upjohn, 7 vols, New York 1972

——, *The Country Builder's Assistant: containing a collection of new designs of carpentry and architecture...*, Greenfield 1797 (^{2}1798; ^{3}1800; ^{4}1805)

——, *The American Builder's Companion: or, a New System of Architecture particularly adapted to the present style of building in the United States of America*, Boston, Mass. 1806 (^{2}1811; ^{3}1816; ^{4}1820; ^{5}1826; ^{6}1827); facs. repr. of 1827 ed., ed. William Morgan, New York 1969

——, *The Rudiments of Architecture: Being a Treatise on Practical Geometry, on Grecian and Roman Mouldings...*, Boston, Mass. 1814 (^{2}1820)

——, *Practice of Architecture. Containing the five orders of architecture and an additional column and entablature...*, New York 1833 (^{2}1835; ^{3}1836; ^{4}1840; ^{5}1847; ^{7}1851)

BERGMANN, L., *Die Schule der Baukunst. Handbuch*, 2 vols, Leipzig 1853

——, *Zehn Tafeln Säulen-Ordnungen nebst Construktion der architektonischen Glieder*, Leipzig n.d. (1853)

BERGMÜLLER, Johann Georg, *Nachbericht zu der Erklärung des geometrischen Maasstabes der Säulenordnungen*, Augsburg 1752

BERKELEY, George, *Alciphron, or the Minute Philosopher*, London 1732

BERKENHOUT, John (?), *The Ruins of Paestum or Posidonia, a City of Magna Graecia...*, London 1767

BERLAGE, Hendrik Petrus, 'Bouwkunst an impressionisme' in: *Architectura* 2, 1894, pp. 93–95, 98–100, 105f., 109f. (repr. in: Manfred Bock, *Anfänge einer neuen Architektur*, 's-Gravenhage-Wiesbaden 1983, pp. 383–90)

——, *Gedanken über Stil in der Baukunst*, Berlin 1905

——, *Grundlagen und Entwicklung der Architektur*, Berlin 1908

BERNINI, Gian Lorenzo (M. de Chantelou), *Journal du voyage du Cav. Bernini en France*, ed. L. Lalanne, Paris 1885 (repr. Clamecy 1981); German trans. by Hans Rose: *Tagebuch des Herrn von Chantelou über die Reise des Cavaliere Bernini nach Frankreich*, Munich 1919

BERRETTINI *see* CORTONA, Pietro da

BERRUGUILLA, Juan Garcia, *Verdadera practica de las resoluciones de la geometria, dobre las tres dimensiones para un perfecto architecto*, Madrid 1747 (facs. repr. ed. Santiago Garma Pons, Murcia 1979)

BERTANI, Giovanni Battista, *Gli oscuri e difficili passi dell'opera jonica di Vitruvio*, Mantua 1558

BERTOTTI SCAMOZZI, Ottavio, *Il Forestiere istruito... della Città di Vicenza*, Vicenza 1761 (facs. repr. Bologna 1974)

——, *Le fabbriche e i disegni di Andrea Palladio*, 4 vols, Vicenza 1776–83 ('1796; facs. repr. ed. J. Quentin Hughes, Venice–London 1968)

BEUTH, Peter (ed.), *Vorbilder für Fabrikanten und Handwerker*, Berlin 1821–37 ('1863)

BICKNELL, Amos Jackson (ed.), *Bicknell's Village Builder. Elevations and plans for cottages, villas, suburban residences, farm houses...*, New York 1870 ('1886); *Supplement to Bicknell's Village Builder, containing eighteen modern designs for country and suburban houses of moderate cost...*, New York (c. 1871); facs. repr. of whole work (New York 1878) New York 1979

BLANC, Charles, *Grammaire des arts de dessin: Architecture, sculpture, peinture*, Paris 1867

BLANKENBURG, Friedrich von *see* SULZER, Johann-Georg

BLONDEL, François, *Cours d'architecture enseigné dans l'Académie Royale d'Architecture*, Part I, Paris 1675; Parts II–V, Paris 1683 (facs. repr. of 2nd ed. of 1698, Hildesheim–New York 1982)

BLONDEL, Jacques-François, *De la Distribution des Maisons de Plaisance, et de la Décoration des édifices en general*, 2 vols, Paris 1737–38 (facs. repr. 1967)

——, *Architecture françois, ou Recueil des plans, élévations, coupes et profils des églises, maisons royales, palais, hôtels et édifices les plus considérables de Paris*, 4 vols, Paris 1752–1756 (repr. Paris 1904)

——, *Discours sur la nécessité de l'étude de l'architecture*, Paris 1754 (facs. repr. Geneva 1973)

——, *Cours d'architecture ou traité de la Décoration, Distribution & Construction des bâtiments*, 6 vols of text and 3 vols of plates, Paris 1771–77 (vols 5 and 6 by Pierre Patte)

BLOX(H)AM, Matthew Holbeche, *The Principles of Gothic Architecture Elucidated by Question and Answer*, London 1829 (up to 1882, 11 constantly enlarged eds; later under the title *The Principles of Gothic Ecclesiastical Architecture*)

BLUM, Hans, *Quinque columnarum exacta descriptio*, Zürich 1550

——, *Architectura antiqua das ist Wahrhaffte und eigentliche Contrafacturen ettlich alter und schönen Gebeuwen...*, Zürich 1561

BÖCKLER, Georg Andreas, *Manuale Architecturae Militaris oder Hand-Büchlein über die Fortification*, Frankfurt 1645

——, *Compendium Architecturae civilis*, Frankfurt 1648

——, *Architectura civilis Nova & Antiqua*, Frankfurt 1663 (repr. 1684)

——, *Architectura curiosa nova. Das ist: Neue Ergötzliche Sinn- und Kunstreiche auch nützliche Bau- und Wasser-Kunst...*, Nuremberg 1664 (facs. repr. with introduction by Renate Wagner-Rieger, Graz 1968); Latin ed. 1664 and 1701; 2nd German ed. 1702–04

——, *Schola Militaris Moderna*, Frankfurt 1668 (^{2}1685, ^{3}1706)

——, *Die Baumeisterin Pallas, oder der in Teutschland erstandene Palladius, das ist: Des vortrefflich-Italiänischen Baumeisters Andreae Palladii Zwey Bücher von der Bau-Kunst...*, Nuremberg 1698 (facs. repr. Nördlingen 1991)

BOETTICHER, Carl, *Die Tektonik der Hellenen*, 2 vols, Potsdam 1844–52

——, 'Das Prinzip der hellenischen und germanischen Bauweise hinsichtlich der Übertragung in die Bauweise unserer Tage', *Allgemeine Bauzeitung* 11, 1846, pp. 111–26

BOFFRAND, Germain, *Livre d'architecture contenant les principes généraux de cet art*, Paris 1745 (facs. repr. with *La figure equestre de Louis XIV* [1743], Farnborough 1969)

BOISSERÉE, Sulpiz, *Ansichten, Risse und einzelne Theile des Doms von Köln...*, Stuttgart 1821; *Geschichte und Beschreibung des Doms von Köln...*, Stuttgart 1823 (Munich ^{3}1842); a combined facs. repr. of eds of 1821 and 1842, Cologne 1979

BORROMEO, Carlo, *Instructiones Fabricae et Supellectilis Ecclesiasticae Libri II*, Milan 1577; Ital. ed. S. Carlo Borromeo, *Arte Sacra (De Fabrica Ecclesiae)*, ed. C. Castiglioni and Ca. Marcora, Milan 1952; crit. ed. by Paolo Barocchi, in: *Trattati d'arte del Cinquecento*, vol. III, Bari 1962, pp. 1–113

BORROMINI, Francesco, *La Chiesa e Fabrica della Sapienza di Roma*, ed. Sebastiano Giannini, Rome 1720 (facs. repr. ed. Alessandro Artini, no place, no date)

——, *Opus Architectonicum (Opera... cavata da'suoi originali cioè l'Oratorio, e Fabrica per l'Abitazione De PP. del'Oratorio di S. Filippo Neri di Roma...)*, Rome 1725; ed. Paolo Portoghesi, Rome 1964

BOSSE, Abraham, *Traité des manières de dessiner les ordres d'architecture antique en toutes leurs parties*, Paris 1664

BOULLÉE, Etienne-Louis, *Architecture. Essai sur l'art*; ed. Helen Rosenau: *Boullée's Treatise on Architecture*, London 1953; ed. Jean-Marie Pérouse de Montclos: Etienne-Louis Boullée. *Architecture. Essai sur l'art*, Paris 1968 (with further writings by Boullée)

BOYCEAU, Jacques, *Traité du jardinage selon les raisons de la nature et de l'art*, Paris 1638

BRAMANTE, Donato (?), ('Prospectivo Melanese'), *Antiquariae Prospettiche Romane*, c. 1500

BRANCA, Giovanni, *Manuale d'Architettura, breve, e risoluta Pratica, diviso in sei libri*, Ascoli 1629 (Rome 1718, 1757, 1772, 1781, 1783, 1784, 1786); facs. repr. of 1772 ed., Florence 1975

BRANDON, Raphael and Joshua Arthur, *An Analysis of Gothick Architecture: Illustrated by a Series of Upwards of Seven Hundred Examples of Doorways, Windows etc.*, 2 vols, London 1847

BRISEUX, Charles-Etienne, *L'architecture moderne, ou l'Art de bien bâtir pour toutes sortes des personnes*, 2 vols, Paris 1728

——, *L'Art de bâtir des maisons de campagne, où l'on traite de leur distribution, de leur construction, & leur décoration*, 2 vols, Paris 1743 (^{2}1761; facs. repr. 1966)

———, *Traité du Beau Essentiel dans les arts Appliqué particulièrement à l'Architecture…*, Paris 1752 (facs. repr. Geneva 1974)

BULLANT, Jean, *Reigle généralle d'architecture des cinque manières de colonnes, à scavoir toscane, dorique, ionique, corinthe et composite et enrichi de plusieurs autres à l'exemple de l'antique suivant les reigles et doctrine de Vitruve…*, Paris 1564 ([2]1568, [3]1619)

BULLET, Pierre, *L'architecture pratique, qui comprend le détail du toise & du Devis des ouvrages…*, Paris 1691 (facs. repr. Geneva 1973); several eds in 18th century

BUNSEN, Christian Carl Josias von, *Die Basiliken des christlichen Roms nach ihrem Zusammenhange mit Idee und Geschichte der Kirchenbaukunst*, 2 vols, Munich 1842–44

BURKE, Edmund, *A Philosophical Enquiry into the Origin of our Ideas of the Sublime and Beautiful*, London 1757; [2]1759 (facs. repr. Menston 1970); ed. J. T. Boulton 1958

BURLINGTON, Richard Lord, *Fabbriche antique disegnate da Andrea Palladio Vicentino*, London 1730 (facs. repr. 1969)

BURNHAM, Daniel H. and BENNETT, Edward, *The Plan of Chicago*, Chicago 1909 (facs. repr. New York 1970)

BUSSLER, Ernst Friedrich (ed.), *Verzierungen aus dem Alterthume*, 21 Hefte, Potsdam–Berlin 1806ff.

CALVO, Fabio (Italian trans. of Vitruvius), (ed.), Vicenzo Fontana and Paolo Morachiello, *Vitruvio e Raffaello. Il 'De Architectura' di Vitruvio nella traduzione inedita di Fabio Calvo ravennate*, Rome 1975

CAMPANELLA, Tommaso, *Civitas Solis ('La Città del Sole')* (1602), in: *Scritti scelti di Giordano Bruno e Tommaso Campanella*, ed. Luigi Firpo, Turin [2]1968, pp. 405–64

CAMPBELL, Colen, *Vitruvius Britannicus, or The British Architect*, vol. I, London 1715; vol. II, London 1717; vol. III, London 1725 (facs. repr. with intro. by John Harris, New York 1967)

———, *Andrea Palladio's Five Orders of Architecture…*, London 1728 ([2]1729)

CANCRIN, Franz Ludwig von, *Grundlehren der Bürgerlichen Baukunst nach Theorie und Erfahrung vorgetragen*, Gotha 1792

CAPORALI, Giovan Battista, *Architettura con il suo commento et figure, Vetruvio in volgar lingua reportato per M. Gianbatista Caporali di Perugia*, Perugia 1536 (facs. repr. Perugia 1985)

CAPRA, Alessandro, *La nuova Architettura civile, e militare*, Bologna 1678 (Cremona 1717)

CARAMUEL DE LOBKOWITZ, Juan, *Architectura civil recta, y obliqua, considerada y dibuxada en el Templo de Ierusalem… promivada a suma perfecion en el Templo y Palacio de S. Lorenco cerca del Escurial*, 3 vols, Vigevano 1678

CASTELL, Robert, *The Villas of the Ancients Illustrated*, London 1728 (facs. repr. ed. John Dixon Hunt, New York–London 1982)

CASTRIOTTO, Jacomo see MAGGI, Girolammo

CATANEO, Pietro, *I quattro primi libri di architettura*, Venice 1554 (facs. repr. Ridgewood, NJ 1964)

———, *L'architettura*, Venice 1567 (facs. repr. Bologna 1982)

CAUMONT, Arcisse de, 'Sur L'architecture du moyen-âge particulièrement en Normandie', *Mémoires de la Société des Antiquaires de Normandie* I, 1824, part 2

———, *Cours d'antiquités monumentales*, Paris 1830–41

CAUS, Salomon de, *Hortus Palatinus*, Frankfurt 1620 (facs. repr. Worms 1980)

CAYLUS, Anne-Claude-Philippe de Tubières, Comte de, *Recueil d'Antiquités égyptiennes, étrusques, grecques et romaines*, 7 vols, Paris 1752–67

———, *Abhandlungen zur Geschichte und zur Kunst*, 2 vols, Altenburg 1768–69

CELLINI, Benvenuto, *Della architettura*, in: *Cellini, La Vita, i trattati, i discorsi*, Rome 1967, pp. 565–70

CENNINI, Cennino, *Il libro dell'Arte*, ed. Licisco Magagnato, Vicenza 1971

CERDÁ, Ildefonso, *Teoria general de la Urbanización y aplicación de sus principios y doctrinas a la Reforma y Ensanche de Barcelona*, 2 vols, Madrid 1867 (facs. repr. Barcelona 1968)

CESARIANO, Cesare, *De Lucio Vitruvio Pollione de Architectura libri decem traducti de Latino in Vulgare affigurati, commentati...*, Como 1521 (facs. repr. Munich 1969; Milan 1981)

CÉSPEDES, Pablo de, *Discurso sobre el Templo de Salomón* (1604); ed. Cean Bermudez in: *Diccionario histórico de los más ilustres profesores de las Bellas Artes en España*, V, Madrid 1800, pp. 316ff.

CHAMBERS, William, *Designs of Chinese Buildings, Furniture, Dresses, Machines, and Utensiles...*, London 1757 (facs. reprs. Farnborough 1970; New York 1980)

———, *Plans, Elevations, Sections, and Perspective Views of the Gardens and Buildings at Kew in Surrey*, London 1763 (facs. repr. Farnborough 1966)

———, *A Treatise on Civil Architecture...*, London 1759; ²1768; 3rd ed. under the title *A Treatise on the Decorative Part of Civil Architecture*, London 1791 (facs. repr. with intro. by John Harris, New York 1968; Farnborough 1969)

———, *A Dissertation on Oriental Gardening*, London 1772 (facs. repr. with intro. by John Harris, 1972); enlarged ed. with *An Explanatory Discourse...*, London 1773; French ed. London 1772

CHANDLER, Richard, *Travels in Asia Minor: or: an account of a tour made at the expense of the Society of Dilettanti*, Dublin 1775 (ed. Edith Clay, London 1971)

———, *Travels in Greece: or an account of a tour made at the expense of the Society of Dilettanti*, Oxford 1776

———, and REVETT, Nicholas and PARS, William, *Ionian Antiquities, published with permission of the Society of Dilettanti*, London 1769; *Antiquities of Jonia, published by the Society of Dilettanti*, London 1797

CHERNIKOV, Yakov G., *Konstruktsiya arkhitekturnykh i mashinal'nykh form*, Leningrad 1931 (excerpts in: John E. Bowlt (ed.) *Russian Art of the Avant-Garde. Theory and Criticism 1902–1934*, New York 1976)

———, *Arkhitekturnyye fantasii*, Leningrad 1933

CHOISY, Auguste, *Histoire de l'architecture*, 2 vols, Paris 1899; several eds; facs. repr. of the 1899 ed., Geneva–Paris 1982

COCHIN, Ch. N. and BELLICARD, J. Ch., *Observations sur les antiquités d'Herculanum*, Paris 1754 (²1755)

COECKE VAN AELST, Pieter, *Die inventie der columnen met haren coronementen ende maten*, Antwerp 1539 (facs. repr. in: Rudi Rolf, *Pieter Coecke van Aelst en zijn architektuuruitgaves van 1539*, Amsterdam 1978)

COLE, Benjamin and HOPPUS, Edward, *Andrea Palladio's Architecture in Four Books...*, London 1733–35 (1736)

COLONNA, Francesco, *Hypnerotomachia Poliphili, ubi humana omnia non nisi somnium esse docet*, Venice 1499 (several modern facs. eds.); crit. ed. by Giovanni Pozzi and Lucia A. Ciapponi, 2 vols, Padua 1964

COMOLLI, Angelo, *Bibliografia storico-critica dell'Architettura civile*, 4 vols, Rome 1788–92

CONTA, Carl Friedrich Anton von, *Grundlinien der bürgerlichen Baukunst nach Herrn Durand*, Halle 1806

CORDEMOY, Jean-Louis de, *Nouveau Traité de toute l'Architecture ou l'art de bastir; utile aux entrepreneurs et aux ouvriers... avec un Dictionnaire des termes d'Architecture*, Paris 1706 (2nd enlarged ed. with replies to Amédée-François Frézier and *Dissertation sur la manière dont les églises doivent être bâties*, Paris 1714; facs. repr. of this ed. 1966)

CORNARO, Alvise (Writings); in: Giuseppe Fiocco, *Alvise Cornaro. Il suo tempo e le sue opere*, Vicenza 1965

——, *Scritti sull'architettura*, ed. Paolo Carpeggiani, Padua 1980

CORNEWEYLE, Robert, *The Maner of Fortificacion of Cities, Townes, Castelles and Other Places* (1559; Ms., British Museum, Add. Ms. 28030), ed. Martin Biddle, Richmond, Surrey 1972

CORTESI, Paolo, *De Cardinalatu, Città Cortesiana 1510* (Latin–Engl. ed. of book II, chapter 2 'De Domo Cardinalis', in: Kathleen Weil-Garris and John D'Amico, 'The Renaissance Cardinal's Ideal Palace...', *Memoirs of the American Academy in Rome* XXXV, 1980, pp. 69ff.)

CORTONA, Pietro da (Pietro Berrettini) and OTTONELLI, Giovanni Domenico, *Trattato della pittura, e scultura, uso et abuso loro*, Florence 1652 (ed. Vittorio Casale, Treviso 1973)

CRANE, Walter, *The Claims of Decorative Art*, London 1892

——, *The Bases of Design*, London 1899

——, *Line and Form*, London 1900

CUVILLIÉS, François, *Morceaux de caprices à divers usages*, Munich–Paris 1738, 1745, 1756 (continued by his son up to 1799); part facs. repr. ed. Norbert Lieb, Munich 1981

DANCKERTS, Cornelis *see* DE BRAY, Salomon

DAVID, Ben, 'Ueber griechische und gothische Baukunst', in: *Die Horen*, vol. III, 8. Stück, 1795, pp. 87–102

D'AVILER, Augustin-Charles, *Cours d'architecture qui comprend les ordres de Vignole...*, Paris 1691 (²1696, 1710, 1720); revised by P. J. Mariette, 1735 (further eds 1738, 1750, 1756, 1760)

——, *Dictionnaire d'Architecture ou explication de tous les termes*, Paris 1693

DE BRAY, Salomon, *Architectura Moderna ofte Bouwinge van onsen tyt...*, Amsterdam 1631 (facs. repr. with intro. by E. Taverne, Soest 1971)

DECKER, Paul, *Gothic Architecture Decorated, Consisting of a Large Collection...*, London 1759 (facs. repr. Farnborough 1968)

——, *Chinese Architecture, Civil and Ornamental, Being a Large Collection...*, London

1759 (facs. repr. Farnborough 1968)

DECKER, Paulus, *Fürstlicher Baumeister oder: Architectura Civilis, wie Grosser Fürsten und Herren Palläste...nach heutiger Art auszuzieren; zusemt den Grund-Rissen und Durchschnitten, auch vornehmsten Gemächern und Säälen eines ordentlichen Fürstlichen Pallastes*, Augsburg 1711; *Deß Fürstlichen Baumeisters Anhang zum Ersten Theil..*, Augsburg 1713; *Deß Fürstlichen Baumeisters oder Architecture Civilis Anderer Theil, welcher Eines Königlichen Pallastes General-Prospect...vorstellet*, Augsburg 1716 (facs. repr. Hildesheim 1978)

——, *Ausführliche Anleitung zur Civilbau-Kunst*, 3 parts, Nuremberg, n.d. (c. 1719/20)

DELAGARDETTE, C. M., *Les Ruines de Paestum ou Poseidonia*, Paris VII (1799)

DE LILLE, J., *Les jardins, ou l'art d'embellir les paysages: poème*, Paris 1782

DELORME, Philibert, *Nouvelles inventions pour bien bastir et a petits fraiz*, Paris 1561 (from 1568 published as appendix to editions of 'Premier tome' as Books X and XI)

——, *Le premier tome de l'architecture*, Paris 1567 (^{2}1568; ^{3}1626, ^{4}1648; facs repr. of 1648 ed. 1894; 1964; ed. Geert Bekaert, Brussels 1981)

DE MARCHI, Francesco, *Della Architettura militare libri tre*, Brescia 1599; *Architettura militare*, ed. Luigi Marini, 6 vols, Rome 1810

DESGODETS, Antoine, *Les édifices antiques de Rome*, Paris 1682 (^{2}1697); a 2-vol. English–French ed. (ed. George Marshall) appeared in London 1771–95; facs. repr. of 1682 ed.: Portland, Or. 1972

——, *Traité des Ordres d'Architecture* (Ms, Paris, Bibl. de l'Institut de France, Ms. 1031)

——, *Cours d'architecture* (Part II: 'Traité de la commodité de l'architecture, concernant la distribution et les Proportions des Edifices') (Ms, Paris, Bibl. Nat., Cabinet des Estampes, Ha 23 and 23a; Paris, Bibl. de l'Arsenal, Ms. 2545; London, library of the Royal Institute of British Architects, Ms 72)

——, *Traité du toisé des bâtiments* (Ms, New York, Columbia University, Avery Library, Ms. AA/3101/D 45; AA/3101/D 451)

DIETTERLIN, Wendel, *Architectura von Außtheilung, Symmetria und Proportion der Fünff Seulen und aller darauß volgender Kunst Arbeit von Fenstern, Caminen, Thürgerichten, Portalen, Bronnen und Epitaphien*, Nuremberg 1598 (in parts from 1593; facs. repr. with introduction by Hans Gerhard Evers, Darmstadt 1965; under the title *The Fantastic Engravings of Wendel Dietterlin* with introduction by Adolf K. Placzek, New York 1968)

DIEUSSART, Carl Philipp, *Theatrum Architecture Civilis, in drey Bücher getheilet*, Güstrow 1682; Bamberg 1697

DOESBURG, Theo van (ed.), *De Stijl en de Europese architectur (1917–1932)*; facs. repr. 2 vols, Amsterdam 1968

——, *Scritti di arte e di architettura*, ed. Sergio Polano, Rome 1979

——, *Grundbegriffe der neuen gestaltenden Kunst* (Bauhausbücher, 1925), ed. Hans M. Wingler, Mainz–Berlin 1966

DOHME, Robert, *Das englische Haus. Eine kultur- und baugeschichtliche Studie*, Brunswick 1888

DONALDSON, Thomas Leverton, *Preliminary Discourse on Architecture*, London 1842

D'ORVILLE, Jacque Philippe, *Sicula, quibus Siciliae Veteris Rudera*, 2 vols, Amsterdam

1764

DOSIO, Antonio, *Roma antica e i disegni di architettura agli Uffizi*, ed. Franco Borsi a.o., Rome 1976 (esp. pp. 109ff.)

DUBUT, Louis-Amboise, *Architecture Civile. Maisons de ville et de campagne de toutes formes et de tous genres...*, Paris 1803 (²1837); facs. repr. of 1803 ed. Unterschneidheim 1974

DU CERCEAU, Jacques Androuet, *XXX Exempla Arcuum, partim ab ipso inventa, partim ex veterum sumpta monumenta*, Orleans 1549

——, *De Architectura... Opus, quo desriptae sunt aedifiorum quinquaginta planè dissimilium ichnographiae, in omnium non modo potentiorum, sed etiam mediocrium & tenuirorum gratiam, quos aedificandi studium oblectat...*, Paris 1558; French ed. *Livre d'architecture... contenant les plans & dessaings de cinquante bastiments tous differens pour instruire ceux qui desirent bastir, soient de petit, moyen, ou grand estat...*, Paris 1559 (facs. repr. including Books II and III, Ridgewood, NJ 1965)

——, *Second Livre d'architecture... contenant plusieurs et diverses ordonnances de cheminees, lucarnes, portes, fonteines...*, Paris 1561

——, *Le premier volume des plus excellents Bastiments de France*, Paris 1576; *Le second volume des plus excellents Bastiments de France*, Paris 1577 (facs. rpr. 1972)

——, *Livre d'architecture... auquel sont contenues diverses ordonnances de plants et élévations de bastiments de Seigneurs... qui voudront bastir aux champs...*, Paris 1582

DÜRER, Albrecht, *Underweysung der Messung mit dem Zirckel und Richtscheyt*, Nuremberg 1525 (2nd ed. Nuremberg 1538)

——, *Etliche underricht, zu befestigung der Stett, Schloß, und flecken*, Nuremberg 1527 (facs. reprs. Farnborough, 1972; ed. A. E. Jäggli, Dietikon 1971); Latin ed. Paris 1535

DUMONT, G. P. M., *Suite de plans, coupes, profiles... de Pesto... mesurés et dessinés par J. G. Soufflot architecte du roy en 1750*, Paris 1764

——, *Les Ruines de Paestum... Traduction libre de l'anglois imprimé à Londres en 1767...*, London–Paris 1769

DUPERRON, *Discours sur la peinture et sur l'architecture dédié à Madame de Pompadour*, Paris 1758 (facs. repr. Geneva 1973)

DURAND, Jean-Nicolaus-Louis, *Recueil et parallèle des édifices de tous genre, anciens et modernes*, Paris 1800 (enlarged ed. by J. G. Legrand: *Raccolta e paralello delle fabriche classiche di tutti i tempi...*, Venice 1833); facs. repr. of French ed. by Legrand of 1842, Nördlingen 1986

——, *Précis des leçons d'architecture données à l'Ecole Polytechnique*, 2 vols, Paris 1802–1805; revised ed. Paris 1817–19; *Partie graphique des Cours d'Architecture*, Paris 1821 (facs. repr. of vols of 1817, 1819 and 1821, Unterschneidheim 1975)

EIDLITZ, Leopold, *The Nature and Function of Art, More Especially of Architecture*, London–New York 1881

ERASMUS, Georg Caspar (anonymous title-page; author identified in foreword), *Seulenbuch Oder Gründlicher Bericht Von den Fünf Ordnungen der Architectur-Kunst... durch Einen Liebhaber der Edlen Architectur-Kunst an den Tag gegeben*, Nuremberg 1672 (²1688)

ERCOLANI, Giuseppe Maria ('opera di Neralco P.A.'), *I tre ordini d'architettura dorico, jonico, e corintio, presi dalle Fabbriche più celebri dell'Antica Roma, e posti in uso con un nuovo esattissimo metodo*, Rome 1744

ERRARD, Jean (de Bar-le-Duc), *La Fortification reduicte en art et demonstrée*, Paris 1600

EVELYN, John, *The Diary of John Evelyn*, ed. E. S. Beer, 6 vols, Oxford 1955
See also FRÉART DE CHAMBRAY

FÉLIBIEN, André, *Des Principes de l'Architecture, de la Sculpture, de la Peinture*, Paris 1676 (^{2}1690; ^{3}1699; facs. repr. of 1699 ed., 1966)

FÉLIBIEN, Jean-François, *Recueil Historique de la vie et des ouvrages des plus célèbres architectes*, Paris 1687; later eds; German trans. Hamburg 1711 (facs. repr. Leipzig 1975); Berlin 1828

FERGUSSON, James, *An Historical Enquiry in the True Principles of Beauty in Art, more especially with Reference to Architecture*, London 1849

——, *The Illustrated Handbook of Architecture: being a concise and popular account of the different styles of architecture prevailing in all ages and countries*, 2 vols, London 1855

——, *A History of Modern Styles in Architecture*, London 1862

——, *A History of Architecture*, 4 vols, London 1865–76

FERRAN, Albert, *Philosophie de la Composition Architecturale*, Paris 1955

FILARETE (Antonio Averlino), *Trattato di architettura*, 2 vols, ed. Anna Maria Finoli and Liliana Grassi, Milan 1972; earlier partial eds. Wolfgang von Oettingen (ed.), *Antonio Averlino Filarete's Tractat über die Baukunst*, Vienna 1890; Engl. transl. with facs. of Cod. Magl. II, I, 140, Florence, Bibl. Nat., ed. John R. Spencer, *Filarete's Treatise on Architecture*, 2 vols, New Haven, Conn–London 1965

FISCHER VON ERLACH, Johann Bernhard, *Entwurff Einer Historischen Architectur*, Vienna 1721 (very reduced-size repr. with afterword by Harald Keller, Dortmund 1978); 2nd ed. Leipzig 1725 (facs. repr. 1964); 3rd ed. Leipzig 1742

FLAMAND, Claude, *Le guide des fortifications et conduite militaire pour bien se défendre*, Montbéliard (Mömpelgard) 1597 (^{2}1611)

FLETCHER, Banister, *History of Architecture on the Comparative Method for the Student, Craftsman, and Amateur*, London 1896 (numerous eds: ^{15}1950)

FONDA, Girolamo, *Elementi di architettura civile, e militare ad uso del Collegio Nazareno*, Rome 1764

FONTAINE, Pierre-François-Léonard see PERCIER, Charles

FOURIER, Charles, *Théorie de l'unité universelle* (1822), in: Fourier, *Oeuvres complètes*, vols. II–V (1841–42), Paris 1966

FRANCINI, Alessandro, *Livre d'architecture contenant plusieurs portiques de différentes inventions, sur les cinq ordres de Colonnes*, Paris 1631 (facs. repr. with Engl. transl. by Robert Pricke (1669), 1966)

FRÉART DE CHAMBRAY, Roland, *Parallèle de l'architecture antique et de la moderne: avec un recueil des dix principaux autheurs qui ont écrit des cinq Ordres...*, Paris 1650 (^{2}1702)

——, (translation) *Andrea Palladio, Les quatre livres de l'architecture*, Paris 1650 (facs. repr., ed. François Hebert-Stevens, Paris 1980)

FRÉMIN, Michel de, *Mémoires critiques d'architecture contenans l'idée de la vray & de la fausse Architecture*, Paris 1702 (facs. repr. Farnborough 1967)

FRÉZIER, Amédée-François, *La Théorie et la pratique de la coupe des pierres et des bois pour la construction des voûtes et autres parties des bâtiments civiles et militaires, ou Traité de Stéréometrie, à l'usage de l'architecture* (Appendix: '*Dissertation historique et critique sur les ordres de l'architecture*', 1738), Strasbourg 1737–39 (facs. repr. Noyent-Le-Roi 1980)

FRISI, Paolo, *Saggio sopra l'architettura gotica*, Livorno 1766; in German trans. included in Herder, ed., *Von deutscher Art und Kunst* (1773) (cf. new ed. by Dietrich Irmscher, Stuttgart 1968, pp. 105ff.)

FURTTENBACH, Joseph, *Architectura Civilis, das ist, Eigentlich Beschreibung wie man nach bester Form und gerechter Regul Fürs Erste Palläst...erbawen soll...*, Ulm 1628 (facs. repr. in: Hans Foramitti, ed., Joseph Furttenbach, *Architectura civilis...*, Hildesheim–New York 1971)

——, *Architectura universalis, das ist von Kriegs-, Statt- und Wasser Gebäwen...*, Ulm 1635

——, *Architectura recreationis, das ist von Allerhand Nutzlich und Erfrewlichen Civilischen Gebäwen...*, Augsburg 1640 (facs. repr. in: Foramitti, ed., op. cit., 1971)

——, *Architectura privata, das ist die gründtliche Beschreibung neben conterfetischer Vorstellung, inn was Form und Manier ein gar Irregular, Burgerliches Wohn-Hauß...*, Augsburg 1641, (facs. repr. in: Foramitti, ed., op. cit., 1971)

FURTTENBACH the Younger, *Joseph, Feriae Architectonicae*, 1649

GALIANI, Berardo, *L'architettura di M. Vitruvio Pollione* (Latin–Ital. ed.), Naples 1758 (Siena ²1790)

GALLACCINI, Teofilo, *Trattato sopra gli errori degli architetti* (1625), ed. Giovanni Antonio Pecci, Venice 1767 (facs. repr. 1970)

——, c.f. also VISENTINI, Antonio

GALLI BIBIENA, Ferdinando, *L'architettura civile preparata su la geometria, e ridotta alle prospettive, considerazioni pratiche...*, Parma 1711 (facs. repr. ed. Diana M. Kelder, New York 1971)

——, *Direzione a giovani studenti nel disegno dell'architettura civile...*, Bologna 1725 (1731, 1745, 1753, 1777)

GALLI BIBIENA, Giuseppe, *Architetture, e Prospettive*, Augsburg 1740 (facs. repr. with introduction by A. Hyatt Mayor under the title *Architectural and Perspective Designs*, New York 1964)

GAN, Alexey, *Konstructivism* (Russian), Moscow 1922

GARBETT, Edward Lacy, *Rudimentary Treatise on the Principles of Design in Architecture as Deducible from Nature and Exemplified in the Works of the Greek and Gothic Architects*, London 1850

GARCÍA, Simón, 'Compendio de Architetura y simetría de los Templos conforme a la medida del cuerpo humano...Año de 1681' (Madrid, Bibl. Nac., Ms. 8884); ed. José Camón, *Compendio de architectura y simetria de los templos por Simón García año de 1681*, Salamanca 1941

GARNIER, Charles, *Le Théâtre*, Paris 1871

——, *Le nouvel Opéra de Paris*, 4 vols, Paris 1878–81

GARNIER, Tony, *Une cité industrielle. Etude pour la construction des villes*, Paris 1917 (²1932)

——, *Les Grands Traveaux de la Ville de Lyon*, Paris 1920

GAUDÍ, Antoni, *La seva vida. Les seves obres. La seva mort*, Barcelona 1926

GEDDES, Patrick, *City Development. A Study of Parks, Gardens, and Culture-Institutes. A Report to the Carnegie Dunfermline Trust*, Edinburgh–Birmingham 1904 (facs. repr., Shannon 1973–New Brunswick, NJ 1973)

——, *Town Planning toward City Development: A Report to the Durbar of Indore*, 2 vols, Indore 1918

GENTZ, Heinrich (ed.), *Elementar-Zeichenwerk zum Gebrauch der Kunst- und Gewerbe-Schulen der Preußischen Staaten*, Berlin 1803–06

GERBIER, Balthasar, *A Brief Discourse, Concerning the Three Chief Principles of Magnificent Building...*, London 1662

——, *Counsel and Advise to all Builders...*, London 1663; facs. repr. (together with Thomas Willford, *Architectonicae, or the Art of Building*, London 1659) 1969

GHIBERTI, Buonaccorso (trans. of Vitruvius); ms in his 'Zibaldone' (Florence, Nat. Lib., Cod. Banco Rari 228); repr. in: Gustina Scaglia, 'A Translation of Vitruvius and Copies of Late Antique Drawings in Buonaccorso Ghiberti's Zibaldone', *Transactions of the American Philosophical Society*, vol. 69, part I, 1979, pp. 19–30

GHIBERTI, Lorenzo, *I Commentari*, ed. Julius von Schlosser entitled *Lorenzo Ghiberti's Denkwürtigkeiten*, 2 vols, Berlin 1912; ed. Ottavio Morisani, 1947

GIBBS, James, *A Book of Architecture containing Designs of Buildings and Ornaments*, London 1728 (facs. repr. New York 1968); London ²1739

——, *Rules for Drawing the Several Parts of Architecture...* London 1732 (facs. repr. Farnborough 1968); London ²1738; ³1753

——, 'Cursory Remarks' and 'A Short Accompt of Mr. James Gibbs Architect And of several things he built in England & affter his returne from Italy', ms., London, Sir John Soane's Museum

GIL, Rodrigo (de Hontañon) see GARCÍA, Simón

GILLY, David, *Handbuch der Land-Bau-Kunst vorzüglich in Rücksicht auf die Construction der Wohn- und Wirtschaftsgebäude für angehende Cameral-Baumeister und Oeconomen*, Parts I and II, Berlin 1797–98; Brunswick ²1800; Part III, Halle 1811; Brunswick ⁵1831; Leipzig–Halle ⁶1836

——(ed.), *Sammlung nützlicher Aufsätze und Nachrichten, die Baukunst betreffend. Für angehende Baumeister und Freunde der Architektur*, vols. 1–6, 1797–1806

GILPIN, William, *A Dialogue upon the Gardens of the Right Honourable the Viscount Cobham at Stow...*, London 1748

——, *Observations...*, London 1782ff.; *Three Essays: On the Picturesque Beauty...*, London 1792 (²1794)

GINZBURG, Moisey Yakovlevich, *Stil' i epokha*, Moscow 1924; Ital. ed. in: Moisej Ja. Ginzburg, *Saggi sull'architettura costruttivista*, ed. Emilio Battisti, Milan 1977

——, *Ritm v arkhitekture*, Moscow 1923; Ital. ed. in: Ginzburg, ed. Emilio Battista (1977)

——, *Zhilishchiy opyt pyatiletney raboty nad problemoy zhilishcha*, Moscow 1934; Ital. ed. in Ginzburg, ed. Emilio Battisti (1977)

GIOCONDO, Fra, M. *Vitruvius per Iocundum solito castigatur factus cum Figuris et tabula ut iam legi et intellegi possit*, Venice 1511

GIOFFREDI, Mario, *Dell'architettura. Parte prima nella quale si tratta degli Ordini dell'Architettura de Greci, e degl'Italiani, e si danno le regole più spedite per designarli*, Naples 1768

GIOLLI, Raffaello, *L'architettura razionale*, ed. Cesare De Seta, Bari 1972

GIORGI, Francesco, *De Harmonia Mundi totius cantica tria*, Venice 1525

——, (memorial volume for S. Francesco della Vigna, 1535), in: Gianantonio Moschini, *Guida per la Città de Venezia*, vol. I, Venice 1815, pp. 55–61; Antonio Foscari and Manfredo Tafuri, *L'armonia e i conflilti. La chiesa di San Francesco della Vigna nella Venezia del '500*, Turin 1983, pp. 208–12

GIRARDIN, René-Louis de, *De la composition des paysages ou des moyens d'embellir la nature…*, Paris 1777 (ed. Michel H. Conan, Paris 1979)

GIUSTINIANI, Vincenzo, *Discorsi sulle arti e sui mestieri*, ed. Anna Banti, Florence 1981

GOETHE, Johann Wolfgang von, *Schriften zur bildenden Kunst*, 2 vols, Berlin ed. vols 19 and 20, Berlin–Weimar 1973, 1974

GOLDMANN, Nicolaus, *Tractatus de usu proportionatorii*, Leiden 1656

——, *Vollständige Anweisung zu der Civil-Bau-Kunst… vermehrt von Leonhard Christoph Sturm*, Wolfenbüttel 1696 (facs. repr. Baden–Baden–Strasbourg 1962); 2nd ed. enlarged with *Erste Ausübung der Vortrefflichen und Vollständigen Anweisung zu der Civil-Bau-Kunst Nicolai Goldmanns… herausgegeben von Leonhard Christoph Sturm*, Brunswick 1699; 3rd ed.: Leipzig 1708

GRAPALDI, Francesco Mario, *De Partibus Aedium. Addita modo Verborum explicatione*, Parma 1494 (numerous eds up to Dordrecht 1618)

GREENHOUGH, Horatio, 'American Architecture', in: *United States Magazine and Democratic Review* 13, 1843, pp. 206–10

——, *The Travels, Observations and Experience of a Yankee Stonecutter* (publ. under the pseudonym Horace Bender), New York 1852

——, *Form and Function. Remarks on Art, Design and Architecture*, ed. Harold A. Small, Berekeley–Los Angeles–London 1947 ([6]1969)

GROPIUS, Walter, 'Die Entwicklung moderner Industriebaukunst', in: *Jahrbuch des Deutschen Werkbundes* 1913, pp. 17–22

——, *Programm des Staatlichen Bauhauses in Weimar*, Weimar 1919

——, *Internationale Architektur (Bauhausbücher)*, Munich 1925; [2]1927 (facs. repr. Mainz 1981)

——, *Bauhausbauten Dessau (Bauhausbücher)*, Fulda 1930 (facs. repr. Mainz–Berlin 1974)

——, *The New Architecture and the Bauhaus*, London 1935

——, *The Scope of Total Architecture*, New York 1955

GRZIMEK, G., *Gedanken zur Stadt- und Landschaftsarchitektur seit Friedrich Ludwig von Sckell*, Munich 1973

GUADET, Julien, *Eléments et théorie de l'Architecture. Cours professé à l'Ecole Nationale et Spéciale des Beaux-Arts*, 4 vols, Paris 1901–04 ([6]1929–30)

GUARINI, Guarino, *Modo di misurare le fabbriche*, Turin 1674

——, *Trattato di fortificazione che hora si usa in Fiandra, Francia, e Italia…*, Turin 1676

——, *Dissegni d'Architettura civile et ecclesiastica inventati, e delineati dal padre D.*

Guarino Guarini..., Turin 1686 (repr. as appendix in: Daria De Bernardi Ferrero, *I 'Disegni d'architettura civile et ecclesiastica' di Guarino Guarini*, Turin 1966)
——, *Architettura civile*, 2 vols, Turin 1739 (facs. repr. London 1964); crit. ed. Guarino Guarini, *Architettura civile*, ed. Nino Carboneri and Bianca Tavassi La Greca, Milan 1968

GUTENSOHN, J. G. and KNAPP, J. M., *Denkmale der christlichen Religion, oder Sammlung der ältesten christlichen Kirchen oder Basiliken Roms vom 4ten bis zum 13ten Jahrhundert*, Tübingen–Stuttgart 1822–27

GWILT, Joseph, *Rudiments of Architecture, Practical and Theoretical*, London 1826 (²1835; ³1839; ⁴1899)
——, *An Encyclopaedia of Architecture, Historical, Theoretical, and Practical*, London 1842 (1945, 1954, 1859; ed. Wyatt Papworth: 1867, 1876, 1899)

HÄRING, Hugo, *Schriften, Entwürfe, Bauten*, ed. Jürgen Joedicke, Stuttgart 1965

HALFPENNY, William, *New Designs for Chinese Temples, Triumphal Arches, Garden Seats...*, London 1750; Parts II to IV (together with John Halfpenny) 1751–52; 2nd ed. entitled *Rural Architecture in the Chinese Taste...*, London 1752 (³1755)
—— and HALFPENNY, John, *Chinese and Gothic Architecture properly Ornamented...*, London 1752
—— and HALFPENNY, John and MORRIS, Robert and LIGHTOLER, Thomas, *The Modern Builder's Assistant*; Or, *a concise Epitome of the Whole System of Architecture*, London 1742; ²1757 (facs. repr. Farnborough 1971)

HAMILTON, William (P. F. H. d'Hancarville), *Collection of Etruscan, Greek and Roman antiquities...*, 4 vols, Naples 1766–67
——, (ed. Wilhelm Tischbein), *Collection of engravings from ancient vases mostly of pure Greek workmanship...*, 3 vols, Naples 1791–95

HARTMANN, Daniel, *Burgerliche Wohnungs Baw-Kunst...*, Basel 1673 (²1688)

HAUSSMANN, Georges, *Mémoires*, 3 vols, Paris 1890–93

HEINRICH VON SACHSEN, *Fürstliche Bau-Lust, nach dero eigenen hohen Disposition*, Glücksburg 1698

HÉNARD, Eugène, *Etudes sur les transformations de Paris*, 8 fasc. Paris 1903–09
——, 'The Cities of the Future', in: *Transactions: Town Planning Conference*, London 10.–15 October 1910, London 1911, pp. 357–67
——, *Etudes sur les transformations de Paris. Et autres écrits sur l'urbanisme*, ed. John Louis Cohen, Paris 1982

HERRERA, Juan de, *Discurso de la Figura Cúbica*; ed. Julio Rey Pastor, Madrid 1935; ed. Edison Simons and Roberto Godoy, Madrid 1976
——, *Sumario y breve declaración de los diseños y estampas de la fábrica de San Lorenzo el Real del Escurial*, Madrid 1589; ed. Luis Cervera Vera, Madrid 1954

HILBERSEIMER, Ludwig, *Großstadtarchitektur*, Stuttgart 1927 (²1978)

HIRSCHFELD, Christian Cay Lorenz, *Anmerkungen über die Landhäuser und die Gartenkunst*, Frankfurt–Leipzig 1773 (²1779)
——, *Theorie der Gartenkunst*, Frankfurt-Leipzig 1775 (²1777)
——, *Theorie der Gartenkunst*, 5 vols, Leipzig 1779–1785 (facs. repr. with intro. by Hans Foramitti, 2 vols, Hildesheim–New York 1973); French ed. *Théorie de l'art des Jardins*, Leipzig 1779–1785 (facs. repr. Geneva 1973)

HIRT, Aloys, *Die Baukunst nach den Grundsätzen der Alten*, Berlin 1809 (later ed.

entitled *Die Geschichte der Baukunst bei den Alten*, 3 vols, Berlin 1821–27)

HITTORFF, Jakob Ignaz, *Restitution du Temple d'Empédocle à Sélinonte ou l'Architecture polychrome chez les Grecs*, Paris 1851

—— and ZANTH, Karl Ludwig Wilhelm von, *Architecture antique de la Sicile ou Recueil des plus intéressants monuments d'architecture des villes et des lieux, les plus remarquables de la Sicile ancienne, mesurés et déssinés...*, Paris 1828

HÖSCH, Hans, *Geometria Deutsch*; published by Carl Heideloff, *Die Bauhütte des Mittelalters in Deutschland*, Nuremberg 1844, pp. 95–9

HOFFSTÄDT, Friedrich, *Gothisches A-B-C-Buch, das ist: Grundregeln des gothischen Styls für Künstler und Werkleute*, Frankfurt 1840–63

HOGARTH, William, *The Analysis of Beauty*, London 1753

HOLL, Elias (family chronicle); Christian Meyer (ed.), *Die Selbstbiographie des Elias Holl*, Augsburg 1873; Christian Meyer (ed.), *Die Hauschronik der Familie Holl*, Munich 1910

——, 'Geometrie- und Meßbuch', ms, Augsburg, Städt. Kunstsammlungen, Graph. Sammlung, Inv. Nr. 11216

HOLLANDA, Francisco de, '*Desenhos das Antigualhas que vio Francisco d'Ollanda*'; ed. Archille Pellizzari, *Opere di Francisco de Hollanda*, II, Naples 1915; ed. Elias Tormo, Madrid 1940

——, *Da Fabrica que falece La Cidade de Lysboa* (1571); ed. Joaquim de Vasconcellos, Oporto 1879; ed. Jorge Segurado, Francisco D'Ollanda, Lisbon 1970

HOME, Henry (Lord Kames), *Elements of Criticism*, 3 vols, Edinburgh 1762

HOPE, Thomas, *Observations on the Plans and Elevations designed by James Watt, Architect, for Downing College, Cambridge, in a letter to Francis Annesley, esq., M.P.*, London 1804

——, *Household Furniture and Interior Decoration executed from Designs by Thomas Hope*, London 1807 (facs. reprs. London 1937 (without text); London 1947 (without text); with intro. by Clifford Musgrave, London 1970; with intro. by David Watkin, New York 1971)

——, *An Historical Essay on Architecture by the late Thomas Hope, illustrated by drawings by him in Italy and Germany*, 2 vols, London 1835 (⁴1843); French ed. Paris–Brussels 1839 (²1852); Ital. ed. 1840

HOUEL, Jean, *Voyage pittoresque des isles de Sicile, de Lipari et de Malta*, 4 vols, Paris 1782–87

HOWARD, Ebenezer, *Tomorrow: a Peaceful Path to real Reform*, London 1898; entitled *Garden Cities of Tomorrow*, London 1902; ed. F. J. Osborn, Cambridge, Mass.-London 1965 (several reprs)

HÜBSCH, Heinrich, *In welchem Style sollen wir bauen?*, Karlsruhe 1828 (facs. repr. with afterword by Wulf Schirmer, Karlsruhe 1984)

ISIDORE OF SEVILLE, *Etymologiarum sive Originum Libri XX*, ed. W. M. Lindsay, Oxford 1911 (several reprs)

IZZO, Johann Baptist, *Anfangsgründe der bürgerlichen Baukunst*, Vienna n.d. (1773); Latin ed. *Elementa architecturae civilis*, Vienna 1784

——, *Anleitung zur bürgerlichen Baukunst. Zum Gebrauche der deutschen Schulen in den kaiserl. königl. Staaten*, Vienna 1777

JAMNITZER, Wenzel, *Perspectiva Corporum Regularium*, Nuremberg 1568 (facs. repr.

Frankfurt 1972)

JANÁK, Pavel, 'The Prism and the Pyramid' (Czech), in: *Umělecký Měsíčník* II, 1911–12, pp. 162–70

JEANNERET, Charles-Edouard *see* LE CORBUSIER

JIMÉNEZ, Fray Andrés, *Descripción del Real Monasterio de San Lorenzo del Escorial...*, Madrid 1764

JOMBERT, Charles-Antoine, *Architecture moderne ou l'art de bien bâtir*, 2 vols, Paris ¹1728 (²1764)

JONES, Owen, *The Polychromatic Ornament of Italy*, London 1846

——, *Grammar of Ornament*, London 1856 (⁹1910)

—— and GOURY, Jules, *Plans, Elevations, Sections and Details of the Alhambra*, 3 vols, London 1836–45 (1842–46)

KENT, William, *The Designs of Inigo Jones...*, 2 vols, London 1727 (facs. repr. 1967); further eds 1735, 1770, 1825

KIESLER, Frederick, 'Kiesler's Pursuit of an Idea', *Progessive Architecture*, July 1961, pp. 104–16

KIP, Johannes and KNYFF, Leonard, *Britannia Illustrata, or Views of Noblemen's and Gentlemen's Seats, Cathedrals and Collegiate Churches...*, London 1707 (facs. repr. ed. John Harris, Farnborough 1970; cf. further John Harris, *Die Häuser der Lords und Gentlemen*, Dortmund 1982)

KLEINER, Salomon, *Representation naturelle...de la Favorite...*, Augsburg 1726; *Representation au naturel des chateaux de Weissenstein au dessus de Pommersfeld, et de celui de Geibach...*, Augsburg 1728; *Representation exacte du chateau...Marquardsbourg ou Seehof...*, Augsburg 1731 (much reduced repr. of all three volumes with afterword by Harald Keller: Salomon Kleiner, Schönbrunn-Schlösser, Dortmund 1980)

KLENZE, Leo von, *Der Tempel des olympischen Jupiter von Agrigent*, Stuttgart–Tübingen ¹1821 (²1827)

——, *Versuch einer Wiederherstellung des toskanischen Tempels nach seinen historischen und technischen Analogien*, in: *Denkschriften der Königlichen Akademie der Wissenschaften zu München für die Jahre 1821 und 1822*, vol. VIII, Munich 1824, pp. 1–86

——, *Anweisung zur Architektur des christlichen Cultus*, Munich 1822 (²1834); facs. repr. of ed. of 1822, ed. Adrian von Buttlar, Nördlingen 1990

——, *Sammlung architektonischer Entwürfe welche ausgeführt oder für die Ausführung entworfen wurden*, Munich 1830ff. (²1847ff.); facs. repr. ed. Florian Hufnagl, Worms 1983

——, *Walhalla in artistischer und technischer Beziehung*, Munich 1842

KNIGHT, Richard Payne, *The Landscape, A Didactic Poem, in Three Books*, London 1794 (²1795; facs. repr. of this ed. Farnborough 1972)

——, *An Analytical Inquiry into the Principles of Taste*, London 1805 (²1805; ³1806; ⁴1808; facs. repr. of the 1808 ed. Farnborough 1972)

KRAMMER, Gabriel, *Architectura Von den fünf Seulen sambt iren Ornamenten und Zierden...*, Cologne 1600; Prague 1606

KRUBSACIUS, Friedrich August, 'Betrachtungen über den Geschmack der Alten in der Baukunst', in: *Neuer Büchersaal der schönen Wissenschaften und freyen Künste* IV,

1747, pp. 411–28

KUGLER, Franz, *Über die Polychromie der griechischen Architektur und Skulptur und ihre Grenzen*, Berlin 1835 (with supplementary material in: Kugler, *Kleine Schriften und Studien zur Kunstgeschichte*, Part I, Stuttgart 1853, pp. 265ff.)

——, *Handbuch der Kunstgeschichte* (1842), ed. Wilhelm Lübke, 2 vols, Stuttgart 1872

LABACCO, Antonio, *Libro appartenente al'architettura nel qual si figurano alcune notabili antiquità di Roma*, Rome 1552

LABROUSTE, Henri, *Temples de Paestum par Labrouste. Restauration des monuments antiques par les architectes pensionnaires de France à Roma*, Paris 1877

LACHLER (Lechler), Lorenz, *Unterweisung* (written in 1516); published by August Reichensperger, *Vermischte Schriften über christliche Kunst*, Leipzig 1856, pp. 133–55

LA FONT DE SAINT-YENNE, *Examen d'un essai sur l'architecture*, Paris 1753 (facs. repr. Geneva 1973)

LA HIRE, Philippe de, 'Architecture civile', Ms. (London, Library of Royal Institute of British Architects, ms. 725)

LANGLEY, Batty, *The Builder's Chest-Book; or a Complete Key to the Five Orders of Columns in Architecture...*, London 1727 (facs. repr. Farnborough 1971)

——, *New Principles of Gardening: Or, The Laying out and Planning Parterres...*, London 1728 (facs. repr. Farnborough 1970)

——, *The Builder's Jewel*, London 1741 (numerous later eds)

—— and LANGLEY, Thomas, *Ancient Architecture, Restored and Improved by a Great Variety of Grand and Useful Designs, entirely new, in the Gothick Mode, for the Ornamenting of Building and Gardens*, London 1741; 2nd ed. *Gothic Architecture, Improved by Rules and Proportions...* (with *Historical Dissertation on Gothic Architecture*), London 1742; 3rd ed. London 1747 (without *Historical Dissertation*); facs. repr. of 1747 ed. Farnborough 1967

LAUGIER, Marc-Antoine, *Essai sur l'Architecture* (1st ed. anon.), Paris 1753; 2nd enlarged ed. Paris 1765 (facs. repr. of this ed. 1966 and, ed. Geert Bekaert, Brussels 1979)

——, *Observations sur l'Architecture*, Paris 1765 (facs. repr. 1966 and, ed. Geert Bekaert, Brussels 1979)

LAUWERIKS, Johannes Ludovicus Mathieu, 'Einen Beitrag zum Entwerfen auf systematischer Grundlage in der Architectur', in: *Ring* I, Heft 4, 1909, pp. 25–34

——, 'Leitmotive', in: *Ring* I, Heft 1, 1909, pp. 5–9

Le Antichità di Ercolano esposte, vols 1–5: *Le pitture antiche d'Ercolano e contorni incise con qualche spiegazione*, Naples 1757–69; *De Bronzi di Ercolano e contorni*, vol. I: *Busti*, Naples 1767; vol. II: *Statue*, Naples 1771; *Le lucerne ed i candelabri d'Ercolano e contorni*, Naples 1792

LE BLOND, Jean, *Deux exemples des cinq Ordres de l'architecture Antique, et des quatre Excellens Autheurs qui en on traitté, Sçavoir Palladio, Scamozzi, Serlio, et Vignole*, Paris 1683

LE CAMUS DE MÉZIÈRE, Nicolas, *Le génie de l'architecture ou l'analogie de cet art avec nos sensations*, Paris 1780 (facs. repr. Geneva 1972)

——, *Le guide de ceux qui veulent bâtir*, Paris 1781 (²1786; facs. repr. of this ed. Geneva 1972)

LE CLERC, Sébastien, *Traité d'architecture, avec des remarques et des observations très utiles pour les jeunes gens qui veulent s'appliquer à ce bel art*, Paris 1714

LE CORBUSIER (Charles-Edouard Jeanneret), *Oeuvre complète*, ed. Willy Boesiger, 8 vols, Zürich 1929–70 (several reprs)

——, *Le voyage d'Orient* (1911), Paris 1965 (Ital. ed. *Il viaggio d'Oriente*, Faenza 1974)

——, *Etude sur le mouvement d'art décoratif en Allemagne*, La Chaux-de-Fonds 1912 (facs. repr. New York 1968)

—— and OZENFANT, Amedée, *Après le Cubisme*, Paris 1918 (facs. repr. Turin 1975)

—— (-Saugnier), *Vers une architecture*, Paris 1923 (³1928)

——, *Urbanisme*, Paris 1925

——, *Précisions sur un état de l'architecture et de l'urbanisme*, Paris 1929 (²1960)

——, *La ville radieuse*, Paris 1935 (new ed. Paris 1965)

——, *La Charte d'Athènes*, Paris 1943

——, *Propos d'urbanisme*, Paris 1946

——, *Le Modulor*, Boulogne-sur-Seine 1948

——, *Modulor 2*, Boulogne-sur-Seine 1955

LEDOUX, Claude-Nicolas, *L'architecture considérée sous le rapport de l'art, des moeurs et de la législation*, Paris 1804; a 2nd ed. with additional plates from Ledoux's papers, ed. Daniel Ramée, 1847; facs. repr. of both eds combined: 2 vols, Paris 1961; facs. repr. of 1804 ed. Hildesheim 1980, Nördlingen 1981

LE MUET, Pierre, *Manière de bien bastir pour toutes sortes de personnes*, Paris 1623; 2nd ed. with *Augmentations de nouveaux bastiments faits en France par les ordres & desseins du Sieur le Muet*, Paris 1647 (facs. repr. with intro. by Anthony Blunt, Richmond, Surrey 1972); Paris 1664 (facs. repr. Paris 1981); slightly enlarged new ed. Paris 1681

——, *Règles des cinq ordres d'architecture de Vignole revues, augmentées et réduites du grand au petit en octavo*, Paris 1632

——, *Règle des cinq ordres d'architecture dont se sont servi les anciens, traduits de Palladio*, Paris 1645

LENCKER, Johannes, *Perspectiva literaria*, Nuremberg 1567 (facs. repr. Frankfurt 1972)

——, *Perspectiva hierinnen auffs kürtzte beschrieben...*, Nuremberg 1591 (²1617)

LEONARDO DA VINCI, ed. Jean Paul Richter, *The Notebooks of Leonard da Vinci* (1883), 2 vols, New York 1970

——, *Codices Madrid*, ed. Ladislao Reti, 5 vols, Frankfurt 1974

LEONI, Giacomo, *The Architecture of A. Palladio; In Four Books*, London 1716 (1715–19) (1720)

——, *Ten Books on Architecture by Leone Battista Alberti*, London 1726; ³1755 (facs. repr. Joseph Rykwert, London 1955, ²1965)

LE PAUTRE, Antoine, *Les oeuvres d'architecture*, Paris 1652 (facs. repr. Farnborough 1966)

LE ROUGE, Georges Louis, *Détails des nouveaux jardins à la mode; Jardins anglo chinois à la mode*, 21 numbers, Paris 1776–87; facs. repr. with intro. by Daniel Jacomot, Paris 1978

LE ROY, Julien-David, *Les Ruines des plus beaux monuments de la Grèce*, Paris 1758 (²1770)

LETHABY, William Richard, *Architecture, Mysticism and Myth*, London 1892 (facs. repr.

with intro. by Godfrey Rubens, London 1974); revised version entitled *Architecture, Nature and Magic* (in *The Builder*, 1928), London 1956

——, *Architecture*, London 1911 (²1929; ³1955)

LIECHTENSTEIN, Karl Eusebius von, *Werk von der Architektur*; repr. in: Victor Fleischer, *Fürst Karl Eusebius von Liechtenstein als Bauherr und Kunstsammler* (1611–84), Vienna–Leipzig 1910, pp. 87–209

LIGORIO, Pirro, *Il libro delle antichità di Roma* (Ms. in Naples, Oxford, Paris, Turin); cf. Erna Mandowski and Charles Mitchell, *Pirro Logorio's Roman Antiquities*, London 1963

LISSITZKY, El, *Proun und Wolkenbügel. Schriften, Briefe, Dokumente*, ed. Sophie Lissitzky-Küppers and Jan Lissitzky, Dresden 1977

——, *Rußland. Die Rekonstruktion der Architektur in der Sowjetunion*, Vienna 1930; new ed. entitled *Rußland: Architektur für eine Weltrevolution (Bauwelt Fundamente* 14), Berlin–Frankfurt–Vienna 1965

LOMAZZO, Gian Paolo, *Trattato dell'arte della pittura*, Milan 1584 (facs. repr. Hildesheim 1968)

——, *Idea del Tempio della Pittura*, Milan 1590 (facs. repr. Hildesheim 1965)

——, *Scritti sulle arti*, crit. ed. by Roberto Paolo Ciardi, 2 vols, Florence 1973–74

LOOS, Adolf, *Ins Leere gesprochen 1897–1900*, Paris–Zürich 1921; Innsbruck ²1931–32; ed. Adolf Opel, Vienna 1981

——, *Trotzdem 1900–1930*, Innsbruck 1931; ed. Adolf Opel, Vienna 1982

——, *Sämtliche Schriften*, vol. I, ed. Franz Glück, Vienna–Munich 1962

——, *Die Potemkin'sche Stadt. Verschollene Schriften 1897–1933*, ed. Adolf Opel, Vienna 1983

LORINI, Bonaiuto, *Delle fortificationi libri cinque*, Venice 1592; *Le fortificationi... nuovamente ristampate... con l'aggiunta del sesto libro*, Venice 1609

LOUDON, John Claudius, *A Short Treatise on Several Improvements, recently made in Hot-Houses...*, Edinburgh 1805

——, *A Treatise on forming, improving, and managing Country Residences...*, 2 vols, London 1806

——, *Remarks on the Construction of Hothouses...*, London 1817

——, *Sketches of Curvilinear Hothouses...*, London 1818

——, *An Encyclopaedia of Gardening...*, London 1822

——, *The Green House Companion...*, London 1824 (²1832)

——, *An Encyclopaedia of Cottage, Farm and Villa Architecture and Furniture...*, London 1833 (several eds)

LURÇAT, André, *Formes, Composition et lois d'Harmonie. Eléments d'une science de l'ésthétique architecturale*, 5 vols, Paris 1953–57

LUTIO, Francesco (Durantino), *M. L. Vitruvio Pollione de Architectura traducto di Latino in Vulgare... da niuno altro fin al presente facto ad immensa utilitate di ciascuno studioso*, Venice 1524

MACHIAVELLI, Niccolò, *Dell'arte della guerra*, Florence 1521 (ed. Sergio Bertelli: *Niccolò Machiavelli, Arte della guerra e scritti politici minori*, Milan 1961)

MAGGI, Girolamo and CASTRIOTTO, Jacomo, *Della Fortificatione della Città... libri tre*, Venice 1564

MAJOR, Thomas, *The Ruins of Paestum, otherwise Posidonia in Magna Graecia*, London

1768 (Fr. ed. London 1768; facs. repr. of Fr. ed. 1969)

MALEVICH, Kazimir, *Die gegenstandslose Welt (Bauhausbücher)*, Munich 1927; facs. repr. with intro. by Stephan von Wiese, Mainz–Berlin 1980

——, *Suprematismus – Die gegenstandslose Welt*, ed. Werner Haftmann, Cologne 1962

——, *Essays on Art and Unpublished Writings*, ed. Troels Anderson, 4 vols, Copenhagen 1968–78

——, 'Suprematistische Architektur', *Wasmuths Monatshefte für Baukunst* XI, 1927, pp. 412–14

MARCHI, Virgilio, *Architettura futurista*, Foligno 1924

MARIETTE, Jean-Pierre, 'Lettre' (on Piranesi), *Gazette Littéraire de l'Europe* 1764

MARINIO, Aloisio, *Vitruvii De Architectura libri decem*, 4 vols, Rome 1836

MARLIANI, Bartolommeo, *Topographia antiquae Romae*, Lyons 1534

MARTIN, Jean, *Architecture ou Art de bien bastir, de Marc Vitruve Pollion... par Jan Martin...*, Paris 1547 (²1572); facs. repr. of 1547 ed. 1964

MARTINI, Francesco di Giorgio, *Trattati di architettura, ingenieria e arte militare*, ed. Corrado Maltese and Livia Maltese Degrassi, 2 vols, Milan 1967; earlier ed.: Carlo Promis and Cesare Saluzzo (ed.), *Trattato di Architettura civile e militare di Francesco di Giorgio Martini*, 2 vols, Turin 1841

——, (ed. Luigi Firpo and Pietro C. Marani), *Il Codice Ashburnham 361 della Biblioteca Medicea Laurenziana di Firenze, Trattato di Architettura di Francesco di Giorgio Martini*, 2 vols, Florence 1979

——, (F. Paolo Fiore), *Città e macchine del '400 nei disegni di Francesco di Giorgio Martini*, Florence 1978

See also PERUZZI

MASI, Girolamo, *Teoria e pratica di architettura per istruzione della gioventù specialmente Romana*, Rome 1788

MASON, William, *The English Garden*, London 1772–81 (London and York 1781; Dublin 1782; York 1783; facs. repr. of this ed. Farnborough 1971)

——, *An Heroic Epistle to Sir William Chambers* (1773); facs. repr. (together with Chambers, *A Dissertation on Oriental Gardening*): Farnborough 1972

MEMMO, Andrea, *Elementi dell'architettura lodoliana*, Rome 1786

——, *Elementi di Architettura lodoliana... libri tre*, 2 vols, Zara 1833–34 (facs. repr. Milan 1973)

MERCKLEIN, Albert Daniel, *Mathematische Anfängsgründe fünffter Theil Darinnen Die Architectura Civilis Oder Die Civil-Baukunst...*, Frankfurt–Leipzig 1737

MEYER, Daniel, *Architectura oder Verzeichnuß allerhand Eynfassungen an Thüren, Fenstern und Decken etc. Sehr nützlich unnd dienlich allen Mahlern, Bildthawern, Steinmetzen, Schreinern und andern Liebhabern dieser Kunst*, Frankfurt 1609

MEYER, Hannes, *Bauen und Gesellschaft. Schriften, Briefe, Projekte*, Dresden 1980

MIDDLETON, Charles Thomas, *Picturesque and Architectural Views for Cottages, Farm Houses and Country Villas*, London 1793 (facs. repr. 1970)

MILIZIA, Francesco, *Le vite de' più celebri architetti*, Rome 1768

——, *Memorie degli architetti antichi e moderni*, 2 vols, Rome 1768 (Parma ³1781; Bassano ⁴1785; facs. repr. of this ed. 2 vols, Bologna 1978); Fr. ed.: Paris 1771 (and 1819)

——, *Principi di architettura civile*, 3 vols, Finale 1781 (Bassano 1785; Bassano 1804, with illustrations by Giovanni Battista Cipriani; Bassano 1813; Bassano 1825); ed. by Giovanni Antolini, Milan 1832 (²1847); facs. repr. of this ed. Milan 1972)

——, *Dell'arte di vedere nelle belle arti del disegno secondo i principii di Sulzer e di Mengs*, Venice 1781 (facs. repr. Bologna 1983); German ed. Halle, 1785; French ed. Paris 1798; Spanish ed. Madrid 1827

——, *Dizionario delle arti del disegno*, 2 vols, Bassano 1787 (²1797; Milan 1802 and 1804)

——, *Notizie die Francesco Milizia scritte da lui medesimo*, Venice 1804

——, *Opere complete... risguardanti le belle arti*, 9 vols, Bologna 1826–28

MILYUTIN, Nikolay, A., *Sotsgorod. Problema sotsialisticheskogo planirovaniya gorodov*, Moscow 1930; Ital. ed., ed. Vieri Quilici, Milan 1971

MÖSER, Justus, *Das englische Gärtgen* (first in: *Wöchentliche Osnabrückische Anzeigen*, 1773), in: Möser, *Patriotische Phantasien*, Part II, Berlin 1775, Nr. 86, pp. 465–67

MOHOLY-NAGY, László, *Von Material zu Architektur (Bauhausbücher)*, Munich 1929 (facs. repr. Mainz-Berlin 1968)

MOLLER, Georg, *Denkmäler der deutschen Baukunst*, 3 vols, Darmstadt 1815–49

——, *Bemerkungen über die aufgefundenen Originalzeichnungen des Domes zu Köln*, Darmstadt 1818 (Leipzig–Darmstadt ²1837)

MONTANO, Giovanni Battista, *Li cinque libri di architettura*, Rome 1691

MONTFAUCON, Bernard de, *L'Antiquité expliquée et représentée en figures*, Paris 1719ff.

MOREL, Jean-Marie, *Théorie des jardins*, Paris 1776

MORGHEN, Filippo, *Sei vedute delle rovine di Pesto*, 1766

MORITZ, Karl Philipp, *Vorbegriffe zu einer Theorie der Ornamente*, Berlin 1793; facs. repr. ed. Hanno-Walter Kruft, Nördlingen 1986

MORRIS, Robert, *An Essay in Defence of Ancient Architecture; Or, a Parallel of the Ancient with the Modern...*, London 1728 (facs. repr. Farnborough 1971)

——, *Lectures on Architecture, Consisting of Rules Founded upon Harmonick and Arithmetical Proportions in Building*, London 1734–1736; ²1759 (facs. repr. Farnborough 1971)

MORRIS, William, *The Collected Works*, ed. May Morris, 24 vols, London 1910–15 (facs. repr. New York 1966)

——, *News from Nowhere or an epoch of rest* (first in: *The Commonweal* 1890), Boston 1890 (London 1891); ed. James Redmond, London 1970 (²1972)

MORUS (More), Thomas, *De Optimo Reipublicae Statu, deque nova Insula Utopia...* (1515), Löwen 1516; Paris 1517, Basel 1518; numerous eds and trans.

MOZZI, Vincenzo (ascribed to), *Ragionamento intorno al formare logge arcate l'una soprapposta all'altra in fabbriche fornite di più ordini di architettura*, Bologna 1778

MUTHESIUS, Hermann, *Die englische Baukunst der Gegenwart. Beispiele neuer englischer Profanbauten, mit Grundrissen, Textabbildungen und erläuterndem Text* 4 vols, Leipzig–Berlin 1900–03

——, *Die neue kirchliche Baukunst in England. Entwicklung, Bedingungen und Grundzüge des Kirchenbaues der englischen Staatskirche und der Secten*, Berlin 1901

——, *Das englische Haus. Entwicklung, Bedingungen, Anlage, Aufbau, Einrichtung und Innenraum*, 3 vols, Berlin 1904–5; ²1908–11

——, 'Die Bedeutung des Kunstgewerbes', *Dekorative Kunst* X, 1907, pp. 177–92

——, *Die Einheit der Architektur. Betrachtungen über Baukunst, Ingenieurbau und Kunstgewerbe*, Berlin 1908

——, 'Das Form-Problem im Ingenieurbau', in: *Jahrbuch des Deutschen Werkbundes* 1913, pp. 23–32

NEALE, John Mason (and John F. Russell), *A Few Hints on the Practical Study of Ecclesiastical Antiquities for the Use of the Cambridge Camden Society*, Cambridge 1839 (^{2}1840; ^{3}1842; ^{4}1843)

——, *A Few Words to Church Builders*, Cambridge 1841 (new eds up to 1844)

——(and Benjamin Webb), *The Symbolism of Churches and Church Ornaments: A Translation of the First Book of the Rationale Divinorum...*, Leeds 1843

NEUFFORGE, Jean-François de, *Recueil élémentaire d'architecture*, 10 vols, Paris 1757–80 (facs. repr. without place or date)

NEUMANN, Joseph, *Art de construire et de gouverner les serres*, Paris 1844 (facs. repr. with intro. by Michel Vernes, Neuilly-sur-Seine 1980)

NEUTRA, Richard J., *Wie Baut Amerika?*, Stuttgart 1927

——, *Amerika, Die Stilbildung des Neuen Bauens in den Vereinigten Staaten*, Vienna 1930

——, *Survival Through Design*, New York–London 1954 (paperback ed. London–New York 1969; several reprs)

——, *Auftrag für morgen*, Hamburg 1962

NICHOLSON, Peter, *An Architectural Dictionary, Containing a correct Nomenclature...*, 2 vols, London 1812–19 (new ed., ed. E. Lomax and T. Gunyon entitled *Encyclopaedia of Architecture...*, 2 vols, London 1852; 1857–62)

——, *The Builder and Workman's New Director...*, London 1824 (^{2}1834)

NORMAND, Charles-Pierre-Joseph, *Recueil varié de plans et de façades de maisons de ville et de Campagne...*, Paris 1815

——, *Le Vignole des ouvriers. Ou la méthode facile pour tracer les cinque ordres d'architecture*, 4 parts, 2 vols, Paris ^{7}1839

OETTINGEN-WALLERSTEIN, Friedrich, *Ueber die Grundsätze der Bau-Oekonomie*, Prague 1835 (author on title-page as: F. Oe)

OPPENORDT, Gilles-Marie, *Livre de fragments d'architecture recueillés et dessinés à Rome d'après les plus beaux monuments*, Paris (c. 1715)

OSIO, Carlo Cesare, *Architettura civile dimostrativamente proporzionata et accrescuita...*, Milan 1641 (1661, 1686)

OTTONELLI, Giovanni Domenico *see* CORTONA, Pietro da

OUD, Jacobus Johannes Pieter, *Holländische Architektur (Bauhausbücher, 1926)*, ed. Hans M. Wingler, Mainz–Berlin 1976

OUVRARD, René, *Architecture Harmonique, ou Application de la doctrine des proportions de la musique à l'architecture*, Paris 1679

OWEN, Robert, *A New View of Society*, London 1813 (^{2}1816); ed. G. D. H. Cole, London 1927; ed. John Saville, Clifton, N.J. 1972

——, 'Report to the Committee of the Association for the Relief of the Manufacturing, and Labouring Poor (March 1817)', in: Owen, *The Life*, vol I A (1858), App. C.

——, *The Life of Robert Owen*, 2 vols, London 1857–58 (facs. repr. New York 1967)

PACIOLI, Luca, *Divina Proportione, opera a tutti glingegni perspicaci e curiosi necessaria que ciascun studioso di Philosophia, Prospectiva, Pictura, Sculptura, Architectura, Musica e altre Mathematicae suavissima, sottile e admirabile doctrina consegui-rà... de secretissima scientia*, Venice 1509 (facs. repr. Urbino 1969); Ital.–German ed., ed. Constantin Winterberg, Vienna 1889

PAGANO, Giuseppe, *Architettura e città durante il fascismo*, ed. Cesare De Seta, Bari 1976

PALISSY, Bernard, 'Recepte véritable' (1563), in: Bernard Palissy, *Les Oeuvres*, ed. Anatole France, Paris 1880

PALLADIO, Andrea, *L'antichità di Roma*, Venice 1554

——, *I quattro libri dell'architettura*, Venice 1570 (numerous reprs.); crit. ed., ed. Licisco Magagnato and Paola Marini, Milan 1980

——, *I commentari di Giulio Cesare*, Venice 1574–75

——, (commentary on Polybius): c.f. J. R. Hale, 'Andrea Palladio, Polybius and Julius Caesar', *Journal of the Warburg and Courtauld Institutes* XL, 1977, pp. 240–55

PALM, G., *Von welchen Principien soll die Wahl des Baustyls, insbesondere des Kirchenbaustyls geleitet werden?*, Hamburg 1845

PANCRAZI, Giuseppe Maria, *Antichità Siciliane spiegate*, 2 vols, Naples 1751–52

PAOLI, Paolo Antonio, *Antichità di Pozzuoli (Avanzi delle Antichità esistenti a Pozzuoli, Cuma, e Baja)*, Naples 1768

——, *Paesti quod Posidoniam etiam dixere rudera*, Rome 1784

PARS, William *see* CHANDLER, Richard

PATTE, Pierre, *Discours sur l'architecture*, Paris 1754

——, *Monumens érigés en France à gloire de Louis XV*, Paris 1765

——, *Mémoires sur les objets les plus importants de l'architecture*, Paris 1769 (facs. repr. Geneva 1973)

PENTHER, Johann Friedrich, *Erster Theil einer ausführlichen Anleitung zur Bürgerlichen Bau-Kunst enthaltend ein Lexicon Architectonicum*, Augsburg 1744 (2nd Part 1745; 3rd Part 1746; 4th Part 1748)

PERCIER, Charles and FONTAINE, Pierre-François-Léonard, *Palais, Maisons, et autres édifices modernes dessinés à Rome*, Paris 1798 (facs. repr. with intro. by Hans Foramitti, Hildesheim–New York 1980)

——, *Recueil de décorations intérieures, comprenant tout ce qui a rapport à l'ameuble-ment...*, Paris 1801; enlarged ed. Paris 1812

——, *Résidences de Souverains. Parallèle entre plusiers Résidences de Souverains de France, d'Allemagne, de Suède, de Russie, d'Espagne, et d'Italie*, Paris 1833 (facs. repr. with intro. by Hans Foramitti, Hildesheim–New York 1973)

PERRAULT, Charles, *Paralèlle des Anciens et des Modernes, en ce qui regarde les arts et les sciences*, Paris 1688–97. (repr. in: *Theorie und Geschichte der Literatur und Schönen Künste*, vol. 2, with essays by H. R. Jauss-Max Imdahl, Munich 1964)

PERRAULT, Claude, *Les dix livres d'Architecture de Vitruve corrigez et traduits nouvellement en François, avec des Notes & des Figures*, Paris 1673 (small format ed. *Architecture generale de Vitruve...*, Amsterdam 1681); 2nd revised and enlarged ed. Paris 1684 (facs. repr. Brussels 1979)

——, *Ordonnance des cinq espèces de colonnes selon la méthode des anciens*, Paris 1683

PERRET, Auguste, *Contributions à une théorie de l'architecture*, Paris 1952

PERRET, Jacques, *Des fortifications et artifices d'architecture et perspective*, Paris 1601

(facs. repr. Unterschneidheim 1971)

PERSICO, Edoardo, *Scritti d'architettura* (1927–35), ed. Giulia Veronesi, Florence 1968

——, *Oltre l'architettura. Scritti scelti e lettere*, ed. Riccardo Mariani, Milan 1977

PERSON, Nikolaus, *Novum Architecturae Speculum*, Mainz (between 1699 and 1710); ed. Fritz Arens (*Beiträge zur Geschichte der Stadt Mainz*), Mainz 1977

PERUZZI, Baldassare (?); cf. Alessandro Parronchi (ed.), (Baldassare Peruzzi) 'Trattato di architettura militare' (*Documenti inediti di cultura toscana*, V), Florence 1982

PEYRE, Marie-Joseph, *Oeuvres d'Architecture*, Paris 1765 (facs. repr. 1967); *Oeuvres d'architecture. Supplément, composé d'un Discours sur les monuments des anciens*, Paris 1795

PHILANDER, Guillaume, *Guglielmi Philandri Castilioni Galli Civis Ro. in Decem Libros M. Vitruvii Pollionis De Architectura Annotationes...*, Rome 1544

PIACENTINI, Marcello, *Sulla conservazione della Bellezza di Roma e sullo sviluppo della città moderna*, Rome 1916

——, *Architettura d'oggi*, Rome 1930

PIGONATI, C. Andrea, *Stato presente degli antichi monumenti siciliani*, Naples 1767

PINI, Ermenegildo, *Dell'Architettura. Dialoghi*, Milan 1770

PIRANESI, F. and P., *Antiquités d'Herculanum (gravées par Th. Piroli)*, 6 vols, Paris 1804–06

PIRANESI, Giovanni Battista, *Della Magnificenza ed Architettura de' Romani*, Rome 1761 (facs. repr. in: John Wilton-Ely, ed., Giovanni Battista Piranesi, *The Polemical Works*, 1972)

——, *Osservazioni... sopra la Lettre de M. Mariette aux Auteurs de la Gazette Littéraire de l'Europe... e Parere su l'architettura con una Prefazione ad un nuovo Trattato della introduzione e del progresso delle belle arti in Europa ne'tempi antichi*, Rome 1765 (facs. repr. in: Wilton-Ely, ed., op. cit., 1972)

——, *Diverse maniere d'ornare i cammini ed ogni altra parte degli edifizj desunte dall'architettura egizia, etrusca, greca e romana*, Rome 1769 (facs. repr. in: Wilton-Ely, ed., 1972)

——, *Différentes vues de quelques restes de trois grands édifices qui subsistent encore dans le milieu de l'ancienne ville de Pesto autrement Posidonia, qui est située dans la Luganie*, Rome 1778 (facs. repr. Unterschneidheim 1973)

PLUCHE, Noël Antoine, *Le Spectacle de la Nature, ou entretiens sur les particularités de l'histoire naturelle...*, 8 parts, 9 vols, Paris 1732ff.

PONZ, Antonio, *Viage de España...*, 18 vols, Madrid 1772–94

POPE, Alexander, An Epistle to the Right Honourable Earl of Burlington..., London 1731; in: Pope, *Epistles to Several Persons*, ed. F. W. Bateson, London–New Haven, Conn. 1956 (²1961)

POZZO, Andrea, *Perspectiva Pictorum et Architectorum*, 2 parts, Rome 1693–98 (Rome 1700–02; 1717–37; 1741; 1764–68; 1793; 1810); Lat.–German ed. Augsburg 1706–19; 1800 (facs. repr. Hildesheim 1981); English-Latin ed. London 1707 (facs. repr. New York 1989)

PRADO, Jerónimo *see* VILLALPANDO, Juan Bautista

PRATT, Roger; cf. R. T. Gunter, *The Architecture of Sir Roger Pratt. Charles II's Commissioner for the Rebuilding of London after the Great Fire. Now Printed for the First Time from his Note-Books*, Oxford 1928

PRETI, Francesco Maria, *Elementi di Architettura*, Venice 1780

PRICE, Uvedale, *An Essay on the Picturesque, as Compared with the Sublime and Beautiful, and, on the Use of Studying Pictures, for the Purpose of Improving Real Landscape*, London 1794

——, *Essays on the Picturesque...*, 3 vols, London 1810 (facs. repr. Farnborough 1971)

——, *A Letter to Humphry Repton Esq.*, London 1795

Procopius, *Prokop, Opera, III, 2*, ed. J. Haury, Leipzig 1913; *Procopius*, ed. H. B. Dewing and Glanville Downey, vol. VII (Loeb Classical Library), London-Cambridge, Mass. 1940

PÜCKLER-MUSKAU, Hermann von, *Andeutungen über Landschaftsgärtnerei*, Stuttgart 1834; new ed. 1933; with intro. by Albrecht Kruse-Rodenacker, Stuttgart 1977

PUGIN, Augustus Charles (and E. J. Wilson, text), *Specimens of Gothic Architecture, Selected from Various Antient Edifices in England and France...*, 2 vols, London 1821–28 (²1838–39)

PUGIN, Augustus Welby Northmore, *A Letter to A. W. Hakewill, Architect, in Answer to his 'Reflections on the Style for Rebuilding the House of Parliament'*, Salisbury 1835

——, *Contrasts: or, A Parallel between the Noble Edifices of the Fourteenth and Fifteenth Centuries and Similar Buildings of the Present Day; Shewing the Present Decay of Taste*, Salisbury 1836; ²1841 (facs. repr. ed. H. R. Hitchcock, Leicester–New York 1969)

——, *The True Principles of Pointed or Christian Architecture*, London 1841 (²1853); facs. repr. of ed. of 1841: London–New York 1973; facs. repr. of ed. of 1853, Oxford 1969

——, *An Apology for the Revival of Christian Architecture in England*, London 1843 (facs. repr. Oxford 1969)

——, *A Treatise on Chancel Screens and Rood Lofts*, London 1851

QUATREMÈRE DE QUINCY, Antoine-Chrisostome, *Dictionnaire d'Architecture I*, Paris 1789; II, 1832

——, *Jupiter Olympien: l'art de la sculpture antique considérée sous un nouveau point de vue*, Paris 1815

——, *Essai sur la nature, le but et les moyens de l'imitation dans les Beaux-Arts*, Paris 1823 (facs. repr. with intro. by Leon Krier and Demetri Porphyrios, 1980)

——, *Histoire de la vie et des ouvrages des plus célèbres architectes*, 2 vols, Paris 1830 (facs. repr. New York 1970)

RABELAIS, François, *Oeuvres complètes*, ed. Jacques Boulenger (Bibl. de la Pléiade, 15), Paris 1955; *Gargantua und Pantagruel*

RALPH, James, *A Critical Review of the Publick Buildings, Statues and Ornaments, In, and about London and Westminster*, London 1734 (facs. repr. Farnborough 1970); 2nd ed. '*A New Critical Review...*', London 1736; ³1763; ⁴1783

RAMSAY, Allan (*The Investigator*, Nr. 332); 'A Dialogue of Taste', London 1755

REICHENSPERGER, August, *Die christlich-germanische Baukunst und ihr Verhältniß zur Gegenwart*, Trier 1845 (²1852)

——, *Fingerzeige auf dem Gebiete der kirchlichen Kunst*, Leipzig 1854

——, *Vermischte Schriften*, Leipzig 1856

REPTON, Humphry, *A Letter to Sir Uvedale Price Esq.*, London 1794

——, *Sketches and Hints on Landscape Gardening*, London 1795

——, *Observations on Theory and Practice of Landscape Gardening, including some Remarks on Grecian and Gothic Architecture...*, London 1803 (²1805)

——, *An Inquiry into the Changes of Taste in Landscape Gardening...*, London 1806

—— and ADEY, John, *Fragments on the Theory and Practice of Landscape Gardening...*, London 1816

——, *The Landscape Gardening and Landscape Architecture of the Late Humphry Repton Esq.*, ed. J. C. Loudon, London 1840 (facs. repr. Farnborough 1969)

REVETT, Nicholas *see* CHANDLER, Richard and STUART, James

REYNAUD, Léonce, *Traité d'architecture contenant des notions générales sur les principes de la construction et sur l'histoire de l'art*, 2 vols text and 2 vols plates, Paris 1850–58

REYNOLDS, Joshua, *Discourses on Art (1769–1790)*, ed. Robert R. Wark, London 1966

RIBART DE CHAMOUST, *L'ordre François trouvé dans la nature, présenté au roi, le 21 Septembre 1776*, Paris 1783 (facs. repr. 1967)

RICCI, Fray Juan, *Tratado de la pintura sabia und Epitome arquitecturae de ordine Salomonico integro* (1663); ed. Elías Tormo Monzó and Enrique Lafuente Ferrari, *La vida y la obra de Fray Juan Ricci*, 2 vols, Madrid 1930

RICHARDS, Godfrey, *The First Book of Architecture by Andrea Palladio*, London 1663; numerous reprs up to 1733

RICHARDSON, George, *A Treatise on the five orders of architecture*, London 1797 (facs. repr. 1969)

——, *The New Vitruvius Britannicus*, 2 vols, London 1802 and 1809 (facs. repr. New York 1970 and 1978)

RICKMAN, Thomas, *An Attempt to Discriminate the Styles of English Architecture, From the Conquest to the Reformation...* (first in: *Panorama of Science and Art*, ed. James Smith, Liverpool 1815), London 1819 (6 further eds up to 1881)

RIVIUS (Ryff), Walther, *M. Vitruvii, viri suae professionis peritissimi de Architectura libri decem... per Gualtherium H. Ryff Argentinum medicum*, Strassburg 1543

——, *Der furnembsten, notwendigsten, der gantzen Architectur angehörigen Mathematischen und Mechanischen künst, eygentlicher bericht...*, Nuremberg 1547 (facs. repr. Hildesheim 1981)

——, *Der fünff maniren der Colonen, sampt aller derselbigen zierung...*, Nuremberg 1547

——, *Vitruvius Teutsch... erstmals verteutscht und in Truck verordnet durch D. Gualtherum H. Rivium Medi. & Math. vormals in Teutsche sprach zu transferiren noch niemand sonst understanden sonder für unmüglichen geachtet worden*, Nuremberg 1548 (facs. repr. with intro. by Erik Forssman: Hildesheim–New York 1973)

ROLAND LE VIRLOYS, C. F. *Dictionnaire d'architecture, civile, militaire et navale... dont tous les Termes sont exprimés, en Francois, Latin, Italien, Espagnol, Anglois et Allemand*, 3 vols, Paris 1770–71

RONDELET, Jean-Baptiste, *Traité théorique et pratique de l'art de bâtir*, 5 vols, 1 vol. of plates, Paris 1802–1817; numerous eds: ⁸1838

ROOT, John Wellborn; Donald Hoffmann (ed.), *The Meanings of Architecture. Buildings and Writings by John Wellborn Root*, New York 1967

RORICZER, Matthäus, *Das Büchlein von der Fialen Gerechtigkeit*, Regensburg 1486; *Geometria Deutsch* both texts (with English trans.) in: Lon R. Shelby (ed.), *Gothic Design Techniques*, Carbondale, Ill.–London 1977

ROSSI, Domenico de', *Studio d'architettura civile...*, 3 vols, Rome 1702, 1711, 1721 (Further: *Disegni di vari altari e cappelle nelle Chiese di Roma...*, Rome n.d., probably 1713); facs. repr. all vols with intro. by Anthony Blunt, 1972

RUBENS, Peter Paul, *Palazzi di Genova, 1622*; repr. with intro by Hildebrand Gurlitt, Berlin 1924 (frequently reprinted)

RUMOHR, Carl Friedrich von, *Fragmente einer Geschichte der Baukunst im Mittelalter*, in: Friedrich Schlegel (ed.), *Deutsches Museum*, vol. III, Vienna 1813, pp. 224–46, 361–85, 468–502

RUSCONI, Giovanantonio, *Della architettura...con Centosessanta Figure...secondo i Precetti di Vitruvio...libri decem*, Venice 1590 (facs. repr. Farnborough 1968)

RUSKIN, John, *The Works*, ed. E. T. Cook and A. Wedderburn, 39 vols, London 1903–12 (Library edition)

SAARINEN, Eliel, *The City, Its Growth, its Decay, its Future*, New York 1943 (Paperback ed. Cambridge, Mass. ³1971)

SAGREDO, Diego de, *Medidas del Romano: necessarias alos oficiales que quieren seguir las formaciones delas Basas, Coluñas, Capiteles y otras pieças de los edificios antiguos*, Toledo 1526 (facs. repr. ed. Luis Cervera Vera, Valencia 1976); numerous further eds

SAINT-NON, Jean-Claude Richard de, *Voyage pittoresque ou description des Royaumes de Naples et de Sicile*, 5 vols, Paris 1781–86

SALMON, William, *Palladio Londinensis, or the London Art of Building*, London 1734 (facs. repr. Farnborough 1969); further eds up to 1773

SALVIATI, Francesco, *Regola di far perfettamente col compasso la voluta del capitello ionico e d'ogn'altra sorte*, Venice 1552

SANDRART, Joachim von, *L'Academia Todesca della Architectura Scultura et Pictura: Oder Teutsche Academie...*, Nuremberg 1675; *Der Teutschen Academie Zweyter und letzter Haupt-Teil...*, Nuremberg 1679 (Latin ed., Nuremberg 1683); an ed. of all Sandrart's writings revised by Johann Jacob Volkmann appeared under the title *Teutsche Academie der Bau, Bild- und Maler-Kunst* in 3 parts and in 8 vols, Nuremberg 1768–75; a brief selection, ed. A. R. Peltzer, *Joachim von Sandrarts Academie der Bau, Bild- und Mahlerey-Künste von 1675*, Munich 1925 (facs. repr. Farnborough 1971)

SAN JERÓNIMO, Fray Juan de, 'Memorias desde Monasterio de Sant Lorencio el Real (1563–91)'; in: *Colección de documentos ineditos para la Historia de España* VII, Madrid 1845

SANMICHELI, Michele, *Li cinque ordini dell'architettura civile*, ed. Alessandro Pompei, Verona 1635 (²1735)

SAN NICOLÁS, Fray Lorenzo, *Arte y Uso de Architectura*, Part I, Madrid 1633; Part II, Madrid 1664; new ed. of Part I: Madrid 1667; both parts: Madrid 1736 (1796)

SANT' ELIA, Antonio, 'Messaggio' without title in cat. *Prima Esposizione d'arte del gruppo 'Nuove Tendenze' alla Famiglia Artistica di Milano*, Milan 1914

——, 'L'Architettura Futurista. Manifesto, Flugblatt', Milan 1914; in: *Lacerba* II, nr.

15, August 1914, pp. 228–31 (facs. repr. Milan 1980)

SANTOS, Fray Francisco de los, *Descripción breve del Monasterio de San Lorenzo el Real del Escorial, única maravilla de mundo...*, Madrid 1657 (1667, 1671, 1681, 1698, 1760; Engl. Ed. London 1671)

SANVITALI, Federico, *Elementi di Architettura civile*, Brescia 1765

SARDI, Pietro, *La corona imperiale dell'architettura militare*, Venice 1618; *Corno Dogale Della Architettura Militare*, Venice 1639

SARTORIS, Alberto, *Gli elementi dell'architettura funzionale*, Milan 1932

SAVOT, Louis, *Architecture françoise des bastiments particuliers*, Paris 1624 (²1632; ed. François Blondel 1673, 1685); facs. repr. of ed. of 1685, Geneva 1973

SCAMOZZI, Giovanni Domenico and SCAMOZZI, Vincenzo, 'Indice copiosissimo' and 'Discorso' in: Seb. Serlio, *I sette libri* (1584)

SCAMOZZI, Vincenzo, *L'idea della architettura universale*, Venice 1615 (facs. repr. Ridgewood, N.J. 1964; Bologna 1982); further eds: Piazzola 1687; Venice 1694; Venice 1714; Perugia 1803; Milan 1811 and 1838; Dutch ed. Amsterdam 1640, 1662, 1686; French ed. Leyden 1713; Paris 1713, 1730

——, *Les cinque ordres d'architecture... Tirez du sixième Livre de son Idée générale d'Architecture*, ed. Augustin Charles d'Aviler, Paris 1685

——, *Grundregeln der Bau-Kunst oder klärliche Beschreibung der fünff Säulen-Ordnungen und der gantzen Architectur*, Amsterdam 1646; Nuremberg 1647; Nuremberg 1678 and 1697

SCHÄFER, Carl, *Die Bauhütte. Entwürfe im Stile des Mittelalters, angefertigt von Studirenden unter Leitung von Carl Schäfer*, 3 vols, Berlin 1893–95

——, *Von deutscher Kunst. Gesammelte Aufsätze und nachgelassene Schriften*, Berlin 1910

SCHEDEL, Hartmann, *Weltchronik*, Nuremberg 1493

SCHEERBART, Paul, *Glasarchitektur*, Berlin 1914; ed. Wolfgang Pehnt, Munich 1971

SCHICKHARDT, Heinrich, *Beschreibung einer Reiß... in Italiam*, Montbéliard (Mömpelgard) 1602; Tübingen ²1603; repr. in: Wilhelm Heyd, ed., *Handschriften und Handzeichnungen des herzoglichen württembergischen Baumeisters Heinrich Schickhardt*, Stuttgart 1902

——, *Etliche Gebey, die ich... zu Itallien verzaichnet hab, die mier lieb send*; in: Heyd, ed., *Handschriften etc.*, 1902

SCHILLER, Friedrich von, *Über den Gartenkalender auf das Jahr 1795*; in: Schiller, *Sämmtliche Werke*, vol. 12, Stuttgart–Tübingen 1847, pp. 342–50

SCHINKEL, Karl Friedrich; *Aus Schinkel's Nachlaß. Reisetagebücher, Briefe und Aphorismen*, ed. Alfred von Wolzogen, 4 vols, Berlin 1862–64 (facs. repr. Mittenwald 1981)

——, *Das Architektonische Lehrbuch*, ed. Goerd Peschken, Munich–Berlin 1979

——, *Reisen in Italien. Tagebücher, Briefe, Zeichnungen, Aquarelle*, ed. Gottfried Riemann, Berlin 1979

——, *Werke der höheren Baukunst. Für die Ausführung erfunden und dargestellt*. 1. Abt.: *Entwurf zu einem Königspalast auf der Akropolis zu Athen*, Potsdam 1840–42; 2. Abt.: *Orianda*, Potsdam 1845–48

——, *Sammlung architektonischer Entwürfe enthaltend theils Werke welche ausgeführt sind, theils Gegenstände deren Ausführung beabsichtigt wurde*, 28 Hefte, Berlin 1819–40; Potsdam 1841–43; 1843–47; 1852; 1857–58; 1866 (facs. reprs Berlin 1973,

1980; Guildford 1989)

SCHMITTHENNER, Paul, *Die Baukunst im Neuen Reich*, Munich 1934

SCHMUTTERMAYER, Hans, *Fialenbüchlein*; with English trans in: Lon R. Shelby (ed.), *Gothic Design Techniques*, Carbondale, Ill. 1977

SCHNAASE, Carl, *Geschichte der bildenden Künste*, 7 vols, Düsseldorf 1843–64

SCHÜBLER, Johann Jacob, *Perspectiva, Pes Picturae Das ist: Kurtze und leichte Verfaßung der practicabelsten Regul zur Perspectivischen Zeichnungs-Kunst*, 2 parts, Nuremberg 1719–20 (further eds 1735; 1749–58)

SCHULTZE-NAUMBURG, Paul, *Kulturarbeiten*, 9 vols, Munich 1901–17 (²1922ff.)

SCHUMACHER, Fritz, *Der Geist der Baukunst*, Stuttgart 1938 (new ed. Stuttgart 1983)

SCHWABE, Hermann, *Der Stand der Kunstindustrie in England und der Stand dieser Frage in Deutschland*, Berlin 1866

SCKELL, Friedrich Ludwig von, *Beiträge zur bildenden Gartenkunst für angehende Gartenkünstler und Gartenliebhaber*, Munich 1818 (²1825); facs. repr. of the 1825 ed. with afterword by Wolfgang Schepers, Worms 1982

SCOTT, Geoffrey, *The Architecture of Humanism. A Study in the History of Taste* (¹1914, ²1924), ed. Henry Hope Reed, New York 1974

SEDDING, John Dando, *Art and Handicraft*, London 1893 (facs. repr. New York 1977)

SEMPER, Gottfried, *Die vier Elemente der Baukunst. Ein Beitrag zur vergleichenden Baukunde*, Brunswick 1851

——, *Wissenschaft, Industrie und Kunst. Vorschläge zur Anregung nationalen Kunstgefühles*, Brunswick 1852

——, *Der Stil in den technischen und tektonischen Künsten oder praktische Aesthetik. Ein Handbuch für Techniker, Künstler und Kunstfreunde*, 2 vols, Frankfurt 1860, Munich 1863 (facs. repr. with intro. by Adrian von Buttlar: Mittenwald 1977); 2nd ed. Munich 1878–79

——, *Kleine Schriften*, ed. Hans and Manfred Semper, Stuttgart 1884 (facs. repr. Mittenwald 1979)

——, *Wissenschaft, Industrie und Kunst und andere Schriften*, ed. Hans M. Wingler (*Neue Bauhausbücher*), Mainz–Berlin 1966

SERLE (Searle), J., *A Plan of Mr. Pope's Garden as it was left at his death, with a Plan and a perspective view of the grotto...*, London 1745 (facs. repr. New York 1982)

SERLIO, Sebastiano, *Regole generali di architettura sopra le cinque maniere degli edifici... con gli essempi dell'antichità, che, per la magior parte concordano con la dottrina di Vitruvio*, Venice 1537; *Il Terzo libro... nel quale si figurano e descrivono le Antichità di Roma*, Venice 1540; *Il Primo libro d'architettura (Geometria)*, together with *Il Secondo libro (Prospettiva)*, Paris 1545; *Il quinto libro d'architettura... nel quale si tratta di diverse forme de'tempj sacri*, Paris 1547; *Extraordinario libro di architettura nel quale si dimostrano trenta porte di opera rustica mista...*, Lyons 1551; *Il settimo libro d'architettura... nel quale si tratta di molte accidenti che possono occorrere all'Architetto...*, Ital.-Latin ed., Frankfurt 1575

——, *I sette libri dell'architettura*, Venice 1584 (facs. repr. Bologna 1978); *Tutte l'opere d'architettura et prospettiva di Sebastiano Serlio Bolognese... diviso in sette libri*, Venice 1619 (facs. repr. Ridgewood, NJ 1964)

——, *Sesto Libro. Delle habitationi di tutti li gradi degli homini* (Ms. Bayer. Staatsbibl., Munich, Cod. Icon. 189), ed. Marco Rosci, Milan 1967; (Ms., Columbia Univ.,

Avery Library, New York) ed. Myra Nan Rosenfeld, *Sebastiano Serlio on Domestic Architecture*, New York 1978

——, *Della castrametatione di Polibio ridotta in una cittadella murata...* (Ms., Bayer. Staatsbibl., Munich, Cod. Icon. 190); c.f. Paolo Marconi, 'Un progetto di città militare. L'VIII libro inedito di Sebastiano Serlio', *Controspazio* I, 1969, n. 1, pp. 51–9; 3, pp. 53–9

SHENSTONE, William, 'Unconnected Thoughts on Gardening', in: *Works in Prose and Verse of William Shenstone*, II, London 1764, pp. 125–48

SHUTE, John, *The First and Chief Groundes of Architecture*, London 1563 (facs. reprs. 1912, 1964); 1579, 1584, 1587

SIGUENZA, Fray José de, *Historia de la Orden de San Gerónimo, libro tercero y cuarto: La Fundación del Monasterio de San Lorenzo el Real*, Madrid 1605 (new ed. in: *Nueva Biblioteca de auctores españoles*, II, Madrid ²1909)

SILENTIARIUS, Paulus, 'Εκφρασις του ναου της Αγιας Σοφιας' (ekphrasis) in: Paul Friedländer, *Johannes von Gaza, Paulus Silentiarius. Kunstbeschreibungen justinianischer Zeit*, Berlin–Leipzig 1912 (facs. repr. Hildesheim–New York 1969)

SINGER, Alexander von, *Krisis der Architektur*, Zürich 1928

SITTE, Camillo, *Der Städte-Bau nach seinen künstlerischen Grundsätzen*, Vienna 1889 (³1901; ⁴1909: facs. repr. Brunswick–Wiesbaden 1983); Fr. ed. Geneva–Paris 1902 (1918)

SLOAN, Samuel, *The Model Architect. A series of original designs for cottages, villas, suburban residences...* 2 vols, Philadelphia 1852 (1860, 1865, 1868, 1873); facs. repr. of 1852 entitled *Sloan's Victorian Buildings*, ed. Harold N. Cooledge, Jr, New York 1980

SOANE, John, *Designs in Architecture Consisting of Plans, Elevations and Sections for Temples, Baths, Cassines, Pavilions, Garden-Seats, Obelisks, and Other Buildings...*, London 1778

——, *Plans, Elevations and Sections of Buildings, Executed in the Counties of Norfolk, Suffolk, etc.*, London 1788 (facs. repr. 1971)

——, *Sketches in Architecture Containing Plans and Elevations of Cottages, Villas and Other Useful Buildings...*, London 1793 (facs. repr. 1971)

——, *Lectures on Architecture, By Sir John Soane...*, ed. Arthur T. Bolton, London 1929

——, *Description of the House and Museum on the North Side of Lincoln's-Inn Fields*, London 1830 (1832, 1835, 1893; ed. A. T. Bolton 1930)

SPECKLE (Specklin), Daniel, *Architectura von Vestungen, wie die zu unsern zeiten mögen erbawen werden, an Stätten Schlössern, und Clussen zu Wasser, Land...*, Strassburg 1589 (facs. repr. Unterschneidheim 1971; Portland, Or. 1972); enlarged ed. Strassburg 1599, 1608; later eds Dresden 1705, 1712, 1736

SPINI, Gherardo, *I tre primi libri sopra l'instituzione de'Greci et Latini architettori intorno agl'ornamenti che convengono a tutte le fabbriche che l'architettura compone (1568/69)*, ed. Cristina Acidini, in: Franco Borsi a.o., *Il disegno interrotto. Trattati medicei d'architettura*, 2 vols, Florence 1980; vol. I, pp. 11–201

SPON, Jacob and WHEELER, George, *Voyage d'Italie, de Dalmatie, de Grèce, et du Levant, fait aux années 1675 & 1676*, 2 vols, Amsterdam 1679 (other eds. Lyons 1678, London 1682)

STEINER, Rudolf, *Wege zu einem neuen Baustil 'und der Bau wird Mensch'*, Dornach

¹1926; Stuttgart ²1957; Dornach ³1982

——, *Architektur, Plastik und Malerei des Ersten Goetheanum*, Dornach ¹1972 (²1982)

——, *Der Baugedanke des Goetheanum*, Dornach ¹1932; Stuttgart ²1958

STEINGRUBER, Johann David, *Practische bürgerliche Baukunst...*, Nuremberg 1773

STICKLEY, Gustav, *Craftsman Houses*, New York 1909 (facs. repr. New York 1979)

STIEGLITZ, Christian Ludwig, *Geschichte der Baukunst der Alten*, Leipzig 1792

——, *Encyklopädie der bürgerlichen Baukunst*, 5 vols, Leipzig 1792–98

——, *Plans et dessins tirés de la belle architecture... accompagné d'un traité abrégé sur le beau dans l'architecture*, Leipzig 1800

——, *Archaeologie der Baukunst der Griechen und Römer*, Weimar 1801

——, *Von altdeutscher Baukunst*, Leipzig 1820

——, *Geschichte der Baukunst vom frühesten Alterhum bis in neuere Zeiten*, Nuremberg 1827

——, *Beiträge zur Geschichte der Ausbildung der Baukunst*, 2 vols, Leipzig 1834

STÖER, Lorenz, *Geometria et Perspectiva. Hier Inn Etliche Zerbochne Gebew den Schreinern in eingelegter Arbait dienstlich...*, Augsburg 1567 (facs. repr. Frankfurt 1972)

STUART, James and REVETT, Nicholas, *The Antiquities of Athens*, vol. I, London 1762; vol. II, London 1787 (finished by William Newton and published in 1788 after Stuart's death); vol. III, London 1794 (revised by Willey Reveley); vol. IV, London 1816 (Stuart's posthumous papers ed. Josuah Taylor and Joseph Wood); later eds London 1825–30; 1849; 1881; French ed. Paris 1818; German ed. Darmstadt–Leipzig 1829–33

STUKELEY, William, *Stonehenge: a Temple Restaur'd to the British Druids*, London 1740

STURM, Leonhard, Christoph, *De Sciagraphia templi Hierosolymitani*, Leipzig 1694

——, *Vademecum Architectonicum bestehend in neu ausgerechneten Tabellen zu der Civil und Militar-Baukunst...*, Amsterdam 1700

——, *Architectonisches Bedencken von der protestantischen kleinen Kirchen Figur und Einrichtung*, 1712

——, *Prodromus Architecturae Goldmannianae*, Augsburg 1714

——, *Vollständige Anweisung alle Art von Kirchen wohl anzugehen*, 1718

See also GOLDMANN, Nicolaus

SUCKLOW (Succov), Lorenz Johann Daniel, *Erste Gründe der bürgerlichen Baukunst im Zusammenhange entworfen*, Jena 1751 (²1763; ³1781; ⁴1798; facs. repr. of 4th ed. Leipzig 1979)

SUGER, Ordinationes; *Libellus Alter de Consacratione Ecclesiae Sancti Dionysii; Liber de Rebus in Administratione Sua Gestis*; Part repr. of Latin texts with Engl. trans. by Erwin Panofsky in: *Abbot Suger. On the Abbey Church of St.-Denis and its Art Treasures*, Princeton, NJ 1946 (ed. Gerda Panofsky-Soergel, ²1979)

SULLIVAN, Louis H., *Kindergarten Chats* (first in: *Interstate Architect & Builder 1901–02*); revised 1918; ed. Claude F. Bragdon, Lawrence 1934; ed. Isabella Athey 'Kindergarten Chats and Other Writings', New york 1947 (several reprs.)

——, *Democracy: A Man-Search* (ms, final version 1908), ed. Elaine Hedges, Detroit 1961

——, 'The Autobiography of an Idea' (first in: *Journal of the American Institute of*

Architects 10–11, 1922–23), New York 1924; ed. Ralph Marlowe Line, New York 1956 (several reprs)

——, *A System of Architectural Ornament According with a Philosophy of Man's Powers*, New York 1924; ed. Ada Louise Huxtable, New York 1967, Tübingen 1990

——, 'The High-Building Question', in: *The Graphic* V, 19 December 1891, p. 405

SULPICIO, Giovanni, ed.: *Vitruvius, De architectura libri decem*, Rome 1486 (?)

SULZER, Johann Georg, *Allgemeine Theorie der Schönen Künste*, 2 vols, Leipzig 1771–1774 (pirate eds. Leipzig 1773–74; Biel 1777; Leipzig 1777–78 and 1778–79); with 'literary additions', ed. Friedrich von Blankenburg: 4 vols, Leipzig 1786–87; 5 vols, Leipzig 1792–94 (facs. repr. Hildesheim 1967–70); the most complete ed. of Blankenburg's '*Literarische Zusätze*' (without Sulzer's text): 3 vols, Leipzig 1796–98 (facs. repr. Frankfurt 1972)

SWAN, Abraham, *The British Architect: or, The Builder's treasury of staircases...*, London 1745 (²1750; ³1758; facs. repr. of 1758 ed., ed. Adolf K. Placzek, New York 1967); Philadelphia 1775

SWITZER, Stephen, *Ichnographia Rustica: Or, The Nobleman, Gentleman and Gardener's Recreation...*, 3 vols, London 1715–18 (²1741–42)

TACCOLA, Mariano di Jacopo gen., (Florence, Cod. Pal. 766) *Liber tertius de Ingeneis ac Edifitiis non usitatis*, ed. J. H. Beck, Milan 1969)

——, (Munich, Cod. lat. 28800) *De Machinis. The Engineering Treatise of 1449*, ed. Gustina Scaglia, 2 vols, Wiesbaden 1971

TARTAGLIA, Nicolo, *La Nova Scientia*, Venice 1537 (²1550)

——, *Quesiti et inventioni diverse*, Venice 1538 (²1554)

TAUT, Bruno, *Glashaus. Werkbund-Ausstellung Cöln 1914*, Berlin 1914

——, *Die Stadtkrone*. Contributions by Paul Scheerbart a.o., Jena 1919

——, *Alpine Architektur*, Hagen 1919

——, *Die Auflösung der Städte oder Die Erde eine gute Wohnung oder Der Weg zur Alpinen Architektur*, Hagen 1920

——, *Der Weltbaumeister. Architekturschauspiel für symphonische Musik. Dem Geiste Paul Scheerbarts gewidmet*, Hagen 1920

——, (ed.), *Frühlicht*, 1920–1922 (1920 as supplement to *Stadtbaukunst in alter und neuer Zeit*; 1921–22 (published separately; repr. of a selection: Bruno Taut, *Frühlicht 1920–1922. Eine Folge für die Verwirklichung des neuen Baugedankens* (*Bauwelt Fundamente* 8). Berlin–Frankfurt–Vienna 1963

——, *Die neue Wohnung*, Leipzig 1924

——, *Architekturlehre aus der Sicht eines sozialistischen Architekten* (Turkish ed. Istanbul 1938); ed. Tilmann Heinisch and Goerd Peschken, Hamburg–Berlin 1977

TEMANZA, Tommaso, *Vite dei più celebri Architetti, e Scultori Veneziani...*, Venice 1778 (facs. repr. ed. Liliana Grassi, Milan 1966)

TEMPLE, William, *Upon the Gardens of Epicurus* (1685), first in *Miscellanea*, London 1690

TENSINI, Francesco, *La fortificazione, guardia, difesa et espugnazione delle fortezze esperimentata in diverse guerre*, Venice 1624

TESSENOW, Heinrich, *Der Wohnhausbau*, Munich 1909

——, *Hausbau und dergleichen*, Berlin 1916 (numerous eds; most recently, Munich 1984)

——, *Geschriebenes. Gedanken eines Baumeisters*, ed. Otto Kindt, Brunswick–Wiesbaden 1982

THORPE, John; John Summerson, 'The Book of Architecture of John Thorpe in Sir John Soane's Museum', *Walpole Society* XL, 1964–66

TIBALDI, Pellegrino, *Discorso d'Architettura* (Ms. der Bibl. Ambrosiana, Milan, Ms. P. 246 sup.)

——, *Regole di architettura* (Ms. der Bibl. Nat., Paris); as Pellegrino Pellegrini, *L'Architettura*, ed. Giorgio Panitta, Milan 1990

TORIJA Juan de, *Tratado breve, sobre las Ordenanzas de la Villa de Madrid...*, Madrid 1661 (1664, 1728, 1754, 1760)

TREILLE, François de la, *La Manière de fortifier villes, Chasteaux, et faire autres lieux fortz*, Lyons 1556

TRISSINO, Giangiorgio, 'Dell'Architettura' (fragment)'; first published 1878 (Nozze Pesaro-Bertolini); most recently in: Lionello Puppi, *Scrittori vicentini d'architettura del secolo XVI*, Vicenza 1973, pp. 82ff.; Paola Barocchi (ed.), *Scritti d'arte del Cinquecento*, III, Milan–Naples 1977, pp. 3032–36

TROOST, Gerdy, *Das Bauen im Neuen Reich*, Bayreuth 1938

UMBDENSTOCK, Gustave, *Cours d'architecture (Ecole Polytechnique)*, 2 vols, Paris 1930

UNGEWITTER, Georg Gottlob, *Entwürfe zu gothischen Ornamenten, zunächst für Decken und Wände*, Leipzig 1854

——, *Lehrbuch der gothischen Constructionen*, Leipzig 1859–64 (^{2}1875); ed. K. Mohrmann, ^{3}1889; ^{4}1901–03

——, *Sammlung mittelalterlicher Ornamentik in geschichtlicher und systematischer Anordnung*, Leipzig 1863–1865

Untersuchungen über den Charakter der Gebäude; über die Verbindung der Baukunst mit den schönen Künsten und über die Wirkungen, welche durch dieselbe hervorgebracht werden sollen, Dessau 1785 (2nd ed. Leipzig 1788); facs. repr. of ed. of 1788, ed. Hanno-Walter Kruft, Nördlingen 1986

VALADIER, Giuseppe, *L'architettura pratica dettata nella scuola e cattedra dell'insegne Accademia di San Luca*, 5 vols, Rome 1828–39

—— and VISCONTI, Aurelio, *Raccolta della più insigni fabbriche di Roma antica*, 7 fasc. Rome 1810–26

VALÉRY, Paul, *Eupalinous ou l'Architecte, précéde de l'Ame et la Danse*, Paris 1923

VALLE DI VENAFRO, Giovan Battista della, *Vallo. Libro continente appartenentie ad Capitanij: retenere et fortificare una Cita con bastioni, artificj de fuoco...*, Naples 1521

VALTURIO, Roberto, *De re militari libri XII*, Verona 1472 (numerous eds and trans in 15th and 16th centuries)

VANDELVIRA, Alonso de, *El tratado de arquitectura*, ed. Geneviève Barbé-Coquelin de Lisle, 2 vols, Albacete 1977

VAN DE VELDE, Henry, *Die Renaissance im modernen Kunstgewerbe*, Berlin 1901

——, *Kunstgewerbliche Laienpredigten*, Leipzig 1902

——, *Vom Neuen Stil*, Leipzig 1907

——, *Essays*, Leipzig 1910

——, *Geschichte meines Lebens*, ed. Hans Curjel, Munich 1962

——, *Zum Neuen Stil*, ed. Hans Curjel, Munich 1955

VANVITELLI, Luigi, *Dichiarazione dei Disegni del Reale Palazzo di Caserta*, Naples 1756

VASARI, Giorgio, *Le Vite d' più eccellenti pittori, scultori e architettori*, Florence '1550, ²1568; with commentary by Gaetano Milanesi (1878–1885), Club del Libri (1962–1966), Paola Barocchi (forthcoming)

VASARI the Younger, Giorgio, *La Città ideale* (1598). *Piante di Chiese (palazzi e ville) di Toscana e d'Italia*, ed. Virginia Stefanelli, Rome 1960

——, *Porte e finestre di Firenze e Roma*, ed. Franco Borsi, in: Borsi a.o., *Il disegno interrotto. Trattati medicei d'architettura*, 2 vols, Florence 1980; vol. I, pp. 293–321

VASI, Giuseppe, *Delle Magnificenze di Roma antica e moderna*, 10 vols, Rome 1747–61

VAUX, Calvert, *Villas and Cottages. A Series of Designs Prepared for Execution in the United States*, New York 1857 (²1864; ³1867; ⁴1869; ⁵1872; ⁶1874); facs. repr. of 1864 ed.: New York 1970

VEGETIUS, Renatus, *Flavius, Epitoma rei militaris (c. 400)*, ed. C. Lang, ²1885 (facs. repr. 1967)

VIEL, Charles-François, *Projet d'un Monument consacré à l'histoire naturelle*, Paris 1779

——, *Décadence de l'architecture à la fin du dix-huitième siècle*, Paris 1800

VIEL DE SAINT-MAUX, Jean-Louis, *Lettres sur l'architecture des anciens et celle des modernes, dans lesquelles se trouve développé la génie symbolique qui présida aux Monumens de l'Antiquité*, Paris 1787 (facs. repr. with intro. by Michel Faré under the name of Charles-François Viel de Saint-Maux, Geneva 1974)

VIGNOLA (Jacopo Barozzi), *Regola delli cinque ordini d'architettura* (1562?); facs. repr. Vignola 1974

——, *Le due regole della prospettiva pratica*, Rome 1583 (facs. repr. Vignola 1974)

VILLALÓN, Cristóbal de, *Ingeniosa comparación entre lo antiquo y lo presente*, Valladolid 1539

VILLALPANDO, Juan Bautista and PRADO, Jerónimo, *In Ezechielem Explanationes et Apparatus Urbis, ac Templi Hierosolymitani Commentariis et imaginibus illustratus*, 3 vols, Rome 1596–1604

VILLANUEVA, Diego de, *Colección de diferentes papales críticos sobre todas las partes de la Arquitectura...*, Valencia 1766 (facs. repr. with intro. by Luis Moya: Valencia 1979)

VILLARD DE HONNECOURT (lodge-book): Hans R. Hahnloser, *Villard de Honnecourt. Critical complete ed. of the lodge-book ms. fr. 19093 Paris, Bibl. Nat., Vienna 1935 (Graz ²1972); J. B. A. Lassus, Album de Villard de Honnecourt, Paris 1968; Theodore Bowie, The Sketchbook of Villard de Honnecourt*, New York 1959 (²1962); François Bucher, *Architector. The Lodge Books and Sketchbooks of Medieval Architects*, I, New York 1979, p. 15ff.

VIOLA ZANINI, Gioseffe, *Della architettura libri due*, Padua 1629 (1677, 1698)

VIOLLET-LE-DUC, Eugène-Emmanuel, *Dictionnaire raisonné de l'architecture française du XIe au XVIe siècle*, 10 vols, Paris 1854–1868 (facs. repr. Paris 1967)

——, *Entretiens sur l'architecture*, 2 vols, Paris 1863–72 (facs. repr. Brussels 1977)

——, *Habitations modernes*, 2 vols, Paris 1875–77 (facs. repr. Brussels 1979)

VISENTINI, Antonio, *Osservazioni, che servono di continuazione al trattato de Teofilo Gallaccini sopra gli errori degli architetti*, Venice 1771 (facs. repr. 1970)

VITRUVIUS, *De architectura libri decem*, ed. Valentin Rose, Leipzig ²1899; Lat.–Engl. ed., ed. Frank Granger, London–Cambridge ¹1931 (several eds); Lat.-German ed., ed. Curt Fensterbusch Darmstadt 1964.

For other eds of Vitruvius, see under names of translators or editors

VITTONE, Bernardo Antonio, *Istruzioni Elementari per indirizzo de' giovani allo studio dell'Architettura Civile divise in libri tre...*, 2 vols, Lugano 1760

——, *Istruzioni diverse concernenti l'officio dell'Architetto Civile...ad aumento delle Istruzioni Elementari...Della misura delle Fabbriche, del Moto, Misura della acque correnti, estimo de'beni...*, 2 vols, Lugano 1766

VOCHS, Lukas, *Allgemeines Baulexicon oder Erklärung der deutschen und französischen Kunstwörter...*, Augsburg–Leipzig 1781

VOGTHERR, Heinrich, *Ein frembds und wunderbars Kunstbüchlin allen Molern, Bildschnitzern, Goldschmiden, Steynmetzen, Schreynern, Platnern, Waffen- und Messerschmiden hochnutzlich zu gebrauchen...*, Strassburg 1537 (other eds 1538, 1572, 1608); facs. repr. of 1572 ed. Zwickau 1913

VOYSEY, Charles F. Annesley, *Reason as a basis of art*, London 1906

——, *Individuality*, London 1915

——, 'Patriotism in architecture', in: *Architectural Association Journal* XXVIII, 1912, pp. 21–5

VREDEMAN DE VRIES, Hans, *Das ander Bucch gemacht auff die zway Colonnen Corinthia und Composita*, Antwerp (¹1565) 1578

——, *Architectura der Bauung der Antiquen auss dem Vitruvius...*, Antwerp 1577, 1581 (facs. repr. of 1581 ed. Hildesheim–New York 1973)

——, *Hortorum Viridariorumque elegantes et multiplices formae...*, Antwerp 1583

——, *Perspective*, Lat.-German ed. Leyden 1604–05 (facs. repr. of Lat. ed. New York 1968)

——and VREDEMANN DE VRIES, Paul, *Variae Architecturae Formae*, Antwerp 1601

——, *Architectura, di köstliche unnd Weithberumbte khunst...*, 1606

WAGNER, Otto, *Moderne Architektur. Seinen Schülern ein Führer auf diesem Kunstgebiete*, Vienna 1895 (²1899; ³1902); 4th ed. entitled *Die Baukunst unserer Zeit. Dem Baukunstjünger ein Führer auf diesem Kunstgebiete*, Vienna 1914 (facs. repr. Vienna 1979)

——, *Die Großstadt. Eine Studie über diese*, Vienna 1911

——, *Einige Skizzen, Projekte und ausgeführte Bauwerke*, vol. I, Vienna 1890; vol. II, Vienna 1897; vol. III Vienna 1906; vol. IV, Vienna 1922; facs. repr. Tübingen 1987

WALPOLE, Horace, A Description of the Villa...at Strawberry-Hill near Twickenham, Middlesex, Strawberry Hill 1774; ²1784 (enlarged facs. ed. London 1964)

——, *On Modern Gardening* (1770), first in vol. 4 of Walpole's *Ancedotes of Painting*, 1771; crit. ed., ed. I. W. U. Chase, *Horace Walpole: Gardenist. An Edition of Walpole's The History of Modern Taste in Gardening*, Princeton, NJ 1943

WARE, Isaac, *The Four Books of Andrea Palladio's Architecture*, London 1738 (facs. repr. with intro. by Adolf K. Placzek, New York 1965)

——, *A Complete Body of Architecture*, London 1756; ²1757; ³c.1758–60; ⁴1768 (facs. repr. Farnborough 1971)

WATELET, Claude-Henri, *Essai sur les jardins*, Paris 1774 (facs. repr. Geneva 1972)

WEBB, John, *The Most Notable Antiquity of Great Britain, vulgarly called Stone-Heng, on Salisbury Plain, Restored*, London 1655

WEINBRENNER, Friedrich, *Denkwürdigkeiten aus seinem Leben*, ed. Aloys Schreiber, Heidelberg 1829; ed. Kurt K. Eberlein, Potsdam 1920; ed. Arthur von Schneider, Karlsruhe 1958

——, *Architektonisches Lehrbuch*, Tübingen 1810–19

——, *Ausgeführte und projectierte Gebäude*, Karlsruhe 1822–35 (part ed. of Hefte 1–3 and 7, ed. Wulf Schirmer, Karlsruhe 1978)

WEINLIG, Christian Traugott, *Briefe über Rom, verschiedene die Werke der Kunst, der öffentlichen Feste, Gebräuche und Sitten betreffenden Inhalts*, 3 vols, Dresden 1782–87

WHATELY, Thomas, *Observations on modern Gardening, illustrated by Descriptions*, London 1770 ([2]1770; [3]1771; [4]1777; [5]1801); facs. repr. of 1801 ed. Farnborough 1970; French ed. Paris 1771; German ed. Leipzig 1771

WHELER, George *see* SPON, Jacob

WHEWELL, William, *Architectural Notes on German Churches*, Cambridge–London 1830 (1st ed. anon.; [2]1835; [3]1842)

WHITWELL, Thomas Stedman, *Description of an Architectural Model from a Design by Stedman Whitwell Esq. for a Community upon a principle of united interests, as advocated by Robert Owen Esq.*, London 1830

WIEBEKING, Carl Friedrich von, *Theoretisch-practische Bürgerliche Baukunde durch Geschichte und Beschreibung der merkwürdigsten Baudenkmahle und ihre genauen Abbildungen bereichert*, 4 vols, Munich 1826

WILDE, Oscar, *Miscellanies*; in: *First Collected Edition of the Works of Oscar Wilde*, ed. Robert Ross, London 1908 (facs. repr. London 1969)

WILHELM, Johann, *Architectura Civilis, Beschreib- oder Vorreissung der fürnembsten Tachwerck...*, Frankfurt 1649 ([2]1654); slightly revised ed. Nuremberg 1668 ([2]1702); facs. repr. of 1668 ed. Hannover 1977

——, *Architecturae Civilis Pars II* (ed. by the publisher Paul Fürst), Nuremberg n.d.; facs. repr. in appendix: Hannover 1977

WILLIS, Robert, *Remarks on the Architecture of the Middle Ages, especially of Italy*, Cambridge 1835

——, *On the Construction of Vaults in the Middle Ages*, Royal Institute of British Architects, London 1842

——, *The Architectural Nomenclature of the Middle Ages*, London 1844

WINCKELMANN, Johann Joachim, *Anmerkungen über die Baukunst der Alten*, Dresden 1762 (facs. repr. Baden–Baden–Strasbourg 1964)

——, *Sendschreiben von den Herculanischen Entdeckungen*, Dresden 1762; *Nachrichten von den neuesten Herculanischen Entdeckungen*, Dresden 1764 (facs. repr. of both writings, Baden–Baden–Strasbourg 1964)

——, *Geschichte der Kunst des Altertums*, Dresden 1764 (facs. repr. Baden-Baden–Strasbourg 1966; ed. Wilhelm Senff, Weimar 1964)

——, *Sämtliche Werke*, ed. Joseph Eiselein, 12 vols, Donaueschingen 1825–29

——, *Kleine Schriften, Vorreden, Entwürfe*, ed. Walther Rehm and Hellmut Sichtermann, Berlin 1968

WOLTERS, Rudolf, *Neue deutsche Baukunst*, Prague 1943

WOOD, John, *The Origin of Building: or, the Plagiarism of the Heathens detected in Five*

Books, Bath 1741 (facs. repr. Farnborough 1968)

——, *An Essay towards a Description of Bath...*, London 1742; ²1749; 1769 (facs. repr. Bath 1969; Farnborough 1970)

——, *Choir Gaure, Vulgarly called Stonehenge...*, Oxford 1747

——, *A Dissertation upon the Orders of Columns, And Their Appendages...*, London 1750

WOOD, John (the Younger), *A Series of Plans for Cottages or Habitations of the Labourer...*, London 1781 (²1792; ³1806; facs. repr. of 1806 ed. 1972)

WOOD, Robert, *The Ruins of Palmyra, otherwise Tedmor, in the Desert*, London 1753 (simultaneous French ed. London 1753)

——, *The Ruins of Balbec otherwise Heliopolis in Coelosyria*, London 1757

——, *The Ruins of Palmyra and Balbec*, London 1827

WOOLFE, John and GANDON, James, *Vitruvius Britannicus, or the British Architect*, vol. IV, London 1767 (facs. repr. in ed. by John Harris, New York 1967)

WOTTON, Henry, *The Elements of Architecture*, London 1624 (facs. repr. with intro. by Frederick Hard, Charlottesville, Vir. 1968; Farnborough 1969)

WREN, Christopher, *Stephen Wren, Parentalia: or, Memoirs of the Family of the Wren*, London 1750; facs. repr. of so-called 'Heirloom Copy' in RIBA, Farnborough 1965; Wren Society, 20 vols, Oxford 1924–43

WRIGHT, Frank Lloyd, *Ausgeführte Bauten und Entwürfe*, Berlin 1910 (²1924); facs. repr. ed. Vincent Scully, Tübingen 1986

——, *Ausgeführte Bauten* (intro. by Charles Robert Ashbee), Berlin 1911 (facs. repr. with intro. by Grant Carpenter Manson, New York 1982)

——, *Modern Architecture. Being the Kahn Lectures for 1930*, Princeton, NJ 1931

——, *The Disappearing City*, New York 1932 (new ed. entitled *The Industrial Revolution Runs Away*, New York 1969)

——, *An Organic Architecture. The Architecture of Democracy. The Sir George Watson Lectures of the Sulgrave Manor Board for 1939*, London 1939 (facs. reprs. 1941, 1970)

——, *When Democracy Builds*, Chicago 1945 (German ed. *Usonien: When Democracy Builds*, Berlin 1950)

——, *Genius and the Mobocracy*, New York 1949 (enlarged ed. New York 1971)

——, *The Future of Architecture*, New York 1953 (repr. London 1955; New York 1970)

——, *The Natural House*, New York 1954 (New York 1970; London 1972)

——, *A Testament*, New York 1957 (repr. London 1959)

——, *The Living City*, New York 1958 (facs. repr. New York 1970)

——, *Schriften und Bauten*, Munich–Vienna 1963

——, *Humane Architektur*, ed. Wolfgang Braatz (*Bauwelt Fundamente 25*), Gütersloh–Berlin 1969

XIMÉNEZ, Fray Andrés *see* JIMÉNEZ

ZANCHI, Giovanni Battista, *Del modo di fortificar le città*, Venice 1554

ZUCCARO, Federico, *L'idea de'Pittori, scultori et architetti*, Turin 1607; c.f. the ed. of Federico Zuccaro, *Scritti d'arte*, ed. Detlef Heikamp, Florence 1961

5. Since 1945

AALTO, Alvar, *Sketches*, ed. Göran Schildt, Cambridge, Mass.–London 1978

ALEXANDER, Christopher, *Notes on the Synthesis of Form (1964)*, Cambridge, Mass.–London 1971 (frequently reprinted)

——, *The Timeless Way of Building*, New York 1979

——, *The Linz Café*, Oxford–Vienna 1981

ALLSOPP, Bruce, *A Modern Theory of Architecture*, London–Henley–Boston, Mass. 1977

ARNDT, Adolf, *Demokratie als Bauherr*. Akademie der Künste Berlin (*Anmerkungen zur Zeit*, 6), Berlin 1961

ARNHEIM, Rudolf, *The Dynamics of Architectural Form*, Berkeley–Los Angeles–London 1977

AYMONINO, Carlo, *Origine e sviluppo della città moderna*, Padua 1964

BAKEMA, J. B., *Thoughts about architecture*, ed. Marianne Gray, London–New York 1981

BLOOMER, Kent, C. see MOORE, Charles W.

BOFILL, Ricardo, *Los espacios de Abraxas. El palacio, el teatro, el arco*, ed. Annabella d'Huart, Milan 1981

——, a.o. (Taller de arquitectura), *La Cité: Histoire et Technologie. Projets Français 1978–81*, Milan 1981

DAHINDEN, Justus, *Versuch einer Standortsbestimmung der Gegenwartsarchitektur*, Zürich 1956

FULLER, R. Buckminster, *No More Secondhand God and Other Writings*, Carbondale 1963

GERKAN, Meinhard von, *Die Verantwortung der Architektur. Bedingungen für die gebaute Umwelt*, Stuttgart 1982

JACOBS, Jane, *The Death and Life of Great American Cities*, New York 1961

JOHNSON, Philip, *Writings*, New York 1979

KRIER, Rob, *On Architecture*, London–New York 1982

KUROKAWA, Kisho, *Metabolism in Architecture*, Boulder, Col. 1977

MICHELUCCI, Giovanni, *La felicità dell'architetto 1948–1980*, Pistoia 1981

MOORE, Charles W. and ALLEN, Gerald and LYNDON, Donlyn, *The places of houses*, New York 1974

—— and ALLEN, Gerald, *Dimensions. Space, Shape & Scale in Architecture*, New York 1976

—— and BLOOMER, Kent C., *Body, Memory and Architecture*, New Haven, Conn.–London 1977

NERVI, Per Luigi, *Scienza o arte del costruire*, Rome 1945

——, *Aesthetics and Technology in Building*, Cambridge, Mass.–London 1965

NIEMEYER, Oscar, *Minha Esperiencia em Brasilia*, Rio de Janeiro 1961

NORBERG-SCHULZ, Christian, *Intentions in Architecture*, Oslo 1963

OTTO, Frei, *Das Hängende Dach. Gestalt und Struktur*, diss. Berlin 1954

——, *Schriften und Reden 1951–1983*, ed. Berthold Burckhardt, Brunswick–Wiesbaden 1984

——, a.o., *Zugbeanspruchte Konstruktionen. Gestalt, Struktur und Berechnung von Bauten aus Seilen, Netzen und Membranen*, 2 vols, Berlin 1962–64

——— a.o., *Natürliche Konstruktionen*, Stuttgart 1982

PRAK, Niels Luning, *The language of architecture. A contribution to architectural theory*, The Hague–Paris 1968

ROGERS, Ernesto Nathan, *Gli elementi del fenomeno architettonico*, ed. Cesare De Seta, Naples 1981

ROSSI, Aldo, *L'Architettura della Città*, Padua 1966

———, *Scritti scelti sull'architettura e la città 1956–1972*, Milan 1975

———, *A Scientific Autobiography*, Cambridge, Mass. 1982

——— a.o., 'Architettura Razionale' (*XV Triennale di Milano. Sezione Internazionale di Architettura*), Milan 1973

SAMONÀ, Giuseppe, *L'urbanistica e l'avvenire della città negli stati europei*, Bari 1959 (²1960); paperback ed. Rome–Bari 1967

SMITHSON, Alison and Peter, *Ordinariness and Light: Urban Theories 1952–1960 and their application in a building project 1963–1970*, London 1970

———, *Without Rhetoric: An Architectural Aesthetic 1955–1972*, London 1973

SOLERI, Paolo, *Arcology: The City in the Image of Man*, Cambridge, Mass. 1969

———, *The Bridge Between Matter and Spirit Is Matter Becoming Spirit. The Arcology of Paolo Soleri*, Garden City, NY 1973

TANGE, Kenzo a.o., *Katsura-Tradition and Creation in Japanese Architecture*, Tokyo–New Haven, Conn. 1960

TIGERMAN, Stanley, *Versus An American Architect's Alternatives*, New York 1982

——— a.o., *Late Entries to the Chicago Tribune Tower Competition*, New York 1980

VENTURI, Robert, *Complexity and Contradiction in Architecture*, New York 1966

——— SCOTT BROWN, Denis and IZENOUR, Steven, *Learning from Las Vegas*, Cambridge, Mass.–London 1972 (²1978)

VILLANUEVA, Carlos Raúl, *La Caracas de ayer y de hoy*, Caracas 1943

Supplement to the Bibliography

Sequence of subheadings follows that of the main Bibliography.

I, 1: General works on art and architectural theory

BARASCH, Moshe, *Theories of Art From Plato to Winckelmann*, New York–London 1985
——, *Modern Theories of Art, I. From Winckelmann to Baudelaire*, New York–London 1990
BIRAL, Alessandro and MORACHIELLO, Paolo, *Immagini dell'ingegnere tra Quattro e Settecento*, Milan 1985
CHASTEL, André and GUILLAUME, Jean (ed.), 'Les traités d'architecture de la Renaissance'. *Actes du colloque tenu à Tours du 1er au 11 juillet 1981*, Paris 1988
FAGIOLO, Marcello, *Architettura e massoneria*, Florence 1988
KRUFT, Hanno-Walter, *Städte in Utopia. Die Idealstadt vom 15. bis zum 18. Jahrhundert zwischen Staatsutopie und Wirklichkeit*, Munich 1989
KULTERMANN, Udo, *Kleine Geschichte der Kunsttheorie*, Darmstadt 1987
LONG, Pamela O., 'The contribution of architectural writers to a 'scientific' outlook in the fifteenth and sixteenth centuries', *The Journal of Medieval and Renaissance Studies* 15, 1985, pp. 265–98
NERDINGER, Winfried a.o. (ed.), *Revolutionsarchitektur. Ein Aspekt der europäischen Architektur um 1800* (cat.), Munich 1990
PEREZ GOMEZ, Alberto, *The Use of Geometry and Number in Architectural Theory From Symbols of Reconciliation to Instruments of Technological Domination (1680–1820)*, PhD thesis, University of Essex 1972
POCHAT, Götz, *Geschichte der Ästhetik und Kunsttheorie. Von der Antike bis zum 19. Jahrhundert*, Cologne 1986
SCRUTON, Roger, *The Aesthetics of Architecture*, Princeton 1979 (²1980)
TATARKIEWICZ, Wladislaw, *History of Aesthetics*, 3 vols, Warsaw 1962–67 (Polish); Engl. ed. The Hague–Paris–Warsaw 1970–74
VEN, Conelis van de, *Space in Architecture: The Evolution of a New Idea in the Theory and History of the Modern Movements*, Assen 1987

I, 2.a. The Middle Ages

Cat. *Les bâtisseurs des cathédrales gothiques*, ed. Roland Recht, Strasbourg 1989
COENEN, Ulrich, *Die spätgotischen Werkmeisterbücher in Deutschland als Beitrag zur mittelalterlichen Architekturtheorie. Untersuchung und Edition der Lehrschriften für Entwurf und Ausführung von Sakralbauten*, diss., Aachen 1989
GÜNTHER, Hubertus (ed.), *Deutsche Architekturtheorie zwischen Gotik und Renaissance*, Darmstadt 1985
PITZ, Ernst, 'Das Aufkommen der Berufe des Architekten und Bauingenieurs. Baubetrieb

und Baugewerbe nach unteritalienischen Quellen des 13. Jahrhunderts', *Quellen und Forschungen aus italienischen Archiven und Bibliotheken* 66, 1986, pp. 40–74

I, 2.*b*. Italy: fifteenth to eighteenth century

Buck, August and Guthmüller, Bodo, 'Die italienische Stadt der Renaissance im Spannungsfeld von Utopie und Wirklichkeit' (*Centro Tedesco di Studi Veneziani. Quaderni 27*), Venice 1984

Gioseffi, Decio a.o., *Trattati di prospettiva, architettura militare, idraulica e altre discipline. Saggi e note*, Venice 1985

Guenzi, Carlo (ed.), *L'arte di edificare. Manuali in Italia 1750–1950*, Milan 1981

Mayer-Himmelheber, Susanne, *Bischöfliche Kunstpolitik nach dem Tridentinum. Der Secunda-Roma-Anspruch Carlo Borromeos und die mailändischen Verordnungen zu Bau und Ausstattung von Kirchen*, Munich 1984

Tafuri, Manfredo, *Venezia e il Rinascimento*, Turin 1985

Wazbinski, Zygmunt, *L'Accademia Medicea del Disegno a Firenze nel Cinquecento*, 2 vols, Florence 1987

I, 1.*c*. France: sixteenth to eighteenth century

Braham, Allan, *The Architecture of the French Enlightenment*, Berkeley, Ca.–Los Angeles 1980

Cat. '*Les architectes de la liberté 1789–1799*', Paris 1989

Cat. '*Architecture et art urbain. Bordeaux 1780–1815*', Bordeaux 1989

Harrington, Kevin, *Changing Ideas on Architecture in the 'Encyclopédie', 1750–1776*, Ann Arbor, Mich. 1985

Szambien, Werner, *Symétrie, goût, caractère. Théorie et terminologie de l'architecture à l'âge classique 1550–1800*, Paris 1986

——, *Les projets de l'an II. Concours d'architecture de la période révolutionnaire*, Paris 1986

Vidler, Anthony, *The Writing of the Walls. Architectural Theory in the Late Enlightenment*, Princeton, NJ 1987

I, 2.*d*. Spain: sixteenth to eighteenth century

Riviera Blanco, José Janvier, *Juan Bautista de Toledo y Felipe II. La implantación del clasicismo en España*, Villadolid 1984

Wilkinson, Catherine, 'Planning a style for the Escorial: An Architectural Treatise for Philip of Spain', *Journal of the Society of Architectural Historians* XLIV, 1985, pp. 37–47

I, 2.*e*. Germany and its neighbours: sixteenth to eighteenth century

Brugerolles, Emmanuelle and Guillet, David, 'Recueils gravés d'architecture et de décoration en Allemagne au XVIIIᵉ siècle: à propos d'un groupe de dessins de l'École des Beaux-Arts', *Revue du Louvre* 38, 1988, pp. 106–16

LÜTTICHAU, Mario-Andreas von, *Die deutsche Ornamentkritik im 18. Jahrhundert*, Hildesheim–Zürich–New York 1983

MELLINGHOFF, Tilman and WATKIN, David, *German Architecture and the Classical Ideal, 1740–1840*, London 1987

SCHÜTTE, Ulrich, *Ordnung und Verzierung. Untersuchungen zur deutschsprachigen Architekturtheorie des 18. Jahrhunderts*, Brunswick–Wiesbaden 1986

I, 2.*f.* England: sixteenth to eighteenth century

ARCHER, John, *The Literature of British Domestic Architecture 1715–1842*, Cambridge, Mass.–London 1985

LEES-MILNE, James, *Earls of Creation. Five Great Patrons of Eighteenth-Century Art* (1962), London 1986

——, *William Beckford*, Montclair, NJ 1979

RUMP, Gerhard Charles (ed.), *Kunst und Kunsttheorie des XVIII. Jahrhunderts in England. Studien zum Wandel ästhetischer Anschauungen 1650–1830*, Hildesheim 1979

STILLMAN, Damie, *English Neo-Classical Architecture*, 2 vols, London 1988

WORSLEY, Giles, 'The baseless Roman Doric column in mid-eighteenth-century English architecture: a study in neo-classicism', *The Burlington Magazine* CXXVIII, 1986, pp. 331–9

I, 2.*g.* Nineteenth and twentieth centuries: general

BRADBURY, Ronald, *The Romantic Theories of Architecture of the Nineteenth Century in Germany, England and France*, PhD thesis, Columbia Univ., New York 1934 (facs. repr. New York 1976)

ISAC, Ángel, *Eclecticismo y pensamiento arquitectónico en España. Discursos, revistas, congresos 1846–1919*, Granda 1987

I, 2.*j.* England: nineteenth century

BROWNLEE, David B., 'The First High Victorians: British architectural theory in the 1840s', *Architectura* 15, 1985, pp. 33–46

I, 2.*k.* United States: nineteenth century

ZUKOWSKY, John (ed.), *Chicago Architecture, 1872–1922: Birth of a Metropolis*, Munich–Chicago 1987)

I, 2.*m.* Italy: 1900–1945

DE SETA, Cesare, *Architetti italiani del Novecento*, Rome–Bari 1982 (^{2}1987)

——, *Il destino dell'architettura. Persico Giolli Pagano*, Rome–Bari 1985

I, 2.*p.* Since 1945

BELLUZZI, Amedeo and CONFORTI, Claudia, *Architettura italiana 1944–1984*, Rome–Bari 1985

DIAMONSTEIN, Barbaralee, *American Architecture Now II*, New York 1985

KAUFMANN, Jacob, *'Post-Modern Architecture': An Ideology*, PhD thesis, Univ. of California, Los Angeles 1982

I, 3.*a.* Theory of the Orders

ONIANS, John, *Bearers of Meaning: The Classical Orders in Antiquity, the Middle Ages, and the Renaissance*, Princeton, NJ 1989

I, 3.*b.* Vitruvian tradition in the Renaissance

CIAPPONI, Lucia A., 'Fra Giocondo da Verona and his Edition of Vitruvius', *Journal of the Warburg and Courtauld Institutes*, XLVI, 1983, pp. 72–90

FONTANA, Vincenzo, 'Il "Vitruvio" del 1556: Barbaro, Palladio, Marcolini', in: *Trattati scientifici nel Veneto fra il XV e XVI secolo. Saggi e studi*, ed. Enzo Riondato, Vicenza 1985, pp. 39–72

LONG, Pamela Olivia, *The Vitruvian Commentary Tradition and Rational Architecture in the Sixteenth Century: a Study in the History of Ideas*, PhD thesis, Univ. of Maryland 1979

PAGLIARA, Pier Nicola, 'Vitruvio da testo a canone', in: Salvatore Settis (ed.), *Memoria dell'antico nell'arte italiana*, vol. III, Turin 1986, pp. 3–85

I, 3.*c.* Theory of proportion

FEINSTEIN, Diego Horacio, *Der Harmoniebegriff in der Kunstliteratur und Musiktheorie der italienischen Renaissance*, diss., Freiburg 1977

JUNECKE, Hans, *Die wohlbemessene Ordnung. Pythagoreische Proportionen in der historischen Architektur*, Berlin 1982

I, 3.*e.* Gothic Revival

HASLAG, Josef, *'Gothic' im siebzehnten und achtzehnten Jahrhundert. Eine wort- und ideengeschichtliche Untersuchung*, Cologne–Graz 1963

MCCARTHY, Michael, *The Origins of the Gothic Revival*, New Haven, Conn.–London 1987

I, 3.*f.* Rediscovery of Classical antiquity

Cat. *'Bibliotheca Etrusca. Fonti letterarie e figurative tra XVIII e XIX secolo nella Biblioteca dell'Istituto Nazionale di Archeologia e Storia dell'Arte'*, Rome 1985

FAGIOLO, Marcello (ed.), *Roma e l'antico nell'arte e nella cultura del Cinquecento*, Rome 1985

GÜNTHER, Hubertus, *Das Studium der antiken Architektur in den Zeichnungen der Hochrenaissance*, Tübingen 1988

RASPI SERRA, Joselita (ed.), *La fortuna di Paestum e la memoria del dorico 1750–1830*, 2 vols, Florence 1986

SETTIS, Salvatore (ed.), *Memoria dell'antico nell'arte italiana*, 3 vols, Turin 1984–86

I, 3.g. Concepts of the garden

BUTTLAR, Adrian von, *Der Landschaftsgarten. Gartenkunst des Klassizismus und der Romantik*, Cologne 1989

STRONG, Roy, *The Renaissance Garden in England*, London 1979

WIMMER, Clemens Alexander, *Geschichte der Gartentheorie*, Darmstadt 1989

II, 2: Anthologies: fifteenth to eighteenth century

Pietro Cataneo, Giacomo Barozzi da Vignola, Trattati con l'aggiunta degli scritti di architettura di Alvise Cornaro, Francesco Giorgi, Claudio Tolomei, Giangiorgio Trissino, Giorgio Vasari, ed. Elena Bassi a.o., Milan 1985

LEFAIVRE, Liane and TZONIS, Alexander (ed.), *Theorieën van het architektonies ontwerpen. Een historiese dokumentatie*, Nijmegen 1984

SCIOLLA, Gianni Carlo (ed.), *Letteratura artistica dell'età barocca. Antologia di testi*, Turin 1983

——(ed.), *Letteratura artistica del Settecento. Antologia di testi*, Turin 1984

II, 3. Anthologies: nineteenth and twentieth centuries

BEYRODT, Wolfgang a.o. (ed.), *Kunsttheorie und Kunstgeschichte des 19. Jahrhunderts in Deutschland*, 3 vols, Stuttgart 1982–85 (vol. II: *Architektur*, ed. Harold Hammer-Schenk)

II, 4: Sources (primary and secondary)

Ashbee, C. R.:
CRAWFORD, Alan, *C. R. Ashbee. Architect, Designer & Romantic Socialist*, New Haven, Conn.–London 1985

Bötticher, Karl:
SKERL, Joachim, 'Zur Architekturtheorie Karl Böttichers', in: *Karl Friedrich Schinkel und die Antike*, ed. Max Kunze (*Beiträge der Winckelmann-Gesellschaft*, vol. 12), Stendal 1985, pp. 85–91

Boffrand, Germain:
GALLET, Michel and GARMS, Jörg a.o., *Germain Boffrand 1667–1754. L'aventure d'un architecte indépendant*, Paris 1986

Boullée, Etienne-Louis:
MADEC, Philippe, *Boullée*, Paris 1986

Colonna, Francesco:
CALVESI, Maurizio, 'Hypnerotomachia Poliphili. Nuovi riscontri e nuove evidenze documentarie per Francesco Colonna Signore di Preneste', *Storia dell'arte 60*, 1987, pp. 85–136

DANESI SQUARZINA, Silvia, 'Francesco Colonna, principe, letterato, e la sua cerchia', *Storia dell'arte* 60, 1987, pp. 137–54

Durand, J.-N.-L.:
VILLARI, Sergio, *J.-N.-L. Durand (1760–1834). Arte e scienza dell'architettura*, Rome 1987

Finsterlin, Hermann:
DÖHL, Reinhard, *Hermann Finsterlin. Eine Annäherung*, Stuttgart 1988

Fontaine, Pierre-François-Léonard:
FONTAINE, Pierre-François-Léonard, *Journal 1799–1853*, 2 vols, Paris 1987

Francesco di Giorgio Martini:
SCAGLIA, Gustina (ed.), 'Il 'Vitruvio Magliabechiano' di Francesco di Giorgio Martini' (*Documenti inediti di cultura toscana*, VI), Florence 1985

Guarini, Guarino:
MEEK, H. A., *Guarino Guarini and His Architecture*, New Haven, Conn.–London 1988
MÜLLER, Claudia, *Unendlichkeit und Transzendenz in der Sakralarchitektur Guarinis*, Hildesheim–Zürich–New York 1986

Hübsch, Heinrich:
HÜBSCH, Heinrich, *Die Architektur und ihr Verhältnis zur heutigen Malerei und Skulptur*, Stuttgart-Tübingen 1847 (New ed., ed. Jürgen Eckhardt und Helmut Geisert, Berlin 1985)

Kiesler, Friedrich:
BOGNER, Dieter (ed.), *Friedrich Kiesler. Architekt, Maler, Bildhauer 1890–1965*, Vienna 1988

Loos, Adolf:
AMANSHAUSER, Hildegard, *Untersuchungen zu den Schriften von Adolf Loos*, Vienna 1985

Loudon, John Claudius:
SIMO, Melanie Louise, *Loudon and the Landscape: From Country Seat to Metropolis, 1783–1843*, New Haven, Conn.–London 1988

Mies van der Rohe, Ludwig:
NEUMEYER, Fritz, *Mies van der Rohe. Das kunstlose Wort*, Berlin 1986
SCHULZ, Franz, *Mies van der Rohe. A Critical Biography*, Chicago–London 1985

Palissy, Bernard:
PALISSY, Bernard, *La Recepte véritable*, ed. Keith Cameron, Geneva 1988
CÉARD, Jean, 'Relire Bernard Palissy', *Revue de l'art* 78, 1987, pp. 77–83

Palladio, Andrea:
PALLADIO, Andrea, *Scritti sull'architettura (1554–1579)*, ed. Lionello Puppi, Vicenza 1988
BATTILOTTI, Donata, 'Villa Barbaro a Maser: Un difficile cantiere', *Storia dell'arte* 53, 1985, pp. 33–48
JACKSON REIST, Inge, *Renaissance Harmony: The Villa Barbaro at Maser*, PhD thesis, Columbia Univ. New York 1985

Perrault, Claude:
PICON, Antoine, *Claude Perrault, 1613–1688 ou la curiosité d'un classique*, Paris 1988

Pugin, A. W. N.:
BLECHER, Margaret, *A. W. N. Pugin: An Annotated Bibliography*, London 1987
WEDGWOOD, Alexandra, *A. W. N. Pugin and the Pugin Family (Catalogue of Architectural*

Drawings in the Victoria and Albert Museum), London 1985

Saarinen, Eliel:

SAARINEN, Eliel, *The Search for Form in Art and Architecture*, New York 1948 (facs. repr. New York 1985)

Schinkel, Karl Friedrich:

SCHINKEL, Karl Friedrich, *Reise nach England, Schottland und Paris im Jahre 1826*, ed. Gottfried Riemann, Berlin–Munich 1986; *Die Reise nach Frankreich und England im Jahre 1826*, ed. Reinhard Wegner, Munich–Berlin 1990

SZAMBIEN, Werner, *Schinkel*, Paris 1989

Serlio, Sebastiano:

GÜNTHER, Hubertus, 'Porticus Pompeji. Zur archäologischen Erforschung eines antiken Bauwerks in der Renaissance und seine Rekonstruktion im dritten Buch des Sebastiano Serlio', *Zeitschrift für Kunstgeschichte* 44, 1981, pp. 358–98

JOHNSON, June Gwendolyn, *Sebastiano Serlio's Treatise on Military Architecture* (Bayerische Staatsbibliothek, Munich, Codex Icon. 190), PhD thesis, Univ. of California, Los Angeles 1984

THOENES, Christof (ed.), *Sebastiano Serlio (Centro Internazionale di Studi di Architettura 'Andrea Palladio' di Vicenza)*, Milan 1989

WISCHERMANN, Heinrich, 'Castrametatio und Städtebau im 16. Jahrhundert: Sebastiano Serlio', *Bonner Jahrbücher des Rheinischen Landesmuseums in Bonn* 175, pp. 171–186

Sullivan, Louis:

ANDREW, David S., *Louis Sullivan and the Polemics of Modern Architecture*, Chicago 1985

TWOMBLY, Robert, *Louis Sullivan. His Life and Work*, New York 1986

DE WIT, Wim (ed.), *Louis Sullivan. The Function of Ornament*, New York–London 1986

Tibaldi, Pellegrino:

TIBALDI, Pellegrino, *L'Archittetura di Leon Battista Alberti nel Commento di P. T.*, ed. Giorgio Simoncini, Rome 1988

Viollet-le-Duc, Eugène:

BRESSANI, Martin, 'Notes on Viollet-le-Duc's philosophy of history: dialectics and technology', *Journal of the Society of Architectural Historians* XLVIII, 1989, pp. 327–50

Vittone Bernardo:

TAVASSI LA GRECA, Bianca, *Bernardo Vittone architetto e teorico del 1700*, Rome 1985

——, 'Considerazioni sull' opera teorica di Bernardo Vittone. Guarini/Vittone: una linea teorica di continuità o di fratture?', *Storia dell'arte* 64, 1988, pp. 249–84

Webb, John:

BOLD, John, *John Webb. Architectural Theory and Practice in the Seventeenth Century*, Oxford 1989

Wood, John:

MOWL, Tim and EARNSHAW, Brian, *John Wood: Architect of Obsession*, Bath 1988

English-language translations of sources

English-language translations of sources listed on pages 633–73 and 678–80, from all periods to the present day, including modern facsimile reprints.

To 1945

ALBERTI, Leone Battista, *The Architecture of Leon Battista Alberti in Ten Books*, trans. James Leoni, 3 vols, London from 1726, (one vol) ³1755 (facs. repr. Alberti: *The Ten Books on Architecture*, ed. Joseph Rykwert, London 1955–New York 1986)
———, *On the Art of Building in Ten Books*, trans. Joseph Rykwert, Neil Leach and Robert Tavernor, Cambridge, Mass.–London 1989
ALLATIOS, Leo, *The Newer Temples of the Greeks*, trans. with commentary by Anthony Cutler, University Park Rome–London 1969
BARTHÉLEMY, Jean-Jacques, *Travels of Anacharsis the Younger in Greece...*, trans. William Beaumont, 7 vols, London ²1794, ⁴1806
BERNINI, Gian Lorenzo (M. de Chantelou), *Journal du voyage du Cav. Bernini en France* trans. in: Cecil Gould, *Bernini in France: An Episode in Seventeenth-Century History*, Princeton, NJ 1982
BLUM, Hans, *A Description of the Five Orders of...Architecture*, London 1678 (facs. repr. 1967)
BORROMEO, Carlo, *Instructions on Ecclesiastical Buildings*, trans. and ed. G.J. Wigley, London 1857
BOULLÉE, Etienne-Louis, *Architecture. Essai sur l'art* trans. in: Helen Rosenau, *Boullée and Visionary Architecture*, London 1976
CORTESI, Paolo, Lat.–Engl. ed. of *De Cardinalatu*, book II, chapter 2 'De Domo Cardinalis' trans. in: Kathleen Weil-Garris and John D'Amico, 'The Renaissance Cardinal's Ideal Palace...', *Memoirs of the American Academy in Rome* XXXV, 1980, pp.69ff.
DESGODETS, Antoine, *The Ancient Buildings of Rome*, plates engraved and text trans. by G. Marshall, 2 vols, London 1771, 1795
DOESBURG, Theo van, *Principles of Neo-Plastic Art*, trans. Janet Seligman, London 1969
———, *On European Architecture: Complete Essays from Het Bouwebedrijf 1924–1931*, trans. Charlotte I. Loeb and Arthur L. Loeb, Basel 1990
FILARETE (Antonio Averlino), *Trattato* trans. in: *Filarete's Treatise on Architecture*, ed. John R. Spencer, 2 vols, New Haven–London 1965
FISCHER VON ERLACH, Johann Bernhard, *A Plan of Civil and Historical Architecture*, trans. Thomas Lediard, London 1730, ²1737
FRANCINI, Alessandro, *A New Book of Architecture...*, trans. Robert Pricke, London 1669 (facs. repr. with original, 1966)
FRÉART DE CHAMBRAY, Roland, *A Parallel of Antient Architecture with the Modern* (appendix contains English trans. of Alberti's *De Statua*), trans. John Evelyn, London 1664 (facs. repr. 1970)

GINZBURG, Moisey Yakovlevich, *Style and Epoch*, with introduction by Anatole Senkevitch, Jr, Cambridge, Mass–London 1982

KUGLER, Franz, *Über die Polychromie* trans. in part by W.R. Hamilton, 'On the Polychromy of Greek Architecture', *RIBA Transactions* I, Part I, 1835–36

LAUGIER, Marc-Antoine, *An Essay on Architecture*, London 1755, 1756

LE CLERC, Sébastien, *A Treatise of Architecture*, 2 vols, London 1723, 1724

LE CORBUSIER (Charles-Edouard Jeanneret), *Complete Architectural Works*, with some English transs. ed. Willy Boesiger, 8 vols, London 1964–70

—— (and Saugnier), *Towards a New Architecture*, trans. Frederick Etchells, London 1927 (facs. repr. New York–London 1986)

——, *The City of Tomorrow and its Planning* [*Urbanisme*], trans. Frederick Etchells, London 1929 (facs. repr. New York–London 1987)

——, *The Radiant City*, trans. Pamela Knight, Eleanor Levieux and Derek Coltman, London 1967

——, *The Athens Charter*, trans. Anthony Eardley, New York 1973

——, *Concerning Town Planning* [*Propos d'urbanisme*], trans. Clive Entwistle, London 1947

——, *The Modulor*, trans. Peter de Francia and Anna Bostock, London 1954

——, *Modulor 2*, trans. Peter de Francia and Anna Bostock, London 1958

——, *Modulor 1 and Modulor 2*, trans. Peter de Francia and Anna Bostock, in one vol, Cambridge, Mass. 1980

LE MUET, Pierre, *The Art of Fair Building*, trans. Robert Pricke, London 1670

LE ROY, Julien-David, *Ruins of Athens*, London 1759 (facs. repr. 1969)

LISSITZKY, EL, *Life – Letters – Texts*, trans. Helene Aldwinckle and Mary Whittall, London 1968, rev. ed. 1980

——, *Russia. An Architecture for World Revolution*, trans. Erich Dluhosch, Cambridge, Mass.–London 1970

LOMAZZO, Gian Paolo, *A Tracte Containing the Artes of curious Painting...*, trans. Richard Haydocke, Oxford 1598

LOOS, Adolf, *Spoken into the Void*, trans. Jane O. Newman and John H. Smith, Cambridge, Mass.–London 1982

MALEVICH, Kazimir, *Essays on Art and Unpublished Writings*, ed. Troels Andersen, 4 vols, Copenhagen 1968–78

MILIZIA, Francesco, *Lives of Celebrated Architects, Ancient and Modern*, trans. Mrs E. Cresy, 2 vols, London 1826

MILYUTIN, Nikolay, *Sotsgorod...*, trans. Arthur Sprague, Cambridge, Mass.–London 1974

MOHOLY-NAGY, László, *The New Vision: From Material to Architecture*, trans. Daphne M. Hoffmann, New York 1932

MUTHESIUS, Hermann, *The English House*, ed. with introduction by Dennis Sharp, trans. Janet Seligman, slightly abridged from 2nd German ed. (1908–11) in one vol., London 1979

PALLADIO, Andrea, *The Four Books of Architecture*, trans. Isaac Ware, 4 vols, London 1737–42 (facs. repr. New York–London 1965)

PERRAULT, Claude, *A Treatise of the Five Orders of Columns in Architecture*, trans. John James, London 1708

Pozzo, Andrea, *Rules and Examples of Perspective*, Latin text with trans. by John James, London 1707 (facs. repr. New York–London 1989)

Quatremère de Quincy, Antoine-Chrisostome, *An Essay on the nature, the end and the means of imitation in the fine arts*, trans. J.C. Kent, London 1837

Rabelais, François, *Gargantua and Pantagruel*, trans. J.M. Cohen, London 1970

Roriczer, Matthäus, *Das Büchlein von der Fialen Gerechtigkeit* and *Geometria Deutsch* trans. (with original texts) in: *Gothic Design Techniques*, ed. Lon R. Shelby, Carbondale, Ill.–London 1977

Scamozzi, Vincenzo, sixth book of *L'idea della architettura universale*, in Joachim Schuym's abridgment, trans. William Fisher in: *The Mirror of Architecture*, ed. William Fisher, London 1669 etc

Schinkel, Karl Friedrich, *Collected Architectural Designs* (without text), London 1982

——, *The English Journey: journal of a visit to France and Britain in 1826*, trans. F. Gayna Walls, ed. David Bindman and Gottfried Riemann, New Háven–London 1993

Schmuttermayer, Hans, *Fialenbüchlein* trans. (with original text) in: *Gothic Design Techniques*, ed. Lon R. Shelby, Carbondale, Ill.–London 1977

Semper, Gottfried, *The Four Elements of Architecture and other Writings*, trans. Harry Francis Mallgrave and Wolfgang Hermann, Cambridge 1989

Serlio, Sebastiano, *The First [Fift] Booke of Architecture*, trans. (from a Dutch trans. from a Flemish or French ed.), London 1611 (facs. repr. *The Five Books of Architecture*, New York–London 1982)

Sitte, Camillo, *The Art of Building Cities…*, trans. Charles T Stewart, New York 1945 (facs. repr. 1991)

Steiner, Rudolf, *Ways to a new Style in architecture: Five lectures*, London 1927

——, *Architectural forms considered as the thoughts of culture and world-perception. Words…on the third anniversary of the laying of the foundation stone of the first Goetheanum at Dornach…* 1916, London 19–

Suger, Abbot, of Saint-Denis, part of *Libellus Alter* trans. (with original text) by Erwin Panofsky in: *Abbot Suger. On the Abbey Church of St.–Denis and its Art Treasures*, Princeton, NJ 1946; ed. Gerda Panofsky-Soergel 1979

Taut, Bruno, *The Crystal Chain Letters: architectural fantasies by Bruno Taut and his circle*, ed. and trans. Iain Boyd Whyte, Cambridge, Mass.–London 1985

——, *Alpine Architectur* trans. Shirley Palmer, ed. with introduction by Dennis Sharp in: Paul Scheerbart, *Glass Architecture*, London 1972

Ungewitter, Georg Gottlob (with A. Reichensperger and V. Statz), *Gothic Model Book*, trans. Möricke, London 18–

Valéry, Paul, *Eupalinos or the Architect*, trans. William McCausland Stewart, London 1932

Vasari, Giorgio, *The Lives of the Painters, Sculptors and Architects*, trans. A.B. Hinds, 4 vols, London 1927, rev. ed. 1963

——, *Vasari on Technique* [introduction to the *Lives*], trans. L.S. Maclehose, ed. G. Baldwin Brown, London 1907

Vignola (Jacopo Barozzi), *Vignola: Or the Compleat Architect* [*Regola delle cinque ordini d'architettura*], trans. (almost certainly from a Dutch version of Pierre Le Muet's reduction published in 1631) Joseph Moxon, London 1655

Villard de Honnecourt, lodge-book trans. (with original text) in: Theodore Bowie, *The Sketchbook of Villard de Honnecourt*, New York 1959, 1962

Viollet-le-Duc, Eugène-Emmanuel, *Discourses on Architecture*, trans. B. Bucknall, 2 vols, Boston, Mass. 1875, 1881; London 1877, 1882 (facs. repr. titled *Lectures on Architecture*, 2 vols, New York–London 1987

——, *The habitations of man in all ages*, trans. B. Bucknall, London 1876

Vitruvius, Lat.–Engl. ed. of *De architectura libri decem* ed. Frank Granger, London–Cambridge 1931

Wagner, Otto, *Modern Architecture: A Guidebook for his students to this field of art*, trans. with an introduction by Harry Francis Mallgrave, Santa Monica, Calif. 1988

Winckelmann, Johann Joachim, *The History of Ancient Art amongst the Greeks*, trans. G.H. Lodge, London 1881

Since 1945

Otto, Frei (with Rudolf Trostel and Friedrich Karl Schleyer), *Tensile Structures: Design, Structure and Calculation of Buildings, nets and membranes*, ed. Frei Otto, 2 vols, Cambridge, Mass.–London 1967, 1969

Rossi, Aldo, *The Architecture of the City*, introduction by Peter Eisenman, trans. Diane Ghirardo and Joan Ockman, rev. by Aldo Rossi and Peter Eisenman, Cambridge, Mass.–London 1982

——, *Selected Writings and Projects*, ed. John O'Regan, London 1983

Tafuri, Manfredo, *The Sphere and the Labyrinth: Avant-Garde and Architecture from Piranesi to the 1970s*, Cambridge, Mass. 1987, ²1990

Index of Names

Notes and captions to plates are indexed as well as the main text. Italicised numbers are those of plates.